HAUNTED SKIES
PRESERVING THE SOCIAL HISTORY OF UFO RESEARCH

VOLUME TWO 1960-1969
REVISED AND EXPANDED EDITION

**JOHN HANSON
DAWN HOLLOWAY
V. J. HYDE**

HAUNTED SKIES VOLUME 2 Revised 1960-1969
Copyright © 2017 John Hanson & Dawn Holloway. All rights reserved.
First paperback edition printed 2017 in the United Kingdom.
A catalogue record for this book is available from the British Library.

ISBN 978-09956428-2-9

No part of this book shall be reproduced or transmitted in any form or by any means, electronic or mechanical,
including photocopying, recording, or by any information retrieval system
without written permission of the publisher.

Published by
Haunted Skies Publishing

For more copies of this book, please email: johndawn1@sky.com

Telephone: 0121 445 0340

Designed and typeset by Bob Tibbitts ~ (iSET)

Printed in Great Britain

Although every precaution has been taken in the preparation of this book,
the publisher and author assume no responsibility for errors or omissions.
Neither is any liability assumed for damages resulting from the use of this
information contained within.

FOREWORD
By NICK POPE

TO this day, the 1960's remain one of the most iconic decades of all time. It's the decade that brought us the assassination of JFK, the Vietnam War, and the Cuban Missile Crisis, which took the world to the very brink of Armageddon. Yet despite this, or – perhaps – because of it, it was also a decade of progress, achievement and joy. The Civil Rights Act and the Voting Rights Act helped put right a great wrong in the US, while the protests against the Vietnam War indirectly spawned the hippie movement, and, in 1969, Neil Armstrong and Buzz Aldrin walked on the moon. Culturally, too, the Sixties is the decade we all secretly wish we had been teenagers in: The Beatles, Mary Quant, Carnaby Street – it truly was the 'Swinging Sixties'. And as the space program took us to the moon, television took us even further afield, with the Sixties bringing us iconic shows like *Doctor Who* and *Star Trek*. This science fiction, perhaps, reflected a profound and mysterious truth, because the Sixties was also the decade that saw some of the most spectacular and intriguing UFO encounters of all time. Many of these events are featured in this book.

As with the other volumes in the *Haunted Skies* series, the cases that are particularly close to my heart are the ones involving the RAF and ones where the hidden hand of the MOD can briefly be glimpsed. I ran the MOD's UFO project for much of the early Nineties, but when I looked back into the MOD's archives, I often thought of the Sixties as being the 'golden years' of British ufology. My predecessors on the British government's UFO project certainly had a busy time of it though, as ever, this was hardly appreciated at the time, due to the MOD's longstanding policy of downplaying the true extent of its interest in and involvement with this subject, with Parliament, the media and the public. Our 'party line' on the subject was always that UFOs were of "no defence significance" – a neat sound bite, but one which – quite deliberately – we never actually defined. The truth can now be told. I've been the public face of a project to declassify and release the MOD's UFO files, and the hidden hand of the MOD that I mentioned earlier can now be seen a little more clearly.

Interestingly, while the MOD remains the villain of the story to many in the UFO community, in one way it's the unsung hero of ufology in the Sixties.

That's because in 1967 the MOD gave a commitment to Parliament that UFO files should be preserved permanently, in view of their historical significance and public interest. Tragically, before this commitment was given, it had been standard practice that files on this subject were routinely destroyed after five years – as was the case with files on many other subjects. So the MOD's 1967 commitment meant that UFO files from around 1963 onwards have survived, whereas with only a few exceptions, those from pre-1963 have been lost. With the declassification and release of most of the MOD's archive of UFO files, the public are finally getting a glimpse into what the media have called the real-life X-Files, and many of the cases featured in these governments UFO files are covered in *Haunted Skies*.

Haunted Skies Volume Two Revised

One of the best things about this book is that it reminds us how multi-faceted the UFO phenomenon is. Of all the decades, perhaps the Sixties best illustrate the point that far from being a homogenous phenomenon, UFOs really do come in all shapes and sizes, and the encounters themselves can range from the bizarre to the downright surreal. There are, for example, cases in this book covering not just lights in the sky, but landings! In addition we are treated to reports from other Countries such as Australia and the USA.

Before the Sixties, the media and public perception was that UFO sightings predominantly involved disc-shaped craft. More recently, reports of triangular-shaped craft are preeminent. One intriguing reason for what I call this faux homogeneity is the tendency of some UFO researchers to focus on cases that fit their perception of what's 'hot' at any particular time. Thus, though they have a wide variety of material from which to draw, what they highlight to their peers and to the media are cases that they think capture the ufological zeitgeist. It's a sort of playing to the gallery. What this means is that cases not seen as fitting the current model get edited out, and thus the true richness and variety of the phenomenon is lost. This isn't the case here, and as with all the Haunted Skies books, one gets a truly faithful representation of what people were seeing and experiencing. As a result, this book is a more honest account than many titles on this subject.

This updated, revised and reissued Volume Two of the Haunted Skies series of books is a 'must have' for any serious student of UFO research. It's a data-rich book, packed with facts about individual cases, and contemporary newspaper accounts that offer a window into the past when it comes to studying the UFO mystery. John Hanson and Dawn Holloway have pieced together a fascinating account of a period of history in which the UFO phenomenon exploded into the public consciousness in a way that has happened few times before or indeed since.

Nick Pope, Ministry of Defence UFO Project (Retired)

INTRODUCTION

THIS was a period in history now referred to as the 'Swinging Sixties' – an era of flamboyance, rampant recreational drug use and casual sex, not forgetting the radical and subversive events which were to influence so many people's lives and see the emergence of many popular musical groups, including *The Beatles and Rolling Stones*.

It also saw the manufacture of the first oral contraceptive pill, felt tip pens, artificial tanning cream and Astro Turf, while scientists in an effort to discover what lay out there in the vastness of space beamed radio messages to the stars in search for intelligent life on other worlds, ignoring what was lying literally in front of their eyes.

This second revised volume of *Haunted Skies* covers the period 1960-1969; a relatively short time, but it is packed with all manner of strange reports relating to unidentified flying objects seen by members of the public from all walks of life. Before we launch ourselves into the next fascinating period of English UFO history, we should – we believe – journey further back into the past and examine the event that many believe started the modern era.

How it all began

Kenneth Arnold (born Minnesota on 29th March 1915, and died on 16th January 1984) is generally considered as being the first widely reported witness to a UFO event. 'His' incident involved nine unusual objects seen flying in a chain near Mount Rainier, Washington, on 24th June 1947, a day often celebrated as a 'Sky Watch Day' by UFO researchers all over the world.

Many people still refer to UFOs as *'Flying Saucers'*, which seems far more appropriate in description than the ambiguous terminology of *Unidentified Flying Objects*. So we should at least count ourselves lucky that the Press labelled what Kenneth Arnold had seen in 1947 as *'Flying Saucers'*, not through visual image because of their movements. However, the popular name for such objects could have been very different.

There is a tape-recorded interview held between English UFO veteran Normal Oliver (ex head of BUFORA) and Mr Arnold, who told him the objects *"looked like 'flying tadpoles'."* It doesn't quite have the same ring to it, does it? There are few people interested in UFOs who *don't* know details of the now famous UFO sighting which took place over Mount Rainer, Washington state.

> "They didn't fly like any aircraft I had ever seen before. In the first place, their echelon movement was backwards, the elevation of the first craft was greater than the last. They flew in a definite formation but erratically, their flight was like speed boats on rough water or similar to the tail of a Chinese kite blowing in the wind, or even like a formation of geese in a chain like line as if linked together."

(Source: *Flying Saucers from other Worlds*, May 1958)

Other descriptions include *"as flat as a pie pan"*, *"shaped like a pie plate"*, *"half-moon shaped"*, *"oval in front and convex in the rear"*, *"something like a pie plate that was cut in half with a sort of a convex triangle in the rear"*, or simply *"saucer-like or like a big flat disc, their erratic motion being like a fish flipping in the sun, crescent or flying wing, or saucer skipped across water."*

The US Air Force formally listed the Arnold case as a mirage – an explanation which should, we feel, be treated with the contempt that it deserves.

UFO sighting over Oregon – Filmed!

What we found odd, if one can apply this trait of human behaviour to subject matter that is already very odd indeed, is the second sighting by Kenneth Arnold on the 29th July 1947, when, while flying over Baker, Oregon, intending to land at La Grande:

> "I noticed a cluster of about twenty to twenty-five brass colored objects that looked like ducks coming straight towards me, at what seemed like a terrific speed. I grabbed my camera and started filming, even though I thought they were ducks. As they came within 400 yards approx. of me, they veered sharply away from me and to their right, gaining altitude as they did so, fluttering and flashing a dull amber color. I was a bit shocked to see that they had the same flight characteristics as the ones I had seen previously. These appeared to be round, rather rough on top, and to have a dark or light spot on top of each one. They disappeared eastwards at a speed far in excess of airplane or ducks."

Mr Arnold, curious as to what was on the film, had it developed. However, it showed *"only one or two of these objects could be found on my film and you could only see them under jeweler's glass"*. Incredibly, what promised to be one of the most important pieces of film appears to have been lost from history. We wrote to Kenneth Arnold's daughter, living in Boise, Idaho, but never received a reply. Likewise, enquiries with a major USA UFO Group, in 2006, were unsuccessful; worryingly they didn't even *know* about the film! We hope that Kenneth Arnold's family will eventually be prepared to contact us, if only to put the record straight; it *has* been over 60 years now!

Back to the 1960s

In our opinion, the facts speak for themselves. The eye-witness evidence contained within the pages of this second volume, covering a mind boggling historical period of only ten years of British /USA UFO history, tells it own story ... but what about the reports we had missed? And what about the sightings never reported at all for fear of ridicule? And we shouldn't forget the thousands of other reports we could have included from other parts of the world never mind from the Unites States. If this had been feasible, would this Volume only cover a few months?

We do not believe, despite the clamour of the sceptics, that people who witness such phenomena are experiencing vivid bouts of hallucination or imagining, however real it appears to them, incidents which have no place in modern-day reality.

The majority of incidents outlined in our volumes involve the appearance of strange saucer or triangular-shaped craft, seen moving across the sky, rather than the movements of strange lights discerned above, which are often judged of no importance to the UFO researcher. However, the discovery of a veritable mass of personal letters, sighting reports, collected painstakingly over the years from groups such as the Isle of Wight UFO Society, who received reports from all over the UK, UFOSIS, and other organisations during this period of time, tell a different story. We should be careful of dismissing such sightings, normally referred to as LITS (lights in the sky), as being of no value to the researcher. Admittedly, while *some* may be explained away rationally, the vast bulk cannot. If we were to include these reports of strange lights, which can and do corroborate other more substantive sightings as additional to the main body of UFO evidence, this Volume would then only cover a mere period of a few years.

In 2009, the MOD declared that they were no longer willing to accept UFO sightings from members of the public and closed Air Desk 2A, as a part of a cost cutting exercise.

We have not included any accounts from the 'Warminster Wave'. Should the reader wish to examine what happened there, including many previously unpublished letters from Arthur Shuttlewood, please see *Haunted Skies Wiltshire* (Wiltshire/Warminster), published in 2017

MOD – UFO records were destroyed from this period of time

If a person was asked to supply details of English UFO sightings from the early 1960s, it is unlikely that he or she would be able to offer few, if any, examples at all, taking into consideration the MOD have stated that *"prior to 1967, all of our records were routinely destroyed"*. However, thanks to a veritable 'army' of UFO enthusiasts, including the Isle of Wight UFO Society – who bothered to catalogue an astonishing number of UFO sightings covering this period, sent to them from many other UK groups and organizations – we can now see for ourselves the extent of many hitherto unpublished UFO reports which are not to be found in the main body of this chapter, but offered as additional reference source material to the reader.

Dr Carl Sagan

The argument continues to fester right up to the present day about the origin of these elusive UFOs. Some believe them to be extraterrestrial; others claim they are from another dimension, while others that they live inside the planet because the earth is hollow. The simple truth is we don't know. Consider the words of Dr. Carl Sagan, noted astronomer from Cornell University:

> *"There are hundreds of people who are reliably seeing lights in the sky. That's ok, so there are lights in the sky. There are lots of explanations for lights in the sky. So I'm perfectly willing to believe the Governor of Ohio that he saw something that was in the sky and he didn't know what it was. That's the definition of an unidentified flying object. But that's very different from saying it has anything to do with being visited by spaceships from elsewhere."*

Words of wisdom – Wilfred Daniels

Wilfred Daniels from 134 Weston Road, Stafford, who has long since passed away, has some words of common sense about the subject matter. They are valid and of interest. Wilfred was a well-respected UFO researcher and was involved in various investigations, including the Jesse Roestenberg incident of 1954 when 'alien' occupants were seen inside a saucer-shaped object over Ranton, Staffordshire, and

Haunted Skies Volume Two Revised

allegations of an object that landed at RAF Cosford. In 1961, he wrote to David Jones – another UFO veteran researcher. This is what he had to say:

Dear Mr Jones,

Aside from, apart from in spite of and without the help of , 'Ufologists', Study Groups, Researchers, Lunatic Fringes, Spirits, Spiritualists, Satanists, etc., etc., the World at large will probably resolve the 'Flying Saucer' mystery for itself in its own time and in its own way. After almost 13 years of 'saucers', even dedicated individuals – not to mention Groups – fight amongst themselves and can give the uninitiated no more now than at the beginning ....The more we protest the truth or that 'hoax' the more we confuse the issue, even amongst ourselves. Small wonder that John Citizen merely shrugs or guffaws when 'Flying Saucers' are mentioned, when even those who profess to know what 'saucers' are all about squabble and bicker amongst themselves.

One believes this, another believes that; some follow Adamski – others say you would be dammed and a fool to follow Adamski, some say it is only a scientific problem, others say it is part of spiritual enlightenment for mankind…Ultimately it will all boil down to one question, for every living soul on this planet, to answer solo: 'Do I believe in 'Flying Saucers' and do I know what they are?'"

[Time may have flowed forward by over 55 years – little has changed!]

We are pleased to introduce the readers to Mrs. Victoria Jane Hyde (neé Hanson), who has, on occasion, assisted us with some of the investigations relating to the work carried out by us. We hope that Vicky will, in due course, hopefully take over the more up to date editions of *Haunted Skies*, as we have no intention of covering the events from 2000 onwards, owing to insufficient resources and time. Vicky is shown with her husband, Steven, at Silbury Hill some years ago. She is a dog lover and shares the family with Abbey, shown with her 'Mum' Bella.

CHAPTER 1 – 1960

UFO REPORTS INCLUDE:

JANUARY:
January 1960 – Spinning object over Suffolk – Local newspaper had a large file of UFO reports!
Mr Arthur Constance writes in the flyleaf of his book.

FEBRUARY:
21st February 1960 – Joseph Perry Photos a UFO!
22nd February 1960 – UFO seen in sky near RAF West Freugh, Scotland
27th February 1960 – Fan-shaped UFO over US Air Force Base

MARCH:
4th March 1960 – Three objects seen over Iowa USA
23rd March 1960 – USA Objects forming an 'X' in the sky seen.

APRIL:
11th April 1960 – Red saucer-shaped object seen over Scotland
12th April 1960 – UFO sighted over California
25th April 1960 – Five UFOs seen over Montana USA

MAY:
25th May 1960 – UFO sighted over Surrey
28th May 1960 – Black sphere seen over Kent.

JUNE:
2nd June 1960 – RAF Jet Fighter scrambled
3rd June 1960 – Crop Circles discovered in Gloucestershire
7th June 1960 – UFO making a whistling sound
19th June 1960 – 'Silver saucer' seen over Dunston Power Station
27th June 1960 – Spinning 'stars' seen over the coast
29th June 1960 – Egg-shaped UFO seen
June 1960 – Cylindrical UFO seen over Gloucestershire.

JULY:
8th July 1960 – UFO sighted projecting three beams of light
13th July 1960 – Silver UFO sighted
19th July 1960 – Single red light seen over St. Charles, Missouri,
20th July 1960 – Orange 'banana' shaped lights seen
30th July 1960 – Bell-shaped object seen over Scotland.

AUGUST:
13th August 1960 – Red Bluff, California – UFO Display
15th August 1960 – Triangular UFO seen over Scotland
23rd August 1960 – Three triangular windows seen in base of UFO over Kansas, USA
28th August 1960 – Spinning top UFO seen

SEPTEMBER:
2nd September 1960 – UFO hovers over Gloucestershire orchard
8th September 1960 – 'Flying Triangle' over Tyneside, showing three lights
10th September 1960 – Two 'boomerang'-shaped UFOs seen over California
11th September 1960 – Three UFOs tracked on radar over East Anglia
25th September 1960 – UFOs over Harlow, Essex

OCTOBER:
28th October 1960 – Cigar-shaped UFO sighted over Cheshire.

NOVEMBER:
11th November 1960 – Fireball over Gloucestershire
12th November 1960 – Cigar-shaped UFO seen
15th November 1960 – Cylindrical UFO over London
17th November 1960 – UFOs follow US jets
30th November 1960 – Ice-blue UFO

DECEMBER:
2nd December 1960 – Cylindrical object seen over Coventry

JANUARY 1960

January 1960 – Spinning object over Suffolk:

Local newspaper had a large file of UFO reports!

At 3.20pm in this month, Mr Tipping of Cransford, Suffolk, was asked by his poultry man to look at something strange in the sky, which he thought might have been a parachute.

> "Through binoculars I saw a circular, apparently spinning object, flashing at great height (50,000ft), with a bright centre portion. After about 20 minutes it disappeared behind clouds."

Mr Tipping contacted the *East Anglia Daily Times*, who told him they had a large file relating to such reports!

Mr Arthur Constance writes in the flyleaf of his book

On the 16h January 1960, the *Cheltenham Echo* published an article about Mr Arthur Constance, *'From another World says Mr Constance'*, in which there is a reference to his investigation into a report made by local woman – retired physiotherapist Miss H. Mckean (77) – who was living in Suffolk Square, Cheltenham, when she sighted a gold coloured object with 'paddle-like wings'

Arthur Constance

flying past her window, at 8.30pm on the 27th December 1959. Mr Constance presented Miss Mcklean with a copy of his book -*The Inexplicable Sky* – and wrote in the flyleaf,

> "I am quite sure that the flying object you saw last Sunday morning was neither an earth aircraft, a drifting balloon, nor an hallucination, and that it came from another world (or probably another dimension)."

FEBUARY 1960

21st February 1960 – Joseph Perry Photos a UFO!

The RAF West Freugh incident, 22nd February, 1960

22nd February 1960 – UFO seen in sky near RAF West Freugh, Scotland

During the afternoon, Mr L. Holmes – an employee for Stranraer Corporation cleansing department – was with three colleagues when they sighted an aircraft from RAF West Freugh Radar Station moving across the sky, followed by what appeared to be a cylindrical shaped object seen heading away towards the direction of Kirkcolm, near Loch Ryan.

(Source: Scottish UFO Research Society)

On the 4th April 1957, a similar incident appears to have taken place. This was covered by the *Sunday Dispatch*, (7.4.1957) -'Clues to radar sky riddle', *The Newark Sunday Newspaper*, (7.5.1957) – 'British hunt flying object', *New York Journal*, (6.4.1957) – 'RAF Radar seeks object', and *London News*, (6.4.1957) – 'Hint plane over Scots was red').

27th February 1960 – Fan-shaped UFO over US Air Force Base

At 6.27pm, Rome Air Force Base, New York control tower officer – Captain J. Huey, and four other tower operators, sighted a 'light', trailing a white fan shape, descending through the sky for 3-4 minutes.

MARCH 1960

4th March 1960: Three objects seen over Iowa, USA

At 5.55pm, over Dubuque, Iowa, three elliptical-shaped objects were seen slightly climbing up into the sky for four minutes.

Film exposed during sighting showed no images of the objects.

23rd March 1960 – USA Objects forming an 'X' in the sky seen

At 3.35am, Indianapolis, Indiana residents – Mr and Mrs E.I. Larsen – sighted a series of 'balls', arranged like an 'X' with one diagonal line, seen for three-quarters of a minute.

APRIL 1960

11th April 1960 – Red saucer-shaped object seen over Scotland

At 8.15pm, a *"red saucer-shaped object"* was sighted by Miss Greig and her family, from Dundee, moving slowly across the sky, heading northwards towards the Grampians, before disappearing into cloud. *"When it emerged, it looked like a large Catherine wheel."* (**Source:** *Dundee Courier & Advertiser,* **14.4.1960**)

12th April 1960 – UFO sighted over California

One wonders what exactly was seen at 9pm on this date by Scientist Monroe Arnold, who told of seeing a fiery-red 'disc' in the south direction over Lacamp, Los Angeles, which was seen to touch the ground about 1,000 feet away, with a loud explosion and flame – heard by many people. It bounced in an east direction for about 1,000 feet – then rose again, turned west, and disappeared. The ground was later examined and found scarred in nine places, and a substance resembling metallic paint was found; analysis inconclusive. (**Source: Berliner; cf. Vallée Magonia 503**)

13th April 1960 – Police sight UFO over Red Bluff, California

The State Police reported having sighted a highly manoeuvrable elliptical object, showing red light beams which swept the ground underneath it. (**Source: NICAP UFOE, V**)

25th April 1960 – Five UFOs seen over Montana

Shelby, Montana resident – Mrs M. Clark – sighted five circular objects moving through the sky, at 7.10pm, one behind the other.

On occasion they were seen to hover, accelerate, and make sharp turns. (**Source: Project Blue Book files**)

MAY 1960

25th May 1960 – UFO sighted over Surrey

Vera Bowden and her son, Nigel, sighted:

> *". . . an elliptical grey shape over Broadwater Lake, a couple of miles away from Godalming. We reported it to the police and kept it under observation for about 18 minutes".*

(**Source:** *The New Daily Mail,* **27.5.1960**)

28th May 1960 – Black sphere seen over Kent

On 28th May 1960, a *'black sphere, surrounded by six bright lights'* was seen at dawn, over Tilehurst, Kent, by Mr C. Coventry, employed at RAF HQ. Shinfield Park, Works Department:

> *"I awoke at 3.50am and went to the bathroom. Looking out of the window, I noticed a black object, about the size of a football, around which were six very bright lights, hardly moving across the sky. I got back into bed and continued to watch it, measuring out some 12-15 inches down the window pane to plot its movement, which took 15 minutes. I last saw it heading towards the north, where I lost sight of it at 4.45 am."*

The story does not end there. While having a drink, later, in a local public house, he discovered that a holidaymaker, from Birmingham, had seen the same *'black ball'* in the sky. (**Source: David C. Jones,** *Cheltenham/Reading* **Mercury, 4.6.1960**)

JUNE 1960

2nd June 1960 – RAF Jet Fighter scrambled

An RAF Jet, from Shawbury, was scrambled to investigate the sighting of an unidentified object, after a police officer originally reported the object hovering in the sky, at approximately 6,000 feet, over Minsterley. It was later explained away as being a weather balloon. (**Source:** *Birmingham Evening Mail*, 2.6.1960)

3rd June 1960 – Crop Circles discovered in Gloucestershire

On or about the 3rd June 1960, two jet black burnt 'rings' (or circles) were found by farmer Bill Edwards in a field at Poplar Farm, Evenlode, midway between Chastleton and Evenlode, near Moreton-in-Marsh, Gloucestershire. This matter was later brought to the attention of the Cheltenham-based UFO researcher, David Jones David who visited the area and interviewed Mr Edwards on the 3rd June 1960, when he was able to confirm the imprints in the ground.

> "They formed two apparently perfect circles, the inner circle being equidistant from the outer. I paced the outer circle and found it to be approximately 23 feet in diameter, the inner 16 feet by four inches across. The grass on the edge of the imprints was showing definite indications of burning, but no burning in the central areas."

David Jones:

> "I estimated the depth of the imprint to be one inch thick, although the eastern side of the imprints were impressed deeply, causing a lip to form. The ground was extremely hard, owing to no recent rain, which led me to believe that whatever had caused the imprints had been very heavy. I could not understand what had caused the marks, since the fields were about half a mile from the nearest road. No vehicle could have reached the spot, without leaving some sign of approach through other fields. My previous crossing through the field had been two days previously, and they weren't there then. I reported it to the police on the 5th June, who was as puzzled as I.

> The incident was first brought to my attention by my sister-in-law, who heard it mentioned on the ITV Midlands News. The following day (the 20th June 1960) I made my way to Poplars Farm, and met up with Mr Bill Edwards. He told me that he had been walking through the field concerned (something he did most days) when he came across the markings – two circles, burnt into the grass."

After Bill told his wife and son, they rang the Moreton-in-Marsh office of the *Evesham Journal*, and sent reporter David Day to cover the story. David tells us that between the date of the discovery and the date of his visit, there were two severe thunderstorms and the grass had grown considerably, and that:

> "following publicity, various people made their way to the scene; one of them was Mr Rutherford, a draughtsman with a local aircraft firm, who made some measurements."

A visit to the scene

When David and Bill Edwards visited the scene, they were unable to see much, other than the outlines of the two circles, and the deeper depression at one side where the field slopes downward. They noticed that the grass still showed the burn marks on some parts, although no signs of burning were found either on the inside or the outside of the circles. The markings were situated towards the corner of the field, about midway between Chastleton and Evenlode – far from any roads or houses. Cattle were using the land when the incident took place, and showed no signs of being disturbed or agitated.

While in Evenlode, David spoke to some of the villagers and one man said he thought he had heard *"a strange whistling sound, one night"*, but whether there is a connection we cannot say, because we don't know the exact date of the incident.

Haunted Skies Volume Two Revised

Ruby Llewellyn showing a photograph of husband, John 'Dennis' Llewellyn

Colour photographs were taken – whereabouts not known

Mr Coles of the 'The Stores', at Evenlode, took some colour photographs and promised to let David have some copies. Unfortunately, this never happened. What happened to Mr Coles, the shop, or the photographs, is not known and probably never will be. Amongst the inevitable rumours was a thinly veiled suggestion that this was the work of Satanists, or people conducting black magic rituals, which was rejected as an explanation by David and Stratford-upon-Avon UFO researchers John 'Dennis' Llewellyn and his wife, Ruby.

David said:

> "I believe the marks were caused by the pressure of something interacting with the ground […], rather than a lightning strike. What it was that actually caused it is anybody's guess."

John 'Dennis' Llewellyn visited the scene of the 'burn marks', together with his wife Ruby, and baby – Janet four weeks after the discovery. They met up with Farmer Bill Edwards of Poplars Farm, and obtained the photographs shown (handed over to us by Ruby, some years after John 'Dennis' Llewellyn passed away.

Although thought by many to be a phenomenon of the 20th Century, crop circles and formations have been around for a very long time. Is there a connection with circles carved into prehistoric stone, and wall carvings, thousands of years ago?

From the 1960s onwards, there has been a steady increase in reports of crop circles, together with an increase in the intricacy of the patterns, with almost 200 formations reported in 1999.

Ruby still remains interested in the UFO subject, and had her own sightings of unusual flying objects over the town of Stratford-upon-Avon during the 1960/1970s.

Maybe Bill had his own views on how they were made. Some people thought it was the work of extraterrestrials; others, black magic. But was there a rational explanation for the appearance of these marks? One should not forget that similar marks were found at a farm in Reading in the 1920s. Despite the passing of over half a century since the Evenlode incident, we still do not know the answers.

John 'Dennis' Llewellyn says that he was most impressed by the integrity of the persons concerned, and pondered whether the marks could have been caused by something from the sky, such as a helicopter or vertical take-off aircraft. John told us that he extracted a small piece of burnt grass from the outer circle and took it to a laboratory in Cheltenham, who advised him to submit it to the Public Analyst at Gloucester for testing.

> "The Public Analyst examined it under a microscope and said the grass appeared to be burnt. He felt the thunderstorms, rain, and delay in getting the sample to him probably had some effect and it would not be worth the two pounds and two shillings to examine it further."

Crop Circle researcher Colin Andrews had this to say about early crop circles:

> "Circular markings in the fields date back to the 1960s and were distinctly different from the typical crop circles of the 1970-80s.
>
> I was the person who created the term 'crop circle' to describe what I was researching during the 1980s. These were plants bent over at right angles and swirled into circles.
>
> While there are reasons to associate the crop circles to UFO activity on some occasions, I am certain that they are not created by landing UFOs. That cannot be said for a number of cases reported during the first half of the 1960s, examples of which included a 'disc' seen to land in grass and leave a 90 feet diameter circle in Argentina, during August 1960, which was witnessed by four engineers, and two circles etched into concrete in different parts of Forestry Camp, Puerta Cruz, Hermitt, California, during July 1962. According to Colonel Steve Wilson (USAF) who investigated the incident, the dust inside both showed higher than normal radiation."

John Hanson

> "In late October 2016 we visited Evenlode again, and attempted to discover what had happened to the 'village' shop or the location of Mr Coles, but we were unsuccessful. We therefore contacted the Evesham Journal, hoping that an appeal to some of the older readers might bring in any new information, but nothing further was heard."

(Sources: *Evesham Journal,* 10.6.1960 – 'Flying Saucer at Evenlode'/*Cheltenham Chronicle,* 2.7.1960 – Circles in Cotswold field, 'Flying Saucer landings'/Personal interviews)

7th June 1960 – UFO making a whistling sound

An object – thought initially to be a satellite – was sighted moving quickly across the sky over Westcliff, Southend, at 11.20pm.

It was described as *"making a whistling sound, leaving a trail of yellow light behind it"*.

At 11.30pm, *"a luminous light green object"* was seen moving quickly across the sky over Retford, Nottinghamshire. It was doubtlessly the same UFO sighted shortly afterwards, by people living in the Essex area, shortly afterwards.

(Source: *London Daily Telegraph,* 15.6.1960/*Colchester Gazette,* 14.6.1960/*Southend Pictorial,* 10.6.1960)

19th June 1960 'Silver saucer' seen over Dunston Power Station

On 19th June 1960, a silver, saucer-shaped, object was seen at 3 30pm, over Dunston, County Durham, by local resident Colin Vince, who had this to say:

> "I was talking to three friends at Benwell, where I lived at the time, when I spotted what I thought was a bird in the distance, heading in from the west. As it grew closer, we were astounded to see a 'silver saucer' glinting in the sunlight. Suddenly, it stopped dead in the sky, over Dunston Power Station, before moving away at terrific speed towards the coast."

(Source: Gordon Creighton/*Newcastle Journal* **28.6.1960** – 'Society probes Mr Vince's flying saucer')

27th June 1960 – Spinning 'stars' seen over the coast

Strange red and green 'spinning stars' were seen moving across the sky, at 10.30pm, over parts of Wales and the West Country, including Mumbles Head, The Lizard and Lamorna Cove, at11pm. Despite a search of the coast, made by search and rescue teams from RAF Mount Batten, Plymouth, no explanation was ever found.

(Source: *The Coachman*, 30.6.1960/*Evening Post* – '*Mystery* in the sky', 28. 8 .1960)

29th June 1960 – Egg-shaped UFO seen

At 4.48pm a resident of Whitley Bay was stood at Backworth, casually watching an aircraft pass over,

> "...when I noticed an object, shaped like a flattened circle, almost the shape of a symmetrical egg with two broad ends. It had a clear outline, was matt white in colour, with no visible protrusions, moving in the sky a short distance away ahead of the plane. As the aircraft approached closer, it took off at fantastic rate, disappearing into infinity in five seconds – like liquid air melting in warm water or ice in boiling liquid. Just before it left, I saw it jump up into the sky."

(Source: TUFOS)

June 1960 – Cylindrical UFO seen over Gloucestershire

Tommy Dunford from Malmesbury, Wiltshire, was cycling along Station Road, Purton, towards Cricklade, when he noticed a curious cylindrical object travelling slowly across the sky at a height of approximately 12, 000 feet.

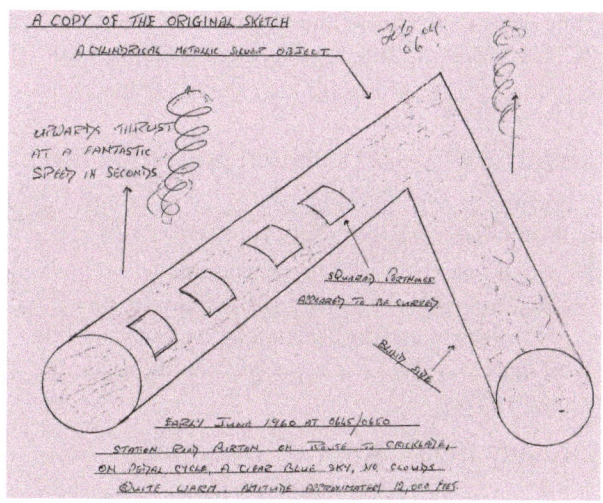

> "I could see what looked like windows, or portholes – square, rather than curved – set into its side, and presumed there was another 'wing', or arm, on its other side. Suddenly, in a matter of seconds, it went straight upwards into the sky and was gone, leaving me bewildered and excited but not frightened. I later reported the sighting to the MOD, who treated the matter with disbelief, although I found out that similar objects had been seen and photographed over Colombus, Ohio, in 1973."

(Source: Personal interview)

Haunted Skies Volume Two Revised

Tommy Dunford

Tommy Dunford, who passed away in 2001, was a member of a group run by Trowbridge couple – Barry and Judy Gooding. According to Tommy, this group came to an abrupt end in the 1970s after they received a threatening visit from 'Men in Black', whom he believed were from the Air Ministry.

JULY 1960

8th July 1960 – UFO sighted projecting three beams of light

Mr George Brown – an employee of Self's Garage, Denton Burn, Newcastle-on-Tyne, was looking out of the window, due north, at 8.30pm, when he saw

> "... a long, pure white object appear, showing illuminated in low cloud towards the north-east, projecting three beams of light. I could see the top but not the bottom of the object; it seemed to be in two parts, with light streaming out of the middle, (like two shallow discs, or saucer shapes), then it tilted and showed a ripple effect on the underside of the top half, before disappearing into cloud."

(Source: TUFOS)

13th July 1960 – Silver UFO sighted

At 6.25pm, a Fleetwood resident – Mr C.O. Harper – was watching a four-engine plane flying between 1-15,000 feet, heading south-east to north-west, when:

> "I saw a silver coloured object flying above the aircraft, in the opposite direction, through a break in the clouds; about a minute later it disappeared into cloud cover."

(Source: LUFORO, July 1960)

19th July 1960 – Single red light seen over St. Charles Missouri

At 8.30pm a round, bright red light was seen moving overhead, which then stopped in mid-air before reversing on its original course 20 minutes later. It is claimed that this phenomena was one of three reported similar sightings over the following nights.

20th July 1960 – Orange 'banana'-shaped lights seen

Between 7-8pm, a number of UFOs – described as looking like comets, rockets with fiery tails, or orange 'bananas' – were seen passing over the town of Sherringham, Norfolk, heading coastward – matters later brought to the attention of *East Anglia TV*, who rushed to the area, eager to interview witnesses.

24th July 1960 – Police sight UFO

At Portville, New York State policeman reported seeing two dumbbell-like UFOs. **(Source: NICAP UFOE, VII)**

30th July 1960 – Bell-shaped object seen over Scotland

Kirkintilloch night-watchman George Jerritt, and sixteen schoolboys from St. Mary's Industrial School, reported having sighted a UFO over Bishopbriggs. They described it as:

> "...bell-shaped, with a red dome on top, showing half a dozen windows on the one side, with a shining cushion underneath, flying at about 600 feet off the ground, and green and yellow lights flashing on and off. It was 'flitting around' for three and a half hours, returning every 15 minutes."

(Source: *The Scottish Daily Mail* – 'I saw a flying saucer – watchman')

1960 – Police Officer escapes electrocution

Ex-Police Constable Roger Crowhurst:

> "In the summer of 1960 I was a Police cadet, stationed at Chiswick in South London. One of our more menial tasks was to do school crossing duty, but because no-one would give us youngsters legal power to stop traffic by hand signals as the Constables had, we had to do so with a 'Stop – Children Crossing' metal board and pole and a white cotton full length coat. Most embarrassing, but the pole was handy for whacking the roofs of cars which failed to stop for us. Lunchtimes were the worst as, though we manned each crossing for over an hour, usually only a trickle of children crossed the road to go home for their lunch.
>
> On this particular day it was dark, raining hard and stormy, with occasional flashes of lightning. A few women were shopping opposite my place on the pavement and I was just five yards from a towering oak tree to my left and I wondered just how long one could put up with this boring and wet job – indeed I wondered if I had actually chosen totally the wrong career.
>
> Suddenly there was the loudest high-pitched screaming sound I had ever heard, coming from the sky above me and to my front. It was similar to the sound of a jet fighter and increasing rapidly in crescendo. I looked up and saw what seemed to be a perfect empty circle in the sky – about the size when a split second away of a football and similar to when one inadvertently looks at the sun and sees an empty circle. It was coming straight for me. My brain screamed 'METAL POLE, METAL POLE!', and I instinctively threw the wet metal sign I was holding into the roadway. As I did so, still watching the phenomenon – which I wrongly assumed was a crashing RAF jet – it veered sharply to my left and struck the wet oak like a white hot flaming cannonball with an ear splitting 'BANG!', and a massive explosion of fire which engulfed the entire tree in total flames, spitting fire and smoke like a huge exploding firework and flinging burning debris in all directions. Almost immediately the torrential rain extinguished the blaze, leaving the old tree smoking, crackling and steaming, almost leafless and black from top to bottom.

I found myself on the pavement, sobbing, shivering in fear, wet and icy cold. Across the road by the shops, several women were sitting on the wet ground, crying and wailing loudly. Pulling myself together and understanding that I was the only authority figure at the scene, I gathered some composure, walked across to the newsagent's and gasped 'call 999 for fire, police and ambulance. We've just experienced ball lightning!' The ambulance took us to Casualty at Hammersmith Hospital, where we were put in separate rooms with the blinds down and in the dark for an hour or two and given hot sweet tea for our shock. The doctor kindly gave me a week off work to get over it. Strangely, I had read Arthur C. Clarke's book on ball lightning only the week before."

(Source: Personal interview)

AUGUST 1960

13th August 1960 – Red Bluff, California – UFO Display

Oddly this took place on the same day as the previous one in April, although this does appear to be two separate reports. California Highway Patrol Officers Charles A. Carson and Stanley Scott were on patrol when they sighted what they thought was an airliner about to crash. When the UFO descended to about 100 or 200 feet, it suddenly reversed direction and climbed to 500 feet. It was described as being *"round or oblong, surrounded by a glow and having definite red lights at each end"*.

They continued to watch the UFO as it performed *"unbelievable"* aerial feats. The local Radar operator confirmed the UFO at this time, but denied it the next day. Other Tehema County Sheriffs' officers also saw this UFO and another similar one that same night.

(**Source:** NICAP 1964/*The Hynek UFO Report,* by J. Allen Hynek (1977), pages 92-94)

15th August 1960 – Triangular UFO seen over Scotland

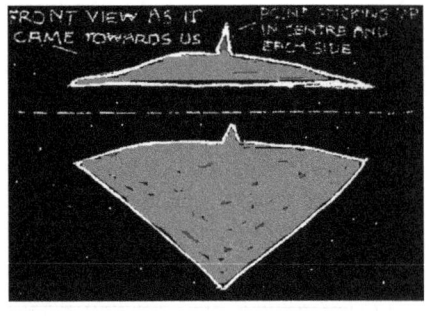

At 2.30am, Mrs Violet Whybrow from Moffat, Dumfriesshire, happened to look out of her bedroom window and saw a grey/amber coloured object, hovering outside the house. The top was surmounted by a brilliant white light with a gauzy band, slowly weaving itself around the object in a corkscrew fashion.

The next day, Mr and Mrs Watson were visiting their daughter, Violet, when a reddish-brown coloured object was seen, shaped like a cigar, showing *'points'* along its centre and sides, which stood out from the main structure. This created a roughly triangular shape, about 4 feet in length, which passed overhead, at 10.40pm, only a hundred feet or so off the ground.

23rd August 1960 – Three triangular windows seen in base of UFO over Kansas

At 3.24am, a Boeing aeronautical engineer – Mr C.A. Komiske from Wichita, Kansas – sighted a dull orange, round object, with yellow lights emanating from what looked like three triangular windows in the base of the object. It flew in an arc across the sky for two minutes, before being lost from view.

At 4.30am, Mrs Aaron from Borehamwood, Hertfordshire, was awoken by a high-pitched vibrating sound, reminding her of a giant tuning fork. Running to the window, she saw a glowing green object, shaped like a child's spinning top, scattering sparks from *"three central openings"* in its 'body', as it rotated across the sky, at a height she estimated to be over a thousand feet. By the time she had alerted her husband, the object had gone. Investigation carried out into the incident by Thelma Roberts, revealed it had maintained a parallel course to the road and railway line from St. Pancras and King's Cross to the North. (**Source:** Thelma Roberts/*LUFORO Bulletin,* No's. 11 & 12, December 1960)

SEPTEMBER 1960

2nd September 1960 – UFO hovers over Gloucestershire orchard

A resident of Gloucester, with nearly 40 years of experience in the aircraft industry, was outside at 9.30pm, when he saw:

> "...an object, 40 yards away, hovering over an orchard; it was dark in colour with no wings or structure, except a strut along its side. From inside came a bright light that flashed white, red, and green. About ten minutes later, it suddenly shot upwards and was just a point of light in the sky in seconds." **(Source: Isle of Wight UFO Society)**

8th September 1960 – 'Flying Triangle' over Tyneside, showing three lights

At 8.15pm, Mr Alfred Miller from Consett – a member of the Tyneside UFO Society – was one of the first people to sight:

> "...four or five small 'lights', with a single 'light' following some distance behind, circling and changing formation as they flew silently, south to north, across the sky."

Alfred Miller

Following a telephone call made to other members of the group, alerting them of the sighting – Eileen Steel, John Booth and Jean Otley, living 16 miles to the north – confirmed they had the 'lights' under observation. According to John Booth:

> "Through binoculars, the three main 'lights' forming the 'triangle' were, in fact, made up of a number of smaller 'lights'. I estimated they were moving at a height of less than 3,000 feet, under cloud cover. After completing a couple of circuits, lasting 25 minutes, they moved off North."

James Leslie Otley and Jean Otley

Mr James Leslie Otley (head of the Tyneside UFO Group) ands responsible for the *ORBIT* magazine was – together with colleague, Andy Steel – coincidently giving a talk on UFOs at the local Conservative Club that evening. Andy Steel, was informed about the sighting, and telephoned the Duty Officer at the nearest RAF station, to report the matter. He was told that others had already telephoned them about this.

Air Ministry explains it away as being refuelling!

Two hours later, at 12.35am, Leslie and his wife, Jean, received a telephone call from RAF Fighter Command HQ, 300 miles away, at Stanmore. They wanted details of the sighting, which had now been reported by others living in the Newcastle-on-Tyne area.

Mr A. Goddard from the Air Ministry later wrote to Leslie Otley, explaining it away as

> ". . . being military aircraft, carrying out a routine air refuelling exercise in the area at the time. The aircraft belonged to the USAF. May I also say that there is no reason why the Royal Air Force stations in the area

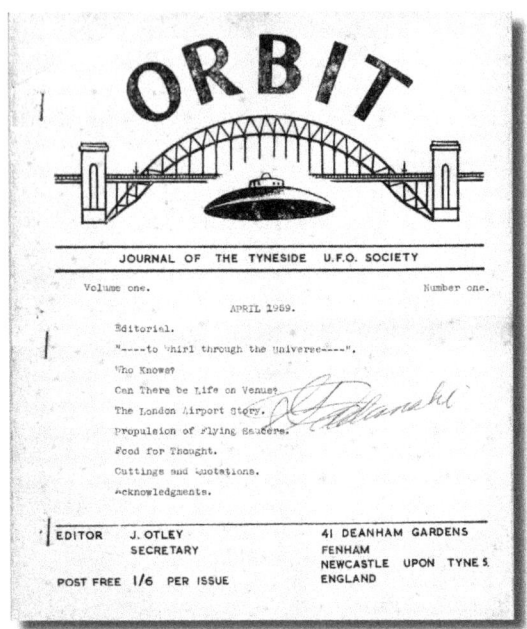

should have known about the exercise and that the air defence of this country does not depend on the investigation by flight stations of events in the air above them; There is no possibility that Russian planes could do likewise".

(Source: Tyneside UFO Society/*Newcastle Evening Chronicle***, 9.9.1960 – 'Mystery Flying Triangle is spotted over the North', Evening Chronicle, 8.10.1960' – Mystery objects seen in the North'/***Newcastle Evening Chronicle***, 10.9.1960 – 'Flying object is still a mystery'/Evening Chronicle, 16.9.1960 – 'Was Flying Triangle a tanker aircraft?'/Evening Chronicle, 17.9.1960 – 'Flying Triangle was not an aircraft')**

Other sightings of Flying Triangles reported over England

During the same year, according to freelance journalist Douglas Lockhart, hundreds of people contacted the authorities after *"three orange triangles"* were seen flying over the town of Coatbridge, Lanarkshire, Scotland.

10th September 1960 – Two Boomerangs--shaped UFOs seen over California

At 9.50pm Ridgecrest, California residents – Mr and Mrs M.G. Evans – sighted:

". . . two light grey, glowing objects, saucer or boomerang-shaped, which swished when accelerating through the sky; seconds later, they were gone."

11th September 1960 – Three UFOs tracked on radar over East Anglia

A number of residents living in the East Anglia region contacted the police, after sighting an object resembling a 'figure 8' – like two glass marbles, placed on top of each other, in the sky. The phenomenon was explained away by a spokesman from RAF Markham, Norfolk, as a special research balloon, released by a research unit from either London or Bristol University. This conclusion was also reached by the Meteorological Officer at RAF Mildenhall, who stated that it had been kept under observation at an estimated height of 60,000 feet. A spokesman from RAF Marham, near King's Lynn, suggested that it was probably a balloon, but remained puzzled why it had remained stationary for so long, adding,

". . . Air Traffic Control had picked up the presence of three objects, on radar, over Thetford".

17th September 1960 – UFOs tracked over Kirksville Air Force Station, Missouri

At 10.13pm CST, Radar returns were detected by the 790th Radar Squadron (SAGE) of what was initially thought to be 8 to 12 aircraft, flying at 95,000 feet. At 10.17pm, they descended to 23,000 feet. At 10.19pm, 6 to 8 objects were picked up at 100,000 feet and were then lost in the weather. At 10.23pm, the first formation started to climb and was tracked until they disappeared off the top of the scope at 100,000 feet. Another formation then appeared at 10.40p.m, at 85,000 feet. **(Source: NICAP)**

25th September 1960 – UFOs over Harlow, Essex

Thousands of mysterious 'parachute-like objects' were reportedly seen flying through the air over Essex, by a number of people, including Maurice Fryer – an Aircraft Engineer, who works at Gatwick Airport – who told us:

"While in Harlow, Essex, on 25th September 1960, at 9.45am, I saw what appeared to be parachutes, between 10-15,000 feet, in the sky. Attached above was what looked like a smaller stabilizing parachute, the length of which was a quarter of the diameter of the main one; it first appeared in the North, about 80 degrees above the horizon, drifting south, but I lost sight of it before it landed. I then saw another group of these objects higher up, still visible to the naked eye. If they had been parachutes, I would have said they were at 20,000 feet.

I fetched a telescope and discovered there were more objects, in layers, at increasing heights, up to the limit of my vision; say, 50,000 feet. There were between 15-20 objects in each group, which appeared like puffs of anti-aircraft fire. The lower groups moved slowly south, but disappeared when approaching the direction of the sun. The groups in the upper layers disappeared while still overhead. While these objects were overhead, I telephoned Stansted Aerodrome to report the sighting, and was told a Met. Balloon had burst at 70,000 feet. I consider these objects were not fragments of a burst balloon. I continued watching until 10.44am – the sky now cloudless, with a light northern breeze. These objects were seen by several people besides me."

(Source: Mr K.A. Lawrence/LUFORO/Personal interview)

OCTOBER 1960

28th October 1960 – Cigar-shaped UFO sighted over Cheshire

Mr and Mrs Cooke were at their home address in Hazel Grove, Stockport, Cheshire, at midnight, when they were astonished to see:

"...a large, golden, cigar-shaped or sausage-shaped object, motionless in the sky, showing blue blurred light at the back, at a height of about 5,000 feet. We watched it until it began to move towards the south-west, where we eventually lost sight of it, five minutes later."

The sighting was explained away by Manchester Meteorological Office as possibly being a weather balloon, sent up from Aughton. **(Source: Personal interview)**

NOVEMBER 1960

11th November 1960 – Fireball over Gloucestershire

During the evening, residents living in Gloucestershire and Bristol contacted the police after sighting what looked like a 'rocket', trailing sparks, falling from the sky, at 8.50pm. One of the witnesses was Maurice Estop (then aged 14), who was cycling home, towards Redmarley.

"The road behind me was flooded with light, illuminating the landscape harshly. It frightened the life out of me. I looked around and saw a 'ball of light' shooting across the sky, at great speed. I think I must have broken any previous records for getting home." Another report from the same date tells of a *"dazzling white object"* seen by an Army officer and four guards, at Warminster, Wiltshire. It was seen to hover for a few seconds before vanishing, leaving a trail of sparks. Apparently, the officer thought that it might have been a satellite coming in to land!

A UFO was also seen hovering over Deepdale Football Club, Norfolk, by a capacity crowd of 11,000 fans, watching Preston play Aston Villa.

(Sources: *Bristol Evening Post*, **12.11.1960/G. Stephenson, London UFO Research Organisation/***Bristol Evening Post*, **12.11.1960 – 'Mystery 'things' observed in Bristol sky'/***Sunday Express*, **13.11.1960 -'Ball in sky puzzles soccer fans'/***Daily Express*, **12.11.1960 – 'Sparks in the sky'/***Gloucester Citizen*, **14.11.1960 – 'The Thing in the sky gave out great heat'/Personal interview)**

12th November 1960 – Cigar-shaped UFO seen

At 8am, Mrs Harold Isles from Uplands, Gloucestershire, sighted:

> "... a large cigar-shaped object in the sky, over Gloucester – just like an airship – resembling a huge mass of light, travelling south to north-east." (**Source:** *Stroud News & Journal,* **18.11.1960**)

Other sightings tell of an aircraft seen at 8am, heading north-east, at an estimated height of 25,000 feet over Wroxall. It was

> "... apparently followed by a round object", later explained away by the Air Ministry as being "possibly a drogue parachute being towed, or an aircraft towing a target for missile or anti-aircraft practice."

Was this the same UFO seen over Keynsham, Bristol, by Gordon Dewey, describing a

> "... long silver cigar, with a white trail ending in red sparks, going with a whoosh across the sky"?

15th November 1960 – Cylindrical UFO over London

Mr David Vessey of Uphill Grove, Mill Hill, Hampstead, London NW7, happened to look outside at 8.30am, when he was stunned to see:

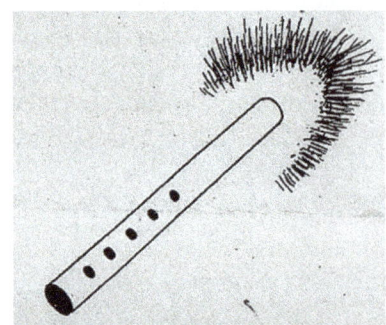

> "... a cylindrical object in shape, showing a row of four or five tiny windows on the side, fairly high up in the sky. It appeared to be silver metal and made a rapid course of about 40 degrees to 60 degrees from the horizontal, before being hidden from view by rooftops. The visibility was clear and the object was silent."

The authors include an illustration depicting a similar UFO as seen by allied serviceman during World War 2.

17th November 1960-UFOs follow US jets

At Lexington, Kentucky, three UFOs were seen to follow two jet aircraft. One object closed-in on the jets and then stopped, repeating this manoeuvre several times. Witnesses described it as being *"round, rotating, changing from gray to silver as it turned"*. **(Source: NICAP)**

30th November 1960 – Ice-blue UFO

An ice-blue object, *"roughly five times the size of a star"*, was seen over Cromwell Street, Middlesbrough. It was swaying to and fro in the sky, during the evening of 30th November 1960. It then moved slowly upwards and westwards, before flying off at terrific speed.

DECEMBER 1960

2nd December 1960 – Cylindrical object seen over Coventry

Several people in the Coventry area contacted the authorities after sighting

> *"... a glowing white, long, cylindrical object, about four times the size of a normal fuselage, emitting puffs of smoke as it passed overhead"*.

Various explanations were offered. They included: the reflected light of the setting sun on an aircraft, the planet Venus, or an American weather balloon. None of these actually appeared to correlate with what was seen. **(Source: Bob Tibbitts, Coventry UFO Research Group)**

As the year drew to a close, the *Eastern Evening News* (1.11.1960) told of a flickering orange 'cone' seen heading across the sky, east to west, over Norwich, followed by a similar sighting, at 4.30pm the next day, over Bungay.

(Source: *LUFORO Bulletin*, Vol. 1, No. 11/12/DIGAP/*Evening Chronicle, Cheshire*)

Left: Arthur Constance with David Jones

CHAPTER 2 – 1961

UFO REPORTS INCLUDE:

JANUARY:
January 1961 – UFO hovers over Shropshire Railway Station
5th-6th January 1961 – Freak storm and UFO sighting
10th January 1961 – Cape Canaveral, Florida
10th January 1961 – UFO seen to land at Texas
16th January 1961 – Did a meteorite fall to Earth?

FEBRUARY:
February 1961 – Evening Standard (7.2.1961) – 'Explosion scare ... it's a mystery'
27th February 1961 – UFO agitates dog at Michigan USA
27th February 1961 – Five 'flying discs' seen over Hull
27th February 1961 – Fiery object in the sky over Michigan USA
27th February 1961 – UFO Display
28th February 1961 – Waverley Air Force Base UFO tracked on Radar.

MARCH:
2nd March 1961 – UFO showing beams of light sighted
Early March 1961 – Rocket-shaped UFO seen

APRIL:
11th April 1961 – Cape Canaveral
14th April 1961 – A lecture on Flying Saucers!
18th April 1961 – Alien man seen at Eagle River, Wisconsin
20th April 1961 – UFO tracked on radar
24th April 1961 – UFO over California

MAY:
2nd May 1961 – Torpedo-shaped UFO sighted
12th May 1961 – Torpedo-shaped UFO sighted
15th May 1961 – Cigar-shaped UFO
19th May 1961, Long Beach, California – Another UFO Display!
20th May 1961 – Tyndale Air Force Base Florida UFO tracked on Radar
22nd May 1961 – UFO sighted over Florida Air Force Base
25th May 1961 – 'Bowler hat' shaped UFO sighted
May 1961 – UFO seen over RAF Bovingdon

JUNE:
June 1961 – UFO over RAF Woodbridge
18th June 1961 – UFO over Airport – tracked on radar
30th June 1961 – Two 'balls of orange light' reported over Essex
Summer 1961 – 'Spinning top' UFO seen by family over Staffordshire.

JULY:
4th July 1961 – Flying Saucer' over the Isle of Wight
5th July 1961 – UFOs sighted over the Isle of Wight
7th July 1961 – Four UFOs flying in formation seen over Michigan
11th July 1961 – Mysterious 'light' seen over Ohio
17th July 1961 – Low flying object over Las Vegas area
20th July 1961 – US Pilot sights UFOs over Texas
Late July 1961 – Police officer sights UFO over Wales

AUGUST:
10th August 1961 – Cyclist sights two UFOs
12th August 1961 – UFO, with 'fin', seen hovering in the sky over Kansas
15th August 1961 – 'Flying Saucer' over Devon
27th August 1961 – UFO over Wolverhampton
28th August 1961 – UFO with 'fins' on the side, seen by night-watchmen
29th August 1961 – UFO with occupants photographed!
31st August 1961 – Were RAF Jets scrambled to intercept UFOs?
Early 1960s – 'Mysterious 'ring' seen over canal
Autumn 1961 – UFO sighted over Birmingham
Autumn 1961 – Cylindrical UFO and UFOs over North Sea
Autumn 1961 – UFOs sighted over North Sea.

SEPTEMBER:
1st September 1961 – UFO display
19th September 1961 – Betty and Barney Hill UFO encounter, USA
23rd September – UFO Discussion, 'Brains Trust'

OCTOBER:
Early October 1961 – Astronomer sights saucer-shaped UFO
2nd October 1961 – US Pilot sights UFO over Salt Lake City
14th October 1961 – Further sightings of UFOs

Haunted Skies Volume Two Revised

NOVEMBER:
9th November 1961 – Lights over Warwickshire
21st November 1961 – UFO over Florida
23rd November 1961 – USA: Red object sighted
25th November 1961 – UFO sighted over Swansea Bay
29th November 1961 – Domed UFO sighted over Wales
Letter to the Prime Minister

DECEMBER:
11th December 1961 – UFOs sighted over Merseyside
12th December 1961 – UFO over Cheshire
13th December 1961 – Diamond-shaped object sighted over Washington
John 'Dennis' Llewellyn – *The Flying Saucer Pilgrimage*, by Bryant & Helen Reeve

JANUARY 1961

January 1961 – UFO hovers over Shropshire Railway Station

The tranquility of everyday life as a porter, working for British Rail at *Woofferton Railway Station, Shropshire, in January 1961, was to be irrevocably changed for Eric Lewis, after what he witnessed.

"I was accompanied by the Station Master and a colleague, at the time, and crossing the platform bridge, at 6pm, on the way home, when, to our amazement, we saw this grey/white object, resembling a double-yoked egg, about 25 feet in diameter and 70 feet in length, hovering a few hundred feet in the air, close to the BBC transmission masts, a couple of hundred feet away, rotating anticlockwise, spilling out constant streams of multicoloured light – like sparks, falling to the ground. A couple of minutes later, there was a subtle change, when the pulsing stopped, allowing us to see a cigar shape, with nine or ten lights across its middle. It slowly moved towards us, beginning to oscillate once more, scattering particles of golden flecks of light, illuminating the landscape below it, now beginning to take on an irregular shape, roughly 90 feet in length by 15 feet wide, looking more like a cloud of gas in a flexible skin.

The Station Master shouted, 'Quick, fetch a camera', at which point a beam of light shot straight at us, for a few seconds, before fading away. It was now pear-shaped, moving over the engine shed and saw mill. Suddenly, in a blur of speed, it shot upwards into the sky and was gone."

(Source: Bob Bierd, Birmingham UFO Society/Personal interview)

*Woofferton Railway Station, now privatized, was a BBC short wave transmitter. It switched from broadcasting *Voice of America* to the World Service during the 1990s and was the cause of problems locally, due to break-through and interference with UHF television, leading to many residents being forced to install early satellite TV. Woofferton was once a candidate for the building of a new town – due to the rail link with the West Midlands (now closed) and the still-running line between NW England and South Wales. It never happened, but there could easily have been a small city here.

Haunted Skies **Volume Two Revised**

5th-6th January 1961 – Freak storm and UFO sighting

A coastguard stationed at Shoreham, Sussex, sighted a brilliant 'white light' travelling eastwards, high across the sky. A few hours later, a freak storm struck Bournemouth, (then in Hampshire, now in Dorset), involving wind speeds of over 60 miles per hour, which caused structural damage to houses, and trees to be blown down. This was no doubt the same storm which hit Norfolk, the following morning – hardly ideal weather conditions for a UFO sighting, one would have thought! (**Source:** *Evening News & Star,* 5.1.1961)

Not so, according to Mr and Mrs Penny, from Swaffham, who were getting ready for work at 6am. As lightning flashed across the sky, through the torrential rain, the couple was shocked to see

"... *an object, about the size of a house, showing three brilliant lights, hovering silently over nearby power cables, crackling and spitting under the object, before shortly disappearing."*

(Source: Eastern Daily Press Norwich 9.1.1961)

10th January 1961 – Cape Canaveral, Florida

During this morning following the launch of a US Navy Polaris missile a 'flying disc shaped object' whose diameter was close to the length of the Polaris, altered its tracking, but did not block the missile firing. The tracking system in operation continued to plot the UFO and later returned to track the Polaris downrange. The diameter of the disc was approximately 20 to 25 feet and about 6-8 feet thick at its centre. It was visually lost to ground observers and primary witness (Clark McClelland with 10x50 binoculars) at the Cape as it continued downrange.

Source, *True Magazine* January 1965/NICAP Fran Ridge/*Flying Saucers Serious Business*, **Frank Edwards**)

10th January 1961 – UFO seen to land at Texas

At 9.12pm on the same day, attorney Mr W.K. Rutledge and his colleague drilling engineer – Mr George A. Thomas – were flying to Abilene, Texas, from Tulsa, at a height of 6,500 feet, when they sighted an odd phenomenon in the sky, about 1,500 feet above them, which they described as being a large, round, luminous craft surrounded by a brilliant glow.

Puzzled, Rutledge flew towards the object in order to obtain a closer look. As he did so, the object began to descend. At the same time a number of people on the ground sighted an orange glowing craft, zigzagging across the sky. One of them was the Guthrie King County Sheriff – Dub Holler; another, wife of Knox County Sheriff – Homer Melton.

The object was then seen to land less than ten minutes later by Mr Rutledge, a short distance west of Benjamin. He then radioed Wichita Falls to enquire about any aircraft trouble in the area and was told there were none. Mr Rutledge then spoke to Sheriff Melton about the incident, who told him he was assembling a search party while he continued to circle the object, which was glowing so strongly that it cast light onto the aircraft now flying at 4,000 feet. At 10pm, when the searchers were within one hundred yards from the object, Rutledge was forced to leave as he was running low on fuel. As he did so, the object shot up into the sky and was lost from view.

The next day Rutledge and Thomas made their way back to Benjamin, hoping to discuss the matter further with the Sheriff and newsmen, but were prevented from doing so by Air Force Intelligence Officers from Sheppard Air Force Base. This seems more like the script from *The Invaders* science fiction TV series, starring Roy Thinness as David Vincent, than reality!

(Source: Dan Wilson, McDonald list, NICAP/*Flying Saucers are Hostile*, **Brad Steiger & Joan Writenour**)

16th January 1961 – Did a meteorite fall to Earth?

Mysterious power failure in the North East – cause unknown. Serious flooding and a freak tornado, lasting five seconds, strikes Egremont, Cumbria, destroying roofs and causing damage along Eden Valley.

Was there a connection with an incident on 13-17th January 1961, when mysterious flashes of light were seen in the sky over the Cumberland area? Pieces of rock, believed meteorite, were later recovered.
(Source: *ORBIT*, No. 2, Nov/Dec/Jan. 1961)

FEBRUARY 1961

February 1961 – Evening Standard (7.2.1961) – 'Explosion scare … it's a mystery'

Police and Fireman were called out, during the late evening, after members of the public telephoned reporting a mysterious explosion, accompanied by a vivid red flash in the sky over Rutland Gate, South Kensington. A police officer said that nothing was found, although similar phenomena had been reported on the previous Saturday evening (4.2.1961).

27th February 1961 – UFO agitates dog at Michigan

At 10.15pm Bark River, Michigan housewife – Mrs Lapalme – sighted a fiery-red, round object, preceded by light rays, slowing down and then descending, causing her dog to howl. The object was last seen at 10.45pm.

27th February 1961 – Five 'flying discs' seen over Hull

An amateur astronomer from Hull was studying the night sky, at 7.15pm, when he noticed *five unidentified 'flying discs'*, heading towards Anlaby. One of these was seen to branch away, at tremendous speed.
(Source: *Hull Daily Mail*, 14.1.1961)

27th February 1961 – Fiery object in the sky over Michigan

At 10.15pm, Mrs Lapalm – a resident of *Bark River*, Michigan, sighted:

> "…a fiery red round object, preceded by light rays in the sky, which then slowed down and descended while my dog, who was with me, howled. Ten minutes later if was gone."

(Source: NICAP)

27th February 1961 – UFO Display

At 10.45pm a USAF Sergeant at Fort Mead Missile Master Center Maryland tracked on radar for approximately 20 minutes a cluster of three objects at an altitude of approximately 6300 feet. The objects had the ability to stand still and had a high rate of change of direction. Their speed was tracked at 900 knots with stops and starts.

28th February 1961 – Waverley Air Force Base UFO tracked on Radar

At 9:16 p.m. local time, a fast moving object appeared on a Mark X radar of the 788th Radar Squadron at 245 degrees at a range of 40 miles and on a SW heading. The object proceeded to a range of 125 miles at 240 degrees then made left turn to 230 degrees at 140 miles. The object turned inbound on a heading of 40 degrees and disappeared at a range of 30 miles. Length of observation was 10 minutes. All the witnesses were employed by the FAA as Flight Followers and considered very reliable.

(Source: Dan Wilson, McDonald List)

MARCH 1961

2nd March 1961 – UFO showing beams of light sighted

A mysterious object, projecting beams of light from its base, was seen travelling slowly north-west across the sky, between the horizon and the visible star-line, at 9.15pm. At the same time and date, Barbara Bowyer of Portchester, Hampshire, sighted:

". . . a white, top-shaped object, heading across the sky in east to west direction, over the Portsdown Hill area."

(Source: Isle of Wight UFO Society)

Early March 1961 – Rocket-shaped UFO seen

In early March 1961, people living in the southern counties sighted objects *"resembling a gigantic light bulb, or rocket in shape"* heading across the sky. This was followed by a report from Rowland's Castle, Hampshire, of a UFO seen at 9.45pm, projecting beams of powerful lights through the sky, as it headed north-westwards. **(Source: Isle of Wight UFO Society)**

APRIL 1961

11th April 1961 – Cape Canaveral

At 9:57 a.m. an object was picked up on ground radar at speeds between 150 knots to 600 knots. The object orbited six or seven times along an azimuth of 126 degrees between 10 and 55 miles from the Cape. The length of the observation was 30 minutes. The UFO was picked up prior to launch of test number 1352, a Polaris Missile. [Was there any connection with the January date?]

(Source: Dan Wilson, McDonald list)

14th April 1961 – A Lecture on Flying Saucers

18th April 1961 – Alien man seen at *Eagle River*, Wisconsin.

At 11am, local resident Joe Simonton heard a whining sound and saw an object, 30 feet in diameter, 12 ft high, with exhaust pipes around the periphery, land near his house. A door opened and a 'man' appeared, about 5 feet tall, wearing a black, turtle-neck pullover with a white band at the belt, and black trousers with a vertical white band along the side.

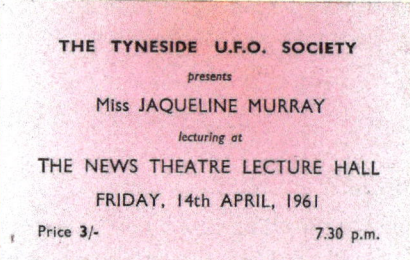

Two other 'figures' were visible inside. Simonton filled a jug with water, returned it to the 'man', who gave him three ordinary pancakes, and the object took off.

(Source: Jacques Vallée, *Magonia*)

20th April 1961 – UFO racked on radar

At 6.20pm, an object (at an estimated altitude of 97,000 feet) was picked up on a ANFPS-6A radar of the 791 Radar Squadron (SAGE), at a bearing of 96 degrees. The object disappeared after 1 hour and 4 minutes at 10,000 feet at a 95 degrees bearing. In the same month, a joint statement by 21 American scientists, released by NICAP, called for open investigation of UFOs without secrecy, the need for a more thorough investigation shown by circumstantial evidence. It was also suggested that the Air Force should have more straightforward information policy, specifically to give out all facts on major UFO sightings.

24th April 1961 – UFO over California

At 3.34am, Captain H.J. Savoy, and navigator – First Lt. M.W. Rand, were flying a USAF RC-l21D patrol plane, when they sighted a reddish-white round object, or light – similar to a satellite in the sky – 200 miles south-west of San Francisco, California, (35' 50' N, 125' 40). The object was observed for eight minutes. (**Source: NICAP**)

MAY 1961

2nd May 1961 – Torpedo-shaped UFO sighted

At 7.58pm a torpedo-shaped object was seen trailing sparks, in the sky over Staffordshire. At 8pm, a flashing object was seen in the sky over the Humber area, Midlands and Nottingham, by numerous witnesses (**Sources:** *Hull Daily Mail,* **15/26th May1961/***Birmingham Mail,* **13.5.1961/***Notts. Evening News*)

15th May 1961 – Cigar-shaped UFO

A *"long cigar-shaped object, showing an orange light"*, was seen by residents in Dumfries, Scotland, just after 9pm. It was – according to the local observatory – extremely unlikely to have been an aircraft or weather balloon.

19th May 1961, Long Beach, California – Another UFO Display!

At 3:50 p.m twelve shiny UFOs were seen manoeuvring erratically over the area and observed to moving with an odd fluttering motion. This was followed by two loud sky quakes (**Source: NICAP**)

20th May 1961 – Tyndale Air Force Base, Florida – UFO tracked on radar

At 5am, a round, rusty-orange coloured, object was observed near the Drone Launching Area. The object moved up and down and would gain altitude rapidly. The object seemed to float. Four Air Policemen saw the object. RAPCON was painting the target that the Air Police at the launching site had called in. An F-102 fighter was scrambled to run on the object. The object was travelling at 2-4 miles per hour and then up to 45 miles per hour. The fighter was getting a sporadic paint on radar. A helicopter was scrambled due to the slowness of the object. AF GCI (Ground Control Information) radar also tracked the object at a height of between 2,000 and 10,000 feet. Total time of observation was approximately 1 hour and 40 minutes. (**Source: UFOE, III; 85 pages of documents by Dan Wilson**)

22nd May 1961 – UFO sighted over Florida Air Force Base

At 4.30pm over Tyndall Air Force Base, Florida, Mrs Jones and Mrs R.F. Davis sighted *"a large, 'silver dollar' disc-shaped object that hovered and revolved in the sky. It then suddenly disappeared, 15 minutes later."* (**Source; NICAP**)

25th May 1961 – 'Bowler hat' shaped UFO sighted

Just after 10pm, Shepperton resident – Julia Cardoza (16) – noticed a brilliant point of yellow light in the western sky.

> *"As it came closer I saw an object, resembling a Bowler hat, the top part of which was glowing like an electric light bulb, but yellow light. Below it was a dark portion, around the edges of which were what looked like portholes glowing with a green light. I last saw it disappear silently behind rooftops towards the north-east direction. I estimated it was 20-30 feet in size and about 150-200 yards away from where I saw it, moving at about 20 mph."*

(**Source: Philip Heselton/***Flying Saucer Review,* **1961, Volume 7, Number 5**)

May 1961 – UFO seen over RAF Bovingdon

Mr Colin Johnson was on his way to work at 6am, when he saw what he first thought was

> ". . . the landing light of an airplane, descending onto the runway at *RAF Bovingdon. When I arrived at the farm, my workmate and boss were stood watching it – now stationary in the sky. As dawn approached, the 'light' moved silently away, until just a tiny 'star' in the sky."

(Source: UFOLOG)

JUNE 1961

June 1961 – UFO over RAF Woodbridge

Gordon Kinsey, in his excellent book – *Birth Of A Beam* – tells of an incident that happened near RAF Woodbridge, Suffolk, on the 9th June 1961, when it was alleged an aircraft was seen to come down by one of the airmen at the base. A full-scale search by military personnel from RAF Bentwaters, and civilian emergency services, failed to find any trace.

Gordon Kinsey died at the age of 92, on the 11th December 2014, after a battle with Parkinson's disease and dementia.

Gordon was "passionate" about aviation and wrote a number of books about its history in Suffolk.

During the Second World War, Mr Kinsey joined the Royal Air Force and served in the Far East as a flight engineer on Dakotas'. Kinsey married Margaret in 1943 in Newark, Nottinghamshire, and they had three daughters, Sallie, Margo and Carolyn. They made their home in Roundwood Road, Ipswich, where he was often visited by people wanting to talk to him about his books. Brought up in Kesgrave, Mr Kinsey was one of the first pupils to go to Kesgrave Secondary Modern School, now Kesgrave High School.

Gordon Kinsey

18th June 1961 – UFO over Airport – tracked on radar

The *London Evening News,* (19.6.1961), told its readers about a mystery object seen hovering over Exeter Airport, for up to an hour, the previous evening. A spokesman from the airport said:

> "It was seen on radar, north-east of Falmouth, and kept under observations for some time. We still don't know what it was. We think it was at 50,000 feet. We've had many calls from the public."

When the Air Ministry was asked for an explanation, they suggested it may have been a Skyhook meteorological research balloon, launched from Bristol. Enquiries made later, by *Flying Saucer Review*, revealed no such balloon had been launched.

A UFO was sighted over the New Forest, Hampshire, on the same day before disappearing in a flash of light.

A green cigar-shaped object was seen at 10.40pm, heading in a west to east direction, over the North East and Scotland.

A large number of people contacted the authorities reporting this phenomenon, which was later explained away as being a meteorite – a likely explanation, one would have thought, from the description.

(Source: LUFORO, Vol. 2, No. 9, September 1961/*The Journal*, 19.6.1960 – 'Green object in the sky starts North mystery')

---

*Royal Air Force Bovingdon, or more simply **RAF Bovingdon,** is a former Royal Air Force station located 2.5 miles (4.0 km) south of Hemel Hempstead, Hertfordshire and 2.5 miles (4.0 km) south-east of Berkhamsted, Hertfordshire, England. During the Second World War, the airfield was used by the Royal Air Force (RAF) and the United States Army Air Forces (USAAF) Eighth Air Force. It was assigned USAAF designation Station 112, station code "BV", later changed to "BZ".

30th June 1961 – Two 'balls of orange light' reported over Essex

On the evening, people living in the Colchester, Brighton and Southend-on-Sea areas, contacted the authorities, after sighting *two brilliant orange 'balls of light'* hovering in the sky, occasionally changing in brightness from yellow to dazzling white, whilst others reported seeing structured objects.
(Source: Alan Watts)

Summer 1961 – 'Spinning top' UFO seen by family over Staffordshire

During the summer of the same year, Josephine Cole and her family were driving in the Staffordshire area, when they saw, slowly descending through the sky, what looked like an old-fashioned spinning-top, shining like stainless steel. Curious, they stopped the car and watched, as the object began to settle over the top of an oak tree, approximately 150 yards away. A few minutes later, whatever it was, took off at terrific speed across the sky and vanished from view. **(Source: Mark Pritchard, UFOSIS)**

JULY 1961

4th July 1961 – 'Flying Saucer' over the Isle of Wight

At 12.35am, Isle of Wight residents – Mrs A.W. Taylor and her mother, Mrs C. Smith – were on the flat roof of Mrs Taylor's house in George Street, Ryde, overlooking *The Solent*. Mrs Smith saw a row of five 'lights' in the direction of Seaview. They looked like a ship, except for the fact that it was in the sky.

> *"The object came towards us and stopped at about eye level. It appeared to have a top and base, rather like a hovercraft, and the whole base emitted an orange light. It then disappeared at high speed, faster than any jet plane, in the direction of Seaview, leaving behind it a ring of smoke, which dissolved into a haze of light."*

According to Isle of Wight UFO Society researcher Mr Leonard Cramp, a world-renowned inventor, Aerospace engineer, and author, to whom we had the pleasure of writing on a number of matters over the years, he told us that in his judgment the two women were sincere and of unimpeachable honesty. He also brought our attention to a report of 'bright lights' seen by a friend of his in a remote field, several miles away. They were preceded by a mysterious whirlwind sometime before this sighting took place.
(Source: *Evening Standard***, 6.7.1961/Personal interview)**

The Isle of Wight UFO Society – Leonard Cramp and UFOLOG

At this point, it seems appropriate, following his death on 7th June 2006, to introduce the reader to the valuable contributions made by Mr Leonard Gordon Cramp, (born 10.12.1919), London, married to Irene Rose Cramp, 28.10.1920-14.11.2006, the holder of a life Presidency with the British Unidentified Objects Research Association and President of the Isle of Wight UFO Society. Len, along with John Feakins, Pat and Fred Smith, and Kath Smith (no relation), were all involved in the production and publication of *UFOLOG* – an early UFO magazine, which ran for over 80 issues. It was simplistic in form, but in its two or three typed pages, catalogued an extraordinary wealth of UFO sightings sent to them by other groups from across the British Isles. They were also members of the Isle of Wight UFO Society, which used to hold monthly UFO meetings at the Unitarian Church Hall, Newport. We felt honoured when Kath handed over the whole of their records, and gave us permission to refer to and investigate many long-forgotten and previously unpublished sightings which were brought to their attention, over the years.

Spacelink Magazine

Len and his wife, Irene, were also involved in the circulation of *Spacelink* – a UFO magazine, produced by Pat's ex-husband – Fred Smith, who now lives in France. Leonard, previously employed by British Aerospace, had worked for most of his life in the Aerospace industry, and was involved in special forward projects, which led to the development of jet propulsion, gas turbines, helicopters, hovercraft, rockets, and more. In 1977, he set up his own company, entitled *Airbilt Ltd.,* in order to conduct private research into vertical take off aircraft, and is best remembered for a number of books produced by him, beginning with the 1954 landmark book – *Space, Gravity and the Flying Saucer* – with an introduction by Desmond Leslie, published by Werner Laurie, for the princely sum of 10/6d (£0.52)

Leonard Cramp

Copy of the book handed in to Buckingham Palace!

According to Derek Dempster the first editor, of *Flying Saucer Review*, a copy of that book was handed in to Buckingham Palace, following which a second copy was requested!

5th July 1961 – UFOs sighted over the Isle of Wight

Several people who were living in the Ryde area reported having sighted UFOs. They included a Commander Mole, who was later interviewed by *Southern Television* and the local Press.

(Sources: *Isle of Wight County Press*, 8.7.1961/Leonard Cramp, Isle of Wight UFO Society, 1961)

7th July 1961 – Four UFOs flying in formation seen over Michigan

At 11pm, waitress Nannette Hilley of Copemish, Michigan, reported having sighted:

> "... a large 'ball', flying slowly through the sky. It then split into four after 45 minutes. The four flew in a close formation, before descending and heading away, westwards, an hour later."

(Source: Berliner)

11th July 1961 – Mysterious 'light' seen over Ohio

At Springfield, Ohio, ex-air navigator – Mr G. Scott, and his wife, along with neighbours, sighted a round, bright 'light', resembling shiny aluminium, passing overhead at 7.45pm, during the 20 minutes observation.

17th July 1961 – Low flying object over Las Vegas area

Two civilians in a car being driven along Highway 95, one mile north of Bonny Spring Ranch, near Las Vegas, saw through the rear-view mirror, at 2am, a low-flying object that overtook their car, followed by a rush of cold air. It was then seen to stop and circle the vehicle, before flying away and then lost to sight behind the mountains. (**Source: Jacques Vallée, Magonia**)

20th July 1961 – US Pilot sights UFOs over Texas

At 9am, Trans-Texas Airlines Captain A. V. Beather, was flying a DC-3, when he saw two very bright white objects straight ahead of the aircraft, hovering between 6,000 and 7,000 feet over Bayton, Texas. The objects disappeared on a heading of between 65 and 70 degrees, at 10,000 feet. The objects followed an erratic flight path. They appeared to be travelling much faster than an aircraft. Weather radar showed small non-persistent blips on the scope in the general area of the sighting, south-west of Orange, Texas. These blips were apparently not ground clutter.

(**Source: Berliner, Sparks, 42 pages of document by Dan Wilson**)

Late July 1961 – Police officer sights UFO over Wales

Police Constable Peter Buford, of the Glamorgan Police, told of sighting something in the sky over Pentre Meyrick,

> "... resembling a full moon, while driving a police car towards Bridgend. Oddly, a UFO was sighted in the same locality by two patrol cars in July 1958."

(**Source: *LUFORO Bulletin*, Volume 3, No. 2, March/April 1962**)

AUGUST 1961

10th August 1961 – England: Cyclist sights two UFOs

At 9.35pm, Peter Kent – a plumber from Harleston – was out cycling near Pulham Market, Norfolk, with his girlfriend, when they saw:

> "...two lights, pointing downwards in the sky, no more than a thousand feet in height. They approached to within 500 yards, before they disappeared in a blue flash of fuzzy light."

(Source: *North Norfolk News*)

12th August 1961 – UFO, with 'fin', seen hovering in the sky over Kansas

At 9pm Kansas City College seniors – J.B. Furkenhoff and Tom Phipps – sighted a very large, oval object, with a 'fin' extending from one edge to the centre – like a sledge, with lighted car running boards. It was seen to hover at a 50 feet altitude for three to five minutes, before flying straight up and eastwards.

15th August 1961 – 'Flying Saucer' over Devon

Mr R.G. Clift of Chelston, Torquay, was studying the night sky through binoculars, at 12.15pm, when he sighted a saucer-shaped object, emitting a faint blue light,

> "... which scintillated in the rays of the sun. The upper part, or superstructure, was of a burnished white colour – almost opaque – in strong contrast to the underneath, before it sped away towards the Berry Head direction. It then accelerated away in a burst of speed and was gone."

On the same day a UFO, described as *"looking like a hand mirror, reflecting in the sky"*, was seen heading westwards in a perfectly straight line, over the coast of Tyneside. (**Source:** *Herald Express,* **16.8.1961**).

Three *"pink objects, resembling inverted saucers, visible for only a few seconds"*, were sighted moving through the sky at incredible speed over Barrow, Lancashire, during the late evening of 15th August 1961. They were heading in a straight line north-west to south-east, according to local resident Mr M. Poland. The sighting attracted the attention of the Meteorological Office, who denied that they were balloons, adding: *"I don't wish to be facetious, but they could have been something from outer space!"*

(**Source:** *Western Evening News,* **exact date not known/***LUFORO Bulletin,* **Vol. 2, No's. 11 & 12, November/December 1961**)

27th August 1961 – UFO over Wolverhampton

At 8pm, a Wolverhampton housewife Mrs Lea, and her husband, sighted a long rectangular strip of brilliant light with a 'ring' at one end. It was motionless in the north-west part of the sky, for half an hour, before it faded away.

(**Source:** *Express & Star,* **date not known**)

28th August 1961 – UFO with 'fins' on the side, seen by night-watchmen

Night-watchman George Parr, from Wednesbury, was 'out on his rounds', at 5.18am, when he saw an object crossing the sky, with what looked like 'fins' on its side.

> *"As it passed overhead, one of the 'fins' fell away, causing me to speculate whether it was an aircraft or rocket, descending to Earth."*

Another witness – Mr Banks Fearon (a resident of West Bromwich) – described seeing an object resembling a military shell, showing three lights, with flames shooting from its rear. To his surprise, it returned over the area a short time later, and appeared to explode in mid-air. Two of the lights then vanished, whilst the other slowly drifted to the ground. (**Source: Personal interview**)

29th August 1961 – UFO with occupants photographed!

Mr N. Simpson was on a caravan holiday at Glasson, near Lancaster, when he,

> "... saw and photographed a circular-shaped object, hovering over a nearby field, at 6.45am; further photographs being taken as the 'craft' moved upwards into cloud."

We spoke to Harold Bunting – former head of DIGAP (Direct Investigation Group on Aerial Phenomena) – in 2006, hoping to glean further information as to the whereabouts of the photos. Unfortunately, he was unable to assist any further, but told us there were at least six other witnesses to this incident, involving *"what appeared to be occupants seen inside the 'craft', moving about."*

31st August 1961 – Were RAF jets scrambled to intercept UFOs?

In the evening, Mr Peter Crump was outside his house, talking to his uncle, on Burley Moor Road,

> "... when three English Electric Lightning jets screamed across the sky, at high speed – so low you could see the glow of their cockpits, as if they were chasing something."

The next day, he picked up the newspaper and saw the headline, 'Mystery plane buzzes Sheffield'. He said:

> "I wrote to the MOD, complaining about the aircraft flying dangerously low over the suburb. They wrote back saying they had no knowledge of any aircraft over Sheffield that evening."

(Source: Personal interview)

Early 1960s – 'Mysterious ring' seen over canal

Mrs Olivia .R. Boyce was living at Turleigh, near Bradford-on-Avon, Wiltshire, in the early 1960s. One day she was walking towards the village, down a narrow lane that runs alongside the Avon Canal.

> "I was with a friend and walking down the road, at about 3pm, when we noticed a large, grey, smoky circle – the shape of a ring doughnut – floating gently 6-7 feet above the canal – possibly 9-10 feet in width. We watched in amazement as it headed out of sight, totally unlike any smoke ring I have ever seen. This one was quite substantial and showed no straggly bits as you might have imagined if it had been a smoke ring." **(Source: Personal interview)**

According to Lionel Beer, founder Member of BUFORA – now (2010) the owner of *Spacelink* Books, to whom we spoke in 2008:

> "All 6,000 copies of Len Cramp's book, offered for sale at the British Book Publishing Centre in New York, were withdrawn from sale and pulped, after the firm went into voluntary liquidation. A year later, the firm was up and running again!
>
> When BUFORA (then BUFOA) was founded in Kensington, on 22nd September 1962, Len gave a talk on his theories to a packed lecture theatre, at an event arranged by me.
>
> There were even people standing in the aisles – something not now permitted under current health and safety rules."

Dawn Holloway seen here with Lionel Beer

"Over the years, Defence spokesmen have denied there was any serious official interest in UFOs.

Files progressively released by the Public Records Office, at Kew, show that there has been ad hoc interest, but few actual cases were investigated with much enthusiasm. It seems to have been general policy to downplay reports and occasionally censor the media."

Lionel told us that Len, (later to become the Vice President of BUFORA), had worked with George Bainbridge – the owner of a Somerton garage on the Isle of Wight – to publish his next book, *Piece for a Jigsaw*, in 1966, (reprinted in 1967), and had appeared at a conference in Birmingham, on 23rd November 1963, when he theorised how the Charlton crater had been formed in July 1963.

Lionel, who took over the magazine *Spacelink*, edited by Fred Smith, in 1967, was to visit Len and his family at his house in Cranmore, Isle of Wight, *"but I never saw inside the garage where the experimental models were kept".*

Piece for a Jigsaw and *UFOs and Anti-Gravity* were republished in 1996, followed by *The Cosmic Matrix*,

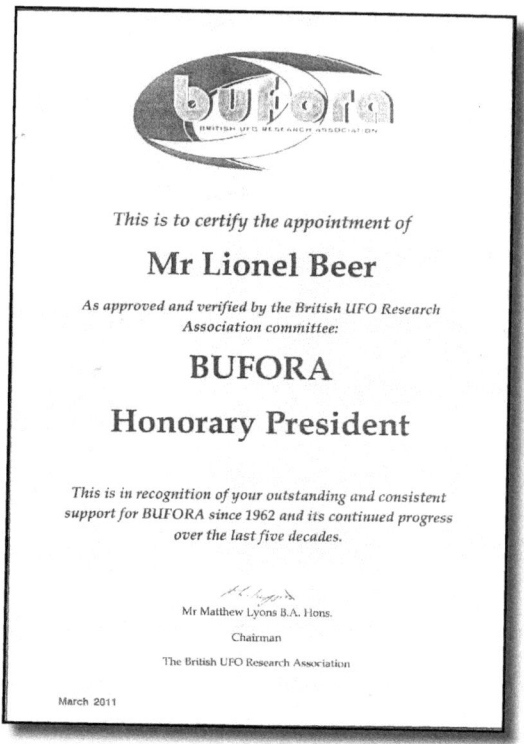

(1999), and the final book, *The A.T. Factor*, (AUP Publisher, 2001), (A.T.=Advanced Time Factor), which includes some of Len's paranormal experiences and encounters with UFOs.

(Source: Lionel Beer/Margaret Fry/Gary Cramp/Fred Smith, Kath Smith and Pat Smith)

Autumn 1961 – UFO sighted over Birmingham

In 1961, on a bright sunny day with a few scattered clouds, (exact date not identified), hundreds of people living in the Birmingham area contacted the authorities after sighting a highly polished object, motionless in the sky, about a mile above the City.

"Suddenly it shot off across the sky, stopped for ten seconds, and then flew into a cloud – never to be seen again." **(Source: Mr A. Cameron, B.A./Isle of Wight UFO Society)**

Autumn 1961 – Cylindrical UFO and UFOs over North Sea

One late evening, Keith Smith was returning from a fishing trip with his father, through Bentley, Warwickshire, close to the A5.

"All of a sudden my dog began to bark, for no apparent reason. I looked upwards and noticed a dim light moving overhead, through which could be seen a large cylindrical object that slowly descended over open land, to our left. Wondering what on earth this thing was, we raced along the road after the object, for a short distance, when it suddenly stopped about a hundred feet up in the air, just a few hundred feet away from us. I could smell something strange and felt nauseous – as if I was recovering from the effects of an electric shock, although I didn't experience the actual sensation. Within a very short time, the 'cylinder' rose upwards and disappeared into the sky. We decided not to tell anybody about the incident, believing nobody would take us seriously."

(Source: Personal interview)

Autumn 1961 – UFOs sighted over North Sea

A pear-shaped silvery object was observed high in the sky over the North Sea by Mr J.H. Upton – a deckhand aboard the British trawler *Lepanto*, during autumn 1961.

> "I called the others to come up on deck and take a look. To our surprise, another similar object appeared next to the first one. Suddenly, both of them shot away across the sky like lightning."

The Chief Engineer – Toby Barnett – confirmed the sighting, adding:

> "It looked like a miniature barrage balloon, pinkish-grey in colour, and appeared to be directly above us, revolving and forming shapes very high in the sky. Then another one joined, before both of them – now looking like parachutes in shape – shot away into the sky. They left no exhaust or smoke." (**Source:** Tyneside UFO Society/*Evening Telegraph*, 29.9.1961)

SEPTEMBER 1961

1st September 1961 – UFO display

Another UFO 'display' took place at 10.10pm over Nottingham. Celia Fox – a local resident – was out walking with a friend, Mr J. Berry of Chilwell. They were glancing up at the stars when they saw:

> "... a number of whitish lights, as bright as car headlights, darting about in the sky, in all directions – not in formation. There were lots of them visible in the northern part of the sky, between 30 degrees and 70 degrees. We watched for about ten minutes, until they became obliterated from view by gathering clouds approaching from the south." (**Source:** *LUFORO Bulletin*, May/June 1962)

19th September 1961 – Betty and Barney Hill UFO encounter USA

American couple Betty and Barney Hill's account of what happened to them during the late night and early morning of the 19th/20th September 1961 has so many parallels with *similar incidents which have been previously outlined by us in the various volumes of *Haunted Skies* over the years. Their encounter with the UFO and interaction with its occupants along with information obtained from later sessions of hypnotic regression is now well known and has been the subject of an enormous number of articles over the many years, reflecting the Publics ongoing curiosity about the event.

John Grant Fuller, Jr. – *The Interrupted Journey*

Their story the first widely publicized claim of what appears to be an alien abduction known initially as the *Zeta Reticuli Incident*, was adapted into the best-selling 1966 book *The Interrupted Journey* by John G. Fuller and the 1975 television movie *The UFO Incident*.

[There appears to be various front cover versions of this book as shown]

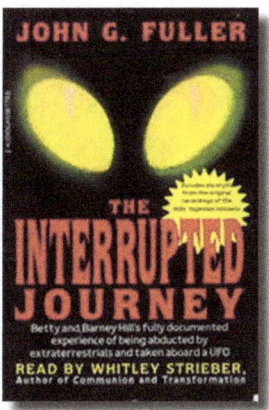
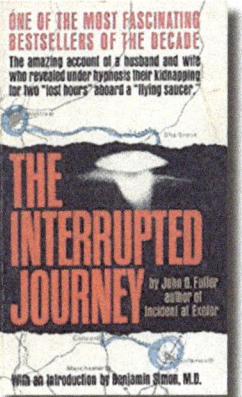

We have to say that were very impressed with the thorough account outlined by Mr Fuller contained in his book of 388 pages. In it John tells of meeting Neuropsychiatrist – Dr Benjamin Simon, in 1964, describing him as a man of impressive qualifications and Director of one of the largest State Mental Institutions in Massachusetts. The subject of their conversation were two of his patients Barney and Betty Hill, who had allowed John – then a reporter for *Look Magazine* – the opportunity to examine their medical reports, which included records and tape of their experience with a UFO, while in the White Mountains of Hampshire, a few years previously.

John Grant Fuller, Jr.

How it all began

At around 10.30pm on the 19th September 1961, the couple was driving back to Portsmouth from a vacation in Niagara Falls, Montreal, and Quebec, Canada.

There were only a few other cars on the road as they made their way home to New Hampshire's seacoast. Just south of Lancaster, New Hampshire, Betty sighted a bright point of light in the sky that moved from below the moon and the planet Jupiter, upward to the west of the moon.

While Barney continued navigating U.S. Route 3, Betty speculated if she had seen a falling star, but remained puzzled why it moved upwards, erratically, like a plane or a satellite, and growing bigger and brighter as it did so. Betty urged Barney to stop the car for a closer look, as well as to walk their dog, Delsey. Barney stopped at a scenic picnic area just south of Twin Mountain. Worried about the presence of bears, Barney retrieved a pistol that he had concealed in the trunk of the car.

A Craft is seen

Betty, fetched a pair of binoculars, and saw an "odd shaped" craft flashing multicolored lights, flying across the face of the moon. Because her sister had confided to her about having a 'flying saucer' sighting several years earlier, Betty thought it might be what she was observing.

Through binoculars Barney observed what he first took to be a commercial airliner, travelling toward Vermont on its way to Montreal. However, he soon changed his mind, when the 'craft' rapidly descended towards their direction. At this point the couple returned to the car and drove toward Franconia, a narrow, mountainous stretch of the road. The Hills continued driving on the isolated road, moving very slowly through Franconia Notch in order to observe

Betty and Barney Hill with their dog Desley

the object as it came even closer. At one point, the object passed above a restaurant and signal tower on top of Cannon Mountain. It passed over the mountain and came out near the Old Man of the Mountain. Betty said that it was at least one and a half times the length of the granite cliff profile, some 40 feet long, and that it seemed to be rotating. The couple watched as the silent, illuminated craft moved erratically and bounced back and forth in the night sky. As they drove along Route 3 through Franconia Notch, they stated that it seemed to be 'playing a game of cat and mouse' with them.

UFO descends over Highway

Approximately one mile south of Indian Head, the object rapidly descended toward their vehicle, causing Barney to stop directly in the middle of the highway. The huge, silent craft, resembling a huge flattened disc, hovered approximately 80–100 feet above the Hills' 1957 Chevrolet Bel Airand filled the entire field of the windshield [windscreen]; it reminded Barney of a huge pancake.

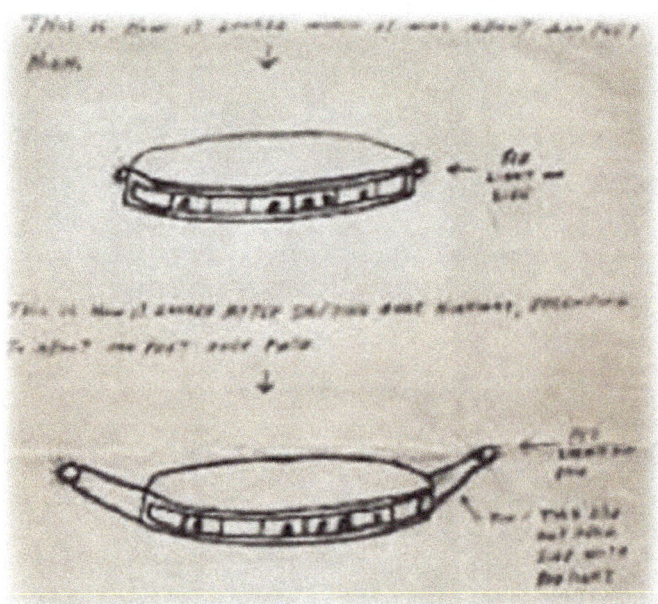

Suddenly, in an arc like movement, it shifted from its location directly ahead, and rested above the tree tops in an adjacent field. Barney pocketed his handgun and walked toward it. The silent enigmatic craft was huge; maybe sixty to eighty feet in diameter.

As he approached it, two red lights at the end of fin-like structures parted from the sides of the craft, and it tilted toward Barney. Lifting his binoculars to his eyes, he noticed a group of humanoid figures – eight or nine of them – moving about with the precision of German officers, wearing glossy black uniforms and black caps.

As the 'craft' tilted downward and began to descend toward him, one of these strange creatures, who remained at the window, communicated a frightening message, telepathically, telling him to *"stay where you are and keep looking"*. Barney had the immediate impression that he was in danger of being plucked from the field. Overcome with fear and with all of the courage that he could muster, he tore the binoculars from his eyes and raced back to the car. Breathless, trembling, and in near hysterics, he told Betty that they needed to get out of there or they were going to be captured. On the 21st October 1961, Barney reported to NICAP Investigator – Walter Webb, that the *"beings were somehow not human"*.

Entities seen inside Craft

Barney tore the binoculars away from his eyes and ran back to his car. In a near hysterical state, he told Betty, *"They're going to capture us!"* He saw the object again shift its location directly above the vehicle. He drove away at high speed, telling Betty to look for the object. She rolled down the window and looked up, but saw only darkness above them, even though it was a bright, starry night. Almost immediately, the Hills heard a rhythmic series of beeping or buzzing sounds, which they said seemed to bounce off the trunk of their vehicle. The car vibrated and a tingling sensation passed through the Hills' bodies. Betty touched the metal on the passenger door, expecting to feel an electric shock, but felt only the vibration.

Haunted Skies Volume Two Revised

The Hills said that at this point in time they experienced the onset of an altered state of consciousness that left their minds dulled. A second series of code like beeping or buzzing sounds returned the couple to full consciousness. They found that they had travelled nearly 35 miles south but had only vague, spotty memories of this section of road. They recalled making a sudden unplanned turn, encountering a roadblock, and observing a fiery orb in the road.

After arriving home

The couple began to experience odd sensations and impulses that they could not readily explain; Betty insisted their luggage be kept near the back door rather than in the main part of the house. Their watches would never run again. Barney noted that the leather strap for the binoculars was torn, though he could not recall it tearing. The toes of his best dress shoes were inexplicably scraped. Barney says he was compelled to examine his genitals in the bathroom, though he found nothing unusual. They took long showers to remove possible contamination and each drew a picture of what they had observed.

Their drawings were strikingly similar. After sleeping for a few hours, Betty awoke and placed the shoes and clothing she had worn during the drive into her closet, observing that the dress was torn at the hem, zipper and lining. Later, when she retrieved the items from her closet, she noted a pinkish powder on her dress. She hung the dress on her clothesline and the pink powder blew away. However, the dress was irreparably damaged. She threw it away, but then changed her mind, retrieving the dress and hanging it in her closet. Over the years, five laboratories have conducted chemical and forensic analyses on the dress.

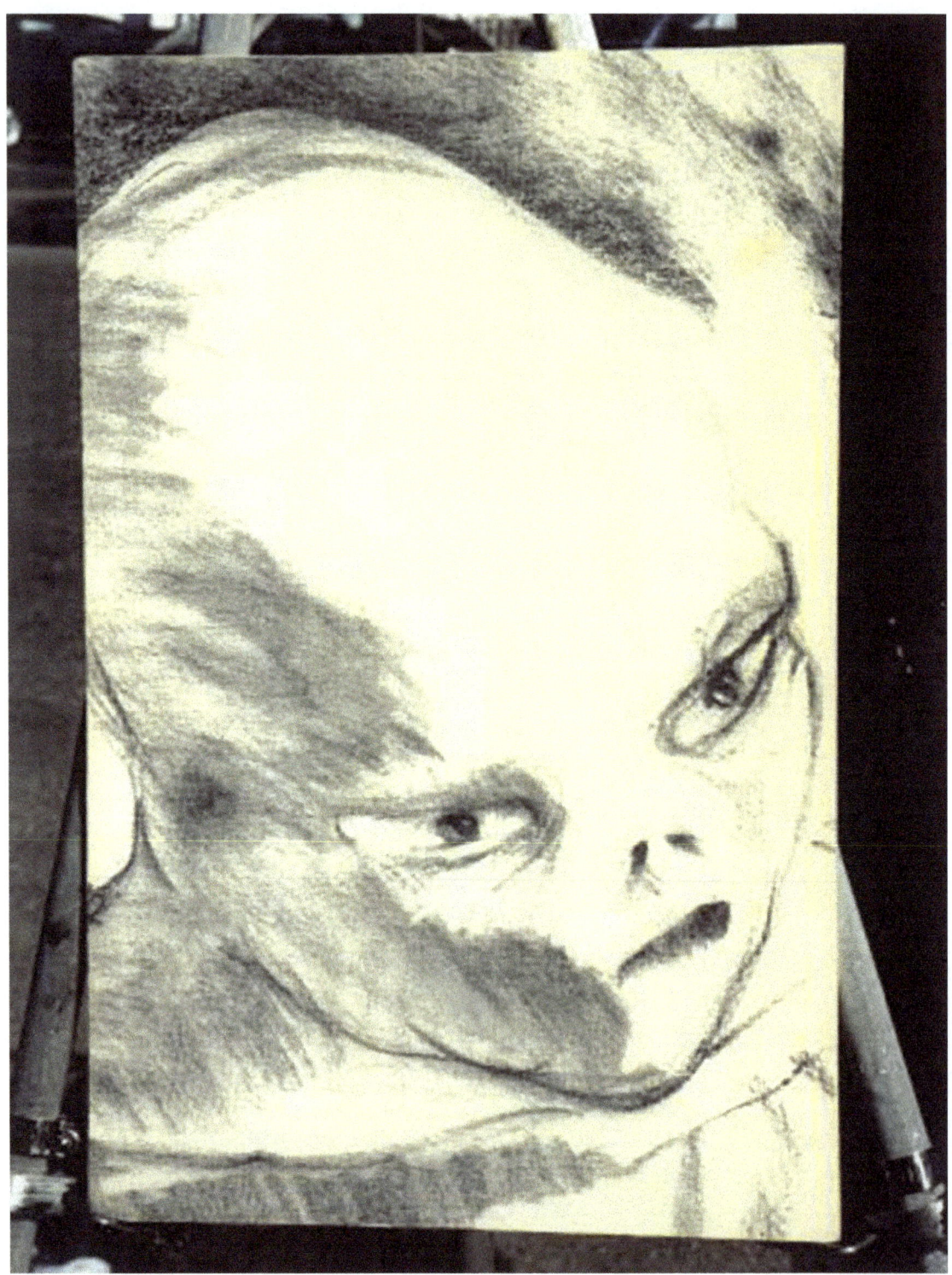

Over the years, five laboratories have conducted chemical and forensic analyses on the dress Betty wore at the time of her abduction

There were shiny, concentric circles on their car's trunk that had not been there the previous day. Betty and Barney experimented with a compass, noting that when they moved it close to the spots the needle would whirl rapidly, but when they moved it a few inches away from the shiny spots, it would drop down.

Incident reported to USAF and NICAP

On September 21, Betty telephoned Pease Air Force Base to report their UFO encounter, though for fear of being labeled eccentric, she withheld some of the details. On September 22nd, Major Paul W. Henderson telephoned the Hills for a more detailed interview.

USAF explanation – Couple had misidentified Jupiter!

Henderson's report, dated 26th September, determined that the Hills had probably misidentified the planet Jupiter. (This was later changed to "optical condition", "inversion" and "insufficient data.") (Report 100-1-61, Air Intelligence Information Record) His report was forwarded to Project Blue Book, the U.S. Air Force's UFO research project.

Within days of the encounter, Betty borrowed a UFO book from a local library. It had been written by retired Marine Corps Major Donald E. Keyhoe, who was also the head of NICAP – a civilian UFO research group.

Haunted Skies Volume Two Revised

To : Betty Hill
Re : Dress Sample

The chromatogram of the dress show a form of degradation that is consistent with high U.V. exposure. As an environmental fate chemistry specialist, I see these types of effects on a number of chemical compounds daily. As to the type of U.V. (nanometer range) an duration of exposure, I can not say with out more indepth testing. I based my finding mainly on the fact that the metals present in both the samples are about the same. As my counterpart has stated in his report there is an organic residue that he can not determine, I find this supportive of the degradation given that the dress is organic and these degrade faster under U.V. conditions.

As more time and resources become available to me, I will try to do more testing. Thank you for time and understanding.

Truly Yours

Matthew Moniz
Scientific Analysis Director

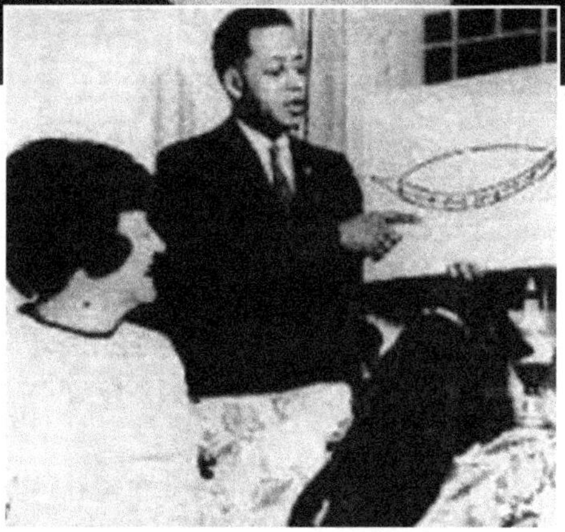

On 26th September, Betty wrote to Donald Keyhoe. She related the full story, including the details about the humanoid figures that Barney had observed through binoculars. Betty wrote that she and Barney were considering hypnosis to help recall what had happened. Her letter was eventually passed on to Walter N. Webb, a Boston astronomer and NICAP member.

Donald Keyhoe.

Webb met with the Hills on 21st October 1961. In a six-hour interview, the Hills related all they could remember of the UFO encounter. Barney asserted that he had developed a sort of *"mental block"* and that he suspected there were some portions of the event he did not wish to remember. He described in detail what he could remember about the craft and the appearance of the *"somehow not human figures"* aboard the craft.

Webb stated that:

> "They were telling the truth and the incident probably occurred exactly as reported, except for some minor uncertainties and

technicalities that must be tolerated in any such observations where human judgment is involved (e.g., exact time and length of visibility, apparent sizes of object and occupants, distance and height of object, etc.)"

Vivid dreams experienced

Ten days after the UFO encounter, Betty began having a series of vivid dreams. They continued for five successive nights. Never in her memory had she recalled dreams in such detail and intensity, but they stopped abruptly after five nights and never returned again. They occupied her thoughts during the day. When she finally did mention them to Barney, he was sympathetic but not too concerned, and the matter was dropped. Betty did not mention them to Barney again.

In November 1961, Betty began writing down the details of her dreams. In one dream, she and Barney encountered a roadblock and men who surrounded their car. She lost consciousness but struggled to regain it.

She then realised that she was being forced by two small men to walk in a forest in the night time, and of seeing Barney walking behind her, though when she called to him he seemed to be in a trance or sleepwalking. The men stood about five feet to five feet four inches tall, and wore matching uniforms, with caps similar to those worn by military cadets. They appeared nearly human, but with bald heads, large wrap-around eyes, small ears and almost absent noses.

Their skin was a grayish colour. In the dreams, Betty, Barney, and the men walked up a ramp into a disc-shaped craft of metallic appearance. Once inside, Barney and Betty were separated. She protested, and was told by a man she called *"the leader"* that if she and Barney were examined together, it would take much longer to conduct the exams. She and Barney were then taken to separate rooms. Betty then dreamt that a new man, similar to the others, entered to conduct her exam with the 'leader'. Betty called this new man *"the examiner"* and said he had a pleasant, calm manner. Though the 'leader' and the 'examiner' spoke to her in English, the 'examiner's' command of the language seemed imperfect and she had difficulty understanding him.

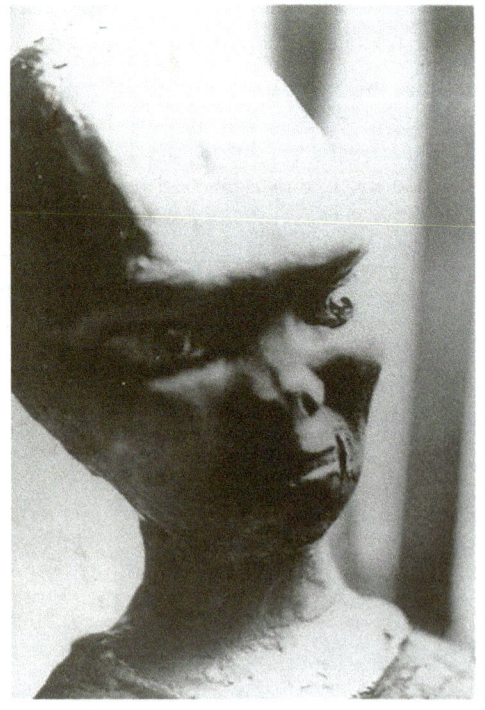

Medical examinations take place in the dreams

The 'examiner' told Betty that he would conduct a few tests to note the differences between humans and the craft's occupants. He seated her on a chair, and a bright light was shone on her. The man cut off a lock of Betty's hair. He examined her eyes, ears, mouth, teeth, throat and hands. He saved trimmings from her fingernails. After examining her legs and feet, the man then used a dull knife, similar to a letter opener to scrape some of her skin onto what resembled cellophane. He then tested her nervous system and he thrust the needle into her navel, which caused Betty agonizing pain, but the leader waved his hand in front of

Haunted Skies Volume Two Revised

her eyes and the pain vanished. The examiner left the room and Betty engaged in conversation with the 'leader'. She picked up a book with rows of strange symbols that the 'leader' said she could take home with her. She also asked where he was from, and he pulled down an instructional map dotted with stars. In Betty's dream account, the men began escorting the Hills from the ship when a disagreement broke out. The 'leader' then informed Betty that she couldn't keep the book, stating that they had decided that the other men did not want her to even remember the encounter. Betty insisted that no matter what they did to her memory, she would one day recall the events. She and Barney were taken to their car, where the 'leader' suggested that they wait to watch the craft's departure. They did so, and then resumed their drive.

Further interview with couple by NICAP

On 25th November 1961, the Hills were again interviewed at length by NICAP members – this time by C.D. Jackson and Robert E. Hohman. Having read Webb's initial report, Jackson and Hohman had many questions for the Hills. One of their main questions was about the length of the trip. Neither Webb nor the Hills had realised that the drive should have taken about four hours, but the couple did not arrive at home until seven hours after their departure. When Hohman and Jackson brought this to the attention of Betty and Barney, the couple was unable to recall almost nothing of the 35 mile journey taken between Indian Head and Ashland.

However, although Betty's recall was somewhat fuller than Barney's, both were able to recall an image of a fiery orb sitting on the ground. Betty and Barney reasoned that it must have been the moon, but Hohman and Jackson informed them that the moon had set earlier in the evening. The subject of hypnosis was mentioned as means of locking some of the unconscious memories. Barney was apprehensive about hypnosis, but thought it might help Betty put to rest what Barney described as the 'nonsense' about her dreams.

By February 1962, the Hills were making frequent weekend drives to the White Mountains, hoping that revisiting the site might spark more memories. (This was actually identified in 1965)

Meeting Captain Benjamin H. Swett at the local Church

On 23rd November 1962, the Hills attended a meeting at the parsonage of their church where the invited guest speaker was Captain Ben H. Swett of the U.S. Air Force, who had recently published a book of his poetry.

After he read selections of his poetry, the pastor asked him to discuss his personal interest in hypnosis. After the meeting broke up, the Hills approached Captain Swett privately and told him what they could remember of their strange encounter. He was particularly interested in the 'missing time' of the Hills' account. The Hills asked Swett if he would hypnotize them to recover their memories, but Swett said he was not qualified to do that and cautioned them against going to an amateur hypnotist, such as himself.

On 3rd March 1963, the Hills first publicly discussed the UFO encounter with a group at their church. On 7th September 1963, Captain Swett gave a formal lecture on hypnosis to a meeting at the Unitarian

Church. After the lecture, the Hills told him that Barney was going to a psychiatrist – Dr. Stephens – whom he liked and trusted. Captain Swett suggested that Barney ask Dr. Stephens about the use of hypnosis in his case. When Barney next met with Dr. Stephens, he asked about hypnosis. Stephens referred the Hills to Dr. Benjamin Simon, of Boston.

Discussing the incident at a UFO group

On 3rd November 1963, the Hills spoke before an amateur UFO study group – the Two State UFO Study Group in Quincy Center, Massachusetts. On 14th December 1963, they met Dr. Simon for the first time. Early in their discussions, Simon determined the UFO encounter was causing Barney far more worry and anxiety than he was willing to admit. Though Dr. Simon dismissed the popular extraterrestrial hypothesis as impossible, it seemed obvious to him that the Hills genuinely thought they had witnessed a UFO with human-like occupants. Simon hoped to uncover more about the experience through hypnosis.

Hypnosis sessions begin

Dr Simon hypnotized Betty and Barney several times. These began on the 4th January and lasted until 6th June 1964. Simon conducted the sessions on Barney and Betty separately, so they could not overhear one another's recollections. At the end of each session he reinstated amnesia. Barney described the beings as generally similar to Betty's hypnotic, not dream recollection. The beings often stared into his eyes, said Barney, with a terrifying, mesmerizing effect. Under hypnosis, Barney said things like *"Oh, those eyes. They're there in my brain."* (from his first hypnosis session) and *"I was told to close my eyes because I saw two eyes coming close to mine, and I felt like the eyes had pushed into my eyes"* (from his second hypnosis session) and *"All I see are these eyes... I'm not even afraid that they're not connected to a body. They're just there. They're just up close to me, pressing against my eyes."*

Barney related that he and Betty were taken onto the disc-shaped craft, where they were separated. He was escorted to a room by three of the men and told to lie on a small rectangular exam table. Unlike Betty, Barney's narrative of the exam was fragmented, and he continued to keep his eyes closed for most of the examination.

Barney recollects physical examination

He told of them applying a cup-like device over his genitals and that a sperm sample was taken, although he did not experience an orgasm. The men scraped his skin, peered in his ears and mouth. A tube or cylinder was then inserted in his anus. Someone felt his spine, and seemed to be counting his vertebrae. While Betty reported extended conversations with the 'beings' in English, Barney said that he heard them speaking in a mumbling language he did not understand. Betty also mentioned this detail. The few times they communicated with him, Barney said it seemed to be *"thought transference"*; at that time, he was unfamiliar with the word *"telepathy"*. Both Betty and Barney stated that they hadn't observed the 'beings' mouths moving when they communicated in English with them. He recalled being escorted from the ship, and taken to his car, which was now near the road rather than in the woods. In a daze, he watched the 'ship' leave. Barney remembered a 'light' appearing on the road, and he said, *"Oh no, not again"*. He recalled Betty's speculation that the 'light' might have been the moon, though the moon had, in fact, set several hours earlier. He also stated that he attempted to produce the code-like buzzing sounds, which seemed to strike the car's trunk a second time, by driving from side to side and stopping and starting the vehicle. His attempt was unsuccessful.

Betty recollects physical examination

Under hypnosis, Betty's account was very similar to the events of her five dreams about the UFO abduction, but there were also notable differences. Under hypnosis, her capture and release were different. The technology on the 'craft' was different. The short men had a significantly different physical appearance

than the ones in her dreams. The sequential order of the abduction event was also different from that in Betty's dream account. She filled in many details that were not in her dreams and contradicted some of her dream content. It is interesting that Barney's and Betty's memories in hypnotic regression were consistent but contradicted some of the information in Betty's dreams.

Betty exhibited considerable emotional distress during her capture and examination. Dr. Simon ended one session early, because tears were flowing down her cheeks and she was in considerable agony. Dr. Simon gave Betty the post-hypnotic suggestion that she could sketch a copy of the 'star map' that she later described as a three-dimensional projection, similar to a hologram. She hesitated, thinking she would be unable to accurately depict the three-dimensional quality of the map she says she saw on the 'ship'. Eventually, however, she did what Simon suggested. Although she said the map had many stars, she drew only those that stood out in her memory. Her map consisted of twelve prominent stars, connected by lines,

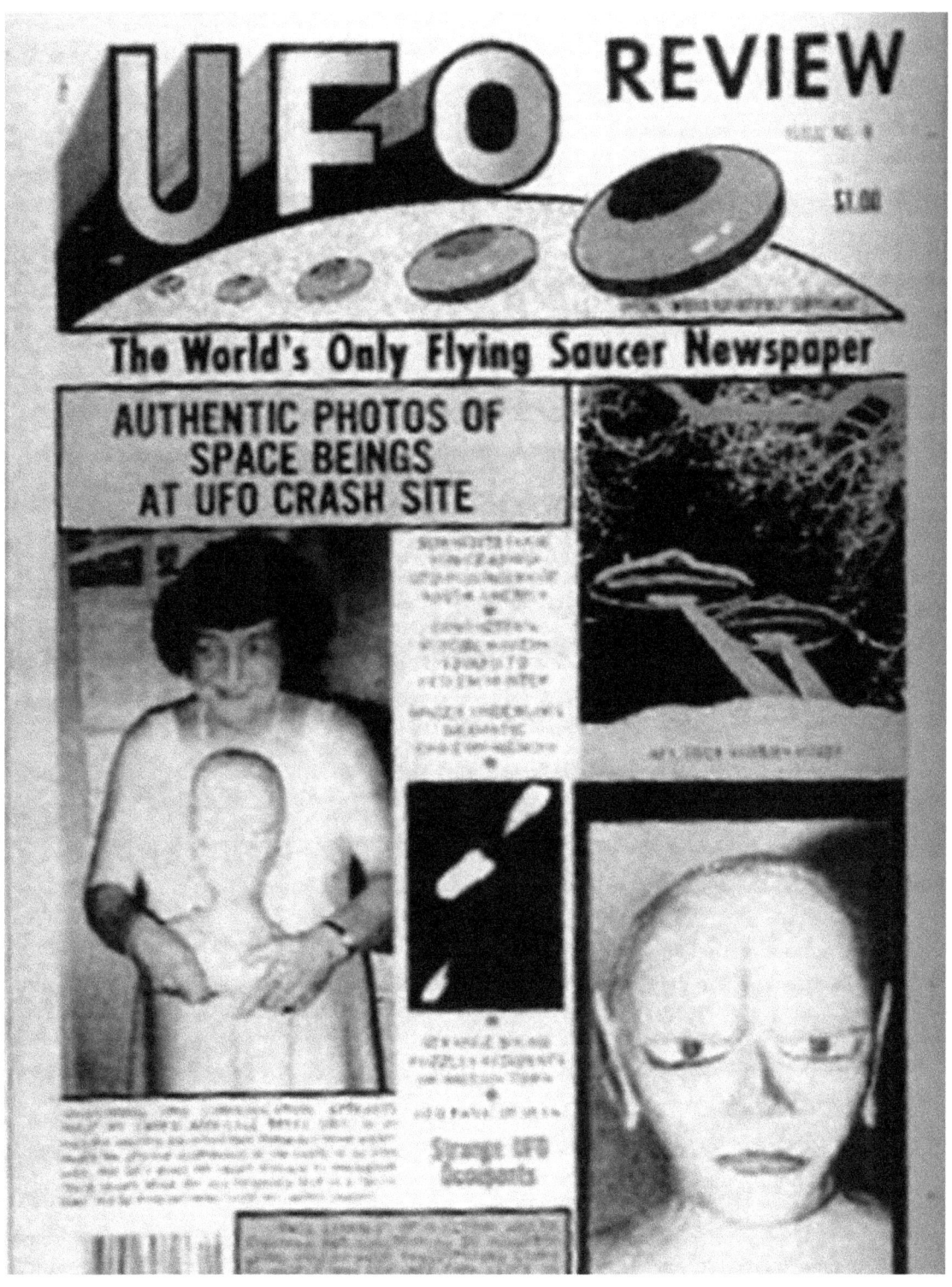

and three lesser ones that formed a distinctive triangle. She said she was told the stars connected by solid lines formed *"trade routes"*, whereas dashed lines were to less-travelled stars.

Dr Simon's conclusions

After extensive hypnosis sessions, Dr. Simon concluded that Barney's recall of the UFO encounter was a fantasy inspired by Betty's dreams. Though Dr. Simon admitted this hypothesis did not explain every aspect of the experience, he thought it was the most plausible and consistent explanation. Barney rejected this idea, noting that while their memories were in some regards interlocking, there were also portions of both their narratives that were unique to each. Barney was now ready to accept that they had been abducted by the occupants of a UFO, though he never embraced it as fully as Betty did.

Though the Hills and Dr. Simon disagreed about the nature of the case, they all concurred that the hypnosis sessions were effective; the Hills were no longer tormented by anxiety about the UFO encounter.

Kidnapped by spacemen

ON the night of September 19, 1961, Barney and Betty Hill were returning by car to their home in Portsmouth, New Hampshire, after honeymooning in Canada. While passing through the White Mountains on the U.S. Route 3 they saw what they thought was a star or strange plane. They stopped the car to investigate. But the object in the sky 'came over' from a star-like position to our area.'

Barney was quite upset so they got back into the car and drove on. Later Betty was again attracted by the strange object and again the Hills stopped to investigate. This time Barney claims, using binoculars, he was able to make out 'a large series of windows with creatures looking towards me on the ground.' Again he became upset and started to drive away. Suddenly there was a series of bleeping sounds and the car shook violently.

Later under hypnosis the Hills revealed that following the bleeps they were overcome by a daze and while in this state they say they were taken aboard the Flying Saucer for a medical examination.

Afterwards, Dr. Simon wrote an article about the Hills for the journal *Psychiatric Opinion*, explaining his conclusions that the case was a singular psychological aberration.

Back to normality – but not for long!

The Hills then went back to their regular lives and, like so many others that we had spoken to, over the years, were willing to discuss the UFO encounter with friends, family, and the occasional UFO researcher, but they made no effort to seek publicity for perhaps understandable reasons.

On 25th October 1965, the *Boston Traveler* (on its front page) asked *"UFO Chiller: Did THEY Seize Couple?"*, following information from news reporter John H. Luttrell of the *Traveler*, who had been given an audio tape-recording of the lecture the Hills had made in Quincy Center, in late 1963. Luttrell learned that the Hills had undergone hypnosis with Dr. Simon. He also obtained notes from confidential interviews the Hills had given to UFO investigators. This seems to be an abuse of confidentiality; surely the Hills should have been pre-warned about this.

[We ourselves learned of a similar incident which took place a few years ago, involving video tape-recorded interviews, conducted in the 1970s, relating to an allegation of abduction being given to a representative of a company that was planning to produce a film about the UFO encounter and sessions of hypnosis carried out later. The woman witness expressed much anxiety about this and, quite rightfully, felt this was a form of betrayal – never mind the awful possibility of seeing those very private images of herself during the emotive sessions.]

The Interrupted Journey

On 26th October, the UPI picked up Luttrell's story, and the Hills earned international attention. In 1966, writer John G. Fuller secured the cooperation of the Hills and Dr. Simon, and wrote the book *The Interrupted Journey* about the case. The book included a copy of Betty's sketch of the 'star map'. The book was a quick success, and went through several printings.

Following its publication various allegations were made by sceptics, who in their boundless enthusiasm to convince others that the world was a sterile place even suggested that the experience encountered by the couple could be explained away as a hallucination, brought on by the stress of being an interracial couple in the early 1960s!

In 1968, artist David Baker interviewed the Hills at length and later drew several sketches, after Dr. Simon placed Barney under hypnosis so he could be questioned about what had occurred.

It has also been claimed that Barney Hill's memories under hypnosis may have been by an episode of the science fiction television show *The Outer Limits* titled "The Bellero Shield", which was broadcast about two weeks before Barney's first hypnotic session. In this edition an extraterrestrial with large eyes was featured who says, *"In all the universes, in all the unities beyond the universes, all who have eyes have eyes that speak"*. It is alleged that similarities can be drawn between the wrap-around eyes, as drawn in the sketch by Barney, and the alien in this film. The less said about this the better.

1975 – Film *The UFO Incident*

Haunted Skies Volume Two Revised

The couple was portrayed by James Earl Jones and Estelle Parsons in the 1975 television movie, adapted by S. Lee Pogostin, *The UFO Incident*, and by Basil Wallace and Lee Garlington in the 1996 television series *Dark Skies*. The Hills were briefly pictured and discussed in the miniseries *Taken*. The book *The Chronologies of Babylon 5*, which describes the fictional timeline of the *Babylon 5* universe, states that the couple was abducted by a race called The Strieb.

The encounter was portrayed in a segment on the 12th episode of Carl Sagan's miniseries *Cosmos*, "Encyclopedia Galactica".

Details of the Hills' case were used in *The X-Files* episode, Jose Chung's *"From Outer Space"*. Certain components of the case were depicted in *American Horror Story: Asylum*.

Barney died of a cerebral hemorrhage on 25th February 1969, at the young age of 46.

Betty Hill died of cancer on 17th October 2004, at the age of 85.

[Authors]

Over the years we were to hear of numerous occasions involving reports of strange 'globes of light' seen by motorists, while driving along lonely country roads. Many of the reports concern an initial sighting of a globe of yellow or white light, approximately the size of a rugby ball/football, which would often fly alongside the vehicle, sometimes for many miles, before inexplicably shooting up into the sky. Sometimes people reported strange medical maladies afterwards which they didn't have before, others not. One cannot help but speculate whether just how many occurrences involving motorist [and human beings] are preludes to what could be referred to as an abduction experience? – A chilling scenario if it is.

Some people suggest encounter with UFOs and 'alien beings' can be explained by an altered state of consciousness, sleep paralysis, hypnagogic states, or misidentification of natural phenomena. We accept that on occasion this may provide some of the answers but not all taking into consideration that some of the incidents involve more than one witness who was present and occur during everyday activities, rather than bordering on sleep.

There is little doubt in our opinion that we were dealing with the same intelligence that was responsible for other interactions with human beings which had been committed all over the World going back many years. Whether it is actually representative of an alien species, indigenous to the planet, or examples of what some people claim to be paranormal or demonic are questions we cannot answer. All we can say is that our heart goes out to people like Betty and Barney Hill who often in the face of anticipated ridicule just tell it how it was- surely some day soon the People will demand an answer to what lies behind all of this – we all deserve that

Letters from Betty to Philip Mantle UK

Whilst space is at a premium, we felt we had to include some images from our colleague Phil Mantle – head of *Flying Disk Press* and a veteran of the chosen subject, who has committed not only time but a great deal of money in ensuring that UFO history is recorded for posterity. An example would be personal letters from Betty Hill to Phil, and other memorabilia.

953 State Street
Portsmouth NH USA
03801-4334

Dear Mr. Hanlte,

K T told me you were in this country, so I have waited until you returned home.

I am sending you three pictures. These are from paintings done by Dave Baker, a well-known artist. At the time, he and Barney were at the home of Dr. Simon. Dr Simon put Barney into a deep hypnotic trance and described several persons he saw. Dave painted these and then Dr Simon had Barney open his eyes and make corrections.

We saw 11 different ufo people, and none were identical, individual differences in each one.

The first picture shows the body build of most of them – not skinny little people but sturdy The person looks very similar to the one we called the examiner, for he did the testing of us

The second picture – of three, shows some of the differences. The one on the left has a round head, smaller in height than the others. I thought this one must have had an accident for the ends of his fingers were missing, with no fingernails.

The third picture is one of the crew members. On the cover of my book is one similar to the one we called the leader, because he spoke English in a limited way with difficulty.

These pictures are for your use only, can not be published. They have never been shown. I am sending them to you because of the alien autopsy.

The part of their anatomy involves the mouth area. If you could get information, it would be appreciated. We were never quite sure if it was their mouth or if they were using some kind of fixture, equipment. I did receive a phone call from a person who described what he had seen, the same as us. No name, but said he had done an autopsy. This was years ago.

After 30 years of travel, which included five years of college lecture tours, I have retired. However my mother and I did a tour of the UK, back in the 1970s. Two of my family lines came from Norfolk County, back in the 1600s; my third line came from there but I am not sure of the original area. He was here in the late 1500s. Then during WW 11, my brother was there, Air Force, bombing Germany.

Sincerely,

Betty Hill
Betty Hill

> 953 State Street
> Portsmouth NH 03801-4334
> 603 - 436-3803 Phone
> February 25, 2003
>
> Dear Mr. Mantle
>
> I have just received your letter of January 30.
>
> I am sending you a picture of a 'head' we made, which is a composite of the different appearances of the ufo people. Unfortunately the picture is not of the best quality. One mistake is the poor lighting of the forehead. Actually the forehead goes straight up and not slanted looking. This area is about th size of the face. The eyes are larger than ours, but not huge. They are wide-spaced and slant slightly upward.
>
> This bust has been studied by several anthropologists. They predict that about 25000 years from now, we will look like this - evolution.
>
> If your friend Rob Townshend wishes to call me, I am usually home. I do not know the number for this country but my phone number is above.
>
> Sincerely,
>
> *Betty Hill*
> Betty Hill

Parallels with the Abduction of Cathie Connolly, Meriden, Warwickshire, 1940

Bob Tibbitts – head of the Coventry UFO Research Group – interviewed Cathie Connolly about her UFO experience, which took place in the summer of 1940 on the outskirts of Meriden (a small village, situated near Coventry) when she encountered....

> "...a dome-shaped object, around which were a number of tall men, dressed in one-piece garments, with unusually high foreheads, strange eyes and tanned skin – very unusual in those days, as most people had pasty skins.
>
> A few months later, I was working in the chain room at Reynold Chains, Coventry, examining the metal links, when all of a sudden I became aware of a man next to me, whom I instantly recognised as being similar in description to one of the persons I had seen near the structure. He said 'It's your war as well. Take me to your King and Queen'. I was stunned. I told him I couldn't do that. The next thing I was aware of was lying on my back in what I took to be a spaceship. I tried to move but couldn't, as I was being held down by a number of strange men who had slits for a mouth, stretching almost to their ears, with cat-like faces and eyes devoid of the white part. One of them said, 'We are not going to hurt you. We just want to know if you are pregnant.'"

Bob:

> "I have to admit that when I first heard of what Cathie claimed had happened, all those years ago, it seemed too incredible to believe, especially when she revealed a number of journeys made in

the 'craft' (UFO) to places like New York and Rhodesia. However, as time went on, I realised I was dealing with a genuine woman who firmly believed, wholeheartedly, in what she had experienced – as opposed to any flight of fanciful imagination."

Kathleen Marsden – niece of late Betty and Barney Hill

Kathleen Marsden is a best-selling author, award-winning UFO researcher, lecturer, and a frequent guest on radio shows. Her expert testimony has been featured on the History, Discovery, National Geographic, and Destination America channels. She is co-author of *Captured! Science Was Wrong*, and *The Alien Abduction Files*.

"The 1961 abduction of Betty and Barney Hill stirred worldwide interest, because of the book The Interrupted Journey (1966), the subsequent media coverage and the 1975 TV movie. The case is mentioned in almost all UFO books. It has also become a target for sceptics and disinformation that has distorted the public's perception of the case. The true and complete story of what happened that day, its effect on the participants, and the findings of investigators has never been told until now.

Kathleen Marsden with Travis Walton (left) and Stanton Friedman

I can now share documented evidence found in government files, insight into the Hill's personalities and character, and their work with the scientific community, the evaluation of their evidence, and Betty's life after Barney's early death in 1969. This book is not a repeat of The Interrupted Journey. It contains never before released information."

23rd September – UFO Discussion, *'Brains Trust'*

There was a UFO meeting at Caxton Hall, London. The 'Brains Trust' panel included: G.F.N. Knewstub, Charles H. Gibbs-Smith, Desmond Leslie, and was reported on BBC Programme *'Today'*, broadcast on 26.9.1961. An Air Ministry employee was invited to attend, but refused. (**Source: LUFORO, Volume 11, No.10, October 1961**)

OCTOBER 1961

2nd October 1961 – US Pilot sights UFO over Salt Lake City

Private pilot Waldo J. Harris, of 631 Garfield Avenue, Salt Lake City – a real estate broker by profession – was preparing to take off in a *Mooney Mark 20A* from the North-South runway at Utah Central Airport, when he noticed:

> "... a bright 'spot' in the sky over the southern end of the Salt Lake Valley. I began my take off run without paying much attention to the bright spot, as I assumed that it was some aircraft reflecting the sun as it turned. After I was airborne and trimmed for my climb-out, I noticed that the bright 'spot' was still about in the same position as before. I thought it must be the sun, reflecting from an airplane, so I made my turn onto my cross-wind leg of the traffic pattern, and was about to turn downwind, when I noticed that the 'spot' was still in the same position. I turned out of the pattern and proceeded toward the 'spot' to get a better look. As I drew nearer, I could see that the object had no wings nor tail nor any other exterior control surfaces protruding from what appeared to be the fuselage. It seemed to be hovering with a little rocking motion. As it rocked up away from me, I could see that it was a disc-shaped object. I would guess the diameter at about 50 to 55 feet, the thickness in the middle at about eight to ten feet. It had the appearance of sand-blasted aluminum. I could not see any windows or doors or any other openings, nor could I see any landing gear doors, etc., protruding, nor showing."

Two miles away from UFO – seen hovering over Utah Lake, Omni Station

> "I believe at the closest point I was about two miles from the object, at the same altitude or a little above the object. It rose abruptly about 1,000 feet above me as I closed in, giving me an excellent view of the underneath side, which was exactly like the upper side as far as I could tell. It then went off on a course of about 170 degrees, for about 10 miles, where it again hovered with that

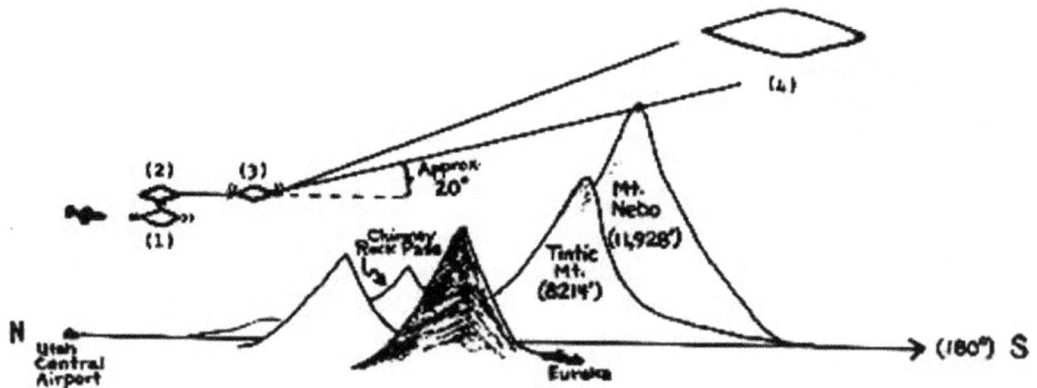

little rocking motion. I again approached the object, but not so closely this time, when it departed on a course of about 245 degrees climbing at about 18 to 20 degrees above the horizon. It went completely out of sight in two or three seconds."

Other witnesses on the ground saw it

"As you know I can keep our fastest jets in sight for several minutes, so you can see that this object was moving rather rapidly. All the time I was observing the object, after getting visual confirmation from the ground, I was describing what I saw on radio Unicom frequency. I was answering questions from the ground both from Utah Central, and Provo. The voice at Provo said that they could not see the object, but at least 8 or 10 people did see it from the ground at Utah Central Airport. As to seeing it again, I was returning to the field after it had departed when I was asked over radio if I still could see the object, and I reported that I could not. They said they had it in sight again. I turned back and saw it at much greater distance, only for about a second or two, when it completely vanished. The guys on the ground said it went straight up as it finally left, but I didn't see that departure."

One of the witnesses was Virgil S. Redmond (Map ref: 6266 S 2005 West Salt Lake City); he had just landed and said it wasn't there when he came in.

"Whatever it was seemed to be rocking while hovering almost stationary just south of the field, at times it turned it almost looked like a zeppelin, we passed the field glasses around and had a good view."

Other witnesses included Jay Galbraith – owners and operators of the Clyde Airport and Duane Sinclair – both of Lincoln, Nebraska, who were preparing for a flight. Robert Butler and Risa Wood nearby also watched it for 15 minutes.

On the later filled out NICAP report form, Mr Harris pointed out that the UFO at one time

"...passed below the horizon in front of mountains to the south. This fact rules out any astronomical explanation".

The incident was reported in the *Salt Lake City Tribune* (3.10.1961 – 'Saucer soars in Salt Lake. Sky-Disc eludes Pilot after chase')

On the same date it was reported by the *Desert News and Telegram,* Salt Lake City, that 'Pentagon calls Utah saucer 'Ballooney'', once again illustrating the need by the authorities to down play such events and offer a rational explanation – (where have we heard that before?!). In this article Air Force Officers at the Pentagon explained the sighting away as being the planet Venus, or a research balloon! Waldo Harris commented:

"If the Pentagon thinks I have eyes good enough to see Venus, at high noon, they are really off the beam. The object I saw was saucer shaped, gray in colour, and moved under intelligent control. I got within three miles of it and that is a lot closer than Venus. I have seen a lot of balloons too, and this was no balloon. It just doesn't make sense for the Pentagon to make such statements. Balloons move with the winds and at terrific speed. I'd like to talk to that Pentagon spokesman."

(Source: *ORBIT,* The Journal of the Tyneside UFO Society)

Early October 1961 – Astronomer sights saucer-shaped UFO

Derek Shelton, from Hull, was scanning the night sky with his 6-inch Newtonian astronomical telescope.

He was attempting to find a red star called Piscium, in the Constellation of Pisces, which was – at that time – observable in the south-western sky. During one 'sweep' of the sky with the 'scope', he noticed an object entering the right-hand of his field of view.

"I watched a saucer-shaped object travelling slowly across the sky and realised I was viewing something out of the ordinary.

Haunted Skies Volume Two Revised

I shouted for my wife to come and have a look, but in my excitement I knocked the telescope out of position and although I spent some time trying to find the object again, I was unsuccessful. I then made a sketch of the object I had seen, together with brief notes, as quickly as possible, while the incident was still fresh in my mind. With regard to the object, I did not see any lights, windows, portholes or other details common to aircraft, but there was seemingly a reflection of light from the upper part, which looked like a glow of some kind. At first I thought it might have been a balloon but there was no mistaking it for a balloon, as I had seen it in such perfect detail."

After careful consideration, Mr Shelton (an experienced astronomer for 48 years) ruled out any other explanation, such as a rocket, aircraft or satellite.

Coincidentally, a considerable time later, he was contacted by someone who corroborated the sighting; his sketch of the object being identical to Derek's and described seeing the UFO change direction several times, while flying through the sky, and occasionally hovering in mid-flight during 15-20 minutes' observation. Unfortunately, the other party was unable to remember the exact date and time.

Source: letter to *Spacelink,* Volume 6, Number 4, April 1971)

14th October 1961 – Further sightings of UFOs

The same newspaper – *Desert News and Telegram,* in their edition of the 15th October – brought the readers' attention to another UFO sighting that took place the previous afternoon – 'Sky scanners spot Weird flying objects at Sunset'.

Mr Remolds Miskin – head of the *Strange Aerial Sights Information Organization* – told of having received a report from Mrs Michele Burson, wife of Sunset's Mayor, who sighted *"four white circular objects, at around 5.30pm"* after her husband saw them minutes before.

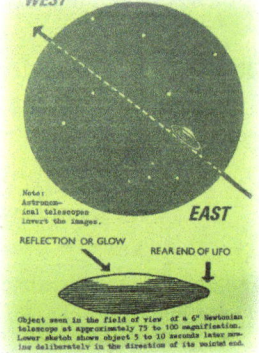

Mr Miskin went to visit the couple and found Mr Burson outside, at 4.20pm. He asked him what he had seen and was surprised when Mr Burson replied:

"There's one coming now."

Mr Miskin:

"I looked up and saw several of them but they had no definite shape – rather puffy and irregular, like puffs of cotton – moving at high speed in the same line of flight as the objects seen on Saturday. They were followed by something that had a far more defined shape to it, was round, and looked like the moon does in the daytime but much smaller."

Mayor Burson:

"They seemed to be attached together with long stringy stuff, and moved silently at terrific speed."

NOVEMBER 1961

9th November 1961 – Lights over Warwickshire

Ruby Llewellyn and husband, John 'Dennis' Llewellyn, living in South Green Drive, Stratford-upon-Avon, watched an intermittently flashing crimson light moving through the sky over the town, heading in a north-west direction.

John said:

"It stopped and dropped a short distance, now appearing smaller and fainter, and then reversed its direction – almost at ground level over open land, dotted with a few trees – before being lost from view behind a small sub Power Station, approximately 200 yards away."

The couple was concerned, believing that it may have been an aircraft in distress, so they telephoned 999. A search of the area revealed no trace of anything that could explain their sighting.

The following morning, Mr Llewellyn telephoned Air Traffic Control, at Gaydon, asking if any aircraft in distress could have accounted for the sighting. He was told they knew nothing about it, although the officer on duty pointed out that American aircraft carried a large red anti-collision light.

Butt of humour

However, if this had in fact been the case, other identification lights displayed by the aircraft would have been seen. The Air Traffic Controller added, humorously, that it could have been a 'flying saucer'. When Mr Llewellyn attempted to take the conversation further, the line went dead!

In the same month

We came across details of a sighting made during the same month at Wood Green, Middlesex, when an unnamed couple, who were standing in the back garden, saw a mysterious 'light', described as:

"...a whitish-yellow circle or fluorescent light pass over a neighbour's house and hover over an apple tree, a few hundred feet off the ground, before returning along its original path; a manoeuvre repeated twice, before disappearing for good." (**Source:** *Isle of Wight UFO Society*)

21st November 1961 – UFO over Florida

At 7.30pm, Mr C. Locklear and his companion – Helen Hatch, sighted a round, red-orange object, flying straight up in the air over Old Town, Florida. It faded away from sight, a few minutes later.

21st November 1961 – *Manchester Evening News* – 'They thought they saw.....FLYING SAUCER' – reports on a sighting from Frank Burrows of 18, Salisbury Road, Chorlton Cum Hardy, Manchester, a security officer who was with a colleague, one night, when they saw:

"...unusual cloud formation – like a sword in the clouds. A moving object came out of the 'hilt', shone like silver in the moonlight, and looked like a submarine in shape, at arm's length, 3 inches long. It disappeared into the darkness 35 minutes later. We saw a smaller one travelling in the same direction."

23rd November 1961 – USA: Red object sighted

Over Sioux City, Iowa a bright red star object was reported by local man Mr F Braunger heading across the sky on a straight and level course at 9.30pm. Fifteen minutes later it was out of sight.

25th November 1961 – UFO sighted over Swansea Bay

Alan Williams of Hazel Road, Uplands, told his headmaster what he had seen. In turn, the police were telephoned. Alan described it as being:

"... luminous, sausage-shaped, with a circular dome on top and two glass cowls fore and aft, with flames issuing from the rear, heading from the direction of the Mumbles towards Port Talbot."
(**Source:** *Herald of Wales*, 25.11.1961 – 'Mystery object over Bay')

29th November 1961 – Domed UFO sighted over Wales

At 6.15pm, Swansea resident – Alan Williams – saw an object flash across the sky, heading towards Port Talbot.

"It was oval, with two windows at the front – one fully in view, the other partly. There was a dome on top. It was trailing red flames, which illuminated the object – out of sight in five seconds. It was not an aircraft, as it had no wings or tail fin."

(**Source:** *Western Mail*, 22.11.1961/LUFORO, Vol. 3, No. 1, Jan/Feb. 1962)

In the same month an object, resembling a 'silver sword' was seen in the night sky over Manchester. A second smaller object was also seen.
(**Source:** *Manchester Evening News*, 21.11.1961 – 'They thought they saw a flying saucer')

A cigar-shaped object, with a dome on top and a 'glass' dome at each end, issuing flames, was seen heading across the sky from Mumbles, towards Port Talbot.
(**Source:** *Herald of Wales*, 25.11.1961 – 'Mystery object over Bay')

Letter to the Prime Minister!

An open letter to Lord Hailsham

The Rt. Hon. Viscount Hailsham, Q.C.,
Lord President of the Council and
   Minister for Science,
Office of the Minister for Science,
2, Richmond Terrace,
Whitehall,
London, S.W.1.

My Lord,

In November, 1961, I submitted to the Prime Minister an open letter drawing his attention to the danger that could arise if an unidentified flying object were to be misinterpreted as a hostile weapon launched by a potential enemy of this country. My letter was also intended as a plea for the ending of secrecy surrounding this phenomenon which has puzzled mankind for the last fifteen years. My letter was acknowledged by the Prime Minister, who informed me that it had been passed to you. Subsequently, after a reminder, I received a bare acknowledgment from you and there the matter was allowed to rest.

I am now writing again to draw your attention to the series of sightings that have occurred this year over the North of England, particularly the Sheffield area. In February a photograph was taken of a number of mysterious objects; in August scores of people saw similar objects and on one occasion a colour film corroborated the testimony of a Sheffield man and his three witnesses. On another occasion, three of the staff of the *Sheffield Telegraph* were able to add their testimony to yet another remarkable occurrence. Full reports are available and the series of events was treated in great detail by the Press, both national and local, and by the B.B.C.

My purpose now is to enquire whether your Ministry is aware of these reports and, if so, whether you and your Advisory Council are studying this matter, which may be of the greatest importance not only to the people of this country but to all mankind.

This letter will be published in the November-December issue of the FLYING SAUCER REVIEW, due for publication during the first week of November. I am reserving space for your reply, which I feel sure will be of the greatest possible interest to my readers.

I am, My Lord,
   Your obedient Servant,
      (Signed) Waveney Girvan,
         Editor.

On September 11, Lord Hailsham's Private Secretary sent the following reply:
      September 11, 1962.

Dear Mr. Girvan,

I am writing to acknowledge receipt of your letter of September 8 to Lord Hailsham about the reports of unidentified flying objects.

The Office of the Minister for Science is not, however, studying this matter.

Yours sincerely,
   (K. R. Mears)
     Private Secretary.

To conclude the matter the Editor sent the following communication:
      September 15, 1962.

Dear Mr. Mears,

I am sorry that you should have been troubled with my letter of September 8 as I now learn that the Ministry for Science is not studying reports of unidentified flying objects. As I explained in my previous letter, the only reason that I approached your Ministry was because last year when I wrote to the Prime Minister on the subject he referred my letter to you. Perhaps you would be good enough to inform the Prime Minister as well that yours is not the Ministry concerned.

Yours sincerely,
   (Signed) Waveney Girvan,
      Editor.

DECEMBER 1961

11th December 1961 – UFOs sighted over Merseyside

Mr Aubrey C Fishel (40) – a decorator's merchant – of Menlove Gardens West, Liverpool, was driving along the main road between Liverpool and Bootle, at 10am, when:

> "I noticed an object ahead of me, about 45 degrees above the horizon. It was elliptical in shape, clearly outlined, reflecting like aluminum, showing a green fluorescent top. Almost immediately, I observed a similar object to my right at a bearing of about 30 degrees, but at a higher elevation of 60 degrees. About 20 seconds later this object departed, northwards, at incredible speed, leaving a thin trail of black smoke as it did so, which quickly dissipated."

Mr Fishel rang the local Press and told them what he had witnessed. They confirmed that no one else had telephoned them about this sighting. (**Source: LUFORO**)

12th December 1961 – UFO over Cheshire

At 9.36pm, Harold Bunting of Hazel Grove, Stockport, Cheshire, was in the process of putting his car in the garage, when he noticed a bright object, low down in the sky, at an estimated height of 2,500 feet:

> "I called my wife, expressing amazement at its size and lack of noise, and watched it for a few minutes until it performed a right-angled turn upwards, and was lost from view behind houses opposite. I am certain this was no balloon, satellite, meteorite or aircraft."

At 10pm on the same date, Jennifer Holberton was travelling in a car on the way back from Chelmsford, Essex. The car was approaching Kelvedon when she sighted two 'lights' in the sky, which vanished one by one, *"leaving a long grey object; this also vanished, a few minutes later."*

Source: *LUFORO Bulletin,* **March/April 1962, Volume 3, No. 2)**

13th December 1961 – Diamond-shaped object sighted over Washington

The crew of an aircraft, Mr C.F Muncy (an ex-U.S. Navy pilot), W.J. Myers and G. Weber, were over Washington, D.C., at 5.05pm, when they saw a dark, diamond-shaped object with a bright tip, flying level in the sky adjacent to them, for a few minutes.

Robin and Gavin Gibbons, 'The Coming Of The Spaceships'

During our research we met Robin Gibbons and his wife, Margaret, who took time to talk about his brother, Gavin Gibbons – author and linguist – who was married to Irene Rosalind Anderson of Aberdeen (a fellow traveller and linguist) at the nearby church on 27th April 1963. Gavin wrote *The Coming Of The Space Ships, Meole Brace Through the Centuries, They Rode In Space Ships, Trains Under The Channel* and a science fiction novel *By Space Ship To The Moon* (1958). He also wrote various letters to *Saucer Forum*, which formed the subject of lively debate during the early 1960s:

> "I think that the 'flying saucers' and their pilots are friendly, or indifferent. The pilots are from another world, probably outside our solar system, and that the subject of saucer research is a completely scientific one, and has nothing to do with religion. I also believe that spirits exist, and that most of them are evil. I do not think those in the 'saucers' are spirits, but do feel that spirits – for whatever reason of their own – do not wish Mankind to have knowledge of the 'saucers'. This is done in various ways; firstly by making enthusiasts lose interest in the subject – the fact that I have been concentrating to write two books on it sickened me of 'saucers' for a long period in 1957-1958, and I did little about them. I am sure that the spirits were behind my temporary loss of interest."

The Influence of Spirits

Gavin goes on to say that he also attributes the influence of the 'spirits' in encouraging enthusiasts to quarrel amongst themselves, and suggests that 'spirits' were responsible for breaking up the West Midlands Flying Saucer Club, commenting that the...

> "'Saucer people' are fallen angels of evil disposition. The spirits cause cases like that of Mrs Appleton, to confuse 'saucer' enthusiasts, and make non-believers scoff. They impersonate 'saucers' occasionally, and destroy aircraft to make people afraid of what are really friendly and benevolent creatures. I am convinced that the 'closing down' of people are due to spirit activity. I used to think that the men in the dark suits [Men in Black?] who closed down Al Bender were bureaucrats. I now think they were spirits disguised as men.
>
> It would have been interesting to have examined the texture and tailoring of their dark suits."

Gavin Gibbons

John 'Dennis' Llewellyn – *The Flying Saucer Pilgrimage*, by Bryant and Helen Reeve:

John 'Dennis' Llewellyn, in a letter to the same journal, complained of the UFO solution being as far away as ever, despite the passing of 14 years, and referred the readers to a book dealing with contactees that he considered a significant contribution to UFO research – *The Flying Saucer Pilgrimage*, by Bryant & Helen Reeve:

> "Space people have been visiting us for a long time now, being physical craft from Mars and Venus, but there are also etheric vehicles or the manifestations of highly evolved personnel themselves, which have tended to cause confusion in UFO reports."

John also believed that 'space people' live and work on the planet.

Mr E.V. Inglesby of Truro, Cornwall, also wrote in the same journal pointing out

> "... that spirits do exist but they are both good and evil, extraterritorial spacecraft exist, too, and they are roughly of two kinds, since we cannot do any good things without thee O God, let us be careful of pointing our religion first and pursue our researches trusting in the spirit to keep us free from harm because, in my opinion, some of us are fishing in very dangerous waters."

Tried to stop the Queen from watching film!

Was this gentleman related to the Reverend Paul Inglesby? Because Lieutenant-Commander the Reverend Paul Inglesby, whom we met some years ago (died in 2010, aged 94) held unconventional views on the origin of Unidentified Flying Objects (UFOs) and was alleged to have tried to stop the Queen watching Steven Spielberg's alien film *Close Encounters Of The Third Kind*, claiming it was a Satanic plot to seize control of her mind!

Wilfred Daniels, Stafford based UFO researcher

"The UFO may not yet be proved to be spaceships from another world, but neither are they to be accounted for by any terrestrial yardstick, and therefore as true 'unknowns' are just as likely to be Venusian spaceships as anything else. While the 'flying saucer' has not been acceptably proved to be a spaceship, emphatically it has been proved to exist – to be a 'something', and not to be categorised with balloons, birds, lights, weather-effects, hoaxes, etc. Some there are, it seems, who 'scream the loudest' just before they are hurt. One might be inclined to wonder how – just after 15 years – the UFO would hurt the USA, for there is no Government that screams louder than that of the US on the subject of 'flying saucers'."

(Sources: *Saucer Forum*, Vol. 2, 3, No. 4, November 1960/1961/*Saucer Forum*, Vol. 2, No. 2, May 1960/*Orbit*, Nov/Dec/Jan/1961)

Obituary on Paul Inglesby

Lt. Cdr the Reverend Paul Inglesby (Father Paul) died on May 26th, 2010, aged 94.

Born Eric Vredenburg in 1915 during a Zeppelin raid over London to a Dutch entrepreneur father and an Afrikaner mother, Eric Paul Inglesby was educated at the NCP with a view to joining the Royal Navy. Failing to get into Dartmouth in 1932 owing to short-sightedness, he joined the Navy in 1933 as a special entry Paymaster Cadet. During World War 11 he saw active service in the Mediterranean and was mentioned in dispatches in February 1941 when a ship he was serving in was sunk. He was one of the last naval evacuees from Crete later that year.

Invalided out of the RN in 1944 he studied at Oxford University 1945-46 where he gained a degree in PPE. Subsequently, reflecting his love of sailing, he moved to Cornwall where he worked for the Cornish education department from 1954-63. At this point he began a religious life, first as a Church of England priest. He was ordained in 1964 and later held church posts in Plymouth, Caythorpe and the Isles of Scilly between 1965 and 1976.

At this point Inglesby's longtime fascination dating back to childhood with Unidentified Flying Objects (UFOs) began to dominate his life. In a book he published in 1978 he argued that UFOs were of satanic origin. Later that year he formed the Christian UFO Research Association. In 1980 he converted to the Greek Orthodox Church and took the name Father Paul. He spent the following two decades alerting the world to the risks of UFOs and in 1996 collaborated with Admiral of the Fleet Lord Hill-Norton to write *"The UFO Concern Report"* which was privately published. Besides books on UFOs Inglesby wrote several religious tracts and was an inveterate letter writer to The Daily Telegraph.

(Source: www. Old Pangbournian Society)

Lt. Cdr the Reverend Paul Inglesby

CHAPTER 3 – 1962

UFO REPORTS INCLUDE:

JANUARY:
January 1962 – 'Flying Saucer' over Sutton Coldfield, Warwickshire
13th January 1962 – Mysterious green fireballs sighted
15th January 1962 – Rotating UFO sighted over Lancashire
18th January 1962 – Blue 'light' over Southampton
19th January 1962 – UFO over Southampton Docks
20th January 1962 – Green 'ball of fire' over Stafford
29th January 1962 – UFO over Bolton, Lancashire

FEBRUARY:
9th February 1962 – England: 'Flying Saucer' over Aston Clinton
9th February 1962 – Mysterious 'light' over Luton, Bedfordshire
16th February 1962 – Aluminum object sighted in the sky over Leeds
28th February 1962 – UFO photographed over Sheffield
February 1962 – USAF attempts to intercept UFO
20th February 1962 – UFO sighting from Mercury Capsule

MARCH:
6th March 1962 – Larger red rotating object seen
17th March 1962 – 'Flying Saucers' over Bristol

APRIL:
15th April 1962 – Nine objects seen over the Northumberland Moors
27th April 1962 – Strange object seen over Dumfries
Late April 1962 – USA: Pilot sights five UFOs while on record-breaking flight.

MAY:
8th May 1962 – Bright object over Newcastle-on-Tyne
17th May 1962 – UFO sighted, and then RAF Bomber appears
19th May 1962 – UFO making humming noise sighted over Scotland
21st May 1962 – Pilot sights UFO over Wales
25th May 1962 – UFO over Lancashire
26th May 1962 – Silver and black UFO sighted over Cornwall.

JUNE:
11th June 1962 – Police Officer sights UFO over Welsh mountain

1962 – Triangular UFO over Newcastle-on-Tyne, England
Summer 1962 – Revolving UFO near airfield
Summer 1962 – UFO over Derbyshire
1962 – 'Flying Saucer' over Smethwick

JULY:
1st July 1962 – Strange phenomena sighted over Grimsby
July 1962 – Triangular UFO over Stratford-upon-Avon
1962 – Vanessa Redgrave sights UFO over Stratford-upon-Avon
11th July 1962 – Red glowing sky and white flashes
18th July 1962 – *The Guardian Newspaper*, 'Object baffles Space Pilot'

AUGUST:
2nd August 1962 – USA: UFOs reported to Central Airlines
4th August 1962 – 'H'-shaped light in the sky
19th August 1962 – Orange glowing 'saucer' sighted
21st August 1962 – Three lights seen over Coventry
26th August 1962 – Tube-shaped UFO over Brands Hatch, Kent
30th August 1962 – UFOs over Taunton
1962 – Silver 'disc' over Tintagel Castle
August 1962 – 'Flying Saucer' seen on the ground at Reigate, Surrey

SEPTEMBER:
8th September 1962 – UFOs sighted over Lancashire
9th September 1962 – UFO reported over Air Show
13th September 1962 – 'Spinning top' UFO sighted over Staffordshire
18th September 1962 – Three strange 'lights' circling the sky
22nd September 1962 – British UFO Association Conference
24th September 1962 – Rectangular object seen
28th September 1962 – 'Ball of blue light' seen
28th September 1962 – UFO over Newcastle

OCTOBER:
1st October 1962 – Three cigar-shaped objects seen by Gateshead lorry drivers
2nd October 1962 – Rectangular UFO over Gateshead
4th October 1962 – Elliptical object reported over Sunderland

16th October 1962 – Swishing UFO over Derbyshire
25th October 1962 – Mysterious siren noise
31st October 1962 – UFO sighted over Isle of Wight

NOVEMBER:
3rd November 1962 – Triangular object over Leicester
6th November 1962 – Orange 'light' over Portsmouth Harbour
13th November 1962 – Saucer-shaped UFO over Nottingham
17th November 1962 – Three 'lights' over Florida
23rd November 1962 – First 'Flying Saucer' Exhibition in Tyneside!
24th November 1962 – Fireball seen
26th November 1962 – UFO reported over Newcastle-on-Tyne

DECEMBER:
4th December 1962 – Three 'rods of light' seen over the sea at Lowestoft
5th December 1962 – UFOs sighted RAF tries to intercept
19th December 1962 – 'Flying Saucer' over Cumbria
21st December 1962 – Three bright lights on UFO over Norfolk
27th December 1962 – Saucer-shaped object seen over Norwich
28th December 1962 – Pilot sights UFO over Lancashire.

JANUARY 1962

January 1962 – 'Flying Saucer' over Sutton Coldfield, Warwickshire

John Shakespeare contacted us about what he saw during January 1962, while living in Mill Street, Sutton Coldfield.

> "I happened to glance out of the window, one evening, and see a metallic grey object with a reddish dome, spinning in the sky, a few hundred feet above the Midland Bank. I just stood there in disbelief, watching it for several seconds, until it shot off across the sky towards the Coleshill Road. After several seconds it moved back to where I had first seen it, but now a little higher in the air, before shooting off across the sky, once again, towards Newhall, and gone. I wrote to the local newspaper, explaining what I had seen.
>
> To my surprise, although they published my story, they deleted my opinions."

13th January 1962 – Mysterious green fireballs sighted

Mysterious green fireballs were sighted flying through the sky over Southampton, in Hampshire, and Stow-on the-Wold, Gloucestershire.

Was there a connection with the similar phenomena reported throughout the United States, during the late 1940s, and then sporadically over the following years?

15th January 1962 – Rotating UFO sighted over Lancashire

A highly polished object, described as *"kingfisher blue in colour and as large as a football, held at arm's length"*, was seen rotating around itself as it flew across the sky over Lincoln Grove, Harwood, near Bolton, Lancashire, at 9am, by Mr Harry Kirkham, who estimated it to be moving at hundreds of miles per hour. It appears that the same object was seen by Mr J. Dawson and Mr S. Liversedge, employed at the Department of Pathology, Bolton Royal Infirmary. (**Source:** *Bolton Evening News, 5.2.1962*)

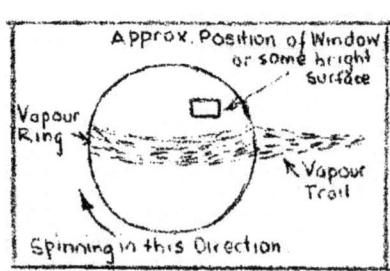

18th January 1962 – Blue 'light' over Southampton

Mr H.J.B House from Bassett, Southampton, was walking home at 10pm, when he saw:

> "...a bright bluish light, travelling south, which dropped down a little before switching off like a fluorescent tube, seconds later".

When he reported it to the newspapers, they suggested he had seen a 'shooting star' – an explanation he rejected.

19th January 1962 – UFO over Southampton Docks

At 9.15am on the 19th January 1962, a circular object was seen travelling through the sky over Southampton Docks. It left a slight smoky trail (or vapour) behind it, before fading away.

(Source: *LUFORO Bulletin*, May/June 1962, Volume 3, No. 3)

20th January 1962 Green 'ball of fire' over Stafford

A green 'ball of fire' was seen heading through the sky over Stafford, by many people, including Police Constables Fox and Parry. They believed it descended towards Seighford Aerodrome.

(Source: *Stafford & Mid-Staffordshire Newsletter*, 20.1.1962 – 'Opinions differ on flying object')

29th January 1962 – UFO over Bolton, Lancashire

Jennifer Bell of 'Broadshard', Holden Road, Leigh, sighted a glowing object flying through the sky, at 9.45am, described as:

> "...round in shape, 20 feet in diameter, with a yellow glow on the other edges, with a deep red centre. It made a faint whirring sound, with intermittent 'pips'. It appeared to slow up over Bolton, as if making observations, and turned off towards the direction of Bury."

Another witness to UFO sightings around the Bolton area was Denise Roberta Harper of Pall Mall, Chorley. She told of seeing what looked like a large firework in the sky with lights flashing on one side, making a 'pipping' noise – as if signaling – (An ex-Girl Guide, who pondered if this was Morse code).

On the same date during the afternoon, over eastern Holland, a pilot with the Royal Dutch Air Force took off in a Sabre F86-K, armed with four 20mm guns and a sidewinder rocket, on a practice flight. During the flight the pilot saw a 'blip' on his radar screen, so he asked the controller whether any other aircraft were up in the air and was told he was the only one. The pilot tried to make contact with the 'plane', but was unsuccessful.

The ground radar was switched on to plot the movements of the UFO, which was moving at 3,500kms an hour. The pilot decided to take action and was about to fire his sidewinder, as he suspected the object was hostile. Before this action could be taken, the object shot off at high speed, in an easterly direction, then disappeared off the radar screen. The ground radar had only been able to follow the object for about six minutes, which was estimated to be 45 feet in diameter and silver-white in colour.

(Source: Netherlands Study Group for Ufology)

FEBRUARY 1962

9th February 1962 – England: 'Flying Saucer' over Aston Clinton, Buckinghamshire

At 3.30am, Ronald Wildman from 42, St. Margaret's Avenue, Luton, in Bedfordshire – employed as a car delivery driver for the Car Collection Company – was driving along the A.41, Ivinghoe Road, through Aston Clinton, Buckinghamshire, to deliver a new car.

He noticed:

> "... a large, metallic-looking object, hovering approximately 30 feet off the ground, over some nearby trees."

Tape-recorded interview

From a tape-recorded interview, conducted by Stratford-upon-Avon UFO researcher John 'Dennis' Llewellyn, a more comprehensive account was obtained.

> "I left home at approximately 3am, as I had a delivery to make in Swansea. I proceeded to Dunstable and was on the Ivinghoe, Aston Clinton Road, going towards Aylesbury. I had just passed some cement works.

(4) CAR DRIVERS AMAZING EXPERIENCE... Credit FLYING SAUCER REVIEW

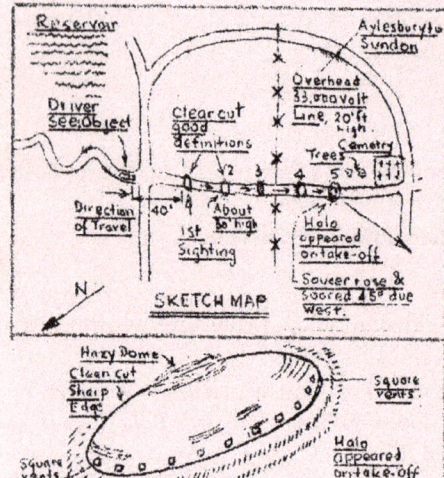

Mr. R. Wildman, of 42, St. Margarets Avenue, Luton, Bedfordshire details below an account of his amazing experience which occurred whilst delivering a new car to Swansea in the early hours of Feb. 9th.

"I left home at 3 am to proceed to Swansea with a new estate car from the factory. I had driven through Dunstable and was approaching the cross-roads at the end of the deserted Ivinghoe road at Aston Clinton, the time now being 3.30 am. Then I saw the object-it was oval shaped and white with black marks at regular intervals round it, which could have been portholes or air vents. It was about 20 or 30 feet above the ground and at least 40 feet wide across....

"When I came within 20 yards of it the power of my car changed, it dropped right down to 20mph. I changed down into second gear and put my foot flat down on the accelerator, but nothing happened.

At the time I had my headlights full on and although the engine lost revs. the lights did not fade. The object which was silent, kept ahead by approximately 20 feet for 200yds, and then started to come lower- it carried on like this until the end of the stretch, then a white haze appeared around it. The object then veered off to the right at tremendous speed and disappeared, at the same time brushing frost particles from the tree tops on to the windscreen.

"It was most certainly a solid object as the reflection of the lights was thrown back from it."

Three investigators, Dr.B.E.Finch, Dr.J.Doel, a radiologist, and Mr.Russel, a photographic expert visited Mr.R.Wildman the day after the incident occurred, and came to the conclusion that he had a genuine sighting, that he was not hallucinated and that he was reliable and honest.

Comment by an Air Ministry spokesman:- "He may have seen a low cloud lit up by headlights, or it may have been a JOKE".
(Eds.comment:- I somehow think Mr.Wildman will not take too kindly to the above statement, as he was in a far better position to make a statement than the Air Ministry.

Scene of the incident

Approximately two miles past this, I rounded a slight bend at 40mph. As I did so, I came across a terrific glare from an object in front of me. It was approximately 30-40 feet across, and 20 feet high. I didn't have time to brake, as I was within yards of it. My engine started to slow up. When I was within 20 feet of it, the car just lost power. I changed down to second gear, but the car didn't pick up any 'revs'. I proceeded at 20 mph. (approximately), with the object in front of me. It was oval in shape, and was – quite honestly – fantastic. It was a clear night. There had been a frost. You could count the stars. There was no cloud, or mist, of any description.

I followed the object 200 or a few more yards. It did appear to come lower at one spot."

Black marks seen on object

"At this spot, a halo appeared around the base; I should say a couple of feet away from the object. On the object itself, I could see what looked like black marks – at regular intervals – which could have been portholes, or air vents. The haze (or halo) could have come from

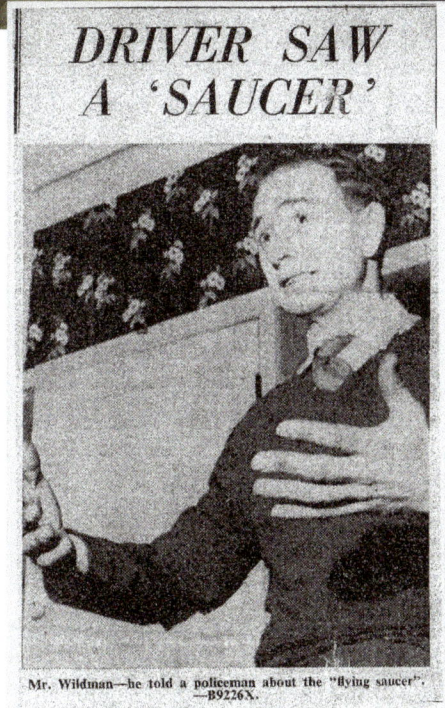

Mr. Wildman—he told a policeman about the "flying saucer".
—B9226X.

that, but I wouldn't like to say. But when the halo appeared near to trees on the left, at this point, (there is a slight bend), the object veered off to the right at fantastic speed. At the time it veered off, I don't know whether it touched the trees, or whether the power of it moving away thrust the particles of frost on the trees onto the car. My car automatically picked-up its 'revs'.

I changed back into top gear, and proceeded as fast as I could to Aylesbury. I didn't pass anybody."

Stopped a Police Officer to report incident

"On the way, I met a Police Constable at Aylesbury lights and explained what had happened. He called over a colleague, and – after explaining to his colleague – he said I had better come down to the Police Station. When the Police Sergeant saw me he said I looked shaken, which I was – rather scared. He said, 'give him a cup'. After they gave me a cup of coffee, half an hour later, I left the Police Station, and proceeded on my way to Swansea."

Mr Wildman was asked if he could explain why the appearance of this object should have caused any engine faults.

"I should have said that the headlights of my car, when coming onto the object, threw back a solid reflection, approximately 40 feet across the clear sky. Knowing it was there 'really put the wind up me'." (End of tape-recording)

Explanations put forward

A number of possible explanations were put to Mr Wildman. They included the possibility that he was delusional through tiredness, that he had seen the headlights reflecting off low cloud, (as suggested by the Air Force), or that it was nothing but a publicity stunt! All of these were dismissed by him. He also denied telling any of the reporters who interviewed him that he had *ever* said that he had seen a *'flying saucer'*. All he ever mentioned was seeing an object.

Mrs Wildman also interviewed

Mrs Wildman was also interviewed. Many reporters came to the house and she felt swamped with people anxious to interview her husband when he arrived home. The following Sunday, three men came down from London to see him – a doctor, a scientist, and 'a man from the Air Ministry'. They asked Mr Wildman a number of questions, and invited him to show them the location of the incident. Following their arrival at the scene, they took a number of photographs and invited him to wait there for the rest of the day, as they were going to check out the ground with a Geiger counter. (These tests proved negative). They also conducted some enquiries with persons living in the vicinity, but failed to find any other witnesses.

Rocket research station a few miles away from the sighting

A search of the area revealed the presence of a large cement works which was lit up at night, a rocket research station a few miles away, and a meteorological station in the vicinity. A few yards from where the object was seen lies a small drinking water reservoir; the top being 20 feet above the road, in direct line with the craft's progress – which may be of some significance.

It appears that the three men were not, in fact, from the Air Ministry, as Mr Wildman believed. They were Dr. B.E. Finch – a regular contributor to *Flying Saucer Review*, Dr. D.G. Doel – a radiologist, and Mr R.R Russell – a photographic expert.

They travelled to interview Mr Wildman at his home address in St. Margaret's Avenue, Luton, in Bedfordshire, after reading a brief account of the incident published on 10th February 1962, by the *Daily Telegraph*, who quoted a MOD spokesman as saying:

"He may have seen a low cloud, lit up by headlights, or it may have been a joke".

> *1*
>
> I left home at 3 A.M. on February 9th 1962 to proceed to Swansea. At 3.30 A.M. as I had driven through Dunstable and was approaching the crossroads at the end of Ivinghoe-road at Ashton-Clinton. Then I saw something. It was about 20 or 30 feet above the ground, and at least 40 feet across. As soon as I came within 20 yards of it, the speed of my car dropped right down to about 20 m.p.h. I changed down to second and put my foot flat on the accelerator — nothing happened —
>
> I got a better look at the thing, it was oval-shaped and white metallic look with black marks at regular intervals round it — (which could have been port-holes or air-vents)
>
> *2*
>
> I was really alarmed now as my car which was a new Estate-car from the factory would not pick up speed. It seemed as the object had control of the car. I had my headlights full on and although the engine had lost revs, the lights did not fade. The object which was silent kept just ahead of me; after approx. 200 yds. it appeared to come lower. As I reached a bend from this straight run, I noticed a halo appear approx. 2 feet away from the base of the object when it suddenly veered off to the right at a terrific speed. The engine of my car immediately picked up. It was definitely a solid object because the reflection
>
> *3*
>
> of my headlights was thrown back from it. And as it moved away, it brushed particles of frost from the tree tops on to my windscreen. Please note it was a very clear night with the stars easily visible in the sky.

As we suspected, the straight stretch of road along which this sighting took place was the old Roman road, now Ayelsbury Road, (formerly Akeman Street, circa 1870s). Close by is Upper Icknield Way and Icknield Way.

A map drawn by Mr Wildman shows the presence of overhead power cables, and a cemetery to his left. An examination of a sketch, provided to the investigators, shows – in contrast to the later illustration – a slightly different image, but this should not detract in any way to the obvious authenticity of what transpired.

Incomprehensibly, the MOD never did send anybody to interview him, although we learnt that the incident was brought to their attention. The investigators judged Mr Wildman's account as being entirely truthful and that he had seen a flying object of an unknown type and origin.

(**Sources:** John 'Dennis' Llewellyn/*Daily Herald*, 10.2.1962 – 'Flying Saucer slows driver'/*Daily Express*, 10.2.1962/Daily Mail – 'I saw IT says scared driver')

9th February 1962 – Mysterious 'light' over Luton, Bedfordshire

Mrs K.J Taber of 42, Pirton Road, Luton, told of being awoken during the early hours of Friday, the 9th February 1962,

"... by a brilliant light shining through the tapestry curtains of the bedroom. As we back onto a country lane, we normally only see dim reflections from the headlights of passing traffic. We expected to hear the crash of an explosion, but only silence. About three years ago (1959) I was with my 14 year-old nephew, in Waller Avenue, when we saw a cigar-shaped object heading across the sky. It had neither wings nor tail fin."

16th February 1962 – Aluminum object sighted in the sky over Leeds

At 11am a dull aluminum object was seen, at a height of between 1-2 miles in the sky, over Pudsey, Leeds. It was heading southwards. **(Source:** *Flying Saucer Review,* **March/April 1962, Volume 8, No. 2/John 'Dennis' Llewellyn)**

28th February 1962 – UFO photographed over Sheffield

A photo taken by Alexander Birch (14) of Mosborough, Sheffield, on 28th February 1962, using a Brownie 'Box' 127 camera became the subject of interest by UFO researchers. At the time the picture was taken, he was accompanied by David Brownlow (12) and Stuart Dixon (16).

The photograph shows not one but five UFOs. Alex said, at the time, that

"... they were vivid, just hanging there after a second or so. Some white blobs started to come out of them, and they seemed hazy and obscured. I got my camera and took a shot of them. A second later they disappeared, at a terrific speed, towards Sheffield."

In the article, entitled 'The Mosborough Incident', published in *Space Bulletin,* Volume 1, Number 2, May-June 1962 (published by Harry Bunting of the Direct Investigation Group of Aerial Phenomena), it tells us that sightings *"appear to be on the increase worldwide, especially in the Teesside area, during April and May".*

A young Alex Birch

Harry Bunting declared the photograph to be genuine, following an *'on the spot'* examination of the negative by his tape librarian and photographic consultant – Mr W. Skellon. Ironically, Alex's mother – Margaret – had previously suggested that her son had been seeing things, but she changed her mind after seeing a photo.

Oddly, the accompanying illustration was taken from the photograph which was not copied into the magazine, probably because even at that stage it was heavily copyrighted, and not to be reproduced in part or whole without permission from the Birch family.

However, our friend (John 'Dennis' Llewellyn) was in possession of a copy of the photograph, which we understand was obtained from Alex [whom we had spoken to ourselves, on many occasions, over recent years].

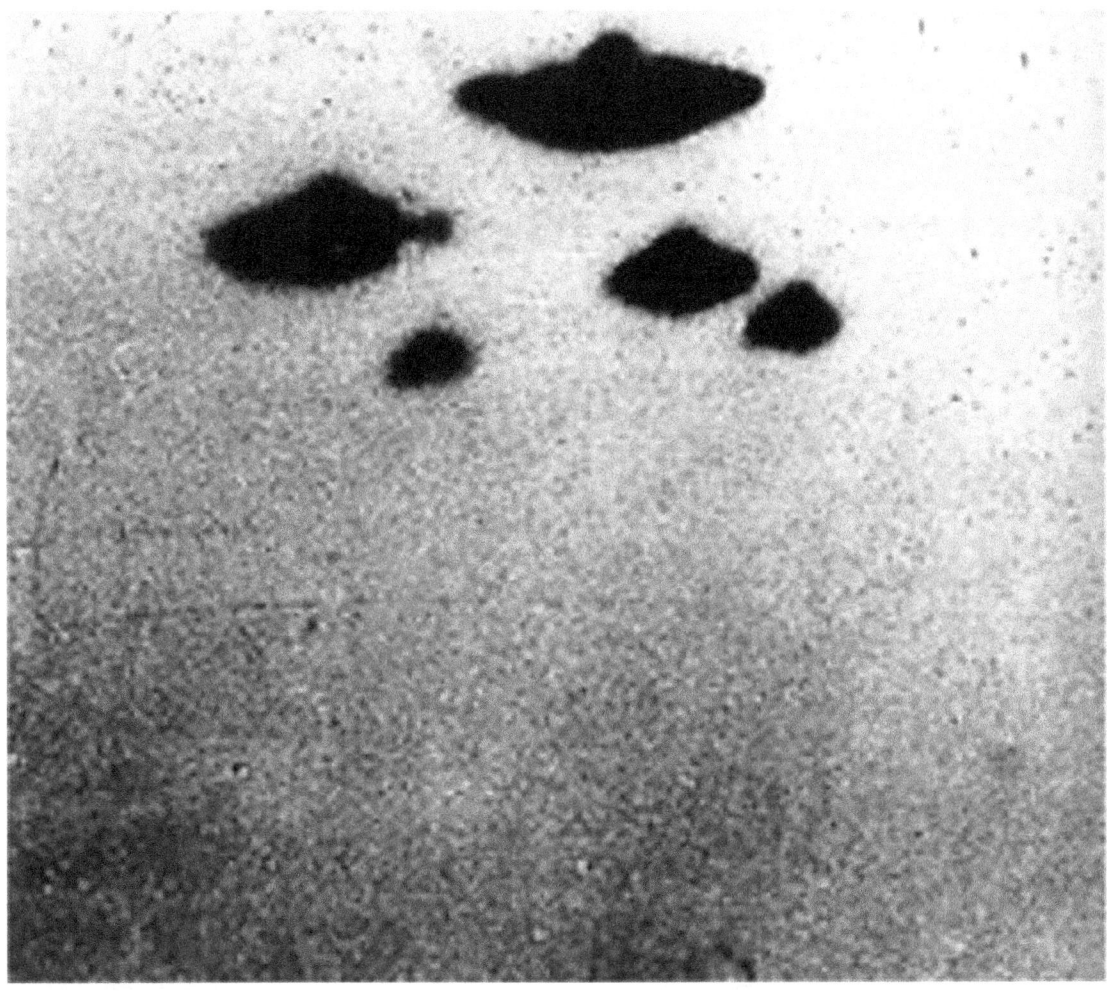

Len Cramp

As usual with photos of this nature, it did not just attract the attention of the media. It drew comments from people within the UFO investigation field, including the well-respected Isle of Wight resident – Len Cramp – who stated, in an edition of *Flying Saucer Review*:

> "There is no doubt that the photographs are completely authentic. It is inconceivable that the youngster or parent could have perpetrated a hoax."

Alan Watts

BUFORA also enthusiastically endorsed his pictures, following an analysis conducted by Alan Watts.

> "If we want the truth, I would say we couldn't do better than take these to be fairly normal Adamski-type 'saucers' and argue it out from there."

Lionel Beer

Lionel Beer of *Space-link* Books (2010), who joined BUFORA in 1961 as their Publicity Officer, after having met Nigel Stephenson and Susanne Stebbing at the first British Flying Saucer convention held

BOY STARTS NEW PROBE INTO FLYING SAUCERS

NEWS OF THE WORLD REPORTER

A PHOTOGRAPH taken by a 14-year-old boy has started Air Ministry experts on an investigation into a new flying saucer riddle. The picture, of five mystery objects in the sky, was taken by Alex Birch while he was playing with friends at his home in Moor-crescent, Mosborough, near Sheffield.

He and his father visited the Air Ministry in London, told officers what had happened and showed them the picture.

"They are very keen to get the exact time and date this took place," Mr. Birch said yesterday.

Alex said: "I think it was Sunday, February 25, we saw them. It was either then or March 4.

Looked up

"Three of us, Stewart Dixon, David Brownlow and myself were in the field at the back of our house taking photographs.

"David bent down and picked up a stone to throw. As he got up he saw the shapes in the sky. He shouted to me and we all three looked up

Alex Birch, the boy photographer whose camera captured the flight of mystery objects in the sky.

Exposed! The great flying saucer hoax

THE FAKE PICTURE

THE Great Flying Saucer Hoax was revealed yesterday....

TEN YEARS after it happened—and by the man who pulled off the spoof.

Alex Birch, now a 24-year-old salesman, confessed how he fooled the world with a box-camera photo that brought him fame.

At the time of his incredible "scoop" Alex was a 14-year-old schoolboy.

Secret

His picture startled scientists. He appeared on TV and made radio broadcasts.

He was even interviewed for three hours by Air Ministry officials.

But yesterday, at his home in Pitsmoor, Sheffield, he told the secret he'd kept so long.

He PAINTED the saucers on to a pane of glass, then photographed through it.

Two school chums helped him. The three of them later vowed not to tell.

"I got the idea," Alex said disarmingly yesterday, "from seeing a fly crawl up a window pane. I realised that on a photo it would be difficult to tell whether the fly was on the glass or in the air."

Alex, now married, with a two-year-old daughter, added: "There was a lot of talk about flying saucers at the time. Things snowballed and it became difficult to back down and admit it was a fake.

"Now I feel I should straighten things out."

Author Leonard G. Cramp featured the fake picture as

HOAXER ALEX

evidence of flying saucers in his book "Piece in the Jigsaw."

He said last night: "I'm astonished. But it does not destroy my belief in flying saucers."

---

at the Russell Hotel, Bloomsbury, London organised by the Aetherius Society, the previous year, was to provide us with much illuminating information relating to the background of BUFORA and its activities during the early years:

> "LUFORO had proposed forming a national and international federation of UFO societies when the committee met at my flat, in Dorset Street. Nigel again advanced his plans for a UK federation and, after being given the go-ahead, it was suggested an inaugural meeting was to be arranged, which took place at 2.30pm on Saturday, 22nd September 1962. When BUFORA held its conference at Kensington Central Library, London, tickets were sold at four shillings, with a buffet tea being offered at three shillings (the price of a cup of British railway tea in those days). The response was overwhelming, and several dozen ticket applications had to be turned away. The speakers included Leonard Cramp, who gave a lecture on his theories and Dr. Geoffrey Doel showed slides. Ray and Rex Stanford, two brothers from the United States, showed slides of a UFO in flight, but the star turn was 12 year-old Alex Birch from Sheffield, who described having photographed a UFO in

February 1962. While the editor of Flying Saucer Review, Waveney Girvan went further, suggesting: 'the 'saucer' pilots were interested in Sheffield, because if there is life of any sort inside these flying objects, it presumably needs water to sustain it...and Sheffield is surrounded by reservoirs'."

Alex Birch's father

In a letter to *Flying Saucer Review*, published in 1963, Alex's father wrote:

"I myself was a non-believer in these objects, but now I am firmly convinced that we are being visited by 'flying saucers' of other planets."

In July 1962, Alex's father contacted the Air Ministry and informed them of the existence of his son's photograph, and said he was *"awaiting instructions"*.

After declining to visit the locality where the photographs had been taken, the Air Ministry agreed to take a look at Alex's photo in the face of mounting public interest.

A trip to London

Subsequently, Alex and his father travelled down to London in a trip sponsored by the *Yorkshire Post*. When the group arrived at the Ministry building, the journalist was carefully separated from the Birch family and taken to visit the Public Relations office. Alex was questioned by the two senior RAF Officers, Flight Lieutenant R.H. White of S6 – a predecessor of Nick Pope's Secretariat (Air Staff) 2A – and a 'technical consultant', Flight Lieutenant Anthony Bardsley of the Air Intelligence department (Tech).

An internal MOD account described the atmosphere at the meeting as

"...cordial, and both Mr Birch and his son were prepared to talk about the photograph at length".

Although perhaps not surprisingly, in *Flying Saucer Review*, Mr Birch claimed his son was

"...sick with fear when the interview began. The officials started what I will call brainwash...asking him wasn't it any reflection that he saw and what was the weather like, what were the formations of cloud...the questions they must have repeated at least thirty times..."

The Air Ministry file on the Birch case, preserved at the Public Record Office, shows us that White and Bardsley did not believe the boy's story, but could not say so publically.

Air Ministry internal memo

In an internal memo, dated 24th September 1962, released in 1993 under the '30 year rule', Bardsley writes to a colleague in S6:

"It is a relatively simple task to reproduce an identical photograph to the one we were shown... The sequence of exposures on the two strips of negatives we saw, do not exactly fit the boy's story."

In a letter sent to Alex's father, and which was subsequently released by the family to the Press, the Ministry suggested that the objects shown in the photograph were *"ice particles in the atmosphere"*.

This explanation was rejected by just about everyone, including Charles Bowen – the editor of *Flying Saucer Review*.

Bowen questioned whether the Air Ministry really believed the explanation.

They probably didn't. One should bear in mind that over the years the Air Ministry/MOD have consistently suggested all manner of apparently ridiculous explanations to explain away what people have seen, knowing that however silly the explanation may be to the actual witness. The majority of the public (who have no interest in UFOs) will accept this as being the answer! To many observers, including Alex's father, the Air Ministry statement simply confirmed their belief in an official cover-up. Birch claimed that it was this statement that actually led him to believe that 'flying saucers' were extraterrestrial in origin, *"and what is more, the Air Ministry knows also, but won't admit it"*.

Haunted Skies Volume Two Revised

The 'stamp of approval' as to the authenticity of the photograph was to lead to an invitation by BUFORA, for Alex to speak about the matter during a meeting at Kensington, on 22nd September 1962. Alex was facing so much ridicule for his pictures that he decided to 'nip the whole matter in the bud'. He contacted the *Daily Express* and admitted that they were hoaxed. They *"were simply cut-out shapes, pasted on a sheet of glass, and re-photographed."*

The *Sheffield Telegraph* then contacted David Brownlow, who confirmed that the whole thing was a joke which had snowballed out of control. In 1998, during a short-lived UFO revival that accompanied the popular TV series *The X-Files*, Alex – now middle aged, and a successful antiques dealer – courted publicity once again. This time his story followed a familiar route taken by *Stephen Derbyshire as a result of his 1959 'confession'; it was the hoax that was in itself a hoax – the photograph was genuine after all!

Alex Birch

> *"I did become internationally famous, but I also faced a lot of ridicule and pressure"*,

Birch told Pete Moxon of Sheffield-based White's news agency.

> *"I decided to claim that it was a fake, in the hope that it would all go away and the pressure would be taken off me, but it didn't work out like that…the UFO fraternity didn't believe me, and they even called a conference in London and came to the conclusion that my change of story was due to pressure from the Government."*

Why had Alex waited until 1998 to tell the whole truth?

> *"The reason I've decided to let the real story be known now is because I think it is important that the public should know."*

Unfortunately, David Brownlow and Stuart Dixon – still resident in Mosborough – both independently dismissed Alex's new claim, although Stuart Dixon was later to retract his original statement, but only after meeting his old friend for the first time since 1962. Brownlow told researchers – Dr. David Clarke and Andy Roberts – in an interview:

> *"It was a hoax. Alex has always run with it more than we have. It was painted on glass. We were just messing around in Alex's dad's greenhouse when we had the idea to do it. We were all into* Quatermass *and* War Of The Worlds *at the time. It was Alex's idea to take the photo but then his dad and a teacher at the school got hold of it and we all got swept along with the hoax, which just snowballed. It was an incredible experience and we had our ten minutes of fame, but I just want to forget about it now.*
>
> *I've been an antiques dealer all my working life and have always retained a great interest in photography, and have toured the UK with a famous photographer, giving lectures – one to the Royal Photographic Society. I am glad that you have contacted me with regard to using my photograph of the UFO taken at Mosborough, as over the years many people have used the photograph without bothering to ask me for permission in books and made money, which is not right as it breaches my copyright. Apart from that I never received a penny from the use of my photograph, which – on one occasion – was used many times over, without consulting me. Is it no wonder I get annoyed*

with people? Worse, the negative was actually stolen and sold in a UFO magazine – so that's why I decided to do something about it. I was so annoyed; I even pursued legal battles against people in the USA, and won the Court cases from improper use of the photo. Incredibly, the American Government was selling it themselves. Ironically the CIA even used it on their opening page on their website about UFOs."

Alex Birch

However, there is much more to Alex than the capture of a UFO on photograph. He retains a love of nature and wildlife, and is passionate about the environment and our planet's wildlife. He is also internationally respected as a photographer of note; his photographs and other work have appeared within numerous publications, including *Time*, *Life*, in hardbacks, newspapers, magazines and on television. We should judge Alex for what he is now and respect him for what he has achieved. As far as the photo is concerned we cannot prove either way, but we did ask Alex the all important question… Did he fake the 1962 pictures?

He replied:

"I have never, not photographed a UFO – this was genuine. I did not – and have never – fabricated anything! I ended up regretting very bitterly having reported this matter in the first place, because of all the nasty, harmful, allegations directed against me over the years. Stuart Dixon and David Brownlow became absolutely sick of it as well. My life did become a misery; everywhere I went some person would call me a nutcase, or worse. When I went into work, people would make cryptic comments to me about 'Martians'. It was a laugh, to begin, but then turned out to be a real pain."

The legacy of the photo and its association with his current business still continues to haunt Alex to this present day. There is no reason to dispute the authenticity of this photo or the man behind taking it. We felt privileged to have entered into a dialogue with him, over the years, and can only wish him and his family the best.

(Sources: Alex Birch/David Clarke/Andy Roberts/ /*Derbyshire Times*, 22.6.1962/*Daily Express* 14.7.1962 – 'WHAT ARE THEY'/*News of the World* 2.9.1962 – 'Boy starts new probe into Flying Saucers')

February 1962 – USAF attempts to intercept UFO

Was there any connection between the saucer-shaped object seen by Mr Wildman, and others, and an object picked-up on radar during February 1962 by the RAF, who scrambled an aircraft, already on patrol, to investigate the matter further? The incident involved (now retired) United States Air Force Major George A. Filer, currently Eastern Director of MUFON (Mutual UFO Network), and Vice President of Sky-watch International (2006).

Major George Filer:

"I was stationed at the 420th RAF Air refuelling Squadron Base, at RAF Scunthorpe, Lincolnshire, in February 1962. I was in orbit over the North Sea in a six engine K5-50 Tanker Aircraft, when we received a call over the radio from London Control, who excitedly asked us to have a look at an unidentified flying object which had been picked-up on radar, hovering between Oxford and Stonehenge. After being given the intercept heading, the aircraft moved in towards the target, with further transmissions from London Control informing us that all commercial aircraft had been cleared from our path, in order that we could intercept safely.

We realised we were exceeding our maximum speed and had great trouble slowing the aircraft down. At about 30 miles, my APS-23 radar seemed to pick up on the hovering, directly ahead of us. It was an exceptionally large radar return, reminding me of a huge bridge or a ship, such as a destroyer – bigger than anything I had seen on radar in the air before.

Haunted Skies Volume Two Revised

Major George Filer

A recent photo of George Filer

The return was sharp and solid, as compared to the fuzziness of a rain cloud. My impression was that this UFO must have been made of something substantive, like metal or steel. As we approached to now ten miles from the target, at a speed of around 425 miles per hour, it apparently sensed us because we could now see a series of dim lights, directly ahead of us, on what was a dark night. At five miles from intercept, the UFO seemed to come alive. The lights brightened and the object accelerated in a launch similar to the Space Shuttle, at night. Within a few seconds, it moved vertically upwards and was gone from sight.

We asked London Air Traffic Control if they had any rocket launches in the area. They replied in the negative and told us we were now clear to return to our mission. The incident was recorded in my navigator's log and mentioned the next day, on Operations, but no intelligence briefings ever took place." (**Source: Personal interviews**).

20th February 1962 – UFO sighting from Mercury Capsule

John Glenn, piloting his Mercury capsule, reported having sighted three objects follow him and then overtake him at varying speeds. Glenn also said that these *"snowflakes"* were small, and seemed to be coming from the rear end of his capsule. Later flights also observed them and were able to create 'snowstorms' by having astronauts bang on the walls of their capsules.

Can any associations be made with an appearance of objects that have plagued the background of the UFO phenomena and the pages of the *Haunted Skies* books? Or is this only speculation?

Footnote: Interesting conversation 10 years later

Somewhat as a footnote to this, we learnt of an interesting conversation that took place between Mike Jaffe and Douglas Cooper, on the 19th May 1972.

During this evening, Mike Jaffe – director of *Data-Net*, the UFO amateur radio network – was aboard his 33 foot motorboat, anchored off Atsena otie Key (a bird sanctuary off the Florida Keys) along with his tom cat 'Beezel'.

At 9.25pm, following a brilliant display of lightning, his attention was drawn to an object in the sky *"like a disc, edge-on"*.

He watched it for about 20 minutes until forced to move the boat, owing to the choppy conditions. Later he found the cat in the bilge that refused to come out – presumably terrified from the storm. While this is of course most interesting, especially as Mike included

John Glenn

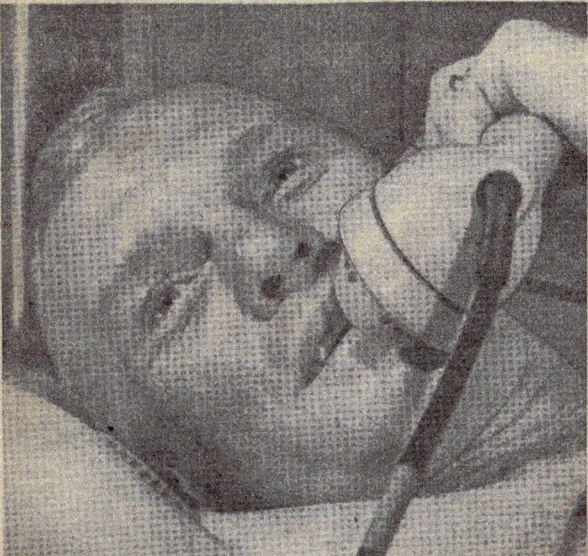

Rocky Mountain News

A Scripps-Howard Newspaper — Colorado's First Newspaper—Founded in 1859

103D YEAR: NO. 305 — DENVER 1, COLO., WEDNESDAY, FEB. 21, 1962

COLORADO SPRINGS HOME EDITION — FORECAST: Light Snow — PRICE 5 CENTS — 88 PAGES

Souvenir Orbit Edition

Glenn Does It!

4 FULL PAGES OF PICTURES BEGINNING ON PAGE 1A

First Photo of Glenn at Journey's End

Astronaut John H. Glenn Jr. talks happily over ship-to-shore radiophone while relaxing on medical examiner's couch aboard the destroyer Noa after his capsule was plucked from the sea Tuesday afternoon. Glenn made three orbits of the Earth and then made a target landing in the Atlantic about 800 miles south of Cape Canaveral, Fla., where crewmen of the Noa lifted his Friendship 7 capsule to the deck and helped the spaceman out of his tight quarters.
—U.S. Navy Photo From UPI Telephoto.

All Denver Joins Astronaut As He Whirls About Earth
—STORY ON PAGE 5

We tell Glenn's triumph in stories and pictures on Pages 3, 5, 6, 10, 12, 13, 14, 15, 18, 20, 24, 26, 28, 36 and 37.

By CHARLES W. CORDRY
United Press International Writer

CAPE CANAVERAL, Feb. 20—Astronaut John H. Glenn Jr. flashed triumphantly around the Earth Tuesday in America's first manned orbital flight and had scarcely splashed down safely in the Atlantic when the nation erupted in joyous celebration.

Blazing a 3-orbit spaceway round the planet in a 4-hour, 56-minute flight, the 40-year-old Marine plopped into the sea near a waiting U.S. destroyer. He was plucked promptly from the ocean by crane before being taken to the nearby carrier Randolph for the night.

President Kennedy immediately telephoned his congratulations to the freckle-faced, grinning pilot and arranged to fly to Cape Canaveral Friday to pay personal homage. The President also publicly expressed the nation's great happiness at Glenn's successful trip.

Mr. Kennedy, who anxiously watched the flight over television, summed up America's reaction after all the weeks of waiting when he said: "Colonel, we are really proud of you and I must say you did a wonderful job."

17,545-Mile-an-Hour Trip

"Thanks, Mr. President," replied the astronaut with the same composure he displayed throughout his near 17,545-mile-an-hour circuit of the world.

Even before emerging from his cramped space capsule, Glenn reported: "My condition is excellent." Climbing from the cabin where he had been strapped down from early morning to mid-afternoon, his first words were: "It was hot in there."

Back at Cape Canaveral, space officials made no effort to hide their jubilation, or their praise of the pilot. Said Project Mercury Director Robert R. Gilruth:

"John Glenn performed all test pilot functions very, very well. He was very sharp through the flight. He felt good and retained his sense of humor."

In Arlington, Va., Glenn's wife, Annie, and their two teenage children joined in a prayer of thanksgiving. They also received a telephone call from President Kennedy offering his congratulations.

Glenn, who whirled around the Earth once every 88.29 minutes, repeatedly sent back reports that his condition was "fine." They were interspersed with progress data he relayed on his flight and the performance of his bell-shaped spacecraft.

Minor Difficulties Brushed Off

He never voiced any complaints and brushed aside "minor" difficulties with a guidance device on the capsule that forced him to take over semi-manual operation of the vehicle.

So overjoyed was President Kennedy with the astronaut's performance that he planned a Washington celebration in Glenn's honor next Monday or Tuesday in addition to the personal visit to Cape Canaveral Friday.

Glenn will visit the White House and then will be honored with a parade to the Capitol where he will be the guest at a congressional reception.

To the acclaim of his elated countrymen, Glenn was plucked from the sea at the end of his mission by a crane on the destroyer Noa, one of the recovery ships waiting to rescue him. He landed only six miles from the vessel.

(Continued on Page 3)

some sketches in the *Data-Net* magazine of the 7th July 1972, even more interesting is what he had to say during a conversation which took place in June of the same year, after having docked the boat at Casey Key, Nokomis, Florida.

> *"It was here that I met Doug Cooper, skipper of the ill-fated Eloise – a 43 feet double-ender, with a cruising range of 3,000 miles.*
>
> *While I was grouper, fishing 80 miles south-west, the Eloise was on her way to Tampa to be cleaned and painted. Two miles off Lido Beach she went down during the night. An investigation later revealed that a thru ball fitting had come off. I immediately checked all the sea cocks.*
>
> *Doug visited me often. We had countless conversations and I learned that Doug was writing a book. We discussed Dr. Hynek's book and we both agreed it was one of the best contributions to the subject. I gave him a copy of the Data-Net report and explained what we were doing. Doug said he couldn't stay too long, as his father – Gordon Cooper – was visiting the area and that we would both get on well. I asked him if he meant the Astronaut. He replied, 'yes, he is in real estate'. I asked him whether he (Gordon) was interested in UFOs. He replied, 'oh yes, all of them are'. I asked him, 'how many is that then'? He replied, 'about fifty that I know of, they are all very concerned. They believe that they are real; some of them feel they come from another planet – the universe is so big. The astronauts are all very concerned. Do you remember when one of the astronauts saw all the little flakes out of the window?'*
>
> *I said that I remembered. He replied, 'well they were concerned about that; also they were followed by an unknown'.*
>
> *I replied, 'wasn't that the satellite Pegasus?' He replied, 'yes, but they still don't know what it was … wow, were they worried then! All of them are concerned with UFOs and try to keep up on all information'."*

MARCH 1962

6th March 1962 – Larger red rotating object seen

At 7.30pm, two unidentified flying objects – described as *"resembling stars, accompanied by a larger rotating red object"* – were seen flying through the sky, at approximately a thousand miles per hour, by people living in the Walton Hall Park Avenue area of Liverpool, at an estimated height of 3,000 feet. **(Source:** *UFOLOG***)**

17th March 1962 – 'Flying Saucers' over Bristol

At 9.25pm, a Bristol resident – Mrs W.J. Cox – was with a Miss Welshman, standing at her front door in Pembroke Road, looking eastwards, when:

"We saw a sharply-defined, circular, pale amber coloured object, hovering 50 feet above the tops of nearby houses, opposite, giving off some sort of vapour from part of its circumference. It seemed to be end-on to us, resembling a full moon in appearance, and occasionally tilted towards us. Five minutes later, it vanished from sight." **(Source: Peter Tate)**

APRIL 1962

15th April 1962 – Nine objects seen over the Northumberland Moors

At 3.05am, following an all night 'skywatch' held on the moors at Kirkwhelpington, Northumberland, by members of the Tyneside based UFO Society – Alan Murphy, John Murphy, and John Elliott,

"... nine star-like objects of different sizes, two being larger than the rest were observed, moving eastwards, which were seen to change into a rough circular pattern while in flight".

(Source: UFOLOG)

27th April 1962 – Strange object seen over Dumfries

During the late evening Mrs Betty McKeown, of Merkland Farm, Dumfries, went to her front door for a breath of fresh air. As she looked across the clear night sky, she saw:

"... a strange object flashing with green and red lights, sweeping back and forwards".

After observing it for over an hour, she called the Police. Police Constable, John Williamson, arrived and watched the object with Mrs McKeown and her husband, John, but was unable to identify it.

(Source: *Daily Mail,* **29.4.1962/** *LUFORO Bulletin,* **May/June 1962)**

At 9.55pm, four people in Jesmond Road, Newcastle-on-Tyne sighted an orange 'light', heading in a south to west direction. From the orange 'light' emerged a small star like object that shot away at speed, leaving the other larger object to promptly vanish from view.

Late April 1962 – USA: Pilot sights five UFOs while on record-breaking flight

NASA pilot – Joseph Walker – claimed to have detected UFOs whilst making a record-breaking attempt at piloting the X-15 Aircraft. He described them as

"... five disc-shaped or perhaps even cylindrical objects. It was impossible to estimate their size or distance from the camera".

During a lecture at the Second National Conference on the 'Peaceful Uses of Space Research' in Seattle, Washington (2008), he said:

"I don't feel like speculating about them. All I know is what appeared on the film, which was developed after the flight."

(Sources: *The Calgary Herald,* **Friday, 11.5.1962/** *Daily Telegraph,* **12.5.1962)**

NASA pilot, Joseph Walker: "... all I know is what appeared on the film, which was developed after the flight."

MAY 1962

8th May 1962 – Bright object over Newcastle-on-Tyne

The Newcastle-on-Tyne based newspaper, The Journal – in their edition of the 10th May 1962, 'Did I see a saucer' – told of being contacted by John Carr (26) who was in his bedroom at Deanham Gardens, Fenham, Newcastle-on-Tyne, with his brother Colin (16), getting ready for bed at 12.45am, when they saw a large, bright, object approach the house, which then moved away.

The same UFO was seen by Mrs Freda Heightley of Westgarth House, Ivesley Villas, Waterhouses. She described seeing it moving slowly across the sky and trailing pale yellow flame.

17th May 1962 – UFO sighted, and then RAF Bomber appears

At 1.05pm, Colin Vince from Benwell, Newcastle-on-Tyne, reported having seen

"...a silvery 'disc' like object, heading in a NNW direction, then change to a south course. Thirty seconds later a Victor Bomber appeared, apparently on the same course of the object. Both of them disappeared into distant cloud." (**Source TUFOS**)

19th May 1962 – UFO making humming noise sighted over Scotland

At 10pm, an object – described as

". . . looking like a hovering red lighted horseshoe, rising and falling in the air, with reddish/blue lights around its outer rim and blue lights in the inner rim, showing a 'ball of fire' between its two ends. . ."

was seen over Solway Firth, Dumfriesshire, by amateur astronomer, James McGill.

"It was humming, like a vacuum cleaner, as it moved across the sky, forwards and backwards, where it hovered for a while and then flew past Criffell – an 1,800 feet hill, on the opposite side of the Nith

Estuary, before stopping and hovering over Loch Kinder. It then reversed and moved northwards, passing over the ICI factory at Drungans, where it passed over the River Nith and continued on its journey towards the north-east, where it became lost from view at 12.15 am."
(Source: *LUFORO Bulletin*, May/June 1962, Volume 11, No. 3)

21st May 1962 – Pilot sights UFO over Wales

Captain Gordon Pendleton – a former RAF Officer – was piloting an Aer Lingus 'Viscount' to Brussels from the UK, at a height of 17,000 feet. He and the First Officer, Peter Murphy, saw:

> "...a circular brown object, with protrusion-like antennae (smaller than a 'Viscount') pass underneath, at 14,000 feet, heading across the sky at 600 knots, 35 miles south-west of Bristol" [Over the Brecon area].

(Source: *Western Daily Mail*, Bristol/*Daily Herald*, London, 22.5.1962)

25th May 1962 – UFO over Lancashire

A round object, constantly changing colour from red to white, was seen high in the sky over Whalley, near Blackburn, Lancashire. (Source: *Irish Times*, 22.5.1962/*Blackburn Evening Telegraph*, 27.4.1962)

26th May 1962 – Silver and black UFO, sighted over Cornwall

Mr H.G. Pryor from Truro, Cornwall, sighted *"a silver and black UFO, resembling a stack of coins"*, led by a small object, heading across the sea. It was 50 feet above the water, at an estimated speed of between 60-70 miles per hour. The appearance of a second object, *apparently not attached* to the main body of the UFO, was to become a familiar background description to other UFO sightings we were to come across, over the years.

JUNE 1962

11th June 1962 – Police Officer sights UFO over Welsh mountain

Retired Police Constable David Harris contacted us with regard to what he saw, while driving through Ogmore Valley, Bridgend, at 11.45pm:

> "I saw this object – the size of a bus, with lights at its front and rear – moving slowly through the sky, about 40 feet above the top of Llangeinor Mountain. It then headed downwards. I braced myself for an explosion, but nothing happened. I telephoned the Police Control Room at Bridgend to report the incident. As a result of what I had seen, I was ridiculed by my colleagues; worse, a Senior Officer took me to one side and suggested, offensively, I had fabricated the report."

1962 – Triangular UFO over Newcastle-on-Tyne England

In (either May or June), 1962 aviation enthusiast Brian Pickering was with a friend in Walbottle schoolyard, Newcastle-on-Tyne, just before 9am, when they saw:

> "...three Day Glo red spherical objects (forming a triangle) stationary in the northern sky, at 88 degrees off the horizon, approximately the size of a Boeing 707 Airliner. About a minute later, they moved silently off towards the east – gone in a few minutes."

1962: Summer – Revolving UFO near airfield

RAF Officer Ernest Scott was parked with his girlfriend, Frankie (an RAF Nurse), on moorland above Holton Airfield.

> "We saw an object in the sky looking like a slowly revolving sphere, almost a whirling mass of light – no other colours, just white – without any apparent heat. It looked like it was on fire and seemed to be revolving vertically in a clockwise direction. We watched, as it passed overhead and apparently descend into trees ahead and below of us."

Haunted Skies Volume Two Revised

By this time Frankie was now almost hysterical, so Ernest decided to leave the locality. When he tried the ignition on the MG sports car, nothing happened, so he got out of the vehicle and – with the help of Frankie – pushed the car down the slope, jumped in, and coasted to the bottom, where the engine burst into life. An examination carried out, the next day, revealed no sight of anything amiss which could have caused the car to cut out.

(Sources: Police Constable John Makin/Wessex UFO Group/'*WATSUP*', Nicholas Maloret)

Summer 1962 – UFO over Derbyshire

Ex-RAF serviceman Mr S. Pilgrim of Selston, Nottingham, was on his round, delivering post to houses in Brookhill Lane, Pinxton, at 8.30am, when he happened to catch sight of

> "... a glowing copper coloured 'disc' – as big as the full moon – 'radiating' or issuing, rather than shining, about 40 degrees elevation, motionless in the sky towards the north-west. After a couple of minutes, it vanished from sight." (Source: UFOLOG)

1962 – 'Flying Saucer' over Smethwick

John Kilworth, from the West Midlands, spoke to us about his own unique experience which befell him, when he was aged 9-10, some time in the summer of 1962. Although he cannot be sure that this was the exact year, he is absolutely sure of what happened. It was to leave (like many others we came across, over the years), an indelible impression that became burnt into his memory.

John explained that at the time, it was his mother's habit, when putting him and his sister to bed, to look out of the bedroom window, overlooking the traffic island at the bottom of Telford Close, Smethwick, Warley, before closing the curtains and allowing the children to switch-on the bedroom light.

> "Things were different that night. She went over to the bedroom window, peered out, and said, 'what the bloody hell is that?' We went into the room, looked out of the bedroom window, and saw a 'light' in the distance on the horizon, moving backwards and forwards in a straight line across the sky. The curious thing was that it never over-ran the end of the 'line'. I asked my sister to put the light on, thinking it might help us, but of course it didn't. However, when I looked out, it had stopped its movements. I told my sister to put the light off, and a curious thing happened. It began to move towards our house.
>
> As it drew closer, I could now see from the underneath that it was shaped like a saucer, with a silver dome in the middle and orange lights at the outer edges flashing on and off, one after the other. It passed overhead slowly, at what I thought was only about 40-50 feet. We could hear this low humming noise as it disappeared over the house. We ran into the back room – just in time to see it vanish over the tops of some other houses, towards a large wooded park."

John was told by his mother not to say anything about the incident, for fear of being disbelieved. Unfortunately, he chose to disregard his mother's advice and became the butt of considerable amounts of humour. From then on he decided to keep quiet.

A week after the incident, his mother showed him an article published by the *News Telephone* relating to a report of a UFO seen by a retired police officer, who was then living on the other side of the hill. Unfortunately, due to the demise of both his mother and sister, John is unable to identify the exact day when this particular incident occurred, but still remains intrigued as to what it was the family saw that night. (Source: Personal interview)

JULY 1962

1st July 1962 – Strange phenomena sighted over Grimsby

People living in the Bridlington area sighted several mirages of *"ships, sailing upside-down and part of the Grimsby landscape, 40 miles away"*. A large number of mysterious coloured stars were also sighted in the sky over Leyburn, the same evening.

(Source: *Space Bulletin*, Volume 1, No. 4, Sept/Oct 1964/*Northern Echo*, 2.7.1962)

July 1962 – Triangular UFO over Stratford-upon-Avon

John 'Dennis' Llewellyn was in the rear garden of his home in West Green Drive, Stratford-upon-Avon, at 10.40pm, when he noticed a bright satellite-like object, with a powerful searchlight on its top, moving slowly from the north-east.

> "As it passed silently overhead, I was able to see three lights; one orange and one green, forming a triangle in the sky."

1962 – *Vanessa Redgrave sights UFO over Stratford-upon-Avon

As a result of an appeal made in the *Stratford-upon-Avon Herald* newspaper, John Llewellyn received a letter from **Mr Gordon Honeycombe – then performing at the Royal Shakespeare Theatre.

> "I read in Friday's 'Herald' that you are seeking further reports of a UFO seen last Monday. Several of us from the theatre saw it.
>
> I can't give an exact time but it would have been about 10.45pm. We had come into the 'Duck' for a meal, after the 'Shrew', and hadn't yet been served. About seven of us were around the table when Vanessa Redgrave came bursting in, asking us to come outside, as there was something in the sky that she needed an opinion on. Four of us went outside with her and stood on the terrace of the 'Duck', facing what I imagine is northwards. She had apparently been watching the moving 'light' for about ten minutes (but it could have been less). She had first seen it directly overhead, when the 'light' from it had seemed to be revolving. All we saw was this planet sized point of light moving slowly down the sky, at the speed of a very slow 'Chipmunk', or training plane.
>
> Yours sincerely,
> Gordon Honeycombe"

We contacted Gordon, then pursuing a career in Australia (in 2008), who confirmed the incident. His account was identical to that of nearly 50 years before, although he pointed out, *"while weird, I never thought of it as anything alien, or from outer space"*.

---

*Vanessa Redgrave, CBE (born 30th January 1937) is an English actress of stage, screen and television, as well as a political activist. She is a 2003 American Theatre Hall of Fame inductee, and received the 2010 BAFTA Fellowship.

Redgrave rose to prominence in 1961 playing Rosalind in *As You Like It* with the Royal Shakespeare Company and has since starred in more than 35 productions in London's West End and on Broadway, winning the 1984 Olivier Award for Best Actress in a Revival for *The Aspern Papers*, and the 2003 Tony Award for Best Actress in a Play for the revival of *Long Day's Journey into Night*. She also received Tony nominations for *The Year of Magical Thinking* and *Driving Miss Daisy*.

On screen, she has starred in more than 80 films and is a six-time Oscar nominee, winning the Academy Award for Best Supporting Actress for the title role in the film *Julia* (1977). Her other nominations were for *Morgan: A Suitable Case for Treatment* (1966), *Isadora* (1968), *Mary, Queen of Scots* (1971), *The Bostonians* (1984) and *Howards End* (1992).

Among her other films are *A Man for All Seasons* (1966), *Blowup* (1966), *Camelot* (1967), *The Devils* (1971), *Murder on the Orient Express* (1974), *Prick Up Your Ears* (1987), *Mission: Impossible* (1996), *Atonement* (2007), *Coriolanus* (2011) and *The Butler* (2013). Redgrave was proclaimed by Arthur Miller and Tennessee Williams as "the greatest living actress of our times", and has won the Oscar, Emmy, Tony, BAFTA, Olivier, Cannes, Golden Globe, and the Screen Actors Guild awards.

A member of the Redgrave family of actors, she is the daughter of Sir Michael Redgrave and Lady Redgrave (the actress Rachel Kempson), the sister of Lynn Redgrave and Corin Redgrave, the mother of actresses Joely Richardson and Natasha Richardson, the aunt of British actress Jemma Redgrave, and the mother-in-law of actor Liam Neeson.

**Ronald Gordon Honeycombe (27th September 1936 – 9th October 2015) was a British newscaster, author, playwright and stage actor. Gordon Honeycombe was born in Karachi, in the British Raj, and educated at the Edinburgh Academy and read English at University College, Oxford. (His degree was later raised (automatically) to an MA). He completed National Service with the Royal Artillery, mainly in Hong Kong, where he was also an announcer with *Radio Hong Kong*. Returning to the UK, he embarked on an acting career, which led to television and public prominence as a national newscaster with *ITN*. He later settled in Perth, Western Australia, where he continued to work in radio, television and theatre, and was regularly engaged in voice-over work for radio and television, and in documentary narrations. (Source: Wikipedia) He was also a prolific author of many books here are some of them.

   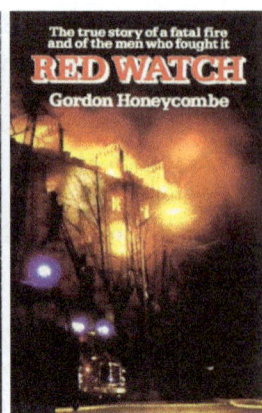
 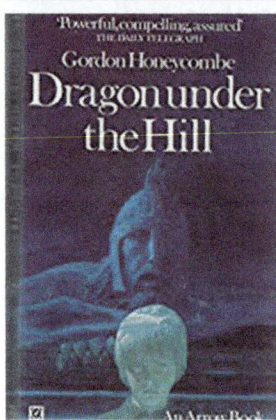  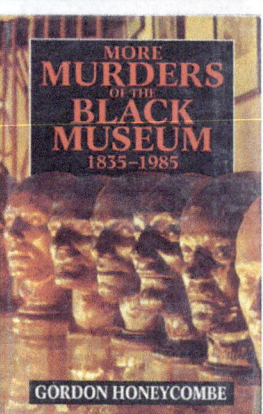

A selection of books written by Gordon Honeycombe

3rd July 1962 – England: Mysterious 'light' seen in the sky by fishermen

Bournemouth grocer – Mr R Cable – was fishing with a friend at Sandbanks, at 1am, when they noticed a 'light' in the sky, which was behaving peculiarly.

> "It moved to the east in short bursts of speed, then stopped and moved back and forth, but it left no trail and was silent. It wasn't a Sputnik or Shooting Star. We watched it for twenty minutes. When I told people, they laughed at me and suggested I had been drinking or was hallucinating."

(Source: *Bournemouth Evening Echo, 3.7.1962* – 'What was happening in the sky in the early hours of today?')

11th July 1962 – Red glowing sky and white flashes

Mrs N. Morris from Rawdon Road, *Wallsend, wrote into the Evening Chronicle, asking if anybody had seen what they had sighted at 11.20pm.

> "The sky went bright red, as though there was a fire. We went to the front door but couldn't see anything. After a while the red glow died down. We then saw white flashes that went off and on. They then died out, the red glow moved to the right of the sky, and the white flashes came on again and lasted fifteen minutes."

(Source: Evening Chronicle, 17.7.1962 – 'There was a strange glow in the sky')

---

*Wallsend, historically Wallsend-on-Tyne, is a large town in North Tyneside, Tyne and Wear, north-east of England. Historically part of Northumberland, Wallsend derives its name as the location of the end of Hadrian's Wall.

18th July 1962 – The Guardian Newspaper, 'Object baffles Space Pilot'

They published a report from USAF Major Robert White, who had flown an X-15 rocket plane at a height of nearly 59 miles. today. The Major told of sighting a mysterious object as he re-entered the atmosphere:

> "... something like a piece of paper. I've never seen anything like this before. As I went over the top I saw a couple of particles go by the plane; they were very small, flaky objects. I thought they were residue from the peroxide which the engine burns. Then, to my left, I saw this large object. It looked like a piece of paper, about the size of my head. It was grey in colour and was visible for 5 seconds, and moved along with the X-15, and was about 30-40 feet away from me."

AUGUST 1962

2nd August 1962 – USA: UFOs reported to Central Airlines

Several UFO reports were made to Central Airlines agent Fred Jones, at Liberal Airport, who himself went outside at about 8pm, when he saw a bright object hovering over a nearby field – its dazzling light strong enough to light up the runway. Some passengers also witnessed this; they told of seeing three objects flying above the airport.

At 8.30pm, Captain Metzger (who was flying between Wichita and Kansas) saw a brilliant object heading swiftly through the sky in an east to west direction. Thirty minutes later, after landing and then taking off at Guymon, Oklahoma, Captain Metzger saw an object flying at high altitude. The pilot dismissed any claims that these were meteors. Following this, he was interviewed by a Colonel from Dayton and by a Lt. Colonel at NORAD HQ, Colorado Springs. (**Source:** *UFO Investigator* **Vol. 11, No. 5, NICAP**)

4th August 1962 – 'H'-shaped light in the sky

At 1.30am, Mr Hector Marr – a steward at the Union Club in Cheltenham – sighted:

> "...a 'brilliant' large, H-shaped sign, high in the sky while in the process of answering a telephone call; excitedly I called my wife, and we watched it hovering stationary in the sky. To the left of it was an exceptionally bright star". (**Source: David Jones/***Gloucestershire Echo***, 4.8.1962)**

Another witness to the phenomenon was Mr D. Attwood. He was with his father of Upper Bath Street, Cheltenham. They described seeing:

> "...a hazy formation, like the Milky Way, which could be said to form a letter 'H', but not well defined, at 1am; Jupiter being clearly visible below the leading stroke of the H".

In the evening of the same day, at 10.42pm, Mr Richard Bury and members of his family were travelling through Lancashire.

His sister brought his attention to something strange in the sky. Mr Bury stopped the car, where they all saw:

> "...an orange coloured, square-shaped, object above a small cloud bank, which changed to dark red at intervals during our observation, as it oscillated in a vertical motion. Suddenly it split into two parts, rapidly diminishing in size, although they later regained their original form – now resembling a crescent in shape. Five minutes later they disappeared from sight".

(Source: *LUFORO Bulletin*, September/October 1962, Volume 3, Number 5)

19th August 1962 - Orange glowing 'saucer' sighted

Mrs Margaret Scowl of Wolsingham, Bishop Auckland, County Durham, was with her husband and neighbours, at about 10pm, when they saw:

> "...an orange coloured, glowing, saucer-shaped, object with a flat base in the sky, about an hour earlier than the Sheffield sighting, heading west to east. It was visible for ten to fifteen minutes and, before disappearing from view, seemed to alter course slightly, showing a black circle in the centre."

Was this the same UFO seen over Sheffield?

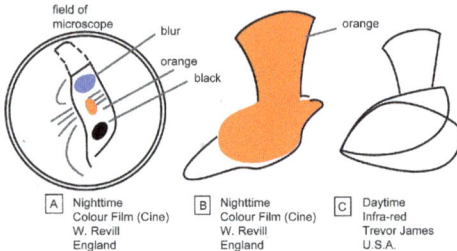

At 11pm, an object resembling a large 'box' in shape was sighted moving across the sky over Sheffield, by Walkley resident – Teresa Spotwood. She then alerted her neighbour – Walter Revill, who dashed outside with his cine camera, and took a short clip of film in the presence of Mr and Mrs Greta Pellegrina.

In an interview held with a reporter from the *Star* newspaper (20.8.1962), Walter had this to say:

> "I could not believe my eyes. It measured about a foot across in the sky, although it was very high up, moving from north to south.
>
> It was like two saucers, one on top of each other, with a horizontal line through the middle, and lit up by a sort of orange colour, moving steadily in a straight-line. I remembered I had a colour film in the house, and filmed the object for some minutes."

Although Walter has now passed away, we were able to contact Greta in 2007, who told us:

> "It was saucer-shaped, orange in colour, showing a number of portholes around its exterior. Somebody must have contacted the local radio station, because I heard it being broadcast when I got up the next morning."

Linda Sanderson, the daughter of Walter:

> "I remember how excited my father was after taking the film. Shortly after the event, two smartly dressed men came to the house and took possession of the film. I don't know who they were, but he never saw them again. It really upset my father, who bitterly regretted letting it go out of his hands."

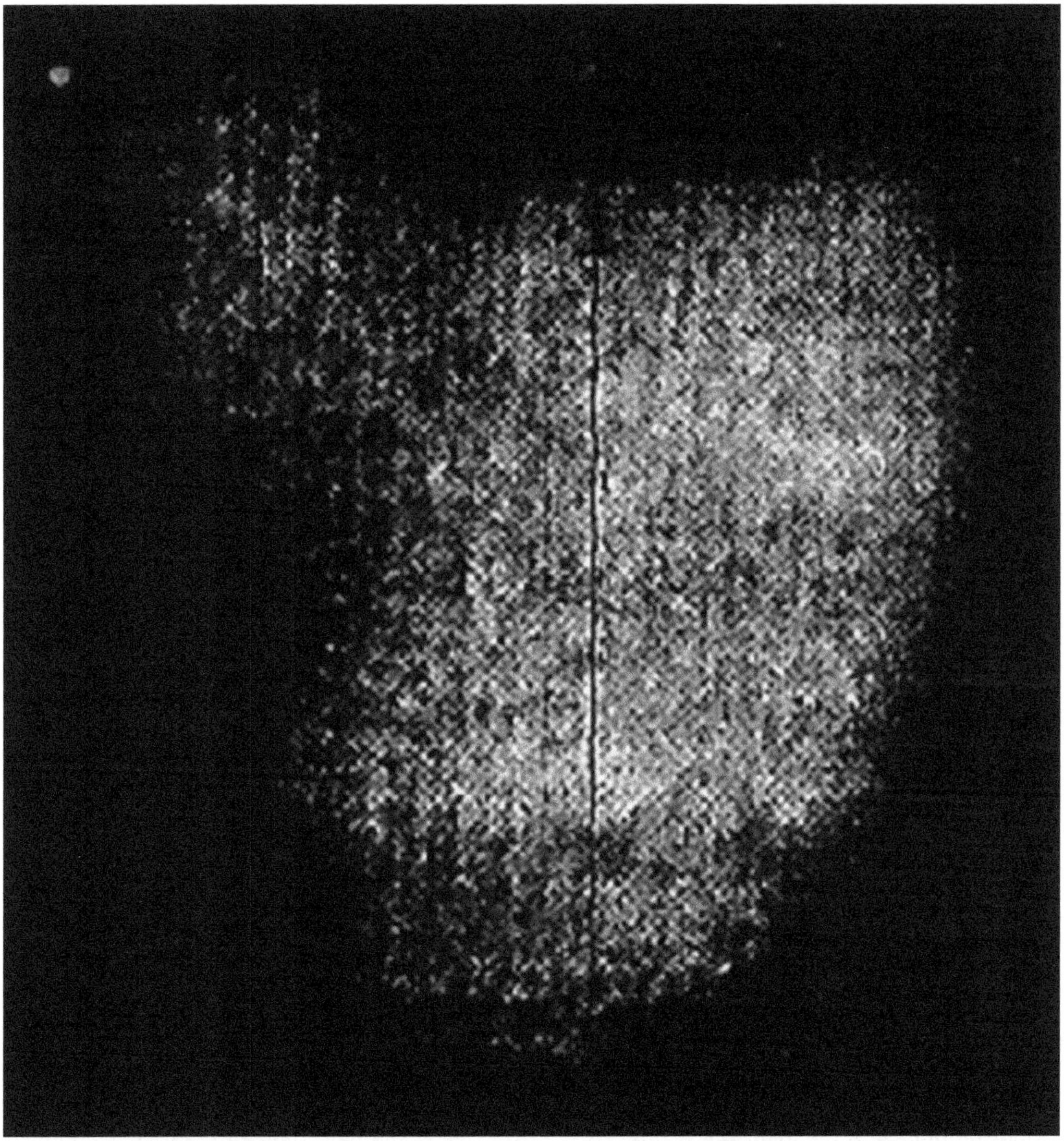

Still from the cine film shot by Walter Revill of the UFO over Sheffield which appeared in the Sheffield Star

Domed UFO sighted

Another witness to the incident was Michael John Waterhouse, who was driving near the City Hospital, with his wife, at 11pm, when they saw what they first took to be the reflection of sodium light in the car's windscreen. Mr Waterhouse pulled-in to obtain a better look, and saw an object – slightly domed at the top and bottom – move away but return a few minutes later, before disappearing for good.

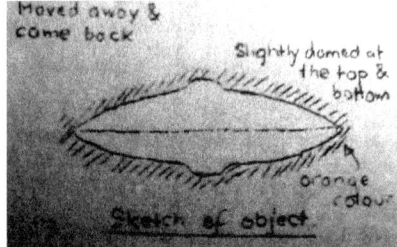

Examination of the film

According to the UFO Magazine *Spacelink*, the film was being developed and examined by experts at LUFORO – (the London UFO Research Organisation), forerunner of BUFORA – and that a report would be given in the next edition of *Spacelink*. This never appeared to have happened. However, we discovered that an examination of the cine film was carried out by Mr Basil Nubel, whose findings were subsequently published in an edition of the London UFO Research Association, Volume IV, No. 4, Sept/Oct. 1963, rather than in the next edition of *Spacelink*, as promised.

Results

The results were quite illuminating.

> *"There is a great variety of shapes. More than twenty have been drawn with the aid of a microscope from the colour film, taken at night, by Mr Walter Revill, in August 1962. No individual one of the shapes in the film can be said to look like a 'scout ship'.*
>
> *'A' these shapes existed in the film for only a fraction of a second before being truly superseded by a new shape. They could not individually have been seen and remembered by the human eye. 'B' has been enlarged by a photographic enlarger. 'C' is a shape from a photograph taken by Trevor James Constable, using infrared film, just before sunrise, over Mount Wilson, USA. This shape has been enlarged, so that it may conveniently be compared with 'B'.*
>
> *It is clear, now, that the film taken by Walter Revill, by use of a cine camera, was while at some considerable height, still close enough to have caught the attention of the witnesses in the first place, and explains the variations of descriptions seen of an object whose metamorphosis is typical of the characteristics of behavior associated with the movement of UFOs.*

On the 29th August 1962, the *Sheffield Star* newspaper showed a still taken from the film, which shows a curious 'duck-like' shape image rather than a 'flying saucer', reminding us of the famous Kenneth Arnold, whose UFO sighting sparked off a wave of interest in the USA during June 1947. Strangely, while many people know of this incident, they seem unaware that he not only saw but photographed similar objects on the 24th July 1947, at 7.50am, over Union, Oregon, as described in the introduction to this present Volume.

(Sources: *The Star*, 21.8.1962/*Northern Echo*, 27.8.1962 – 'Did anyone else see orange Saucer?'/*Sheffield Telegraph*, 29.8.1962/*The Star*, 30.8.1962/Trevor James Constable/*Flying Saucers from Other Worlds*, May 1958)

21st August 1962 – Three lights seen over Coventry

Mr Arthur Freeman from Green Lane, Coventry, was told by a member of his family about an unusual 'light' seen at 10pm, moving slowly across the sky. Through binoculars, he saw a large 'light', with two small ones directly behind it. After keeping the 'light' under observation until 10.30pm, he then telephoned the Duty Officer at RAF Church Lawford, who confirmed they had also seen it pass over. The sighting was later explained away by the Warwickshire Astronomical Society as being Pluto, with its two smaller moons prominent in the night sky. If this was the case, one would have thought the RAF would have known this!

(Source: Bob Tibbitts, Coventry UFO Research Group)

26th August 1962 – Tube-shaped UFO over Brands Hatch, Kent

David Venables was attending a motor racing meeting at Brands Hatch, Kent, when he and a number of others noticed what they thought was an aircraft towards the north direction, glinting in the sun at, 4.30pm. He looked at it through binoculars, and saw:

> *"...a tube with a black end, light grey in colour, stationary in the sky despite a strong wind blowing. Five minutes later it disappeared from sight."*

Mr Venables estimated the height was between 5-7,000 feet. He wondered if there was any connection, later, after having heard a BBC news item about a 'Flying Saucer' being captured on cine film by a man living on the Isle of Sheppey, about 15 miles away from Brands Hatch, during the same afternoon.

30th August 1962 – UFOs over Taunton

Anne Henson (16) was living with her parents at Chilliswood Farm, situated four miles south-west of Taunton, Somerset, in 1962.

> "Between 10.10pm and 10.30pm, I opened the window of my room overlooking the NNE direction and saw a star-like object with red and green flames coming from it in the sky. It was slightly larger than a star and appeared round. After two minutes it was very small and could only be seen through binoculars. I am sure it wasn't the navigation lights of an aircraft, as I had seen many of these before.
>
> I made an entry into my diary. On the 17th October 1962 I saw it again, partially obscured by fog but clearly red and green and not flashing. The colours appeared mixed together, as if something was burning and giving off the flame. Near to it and above was a similar smaller object. I then lost sight of them as the fog closed in."

Incredibly Anne was to witness another sighting, the following evening, at 7.30pm, involving the same, if not similar pair of objects.

Anne wrote a letter to RAF Chivenor about her sightings, which was forwarded onto Wing Commander C.M. Gibbs. After reading it, he contacted the RAF's *Provost and Security Services at Government buildings, Acton. In turn they allocated the investigation to Sergeant J.W. Scott, who visited Anne on a number of occasions, and although he didn't witness anything untoward himself, the case file was classified 'Staff Confidential'. No doubt this was the same officer that warned her not to talk about what she had seen. [The official files on her experience runs to 17 pages]

1962 – Silver 'disc' over Tintagel Castle

Henry Wharton – a resident of Luton, Bedfordshire – spoke about a visit to Tintagel Castle, Cornwall (believed, by many, to be the legendary home of King Arthur and the Knights of the Round Table) in 1962, which changed not only his mind but also his whole outlook on life.

Tintagel Castle

> "I met a couple, who told me they were conducting some research into paranormal phenomena, and asked me if I wanted to accompany them on a night-time vigil to the Castle. I agreed – my curiosity aroused. By the time we arrived at the locality, darkness had fallen. I selected a sheltered area to watch-out, and settled down for the evening; the moon a narrow slit in the sky.
>
> After a time, I became restless, straining my eyes to see, and was grateful when it was suggested we take a break and have some nourishment.
>
> Ten minutes later, I resumed the vigil. All of a sudden, a bright light appeared above us. I looked upwards and saw a spinning silver 'disc'. I looked around and saw the couple running, so I did the same."

---

*The P&SS is the equivalent of the United States' Air Force Office of Special Investigations (AFOSI). Its work includes espionage, counter-espionage, and disinformation – and deception-based programs that have a bearing upon national security and the defense of the realm. The official verdict was that Henson had likely seen nothing stranger than a planet or a star. That may very well have been the case, although we doubt it!

1962 August – 'Flying Saucer' seen on the ground at Reigate, Surrey

Paula Mandham was walking along a narrow lane, close to the main A25 at Reigate, Surrey, accompanied by her friend, Bruce, in late August 1962.

> "It was getting dark about 8.45pm, when I noticed some colourful lights in a field, not too far away. 'Look, it's a fair', I shouted to Bruce. He replied, 'That's no fair'. I ran along the lane and eventually reached a hedgerow bordering the field. On the ground was what I can only describe as a very big 'flying saucer', with a flashing red light on its dome. Running down its sides were these flickering coloured lights, like the ones you see at a fairground. It also had a single light, which flickered around the widest part of its body. At this point our attention was caught by movement in the sky above us. When we looked up, we saw at least six other similar 'crafts', showing gigantic spotlights projecting downwards. I looked back into the field. The first 'saucer' was still there, now approximately a hundred feet above us, but a section of it, which I hadn't noticed, was now closing. I heard the sound of rushing air, and then it shot away – too fast for the eye to register properly, and was gone. When we arrived back home, I thought it was about 9.30pm. Imagine our shock to learn it was now 3.30am!" (**Source: Graham Birdsall, Editor of** *UFO Magazine*)

SEPTEMBER 1962

8th September 1962 – UFOs sighted over Lancashire

At 6.40pm, Mrs Ellen Jordan from Nelson, Lancashire, happened to glance out of the window across a deep blue sky and see two red objects – like saucers on edge – hovering in the air. Ellen awoke her husband, Ernest, and while he was getting dressed went back to the window, where she was just in time to see them swoop down and disappear. (**Source: Personal interview**)

9th September 1962 – UFO reported over Air Show

A number of spectators attending the Farnborough Air Show reported having seen a long silver coloured object, rising upwards into the sky, completely unnoticed by five RAF Jets flying in the near vicinity. (**Source:** *UFOLOG*)

One of the witnesses was Susanne R Stebbing – Editor of Space Review, from Aldershot, in Hampshire, who contacted the Air Ministry about this matter. Mr B.D. Goodfellow, of the information office, told her it was one of the aircraft participating in the display, or might have been one of the air balloon toys on sale at the show.

Susanne:

> "At about 3.10pm, along with at least three other people, an object was sighted in a NNW direction, at an altitude of 50 degrees above the horizon. It appeared long shaped and silver. No wings could be seen through binoculars. After twenty seconds later, it rose upwards and out of sight. There were five other Jet aircraft in the area at the time, but they were flying in formation at a much lower altitude than the UFO."

13th September 1962 – Spinning top UFO sighted over Staffordshire

Myra Jones, of Norris Hill, Burton-on-Trent, was a passenger in a Morris Minor car being driven home from Overfield, by her husband, at 11.20pm, when she noticed a luminous object hovering above the car, at what she estimated to be telegraph pole height.

> "The object was in view for 30 seconds, appeared bigger than the car and was following us, the underneath part being slightly rounded, with a cone-shaped top – like a child's spinning top. I was able to see the upper and lower parts as it tilted on its side. Around the edge there appeared to be

three bulbous markings, which could have been mistaken for windows. It looked quite solid and seemed to be revolving slowly. It was aluminum coloured. All of a sudden, there was a swishing noise – like a rocket taking off – and it was gone."

(Sources: Ivan W. Bunn, author of the *'Lantern' series*/Mr W. Franklands, Investigator for the London UFO Research Organisation/BBC 4 Broadcast News Bulletin, 14.9.1962/*Times* and *Daily Mirror* – 'Woman in car buzzed by flying saucer')

18th September 1962 - Three strange 'lights' circling the sky

Mr C.A. Roberts from Southampton was looking out of his window when he saw:

"...three strange 'lights' in the sky, over Fawley; one seemed stationary, the other two kept circling for about an hour and-a-quarter".

A mysterious, glowing white, pearl-shaped, object was seen in the sky over Worksop and Manton Colliery, by at least twelve people. Some of them described it as resembling *"a white football in the sky."*

(Source: *Sheffield Star*, 22.9.1962)

22nd September 1962 – British UFO Association Conference

On Saturday, 22nd September 1962, people from all over the world made their way to the Kensington Central Library, London, where they were met by Mr G.N.P. Stephenson – Chairman of the London UFO Research Organisation. He began the conference by speaking optimistically about the serious attitude displayed towards the UFO subject and hoped this might lead to greater co-operation between the Government and UFO Societies.

Guest speaker Mr Leonard G Cramp – author of *Space, Gravity and the Flying Saucer* – gave a fascinating lecture on the subject.

During the afternoon, Alex Birch (14) from Mosborough, Sheffield, addressed the 200 people audience for four minutes, explaining how he had taken five UFO photographs in May of the same year. The afternoon ended with the showing of a selection of photographs and slides by Dr. Geoffrey G Doel, followed by the showing of two short cine films of UFOs seen over Corpus Christi, Texas, by Ray Stanford.

24th September 1962 – Rectangular object seen

At 6.45am, a *bright red rectangular object, occasionally pulsing or flickering, was seen hovering in the eastern sky, just above the sea, over Horden, County Durham.*

28th September 1962 – 'Ball of blue light' seen

A 'ball of blue light' was seen heading across the sky over parts of the East Midlands. One explanation was a high flying RAF Jet. Major John Baggart of Terry Farm, Sandiacre, saw it go over.

He said:

"It was like a ball of blue fire, making a roaring noise; windows shook and TV aerials rattled in Station Road, Borrrowash."

The Air Ministry denied any aircraft were in the area and had no knowledge of 'Blue Streaks' used in any exercise.

28th September 1962 – UFO over Newcastle

A round object – about half the size of a full moon – surrounded by lights, *"resembling points or blunt arms"*, was seen flying across the sky over Newcastle, at 12.40am, by Mrs Tubby of Choppington.

(Source: *Newcastle Evening Chronicle*, 10.10.1962)

OCTOBER 1962

1st October 1962 – Three cigar-shaped object seen by Gateshead lorry drivers

Gateshead lorry drivers – Mr Bellerby and Mr Cowell – sighted:

> "...five circular, silver, and three cigar-shaped objects, motionless in the clear sky, forming a circle with one in the middle, over the Team Valley Trading Estate, Gateshead, before moving away eastwards and vanishing from view at 8.56am".

Enquiries with RAF Acklington proved negative.

(Sources: TUFOS/*Evening Chronicle, 1.10.*1962 – 'Lorry drivers see mystery objects flying over North')

2nd October 1962 – Rectangular UFO over Gateshead

At 11.45pm, a bright, gold coloured object was seen by Miss E. Burn, and her sister, from Gateshead. They described it as:

> "...shaped like a rectangle, but with the corners cut-of, and the sides slightly curved, travelling at about 700 miles per hour".

4th October 1962 – Elliptical object reported over Sunderland

At 6.40pm, a deep glowing streak of golden light – one end brighter than the other – was seen over Berkhamstead, by a couple returning home. This was quite possibly the same UFO seen as a bright red object – this time over the M10 – by another Berkhamstead resident. Ten minutes later, Mr and Mrs Wood from Copsley, Surrey, noticed an elliptical *"thing"* hovering in the sky, ten degrees above the horizon, at 6.50pm.

At 10pm, Nurse Judith Loftus was looking out of a window at Ryhope General Hospital,

> "... when I saw what I thought was a parachute, at first, but there was no man hanging from the straps. The object remained poised over the grounds of the hospital for some seconds, shimmering in the sunshine. It then raced behind a cloud."

(Source: *Sunderland Echo,* 2.10.1962 – 'Flying Saucer seen by three Nurses')

It appears that this was not the only sighting reported from the locality. Sunderland housewife – Rita Hodgson – spoke of having seen a 'flying saucer' hovering over the sea, whilst another resident told of watching *"a weird illuminated object, dancing in the sky".* (**Source: Isle of Wight UFO Society**)

On Friday the 5th of October the *Evening Chronicle* told of a weather balloon recovered from a barley field in Durham. This appears to have explained away the UFO sighted on the 2nd of October 1962. However Lesley Otley the Honorary Secretary of the Tyneside Unidentified Flying Objects Society pointed out that the balloon found by a Mr Amos was released from Berkshire at 11.20pm on the 1st of October 1962 and could not have been the answer for the UFO sightings as they had taken place at 8.56am that day.

16th October 1962 – Swishing UFO over Derbyshire

Police in the North Derbyshire area were inundated with late night calls from the public, reporting a 'flying saucer' seen moving across the sky. One of the witnesses was ice-cream salesman James Hardwick (20) of Withens Avenue, Sheffield.

> "I was travelling through Grindleford when I saw a glowing yellow object in the sky, making a swishing sound, and moving at the speed of an aircraft."

Another witness was Eric Durward of Fern Square, Eyam, near Sheffield. He attempted to give chase to the UFO. (**Source:** *Nottingham Evening Post,* **17.10.1962 – 'Many report new Saucer over Derbyshire'**)

25th October 1962 – Mysterious siren noise

Isle of Wight resident Ken Onslow was at Binfield Corner, at 10.45pm, when he heard a high-pitched siren-like noise, followed by the appearance of a bright yellow 'light' – larger than the moon. It was moving in the east across the sky.

> *"The 'light' went out. As it did so, the siren stopped but came on again. I experienced an eerie feeling and thought of running away."*

31st October 1962 – UFO sighted over Isle of Wight:

At 11.15pm, Mr Waplesworth from Wootton Bridge, Isle of Wight, sighted an object, showing a purple centre with an orange-red fuzzy surround, approximately half the size of a full moon, heading north-west, leaving a distinctive white trail behind it. It was *"gone in a second"*. **(Source: Kath Smith, Isle of Wight UFO Society)**

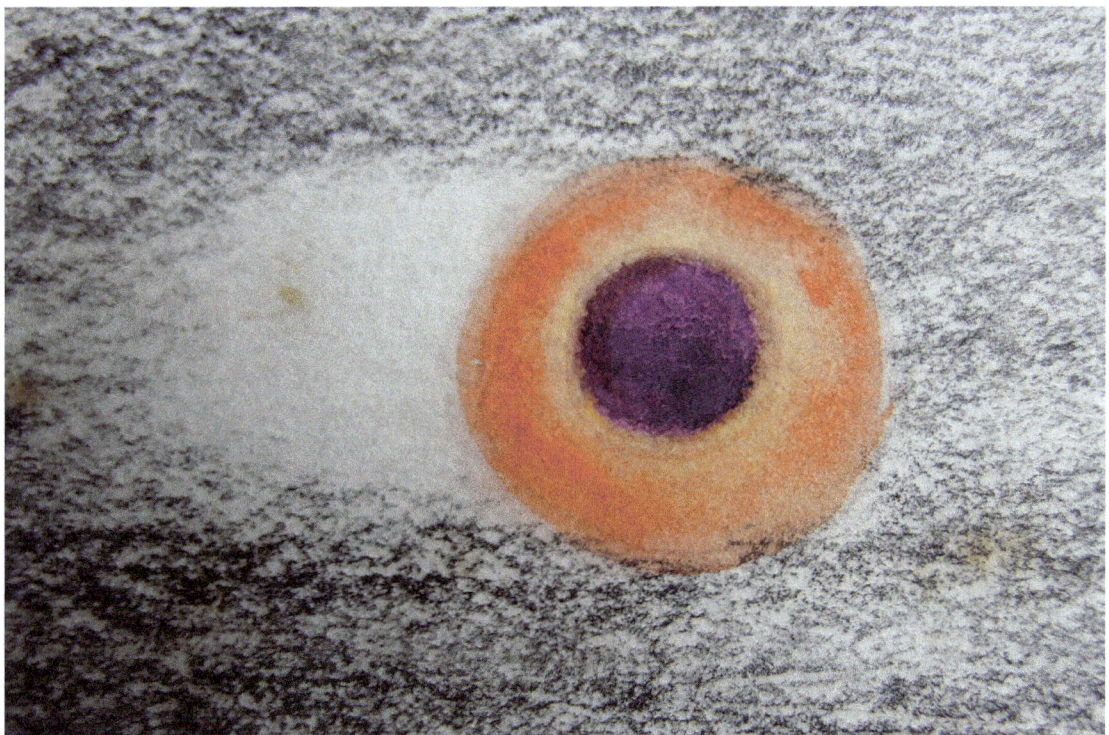

NOVEMBER 1962

3rd November 1962 – Triangular object over Leicester

Mr Eric Adkins – a draughtsman and engineer – was walking towards his house on the Eyres Monsell estate, Leicester, at 4.28pm.

He noticed a couple in front of him, were gazing up into the sky.

> *"I looked up, and was surprised to see a blinding yellow light, with an orange centre passing overhead, at a height I estimated to be 16,000 feet, at a speed of 600 miles per hour. I watched it fly across the darkening sky, and could just make out an elliptical form – flat on three edges, like a triangle. It then flipped and drifted at right angles to its original course, presenting as it did so a*

side view, allowing one to see a light on top, and one below. When it reached a position in the sky south-east over the direction of Oadby, it halted and began to hover, before finally disappearing north-east as twilight fell. I wasn't the only one to see; at least two dozen others saw its passage through the sky." **(Source: *LUFORO Bulletin*, May/June 1962)**

6th November 1962 – Orange 'light' over Portsmouth Harbour

At 8pm, an orange 'light' – approximately 15 feet in diameter – was sighted at an estimated height of 50 feet above the ground, close to Portsmouth Harbour, by Mr P. Thorne and his wife.

"It was completely still and remained in the same position for ten minutes, before disappearing from view." **(Source: Letter to Kath Smith, Isle of Wight UFO Society)**

13th November 1962 – Saucer-shaped UFO over Nottingham

A saucer-shaped object with a bright gold centre, and edged with a lighter shade, was seen over Nottingham, at 4pm, by local resident – Mrs M. Bashford. It then entered the clouds and was lost from view.

17th November 1962 – Three 'lights' over Florida

Three bright 'lights' were seen moving through the sky over Tampa, Florida, by Mr F.L. Swindale and ex-USMC Captain.

"After approaching, they hovered and bounced – then faded away after 11-15 minutes."

23rd November 1962-First Flying Saucer Exhibition in Tyneside!

The *Evening Chronicle,* in their edition, told the readers of the north-east's first 'flying saucer' exhibition, held in a Newcastle public house, (Univision gallery of the Royal Court Grill). It was organised by the Tyneside Unidentified Flying Object Society. Their chairman, Leslie Otley, explained that on display *"were photographs, books, and magazines on the subject."*

Two days later (25.11.1962) the *Sunday Post* put everything in the right perspective, 'They keep seeing Flying Saucers' –

'Regulars at the Royal Court Grill in Newcastle might think they have had a drop too much to drink when they begin to see flying saucers. But they have nothing to worry about; it is only the Tyneside Unidentified Flying Objects Society holding the first flying saucer exhibition in the public house'.

24th November 1962 – Fireball seen

A bright fireball, trailing yellow vapour, was seen passing over the counties of Gloucestershire, Middlesex and Devon, illuminating landscape with its brilliance, during the late evening. Other reports told of a large pale blue, moon-sized object, seen moving over the counties, which was brought to the attention of the *BBC Bristol* Newsroom, who interviewed one of the witnesses involved.

26th November 1962 – UFO reported over Newcastle on Tyne

An object – described as resembling *"a tall candle flame, red-gold in colour, with a lighter coloured centre, and a flat base"* – was seen suspended in the sky over Gosforth, Newcastle-upon-Tyne, at 3pm, by local resident – Mrs R. Cassie. By the time she called to her friend, it was gone from view. **(Source: TUFOS)**

DECEMBER 1962

4th December 1962 – Three 'rods of light' seen over sea at Lowestoft

At 6.15am, Mrs Agnes Blanchflower from Lowestoft, Norfolk, happened to glance through the window overlooking the ocean, when she saw what she took to be the head of a whale floating above the sea:

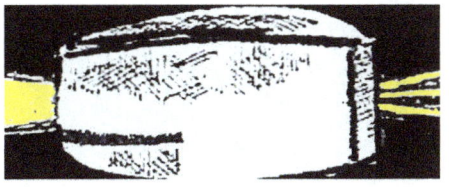

"At first I thought it was a bright star, then the head of a whale. When I looked closer, I was shocked to see it resembled a pillbox, showing a band of generated light at the rear, with three bright 'rods of light'. Every few minutes, it pulsated. When this happened more 'rods of light' appeared, followed by a bright beam – like a searchlight. On two occasions, I saw an extra piece at the top – as if seeing it at a different angle. When it pulsed with light, all the luminous parts shone brighter. As dawn began to break, the object faded away." **(Source: Ivan W. Bunn/Personal interview)**

5th December 1962 – UFOs sighted RAF tries to intercept

A circular, silvery-white, object was seen moving quickly across the sky, at an estimated height of 5,000 feet, three miles away, over Stockport, at 1.15pm, by Mr and Mrs F. Foley of Cheadle. **(Source: *ORBIT,* Vol. 4, No. 4)**

A similar (if not the same) silver object was seen moving west to east over Prestwich, near Manchester, at 4pm on the same date, according to Mr D. Ireland from Prestwich, who told of seeing:

"...six RAF Jets thundering across the sky, and converging on the object, which did a U-turn, and headed off across the sky at a speed, ruling out any pursuit".

(Sources: *UFOLOG,* Isle of Wight Investigation Society/*Space Bulletin,* DIGAP, Volume 2, No. 1, Jan/Feb/March 1963)

At 6.45pm, Manchester resident – John Chapman – sighted a silvery coloured object, *which appeared to be*

". . . five times the size and brightness of Venus, hovering in the sky at a height of some 500 feet, from a distance of five miles. It then moved slowly away, gaining speed". **(Source: *ORBIT,* October 1964, Number 4)**

19th December 1962 – 'Flying Saucer' over Cumbria

Mr Harold Threkeld of Grassgarth Cottage, Staveley, near Kendal, was walking along a fell, half a mile away from the village of Elterwater, Langdale, Cumbria, and picking holly at 4pm, when he heard a buzzing noise. He paid little attention, to begin with, but when it increased in volume, he told us:

"I saw this huge great thing in the sky, 'disc' shaped – like an upside-down saucer – hovering about 700 feet off the ground. It then came down to about 150 feet. After a couple of minutes, it swished away at tremendous speed and disappeared in the direction of Wrynose Pass. As it moved away, I was able to see the underneath very clearly. It had three projections – like beer barrels underneath – and a transparent dome, glowing with blue radiant light, with what looked like tables or benches inside. I also saw what looked like spars all around the rim, with slats or fins. I estimated the 'saucer' to be 60 feet in diameter."

We were intrigued with the UFO illustration (as sketched by Harold Threkeld) because of its similarities with that most famous of American UFO contactees – George Adamski, whose controversial claims of encounters with 'Venusians', and the saucer-shaped 'craft' with three hemispherical globes set into the base. This cultural archetype, often referred to as an 'Adamski-type saucer', has captivated worldwide audiences for over half a century.

Some regard him as a hoaxer, accusing him of having photographed hubcaps, street lamps, and chicken feeders hung from a wire, and then presented them as authentic. These are matters upon which we are not qualified to cast any judgment. However, one cannot help but notice the striking similarities between what Adamski described, and the 'craft' seen by Margaret Fry and many others, whom we were to meet

personally, over the years, and whose integrity has never been in question. Coincidentally, Harold was employed at Croppers Paper Mill, Burneside, a short distance away from where local man – Mario Luisi – was to experience an incredible 'close encounter' in November 1980.

(Source: Personal interviews/*Lakeland Evening Post* 21.12.1962 'Walker tells of 60' Phenomenon on the Fells')

Cluster of 'lights' seen over Lowestoft

One hour later, at 5pm, Mrs Avis Hall of Windsor Road, Lowestoft, saw what she took to be a cluster of stars, low in the sky over the Grand Cinema, moving slowly from the direction of the sea.

> "I've seen aeroplanes with lights, but this was nothing like that; it was so low and quiet, my knees felt weak with fear – really eerie sensation. I called for the rest of the family to come and have a look as it passed over the housetops, towards the north of the town.
>
> It wasn't a mass but appeared to consist of seven or eight stars, fixed onto some kind of frame."

(Sources: Personal interview/*Space Bulletin*, Volume 2, No. 1, Jan/Feb/March 1963/*Lancashire Evening Post*, 21.12.1962 – 'Walker tells of phenomenon on the fells'/*UFOLOG*)

In the same month, Manchester pensioners – Mr and Mrs Longshaw – were on their way to Church, at 6.15pm, when they sighted a large circular object low down in the sky, showing a number of lights around its edges, passing across the main football ground. Within 4-5 minutes, it had disappeared from sight.

21st December 1962 – Three bright lights on UFO over Norfolk

At 7.15am, Mr Harold Mayhew of Hempnall, Norfolk, was riding to work when he was stunned to see a peculiar object, hovering silently above a field. It was 500 yards from the village, at a distance of some 200 yards.

He said:

> "...It was like a thin bar, giving off a faint light, with three bright lights hanging underneath – one at each end, and one in the middle. It was making no sound and moving very slowly. As I cycled past, I got ahead of the object and lost sight of it".

(Sources: *ORBIT*, Vol. 4, Number 4/*Eastern Evening News*, 27.12 1962)

27th December 1962 – Saucer-shaped object seen over Norwich

Other witnesses of strange objects seen during this month included Norwich couple – Mr and Mrs Mann – who sighted a number of saucer-shaped objects, at 9.45pm, which they described as:

> "...having a much brighter light in their centre and moving over the town, before being lost from view amongst the city lights." (**Source:** *Eastern Evening News*, 28.12.1962)

28th December 1962 – Pilot sights UFO over Lancashire

During the late evening, an unidentified 'white light' was sighted off Morecambe Bay, Lancashire, by a member of the public.

A short time later, the Air Ministry Air Traffic Control Centre, near Preston, told police that a pilot had reported seeing something similar, travelling east to west, at a speed of between 7-800 miles per hour, at an altitude of 6,000 feet. This was later explained as possibly being a large meteor, after coastguards dismissed any suggestion it had been a distress rocket.

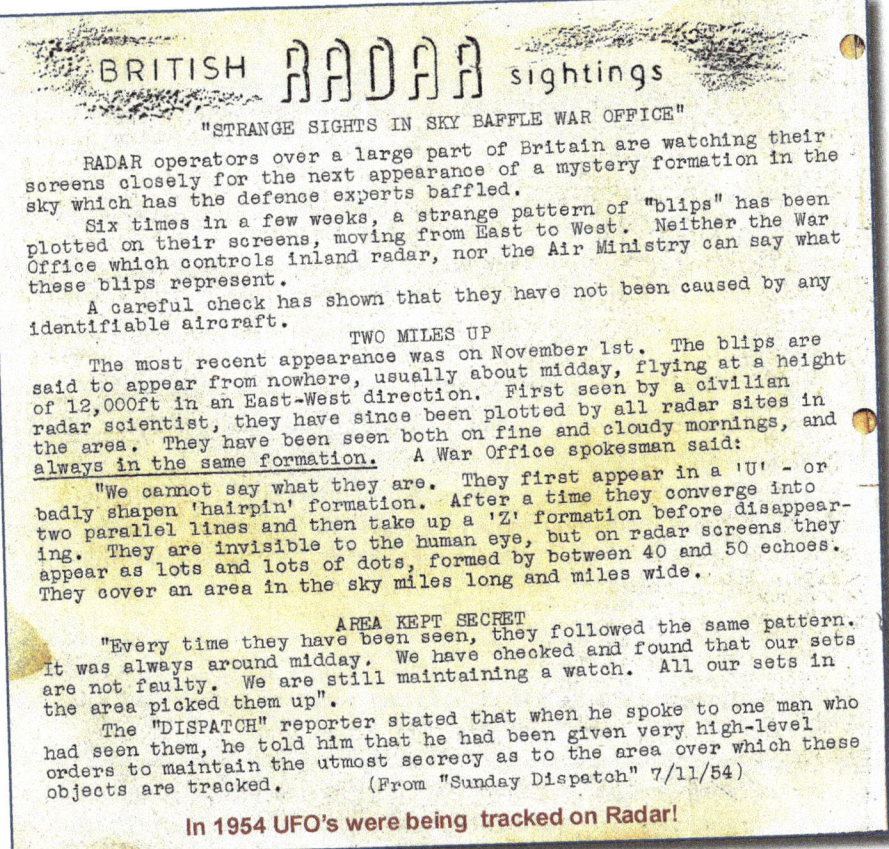

Rendlesham Forest, May 2017: Left, retired Colonel Charles Halt with David Young (centre) and Gary Baker

UFOs captured on radar evidence removed

UFOs – undoubtedly the greatest phenomena (and conundrum) of modern day times, with reports of inexplicable events stretching back throughout history – still continue to be the focus of attention in 2017 – now over fifty years later. The anticipated evidence of anomalous objects caught on radar has always been the subject of controversy, and discussion. In 2017, we met Gary Baker (who was a radar operator at RAF Neatishead, between 1978 and 1980, during a visit to the UK by Colonel Charles Irwin Halt – the former Deputy Base Commander at RAF Bentwaters/Woodbridge, Suffolk.

His famous 'Halt Memorandum', relating to UFOs sighted in the nearby forest, is still the subject of enormous controversy to the present day!

In the face of opposition by those who seek to prevent any of the 'real truths' getting out, with continuing bombardment by the National media of sensational articles on the internet-based newspapers (which only denigrate the subject), we should be grateful for people like Gary Baker, who still finds the courage to come forward to report the truth.

His account contained in *The Halt Perspective* is summarised.

Gary:

> "I was told that it never happened, by RAF Officers who came to the station and presumably were the ones who seized the radar tapes and bridge logs. It would have been sensible to quash any evidence. If something happened and it wasn't picked up, it would have shown we weren't capable of dealing with something from 'above'. Later I read the MOD claimed the radar had been switched off at the time, which is rubbish. I'm no UFO researcher but something extraordinary happened there outside the parameters of manned aircraft."

CHAPTER 4 – 1963

UFO REPORTS INCLUDE:

JANUARY:
8th January 1963 – UFO over Hulver
28th January 1963 – Cigar-shaped UFO over Coventry

FEBRUARY:
5th February 1963 – UFO over US missile site, aircraft scrambled
6th February 1963 – US Pilot sights UFO
February 1963 – Girder-like object over Bournemouth
10th February 1963 – 'Flying Saucers' over Lancashire
15th February 1963 – Domed UFO over Victoria Australia,
21st February 1963 – 'Globe of fire' strikes car at Montana
27th February 1963 – USA: Crescent-shaped UFO seen over California,
February 1963 – Royal Navy: UFO seen entering Arctic Ocean
28th February 1963 – Smoke rings seen over Northern Arizona
What was seen by the crew of the British Trawler, St. Chad, off Norway?
UFO sighting – Three UFOs over Kent, RAF scrambles fighters

MARCH:
6th March 1963 – Bright flash seen near US Air Force Base
8th March 1963 – Two 'discs' seen over Northumberland
11th March 1963 – USA: UFOs sighted by US pilots
15th March 1963 – Member of Parliament quizzed about UFOs
18th March 1963 – USA: Did UFO cause missile to change direction?
26th March 1963 – Rectangular UFO seen over Illinois
28th March 1963 – Incident at Britannia Barracks, Norwich.

APRIL:
4th April 1963 – Silver UFO reported
8th April 1963 – Black 'wagon wheel' shaped UFO
April 1963 – Strange 'lights' sighted over Wales
14th April 1963 – String of orange objects seen in the sky
19th April 1963 – Looking out to sea
29th April 1963 – Cigar-shaped UFO over Isle of Wight

MAY:
3rd May 1963 – Dark UFO seen ejecting vapour over Warwickshire

15th May 1963 – Astronaut sights UFO
22nd May 1963 – Air Training Corp sight unusual object seen in sky.

JUNE:
6th June 1963 – "They looked like flying saucers"
8th June 1963 – Domed UFO over Isle of Wight
9th June 1963 – UFO over Chelmsford, Essex
10th June 1963 – Similar phenomena sighted
19th June 1963 – Spinning UFO sighted
24th June 1963 – Top secret report of UFO plotted on radar over UK
28th June 1963 – Oval UFO reported
Summer – 'Wobbling' UFO over Lincolnshire

JULY:
6th July 1963 – RAF Open Day UFO sighted
7th/8th July 1963 – 'Globe' seen over Charlton area of Wiltshire
10th July 1963 – The Charlton crater and UFO activity, Police Officer sights orange object
11th July 1963 – Blowlamp-shaped UFO hovers over house
13th July 1963 – Red twinkling 'light' sighted over UK
14th July 1963 – Huge cigar-shaped UFO seen over Dorset
22nd July 1963 – 'Flying Saucer' over Lancashire
23rd July 1963 – 'Flying Saucer' over Gloucestershire
24th July 1963 – 'Spinning Top' UFO, Lancashire, UFO seen over Leeds, the same day
25th July 1963 – Seven objects sighted, Orange object seen over Malvern
28th July 1963 – Green object with aerial
29th July 1963 – UFO over Chelmsford, Essex
30th July 1963 – Four red 'lights' seen over Tipton
31st July 1963 – UFO seen over Somerset
July 1963 – RAF Pilot sights UFO over Lake District

AUGUST:
1st August 1963 – The fishermen's tale
5th August – 'Flying Saucer' over Blackburn, Lancashire
5th August 1963 – Motorist chased by UFO over Illinois, USA
6th August 1963 – 'Wheezing' UFO over Edinburgh

7th August 1963 – USA: Diamond-shaped UFO sighted in sky over Fairfield, Illinois
7th August 1963 – Unusual object sighted in the sky
12th August 1963 – UFO seen over Wolverhampton
17th August 1963 – Three flashes of light over Nottingham, then orange 'disc' seen
20th August 1963 – Strange lights over Gloucester
22nd August 1963 – 'Jellyfish' UFO sighted by ex-RAF Officer
26th August 1963 – UFO with 'aerial' sighted over London
31st August 1963 – 'Flying Saucer' over Croydon

SEPTEMBER:
6th September 1963 – 'Flying Saucer' over Southampton
14th September 1963 – Heart-shaped UFO sighted
14th September 1963 – USA: Strange object in the sky over California
15th September 1963 – Pulsating crescent-shaped UFO sighted
15th September 1963 – USA: Golden UFOs over Ohio
September 1963 – 'Ice-cream cone' shaped object over Kent
Late September 1963 – Silver object over Nottingham
27th September 1963 – Two UFOs attached to each other

OCTOBER:
1st October 1963 – UFO over Manchester Airport
2nd October 1963 – Was this the same UFO?
4th October 1963 – Spinning UFO over Cheshire
7th October 1963 – Strange phenomena over Southampton
October 1963 – UFO over Romford, Essex

14th October 1963 – Fireball over Sussex
20th October 1963 – UFOs seen over Leeds and Suffolk
21st October 1963 – 'Discs' of orange light reported in the sky
23rd October 1963 – Football-shaped UFO seen over Ohio
24th October 1963 – Strange 'light' in the sky over Scotland
29th October 1963 – Silver object over Devizes

NOVEMBER:
13th November 1963 – Pulsating object seen over Isle of Wight
18th November 1963 – Silver 'disc' seen. Did RAF respond?
20th November 1963 – Flashing 'red light' seen by crew of trawler
November 1963 – Four cylindrical objects sighted over reservoir
27th November 1963 – Silver 'ball' sighted over Cornwall
29th November 1963 – UFO with three 'spikes' sighted in sky

DECEMBER:
1st (provisional) December 1963 – UFO landing at RAF Cosford, Staffordshire
5th December 1963 – Blazing 'ball of fire' sighted over Isle of Wight
7th December 1963 – Fiery object seen by mother and daughter
11th December 1963 – Flashing UFO
12th December – UFO making warbling noise
14th December 1963 – Cigar-shaped UFO seen over Margate
24th December 1963 – Car battery flattened by UFO
27th December 1963 – UFO landing at Buckhurst Hill, Epping

JANUARY 1963

8th January 1963 – UFO over Hulver

Beccles Ambulance driver – Alfred Crisp, and his attendant – Charles Bennett, were driving towards Hulver Street, Norfolk, along the B.1127, at 5pm. They noticed a long, dark object, motionless in the sky.

Alfred:

> "When we arrived at Hulver Street, we stopped on high ground near the disused Ellough Airfield, to obtain a closer look. Could it have been a man, suspended from a parachute, we wondered, or a kite? Suddenly, without any warning whatever, it shot off across the sky, at speed, which ruled out any such ideas." (**Source: Ivan W. Bunn, 'Lantern' Series**)

Puzzling characteristic

Ivan W. Bunn

Another puzzling characteristic is the similarities in description of the external structure of UFOs, often referred to as resembling: *"a ladder"*, *"steel girder-like beams"*, or *"square"*, or *"oblong rectangular panels or markings"*, which may seem odd, bearing in mind the stereotyped perception of *'Flying Saucers'*. *However*, sightings of triangular, pyramidal and box-shaped objects, seen in the skies, can be traced back to the 1940s. This may indicate the possibility that while descriptions of UFOs appear to be varied, we should bear in mind that we may not be seeing all of the UFO but just a tantalizing part of it. One senses that whatever it looks like to the observer, they all originate from the same source, wherever that may be.

28th January 1963 – Cigar-shaped UFO over Coventry

At 5.20pm on the same date at Shilton, Coventry, Mary Sharp and her mother sighted a yellow-orange cigar-shaped object, showing four portholes, lying on the ground. It left a short time later and headed away, at speed, towards Rugby. (Source: Bob Tibbitts, CUFORG)

FEBRUARY 1963

5th February 1963 – UFO over US missile site, aircraft scrambled

At 11.45pm, following a report of a yellow-white glowing UFO, about 3 feet in diameter, seen over a missile site at Charlottesville, (located in west Central Virginia, approximately 100 miles south-west of Washington DC), aircraft were scrambled to respond. It appears that a pulsating yellow *'light'* was also seen to manoeuvre around their plane, by a private pilot and a newsman passenger.

6th February 1963 – US Pilot sights UFO

A pilot of a C-46 aircraft was flying 15 miles south-west of Montebello, on a 40 degrees heading, at 12am, when the pilot sighted a large, round, very bright star-like object at the one o'clock position, at 3-5 degrees above the horizon. The object appeared to vary in size during observation, and gain in elevation to 15-30 degrees above the horizon. The object was last sighted at 3-5 degrees above horizon at the 4-5 o'clock position. The length of the observation was approximately 45 minutes. (Source: Dan Wilson)

February 1963 – Girder-like object over Bournemouth

Ex-RAF serviceman Mr C. Barnes, from Bournemouth, was cycling home along the main Wimborne Road, towards Moordown, in February 1963, when he saw:

> *"...a girder-like object, aluminum in colour, about the size of a large aircraft, of lattice-like construction moving across the sky in a see-saw action, which formed a large semicircle two miles away."*

The UFO was kept under observation for 20 minutes before it moved out of view. Enquiries into the matter by Fred and Pat Smith, of the Isle of Wight UFO Society, established the object was 75 feet long by 15 feet high, moving at approximately one hundred miles an hour, at a height of 3,000 feet.

(Source: *Spacelink*, F.W. Smith, May/June 1964, Volume 1, No. 3)

10th February 1963 – 'Flying Saucers' over Lancashire

Retired psychiatric Staff Nurse Bill Cassidy from Eccleston, Lancashire, now (2010) in his mid 80s, contacted us in 2006, after reading an appeal made by us in the local newspaper, requesting any information on UFOs seen in the locality.

Bill told us that he was living in a flat, overlooking wasteland near to an old coal tip, in February 1963, when – while looking through the window, at midday – he saw five objects, heading across a blue sky.

It was a cold day – cold enough for the *River Mersey* to have frozen over.

> *"As they approached closer, I was able to see they were silver metallic 'saucers' in appearance. The 'craft' on the outside of the formation was much smaller than the one in the middle. I shouted to my wife. We watched in stark disbelief, as they moved overhead, at a height of about 300 feet off the*

Haunted Skies **Volume Two Revised**

ground. We rushed to the other side of the house and saw them heading towards RAF Burtonwood Airbase – then closed. My wife rang the Liverpool Echo, who contacted the MOD. They were told we must have seen weather balloons, released from Preston!" (**Source: Personal interview**)

15th February 1963 – Domed UFO over Victoria, Australia

This was such an interesting report which we felt was well worth including, irrespective of the fact that it took place in Australia.

At 7am, Charles Brew and his 20 year-old son, Trevor Brew, were at work in the milking shed on their farm, 'Willow Grove', near Moe, Victoria. It was daylight, but rain clouds lay overhead.

Object appears in the sky

Charles Brew was standing in an open area, with a full view of the eastern sky, when he saw a strange object appear and descend very slowly towards the milk shed. As it did so, livestock in the area – which included a pony and nearby cows and two farm dogs – fled in fear. [A local newspaper was to later report that the cows turned somersaults, which the Brews' later denied.]

UFO hovers over farm

The UFO descended to a height of about 30 metres, hovering over a stringy-bark tree, and was described as being:

> "...about eight metres in diameter and three metres high. The top section appeared to be a transparent dome of a glass-like material, from which protruded a two metre high mast or aerial. The 'aerial' appeared to be as thick as a broom and resembled bright chrome. The top portion of the 'disc' itself was battleship grey in colour and appeared to be of metallic lustre. The base or underside section glowed with a pale blue colour and had 'scoop-like protuberances around the outside edge'. This section rotated slowly at about one revolution per second".

Rotated slowly

This spinning motion apparently caused the protuberances to generate a swishing sound – somewhat like a turbine noise – that was clearly audible not only to Brew but also to his son, Trevor, who was located inside the shed, near the operating diesel powered milking machine units.

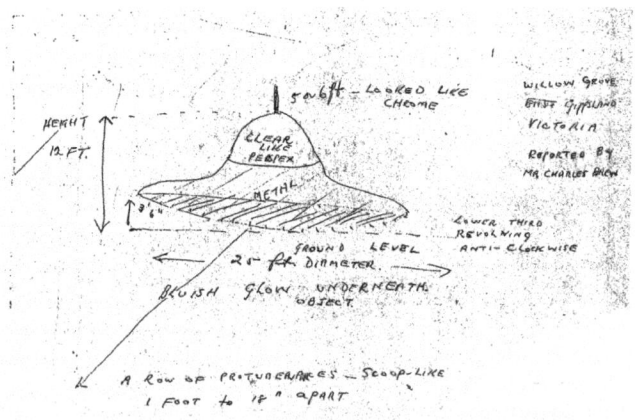

Strange sound heard

Charles Brew felt his eyes were drawn towards the object *"as though beams of magnetic current"* were between it and him. He also experienced a peculiar headache, which came on with the approach of the object. After hovering for a few seconds the object began to climb, continuing on its westward course and passing up into the cloud deck again. Trevor did not see the UFO, but confirmed the unusual sound – like a didgeridoo or bullroarer [aboriginal artifacts which can produce pulsating, wind-rushing noise].

Royal Australian Air Force sends investigators

Flight Lieutenant N. Hudson and Squadron Leader A.F. Javes, of the RAAF, interviewed Mr Brew. While impressed with his credibility, the weather at the time of the sighting – heavy continuous rain, with very

The Advocate, 20/2/63

"Flying saucer" sends cattle into panic

A "flying saucer" — or something — sent a horse and a herd of cows into a panic at Mr. Charlie Brew's farm at Willow Grove on Friday morning.

FROM MARS TO MOE (MO) — HERESY IN VERSE

The following heretical ballad has been submitted by a Moe resident who asks us to preserve his anonymity as he is "strongly against capital punishment."

FROM MARS TO MOE (MO)

At Willow Grove, north west of Moe,
One starry summer's night,
A flying saucer 'peared on high,
And gave the cows a fright.
Don't scoff or scorn at Willow Grove,
Or throw jokes at its face,
For Willow Groves' not far from Moe
And Moe's the queerest place.

For we who've lived here long enough
Are not surprised one bit
That men from Mars should visit us,
And give the cows a fit.
You listen to a Moe bloke,
Tale - telling of his town —
You'd like to hear a tale or two?
I'll write a couple down.

We live down south of Moe,
Yet our shops are in the north.
The railway line runs through the town —
Briquette trucks back and forth.
Our bridge is feared throughout the State,
A monstrous sight to see.
Most here are Labour-minded folk —
We've a Liberal M.P.

Moe advances to a City, on a Wednesday very soon,
But we celebrate the holiday,
The previous afternoon.
For it's then they run the Moe Cup
(A more important day).
We'd have had a cup and saucer,
But the Mars men went away.

A Nyaalinga show's arranged
(That means "come back to Moe") —
Perhaps these Mars mens' grandads,
Used to live here long ago.
Or perhaps these saucer jokers,
Wandering lost amongst the stars,
Thought Moe's like nothing else on earth,
And reckoned it was Mars.

From Mr. Brew's description it sounded like a fairly thick disc.

Mr. Brew said it was battleship - grey, and appeared to have a band of glass or perspex around the circumference and a number of protusions which looked like scoops. He thought it was about 25 feet across.

Mr. Brew and his son Trevor were milking at 7.10 a.m. It was raining heavily.

Mr. Brew happened to be looking out at the cows when the thing appeared from the east, came down fairly slowly and steeply to perhaps 75 or 100 feet, as if it were going to land, he thought.

Then it shot off westward "two or three times as fast as a jet," and disappeared in cloud.

He said Trevor was at the "blind" end of the bail and did not see the object, but he heard it.

There was no engine noise, but kind of pulsating, whooshing sound, as might be made by the scoops.

Mr. Brew said the thing was revolving slowly, though travelling very fast.

He said he would not have seen it if he had not happened to be looking in the right direction — the whole "visit" lasted only about the time it would take to turn your head.

low cloud and poor visibility, and with a fresh wind in an easterly direction – seems to have led them to consider that it might have been a tornado!

Explained away as a tornado!

On 6th March, Dr. Berson and a Mr Clark – Commonwealth meteorologists – were interviewed to ascertain if clouds could produce this type of phenomenon. They agreed that tornado conditions could cause this effect. According to them, the only difference in Brew's report was that the object moved from east to west because, in all their previous reports of this nature, have been from west to east. [Mr Brew stated that the wind was fresh, from an easterly direction.] However, a meteorological report states that wind was westerly at eight knots. Despite this lack of rigour in determining how relevant their hypothesis was, the RAAF officers' report concluded:

> "There is little doubt that Brew did witness something, and it is most likely that it was a natural phenomenon. The phenomenon was probably a tornado. There was no reported damage along its path; therefore, one could assume that it was weak in nature."

The Department of Air

The Department of Air responded to a civilian UFO group enquiry about the incident, with the following statement:

> "Our investigation and enquiries reveal that there are scientific records of certain tornado-like meteorological manifestations, which have a similar appearance in many ways to whatever was seen by Mr Brew. The information available is such, however, that while we accept this is a possibility, we are unable to come to any firm conclusion as to the nature of the object or manifestation reported."

The official sighting summaries removed any such doubt. By then, the 'possible cause' was listed as 'a tornado-like meteorological manifestation'.

Dr. James McDonald

Dr. James McDonald visited Charles Brew during his 1967 Australian trip, interviewing him at the site of the 1963 incident. McDonald concluded:

> "Like that of many other UFO witnesses, it is extremely difficult to explain in present-day scientific or technological terms."

Summary of Unidentified Aerial Sightings reported to Department of Air, Canberra, ACT, from 1960

Despite the extraordinary nature of the 'Willow Grove' incident, and the high level of official interest in it, the sighting was listed in a subsequently released *"Summary of Unidentified Aerial Sightings reported to Department of Air, Canberra, ACT, from 1960"* as having a possible cause of *"tornado-like meteorological manifestation"*. Are we really expected to believe that what the men saw was a tornado?

If the illustration (which is shown here) is typical of a tornado in action, then this would suggest that the thousands, if not millions, of other cases involving similarly described objects, reported all over the world, is the answer to the UFO phenomena! This is, in our opinion, a preposterous explanation. As we have said before, all the authorities have to do is supply an explanation – no matter how ridiculous it is – purely because the majority of people will accept it as a rational answer, without question, knowing that UFOs cannot exist.

(Sources: *Auckland Star*, 16.2.1963/*Australian Flying Saucer Review*, No. 8, June 1965/*Flying Saucer Review*, 29.5.1961/Bill Chalker, 1996/NAA, File series A703) [15.3.1963 – *The Wimbledon Borough News*, **London, reported on a gleaming silver, circular object, seen in the sky over Wimbledon Common on this date.**]

21st February 1963 – *'Globe of fire'* strikes car at Montana

A motorist was driving his car through Belgrade, Montana, at 2.30am, when his car was struck by a strange *'globe of fire'*, and several people called the authorities to report that they had been awakened by a peculiar object crossing the sky. (Source: *Magonia 565*)

27th February 1963 – USA: Crescent-shaped UFO seen over California

A large crescent-shaped object, with what appeared to be portholes set into its structure, was seen over Modesto, California, by seven people, who told of watching it descend to about a 1,000 feet and project a bright beam of light, before moving away. (Source: *Anatomy of a Phenomenon,* Jacques Vallee)

28th February 1963 – USA: Smoke rings seen over Northern Arizona

A number or mysterious *'smoke ring'* cloud effects were seen in the sky over Northern Arizona, which, according to *Science* – the American association for the advancement of Science – was unprecedented in years of sky watching. (Source: NICAP)

February 1963 – Royal Navy: UFO seen entering Arctic Ocean

A contingent of the Royal Navy's North Atlantic Fleet was participating in exercises off Norway. At 3.15am, between Spitzbergen Island and Norway – 30-50 miles off the Norway coast – an object was tracked on the ship's radar, at 35,000 feet, and by sonar after it entered the water. It was then tracked at 50 feet below the surface and continued into deep water at a range of 20,000 yards. The radar signature indicated it was 100 feet-120 feet in diameter. The object was also tracked by other ships and the order was issued for the fleet to execute an evasive 'Z' pattern maneuvers. Jets were scrambled. The duration of the alert was at least 15-20 minutes. (Source: *MUFON Journal*, 1984)

What was seen by the crew of the British Trawler, St. Chad, off Norway?

It is of interest to mention, at this point, another incident involving the appearance of a UFO followed by Air Force Jets that took place off the coast of Norway, which took place in the previous year, although no precise date has been given. William Jefferson, who served in a British Army 'Defence' Regiment from 1977 to 1991, commanding a sophisticated missile system, contacted us with regard to what his father, Bill, had seen while aboard the fishing trawler *Saint Chad,* off the Norway Coast.

> *"My Dad told me that it was an extremely calm day and that he had turned in after his four hours on four hours off shift, only interrupted normally when fish were picked up by the fishing trawl. The skipper ordered that the trawl be brought back on board, as nothing was being picked up. Suddenly Bill and the rest of the crew were ordered to go up on deck. Wondering what was going on, he made his way onto the deck and was stunned to see a huge grey 'disc' shaped craft – bigger that the trawler – hovering a few feet above the funnel. It was so close you could see the panels were joined with small squares and strange writing. There were different coloured lights also visible, but none were illuminated. The skipper ordered the radio operator to contact the authorities.*
>
> *About thirty minutes later, three low flying Norwegian Jets appeared – at which point the craft inexplicably disappeared from view."*

We understood that all of the crew was told not to say anything to anybody about the sighting.

The Saint Chad was built in 1956 for the St. Andrews Steam Fishing Company and sold to Boston Deep Sea Fisheries Ltd. on the 30th March 1973, under the command of Skipper Neville 'the devil' Beavers. It was driven ashore and wrecked at Ritur Huk Isafjordur, North West Iceland, while sheltering in a blizzard and gale conditions; the crew took to the life rafts, and after reaching the shore were picked up by the support tug – the Statesman – before being transferred to the mother ship – Othello H389.

Enquiries were made, in 2007, by our colleague – David Sankey [whose wonderful art work still provides a backcloth in 2017] with Arthur Credland at the Hull local Libraries to identify from maritime records that Mr William Jefferson served aboard the Trawler – Saint Chad – between 1961 and 1963.

Mysterious disappearing public house

The story of strange phenomena does not end here. On one occasion, the three men were visiting Norman's nephew – Ronny Hill, who was then living in Anglesey, at Black Horse Lane, Pen-Y-Garnedd. On their return home, they decided to take the B5109 from Blackthorne Lane. Mark left his dog, Toby, in the car and they sought refreshment in the main lounge at a smart hotel. During conversation with the barmaid, after consuming some delicious beer and ham sandwiches, she told them they had their own farm behind the pub and that they cured and baked all the produce. On a return visit to the locality they were shocked to find no trace of the public house!

UFO sighting – Three UFOs over Kent, RAF scrambles fighters

Mr Dennis Wright, from Kent, was installing new hoppers at the Dover Gasworks (now demolished), accompanied by his two brothers, in the early 1960s, (although the exact date eludes him), unloading reinforcing bars from a railway truck, at the time, when an object appeared in the sky – transparent in colour and cigar-shaped – closely followed by two others, moving from the direction of France.

> "I shouted out to my brothers. We watched as they moved over. The first one flipped on end and went straight up at a 90 degree angle, followed by the other two, perfectly round and metallic silver in appearance. To our amazement, they began some sort of 'aerial display' above us. A twin-engine plane appeared; one of the 'saucers' flew directly at it. The pilot must have been terrified. The object was so big in comparison to the aircraft."

Telephoned RAF Manston

Dennis made a telephone call to the nearby RAF Manston Airbase to report the incident, when – all of a sudden – the three 'saucers' shot off in the direction from which they had come. They were gone in seconds.

> "About a minute later, two RAF Jet fighters appeared, and began a search across the sky – presumably looking for the 'saucers'.
>
> Over the years I have told a number of people about this sighting, but very few believe me, yet the report the pilot made to RAF Manston Airbase must be on record somewhere. The odd thing is that out of twenty other workmen who were there, at the time, we were the only three to see them."

(Source: Probe/Peter Tate)

MARCH 1963

6th March 1963 – Bright flash seen near US Air Force Base

At around 10.37am, a bright flash was observed by numerous witnesses from Louisiana to Texas. One report said a large bright flash was seen 20 miles north of Barksdale Air Force Base. It was also seen by two light aircraft and a SAC Bomber.

Another report stated that there was on observation of a bright flash and metallic falling object, 40 miles north-north-west of Chennault Air Force Base, at 10.55am.

(Source: *McDonald list*, Dan Wilson)

8th March 1963 – Two *'discs' seen over Northumberland*

Mr William Muir of Rowanberry Road, Longbenton, was out walking in High Heaton when he saw,

> "...An object shaped like two discs joined together by a grey blue colored tube. Hovering in the sky I watched it for about three minutes before it disappeared from view." (Source: *Evening Chronicle*, 21.3.1963 – 'Another Flying saucer claim')

11th March 1963 – USA: UFOs sighted by US pilots

Just after 8pm, a brilliant 'light' was seen heading westwards over Oahu, Hawaii, leaving a trail observed by many people.

Two National Guard pilots, flying jets about 40 miles west of Honolulu, reported the UFO was *"much higher"* than their altitude of 40,000 feet and moving *"very fast"*. (At 7.28pm, a newsboy, in El Sobrante, California, saw two oval, yellow, 'lights' pass over the San Francisco Bay area, from North to South, travelling at high-speed.) (**Source: NICAP**)

15th March 1963 – Member of Parliament quizzed about UFOs

At a public meeting held in Frimley, Surrey, Member of Parliament, Harold Watkinson (Tory Member of Parliament for Woking), was asked by a woman in the audience:

> *"Why is the Government trying to hush up the sightings of 'Flying Saucers'? Whenever these visitors from space are sighted, newspaper and television are ordered not to report the fact. Why is the public not kept informed?"*

Mr Watkinson, who resigned as Minster of Defence in last year's cabinet reshuffle, said:

> "Before I left the Ministry I had to sign a large number of papers, promising never to reveal certain facts I had learned as Minister of Defence. The subject of 'Flying Saucers' may be included." (**Source:** *Camberley News*, **15.3.1963**)

18th March 1963 – USA: Did UFO cause missile to change direction?

A strange object was sighted over the Atlantic coast of Florida, a few moments before a Minuteman missile launched from Cape Canaveral, which then veered off course and had to be destroyed.

(Source: *UFO Investigator,* March-April 1963, page 4 – 'UFO SEEN AS ROCKET VEERS OFF COURSE')

26th March 1963 – USA: Rectangular UFO seen over Illinois

At 11.40pm, Mrs D. Wheeler and Claudine Milligan from Naperville, Illinois, saw 6-8 'red *balls*', arranged in a rectangular formation in the sky, which changed into two objects, with lights, by the end of the sighting. (**Source: Berliner**)

28th March 1963 – Incident at Britannia Barracks, Norwich

Norwich resident – Miss I. Duffield – was sitting near the Britannia Barracks, Norwich, with her boyfriend, at 8pm, when a van pulled-up. Two men alighted, and proceeded to set up a tripod on the ground. From out of the tripod came a yellow and red 'light' which shot up into the sky, moved over the barracks, and disappeared.

A second light then came out of the tripod, at which stage the couple – now feeling rather frightened – decided to leave.

The next day, they read in their local newspaper that similar lights had been seen over the town, the same evening. Was this some exercise, involving the discharge of flares, or is there a more mundane explanation? Enquiries with the MOD and the local newspapers failed to obtain any explanation.

(Source: *Norwich Evening News,* 30.3.1963)

APRIL 1963

4th April 1963 – Silver UFO reported

At 10.30pm, a silver shining object, resembling an arrowhead, was seen over Blackburn, Lancashire.
(**Source:** *Blackburn Evening Telegraph,* **5.4.1963**)

8th April 1963 – Black 'wagon wheel' shaped UFO

Mr Peter Finlay – an engineer from Stakeford, Newcastle-upon-Tyne – was driving between Rothbury and Whittingham. He noticed, through his windscreen, an object reminding him of: *"... a black wagon wheel"* moving across the sky, at a height of approximately 800 feet high, and two to three miles away; *"Minutes later, a RAF jet shot across the sky".*

Mr Finlay rang the Duty Officer at RAF Boulmer, to report the incident, but was told by the man that *"he was not prepared to comment on the matter".* (**Source:** *Newcastle-upon-Tyne Journal,* 9.4.1963)

April 1963 – Strange 'lights' sighted over Wales

Miss Susan Mitchell of Wilmslow, Cheshire, was walking along the promenade at Criccieth, in Wales, with her companion.

They were looking out to the south-west part of the sky, at 9pm, just after the sun had set, when they saw:

> *"...a very steady brightness, and quite large; it appeared to be drifting slowly across the sky. Suddenly, a smaller 'light' detached itself from the main one, and fell behind, disappearing from view. Then the main object ejected further lights at one or two second intervals, in the following pattern, 1, 1,2,1,2 – until there were fifteen of these 'lights' in the sky, which themselves disappeared from view. A short time later, the main object itself inexplicably vanished from view."* (**Source: UFOLOG**)

14th April 1963 – String of orange objects seen in the sky

A retired couple from Fitzwilliam Street, Cambridge, was walking through the grounds of Downing College, at 7pm, when they noticed:

> *"...a string of between five and nine flame-coloured orange objects in the sky, completely stationary. It was twilight, at the time, with some stars visible after a hot day; they were one behind the other, forming a curve in the sky. Eight seconds or so later, they vanished from sight."*

The description would fit perfectly into modern-day reports of Chinese Lanterns, except for the fact that this was, after all, over fifty years ago! As for explanations, the Isle of Wight UFO Society wondered if it could have been attributed to temperature inversion, reflecting the sodium street lights on a nearby road.

(**Source: Isle of Wight UFO Society**)

19th April 1963 – Looking out to sea

Mr A.J. Rawden (35) of High Street, Ryde, was looking out to sea from the top of Brading and Ashey Down, just after 7.15pm, when:

> *"I saw a whitish coloured area – oblong in shape – motionless in a belt of sea mist, between the sea and the brilliant blue sky."* (**Source: UFOLOG**)

29th April 1963 – Cigar-shaped UFO over Isle of Wight

At.10.45pm, a cigar-shaped object was seen in the sky, 55 degrees off the horizon, by Isle of Wight housewife – Mrs Spanner, and daughter.

> *"At 1am, a small red 'light' came out and headed off north-east. Through binoculars, two long, narrow cylinders, vivid bright green in colour, showing brilliant red light at the forward travel end, could be seen – like two cigarettes, held together, which slowly moved out of sight."*

(**Source: UFOLOG/Personal interview, Eric Spanner**)

MAY 1963

3rd May 1963 – Dark UFO seen ejecting vapour over Warwickshire
At 9pm, a dark object was seen stationary in the sky over Alveston, Warwickshire, ejecting a grey vapour.
(**Source: Cheltenham Flying Saucer Group**)

15th May 1963 – Astronaut sights UFO
During the final orbit, Major Gordon Cooper – one of the original Mercury astronauts – told the tracking station at Muchea, near Perth, Australia, that he could see *"a glowing greenish object ahead of him, quickly approaching the capsule"* (which had been tracked on radar). When Major Cooper landed, reporters who had learnt of the sighting from NBC were instructed they would not be allowed to interview him.

22nd May 1963 – Air Training Corp sight unusual object in the sky
Seven members of the Bebington 1123 Air Training Corp sighted something unusual in the sky, at 9.15pm. One of them – Cadet Warrant Officer, Jeffrey Green – described what happened:

"I should imagine it was at an altitude of about 50,000 feet, possibly more. It seemed to hover, and then disappeared very quickly – too fast to be an aircraft. As it went from sight, it seemed to be climbing in a westerly direction, quite unlike anything I have ever seen before in aircraft recognition classes." (**Source:** *The Liverpool Echo, 22.5.1963*)

JUNE 1963

6th June 1963 – *"They looked like flying saucers"*
An object – resembling a *'lantern hanging in the sky'* – was seen over Whyteleafe, Surrey, at 11.40pm, by Mrs Phyllis Watters, who watched it for thirty minutes, before it moved away gradually into the distance.

"They looked like 'flying saucers' to me. I was hoping someone else had seen it because my husband and people I have told think I am mad. There was a plane about, because I could hear it and wondered if it was keeping observations on them.." (**Source:** *Couldson & Purley Times,* **14.6.1963**)

8th June 1963 – Domed UFO over Isle of Wight
A retired music teacher – Doreen Waddell, from the Isle of Wight – had just finished feeding the swans which frequent the shores off the Solent, at Gurnard Bay, one afternoon, when she was astonished to see

"...a dome-shaped, circular, object – motionless in the sky, opalescent, or translucent in appearance – shimmering as it caught the rays of the sun – an effect emphasised by the clear blue sky behind it. It appeared to hover and then move away in a straight line, towards the direction of Portsmouth. I felt a great sorrow as it left, feeling that nothing else seemed as important."
(**Source: Kath Smith, Isle of Wight UFO Society**)

9th June 1963 – UFO over Chelmsford, Essex
At 11.10pm, a luminous object was observed in the sky over Chelmsford, by Mr H. Cafferata, and his friends – Mr and Mrs Alan Woods. They saw it for a period of between 10-15 minutes.

"The object was first seen at an angle of 60 degrees elevation and then changed course, gradually, by as much as 45 degrees, taking a wide curving path to the east – until lost from view, at an elevation angle of about 30 degrees. While travelling along this course, it seemed to vary in speed considerably; sometimes appearing to move very slowly, at other times very quickly. Relatively small 'lights', or luminous objects, were seen emerging from it, one after the other, about five or six in number, which moved away and out of sight." (**Source: BUFORA**)

10th June 1963 – Similar phenomena sighted

Incredibly, but not uncommonly, during a visit to discuss the matter more fully with his two friends, the following evening (10.6.1963), a similar phenomenon was sighted at l0.10pm, high in the sky, approaching from the south-west, at an elevation angle of about 70 degrees. On this occasion, no 'navigation' lights were displayed. The object was seen to take a somewhat curved course – like a long letter 'S', only reversed. (**Source: Letter to** *Flying Saucer Review,* **Gordon Creighton**)

17th June 1963 – UFO sketch from the Ron West archives – no other details available

19th June 1963 – Spinning UFO sighted

At Newton Heath, Manchester, a spinning object, showing a white light, was reported in the sky.
(**Source:** *Manchester Evening News***, 19.6.1963**)

24th June 1963 – Top secret report of UFO plotted on radar over UK

According to Fred Smith (known to the authors personally) in an edition of Space-link (September/October 1964) he said he had been contacted by a radar operator in the UK, who told him that at 8.36pm on this date, a target was sighted at 12miles on a bearing of 130 degrees magnetic.

> *"The echo had the appearance of several thin parallel lines of unequal length in the direction of movement, the lines being very close together and thinner towards the 'tail' end. Its length was indicated at approximately 8 miles and its speed measured at 5,400 miles per hour. The echo was observed at a range of 29 miles. Over a period of 5 seconds it assumed zero velocity. It then changed aspect, becoming a square with sides approximately 1.2 miles. The echo remained stationary for almost 18 seconds; it then reversed course for four miles, veering off in a an arc to North of radius 5 miles. Its speed now measured approximately 450 miles per hour and the echo slowly became elongated at right angles to its course, as for a normal aircraft aspect change. At a distance of five miles the echo diminished in intensity, finally receding into normal background noise."*

28th June 1963 – Oval UFO reported

An oval object was seen hovering 150 feet in the sky over Royton, Lancashire.
(**Source:** *Oldham Chronicle,* **29.6.1963**)

Summer – 'Wobbling' UFO over Lincolnshire

Mrs Stapling and her young daughter, from Stamford, Lincolnshire, were in the kitchen when Mrs Stapling noticed a bright object in the sky,

> "... like a fluorescent light, but more golden in colour – the same size of an aircraft, but oval with no wings. We watched the object as it flew along in wobbly up and down movements before it entered clouds, although we could still see the object shining through".

(Source: South Lincolnshire UFO Study Group)

JULY 1963

6th July 1963 – RAF Open Day, UFO sighted

Anthony John Walker from Coalville, Leicestershire, was with his wife and a group of friends, attending the Royal Air Force Open Day, at RAF Waddington, near Lincoln. Towards the end of the afternoon, following a lull in aircraft activity, John's attention was drawn to a number of people in the crowd looking upwards and pointing in the sky. Wondering about the source of their interest, he glanced up and saw what looked like a smoke ring, motionless in the air, about a hundred feet above their heads. It was sharply defined against the background of an overcast but bright day. Reacting quickly, John took a photograph of the object (later shown to a number of RAF personnel), who were unable to offer any explanation.

7th/8th July 1963 – 'Globe' seen over Charlton area of Wiltshire

A white, incandescent 'globe' was seen on one of these two dates by Mrs Martin of Pythouse, Tisbury, at 3am, heading north-west across the sky, just above the horizon, towards Donhead, approximately one and a half miles from Charlton, Wiltshire.

July 1963 – The Charlton crater and UFO activity

In July 1963, a 'wave' of excitement caught the attention of the media after a number of saucer-shaped craft were reported seen over the UK. They were accompanied by seemingly unconnected reports of strange impressions found in farmers' fields, believed – by some – to be the result of 'flying saucers' having landed. Others, however, suggested they were caused by lightning striking the ground, whilst some claimed they were just hoaxes.

Following an article published in the *Daily Express*, relating to a mysterious hole found in a farmer's field in Charlton, Mr Charles Stickland – editor of *LUFORO* magazine – made his way to the area, accompanied by Mr Nigel Stephenson, who later wrote an excellent description of what they found:

> "The place is a field at Manor Farm, Charlton, Wiltshire, a little to the east of Shaftsbury, Dorset, owned by Farmer Roy Blanchard. When we arrived on the 18th, Captain John Rogers – head of the Bomb Disposal Squad – was in attendance. He confirmed they had been called out on the 10th of July. The field is divided into two crops – barley and potatoes. The site is on the boundary between the two crops, the measurements are probably close to the original, but bear in mind that others had visited the site before we had arrived, and may have disturbed it to some extent. The central hole was about five feet across and three feet deep. It was not completely empty but had some loose rocks in it and was situated in a shallow depression 8 feet in diameter, not more than three or four inches below the surrounding ground and from which the potato plants had disappeared. In the barley were three gaps which did not extend to the boundary of the planted area. When they were discovered, all of the barley had disappeared, and only loose soil remained. The cutting in the potato ridges was very ill-defined by the time we had reached the site; only a few potato plants were seen within a roughly circular area of about 12 feet radius from the centre. The bomb disposal

Haunted Skies **Volume Two Revised**

FLYING SAUCER REVIEW

SEPTEMBER—OCTOBER 1963

VOLUME 9, No. 5   **9th YEAR OF PUBLICATION**

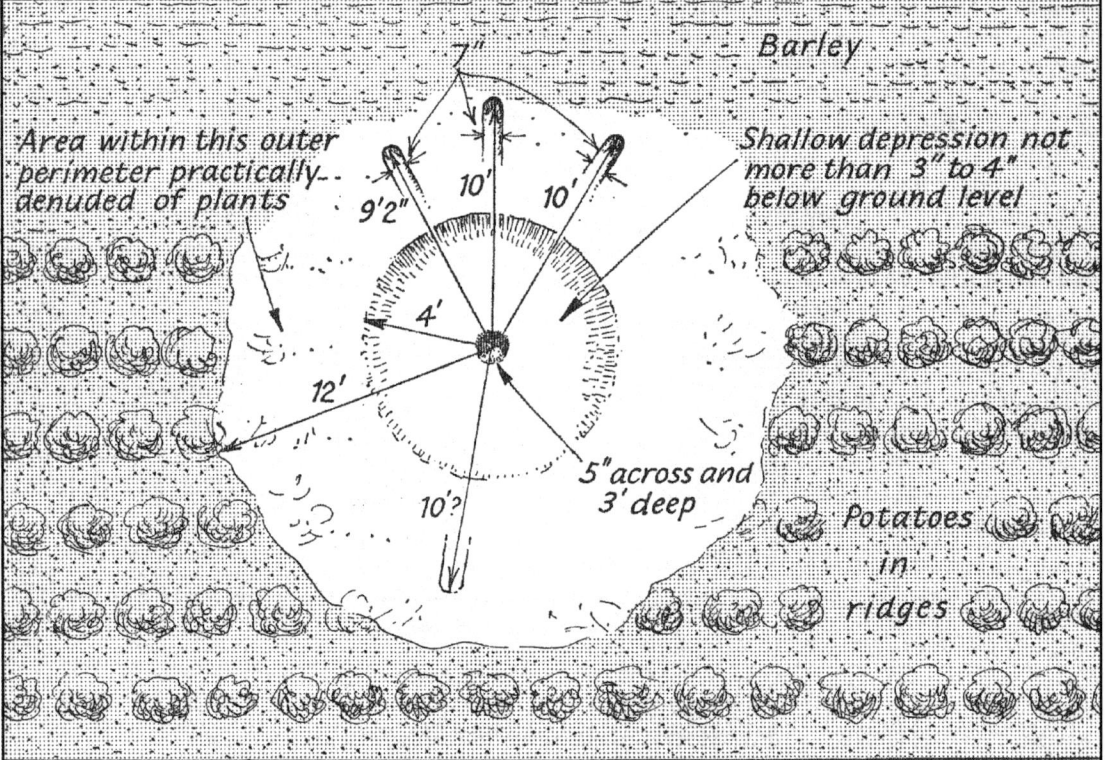

THE WILTSHIRE CRATER
FULL INSIDE STORY

squad continued their examination of the site until the 25th July, when their metal detectors picked up an object subsequently identified by the British Museum as being an 'iron pan'; a hard cement like layer made up of iron hydroxide, as a result of chemical reaction caused by water percolating through the uppermost layer of the soil, which could not have caused the hole and markings."

Farmer Roy Blanchard – "It was a flying saucer"

Some people suggested the crater had been caused by an unexploded wartime bomb. However, the Army bomb disposal squad determined there was no bomb, nor remains of any meteorite. Major H.P. Qualtrough, from Horsham Bomb Disposal Unit, pointed out that six men had been deployed for ten days on this task. Roy Blanchard was convinced there was only one explanation as to the crater's origin, a 'Flying Saucer'! He admitted:

"I didn't actually see it, but what else could it have been? Obviously some craft from outer space, since it sucked out my barley and potatoes when it took off."

Dr. Robert Randall – claimed to be an Astrophysicist

A rather curious character by the name of D. Robert Randall, who claimed to be an astrophysicist, informed the Press that the crater had been formed by a 'flying saucer' from Uranus! The Press reported the doctor's claims and so fuelled speculation about the strange nature of the crater, with questions about the crater being raised later in the House of Commons.

The *Daily Telegraph* – 'Three-legged spaceship from Uranus'

Incredibly the *Daily Telegraph*, on the 24th July 1963, published his theory *"...that the culprit was a three-legged spaceship from Uranus!"* On the 24th and 25th July, Mr Stephenson paid a second visit to the locality. It was now very much trampled, due to the number of visitors making their way there. He discovered that:

"Beyond the potato and barley field – a grass field. And beyond that, some distance from the original site, another field of barley – of which I noticed two things: firstly the stalks were not lying flat, but lying in the direction indicated. Secondly, beyond that area was a line almost of single stalks with the ears bent over (extended over an area of 17 feet.)"

(Sources: *LUFORO Bulletin*, July/August 1963/*LUFORO Bulletin*, September/October 1963/*Spacelink*, Volume 1, No. 1, January/February 1964/*News of the World*, 25.8.1963 and *Daily Mail*, 26.8.1963/*Daily Mirror*, 27.7.63/ *Daily Sketch*, 17/30th July1963/*Daily Express*, 23.7.1963/*Daily Telegraph*, 27.7.1963/*Southern Evening Echo*, 17th/19th July 1963/*The Times*, 19th July/*Yorkshire Post*, 19/24/27th July/*The Guardian*, 18/23/24th July/ *Western Daily Press*, 27.7.1963/National Archives, AIR2/17318/*Flying Saucer Review*, Volume 10, No. 2/4)

7th July – Craters found after storm

Following freak thunderstorms over Dufton Fell, Westmoreland, two craters were found with a diameter of 200 feet and depth of 2-3 feet, found at the end of same month, by farmers Bill Richardson of Ghyll House, Dufton, and John Rudd of Dufton Hall.

10th July 1963 – Police Officer sights orange object

On July 10th 1963, according to the village policeman – PC Anthony Penny – who made his report after returning from holiday, an orange object was seen to flash through the sky and vanish near the field where the strange marks had been found.

10th July 1963 – Star shaped craters found in land on Edinburgh farm

On the same day, many hundreds of miles to the North, two star-shaped craters were discovered in a field belonging to Mr James Brown, at Middle Moneynut Farm, Edinburgh. They had a diameter of 16 feet, a depth of 2-3 feet and were 12 feet apart, with 12 channels, varying in length up to 44 feet, radiating outwards. Around the craters, large blocks of earth had been scooped from the ground and scattered over an area of 40 yards. The Police and Bomb Squad arrived, but found nothing.

The site was later visited by Frank Satterthwaite, Mr S Stevens, Bill Muir, Miss O' Harrow and Harry Lord – all members of the Tyneside UFO Society – who concluded, *"an unknown object had landed, causing the craters"*, discounting any possible hoax.

1913 – Claims that sheep went missing!

It is alleged forty sheep were found to be missing by the farmer that owns the field. Was there any truth of a similar occurrence that took place over 50 years previously, in 1913?

The War Officer explained it away as being a meteorite that had crashed into the field, believing that part of it had been found, but who or what had taken the sheep? Was it sheer coincidence that another set of 'craters' were found in a field at Dumfries around the same time?

The *Evening Chronicle* (24.10.1963) 'The Craters are still without explanation', also published a letter from Mr S. Stevens of 41, Chirton West View, North Shields, who rejected the explanation of it being a meteorite, and that he had himself examined the scene carefully with others and that a conventional explanation could not be found. Another person who objected to the official statement was Harry Lord, 101, Mowbray Street, Heaton, in Newcastle-on-Tyne. He dismissed the 'meteorite' claim as rubbish and misleading.

> *"It is obvious that my report has been confused with the mystery crater found at Charlton, Wiltshire. In this case a half pound object was discovered and thought to be part of a meteorite at the time. However, after inspection by Dr. G. F. Claringbull, keeper of the department of the Natural History Museum, it was found it was a piece of ironstone characteristic of the region."*

Once again, there were the inevitable quips made by one reporter at the tail end of the letter referring to beings and spaceships having the sense to head north!

(Sources: *Yorkshire Post*, 1.8.1963/*Orbit*, The Journal of the Tyneside UFO Society/*Evening Chronicle*, 18.10.1963 – 'Flying Saucer or just a meteorite?')

11th July 1963 – 'Blowlamp' shaped UFO hovers over house

At 3am, Captain Cornelius Buck, resident of Rownhams Mount – a large isolated house, situated to the North of Southampton – was awoken by the sound of dogs, barking frenziedly. On looking out of the window, he saw a curious glow over the roof of one of the wings of the house, and thought a fire could have broken out.

> *"I then became aware that the light was coming from above. Glancing upwards, I saw what looked like a blowlamp, with a flame directed downwards, giving off an orange glow, surrounded by what appeared to be clouds of smoke. After a short time, the orange glow turned to bluish-white, and the whole contraption appeared to go straight up."* **(Source: Norman C. Toogood)**

13th July 1963 – Red twinkling 'light' sighted over UK

At 8.30pm, Mr C. Palmer was travelling home in the car to London from Cornwall with his wife, brother in-law, and three children. He decided to take a rest in a lay-by along the A30, between Crewkerne and Chinnock.

> *"It was a brilliant night; the moon had just risen, and was low in the sky. Suddenly, I noticed a red, twinkling 'light' heading across the sky, and thought it my imagination to begin with. I pointed it out to the children. I got out of the car for a better look, and we watched it head across the sky in an occasional erratic movement. It then crossed the road in front of us, and turned towards our direction, at an angle of one o'clock position."*

14th July 1963 – Huge cigar-shaped UFO seen over Dorset

At 3am, Frank Selwood of Parkstone, Dorset, awoke and looked out of the bedroom window. He saw:

> "...towering over a large gasholder at the rear of the house, a huge cigar-shaped object – as big as four terraced houses – about 300 feet up in the air, showing an intermittent flashing wavy blue-green light. I could hear a quiet sort of whistle coming from it, and flapping sounds. It sounded like its engine (or whatever it was), running rough. It then seemed to spring into life; the motor changed, the lights became continuous along its length, and it shot away towards the west at a fantastic speed." (**Source: Frank Marshall, BUFORA**)

At Flamborough Head, Yorkshire, a hole – 6 feet in diameter by 12-18 inches deep – was found with radiating cracks. (**Source:** *BUFOA Journal,* **Summer 1963**)

16th July 1963 – Landed object seen at 9.15pm, Brooks Farm, Wisbech, Cambridgeshire

22nd July 1963 – 'Flying Saucer' over Lancashire

At 8.30pm, schoolboys – William Holland, Paul Lightfoot and Keith Kerfoot, from Redgate, Parr, St. Helens, Lancashire – were playing on the nearby tip when they noticed a shining spinning object, descending from the sky, which came to a stop approximately 70 feet above their heads. William said at the time:

> "It had a red flashing light and was spinning. It stopped dead, and the red light went out. Something slid back and what looked like a periscope came out and swivelled, pointed at us, and went back inside the object – which then shot upwards into the sky and vanished into a strange coloured cloud, a few seconds later."

We traced two of the boys concerned, and spoke to them regarding the incident, after launching an appeal for any other witnesses to come forward, but no additional information was forthcoming. We were, however, contacted by at least two members of the public, who suggested the boys had seen a 'Vulcan' Bomber, with its refuelling probe hanging down – an explanation put to Keith (now licensee of a public house), who agreed that the illustration, prepared by David Sankey from the original sketch, was accurate.

"This was no refueling aircraft. It hovered silently over our heads. There were no identifying markings on it – just this silver body.

It flashed away at an incredible speed. I've never seen anything like it before, or since. It was quite frightening. I can't give any answers. I just know what we all saw."

At 9pm on the same date (22.7.1963), Mr and Mrs Dickenson from Strood, Kent, were watching television in the kitchen of their bungalow, when she became aware of her husband gazing intently up into the night sky. She asked him what he was looking at, and he replied *"a flying saucer"*. She continued:

"I thought he was joking and looked out and saw a pale yellow dome-shaped object, surrounded by an orange glow, moving northwards across the sky, over the end of the new M2 Motorway. It was very high up, but there was no mistake about what it was.

It's funny, but when the subject has come up before, we used to laugh at people who had seen 'flying saucers'." **(Source: Anglo-Polish UFO Group/Isle of Wight UFO Society)**

23rd July 1963 – 'Flying Saucer' over Gloucestershire

At 10.45pm the same day, a UFO was sighted by an unnamed ex-RAF Cadet, from Hinton Green, who was travelling along the main Cheltenham to Evesham Road, when he saw some lights in the sky. He stopped the car and got out in time to see an object:

"...shaped like an inverted dessert dish, with three tiers of lights – yellow, orange and red, around the outside – crossing the main road, at a speed of about l00 miles per hour, heading north-west."

(Source: *Gloucestershire Echo,* **23.7.1963)**

24th July 1963 – 'Spinning Top' UFO, Lancashire

At 2am, a UFO – described as looking like *"a gigantic spinning top, with a shimmering gold centre, red top and blue/green base"*, was seen by Mr Robert Armitage – the Manager of a petrol filling station at Accrington, Lancashire:

"It was a clear night when I saw the object stationary in the sky, east, towards Burnley. Suddenly, it arced across the sky, towards Bacup, stopped, and began to shimmer. I watched it for about 15 minutes, as it flew silently across the sky. It was a beautiful thing to look at."

A RAF spokesman at Barton Hall, near Preston, was unable to identify the object.

"This is the first time we have heard of it."

(Source: *Lancashire Evening Telegraph,* **24.7.1963 – 'Mystery flying object hovered in sky')**

At 8.45am – this time over Staffordshire – *"a silver grey buzzing circular object was seen in the sky, with a 'cockpit' on top."* **(Source:** *Orbit***)**

UFO seen over Leeds, the same day

Later that morning, Leeds schoolboys – Michael Lee and John Duffy – were on their way to school, at 8.45am, when they noticed a silver-grey circular object, with a cockpit on top, hovering over Roundhay Park Wood. It flew away, making a 'buzzing' noise. The boys were too frightened to bring the matter to the attention of their teachers, but told their uncle (Donald Foy), who contacted the *Yorkshire Post*. Strangely, Mr Foy admitted to having seen a similar object over Leeds, six years before.

(Source: *Yorkshire Post,* **25.7.1963)**

25th July 1963 – Seven objects sighted

Mr L. Booth from Blackpool, Lancashire, was walking home to Anchorsholme, at 12.05am, when he looked up into the sky and saw a formation of seven objects, *"passing silently over and out to sea, low, but moving fast, apparently round in shape, emitting orange light and only visible for about ten seconds"*.

'Flying Saucer' over Coatbridge, Scotland

At 9.45am, Councillor John Gallagher was on duty at Whifflet North signal box, Coatbridge, when he noticed an aircraft heading towards Renfrew.

> "Just as it disappeared, a 'flying saucer' came into view, which stopped and hovered over the town centre, at a height of about 100 feet, before heading to the north side of the Parish Church. When I looked back again at10am, having attended to a passing train, it was nowhere to be seen."

The same day, a doctor's wife – Ruth Scott, from Roslin, Midlothian – was in the garden, with her son, Simon (10), and university student, Ben Oddotte, when Simon drew their attention to something in the sky:

> "It looked like two saucers, one on top of each other, with a hump on top, a dark underneath and grey top, travelling south."

A similar object was seen over Clermiston, Edinburgh, by Elizabeth Potts and her two children.
(Source: *Scottish Daily Mail*, 27.7.1963 – 'We saw 'flying saucer' over City, say six')

Flashing red light in the sky

At 11.30pm, a *large flashing stationary red light was* seen over Walsall, Staffs.
(Source: *Wolverhampton Express & Star*, 26/30th July/1.8.63)

26th July 1963 – UFO and scorched circles

Mrs Kathleen Smith, from Heytesbury Road, Yarmouth, Isle of Wight, was standing at the bottom of her garden, overlooking a railway track and open countryside, just before midnight on 26th July 1963, when she saw:

> "...a bright elliptical object, stationary in the night sky, about the same size of a full moon, which suddenly shot forward, and headed off towards the south."

Two days later, she was to find herself in the middle of another mystery, when – while walking over the Downs with her son, Clive, and nephew, John – they came across a scorched circle in the grass on Afton Down, Isle of Wight, roughly 30 feet across, with a rim 8 inches thick.

> "Each blade of the grass was brown, except for half an inch at the bottom – as if it had grown out. I discovered another similar circle about a hundred yards away, near the golf links. I paced both circles. They appeared to be the same diameter. I looked for some kind of landmark and saw a very thick hedge in a field below where we were, which ran towards the road."

(Sources: Kath Smith, Isle of Wight UFO Society/Personal interview)

27th July 1963 – Red UFO with a 'V' type centre sighted

The *West Cumberland Times* (3.8.1963), told its readers about a strange object seen by Harry Stalker, from Distington – described as: "...a tumbler-shaped object, glowing brightly in the northern sky" – on the late evening. Another witness was Mr C. Hetherington, from Wigton, who managed to look at the object through binoculars, when he saw:

> "...a metallic object, very high, surrounded by a red ring, apparently winged, with a 'V' type centre, which reflected the sun's rays". (Source: *The Guardian*, 30.7.1963 – 'The glow in the sky')

Orange object seen over Malvern

Malvern couple – Donald Lloyd and his wife – were in the process of retiring to bed, when the bedroom was illuminated by a burst of harsh light – strong enough to penetrate the closed curtains of the room. The couple rushed to the window and saw a large *"ball of light"*, moving towards Malvern, from the direction of Old Hills, changing to orange in colour before it disappeared. Incredibly, the same object (or an identical one) was seen, a short time later, heading away from the Old Hills, dimming as it apparently climbed upwards, at an angle of 45 degrees. (**Source:** *Worcester Evening News,* 27.7.1963 – 'Mystery object over Malvern')

A "tumbler shaped object" was reported in the night sky, over West Cumberland.
(**Source:** The *Guardian,* 30.7.1963/*West Cumberland Times,* 3.8.1963)

28th July 1963 – Green object with aerial

At 8.35pm, John White (19) from Providence Lane, Long Ashton, Bristol, and his next door neighbour, Howard Williams, sighted:

> *"...a green, oval shaped object, with an aerial, making a whistling noise – like a radio being tuned in – approaching from the direction of Weston-super-Mare and flying approximately one hundred feet along the top end of the lane, near Long Ashton Golf Course."*

(**Source:** *Bristol Evening Post,* 29.7.1963 – 'Riddle of a Saucer')

29th July 1963 – UFO over Chelmsford, Essex

An orange coloured *'short stick' was* seen in the sky over Chelmsford, at 9pm.

(**Source:** Flying Saucer Review, November/December 1963)

During the early hours of the next morning, a glowing object was seen moving at speed across the sky, over Bristol – later explained away as being a weather balloon on fire.

(**Source:** *Worcester News and Times,* 30.7.1963)

30th July 1963 – Four red 'lights' seen over Tipton

At 11.35pm, a flashing red light was seen directly over the Patent shaft works at Tipton, by Mr K.C. Martin. He spoke of:

> *"...seeing it move very slowly in one direction, and then back to the same position. It then moved, and stopped, before finally disappearing behind a row of houses."*

Another witness – amateur astronomer Nigel Neale, from Lanesfield, Wolverhampton – was able to observe it through a telescope.

> *"The object was 'winking' once every three seconds, and looked a brilliant red. I could see four lights. It did not appear to be an aircraft, because of its phenomenal speed and twisted path."*

31st July 1963 – UFO seen over Somerset

Shortly after midnight, Mrs Alice Chiswell from West Huntspill, Burnham-on-Sea, alerted her husband after sighting:

> *"...a large glowing light, oval in shape, glittering with streams of red and orange light, descending through the sky, 'quivering' like a jelly, for about a quarter of an hour, until it faded away."*

Source: *Burnham-on-Sea Gazette & Highbridge Express,* 1.8.1963)

6.30pm

Frank Pearson from Wallington, Surrey, was enjoying a week's holiday at Clacton-on-Sea, and lying on the beach at 6.30pm, looking upwards, when something over the sea caught his attention:

> *"It wasn't very big and moved slowly across the sky. I watched it, trying to make out what it could be, but it was quite a distance away – roughly the size of a sixpence. It then moved in a swaying motion and came to a stop, now much lower, over the sea. As it sunk lower, it now resembled an aircraft, without wings – then it rose upwards into the sky and headed off over Clacton, where I lost sight of it. I decided to go in for tea. When I came out, at 7pm, I could see it again in the sky."*

The following day, Mr Pearson learnt, through newspaper reports of UFOs, that other people had sighted a similar object over the Clacton area.

(Source: Isle of Wight UFO Society)

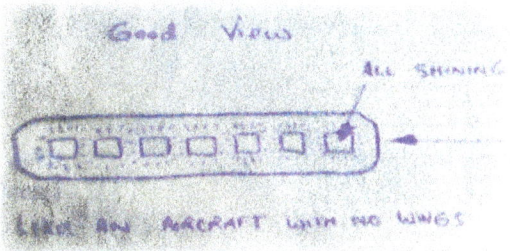

8.30pm

On the same evening, an unidentified object – described as 'V'-shaped – *"like a shiny plastic triangle, with red glow at the bottom, which was seen to change into a circular shape"* – was seen moving slowly across the sky heading north to south over Gillingham, Kent, at 8.30pm, before going upwards and out of sight.

(Source: *Chatham, Rochester & Gillingham News, 2.8.1963* – 'Was it a 'Flying Saucer' over Medway towns?')

Later the same evening – Triangular UFO reported

The *Chatham, Rochester & Gillingham News* (2.8.1963), asked its readers: *"What was the object which hung for two hours in the sky over Gillingham, on Wednesday night, 31st July 1963?"*

They described it as looking like a triangle, shining in the sunlight, with a red glowing base.

Another man spoke of seeing – through a 60x magnification telescope – what looked like:

> *"... an old-fashioned humbug, 8-10 thousand feet up and apparently constructed of shiny plastic, although, with the eye, it could have been mistaken for a plane, glinting in the sun."*

The *Southend Standard* (1.8.1963), reported that a number of people living in the town had contacted them about a triangular object seen in the sky on early Wednesday evening, some of whom described it as 'kite-like' in appearance. The Air Ministry explained away the sightings as:

> *"...probably being one of many varieties of meteorological, radiosonde balloons, made of plastic, which, when inflated, look like an inverted pear. At certain altitudes, they burst and parachute down equipment used for examining the atmosphere".*

We interviewed a number of witnesses, including RAF servicemen who had attempted to unsuccessfully climb up to the object in their aircraft. One of these was Mr John Nightingale, who had photographed the object (which we later confirmed to be a French weather balloon, adrift from its moorings) but was this what was seen, bearing in mind the other sightings?

July 1963 – RAF pilot sights UFO over Lake District

In the same month, an unnamed RAF Pilot, with over 24 years of flying, was on holiday with his family in the Lake District, Cumbria, when a silver object – resembling an airship, but without any markings, fins or engines – was seen at 8am, three to four miles away, between 2,000 to 3,000 feet above them.

The Daily Telegraph and *Morning Post* (30th July 1963) told its readers about a mysterious object, seen twice, high above Bristol, late last night and again early today. On the first occasion, an orange 'ball of fire' was seen motionless in the sky, for ten minutes, before disintegrating. An hour later, a similar glowing object was seen – this time moving at terrific speed, upwards, over the Bristol Channel.

AUGUST 1963

1st August 1963 – The fishermen's tale

At 2am, three men – out night fishing near the suspension bridge at Trent Bridge – saw something unusual in the sky at 2am, while in the process of packing up their equipment to go home. According to Mr Edward O'Dowd, who was accompanied by his two younger brothers, Peter and Barry:

"We saw this light in the sky coming towards us, at fast speed, and then it disintegrated? About fifteen minutes later, we saw it again. I don't believe it was a Shooting Star, or a satellite."

At 8pm on this date, Mr D.F. Ogilvy (who we spoke to) saw something very unusual – although in later years he believes it may have been a French weather balloon that had escaped from its mooring. Whilst that of course may be the case, it is intriguing to contrast the photo and illustrations with contemporary reports of what many people describe as triangular UFOs – the scourge of our skies in the later part of the 20th century.

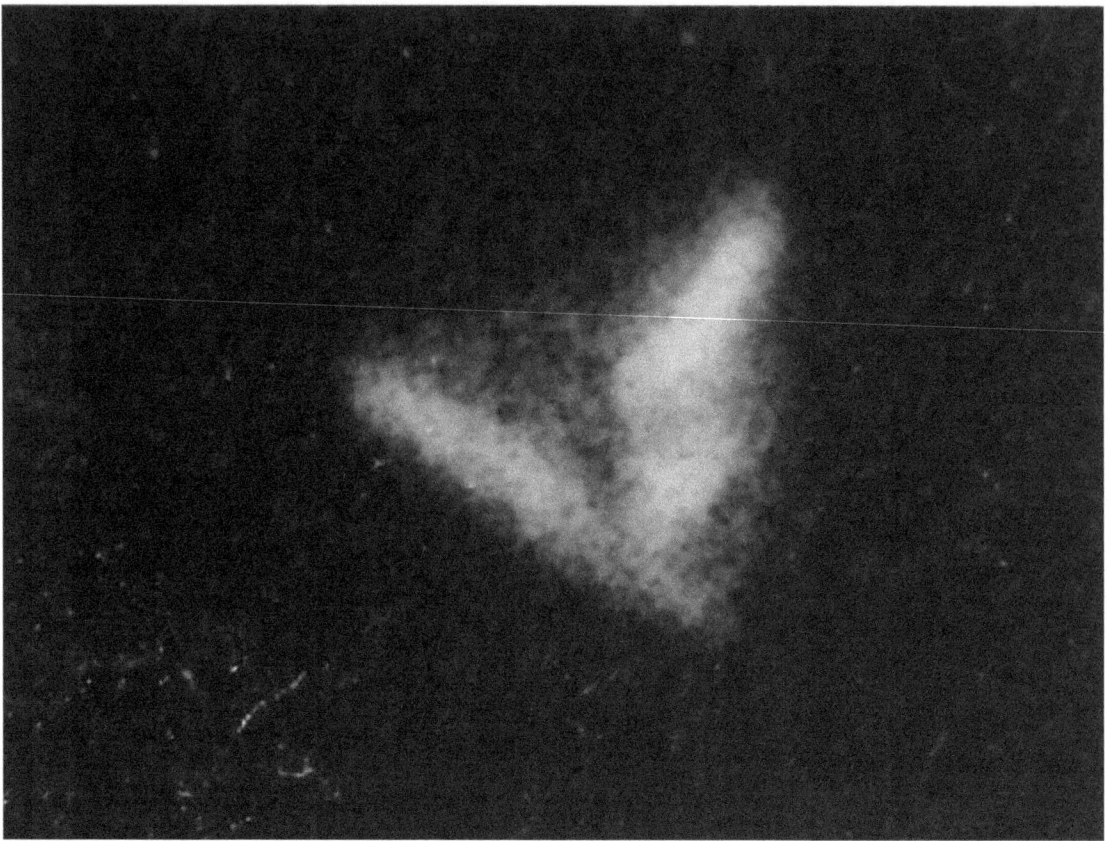

Veteran UFO researcher, internationally known, and author of some excellent books on the UFO subject – Tim Good – was a witness, along with four other people.

"We saw a triangular-shaped object, with a width of about 400 feet. It seemed to be made of either polished metal or height reflective material. It seemed to be about 90,000 feet high and was enormous."

We interviewed a number of witnesses, including RAF servicemen who had attempted to unsuccessfully climb up to the object in their aircraft. One of these was Mr John Nightingale, who had photographed the object.

At 11.30pm, a mysterious red 'beam of light' was again seen in the sky over Walsall, West Midlands, by Mr E. Dunn and Mr G. Cope, who called the police. Following the attendance of an officer, the two men told him:

"It was flying at about 600 feet, and circled over the Beechdale Estate, three times, changing in colour from red, to blue and white, sometimes stationary in the air for a period of up to 20 seconds, before vanishing behind Bloxwich Fire Station."

At 11.40pm, Mr R. Martin from Rowan Road, Walsall, dialled 999 after seeing a strange object circling over the Bescot area. By the time an officer arrived (as in the previous incident), there was no sign of the UFO – which was explained away by the officer as likely to have been an aircraft!

(Source: *Walsall Observer*, 2.8.1963/*Daily Express* 1.8.1963 – 'Flying Triangle'/*Daily Sketch*, 2.8.1963 – '100 phone over a thing in the sky'/*Daily Mirror*, 2.8 1963 – 'It was only a balloon')

5th August 1963 – 'Flying Saucer' over Blackburn, Lancashire

In 1968, Mrs E. Winstanley of Bolton Road, Crown's Brow, Blackburn, Lancashire, wrote to Lionel Beer, head of BUFORA, about a frightening experience which befell her teenage son – Christopher Roy – while living at Crown's Brow, Blackburn.

Mrs Winstanley:

"I was out fetching some coal, at 10.30pm, when I saw a greenish coloured 'light' hovering over the wood at the back of the house, which I first took to be a star, until it made a noise I likened to a wireless, oscillating, followed by its flight across the sky in a rotating manner, involving jumping up and down as it moved forwards."

Mrs Winstanley brought the matter to the attention of her daughter, son-in-law and husband, who laughed at her, making comments about her state of mind.

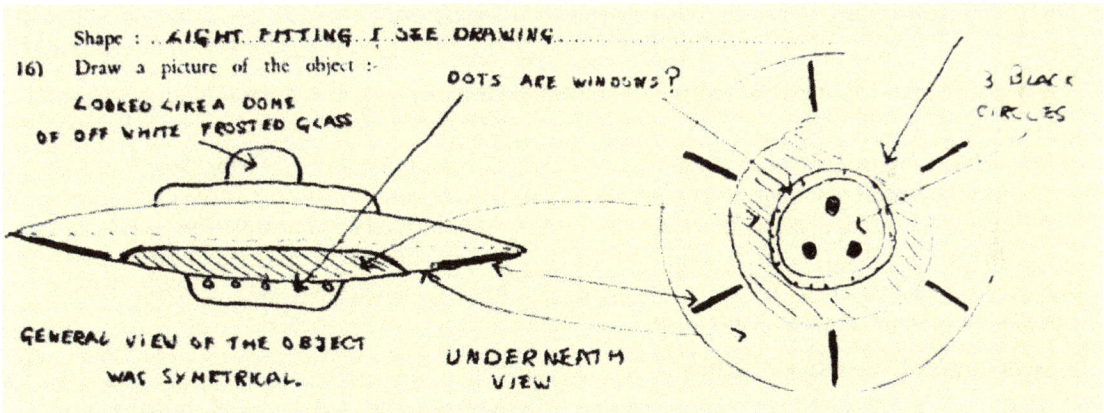

At 11.30pm. Christopher arrived home, after having been to see his girlfriend Barbara. After some conversation, during which they periodically looked out of the window, hoping to see the 'light' again, she went to bed at 12.30am.

At 1.55am, Mrs Winstanley was awoken by Christopher, who told her

"...about a strange 'light' he had seen hovering over the lawn at the back of the house from his bedroom, which faces the rear of the property".

She dismissed the incident as being of no consequence, and suggested he get back into bed, although she wondered if it was the same 'light' she had seen earlier, hovering over the wood at the back of the house, but presumably she didn't want to alarm him.

At 3.00am. Mrs Winstanley was awoken, once again, by her son, who said:

"He was in quite a state. His face was ashen. He was trembling all over and was soaking wet. It took him half-hour before he was able to tell me what had taken place".

Chris:

"I had been in bed for about half an hour but was unable to sleep, as the room was lit up from what I took to be the full moon.

My curiosity aroused, I looked out and saw not only the full moon but a sphere, about a foot in diameter, hovering ten feet off the ground. Wondering what it was, I went to the kitchen and opened the door but could see nothing, apart from the feeble light thrown off by some street lamps. I decided to investigate further; I checked it wasn't any reflection. I immediately got dressed and went outside. By now it was 2am when I saw a football-sized light, giving off a pale green glow, hovering about 8 feet off the ground, some 50 yards away."

Went outside to investigate further

"Curious as to what it was, I walked towards it. When 30 yards away, it began to increase its speed so I decided to give chase, and followed the 'light' over a sandpit and four fields, before it disappeared behind a wall, about a quarter of a mile away. When I arrived at the location, there was no sign of it. Looking around, I saw it travelling towards the brickworks at the top of the quarry, at a speed I estimated to be 80 miles per hour.

When I arrived at the quarry, 20 minutes later, there was nothing to be seen. I walked about for ten minutes – still nothing.

All was in darkness. I stood still, and looked up into the night sky, and was amazed to see this dustbin sized 'light', circular in form, hovering there. I ran over to a farmer's hut and watched it through the holes in the roof and wall, when – all of a sudden – it moved towards my location and took up a hovering position, 200 feet above my head. Flames came out of the base – like a rocket taking off.

I ran out of the hut, climbed down a nearby wall, and headed home. No sooner had I done this, when I saw a beam of light project from the 'disc', lasting two seconds, which appeared to light up the ground six feet away from where I stood, making a noise like a high voltage discharge, before disappearing from sight."

Blackened circle found next morning

Roy returned to the location, the following morning, with two of his neighbour's sons, and discovered a blackened circle, some six feet in diameter, on the stone wall – as if caused by smoke from a candle being held against it, but without any sign of soot or carbon on the surface. Rather oddly, he noticed later, that the rock gave off a feeble pale green light in darkness. This matter was eventually brought to the attention of Lionel Beer (head of BUFORA), by Ken Rogers, who judged that there was no reason to suppose this was none other than a genuine sighting. What a pity this matter was not brought to the attention of the researchers until 1967/8.

Christopher, who worked as Technical Director for a Blackburn Electronic Company, was to take an active part in BUFORA during the 1960s, after being appointed their Northern Communications Officer and research coordinator.

As the incident was reported to have happened on a full moon, we were able to calculate that it occurred around the 5th August (Monday). The moon was at its fullest on the (waxing gibbous), illuminated to 99.8% on that day, having started around Saturday, the 3rd, until Wednesday, the 7th, on the 5th August 1963, sunrise being at 5.27am.

5th August 1963 – USA: Motorist chased by UFO over Illinois, USA

Ronnie Austin (18) and his girlfriend Phyllis Bruce (18), from Fairfield – a market town that straddles Illinois Route 15 with (then) 6,400 persons – had been driving home Sunday night, after seeing *The Great Escape* at the Kerasota Drive-in Theater in Mount Vernon, 32 miles west of Fairfield. At about 11.30pm, as they drove east along Illinois Route 15, past Mount Vernon Airport, Ronnie leaned over to speak to Phyllis, at which point he noticed 'a round ball of bright white light' just above treetop level, about 20 degrees above the horizon, to the south-west. The 'light' had a fuzzy outline and appeared to be the size of a washtub. He asked Phyllis, *"Look there at that thing! What is it? Is it an airplane?"*

Phyllis looked and answered slowly, *"No, it's not an airplane; it doesn't have flashing red and green lights"*.

They then discovered that the 'light' seemed to be keeping pace with them. When they decreased speed, the 'light' decreased its speed, always keeping in the same relative position. When they increased speed, the object still seemed to keep pace. At one time Ronnie's car – a 1956 Ford Victoria, souped up for racing – was going 120 mph, but the 'light' stayed right with them.

When they arrived home, the strange 'light' was still with them. (His report was the first of many reported over Southern Illinois during that period of time.)

Ronnie Austin arrived home at the family farm in Keenes (about twenty miles from Fairfield) shortly after midnight, so shaken that he could hardly say more than half a dozen words. Ronnie told his father, Orval, what had happened – who then fetched a shotgun, but Ronnie advised him against this. His agitation was such that his parents phoned Dr. S.W. Conarski, in Fairfield, who instructed them to give Ronnie a sedative which they had in the house. Ronnie, his father, mother, brother, and sister – Roxie (15), then began to observe it from their kitchen windows. By this time it was about 12.25am. Mr Austin decided to call Jefferson County authorities to have them notify Scott Air Force Base, 80 miles away. Jefferson County authorities instead called Deputy Lee, who arrived

Ronnie Austin

on the scene about 1.10am. Before that though, State Trooper Richard Gidcumb of McLeansboro and George Sexton – Village Marshal of Wayne City, had come by at about 12.45am, having heard the call on their radios. The neighbours, Mr and Mrs Dwight Withrow, were also called and they, too, went out and observed the 'light'. The Austins' watched the object as it slowly faded higher into the sky, toward the south, and by the time Deputy Lee arrived it appeared like an extremely bright star in the south-eastern sky, where it remained until it faded out of sight at dawn.

Several other persons, including a deputy sheriff and a police radio operator, witnessed the strange 'light' in the sky that night and the story appeared in newspapers across the Midwest. The *Chicago Tribune* gave it 15 inches of space on page one. Deputy Sheriff Harry Lee, who handled his department's reports, visited the Austin home within an hour after Ronnie reported the matter. He said later:

> *"I'm sure he saw something. He was in pretty bad shape when I saw him; he looked scared to death. The parents were real shook up, too. They had seen it up close and knew there was something to it."*

Not unusually for matters such as this the family was inundated by people, including reporters, eccentrics, and curiosity seekers, eager to interview them about the incident. They declined to get involved.

Explanations for the sighting

Various explanations were offered from the Air Force investigators. They included the moon partly hidden by fog, or the planet Jupiter. At that time of year, according to the Adler planetarium, in Chicago, Jupiter was the brightest object in the sky, rising almost due east at about 11pm, and ascending to about 50 feet – 60 feet above the horizon in the south, before it sets in the west at about 5am. At midnight it is about 30 feet above the horizon, a little south of east.

A distant object will appear to move parallel with a moving vehicle. Yet, if the light was Jupiter, how was it able to appear in so many different directions and pass in front of and over Ronnie's car? Moreover, Jupiter sets in the west; this 'light' disappeared in the south-east. What would have been the attitude taken by the media *now* if they had known that this was not an apparent singular incident but one of many thousands, if not millions, which had taken place over the years. But of course it appears that media interest only relates to an individual incident, rather than attempting to deal with any seriousness – something that prevails to this present day! **(Source: NICAP)**

6th August 1963 – 'Wheezing' UFO over Edinburgh

Robert Brown – a van boy with Smiths Bakeries at Hawkshill, Edinburgh – sighted a silver coloured object, resembling a child's spinning top with a flat bottom, hovering over the city, at 4am, accompanied by *"a strange wheezing noise"*, before going out of sight a few minutes later.
(Source: *Evening Dispatch,* **6.8.1963 – 'Another saucer seen in Edinburgh')**

7th August 1963 – Unusual object sighted in the sky

Bilston Grammar schoolboy – Peter Jones – was in Parkfield Road, Ettingshall, at 10.30pm, with three other friends, when they saw an object, slightly smaller than the moon, changing colour from red to pink, to white, occasionally ejecting a bright rocket-like trail, travelling towards Bilston.
(Source: *Wolverhampton Express and Star,* **8.8.1963 – 'Thing in the sky')**

7th August 1963 – USA: Diamond-shaped UFO sighted in sky over Fairfield, Illinois

Between 8.45pm-9.10pm, Chauncey Uphoff, who operates a farm on Highway 15, four miles east of Fairfield, and Mike Hill – operator of the Hill cleaning plant – were sat in the yard, talking. All of a sudden Mike said:

> *"Did you turn your porch light on? Look at that up there; it looks like a big diamond, moving from the west over the railroad track to the east".*

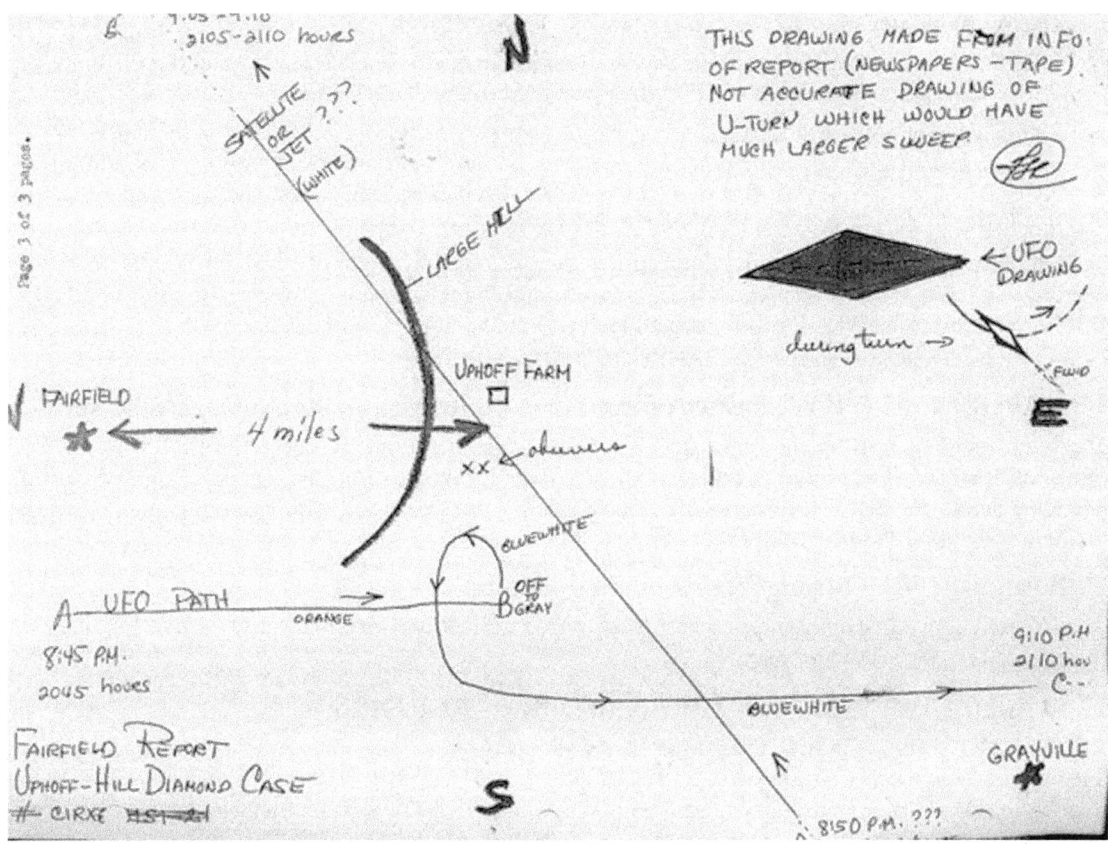

Chauncey:

> "I had never seen anything like it before. I ran inside and called the police station. It was a silent, yellowish-orange, diamond shaped object in the south-west part of the sky, at about 1,000 feet altitude, moving east, joined by what looked like a possible aircraft white light that went from south-east to north-west, climbing, with a drumming sound. When it neared the first object, the latter blinked out. After the white light disappeared to the north-west, the diamond-shaped object reappeared as dim gray to the south-west, and headed straight towards us. It looked like a ball diamond, sideways, with a 'tail' – more like a fluid dripping off than a solid protuberance object – then changed colour to orange, then brilliant blue-white, before making a U-turn and heading south-east towards Grayville." **(Source: NICAP, Dan Wright)**

12th August 1963 – UFO seen over Wolverhampton

At 10.24pm, Mr J. Challenger from Sedgley, Wolverhampton – a bus inspector, who had previously treated the UFO subject with suspicion – was walking along Wolverhampton Road, towards his home, at 12.40am, when he saw:

> "...a large white stationary 'light' in the sky – much larger than any star – towards the south-east, underneath low cloud, appearing to drop other smaller 'lights' as it moved along."

When he arrived home, his 12 year-old daughter told him she had seen something similar on Saturday evening, the 10th August.

Two minutes later

At 10.26pm, Mr S. Day was sitting in his back garden in Highfield Road, Dudley, watching the night sky with binoculars, following reports of UFOs being sighted in the Dudley area.

"While looking towards the east, I saw a bright pear-shaped white light – blue at the bottom – which appeared to be dropping other lights. I counted eleven of these dropping from the bottom, before it headed northwards. One and half minutes later, it disappeared from view but reappeared in a bright flash, followed by a dull bang in the sky."

According to the police at Walsall, other reports were received by them of similar accounts, including sightings of 'strange lights' over the town, and an orange 'light' seen hovering over Birchills and Ocker Hill Power Stations by Walsall residents, Kathleen Edwards and Raymond Laban.

(Source: *Wolverhampton Express & Star,* **13.8.1963/UFOSIS/Alan Poyner)**

17th August 1963 – Three flashes of light over Nottingham, then orange 'disc' seen

Three flashes of light lit up the night sky over Bilborough, Nottingham. These were followed by *"two beams of light"* seen to cross each other's path, and the appearance of an *"orange disc"*, sighted rushing headlong across the sky, according to Mr Ronald Atkin, who was stood with two other men when the incident took place. **(Source: UFOSIS)**

20th August 1963 – Strange lights over Gloucester

A cluster of eight, to ten 'lights' were seen manoeuvring in the sky over Gloucester.

(Source: *Gloucester Citizen,* **21.8.1963)**

22nd August 1963 – 'Jellyfish' UFO sighted by ex-RAF Officer

Retired RAF Officer – Mr W.D. Evans – sighted an object *"resembling a jellyfish or shuttlecock in shape, pulsing with orange lights, crossing the sky over Langland, Swansea".* This was later explained away as being a rocket, or flare, although the Coastguard denied any knowledge of such an incident.

(Source: *South Wales Evening Post,* **23.8.1963)**

26th August 1963 – UFO with 'aerial' sighted over Lndon

David Anthony Mohan (10), living on the top floor of Grantley House – a block of flats on the Ackroydon Estate, Wandsworth – noticed something glistening in the sky, at 7.45am. It was flying silently northeastwards.

"As it passed over the nearby Timperley Court, I had a very good view. It seemed to be moving at about 60mph, and was far too big to be a balloon, and about a hundred feet in diameter. The object was round, with a flat top, like a platform. Underneath was this 'thing', like a wireless aerial sticking out quite straight. It went behind a small cloud, and that was the last I saw of it."

(Sources: UFOLOG/*Wandsworth Borough News,* **28.8.1963)**

31st August 1963 – 'Flying Saucer' over Croydon

Mrs Marie Rogers – ex-District Councillor for 13 years, and County Councillor for 18 and a half years in the local community – spoke to us about an extraordinary sighting which happened when then living near Mitcham Common, Croydon, Surrey.

"I was in the kitchen, when my son burst into the house and asked me to come and have a look at something strange in the sky.

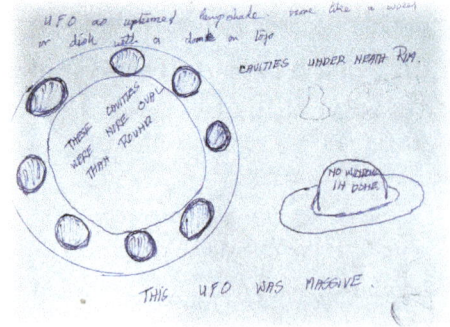

Haunted Skies **Volume Two Revised**

I went out with him and saw this dome-shaped object, hovering over trees at Mitcham Common. I stood there, mesmerised, looking at this thing, which reminded me of an upturned lampshade, with cavities below it. Suddenly, it pulsed with light, veered away, and was out of sight. I asked around, afterwards, if anyone else had seen it. They hadn't – which I thought very odd, as it had been a Bank Holiday, with crowds of people on the Common, including many police officers."

Telephoned the *Daily Mail*

"I telephoned the Daily Mail *Newspaper, who told me they had received a number of calls from the public about the UFO, and would get back to me. I'm still waiting for them to ring, over 45 years later!"* (**Source: Personal interview**)

SEPTEMBER 1963

6th September 1963 - 'Flying Saucer' over Southampton

Southampton schoolboy, Michael Blake – a fifth former at Testwood School – was walking along Houndsdown Avenue, Houndsdown, when he noticed an oval, red object in the sky, towards the south-east, at an angle of some 60 degrees.

"As it descended, it oscillated from side to side, following an S-shaped course, alternating in colour from dark to light red.

After reaching a height of about 200 feet in the air, it hovered over the electric power station at *Marchwood, three miles North of Hyde, enabling me to see a superstructure. I went indoors to tell a friend. When I came out, it had gone."

*Marchwood Power Station is located on the site of a former oil-fired power station within Marchwood Industrial Park, adjacent to the River Test and overlooking the Port of Southampton. Since the late 1980s, the site had remained largely unused, apart from some vehicle storage. The site was selected primarily because of its previous use as a power station..

14th September 1963 – Heart-shaped UFO sighted

At 5am, an amateur astronomer – Frederick Parker, from Goldthorpe (who had previously been sceptical about reports of *'flying saucers'*) – was in his garden, intending to look at the constellation Orion, when he noticed:

> "...a *'flying saucer'*, moving on a very low course before disappearing in seconds over adjacent buildings. It was almost identical to what other people (whom I have never believed) described. It was spherical in shape, surrounded by a metallic *'tyre'* and spinning as it flew silently across the sky."

(Source: *South Yorkshire Times*, 5.10.1963)

At 9pm, Vivienne Taylor – a second form schoolgirl at Testwood School – was with her father when the couple saw a glowing bright red, oval object, heading northwestwards. It disappeared into a cloud, and then emerged almost at the point where it had entered. It then travelled back along the direction from whence it had come, but now showing a heart or 'B' shaped, dark marking in the middle. The 'mark' was not evident before the object entered the cloud.

14th September 1963 – USA: Strange object in the sky over California

Mr E.A. Grant – veteran of 37 years, training forest fire lookouts for the U.S. Forest Service – was in Susanville, California, at 3.15pm, when he sighted a round object in the sky that joined up with a longer one, before disappearing from view 10 minutes later,

15th September 1963 – Pulsating crescent-shaped UFO sighted

At 3.30am, Joan Allinson and her father from Alnmouth, Northumberland, were approaching Shilbottle, when they saw:

> "...a pulsating golden crescent-shaped object, with a halo of light, hovering at an estimated height of 1,000 feet; suddenly, it swooped down and hovered in front of the car, darting backwards and forwards – always on the left hand side – occasionally travelling ahead."

It was a traumatic experience, from which it took Joan a few weeks to recover.

(Source: Tyneside UFO Society)

Seen over Hampshire, the same day

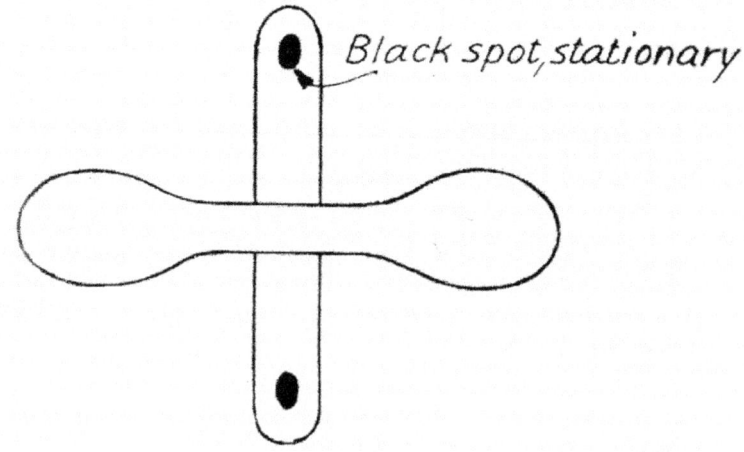

At 4.45pm, James Poulton – a sixth form pupil at Testwood School – was with his parents, sister, and brother-in-law, five miles North of Barton-on-Sea, Hampshire, when they noticed an object high in the air. It resembled a silver gyroscope, with a very thick spindle, showing prominent black spots, travelling at moderate speed. It appears this was the same UFO seen minutes later, by Michael Blake, who watched it heading across the sky towards Southampton, between 5am-6am. **(Source: Peter I. Kelly)**

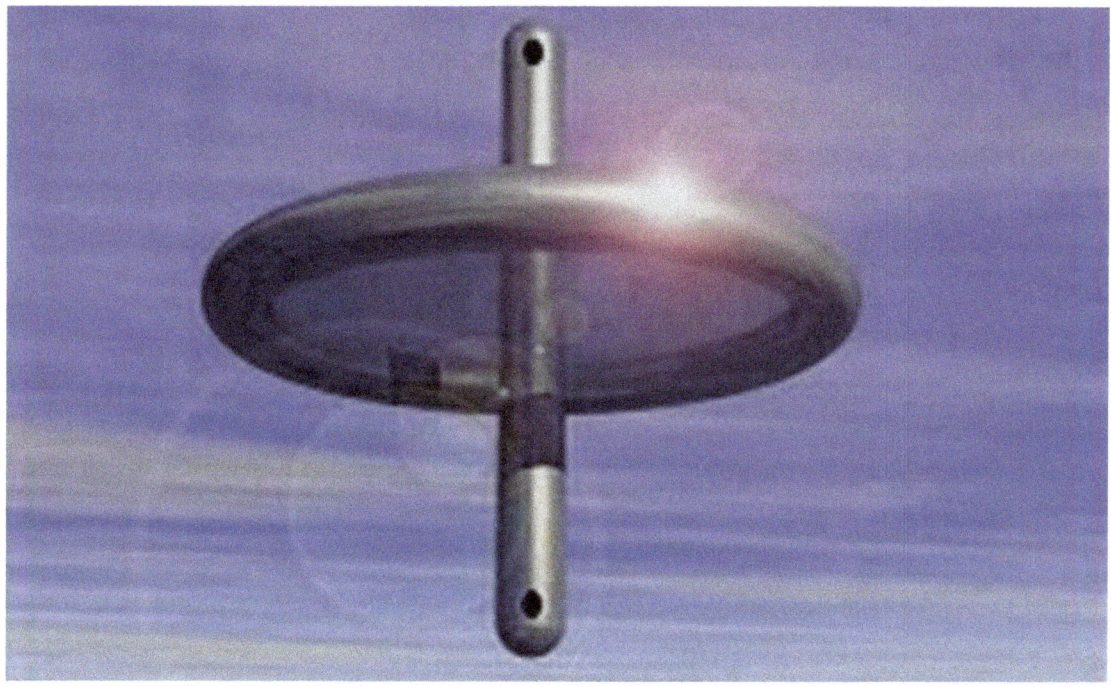

15th September 1963 – USA: Golden UFOs over Ohio

Two bright golden objects – one like a banana; the other, like an ear of corn – were seen in the sky over Vandalia, Ohio, at 6pm, by Mrs F.E. Roush. One was stationary; the other headed away in a west to north direction, during the 10 minutes observation. (**Source: Project Blue Book unknowns**)

September 1963 – 'Ice-cream cone'-shaped object over Kent

Ex-RAF serviceman Stanley Richardson was to witness something strange, during September while living in Maidstone, Kent:

> "My three young children were playing outside, when they told me about something in the sky. I picked up my binoculars, and looked at the area of sky where they were pointing, and saw an object shaped like an ice-cream cone, completely stationary in the sky, with two fluted shapes running along its length. It was at a very great height – probably too high for aircraft, despite a strong wind blowing. It was metallic grey in colour, with the sun reflecting off some of its surface – then small amounts of cloud passed below it, but it was still visible in the gaps. After about 35 minutes I lost sight of it, as it became covered with cloud. I later found out dozens of people had telephoned the authorities to report the sighting, which was explained away as being a balloon."

(**Source:** *Fountain Journal,* No. 9, 1977, Peter and Jane Paget)

Late September 1963 – Silver object over Nottingham

John Derry from Bobbers Hill, Nottingham, was in the backyard, playing with his two-year-old daughter, at 5.45pm, when he sighted a silver object moving fairly swiftly across the sky. At first he took it to be a weather balloon, but discounted this idea as it looked far too large. Enquiries made with the local weather station revealed that none of their equipment fitted the description, although they suggested it could have been a Radiosonde balloon, launched from Liverpool, or Cardington, Bedfordshire.

(**Source:** *Nottingham Evening Post,* 16.9 1963)

27th September 1963 - Two UFOs attached to each other

Ex-RAF employee – James Brooke of Lodge Road, Huddersfield – was in his garden at 7.30am, when he saw:

> "...two strange circular objects, apparently attached to each other, flying slowly across the sky, heading eastwards – like nothing I had ever seen before".

(Source: *Huddersfield Examiner*, 27.9.1963)

OCTOBER 1963

1st October 1963 – UFO over Manchester Airport

At 5.50am a local resident, living near Manchester Airport, was awoken by the sound of powerful engines. On going to the window, he saw a brightly-lit object descending through the sky, over the direction of Manchester Airport. He initially thought it was an aircraft about to crash-land – until it stopped falling, and hovered in the air, while aircraft began to take off from the airport, passing underneath it. Suddenly, it shot straight upwards and could only be seen as a 'star' in the sky. By 7.00am, it had gone.

(Source: *Manchester Evening News*, 1.10.1963 – 'Mystery of the thing in the sky')

2nd October 1963 – Was this the same UFO?

At 6.45pm, a glowing object was seen to exit a cloud over Manchester, and hover a while, before climbing back into the cloud – its glow diminishing to reveal a black, oval, object. **(Source: UFOSIS)**

4th October 1963 -: Spinning UFO over Cheshire

At 1.30pm, a coloured spinning object was seen hovering thousands of feet up in the sky, over Cheadle, giving out a white flash of light every few minutes. It was seen by Stuart Scully (then aged 13), who wrote a letter to the local newspaper.

Similar objects were also reported on the 5th and 8th October, over Teesside.

(Source: *Manchester Evening News*, 8.10.1963)

7th October 1963 – Strange phenomena over Southampton

John Baker – a sixth form prefect at Testwood Secondary Modern School, Southampton – was fishing on the *River Test*, near Totton, at 11.30pm, with three friends, when they noticed an extremely bright glow towards the east, about three times the size of the sun, *"so bright, we had to look away. It resembled burning magnesium – then faded from sight."* **(Source: Peter I. Kelly)**

October 1963 – UFO over Romford, Essex

John Rollington, aged 12, was out playing with his friends – Colin Wright and another boy, with the surname Gunn – in the Romford area of Essex, one evening, when they saw what looked like:

> "...two soup plates, joined together, orange-white in colour, with silvery ends, moving through the sky".

The incident was brought to the attention of the Essex UFO Study Group, in 1975.

(Source: Original file, Essex UFO Study Group)

14th October 1963 – Fireball over Sussex

Mrs Joan Child was preparing breakfast at her Woodingdean home, at 6.45am, when she heard a *"whooshing"* noise – strong enough to rattle the windows in the house. Looking out of the window, she saw a 'ball of fire', of about 12 inches in diameter, flashing past the house, a few feet off the ground. A search of the locality by Mrs Child and her neighbours, who came rushing out, failed to reveal anything out of the ordinary. **(Source: Personal interview)**

20th October 1963 – UFOs seen over Leeds and Suffolk

At 2am, Leeds housewife – Mrs M. Foster – happened to look out of the bedroom window and see *"a large star, blue-green in colour, moving from side-to-side in the sky"*, and awoke her husband. The couple watched it for twenty minutes, until it disappeared from view behind a row of houses.

Also seen in Suffolk

At about the same time, Mr C. Lambert, from Ipswich, noticed *"…two objects, at great height in the sky – one brighter or larger than the other – connected by a 'line', or something similar, weaving from side to side in level flight, circling, hovering and spiralling overhead, for about ten minutes"*, before heading towards Ipswich. (**Source:** *East Anglian Daily Times*, 29.10.1963)

21st October 1963 – 'Discs' of orange light reported in the sky

A UFO was reported over Harrogate, at 6.45am, by Mrs D. Cook. (**Source:** *Yorkshire Post*, 24.10.1963)

Later that evening, strange 'discs' of orange light were seen by several people living in Bilborough, Nottingham, at an estimated altitude of between 8-10,000 feet. (**Source:** *Nottingham Evening Post*, 23.10.1963)

23rd October 1963 – Football-shaped UFO seen over Ohio

On the evening of this day, several unnamed students from Meridian, Ohio, sighted an object shaped like a circle from below, and football-shaped from the side, hovering low in the sky. It was making a deep, pulsating, loud, extremely irritating sound, for six minutes. (**Source: Project Blue Book unknowns**)

24th October 1963 – Strange 'light' in the sky over Scotland

Over Cupar, Fife, young boys – A. McLean (12), and his brother G. McLean (8) – sighted a strange 'light' in the sky. No other details are available. Interestingly, it appears the incident was later brought to the attention of Project Blue Book chief – Major H. Quintanilla – who told the youngsters, in a letter, that this was *"one of the most complete"* of the unexplained cases for the year!

29th October 1963 – Silver object over Devizes

An object, "highly polished, silvery metallic in appearance", was seen hovering over Roundway Hospital, Devizes, by hospital orderly – Martin Tucker. (**Source:** *Bath & Wiltshire Chronicle*, 29.10.1963)

NOVEMBER 1963

13th November 1963 – Pulsating object seen over Isle of Wight

At 10am, a schoolboy was walking down The Fairway, towards Fairway School, Sandown, Isle of Wight, when he noticed an aircraft crossing the sky. It was followed by the sight of a lightly pulsating, circular object, climbing upwards through the air in an easterly direction. (**Source: Isle of Wight UFO Society**)

18th November 1963 – Silver 'disc' seen. Did RAF respond?

Shanklin resident – John Kimber – was watching a number of Westland 'Whirlwind' helicopters and 'Seahawks' flying over the Isle of Wight, at 10.30am. Weather conditions were described there as being a dark and misty sky to the east, but blue sky with small clouds to the west

"I was just in time to see a small silver 'disc' disappear into a tiny cloud – I waited for it to come out, but nothing appeared. The puzzling thing was that the 'cloud' had been moving in the opposite direction to the UFO."

The next day, Mr Kimber discovered a number of people had seen a similar UFO while on Sandown Golf Course. Incredibly, during another period of intense aerial activity over the island, he saw a small white, dome-shaped, object appear in the sky during that afternoon. He said:

"No sooner had it gone out of sight when the RAF 'Seahawks' flew over once again."

(**Source: Isle of Wight UFO Society**)

20th November 1963 – Flashing 'red light' seen by crew of trawler

At 6pm, Captain Murray and his crew, aboard the Aberdeen collier – *Thrift* – sighted a flashing *'red light'* pass within a mile of port side, 20 feet above sea level, off Girdle Ness, and disappear (showed on radar). A search was made – no trace. (**Source:** *Northern Echo,* **22.11.1963**)

November 1963 – Four cylindrical objects sighted over reservoir

Other reports for the month of November 1963 told of four cylindrical objects, with black globes on top, seen descending through the sky at 6.30pm, over Colt Crag Reservoir, Watling Street, Northumberland, by Otterburn resident – Mr J. Wood.

27th November 1963 – Silver 'ball' sighted over Cornwall

A silver 'ball of light' was seen over St. Austell, Cornwall, at 5.45pm, by Mrs C.L. Hancock.

> *"It was heading west to east. Suddenly, it changed course to south and just 'snuffed out' like a candle. Fifteen minutes later an aircraft was seen following the same course in the sky."*

29th November 1963 – UFO with three 'spikes' sighted in the sky

Miss Valentine, from Falmouth, wrote to the Tyneside-based UFO group (TUFOS), telling them about

> *"a long, brightly-lit, object seen stationary in the sky over The Lizard Peninsular. A short time afterwards, it began to move across the sky in a series of 'stop and start' movements, before being lost from view as it entered cloud."*

During the later part of the same day, a shining object was seen by pupils at Cradle Junior School, Fforestfach, near Swansea, described as, *"looking like a hovercraft, with three spikes sticking out, and a propeller turning around underneath it"*.

DECEMBER 1963

1st (provisional) December 1963 – UFO landing at RAF Cosford, Staffordshire

A report of a landed UFO, at RAF Cosford, was initially brought to the attention of Leslie Otley, of the Tyneside UFO Society, on the 10th December 1963, by a colleague, who told him of an incident which had taken place at a RAF Base approximately ten days earlier, indicating the end of November/or possible the 1st of December 1963, although, at this stage, the location was not given. This means the 'universally accepted date' of the 10th December 1963, is wrong.

Leslie:

> *"The details were exactly the same as our typed-up report of the 14th December, 1963. His information related to a matter at least ten days earlier."*

Details passed to Harry Bunting, of DIGAP

The information was passed onto Harry Bunting – President of DIGAP – who contacted Staffordshire based investigator – Mr Wilfred Daniels, who in turn

wrote a letter to the *Express and Star,* which was published on the 7th January 1964, quote:

> "Reports of a 'flying saucer' having landed at RAF Cosford have been discounted after an investigation. Two boy entrants and a signalman were thought to have seen an unidentified object on the station two weeks before Christmas. A report in the Tyneside Unidentified Flying Objects Journal claims that it was seen by several RAF men, and after flashing green lights around the airport, took off again. Mr Wilfred Daniels of 134, Weston Road, Stafford, a member of the British Flying Saucer movement and the British Unidentified Flying Objects Association, has been seeking the help of airmen and civilians in the Cosford area about the report."

Wilfred Daniels

Wilfred Daniels

Wilfred received a letter from a Stockport colleague (Harry) saying there were two RAF witnesses and a British Railways signalman near to the spot where the 'saucer' was said to have landed, and contacted Flight Lt. Stevens' station officer, at RAF Cosford, who told him that Wing Commander Wolsey – in charge of boy entrants – had investigated this matter and found no substance to it.

Newspaper account – mistaken identity!

According to the newspaper:

> "Mr Cecil Evans, the signalman concerned, laughed at his home today when asked about the report of a 'flying saucer'. A RAF Flight Lt. called to see me the day after the object was supposed to have been seen. He said that two boy entrants had seen a blue flashing light on the end of the clothing stores at the station, opposite my signal box, at 11.45pm, the previous night. At that time I had been looking out of the signal box and saw nothing unusual. Later, it occurred to me that what the boys might have seen were the reflections in the clothing store windows of lights on the Air Ministry estate at the bottom of Elm Lane – the reflections seemed to be dancing in the windows. Had a 'flying saucer' landed, I would have certainly known about it. It is just another case of mistaken identity; we had a good laugh about it."

On 9th January, retired British Army Royal Electrical and Mechanical Engineers (REME) Captain Wilfred Daniels, drove to Albrighton, close to the RAF Technical Training Establishment (RAF Cosford), on the west side of the A41 Wolverhampton to Salop road. First, he made some enquiries at Cosford Road Garage, about whether they had heard any rumours of any UFO landing at the camp. He was told they had no such knowledge.

Wilfred encounters the chaplain – it happened!

While walking along the High Street, he came face-to-face with a young man in clerical garb. It was the chaplain at the RAF Station, (Flt. Lt. Reverend Brian George Henry, Service number 507521, discharged 26th June 1981 with rank of Wing Commander).

After identifying himself, Wilfred asked him a number of questions about the incident, including his personal knowledge of the two boys involved, and received the following reply,

> "Oh yes, I've talked about it to them and they really believe they saw it."

When asked how they described it, and about their reactions, he answered:

> "They said it looked like what you would take for a 'flying saucer' down on the ground, as they watched a trapdoor in the upper part slowly open. Frightened, they ran away and, after telling someone what they had seen, they were told to sober up. But they were not drunk – quite sane and sensible."

> Reference:- AIR 2/17527
>
> PUBLIC RECORD OFFICE
>
> COPYRIGHT - NOT TO BE REPRODUCED PHOTOGRAPHICALLY WITHOUT PERMISSION
>
> From: Mr. B.E. Robson (S4(Air))
>
> 20th October 1964
>
> Your letter of the 15th October to RAF Cosford has been passed to me to deal with.
>
> After careful investigation, the Air Force Department is satisfied beyond any reasonable doubt that no unidentified object was either seen or landed at Cosford last year, and that the whole affair was merely a piece of high spirits by the apprentices concerned. This has been made quite clear to previous enquirers on the same subject.
>
> In these circumstances, the question of photographs, drawings, details of movement etc. does not arise.

Wilfred asked him if he was willing to arrange an interview with the two boys. The chaplain refused, and asked that his name be withheld. Wilfred then went to see the signalman – Mr Evans – but, although spending over an hour with him, learnt nothing of any value. Interestingly, Leslie Otley discovered that one of the boy entrants came from the Newcastle-on-Tyne area, and pondered whether he was responsible for leaking the information relating to the UFO landing in the first place.

On 14th January 1964, Leslie Otley wrote to Wilfred Daniels, suggesting the real date of the landing was between 17th November and 1st December, 1963. Wilfred contacted the RAF Station and spoke to the Station adjutant, who said:

> *"The story came out on the 14th December 1963, but it did not really happen; several of the trainees conspired together to 'cook up' the yarn of the 'flying saucer', but what started as a joke, got out of hand. It was the 14th December 1963, when it emerged."*

**ROYAL AIR FORCE
PERSONNEL MANAGEMENT AGENCY
ROYAL AIR FORCE INNSWORTH
GLOUCESTER GL3 1EZ**

Telephone Gloucester (01452) 712612 Ext. 7617

Mr C A H

Stafford

Your Reference

Our Reference
PMA/132104/5/W/97106/2a2b
Date
18 January 1999

Dear Mr H

RE RAY WARDLE

Thank you for your recent letter.

Unfortunately I have been unable to identify the above named from our records with the information provided. To make a positive identification we require either a service number or a date of birth.

I am sorry to send what must be a disappointing reply.

Yours sincerely

J A Mortimer
MRS J A MORTIMER
ADMIN OFFICER
for Air Secretary

Letter from RAF Cosford to the Air Ministry

A letter from Flying Officer Robert Alan Roberts (Service number 2201456 D, discharged 29th April 1964) at Cosford, to the Air Ministry, at Whitehall, stated that Flight Lieutenant Henry, *"categorically denies all statements attributed to him"*.

Flying Officer Roberts further added that the chaplain was *seriously considering taking legal action.*

In a letter sent to Waveney Girvan – editor of *Flying Saucer Review* magazine – on 13th April 1964, Wilfred Daniels reported:

"Flight Lieutenant Henry said that publication of his name would cause him trouble; that it was 'more than his job was worth' to arrange a meeting between me and the two RAF apprentices. He really ought not to be talking to me about it at all; that security had dropped right down on the whole thing."

Waveney Girvan – editor of Flying Saucer Review

Waveney Girvan resolved to get to the bottom of the mystery, and wrote a number of letters to both RAF Cosford and the Air Ministry, following the disclosure of several contradictory explanations offered by the authorities to explain the encounter: including, *"Nothing at all"*, *"two drunk apprentices"*, *"a hoax"*, and – somewhat amusingly – *"a British Railways steam train"*. These were the various theories offered by the Air Ministry in its attempts to 'kill' interest in the case.

He also wrote an article in *Flying Saucer Review*, the *Kensington News* and *West London Times* about the incident – 'AFFAIR AT COSFORD', in which he challenged (on behalf of the *Kensington News* and *West London Times*) Flt. Lt. Henry to: *"come forward and swear an affidavit that he did not say what Mr Daniels swears he did when they met in Albrighton last February"*.

Waveney identified one of the RAF trainees as Ian Jones, and commented on the Government's self-contradictory explanations, *"What is it that the Air Ministry is trying so desperately to hide?"* Later, following further enquiries into the incident, he established the identities of both of the witnesses as being Ian Jones and Ray Wardle.

UFOs reported over the M6 Motorway

In correspondence with Flt. Lt. Stevens, on the 3rd January 1964, Wilfred Daniels, told him:

"On the 12th and 14th November (1963) last, there were UFOs over the M6 Motorway, at Warley, (my own sighting), and at Tittensor, Manchester, (lorry driver witness). There were two UFOs between Preston and Southport on Wednesday, 12th November 1963."

Nick Redfern

In 2009, we spoke to British born UFO author Nick Redfern – now living in Dallas, Texas – after having read his book, *Cosmic Crashes – the incredible stories of the UFOs that fell to earth*, published by Simon and Schuster, in 1999, which included a chapter relating to his investigation into this incident, following his examination of the declassified file, that contained over 60 pages.

As a result of an article submitted by Nick, published by *UFO Magazine* in their Christmas edition, relating to the Cosford incident, he was contacted by Wolverhampton resident – Barry Green, who told him the following:

"At the time of the 'encounter' (RAF Cosford incident), I was living with my family near Tettenhall Wood, some four miles away from RAF Cosford. One evening, my father and brother, who were in the kitchen, shouted out they had sighted an object in the night sky, displaying flashing lights with a larger green light. I rushed into the room and remember how nice the colours were. The next thing is that it shot off, at great speed, towards the direction of RAF Cosford. It's made us all wonder if this was the one seen at RAF Cosford."

Telephone call from Graham Birdsall

In 1997, Nick received a telephone call from Graham Birdsall, of *UFO Magazine*, who told him he had been contacted by Ray Wardle. As a result of this, Nick conducted an interview with him:

"My friend and I went out for the evening. We had passes that covered us until 9pm, but by the time we got back to Cosford, it was 9.15pm, so I said, 'the best thing we can do is to climb the fence'. We

walked alongside the chain-link fence, near the hangars, close to a railroad track outside the Camp site, and climbed over the fence, took a few steps, and there was this object. I'm not going to say it was a 'flying saucer' because it wasn't. It wasn't shaped like one – it didn't look like one. It was very bright, mainly orange, with white lights, and reminded me of a church organ. It appeared to have pipes on it – things like that in the centre of it – but there was no distinct outline to the object at all, and I couldn't tell if it was on the ground or just above it."

Graham Birdsall

During further conversation, Ray told Nick he estimated the size of the object as being:

"…twenty feet across, by thirty feet high, and that he and his companion were probably a hundred yards away from it."

Although Ray wanted to investigate further, Ian ran away. Ray deliberated and then caught up with Ian, between two hangars, where they discussed what they should do about the sighting. After some conversation, they decided to report it.

Ray:

"What bothered me was that they refused to come back with us. Nobody would go to the spot that we were telling them about.

It was frustrating. I suppose we were humoured. I really don't know. Nobody said, 'Oh, you're lying'. They just wanted the facts and that was it. It was quite strange."

Ray confirmed he had made a written statement to the officer in charge, but couldn't recall having signed it. (There was no trace of this document in the MOD file.)

Chris Holton – reply from Gaynor South, of the MOD

This is not, of course, the whole story. Somebody else who took an interest in the events at Cosford was Chris Holton, from Stafford, whom we met some years ago. Chris wrote to the MOD in October 1997, asking them for details of the other serviceman -

Ian Jones – but was told that this was not possible without his date of birth and service details.

In July 1996, Chris received a reply from the MOD, after enquiring about unexplained aerial sightings over RAF Cosford, when he received the following answer from Gaynor South:

"Unfortunately we maintain our records in date order, so I am afraid it would be too time-consuming a task to sift through all the files to pick out sighting reports in any one area.

From 1960, the MOD has received nearly 9,000 UFO sighting reports. All MOD and Government files generally remain closed from public viewing for 30 years after the last action has been taken. It was generally the case that before 1967 all 'UFO' report files were destroyed after 5 years as in the context of limited archive space, and that due to insufficient public interest in the subject, there was no reason for them to be retained.

Since 1967, due to an increase in public interest, these files are now preserved. However, a few files from the 1950s and 1960s did survive, and maybe viewed by members of the public at the Public Records Office. The files are AIR.16/1199- Air 20/9322- AIR 2/16918-AIR 20/ 7390- AIR20/ 9994- AIR 2/17318-AIR 20/ 9320- PREM 11/855- AIR2/ 17318-AIR 2/17526-AIR 20/9321/"

Ray Wardle

In November 2009, we spoke to Ray about the 'Cosford' incident. He still remembered it but said that it was insignificant in contrast to some harrowing experiences he was to have, while living in Nevada.

These involved a variety of strange phenomena, which included a weird siren noise, heard on two occasions, while driving through the desert in the late 1980s. He said:

> "Each time I thought I was being pulled over by the police. When I stopped and got out, there was nothing there."

Another time, he and his wife were travelling along Highway 168, which runs between Route 193 and 115, when they heard a mysterious electronic sound, which pervaded the atmosphere within the car, frightening them both. Fortunately, the sound faded away. However, this was not the end of the story. When they arrived home, Ray discovered a scar on his left shoulder which wasn't there when he went out.

Understandably, incidents of such nature culminated in Ray carrying a firearm for protection.

> "At the time I was employed in setting up surveillance in the casinos at Las Vegas, so I decided to set up some electronic equipment in the house for protection, but was astounded to find the batteries from the microphone had gone (in plain view of the camera), but later found them in a bag ... it didn't make sense."

Area 51

Ray believes he was singled out by the authorities, after capturing UFOs on film and visiting such locations as Area 51 (or at least the perimeter), while living in Nevada. He claims that on another occasion he filmed someone in a helicopter, shooting at him. Details of this incident were sent to the FBI, but they told him that they would not be investigating it!

It appears that Ray is a genuine man, who has suffered both physically and mentally through his involvement with UFOs. He tells us that he is still unable to sleep properly, after having undergone some horrific traumatic experiences which may or may not be connected with the original incident, all those years ago.

If you judged a case like this on its merits, without having ever listened to other people's stories, it would be so easy to dismiss it as a flight of fancy, or even fabrication, as it sounds too unbelievable to credit, purely because it doesn't fit into what we perceive as rational or logical parameters of normal human behaviour.

We wish the best to Ray and his partner, Sue, and apologise for resurrecting something which has caused anxiety, but we appreciate their courage in allowing us to share in what is, after all, a very personal and private part of their lives. Without them, and so many others, we would not have any book at all.

(Sources: As above/Wolverhampton *Express and Star,* **12.3.1964/Declassified MOD records/Nick Redfern/ Matthew Williams /Chris Holton)**

5th December 1963 – Blazing 'ball of fire' sighted over Isle of Wight

Mr H.J. Wells of Wroxall, Isle of Wight – a brick kiln setter by occupation – was waiting for a friend to pick him up for work, at 7am.

> "I noticed what I took to be a large star moving across the sky, travelling in a west from south-east direction. I waited, thinking it was going to 'shoot and disappear'. This didn't happen. It resembled a blazing 'ball of fire', red-yellow in colour, which occasionally flashed a light – like that seen on an aircraft." **(Source: Isle of Wight UFO Society)**

On the same date, Lorry driver – Tom Walker – reported being followed by a UFO, between Callow and Wormelow, Herefordshire. Upon arriving home, the object shot up into the sky and disappeared.

(Source: *Hereford Citizen & Bulletin,* **6.12.1963)**

7th December 1963 – Fiery object seen by mother and daughter

As a result of some publicity given to the UFO subject in the *BBC Round-up* programme, Newport resident – Mrs Monica Allpress, wrote to the Isle of Wight UFO Society about what she and her daughter, Sarah (11), saw at 5.40pm, while visiting Farmer Alan Wood – then owner of Rookley Farm:

> "Our attention was caught by a very large, fiery object, which shot across the sky, heading east to west, travelling parallel to the Earth, before inexplicably vanishing halfway across the sky. The shape of the object was vaguely reminiscent of an aircraft, with body and wings, but its edges were ragged, as fire might be. It looked like a cross between a meteor and aircraft."

(Source: Isle of Wight UFO Society)

11th December 1963 – Flashing UFO

Over McMinnville, Oregon, Mr W.W. Dolan – professor of mathematics and astronomy, and Dean of the faculty of Linfield College – sighted a bright, star-like object in the sky, at 7am, which hovered, slowed, dimmed and flashed, over the minute's duration.

12th December – UFO making warbling noise

Mr Norman. Sachs was walking his dog along the beach at Polperro, Cornwall, at 10.35pm, when he saw what he took to be a fireball dropping down through the sky. To his amazement it stopped overhead,

> "...making this warbling noise, flashing green and orange lights, before slowly rising upwards, and disappearing from sight."

He was later interviewed by Mr David Lomax for the BBC West region.

(Source: British Flying Saucer Bureau) [Some accounts give this date as being the 28th December 1963]

14th December 1963 - Cigar-shaped UFO seen over Margate

A huge cigar-shaped object, with lights streaming out of it – showing four rectangular dark patches, resembling windows on its body – was seen over Margate, at 11.35pm.

(Source: Cambridge University for the Investigation of UFOs)

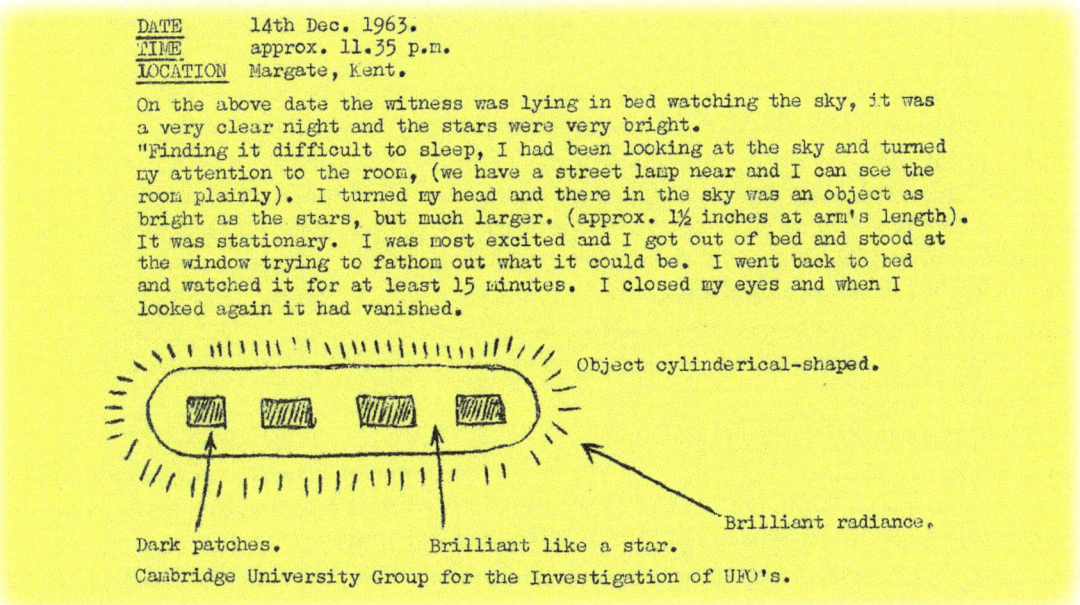

24th December 1963 – Car battery flattened by UFO

Mr Raymond Chandler of Mottram, Cheshire, was driving his Landrover, near Rowarth, in the Glossop area, at 7.25pm, when he saw a brilliantly coloured object hovering near his car. This frightened him, and his recently purchased new battery was considerably flattened. According to Mr Chandler, cows in the area were agitated and did not give milk for a few days. (**Source:** DIGAP)

27th December 1963 – UFO landing at Buckhurst Hill, Epping

Following reports of UFOs being seen in the Essex area, Pauline Abbott (then aged 17) – a trainee riding instructor at the Ivy Chimneys Riding School, Epping – was exercising her horse, 'Leberstram', in the yard of the riding school, at 4pm, on a misty afternoon, on 27th December 1963. She heard a squelching noise coming from the nearby field – which she took to be a duck, quacking – then wondered if there was somebody in the field itself, and shouted out, *"Who's there?"*, but received no answer.

Looking over towards the field:

> *"I saw this thing on the ground. It was about three feet high and eight feet wide, greyish in colour, with a glow coming from the one end. I sat on the horse, too frightened to move. Whatever it was took-off slowly and disappeared into the distance. When I later went to have a look in the field, I found a number of deep indented marks in the ground, approximately 8 feet across, by one and a half feet deep, with four lines radiating outwards from the circular marks, with 'cup' marks at the end of each line."*

As a result of subsequent further publicity in the local newspapers – *The Times* and *Wessex Star* (3.1.1964) – two girls contacted them to report having seen a dome-shaped, shiny, object in the sky, during the morning. One of them mentioned that it was common knowledge, locally, that other 'strange marks' and ground traces had been found in the locality, *'when something had crash-landed'*, in 1958.

Dr. D.G. Doel, who was to become involved in a number of UFO investigations, during this period, heard about the matter and paid a visit to the area, together with his daughter, Diana, (unaware of the incident until March 1964), where they met up with the owner of the riding school and Mr Banks, who then directed them to the riding stables where Carol Foster (18), Robert Ewing (13), and Pauline Abbott, were waiting.

In a tape-recorded interview, the couple told of arriving at the stables at 8am, on the 26th December – a dry but overcast day – when they saw an unusual object crossing the sky. They described it as being:

> *"…long and flat, with a dome-like protuberance, without visible windows at the end, silvery-white in colour, and bright"* (presumably self-illuminating, as there was no sun). When they took their eyes off the object to look around for any other witnesses, and looked back again, it had gone. Dr. Doel then interviewed Pauline Abbott, who told of arriving at the stables at 4pm, on the 27th, and riding the horse to the field concerned, when she heard a squelching noise.

Thinking it was a man, walking over the mud (not forgetting the previous day's UFO sighting, which had been brought to her attention), she looked out and saw a peculiar object on the ground in front of her and shouted:

> *"Mr Banks, there's a UFO in the field"*.

In a later interview, she described it as being … *"eight feet long, three feet high in the middle, tapering down to a point at each end, bright and white in appearance. Towards the left of the object was a feature that looked like a car windscreen, or panel, glowing much brighter than the rest."*

After calling out, the object took-off in a shallow climb, where she lost sight of it as it passed behind a haystack.

The next morning, some of the occupants of the riding stables went to the scene and examined it, finding the previously described 'marks' on the ground, *"...as if a blunt knife had been dragged across the grass."*

Mr Banks was also interviewed. He told Dr. Doel that by the time he arrived at the scene there was no sign of the UFO, although he did see some vague marks in the ground. However, he did tell them of an earlier incident which took place, in 1958, brought to his attention by a Major Frank Collins, whom he had telephoned.

Retired Major Frank Collins

Mr Collins then arrived and had this to say:

> *"I was in my garden one day, in June or July 1958, when I heard a rendering, tearing noise – like a jet plane out of control. There was a brilliant green light, which outlined the object in the room of the house, and then something crashed behind me. I turned around, and saw that the bushes were alight and smouldering a little.*
>
> *When I arrived at the spot, I found an area of about 30 square yards, burning. Many people had rushed out of their houses to have a look. The police and fire brigade were in attendance. One of the officers began to probe a small hole in the centre, some 7 inches in diameter and 14 inches deep."*

Material recovered from the scene – incidents later dismissed

After the emergency services had left, Major Collins went over and scraped around the side of the hole and retrieved some pieces of silvery material, resembling fused plastic. Photographs were then taken of a Mrs Hutton, holding a few of these fragments. When this matter was brought to the attention of John Cleary-Baker, the Editor of BUFORA, he concluded that the initial sighting on the 26th December 1964,

> *"... was possibly an aircraft, and that the later incident, involving Pauline, was a reflection of light",*

and suggested, *"the marks in the ground were lightning, striking the ground."*

In his summing-up of the three individual cases, as forwarded to him by Mr D.G. Doel, John Cleary-Baker, PhD., appears to have dismissed all three incidents as offering any evidence of UFO activity at all, which seems rather strange.

With regard to the second incident involving Pauline Abbott, Dr. John Cleary-Baker concluded:

> *"The evidence of a single witness, described by a responsible person well acquainted with her as 'imaginative', is a somewhat precarious foundation on which to erect a narrative of a UFO landing. I will not go so far as to accuse this young lady of hoaxing, but I feel that a pennyworth of fact has been augmented by a pound's worth of invention. The evening was misty and a light reflection from a vehicle on the road nearby, distorted by a swirl of vapour, could afford a fanciful mind all the prerequisites for a UFO landing story. Miss Abbott's story impresses me as representing much ado about little."*

Is it any wonder that Pauline Abbott became the subject of much ridicule to the extent that she regretted intensely having ever reported the matter in the first place? We doubt very much that the object she saw and drew was a swirl of vapour, caused by a passing motor vehicle!

This was one of those cases where the reader was left with a number of unanswered questions, such as: Where exactly did the 1958 incident take place? What happened to the photos taken? Was it reported to the newspapers? What happened to the material recovered from the scene? Was it ever analysed? What were the views of the original BUFORA Investigator – Mr Paul Webb? He attended the scene and discovered a thick, silvery, slimy, deposit on top of a fence post, in 'line of flight' identical to what was found on the ground where the object had landed. (**Source:** *BUFORA Journal***, Vol. 1, No. 1, summer 1964)**

Pauline Abbott points to the spot where she saw the 'flying saucer'.

Further developments

In the August 2017, I received a telephone call from London resident Ron Clarke (69) – a retired Trading Standards Officer. He said he had been in touch with Gary Heseltine about a UFO seen at Ivy Chimneys, Buckhurst Hill, many years ago, by his colleague, Terry Payne (72) – a retired Epping Police Officer, then (18). First of all we cannot categorically say that this is the same incident, as we do not have a precise date – other than around 1963 – but it appears, bearing in mind the location, that we would be dealing with the same incident.

Terry:

> "The sergeant asked me to go to Ivy Chimneys, as the police had received a report of a UFO seen there. I drove the Wolsey police car down to the location. When I arrived I was staggered to see a light-blue, banana-shaped object – which had what looked like windows, although you couldn't see inside it – hovering a few feet off the ground. We got out of the car. By this time about a dozen officers were there at the scene. 'It' then made a 'voom', 'voom' noise and shot away into the sky, leaving a strange smell behind – like that given off by an electrical board. The next thing that happened was that a digger appeared with a pointed shaped implement at the front. They dug out a three feet wide circle around where the object had been, and took the earth away. A short time later some low loader lorries arrived, bearing the 'HALLS' insignia, and filled in the hole with fresh soil. I was told to keep my mouth shut, which I have for many years."

Then suddenly I saw this 'thing' on the ground in the field. It was about three feet high and eight feet wide and was greyish-white in colour and rather shiny. Also, there was a kind of glow coming from one end."

Pauline borrowed my pencil and did a rough sketch of what she saw. (Fig. 1.)

I was almost mesmerized and just sat on Leberstram and looked at it. It was a bit like a dream. And as I watched, it took off very slowly and disappeared into the distance.

"I realized what it was because U.F.O.s had been sighted around the area, and I notified the local paper. But I didn't mention it to any of my friends, because I was afraid they would laugh at me and think I was nuts. Then, the next day, we found

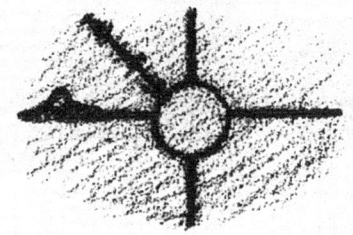

some strange marks on the ground which looked like this . . ." She did another quick drawing (Fig. 2), ". . . and I knew they had been left by the saucer."

She went on: "But even now I still get teased by people who read the reports. Bus conductors grin at me and say: 'Seen any flying saucers lately?' Nobody seems to take the subject seriously!"

I was impressed, and got in touch with the Ministry of Defence (Air) for their views. "Well, we haven't actually investigated this particular incident," a spokesman told me, "we only look into these sightings if we're asked to. And, over the last 12 years, 90 per cent of the U.F.O.s we've investigated have turned out to be weather balloons, aircraft,

CHAPTER 5 – 1964

UFO REPORTS INCLUDE:

JANUARY:
10th January 1964 – Mystery hole found in field at Isle of Wight
27th January 1964 – BUFORA formed (British UFO Research Association)

FEBRUARY:
5th February 1964 – Rectangular UFOs over North Sea
19th February 1964 – Black cylindrical object over North Sea
1964 – Naval sighting of a UFO
February 1964 – Did a UFO 'crash-land at Penkridge, Staffordshire?

APRIL:
10th April 1964 – Object over Northumberland
11th April 1964 – UFO over Walthamstow
11th April 1964 – USA: Cloud-like objects over New York
12th April 1964 – UFO over Croydon
13th April 1964 – USA: Four red lights seen over Wisconsin
24th April 1964 – USA: Socorro Police officer sights UFO
29th April 1964 – 'Disc' shaped cloud seen over Southampton
30th April 1964 – USA: Did a UFO land at Holloman Air Base?

MAY:
7th May 1964 – UFO over Luton, Bedfordshire
9th May 1964 – USA: Three lights seen over Chicago
17th May 1964 – UFO sighted over Kirby, Liverpool
20th May 1964 – Silver rectangular object over Middlesex
26th May 1964 – USA: Pleasant View, Pennsylvania
31st May 1964 – Unusual lights seen in sky over Gateshead

JUNE:
1st June 1964 – Fiery object sighted over Isle of Wight
2nd June 1964 – Silver domed object, showing three legs, at Gateshead
2nd June – Entities seen at Leam Lane Farm
12th June – Three glowing spheres over Ohio
26th June 1964 – UFO over Northumberland
29th June 1964- Object sighted over Salford,

JULY:
1st July 1964 – Liverpool leprechauns and 'little green men'!
1st July 1964 – Bright yellow object sighted. Were RAF scrambled?
3rd July 1964 – Massive object seen over Liverpool
6th July 1964 – Silver cigar-shaped object seen
8th July 1964 – Two bright objects sighted over Liverpool
8th July 1964 – England: Three 'flying discs' seen over London
10th July 1964 – Liverpool leprechauns sighted – Mass hysteria sweeps local children
12th July 1964 – UFO seen – then aircraft circles the sky
13th July 1964 – Black, round, machine showing rod on top, sighted over Essex
15th/16th July 1964 – Amateur astronomer sights UFO
16th July 1964 – USA: Four white 'lights' sighted over Michigan
17th July 1964 – UFO sighted over forest
23rd July 1964 – Bright object seen
26th July 1964 – UFO display over Liverpool
30th July 1964 – Glowing object over West Midlands

AUGUST:
1st August 1964 – UFO over Jersey
3rd August 1964 – White 'disc' seen in the sky
4th August 1964 – UFO making strange noise heard and seen, Scotland
5th August 1964 – Three orange lights seen in sky over Yorkshire
6th August 1964 – 'Bright light' seen over Lowestoft
7th August 1964 – 'Cottage loaf' UFO sighted
8th August 1964 – Cheshire motorist reports being followed by UFO
9th August 1964 – UFO over Littlehampton, Essex
10th August 1964 – USA: Wake Island: 'Red light' approaches runway
1964 – Birmingham: UFO seen carrying out a 'search' of the locality
14th August 1964 – UFO sighted over Wales
15th August 1964 – USA: Bullet-shaped UFO over New York
18th August 1964 – UFO displays observed over the UK
1964 – Landed 'Flying Saucer' over Cannock Chase, Staffordshire
21st August 1964 – 'Flying Saucer' seen by fisherman

22nd August 1964 – 'Ball of light' over Cheshire
23rd August 1964 – Black cross-shaped object sighted over Cheshire
27th August 1964 – Blinding light over Tyneside
31st August 1964 – UFO over Manchester, showing three lights

SEPTEMBER:

1st September 1964 – Red 'ring', with flashing lights, sighted over Isle of Wight
2nd September 1964 – Red-orange flickering 'light' seen over Cheshire
6th September 1964 – Flashing object seen over Lancashire
10th September 1964 (approx.) – Leprechauns sighted in Belfast!
10th September 1964 – Wingless UFO sighted over Manchester
11th September 1964 – Flashing lights over Huddersfield Yorkshire
12th September 1964 – Red 'globe' seen over Portsmouth
14th September 1964 – Silver rotating object over Manchester
15th September 1964 – Egg-shaped UFO seen over the Manchester area
20th September 1964 – Luminous 'disc' over Buckinghamshire
21st September 1964 – Silver 'disc' sighted over Nottingham
30th September – Red/orange sphere sighted

OCTOBER:

2nd October 1964 – Bright 'disc' seen, RAF respond, Space monsters reported at Manchester!
3rd October 1964 – White 'dots', forming 'V' shapes in the sky
7th October 1964 – UFOs over Stafford
10th October 1964 – Dinner plate UFO
12th October 1964 – Loud humming noise … then two pink 'discs'
17th October 1964 – 'T'-shaped UFO
19th October 1964 – Struck by a meteorite?
22nd October 1964 – Cross-shaped UFO over Southampton
24th October 1964 – Revolving red light in the sky
25th October 1964 – Somerset fisherman reports dazzling red 'light'
26th October 1964 – Unusual 'lights' seen over Hampshire
27th October 1964 – Two shapes seen in the sky
31st October 1964 – Police Officer sights 'flying cone' over Southampton.

NOVEMBER:

6th November 1964 – Elliptical UFO over Gateshead
8th-16th November 1964 – 'Spinning top' UFO

DECEMBER:

1st December 1964 – Brownies sight cylindrical object in the sky
BUFORA formed – (British UFO Research Association)
9th December 1964 – USA: UFOs tracked on radar Patuxent River, Maryland
24th December 1964 – Cone-shaped UFO, with concentric rings seen
29th December 1964 – USA: Three objects detected by radar Isle of Wight UFO Society contacts US Naval Air Station

JANUARY 1964

10th January 1964 – Mystery hole found in field at Isle of Wight

Farmer Roy Peach of Puckwell Farm, Niton, Isle of Wight, was ploughing 'Ridges' – his 13 acre field – when he came across a hole, fifteen feet in depth, by two feet wide. An examination of the hole revealed that it turned off at a sharp angle.

Thinking that it might have been caused by a Second World War unexploded bomb, he contacted PC William Donovan, from Ventnor Police Station. PC Donovan arrived at the scene and then reported it to the Bomb Disposal Squad, from HMS Vernon, who – after a preliminary examination of the scene – felt unable to commit their selves as to any explanation. They later handed over the matter to the Army Bomb Disposal Squad at Horsham, who spent two weeks on the site, before eventually filling in the hole, now 20 feet deep.

They believed that the hole had been caused by the movement of an unexploded wartime bomb.

Records from the Isle of Wight UFO Society reveal that the hole was no simple circle in the ground. It was irregularly shaped, and measured 23 inches across by 12 inches wide, and 12-15 feet deep.

Len Cramp and John Feakins

A visit was made to the scene by Len Cramp and John Feakins – members of the Isle of Wight UFO Society.

(Sources: Isle of Wight UFO Society/*Isle of Wight County Press*, 1.8.1964 – Mystery hole, Niton/*Portsmouth Evening News*, 12.1.1964 – 'Mystery of 20 foot hole in Niton field'/*Isle of Wight County Press*, 25.1.1964 – 'Mystery hole probed'/*Isle of Wight County Press*, 8.2.1964 - 'Niton hole mystery unsolved')

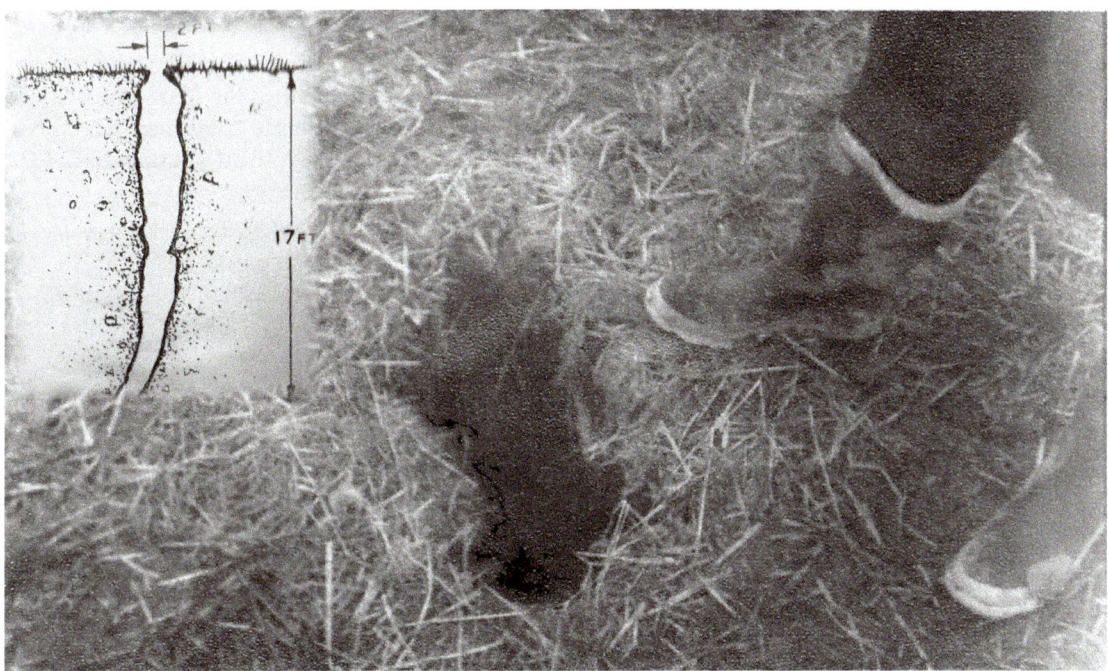

Fred Smith

Fred Smith – Honourable Secretary of the Isle of Wight UFO Society – was to write up further details regarding this case, which were published in an edition of *Space-link*, Volume 1, Number 2, March/April 1964, in which he described the impression in the ground as being 2 feet across by 12 inches wide:

> "It widened out under the surface to about 3 feet and went almost straight down for about 12 feet, narrowing slightly, before turning and disappearing around a bend. The sides were slightly irregular and a large stone or flint jutted out of the wall, 6-7 feet down.
>
> Mr Peach told the Portsmouth Evening News that he had found a 'thunderbolt' in the same field, but that it was very much smaller than whatever caused the present hole."

Lightning strikes – Fulgurites

One is bound to wonder if these were the result of a lightning strike. These can travel at speeds of 130,000 miles per hour, and reach a temperature of 30,000° C. This is hot enough to fuse sand into glass, forming channels known as fulgurites, which are normally hollow, and can extend deep into the ground.

Because of the irregular outline of the holed entrance and the top of a large fulgurate, we considered the possibility that the holes found at Niton and Silkstead, near Hursley, in Hampshire (December 1963, found in February 1964) were produced as a result of lightning strikes.

27th January 1964 – BUFORA formed (British UFO Research Association)

On the 25th January 1964, BUFORA came into being. The first edition of the new *BUFORA Journal*, Volume 1, No.1, was also published. Its board of members more or less remained the same and included president Mr Graham, F.N. Knewstub, Vice president Mr Leonard Cramp, Chairman Mr G.N.P. Stephenson, Vice-chairman Mr D.G. Doel, Editor Mr C.A Stickland, and Evaluation Officer Mr John Cleary-Baker. It was founded with the following aims:

> "To encourage, promote, and conduct unbiased scientific research into UFO phenomena throughout the United Kingdom: To collect and disseminate evidence and data relating to UFOs: To co-ordinate UFO research throughout the United Kingdom and to co-operate with others engaged in such research throughout the world."

FEBRUARY 1964

5th February 1964 – Rectangular UFOs over North Sea

At 3.24am, a British Rail signalman – Gerard O'Flynn – sighted:

> "...a silver, long, rectangular object (like a plank) projecting upwards at an angle in the sky, at an estimated height of two miles, which I thought was observing a Jet fighter. Fifteen seconds later, it was gone." (**Source: DIGAP, Harry Bunting, *UFOLOG*)**

19th February 1964 – Black cylindrical object over North Sea

Mr L. Henderson was a passenger in a DC3 returning to the UK from Germany, at 5.55pm GMT. It was flying over the North Sea, above a solid layer of cloud, extending to the horizon, when he sighted:

> "...a dark grey (almost black), cylindrical object, inclined at a slight angle, appearing solid (although fuzzy in outline) and – apparently – below, and to the left of the sun. Its size in contrast to the sun was approximately three times its length. At the base or lower end could be seen what looked like a small grey cloud. The object remained in this position for about five minutes.
>
> I moved my hand about, while observing, to ensure this was not any reflection, and asked the passenger sat behind me to confirm he could see it as well. At this point, the object started to move away to the left of the sun's disc, and also changing its angle, until about horizontal, then appearing to fade away as it moved off at a tangent to the Earth's curvature; now appearing to be a quarter of the size of the sun's disc."

Was it possible that this could have been the object described by the earlier witness? If so, what was the purpose of the visit? (**Source: *Orbit*, November/December 1963; January 1964, Volume 5, No. 4**)

1964 – Naval sighting of a UFO

Mrs Margaret Fry is a founder member of the Contact International UK (1967) based in Oxford, and also co founder of the Wales Fellowship of Independent Ufologists in 1993. She has been researching the UFO subject since 1965, having experienced a spectacular close encounter in 1955 and is known to us personally.

Margaret told of being contacted by Mr Mark Andrews of Wallasey, Merseyside, in 2013, who disclosed what he saw in 1964, while a radio operator aboard the motor vessel *Azmaut*, of the Atid Shipping Company, while anchored one-and-a-half miles off Jaffa, discharging cargo into lighters.

Margaret Fry

Mark:

> "The lighters were warning us of an impending severe storm and sailed away to Jaffa Harbour. Foolishly, we remained at anchor. As predicted the wind blew with hurricane force, creating huge seas. We were pounded all night. As dawn broke, the ship parted its cable and drifted onto rocks. I sent out a SOS. By this time the ship was completely waterlogged and solidly bedded into ground under its keel.
>
> The following morning, I went and sat on deck; the sea was calm with a blue sky, like a summer's day. I looked up into the sky and saw – no more than a mile away, about 8-9,000 feet up in the air – a silver 'oblong box' shaped object, reflecting the sun's rays.
>
> It was covered in criss-cross trellising and had a short 'leg' at each corner; it then manoeuvred itself until it was over the ship.
>
> Then the unbelievable – the ship lifted off the rocks and started to bump along the seabed, at about four miles per hour, until coming to a rest at the end of the concrete jetty. The deckhands – a skeleton crew of five, the rest Israeli – ran a short plank as gangway.
>
> I ran to get my binoculars, but by then it was gone."

Margaret informed us that, on retirement, Mark took up the hobby of dowsing and plotting ley lines with his two friends – Ronnie Cady and Norman Hill – both retired merchant navy men. Margaret remained staunch friends with Mark, until he passed away some years ago, but continued to stay in touch with Ronnie Cady afterwards.

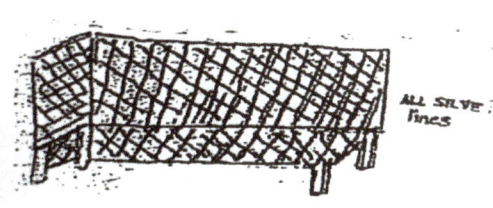

February 1964 – Did a UFO 'crash-land' at Penkridge, Staffordshire?

We weren't sure what to make of an incident alleged to have happened at Penkridge, Staffordshire, during February 1964, in an area of forest known as Cannock Chase. An object allegedly 'crash-landed' and

Haunted Skies Volume Two Revised

This week we uncover the Cannock-Files

Was there a Chase UFO crash cover-up?

WHILE FBI agents Mulder and Scully are merely fictional characters in TV's most paranormal and paranoid programme, we have found time and again that life has an uncanny knack of imitating art. Or is it the other way around?

During our investigations into the X-Files of Staffordshire, we have found ourselves following many of the UFO and conspiracy related paths already trod by our TV counterparts.

For example, what was surely one of the weirdest C-Files that we investigated took us back in time to the Cannock Chase of the 1960s and plunged us into a bizarre mystery involving the retrieval by the military of a strange aircraft that had crashed on the Chase, the silencing of a key witness, rumours of alien bodies found in the wreckage of the vehicle and the deep involvement of the Ministry of Defence!

It began when Leonard Stringfield, a US Air Force officer, revealed that in 1964 a UFO piloted by three alien creatures crashed on the edge of the Cannock Chase and was recovered by elite forces from NATO.

Despite the incredible nature of this account, we located a source who was intimately involved.

He had been driving through the Chase on that fateful day in 1964 and had come across a cordon manned by military personnel.

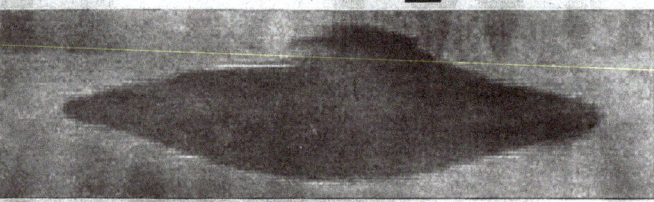

Local paranormal investigators Nick Redfern and Irene Bott look into a bizarre 1960s mystery

Ordered to turn his vehicle around, he drove several hundred yards up the road, pulled over and, with camera in hand, stealthily headed through the trees to see what the fuss was about.

He soon found out.

Sitting on the trailer of a military transporter was a small triangular-shaped object that looked like nothing on Earth...

The witness told us that his camera was confiscated and he was asked about his reasons for being in the area. It was made clear to him that speaking out publicly would not be in his best interests.

But that was not all.

On the day we went to interview him, he told us that he had received a strange telephone call from the MoD that had unnerved him considerably.

We looked at each other and questions flooded our minds: Was he a hoaxer?

Were we in the middle of an investigation worthy of an entire episode of the X-Files? And was our witness really being kept under apparent surveillance more than 30 years on?

We asked if we could dial 1471 to see if he was being honest. Sure enough, a number was available and it was the MoD. We were put through to a military operator and eventually traced the call to the MoD Guards Service at Whittington Army Barracks. From there, however, the only response was a deafening silence.

To this day, the origin of the mysterious object found on the Chase in 1964 remains unknown.

Was it a crashed UFO? Or was it perhaps a prototype aircraft that the military and the MoD wished to keep under wraps? At this stage the C-File on this case remains open.

Do you know what the object was? Were you part of the retrieval team? If so, give us a call.

– together with its occupants – was recovered by H.M Armed Forces. This matter was first brought to the attention of (then) Staffordshire based UFO investigator – Nick Redfern, following communication with retired US Air Force intelligence officer – *Leonard Stringfield, who – just before his death in 1994, said:

> "Having learnt from an informant of a decoded report revealing a UFO had crashed in two parts: the main section was in Penkridge, Staffordshire, the remainder in West Germany, and that artifacts had been recovered with three dead alien personnel. The top secret decoded radio message stated that wreckage and the bodies were shipped to Wright-Patterson Air Force Base in the States."

After discussing this with Nick, Irene Bott, and Graham Allen – then head of the Staffordshire UFO Group (SUFOG) based at Rugeley – contacted the *Burntwood Post*, and placed an appeal in the newspaper seeking any information on the incident.

Irene Bott receives a letter

As a result, Irene received a letter from a Mr Harold South, a week later, who claimed:

"I had been driving across the Chase, when I came across a Military cordon and was ordered to turn my vehicle around and find an alternative route. I did as I was told; however, when out of sight of the Military, I parked my van on the side of the road and stealthily crept through the forest on foot back to the area that had been cordoned off, when I was shocked and fascinated to see some form of small triangular shaped object that did not look man-made, being loaded aboard a Military transport vehicle. As I always carry my camera with me, I took a couple of photographs of the object".

When Harold arrived home, his mother told him that the local police had been looking for him. After attending the local police station, he was subsequently interviewed by officers, who told him he had been seen taking photographs and demanded the camera and film. He never saw them or the camera again. Nick Redfern and Irene Bott considered him to be a credible witness, and during the course of an interview held with Harold, in December 1996, he told them that only minutes after speaking with them on the telephone to arrange the interview, he received a strange and disconcerting telephone call from the MOD Police, warning him not to speak with the investigators.

Nick and Irene wondered if the man was fantasizing or lying, but ascertained through the telephone 'ring back' system that the call had originated from the office of the Ministry of Defence Guard Service at the nearby Whittington Army Barracks, Lichfield. This would appear to prove a phone call was made from someone there, but not necessarily the content of the alleged conversation.

Nick Redfern

"The investigation from 1996 onwards was very much SUFOG's – my only active role was to go along on the interview. I didn't take part in any other follow-ups/leads, but I seem to remember that other witnesses were traced. One was something to do with the road-block (someone else who had some knowledge of it, and I recall there was a link with the Fire Brigade here) and someone who looked into the issue of the police involved."

Graham Allen

In conversation with Graham Allen about this matter, in February 2010, he confirmed that as a result of a newspaper appeal by Irene, a number of people had come forward in support of the claims made by Mr South, including a fireman and police officers. Unfortunately, the whereabouts of these documents and their all important testimonies are not currently known. Graham has, however, promised to discover their current whereabouts, and let us know.

(Sources: Staffordshire UFO Group/Graham Allen/Irene Bott/Nick Redfern)

---

*Leonard Stringfield (1920–1994) was an American Ufologist, who took particular interest in crashed 'flying saucer' stories.

He died in 1994. Stringfield was director of Civilian Research, Interplanetary Flying Objects (CRIFO), and published a monthly newsletter, *ORBIT*. In 1957 he became public relations adviser for the civilian UFO group NICAP under the direction of Donald Keyhoe, a friend of his since 1953. From 1967-1969, Stringfield served as an "Early Warning Coordinator" for the Condon Committee. During the 1970s, he wrote a number of books about alleged recoveries of alien spaceships and alien bodies.

In 1978, Stringfield served as UFO research adviser to Grenada Prime Minister Sir Eric Gairy. Privately, Stringfield worked as Director of Public Relations and Marketing Services for DuBois Chemicals, a division of Chemed Corporation, Cincinnati. He self-published "Status Reports" on alleged UFO "crash-retrievals" until his death. He died December 18, 1994 after a long battle with lung cancer.

APRIL 1964

10th April 1964 – Object over Northumberland

Mr A. Lawler, Mr D. Carter, and Mr J. Rafferty were in Wallsend Park, Northumberland, at 8pm, when they sighted an orange coloured object moving through the sky, in a peculiar sequence of forwards and backwards in flight, before disappearing towards the direction of Durham City. (**Source: UFOLOG**)

11th April 1964 – UFO over Walthamstow

Another matter brought to the attention of Dr. D.G. Doel, (by BUFORA member, Paul Webb), related to a report from Mr Bob Fall of Upper Road, Walthamstow, who was driving a passenger bus, No.123, along Ferry Lane, at 8.43pm. As he neared the bridge by the *River Lea*, he saw a gleaming, cylindrical or cigar-shaped, object fall out of the sky and strike the telephone wires with a crash, before hitting the concrete bank and dropping into the deep river. In an interview conducted with one of many newspapers, Bob told them:

> "I glanced into the sky and saw something coming towards me, very fast. It flew straight across the road. Had it been a few yards further forward, it would have hit the top deck of the bus. I saw it cut through the telephone wires. There was a loud crash as it struck the bank. I thought the back windows of the bus had come in. Stunned, I glanced around and saw all the passengers looking out over the river. I stopped and reported it."

Police in attendance

When he drove past the scene on the way back, at l0pm, he noticed a police van and officers in attendance. According to the police nothing was found initially. However, a police spokesman later suggested that while making a search of the area, *"the officers had disturbed four ducks. He thought these, flying in formation, were what Mr Fall had seen!"* This theory was soundly rejected by Mr Fall, who declared what he had observed was at least nine feet long, cigar-shaped, and silver in colour. If it had been birds, he would have seen the wings. Mr Fall told Dr. D.G. Doel – who was accompanied by his daughter, Diane – during an interview on the 19th April 1964, that he heard a loud fizzing noise as the object passed over.

We felt the explanation offered by the police was ludicrous. Whatever struck the wires had also gouged out a chunk of concrete. Was it possible it could have been either a piece of ice falling from an aircraft, or a piece of ice formed in the upper atmosphere? These are known as megacryometeors, and have been known to punch through metal, but they melt. Could this explain why the police found nothing? Dr. Doel pondered whether the object could have been a fuel tank, or dummy aerial torpedo, dropped accidentally by an F-101 Voodoo Jet fighter from Bentwaters Airbase, Suffolk, taking part in a training exercise, (as was shown on television, the same week). Doel wrote to the Base Commander – Colonel Robin Olds, but did not appear to have received any reply. This was not the first time we were to come across Colonel Olds, who – according to Jenny Randles – had sighted a UFO while flying over the UK.

We wrote to General Olds, asking for further details, but never received any reply. We then wrote to his biographer, who told us he had no knowledge on any UFO incident ever having been witnessed by Olds – a much decorated World War Two hero. (**Source:** *Walthamstow Guardian,* **17.4.1964**)

11th April 1964 – USA: Cloud-like objects over New York

A physiotherapist W.B. Ochsner, and his wife, from Homer, New York, sighted two cloud-like objects in the sky – one of which darkened and shot away, but returned during the 30-45 minutes' sighting.
(**Source: Project Blue Book unknowns**)

12th April 1964 – UFO over Croydon

Mrs May Church of Fir Tree Gardens (a fourth floor flat in Shirley, Croydon) was looking out of the window, at 11pm, with her husband – Albert, and son – Roy, when they saw:

> *"...a large, red glowing object, moving slowly through the sky over Crystal Palace Parade, heading towards the direction of London Airport; it was no aircraft and resembled a brilliant star. It took an hour to go out of sight and I am sure there was an aircraft circling it."*

It appears that a similar object was seen, a week previously, by Lee Turner (14) of Livingstone Road, South Norwood, and his father, Anthony – a keen amateur astronomer – who said:

> *"I have never seen anything like it before."*

(**Source:** *Croydon Advertiser,* **17.4.1964** – 'A glowing object in the sky')

13th April 1964 – USA: Four red lights seen over Wisconsin

At 9pm, four huge red lights in a rectangular formation, with a white light above, were seen near the ground over Monticello, Wisconsin, by Mr Wold, (who was a graduate student in anthropology), and his wife. It then tilted and flew away, three to four minutes later.

24th April 1964 – USA: Socorro police officer sights UFO

Socorro Police Department patrol officer Lonnie Zamora, while chasing a speeder heading south, heard a roaring sound and saw a bluish-orange funnel of flame in the sky to the south-west, slowly descending, possibly half to one mile away; bottom of flame hidden behind a hill. He tried to pursue the flame,

Modo's hand-painted image depicting the object seen at Socorro by Lonnie Zamora

turning off to the right on a rough gravel road to the south-west, but lost sight of the flame while trying to get the car up a steep rough hill. At the top, after 10-15 seconds of continuing along the gravel road, he suddenly noticed a shiny, whitish-aluminum colour 'landed' object, approximately 12-15 feet tall, some 800 feet away to the south-west, down in a gully. At first he thought it looked like an upturned car, oval in shape (long-axis vertical) standing on two 'legs'.

A few seconds later he saw two small, adult-like figures in white coveralls near the object; one turned towards him, seemingly startled, and began jumping. He lost sight of the object as he drove about 1,000 feet further, west-south-west.

Lonnie then radioed headquarters that he was investigating a possible car accident and stopped at the top of the ridge, about 103 feet from the landing site down in the gully to the south-east. He got out, and heard two or three loud thumping noises – like a door shutting hard. He walked a few steps to the front of the car, to possibly 90 feet distance away from the object, when he heard a very load roar, increasing in volume, and saw a smokeless blue-orange flame coming from beneath the oval object – now seemingly long-axis horizontal at this angle (about 120 degrees from the previous sighting), with a red insignia or lettering in the middle, about 2 x 2.1/2 feet, and slowly rising.

He thought it was going to explode and ran away, some 25 feet, putting the car between him and the object. He glanced back and saw that the object had risen about 20-25 feet to the level of his car. Lonnie ran another 25 feet and 'ducked down' below the edge of the ridge. The roaring noise stopped, and he looked up and saw the object heading to the south-west (towards the west end of Socorro Municipal Airport, one mile away) at level height, just clearing an eight feet dynamite shack by about three feet, moving "very fast" – no flame or smoke, or noise. He ran back to the patrol car, radioed headquarters, and saw the object climbing slowly and "get small" in the distance, just clearing Box Canyon or Six Mile Canyon Mountain (about 6 miles to the west-south-west).

Immediate police and military investigation found physical traces, burning brush and indentations in the ground, and several other more distant witnesses.

(Source: *UFOE, Section V*; Hynek UFO Report, pp. 223-9 etc)

[We have fully covered this incident in a previous volume of *Haunted Skies*]

29th April 1964 – Disc-shaped cloud seen over Southampton

Local science teacher Patrick I. Kelly, of Testwood School, Southampton – was contacted by pupil David Lawrence, who told him that while watching a game of football, he heard a woman asking her husband: *"What's that?"* pointing upwards into the sky.

Her husband replied, *"It's a cloud."* David:

> *"I looked up and saw a small, grey coloured, regular cloud moving across the sky. It was shaped like a 'disc' and shimmering. It then tilted and moved, increasing in brightness, until lost from view."*

Flying saucers: They're no threat, U.S. verdict

WASHINGTON, Thursday. —The United States air force says it has investigated more than 8000 reported unidentified objects (UFOS) in 16 years "and has yet to discover evidence that they represent a threat" to U.S. security.

Probes of such sightings back to 1947 have failed to turn up any evidence that "UFOS" are "alien interplanetary space vehicles under some form of intelligent control."

This report was given as the Air Force looked into a new epidemic of strange sightings over New Mexico.

One of the Air Force's leading civilian consultants on UFOS has gone to Socorro, New Mexico, to investigate the latest reports.

He is Dr. J. Allen Hynek, director of the Dearborn Observatory at North-Western University.

The latest report on Project Bluebook, the congressionally-ordered air force study of UFOS, shows that in a 16-year study, 7.7 per cent of the 8128 reported cases have remained unidentified.

George Mitropolis, of Albuquerque, New Mexico, was emphatic about both seeing and hearing an unidentified flying object last week-end and he was not alone.

The week-end reports also included: Policeman Lonnie Zamora reported seeing an egg-shaped flying object near Socorro. It hovered at 20ft., then flew away.

Orlando Gallegos, 35, of Santa Fe, saw a similar craft north of La Madera. Two motorists said such an object swooped down towards their car in the Espanola area.

State police and military officials are checking.

The reports were similar in that they described oval or egg-shaped objects.

State police and military officials have confirmed finding scorched earth at the sites, and wedge-shaped depressions that appear to have been left by some type of landing gear.

Said one eye-witness "I wasn't just seeing things because I stopped the car. This thing was glowing like it was luminous."

30th April 1964 – USA: Did a UFO land at Holloman Air Base?

On this day, the news media was buzzing with rumours of a 'flying saucer' having been captured and stored in a hanger at Holloman Air Force base. Coral Lorenzen – author of *The Great Flying Saucer Hoax* and Director of the Aerial Phenomena Research Association (APRO) – telephoned Terry Clarke of *KALG Radio* in Alamogordo, nine miles east of Holloman. He told Coral that he had been monitoring the range communication on that day, when he had picked up the following from a lone B57 Bomber, flying a routine mission in the vicinity of Stallion, a few miles east of San Antonio in Northern Mexico. *"I've got a UFO"* he said.

The Controller asked him *"What does it look like?"* The pilot said *"It's egg-shaped and white"*.

Minutes later, the pilot contacted the controller and said *"It's on the ground"*. At this stage photo crews were instructed to stand by, just before radio communications ceased and a security clampdown began. Coral was unable to establish what had occurred, but she did learn of a report by a security guard on the range, the same night, who spoke of seeing a UFO on the ground.

(Source: Coral Lorenzen, *Fate* Magazine, October 1964)

MAY 1964

7th May 1964 – UFO over Luton, Bedfordshire

An object – resembling a bright 'headlamp', with what looked like a single light on its side – was seen in the sky over Warden Hill, Luton, Bedfordshire, at 10pm, by members of the Payne family. They told of seeing it,

> *". . . swinging like a pendulum and apparently rotating in the sky, constantly dimming and becoming bright. When it appeared, a strong wind blew up."*

An Air Ministry Official, who was consulted, suggested that:

> *". . . it might have been a weather balloon, with its lights on, or even the planet Venus, which sometimes behaves in an extraordinary manner".*

(Source: Aerial Research Centre, Luton) [Some accounts give the 13th May 1964]

9th May 1964 – USA: Three lights seen over Chicago

At 10.20pm, Chicago, Illinois U.S. District Court reporter – Mr J.R. Betz – sighted:

> *"...three light-green crescent-shaped objects, about half the apparent size of the moon, flying very fast in tight formation across the sky, in an east to west direction, oscillating in size and colour for three seconds".* **(Source: Project Blue Book unknowns)**

20th May 1964 – Silver rectangular object over Middlesex

On the 20th May 1964, Mr Alan Bissett, from South Harlow, was visiting the annual Pinner Fair, in Middlesex, when he noticed:

> *"...a silver rectangular shaped object, resembling a helicopter blade, with a halo around it – unlike any helicopter I had ever seen, and at a height where a helicopter could not have operated".*

The Isle of Wight UFO Society, DIGAP and the Torbay Astro Research Society, reported:

> *"...several dozen sightings involving UFO landings, during this period, including reports of an orange glowing 20 feet 'flying saucer', with several landing lights underneath, seen to land by at least six people on Berry Head, before shooting upwards at terrific speed and disappearing".*

Another sighting tells of a *"100 feet in diameter, metallic grey 'flying saucer', with three sliding doors on the outer surface, seen to land on the moor, at Ashburton"*, where there have been as many as eighteen separate reports of large glowing 'discs' observed in the same area.

17th May 1964 – UFO sighted over Kirkby, Liverpool

A UFO, described as *"16 feet in length, showing two aerials, and a flashing red light, making a buzzing noise"*, was seen hovering over the garden of a house in Kirkby, Liverpool, on the evening of 17th May 1964, before taking off over nearby rooftops, by Mrs Margaret McCutcheon and her son, Robert Hirst (13) – then living in Mottram, Liverpool. We traced Robert and spoke to him about the incident – a matter which provoked great curiously up until his death. We were also contacted by a relative of Robert's, in 2009, who told us that *"trees and bushes in the back garden were discovered burnt after the UFO left."*

(Source: Personal interview/*Daily Express*, 8.5.1966/UFOs over Kirkby, John Parkinson)

26th May 1964 – USA: Pleasant View, Pennsylvania

At 11pm, the Reverend H.C. Shaw sighted a yellow-orange light in a field (shaped like the bottom of a ball), which he chased down the road for two miles.

31st May 1964 – Unusual lights seen in sky over Gateshead

Leslie Otley – secretary of the Tyneside UFO Society – and his wife, Jean, first heard of some strange events which had taken place in Leam Lane, Gateshead, County Durham, after being contacted by a member of the group – Joe Lee, (then living in the locality).

Lee asked him to investigate further, and they obtained the following account:

On May 31st 1964, schoolboy Keith Bell of Hopedene, Leam Lane, Gateshead, was at home making a cup of tea, when he sighted *"three luminous egg-shaped flashes"*, each of approximately three seconds' duration. They were crossing the sky in an east to west direction, at 11.35pm. They were also witnessed by his parents, who were upstairs at the time. Unfortunately, as their view through the widows was restricted by frosted glass, they only saw 'flashes'.

Humming noise heard

Other people living in the street, nearby, later complained of having heard an unusual humming noise, which went on until 1am.

A fiery white spherical object, about half the size of a full moon, trailing a *'streaky flare'* behind it, was seen moving in an arc across the sky over the Isle of Wight, in an east to south-west direction, at 9.30am on 1st June 1964, by Shanklin teenager – Richard Abell.

JUNE 1964

1st June 1964 – Fiery object sighted over Isle of Wight

Mr R.A. Bell (15) from 12, Furze Hill Road, Shanklin, Isle of Wight, was outside at 9.30pm when he saw:

"...a fiery yellowish spherical object – about half the size of the full moon – showing a long streaky flame heading silently across the sky, in an east to south direction, over Shanklin Downs. It then vanished before dropping down past the horizon in an arc of movement, a few seconds later."
(Source: *UFOLOG*)

2nd June 1964 – Silver domed object, showing three legs at Gateshead

At 4.10pm, Raymond Varty, Jim Berry, Raymond Bell and Brian Powell from Woodwynd Lane, Leam Lane Estate, Gateshead, reported having sighted

". . . a silver, domed, object – about the size of a dining table – with portholes around the top, with three legs", which was seen falling like a leaf through the sky, making a low buzzing noise, descending approximately 120 yards away from where they were stood".

(Source: UFOLOG)

2nd June – Entities seen at Leam Lane Farm

At 5.30pm, David Wilson (then aged 14) decided to walk down to Leam Lane Farm to collect some straw for his rabbits. When he arrived, he saw a group of about ten children, standing about twenty yards away from a haystack, followed by the startling sight of:

> "...six or eight small human beings on top of the stack; they were about two and half feet tall and dressed in bright green suits.
>
> They appeared to be digging into the haystack, as if searching for something. Their hands seemed like lighted electric light bulbs".

David went home and told his parents what he had observed and decided to make his way back to the scene, but was stopped by the farmer. David says that in conversation with another child, he was told that she had seen

> "... a circular, silvery object take off from the ground in a spinning motion, giving off an orange glow".

Leslie Otley then rang the local Press, who told him they had no knowledge of the occurrences. Following a conversation with him, they contacted the persons involved. On the 9th June they published an article in the *Newcastle Journal*, 'Spacemen of Felling – 'Flying Saucers' and 'Green Invaders' have split the whole neighbourhood'. It included a quote from local headmaster, Mr M Coates, of Roman Road Junior School, who denied that he had called a special assembly of the children to discuss the 'little green men', or that he had told the children to keep away from the farm. *"There is no truth in these silly rumours"*, he said.

Interviews conducted with witnesses

On 6th June 1964, several members of the UFO organisation visited the locality concerned and spent some considerable time speaking to many of the residents and children about the matter; one child, who admitted having seen the 'little green men', told them:

> "The leader of the men was dressed in black and carried a baton with pink stripes".

One girl claimed that 'he' *"was sitting on the roof of a barn, watching us"*. Another girl told them she had seen 'him' *"riding on the back of a cow"* whilst others claimed the whole thing was a hoax.

To complicate the matter further, there was also a rumour that an aircraft had dropped something accidentally into the field, and the airmen had gone searching for it. This was possibly connected with another story of police officers having collected something from the same field.

An examination of the haystack was carefully carried out but nothing untoward, such as landing marks or strange footprints, were found. They spoke to the farmer who owned the land. He told them:

> "The claims are a load of nonsense; if anything had landed I would have known about it. I have a dog kept in the yard; he would have warned me if anyone had been prowling around the farm."

The investigators concluded that whilst there was no reason to doubt the validity of the reports concerning the strange noises and flashes, they felt that under the circumstances one should treat reports of *'little green men'* with some misgivings – taking into consideration the problems involved with accepting evidence verbatim from young children, whose behaviour may have been influenced by fear or panic following the 'wave' of uncontrolled excitement which spread through out the community, after the sightings became public knowledge.

(Source: Harry Lord, April 1964)

UFO over Isle of Wight

Between the 3rd and 8th June 1964, Mrs D. Wadell, L.R.A.M., of Greenmore Park, Cowes, Isle of Wight, sighted a silver, translucent, dome-shaped, shimmering object, hovering in the sky during the late afternoon. *It then moved away towards the direction of Portsmouth, and that was the last she saw of it.*
(Source: UFOLOG, Kath Smith, Isle of Wight)

12th June 1964 – Three glowing spheres over Ohio

At 9.15pm, Toledo, Ohio man – Mr B.L. English (employed as an announcer for radio station *WTOD*) sighted three white spheres, glowing red on their sides, moving slowly through the sky, which were seen to hover and then move in circles very fast, all the while making a low, rumbling sound. On the same night, Richard Crawford (who was then Chief of Police at Elmore, Ohio, located twenty miles south-west of Toledo) was driving towards the town, when he noticed a brilliant light off the side of State Route 51 and pulled the car over to obtain a closer look.

Thinking he was looking at an illuminated blimp, Richard switched on his spotlight and aimed it at the light in the sky; he flashed twice. Immediately afterwards, the light flashed back twice – as if in response. Puzzled, he put it to the back of his mind and continued his night patrol.

At 11.30pm, after checking the Harris Elmore School, he noticed the light again, which appeared to be closer to the ground.

He flashed the spotlight at it – there was no response. The light then moved away, followed by a soft swishing sound. He then radioed his deputy Carl Soenichsoen, who was also out on patrol, and arranged a rendezvous at a local food marked on the outskirts of the town. When Richard arrived, Carl ran over to him and pointed at the light in the sky, which was now blinking at one second intervals.

As the two men watched, the object began moving towards them, picking up speed.

Crawford said:

> *"I'm going to notify the Highway Patrol. They have a plane; maybe they can figure this out."*

While the Chief radioed the State Highway Patrol, Soenichsoen continued to watch. The object appeared to be just beyond the Ohio Turnpike (a distance of about a mile) and glowing in brightness and size.

From Globe to 'V'-shaped UFO

Suddenly, without warning, it gained speed rapidly, and changed from a globe to a wedge or horizontal 'V'.

"Look at that", cried Soenichsoen.

It then changed course abruptly and headed south-west, passing about 500 feet in front of the men. Both men saw clearly what now appeared to be a 'flying wedge'. The upper part of the craft was about a third longer than the lower part; the lower part consisted of a series of closely placed lights. No other lights were visible; neither man could see anything indicating additional structure.

Whether the object had actually changed shape the men could not say. The UFO headed away at *"a fantastic rate of speed"*, making a loud roaring noise – like a jet – and was out of sight in seconds.

Within minutes, two more officers arrived on the scene – one from Genoa, the other from the State Highway Patrol. The officer from Genoa had heard Chief Crawford's call. Both men, however, were too late; the object had disappeared over the horizon.

The State Highway Patrolman immediately put in a call to the Toledo Express Airport (10 miles west of Toledo), explaining what Chief Crawford and Officer Soenichsoen had seen, and asking for a radar check of the vicinity. The operator on duty reported the sky clear. *"There's nothing in your area within a radius of 45 miles"*, he said. Either the object was too low, or it was miles away.

Haunted Skies Volume Two Revised

Interestingly, the Police Chief wondered if the UFO had been attracted to a local plant that produces *Beryllium.

(Sources: *FATE* Magazine, November, 1964 - Richard D. Osborn/*Strangers from the Skies*, Brad Steiger, 1966)

26th June 1964 – UFO over Northumberland

At 2am, Mr Edwin Vipond and his wife, Elaine – licensees of the *Moor House Inn*, Seaton Burn, Northumberland, were asleep with the bedroom window open (as it was a hot night). They were awoken by a high-pitched buzzing – like a 'spinning top'.

The couple went to the window and looked out, seeing:

> "...a pulsating, saucer-shaped object, ringed with electric blue lights, moving up and down in the sky, heading westwards. Suddenly, it shot upwards and out of sight".

(Source: *Evening Chronicle*, 26.6.1964 – 'North couple report Flying Saucer')

29th June 1964 – Object sighted over Salford,

John Chapman – a design engineer from Salford – happened to look through the window of his house, at 9pm. He saw a grey saucer-shaped object, with a domed top, crossing the sky, at a height of about 500 feet, approximately 5-10 miles away. It was heading in a south-easterly direction.

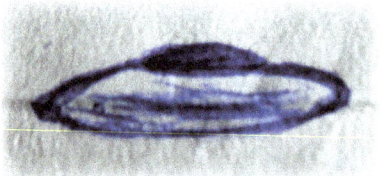

> "The object moved under cloud and then into it. All of a sudden it reappeared, but flew away in the opposite direction." **(Source: DIGAP, H. Bunting/*UFOLOG*, Issue 8, 30.10.1964)**

JULY 1964

1st July 1964 – Liverpool leprechauns and 'little green men'!

Oddly, a few weeks later, there was to be a 'repeat performance' in Liverpool. This followed a number of UFO sightings, which were alleged to have fuelled a 'wave' of (what was claimed to be) mass hysteria on the 1st July 1964. Local newspapers claimed:

> "...thousands of children joined in the hunt, after reports of 'little green men', or leprechauns, had been seen near the Bowling Green, Jubilee Park, Jubilee Drive, Liverpool, east of the city in the Edge Lane district and that the police were called in to control the crowd."

Bowling Green, Jubilee Park, Jubilee Drive, Liverpool

According to the *Liverpool Daily Post*, dated 2nd July 1964, leprechauns were first seen on the night of Tuesday, 30th June. Nobody knew how the rumours started, but one nine year-old boy told the *Post* reporter – Don McKinley – that

> "last night I saw 'little men' in white hats, throwing stones and mud at each other, on the bowling green. Honest mister, I did."

Also, local boy – David Wilson (14) – claimed to have seen

> "... several small, green creatures, about two feet high, running around a haystack on a farm near the estate".

---

*Beryllium is the chemical element with the symbol Be and atomic number 4. Because any beryllium synthesized in stars is short-lived, it is a relatively rare element in both the universe and in the crust of the Earth. It is a divalent element which occurs naturally only in combination with other elements in minerals. Notable gemstones which contain beryllium include beryl (aquamarine, emerald) and chrysoberyl. As a free element it is a steel-gray, strong, lightweight and brittle alkaline earth metal. Beryllium is also a quality aerospace material for high-speed aircraft, missiles, spacecraft, and communication satellites

Police called in to control crowds

On the evening of the 1st July, the bowling green was so crowded that the police had to clear the park and guard it from bands of children, who were tearing up plants and turf in their search for the little creatures.

A rather bewildered Irish park constable – James Nolan – who had to wear a crash helmet to protect him from the children's stone throwing, told the reporter:

> "This all started on Tuesday. How? I just don't know, but the sooner it ends the better. Stones have been thrown on the bowling green, and for the second night running no-one has been able to play. The kids just won't go away. Some swear they have seen leprechauns. The story has gone around and now we are being besieged with leprechaun hunters."

Such was the desperation of the children's search that the police had to set up a temporary first-aid shelter to treat at least a dozen children who suffered from cuts and bruises. The *Liverpool Echo* and *Evening Express* for the 2nd July 1964, described the strange visitors as: *"little green men, in white hats, throwing stones and tiny clods of earth at one another."*

Liverpool Echo – Leprechaun identifies himself!

In the 26th January 1982 edition of the *Liverpool Echo*, a man called Brian Jones – short in stature and a pipe smoker – claimed that *he* was the 'leprechaun' responsible for sparking off a 'wave' of hysteria which swept the locality. He claimed that he had been seen by local children wearing a red waistcoat, a pair of navy-blue trousers, Wellington boots, a denim shirt and a woollen hat with a red bobble on it, while tidying up his grandfather's garden in Edge Lane which backs onto the park.

He said:

> *"I bounded into view, babbling made-up words; I jumped up and down, picked up turfs and threw them at the children. Not surprisingly, the children ran away in a 'blind panic'."*

Over the course of the next few days, further 'confrontations' took place between him and large groups of children, who came to see the leprechaun – actions which necessitated the intervention of the police. A similar bout of hysteria appears to have erupted several miles to the north-east of the city, in the overspill town of Kirkby, when 'flying saucers' and leprechauns were reportedly seen by local children.

1st July 1964 – Bright yellow object sighted. Were RAF scrambled?

At 2am, a bright yellow star-like UFO was seen moving north-east over Newcastle-on-Tyne by three local residents – Mr R. Mooney, Mr F. Thompson of Wallsend, Northumberland, and Mr F. Alderson of Newcastle – before vanishing. A few minutes later, an intense white object appeared in the sky, heading south-west (possibly the same one returning?). (**Source: TUFOS**)

At 9.45pm on 1st July 1964, a thin grey line appeared in the orange sunset over County Durham. It gradually grew thicker, and changed colour to dark grey. Clouds were seen to move around it, but the object remained perfectly still. Two aeroplanes arrived and began to circle in the sky. The UFO faded away, but reappeared for a few minutes before finally disappearing. (**Source:** *UFOLOG*)

At 10.55pm, a white 'disc of light' – far larger than Venus – was seen moving through the sky against a strong wind, at an estimated speed of 7,000 miles per hour, from east to west, over Newcastle-on-Tyne.

3rd July 1964 – Massive object seen over Liverpool

At 11.15pm, a massive 'star', flashing intermittently, was seen travelling in the sky over the Hunt's Cross area of Liverpool. According to the witnesses – a woman and her son – it was heading towards Runcorn, changing colour from brilliant silver to red, as if *'signalling'*. (**Source:** *Liverpool Echo,* **9.7 1964**)

At 11.28pm, a similar object was seen from Birnham Road, Wallasey, Cheshire, by Mr and Mrs Oldrid.

A few hours later, a mysterious bright 'star' was seen, at 2am. It was low down in the sky, heading towards Aintree, by Miss R. Broadbent of Stuart Road, Walton. (**Source:** *Liverpool Echo,* **8th & 9th July 1964/Isle of Wight UFO Society/***Liverpool Echo,* **July 6th 1964**)

6th July 1964 – Silver cigar-shaped object seen

At 8.50pm, Jean Jarvis from Homefield Road, Heavitree, Exeter, was in her garden, talking to a neighbour – Betty Leaworthy, when they noticed:

"...a bright silver 'cigar', moving silently through the air, from the direction of the setting sun. It was so bright you couldn't look at it for too long. By the time we even thought about fetching a camera, it had gone. This was no airplane. We are used to seeing them pass over."

Enquiries made with Exeter Airport revealed no flights were listed for that time.

(**Source:** *Express and Echo, 7.7.1964* – 'Uncanny object flew over, say Exeter women')

8th July 1964 – Two bright objects sighted over Liverpool

Two bright star-like objects – one of them making a slow, jerky, movement – were seen in the sky above St. George's Hall, Lime Street, Liverpool, at 11.25pm. It was heading towards the direction of Bootle.

(**Source: Mr R. Donnelly and Mr R.D. Hughes, MUFORG**)

At 3.40pm, Mrs W.A. Madge from Hayes, Middlesex, was sitting in Rosedale Park, with friends, when their attention was directed to a minute 'circle of light' – almost a pinpoint in the sky.

"At first I was unable to see it, because of its extreme height, but when my eyes became focused I could see it moving at high speed in a west-south-west direction. I thought it was a satellite – an idea quickly dismissed when it slowed down and stopped in the sky for about 30 seconds, before heading off towards the south-west, where it disappeared behind cloud."

(**Source:** *Flight International,* **30.7.1964**)

8th July 1964 – England: Three 'flying discs' seen over London

Well respected UFO researcher Ananda L. Sirisena, (pictured here in 2016, following a visit to see us) had this to tell us what he witnessed:

"Something very strange and unexpected happened to me. I was on my way to school in south-west London with two of my friends, when we saw three 'flying discs' in the sky. It was a bright, sunny morning with white fluffy clouds being driven by a steady breeze. The three of us were walking along the road at about 8.50am, engaged in a scholarly discussion about the merits of the song-writing of the Beatles versus the raucous singing of the Rolling Stones, or we might have been extolling the pugilistic skills of one Muhammad Ali, who had recently changed his name from Cassius Clay and was creating a sensation in the boxing world.

Suddenly, a 'mental hook' pulled my eyes upwards. I stopped walking – in utter amazement. My two friends also stopped because I had pointed to the sky. The younger one of the two brothers said excitedly, 'Flying saucers!' I turned around to him and said, 'I don't think 'flying saucers' exist'. In the next sixty seconds I changed my mind, for clearly visible in the blue skies were three very large 'discs' – apparently metallic – gleaming in the daylight, forming a triangular pattern and moving very slowly.

I then went through a process of wanting to eliminate all possible phenomena to explain away this spectacle – planets, moon, birds, airplanes, sun, and weather balloons. So I made a note of the direction in which the wind was moving the clouds and realised that these three 'discs' seemed bolted together by invisible rods and moving solidly, traversing against the wind. As my theory about weather balloons faded into dust, it dawned on me that we were, indeed, witnessing metallic 'flying discs' – the proverbial 'flying saucers'. I could not understand how such large objects stayed aloft. They had no wings, appendages for engines, or seemingly any motive power. I got the impression of great prowess and exactitude. I was thrilled. I felt a Holy Presence. It was as if the 'flying discs' were just not spacecraft, they were holy vehicles.

So astounded was I by this first shock of the sighting that I next did something that resulted in the second shock of the day.

I formulated a question in my mind and projected it at the trio of 'saucers'. Then the second shock of the day! I received an answer to my question, direct into my mind. It was not outside of my head but traversed right into my brain. In less than a minute, on this weekday morning, my concept of reality was totally shattered. Everything that I had heard from scientists about the existence of terrestrial life was proven wrong. If any scientist said 'telepathy does not exist', from now on I would not believe them because my own, personal, experience said otherwise. To this day I marvel that a teenage boy, like me, could have asked such a profound question and received a reply – so deep and all encompassing. Not that I fully understood the reply at the time. It was much later that part of the mysterious reply made any sense to me.

In 1964, I was in the lower sixth form, studying mathematics and physics. I was no day dreamer or fantasist. Up until this time, I had thought that 'flying saucers' did not exist, but my experience forced me to change my mind. I would have been a fool to deny this outstanding sighting. The three of us watched the trio of 'discs' moving towards a bank of cloud. The cloud was moving toward the unidentified flying objects, thus negating my earlier theory of weather balloons. The 'saucers' moved into the cloud but did not come out the other side. All three of us were now excited. We waited for the triangular pattern to emerge out of the bank of cloud but they did not do so. We wanted to see where they were going next, but it seemed that they were swallowed up by the 'cloud'. As a result of waiting for them to show themselves again, we were late to school that morning. That was a personal embarrassment to me as I was a sub-prefect at the school and one of my duties was to note down the names of pupils who were late! I was always punctual – except on this fateful day.

I recall that because I was late to school, I went straight to my classroom and bypassed the daily service, which usually included a pep talk from the headmaster. My school was, at that time, known as the Wimbledon County Boys Secondary School. I avoided any disturbance to the morning service by going directly to the sixth-form classroom, where I found another student who had also just arrived late. I blurted out to him – a boy by the name of Martin J. – that I had 'just seen three flying saucers'. He burst out laughing and retorted, 'Don't be silly. Flying Saucers don't exist'. I felt deflated. His reaction was not one of curiosity but a rigid denial. Later that morning, I spoke to another pupil – David M. – who was a lot more thoughtful and enquiring. David even asked me to sketch the objects and was curious about their shape, colour, speed, and whether they emitted any sound. He wanted to know if they made any engine noise. The 'saucers' were totally silent. From the clouds in the sky, we surmised that the three objects must have been at an altitude of between 1,000 and 2,000 feet. From the apparent angle subtended by the objects, I calculated that each 'disc' was about 70 feet in diameter. I was studying mathematics and physics, so this was an easy task for me to do."

10th July 1964 – Liverpool leprechauns sighted – Mass hysteria sweeps local children

Scores of excited youngsters contacted the newspaper and police on Friday, eager to tell that they had seen both these things, which included *"a strange object in the sky"*, which changed the colour of its lights from red to silver, seen moving slowly at first – then very fast, across the sky.

So convinced were local children that hundreds of them plagued the vicar of Kirkby (Rev. J. Lawton) by invading St. Chad's churchyard in search of the little people. At times the numbers were such that the police had to chase the children away.

According to the *Liverpool Echo*, (13th July 1964), scores of children began searching the churchyard at St. Chad's for leprechauns. After what was described as two days of hectic activity, relieved Rev. Canon John Lawton told the *Echo's* reporter on the night of Sunday, 12th July, that: *"The children seem to have been convinced, at last, that there are no leprechauns."*

Incredibly, during the same period, children had also searched the grounds of St. Marie's Roman Catholic School and Mother of God Church, Northwood, Kirkby.

The truths behind what exactly happened are unclear, even today. It was not the first or last time we would come across instances of what *appeared* to be mass hysteria, which swept the area, influencing children's minds. These all followed wild unsubstantiated claims which should have no place in today's modern society. But once upon a time, we would have laughed at the very prospect that 'flying saucers' even existed, let alone they had occupants.

(Sources: *Liverpool Daily Post*, **Thursday, 2.7.1964**/*Liverpool Echo*, **2.7.1964**/*Echo*, **26.1.1982**/*Kirkby Reporter*, **17.7.1964**/*Echo*, **13.7.1964** – 'Little folk and Flying Saucers')

Mrs Reginald Smith from Blackheath, London, was driving home at 10.40pm, when she and her friends noticed two 'lights' – motionless in the sky. One of them was glowing green. When she arrived home, she alerted her husband. The couple then watched as the two lights headed away, in what appeared to be a smooth and controlled manner.

Mr Smith rang the MOD, who told him they had received no other reports.

12th July 1964 – UFO seen – then aircraft circles the sky

An orange-white oval object was sighted over Park Avenue, Washington, County Durham, at 8.20pm, flying in a north-east to south-west direction. According to the witness – Mr W.D. Muir, a member of the Tyneside UFO Group:

> *"The object flew back along its original course, at a height of between 1,000-1,500 feet. A few minutes later, an aircraft appeared and circled the sky."*

13th July 1964 – Black, round machine, showing rod on top, sighted over Essex

What was described as *"a dull coloured, black, round machine, making a swishing noise, showing a thin rod on top with a flashing small white light"*, was seen heading north to south over Worthing, Essex, at 5.30pm, by Miss Louise Franklin. It was gone in a few seconds.

15th/16th July 1964 – Amateur astronomer sights UFO

Mr R.M. Glazier from Edgware, Middlesex, reported:

> *"At 1.31pm, I saw what appeared to be a star crossing the sky, followed by a similar object at 12.30am on 16th July 1964, which came to a sudden stop in the sky, before proceeding forwards in a sweeping 'S' movement of flight. Through my 60mm. telescope, it resembled a bicycle wheel."*

(Source: *UFOLOG* **Information Sheet, No. 3, 9.9.1964, handwritten**)

Later that day, *"a brilliant cone-shaped object was seen hovering over the sea"*, about three miles west of Point of Ayr, by observers from Wallasey Coastguard Station, Cheshire, including Mr R.W Lambert, at 3.45pm.

> *"After five minutes, the 'cone' inverted and moved out to sea, where it was soon lost from view."*

(Source: Isle of Wight UFO Society)

16th July 1964 – USA: Four white 'lights' sighted over Michigan

At 11.15pm, Northern Air Service pilot Mr K. Jannereth was 15 miles south of Houghton Lake, Michigan when he sighted:

"...four white lights in a stepped-up echelon formation, moving through the sky. They were then joined by two more. They closed-in on the airplane, rapidly slowed, and flew along with it for a total of five minutes."

17th July 1964 – UFO sighted over forest

At 6.45pm, Mr C. Wood from East Woodhorn, Northumberland, was looking across the sky, towards the north-east, when he noticed:

"...a petal shaped object, smoky-grey in colour, apparently hovering over Harwood Forest, Bellingham area."

20th July 1964 – Mystery object over Illinois

At 4.45am over Littleton, Illinois, Mr J.J. Winkle sighted:

"...a 60 feet diameter round-topped, flat-bottomed object, with a long acetylene-coloured flame shooting downwards, flying on a straight and level course, which then made a half loop – then rose upwards a minute later."

23rd July 1964 – Bright object seen

Mr William Elrick and his wife, from Uddington, were returning home from holiday, at 1am, driving along the moors, between Rochester and Jedburgh, when:

"We saw a bright object approaching from the north. We took it to be an aircraft. As it came level with us, we saw it had no tail, nose, or navigation lights, and was aglow with lights that seemed to shine from the inside, and had about four or five windows."

(**Source: Orbit, Volume 6, October 1964**)

26th July 1964 – UFO displays over Liverpool

A spate of UFO activity occurred at 11pm over Lees Road, Kirkby Industrial Estate, Liverpool, when *"six dazzling 'balls of light'"* were seen hovering and flashing across the sky in a display, attracting the attention of the workers who telephoned the police.

Two of the witnesses – night watchmen, John Parkinson of 7, Fern Grove, Princess Park, Albert Sanderson and Alan Cash, 6, Cristowe Walk, Croxteth, Liverpool – spoke of seeing a similar phenomenon having taken place at 11pm, and that it was *"a regular occurrence"*. By the time police arrived, there was nothing to be seen.

John Parkinson:

"Nearly every night we have seen these objects appear over the estate, at about 11pm, and move around the sky at varying speeds, before they finally disappear in the early morning. We have told everyone, including our family and friends, but they just laugh and shrug it off as if 'we have had one over the eight'. Last night there were six of the things stopping and moving in the sky – just as though they were being controlled. We couldn't stand it any longer and told the Police, so they could see for themselves."

Albert:

"We went to the local Birds Eye factory and told night security staff; they watched one of the objects moving down the length of Lees Road."

The Police later suggested that the men had seen *"a collection of stars"*.

A number of people, who also telephoned the Meteorological Officer at Liverpool Airport and Bidston Hill Observatory, to report seeing UFOs, were advised *"they had seen a collection of bright stars"*.

(Source: *Liverpool Echo, 27.7.1964*)

Late July – Mr D C Hogg (an investigator for BUFORA) told of *'Flying Saucers'* being sighted over the north approach of Abbotsinch Airport, Glasgow.

> *"One saucer-shaped craft approached the small plane and then returned to its original position, before speeding out of sight, followed by a small aircraft circling the area for some time afterwards."*

(Source: *UFOLOG*)

30th July 1964 – Glowing object over West Midlands

At 2am, Mrs Catherine Walsh from Pelsall, West Midlands, was looking out of her bedroom window, unable to sleep, when she saw *"a blue, yellow and green, oval glowing object"*, heading across the night sky.

(Source: *Walsall Observer, 7.8.1964*)

AUGUST 1964

1st August 1964 – UFO over Jersey

At 1.40am, Jersey resident Miss McLeod – whose house overlooks the bay approximately half a mile from Gorey Pier – noticed a bright object, *"looking like a light bulb, with a sharp point rather than circular"*, descending into the sea off Gorey Pier.

(Source: *UFOLOG, Issue 4, 16.9.1964*)

3rd August 1964 – White 'disc' seen in the sky

Between 8pm and 9pm, a white shining 'disc', with sharp edges, was seen by Monmouthshire resident – Andrew Coldrige. He and his brother were travelling along the A470 road in the Brecon area, when they saw it *"shooting across the sky and stopping in mid-flight – then became lost from view as we went past the sides of a mountain."*

4th August 1964 – UFO making strange noise heard and seen Scotland

At 6am, *"a bright circular 'disc', with a flashing red light on top, making a queer noise"* was seen passing through the sky by two men. It then apparently settled on a distant hilltop over Longwood, outside Dumfries.

(Sources: *UFOLOG, Issue No. 7/21st October 1964/Dumfries and Galloway Standard, 8.8.64*)

5th August 1964 – Three orange lights seen in sky over Yorkshire

Mr and Mrs Hurst were watching TV at their home address in Dalton, near Huddersfield, Yorkshire, when they were astounded to see *"three orange lights, forming a triangle, one of which appeared to be revolving, moving slowly across the sky."*

(Source: *Huddersfield Examiner, 5.8.1964/UFOLOG, Issue No. 2, 31.8.1964*)

6th August 1964 – 'Bright light' seen over Lowestoft

Doctor M. Carter of Corton Road, Lowestoft, was visiting Mr and Mrs Neal of Wegnalls Mill, a quarter-of-a-mile south from Presteigne, when they sighted a 'bright light' moving overhead, in irregular surges of movement, travelling one degree of 'arc' in three seconds, which was later suggested *"may have been"* the Polyot 2 or Cosmos 36 satellites, according to the Isle of Wight UFO Society.

7th August 1964 – 'Cottage loaf' UFO sighted

At midnight, Colin Reed and Paul Joy of All Saints Crescent, Hastings, sighted an object

> *". . . resembling a cottage loaf – black or dark red in appearance – with beams of light projecting from the top and bottom. . ."*

moving across the sky, a few hundred feet away from them, heading towards the south-east. They reported the matter to the police, who suggested they were '*seeing things*'.

(Source: *UFOLOG*, 12.4.1965, Issue 14, Kath Smith)

8th August 1964 – Cheshire motorist reports being followed by UFO

A yellow/white, oval, object was seen hovering over Wellington Road South, Stockport, by housewife – Ruby Roe, at 1.30am.

Ninety minutes later, at 3am, Mr Ernest David Hopkins from Hazel Grove, Macclesfield – an aircraft engineer by occupation – was driving his 1961 Ford Zephyr, accompanied by his wife and two sons, Christopher and Mark, on their way back from a holiday in Cornwall. They noticed a *"brilliant pure white light"* at the side of the road in front of trees. As they turned into the junction with the A34 Wilmslow Road/A536 Macclesfield Road, they were surprised to see the glowing object was now following.

After keeping pace with them for nearly an hour, at 50 miles per hour, it suddenly shot up in into the sky and disappeared from sight.

(Source: DIGAP, Harry Bunting/*UFOLOG*, Issue No. 9, 5.11.1964)

9th August 1964 – UFO over Littlehampton, Essex

During the early hours, a brilliant neon red light was seen hovering in the air, approximately 2,000 feet above the ground, over the town of Arun, Littlehampton, Essex. The witnesses were three local men – Brian Mills, P.J. Homer, and Mr Smith – who were out fishing on West Works Pier, close to the English Channel.

In a letter written to Kath Smith, of the Isle of Wight Society, Brian described what happened:

> *"After setting our eyes on the object, it appeared to be in two halves; the top cone or triangle having a more intense glow than the lower crescent, seen for approximately two minutes. The object then*

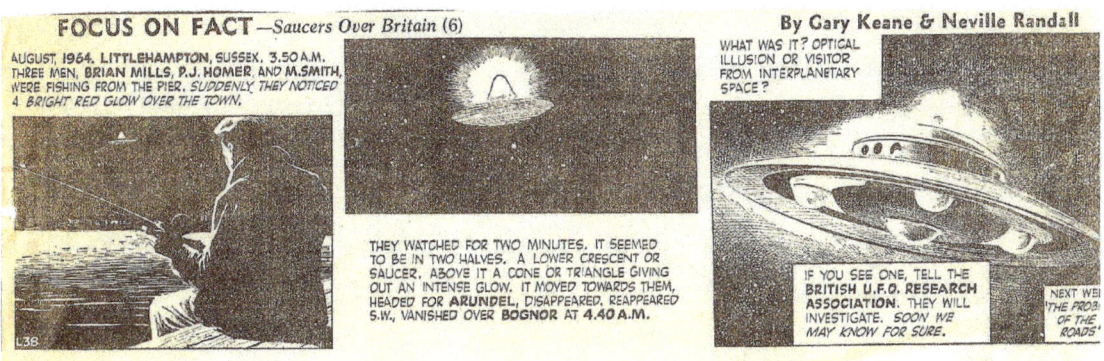

enlarged slightly for a few seconds. We immediately switched off our torches. It appeared to come towards us, but then altered its direction northwards toward Arundel for a second or two, and then faded away completely, before reappearing a few seconds later – still heading towards the North. After 30 seconds, it changed direction and headed towards Bognor Regis. Five minutes later it faded away. We returned to our fishing, facing directly westwards, where we thought it had disappeared. Within 2-3 minutes it reappeared above the skyline, at Bognor. By 4.40am, it had gone for good."

The same object appears to have been also seen by Mrs R. Baker, from Hove, who sighted what she described as:

"...a bright neon red 'flying saucer', travelling through the sky over the Downs, during the early morning, its red lights blinking on and off while it hovered or stalled between Hove and Brighton railways stations."

(Source: Isle of Wight UFO Society/*Evening Argus, Brighton,* 14.8.1964 – 'What a relief to see flying saucer report')

EXTRACT FROM "DAILY EXPRESS" 26/10/64

THE ONE THAT GOT AWAY   -   A FLYING SAUCER

Four anglers spoke with relief last night of the one that got away.

The men from Sheffield and Accrington said of the "thing" hovering 12 ft above the silent waters of Kings Sedgemoor Drain in Somerset:-

"It must have been a flying saucer". Within seconds of seeing the mystery object, a half crazed herd of cows stampeded towards them. Said one of the anglers, coal merchant Mr. Jim Sharman, 21, of Jefflock Road, Sheffield "We saw a red light approaching up the drain. It was just like the red light on an aircraft and as it got nearer, it was so bright it lit up the banks and surrounding fields. The light tapered to the rear about 12 ft away and when it got overhead, it hovered, flashing on and off". Added Mr. Sharman "It was weird and frightening - after about 15 minutes, the light suddenly accelerated and disappeared".

Said another of the anglers, Mr. Walt Depledge, 21, of Shirland Lane, Sheffield "I have never seen anything like it before. It really put the wind up me".

Later the same day, Frank Peake – then a young man from Hollywood, near Birmingham, West Midlands – contacted us, after a newspaper appeal with regard to what he saw, many years ago. At the time he considered it important enough to record in his personal diary – still available for scrutiny, over 35 years later.

> "It was on 9th August 1964. I was walking along Broad Street, Birmingham past the Hall of Memory, at 8.15pm, when I was stunned to see a light coloured grey/silver object, with a dome or conning tower on its top, darting in and out of broken cloud over where a rainbow had formed. I watched as it stopped and started in the sky, at a height of about 5,000 feet, approximately a quarter of a mile away. When I arrived home I eagerly read the newspapers, believing hundreds of people must have seen this object in the sky. There was nothing – apart from a report, a few days later, of a UFO sighted by three schoolboys from Sutton Coldfield, who said they had seen a UFO land and take off from a wooded area in the nearby park."

'SAUCER' STAMPEDE
Anglers nearly trampled to death
Yorkshire Post Correspondent

A MYSTERY aerial object, thought to be a flying saucer, has been seen by four anglers on a night fishing trip in Somerset. "It was weird and frightening," said one of them yesterday.

The men narrowly escaped being trampled to death by a herd of 50 cows terrified by the object. "It was like all pandemonium let loose and we hid behind a car in case the cows swept us into the water," commented Mr. Jim Sharman.

It happened soon after midnight as the party were fishing the King Sedgemoor Drain, Bridgwater. Mr. Sharman, 21, a coal merchant, of Jeffcock-Rd., Sheffield, said they first noticed something unusual when they saw a red light approaching up the drain.

"It was just like the red light on an aircraft and as it got nearer it was so bright it lit up the bank and surrounding fields. The light tapered to the rear about 12ft. away and when it got overhead it hovered, flashing on and off.

'BRIGHT LIGHT'

The anglers shone two spotlights towards the object but the light was so bright they could not see where it was coming from. "It became so bright that the cows started making a heck of a noise and chased round the field."

After about 15 minutes the object suddenly accelerated quickly and soon disappeared. "There was no sound and we don't know whether it was a flying saucer, space ship or a secret craft from a nearby airfield.

A spokesman at Bridgwater Police Headquarters said: "We have not heard of any more cases like this. It is a complete mystery." The others in the party were Mr. Weil Deplodge, 21, of Shirland-Lane Sheffield, and two men from Accrington.

Haunted Skies Volume Two Revised

At 10.13pm on 9th August 1964, Mr M. Harrison from West Bridgford, Nottinghamshire, was outside looking for the Perseid meteor shower, when he noticed an object in the sky to the north, described as being

> "... a large yellow 'disc', flying at a height of 150 feet off the ground, north to east. As it went into the distance, I saw it roll from side to side; a few seconds it had gone [sic]."

(Source: William Blythe/*UFOLOG*, Issue 2, 31.8.1964)

10th August 1964 – USA: Wake Island: 'Red light' approaches runway

At 5.16am, Captain B.C. Jones, and navigator First Lt. H.J. Cavender, were in a parked USAF C-124 transport plane, when they saw a red blinking light approach the runway, stop, and make several reverses during 2 minutes of observation.

1964 – Birmingham: UFO seen carrying out a 'search' of the locality

In the same year, Mr and Mrs Harris, living in Alcester Road, Hollywood (just outside Birmingham), were aroused from sleep at 1am, by the sound of dogs' barking. On going to the window to look out, they saw a saucer-shaped brilliant light in the sky, accompanied by the sound of a whirring noise.

> "The object appeared to be projecting a beam of light from underneath it, moved along in a queer jerking motion across the sky, and appeared to be carrying out some sort of 'search' of the ground with its torch."

An examination of the area revealed an underground lake, with several openings, or holes, in the nearby field, and the presence of an old burial ground, known as Berry Mound. This was previously known as the Danes Camp – an early Iron Age earthwork, which may once again illustrate the association between ancient sites and UFOs. **(Source: Derek Samson, NICAP)**

14th August 1964 – UFO sighted over Wales

At 4.45am, *"a perfectly round shape, containing dozens of lights inside"*, was seen in the north-eastern part of the sky, by Mr and Mrs Cyril Harry, of Caerwent. It appears that the same object was also seen by another Newport couple, at 5am, who said:

"It was as brilliant and three times the size of a star. At 6am, it disappeared behind a cloud."

(Source: Chepstow Weekly Argus, date not known)

On the same day, a bright disc-shaped object, with a red light on top, passed over two men, who were walking along the Dalbeattie Road, Dumfries. The object was *"making a queer noise,* [and was] *resembling a 'flying saucer' in shape, before appearing to settle on top of a distant hill"*.

(Source: UFOLOG/*Dumfries & Galloway Standard*, 8.4.1964)

15th August 1964 – USA: Bullet-shaped UFO over New York

At 1.20am, Mr S.F. D'Alessandro sighted a 10 feet x 5 feet bullet-shaped object, with wavy lines on the rounded front part and six pipes along the straight rear portion, which made a *"whishhh"* sound, as it passed through the sky.

At 8.15am on the same date at Yosemite National Park, California, Mr E.J. Haug, of the San Francisco Orchestra, and C.R. Bubb – a high school mathematics teacher – sighted:

"…three, bright silver, round objects in a stack formation, flying very fast through the sky and changing positions within the formation. The sound of rushing air was heard during the 3-4 seconds' sighting."

18th August 1964 – UFO displays observed over the UK

At 5.20am, Mrs B. Byron, was looking out over the docks and Channel when she saw a bright 'light' appear in the sky. Strange tiny 'spots of lights', were then reported being seen travelling through the sky at fantastic speeds, by many people (including the local post of the Royal Observer Corps). They were even seen high in the sky over the Cheviots, Northumberland, above the small village of Elsdon, and were seen to change direction at impossible angles, sometimes flying in formation.

(Source: John Ogilvy/*News Daily*, 20.8.1964)

19th August 1964 – Brilliant object over Birmingham

Mr and Mrs Derek Samson from St. Margaret's Road, Olton (just outside Birmingham), were in their garden, at 10.35pm, when they saw what they took to be a satellite, heading south-west to south-east.

"Suddenly another brilliant object appeared and overtook the first one, which halted in mid-air for a short while, before gaining speed and moving direction – now due south."

(Source: Derek Samson)

1964 – Landed 'Flying Saucer' over Cannock Chase, Staffordshire

Dennis Bills from Huntington, near Cannock, Staffordshire, contacted Irene Bott and Graham Allen, of the Staffordshire UFO Group, in 1978, wishing to bring their attention to an incident that he witnessed, while walking through Cannock Chase, at 1am in (he thinks) in 1964.

"It was an overcast night, and I had trouble keeping to the trail which led to a clearing near my home in Stanley Croft, when I noticed a neon green and red light, about 200 yards away, which I took to be someone using a child's multicolour torch, which were quite popular then. As I approached closer, now some 50 yards away from the clearing known as Cavans Wood, I saw what looked like a board lit up with luminous paint, standing on the edge of the clearing. I thought … why would someone put that up? … and carried on walking towards it. When about 10-15 yards away, I realised that

Haunted Skies Volume Two Revised

it was reflecting some sort of colour, rather than being self-luminous, and began to feel frightened, but plucked up the courage to walk closer when I saw it was – in fact – circular, about 15 feet in diameter, and just less than six feet high."

Dennis decided not to walk past, fearing what might happen, and took a different path home. Despite much 'leg-pulling' from the people in whom he confided, he is adamant that there was no mistake in what he saw, and it remains perfectly clear in his mind to this present day.

"I don't know if it is of relevance, but the street lights and house lights were all out because of a power cut. For some years after, the grass would not grow over the area in the field where I had seen the object."

(Source: Staffordshire UFO Group, Irene Bott/Graham Allen/Personal interview)

21st August 1964 - 'Flying Saucer' seen by fisherman

As dusk fell by the dam, between Macclesfield and Leek, Eric Bridge – a Company Director, from Macclesfield – was out, trout fishing. It was 9.15pm.

"When I first saw this object over Rudyard, it veered to the right and started to approach my position, allowing me to see a large half-round contraption along the outer edge, with an orange coloured rim. There was a quadrant on it, and lights kept going on and off. I thought it was

looking for a place to land. I was shaking like a leaf and telephoned the police, who contacted the Manchester Evening News."

(Source: *Daily Express,* **22.8.1964/Harry Bunting, DIGAP, Issue 7/***Manchester Evening News*)

At about the same time, schoolgirls – Loraine Cunningham (11) and Julie Powell (16) from Brocklehurst Avenue, Macclesfield – sighted a silver, saucer-shaped object, with what looked like aerials at each side. It was flying through the clear night sky at a height they estimated to be only a couple of hundred feet.

"It was rotating very fast, then stopped, turned on its side and headed off towards the direction of The Hollies – gone in two minutes."

(Source: *UFOLOG,* **21.10.1964)**

At 9.47pm, members of the Gingele family were standing outside their house at Chadwick Road, Falcon Lodge, Sutton Coldfield, when they saw a yellow 'disc', described in size as being:

> "...small, but larger than Venus in comparison, moving across the sky; as it approached closer, the yellow changed colour to red. Behind it was seen a smaller, fainter yellow light, following the larger. We watched it for two minutes until it was out of sight." **(Source: UFOLOG, Issue 5, 28.9.1964)**

At 11pm on 21st August 1964, an object – resembling *"a large electric light bulb with frosted glass, seven or eight times the size of a sixpence as seen from the ground"* – was observed flying through the air. It was at the same height of nearby flats in Nicholson Avenue, on the junction with Queens Drive, Macclesfield, and was reported by resident William Cumberlidge. **(Source: DIGAP, Harold Bunting)**

22nd August 1964 – 'Ball of light' over Cheshire

A shimmering, small *"ball of light"* was seen in the sky over Heaton Moor, Stockport, heading towards the direction of Reddish, at 3.10am, by Mr Harrison, who reported it being motionless in the sky for seven minutes, before disappearing from sight.

23rd August 1964 – Black cross-shaped object sighted over Cheshire

A black cross-shaped object was seen motionless in the sky over Mobberley, Cheshire, at 4.30pm, by Mr A.M. Johnson. It was at an estimated height of one thousand feet, and two miles away. After ten or fifteen seconds, it vanished from view. **(Source: Harry Bunting, DIGAP)**

27th August 1964 – Blinding light over Tyneside

At 3.50am, Mrs Kathleen Shard from Woodford, near Stockton, was awoken by flashing lights. Rushing to the window, she looked out and saw:

> "...this huge blinding light, apparently coming towards me. It then receded, but approached again and vanished seconds later."

At 8pm, the same day, a curious white object was seen moving over Low Fell, Gateshead, heading south to north. **(Source: Harold Bunting)**

31st August 1964 – UFO over Manchester, showing three lights

At 9.10pm, an object was seen by Mr Burrows – a resident of Chorlton-cum-Hardy, near Manchester – travelling at fantastic speed, from north to south through the sky, rushing past an aircraft which had just taken off from Manchester Ringway Airport.

At 11.05pm, Mr and Mrs Hankinson of the Queensway, Heald Green, Cheshire, sighted what appeared to be two lights following each other across the sky, heading north-west to south-west at considerable height. They were far too fast to be satellites. They went out of sight 30-45 seconds later.

At 11.10 pm, Mr Burrows saw a second object appear in the sky, described as resembling

> "... a wasp in shape, with lights on the front – so strong they would have blinded you had it been lower. It had three windows on the side facing me, lighting up the interior. My compass went wild as it passed overhead, at a speed much faster than an aircraft. I estimated it was probably at a height of some 30,000 feet."

A report of this incident submitted to the MOD attracted the following response from Mr R.A. Langton of the MOD, who wrote back on the 2nd December 1964, suggesting the object seen by Mr Burrows was an aircraft.

> "All we can say at this stage is that our radars did not produce any reports which could not be accounted for, at the time, and that an aircraft in the Manchester Air Traffic control zone might well have had its landing lights on."

The same MOD official also wrote again on the 6th October 1964, explaining away the sighting at 11.05pm on 31st August 1964, as being the satellites 64/28A and 64/53A, which were later dismissed by DIGAP's satellite officer.

> "Two lights travelling and staying together definitely eliminates satellites. They could not have been the 53A and 28 as these are Russian Cosmos satellites west to east orbits and 62/28A was not visible on 31st August 1964."

Enquiries made by the Isle of Wight UFO Society with Ringway Airport revealed no aircraft were flying over the locality at the time in question. **(Source UFOLOG, No. 6, 13.10.1964)**

Autumn 1964 – Triangular UFO, Stoke-on-Trent, Staffordshire

Mrs Mabel Till – a designer by occupation, then living in Stoke Road, Baddeley Green, Stoke-on-Trent – was just getting off to sleep when she heard a noise – like an electric motor – just before 1am, which was most unusual, bearing in mind the rural location of the property concerned. After getting dressed, she went out into the back garden and stood there listening. There was nothing to be seen, or heard – just the glow of lights from a nearby town on the horizon.

> "Suddenly, without warning, a black triangular craft, showing a solitary red light, approximately 35-40 feet in length, swept up from behind a line of damson trees at the end of the garden some streets away, and slowly moved over the house, clearing the TV aerial.
>
> It was dark metallic grey in colour, showing streaks in its paintwork – as though a coat had been applied too thickly."

Mabel was employed by Shorter and Son (a company first set up in 1878 by Arthur Shorter and his partner, James Boulton, at Stoke-on-Trent). Mabel was involved in producing an extensive and exciting range of 'period pottery', based on ethnic designs from around the Mediterranean, Africa and Central America. Even though she left the firm in 1935, her design ware continued to be produced for years afterwards. As her UFO sighting demonstrates, this was a woman who had an eye for detail.

Mrs Till – a woman of considerable artistic skill, according to her lifelong companion Jackie Hepworthis – is to be congratulated for her excellent description of the UFO, meticulously written down after the event, allowing us the opportunity to see for ourselves something which cannot be explained away rationally. (**Source: Gordon Creighton,** *Flying Saucer Review*)

Autumn 1964 – Landed 'flying saucer', Cornwall

Joan Vincent – who has served in Local Government in a variety of positions, including Chairwoman of the County Planning Office, a long standing Borough Councillor, and Governor of her local school – decided to pluck-up the courage and tell what she and her husband, Roy, saw over 40 years before, in the Karslake area of Cornwall, during the autumn of 1964.

Roy and Joan Vincent

> "We read about some students from Fowey College, who reported having seen 'flying saucers' over Carloggas Downs, and decided to go out and have a look for ourselves. After driving for a short time, we stopped at 5pm in Karslake, where we scanned the surrounding skies, hoping to see something. Ten or fifteen minutes later, the whole of the open countryside was enveloped in brilliant light. Startled, we stood there trying to identify the source of this light, and realised it was coming from a field behind a hedge, about 50 yards away from our position. We walked over and peered behind the hedge, and were flabbergasted to see a large dome, with an upper surface that appeared to be translucent – like glass – with a lower solid body, grey or green in colour, about 6 feet in length and 3 feet in height. Unfortunately, as our view was restricted by another hedge, we were unable to determine whether the craft was actually resting on the ground, although it appeared that way. We could see what looked like a large cabinet, with dials inset around the outside with what looked like portholes. At this stage, I felt frightened and asked Roy to take us home. We decided to keep quiet, knowing we would be the subject of ridicule."

We asked Joan if she had noticed any unusual medical symptoms that had occurred after the UFO experience. She told us about a small lump on her right leg, out of which – to her horror – grew something resembling a blade of grass that could only be cut off using scissors.

Despite seeking medical advice over the years, the condition remained undiagnosed until it stopped growing, leaving a small scar. We asked her if she had discovered any unusual marks, or scars, following the event, knowing that 'close encounters' can seem to result in all manner of peculiar physical ailments. She confirmed she had found some

Dawn Holloway with Joan Vincent

Haunted Skies **Volume Two Revised**

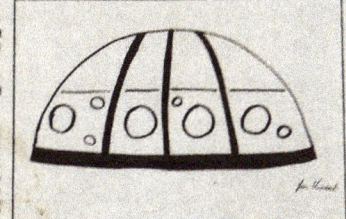

LEFT: Vernon Salmon's drawing of the object he is convinced was a UFO.
RIGHT: Joan and Roy Vincent (below) drew this flying object they saw one night over the clay district.
"Maybe one day we shall all know what it was now," Mrs Vincent said this week.

Orange ball in sky was not from Earth

by IAN SHEPHERD

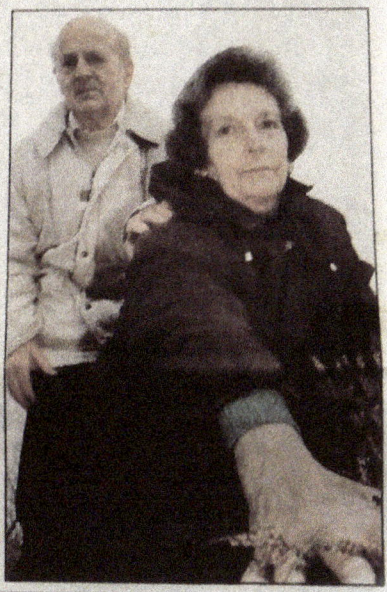

MORE people have broken a silence surrounding widely-witnessed UFO activity over the clay country more than 30 years ago.

They decided to talk about their experiences after former head of county planning, Mrs Joan Vincent, told the Cornish Guardian how she and her husband Roy had a close encounter with what they firmly believe was a flying saucer in 1965 at Karslake, between St Dennis and Carthew.

Following publication of Mrs Vincent's story, Vernon Salmon, a 67-year-old retired lorry driver, said that he and his son Glen, now 42, had also seen a UFO, which flew directly over the house in Carthew where they were living in 1965.

"The house was within about a mile of where Mrs Vincent and her husband had their sighting," said Mr Salmon, who now lives at Polruan.

"It was a summer evening, about eight o'clock and it was a fairly clear night," he said. "I went into the back garden to get some logs for the fire, then I saw what looked like a star in the distance, but it was moving in my direction.

"I called my eldest son Glen. We were both amazed because as it passed over where we were standing we could see that it was some sort of machine. It was showing coloured lights, not flashing ones that you see on aeroplanes. And it was absolutely silent, even though it could have been no more than 200 feet above us.

"It was moving very slowly and it was ball-shaped, orange in colour, with a dark, cross-shaped structure underneath (SEE DRAWING). There was a type of turret on the front with what looked like a window and as it passed I thought there was movement in the turret, as if someone was in there.

"I've seen many things in my life but never anything like that. One thing I am quite certain about, it was not an aeroplane or a balloon. Whatever it was, I don't think it came from earth."

Flying saucer like the ones in films

A BUGLE man, who wishes to remain anonymous, produced a remarkable account of a UFO sighting at around the same time. But his description of the object that he saw fits the typical "flying saucer" shape, as witnessed by Mr and Mrs Vincent, rather than the "orange ball" seen by Mr Salmon and his son.

He said: "I was between 11 and 14 at the time and went down to the field behind Bugle Chapel where we used to play.

"Some of my friends there said that they had seen a flying saucer and were very excited about it because it had landed them with a beam of light. I thought they were talking rubbish and said so.

"But as I was leaving, it came back and I saw it for myself very clearly. It was just like the flying saucers that were shown in films years afterwards. It was moving slowly and was absolutely silent, probably about 250 feet above the ground.

"It was a summer evening with good visibility. We all knew what we had seen, even though RAF St Mawgan told our parents that it could have been an aircraft carrying out mid air refuelling. It was no such thing. It was a flying saucer. Mrs Vincent was very brave to go public with her account."

Mrs Vincent, chairman of the County Planning Committee for nine years until last May and now a long-serving County and Restormel Borough Councillor, said that, following publication of her account in the Cornish Guardian, she had received several phone calls from people who had seen UFOs.

"Most were people who had had similar experiences at around the same time."

marks on her leg identical in size and depth to other marks and scars brought to our notice by people who believe such 'scoop marks' are evidence of alien surgery carried out following 'abduction'. We cannot say, without any proof, that these marks are caused by Aliens, but the presence of them following a UFO encounter is puzzling to say the least. (**Source: Personal interview**)

SEPTEMBER 1964

1st September 1964 – Red 'ring', with flashing lights, sighted over Isle of Wight

At 9.30pm, Mrs B. Morris of St. Mary's Place, Ryde, on the Isle of Wight, sighted:

> "...a rich red coloured, pulsating object – resembling a circus ring – about 45 feet in circumference, showing double blinking lights on one side, moving through the night sky, flying along a straight line from the direction of Cowes to St. Catherine's Point. Five minutes later it had gone from view."

(**Source: UFOLOG**)

2nd September 1964 – Red-orange flickering 'light' seen over Cheshire

"A reddish-orange flickering light, rotating around its central axis", was seen moving no more than a few miles per hour across the sky over Hollins Farm, Macclesfield, Cheshire, heading towards Macclesfield, at 8.50pm, by Elizabeth Astle (aged 16), and her friend – Gillian Bailey of High Street, Macclesfield.
(**Source: DIGAP/UFOLOG, Issue No. 6, 13.10.1964**)

4th September 1964 – Glassboro, New Jersey

Shortly before 8:00 p.m. two teenagers in Glassboro, New Jersey were approached by two tall blond men, who were described as having long hair and barefoot. They asked the boys if they were interested in

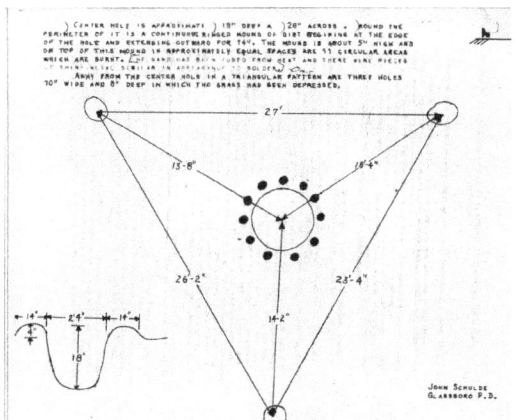

seeing a UFO. They walked to an apple orchard, where they saw a 'red light' land in the woods and then take off. A burnt crater was found later by a NICAP investigator, with tripod indentations. The US Air Force was called and performed a perfunctory investigation of the case, but NICAP did a more thorough job. In addition to the burnt area and ground marks, some white powdery 'balls' were found – cold to the touch.

Upon touching them, the witnesses complained of numbness in their hands which lasted for 24 hours.

6th September 1964 – Flashing object seen over Lancashire

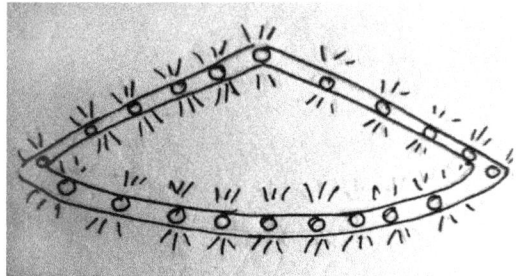

Michael Hallowitz, 18 (right), accompanied by Capt. Philip J. Coppolino, of Glassboro police, leaves police hearing after admitting spaceship hoax.

$50 Fine Suspended

Jersey Youth Pays $10 Court Costs for Space Landing Hoax

The 18-year-old perpetrator of the Glassboro (N. J.) Great Spaceship Hoax got off with paying $10 court cost Monday night after a police official expressed his awe at th

Ivy Harrison, S.R.N., and her husband, Percy – a plant supervisor from Salford, Lancashire – were outside at 11.30pm, when they saw a 'star', shaped like a conical sea buoy, with lights that changed from red, to green and white, moving through the sky.

Investigations carried out by the Isle of Wight UFO Society revealed the object was seen to *"silently hover and rotate; presenting what looked like a hard blue exterior through binoculars."*

On the same evening, amateur astronomer – Mr R. Glass, was observing the Cygnus constellation when he noticed *"a foggy white object, flying in a zigzag across the sky, heading north-east",* which he thought might have been a meteor – until he focused on it and saw a blurred cigar-shaped object that changed from an 'on edge' view to vertical. He believes the object was outside the Earth's atmosphere.

(Source: Personal interview/*Daily Express,* 8.9.1964 – 'The star that wasn't what it seemed')

Another witness to unusual things seen in the sky on the 6th September 1964 was schoolboy P. McCourt of West Bridgford, Nottingham, who reported having seen:

"...a silvery, oval, object – like a 'metallic' rugby ball flying through the sky – at a height of 500 feet off the ground, about two miles away, heading in a south to north direction, at 5.50pm."

Was this a balloon, reflecting sunlight? One was released from Hucknall Weather Station at 6pm everyday, to check wind speed.

10th September 1964 (approx.) – Leprechauns sighted in Belfast!

Although we cannot be sure of the exact date, we were fascinated to learn of yet another incident involving a frenzy of excitement which swept the locality, after it was claimed a *leprechaun* had been sighted in Tamar Street, East Belfast, on or about the 10th September 1964.

The fact that the culprit was later identified as six year-old Jimmy Hughes, playing in a derelict house – dressed as Robin Hood, who was chased away by police after fears for his safety – appears to have triggered off, once again, that insatiable 'spark' which ignited the population's imaginations and desire to descend onto the street, causing massive disruption.

Ironically, the crowds that gathered there included many adults.

The incident – which involved the attendance of the Police and Fire Service – also attracted the interest of David Bleakley, Labour MP for Victoria, who handed over a petition to Belfast Corporation, demanding action to keep the crowds and children away from the embankment and derelict houses.

One senior police officer was quoted as saying:

"A grown man, cold stone sober, insisted to me he had seen a leprechaun!"

10th September 1964 – Wingless UFO sighted over Manchester

The Manchester Evening News (10th September 1964) told of a 'Flying Saucer' seen by hospital worker – Elgar Thomas, Lower Crumpsall, Manchester, who said:

"It was about three times the size of an aircraft, without wings; it stopped dead in the sky and then shot skywards and disappeared."

11th September 1964 – Flashing lights over Huddersfield, Yorkshire

A flashing light was seen in the sky over Huddersfield Road, Halifax, at 11.25pm, by Trevor and Doreen Whittaker.

"It was bigger than a star, moving from north to south in the eastern sky.

On going outside to have a look with binoculars, we saw it was two orange flashing lights, one above the other, the lower being smaller than the above."

The sighting was the trigger which led to Trevor developing a keen interest in the UFO subject and – after joining BUFORA – he was to investigate a number of sightings in West Yorkshire, during the 1970s.

12th September 1964 – Red 'globe' seen over Portsmouth

Mr E. Ford of Southsea, in Hampshire, was scanning the sky for the Echo 2 Satellite, at 3.48am, on 12th September 1964. Together with Mr C. Lucas and another colleague, he was stood at the main gate at Hilsea Depot (old ordnance depot) opposite Old London

Road, Portsmouth, when they saw:

> "...what looked like a small, dull red 'ball', travelling along a flat trajectory from the south-west direction, heading quickly towards the north-east; as it approached closer, we saw it was emitting a bright red light every few seconds. At 3.54am it had gone." **(Source: UFOLOG, John Feakins)**

14th September 1964 – Silver rotating object over Manchester

At 5.15pm, Mrs Ann Powenall and her daughter – Valerie of 47, Stovell Avenue, saw a silver rotating object speeding across the sky, travelling towards Belle Vue, Manchester, from the direction of the Ringway. Within seconds, it became lost from view. **(Source: UFOLOG, Issue No. 6, 13.10.1964)**

15th September 1964 – Egg-shaped UFO seen over Manchester area

At 4.50pm, Frank and Alice Borrows – residents of Chorlton-cum-Hardy, (near Manchester) – were at the junction of Egerton Road, talking to a Miss J. Parker, when they noticed a shining silver object in the sky. It was moving very slowly southwards.

Frank Borrows

> "Through binoculars, the egg-shaped object was now seen as two half-moon-shaped objects, one overhanging the other. We watched it for about forty minutes, before it went out of sight. I contacted the Manchester Evening News and explained what we had seen. They suggested it was an American spy plane, although I discovered later – while it was calm on the ground – that due to gale force winds above, no aircraft were flying over the locality concerned." **(Source: UFOLOG)**

20th September 1964 – Luminous 'disc' over Buckinghamshire

At 11.20pm, **a** schoolboy – Martin Page from Bletchley, Buckinghamshire – happened to look out of his bedroom window.

> "I saw an elliptical, luminous white object, divided by a straight line, with a number of 'dots' along its length, the bottom part of which was rotating. It then tilted and headed away in the direction of north-west from south-east." **(Source: Bletchley Evening Gazette/Isle of Wight UFO Society)**

21st September 1964 – Silver 'disc' sighted over Nottingham

At 3am, "*a silvery, oval 'disc' of flickering light, as bright as a car headlamp, occasionally stationary for a short period*", was seen towards the north-east over Beeston, Nottingham, by Miss S. Hind and her sister. **(Source: Isle of Wight UFO Society)**

22nd September 1964 – White 'light' circles the sky

At 9.15pm, an intermittent light, flashing red and green, "*under some sort of apparent control*", was seen over Wilmslow, Cheshire, through binoculars by Mr P.A Power his daughter Leslie and young son living in Stanneylands Road. After an hour, the size reduced to that of a star in visual image.

A white 'light' was seen circling the sky over Bletchley, during the evening of the 22nd September 1964

Haunted Skies Volume Two Revised

"... as though it was fixed to the edge of something rotating, before heading off west towards the direction of Stony Stratford, at great speed – still rotating."

(Source: Isle of Wight UFO Society/*Bletchley Gazette*)

23rd September 1964 – 'Disc' reported

At 9pm, a disc-shaped red and green object was seen in the sky over Leicester Road, Salford, occasionally halting in mid-flight. (**Source:** *UFOLOG*)

28th September 1964 – Bright red/orange object

At 9.30pm, *"a bright red/orange object"* was seen silently crossing the sky over Woodford Road, near Woodford Aerodrome, Stockton, Cheshire, by John Stott (aged 15).

(**Source: DIGAP, Mr H. Bunting/*UFOLOG*, Isle of Wight UFO Society, Issue 6**)

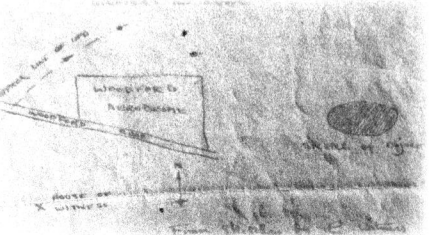

30th September – Red/orange sphere sighted

At 11.45pm, a sharply defined, flickering, red orange sphere was seen over Newcastle-on-Tyne. Was this a fireball?

Our enquiries revealed another report, on the same day, involving a star like object seen heading over Bletchley, before disappearing behind a block of nearby flats. (**Source:** *UFOLOG*)

In this month a veritable blitz of UFO activity was to take place around the Southampton area, reminiscent of the October 'wave' of 1967 – which was later explained away as hot air balloons, launched by Scouts, on the 2nd and 9th November.

OCTOBER 1964

2nd October 1964 – Bright 'disc' seen, RAF respond

M.G. Hastings from Heaton, Newcastle-on-Tyne, was walking home, at 5.55pm, when he saw:

"*...a bright 'disc', hanging in the sky. About five minutes later, two RAF Jets appeared and headed toward the UFO – which then flew away, leaving the Jets standing.*"

(**Source:** *UFOLOG*, Issue No. 9, 5.11.1964)

Space monsters reported at Manchester!

Another example of 'public hysteria' for 1964, included an incident at Stretford School, Manchester, which told of children weeping hysterically, after word went around that 'space monsters' had landed in the playground. The matter was reported to the police. (**Source:** *Manchester Evening News*, 2.10.1964)

3rd October 1964 – White 'dots', forming 'V' shapes in the sky

Just after 10pm, a group of *"white 'dots', forming two 'V' shapes, looking like an 'M', or upside-down 'W', with seven or eight objects in each"*, were seen crossing the south-western sky over Bridgford, Nottingham, by Mr M. Harrison. Enquiries made with the Meteorological Office, and three RAF Stations, failed to obtain any satisfactory answers. (**Source:** *UFOLOG*, Issue No. 10, 30.11.1964)

7th October 1964 – UFOs over Stafford

Four days later, at 5.40pm, Mr and Mrs T. Moore from Brocton, near Stafford, sighted a pulsating, golden-yellow ball-shaped 'craft', heading eastwards, showing two distinctive 'bumps' underneath it. When they arrived home and switched on the TV, it showed a split picture and the radio apparently gave-off a high-pitched humming noise. (**Source: Wilfred Daniels**)

10th October 1964 – Dinner plate UFO

At 11.30am, *"a golden coloured metallic object, resembling a dinner plate in appearance"*, was seen flying slowly across the sky over Testwood, heading towards the Southampton direction. It was witnessed by Mrs G. Worthington, and her daughters – Jane and Sandra. The object then moved from the vertical position, showing what appeared to be a dome-shaped superstructure.

At 10.30pm, the same day, *"a clearly defined triangle of blue light"* was seen in the sky slightly north of due east, over Lyndhurst, by Totton Grammar Schoolboy – David Demant. **(Source: Peter J. Kelly)**

12th October 1964 – Loud humming noise … then two pink 'discs'

At 9.30pm, a loud humming noise was heard over Whitehall Road, Gateshead, Newcastle-on-Tyne, by Arthur Toogood.

He rushed outside, just in time to see *"two pink 'discs', like full moons, one bigger than the other, pass overhead"*. A neighbour – Mrs Olive Turnbull, living in Bewick Road – also sighted the objects.

The matter was later brought to the attention of the Acklington Meteorological Officer, who suggested that *"they had seen a Shooting star in the vicinity. Looked at from an angle, it may have seemed strange"* – an explanation which cannot be taken seriously! **(Source: *Orbit*, Volume 6, October 1964)**

17th October 1964 – 'T'-shaped UFO

A brilliantly-lit 'T'-shaped UFO was seen in the east of the sky, over Oldham, Lancashire, between 11pm-11.30pm, by retired postmaster – Mr Thompson Browne of Prestwick, Lancashire. He saw it, together with his wife, and described the object as:

> *"…changing colour from white to green at times, and hovering at an estimated height of under 2,000 feet. I had seen the same object three weeks previously, and believed it to be an aircraft, used for carrying out some sort of check of TV and wireless apparatus"*. Incredibly, Mr Browne reported having sighted this object nightly for over three weeks prior to the sighting of the 17th October, when it moved from its regular position in the sky, towards the south, at 11pm. This spurred him to write to the local newspaper, appealing for any other witnesses to the phenomenon.
>
> *It would be interesting to learn what the brightly illuminated object is, which is seen nightly and fairly high in the sky, looking eastwards from Prestwick. The object appeared to be in the form of a cross, or part of one, and illuminated"*.

Was it an early appearance of the *'Flying Cross'* UFO that was to plague the skies of the UK, during a short period in late autumn 1967? **(Source: Harold Bunting, DIGAP)**

19th October 1964 – Struck by a meteorite?

At 9.40pm, Mr G. Morton-Sooley was cycling home near Emneth Tunnel, near Wisbech, Cambridgeshire, when he saw green, red, and yellow lights, moving horizontally across the sky. He was hit by something which burnt its way through six layers of outer clothing and left a small burn mark on his skin. The raincoat was later examined and found to have a rectangular burn measuring 2 inches x 4 inches, 60 degrees to vertical sloping down from right to left. The top button was burnt on one corner. His pullover also had a rectangular hole, 6 inches x 2 inches, centred over the solar plexus. The tie, which was synthetic fibre, was melted in the lower right-hand corner. The jacket had a rectangular hole, 4 inches x 2 inches axis, situated at the base of the lapel. **(Source: Cambridge UFO Group)**

22nd October 1964 – Cross-shaped UFO over Southampton

A Southampton housewife – Mrs Evelyn Vickers – wrote to Fred Smith, of the Isle of Wight UFO Society, about what she witnessed between 6pm and 7.30pm.

Haunted Skies Volume Two Revised

"It was an oval object, quite large in size, through the centre of which ran a long cross. Both the 'cross' and the oval were pink – as if the setting sun had etched the peculiar pattern in the sky. I was impressed. I called the neighbours to witness it."

At 8pm later that day, a silver sphere – twice as bright as Venus – was seen descending through the sky over Heaton, Newcastle-on-Tyne, by Mr W.J. Dunbar, before changing course at a sharp right angle, and then disappearing behind the moon.

(Source: CUGIUFO [Cambridge University Group Investigation of Unidentified Flying Objects]/Isle of Wight UFO Society)

Editor of *Flying Saucer Review* passes away

On the same day, sadly, Waveney Girvan – Editor of *Flying Saucer Review* – passes away.

24th October 1964 – Revolving 'red light' in the sky

At 10pm, British Rail worker, Robert Britland – then living at Helsby, Cheshire – noticed a revolving 'red light', hovering approximately 600 feet in the air, towards Frodsham Marshes.

He said:

"I could make out a big saucer shape, with a dome on top. It made off toward the south-westerly direction".

At 10.45pm, Robert noticed a wide beam of light appearing over the top of Helsby Hill, stretching to the horizon, which became thinner in the distance towards the direction of Liverpool.

"About five minutes later, a red revolving light – like the one on Saturday night – passed overhead. As it did so, the beam of light cut out, almost creating the impression that the red light was utilizing, or feeding off, the beam in some way."

(Source: *Runcorn Weekly News/Liverpool Echo*, 27.10.1964 – 'Riddle of the night sky')

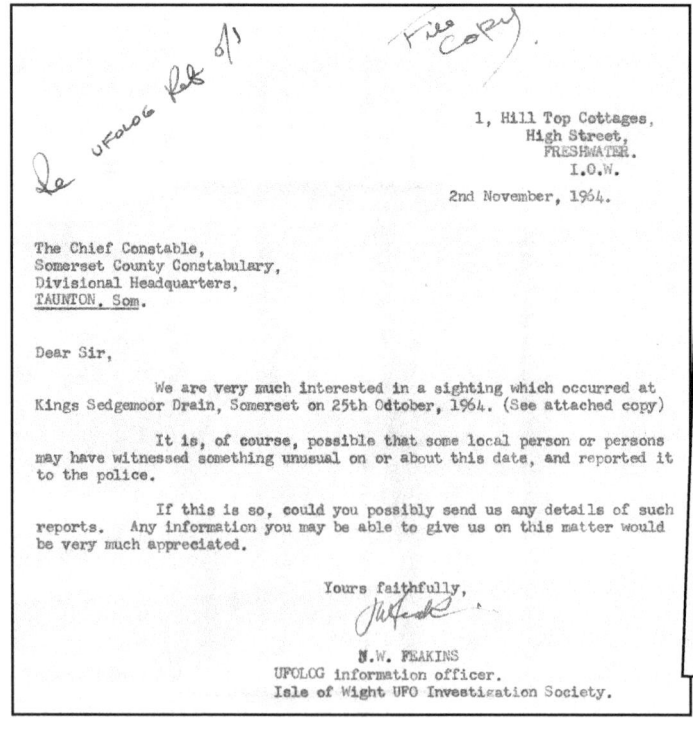
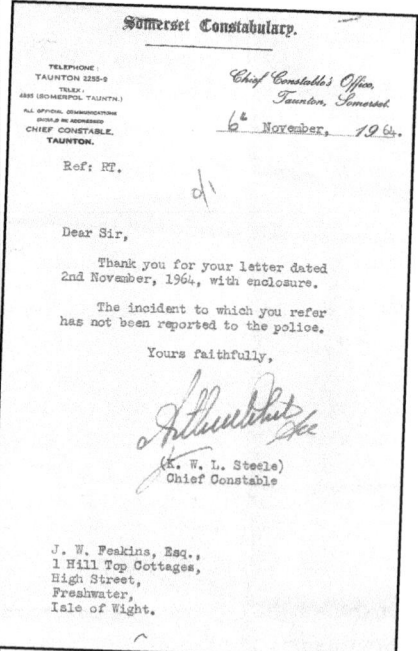

25th October 1964 – Somerset fisherman reports dazzling red light

Sheffield coal merchant – James Sharman, Walt Depledge, and two friends, were out night fishing in Somerset, shortly before midnight, when an object with a dazzling red light appeared overhead, illuminating the landscape and frightening a herd of cows in a nearby field, before accelerating and vanishing from view. (**Source:** *UFOLOG/Daily Express*, **25.10.1964** – 'The one that got away')

26th October 1964 – Unusual 'lights' seen over Hampshire

At 7pm, schoolboys – John Stuart McDougall and John Russell of Ringwood Road, Totton, in Hampshire – noticed an unusual 'bright light' moving across the sky outside their house, and called Mrs McDougall. By the time she had arrived, there was no sign of it.

As she was about to return into the house, another 'light' appeared in the sky. Instead of continuing on its journey, *"it stopped and jerked backwards and forwards"*. Knowing that James Russell (a school friend of the family, who was living a short distance away in Calmore Road) was interested in UFOs, they went off to tell him about the incident. However, by the time they arrived, the second object had faded away from view. Suddenly, a pair of 'lights' – apparently in formation – appeared in the sky in the same direction, and at approximately the same height as the previous ones seen.

After discussing what had been seen, the two boys – James and John – set off to walk back to John's house, when they saw a single 'light' heading across the sky, followed by the solitary appearance of an aircraft, its lighting pattern totally unlike what they had seen before. This was followed by another pair of 'lights', a few minutes later, and then a single one.

Some days after, details were given to the local newspaper – the *Echo* – and a woman rang the McDougall's house, saying that her husband had seen *"an object, with 'flaps', hovering in the sky"*, at about the same time as the sightings had taken place.

(**Source:** Isle of Wight UFO Society/*Southern Evening Echo*, 5.11.1964)

27th October 1964 – Two shapes seen in the sky

At 5am, Miss Josephine Stirling – a nursing sister at a Liverpool factory – said that she saw two mysterious shapes; one brilliant, the other less intense but 'twinkling', from her home in Croxteth Road.
(**Source:** *Liverpool Echo, 27.10.1964* – 'Riddle of the Night Sky')

On the same date, police searched an area near Biggin Hill Aerodrome, in Kent, after a report of a parachutist was seen to fall from an aircraft – explained away as being an illusion, caused by fog.
(**Source:** *Daily Mail*, 28.10.1964)

31st October 1964 – Police Officer sight 'Flying cone' over Southampton

David F. Smith – a PC with the Hampshire Constabulary – who was familiar with aircraft recognition (having served with the ATC), was having trouble sleeping, at 2am, and decided to go for a walk along Green Lane – a high point, overlooking the Millbrook Estate, Southampton.

> *"It was fairly cloudy, with about three-quarters of the sky covered. I looked for the Plough constellation when I saw a rather bright, pulsating, pale green 'star' in the sky, towards the south-west. I looked closer, and was stunned to see a huge inverted 'cone' underneath, tilted slightly to the right. I watched it for about 20 minutes, during which time the 'cone' slowly faded, leaving the bright object. It, too, grew smaller as it moved away, before being obscured by clouds."* (**Source:** UFOLOG)

THE BRITISH U.F.O. ASSOCIATION PRELIMINARY SIGHTING REPORT FORM

(Subject: Unidentified Flying Objects)
In the interests of science, you are requested to give a
detailed report describing the strange thing that you saw in the sky.

Member Societies:
British Flying Saucer Bureau
Anglo-Polish U.F.O. Research Club
Tyneside U.F.O. Society
Scottish U.F.O. Research Society
London U.F.O. Research Organisation
Stratford-on-Avon U.F.O. Group
Direct Investigation Group on Aerial Phenomena
Cheltenham Flying Saucer Group
Isle of Wight U.F.O. Investigation Society
Cambridge University Group for the Investigation of U.F.Os.
Oxford University U.F.Os Study Group

Name: Mr. /~~Mrs.~~ /~~Miss~~ David F. Smith
Address: 34, Clarence Road, Newport I.W.
(Age: 20.) (Tel. No.: ....)
(Occupation: Police Officer.)
Place: Where were you at the time?
Green Lane, Millbrook, So'ton
Date: What was the date and the day of the week? Saturday 31st October 1964
Time: What time was it? 2.5 a.m. /~~p.m.~~
Names and addresses of any other witnesses: ....

UFOLOG
REF NO 8/188   2 FEB 1965
I.S. ISSUE NO 12

Please write your story below, and make a drawing of what you saw, if you can;
then post this form back to us in the enclosed stamped addressed envelope.

I was spending the weekend of Oct 31st - Nov 1st with friends who live on the Millbrook Estate Southampton. Being unable to sleep I decided to go for a walk the time about 2AM. I reached Green Lane the highest point in the area at about 2-5 AM. The sky was fairly cloudy about 3/5 coverage. With no thought of UFO's I scanned, looking for the Plough in order to find compass directions as I did my attention was attracted to what was later found to be the South West and a rather bright star (first magnitude) it was of pale green colour and pulsating slightly. On closer study it became evident that beneath the "star" was an inverted faintly glowing cone of huge dimensions approximately six inches at arms length. The cone was tilted slightly to the right.

I surveyed the phenomenon for some twenty minutes during which time the cone slowly faded leaving the bright object which slowly grew smaller until it was obscured by clouds. There was no noise from the object at any time. In concluding I feel I should add that for two years I was in the aircraft Recognition team

(Continued overleaf if necessary)

(Please sign at the end of your written report, and give the date of your signature.)
Date received by regional organiser: .... Investigator's Ref.: ....
Regional Ref.: .... Date investigations completed: ....
Possible/probable/certain explanation or UFO type:

NOVEMBER 1964

6th November 1964 – Elliptical UFO over Gateshead
At 5.50pm, a half saucer-shaped object was seen in the sky over Gateshead, by Mrs S. Kerrison, for two minutes. (**Source:** *UFOLOG*)

8th-16th November 1964 – 'Spinning top' UFO
At 6.50pm, a strange 'star-like' object was seen passing through the sky over Old Trafford, Manchester, by local resident Christopher Ridgeway. After ten minutes it was lost from view.

13th November 1964 – 'Spinning top' UFO seen by motorist
Mrs Olivia Heppell, from Newcastle-on-Tyne, was travelling westwards along the coast road, at 8.45pm, when she saw a 'bright light',

> "... shaped like a spinning top, at an angle of 45 degrees elevation, about 200 yards away from me. Five minutes later it was gone".

16th November 1964
At 4pm, Anita Booth from Whalley Range was one of several people who sighted a strange silver object in the sky above Barlow Moor Road, Chorlton-cum-Hardy.

> "It was roughly three times higher than a plane, which was hovering and rising. It was visible for 10-15 minutes, until disappearing from view."

A spokesman for the Meteorological Office suggested they had seen the reflection of the setting sun on a satellite. (**Source:** DIGAP/*Manchester Evening News & Chronicle* – 'Mystery light in the sky')

In November 1964, Dr. Geoffrey Doel took over as chairman, replacing Nigel Stephenson who remained in charge of research and investigation. A new booklet was produced *UFO HANDBOOK No. 1*, edited by Malcolm Bull. In the spring of 1965, John Cleary- Baker took over as editor from Charles Stickland.

From 1964 to 2005, BUFORA published a variety of publications, including the *BUFORA BULLETIN* and *UFO TIMES* (a glossy magazine, which was published from 1989 through to October 1997). From 1979 to 1989, BUFORA also produced the *Journal of Transient Aerial Phenomena* (JTAP) – an attempt to create a scientific Ufology journal. In 2005, BUFORA suspended publication of the *BUFORA BULLETIN* to focus on presenting articles and sighting-accounts on its website.

In November 2005, the membership voted to restructure the Association in a way that would reflect the changing attitudes and habits of those interested, discontinuing paid membership and the printed Journal. BUFORA is now concentrating its efforts and resources on its website, now the sole vehicle for disseminating research, investigation reports, news, and articles.

Over the years we were to speak to many ex-BUFORA members, who were more than willing to assist us with information relating to investigations carried out by themselves into all manner of UFO accounts brought to their attention.

Norman Oliver
We asked him what had triggered off his interest into the UFO subject:

> "As a child, I became interested in Astronomy from the mid-1930s and knew the various constellations in detail – indeed, everything that was visible in our night skies. It was not until a decade or more after WW2, however, when I was – for some years – also a member of The British Interplanetary Society, that my attention was drawn to UFOs – then, of course, known as 'Flying Saucers', following Kenneth Arnold's June 1947 sighting. His oft-repeated description of the objects

he saw, incidentally, was not 'like saucers skimming over water'; this was purely related to their movement."

Tadpole-shaped

"He actually described them as 'tadpole-shaped.' (I have him on tape saying this!) I subsequently subscribed to that excellent magazine Flying Saucer Review (one wonders how long it would have lasted had it been called Flying Tadpole Review!) and from a reference to BUFORA – then LUFORO in its pages subsequently joined BUFORA in 1964, holding a number of different positions on its Committee – later Council, being Editor of both The BUFORA Journal, and later The New BUFORA Journal, for some 30 issues or more, covering three 'stints' between the 1970s and the first decade of the present century."

DECEMBER 1964

1st December 1964 – Brownies sight cylindrical object in the sky

A UFO was seen in the sky by Handforth Cheshire Primary schoolgirls – Marion Muir and Christine Bell – while returning home from a Brownie meeting, at 8pm. According to Marion's mother:

"My daughter (9) came running home from Brownies, petrified, to tell me she had seen a strange cylindrical object in the sky.

At the one end was a bright white pinpoint of light. Her face was ashen. When I asked her if she had seen a 'shooting star', she told me it couldn't have been one, as it was far too big and the wrong shape. When she went back to school, the headmaster – Mr Ringham, asked her to write the sighting out for the class". (**Source:** *Wilmslow County Express,* 3.12.1964 – 'Handforth children see flying object')

9th December 1964 – USA: UFOs tracked on radar Patuxent River, Maryland

The *Washington Star* (19.1.1965) – 'UFOs identified as Radar Errors'. Quote:

"The Air Force says it has identified those mysterious objects reported seen last month on a radar scope at Patuxent Naval Air Station. Two radar operators described them at the time as objects travelling at about 4,000 miles per hour and said one made 180 degree turn within a five mile stretch. The Air Force said Saturday 'a study showed that the radar was merely reacting to some other electronic device at the station or circuit trouble within the radar set itself.'"

The truth appears to be a different matter!

At 3.30am Radar Operator Bernard Sujka and two other Radar specialists tracked two large targets ten miles apart, heading directly toward the radar USN Patuxent River NAS control tower. They were moving at about 7,000 miles per hour, before swerving off at 15 miles range, then approaching again to ten miles. Then one target returned to eight miles range and made a high speed 160° turn. The sighting was confirmed visually by three persons one of them an experienced observer at an airfield.

24th December 1964 – Cone-shaped UFO with concentric rings seen

Horace Burns of Grottoes, Virginia, was driving along Highway 250 when he sighted a huge cone-shaped object, which was gliding across the road in front of him – big enough to fill the windscreen of his car. Horace felt that some sort of force had stalled his car. He then observed the object – estimated to be about 75 feet high and 125 feet at the base – which had settled onto a meadow about a hundred yards away, describing it as

"...having six concentric rings that diminished in diameter towards the top of the bluish glowing cone, on which was housed a dome. I could not see any openings or seams on the object. It then took off squarely at a terrific speed."

29th December 1964 – USA: Three objects detected by radar

Three objects were detected by radar over the Washington area, flying at a speed of 4,800 miles per hour. The incident was later explained away as being defective equipment.

Isle of Wight UFO Society contacts US Naval Air Station

Mr J.W. Feakins, of the Isle of Wight UFO Society, read this and, intrigued, wrote to the US Naval Air Station Patuxent River,

Maryland. On the 27th January 1965, he received a letter back from Commander R.W. Corson, Air Operations Officer, who had this to say:

> *"This is to acknowledge receipt of your request of 14th January 1965. The initial information released from this activity was greatly in error. The unknown informant made many surmises which were not factual. Investigation revealed the radar scope indications as electronic freaks. A newspaper report of the US Air Force study is attached for verification.*
>
> *Thanks you for your interest."*
>
> Signed,
> R.W Corson.

Artist's impression of a UFO sighted on June 17 1964 over a highway in the USA

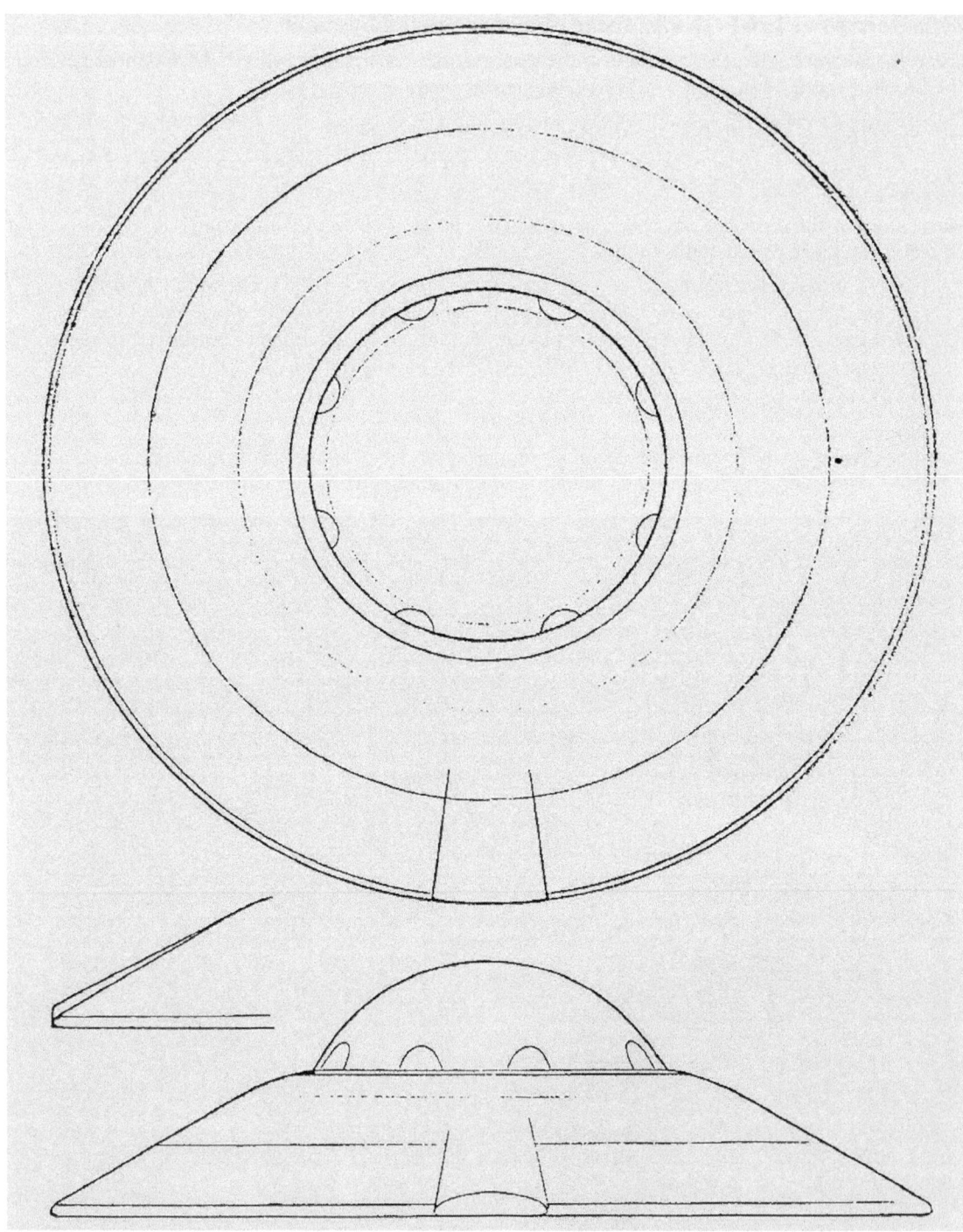

Line drawing sent to Mr Wendelle Stevens and August Roberts and used in the book 'UFO Photographs Around The World' Volume 1. – relating to the sighting by Mr Arthur Strauch, Deputy Sheriff of Sibley County (USA), over Minnesota on 21st October, 1965. See page 239.

CHAPTER 6 – 1965

UFO REPORTS INCLUDE:

JANUARY:
3rd January 1965 – Two UFOs seen over the English Channel
3rd January – Pilots sight UFO over Washington
4th January 1965 – Landed UFO, Theydon Bois
4th January 1965 – Motorist sights UFOs over Vermont
5th January 1965 – Metallic object, with sharp edges, over Newcastle
5th January 1965 – UFO tracked on radar over NASA Station
12th January 1965 – 'Flying disc' hovers over Washington police officer
13th January 1965 – Silver-grey UFO seen over Midlands
15th January 1965 – UFO over Ohio
16th January 1965 – Cone-shaped UFO sighted
18th January 1965 – Unusual 'light'
23rd January 1965 – Mushroom-shaped object over Virginia
24th January 1965 – UFO over Army camp
26th January 1965 – Three 'globes of light' seen over Manchester.

FEBRUARY:
5th February 1965 – Motorist sights UFOs over Kansas
9th February – Saucer-shaped UFO over Illinois
12th February 1965 – Unusual aircraft
14th February 1965 – Dark shape over Dover
15th February 1965 – Aircraft 'paced' by three UFOs

MARCH:
4th March 1965 – Three 'lights' seen rising from the ground over Oregon, West Virginia
6th March 1965 – Lecture on the UFO subject
7th March 1965 – Small orange 'lights' over Isle of Wight
8th March 1965 – Four 'lights', forming a square, seen
11th March 1965 – UFO activity during this day over Northern England
28th March 1965 – Triangular UFO seen over Yorkshire
29th March 1965 – Luminous object sighted.
29th March 1965 – UFO display, Worcestershire

APRIL:
4th April 1965 – Black oval object passes over Keesler Air Force Base, Mississippi
10th April 1965 – Circling 'lights' over Hertfordshire
13th April 1965 – Two 'golden objects seen in the sky
21st April 1965 – UFO over runway at Gatwick … tracked on radar
26th April 1965 – 'Bleeping' UFO
27th April 1965 – Delta-shaped UFO seen
30th April 1965 – Red pulsating object seen

MAY:
7th May 1965 – UFO sighted over Michigan, USA
9th May 1965 – "Like a bunch of bubbles"
20th May 1965 – Another UFO reported over Army camp
24th May 1965 – Red 'disc' in the sky over Nottinghamshire

JUNE:
13th June – 27th July 1965 – UFO activity over Birmingham area
14th June 1965 – UFOs over County Durham
19th June 1965 – 'Flying train' over English Counties
21st June 1965 – Holes found in barley crop
27th June 1965 – Black object over Birmingham.

JULY:
10th July 1965 – Unidentified noises on the Isle of Wight, Miss P. Pearson writes to Kath Smith
19th July 1965 – Cigar-shaped UFO over Bath
21st July 1965 – Mysterious noise over Isle of Wight
26th July 1965 – 'Bright light' seen over TV mast
31st July 1965 – Bleeping noises heard over Isle of Wight
July 1965 – Rocket-shaped object reported over Andover
July 1965 – UFO landing, Hampshire
July 1965 – Cigar shaped UFO seen over Mousehole, Cornwall.

AUGUST:
3rd August 1965 – Strange 'star' over Nottingham
3rd August 1965 – UFO displays over Oklahoma
4th August 1965 – Three 'lights' seen moving across the sky
6th August 1965 – Rotating UFO over Cumbria
13th August 1965 – Three objects sighted over Lanarkshire
14th August 1965 – Cigar-shaped object over Cumbria
16th August 1965 – Cigar-shaped object and two lights

17th August 1965 – Four spinning 'discs' over Sunderland
19th August 1965 – Cylindrical UFO over West Sussex
19th August 1965 – UFO landing at Cherry Creek, New York
21st August 1965 – UFO over Birmingham
23rd August 1965 – Large 'golden ball'
25th August 1965 – Mysterious 'red light' over Isle of Wight, Black 'discs' over Stonehenge
27th August 1965 – 'Red light' over TV masts
29th August 1965 – Were RAF scrambled?
30th August 1965 – Cigar-shaped UFO over Nottingham
30th August 1965 – Motorist encounters strange light, Urbana, Ohio
August 1965 – 'Black Triangles' seen over Lincolnshire mudflats
Summer 1965 – UFOs over Diglis Weir, Worcester
August 1965 – UFO seen over Kidderminster firing range

SEPTEMBER:
1st September 1965 – Bell-shaped UFO, Nottingham
3rd September 1965 – Police encounter UFO
9th September 1965 – 'Rugby ball' shaped UFO
10th September 1965 – Mystery noise, Birmingham
11th September 1965 – UFO over Poole, Dorset
12th September 1965 – Cigar-shaped UFO over Yorkshire
14th September 1965 – Close encounter, Mersea
15th September 1965 – Landed UFO, Lulsgate Bottom, Somerset
16th September 1965 – Black domed object seen
19th September 1965 – 'Straight lines' moving through the sky
20th September 1965 – Close encounter at Felixstowe
22nd September 1965 – Air Traffic Controller sights UFO
24th September 1965 – Huge object over South Wales
25th September 1965 – Motorist paced by UFO over New Mexico
27th September 1965 – 'Flying Saucer', Andover
27th September 1965 – UFO display Isle of Wight
31st September 1965 – Two objects seen over Surrey
September 1965 – Mysterious 'capsule' in the sky over Essex
September – Bell-shaped UFO, showing three globes
September 1965 – Disc-shaped UFO over Indiana

OCTOBER:
1st October 1965 – Sighting by Royal Navy Auxiliary Squadron, Scotland
12th October 1965 – Pink 'discs' over Gateshead
16th October 1965 – Rocket-shaped UFO
22nd October 1965 – UFO with antennae,
22nd October 1965 – 'Flying Saucer', Monmouthshire
25th October 1965 – Dazzling blue UFO
27th October 1965 – 'Spinning top' UFO over Isle of Wight
28th October 1965 – UFO display, Cleethorpes.

NOVEMBER:
3rd November 1965 – Silver triangular objects over County Durham
4th November 1965 – Cigar-shaped UFO over Berkshire
8th November 1965 – UFOs reported
23rd November 1965 – Sixteen objects over West Midlands.

DECEMBER:
2nd December – Dome-shaped UFO sighted
3rd December 1965 – Villagers report sighting UFOs
9th December 1965 – Mysterious object crash-lands in woods at Pennsylvania
10th December 1965 – Girl Guides sight UFO
13th December 1965 – UFO splits into three lights
15th December 1965 – Triangular object over London
16th December 1965 – Red pear-shaped UFO
20th December 1965 – 'Ball of fire'
22nd December 1965 – Tadpole-shaped UFO
23rd December 1965 – 'Cone-shaped' UFO
27th December 1965 – Box-shaped UFO seen
29th December 1965 – 'Cone of light'

JANUARY 1965

3rd January 1965 – Two UFOs seen over the English Channel

Mr John Hart was travelling on a Calais to Dover ferry in the middle of the English Channel, when he saw:

> "...two reflecting objects in the sky, at an angle of 60 degrees off the horizon – just like silver dots – but soon lost from view as cloud obscured them, at 12.30pm; they were not balloons or aircraft."

(Source: *Letter to Flying Saucer Review,* May/June 1965, Volume 11, No. 3)

3rd January – Pilots sight UFO over Washington

Brief details but of interest was a report of a strange flying object that was seen by the crew of an Electra Aircraft approaching their aircraft, while preparing for a landing at Washington. Suddenly it veered away – much to the relief of the Captain and his crew, who thought that this was their final moment. (Source: NICAP)

It is claimed that this was the beginning of a huge 'wave' of UFO sightings which took place in 1965.

4th January 1965 – Landed UFO, Theydon Bois

At 9.15pm, an engineer from Hackney, London, was parked under trees, just off the road near Theydon Bois, with his girlfriend, when he noticed a 'bright light' in the sky, heading slowly towards his position. However, he put it to the back of his mind, after it disappeared from view. Some 30 minutes later he had occasion to get out of the car, when he was shocked to see a brilliant white object – *"like an igloo in appearance, resting on the ground, about 12 yards from the car"*.

Reacting quickly, he jumped into the car and turned it around with the headlights on, but there was nothing to be seen.

Enquiries made into the incident revealed that another strange object was also seen by a couple in the same area, at 5.30pm.

(Source: Mr Paul Webb, BUFORA)

4th January 1965 – Motorist sights UFOs over Vermont

Dr. R.S. Woodruff – a Vermont State pathologist and state trooper – reported having sighted three UFOs between 4.30pm and 5pm, while driving between Bethel and Randolph. Each object carried an orange-red light and was the size of a football in the sky. It left and another appeared, then a third one.

(Source: Space-link, 1965)

5th January 1965 – Metallic object, with sharp edges, over Newcastle

At 6.05am, *"a blue fluorescent oval object, metallic in apparent construction, with sharp edges"*, was sighted by Mr Hall. The object was heading northwards across the sky, over Newcastle, at an estimated speed of 200 miles per hour, and at a height of 2,000 feet. **(Source: TUFOS)**

Bob Tibbitts

According to Bob Tibbitts, of the Coventry UFO Research Group, a number of mysterious lights were reported over Nuneaton, Grendon and Corley on this day, involving the sighting of

> "... two lights – like car headlamps – seen stationary in the sky for long periods, and a circle of about a dozen lights moving towards the direction of Coventry".

Bob Tibbitts

Later that evening, a noise – like a two-stroke engine – was heard, and lights were seen over Grendon. The official explanation was that they were meteorites or satellites burning up!

5th January 1965 – UFO tracked on radar over NASA Station

Scores of reports began to flow into the various US agencies and UFO groups on this day; a huge 'flying disc' was reported heading across the sky over the NASA Station at Wallops Island, Virginia, moving at an estimated speed of 100 miles per minute.

On the same day the Navy disclosed that two UFOs had been tracked on radar at the Naval Air Test Centre in Maryland; one was seen to make a sharp turn at 4,800 miles per hour. Not surprisingly, following the excitement, logical explanations were tendered, such as faulty radar at Wallops Island, and mistakes or hoaxes.

12th January 1965 – 'Flying disc' hovers over Washington police officer

Just after midnight, a Police Inspector (28) was on patrol, driving a department of justice car equipped with a two-way radio, north of Lynden, Washington. The officer was carrying a .357 Magnum revolver.

He headed along a tree-lined road at 40 miles per hour, listening to radio chatter, when a bright glow suddenly hit the ground.

> "It was so powerful. I could see farm buildings in the distance. I was about to stop and get out, when this huge shining thing swooped down right over the car. It scared me half to death; I was almost paralysed. The thing was round, about 30 feet in diameter. The glare was so blinding I couldn't see any details. It stopped just above the road, less than fifty feet away from me; I hit the brakes and thought I was going to ram it. I braced for the collision, when it shot upwards out of the way. I jumped out and saw it hovering above me. I pulled out my revolver but something kept me from firing. It remained above me for a few minutes. I was able to see in the centre of the object a round, dark area. It hung there. I had a feeling I was being watched. I reached for the mike to radio HQ when it began to move away, and then climbing faster than any jet disappeared into the clouds."

Enquiries made after the incident revealed that it had been tracked on radar. The man was warned to keep quiet, but chose to speak to Donald Keyhoe about the incident. He allowed Donald access to the report but asked his name be kept confidential, although in the book – *Aliens from Space* by Donald Keyhoe – the name Robert E. Kerringer was used.

13th January 1965 – Silver-grey UFO seen over Midlands

A silver-grey UFO was sighted in the sky over Solihull, West Midlands, by NICAP UFO investigator – Derek Samson, who observed it

> "...moving west, at 8.12pm. It then tilted at an angle of 45 degrees and moved slowly into cloud cover, when I lost sight of it five minutes later."

15th January 1965 – UFO over Ohio

At 10pm, a former Manchester newsman – Mr Charles Knee, Jr. – was driving on Route 4-A, between *Wilmot and Enfield, when the radio suddenly stopped, the lights on the car went out and the engine quit. He lost control of the car and pulled to the side of the road and then heard a loud humming sound – like a high frequency electrical whine. He then opened the car door and stepped out.

He glanced up and saw a very bright 'light' below the cloud cover, at around 2,000 to 5,000 feet altitude, which looked about the size of a flashlight, held at arm's length, pointed towards his face. It seemed to hover for a moment and then it took off to the south, travelling very fast. As the 'light' left and the whine died away, the car's lights and radio came on and the motor started. The whole thing lasted about 15 or 20 seconds.

(Source: *Manchester (NH) Union Leader,* **22.1.1965/Dan Wilson, BB files)**

16th January 1965 – Cone-shaped UFO sighted

An 'ice-cream cone'-shaped object was seen over a cornfield, causing cars to stall. The location was not identified.

(Sources: Patricia Young/Richard Young)

17th January 1965 – *Manchester Guardian* – 'Good year for Saucers – business booming' [reference to Ford hubcaps!]

18th January 1965 – Unusual 'light' over Gateshead

At 8pm, an unusual 'light' was seen over Sheriff Hill, Gateshead, before vanishing 30 seconds later.

---

*Wilmot is a village in Stark County, Ohio, United States. The population was 304 at the 2010 census. It is part of the Canton–Massillon Metropolitan Statistical Area. Wilmot was originally called Milton, and under the latter name was laid out in 1836.

23rd January 1965 – Mushroom-shaped object over Virginia
At 8.40am, Williamsburg resident – Mr T.F. Mains – sighted:

> "...a metallic grey in colour, mushroom or light bulb-shaped object, estimated to be 75-80 feet in height, 25 feet in diameter on top, tapering to 10 feet at the bottom. It showed a red-orange glow on the near side and a blue glow on the far side, and made a sound like a vacuum cleaner."

Mr Mains stated that the car's electrical system was affected during the sighting, which lasted for 25 seconds. (**Source:** *Project Blue Book*)

24th January 1965 – UFO over Army camp
At 8.45pm, *"a spherical object, surrounded by green, orange, and blue lights"*, was seen motionless in the sky over Catterick Army Camp, by Mr and Mrs G. Gallimore from Scotton.

26th January 1965 – Three 'globes of light' seen, over Manchester
The *Manchester Evening News*, in its edition of 28th January 1965, under the headline – 'Mystery of the falling fiery star', told of being contacted by Mrs Beatrice Hardman, who sighted:

> "...two bright yellow objects in the sky, which appeared to collide – one of them fell down onto the roof of a house opposite, in Abbotsbury Street, and split into three 'balls of light'; two of them rolled along the roof of number 13, glowing briefly for a minute".

A check, the next morning, revealed no sign of any marks or debris. Weather experts at Jodrell Bank were unable to give any satisfactory explanation for the incident, but suggested it may have been a fireball.
(**Sources: As above/DIGAP, Harold Bunting**)

FEBRUARY 1965

5th February 1965 – Motorist sights UFOs over Kansas
On the 5th February, Mr and Mrs G. Heim were driving to Topeka, Kansas, at 3.30pm, when they sighted two blurred grey objects in the sky, about the size of a small airplane, flying in very tight manoeuvres. Checks, made later, revealed no aircraft were logged in that area. The following day, an object was seen over Cleveland, Ohio, heading eastwards in a zigzag path through the sky.

9th February – Saucer-shaped UFO over Illinois
Mrs Susan Crowley of Elk Grove Village, Illinois, was outside at 12.47am, when she saw:

> "...a soft white coloured, saucer-shaped, object rocking from side to side in the sky."

The next day (the 10th), six white football sized objects were seen flying across the sky, at high altitude, heading in a south-east to south-west direction. According to the witness:

> "They had inverted 'V' wings and no tail section; the rear two suddenly jerked out of formation at a right-angle of movement."

Documents preserved for this period show that approximately 100 UFO sightings over the United States were recorded between January and March 1965. The majority are very brief with sparse details. Although some may be attributed to natural phenomena, others (from their description) do not appear to fit into this category. (**Sources: NICAP/UFOLOG**)

12th February 1965 – Unusual aircraft
Mr A. Philips, and his wife, sighted an unusual aircraft flying low through the sky, over Swainswick, near Bath (time not given), described as:

> "...an ash-grey plane flying through the sky, about 100 feet above the road, heading west to south-west; it had a misty appearance but there was no fog or mist about. Suddenly, it disappeared in front of our eyes."

Later the same day, Mr Reginald Eaves and his wife, Myrtle, saw what they took to be a plane crashing into the sea, about a mile offshore, as they drove through Exmoor. Despite a search of the area by RAF helicopters and the Minehead lifeboat, nothing was found.
(**Source:** *Bristol Evening Post,* 13.2.1965/*Western Daily Press,* 15.2.1965 – 'Ghost Plane riddle grows')

14th February 1965 – Dark shape over Dover

Mr C. Watson and Mr F. Pursey were driving home from Whitstable, up an incline, after having just left Dover at 7pm, when:

> *"We saw a dark shape (which I thought was a van, without lights) cross the road from left to right. It seemed to disappear into the churchyard. I thought that perhaps I had imagined the apparition, but my friend remarked he heard no lights or engine noise. I later discovered that others had seen something similar in the locality."* (**Source: Kentish Gazette, date of publication not known**)

15th February 1965 – Aircraft 'paced' by three UFOs

According to retired Major Keyhoe in his book Aliens from Space, a Flying Tiger airliner was cruising over the Pacific, transporting an Army and Air Force group to Japan, on an hour's flight, when the radar picked up three large, fast moving objects. The crew thought, at first, that the set was malfunctioning, as they had never seen such large objects plotted on the scope before …then a reddish glow appeared above them, to their left.

Looking upwards, the Captain was stunned to see three enormous oval objects, which appeared to be heading towards the aircraft. The Captain started to turn the plane – then stopped. The UFOs veered to one side, reduced their speed, and levelled out at the same altitude. The radar showed them to be five miles away; even at that distance they looked enormous in size.

For several minutes the crew watched the objects, which made no attempt to approach closer, before they suddenly shot away, disappearing in seconds. After the matter was reported, it was established that the size of the UFOs had been nearly 2,000 feet in length. Despite some attempts to keep the story hidden, the Captain wrote to NICAP and they in turn contacted Donald Keyhoe.

MARCH 1965

4th March 1965 – USA: Three 'lights' seen rising from the ground over Oregon, West Virginia

At 9.23pm, Corvallis, Oregon resident – Mr W.V. Harrison – reported having sighted three 'lights' rising from the ground, several seconds apart. The next day, an oily spot was found at the location.
(**Source:** *Project Blue Book*)

6th March 1965 – Lecture on the UFO subject

Mr J. Otley secretary of the Tyneside Unidentified Flying Objects Society lectured on *'Flying Saucers are fact'* at the Newcastle Arts festival in the Physics Auditorium, which was packed with people. He alleged that the Government was suppressing the facts on 'Flying Saucers'.
(**Source:** *The Journal,* 6.3.1965 – 'Saucers lecture is festival hit')

7th March 1965 – Small orange lights over Isle of Wight

At 7.35pm, Mr and Mrs J. Linnet from Carisbrooke, Isle of Wight, sighted a small orange light crossing the clear frosty night sky over the direction of Cosham, Portsmouth. It was followed by another identical object, five seconds later, moving in the same direction as the previous one. (**Source:** *UFOLOG*)

8th March 1965 – Four 'lights', forming a square, seen

At 7.15pm, Mrs Yvonne Wright from Kingswinford, West Midlands, was standing outside, talking to her neighbour.

It was a beautiful evening and they were admiring the new moon, when suddenly they saw:

> "...four 'lights' – two red and two white, forming a square – passing low, overhead, on a westerly course across the sky. Two of the 'lights' then became lost from view as they changed direction".

Excited, she dashed to the front of the house with her neighbour and gazed across the sky, but there was no sign of the UFOs.

At about the same time and date, a *"silver, flickering, disc"* was seen over Falcon Lodge, Sutton Coldfield, Warwickshire, on the outskirts of Birmingham. It was travelling from the north-east to south-west, before making a sharp turn on the horizon, 30 seconds later, and disappearing from view. A check with Birmingham Airport revealed no flights logged over the locality. (**Source:** Derek Samson, NICAP, GB)

11th March 1965 – UFO activity during this day over Northern England

A mysterious object – described as *"resembling a ball of twine, with a tail of flame"* – was sighted hovering in the sky over Halifax, West Yorkshire, between 7.30pm and 8.30pm on this date. Several people telephoned the police.

At 8.10pm, *"a golden yellow globe, twice as bright as the full moon, with a blue green trail"*, was seen flying through the sky, south-east, some 40 degrees off the horizon, by Kenton, Newcastle on Tyne resident – Mr T. Buffey. At about the same time, *"a red sphere, with a greenish-yellow tail"*, was seen by Howden-on-Tyne residents – Mr R. Moule and Mr Bird.

Mr Andrew Steel was riding a motor scooter along Shields Road, Newcastle, at 8.10pm, when he sighted *"a pearl coloured object – the size of a full moon – flying across the sky"*, heading westwards at an angle of 45 degrees off the horizon. Seconds later, it had disappeared from view. It appears likely that this was the same UFO seen by Mr G. Hickson of Darlington, County Durham, five minutes later, who described it as *"a white sphere, with a bright red tail, that appeared to land behind nearby houses"*.
(**Source:** *UFOLOG*)

28th March 1965 – Triangular UFO seen over Yorkshire

Geoffrey Brown:

> "At 9.30pm I was driving through the village of Skeeby, near Richmond, North Yorkshire, when the engine of the car began to splutter and came to a halt. I got out of the car, to attempt to locate the

problem, when I noticed a 'light', which I took, initially, to be a weather balloon, but then discounted this as an explanation when I saw it was milky-white in colour, with rounded corners, making a low humming noise, approximately 100 feet across, hovering a few hundred feet above the ground.

It then approached closer, but stopped about 200 yards away from me – then began to move over the moors, pulsing with light underneath, before shooting away at an angle across the sky, at fantastic speed.

I was amazed to notice, high above it, about 9 or 10 similar objects, grouped in a triangular **'V'** *shaped formation that slowly moved out of sight."*

The report makes interesting reading, especially as the description of the 'craft' seen by Mr Brown appears to have much in common with a spate of UFOs – now referred to as 'Triangular UFOs' – which began to appear in the skies over Europe, during 1989.

Red marks noticed in the sky, followed by intimidating phone calls

After reporting the matter to the MOD, Geoffrey noticed some odd red marks appearing on his skin. They resembled *'stretch marks'* but soon faded away, although they reappeared on a number of other occasions. He was also to receive numerous telephone calls made to his house, every few months, by callers who declined to identify themselves. These mystery callers unsettled him by asking questions about what he had seen. (**Source: Personal interview**)

29th March 1965 – Luminous object sighted

At 5.55am, Robert Knight and his wife from Heswall, Liverpool, noticed a luminous object in the sky, surrounded by smaller 'lights', hovering in the south-western sky above the horizon, for ten minutes – until disappearing from view. (**Source:** *Liverpool Echo*, 29.3.1965)

29th March 1965 – UFO display, Worcestershire

At 9.20am, NICAP UFO investigator – Derek Samson, from Shirley, near Birmingham – was driving from Birmingham to Cardiff.

He was passing the Malvern Hills, to his right, when he felt an intuitive urge to stop the vehicle.

"I pulled into the side of the road and was astonished to see what I can only describe as some sort of celestial display above the hills, involving four, long, glowing cigar-shaped objects, above which could be seen five smaller ones. Another three objects then appeared to the left of the first group. I was amazed and felt huge excitement. The small escort ship tilted and moved downwards, before levelling up again. I realised I had been watching the display for some forty minutes, which meant I was going to be late for my appointment! Reluctantly, I continued on my journey, pondering on the significance of what the thirteen 'flying saucers' were doing there."

(**Source: Personal interview**)

Derek Samson (centre of group)

APRIL 1965

4th April 1965 – Black oval object passes over Keesler Air Force Base, Mississippi

At 4.05am, a weather observer USAF A/2c Corum sighted a 40 feet black oval object, showing four lights along the bottom, flying in and out of clouds for 15 seconds. (**Source:** *Project Blue Book*)

AUTHORS AMAZING SIGHTING AT MALVERN HILLS ENGLAND 1965.

On the morning of March 29th,1965,I was motoring from Birmingham to Cardiff,it was a beautiful sunny day with a clear blue sky,and very little cloud,the time was 9.20.am,and I was passing the Malvern hills which lay on my right.Suddenly,intuition made me glance to the right towards the hills,I braked and parked on the grass verge,there I witnessed a fantastic celestial display,lying low over the hills were four long cigar shaped objects,known as Mother Ships,carriers of the small scout ships or saucers,above the Mother Ships lay five medium command craft,to the right of these hovered a small scout ship.As I watched,another three command craft suddenly appeared to the left of the first group of command craft,by now I was overcome with a feeling of greatness,and it was then that the small scout ship moved,it tilted down and forward,then upwards and leveled off then stopped and remained stationary.Having watched this spectacle for forty minutes I began to think of my appointment in Cardiff,reluctently I continued on my journey pondering over in my mind at what significance could thirteen flying saucers in cloud form relate to ?.

10th April 1965 – Circling 'lights' over Hertfordshire

At 11.45pm, a *strange 'light' was seen moving across the sky over High Street, Bushey, in Hertfordshire, by Colin Johnson and his friend, which circled a second object before moving slowly away.*
(Source: Letter to Kath Smith, Isle of Wight UFO Society)

13th April 1965 – Two golden objects seen in the sky

Maud Irving, of Great Corby, was up at 3am when she sighted what looked like:

"*...two 'gold balls', one above the other, in the northern part of the sky, for over an hour*".

The incident was later explained away as likely to have been the reflection of a cloud base searchlight, or a weather balloon! **(Source: *Cumberland Evening News*, 13.4.1965)**

21st April 1965 – UFO over runway at Gatwick ... tracked on radar

At 11.40am, two aircraft were on their final approach to Gatwick Airport, in Sussex. The first, from Dover, was preparing to line-up with the runway; the other, on a heading of 120 degrees, under Southern ATC London Airport Radar, "*when an object was plotted on the radar, 16 miles to the north-east, at 10,000 feet*", causing the approaching aircraft to abort their landings. The UFO then lined-up with Gatwick runway, at a distance of between 3-9 miles, moving at 60 knots, and made a 90 degree turn northwards, before disappearing into ground radar clutter, about 2 miles away. **(Source: Arnold West, BUFORA)**

26th April 1965 – 'Bleeping' UFO

A 'bleeping' object was seen for a minute, moving backwards and forwards on a circular course – but never completely finishing a circle – over Ovenden, near Halifax, during the evening.

27th April 1965 – Delta-shaped UFO seen

At 5.24pm, a white, glistening, delta-shaped, object was seen heading North-north-east, 70 degrees off the horizon, over South Shields, County Durham.

30th April 1965 – Red pulsating object seen

At 10.35pm, two Bucksburn teenagers – Ramsay Tosh and Allan Kelman – were walking along the Northfield-Bucksburn road, when they saw a bright object moving across the sky in a '*jerking movement*', before dropping below the horizon twenty minutes later – explained away as likely to have been a satellite.
(Source: *Aberdeen Press & Journal*, 6.5.1965)

Five minutes later, Mr R. Sadler and Miss J. Wedgewood were between Newmarket and Fordham, when they sighted a red pulsating object in the sky, at 10.40pm.
(Source: Cambridge University Group Investigation UFO)

MAY 1965

7th May 1965 – UFO sighted over Michigan

At 7.30pm, Mr Marshall from Oxford, Michigan, sighted a 'light', resembling a satellite, which was seen to split into two parts; one a copper colour, then two more appeared. One of the objects was believed to have been tumbling, before being lost from sight a minute later. **(Source: *Project Blue Book*)**

9th May 1965 – "*Like a bunch of bubbles*"

At 10.05pm, a small cluster of various coloured spheres – "*like a bunch of bubbles*" – was seen moving slowly through the sky over Ovenden, near Halifax, by local resident – Miss E. Holden.
(Source: John Feakins)

20th May 1965 – Another UFO reported over Army camp

At 8.22am, another UFO sighting was reported from Catterick Army Camp, Yorkshire.

A glittering silver UFO – *"like two inverted soup plates"* – was seen in the north of the sky, about a mile from the camp, by Mr B. Redhead of Northallerton, and Mr M. Coulthard. According to the two men, the object was estimated at only 100 feet off the ground, and disappeared from view ten seconds later. **(Source: UFOLOG)**

24th May 1965 – Red 'disc' in the sky over Nottinghamshire

A red 'disc' was seen moving in and out of cloud over Arnold, Nottinghamshire. This was followed by a report from Mr Nicholls and his son, of Newcastle-on-Tyne, who sighted a moving yellow 'light', with a faint blue tinge, in the south of the sky over Newcastle, at 10.15pm. **(Source: TUFOS)**

Summer – *"Like two soup plates"*

Brian Gibbs contacted us with regard to what he saw over 40 years ago, while walking home to Leamington Avenue, Walthamstow, early one evening, accompanied by his son.

> *"We saw this object in the sky – resembling two soup plates, joined together – with flashing lights running all around its exterior.*
>
> *I shouted to my son to fetch his mother. By the time she came running outside, it had gone. I looked around and saw it moving in the opposite direction, many miles away. I later worked out that it had moved a hundred miles in 2-3 minutes."* **(Source: Personal interview)**

JUNE 1965

June 1965 – Astronaut photographs UFO

In June 1965, Major James McDivitt saw, filmed, and photographed an object, which approached the Gemini IV (3rd June – 7th June 1965) capsule in which they were orbiting the Earth, passing over Hawaii. The UFO had a long arm sticking out of it.

Major James McDivitt:

> *"I was flying with Ed White. He was sleeping at the time so I don't have anybody to verify my story. We were drifting in space with the control engines shut down and all the instrumentation off when, suddenly, an object appeared in the window. It had a very definite shape – a cylindrical object – it was white – it had a long arm that stuck out on the side. I don't know whether it was a very small object up close, or a very large object a long way away. There was nothing to judge by. I really don't know how big it was. We had two cameras that were just floating in the spacecraft at the time, so I grabbed one and took a picture of the object and grabbed the other and took a picture.*
>
> *Then I turned on the rocket control systems because I was afraid we might hit it. At the time we were drifting – without checking I have no idea which way we were going – but as we drifted up a little farther, the sun shone on the window of the spacecraft. The windshield was dirty – just like in an automobile, you can't see through it. So I had the rocket control engines going again and moved the spacecraft so that the window was in darkness again – the object was gone.*
>
> *I called down later and told them what had happened and they went back and checked their records of other space debris that was flying around, but we were never able to identify what it could have been. The film was sent back to NASA and reviewed by some NASA film technicians. One of them selected what he thought was what we talked about, at least before I had a chance to review it. It was not the picture – it was a picture of a sun reflection on the window."*

Haunted Skies Volume Two Revised

During the production of this book we came across a letter sent to Stratford-upon-Avon UFO investigator – John 'Dennis' Llewellyn, following his enquiry made to the American Embassy, in London, about obtaining a copy of a photograph taken by Astronaut James McDivitt. He received a letter from them, along with a photograph showing what at first glance looks to be two frames of a luminous object in flight (others may see it differently). Now confused, taking into consideration the many faked images shown on the internet of what is claimed to have been taken by him, we contacted *David Bryant, of Spacerocks UK – the only full-time professional meteorite dealership in Britain, owned by him and his wife, Linda, who incidentally both have degrees in Astronomy with Biology.

David has been a source of inspiration to us both and has supported the *Haunted Skies* books. David has, over the years, also met many of the astronauts, one of whom was Edgar Mitchell – a man that I (John) had the pleasure of meeting, some years ago, presenting him with a copy of the *Haunted Skies* book that he told me he was impressed with!

David Bryant:

"During his Gemini IV mission, in 1965, Gen James McDivitt witnessed an apparently metallic cylinder with antenna-like structures, which he attempted to photograph; on the first of two occasions when we met (and enjoyed a jug of margaritas together!) I asked why he hadn't woken his fellow crew-member, Edward White. He replied that '...it wasn't in the mission profile. I was on watch. Ed was scheduled for a sleep period. You have to understand the military way of things: you do what's in the profile.' Later, however, both astronauts reported two egg-shaped objects leaving glowing trails. McDivitt told me that the photographs of these on many websites are either fakes or merely show reflections in Gemini IV's window: he has never seen prints of the exposures he made, and feels it is likely they were over exposed, due to the UFOs proximity to the sun. He is, however, adamant that these objects were artificial structures that bore no resemblance to any US or Soviet spacecraft."

David believes that McDivitt's opinion was that all the published photos are fakes: he saw a UFO, but didn't manage any images of it. The letter, of course, doesn't specifically refer to a UFO photo.

General James McDivitt with David Bryant

David Bryant:

"I've had lots of similar letters. When I was a teacher, I subscribed to the NASA school's education program, and received regular info sheets, photos, profiles; I still have carrier bags full of them!"

It appears that a still from the movie camera (which McDivitt insists he never touched during the sighting) was mistakenly released without the astronaut's review, showing what turned out to be a light reflection off his co-pilot's window, according to McDivitt.

UFO buffs took this photo and acclaimed it as one of the best UFO photos ever taken, showing (they claim) a glowing object with a plasma tail. McDivitt never saw anything like that in space. **Verdict:** Gross exaggeration and distortion on the part of UFO writers.

---

* *"Following a less than illustrious career as a naval pilot, I taught and lectured across all phases in education for 45 years. I now run the UK's only full-time meteorite dealership and lecture widely about meteoritics and the paranormal. I have been a student of the UFO phenomenon for nearly 60 years and of astronautics for over 50. Through the connections I've made from my meteorite and space memorabilia businesses, I have been fortunate enough to meet more than 30 astronauts, including seven of the twelve Moonwalkers. My spare time is mostly spent walking five miles a day trying to keep fit and photographing wildlife.*

My second wife Linda and I have been married over twenty years, share all the same interests as well as four children and five grandchildren!"

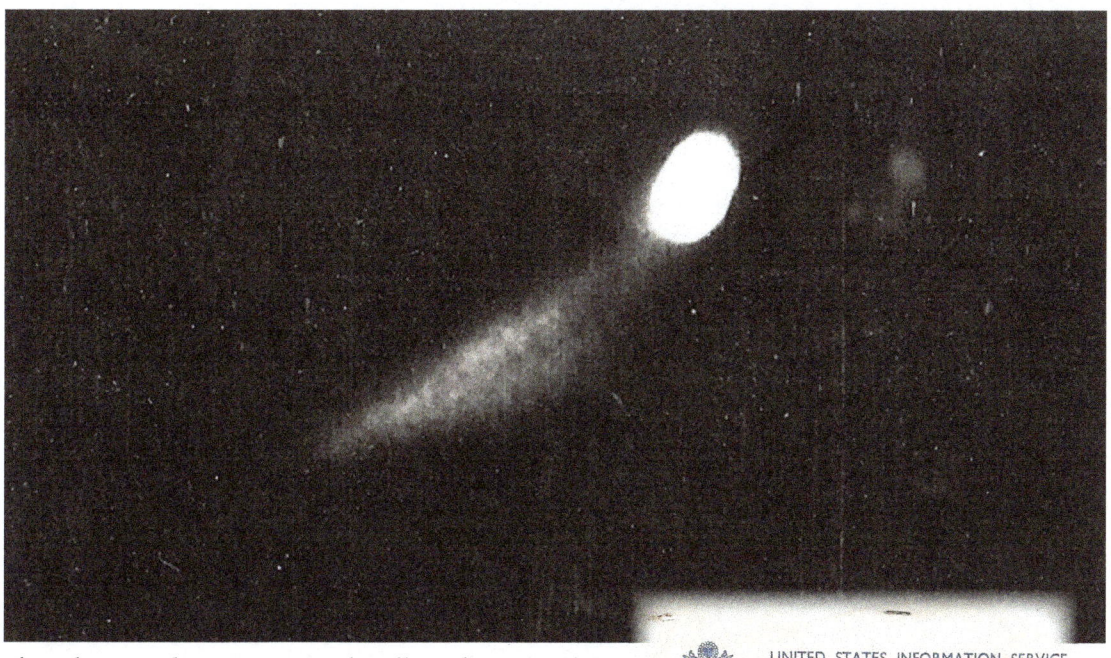

This photograph, sent to Mr Llewellyn, showing what appears to be a glowing object with a plasma trail, reproduced twice on the photo (or two separate objects) is, of course, misleading and in all probability nothing to do with the strange object sighted by General McDivitt, illustrating once again the dangers of automatically believing everything you see and hear as being gospel!

David has also published some interesting books, including *Danger From The Skies* and *Our Forbidden Moon*, which has taken fifteen years of meticulous planning and research to write. During meetings with over thirty astronauts and cosmonauts, including seven of the twelve alleged Moonwalkers, he gradually became aware of a number of major inconsistencies in their recollections of the Apollo program. Furthermore, in occasional unguarded moments, several space travellers have revealed personal experiences of the UFO phenomenon and hinted at even

The Gemini IV Photograph

IN a report which appeared in *The Times* of June 5, it was disclosed that:

"America's Gemini IV spaceship sighted another winged object hurtling along in space above the United States this evening. It could not be immediately identified, although one official said it might be another satellite and Major James McDivitt, the Gemini commander, reported that he had taken photographs of it."

One of the frames from Major McDivitt's film is reproduced on this page.

Later in the same report, we read that:

"Major McDivitt, when he reported the sighting of the other object in space during the twentieth orbit, said his attempts at photography had been complicated by the position of the sun. Several of America's satellites employ large booms extended outwards from the main body and there was speculation that the astronauts had seen one of these. In any case visibility is apparently good in space."

According to a report in the *Daily Mirror* of June 5: "The discovery started frantic efforts by U.S. Space experts to track the object, and to guess its origin. A top official said the paths of all orbiting objects were known, and none of them was on a collision course with Gemini IV."

Elsewhere we had heard speculative suggestions that the object was the Pegasus satellite. To the best of our knowledge, Pegasus is in an orbit hundreds of miles farther out into space than that occupied by Gemini. Again, the object shown in the photograph seems to bear absolutely no resemblance to Pegasus, or other satellites which are equipped with booms carrying solar "sails" and antennae. In fact we feel inclined to ask what has happened to the arms which were reported to have been seen, and, as an afterthought, what is the wispy trail behind the photographed object?

This photograph which was taken from a strip of three issued by the United States Information Service, London, was loaned to the REVIEW by reader John D. Llewellyn. It is part of a 16 mm movie film exposed by Astronaut James McDivitt during the twentieth revolution of his four-day space flight with Astronaut Ed. White. Gemini IV was over Hawaii when the object was sighted (according to official caption), and 16 mm Eastman colour film was used at six frames per second. The camera had a 5 mm, 160° field of view lens.

more dramatic encounters. *Our Forbidden Moon* examines these revelations and considers whether there might be a link between UFOs, extraterrestrial races, and mankind's forty-year failure to travel beyond low Earth orbit. David Bryant uses his knowledge gained during forty years as a teacher, lecturer, and respected authority on spaceflight to ask controversial questions and provide convincing solutions.

13th June-27th July 1965 – UFO activity over the Birmingham area

A further spate of UFO activity was reported around the locality of 9, Alcester Road, South Hollywood (near Birmingham) – the home of Mrs Harris – covering the period from the 13th June-27th July 1965, involving the sighting of a number of 'bright lights' seen circling around the electricity pylon directly in front of her house – matters she brought to the attention of the *Birmingham Evening Mail*, who declined to publish her letter! (**Source: Derek Samson, NICAP, GB**)

14th June 1965 – UFOs over County Durham

At 5am, from a distance of about one and a half miles, a bluish-white disc-shaped object, surrounded by a halo, was seen flying through the air at a height of about 800 feet, over Usworth Colliery, Washington, County Durham, by Mr J. Trevor, and his colleague Mr J Lamb. Ten seconds later, it faded from sight.

Later the same day, at 10.35pm, a bright oval object was seen moving across a clear sky over Railway Terrace, Washington, County Durham, by resident Mr A. Lowdon. When over a local wood (known as The Dene), it vanished from sight. (**Source: TUFOS**)

19th June 1965 – 'Flying train' over English Counties

A large rocket-shaped object, trailing orange flames – described as *"resembling an eel, illuminated along its length" and by* others as *"a flying train"* – was seen moving across the sky over Exeter, Wakefield and Bradford, between 10.30pm-10.50pm. (**Sources: Frank Marshall, BUFORA/***Exeter Express & Echo*)

21st June 1965 – Holes found in barley crop

A crater was found in a field of barley at farmer J.W. Black's Rockinghams Farm, Layer Marney. It was approximately five feet, by three feet six inches, consisting of three three inch holes arranged *"in a triangular shape near one side, extending three feet into the ground"*.

The Army bomb disposal squad visited the scene but found nothing. They suggested it may have been caused by a natural gas explosion under the ground. Others thought it might have been a meteorite.

(**Sources:** *Colchester Gazette*, **1.6.1965/21.6.1965/***Devizes Gazette*, **24.6.1965/***Bath & Wiltshire Chronicle*, **21.6.1965/***Telegraph & Argus*, **6.7.1965/***The Surrey Comet*, **23.6.1965**)

27th June 1965 – Black object over Birmingham

Mr Derek Samson was gardening at 70, Wellington Road, Handsworth, Birmingham, at 4.05pm, when he heard the sound of an aircraft passing overhead. Glancing upwards, he was astonished to see what looked like *"a black penny, flying edgeways on"*. He watched it for about 20 seconds, until it entered cloud cover and became lost from view. (**Source: Derek Samson, NICAP, GB**)

In the same year

Douglas Ellwood from Hertfordshire (then aged 10 or 12) was travelling back from Closeburn (a village 11 miles north-west of Dumfries), after having visited relatives – an annual holiday made by the family.

"As we neared Closeburn, we noticed a circular object in the sky above the village. By the time we arrived, there were a number of people watching the object, which was silver in colour, with darker circles around its outer rim. Some of the people fetched binoculars to look at it, as it remained stationary in the sky for a quite a long time. When somebody went to telephone the authorities, it shot off across the sky and disappeared at a speed that left us speechless. The local newspaper covered the story. A few days later, the RAF suggested we may have seen a weather balloon."

(**Source: Personal interview**)

JULY 1965

10th July 1965 – Unidentified noises on the Isle of Wight

A strange, high-pitched whining noise, which was apparently passing through the sky, was heard by Mrs Evelyn Harman of Falcon Cross Road, Shanklin, Isle of Wight, between 1.15am to 1.30am.

Evelyn:

"It seemed to hover with a lower pitch – then stopped. I looked in the sky, but couldn't see anything. I had an impression it was heading from inland, towards the sea."

Mrs Catherine Powell of Prince Street, Ryde, Isle of Wight, was lying awake at 2.15am on 10th July 1965, when she heard a queer humming noise, which increased in intensity as it approached closer. She rushed to the window, believing a 'Flying Saucer' was overhead, but saw nothing. Was it a Jet aircraft or UFO?

Haunted Skies Volume Two Revised

Miss P. Pearson writes to Kath Smith

Another witness was Miss P. Pearson, of Sandown. She wrote to Kath Smith, of the Isle of Wight UFO Society, on the 23rd July 1965.

Kath pictured here with Pat Pearson

"Dear Sirs,

I read in the County Press of last week about the strange noise heard on the night of the 9th/10th July. Don't know if it would interest you to know that I heard it. It aroused me at 2.20am. I find it rather difficult to describe, but it sounded like something diving out of the sky. The sound started on a high note and gradually lowered as the 'thing' neared the ground, until it became very low, and there were two bumps – as if it had bounced on landing. The sound was much too light for any engine or machinery to be involved, in my opinion, and the bumps were also light – as if it had not been anything heavy that had landed. It was a very quiet night, and there was no further sound after the bumps.

Yours truly, P. Pearson, (Miss)" **(Source: Isle of Wight UFO Society)**

19th July 1965 – Cigar-shaped UFO over Bath

Railway worker Ron Wakefield of Weston, Bath, was getting ready for bed, at 10.30pm. As he opened the bedroom window, he was surprised to see a cigar-shaped object come into view. It was over Lansdown, at a height of between 4-5,000 feet, *"shining like a sparkler, resembling a train but going much faster"*.

Another witness was Mr D. White, living in Twerton. He spoke of seeing:

"...six 'lights' in line, travelling across the sky, accompanied by the glow – like a spacecraft – in view for ten seconds". **(Source: *Bath & Wiltshire Chronicle*, 21.6.1965)**

21st July 1965 – Mysterious noise over Isle of Wight

Mrs Doreen Waddell was at her home address in Cowes, Isle of Wight, which overlooks *The Solent*, when she was awoken by an intense buzzing noise, at 2am.

"The sky was cloudy, with the moon visible. I couldn't see anything, but I could hear a noise – as if something was revolving in the sky; a bit like a vacuum cleaner. However, I was able to make out a very red glow in the sky – like a reflection from a fire – over the Radar works. I put this down to refraction from lights on the ground. Eventually the sound faded away, and I went to bed."

(Source: Kath Smith, Isle of Wight UFO Society)

23rd July 1965 – Three 'lights' over Nottingham

Mr W.L. Freitag – headmaster of Angela House School, West Bridgford, Nottinghamshire, was exercising the dogs at 11.20pm, when he saw:

"...three lights, travelling from the north-west to the north-east. They cruised majestically overhead, before I lost sight of them. One of them seemed to glow brightly and then dimly in flight".

A few minutes earlier they were seen over Long Eaton, by two young men – one of whom was Mr A Sheldrick (19) of Florence Avenue, Long Eaton. **(Source: *Nottingham Weekly News*, 24.7.1965)**

26th July 1965 – 'Bright light' seen over TV mast

A 'bright light' was seen stationary in the sky next to the Sutton Coldfield television transmission mast, at 10.30pm. It was witnessed by Mr Hicken and his friend – residents of Water Orton, Warwickshire – who were out walking. The two men speculated that it was Venus, but rejected the idea as it was in the wrong position.

"Suddenly the object moved and seemed to pulsate, the colour changing from silver to red, before shooting upwards into the sky, changing direction and disappearing from view."

Bright green 'ball of light'

The couple made their way back home and were discussing what they had seen, when Mr Hicken's sister arrived home with her fiancé. They had also just seen an unusual glow in the sky. Some time later, Miss Hicken went to the back door and, on opening it, sighted *"a bright green 'ball of light', which appeared to fall from the sky into nearby fields at the rear of the house"*.

Cylindrical object

Fifteen minutes later, an unidentified cylindrical object was seen hovering for almost 20 minutes over Walmley, Sutton Coldfield, by local butcher – Barry Cox, his wife, and two friends. Mr Cox reported:

"It hovered above the houses, showing a brilliant white light, for about 5 minutes – then moved away towards Minworth. As it did so, the light changed to red in colour – like 'live coals' – and moved out of sight. I could hear an aircraft flying overhead".

Over Bromsgrove on the same date

On the same date, two people from Bromsgrove (and another at Aston) sighted an object – about the size of the moon – emitting a grey vapour trail as it passed over Birmingham. According to Elmdon Airport, nothing was seen overhead (or presumably tracked on radar).

(Sources: Derek Samson, NICAP, GB/Bob Tibbitts, Coventry UFO Research Group)

31st July 1965 – Bleeping noises heard over Isle of Wight

Mrs Cecily Tait and her husband, Jack, of Orchardleigh Road, Shanklin, were disturbed by a strange warbling sound, just after midnight. They believed it was far too evenly pitched to be a bird. Within the next 30 minutes, they heard the noise (lasting half a minute, or so) on three other occasions, apparently emanating in a west to east direction. Mr Tait described the sound as, *"more like a bleeping noise, contrasting it to Middle C on the piano"*.

Neither he nor his wife attempted to look out of the window to identify the source of the noise.

(Source: *UFOLOG*)

July 1965 – Rocket-shaped object reported over Andover

At 11.10pm one evening, during the same month, Mr and Mrs L. Shipsey living in Weyhill, near Andover, Hampshire, were in bed with the curtains open, when they saw a rocket-shaped object, flying in a 'jerky' motion across the sky. It flew towards the east, ejecting a stream of silver and orange sparks. According to Mr Shipsey, a Mrs Barlow from Middlecote, in Hampshire, also saw the object pass overhead.

(Source: *The Sunday Post*, 26.7.1965 – 'Youths see Flying Saucer over Rocket Test site')

July 1965 – UFO landing, Hampshire

Just as strange was a report from Peter Willmott, whom we contacted after learning of his investigation into an incident which took place at Kempshott, near Basingstoke.

> "The couple concerned – Mr and Mrs Ralph Croft – came to see me and explained how they had observed a flat, silver coloured UFO, about 10 feet in diameter, internally lit with green light, fly past their house at 2am, making this weird 'whooshing' noise.
>
> To their amazement, it landed a couple of hundred feet away in nearby farmland, owned by their neighbour – Mr Gibbons.
>
> While they were debating who to call the object took off, trailing an orange flame, heading northward.
>
> The next day, when they went out to have a look, they discovered a burnt patch in the field, 15 feet in diameter."

July 1965 – Cigar-shaped UFO seen over Mousehole, Cornwall

Mr William Cornish of 3, Jamaica Cottage – a Post Office worker at Mousehole, Cornwall – wrote to the Essex UFO Society, telling them what he saw in July of this year, although the actual date was not given. It took place on a fine summer's evening, when he happened to look up into the sky, at 9.30pm, and see *"a yellow cigar-shaped object, moving through the sky, heading in an east to north-west direction. I estimated the distance may have been 15 miles away and wrote to* The Cornishman *Newspaper."*

AUGUST 1965

3rd August 1965 – Strange 'star' over Nottingham

James Johnson from Seely Avenue, Calverton (8 miles outside Nottingham), contacted the newspaper after sighting what looked like a brightly illuminated 'star', flying westwards over the town at 10.50pm,

> "... which disappeared but reappeared, seconds later, and made off southwards towards the Arnold and Nottingham areas, where it once again vanished from sight. Incredibly, I saw the same UFO the next evening, at the same time, but it was heading northwards towards Nottingham".

(Source: Alex Kenyon, Nottingham UFO Group)

3rd August 1965 – UFO displays over Oklahoma

The Bridgeton Evening News (4.8.1965), told its readers under the headline – 'Thousands report seeing mysterious objects in the sky'. Apparently thousands of people across the Midland area sighted mysterious flashing, winking and sparkling phenomena, speeding and zigzagging across the skies. This was the fourth consecutive night of UFO sightings which harried the police, who referred all enquiries to Air Force bases. Once again, we can see what should now be an all too familiar description of these objects to the reader, as exampled by one witness – a 23 year-old Sioux City, Iowa, English schoolteacher:

> 'I first spotted them while out in the car with my wife. Something zipped overhead; it was bright yellow and zigzagged slightly. This was replaced by a red light, surrounded by three white lights."

Others told of seeing what looked like a flat topped object, with two rings around it. It appears a similar phenomenon was reported in the skies over Tinley Park, Illinois, at 11.35pm.

4th August 1965 – Three 'lights' seen moving across the sky

At 9.45pm, Mrs Rosanne Bruce of Erdington, Birmingham, was out walking with her friend, Alison, when their attention was drawn to three 'lights' moving in a line across the sky. They watched as the 'lights' changed position, doubled in number to six (three above and three below) then altered colour to red and moved quickly away. (**Source: Birmingham UFO Group**)

6th August 1965 – Rotating UFO over Cumbria

Shortly after 11pm, Michael Dean – a clerk from Bradford – and his Keighley girlfriend, Molly Petherick, were on holiday, walking to a youth hostel near Ambleside, when the cattle in an adjacent field began to make a loud noise – as if alarmed by something.

The couple looked around, seeking the cause, and noticed an object rotating in the sky over Loughrigg Fell, which they described as:

"...domed, with a number of square windows set into the side, descending downwards, making a deep droning noise".

Molly became frightened and returned to the hostel, followed by Michael, who telephoned the police.

They arrived half an hour later, accompanied by a team from RAF Mountain Rescue, who made a search of the area using their headlights, but found nothing.

(**Sources:** *Newcastle Journal*, 9.8.1965/*Daily Express*, 9.8.1965/*Newcastle Evening Chronicle*, 7.8.1965/8.8.1965/ *Northamptonshire Evening Telegraph*, 7.8.1965 – 'Cigar shaped object spotted'/*The Sunday Sun*, 8.8.1965 – 'Mystery object buzzes couple')

13th August 1965 – Three objects sighted over Lanarkshire

Lt. B.G. Gunter of the Royal Naval Air Squadron, based at Milltown, was staying overnight, with his wife, in a holiday cottage at Abington, Lanarkshire.

At 7pm, he was approached by the owner, who asked him to go outside and have a look at a strange object in the sky:

"It was obvious, from its brilliance, that this was no star – so I fetched a pair of binoculars and looked through, seeing what looked like a silver, metallic, wartime barrage balloon, showing a corona of colour over the top half, a red/orange flame near the base, and two brilliant white lights. I watched it for about 30 minutes, noticing that on occasion it seemed to spin like an old-fashioned humming top. As daylight faded, the object disappeared."

Mr Gunter mentioned (in his sighting report to the Isle of Wight UFO Society) that the object was seen by a number of families nearby, and the incident was later published in the local newspaper.

(**Source: Isle of Wight UFO Society**)

14th August 1965 – Cigar-shaped object over Cumbria

We came across details of another UFO sighting, which took place over Westmorland (now Cumbria). This time it involved three girls, staying in a cottage at Windmore Green. They were awoken from sleep, at midnight, by the sound of sheep that were clearly disturbed by something. One of the girls looked through the window and noticed a cigar-shaped object, hovering vertically in the sky,

500 yards away, only 25 feet off the ground.

"The object was black, with vivid orange lights at each end, and emitting noise – like a propeller rotating, but without any engine (a description brought to our attention a number of times, over the

Cumbria

years) – and was rotating around its central axis. At one point, the lights faded and a white beam came up from the ground, the object being visible in the beam.

We watched it for about an hour and then got bored and went back to bed."

(Source: *UFOLOG*, Issue No. 18, 27.8.1965)

16th August 1965 – Cigar-shaped object and two lights

A vivid orange 'light', flashing intermittently and emitting a strange humming noise, was seen flying through the sky over Brough, Westmorland, at 00.37am, by Stephanie Collins and her friend – Belinda Clarke. Further observation revealed that it *"consisted of two lights, connected to a cigar-shaped object"*. It moved over cattle, which scattered in alarm.

(Sources: *Daily Express/Newcastle Journal*, 18.8.1965)

On the same day

At 11.30pm the same day, Mr C. Duckworth, his wife – Mary, and two friends from London, who were on holiday at St. Lawrence, Isle of Wight, sighted

". . . a bright object with a yellow-orange aura around it, moving irregularly through the sky, northwards, for approximately ten minutes, till it disappeared from view".

(Sources: Isle of Wight UFO Society/*Southern Evening Echo*, 17.8.1965 – 'Mystery object over Island'/*Isle of Wight County Press*, 21.8.1965 – 'Mystery object seen over St. Lawrence'/*Portsmouth Evening News*, 17.8.1965 – 'Mystery object over Isle of Wight'/*Isle of Wight Guardian*, 19.8 1965 – 'Strange object'/*Yorkshire Post*, 17.8 1965 – 'Mystery object sighted')

17th August 1965 – Four spinning 'discs' over Sunderland

Mr and Mrs Jamieson were walking along the seafront at Sunderland, at about 9.45pm, when they saw an orange 'disc of light' moving inland from the sea, heading north-west. As it disappeared from view, a second 'disc' appeared moving in the same direction, followed by a third one going in the opposite direction. A fourth 'disc' was then seen revolving at a tremendous pace. It was: *"seemingly some sort of machine"*, according to the witnesses. (**Source: Harry Lord/***Sunderland Echo,* **18.8.1965**)

19th August 1965 – Cylindrical UFO over West Sussex

Mr P. Harris, from Shoreham, sighted:

> *"... a huge, shiny, cylindrical object, hanging over the moon at an angle of 45 degrees, accompanied by four smaller 'disc'-shaped craft – two of which were lit on the top. The smaller objects then disappeared north, one by one. Ten minutes later, the larger object also headed off in the same direction".*

(**Source**: *Brighton & Hove Argus*)

19th August 1965 – UFO landing at Cherry Creek, New York

At 8.20pm, Mrs William Butcher, her son – Harold (17), and other children, sighted a large elliptical object with a red vapour underneath, which descended onto to the ground making a steady beeping sound, before then shooting straight up into the clouds seconds later. Side effects reported were interference with a local radio, and a tractor engine stopped.

A strange odour was noticed, also followed by the discovery (the next day) of a purplish liquid, two inches x two inches, and marks and patches of singed grass were found at the site.

21st August 1965 – UFO over Birmingham

Mr A.P. Scott of Harborne Lane, Selly Oak, Birmingham, was in the rear garden of his house, at 9.40pm, when he sighted a round, rotating, glowing yellow *'disc of light'* with a flat base, moving across the sky,

> *"...about the size of a car tyre, making this queer fizzing noise, heading east to south-west, before making a distinctive turn".* (**Source: Derek Samson, NICAP, GB**)

22nd August 1965 – *The Sunday Sun* publishes a letter from Mr William Muir

23rd August 1965 – Large 'golden ball'

At 9.30pm, Mr D. Gray and his wife, and a Mrs Joan Frost, were travelling towards Bournemouth, from Winton, along the road leading past the cemetery. They saw a distinctive 'golden light' moving across the sky, over the Boscombe area.

> *"It looked like a large 'golden ball', but didn't throw off flames; it reminded us of a golden Christmas tree decoration, but huge and rather mistier. It was not a firework, or lightning. I saw it in three different places as we continued on our journey. I estimated it was about 20-30 feet across in size, and travelling at an erratic but beautifully controlled course, in a straight line across the sky, before disappearing behind trees".* (**Source: Leslie Harris,** *Scan*)

25th August 1965 – Mysterious 'red light' over Isle of Wight

A mysterious 'red light' was seen moving across the sky over Shanklin, Isle of Wight, at 2.05am, by resident Jack Tait. He had been observing the passage of a satellite through a pair of binoculars, when he noticed a 'red light' low down on the northern horizon, which,

> *"... 'blinked' for a short time, at regular intervals, then changed to an erratic flashing. When it did this the light faded.*

I watched as a satellite actually passed behind the 'red light', which shortly disappeared from sight".

Black 'discs' over Stonehenge

On the same date, a number of strange black 'discs' were seen in the sky over Stonehenge, Salisbury Plain, by a couple from Southend-on-Sea.

26th August 1965 – Red object

At 10.30pm, a red spherical object was seen in the sky, at an angle of 90 degrees, flying south to north over Jarrow, County Durham.

27th August 1965 – 'Red light' over TV masts

At 9.30pm, Robert John Smith from Newport, Isle of Wight, sighted a revolving, oval, object inside a bright red glow – visible in the clear sky, apart from one or two large clouds hovering between the two television transmitter masts.

A minute or so later, the object took off and was soon lost from view as it entered a cloud bank.

At 12.30pm, a *glowing, red-hot,* disc-shaped object was sighted over Lansdowne, Bournemouth, by Doris Le Page, descending slowly in a floating movement towards Parkstone, before tilting and showing an elliptical object with a turret on top. **(Source: Kath Smith, Isle of Wight UFO Society)**

During the same evening, Miss C.H. Jones of Hales Road, Wood Green, Wednesbury, sighted what she took to be a star – until she realised that it was much larger than a star and bright yellow in colour.

"It seemed to be moving backwards and forwards, as though observing the city below. It was making sharp turns – far too sharp to be any aircraft." **(Source: Isle of Wight Society)**

The Evening Chronicle, in their edition of the 27th July 1965 – 'Its flying saucer season' quote: *The US Air Force has investigated more than 9000 sightings since 1947. They are usually balloons, birds, searchlights, jet exhausts, or kites. A USAF spokesman said, 'Only 667 remain unidentified, and most of these could be explained if more information could be given to the Air Force'.*

29th August 1965 – Were RAF scrambled?

At 9.25pm, Mr W.G. Olive – an inspector at a local car factory from Wilton Street, St. Mary's, Southampton – and his wife and son, watched a steady white object moving south to north – unlike any star or aircraft they had ever seen before. Interestingly, an aircraft was seen *"chasing around in the sky, showing a red light".* Was there a connection? Had the RAF been scrambled? We shall never know.

30th August 1965 – Cigar-shaped UFO over Nottingham

At 9.35pm, a light grey cigar-shaped object, with a red centre light, was seen over Bilborough, Nottingham. It dropped two '*sparks*' and moved slowly north-east to north-west. **(Source: Isle of Wight UFO Society)**

30th August 1965 – Motorist encounters strange light, Urbana, Ohio

At 10.30pm, M.A. Lilly, N. Smith, and T. Nastoff were being driven in a vehicle, when a white 'ball', 5-8 feet in diameter, trailed by a 2-3 feet light, hit the road 100 feet in front of the car, which bounced and flew away three or four seconds later. **(Source: *Project Blue Book*)**

August 1965 – 'Black Triangles' seen over Lincolnshire mudflats

During conversation with veteran UFO Researcher 'Dick' Thompson from Saxilby, Lincolnshire, he spoke lovingly about his late wife, proudly showing us the beautiful handmade tapestries adorning the walls of his small house. He then outlined what he considered to be one of the most extraordinary incidents he had ever come across. It involved the sighting of a black triangular object over the Wrangle mudflats, by Mr Peter Howard from Woodall Spa, Lincolnshire. He had been out walking, one afternoon, accompanied by his wife and sister-in law.

'Dick' Thompson

"As we looked out over the seawall, we noticed two black cigar-shaped objects, just above the horizon; the first was clearly visible, moving slowly northwards at a 45 degrees angle to the horizon, the second one travelling in the opposite direction. As the first passed out of sight, the second turned on its axis, presenting a narrow triangle in appearance – then full triangle, before resuming its original cigar shape. Within a few minutes, it was lost in the haze. At this point, we decided to leave, feeling distinctly uneasy about what we had witnessed."

Summer 1965 – UFOs over Diglis Weir, Worcester

Ray Badger from Acocks Green, Birmingham, admits that while his memory is not as good as it used to be, the events he witnessed during a night-time fishing expedition, remain crystal clear.

"I was with my wife, at the time, and decided to visit Diglis Weir on the River Severn, in summer 1965, for some night fishing, on what was an extremely clear, bright, night. We were talking in hushed tones at 2am, when – without any prior warning – a 'block of intense white light' switched on above our heads, no more than a couple of hundred feet above us. We staggered back in alarm on the river bank, unable to comprehend as to the source of this 'light', which was fluorescent rather than dazzling. After a few minutes, the 'block' switched off, and then a second identical 'block' appeared close to where the first one had been.

Haunted Skies Volume Two Revised

Diglis Weir, Worcester

The incredible thing about these weird 'rectangular blocks' was they didn't project any light onwards and failed to reflect in the water below.

A short time later, the 'block of light' switched on and off in the sky a bit further away from us – now pointing in a different direction.

At this stage, we started to pack up our fishing tackle, because we were becoming very frightened. Suddenly, one of 'them' appeared over the gasometer on the other side of the river – this time much higher in the sky. Just before it disappeared, there was the arrival of a huge shower of what looked like 'sparks of light' – similar to a garden bonfire, but much bigger. As these 'sparks of light' slowly fluttered downwards over the gasometer, they faded away, leaving darkness to close-in.

Although I continued to occasionally fish from this place over the forthcoming years, my wife refused to accompany me as she was too frightened."

August – UFO seen over Kidderminster firing range

Pete Drummond, whose house overlooked the Army firing range on the outskirts of Kidderminster, was getting ready for bed at 9.30pm. He happened to look out of the bedroom window, when he saw:

"...the unbelievable sight of a dark coloured 'Saucer' with cream windows, hovering over some trees about a quarter of a mile away from the house. I stood there, astounded, my heart thumping with excitement. After five minutes or so, it slowly moved away northwards, ascending upwards into the sky."

SEPTEMBER 1965

1st September 1965 – Bell-shaped UFO, Nottingham

At 1am, Mrs Poyser from Mere Avenue, Calverton, in Nottinghamshire, heard a noise like a vacuum cleaner.

On going outside to investigate, she saw:

"...a bell-shaped object, swaying in the clear sky, at an elevation of about 50 degrees, showing a red/green light on top and a blue/white haze around its centre, with what looked like a huge ring of stars underneath".

Mrs Poyser wrote a letter to the local newspaper – 'Now will they believe?' in which she outlined what had happened, adding:

"However, I really did see 'The Thing'. I do not drink and I wasn't dreaming, because I had not been to sleep. If it was over Calverton at 10pm, it must have landed somewhere, or else a lot of other people must have seen it."

At about the same time, a short distance away, Mrs Mills was awoken by an intense buzzing sound. Frightened, she awoke her husband. They looked outside, but saw nothing. (**Source:** *UFOLOG*)

Over Carlisle

At 2.45pm, a white-silver coloured 'disc', showing a dome on top, was sighted travelling west to east over Carlisle, which was apparently photographed by Penrith resident – Mr Malpos.

At 8.30pm the same day, over Ryton, County Durham, a silver cigar-shaped UFO, with a red flashing light on either side, was seen slowly moving through the sky before turning black.

2nd September 1965 – Spinning orange 'light' over Berkshire

At 10pm, Mr and Mrs Holliday from East Hagbourne, Berkshire, were sitting in the dining room of their house. They noticed:

"...an orange 'light', spinning in the sky, over the Chilton area."

Within a minute or so, it suddenly came to a halt and vanished from sight.

(**Source:** *Reading Mercury*, 4.9.1965 – 'Mysterious object in the sky')

3rd September 1965 – US Police encounter UFO

At approximately 2am on 3rd September 1965, Norman Muscarello (18) was hitchhiking to his parents' home in Exeter, along Highway 150. (He had recently graduated from high school and was about to leave for service in the US Navy.)

Five flashing 'red lights' appear

As he walked along the highway, with little traffic on it, he noticed five flashing 'red lights' in some nearby woods. The 'lights' illuminated the woods and a nearby farmhouse. (The farm belonged to the Dining family, who were not at home at the time.)

Norman Muscarello

The 'lights' soon moved towards him, and Muscarello became terrified and jumped into a ditch; the 'lights' moved away and hovered near the Dining farmhouse, before going back into the woods. Muscarello ran to the farmhouse, pounded on the door, and yelled for help – but no one answered.

Forced a car to stop ... took him to the Police Station

Two UFO witnesses: Lt. Joseph V. McCarthy (left) and Patrolman Louis Spence, were two of the 17 policemen who spotted the strange unidentified flying object.

When he saw a car coming, he ran into the road and forced it to stop. The couple in the car drove him to Exeter Police Station. At the station, Muscarello told his story to Police Officer Reginald Toland, who knew Muscarello, and was impressed by his obvious fear and agitated state. Toland radioed police officer Eugene Bertrand, Jr., who had coincidently (earlier in the evening) come across a distressed woman sitting in her car on Highway 108. When Bertrand asked her what the problem was, the woman told him that a *"huge object, with flashing red lights"* had been following her car for 12 miles (19 km) and stopped over her car before flying away.

Police return to the scene

After arriving at the police station and hearing Muscarello's story, Bertrand decided to drive back to the Dining farm with Muscarello to investigate the field where he had seen the UFO.

Bertrand drove Muscarello back to the place of his sighting. From Bertrand's patrol car they saw nothing unusual. However, when they left the car and walked towards the woods where Muscarello had first seen the objects, some horses in a nearby corral began kicking their stalls and making loud, frightened noises. Dogs in the area also began howling.

Bertrand and Muscarello both saw an object rise up from the woods beyond the corral. Bertrand described the UFO as *"...this huge, dark object, as big as a barn over there, with red flashing lights on it"*.

The object moved slowly towards them, swaying back and forth. Instinctively remembering his police training, Bertrand dropped to one knee, drew his pistol, and pointed it at the object. He then decided that shooting would not be wise, so he re-holstered the pistol, grabbed Muscarello, and both men ran back to the patrol car. Bertrand radioed another Exeter policeman – David Hunt – for assistance, and while the two men waited for Hunt to arrive, they continued to watch the object.

UFO historian – Jerome Clark

According to UFO historian – Jerome Clark, Bertrand and Muscarello observed the object as it hovered 100 feet away and at 100 feet altitude. It rocked back and forth. The pulsating red lights flashed in rapid sequence, first from right to left, then left to right, each cycle consuming no more than two seconds...the [local] animals continued to act agitated. When Hunt arrived, he also watched the strange object. The object finally flew away over the woods and disappeared. Hunt soon saw a B-47 bomber fly overhead, and he later told journalist John G. Fuller that *"You could tell the difference"* between the UFO and the bomber – *"there was no comparison"*.

All three men drove back to Exeter Police Station and immediately filed separate reports on what they had seen. Bertrand then drove Muscarello home and told his mother what had happened.

At 11pm that evening, Brazoria County Chief Sheriffs Deputies – Billy .E. McCoy and Robert Goode – sighted a large oval UFO, about 200 feet wide, hovering in the sky. Through binoculars it was seen to move swiftly towards their police car, casting a shadow onto the ground illuminated by the moonlight; when approximately fifty yards away, the police officers left the scene at speed.

According to the officers

"We saw a dark grey triangular object, 150-200 feet long, 40-50 feet thick in the middle, with a long, bright, pulsing, purple light on the right side and a long blue light on the left side. It approached us from a distance of about 150 feet off the highway and 100 feet in the air. Purple light illuminated the ground beneath, lighting up the interior of the police vehicle – warm enough to be felt. It left ten minutes later." (**Source:** *Aliens from Space*, **Donald Keyhoe**)

Although we cannot be sure exactly when the following incident took place (it may have been in the early 1970s), it is worth recounting, as it happened in New Hampshire. To the south lies Exeter where, in 1965, there were a number of UFO sightings.

The New Hampshire incident involved seventeen police officers, who reported seeing orange UFOs *"dancing around"* in the sky.

One of them was Sergeant Hollis Whalen (61) – a 17 year member of the Somersworth, New Hampshire Police.

He described what happened just before dawn, on 4th November.

"There was a loud crashing explosion just before it appeared. I saw this orange light 'dancing around' in the sky. Then it darted one way and back again. I was amazed. It was a clear night and I just could not believe this 'dancing balloon'. It carried on for about five minutes and then vanished. A few minutes later it reappeared and went through the same dancing motions. Once again, it vanished."

In nearby Dover, Lt. Joseph McCarthy (48) – a police officer for 13 years and a former US Air Force Bombardier – went outside to have a look, after learning of reports of UFOs seen.

"It was eerie. There was this bright orange light, pulsating and kind of dancing around in the sky. I called Officer Louis Spence to take a look. We drove to a better location and saw this thing jigging around. It would zip backwards till it became a pinpoint of light and then come back again. I'm glad Spence was with me."

Spence (42), an Air Force veteran, had this to say:

"I wouldn't like to say it was a spacecraft, but it was something I have never seen before."

Somersworth Police Officer – Robert Adams (27), who first saw the glow at 4.10am, said:

"It was bright orange and not quite as big as a full moon. There was an explosion, a short time

Haunted Skies **Volume Two Revised**

before, and then it appeared from nowhere. I saw it for maybe 45 seconds, and then it zipped away. I saw it again a few minutes later, and it went through the same up and down, sideways motions."

Dispatcher Richard Moreau told of relaying the information to Sgt. Merill Rinfret (24) and officers – Edmund Bressler (25) and James Gatcomb (26).

Officer Rinfret:

"I was baffled but wasn't scared; it didn't make a sound. I saw it in about six different directions as I drove around, and so did Bressler and Gatcomb who were in the other cars. I'm not a 'flying saucer nut' but there was certainly something unexplainable there."

(Source: The *Enquirer* – '17 Policemen in New Hampshire see bright orange UFO dancing around in sky – in same area where famous sightings took place in 1965' – Edward B. Camlin)

9th September 1965 – 'Rugby ball' shaped UFO

At 5.30am, Mrs D. Stevenson from Basingstoke, Hampshire, sighted an object shaped like a rugby football, hovering over her house in Paddock Road, towards the direction of Thorneycroft. She took it to be a red flare, until:

"…gaudy red streamers appeared to shoot out of it. It then increased in brightness, accompanied by a high-pitched whining noise".

(Source: *Hampshire and Berkshire Gazette*, 10.9.1965)

Over Kent

On the same date, Stephen Oddy and his friend, Graham Blow – members of the Air Training Corps from Leigh, in Kent – were on a visit to RAF Kidbrooke, when they sighted a silver 'triangle', motionless in the sky. The incident was brought to the attention of the *Kentish Times*, who contacted the RAF Station. A spokesman there told the newspaper that they had no reports, and suggested *"it may have been an airman, flying a silver kite!"*

Over County Durham

A whitish-silver object, *"looking like a dinner plate, with one edge cut-off, surrounded by a white aura"*, was seen in the north of the sky, by Mr J. McCerlane, over Jarrow, County Durham, for a few seconds between 10pm and 11pm.

10th September 1965 – Mystery noise, Birmingham

What was the cause of a mysterious noise – like thousands of roof tiles being flung violently about – accompanied by a clattering of what sounded like breaking glass? It awoke Mr L. Darrel and his wife, at their Church Road, Sheldon, Birmingham, address, at 3.30am. The noise continued for several minutes before terminating in a terrific crash, right underneath the bedroom occupied by the couple, causing the cast iron guttering to fall to the ground.

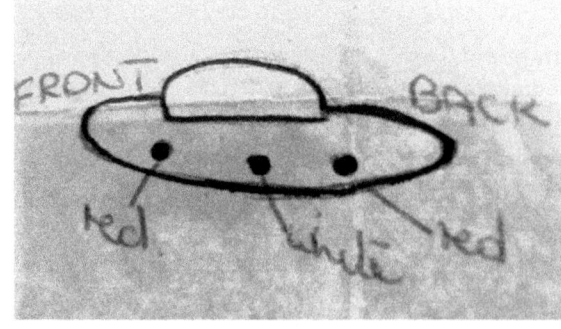

The couple later discovered that their next door neighbour had also shared the experience.

Was there any connection with what appears to be an identical phenomenon that took place in Warminster, beginning on Christmas Day 1964?

On the same day, Elizabeth Parry-Jones (12) of Broadstairs Road, Leckwith, Cardiff, wrote to the Isle of

Wight UFO Investigation Society, in December 1965, about what she saw, at 9pm, on this date.

> "It was a cold day but clear when I saw an object crossing the sky, heading west to east, oval or saucer-shaped, smaller that a sixpence held at arm's length. It had three lights; one red, the middle white, and the end red. A few minutes later it was gone from view."

11th September 1965 – UFO over Poole, Dorset

At 12.25am, Eddy Harvey from Oakdale Road, Poole, was in the process of locking his garden shed before retiring for the night, when he happened to glance upwards into the sky and see a bright blue 'light' approaching his position, about 500 feet off the ground, heading east to south-west.

> "It had a blue-white ring or halo around it, showing a circle of red lights or spots around its centre, with a tapered end on each side, and was rotating as it moved overhead, accompanied by this hissing noise – like a leak of compressed air.
>
> I watched it for about five minutes, until it became lost from sight."

(Source: Frank Marshall, BUFORA, Weymouth, Dorset)

12th September 1965 – Cigar-shaped UFO over Yorkshire

At 11.15pm, a cigar-shaped object with yellow and blue flames shooting out of the back, occasionally stopping and hovering in the sky, was seen over Cleckheaton, Yorkshire, by Mr Frank Holden.

Haunted Skies Volume Two Revised

Over Halifax, Yorkshire, on the same day

At 8.40pm on the same day, Heptonstall residents – Peter Coning and Dudley Yates – sighted:

> "...what looked like two car headlights, stationary in the sky over Stoodley Pike, with a 'red light' below; as the object disappeared over Hardcastle Crags valley, the 'red light' became more intense and increased in length. After the object had passed, there came a white light across its path; it looked like a 'shooting star' but it didn't drop."

(Source: *Halifax Courier and Guardian*, 14.9.1965 – 'Saucer seen at Hebden Bridge')

14th September 1965 – Close encounter, Mersea

We spoke to Paul Green about his memorable UFO encounter. He was initially wary about discussing the matter, after disclosing that he had been approached by two unidentified men, who warned him about the dangers of continuing to talk about his sighting, despite it having occurred over forty years ago – (a threat he didn't take lightly).

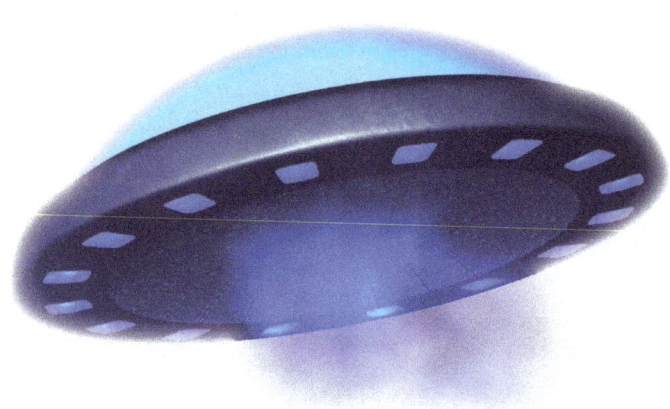

> "At 1am I was motorcycling home, towards West Mersea, after having visited my fiancée in Colchester, and riding along a stretch of straight road, south of Langenhoe Hall. I had just overtaken a motor scooter, when I heard a high-pitched humming noise to my left.
>
> I looked around, expecting to seen an aircraft, but saw nothing – apart from a tiny blue light in the distance, towards Brightlingsea, about five miles away. The light approached my position, winking on and off, crossing over Langenhoe Marsh – the humming noise I had heard previously, now changing to a high-pitched buzz. The engine on the motorcycle began to cough and splutter, and then stopped altogether.
>
> The blue flashing light was now roughly a mile away to the east. All of a sudden, an enormous object loomed into view. It reminded me of the underneath of a large spinning top, about the size of a gasometer. There appeared to be a dome on top, with a flashing blue light inside. It slowed, descended, tilting as it did so – allowing me to see part of the base, which was rimmed by numerous round objects, resembling a ball race in appearance.
>
> I walked towards the object and then felt paralysed, unable to move. The flashing blue light became so bright that it appeared to fluctuate in rhythm, with my heart against my chest. I could feel this tingling all over – like an electric shock.
>
> The buzzing became quieter, as the object descended over several houses at Wick. At this point, a scooter drove up with the engine spluttering. The rider – a young lad in a leather jacket – alighted. He stood there, petrified, unable to speak. I tried my bike. It started. Grateful, I rode away, arriving home at 2am, when I then awoke my invalid mother to tell her what I had experienced.
>
> The next morning, I noticed my hair and clothes were crackling with electricity."

(Sources: Essex UFO Group/Ron West/Unidentified newspaper – 'Man tells of seeing 'flying saucer' land.')

MAN TELLS OF SEEING 'FLYING SAUCER' LAND

Paxman worker says it stopped his motor-cycle

WAS it a flying saucer from another planet which 29-year-old Paxman fork lift truck driver Mr. Paul Green, of Ferndale, Mill Road, West Mersea, saw as he rode his motor-cycle home late one night recently? "I'm not a crank, but I think it was something from another planet," said Mr. Green, who described the mystery object as "about the length of two houses."

His motor-cycle cut out as he received a kind of electric shock from the handlebars of the machine as the "flying saucer" glided in from the east and apparently landed on the marshes by Fingringhoe Wick, he said. Although he admitted afterwards that he was "scared stiff", Mr. Green said he noticed that the object had a dome emitting a blue light, and that there seemed to be a blue light from a band around the machine and also from a cut-away portion underneath.

Also underneath were what looked like landing wheels on two large balls.

The machine disappeared from his view behind a clump of trees, but Mr. Green

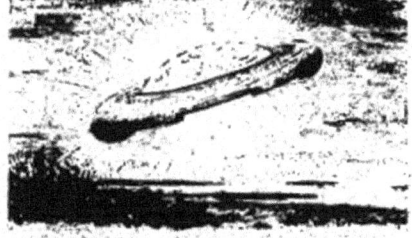

Our artist's impression of the "flying saucer" described by Mr. Green.

said he could still see the blue light over the trees for a while.

HUMMING NOISE

"I was riding past the home of Mr. Antony Buck, M.P., at Peldon, when I heard a strange humming noise, rather like the noise one hears from a kid's spinning top—but much louder and more piercing," he told a reporter.

"I had just overtaken a scooter when I heard this noise, and looking to the sky, saw a saucer-shaped object, with a dome at the top. Then my machine stopped just as if I had run out of petrol.

"I was dumbstruck. The object was about two miles away and about 100ft. up. It appeared to land on the Colchester side of Mersea Marshes.

"Then when I touched the throttle of the bike, it was as if I'd put my hand on a live cable—there was a stinging sensation all over me.

"I kept looking and there appeared to be a pulsating bluish light flickering on and off. I walked on a bit, push-

ing my bike, and then I kicked it and the engine burst into life immediately.

'NUMBED'

"The strange thing is that the scooter rider experienced the same as I did. But neither of us spoke; not one word was said—it was as if we had been numbed."

Mr. Green told a reporter that he hoped the young scooter rider would come forward to describe what he had seen.

Mrs. Russell Walker, of Peet Tye Cottage, Mersea Road, Abberton, a neighbour of Mr. Buck's, said that she had heard nothing of the incident but many people had commented on low flying planes in the area.

Mr. Paul Green

Lorry driver sights UFO

Just after 5am on the same morning, Stewart Mardle – a lorry driver, from Hatfield – was driving along the London to Gloucester Road, when he noticed a bright-red 'light' in the sky and a number of other Lorries parked at the side of the road. He pulled up and watched with amazement, at the sight of:

> "...a glowing red, oval, dome-shaped object, speeding across the sky, heading westwards, which suddenly stopped and hovered in mid-air to the consternation of the assembled crowds, before moving away and out of sight."

(Sources: *Gloucester Citizen/Gloucester Echo*, 14.9.1965)

15th September 1965 – Landed UFO, Lulsgate Bottom, Somerset

Insurance consultant – Kenneth Kimberley – was driving his Bentley along the A38, near to Lulsgate Bottom, during the early hours, when he noticed a patch of odd greenish-blue light across the road, roughly fifty yards in width:

> "I carried on thinking it was a patch of mist on the road – then the engine cut out and the lights failed. I immediately braked and sat there, trying to work out what the problem was, surrounded by this blue light. I then heard this shrill and high-pitched sound – like a jet engine apparently close and yet distant at the same time. I felt frightened. The back of the car then began to vibrate. I thought to myself, was it an earth tremor? I opened the door and got out of the car. As I did so, the 'light' switched off and the noise stopped.

I tried the engine. It worked. The lights then came on. I drove to the nearest telephone box and called the police. A short time later, two police officers arrived. I explained what had just happened. They seemed baffled by the incident and could offer no explanation." (**Source: Frank Marshall**)

16th September 1965 – Black domed object seen

At 9.13pm, a black dome-shaped object, showing a number of scarlet windows, was seen over Gateshead, heading westwards, low in the sky. Two minutes later it was out of sight. (**Source: TUFOS**)

19th September 1965 – 'Straight lines' moving through the sky

At 6.10am, at sunrise, Mrs Webley from Bembridge, Isle of Wight, saw something strange in the sky –

"...thin vertical straight lines, brilliant – like lightning – golden, rather than yellow, reminding me of a full length pencil, upright in the sky, moving slowly eastwards, past trees in the distance, and gradually changing from vertical to almost horizontal. I watched it for 30 minutes, before it was lost from view".

At 8.15pm, a bright yellow object was sighted in the sky between Alston and Westfield. It was *"moving in a number of peculiar hops, or arcs"* over the sky, according to Mr F. Powell of Sandown Court, Sandown, and others. (**Source:** *UFOLOG*, No. 20, 29.10.1965)

20th September 1965 – England: Close encounter at Felixstowe

We came across an extraordinary version of events, involving an encounter with a UFO and its occupants, at Felixstowe. It is still the subject of local gossip and speculation, over 46 years later, and we decided to conduct our own investigation, rather than accept the many garish accounts written in a number of UFO publications showing an orange glowing man, covered in flames, supposedly encountered by local man – Geoffrey Maskey, whom we spoke to some years ago.

"I was with my girlfriend – Mavis Forsyth, driving along Walton Avenue, Felixstowe, at 10.30pm, with my friend – Michael Johnson. 'Mick' asked me to stop the car, because he needed to attend to a call of nature."

Weird noises heard

"After a few minutes had elapsed, I began to wonder what had happened to him, especially when we heard what sounded like a mixture of very weird noises and a high-pitched humming sound, followed by the appearance of an orange, glowing, object lighting up part of the road as it headed off eastwards, over Walton Avenue, towards the coast. Now worried, I reversed the car up and down the road, with the window open, calling out his name."

Michael staggers out of a hedge, and taken to hospital

"About fifteen minutes later, 'Mick' staggered out of the hedge at the side of the road, clutching the back of his neck, and fell onto the ground – apparently unconscious. We managed to put 'Mick' – who had a noticeable burn mark on the back of his neck – into the Vanguard car, and rushed him to Felixstowe Hospital.

After arriving at the hospital and explaining to the casualty staff what had happened, he became the butt of much humour – being referred to as the 'Martian' by his friends. 'Mick', who seemed completely oblivious to what was going on, seemed to have some sort of fit and tried to take his clothes off, flaying his arms about. It required the strength of three or four members of staff to restrain him, before he was taken away for treatment."

When Geoff telephoned the hospital, the next morning, enquiring about his friend's condition, he was told that 'Mick' was being treated for severe shock and that nobody was allowed to visit him.

TRANSCRIBED FROM A TELEDIPHONE RECORDING FROM GENERAL DIVISION — B.9.AB

SPEAKER'S COPY

SIGNED ....

Extract from "Woman's Hour"

FLYING SAUCERS

B.9.   14.00   4th March, 1966.

ANDERSON: Hello everyone. We are starting today with a look at something which turns up every now and again in the newspapers - flying saucers, or identified flying objects as they're called. John Pyper has been investigating. But first, from a box labelled for us from the Radiophonic Workshop Woman's Hour's Flying Saucer. Listen to this:

"FLYING SAUCER"

MASKEY: Mavis and I were sitting in the car and we heard this high-pitched humming sound. It was really a ghastly sound, you know, and she was terrified by it. She didn't know what it was and I didn't know what it was. And all of a sudden we saw this light coming towards us. It was orange in colour, it was about 100 feet high near enough above the trees, and this passed right over the lane. And all the time it was emitting this orange glow, and the sound was coming from it and it lit the complete lane up as it passed overhead.

PYPER: Geoffrey Maskey describes what happened when he and a girl-friend were parked in a lane in Felixstowe one night last September. The third member of the party, Michael Johnson, had already left the car and then:

MASKEY: I wondered where Michael had got to. I shouted to him from the car but there was no reply, so I reversed the car a bit, calling his name from the car. There was still no reply from him. And all of a sudden he came through the hedge, clutching the back of his neck and his eyes. And I went up to him and he lay there on the ground. I was he was having some sort of a game, you know. But he was definitely unconscious. We picked him up and put him in the back of the car, took him to Felixstowe Hospital.

PYPER: Michael is still very confused as to what happened to him:

JOHNSON: I left the car and this thing come right over, and it seemed to attract me, you know. And all the humming row drawed me nearer and nearer, until I ended up in the field. And when I tried to look back it just got me so I couldn't move nothing. You know, I couldn't move my legs, I couldn't move nothing you know at all. I just stood there looking at it.

PYPER: He seems to think he was attacked by some sort of person dressed in green, with long steel talons on the end of his fingers which he revolved in circles in front of Michael's eyes. Michael doesn't know if it was this being that hit him, but he was hit on the back of the neck and he still has headaches. And the doctors have never explained to him exactly what was wrong. He was severely shocked, there were some red marks on the back of his neck which might have been burns, and a bump below his right ear. There were two other points which ought to be born in mind. Firstly, a nearby gasworks sent up a jet of propane gas at about that time. But the witnesses insist the light they saw was quite different, and quite simply Geoffrey has always been interested in in unidentified flying objects, known as UFOS. But Geoffrey isn't the only one who is interested in these phenomena. Many thinking men have been studying them for years. Like Gordon Crichton, a retired member of the Foreign Office, who serves on the unofficial National Investigation Committee on Aerial Phenomena in Washington.

CRICHTON: I haven't a clue as to where they come from and I have very good relations with prominent astronomers and I know that they don't know either. And where they come from is not really very important, because the universe is a rather large place. I suspect that some of them come from near indeed, and others may well come across what we think of as light years. I think it's highly likely that they come from many places, if one calls it that, or levels, and that there are many types of entity involved. I would say that at least five types of entity have been seen and possibly as many as 8 or 9. These beings are more or less humanoid, and if anyone comes up - as they always do - with the argument that this is impossible and say that man evolved here the only reply that I can give is that the evidence is quite overwhelming that these entities are appearing here, that they are humanoid generally, and it may well be that we didn't originate here anyway, and that some of these beings are our kin. I think it quite probable, we don't know anything about our origin.

PYPER: Another is Charles Bowen of the Flying Saucer Review.

BOWEN: A number of sightings have quoted materialisations and instant de-materialisation of the objects. Now then what were they doing? They go, say, 20 metres and then they're not there any more. It's not a case of them travelling too fast to be seen by the human eye. They are just not there, and yet traces of their passage has been found over, say, 400 metres whereas they disappeared in 20 metres. Now then where are they going? Are they going to another plane of matter? This is an idea which is occurring to a lot of people now.

PYPER: Jackie Wingfield had never been interested in UFOS until:

WINGFIELD: Myself and a girl-friend were driving along a road in County Waterford, Ireland, on Boxing Day and we saw this extraordinary thing travelling along from right to left which obviously wasn't an aeroplane but we..we couldn't say what it was. It was a bullet-shaped object which was metally and shiny and had a bright flame coming out of the back of it which trailed along with it, without leaving any mark on the sky. It was in view for approximately 3 to 5 minutes. I couldn't say how fast it was travelling. When we stopped the car it was obviously something which one had to photograph and we had cameras with us, and Elizabeth was able to take it. Although a lot of people have seen these photographs as yet there's been no explanation.

PYPER: The photos show a bright round object with a cloud of eflux streaming out behind. It's come out round because it was going away from the camera, which must have swung slightly. A colleague of Jackie's, aviation historian Charles Gibbs-Smith, describes it in more detail:

SMITH: This is the first photograph in the whole of this saucer business that I personally can guarantee has not been tinkered with in any way at all. If you look at the granulation - our technical photographic people say that this granulation has nothing to do whatever with the granulation of the photographic emulsion, but they also point out that it's very interesting because just after the object it streaks out, it's rather like tapioca, then it bunches together into a hard great white mass and then it tails off again. There is obviously a pattern behaviour there of some kind. And we haven't got anybody that can explain. There was one learned character who said it was sun phenomena; he's now taken that back when I pointed out where the sun was. And he said it was an ice-cloud pheonomena and we've knocked that one completely out.

PYPER: The pattern of this eflux behind it. Would this be the pattern of a motor?

SMITH: I've had it put up to me that it might be an electro-magnetic phenomena which would account for the fact that the photographic emulsion on the plate and through the lens could pick up something Jackie didn't see. This is, I believe, possible.

PYPER: Of course this eflux was much greater than she saw.

SMITH: Much greater. Much greater. And that may be because it's nature beyond the ordinary spectrum of the human eye which the camera of course is free of.

PYPER: I borrowed the prints and asked for comments from Professor Robert Boyd, Director of the Mullard Space Science Laboratory at University College, London. And he thought it might possibly be a rocket from the Alexforth Rocket Range, but the Ministry of Aviation informed us that no rocket was sent up on Boxing Day last year. You know the trouble with people who research into the origins of these objects is they start seeing the finger of the saucer everywhere. I've read articles claiming that everything from angels in the Bible to poltergeists and the recent New York blackout was attributable to their machinations. You name it, the saucers did it so to speak. I asked Gordon Crichton, whom you heard earlier, what were the findings of his Committee in Washington.

CRICHTON: I can only say that the evidence given in it about these flying saucers is quite overwhelming. There are many cases listed where motor vehicles were stopped by them, where there were radiation effects, and we think that these stopping of vehicles and the helium effects generally as we call them are very important, because this sort of thing cannot be attributed to imagination. It cannot be laughed off.

PYPER: Are they kindly disposed towards us?

CRICHTON: I think that some are. I'm quite certain that some are not.

PYPER: Can you enlarge on that slightly?

CRICHTON: No, because this could involve knowing what and who they are, and where they're from and what their motives are. And these things we don't know. I feel certain that this massive arrival here since 1947 is certainly in some way connected with the very dangerous phase into which the development of our race is now entering – namely the nuclear age.

PYPER: You mean that they're frightened we'll inundate space with nuclear fall-out.

CRICHTON: It's possible.

PYPER: Would they perhaps be more interested in us now that we're beginning to probe space ourselves?

CRICHTON: I don't think they are interested in us in the sense that they're longing to contact us. But that they are observing us, very closely. This is so.

PYPER: In a sort of Big Brother way.

CRICHTON: I think that some may be in a Big Brother way, and I think some in a more hostile way. I'm certain that quite different entities are involved. Some of them very much taller than we are, and some of them are only about one metre 20 in height. We've got reports of those from all over the world.

PYPER: How tall is one metre 20 in inches?

CRICHTON: Well it's not very much over three feet. I suppose you might say it's about three and a half feet.

PYPER: When do you think we shall know the worst or the best?

CRICHTON: Within the last year I've spoken with a very distinguished astronomer who is investigating this subject on behalf of his own government, and has been doing so for many years, and he agreed with me firstly that the landings last year were more numerous than ever before; that the whole phenomenon is reaching a point of crescendo, and he agreed that it looked as if something very dramatic was going to occur in the near future.

PYPER: How near?

CRICHTON: I don't know. But I think in the next decade. Something every extraordinary is going to occur. We do know that the astronauts have all seen them, we have evidence that in one case one of the Russian craft may have been forced down by them, our Committee in Washington know that one of the Gemini capsules – it was an unmanned capsule – was accompanied throughout the whole of its first orbit by several of these craft which bunched themselves round it, and were evidently studying it. And if you ask how do we know this, the answer is that we have members of our Committee who are among the scientists who are engaged in this work. And we certainly will not reveal their names, but we do believe these reports are entirely genuine.

PYPER: Well I'm not really worried. Earth is probably included in their packaged holiday tours. But here are Professor Boyd's comments on the interviews you've just heard.

BOYD: I believe in unidentified flying objects in the sense that I think there have been many flying objects which have not been satisfactorily identified by those who saw them. I don't at the moment see any reason at all to think that these various objects are not of terrestrial origin or something to do with our own atmosphere or local part of the universe. One of the most disturbing things about this kind of discussion is the fact that the people who are taking part in it always seem to want to keep the names of the folk involved silent, and they never produce evidence of the kind that would make a scientist come to so drastic a conclusion as a visitation from another planet. They use, for example, a lot of unscientific terms – like humanoid, matter on another plane. Matter on another plane isn't matter.

PYPER: Do you, Professor, accept the premise of people who believe that the trouble with earth is we are so conceited we think we know the lot and therefore anything that is fantastic is outside of the way we think?

BOYD: No, in fact this is not at all the scientist's attitude. The scientist's attitude is the humble attitude: simply to say we don't know and therefore don't let's come to fantastic conclusions, let's remain agnostic on these matters. But there is of course some positive evidence that we ought to look at. The state of this world can be studied back to a thousand million years by looking at geological evidence, and it seems to me very significant that there is no trace, and never has been reported any trace, of visiting machines, or visiting humanoid – what is the word that one of the speakers used? – visiting humanoids from other parts of the universe; there is no trace of this in the fossil records, there's no trace in more recent times of any parts or bits or pieces and one would have expected at some time there would have been failure, disasters, or even just probes just sent to the ground to leave traces. The curious thing is that all the physical evidence that one gets shown is extremely hazy in the form of photographs or black clouds in the sky, and never is any real hardware produced.

PYPER: Do you accept that the astronauts have all seen them?

BOYD: Oh no, this is simple nonsense. If the astronauts had seen them then we would most certainly have heard about it. There's no question at all. There's no veil of secrecy about this. The matter is simply not thought of in some scientific quarters. It's regarded as rather foolish.

PYPER: The scientists who are engaged in space research then are not either sworn to secrecy or frightened of revealing the truth.

BOYD: I have never heard it discussed amongst them. I'm quite sure they're not frightened of revealing the truth. They simply don't believe in it. They think it's sheer nonsense.

PYPER: And Gordon Crichton's answer to that was – and I quote – "the British public are being hoodwinked and humbugged, bamboozled and brainwashed by those who are anxious to hide the truth. But if you read serious literature on the subject you can judge for yourselves." And of course we must judge for ourselves.

ANDERSON: Joan Pyper report on UFOS.

Glowing Object Mystery

STAR 21/9/65

The story was told late last night by Mr. Maskey who, looking shaken, told an "Evening Star" reporter that neither he nor his friend had been drinking.

Here is the story in Mr. Maskey's words: "At about half past ten I drove my car down Walton Avenue, Felixstowe, and stopped about 50 yards past the last street-lamp.

"My girl-friend, Mavis Forsyth, who lives in Granville Road, Felixstowe, was also with me. Mick got out and went for a walk, leaving Mavis and myself in the car.

"After about five minutes, there was a noise. It was just like something out of a space fiction film—a high-pitched humming sound. A few seconds later we saw a long oval object in the sky. It was glowing a dull orange colour, and the light from it lit up quite a large part of Walton Avenue. It was in view for about half a minute and moved across the sky from west to east.

"Nothing happened to us, but I was worried about Mick. Mavis was petrified and grabbed hold of my arm. We called Mick from the car, but there was no answer. After a few minutes, I reversed the car, and we called again.

GEOFFREY MASKEY

"Suddenly, he staggered out of the hedge at the side of the road, clutching the back of his neck. Then he fell to the ground near the car. We thought he was playing games, but he was unconscious. We took him to Felixstowe Hospital.

Last night, a doctor at Felixstowe said Mr. Johnson had definitely suffered something akin to a very severe shock. He was transferred by ambulance to Heath Road early this morning.

Mr. Maskey was forbidden to visit his friend in hospital last night, but he hopes to discuss their experience later today.

FRIGHTENED

Miss Forsyth, who is 18, said: "I've never been so frightened in all my life. This light came over from the Harwich direction, and followed Mick up the road. He was out of sight but we saw the light pass that way, and there was a rustling in the bushes and then Mick staggered back."

Miss Forsyth told an "Evening Star" reporter, "Mick staggered back and collapsed outside the car. There was a lump and marks on his neck and he was mumbling something about a man in the flames getting him.

"We thought he was playing some sort of joke at first but then we realised something was wrong and took him up to Felixstowe hospital. Even the doctors seemed to think our tale was a bit of a tall story, and laughed about it saying the Martians must have come, but they arranged for Mick to be transferred to hospital at Ipswich," added Miss Forsyth.

"It seems all so unbelievable. I know everybody is laughing about it, but I have never seen anything like it," went on Miss Forsyth.

Mr. Maskey and Miss Forsyth agreed that it could not have been the flare stack at the propane gas depot nearby. They saw the stack flaring normally.

Mavis Forsyth

After being discharged, he tells of seeing two humanoid figures

Following his discharge from hospital, five days later, Geoff spoke to 'Mick' and asked him what had happened. He told him:

> "I remember seeing a glowing, silver/orange object, descending next to where I was stood – about twelve feet above me. Standing on the side of this 'craft' were two humanoid figures, wearing steel coloured suits, with arms outstretched at chest height, showing long pointed fingers. I saw them go back into the 'craft', and the next thing I remember was waking up in hospital."

Burn mark

Geoff discovered the burn mark had now disappeared from the back of 'Mick's neck. Although the police found nothing at the scene, a number people in the Suffolk area reported sighting UFOs moving over the coast, during the later part of the same evening.

22nd September 1965 – Air Traffic Controller sights UFO

At 9.10pm, Mr G. Auld – the duty controller at Woolsington Airport, Northumberland – sighted a bright object, surrounded by a white halo, zigzagging across the sky. It was under cloud, towards the north-east, at an elevation of 60 degrees off the horizon, and was lost from view in five minutes.

24th September 1965 – Huge object over South Wales

Kenneth David, and his brother – Michael, of Gorseinon, South Wales (then in their early teens), were playing in the street at 12.35pm, when they heard a peculiar engine noise.

> "Looking upwards, we were astonished to see, instead of a conventional aircraft, a huge object with a long slender 'nose', and the smallest suggestion of a 'tail'. Two parallel cylinder-shaped black marks ran the length of the 'squarest' underside of the machine, silver/grey in colour."

25th September 1965 – Five orange lights seen over Chisholm, Minnesota

At 9.55am, five orange lights in a row were seen flying across the sky, at speed, before making an abrupt turn during the minute's sighting.

25th September 1965 – Motorist paced by UFO over New Mexico

Dr. George Walton – a physical chemist – and his wife, sighted two round objects in the sky, at 10pm, flying side by side at 30-50 degrees altitude, which paced their vehicle while driving through Rodeo, New Mexico, for about six minutes. **(Source: Project Blue Book unknowns)**

27th September 1965 – 'Flying Saucer', Andover, Hampshire

At 4.15am, Janet Philpot – then a young trainee schoolteacher from Andover, Hampshire – was having difficulty in sleeping.

Looking through the open window, she noticed a star – brighter than the others in the sky. She watched as it began to increase in size, now showing some shape to it. Thinking her eyes were playing tricks, she turned away. Curiosity got the better of her and she got out of bed and watched the 'star' (which had stopped moving towards her) change its direction. It was now heading south-west to north-east – close enough for her to see quite clearly an object resembling two soup plates, one on top of the other.

> "The object was a gleaming metallic colour. The bottom of the 'saucer' was more rounded than the top. No windows, or portholes, were visible; it then vanished behind St. Mary's Church."

Terrified, she ran into her parents' bedroom, alerting them. They rushed to the window, but there was nothing to be seen.

(Source: Omar Fowler, PRA, from *UFOs: Guardians of the Planet Earth/Andover Advertiser*, 1.10.1965)

27th September 1965 – UFO display Isle of Wight

At 4.15am, an unusual 'light' was seen fairly high in the sky over Parkhurst Forest, Isle of Wight. It was constantly dimming and brightening for about 15 minutes.

At 10.30pm the same day, three red 'discs', forming a triangle in the sky, were seen heading towards the seafront at Great Yarmouth, just under cloud cover, by Mr Rutledge Rutter and Mr H. Morris, who were on holiday from Washington, County Durham. According to the men, the objects carried out a display of acrobatic manoeuvres across the sky, before eventually leaving in the south-east direction.

31st September 1965 – Two objects seen over Surrey

At 5.15pm, a woman from Echo Pit Road, in Guildford, contacted the police after sighting two objects flying through the sky, heading east to west, one of them trailing smoke. The police suggested *"they were probably high flying birds"*! (**Source:** *Surrey Advertiser*, 2.10.1965 – 'Birds with pipes')

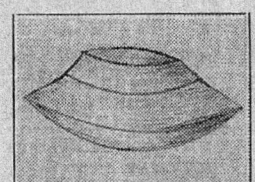

At 9.30pm, Wellingborough teenagers – Susan Foster and Janet Jacques – were out walking when they sighted two bright, pulsating, orange coloured objects, flying across the sky – *"like two pencils at an angle to each other"* – before they disappeared from view. (**Source:** Mr R.A. Jahn, BUFORA)

September 1965 – Mysterious 'capsule' in the sky over Essex

Former Royal New Zealand Air Force navigator – Martin Westgarth, and his son, from Upshire, Essex, were outside their home, at 10.08am, when they saw an object travelling towards the village:

> *"When almost overhead, it silently veered off towards the west, increasing in speed, at a height of between 5-8,000 feet, changing direction and colour, from grey to silver metallic, as it caught the sun's rays. Underneath I could see what looked like a jet of intense heat with a small turret on top. It looked more like a space capsule than a 'Flying Saucer'."*

September – Bell-shaped UFO, showing three globes

On a warm but overcast evening in early September 1965, Kenneth and Jennifer Williams from Gosport, Hampshire, together with another person, decided to visit Gilkicker Point, overlooking *The Solent* and Isle of Wight.

At 7pm, Kenneth noticed an object in the sky. It was heading south-west, towards Ryde, and then suddenly stopped in mid-air – much to the excitement of the party. They could clearly make out a bell-shaped object, now a few thousand feet away in the sky.

Jennifer decided to seek the safety of the car, as she was becoming frightened. The others continued to watch. Kenneth later reported:

> "It was dull bronze in colour, with a number of aligned horizontal grooves covering its surface as it spun in the sky, pulsing once every second. Gradually the rotations slowed, allowing us to see what looked like fluorescent green portholes, visible on the lower part of the 'body'. It then tilted at an angle, enabling us to see three bronze coloured spheres or globes, set into its underside, before shooting upwards into the sky and out of sight. Without doubt, this was the greatest experience of my life."

The purpose of the 'globes', set into the underside of the craft, can only be guessed. Were they part of some sort of drive mechanism? **(Source: Nicholas Maloret, WATSUP)**

September 1965 – Disc-shaped UFO over Indiana

In the same month, we learnt of a UFO sighting which took place, at 8.30pm, in Indianapolis, Indiana. It involved a mother and her two sons (7) and (9). She was driving home from a Cub Scout meeting, held at the White River Elementary School. The evening was warm and the sky was very clear. Several airplanes were in the air. Due to recent publicity about UFOs having been sighted, they kept their eyes on the sky. Just as they negotiated a curve at Haynes Avenue, they saw a 'band of light' in the sky – as large as a house – moving very fast, which then stopped and hovered, bobbing around like a small boat in choppy water.

The mother stopped the car and they all got out, watching what appeared to be a disc-shaped object with lights around the edge.

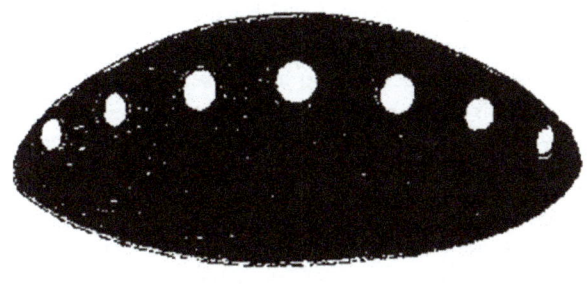

A group of aircraft was seen to head towards the 'disc', which took off southwards over the Glendale area few minutes later.

Afterwards on the evening, they watched Frank Edwards on the TV news, talking about what they had seen, witnessed by hundreds over the Glendale Shopping Center. He reported that witnesses described the object as a large 'disc', showing red, white, blue, and green lights around the edge, that was seen to head off eastwards, before halting and hovering over some radio towers, knocking a radio station off the air for a short time.

(Source: NICAP/Norman Croder)

OCTOBER 1965

1st October 1965 – Sighting by Royal Navy Auxiliary Squadron, Scotland

12th October 1965 – Pink 'discs' over Gateshead

A number of glowing pink 'discs' were seen heading across the sky over Gateshead, Newcastle-on-Tyne, accompanied by a humming noise.

16th October 1965 – Rocket-shaped UFO

A rocket shaped object – described as *"brown at the back, with strips of orange, yellow and green, with a blue point"* – was seen flying through the eastern sky over Southwold, Suffolk, at 5.15pm, by portrait painters – Mr and Mrs Harvey Bloom.

At 7.55pm on the same date, teenager Brian Capon was cycling down New Street, in Earls Barton, with a friend, when they saw a pulsating, deep-red, oval object, with a bright inner core, heading across the sky in a west to east direction.

(Source: R.A. Jahn, BUFORA)

21st October 1965 – UFO photographed over Minnesota

Mr Arthur Strauch (47), Deputy Sheriff of Sibley County, Minnesota, in the company of his wife, Mrs Katherine Strauch (44), housewife; Gary Martin Strauch (16), high school student and son of Mr and Mrs Strauch; Donald Martin Grewe (26), a technician, and his wife, Mrs Retha Ann Grewe (25), a registered nurse, were in the Strauch family car, returning to their homes in Gibbon, Minnesota, from a bow-hunting trip, at 6.10pm. Arthur

Strauch was the first to spot a strange object, which seemed to be 2,000 feet above the ground and a quarter of a mile distant, in the direction of the north-west. After watching for about ten minutes from the car, the group drove down the road about a half-mile and stopped. Mr Strauch observed it both with the naked eye and through 7 x 35 binoculars; therefore, his description was the most detailed. At first they heard no sound but then, as the object flew over them, Grewe described the sound as a *"whistling whine"*. Strauch, from out of the car, snapped a photograph just as the object began to move.

The object then moved into the wind for what appeared to be several hundred feet and stopped, for a few seconds, at which time its lights changed from a bright white to a dull orange, alternating several times. It then moved toward the south-east at a high rate of speed and disappeared out of sight.

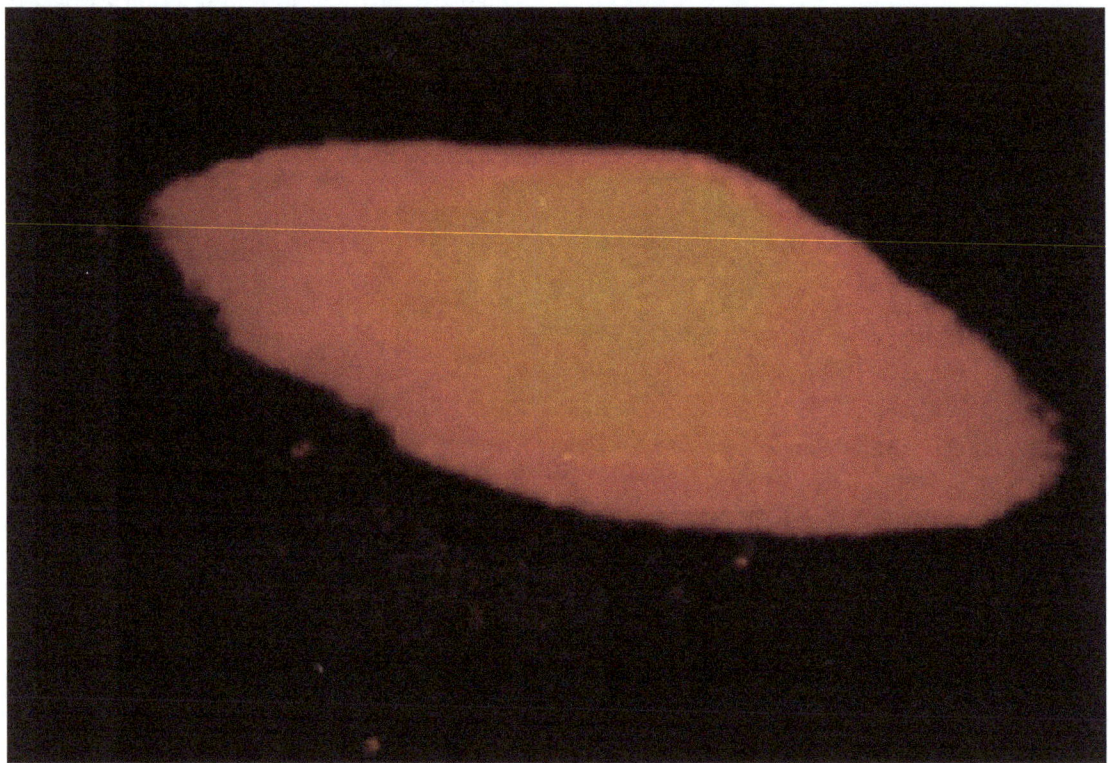

22nd October 1965 – UFO with antennae

Ex-RAF Photographer – John Holden, and his wife – residents of Abbots Langley, Hertfordshire, sighted an object resembling:

> *"...a very large pale star, electric-blue in colour, motionless in the sky over the town, with an impression of three or four 'arms' or antennae appearing to elongate and retract at two second intervals".*

Mrs Holden had the impression that the object was slowly rotating, with fixed antennae. The couple momentarily lost sight of the UFO. When they returned their gaze, the object had gone. All that remained were two bright but diffuse circular white patches, to the left of their position.

> *"Our first impression was that the object had split into two, although we didn't see this happen. The two 'patches' then moved away from each other, leaving a straight white contrail linking them*

together. The straight 'tail' and the lower 'patch' faded fairly rapidly. The other 'patch' enlarged, and moved to the left and appeared to pulsate and decrease in size, until fading away."

22nd October 1965 – 'Flying Saucer', Monmouthshire

Bruce Fielding – an amateur astronomer (12) from Cwmbran, Monmouthshire – was 'sky watching' with a friend, at 6.20pm, using a 4-inch Newtonian reflector telescope, when they saw a saucer-shaped 'craft' heading north-west to south.

"It was first seen 20 degrees above the North-north-west horizon, and travelled uniformly across the sky to a similar elevation in the south, in 60 seconds, on a clear night with slight mist."

25th October 1965 – Dazzling blue UFO

At 4.24am, a dazzling blue lit object – described *"as big as a dustbin lid in the sky"* – was seen over Walton Lane, Shepperton, by a postman. Later that day, at 11.50pm, Mrs V. Francis of Trewyddfa, Morriston, Swansea, was stood in the kitchen when she saw a bright 'light' in the sky.

"The kitchen was illuminated by the glare and heat. I had great difficulty in breathing and became frightened." (**Source:** *South Wales Evening Post,* **3.9.1965**)

27th October 1965 – 'Spinning top' UFO over Isle of Wight

Mr Mrs H.G. Cooper of 'Roselea', Green Lane, Lake, Isle of Wight, were walking along the cliff path between Shanklin and Lake, at 6.35pm, on what a was a clear night with light scattered clouds, when they saw

"a brilliant blue glowing object, with a white centre, falling from the sky – similar to a spinning top. It then stopped and moved along the sky, stopped again and corkscrewed upwards at fantastic speed, and was gone." (**Source: Letter to Mrs Kath Smith Isle of Wight UFO Society**)

28th October 1965 – UFO display, Cleethorpes

At 6.55am, a bright 'light' was seen over Cleethorpes, through binoculars. One of the unnamed witnesses had this to say:

"Four or five groups of 'lights' could be made out, surrounding a larger object. One of these 'lights' detached and descended, causing the rest to disintegrate, and began to perform the most fantastic of designs over the town."

The other objects then dropped downwards, a short distance, and reassembled – beginning the display, once again. These events continued until 7.10am.

At 9.45pm, what appears to have been the same UFO was seen over Cowes, Isle of Wight, by Mr T.G. Clapton, which he thought may have been *Telstar* or the *Echo 2* satellite. (**Source: BUFORA**)

NOVEMBER 1965

3rd November 1965 – Silver triangular objects over County Durham

Joseph Hyde (13) of Albert Road, Jarrow, sighted:

"...several silver, triangular objects, making a roaring noise, circling low over the town. Some of them were flying backwards (rather than point first), north-west to south direction, at 7.15am, over Jarrow, County Durham."

He rushed into the house and told his mother, Maureen, who initially thought he was making it up, but soon changed her mind when she saw them for herself. Her husband, who used to be in the Fleet Air Arm, was convinced they were not aircraft.

(**Source:** *The Journal,* **8.11.1965** – 'Flying Saucers buzz Jarrow once again'/TUFOS)

4th November 1965 – Cigar-shaped UFO over Berkshire

A cigar-shaped object was seen moving through fog over Reading, Berkshire. It was described as showing *"two square, brightly lit portholes, with flames emitting from the back"*. When the UFO passed overhead, triangular shapes were seen above and below. This was no firework!

8th November 1965 – UFOs reported

At 8pm, two white/silver elliptical objects were seen moving eastwards slowly through the sky, by Mr M. Carlisle of Holly Avenue, Wallsend-on-Tyne. He estimated them to be twice the size of the moon, at an unknown height, speed, or elevation. In five minutes they were out of sight.

23rd November 1965 – Sixteen objects over West Midlands

Birmingham man – Stephen Dale (member of NICAP) – told of sighting sixteen oval objects, moving in groups of four across the sky over Earlswood, near Solihull, West Midlands.
(**Source:** *Sunday Mercury,* **22.8.1971 – 'Mr Dale and the Alien visitors')**

DECEMBER 1965

2nd December – Dome-shaped UFO sighted

At 11.20pm at Sheriff Hill, Gateshead, County Durham, a pale blue object was sighted flying across the sky, south-east to north-west. It had a dome on top, flashing with red light. According to witnesses – Mrs M. Richards, and her son – the object disappeared but reappeared (now white in colour) in the same position of the sky, only 30 feet above the rooftops of nearby houses. (**Source:** *UFOLOG*)

3rd December 1965 – Villagers report sighting UFOs

What lay behind a number of sightings reported by villagers from Yardley Hastings, situated between Northampton and Bedford, during the first few days of December 1965? They described *"a red 'ball of fire' in the sky, dome-shaped, with slats underneath"*, which was seen, on at least four occasions, hovering over a wood on the outskirts of the village. It sometimes shot out powerful beams of light and appeared at 6.30pm, before disappearing from view by 8pm. On another occasion, the object was claimed to have disappeared when an aircraft flew near it.
(**Source:** *Chronicle & Echo, 4.12.1965* – 'Great Thing mystery reaches Yardley')

9th December 1965 – Brilliant fireball seen over US and Canada

A large, brilliant fireball was seen by thousands in at least six US States and Ontario, Canada. It streaked over the Detroit, Michigan – Windsor, Canada localities, reportedly dropping hot metal debris over Michigan and northern Ohio, starting grass fires and causing sonic booms in the Pittsburgh metropolitan area. It was generally assumed by the press to be a meteor, after authorities discounted other proposed explanations – such as a plane crash, missile test, or satellite debris falling to earth.

> **Mysterious object seen to crash-land in woods at Pennsylvania**
>
> **Nevin (9) and Nadine Kalp (7)**

Nevin and Nadine Kalp, who were living on a farm about half a mile from Kecksburg, were playing outside at approximately 4.50pm. Nevin, who was riding his bike, saw a strange object moving through the sky overhead, described by him as a *"star on fire"*.

This was then seen to crash into a wooded ravine, about half a mile away. Nevin told his mother, Frances, who was visiting the next door neighbour. She looked out to see a column of blue smoke rising from the trees. [It is also claimed by other witnesses to the event that an object – described as a four pointed star – was seen above the trees, and to the left of the smoke. Another witness reported feeling a vibration and *"a thump"* at about the time the object landed.]

Haunted Skies Volume Two Revised

While Frances was on the phone to the *WHJB* Radio Station her call was interrupted by the operator, who put her in contact with the State Police. They asked her to meet them at the *Pepsi Cola* plant, in Kecksberg, and show them the location of where it had happened.

John Murphy – a reporter for Greensburg Radio Station *WHJB* – was directed to the scene after being told of what happened.

He spoke to one witness and her son (presumably Mrs Kalp and her son) at the scene, who had arrived in a State Police car.

After questioning them, he saw a Fire Marshal and another investigator walk out of the woods, some 15 minutes later.

He asked the Fire Marshal if anything had been found and was told:

"You will have to talk to my lawyer".

After finding nothing of note, John returned to the radio station.

Fire Department

The Elyria Fire Department, Kecksburg, dispatched two trucks to extinguish 10 small fires in a 1,000 feet square area on West River Road North. One of the volunteer firemen was *James Romansky (19), who reported finding an object in the shape of an acorn and about as large as a *Volkswagen 'Beetle'*: [His testimony wasn't made public until he came forward in 1987]

Jim:

"...a humongous metal object, half buried in the ground, about 6-7 feet in diameter, 8 to 10 to 12 feet long. To me, the object looked like a fresh acorn that you would pick off a tree. There were no propellers, no identification whatsoever that would identify it as an aircraft. There was a bumper on the bottom part of it. On that bumper there was what looked like ancient Egyptian hieroglyphics.

It had markings – like stars and shapes and figures and circles and lines. To this day I've never seen anything like it. We were all standing around this thing, wondering what the heck it could be, and finally two men came down through the woods and, after taking a look at it, told us to leave, saying 'We are in charge. We're taking command. Get out of here.' – so we left and by the time we got back to the fire hall, the place was wall to wall with military."

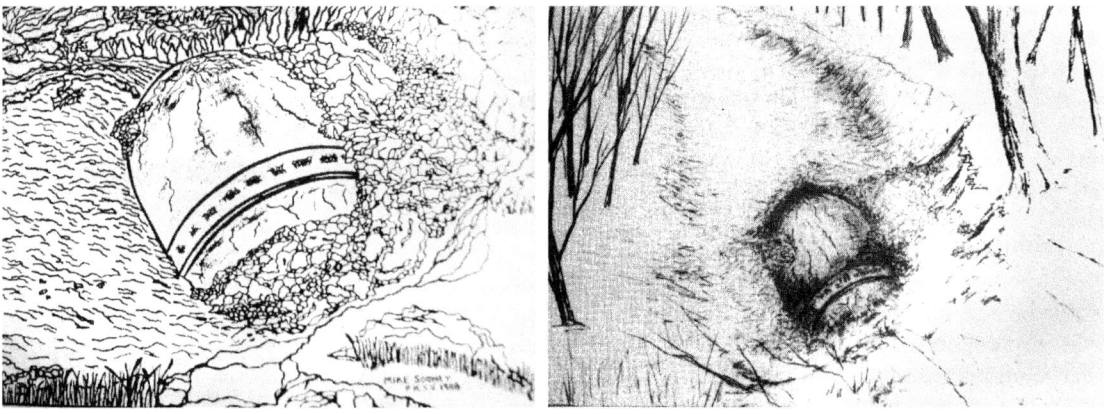

*Romansky was later diagnosed with two types of skin cancer. It is claimed that the analysis of the medical condition baffled local doctors, who had to consult out of state specialists. Jim has always considered the possibility of a link between this medial condition and the object, but of course proof is another matter.

Haunted Skies Volume Two Revised

Jerry Betters

Jerry Betters heard about the sighting over the radio and decided to head out to the area with a few people.

> "The military was already on the scene, blocking the main roads, but I knew the community well and took the back roads. I saw steam emerging from the woods, like there was a fire. There were also a lot of soldiers, what could have been top military brass, people in lab coats and something I will never forget – an object on a flat-bed truck with hieroglyphic writings on it that was leaving the woods. Armed military personnel yelled at us to leave the scene but I wasn't scared, just very excited. It was a really good feeling; my heart was beating really fast. That was no meteorite … it was something I'll never see again, but I'm glad I saw it."

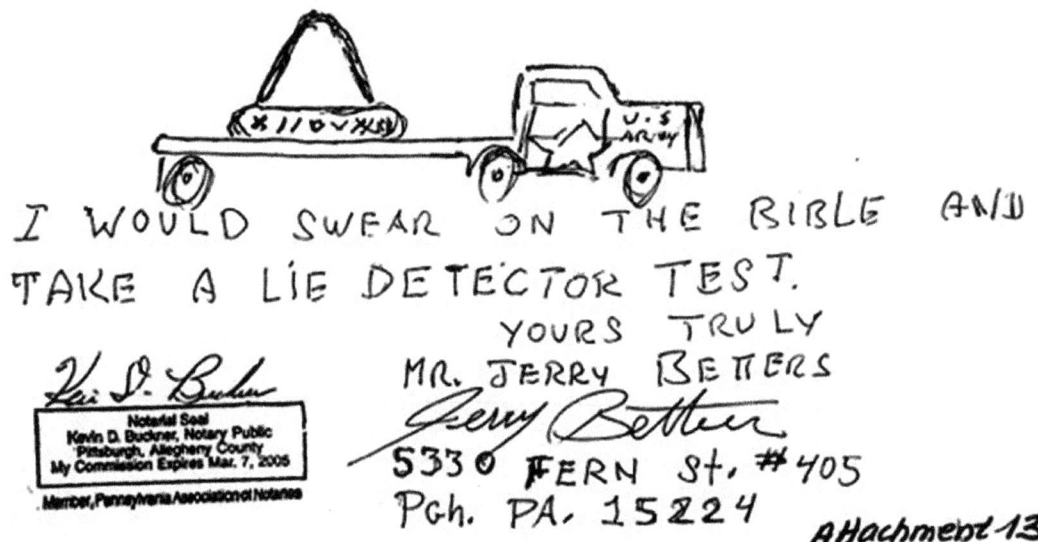

Military removed object

Jim Romansky then tells of seeing a jeep arrive down the hill with its red light on. Behind it was a large flatbed truck, on which was an object that was covered over. Other witnesses included John Hays (10), who also confirmed having sighted a flatbed truck with a large covered object – the size of *Volkswagen 'Beetle'* on it – trundling past his bedroom window.

UFO researcher Stan Gordon

UFO researcher Stan Gordon (then 16, at the time) was to later interview dozens of Kecksburg witnesses. He has examined several theories explaining away what had occurred here; the first was a suggestion

Jim Romansky shown stood next to a life-size model created for the TV program 'Unsolved Mysteries' 1991, as reproduced in 'UFO Magazine', Volume 6, Number 1, 1991, Vicki Cooper Sherie Stark

that it was a Bolide. Stan rejected this, knowing (as we do) that Bolides do not make turns and descend at slow speed through the air.

> *"I made a number of Freedom of Information requests to the Government about this matter, and discovered that there was a lot of interest displayed with memos and requests for information from Houston Space Centre, NORAD, Air Force Command Posts, the Pentagon – even the Chairman of the Office of Emergency Planning. Officially it was explained away as a meteor and that although a search was made, nothing was found. Clearly this is not the case."*

Space Debris

Stan Gordon

Another theory put forth by Stan Gordon is whether the object was space debris.

> *"The government has always monitored not only US space activity, but also launches from other countries. Going back into the records we have from NASA, and documents from other agencies, they apparently had nothing recorded for any type of space debris on that date and the time of this observation, so we also have to look to the other possibility – Could this, indeed, have been an extraterrestrial spacecraft?"*

Freedom of Information Act

Stan Gordon obtained, through requests made under the Freedom of Information Act, the official Air Force record of the Kecksburg incident:

Stan:

> "Eyewitnesses identified the military unit as an Air Force radar squadron, based in Pittsburgh. I believe the unit was part of a Top Secret operation investigating UFOs. There is no entry at all for December 9th of 1965 in the December log of all activities for that squadron. This tells us that somebody apparently wanted to keep all the information associated with the unit's involvement in that site away from public information. We can see that the government has not told us everything they know about the Kecksburg case."

James Romansky:

> "Official reports that the military and the government put out, as far as I'm concerned, are a bunch of bull. If this thing was a meteorite, then why didn't they just bring it out and say, 'Here it is', let the reporters take pictures of it, let the firemen see it, let the people in this area see it… why the big mystery?"

Stan Gordon:

> "Either, one, we're dealing with some highly advanced space probe, probably of a foreign nation, that appears to be very highly technical for what we knew about in 1965, or, the possibility exists that we may indeed be dealing with an extraterrestrial spacecraft."

The *Tribune-Review*

The *Tribune-Review* from nearby Greensburg, which had a reporter at the scene (Robert Gatty), ran an article, the next morning, quote: "Unidentified Flying Object falls near Kecksburg – Army ropes off area. The area where the object landed was immediately sealed off on the order of US Army and State Police officials, reportedly in anticipation of a 'close inspection' of whatever may have fallen … State Police officials there ordered the area roped off to await the expected arrival of both US Army engineers and possibly, civilian scientists."

However, a later edition of the newspaper stated that nothing had been found after authorities searched the area.

Kosmos 96 – one explanation!

The official explanation of the widely seen fireball was that it was a mid-sized meteor. Speculation as to the identity of the Kecksburg object ranged from alien craft to debris from Kosmos 96 – a Soviet space probe intended for Venus, but which failed and never left the Earth's atmosphere, taking into consideration that Kosmos 96 had a 'bell' or 'acorn-like' shape similar to the object reported by eyewitnesses – though much smaller in size.

In a 1991 report, US Space Command concluded that Kosmos 96 crashed in Canada at 3.18am on December 9th, 1965, about 13 hours before the fireball – thought to be the Kecksburg object undergoing re-entry – was recorded at 4.45pm.

In addition, in a 2003 interview, Chief Scientist for Orbital Debris at the NASA Johnson Space Center – Nicholas L. Johnson, stated:

> "I can tell you categorically, that there is no way that any debris from Kosmos 96 could have landed in Pennsylvania anywhere around 4.45pm – that's an absolute. Orbital mechanics is very strict."

Leslie Kean – her search for the truth

In 2003, as part of the new sci-fi investigation, Journalist Leslie Kean asked Nicholas L. Johnson – NASA's chief scientist for orbital debris – to recheck orbital paths of all known satellites and other records from the 1965 period. Johnson told Kean that orbital mechanics made it absolutely impossible for any part of the Cosmos 96 Venus probe to have accounted for either the fireball or any object at Kecksburg. Johnson also stated there were no other known man-made satellites or other objects that re-entered the atmosphere on that day.

In December 2005, a lawsuit was filed to get NASA to search more diligently for the alleged lost records.

On 26th October 2007, NASA agreed to search for those records, after being ordered by the court. The judge, who had tried to move NASA along for more than three years, angrily referred to NASA's previous search efforts as *"a ball of yarn"* that never fully answered the request, adding, *"I can sense the plaintiff's frustration, because I'm frustrated"*.

Author and researcher, Leslie Kean

Papers missing

During the hearing, Steve McConnell – NASA's public liaison officer – admitted that two boxes of papers from the time of the Kecksburg incident were missing. Stan Gordon – principal investigator of the Kecksburg incident for several decades – stated:

"I have no doubt the government knows a lot more about this than it has revealed to the public".

In November 2009, Leslie Kean filed a report on the results of the NASA search. Documents were still missing or reported destroyed, and little of interest was turned up relevant to the Kecksburg case. Of particular interest was a missing box of 'fragology' files, reported destroyed, related to recovery and examination of space debris. Kean said the missing files could be due to a number of reasons, including a poor filing system, misplaced records or records filed outside of the parameters of the search, deliberately concealed records, perhaps still classified, files removed by NASA employees but never returned (one such individual was named), files that were indeed destroyed as reported, and archivists unfamiliar with what was being searched for. In addition, the plaintiffs had to trust that NASA carried out the search as they reported to the court, since the plaintiffs were not allowed to examine the search materials for themselves; despite reservations about the thoroughness or accuracy of the search, Kean said they felt they had exhausted their legal remedies and ended the lawsuit against NASA.

Leslie noted that some items of interest did turn up, such as NASA's general involvement in collecting space debris and analyzing it, including interest in sightings of lesser meteor fireballs seen at about the same time. In addition, NASA sent out press releases to news agencies about these other fireballs, but NASA had nothing on the very widely reported and seen fireball associated with the Kecksburg case and issued no stories on it.

Pieces from the object taken away as souvenirs

She tried to get more information from David Steitz, the NASA spokesperson who issued the surprising statement in 2005 that NASA had indeed examined debris related to Kecksburg, supposedly from a Russian space probe. However, Steitz never responded. Kean was particularly interested in Steitz's source of information to make such a statement, since he also indicated there were no surviving records and the court-ordered search also turned up no relevant records. There are also records of eyewitnesses saying that they had "chipped off" pieces of the artifact – described as being a piece of semi-burnt metal,

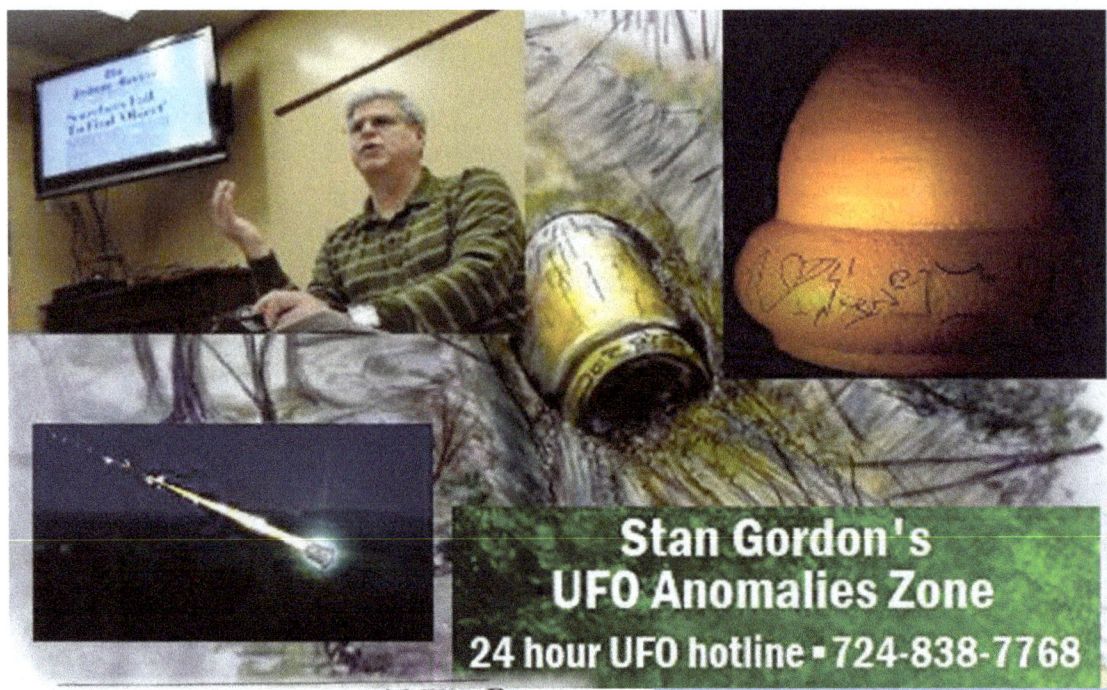

about 10 inches in diameter and warm to the touch. Photos were taken but when developed showed overexposure. Apparently, the unnamed witness who took the photos and then handed over the piece of 'metal' to the authorities died some years ago.

Stan Gordon:

"Whatever came down in Kecksburg, that night, is of high importance to the military agencies. The most mysterious thing about the whole case is the fact that, after 25 years, the government still refuses to give us any actual information on what occurred."

© 2006 Spectre Artwork Studio

Reported as a fireball

The February 1966 issue of *Sky & Telescope* reported that the fireball was seen over the Detroit-Windsor area at about 4.44pm, EST. The Federal Aviation Administration had received 23 reports from aircraft pilots, the first starting at 4.44pm. A seismograph, 25 miles south-west of Detroit, had recorded the shock waves created by the fireball as it passed through the atmosphere. The *Sky & Telescope* article concluded that *"the path of the fireball extended roughly from north-west to south-east"* and ended *"in or near the western part of Lake Erie"*.

A 1967 article by two astronomers in the *Journal of the Royal Astronomical Society of Canada* (JRASC) used the seismographic record to pinpoint the time of passage over the Detroit area to 4.43pm. In addition, they used photographs of the trail taken north of Detroit, at two different locations, to triangulate the trajectory of the object. They concluded that the fireball was descending at a steep angle, moving from the south-west to the north-east, and likely impacted on the north-western shore of Lake Erie, near Windsor, Ontario.

The JRASC trajectory was at nearly right angles to that proposed earlier by *Sky & Telescope*, or a trajectory that would have taken the fireball in the direction of western Pennsylvania and Kecksburg. Thus, if the calculation was correct, this would rule out the fireball being involved in any way with what may or may not have happened in Kecksburg. The JRASC article is often cited by sceptics to debunk the notion of a UFO crash at Kecksburg.

However, the JRASC article has been criticized as lacking any error analysis. Since the triangulation base used by the astronomers in their calculations was very narrow, even very small errors in determination of directions could result in a very different triangulated trajectory. Measurement errors of slightly more than one-half degree would make possible a straight-line trajectory towards the Kecksburg area and a much shallower angle of descent than reported in the JRASC article. It was also pointed out that the photos used actually show the fireball trail becoming progressively thinner, suggesting motion away from the cameras, or in the direction of Pennsylvania. Had the trajectory been sideways to the cameras, as contended in the JRASC article, the trail would likely have remained roughly constant in thickness.
(Sources: MUFON and WWW, 2017)

2005 Conference

*Stan Gordon's interest into this highly fascinating incident has developed over the years. He was the organiser of a special event to commemorate the 40th anniversary of the Kecksburg incident, to bring more witnesses together and even attract new witnesses who may be now willing to tell the group what they saw. *"Some still wish to remain anonymous."*

The program included the following speakers:

Stan Gordon – who held an illustrated talk about the incident based on the information he gathered from 40 years of research.

Robert Gatty – a reporter for the *Tribune-Review*, in 1965. He described his assignment that night and how he was prevented from approaching the object by numerous Army personnel on the scene.

Larry Landsman – the director of special projects for the Sci-Fi Channel. He discussed the channel's UFO Advocacy Initiative that supported a recent investigation of the Kecksburg case by the Coalition for Freedom of Information. The cable channel also produced two TV documentaries on Kecksburg that aired in 2003.

Leslie Kean – a journalist. She spoke on the forensic evidence recently discovered at the crash site and her interviews with Air Force personnel involved in the search of the UFO.

Lee E. Helfrich – an attorney. He spoke about the current status of the lawsuit filed against NASA, in 2003, to gain access information about the Kecksburg incident.

Robert Gatty

2003: Sci-Fi Channel reinvestigates case

In 2003, the Sci-Fi Channel sponsored a scientific study of the area and related records by the Coalition for Freedom of Information; the most significant finding of the scientific team was a line of damaged trees, broken at the top, leading to the site where some eyewitnesses said they saw the object embedded in the soil, along with associated fresh tree damage. Furthermore, tree core samples dated the damage to 1965. This provided physical evidence that something airborne may have come crashing through the trees and landed in the woods there at the time, which would contradict the military's official story of nothing being found. (However, one of the scientists instead suggested ice damage to the trees.) Minor soil disturbance was also found at the alleged landing site.

There was also a push for NASA to release pertinent documents on the subject. Some 40 pages of these documents were released on 1st November 2003, but were unrevealing. However, there are Air

*UFO/Bigfoot research Website: www.stangordon.com

Force Project Blue Book documents indicating that a three-man team was sent from an Air Force radar-installation, near Pittsburgh, to investigate the Kecksburg crash. (This was also reported in some newspaper articles at the time, also that Blue Book was looking into it but had no comment.) They reported back to Blue Book that nothing was found.

2005: NASA changes story to "Russian satellite"

In December 2005, just before the 40th anniversary of the Kecksburg crash, NASA released a statement to the effect that they had examined metallic fragments from the object and now claimed it was from a re-entering *"Russian satellite"*. The spokesman further claimed that the related records had been misplaced. According to *The Associated Press* story,

> *"The object appeared to be a Russian satellite that re-entered the atmosphere and broke up. NASA experts studied fragments from the object, but records of what they found were lost in the 1990s. As a rule, we don't track UFOs. What we could do and what we apparently did, as experts in spacecraft in the 1960s, was to take a look at whatever it was and give our expert opinion".*

10th December 1965 – Girl Guides sight UFO

Two Girl Guides – Sandra Page and Kathleen Clarke – were returning home to Enfield, Middlesex, at 9pm, when they noticed an orange 'disc' moving across the sky. As it passed overhead, they saw an oblong shape, with a ridge running along either side.

(Sources: Ken Rogers, Enfield UFO Investigation Society/*Enfield Gazette***/John Feakins, UFOLOG/Personal interview)**

13th December 1965 – UFO splits into three lights

At 6.30pm, a strange 'star' was sighted crossing the sky over Morpeth, Northumberland, by Mr M. Turner. Suddenly, it made a 90 degrees turn and headed off westwards, splitting into three separate lights – which moved away in different directions.

15th December 1965 Triangular object over London

Mr C.M.W. Martyn from Worcester Park, London, was outside his house, at 8.45pm, when he saw:

> *"...a candle wax coloured triangular object in shape, skimming across the sky just under the clouds, heading towards Heathrow Airport at a speed I estimated to be in the region of hundreds of miles per hour."*

16th December 1965 – Red pear-shaped UFO

At 10pm, over Gateshead, a red pear-shaped object was sighted stationary in the sky, by up to ten people.

(Source: *UFOLOG*)

20th December 1965 – 'Ball of fire'

At 7.25pm, a 'ball of fire', with a burning trail, was seen over Blackgang, Isle of Wight, heading south-west to north-east through the sky, by Mr C. Young, and Mr P. Darby, before being lost from view 30 seconds later as it entered cloud cover.

22nd December 1965 – Tadpole-shaped UFO

A queue of people were standing at a bus stop in Stroud, Gloucestershire, when *"an orange square-shaped object passed silently overhead"*, at 5.41pm.

A huge green tadpole-shaped object, with a flaming 'tail', was seen crossing the sky over Bournemouth, by a Miss Hussey, during the early evening of what was believed to have been the same day.

Another possible witness to this phenomenon was Edgar Shepherd – a retired headmaster from Abbots Langley, Hertfordshire, who described seeing *"a huge green dome, with a red 'tail' – like a tadpole – flying overhead from south to north"*.

23rd December 1965 – 'Cone-shaped' UFO

Police Constable Harwood, and a Mr Gibbons, told of sighting a green object with a red tail, moving rapidly through the sky, east of Warminster.

"It lit up the clouds, and when it went through them it looked more like a cone instead of dome-shaped." **(Source: John Feakins, Isle of Wight UFO Society)**

27th December 1965 – Box-shaped UFO seen

"A white 'disc', surrounded by coloured lights, positioned on top of what looked like a box, and appeared to be some sort of 'curtain' rotating over it every few minutes", was seen over Newton Aycliffe, Durham, at 4.45pm. It was travelling slowly at about 10 miles per hour, north to east, by Darlington man – Mr A. Parks, who estimated the height as being 4-5,000 feet. Fifteen minutes later, members of the Lunn family, living in Washington Crescent, Newton Aycliffe, County Durham, sighted a bright white 'globe', *"as big as a full moon, surrounded by red and orange lights, making a noise like a humming top"*, before it disappeared eastwards. **(Sources: Isle of Wight UFO Society/Tyneside UFO Society)**

As reported in 1978 over Barking, Essex, during a wave of UFO activity – was there any connection?

29th December 1965 – 'Cone of light'

At 6am, Mr Fairbrother, from Birmingham, was driving along the A5 towards Bletchley (on his way to London), when he sighted a red-orange oval 'bright light' in the sky, towards the south-west. Underneath this was positioned a bright 'cone of light'. Within minutes, it was gone from view.
(Source: Derek Samson, NICAP, GB)

Empire Film Studio, Hollywood, announce forthcoming film

In this year it was announced that a new 80 minutes documentary film on UFOs, entitled *Phenomena – Seven Point Seven*, was nearing release date. A company official explained the tile, *"Seven point seven means the 7.7% of an estimated 8,000 sightings classified as UFOs by the Air Force"*. (This figure is close to the latest Air Force admission of 663 unknowns out of 8,908 cases, which works out at 7.44 per cent.) One of the main sequences of the film includes the Socorro case.

CHAPTER 7 – 1966

UFO REPORTS INCLUDE:

JANUARY:
2nd January 1966 – Three 'flying discs' sighted over Cumberland
3rd January 1966 – Silver domed object over Sussex
6th January 1966 – Red sphere sighted over County Durham
6th January 1966 – 'Flying Saucer' landing, Cheshire
7th January 1966 – Mysterious contraption discovered in Hertfordshire
11th January 1966 – 'Flying Saucer' seen by housewife
18th January 1966 – UFO over Cheshire
19th January 1966 – UFO over Hampshire

FEBRUARY:
2nd February 1966 – UFO over Weymouth
2nd February 1966 – Diamond-shaped UFO seen over Carolina, USA
3rd February 1966 – Luminous globe
4th February 1966 – Spinning UFO – Did RAF jets respond?
4th February 1966 – Schoolchildren sight 'Flying Saucer' over Madams Wood, Manchester
6th February 1966 – Pulsating UFO over Texas home
22nd February 1966 – Leonard Cramp lectures
24th February 1966 – Object seen by Cambridge undergraduate
MOD UFO figures for February 1967

MARCH:
3rd March 1966 – Silver, triangular object over Northumberland
5th March 1966 – Yellow/white 'globe' over Tyneside
8th March 1966 – Chesterton, Indiana, USA
10th March 1966 – UFOs over Lancashire
11th March 1966 – Glowing UFO seen, Lancashire
12th March 1966 – Bright star-like object reported, Tyneside
13th March 1966 – Saucer-shaped object photographed by fisherman
14th March 1966 – UFO display was marsh gas!
14th March 1966 – UFO displays over the United States
20th March 1966 – Pulsating light over Miami
20th March 1966 – UFO lands in swamp
22nd March 1966 – Dark elliptical object over Northumberland
23rd March 1966 – Report of a strange craft parked on the Highway
28th March 1966 – UFO display over Washington DC, USA
28th March 1966 – UFOs photographed over South Yorkshire
28th March 1966 – UFO display over Washington DC, USA
30th March 1966 – UFO display over Long Island, New York, USA
31st March 1966 – 100,000 Americans say they have seen UFOs!
31st March 1966 – *Evening Standard* – 'Flying Saucers'

APRIL:
2nd April 1966 – UFO over Cumbria
3rd April 1966 – Similar UFO seen
6th April 1966 – UFO seen to descend at Melbourne Victoria Australia
10th April 1966 – Flashes of light over Northamptonshire
17th April 1966 – Police officers sight a UFO over Ohio
18th April 1966 – Strange noise over Isle of Wight
18th April 1966 – *Daily Telegraph*, 'Flying Object – 85 mile chase'
20th April 1966 – Elliptical object seen over County Durham
23rd April 1966 – Mysterious 'bubble' sighted in a field with occupant, at Maine, USA
28th April 1966 – Close Encounter, Cambridgeshire
30th April 1966 – Triangular lights sighted over a field near Warminster
April 1966 – Triangular UFO over Warwickshire

MAY:
3rd May 1966 – Three propellers on 'golden disc' UFO
7th May 1966 – UFO sighted over Goodfellow Air Force Base, Texas, USA
10th May 1966 – Six objects seen over Lancashire
17th May 1966 – Red flashing light and humming noise heard
18th May 1966 – Three or four objects sighted in the sky
23rd May 1966 – RAF Jet crashes – was a UFO the cause?
27th May 1966 – Prime Minster's Question Time
30th May 1966 – British ship sights 'globe

Haunted Skies Volume Two Revised

JUNE:
3rd June 1966 – Two white 'lights' over Bournemouth
5th June 1966 – UFO over South Birmingham
6th June 1966 – Domed 'discs' over Wisconsin, USA
8th June 1966 – Cigar-shaped UFO over Ohio, USA
17th June 1966 – UFO over Abingdon, Oxfordshire
18th June 1966 – Boy Scouts sight bell-shaped UFO over North Carolina, USA
June 1966 – UFO display over Bristol
22nd June 1966 – Prime Minister's Question Time
24th June 1966 – Four UFOs sighted
June 1966 – Close encounter, Cheshire occupants seen

JULY:
11th July 1966 – UFO over Pennsylvania, USA
19th July 1966 – Prime Minster Harold Wilson answers questions on UFOs
Mid-July 1966 – UFO hovered near Missile Launch Control Center at Minot AFB, USA
20th July 1966 – Close encounter, Isle of Wight
21st July 1966 – Scottish UFOs
22nd July 1966 – Triangular UFO over Wales
25th July 1966 – Carolina student chased by UFO
July 1966 – UFO display over Bolton
July 1966 – Silver UFO over Scotland
31st July 1966 – UFO lands at Carolina, USA

AUGUST:
1st August 1966 – UFO display over Maryland, USA
2nd August 1966 – 'Flying Saucer' over Lincolnshire
4th August 1966 – Cone-shaped UFO over Manchester
August 1966 – 'Flying Saucer', Coventry
14th August 1966 – Black elliptical object
15th August 1966 – UFO crashes into London suburb … causes burns
19th August 1966 – Domed 'disc' seen over Donnybrook, Dakota, USA
20th August 1966 – Object showing three lights
21st August 1966 – 'Flying Saucer', Penge, Kent – Three strange noises heard
21st August 1966 – Strange object seen over Isle of Wight
23rd August 1966 – UFO splits into five over Ohio, USA
25th August 1966 – UFO interacts with US missile crew and then lands!
26th August 1966 – Triangular formation of lights over Alabama, USA
31st August 1966 – Two lights joined by a bar, seen over Lancashire

SEPTEMBER:
1st September 1966 – UFO over New York, USA
3rd September 1966 – Three circular objects seen over Leicester
4th September 1966 – UFO display over Great Yarmouth
6th September 1966 – Three objects sighted, resembling 'flying crosses'
6th September 1966 – UFO sighted over Suffolk County Air Force Base, USA
7th September 1966 – Rocket-shaped object, Leicestershire
8th September 1966 – Eight to twelve objects sighted over Leicester
9th September 1966 – Object seen over Franklin Springs, New York, USA
Middle of September 1966 – Glittering red crescent-shaped object
13th September 1966 – UFO lands at North Dakota, USA
19th September 1966 – Strange object seen in the sky
20th September 1966 – Pilot sights UFO over Florida, USA
21st September 1966 – 'Thing' seen in the sky
22nd September 1966 – Chevron-shaped lights over Essex
24th September 1966 – UFO with 'fin', seen over Epping
September 1966 – Three UFOs sighted over Staffordshire
28th September 1966 – 'Bar of orange light' seen in Worcestershire.

OCTOBER:
October 1966 – 'Flying train' over Norfolk
11th October 1966 – Oval object showing lights
15th October 1966 – Grey UFO seen in Warwickshire
17th October 1966 – UFO over Canterbury
20th October 1966 – UFO over Bradford
22nd October 1966 – Solid white 'tube' moving over Lancashire
23rd October 1966 – UFO display
29th October 1966 – Red glow in the sky
31st October 1966 – Two 'discs' sighted over Lancashire.

NOVEMBER:
4th November 1966 – UFOs over Reading, Berkshire
7th November 1966 – Cigar-shaped UFO over Reading
8th November 1966 – Schoolboys sight two objects
8th November 1966 – Encounter with UFO, Shropshire
15th November 1966 – UFO with four antennae over Guildford, Surrey
Early November 1966 – Crater discovered at Chard, Somerset
16th November 1966 – Blue object in the sky over Reading
17th November 1966 – White UFO, November 1966
17th November 1966 – 'Octopus' UFO over Didcot, Berkshire
November 1966 – Strange phenomena over Essex
21st November 1966 – 'Flying bomb' UFO
24th November 1966 – Pale yellow UFO and three 'stars' seen
24th November 1966 – *Migel 5* singer sights 'lights' in the sky
25th November 1966 – A strange pulsating 'light' over Yorkshire.

DECEMBER:
3rd December – Drifting blue light and red light
4th December 1966 – Seen by motorist
10th December 1966 – Glowing object seen chasing another
13th December 1966 – Star-like object over Isle of Wight
14th December 1966 – Silver 'ball' seen over Isle of Wight
15th December 1966 – UFO captured on photograph, London
20th December 1966 – Glinting UFO
25th December 1966 – 'Flying Cross' UFO.

JANUARY 1966

2nd January 1966 – Three 'flying discs' sighted over Cumberland

One of the earliest sightings we came across took place at 3pm, when *"three crystal coloured 'discs', containing ten smaller objects inside each one"*, were seen crossing the sky over Carlisle, Cumberland, at an estimated height of a mile, by Mrs Haugham and her sons. (**Source:** *UFOLOG*)

UFO over London

At 6.31pm the same day, Robert Langley, Stephen Odd, and teenager Ken Rogers – members of the Enfield UFO Investigation Society – set up their 8-inch magnification telescope outside the Society's observatory in Boleyn Avenue. They saw an object moving across the sky.

Ken later said:

> *"We thought it was a satellite, to begin with. Suddenly, it began to veer from side to side.*
>
> *When Robert looked at it through the telescope, he saw it split into two, but the parts did not move away from each other.*
>
> *By the time it disappeared, we had watched it for 16 minutes."*

Four photographs taken of the object were later examined by BUFORA's Research Officer – Mr Nigel Stephenson, who said that he was unable to offer any rational explanation. They were also examined by the Midland Planetary Association, who promised to publish a detailed report of their findings in the next issue of their magazine. Unfortunately, the whereabouts of the magazine, like the photos, remain currently unknown. (**Source: Ken Rogers/The Dewey Museum, Warminster**)

Yarmouth, Isle of Wight

At 8.15pm, *"a pinkish-red coloured, oblong-shaped object, with a square end"* was seen moving across the sky over Yarmouth, Isle of Wight, by Steven Green (17) of Station Road, Yarmouth.

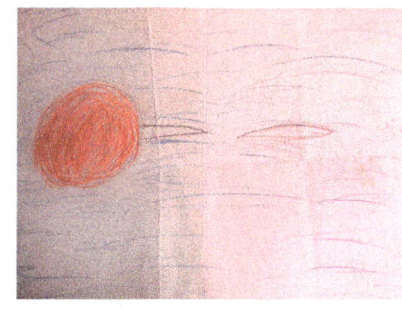

Just after 9pm, Miss D. Bennett and Miss S. Richard from Southwick, Sussex, were walking along Kingston Lane with another witness, when they saw:

> *"...a silvery dome-shaped object – larger than the moon – showing four large square lights revolving around it in the sky, moving west to east, before being lost from view as it went behind trees".*

(**Source:** *UFOLOG*)

UFO sighted over Broadwater, West Sussex

They were not the only ones to sight something unusual that evening. A woman from Broadwater contacted the authorities, after seeing something unusual move across the sky. Enquiries made with the local airport, at Shoreham, revealed the last flight had been at 5pm, and no weather balloons had been launched off the south coast which could have been used to explain the incident away.
(**Source:** *UFOLOG/Worthing Gazette,* **12.1.1966**)

3rd January 1966 – Silver domed object over Sussex

Between 9pm and 9.30pm, a woman from Southwick, Sussex, and two girls, independently sighted *"a silvery dome-shaped object – larger than the moon – showing four red square-shaped lights around its base"*, which was apparently revolving as it moved through the sky in a west to east direction. (**Source:** *UFOLOG*)

Haunted Skies Volume Two Revised

6th January 1966 – 'Flying Saucer' landing, Cheshire

PC Colin Perks

At 4.10am, Police Constable Colin Clive Perks (aged 28), with four years service in the Cheshire Constabulary, was checking the back door of a shop behind Finnegan's shop (now Hoopers) in Alderley Road, Wilmslow, Cheshire, near the A34, when he heard a high-pitched whining noise. He said:

> "I was amazed to see a greenish-grey flying object, hovering about 35 feet off the ground, about a hundred yards away, above the grass of a meadow. It was approximately twenty feet in width and thirty-five feet in length, elliptical in shape and emanating an eerie glow."

After a few seconds the object then moved quickly away, heading in an east to south direction, where it was soon lost from sight.

Mrs Amy Walker – then living on the A538 Altrincham Road, Morley, Wilmslow – was retiring to bed, at 4.30am on the 7th January 1966 (twenty minutes after PC Perks sighted the UFO), when she saw:

> "...a pearly-green coloured object hovering over the Lyndon garage, 50 feet away, opposite my house – as big as a shilling at arm's length – just at the side of the garage roof. It then shot away, moving at a speed I estimated to be 70 miles per hour".

---

*Ministry of Aviation was a department of the United Kingdom government, established in 1959. Its responsibilities included the regulation of civil aviation and the supply of military aircraft, which it took on from the Ministry of Supply.

In 1967, the supply of military aircraft was switched to the Ministry of Technology, while the Board of Trade took on its regulatory responsibilities. This is not to be confused with the Air Ministry, which was purely for the RAF and existed from 1918 to 1964.

Haunted Skies **Volume Two Revised**

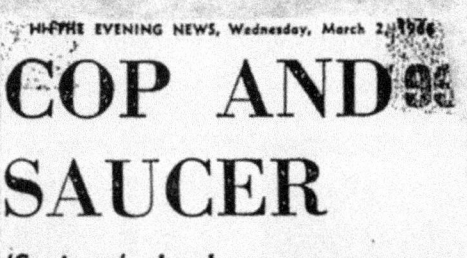

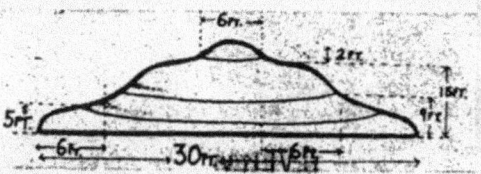

His official report into the matter was later sent to the Ministry of Aviation by the Deputy Chief Constable, and filed as secret until declassified, over 30 years later – although some details were initially released to newspapers, a few months after the sighting.

Gordon Creighton visits Colin

We discovered that Gordon Creighton – a consultant for *Flying Saucer Review* – and his colleague, Mr R.H.B. Winder, B.Sc., interviewed Police Constable Perks on the 10th March 1966, who then showed them the scene of where the incident had taken place.

Mr Winder later reported:

> "We understand that a colleague of PC Perks had looked over the northern end of the car park (behind the Rex Cinema) shortly after the event, and found it thinly covered by glass-like particles. After the departure, Perks hurried to the police station and wrote a report. He also telephoned Ringway Airport and Jodrell Bank, but they were unable to help him. His report was not published until the 2nd March 1966. In the meantime two Ministry of Aviation representatives interviewed him and inspected the location.
>
> After publication, a Mrs Amy Walker claimed to have seen a pearly-green object over a London garage during the same evening."

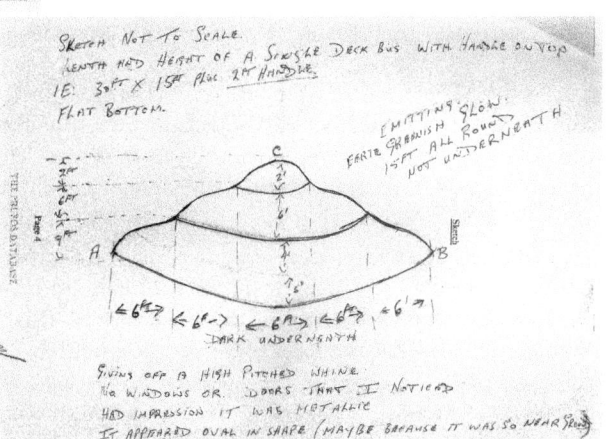

Although we never had the opportunity to speak to Colin (who passed away a few years ago), he was, in recent years, interviewed by Gary Heseltine – an ex-CID officer with the British Transport Police – from which the following account was obtained:

> "On Thursday evening, 6th January 1966, I was posted to night shift, working the town centre beat; my only means of communication being ten minute checks in from a telephone box every 30 minutes, situated along my beat. [Police personal radios not issued then]
>
> At 4.05am I was checking the rear of property on the east side of Alderley Road from north to south, behind the Rex Cinema – the car park being empty, as was the Finnegan's car park (situated a short distance from the A34 Manchester to Alderley road). I walked over the narrow service road and made my way to the rear of the first shops' back yards and had taken just a couple of steps, when I heard this high-pitched whine, at about 4.10am. My first instinct was to suspect intruders at the jeweller's or other close shops along the route. I stood still and analysed the situation, and then decided to make my way to the jewellers.
>
> I turned around and was literally stopped in my tracks, when I saw an apparent metallic object – about the size of a single-decker bus – approximately 30 feet by 18 feet, symmetrical in shape, appearing elliptical (though this appearance may have been due to the object being so low). It had a flat bottom and was quite dark underneath; I could see two tiers, plus what looked like a handle on top, like a dustbin lid. It was emitting this greenish-grey 'ghoulish glow' about fifteen feet all around, except for the bottom. I did not notice any windows, doors, aerials or portholes; neither did I see anything resembling an undercarriage. The object was about 100 yards away, appeared stationary, and approximately 35 feet above the ground. It remained in this position for about five seconds, although it seemed like a lifetime. Then, without any change in the sound, it moved at incredibly fast speed in an east-south-east direction and was lost from view before it reached the treetops and houses, some 500 yards away."

Officers returned to the scene

When PC Perks arrived back at the Police Station, he told a fellow constable and sergeant what he had seen – as a result of which the three of them, at first light, returned to the scene of the incident, where they discovered the car park of Finnegan's (now Hoopers) covered in 2-3in of what looked like broken windscreen glass, that disappeared from view one-and-a-half hours later.

Another possible witness found

MAPIT UFO researcher Derek Woods from Sale, Manchester, told us of being contacted by a local farmer from Alderley Edge (two miles from the town centre). The farmer said he knew of a nurse who was near the *Rex* Cinema, Wilmslow, on the same date, when she sighted what she believes to have been the same saucer-shaped object moving through the air, but – fearing ridicule – chose to keep quiet.

According to Nick Redfern, there was a considerable file relating to this matter held at the Public Records Office. The file was available for public scrutiny and revealed a visit made to the location by two MOD officials, who recovered some of the 'glass debris'. This was later analysed but found not to be of any significance. But what was it? A lot of people would love to know the answer.

(Sources: *Evening News*, 2.3.1966 – 'Cops and Saucers'/*Daily Mirror*, 3.3.1966 – 'Beg to report sir, one Flying Saucer'/*Daily Sketch*, 3.3.1968 – 'PC claims he saw a Flying Saucer'/Gary Heseltine, PRUFOS/*Flying Saucer Review*, March/April 1966, Volume 12, No. 2, 'Wilmslow PCs Report' – R.H.B Winder/Mrs Bridie Perks/Joan Nelstrop, DIGAP)

6th January 1966 – Red sphere sighted over County Durham

At 8pm, a red sphere was seen in the western direction of the sky, over Usworth, Washington, County Durham, by Mr and Mrs Lowdenson, who reported it as: *"flashing intermittently with light, followed by the sound of rushing wind"*, before disappearing behind adjacent houses.

Ted Holiday sights UFO

At approximately the same time and date, Frederick 'Ted' William Holiday – well-known journalist for the *Western Mail*, angler, author and cryptozoologist, who had served in the RAF between 1939 and 1950 – was with several other anglers, out fishing at Saundersfoot, when their attention was drawn to an object moving rapidly from left to right over the sea, at a height of about 500 feet.

"At half-second intervals it emitted a pulse of light, which lit up the surrounding cloud base."

In the same month, a dim yellow disc-shaped object was seen by Mr J. Cram over Rowlands Gill, County Durham, at 7.10pm. It was 80 degrees off the horizon, heading eastwards, at approximately 2,000 feet.

'Ted 'Holiday

7th January 1966 – Mysterious contraption discovered in Hertfordshire

Dame Rebecca West

At 2.45pm well-known writer *Dame Rebecca West, living at Ibstone House, in Hertfordshire, was in the grounds of her home when she noticed a man walking on her property, some distance to the right of the path she was following. Her curiosity aroused, she watched as he reached a point where the wood ended, near a hedge running down the valley along a sharp ridge, and stopped just past a gap in the hedge, allowing her to see what appeared to be some form of strange aerial contraption.

Ibstone House,

"It seemed to descend quite rapidly on the other side of the hedge from the man, but close to it. It consisted of something like a metal band, grey-blue in colour, flattened at one point so as to seem almost leaf-like, crossed with a herringbone system of metal strips. There was also, somehow attached to these, an odd object – like a bag, with an opening that had points of yellowish material. As I looked, the whole thing collapsed to the ground. I saw it crumple, but crumpling is not the right word. The metal band seemed to curl backwards and disappear, while the curious 'bag', about six feet tall, looked as if someone was squeezing the air out of the lower portion – so that all the points stood up and fell back."

The mystery man was then seen to turn around and follow the hedge track down to the valley, looking once or twice to his left – as if he was scrutinising the valley, seemingly unaware of her presence – but at

---

*Rebecca West – the writer and journalist – was born Cicely Fairfield, in 1892. She has been an irresistible subject for biographers since her death in 1983. Her talent was prodigious, her journalism outstanding, and her private life full of drama. She left much revealing personal material behind, but she has proved a curiously intractable subject – a brilliant, demanding woman who it is hard not to admire but also hard to like.

the bottom of the track he stopped again and looked around the slope where she was standing, this time as if he had suddenly become aware of her.

> "We stood and looked at each other for quite a long time and I had an uncomfortable feeling. I felt uneasy and went home. Later that day I spoke to one of the farm workers, who told me that he had seen what he believed to be a helicopter flying in the vicinity earlier."

Dame Rebecca wrote to the MOD

Dame Rebecca wrote to the MOD, explaining what had happened, and later received a reply from Mr L.K. Akhurst, suggesting she *"...may have seen a helicopter, possibly the Bell 47, or similar type, which in conditions of poor visibility, appears to have some unusual characteristics"*.

If this was the case, why did the MOD deem fit to classify this sighting as restricted?

Surely enquiries could have been made to trace the helicopter responsible, if it had made an unscheduled landing in that locality on the day in question?

Dame Rebecca wrote back to the MOD, denying she had seen a helicopter.

> "To have appeared where I saw it, a helicopter would have had to fly 20 to 30 yards with its lower half deeply embedded in the earth and of the fact that there was, at the time, complete silence and that visibility seemed, to me, not poor at all – for I spotted several birds at a considerable distance. I do not expect an answer to this letter. I reported the incident partly because I feared the object might be a parachute, or some such construction, which was being used to drop somebody, or something, for criminal purposes, and partly because the construction I saw, or thought I saw, puzzled me, as I could not conceive how it could have got into the air, could stay in the air, or could be brought down out of the air."

The response of this letter was short and to the point.

> "No further evidence has become available concerning this particular sighting, so there is nothing to add.
>
> Signed,
>
> L.K. Akhurst."

Was there was a connection with a report from Mr and Mrs Woolford living at Minety, near Salisbury, Wiltshire? They contacted the police, after coming across *"a metallic contraption, surmounted by a wheel, supported by a form of parachute, with an arrangement of metal rods and fabric attached to a balloon, lying on the ground"*, and were later told by them that the object had been launched from a Government Establishment, at Larkhill.

11th January 1966 – 'Flying Saucer' seen by housewife

Mrs Margaret Hards of Somer Road, Leyton, in East London, glanced out of her window during the early morning, and was shocked to see:

> "...a 'square' starting to appear and then it changed to a sky-blue saucer-shaped object, resembling a child's humming top, about 75 yards away in the sky. Before I could awake my husband it vanished."

(Source: *Interplanetary News,* No. 12, Volume 3/*The Guardian*)

18th January 1966 – UFO over Cheshire

John Wright – a schoolboy from Dean Low Road, Wilmslow – was standing near the Bluebell Garage, at 7.45pm, when he saw a pinpoint of light approaching in the sky. As it moved closer, he saw:

"...a silvery-grey object with a lighted porthole, flying through the air towards the direction of the Bluebell Hotel, on the opposite side of the road, close to Manchester Road, about 60 feet in the air and 20 yards away from where I was standing". **(Sources:** *UFOLOG/***Joan Nelstrop, DIGAP)**

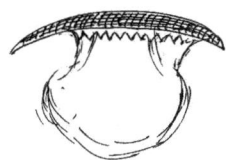

19th January 1966 – UFO over Hampshire

Mr J. McFarlane from Bournemouth, Hampshire, was lying in bed when he saw:

"...what appeared to be two bright yellow circles, joined by a pole around a gleaming red circle, motionless in the sky; I alerted another tenant in the building and we watched it for a while, but eventually decided to go back to bed". **(Source: Isle of Wight UFO Society)**

FEBRUARY 1966

2nd February 1966 – UFO over Weymouth

We spoke to Jeffrey Wontoon about what he and a number of other pupils had seen, while in the playground at Thornlow School, Barton Road, Weymouth, Dorset, at 10.45am.

"We saw this orange sphere, heading slowly across the sky in front of the clouds. As it moved over, an occasional puff of smoke, or flame, appeared. Within four or five minutes, it became lost from view. To this day I don't know what it was, but I am sure it wasn't any weather balloon, because it moved rapidly on a straight course."

2nd February 1966 – Diamond-shaped UFO seen over Carolina, USA

At 11.15pm, Mr and Mrs L.J. Wise sighted a silver, diamond-shaped, object with several 'globes of light' revolving constantly in very fast motion around it, hovering over trees for three to four minutes, presumably agitating a dog nearby which constantly barked, before moving away and eventually out of sight, one hour later. **(Source: NICAP)**

3rd February 1966 – Luminous globe

At 11.30pm, a luminous 'ball' – brighter than the full moon, and as large as the sun in size, with solid sharp edges – was seen over Bootle, Merseyside, at an elevation of 30 degrees North, visible for a few minutes before disappearing northwards.

4th February 1966 – Spinning UFO – Did RAF jets respond?

At 6pm, a spinning object was seen motionless in the sky above the town, at an elevation of 60 degrees, before heading off towards the North at high speed, leaving a trail of white light. Thirty minutes later, an apparently solid object, resembling: *"a white cigar, with the end chopped off, showing blurred edges, a hazy blue line running through the centre, and an orange light at one end – brighter than the moon – making a throbbing noise"*, was seen in the sky west of the town, before disappearing in a 'flash of light', eastwards, at an elevation of approximately 50 degrees. Shortly afterwards, three jet aircraft appeared and went off in the same direction taken by the UFO. **(Source: Merseyside UFO Research Group)**

4th February 1966 – Schoolchildren sight 'Flying Saucer' over Madams Wood, Manchester

On the 4th February, pupils attending R. Peel Junior School, Little Hulton, Manchester, told of seeing a cigar-shaped object hovering over Madams Wood, followed by an even stranger report from another schoolboy, who described sighting:

"...a saucer-shaped object descend and pick-up a cow from a field, by means of a grab, and then head off across the sky".

We spoke to one of the boys from the first incident – Brian Fenlon – a police officer, (working at Kent Constabulary Federation Office), who confirmed:

> "We did see what looked like a 'Flying Saucer', hovering over Madams Wood, although I have no knowledge of the second incident, or the boy concerned. Whatever it was, it didn't appear to be an aircraft or man-made, but I still remember it clearly."

As a result of newspaper publicity, we managed to identify the witness to the afternoon's event and wrote a number of letters to him, hoping to learn more. Disappointingly, we never received any answer – which indicates the event was probably a hoax, stimulated by the earlier sighting. Apart from that, it was reported that no livestock were found to be missing from the field concerned.

(**Source:** *Farnworth and Worsley Journal,* 5.2.1966)

6th February 1966 – Pulsating UFO over Texas home

At 5.45am, Mr and Mrs K.R. Gulley from Nederland, Texas, sighted a yellow object hovering about 500 feet above their property, casting a pulsating red glow onto their lawn. The house lights then went out, followed by a high-pitched frequency which was painful to the ears. Five to ten minutes later, the object moved away and out of sight. (**Source: NICAP**)

22nd February 1966 – Leonard Cramp lectures

Isle of Wight UFO Society President – Mr Leonard Cramp – gives a talk at the Unitarian Church Hall, Newport, on the Isle of Wight.

24th February 1966 – Object seen by Cambridge undergraduate

At 4.30pm, an undergraduate at Cambridge University sighted:

> "…a whitish-silver object, shaped like a slipper in the sky, moving from the North, at an estimated speed of 120 miles per hour, increasing in size as it did so." (**Source: UFOLOG**)

MOD UFO figures for February 1966

The MOD confirmed they received a total of 10 reports, of which they judged three to be satellite debris, two to be aircraft, one meteorological phenomenon, one unknown and four unidentified (insufficient information), but nothing earmarked for investigation.

MARCH 1966

3rd March 1966 – Silver, triangular object over Northumberland

At 11.45pm a silver, triangular, object was sighted moving across the sky, at an estimated height of 40,000 feet, over Bainbridge, Northumberland, by Mrs S. Henderson, accompanied by the sound of a jet aircraft. Was there a connection? Had the RAF been scrambled to intercept the object? (**Source: TUFOS**)

5th March 1966 – Yellow/white 'globe' over Tyneside

At 12.21am, Tyneside UFO Society member – Frank Satterthwaite from Fenham, Newcastle – and Mr and Mrs Muir, of Jesmond, sighted a yellow/white 'globe', flying silently across the sky, heading in a west to north direction – out of sight in a few minutes. (**Source TUFOS**)

8th March 1966 – Chesterton, Indiana, USA

At 2.30pm a UFO, surrounded by a bright misty haze, was seen hovering above a cloud bank for 4-5 minutes. It then changed angles and sped away. (**Source: NICAP**)

10th March 1966 – UFOs over Lancashire

Two objects were sighted in the sky by rugby players at Saddleworth, near Oldham, and initially thought them to be meteors – until they *"turned around and flew back along the path taken"* – later explained away by Manchester Weather Centre as balloons, released from the Radiosonde Station at Aughton, near Liverpool. (**Source: TUFOS**)

11th March 1966 – Glowing UFO seen Lancashire

During the early morning, a glowing object was seen by Mrs Faith Hudson, her daughter – Pauline, and boyfriend – Frank Round, described as *"flying up, down, and sideways in the sky"*, over Shevington, near Wigan, before flying off towards the direction of Gathurst. (**Source:** *Liverpool Daily Post* – **date not known**)

12th March 1966 – Bright star-like object reported Tyneside

A bright star-like object was seen by Mr R. Leighton, at 9.20pm, moving slowly through the sky over the Albert and Edward Dock, Gateshead, heading north-west, before silently fading in brightness.
(**Source: Tyneside UFO Society**)

13th March 1966 – Saucer-shaped object photographed by fisherman

Brian Wilson from Albert Road, Morecambe, Lancashire, was out fishing during the afternoon, when he happened to glance upwards and see a dull black shape gliding across the sky. Reacting quickly, he picked up his camera and managed to take two photographs, before it vanished behind clouds in the direction of Morecambe Bay; the first photo showed a dark flat looking 'blob', while the second image showed a saucer-shaped object, with a dome.

Brian said:

> *"I don't know what made me look up in the first place. I suppose I wasn't concentrating on fishing. It didn't make any noise. There was no rush of air, or anything like that. I don't know what it was. I've never really believed in 'Flying Saucers' before".*

(**Source:** *Flying Saucer Review*, **July/August 1966, Volume 12, No. 4**)

On the same evening

Norman Comber – licensee of the *Plough & Harrow* Inn, Ormskirk Road, Up Holland, described seeing an object, *"about 15 feet long, dark orange in colour, round and flat, moving low down in the sky, leaving a thin trail behind it"*, which was later explained away as being a fireball. (**Source:** *Liverpool Echo*, **24.3.1966**)

14th March 1966 – UFO display was marsh gas!

At 3.50am, Deputy Sheriffs B. Bushroe and J. Foster sighted several 'discs' manoeuvring above Dexter. Four UFOs were then seen flying in a line formation. Other Police agencies also reported similar sightings, which were tracked on radar by Selfridge Air Force.

Deputy Bushroe:

> *"This is the strangest thing that Deputy Forrest and I had ever witnessed. These objects could move at fantastic speeds and make very sharp turns, dive and climb, and hover with great manoeuvrability."*

The explanation was rejected by the media and led to a plethora of articles on the UFO incidents, many of which demanded a full-scale enquiry, which became convoluted by all manner of other sightings brought to the attention of the authorities, including a claim by motorist John T. King, who said he was driving near Bangor, Maine, when he saw a 'flying disc' on the ground. He got out of the car and opened fire with his Magnum revolver, discharging three shots after the object moved closer, causing the car lights to dim and the radio to cut out. (**Source:** *Aliens from outer Space* – **Donald Keyhoe**)

14th March 1966 – UFO displays over the United States

During the early morning hours of 14th March 1966, Washtenaw County sheriff's deputies reported sighting *"four strange flying objects"* in Lima Township. Soon police agencies from Livingston County, Monroe County and Sylvania, Ohio, were also reporting *"red-green objects . . . moving at fantastic speeds"*. By the end of the day the Civil Defense and US Air Force were called in to an investigation that has never really ended for many of those involved.

The UFO story provides an interesting look at the way news events affect the lives of the participants and their communities. The Dexter family that reported the UFOs near their farm was overwhelmed by the coverage, became victims of vandalism and eventually distanced themselves from the story. The UFO sightings proliferated and swept Washtenaw area communities into a worldwide news event.

20th March 1966 – Pulsating light over Miami

USAF Reserve Major K.C. Smith – an employee of NASA, at Cape Kennedy – reported sighting a pulsating light, which varied from white to intense blue in the sky, at 12.15am. It was then seen to make a jerky ascent before rapidly accelerating away, northwards, five minutes later. **(Source: NICAP)**

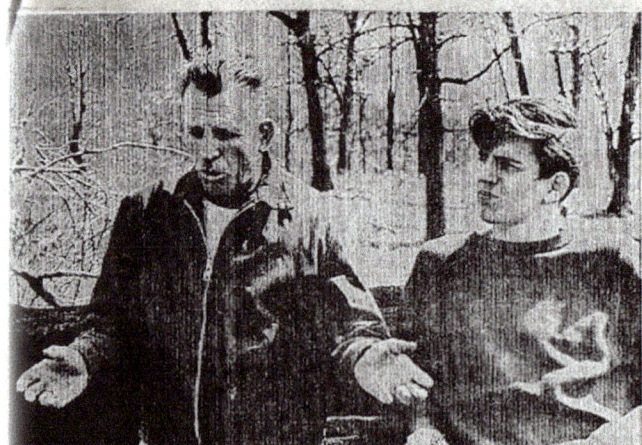

20th March 1966 – UFO lands in swamp

At 8pm, truck driver Frank Manor (47), stepped out of his rented house, located in a 90-acre cattle farm at the end of a dirt road at 10600 McGuiness, close to Territorial Road, with Peach Mountain in the background. He said:

> "I was walking outside on the Sunday evening, when I saw what looked like a falling star; it went to the top of the trees – all red, then blue lights, then a white light rotating."

He shouted for his wife, Leona, 19 year-old son Robert, and daughter Diana (18), and her husband – Donald Merkle, to come and have a look.

Mrs Manor:

> "You could see it rise from the ground and hit the treetop awhile, and fall back to the ground. There were different colours – white on ground, blue, and then red in the trees, come back down again and change colour."

Mrs Manor also mentioned that one of her married daughters (who lived nearby) heard a strange noise – like the roar of a train – at 8am, the previous day.

Police called out

After the police were called, Frank and Robert went back outside to investigate further.

Frank:

> "We got within 500 yards of that thing, which looked pyramid-like. It had lights here and there, and a white light that looked like a porthole. It didn't look like a saucer; it was pyramidal shaped, with a coral surface."

His son said to his father *"Look at that horrible thing, Dad!"* As he did so, the lights went out. Frank and his son jumped a fence and ran across the creek towards the object, as fast as they could cover swampy ground. They looked, but there was nothing to see – only a light about half a mile away. Frank estimated the length of the object to be similar to a car, with a quilted surface and something turning underneath – like a heat wave – brownish surface.

By this time Dexter Police Chief Robert Taylor and Patrolman N.G. Lee had arrived.

Robert Taylor:

> "We saw it from the hills and it looked like it was down in the swamp. Through binoculars we could see it was a pulsating red light. We heard a noise."

Frank Mannor and son at landing site, M1 1966

UFO expert Dr. J. Allen Hynek (left) and Dexter Police Chief Robert R. Taylor go over the map of UFO sightings in the area

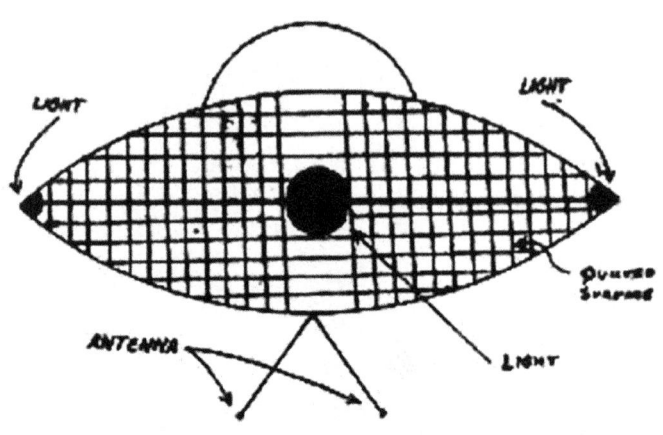

After the sightings, the witnesses put together this composite drawing at the Washtenaw County sheriff's headquarters, showing the lights, surface and antenna.

Lee:

"When we got down into the swamp there wasn't anything there. When our flashlights came in towards it, it disappeared.

The noise it made was like an ambulance."

Leona:

"We were inside when the sound went off and we heard a screeching."

Frank:

"The only sound we heard was the high frequency sound over the house – like the ricochet of a bullet. Down in the swamp they said it was like a siren."

Police 'back up' requested

Washtenaw County Sheriff – Douglas J. Harvey – also arrived at the scene. He had dispatched all available deputies to the scene.

Six patrol cars, carrying 12 men, rushed to Dexter. A Dexter patrolman later reported he had seen what appeared to be a flying object, showing red and green flashing lights. Deputy Sherriff – David Fitzpatrick (24) – told of responding to the scene and then making his way on foot into the swamp with a colleague. He said:

"The only thing we saw was a brilliant light. By the time we got there, it had gone. While we were in the swamp, we were advised it had been seen to hover above a car."

Later at Police HQ, the officers sat down and compiled a record of what had taken place. Sketches were put together of the various descriptions. It was a convex shape with a light at each end, a light in the centre, two antennae from the bottom, and a grill-work pattern on the surface resembling a quilt.

Police Officers chase a UFO

Washtenaw Deputy Sherriff – Ford Bushroe:

"I didn't see the one that landed on Sunday night, but at 11.15pm we were heading back into Ann Arbor from Dexter. I looked up to the south and saw this bluish-green, brilliant red and white light. It looked like an arc; it was rounded. We turned around and started following it back through Dexter for five miles, heading west. We lost it in the trees. Either the lights were off or it took off with a tremendous burst of speed. It was about 1,500 feet above the ground, moving at about 100 miles per hour. We were doing 70 miles per hour and stayed well ahead of us."

The pursuit took them along Dexter Ann Arbor Road and Island Lake Road to the intersection of Wylie Road.

Robert Douglas Taylor (16), son of Chief Taylor, was at his home on Island Lake Road when, at 10.30pm, he sighted a flashing red and white light, heading in an eastwards direction in the sky, and watched it through binoculars.

Not surprisingly, once the news spread about the incident, sightseers arrived. They included one man who played the fiddle, hoping to lure the 'saucers'; another, who claimed he was a University Professor. He spent some time in his car, flashing the letter 'Pi' in Morse code, in the hope of starting a universal dialogue!

The Detectives spent the day checking the area for radioactivity, but found none. By this time Selfridge Air Force Base had been forwarded the reports of the Sunday night sighting.

21st/22nd March 1966 – Michigan College students sight UFOs

65 miles south-west of Ann Arbor, at Hillsdale, about 30 students at the college, together with an assistant Dean, and the Hillsdale County Civil Defense Director – William Van Horn – watched the strange sight, involving a 'pyrotechnic display of changing lights in a swamp, about 1,500 yards from the campus, including what some described as shifting shapes, following a thunderstorm, between 10pm and 2am.

Dr. J. Allen Hynek asked to investigate the incidents –

Explanation: It was swamp gas!

On Tuesday, 22nd March, the Air Force announced that Dr. J. Allen Hynek – scientific consultant, would investigate the Dexter sightings.

He arrived at the Detroit Press Club on 25th March, when the room was jammed with newsmen. He said:

"I have had time to determine that in Hillsdale, over and above the sincere and honest reporting of the young ladies concerned, of a very puzzling sighting. Certain young men have played pranks with flares. As to the photographs published the previous day, of a sighting at Michigan on the 17th March, there were trials made as the result of a time exposure of the rising crescent moon and the planet Venus.

The majority of observers in both cases have reported only lights – red, yellow and green, silent glowing lights near the ground. They have not described an object. Even the only two observers who did describe an object have stated they were no closer than 500 yards, a quarter of a mile away – a distance which does not allow details to be determined."

Dr. Hynek mentioned that witnesses pinpointed the glowing lights in both cases in swamps and said:

"A dismal swamp is a most unlikely place for visitors from outer space! It is not a place where a helicopter would hover for several hours, or where a soundless secret device would be tested".

He then quoted from the Dutch astronomer Marcel Minnaert's – *The Nature of Light and Colour in the Open Air* – [in which he describes lights resembling tiny flames, sometimes on the ground, sometimes floating above it, sometimes red, yellow, or blue green flames, that go out in one place and appear in another, giving the appearance of motion. They give off no heat and do not char the ground. They may stay the whole night with no sound, except the popping sound of little explosions such as when a gas burner ignites.]

Dr. Hynek also said:

"Rotting vegetation in the swamp produces a marsh gas, which can be trapped by ice and released when spring thaw occurs. The flame that sometimes results is a chemical luminescence and of low temperature. The glowing lights on the swamp near Dexter and Hillsdale were observed for two or three hours. No sounds were heard, except for popping sounds. The lights were red, green or yellow, and they appeared to move sideways and to rise a short distance."

Effectively this was a death knell sentence, pronounced on what had taken place, relegating it as being of no importance when, in fact, history was to show the opposite!

(Source: *Fate Magazine***, October 1966 – 'Witnesses galore have versions of the year's most undeniable UFO sightings: so many that marsh gas won't hold up – 'THE GREAT UFO FLAP AT ANN ARBOR')**

Washtenaw County Sheriff – Douglas J. Harvey – did not immediately dismiss the sightings. In fact, he demanded a top-level investigation and challenged the US Air Force's conclusions. Equally persistent was Bill Treml – the legendary and intrepid police beat reporter for the *Ann Arbor News*. His stories dominated the local pages of the paper with in-depth interviews with witnesses, seemingly 24-hour coverage of police operations in tracking the UFO sightings, and a dogged pursuit of US government officials investigating the sightings.

Moving ahead into time!

Somewhat as a footnote to this was a UFO sighting over Ann Arbor on the 19th August 2004, 38 years later. It involved a motorist, who was driving along the M-14 Expressway at 10pm, (he was the only car at the time), when he noticed a large, bright, object just over trees to his left.

"As I got closer, I saw three large circles just above the trees up ahead. I slowed down to about 15 miles per hour to look at the object which was flying about 200 feet off the ground, just past the Gotfredson exit, about 50 yards off the expressway. As I approached closer, I saw that the intense lights were attached to the structure of a triangular shaped object that was slightly darker than the night sky. I couldn't understand why the ground below the objects wasn't lit up by the strong lights. The ends of the 'Triangle' were blunted, not crisp. It made no sound as it hovered over crop fields and a wood. I watched it for two more minutes and it never moved. The only motion was the orange light blinking in the middle of the other three lights."

(Source: www.ufocenter.com/*FSR***, autumn 2004)**

22nd March 1966 – Dark elliptical object over Northumberland

At 10pm, a dark elliptical object - *"ten times the size of the sun"* – displaying red and white lights, was sighted by local resident – Mr Bird of Ridley Avenue, Wallsend, moving slowly across the sky over Northumberland, for 20 minutes. **(Source: Tyneside UFO Society)**

23rd March 1966 – Report of a strange craft parked on the Highway

At 5.05am, a huge object – resembling a wingless C-124 Transport airplane – was sat on the Highway at Temple, Oklahoma, by Mr W.E Lawson. He said:

"I estimated it to be 75 feet long, 8 feet in height, and 12 feet wide. It had a bubble canopy on the top. A man dressed in military style clothes entered the craft, which took off about 40 seconds later."

Later that same day, Mrs P.N. Beer and Mrs E. Smith complained that their vehicle had been 'buzzed' by a flashing light, which was seen to hover above the vehicle over a ten minute duration, while driving through Texhoma, Texas. **(Source: NICAP)**

28th March 1966 – UFOs photographed over South Yorkshire

A photograph taken on the 28th March 1966, by schoolboy Stephen Pratt (15) from Leslie Avenue, Conisbrough, is still a subject of curiosity, over fifty years later. It shows not one, but three peculiar shaped objects in the sky.

At the time Stephen lived with his parents and two brothers, Kevin (10) and Gary (16).

This highly unusual photograph has attracted the attention of many people over the years. Unfortunately, it has also attracted a number of scurrilous remarks directed at the integrity of the witnesses involved, by those who find it easier to form a snap judgement, rather than bothering to examine the circumstances behind which the photograph was taken, when they would have discovered both camera and negative had been examined by Kodak, who felt there was no reason to believe the negative had been tampered with in any way.

We met up with Stephen's brother - Kevin Pratt, who showed us his collection of memorabilia pertaining to that never-to-be forgotten day, which was to change his whole outlook on life. Kevin told us that out of the original strip of twelve negatives, the fifth was the one showing the distinctive triple images, after being developed by E.H. Dickinson's Chemists, in Conisbrough, before being sent with the camera (still in his possession to this present day) to Kodak Laboratories.

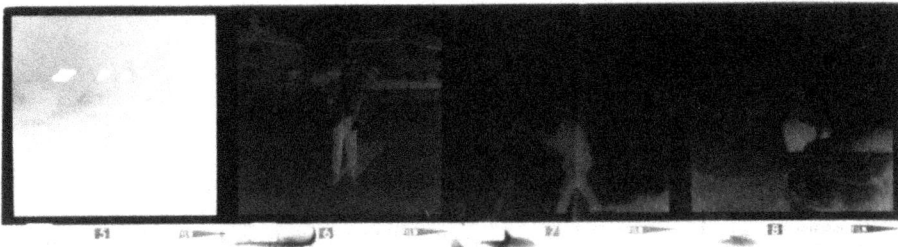

White rocket seen in the air over Conisbrough Crags

Statement From Mr Kevin Pratt: "A few hours before the photo was taken, I was walking home from Balby Street School, Denaby Main, over Conisbrough Crags (an eerie quiet place), when I saw what looked like a white rocket, silently rising slowly over some trees, emitting a white plume of smoke from its tail. It then tilted and headed towards the north-west."

After arriving home and eating his tea, Kevin decided to go and have a look at the area concerned, believing that he had seen a rocket leaving a mobile launching facility. To his surprise, the earth lay undisturbed, with no tyre tracks or sign of any human presence at all. Disappointed, he returned home.

Some time around 8.30pm, Stephen came rushing into the house, urging his father - Walter, and brothers, to come outside and have a look at a strange orange glow that he had seen in the sky. Walter, sensing his son was 'pulling his leg', stayed put until the agitated look on Stephen's face told him that he was serious.

Kevin rushed outside and saw his mum - Teresa, standing at the junction with Montague Avenue (opposite the house), looking upwards at an object resembling a glowing ember in the sky.

Kevin later said: "It resembled a drum kit cymbal, on a dining plate. I could hear a low drone or whirring sound, barely audible, while the massive object hovered motionless in the twilight sky."

Stephens father Walter shouted for Stephen to get the camera. Stephen ran into the house to fetch the Kodak Instamatic and took a photo, as the light began to fade. He then manoeuvred to try and obtain a better vantage point for the next shot, but then missed seeing the object shoot off across the sky in the direction of sheffield, at fantastic speed, and out of sight in a fraction of a second. As the family discussed the event they were joined by the Dainty family who were on their way up the Conisbrough Crags where they also saw the object as they were on their way home on Thirlwall Avenue Conisbrough, they told us that they had seen three of these objects earlier that afternoon accompanied by a cigar shaped object as they were on their way to Denaby down the Conisbrough Crags.

Stephen, who was to find that his way of life was also to become changed (for the worse) by the continual attention of the press (not forgetting all of the ridicule), explained he was on his way home from a fish and chip shop with his mother.

Statement From Mr Stephen Pratt: "It was on a cloudy and overcast evening, the time was between 8pm and 8.30pm when my mother brought my attention to a bright, pulsating reddish/orange 'light' in the sky, towards the north-east. We kept it under observation, while we carried on walking; noticing it had begun to move slowly up and down, as it moved across the sky. My mother told me to fetch the family outside - which I did - then being joined by my father, Gary, and Kevin. My father asked me to go and pick up the camera from the house and take a photo - which I did, Mr Jimmy Dainty and family joined us on the street Mr and Mrs Dainty told us they had seen the same object earlier, accompanied by a cigar-shaped object.

The photograph was taken on the fifth frame of the film, and I thought there was no way it was going to turn out. much to my surprise, when the film was processed, it showed three domed objects. Although I never saw three objects in the sky, my father said that he thought he could make out two objects, which went off westwards towards Rotherham. Despite to the reported contrary, I have never referred to UFOs as Flying Saucers." When the film was processed, eleven out of twelve exposures were perfect and showed everyday photos, apart from the fifth, nearly transparent negative, showing the saucer-like 'blemishes' - which he thought astounding, because he had only seen the one image in the sky"

After Stephen showed the negative to his headmaster at Northcliff High School (Conisbrough) Mr. Arthur Young CBE, who was a ex-RAF officer, took the negative to RAF Finningley to be examined by his ex-colleagues, as a result of it being labelled 'UNEXPLAINED'. Stephen was advised to send the negative to BUFORA (British UFO Research Association).

Gary then sent the negative to Granada Television Studios, asking them, in a letter, what they made of the picture, which was shown on 12th April 1966 - the story then being published, the next day, by the Sun newspaper (Manchester edition) in a half-page spread.

Gary Pratt confirmed the account given by his brothers, although he believed the reddish/orange glowing 'light', apparently hovering motionless in the sky above the house opposite, was a helicopter and went back inside the house to continue watching TV.

Statement From Mr Gary Pratt: "I have to say that none of us really knew what UFO stood for. I thought it was something disrespectful. About a week later, while watching TV with my brother, Stephen, the newsreader - Bill Grundy - read out a news item about people on an airplane seeing a UFO, which was later explained away as being a reflection of the tail, throwing a false reflection into the cabin windows. What annoyed us was that we rather naively asked Granada what they thought of it (our UFO photograph), never expecting them to publish the incident, as shown on TV. As a result of this publicity, many reporters kept coming to the house asking for interviews. I kept out of the way, fearing ridicule, which did eventually happen."

Statement From MrsTeresa Pratt: "The time was between 8pm and 8.30pm, when my son Stephen (15) and myself, were returning home from our local fish and chip shop. We were walking through the alleyway that joins onto Leslie Avenue, when I noticed an orange glow in the sky, I pointed it out to my son Stephen and we kept looking at it till we reached our home. It was so unusual - this strange orange glow that hovered, motionless, to the north-east - that I told Stephen to go into the house to tell his dad to come out quickly, to see the strange phenomenon in the twilight sky. The rest of the family at home, Gary (16) and Kevin (10), along with Stephen and Dad (Walter), joined me to gaze in amazement at the strange orange glow. Stephen was told by his father to get the camera quickly and take some photos. Unfortunately, he only took one photograph because it was getting too dark; Stephen took the camera back indoors, but before he could rejoin everyone, whatever it was that hovered in the sky suddenly shot off at amazing speed, westwards. Stephen was disappointed at missing this departure. We were not the only witnesses to see it.

The Dainty family, from nearby Thirlwall Avenue, also witnessed it but they refused to have anything to do with the Press."

Kevin, holding the same camera, during a visit to his house in Staffordshire.

Kevin told us: "It is worth noting that the type of camera used was a Kodak Instamatic 50 camera, with a fixed focus set for cloudy. The camera is a cartridge loading type. Due to the parallax effect and the lack of double exposure facilities, the camera is useless for producing fake shots (as was suggested in the Alex Birch case, where he admitted to painting images on glass and photographing the objects through the glass showing the background sky). If you tried the same method with the instamatic 50, the focus would obliterate any such object; also, if you attempted to view the object through the viewfinder, the lens (being about an inch below the viewfinder) would miss the close-up images on glass. If you wanted to fake a photograph, the Kodak instamatic 50 is the worse tool for the job and, on top of this, even with the right tools, the photographer would have to be very talented indeed to produce such results."

The Dainty family joined us after the UFO left. However, I can confirm they watched the event at the same time from the top of the Conisbrough Crags. After joining us at the top of Montague Avenue, they described seeing three objects earlier in the day, along with a cigar-shaped object, as they were going down the crags to Denaby.

Incidentally, Gary hardly looked at the object, because he assumed it to be a helicopter, and shrugged it off and went back indoors. Gary seemed to be more interested in getting back to the TV programme he was watching and tucking into his fish and chips. We, on the other hand, could see that this was no helicopter and it was almost totally silent. I could make out a faint whirring sound. I am not 100 per cent sure whom it was that sent Stephen into the house for the camera. I always assumed it was my father. I know it was one of my parents. Stephen was forced to discontinue his communication with people regarding his UFO sighting name, due to the problems the kids were having at school following the level of attention and ridicule directed at them - not forgetting all the rubbish, published by so called UFO investigators and writers. However, he couldn't do anything about these issues without drawing attention to himself.

I became so fed-up with the lies and rubbish published about the sighting that I produced a booklet, called UFODATA and sent a copy of UFODATA to Graham Birdsall, after seeing an article in one of his publications – 50 Years of Unidentified Flying Objects. The article, by Jerome Clark, mixed up Stephen Derbyshire and Alex Birch accounts, using the Conisbrough UFO photograph. This wouldn't have been too bad, but they quoted Stephen Pratt as saying he had admitted the photograph was a hoax.

As you can imagine I was furious and threatened legal action against Graham Birdsall, who advised me to contact Jerome Clark, as a result of which I did and subsequently obtained an apology, but the damage was done and has caused us a lot of pain and aggravation."

The matter was thoroughly investigated at the time, by Mr. John M. Stear and Mr. F. Malcolm Bull - representatives of the British UFO Research Association, who concluded: "it was a genuine sighting of an alien spacecraft, substantiated with a good photograph".

Stephen also wrote to Gordon Creighton, living at 16, Cedars Avenue, Rickmansworth, Hertfordshire, on 11th July 1966, enclosing his report and negative.

Gordon wrote back to him on the 16th, saying: "I am arranging for the photograph to be seen by a very famous expert, not that I disbelieve you, because I don't . I know your picture is genuine, but if we publish it and we can say that so and so, a very famous expert has seen it, then it makes a much better and more impressive effect. We shall be mailing it back to you shortly and if - as I feel he will, pretty sure he will do - the editor Mr. Bowen decides to publish it, then you will be paid the standard reproduction fee payable in such cases. He will also send you a copy of the review containing the article.

Yours sincerely,

Gordon Creighton."

(Sources: As above/Fortean Picture Library/Janet and Colin Bord)

U.F.O. DATA 1966 to 1996.

Volume 1. No.1 Rev.1   October 1, 1996.

The South Yorkshire Sighting, March, 28, 1966.

Mr and Mrs Dainty

Kevin Pratt 2017:

"Hi John, Please find the attached PDF with the amendments. [Seen on previous four pages]. I sent a copy to Stephen and he says it's ok; there were only minor errors here and there. I also included the father of the Dainty family's first name … (Jimmy).

Unfortunately, I couldn't find the mother's name but a little research into the housing records of 1966 should throw up all the family names from the 1966 census. I will do my best to delve more into this to see if I can track any of them down, but someone told me that Mr & Mrs Dainty has passed away and the toddler (son) can't remember anything, so it may be a dead end unless the parents spoke to him about the event. I will do what I can to track him down. I added a few graphics for your viewing but you do not need to use any of them. If you need further graphics, or documents pertaining to the event, I will sort some out for you.

I hope you are well and your books are a great success.

All the very best,

Your friend,

Kev.

Stephen and Kevin Pratt

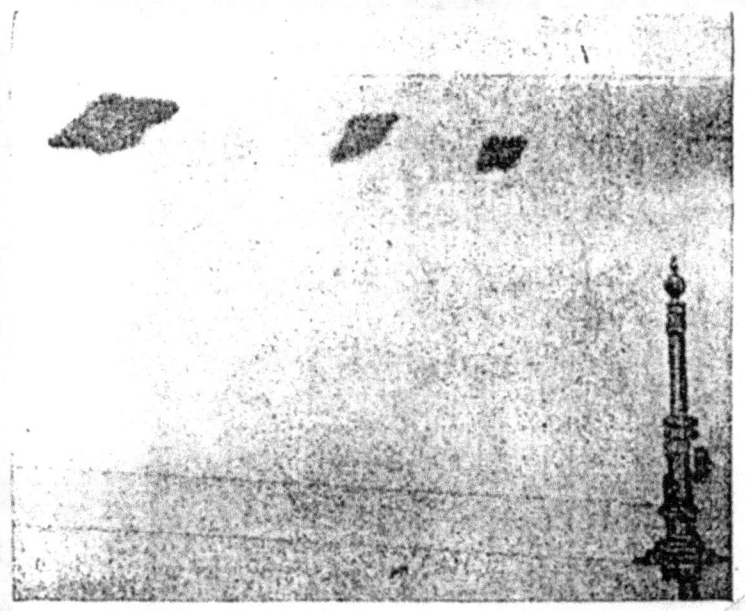

DAILY SKETCH 17 NOV 66

This is Stephen's picture, which experts studied for six months.

STEPHEN, 15, ASKS: DID I SNAP FLYING SAUCERS?

STEPHEN PRATT
"Not a fake."

SCHOOLBOY Stephen Pratt sent this picture, taken with his box camera, to the British Unidentified Flying Objects Research Association and asked: "Are they flying saucers?

After a six month investigation, the association's chairman, Dr. Geoffrey Doel, said last night: "We firmly believe the picture to be genuine.

"It will go down on our records as such."

"I do not believe this photograph is a fake. It is most unlikely that a young boy, using a cheap camera, could have made a fake negative like this."

Dr. Doel is a member of the Royal College of Surgeons and an expert radiologist.

SCEPTICAL

Stephen, aged 15, took the picture in March near his home at Leslie-avenue, Conisbrough, near Doncaster.

Mr. Kenneth Gatland, vice-president of the British Interplanetary Society, said last night: "I would regard any picture of unidentified flying objects with a degree of scepticism.

"So many things can cause a camera to pick up a strange object that, in fact, is a familar one seen from an unusual angle, or atmospheric disturbances, or a trick of the light."

28th March 1966 – UFO display over Washington DC, USA

An object with multicoloured lights was reported to have paced a truck over Niles, Michigan, and flashed back when the truck lights were blinked on and off! On the same date, an oblong object was seen in the sky by control tower operators at an airfield in Columbus and Atlanta. Over Washington DC, a red and green flashing object was sighted performing manoeuvres in the sky, by a radio station announcer and other witnesses.

30th March 1966 – UFO display over Long Island, New York, USA

Numerous reports for this day involved sightings of oblong glowing objects, seen manoeuvring in the sky, flying out to sea and causing interruptions to power supplies and domestic TV sets.

31st March 1966 – 100,000 Americans say they have seen UFOs!

31st March 1966 – *Evening Standard* – 'Flying Saucers'

In the same year

Mrs Kathleen Dickson, from Little Hulton, wrote to us about what she saw, during the early to mid part of the same year.

> "I was sat in the back garden, after having had an argument with my husband, at 1.45am. All of a sudden, I heard this humming noise and what sounded like voices. I looked up and saw a white 'ball of flame' approaching the house, which landed in a field on the other side of the railway line at the bottom of the garden. It then took-off again – now cigar-shaped and enormous in size – and went off across the sky, leaving me shocked." **(Source: Personal interview)**

APRIL 1966

2nd April 1966 – UFO over Cumbria

At 9.10pm a brilliant green oval object, showing orange outer edges and tail, was seen flying across the grey, cloudless, sky in an east-to-west direction by Mrs P Little, from Carlisle, who was visiting a sick relative, seconds later it was out of sight.

2nd April 1966 – UFO Photo, as seen over Australia … any connection?

3rd April 1966 – Similar UFO seen

A similar object was seen from the seawall at Silloth, Carlisle, Cumbria, at 10.23pm, by Mr B. Bamber, who described it as:

> "...a brilliant emerald-green sphere in the west-north-west direction, showing an apparent solid tail of golden flame moving vertically downwards through five degrees of arc in two seconds, before burning out".

6th April 1966 – UFO seen to descend at Melbourne Victoria Australia

Some things cannot be left out irrespective of where they took place in the world, although space is at a premium!

At approximately 11am on Wednesday, 6th April 1966, a class of students and teacher from Westall High School (now Westall Secondary College) at Clayton, close to Melbourne, were outside on the main oval when a 'round' grey saucer-shaped object with a slight purple hue and estimated to be approximately twice the size of a family car, was seen moving through the sky.

The following contains *Shane Ryan's report into what is still a very intriguing case, despite the well-oiled machinery of officialdom that tries to convince us of a mundane explanation! Thanks also go to Philip Mantle of *Flying Disk Press* for his assistance.

Shane:

"According to witnesses, the objects were seen descending before crossing over each other and then fly over the High School's south-west corner, going in a south-easterly direction, before disappearing from sight as it descended behind a stand of trees and into a paddock at The Grange, in front of the Westall State School (primary students). The main and biggest object had landed on the ground. After a short period (approximately 20 minutes) the object – with witnesses now numbering over 210 – then rose and climbed at speed and departed towards the north-west."

[None of the witnesses said that they saw any aliens or any people in or around any of the craft. It was suggested that if there were, in fact, any (people) they would not have been able to stand up, as the height of the craft was no higher than an average family car, the craft being round and large at the base but lacking in height – like the saucer of an upside-down tea cup.]

---

*Shane Ryan is a teacher of English as a Second Language, researcher and former federal public servant. He has worked at Charles Sturt University, University of Canberra, and the Australian National University, all in Canberra. Shane has worked as an information officer and researcher at the Embassy of Japan in Canberra, and he has also taught in schools in Japan and Australia. Shane completed a Diploma of Japanese Studies at Nanzan University, Nagoya; a Bachelor of Theology at Sydney College of Divinity, Sydney; a Master of Arts at Australian Catholic University, Canberra; and a Graduate Certificate in Teaching ESL at University of Canberra. He was working as a barristers' clerk in Melbourne when he first heard about the Westall Incident. Shane lives in Canberra with his wife and son. To contact Shane, or for more information about the Westall Incident, visit: www.westall66ufo.com.au, or the Westall Flying Saucer Incident pages on Facebook and Yahoo Groups, or email: shaneryan@velocitynet.com.au.

Dandenong Journal reports on this incident on the 14th of April 1966

FLYING SAUCER MYSTERY: SCHOOL SILENT
What was it?

CLAYTON. — After more than a week of investigation, mystery still surrounds the reported sighting last Wednesday of a flying saucer near the Westall High School, Clayton.

Investigations of the report have been hampered by the reluctance of school authorities to permit interviews with eye-witness students and staff members.

Several children attending the school and at least one staff member are reported to have seen the unidentified flying object.

They are believed to have given corroborating descriptions of the object as "a round humped object with a flat base being circled by what appeared to be light aircraft."

It was described as grey or silver grey in color, but it is not known whether the object appeared high or low in the sky or for how long it was observed.

One report said several children who saw the object collapsed and became ill with fright.

There have been a number of attempts to explain the sighting as a product of natural causes.

However, The Victorian Flying Saucer Research Society has taken the report so seriously, that it has inserted an advertisement in a daily newspaper seeking descriptions from eye witnesses.

Vice-president of the society, Mrs. Judy Magee, said yesterday that all attempts to obtain information from students or staff members at the school had failed.

"We have only second-hand reports of the sighting, but we believe it could be an important one, Mrs. Magee said.

She said she and two other members of the society last Friday went to the scene of the sighting and discovered "a couple of circular patches" where the grass had been flattened.

These could have been formed by an object landing or taking off.

Army report

However, Mrs. Magee said strong winds had been blowing during the week, and these could have caused the grass to be flattened.

It was also reported that military personnel had been in the area on Saturday.

If this was the case, the area would have been heavily trampled and further investigation of the flattened patches would be useless.

An Army spokesman said yesterday there was no record of personnel in the area on Saturday.

Mrs. Magee said she understood that children at the school had been instructed to talk to no one who asked questions about the sighting.

This was why the society had made its independent appeal for eye-witness accounts.

She said she believed some of the children had also heard the sound of engines as what appeared to be light aircraft circled the object.

Department of Civil Aviation officials have checked for reports of strange aircraft in the area, but none has been made.

A spokesman for the Bureau of Meteorology said a weather balloon equipped with a radar reflector and radiosonde transmitter was released from Laverton last Wednesday morning.

Under the influence of rising winds, it could have drifted to the Clayton region.

This could have explained the reported sighting of a flying saucer, he said.

However, the Victorian Flying Saucer Research Society will continue its investigations.

Investigators call for eye-witnesses

A cold start to 28 mile push

DANDENONG. — Biting winds and lashing rain on Good Friday failed to dampen the enthusiasm of the Dandenong Dodgers Basketball team members when they conducted their annual 28-mile wheelbarrow push from the Town Hall to Melbourne to raise money for the Royal Children's Hospital.

Their efforts were well rewarded. Thanks to the generosity of householders en-route from Dandenong to Melbourne, they raised a record $2061.44 — almost double last year's collection of $1086.

A barbecue and cabaret dance held prior to Good Friday, gave them an excellent start.

The Mayor, Cr. Eric Hill, received an enthusiastic reception as he pushed the first barrow from the starting tape to honorate St. outside the Town Hall to the child at the early members.

The "Big Push" is sponsored by Dandenong Lions Club as one of its varied community projects. Lions joined the Dodgers in the important convoy which was highlighted by horn-blowing and the use of loud hailers.

Alan Coffey Motors loaned their vehicles for the day, and the barrow was followed by a sports saloon, a tractor and trailer and a number of sedans.

Mr. Eric Riddell's van, used as a travelling bed, brought up the rear.

Members sorted and counted dollars and cents in the drive pro-vided.

Volunteers

Mr Doug Wilde, manager of Coffey's, and members of his staff were the volunteer drivers.

Lions Club members assisted as sprinklers, dispensed the refreshment vans and were volunteer assistant collectors.

Patrons, Messrs Morris Buchanan, Alan Blignaut and Bert Edgecoe, acted as tellers in the travelling bank.

Lions ladies prepared the lunch.

They also prepared the evening meal at the Windsor, for 60 cold and hungry workers after the "push."

Spokesmen said members of the Dodgers deserved real praise.

The original concept of the "Big Push" was theirs and their enthusiasm keeps it alive.

RECORD TALLY

They push the wheelbarrow, run in and out of houses, run up side streets and main streets and chase the elusive cent.

Dodgers President, Geoff Tucker, was interviewed on 3DB and, assisted by Ron Casey Downard, thanked everyone who contributed.

ABOVE: The Mayor, Cr. E. Hill, in biting winds gives the barrow its first push on the way to Melbourne. (Other picture on page 6).

ABOVE: Dodgers' collectors who accompanied the push, from left to right: Robyn Martin (Queen of Commerce in the 1965 Lions Carnival), Barbara Melford, Graeme Howard, Rev. Howard and Carol Bird.
(Pictures by Graham Southam).

Vandals ruin Easter lighting

CLAYTON. — Since Christmas last year, vandals have destroyed or stolen more than 50 street decoration lights in the Clayton Rd. shopping centre.

Vandals' activities culminated shortly before Easter when an entire section of the lights wiring system was damaged, ruining what traders had hoped would be a colorful Easter display.

President of Clayton Chamber of Commerce, Mr S. Smith, said the decorations had cost traders more than $2500 to install.

The thefts and damage would probably add another $100 to the cost.

In addition to damaging lights, vandals gashed both front wheel tyres on a tractor's truck which was parked in Clayton Rd.

Mr Smith said many shops in Clayton Rd. had been broken into in the last 12 months.

He blamed a lack of adequate police patrols.

"More snap patrols by police are needed", he said. "Some traders in the area use a private security firm, but as checks are made at regular three-hour intervals, there is really little deterrent value."

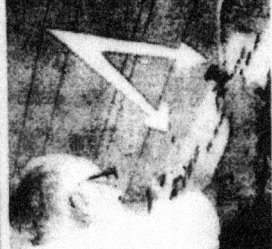

ABOVE: Clayton Chamber of Commerce president, Mr. S. Smith, examines the damaged lighting. Arrows show where the wiring was cut by vandals.
(Picture — Renown Studios, 544-4103).

NISSEN'S Stock Complete Range of Regulation Winter uniforms for
HAILEYBURY COLLEGE

Stamina Pin Head Youth Suits
Sizes 10 to 17
$31   £15/10/-
Extra trousers $11, £5/10/-

Stamina Pin Head Knicker Suits
Sizes 6 to 13
$18.90   £9/9/-
Extra knickers $3.15, £1/6

Althea "Schule" Pullover
Pure wool reinforced with nylon. Sizes 30 to 46
From
$5.25   52/6

School Track Suits   From $8.95

Ties 7/11; School Sox 13/11; Plastic Pants, all sizes.

NISSEN'S 122 Foster St, Dandenong

Registered at the G.P.O., Melbourne, for transmission by post as a newspaper.

Haunted Skies Volume Two Revised

LYING SAUCER MYSTERY: SCHOOL SILENT
What was it?

CLAYTON.— After more than a week of investigation, mystery still surrounds the reported sighting last Wednesday of a flying saucer near the Westall High School, Clayton.

Investigations of the report have been hampered by the reluctance of school authorities to permit interviews with eye-witness students and staff members.

Several children attending the school and at least one staff member are reported to have seen the unidentified flying object.

They are believed to have given corroborating descriptions of the object as "a round humped object with a flat base being circled by what appeared to be light aircraft."

It was described as grey or silver grey in colour, but it is not known whether the object appeared high or low in the sky or for how long it was observed.

One report said several children who saw the object collapsed and became in a state of shock.

There have been a number of attempts to explain the sighting as a case of mass hysteria.

However, the Victorian Flying Saucer Research Society has taken the report seriously, and it has inserted an advertisement in a major newspaper seeking descriptions from eye witnesses.

Vice-president of the society, Miss Judy Magee, said yesterday that an attempt to obtain statements from six students in the presence of the school headmaster had failed.

"The boys were ordered..."

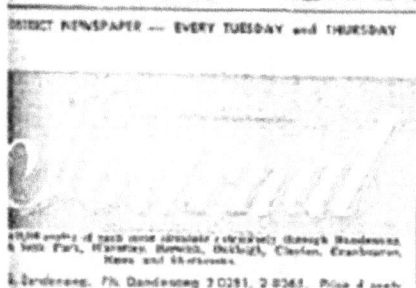

cold start to 28
le push

NDENONG.— Biting winds and rain on Good Friday failed the enthusiasm of the Dandenong Dodgers Basketball team when they conducted their 33-mile wheelbarrow push from Town Hall to Melbourne to money for the Royal Children's...

RECORD TALLY

This puts the school between run in and out of business, not up side streets and main streets and closed the doors

Dodgers' President, Geoff Epstein, was to devised his 28lb shift, assisted by Chris Clark Stewards, Barwick and various other sympathies.

ABOVE: The Mayor, Cr F. Bill, in taking some gives the barrow its first push on the way to Melbourne. Other stories on page 45.

ABOVE: Dodgers' collectors who accompanied the push, from left to right: Helen Hunter, Eileen of Commerce in the 1966 Lions Carnivals, Barbara McLeod, Graeme Howard, Bev. Howard and Carol Bird.

Vandals ruin Easter lighting

CLAYTON.— Since Christmas last year, vandals have destroyed or stolen more than 50 street decoration lights in...

Investigators call for eye-witnesses

young reports of the object, but we believe it could be brighter than was first stated.

She said the most other members of the party left Friday night in the area of the sighting and discovered a sample of burned paddock where the grass had been flattened.

"Others could have been burned by an object landing or taking off."

Army report

Moreover, Mrs. Magee said strong winds had kept flattening devices she went and there would have been fall and the grass in the flattened.

It was also reported that military personnel had been in the area on that morning.

If this was the case, the men would have been heavily armed, and further investigation of the flattened spot patches would be useless.

An Army spokesman said yesterday there was no chance of personnel in the area on Saturday.

Mrs. Magee said investigators would..."

NISSEN'S Stock Complete Range of Regulation Winter uniforms for
HAILEYBURY COLLEGE

Haunted Skies **Volume Two Revised**

Flying saucer mystery deepens

WHO WERE 5 PILOTS?

CLAYTON.— The unidentified flying object reported over the Clayton area on April 6 was almost certainly observed by the pilots of several light aircraft which flew close to and chased the object for a considerable time.

A detailed description of the object given by a science teacher at the Westall High school has discounted theories that the object was a weather balloon, an aircraft or a flock of birds.

Descriptions obtained from eye-witness students at the school and reports of sightings from other nearby locations have confirmed that an object or objects of inexplicable origin have appeared in the sky over this district in the past few weeks.

These facts have been uncovered by Journal reporters in their efforts to penetrate the wall of secrecy which was hastily thrown up after the sighting by students and staff at the Westall school on April 6.

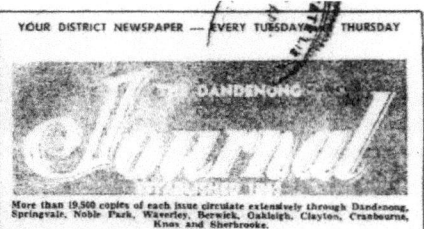

YOUR DISTRICT NEWSPAPER — EVERY TUESDAY & THURSDAY

The Dandenong Journal

More than 19,500 copies of each issue circulate extensively through Dandenong, Springvale, Noble Park, Waverley, Berwick, Oakleigh, Clayton, Cranbourne, Knox and Sherbrooke.

1 Scott St., Dandenong. Ph. Dandenong 2 0251, 2 0365. Price 4 cents

Vol. 105, No. 30   THURSDAY, APRIL 21, 1966   52 Pages

Hospital casualty department—'68

DANDENONG.— A casualty department at the new Dandenong Base Hospital will not be completed before October 1967, and will not be ready for use before June or July, 1968. This has been made clear by the Hospitals and Charities Commission in a letter to the Dandenong and District Hospital Committee.

Only emergency casualty facilities are provided at the hospital at present, because of the absence of resident medical officers.

The commission's letter setting out the expected completion and occupancy dates for the casualty department was discussed at the committee's meeting last week.

Dr. Tunbridge told the committee that the problem of how the casualty department should be staffed when completed, needed some clarification.

Committee president, Mr. McKeon, said this was a matter largely dependent on Commission policy and on discussions between Dr. Lindell, the commission chairman, and representatives of the Honorary Medical Board. "That is the 64-dollar question," he said.

'Different'

He suggested that the matter was one that could be mentioned at the medical board's representatives conference with the steering committee of the proposed Public Obstetric Patients' unit in the new hospital.

The Hospital Committee had to face up to the development of a casualty department. Before it was

Basis for experiment

functioning there were problems that would have to be ironed out, and much depended on commission policy he said.

It appeared that the new base hospital was to be developed as experimental lines and would be different from any other hospital in Victoria.

Even the committee was unaware at this stage of what form it was going to take.

Only Dr. Lindell, chairman of the commission, knew the details.

The medical board's representatives at the conference with the steering committee might be able to learn something of the commission's policy when they were discussing the public obstetric unit he said.

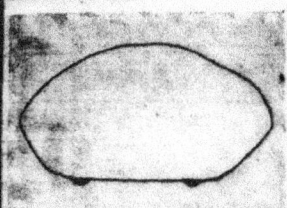

MARYLIN EASTWOOD (pictured) a second-year student at Westall High School, is one of the youngsters who watched the unidentified flying object from her school playground on April 6.

The object left a clear impression on Marylyn's memory, and her description of it tallies with those given by other students and staff members who saw it.

For The Journal, she drew a sketch of the object, reproduced above.

Marylyn described the object as "round, with a bump on top and round things underneath." Her sketch closely resembles sketches and photographs of other unidentified flying objects reported from many parts of the world.

'This wasn't one' ▼

Red and blue

Silver

AN INDICATION of sightings which can be attributed to known causes is the case of a sighting by 18-year-old Neil Dave, of Camelia Crt. Doveton.

On Tuesday, April 12, between 4 and 4.30 a.m., Neil was travelling in his father's car in Wellington Rd. from Stud Rd.

He noticed a round, glowing object hovering above the SEC terminal station in Wellington Rd.

Neil drew a sketch of what he saw (reproduced at right).

At first, this was regarded as a possible UFO sighting, but comparisons between Neil's sketch and Meteorological Bureau photographs confirmed that Neil had almost certainly seen a weather balloon.

'Beam of light like a disc'

The Journal reported the sighting last week, but attempts to obtain detailed accounts were hampered by school authorities. Students and staff are understood to have been instructed to "talk to no-one" about the incident.

Last week The Journal was able to obtain only the information that the object sighted was "round and humped with a fat base grey or silver grey in color and being circled by what appeared to be light aircraft."

It has now been reliably established that the object was in fact chased by five light aircraft, and that the pilots were obviously in a position to observe it.

However, the absence of any record of this number of aircraft operating from airstrips in the vicinity at the time of the sighting, has deepened the mystery.

Officials at Moorabbin airport say a dozen aircraft took off from there on the morning of April 6, one of which was on a cross-country flight.

Other craft were on circuits and bumps training flights but were flying to the south-east of the strip. (The Westall school is three and a half miles to the north-east.)

The RAAF had no aircraft operating in the area at the time.

One plane, piloted by Mr. Bob Ford, of Smith St., Thornbury, was flying "somewhere in that area" at the time of the sighting, but Mr. Ford said he didn't notice anything unusual in the air.

A science teacher at Westall High School, Mr. Andrew Greenwood, who this week because one of the first to help break the silence surrounding the incident, said he had observed the object clearly.

He said five light aircraft were circling the object and were flying at a relatively low altitude.

The aircraft had played a "cat and mouse" kind of game

MR. GREENWOOD

with the object, Mr. Greenwood said.

He described the object being chased by the aircraft as:

"Like a thin beam of light, about half the length of a light aircraft.

"It was silvery-grey and seemed to 'thicken' at times.

"The thickening was similar to when a disc is turned a little to show the underside.

"The object was never really stationary, Mr. Greenwood said. It seemed to move from side to side and up and down.

"At first there was one plane apparently observing the object.

"Later, Mr. Greenwood noticed five aircraft which attempted to follow the object as it occasionally accelerated back and forth from east to west.

Mr. Greenwood first saw the object when it rose into the air from behind pine trees near the school. After about 20 minutes or about the end of morning recess, Mr. Greenwood looked away, and when he looked back, it had disappeared.

All details of interviews conducted by The Journal during its investigation of the Clayton sighting have been passed on to the Victorian Flying Saucer Research Society.

● CONTD. ON P.2

(Photographs on this page by Renown Studios, Clayton, 544-4103).

...BUT WHAT DID THE FISHERMEN SEE?

Dandenong.— Journal reporters investigating the Westall High School sighting, have unearthed reports of several other sightings by local residents.

Some can obviously be explained as sightings of satellites, particularly bright stars or aircraft. However, one of the most intriguing reports comes from Chelsea estate agent, Mr. John McConchie.

He was one of a group of 14 who saw two unidentified flying objects while on a fishing trip near Taggerty over the Easter holiday.

Mr. McConchie says he doesn't believe in flying saucers, but he "knows what he saw."

At about 11 am on Easter Monday, a member of the fishing group looked up at a plane flying overhead and noticed two bright, round objects high up over to the west.

He called the attention of the other fishermen and as they watched, one of the objects took off at high speed to the west.

Mr. McConchie, who was last of the group to "pick up" the objects, trained his field glasses on the remaining object, which was still stationary.

He said: "Thinking it was a weather balloon, I trained my glasses on it, but saw that it was made of a metallic substance.

"Looking longer, I saw that it seemed to sprout a tail, similar to shuttle-cock feathers.

"The tail wasn't there to come and go all the time, but seemed

Mr. McConchie described the objects when first seen as similar to stars.

"But it was 11 o'clock in the morning on a bright sunny day. I know they were not stars," he said.

AVONDALE MOTORS PTY. LTD.

36 LONSDALE STREET, DANDENONG. Tel.: 2 0495.

and at 485 Hampton Street, Hampton.

YOUR LEADING VOLKSWAGEN DEALER!

Six months ago Avondale Motors promised the BEST VW SERVICE available
WE ARE GIVING THIS SERVICE!

● Are YOU taking advantage of this
● Are YOU profiting from our skills and efficiency

1196 VW owners in this area are!

This is NOT Lip Service — This is service ... to YOU the CUSTOMER.

YOU ARE OUR BUSINESS!

USED CAR SPECIALS

1965 VW1500 Twin "S". New car terms
1966 H.D. Holden. $100 off list.

Registered at the G.P.O., Melbourne, for transmission by post as a newspaper.

Haunted Skies Volume Two Revised

Miss Jeanette Muir
Shane:

> "At about 10.15am that morning, two groups of students were involved in Physical Education classes on the school's playing field. One of the teachers – Miss Jeanette Muir, from New Zealand – was probably the first adult to notice the object, alerted by the cries and shrieks of her students. As the object had made no sound as it approached the school oval, it was right overhead when it was spotted. For several minutes about fifty Form 1 and Form 3 students, and their two teachers, watched as this silver/white, shiny, metallic-looking flying object, about the size of one or two cars and shaped like an upside-down bowl, flew low over their heads. It flew so low – as low as the tops of nearby gum trees and football goal posts – that many students thought it was readying to land, or feared an imminent impact with the ground."

> "Some of the students reacted with panic, and many became distraught. Miss Muir and another male teacher attempted to gather the students and shepherd them back towards the safety of the school buildings. The sight of this strange craft was overwhelming for many. It had appeared seemingly out of nowhere, but it seemed to be flying and hovering with intent – as if it was under control – indeed, as if it was a vehicle with something inside. Mystifying for those watching, however, was the fact that it was clearly not an aircraft or a balloon: there were no windows; no visible engines or propellers; no wings or fins; no flashing navigational lights; no markings, or letters or numbers of any kind; no ropes or strings. Its shape was clear, its lack of sound obvious, but both incongruous; it was flying, not floating. For others, something else was startling: there seemed to be one, perhaps two other objects just like it, but further up in the sky, keeping their distance."

Science teacher Andrew Greenwood

By this stage, one extremely agitated Form 1 student had broken away from her class and the control of her teacher, and had run back into the school building, bursting in on a Form 2 science class under the control of science teacher – Mr Andrew Greenwood, blurting out that there were, *"'flying saucers' outside,*

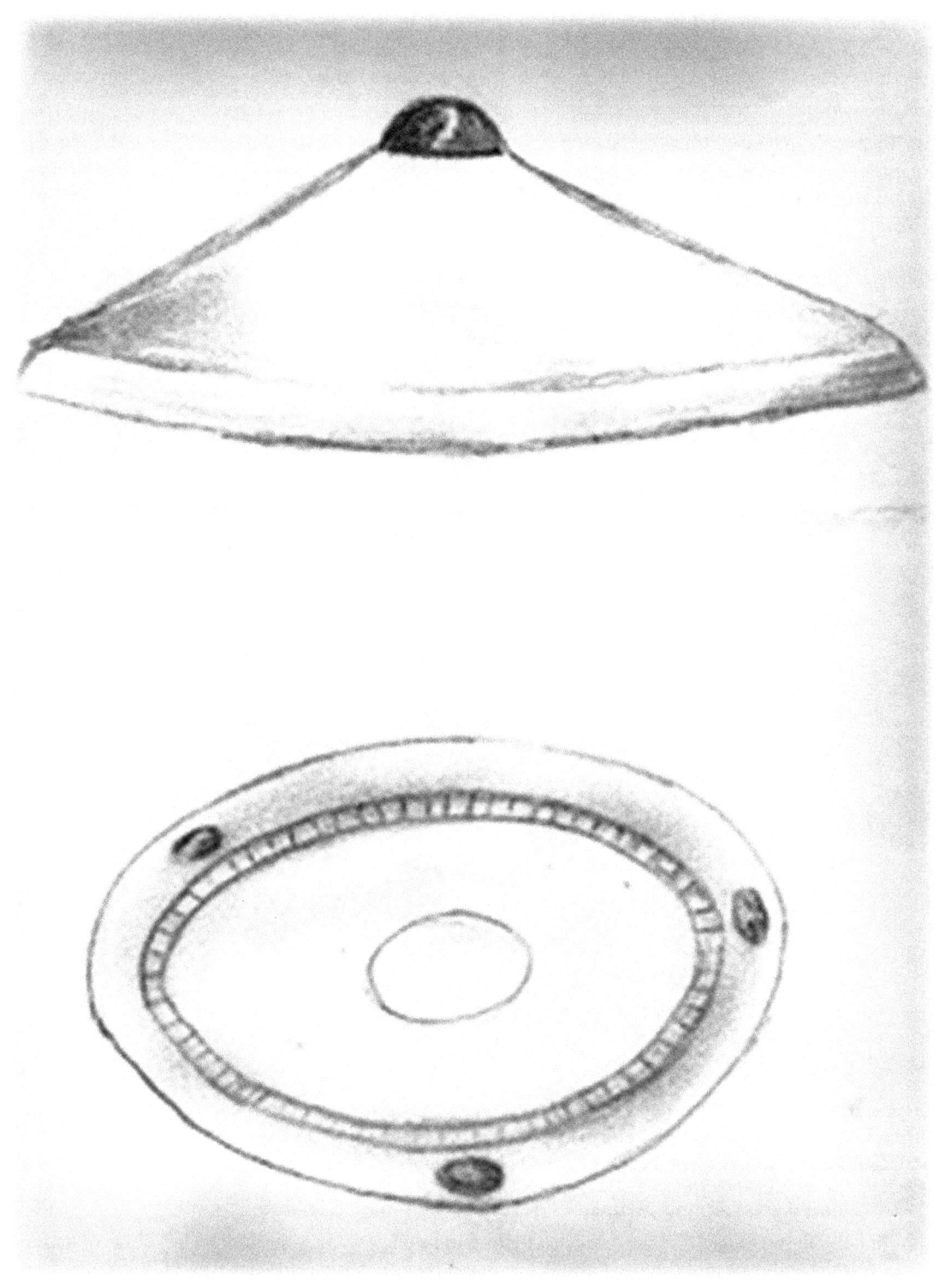

Haunted Skies Volume Two Revised

'flying saucers' outside!" Mr Greenwood reacted harshly to the intrusion and attempted to settle his class, who were by now craning their necks at the windows which looked out towards the oval. A few minutes later the recess bell sounded, and Mr Greenwood with students in tow, went to look for themselves.

Mr Greenwood:

"I was able to observe the object clearly. Five light aircraft were circling the object at relatively low altitude. They seemed to be playing a 'cat and mouse' game with the object, which was like a thin beam of light about half the length of a light aircraft. It was silver-grey and seemed to thicken at times. The thickening was similar to when a disc is turned a little to show the underside; it was never really stationary. It seemed to move up and down and from side to side as it occasionally accelerated back and forth from east to west."

When the excited student ran past the ablution block to burst in to the science lab with the amazing news, she had run past another Form 1 student who was standing nearby. This girl had a sick note, so wasn't doing PE, but was watching from the sidelines. She watched in utter amazement as the objects appeared and silently flew in, sure that at least one of them flew down so low over the oval that it

disappeared behind the wooden paling perimeter fence where, she presumed, it landed in the grassy paddock adjacent to the school. Later, classmates would lead her to that fence so that she could see the marks left behind from where the 'flying saucer' had touched down.

Discoloured grass around perimeter – Three indentations left behind

Although the 'flying saucer' had departed, left behind in its place was a huge and perfect circle of flattened grass, with the stalks of grass swirled around in one direction, with a distinct ring of discoloured grass

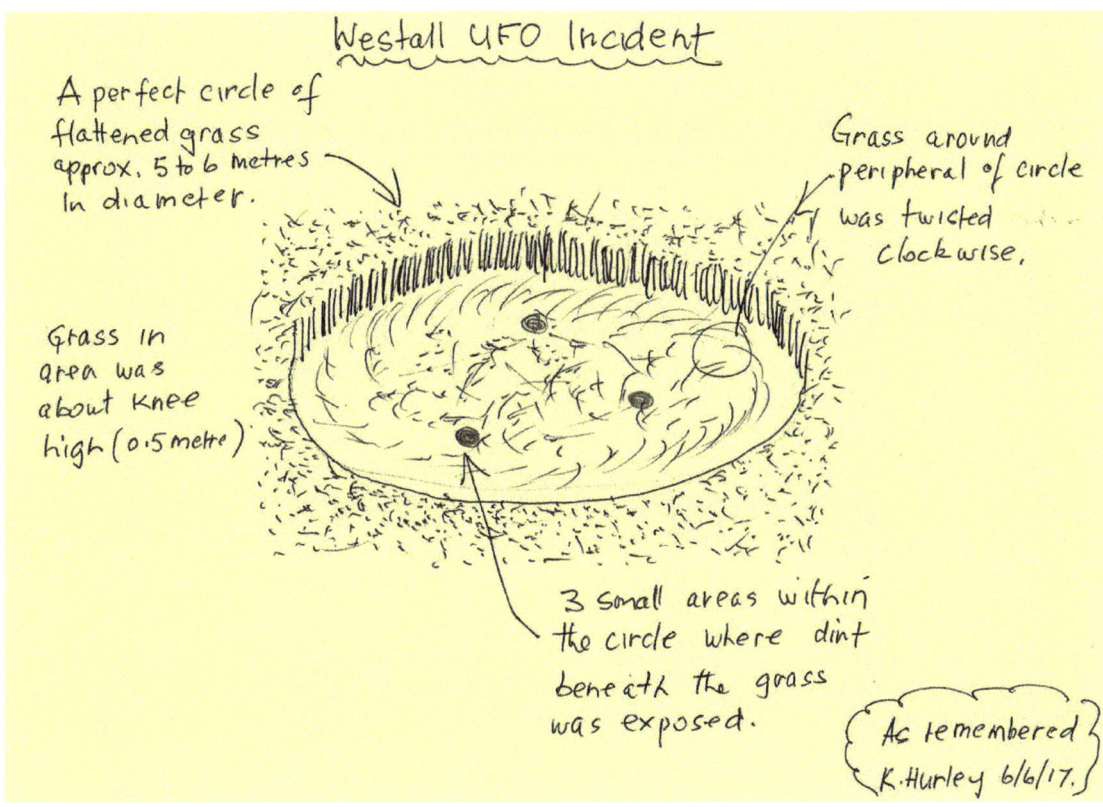

around the perimeter. Many recall that the perimeter seemed to be singed, or a little burnt, or scorched. Others also recall three indentations in the grass around the circle. Strangely, for those who first arrived, there seemed to be no vehicular, animal or human tracks in the grass surrounding the circle. For these witnesses there was no doubting the obvious correlation between the bowl or saucer-shaped craft they had seen in the sky, and then descending to this spot behind the trees, and the tightly wound circle of flattened grass before their eyes.

Lyn:

"As I recall we did see a large area of flattened grass, which looked as though the grass had been flattened all the same way in a circular fashion. By memory it was about 20 feet across. At the time we informed the teachers. Not much interest was shown, although I think a local newspaper came along. Teachers were not impressed." (**Source: Letter from Lyn to Keith Basterfield, 14th May 1990**)

Threats and Intimidation

[It is has been claimed that Andrew Greenwood – the science teacher whose picture appeared in the local newspaper with the story – was visited a few days later, at home, by two people who announced themselves as from the RAAF. They told him that if he made any more public statements, they would "leak out" that he had a "drinking problem" and that would mean the end of his career as a teacher.]

Pandemonium breaks out and an example of UFO display

On the grassy oval, and in the adjacent asphalt quadrangle, pandemonium broke out; word of the arrival over the school of between one and three 'flying saucers' spread like wildfire. Boys were shocked to see girls, still in their PE uniforms, hanging off the fences! When Andrew Greenwood and his class arrived, the closest 'flying saucer' had begun to move away from the school, but was still very visible in the sky above a copse of pine trees at a property called *The Grange,* about 400 hundred metres away.

To the amazement of everyone watching, the larger (or closest) 'flying saucer' flitted from one side of the sky to the other – as if it was just blinking off and then on again at spots hundreds of metres away. It then ascended and descended and turned at incredible speeds. It was like watching a dragonfly trapped in a bottle, except this dragonfly had no wings and the bottle was the size of the sky – a cool blue autumn sky, with nothing but a few white fluffy clouds in the distance.

Aircraft arrive

The silence was then broken by the sound of five small planes suddenly appearing. This was a regular sight, as one of Australia's busiest airports – at that time Melbourne's second main airport, Moorabbin Airport – was a mere four kilometres away, and were presumed to be light aircraft – totally different in shape and characteristics to the 'flying saucers'.

These aircraft were seen to fly low, down towards the 'flying saucer'. Every time they seemed to approach closer towards the object, 'it' just flitted away – as if playing a bizarre game of 'cat and mouse' – then, without warning, the 'flying saucer' descended behind the copse of pines and vanished, temporarily, out of view.

Seen over power lines

By this time about 300 of the High School's 485 students had gathered on and around the oval, many climbing the high wooden fence on the school's western boundary, and the wire fence at the foot of the huge high-tension electric power pylon that stood in the school's south-western corner, where the 'flying saucer' had lifted off and over these power lines as it ascended into the sky from the school, before moving south towards The Grange.

As the 'flying saucer' disappeared behind the pine trees, a huge number of children who had been watching – clearly against school rules [when school rules for kids carried the weight of law] – jumped the low wire fence that separated the school from the drainage ditch that ran alongside the dirt Fairbank Road on the schools' southern flank, and ran towards The Grange in hot, excited pursuit of the 'flying saucer'. The cries of several teachers, warning the children to return to the school, was ignored, as dozens of them traversed dirt tracks and paddocks in search of the elusive 'flying saucer'.

One Form 1 witness remembers arriving in time to see the 'flying saucer' lifting off from where it had settled, or perhaps had been hovering. On the ground were two other girls – one of whom had fainted; the other, just getting up but still dazed. While she tried to comprehend all of this, the 'craft' ascended, turned onto its side, and then flew up and away at a great rate, vanishing from view.

Another Form 2 student told of running after her Form 1 friend, who was in front, and finding her three-quarters of the way between the school and where the craft appeared to have landed. Her younger friend was hysterical and had already started running back towards the oval; she tried to calm her and question her, but the girl was too wrought and broke free from her friend's worried embrace.

The Form 2 girl then decided not to venture any further into The Grange and returned to school, in time to see her friend overcome, falling into the arms of a teacher. Shortly afterwards she watched as an ambulance arrived, drove onto the playing field, and transported her friend away. Forty-five years later she still wonders about her friend, as she never returned to school and was not sighted again.

Kris:

> "I was in the second intake of students at Westall High and in 1966 was in my third year there. The school had been built on vacant land, approximately 19 kilometres south-east of Melbourne.

Westall was a new suburb in an industrial area. Moorabbin Airport is perhaps 7 kilometres away. During the morning tea break, one of the kids told us that there were 'flying saucers' down at the oval.

My friends and I raced to the far corner of the oval, and by this time there were quite a lot of other kids there. We didn't see them immediately, as they were quite high, and apart from that, we didn't expect to see anything! What I saw was several objects that appeared as one 'saucer', inverted on another; they were perhaps white or shiny in colour and maybe there were about 7 of them.

It was difficult to tell how big they were, as I had no way of knowing how high they were, but they were whizzing back and forward across the sky at a rapid pace.

The UFOs appeared to come down behind some trees, not too far from the school ground, and some of the children climbed the fence to go over there ... I didn't. Perhaps they appeared to come down, then up again. I find that part hard to remember. I think we may have had a twenty minute break for morning tea and we saw the UFOs soon after the break began. We watched them until the bell to return to class had sounded. Some of the children returned to class immediately, but I stayed for probably another ten minutes; by this time the teachers were rounding up the kids. The teacher we had (for Library) was intent on telling us we had made the lot up, stop the nonsense and get into class! When the lunch break arrived, I immediately looked skyward but saw nothing. There was talk of reporters being at the gate but teachers on duty told all the children to keep away. After lunch a special assembly was called, where the principal informed the children that they had seen nothing and to talk to no-one about it! I couldn't believe it; there were so many children that did see this event.

When I returned from school I told my mother about the day's events and she mentioned that my brother, Ken, had ridden on his bike somewhere near Westall High. When he returned, much later, he told of the flattened grass circles and of the Army and Air Force taking photos; there were lights set up and a lot of personnel. They were trying to keep onlookers away.

That night there was a short article on the evening news. I think there may have been some film of the school, taken at lunchtime – I'm not sure. Every time I was outside, for days after, I looked for these UFOs but saw nothing – until the following Saturday, when my girlfriend and I were at the local park at the end of our street. The park was alongside a railway line and in a direct line from our homes to the school. We looked toward the direction of our school but a little to the right, and again saw the same type of UFO moving rapidly back and forward in the sky. We watched for only a few minutes before racing back to my friend's house to get her father, who had been very sceptical. They only lived a few hundred metres from the park, and when he saw them he scratched his head and agreed they were not planes and that he had no idea what they were; he wouldn't admit they could be UFOs. The UFOs did not stay around for long, but I remember that when they went it was extremely quickly. That was the last time I saw them.

Some information that could be of value is: Principal: Mr Samblebe, Form teacher: Ms. I.J. Brown."

(Source: Letter from Kris to Keith Basterfield, 1 May 1990)

'Flying Saucers' do not exist!

Although teachers – and prefects – soon arrived on the scene to escort the students back to the relative safety of the school grounds, they also became witnesses too. One of them, woodwork teacher – Mr Gerry Shepherd, found it difficult to believe the stories of 'flying saucers'. He had not seen anything himself, but he could not deny the sudden and unprecedented appearance of this circle in an area he knew like the back of his hand. In the two decades that Mr Shepherd taught at the school, he had never before, nor since, seen such a perfectly formed circle in such an unlikely place. Nor was the pandemonium of that day ever to be repeated in his career. As he described it, *"Westall High School, as a teaching institution, ceased!"* in the immediate wake of these extraordinarily unexpected events.

At a school assembly called after all the students had been returned to the school grounds, headmaster – Mr Samblebe, made it clear to the student body that 'flying saucers' did not exist and that they had not seen anything of importance, and that, despite this, they were not to speak again of the day's events. Most importantly, they were not to speak to the media, which had begun to gather at the school's front gates in Rosebank Avenue.

Men in dark suits attend school assembly

Several students recall that standing alongside the headmaster at the assembly, that day, were several people they had never seen before. Some recall that they wore dark suits; others, that they were in dark blue uniforms. All agree that they were *"from the Government"*. Several students were to meet up with these officials in Mr Samblebe's office over the following hours, presumably in a bid to keep the 'lid on'.

Visitors arrive to the newly-formed impressions in the ground

Over the coming hours that day, and especially after school, many people – including students from the primary and high schools, their families and neighbours – travelled to The Grange to see the circle. They were stunned by what they saw, and for those students now accompanied by their parents, relief that their parents now believed their stories. Unfortunately, for most of the Westall students, that wasn't their experience…and to this day, after 45 long years have passed, many are still hurt that their own parents and siblings refused to believe them, or at least were reluctant to.

Fire Service attended

Albie – a firefighter from nearby Springvale Fire Station, and his crew, tells of being directed to a report of something strange crashing or coming down amongst the trees at The Grange.

> *"The fire crew did not have exact coordinates, so we drove around looking for the 'crash site'. When we arrived, we found a swarm of school kids running around, looking for where the 'craft' had gone to; someone said it had skipped over the fence and into the adjacent Spring Valley Golf Course, but no such reports came in of that happening."*

Civil Defence also alerted

David – then Deputy Controller of the Civil Defence Organisation (now known as the State Emergency Service) – informed Shane that they, too, had received a report of something in trouble – perhaps a crash – at The Grange. A crew was dispatched from the Oakleigh depot, but they also arrived too late to see any 'craft', but in time to see the melee happening in and around The Grange.

Both emergency crews returned to their respective stations with many unanswered questions.

Twenty-four witnesses and what they saw

Shane:

> *"Twenty-four of the witnesses, including a teacher, have recounted memories of people in police and/or military uniforms (some say Army, others Air Force, some aren't sure) coming to the school or to the site of the circle at The Grange. Some recall police, Army and fire vehicles responding within twenty minutes, and still remember the sight of their small convoy raising dust as they raced along what were mainly unsealed roads at the time. Another witness recalls about twenty soldiers dressed in khaki uniforms alighting from two jeeps and two long-bed trucks with camouflage tarpaulins over the top, taking charge of a paddock containing a circle. Another, an apprentice, who had two younger siblings at the school, remembers taking cover behind pine trees as he and his high*

school sister watched four soldiers – two enlisted men in camouflage and two others in officer dress – examine the circle with special equipment. Another, who was an electrical engineering student at nearby Monash University, rode down and met his uncle at The Grange, who showed him the circle.

The following day he returned with mates from university, and was surprised to find the same place completely sealed off with barricades and soldiers on point duty. In the distance, however, near the paddock containing the circle, he could see soldiers alighting from trucks wielding what appeared to be Geiger counters and metal detectors. They were told to 'piss off' by the guards in no uncertain terms!

A week later he went back again. The barricades and the soldiers were gone, but so was the circle! At first he noticed that the grass had been cut between the road and the paddock, and then, in the paddock itself, the whole area had been burnt, leaving no trace of the remarkable circle he and his uncle, and hordes of others that day, had clearly seen. Several boys from the high school, who, a few short years later became police officers themselves, clearly recall seeing two types of uniforms present around the school on the day of the sighting. One of the students was the son of a serving police officer and knew the uniforms well. Cleary, some were police and some were military. They were working together, or at least, alongside each other."

TV Station called ... Media responds

Following calls made to the emergency services, two girl students ran down the street to the phone box outside the Westall shops in Rosebank Avenue and telephoned a TV station. In addition, some residents contacted the district newspaper – *The Dandenong Journal*.

By the afternoon a TV crew from *Channel Nine* was at the front gate, attempting to interview excited witnesses. Several students managed to give their version of the events, before a police officer and a teacher intervened and ordered the students back inside. The story, including vision of the interrupted interview, aired on Melbourne TV news that night. *The Dandenong Journal* was able to interview Mr Greenwood and a Form two student – Marilyn Eastwood. [Both teacher and student were severely reprimanded by the headmaster for doing this.]

Shane:

"The story was to become the leading front-page story for two weeks running, and remains an important primary document from the event. Strangely, even though the newspaper's contract photographer is sure he took photos of the circle at the time, they were not published as part of the articles. Even more strangely, the local government archive that has been entrusted with the newspaper's photographic collection, recently found that the box for April 1966 was now missing from its collection!"

7th April 1966 – It might have been a weather balloon!

The Age, 7th April 1966 – Object Perhaps Balloon – *"An unidentified flying object seen over the Clayton-Moorabbin area yesterday morning might have been a weather balloon. Hundreds of children and a number of teachers at Westall School, Clayton, watched the object during morning break."*

Sue Savage, who now lives in Springvale North, was 13 at the time of the encounter. She was in science

---

*According to the *Dandenong Journal*, further enquiries made into initial reports of the event revealed the object had been chased by five light aircraft and that the pilots were clearly in a position to see it [Authors: not necessarily so, bearing in mind that we have come across occasions when ground observers have seen a UFO in the sky, which has not been seen by pilots who have been asked to investigate such phenomenon].

Enquiries made with Moorabbin Airport disclosed that on 6th April, a dozen aircraft took off, one of which was on a cross-county flight, and that the others were on circuit training to the south-east of the airstrip. (The school lies three and half miles to the north-east.)

class at Westall High School when a fellow student ran into the classroom, shouting *"there is a 'flying saucer' outside"*.

Witness – Suzanne Savage:

> *"The UFO was like two saucers – one on the bottom and one turned upside-down on the top. Some people say there was just one, but I reckon there were three. They were hovering over the trees and then went down into the trees and disappeared for a minute or two, then rose back up, sort of banked on their side and then took off at a 1,000 miles per hour. We were too young to be sceptics ... we know what we saw. It really makes me very angry to hear people say there's nothing else out there and I know there is. Even mum and dad both said it was a load of rubbish and I told my children, years later, and they thought I was crazy until the first reunion was held."*

Witness – Kevin Hurley was 21 at the time of the incident and rode his bike to the school from Murrumbeena, after being alerted to the UFO sighting. He never saw a UFO but he walked through tall grass to the spot behind the trees where the students said the UFO touched down for a couple of minutes.

> *"I saw a whole lot of people in a group huddle; they were all looking at the ground and there in 2 feet high grass was a big perfect circle of absolutely flattened and twisted grass. In that circle there were three distinct impressions where the grass has been penetrated down to the dirt. I returned to the site the next day, with a group of friends, but said it was cordoned off and a military officer ordered me away from the area."*

Joy Tighe interviewed ... film goes missing!

GTV Channel 9 television also ran a news report about the encounter. A student – Joy Tighe, described the event for the reporter. However, a copy of this film is not available. *Channel 9* reports that it was removed from their archive and not returned. Incredibly frustratingly, *Channel 9*, after a search in both its Melbourne and Sydney film archives, was not able to locate the original news story which all of the witnesses recall watching that April night. Shane contacted the original news reporter, who had clear memories of the story, as although 'flying saucer' reports were fairly common at the time, he had never covered one then, or since, that involved schools and with so many witnesses – and in broad daylight. He put the loss of the film containing his news story down to the vagaries of time.

Victorian Flying Saucer Research Society arrived

Investigators from the Victorian Flying Saucer Research Society arrived on the scene, two days later – Good Friday. By this stage however, the school was closed for the vacation, and the students had dispersed for the Easter break. They did manage to speak to some locals, however, and take photos of the circle in the grass. The Society now says it cannot locate those photos, or any investigation notes that may have been taken.

The Dandenong Journal writers – Des Carroll and Dave Oakley – as well as a government meteorological physicist – Dr F.A. Berson, attempted to follow the incident up with the school authorities, local residents, Moorabbin Airport, the Department of Air, and the Army, but were told they knew nothing.

Victorian researchers – Paul Norman and Peter Norris – contacted American atmospheric physicist and researcher – Professor James McDonald, and he interviewed both Andrew Greenwood and Dr. Berson, in 1967, whilst visiting Melbourne, and his notes have become an important source of information about their reflections on the incident. Andrew Greenwood has always stood by his story, without being able to offer an explanation for what he saw. He told Professor McDonald that Miss Muir had also seen the object when it first appeared, but that she had clammed up about it and would not talk. He believed three teachers in total had seen the object, and would not have been surprised if there had been more, but that such was the adverse reaction from Headmaster Samblebe, and others, towards those who spoke up, nothing more would probably be said.

2006 – 40th Anniversary of event

From time to time over the subsequent years, researchers, such as John Pinkney, Bill Chalker and Keith Basterfield, looked at the case, and wrote about it, but for the most part it was left as an indelible and mystifying memory in the minds of those who were there.

In 2005 Shane set up a Yahoo Groups web site (http://tech.groups.yahoo.com/group/Westallhighschoolufo/) in an attempt to encourage people who had memories of the event, to come forward and share them. That led to a reunion to mark the fortieth anniversary of the 'flying saucer' event, in 2006, at The Grange at Westall, in which fifty people gathered, including former high and state school students, the former state school deputy principal, and other Westall residents who had been witnesses. The reunion also marked the first film shoot by *Endangered Pictures*, who had decided to make a documentary about the incident and Shane's research into it, which was released in 2010 as *Westall '66: a Suburban UFO Mystery*.

When it aired in June on the Australian Sci-fi Channel, it was the highest rating programme for that day and for that week on the channel! The broadcast resulted in many more people making contact with him via the film's web site (http://www.westall66ufo.com.au) and many joined the Westall Incident Facebook page, which he had also established (http://www.facebook.com/group.php?gid=7613851618). This has resulted in the uncovering of new details to the story, and many more witness accounts. His original intention, which was to bring this story out into the light of day, from under the carpet where it had been swept, or otherwise found itself, was meeting with some success.

Shane:

> "A conspiracy of silence continues to shroud the events of Westall 1966. There are people who still refuse to talk about it. After the film screened, the daughter of a former senior federal public servant, working in the area of air weapons development, emailed me to say her father had been a witness to what happened at Westall. She remembers that a great deal of pressure was brought to bear on her father to not disclose what he had seen, and this contributed to his early death four years later. He himself had forbidden his daughter from talking about it. She wanted me to know that she felt relief that so many others had seen what her father had seen, and that this was validation for his efforts to deal with whatever was flying over Westall that day. And whatever it was, surely, after the passage of 45 years, there can no longer be valid continuing national security implications. It was all a very long time ago – it is time for the full truth about Westall to see the light of day. For further information go to: www.westall66ufo.com.au or **email**: shaneryan@velocitynet.com.au."

New Information and further leads

In 2011, events from 45 years before led to some new information and leads. One student, Victor – then a student at the school, who had leapt a fence to stand next to two 'flying saucers' on the ground immediately in front of him, so close that he could feel their heat – confided in Shane, a memory he had kept to himself, out of fear, for all of these years.

Form 3 student, Brendan, indicates to Shane Ryan where he saw the 'flying saucer' above the Westall High School oval. (Credit: Carmel McAloon)

> "I had also been summoned to the headmaster's office, and approached it with particular trepidation after having just witnessed the headmaster's rant at the school assembly where the students had been reprimanded for chasing the 'flying saucers' and leaving the school grounds, and for telling tall tales about something which clearly did not – could not – exist. The headmaster forbade any discussion about the incident with anybody, and in particular with the media gathering outside the school gates. He told me that I had been observed jumping the boundary fence and standing next to the 'flying saucers'. I was surprised to learn, in conversation with the

Shane Ryan looks towards where Form 2 student, Victor, in background, saw two flying saucers at Westall. ©Carmel McAloon.

headmaster, that when he had been in the Army as a younger man, something similar had once happened and he understood how the Army handled such matters. The Army, he warned, had ways of ensuring people didn't speak about things they wanted kept quiet. Out of a real concern for Vic, and for his aspirations to one day be an artist, he pleaded with him to keep what he had seen to himself – that was the best course for him, and indeed for the school. Vic soon realised that the demeanor the headmaster had adopted minutes earlier at the assembly was seemingly at odds with his greater recognition of the strange incident taking place outside his office windows. For Vic, the headmaster's words haunted him down the decades, and he indeed remained tight-lipped about Mr Samblebe's exchange with him, for fear that, one day, somehow, the Army would come a-knocking. It took him 45 years to free himself from that fear instilled in him as a fourteen year-old boy, behind the headmaster's office door."

Paul was working with two others in a nearby market garden between the High School and The Grange, when he saw the 'flying saucer'. Here he describes to researcher Shane

Shane Ryan listens as former Westall State School student, Tony, describes the drama of the sighting. He saw the 'flying saucer' from the school and later saw the circle at The Grange with his mother and many other locals. (Credit: Carmel McAloon)

(Credit: Carmel McAloon)

Ryan, the arrival of the Army soon afterwards in trucks and jeeps.

Brady Avenue runs along where the paddock used to be, adjacent to the High School's western boundary. The high wooden fence has been replaced with a low mesh one. This is looking south, towards The Grange (pine trees of which are just visible in the background). The street now covers

Form 2 student, Victor, explains his sighting to the documentary film crew. (Credit: Shane Ryan)

where some students remember seeing 'flying saucers', or the marks left behind by them.

Keith Basterfield unable to trace Government files

Another interested party was Keith Basterfield, living in Adelaide and a member of the Australian UFO Research Association (AURA) involved with Project Disclosure in more recent years, which has spent considerable time tracking down UFO documents held by various Government Departments through both the Archives Act and the Freedom of Information Act.

They have located and examined dozens of Government UFO related files and been through thousands of pages of material – some previously known, but some never seen before by civilian researchers.

Brady Avenue (Credit: Shane Ryan)

Keith:

"In 1966 Clayton, and particularly Westall, was almost country. The paddock the 'saucers' landed in was remote from houses and surrounded by tall pines. The area had the grass flattened and 'tufted' in circles about 60 feet to 120 feet diameter. The rest of the long grass was undisturbed. No circles overlapped. We thought and talked of ways you could make such circles, such as walking with a rope or a tractor and a slasher. They didn't look like they were made by a method we could think of. I remember the circles were like the circles pictured in the newspapers around this time of the 'saucer nest' in Tully N.Q. I don't know if this was before or after what we saw. I know time dulls memories.

I am reminded of various incidents that vary in the way I and other people remember them. I looked for any information on the 1966 Westall event in these Government documents and found nothing at all on it. No record in the RAAF files. CSIRO files have located my sparse personal papers on this incident, which contain the following information from witnesses who were present on that day."

Shane:

"There were two further leads. One was the friend of a high school witness who told of a recent conversation she had with a man who, as a boy, had sat in a car with his father, parked outside the school. The father had noticed the presence of the military and got out of the car to approach an officer he saw nearby, to find out what was going on. The boy couldn't hear what the two men said to each other, but when his dad returned to the car he was ashen-faced, and quietly drove his son home. His father would never reveal what the soldier had said to him, and why the incident at Westall was now off-limits as a topic of discussion. And a former state school witness revealed he had recently come across a man whose father had been one of the pilots of one of the five planes flying around the 'flying saucers' that day at Westall. Nearby Moorabbin Airport, and the Air Force, had both stated that no planes they were responsible for were at Westall that day – but the witnesses had clearly seen the planes...and now a possible contact for one of those pilots.

And so, the search continues. It seems that the answers to the mystery of Westall 1966 lie within the memories of a few remaining people who were in charge that day...and that only their willingness to talk will break the back of this 45-year-old riddle. As always, we rely on fellow citizens to be honest and courageous, open and transparent...as the witnesses have been... for knowledge – of ourselves, and our world – to progress, and for truth to prevail."

Little changes over the years

[Authors: The events outlined by Shane Ryan and others once again show us that despite the clamour of those that feel Governments should come clean about their knowledge of the UFO presence, which has and still continues to form the backcloth of human existence, very little has been released other than periodical admissions of the existence of a phenomena that has been with us for a very long time ago. Unfortunately, we are no further to the truths of knowing what these things are and where they come from, and whether they have an agenda. What should worry people is that, over the years, there has been a concerted campaign to denigrate reports from the public by the media, who often see them as a form of entertainment, often accompanied by images of aliens abducting the luckless victims or

Sue

man's battle against the alien hordes. Very few journalists have the courage to 'tell it how it is', based on thousands – if not millions – of reports worldwide, which demand some answers, rather than a concerted effort to hide the truth and, occasionally, threaten those who have had the courage to come forward simply to tell what they have seen or experienced. This is a shocking indictment on us as a human race that often boasts of our exploration of space but balk at even accepting the validity of a phenomenon which won't go away.]

TERM ONE EDITION

Inside ... STORIES — POEMS — CRYPTIC CROSSWORD FOR PARENTS

Special .. EYE WITNESS ACCOUNT OF A FLYING SAUCER.

EDITORS' COLUMN

We hope you enjoy reading the Clayton Calendar.
Inside you will find many interesting articles.

Karen Ansell
Peter Farrell   *Editors*

(Sources: As above/*The Dandenong Journal*, 14.4.1966/21.4.66 – 'Clayton object and mystery aircraft'/ Judith Magee, Victorian Flying Saucer Research Society/Brian Boyle, PRA/*Australian Flying Saucer Review* (Melbourne, Victoria) Vol. 5, Jul 66/*FSR*)

Haunted Skies **Volume Two Revised**

10th April 1966 – Flashes of light over Northamptonshire

At 9.15am, newspaper employee – Mr Bob Peacock of Cheyne Walk, Kettering, in Northamptonshire – was sat in his living room, when he saw a brilliant, circular, whitish-yellow object flash by. It was visible for a couple of seconds, heading in a south to north direction.

Teenagers sighted it

Other witnesses were teenage cyclists – John Panther and Ian Houghton – who were riding along Cheyne Walk, Kettering, Northamptonshire, at 9.30am. They described:

> "...several flashes of brilliant light in the eastern part of the sky, moving towards the south-east. Through a break in the clouds, we saw a white 'ball of light' with strange edges, moving parallel to the ground, heading south to north."

At about the same time, two girls from Wellingborough noticed what they presumed to be lightning in the sky, after a bright 'flash of light' revealed "...*four horizontal, red, straight lines – the phenomenon being repeated four times, at 3-4 minute intervals*".

(Sources: Mr R.A. Jahn, BUFORA/Birmingham University Group)

17th April 1966 – Police officers sight a UFO over Ohio

At 5am, the police dispatcher from Ravenna, Ohio, radioed that a lady in Summit County (located west of Portage County) had called in with a report of seeing a brightly lighted object, *"as big as a house"*, flying over her neighbourhood. Deputy Sheriff Dale Spauer and Mounted Deputy Wilbur 'Barney' Neff were on patrol at the time. On Route 224, they saw an abandoned car on the side of the road and stopped to check it out. As they walked up to the car, Spauer looked into the wooded area behind them and saw *"this thing"* that rose up out of the woods, a hundred feet or so, and started moving towards them. The trees that the object cleared were on top of a rise in the ground right beside the roadway,

> ". . . so you couldn't see it until it was right on top of you. I looked at Barney and he was still watching the car, the car in front of us, and the 'thing' kept getting brighter and brighter and the area started to get light.
>
> I looked at Barney this time, and then told him to look over his shoulder – so he did. He didn't say anything. He just stood there with his mouth open for a minute, and looked down. I then started looking down and glanced at my hands, and my clothes weren't burning or anything, when it stopped right over us. The only thing, the only sound in the whole area, was a hum – like a transformer being loaded, or an overloaded transformer when it changes."

The officers, now frightened, made their way back to the patrol car and sat there for a while to recover their composure. [They were unaware of how long they sat there. It could have been ten seconds, or three minutes.] The object continued to hover, and then started moving to the east, and stopped again. Spauer picked up the microphone and reported to his dispatcher. At this time the object was brilliantly lighting up the area and it was about 250 feet away.

Spauer reported,

> "This bright object is right here; the one that everybody says is going over. The dispatcher told us to shoot it!"

They were then ordered to follow the object and thus began the wildest UFO chase on record. For more than seventy miles the object was chased, sometimes at speeds as high as 105 miles per hour.

As the sky became lighter with pre-dawn light, Spauer and Neff saw the UFO in silhouette. It had a vertical projection at the rear and it began to take on a metallic appearance as the chase continued and the daylight increased.

Haunted Skies Volume Two Revised

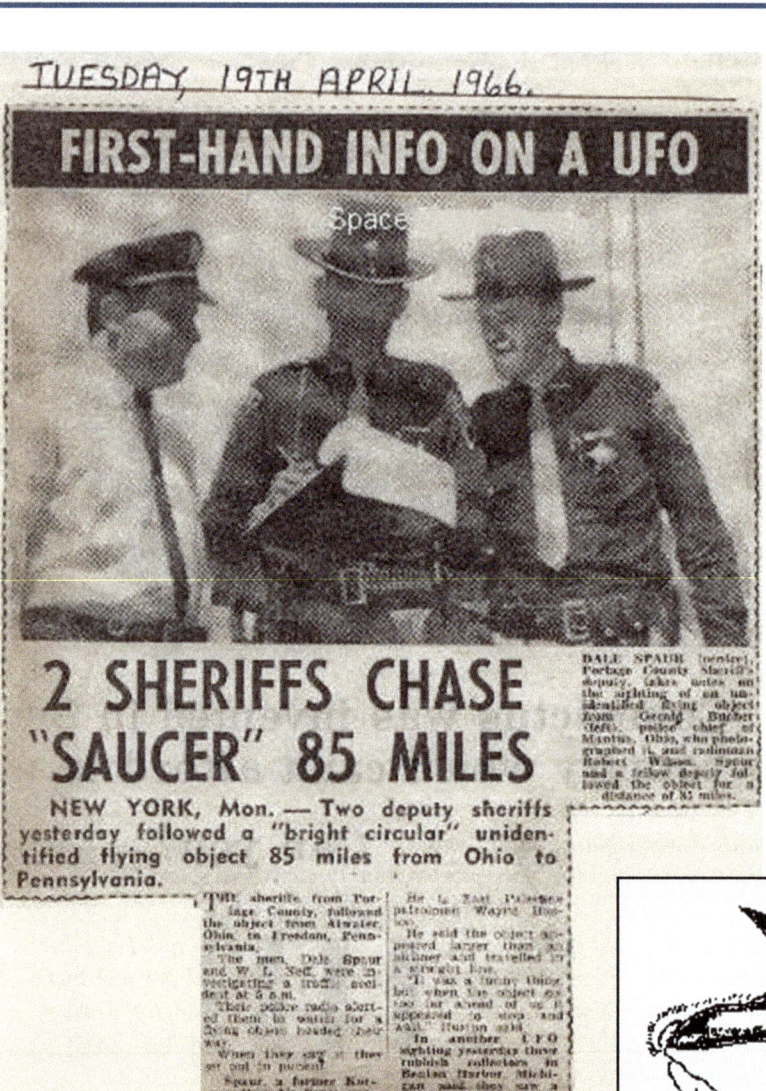

TUESDAY, 19TH APRIL, 1966.

FIRST-HAND INFO ON A UFO

2 SHERIFFS CHASE "SAUCER" 85 MILES

NEW YORK, Mon. — Two deputy sheriffs yesterday followed a "bright circular" unidentified flying object 85 miles from Ohio to Pennsylvania.

While the chase was in progress, Officer Wayne Huston was in his police cruiser near East Palestine, Ohio, some 40 miles to the east, and monitoring the radio conversation between Spauer and his office in Ravenna.

"I talked with Spauer by radio. I met him at the north edge of the city on Route 14. I saw the 'thing' when Dale was about five miles away from me. It was running down Route 14, about 800-900 feet up, when it came by. This was the lowest I ever saw it. As it flew by, I was standing by my cruiser; I watched it go right overhead.

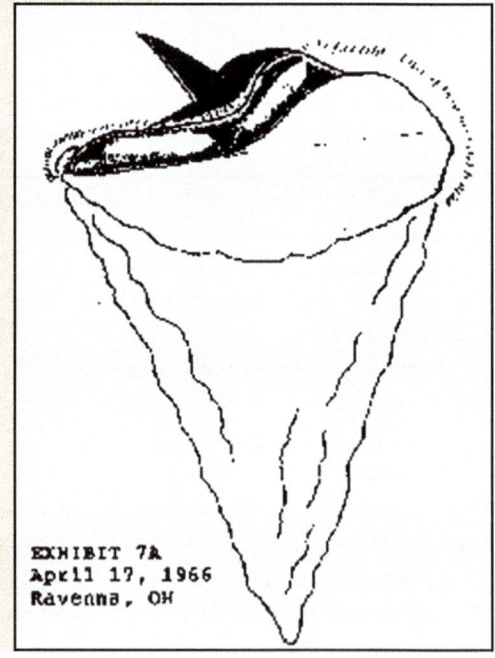

EXHIBIT 7A
April 17, 1966
Ravenna, OH

It was shaped something like an ice-cream cone, with a sort of partly melted down top. The point of the cone was underneath. The top was sort of like a dome. Spauer and Neff came down the road right after it. I fell in behind them. We were going 80-85 miles per hour; a couple of times around 105 miles per hour. At one point, at least, I was almost on Spauer's bumper and we checked with each other what we saw. It was right straight ahead of us, a half to three quarters of a mile ahead."

They were now in Pennsylvania, some fifteen miles east of the Ohio border.

"I guided him by radio. All the way we were trying to get contact with a Pennsylvania car. We had the base call the Chippewa State Police station to see if they had a car on 51. They didn't. The first state police car they saw was at Conway, near Rochester. Dale was low on gas and we stopped where Frank Panzenella was parked."

Panzenella had left a hotel in Conway, after getting some coffee, and was coming down Second Avenue. He looked to his right and saw a shining object. He thought it was a reflection off an airplane. He had been watching it for ten minutes when the two other patrol cars pulled up.

"The object was the shape of half a football, was very bright and about 25 to 35 feet in diameter. The object then moved out toward Harmony Township, approximately 1,000 feet high – then it stopped and went straight up, real fast, to 3,500 feet and then stopped.

It continued on upward until it got very small and disappeared."

All four saw the object shoot straight up and disappear. The object was hovering when an airplane taking off from the airport passed under it. It then took off directly upward, according to all witnesses.

18th April 1966 – Strange noise over Isle of Wight

Carisbrooke, Isle of Wight resident – Mrs C. Carter – was awoken by her alarm clock going off at 3.15 and 3.30am, followed by:

"...the sound of a frightening, whining, noise above the bungalows – the likes of which I had never heard before. I prayed to God, thinking it was going to crash on top of the building, but nothing happened and the noise stopped. When I looked outside, there was nothing to be seen."

At 1pm, the same day, three or four dull silver-coloured objects, triangular in shape, were seen in the sky over Barnsley, Yorkshire, before being lost from view behind cloud. **(Source: Isle of Wight UFO Society)**

18th April 1966 – *Daily Telegraph*, 'Flying Object – 85 mile chase'

The newspaper told its readers about two deputy Sheriffs who had chased a 35-40 feet in diameter UFO for 85 miles to Freedom, Pennsylvania, around this date.

Two 'discs' seen in the sky

At 9am, Mr K. Hetherington was at the GPO building in Gateshead, County Durham, when he sighted:

"...two white circular 'discs', one behind the other, the rear one moving in a wavy motion in the sky towards the North-north-east, at an angle of 50 degrees off the horizon".

Within five seconds, the objects – totally devoid of any markings, protrusions or sound – disappeared out of sight, northwards.

UFOs nonsense!

The *Evening Sentinel* (Montreal) (18.4.1966) brought its reader's attention to a statement made by Sir Bernard Lovell – head of Jodrell Bank radio astronomy observatory in Britain:

"Unidentified Flying Objects, reported over North America recently, were really bits of meteors burning up as they entered the Earth's atmosphere. I am always surprised by the great amount of

discussion which goes on in North America concerning these objects. They do not concern science but science fiction. Scientists have been able to explain every UFO they investigated. Any suggestion that UFOs are visitors from outer space is nonsense."

20th April 1966 – Elliptical object seen over County Durham

On the same day, at 10.20pm, a white elliptical 'craft' was seen moving southwards across the sky from the direction of Leam estate, towards Washington, by a local resident – Mr R. Maddison, who said:

"Sometimes it stopped and moved backwards, retracing its steps, before finally disappearing from view".

During the end of April 1966, one of a number of UFOs was reported in the skies over Wellingborough, Rushden and Kettering areas, between 9pm and 10pm. In an interview held with the local newspaper, a member of the UFO group at Cambridge University added, rather intuitively:

"This seems to be the start of something. A lot more will be seen in the coming weeks, if people keep their eyes open."

(Source: *Wellingborough News,* 22.4.1966 – 'Richard investigates mystery objects')

22nd April 1966 – UFO sighted over Ohio

23rd April 1966 – Mysterious 'bubble' sighted in a field with occupant, at Maine, United States

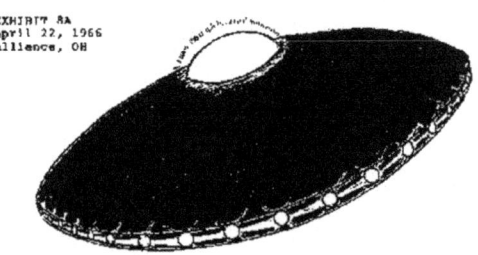

Between 1pm and 3.30pm, Bingham, Maine, resident – Kimberley Baker (6), was out with her cousins, Wendy and Bruce Higgins, picking pussy willows in a large field south of the family home, back of Kennebec Mill, near to the house of Mrs Paul Matheson, when she witnessed something very unusual in a field. [At this stage the cousins had left to go back to the house to get some scissors, as they were finding it difficult to cut the stems]. She later told her mother – Mrs 'Joyce' Wesley Baker – that she had seen:

"...a big 'ball' or 'bubble' showing red lights near the bottom, and a single green light on top that blinked on and off. I walked right up to it although I was afraid someone might come out of the door. The 'bubble' then started to spin around and then went right up and over the house of Mrs Matheson".

Kimberley was asked if she had seen anybody. She answered:

"I saw a man in it, with something on his head; he took it off and smiled at me. He said something. I saw his lips move. He had a white suit with black buttons down the middle".

This matter was brought to the attention of a family acquaintance, Mr Allie King – a representative of the *Gannett Publishing Company* – who made many visits to the Bingham area in order to pick up collections for the *Morning Sentinel*. He repeatedly tried to shake Kim's story by deliberately confusing details, but Kim invariably corrected them so that, accordingly, no inconsistencies could be detected.

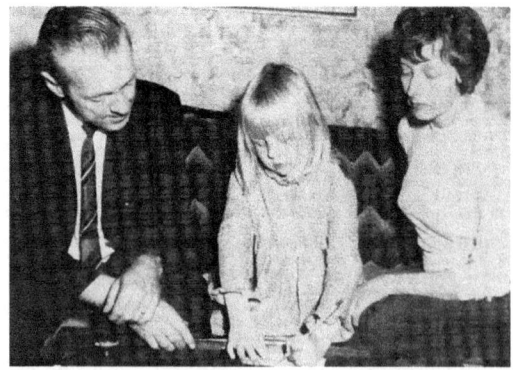

Mr Allie King, Kimberley Baker and Mrs Joyce Baker. Photo taken by Mr Richard Plummer at the home of the witnesses on May 4, 1966

In May 1975 this incident was brought to the attention of Richard Bonenfant, who had a MA in anthropology and was a scientist in the study of birth defects at the New York State Department of Health. He conducted a thorough investigation into the matter, involving interviews with the family and visit to the location in 1975 – 9 years after the event. (Kim would have been 15)

Richard:

"The crux of this report lies in the witness's reliability. Can the testimony of a six year-old girl be accepted at face value, especially when it concerns such an unusual event? Two legitimate objections may be raised against acceptance: First, that there were no other witnesses present during the encounter, and secondly, that the girl's age at the time suggests either exaggeration or misinterpretation. These are valid considerations which must be weighed in evaluating the case. However, there are also several factors which tend to support the witness's description of her experience. One of these factors is her own history of reliability. The witness's mother impressed on me that her daughter was not the imaginative type and had never entertained the habit of exaggeration."

(Sources: *The Baker Sighting: A retrospective investigation*, Richard Bonenfant/*Morning Sentinel*, Waterville, 6.5.1966 – 'Bingham girl says she observed UFO/*FSR*, Volume 22, No. 2, 1976)

28th April 1966 – Close encounter, Cambridgeshire

Ex-RAF Fireman, Peter Rushton – who had seen for himself the devastating effects of atomic bomb testing at Christmas Island, in May 1957 – described an experience that still continues to haunt him, all these years later.

Peter was working as a driver for a removal firm and was on his way back from a delivery, accompanied by fellow employee – Derek Robinson. The men, tired after their long journey, decided to park overnight, using a car park at the small village of Sawtry (just off the A1, between Huntingdon and Peterborough) and had just time to purchase a couple of pints before the pub shut.

Vivid dream

Peter settled himself down in the rear of the Luton van, using a bed which was being delivered, erected over the wheel box of the rear axle, about eight feet away from the roller shutter door, while Derek settled down on the other bed, made up on the top of the cab.

"I set the alarm clock for 7am and went to sleep. The next thing I became aware of was a bang and flash of light that awoke me. I glanced over to the clock. It showed 5am. Straightaway I remembered a vivid dream, involving the appearance of a person, wearing a silver space suit, who discharged a beam of light at my forehead. How weird, I thought. Then I felt a sensation – as if the van was moving at speed, frightening me. Had I left the handbrake off? Was the van out of control? I heard a voice saying, 'Look outside', so I got out of bed and found it was like walking up a steep hill, pulling a heavy weight behind. The air around me seemed charged with electromagnetic energy. I could taste it in my mouth, like lead, and my hearing seemed magnified. The birds were screeching outside."

Orange 'ball of light' seen – then UFO display

Eventually, Peter managed to open the shutter door and looked out. He saw a large orange 'ball of light' in front of him. Frightened, he first thought there had been a major catastrophe. Had the Earth been knocked out of orbit? He struggled to get to grips with what was happening and woke up Derek, and pointed out the orange 'ball of light' to him – now a speck of light in the sky.

Derek suggested they line-up the object with a metal pole. When they did so, they established it was the object hurtling away from them, and not the other way around.

"Suddenly the 'star' halted in the sky, conjoined by another one – the two of them changing places with each other and beginning to move in a series of semicircular patterns, rotating in an anticlockwise movement across the sky. I kept repeating under my breath, many times – 'go away, go away'. By now, it was 6am. Derek decided to go back to bed. I did the same, waking up at 7am. After packing up and leaving, we made our way to 'Kate's Cabin' for breakfast. When we entered the café, there were about 20 drivers in there. The noise was deafening. It sounded like a hundred people. I realised my ears were still very sensitive."

Aftermath of sighting

During the following months, Peter was to relive his experience over and over again, and have a recurring dream involving little silver arrows, floating upwards, interchanging with each other, followed by some form of examination on a table by Alien beings.

"As the years went by the dreams became less vivid, although the experience remained very clear in my memory. The worst of it was that when I saw arrows on street signs, it seemed to trigger-off the memories again."

Reliving memory of event

One day in 1993, Peter was due to have an operation on his left shoulder. On the day of the operation, he asked the anaesthetist to put him to sleep before being taken into the operating theatre, knowing he would have panicked when put onto the table.

All went well until the night before he was due to be discharged, after being given a drug for the pain. He relived the experience so much that the nurse called the psychiatrist to examine him, who advised the nurse (after the examination) that Peter was not suffering from any psychiatric disorder.

The chilling experience, described by Mr Rushton, involving an encounter with a UFO and its traumatic aftermath, forms the background to many other similar reports we were to come across. Once again, there are plenty of questions but too few answers.

Peter refused to take part in hypnotic regression, preferring that the memories of what happened should be released normally, his curiosity sacrificed against the fear of further disruptions to his life. He strongly rejected a suggestion made to him that the experience was illusionary and had been triggered by exposure to powerful electromagnetic fields, rather than interaction with any Alien species.

Contrary to popular belief the Christmas Island concerned is not the one in the Indian Ocean, presently a dependent territory of Australia. It is the one now called Kiritimati, and part of the independent nation of Kiribati, which until 1971 were the British colony of the Gilbert and Ellice Islands. Nuclear tests were conducted in the region around Christmas Island by the United Kingdom, in the late 1950s, and by the United States in 1962. During these tests, islanders were not evacuated. Subsequently British, New Zealand, and Fijian servicemen, as well as local islanders, have claimed to have suffered from exposure to the radiation from these blasts.

Coincidentally, some years ago, we spoke to an ex-serviceman who had been present during one of these tests. His account is chilling:

"We were not given any protection – just ordered to stand with our backs to the anticipated explosion, and place our fists in our eyes. When the bomb went off, the light was so bright it was like looking at an X-ray. I could see all the bones and blood vessels in my hand".

His American counterparts, however, did have protection.

Whatever the reason, *something*, or *someone,* was responsible for implementing this incident to occur in the first place. (**Source: Personal interview/Peter Johnson, BUFORA**)

29th April 1966 – Isle of Wight UFO Society

The Isle of Wight UFO Society held their second annual dinner at *The Wheatsheaf* Hotel, Newport on this date. Charles Bowen – editor of *Flying Saucer Review* – was guest of honour. He was introduced by Leonard G. Cramp – President of IWUFOIS. Some 30 members attended and thanked Mr Bowen for an interesting and sometimes amusing talk, in which he praised the work of the Society.

30th April 1966 – Triangular lights sighted over a field near Warminster

At 11.30pm, Dennis Tilt – a local building contractor – and his wife, Jean, from Warminster, Wiltshire, was driving past Chitterne on the B.390 – a clear night, no wind, with a nearly full moon – when they noticed three luminous 'beams of light', forming a triangle, a few feet off the ground in a nearby field.

Ken Rogers

"We stopped the car and got out to have a closer look. To our amazement, the three 'lights' merged into one 'ball of light', changing into what looked like a frying pan, without a handle – now hovering 50 feet, or so, off the ground. We felt very nervous and decided to leave.

Upon our arrival, at Battlesbury, we were surprised to see what appeared to be the same object passing overhead, going towards Chitterne."

We were unable to speak to Mr Tilt, but his wife confirmed the sighting and told us:

"The next day, Dennis reported the incident and took Ken Rogers to the scene to have a closer look. He later told me they had found a burnt patch on the ground, some 50 feet in diameter, near to where we had seen the UFO – completely out of character for the geology of the area.

To the best of my memory, we weren't physically or mentally scarred by what happened, although, very oddly, Dennis brought my attention to a peculiar red mark on his chest (about the size of a ten pence piece), a few hours after the sighting. This mark was the source of occasional irritation and was still there right up to his death."

Scientific analysis of soil control samples taken from *outside* the burnt area revealed the presence of tin, flint, and an absence of mineral or organic matter. Samples of soil taken from *inside* the burnt area revealed: Lime, Wolfram 2%, Carbon 3%, Tin 1%, Cassiterite 1%, Organic matter, flint and traces of silver …suggesting the surface area of the ground had been subjected to an estimated heat of 12,000 degrees centigrade, or more, and that the elements of Tin, Wolfram and Carbon, had been created by flint being fused together by a tremendous heat source.

(Sources: William Trevor Selby, Contact UK/Ken Rogers/Arthur Shuttlewood)

April 1966 – Triangular UFO over Warwickshire

At 10.30pm, Mr Michael Corns from Ebrington Avenue, Hob's Moat, close to Birmingham Elmdon Airport, West Midlands, was stood looking out of the bedroom window, having a cigarette.

"I saw these flashing coloured lights appear in the sky, at a height of between 2-3,000 feet, forming a well-defined triangular shape; the red, yellow, and pulsating lights then appeared to merge into one another – totally unlike the navigation lights we were used to seeing fly over. I watched, mesmerised, *for about five minutes, as it hovered in the sky. Suddenly, it shot upwards vertically and was gone seconds later."* (**Source: Staffordshire UFO Group, Graham Allen**)

Arthur Shuttlewood's invitation to the MOD

Although hoaxing was rife to the Warminster locality during this time, it was clear there were many sightings of unidentified flying objects which could not be explained away rationally. Arthur Shuttlewood himself wrote to the Minister of Defence – the Rt. Honourable Denis Healey, explaining the result of his findings, during spring 1966, and asking him to come and have a look for himself.

Arthur received a reply back from Ministry official – Mr H. Toft, who thanked him for the invitation, but said *"Mr Healey was too busy to make the trip"*, followed by the now all too familiar suggestions made by a government department following any enquiry about UFO activity, *"that the majority of UFO sightings could be explained away as either Venus, atmospheric disturbances, balloons, or high flying birds"* (and all of the other cacophonic myriad of ridiculous explanations put forward by those sceptical of such matters).

MAY 1966

3rd May 1966 – Three propellers on 'golden disc' UFO

Just before 7am, a resident of Colwyn Bay, North Wales, was looking out of his bedroom window when he noticed an object approaching his position, at an estimated distance of 2,000 yards.

> *"The outer rim, estimated to be some 130 feet in diameter, consisted of what looked like 'a ring of golden discs' around a centre cabin or control room, showing what appeared to be three propellers of a greenish-purple hue, and the object hovered a few feet above the ground for half-an-hour."*

As the sun rose, the 'craft' almost violently shot up into the sky, making a 'V'-turn, and became redder in colour as it disappeared into the sky. What struck the witness as being odd was the terrific whirling of a nearby cloud bank as the 'thing' rose upwards, despite an absence of wind.

(**Source: Anglo-Polish UFO Research Club**)

7th May 1966 – UFO sighted over Goodfellow Air Force Base, Texas, USA

A short cylindrical object, showing a blue light at one end with a yellow at the other, was seen flying through the sky for half a minute, over Goodfellow Air Force Base, Texas, at 9.55pm, by Aircraftman Third Class W.L Whitehead.

10th May 1966 – Six objects seen over Lancashire

At 10.30am, off-duty police officer – Gordon Cameron, was at his home address at Parr Street, St. Helens, in Lancashire, when he happened to glance through the window and asked his wife to take a look at:

> *"…six objects, moving from right to left across the sky, at a steady speed – their angle of elevation dropping. Fifteen seconds later, they stopped in mid-air for about 15 seconds, before moving rapidly away – their size reducing – and were lost from view as they dropped down in the sky, behind a house."*

It was later calculated that the objects were seen between 3 to 6 miles away, against the clouds, flying at 700 miles per hour; the largest being 80 feet in size, the smallest 40 feet, at a height of approximately 2,000 feet.

Enquiries into the incident, conducted many years later, revealed some discrepancies between what actually took place and what the *St. Helens* reporter wrote in their edition of the 17th May, when the officer and his wife were described as reliable witnesses by the Chief Constable of St. Helens – Mr A. Atherton. (**Source: Personal interview**)

17th May 1966 – Red flashing light and humming noise heard

Janet Cox of West Wickham, near Cambridge, had a background in music. She was in her bedroom, at 12.15am on 17th May 1966, when she heard a humming noise that she identified as 'G' above middle 'C', followed by light flooding into the room. Looking out of the window she saw a bright red flashing 'light' heading westwards across the sky, illuminating the ground below it.

Janet firmly rejected an explanation put to her that she had seen an aircraft.

> "The humming noise was constant in pitch and, since a velocity of recession of only 60 miles per hour would cause – by The *Doppler effect – a change in pitch of one semitone, this indicates it was hardly an aircraft."

Cambridge University Group

Stewart Miller was the Secretary of the Cambridge University Group for the Investigation of Unidentified Flying Objects – an organisation that was to record thousands of UFO reports sent in by members of the public and various UFO groups. All this material was then catalogued with the use of an early computer, and the present authors would love to know what happened to all that material.

Miller wrote to the *Sun* newspaper, appealing for any other witnesses with regard to the sighting made by Mrs Janet Cox, which he considered to be genuine.

Media's humiliation of the witness

Subsequently the lady was depicted as a caricature, listening intently, underneath a globe containing a mechanical robot, playing a piano – simply because, during the interview, Mrs Cox had disclosed she had a musical background! **(Source: *UFOLOG*)**

18th May 1966 – Three or four objects sighted in the sky

At 1.15pm, *"three or four dull silver objects, spearhead-shaped – one larger than the rest"*, were seen in the sky over Barnsley, Yorkshire, at a height of approximately 12 miles, by Mr W.H. Parker, of Kendray – an amateur photographer (who was sat in his van, at the time) – before climbing rapidly upwards and disappearing into cloud. **(Source: Trevor Whittaker, BUFORA)**

During the same month, Hilda Hensall and Dorothy Clarke from Denby Lane, Heaton Chapel, were out walking, at 6.30pm, when they sighted a saucer-shaped object moving across the eastern sky.

(Source: DIGAP)

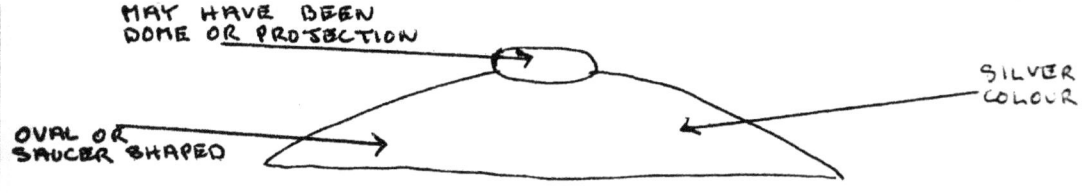

---

*The Doppler effect (or Doppler shift), named after Austrian physicist Christian Doppler who proposed it in 1842 in Prague, is the change in frequency of a wave for an observer moving relative to the source of the wave. It is commonly heard when a vehicle sounding a siren or horn approaches, passes, and recedes from an observer. The received frequency is higher (compared to the emitted frequency) during the approach, identical at the instant of passing by, and lower during the recession.

23rd May 1966 – RAF Jet crashes – was a UFO the cause?

Another matter brought to our attention involved an allegation that a 'Gnat' RAF Jet XR570, from RAF Valley, had crashed after striking an unidentified object, while flying over Lake Llyn Celyn – (a then recently constructed reservoir in North Wales) – some time in mid-1966.

According to the person concerned, there were two witnesses to the crash – Mr Robert Jones, of Lakeside Ty Nant Farm, who was out fishing on Tryweryn Reservoir with his friend – Evan Ellis of Blaenau Ffestiniog.

"All of a sudden, he dipped down and the shining object fell into the lake. It was not a seagull."

Although we were unable to trace the men concerned, we discovered details of an incident which took place over Lake Llyn Celyn, involving Pilot Officer Terrence Jones, from RAF Valley, contained on an accident card archived with the Air Historical Branch, after writing to the MOD.

"The officer was conducting a low sortie and authorised to fly at 200 feet above ground. After setting the correct regional pressure, the pilot entered the low flying area. Whilst flying across Lake Llyn Celyn, the aircraft struck and severed two high-tension cables. The canopy disintegrated and the pilot was unable to see. He then ejected. The aircraft crashed into a hill and disintegrated on impact. The pilot was recovered and retired to RAF Valley by helicopter."

Enquiries to trace any Board of Inquiry (which one presumes was later convened to examine the cause of the accident) were unsuccessful. According to the MOD, to whom we wrote, a search of the National Archives and MOD archives, failed to locate the Board of Inquiry file. They suggested that it had not been selected for permanent retention – which we thought rather odd, bearing in mind the cost of these aircraft and the importance of keeping such information on file. It appears likely that the accident was caused as stated, through some form of pilot negligence rather than a collision with a UFO. It is logical to presume the witnesses on the ground may not have seen the high tension cables, although they clearly saw the aircraft moving across the sky.

27th May 1966 – Prime Minster's Question Time

At Prime Minster's Question Time, Mr Edwin Brooks asked the Secretary of State for Defence, Merlyn Rees:

"How many reports of unidentified flying objects were received by his department throughout Great Britain, during 1964 and 1965, and of these how many have not been satisfactorily explained?"

Mr Rees:

"74 in 1964, of which five cannot be explained, and in 1965, 56 of which 14 cannot be explained", adding, that in the cases that have not been satisfactorily explained, the information given has generally been too imprecise or inadequate to support any further investigation."

30th May 1966 – British ship sights 'globe'

According to the Captain's log, aboard the ship *British Cavalier*, sailing between Malta and Messina, *"a green and yellow 'globe' was sighted flying through the sky in an east to west direction"*, by the Captain, Radio Officer, The Third Mate and helmsman.

JUNE 1966

3rd June 1966 – Two 'white lights' over Bournemouth

At 10.15pm, two bright 'white lights' were observed through a telescope in the southern part of the sky, over Bournemouth, heading northwards, by Richard Taylor – head of a local International Sky Scouts Association – who dashed out into the garden, but by then it had disappeared from view.

Over Sutton Coldfield

At 10.50pm on the same date, Valerie Foster, of Sutton Coldfield, sighted a football-shaped object, changing colour from red to white, moving through the air in the south-east direction, before it rose rapidly upwards and out of sight.

Valerie telephoned the Air Traffic Control at Elmdon Airport, who confirmed that they had received reports from two others regarding this. When Derek Samson of NICAP GB spoke to them, they refused to make any comment.

(Sources: NICAP, GB/International Sky Scouts Association)

5th June 1966 – UFO over South Birmingham

At 11.05pm – a dry and warm night – a star-like object was sighted, heading slowly through the sky towards the direction of West Heath, by Mr R. Medhurst and his wife from Tristram Avenue, West Heath, Birmingham, and nearby neighbour – Mr R. Bradshaw.

"It was in sight for about ten minutes, and stopped dead for a few minutes, above us, before moving on again." **(Source: Derek Samson, NICAP, GB)**

6th June 1966 – Domed 'discs' over Wisconsin, USA

Dorothy Gray – a resident of Spooner, Wisconsin – reported seeing two domed 'discs' with sparkling upper surfaces, with square windows in the tops, revolving above a lake during a 25 second sighting, at 9.30pm.

8th June 1966 – Cigar-shaped UFO over Ohio, USA

Two days later, on the 8th June, Mr Max Baker from Kansas, Ohio, was motoring in his car, at 6.45am, when he was 'buzzed' by a *"cigar-shaped object, for about a minute"*. **(Source: NICAP)**

17th June 1966 – UFO over Abingdon, Oxfordshire

In 2006, we spoke to retired nuclear scientist – Peter Dowling Wroath, with regard to a UFO that had been sighted by him and another scientist.

Peter Dowling Wroath

Over the years we had spoken to many people, from all walks of life, who had sighted UFOs. They included Police Officers of different ranks, RAF service personnel, and numerous people with scientific qualifications, but only *one* Nuclear Scientist! We found this particularly interesting, as – generally speaking – while UFOs have been the subject of extensive investigation by various governments, over the years, few scientific papers have been published. This is an attitude apparently dictated by a belief system which feels such investigation is unwarranted.

However, Peter had no qualms about reporting what he saw. Like so many others, he did not claim that these objects were of extraterrestrial origin, or that they were piloted by Aliens – just that *"this is what we saw. Make of it what you will"*.

Thanks to Peter's daughter – Jenny, we learnt that he had originally trained for the Church, but just before taking his vows decided he would rather pursue a scientific path. We found him to be an extremely intelligent, friendly man, well-versed in astronomical matters, an accomplished yachtsman, musician and tennis player, and who had, on occasion, become involved in carrying out investigations into reports of UFO activity around the Berkshire area. In addition to these attributes, we were amazed to discover that Peter – who had started his career at the Atomic Energy Research Establishment (AERE) – had originally been taken on without any scientific qualifications, but despite this became a member of the team building the new Proton Linear Accelerator.

It soon became clear that Peter had an aptitude for building experimental equipment, and making it operate reliably. When the Rutherford High Energy Laboratory (now known as the Rutherford Appleton Laboratory) was formed under the auspices of the National Institute for Research in Nuclear Science, to take forward the UK particle physics research programme, Peter transferred across with the entire PLA team.

He also helped to build and run a series of particle physics experiments on the Proton Synchrotron at Rutherford, at the DESY laboratory in Hamburg and at CERN in Geneva.

However, despite his impressive scientific background, Peter still pondered as to the nature of what had been seen by him and his colleague, Dr. R.S. Gilmore, at 8.05pm on 17th June 1966:

> *"We first saw the object as a very bright yellow spot, above a bank of glowing cloud on the western horizon, moving slowly. It then accelerated and disappeared behind a tall bank of cloud, near the northern horizon. After about ten minutes, what appeared to be the same object reappeared, travelling in the opposite direction, until it reached a position intermediate between north and west, where it remained stationary for about half-an-hour before receding, approximately in line of sight. Half-an-hour later, it was finally hidden in a bank of cloud off the horizon. Viewed through 10 x 60 binoculars, the object appeared to be triangular in shape and very bright.*

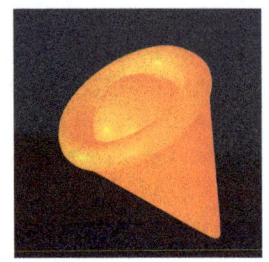

> *Through a 6-inch Newtonian telescope, the object looked like a shining cone of light – its appearance resembling the shape of a bell, with the 'mouth' inclined towards the observer, with a central dome like structure. The periphery of the 'mouth' looked to be toroidal, with three equally spaced 'headlights', and was obviously reflecting sunlight, as it showed shadow and contrast as a solid body would. Taking into account the inverted view of the reflector telescope, the 'mouth' of the bell-shaped object pointed upwards, with the top tapering down to Earth. Eyepieces to give a magnification of 80 and 200 times were used. From the fact that the object was still illuminated by the rays of the sun, forty minutes after sunset, and from the angle of elevation of 25 degrees, its minimum distance in line of sight was calculated to be 28 miles, at an altitude of 7.5 miles, indicating the minimum length to be 60 feet along its major axis."*

In a letter written to Gordon Creighton, Dr. Gilmore added:

> *"The object appeared to be brightly sunlit some forty minutes after sunset. From this fact and its observed position, one may estimate a minimum distance which will keep it out of the Earth's shadow. I estimated this as 28 miles off, with an altitude greater than 7 and- a-half miles. The angle subtended by the object was estimated in the telescope to be some 4 mill radians, suggesting a minimum length of 60 feet."*

(**Sources:** *Flying Saucer Review,* September-October 1966, Volume 12, No. 5/ *The Observer,* 19.6.1966/Personal interview/Wikipedia/British Astronomical Association)

18th June 1966 – Boy Scouts sight bell-shaped UFO over North Carolina, USA

At 12.30am, members of a Boy Scout group at Burnsville, North Carolina, out camping, were astonished to see a bell-shaped object, showing three flashing red lights, hovering in the sky for five hours, during which time six other objects were seen to appear. (**Source: NICAP**)

June 1966 – UFO display over Bristol

Denis Plunkett – Head of the Bristol based British Flying Saucer Bureau – was preparing for bed, one evening, in June 1966, and went to draw the curtains, when he saw:

> *"...a total of nine 'brilliant white lights', dancing in the sky; I shouted to Maureen to come and have a look and we stared in wonderment, transfixed by the 'lights', which flashed on and off – like lights*

on a Christmas tree – for about an hour. Initially, I assumed it was an aircraft, but I soon dismissed this theory because the patterns they were making were too irregular. Suddenly, one 'light' left the group and remained in the same position for ten minutes, before rejoining the main pattern – which was a loose formation, with the 'lights' constantly changing positions. They then disappeared, never to be seen again. Maureen and I tried to explain away what we'd seen."

The next day, Denis discovered local newspapers reported that other people had spotted the lights.

22nd June 1966 – Prime Minister's Question Time

Sir John Langford-Holt asked the Secretary of State – Mr Merlyn Rees:

"What arrangements are made for the reporting and receipt of reports of sightings of unidentified flying objects? And how many of these reports have been received in the last ten years from civilian and service source?"

Mr Rees replied:

*"Reports of unidentified flying objects are received by my department from both service and civilian sources and are investigated. Between 1959 and 1965, **351** reports were received. I regret that earlier figures are not available."*

Sir John also asked Mr Rees:

"What estimate he has made as to the value courses, and origins of reports of sightings of unidentified flying objects as well as the objects themselves?"

Mr Rees replied once more:

"Reports are examined at their face value in the light of their possible air defence implications and we do not carry our study beyond this point. No Defence implications have been found."
(Source: AIR21/19126)

24th June 1966 – Four UFOs sighted

Shirley Andrews (formerly a sceptic in such matters) was travelling from Weymouth to Yeovil, during the evening, when she saw four objects of enormous size – apparently rotating – moving eastwards, a few hundred feet off the ground.

June 1966 – Close Encounter, Cheshire – occupants seen

Peter Leather – a retired professional jockey (then aged 10) – had a sighting with uncanny similarities to what Jessie Roestenberg witnessed on the 21st October 1954 (see *Haunted Skies* Revised Volume One). It occurred over Northwich, Cheshire, during June 1966. He told us:

"I was chatting to my grandfather in the rear garden, on a hot summer's day in June, when, 'out of the blue', appeared a gleaming metallic cigar-shaped object, just hovering above our heads, with the top and base constantly spinning. We stood there, shocked, hardly able to move.

I looked up and saw what appeared to be a woman, with long blonde hair, looking out of one of the windows, set into the centre section of the UFO. Time seemed to stand still. We gazed at each other. She raised her right arm, as if acknowledging our presence – then the 'craft' moved slowly away and was soon out of sight. We raced into the house, so excited we could hardly get our words out, and told the rest of the family what we had just seen. They laughed at us, but changed their attitude, a few days later, when they read about a UFO being sighted over the Manchester area, on the same day as our experience." **(Source: Personal interview)**

JULY 1966

11th July 1966 – UFO over Pennsylvania, USA

At 7.45pm, Carl Wood and Charles Hawthorne from Union, Pennsylvania, sighted a large object hovering in the sky, which they estimated to be 100 feet wide and 20 feet in height, showing small windows filled with yellow light.

> "It was making a humming noise and an occasional grinding noise coming from inside. We watched it for about an hour." (**Source: NICAP**)

Mid-July 1966 – UFO hovered near Missile Launch Control Center at Minot AFB, USA

Robert Hastings

According to retired USAF Captain David D. Schindele, who was interviewed by him in September 2012, he told of an incident involving several nuclear missiles.

> "My recollection of a 'UFO incident', while serving in the US Air Force, has diminished with time and it has been difficult to recall some of the specific details of what I experienced. I attribute this lack of memory to the fact that it occurred some 44 years ago and also because I was officially told to forget what I experienced and to never speak of it.
>
> At the time, I was a First Lieutenant and Deputy Missile Combat Crew Commander in the 742nd Squadron of the 455th Strategic Missile Wing at Minot Air Force Base, in North Dakota. As a Launch Control Officer, I was part of a two-man crew that monitored and controlled ten nuclear-armed Minuteman Intercontinental Ballistic Missiles. My commander and I were together for about a year and a half, from January 1966 to August 1967. In the back of my mind, it seems that the incident occurred not long after I married my wife in mid-July 1966."

Mike Flight

> "My primary duty site was at a Launch Control Center called 'Mike Flight', which was designated as the Squadron Command Post and one of five Launch Control Centers in the squadron that included Kilo, Lima, November, and Oscar. Each of these was located 60-feet below ground, underneath their respective Launch Control Facility, which housed the topside support and security personnel.

The following is what I remember:

Strange lights over Mohall, North Dakota

"I lived in town (Minot, North Dakota) and awoke early in the morning to get ready for my scheduled duty at November Flight, which was a change from my regular duty at Mike Flight. As usual, I had the TV on while having breakfast and heard on the local news that residents of Mohall, North Dakota, had witnessed strange lights near their town during the night that was attributed to a UFO. This caught my attention, because November Flight was only about three miles west of this town."

Robert Hastings

Crew Briefing

"At the pre-departure crew briefing on base that morning, where all 15 missile crews were gathered before departing for their assigned Launch Control Centers, we were told that the crew at November Flight had experienced some unusual circumstance and a situation where some missiles came 'off alert'. This general statement was made without undue detail, but there was a suggestion that some unexplained, mysterious, event was connected with this. I then recalled the TV news report that morning and immediately linked that with what I heard in the crew briefing. As my commander and I travelled to the Launch Control Facility, we were anxious and curious as to what we would discover upon arriving. The normal procedure upon arriving at the Launch Control Facility was for us to first inspect the facility and to also debrief 'topside' personnel."

Site Manager tells of hovering UFO seen

"While inspecting the facility I talked with the Site Manager, who detailed to me his unique and bewildering experience of that evening. He indicated that a large hovering object was sighted close by, out of the windows on the west side of the facility in the dark of night, and it had bright, flashing lights. I queried him on what this object looked like, but he was unable to discern its shape (perhaps because of the flashing lights), but he knew it was not a helicopter because the object was much larger and did not have the associated noise. He also could not adequately explain to me what the flashing lights really looked like; he could not put it into words. He then said that the object proceeded to move to the front right side of the facility, but it was not completely visible then, because the view was partially obstructed by the on-site garage. All of this activity transpired for quite some time; a matter of minutes. I also talked briefly to security personnel about their experience and they essentially confirmed what the Site Manager told me. My crew commander was more involved with debriefing security, and I was more involved with talking with the Site Manager."

Missile had gone off alert – monitoring of them lost!

"The first thing that caught my attention when I arrived at the capsule below ground was the launch control console. The two-man officer crew provided my commander and me a thorough briefing of the past evening's events and current status. I still recall the feeling of awe and wonder, the concern for the situation, and the feeling of helplessness that the crew had experienced. They related that lights on the missile console had illuminated – the ones you would not normally expect to see – and then missiles had gone 'off alert' – (monitoring of them was lost).

It concerns me that I can no longer remember much of my duty on this day in the Launch Control Center; it is like a mental block, but I do remember that our duty shift consisted of controlling communications and monitoring a missile console that showed little missile status. It was like there was nothing to do. In the back of my mind, my feeling is that a majority of the ten missiles were 'off alert' (if not all of them) when we relieved the crew, and that a majority of them remained 'off alert' during our 24-hour duty there.

I remember that when we were relieved, the next morning and arrived topside I attempted to query the Flight Security Controller, who told me he could not speak about the incident. It was then that my commander also informed me that he had received word, during my rest break below, that we were to never speak about the incident.

My recollection of this experience is that it was unique, and that it was not shared at any other Launch Control Center at the time. From my memory of the morning crew briefing, only November Flight was mentioned and involved. After returning to base, and from that time on, no further discussion or reference to the incident was ever made, that I can remember. The incident was, however, high on our minds and we were always keeping our ears open to find out if there was ever any resolution or answers to it. I have no other recollection or knowledge of any other such events taking place at Minot Air Force Base during my time of duty there, although I've learned since then that my experience was not unique."

Robert recently asked Schindele if he had ever spoken with his former missile commander after retiring from the Air Force. He responded:

"I did manage to contact T------- on March 24th, 2011, but actually talked to his wife most of the time. She mentioned that he was 85 years-old, had Alzheimer's since the mid-to-late 1990s, and had difficulty remembering much of anything. She said that he retired in his 60s as a Lieutenant Colonel. Last November 1st, I received word from his family that he had passed away on October 23rd."

19th July 1966 – Prime Minster Harold Wilson answers questions on UFOs

Harold Wilson

Sir John Langford-Holt asked the Prime Minister:

"Whether in view of the fact that the Secretary of State for Defence is responsible only for the air defence implications of the reports of unidentified flying objects, he will allocate to a department the duty of assessing the wider implications of these reports."

Prime Minster Harold Wilson replied: *"No Sir."*

Sir John continued:

"Is the Prime Minister aware that enormous numbers of reports are coming into the Government from people not all of whom are cranks? Would it not be appropriate without me knowing very much about the origins or significance of these items that somebody in the Government should at least take a serious interest in them?"

The Prime Minster replied:

"These matters are taken seriously when the reports which are received are sufficiently detailed to enable a check to be made. In very many cases there are natural phenomena such as balloons, aircraft, and so on. Where it has not been possible to get a satisfactory explanation, it is usually because the information has been too inadequate or imprecise for investigation."

20th July 1966 – Close encounter, Isle of Wight

Isle of Wight couple – Angela L. Cotton, and her boyfriend (at the time), John – were sat in a car on the Blackgang side of the Landslip car park. At 9.30pm, Angela sensed something, or someone, was close to them. Looking out of the window they saw a yellow glow, towards the hills, blocking their view of the sea. Curious, they wound-down the windows and were almost immediately aware of a vibrating sound, apparently coming from the same direction where the glow was situated. John decided they should return home and they set off along the country lane, about a quarter of the way along, before joining the main road.

Angela:

"Suddenly, John doubled over the steering wheel, clutching his stomach. He gripped his right arm on the inside of the elbow joint and his foot began to slip off the accelerator. His face went white, almost blue. I told him to put his foot back and I would steer the car to the main road – which I did. After arriving home, John told me he felt as if his stomach had been gripped in a vice, and rolled up his right sleeve. On the inside of the elbow joint, there was a mark, like a bruise – about the size of a penny – showing numerous holes, like the punctures made by a test vaccine. The next day, he told me he had similar marks on his stomach. By the weekend, these marks had gone."

The following day, they drove to the Blackgang side of the Landslip, and noticed what looked like a furrow on the side of the hill – as if the earth had been scooped out of the ground. After making their way there on foot, they examined the area.

"It looked as if something had been rubbing against the earth to produce the effect – like a large wheel, some six feet in partial radius. The earth around the edges of this furrow was very dry and the grass around the edges was not charred but brown – as if heat had been applied.

I don't know what the 'glow' was. It certainly wasn't the beam of St. Catherine's Lighthouse, or the sunset. I can't explain what happened.

I have never forgotten the incident you mentioned, as it is one of the few moments in my life for which I could 'kick myself' for not having the courage to walk to the edge of Sugar Lump Hill (as it was known then), and look down at the source of the light. If I had seen what was causing the light, I would have perhaps known what caused the scuff marks on the side of the hill that we viewed, the following evening, from the opposite side of the Landslip.

In answer to our questions about the discovery of the mysterious strange marks found on her boyfriend's stomach, she replied:

"They looked like weal marks. I have no idea what caused them, although I do wonder if some form of hysteria could have induced them to occur, rather than through physical assault."

(Sources: Fred Smith, *UFOLOG*, Isle of Wight UFO Society/Personal interview)

21st July 1966 – Scottish UFOs

Charles Ogilvy MacLean from Glen Prosen, Forfar, in Scotland, was driving home (accompanied by his farmhand), between Perth and Blairgowrie (three miles from Perth), at l0pm. The two men saw what they took to be at least three or four helicopters (there may have been more), between three to five miles away.

"I'm sorry I can't be more specific, but the 'helicopters' seemed to change shape drastically in a way which left us very puzzled.

We continued on our journey along the twisting roads, for a few miles, and then stopped the car so as to have a closer look.

We saw what appeared to be a large cloud with another smaller one next to it, increasing in size. At the end of the large cloud could be seen something like a short pillar, rising out of the top, which was level with the smaller cloud. At this point, a car passed.

When we looked upwards, there was nothing to be seen." **(Source: Charles H.O. McLean)**

22nd July 1966 – Triangular UFO over Wales

At 9pm, Mr W.J. Norton (then curator of the Ludlow Museum, in Shropshire) was out walking with his son (5), and wife, over Penybont Common, Llandrindod Wells, in Radnorshire.

> "My son pointed out a shining object, apparently near the eastern horizon, before it vanished a short time later. We stopped to eat a snack, wondering if it would reappear. A few minutes later, we heard a local farmer – Mr Reynolds of Talfryn, Dolau, Knighton – calling out and directing our attention to an object which appeared almost overhead, making a low humming noise. The shape was of an isosceles triangle, or low cone, highly polished, silver, and shining brilliantly. It seemed to 'drift' out of sight in a very strange manner, before vanishing from sight suddenly".

(Source: Letter to Gordon Creighton, *Flying Saucer Review*)

'Flying Saucer' over Lowestoft

At 9pm, just before sunset, Mr H. Breakwell – a resident of Coventry – was on holiday in Lowestoft. He was strolling down the promenade with his wife, when they noticed a flame-coloured, saucer-shaped, object in the sky.

In a letter written to Coventry UFO Researcher – Bob Tibbitts, he said:

> "A sort of 'chandelier' dropped from its centre and slowly rose up again – like a magnesium flare. When we read the local newspaper, the following day, we saw that others had also sighted a similar object further down the coast." **(Source: As above)**

25th July 1966 – Carolina student chased by UFO

Yet another report from a member of the public, involving what appears to be an interaction between a motorist and UFO. On this occasion, college student – James Clarke of Vanceboro, North Carolina, was out at 1am, when he saw an object in the sky which was seen to change colour from red to blue to green, and then orange, which followed his car and then took up a hovering position above the vehicle for over an hour, before flying upwards and out of sight in seconds. **(Source: NICAP)**

July 1966 – UFO display over Bolton

Carol Vickers – a long-term resident of Breightmet (two-and-a-half miles east of Bolton) – wrote to us. She described a mysterious yellow glowing 'ball of light' that she saw, whilst aged 14. At the time she was living in Greenroyd Avenue – an elevated position, with unrivalled view of the countryside overlooking Winter Hill, Rivington, and the *White Horse* public house, Haslingden. The area has since been developed and covered with housing estates.

> "It was a hot summer's night, in July 1966. I couldn't sleep and got up at about 3.30am. Glancing through the window I saw what I thought to be a really bright star, over the White Horse pub, when, all of a sudden, it darted downwards onto the car park and began moving up and down, changing speed and going from one place to another – so fast, my eyes could not keep up with it. It then moved to the field opposite, and hovered above the tall grass for about twenty minutes. I became frightened when it began to move towards the house, and hid under the covers."

Carol decided to keep quiet about what she had seen for over 30 years, until speaking to us.

July 1966 – Silver UFO over Scotland

Douglas Elwood, from Hertfordshire (then aged 12), was travelling back from Closeburn, Dumfries, after having visited relatives, (an annual holiday made by the family), in 1966.

"As we neared Closeburn, we noticed a circular object in the sky above the village. By the time we arrived, there were a number of people watching the object, which was silver in colour with darker circles around its outer rim. Some of the people fetched binoculars to look at the object – still stationary in the sky for quite a long time. When somebody went to telephone the authorities, it shot off across the sky and disappeared at a speed that left us speechless."

Following publication of the incident by the local newspaper, a few days later, the RAF suggested they may have seen a weather balloon! **(Source: Personal interview)**

31st July 1966 – UFO lands at Carolina, USA

Pennsylvania appears to have been the continued source of UFO interest. At 7.25pm, Douglas Tibbetts (16), Betty Klem (16), Anita Haifley (22), and Gerald Labelle (29), was out at Presque Isle State Park, when they saw:

"...a hexagonal object with edges lit by light, or reflective edges, tumbling down from the sky in a right to left movement. It then halted in mid-air about 5-10 feet off the beach, and then settled down onto the ground, showing a circle of spotlights on the top. Five minutes later (presumably) it took off." **(Source: NICAP)**

During the same year, Christopher Chesters from Nantwich, Cheshire, was walking through Cholmondeston, accompanied by his girlfriend, when they saw *"a silver coloured, egg-shaped object"* hovering in front of them, about 60 feet off the ground, followed by the appearance of a second smaller object, which rose up from behind a nearby barn and merged into the first, before heading westwards.

AUGUST 1966

1st August 1966 – UFO display over Maryland, USA

During the late evening, high-speed objects performing manoeuvres in the sky were reported by Police Officers, State Troopers and civilians, over Prince George County, Maryland. One witness was physicist and electronics expert – Dr. Vasil Uzunoglu. He was driving on the Capital Beltway, at 11pm, near Washington, when he noticed an unusual object in the sky, about 18,000 feet above the highway. It then began to descend and was next seen by him about 200 feet above a house, approximately 200 feet away from the Beltway. He was going to stop and get a closer look but, shaken by the sighting, changed his mind and drove away. He later reported the matter to Andrews Air Force Base.

Jamestown, New York – 'creature' seen

During the same evening, the police were contacted after a group of young people – who had been picnicking on Erie Peninsula – reported having sighted a UFO, which landed not far away from where they had been sitting. As some of the group watched to see what was going to happen next, one of the girls (who had returned to her car) saw what she described as:

"...a strange 'hairy creature' that tried to break into the car and then climbed onto the roof. I sounded the horn and the 'creature' jumped down and then disappeared." **(Source: NICAP)**

2nd August 1966 – 'Flying Saucer' over Lincolnshire

At 10.30am, Andrew Hyde (aged 8) was in his back garden in Stamford, Lincolnshire, when he noticed an object moving quickly through the sky, above cloud, heading north-west. Ten minutes later the UFO returned, going towards the south-east direction.

"It was round, with black circles – like a ship's portholes, around its middle. I could see what looked like landing wheels on the bottom, with a cloud of yellow stuff coming out of the back."

(Source: Lincoln UFO Study Group)

4th August 1966 – Cone-shaped UFO over Manchester

At 8pm, a motorcyclist and his passenger were riding along the Middleton to Ashley road, Manchester, when they sighted *"a cone-shaped, whitish or pale grey light"*, moving across the sky. Within seconds, it had vanished behind cloud. (**Source: BUFORA, Mr R.A. Jahn**)

At 10.45pm the same day, *"a large cigar-shaped object, showing two orange lights"*, was seen passing through the sky over Waltham Cross, in Hertfordshire. (**Source: International Sky Scouts**)

August 1966 – 'Flying Saucer', Coventry

We spoke to Stanley Maddocks, a former Royal Navy diver and decorated Second World War hero, who had been employed in underwater mine clearance from various harbours – surely one of the most hazardous jobs in existence!

Ironically, it was not the murky depths and the danger of being 'blown to pieces' that frightened him. It was what he saw, over 25 years later, while standing outside the Hawker factory at Whitley, Coventry, in August 1966.

> *"I was stood outside the factory gate, at 9.30pm, talking to the security officer, when we saw some flashing 'lights' over Baginton airfield. A few minutes passed, then the 'lights' came towards us. When they came closer, we could clearly see they were part of a fan-shaped object, which had now stopped overhead, only a few hundred feet above us. It had three strips of light in the underside and portholes around the 'craft'. Suddenly it shot upwards, in complete silence, and was out of sight in seconds. The following night, I met a fellow workman from the factory. Without telling him anything, I casually asked if he had seen anything the previous evening. I was so excited when he described having seen a similar object in the sky at the time we saw it. Over the years I've wondered what the attraction was. Could it have been anything to do with the treatment of depleted uranium tips, used in the manufacture of ammunition at the factory?"*

In 2010, we spoke to John Maddocks (the son of Stan), who told us his father had passed away a few years ago, but that his mother remembered, vividly, the agitated state of her husband when he had arrived home following the UFO sighting. (**Source: Bob Tibbitts**)

14th August 1966 – Black elliptical object

Mr D. Carter of Chester-le-Street, County Durham, contacted the Isle of Wight Society after having sighted a jet-black elliptical object, at 8.40pm. The object was seen to change image as it went over, westwards, towards the setting sun, at a height he estimated to be 250-300 feet. Within 45 seconds, it disappeared out of sight. (**Source: *UFOLOG***)

15th August 1966 – UFO crashes into London suburb ... causes burns

Keith Palmer – a UFO researcher from Wood Green, London, who was responsible for organising a number of 'sky watches' both in the London and Banbury areas, during the 1960-70s – wrote to Prime Minister Harold Wilson, telling him of:

> *"...a very nasty experience my wife and I had, at 2am, when we saw a large UFO with flames shooting out of it, about 800 yards away, approaching the house. It suddenly came right at us and whizzed over the house, showing rows and rows of little lights underneath, as a result of which I suffered a number of burns – about the size of a sixpence – on my body."*

Colin McCarthy of *Flying Saucer Review*

In an interview conducted by Colin McCarthy, of *Flying Saucer Review*, Keith told him:

"I had to visit the bathroom. On the way back to my bedroom, I just happened to glance out through the net curtains, when I saw a bright white light at eye level. I pulled back the nets and opened the window to a beautiful North London night sky – warm and full of stars – but the light I saw was about 500 yards from my window, just stationery and so very brilliant it almost dazzled me. As I watched I could not hear anything, apart from some slight traffic sounds in the distance. Suddenly, two smaller lights then shot out from both sides and a very, very, brilliant cone-shaped beam appeared. It was then that I noticed through the beam – bright enough to see the time on my wristwatch, at 2.10am – an oak tree in the field below the object. I had to partially shield my eyes from the brilliance, but I could still see the almost plasma type 'balls of light', consisting of a big one in the centre and two smaller ones on either side. After maybe a minute or two, suddenly, the two smaller lights went out – then the centre main light started to move, wobbled slightly and rose, moving in my direction, slowly and silently – just a huge brilliant light. As it came towards me the brilliance seemed to dim, until I realised the bottom part up of the object was tilting at a 20 degrees angle. It came directly over the house, losing its dazzle. I looked up to see a huge pear-shaped object, with thousands of small lights haphazardly turning around on the underside of the 'craft', as high as a 20 storey building. I felt a tingling sensation as the 'craft' – approximately 300 feet in width, longer in length – slowly drifted over from the back of the house to the front, going out of view over the roof, so I rushed out of my bedroom to the room in the front, hoping to see the 'craft' as it passed over …but there was nothing to be seen."

Keith ran into the street, still in pyjamas, but nothing could be seen. Worried and concerned, he called the local police, only to be greeted with the words: *"Oh, no! Not another one"*.

The officer took his phone number and said they would make a note of it, without bothering to ask for any details. Keith, now unable to sleep, spent some time looking up into the sky, hoping to see something, but then decided to go indoors, where he happened to look in the mirror and notice that, *"the right side of my face, hands and right arm, were covered in reddish-brown flaky patches"*.

Asked to go to Police Station – then to MOD

At 5.30am the police called him, wanting to know what he had seen, and asked him to go the police station to fill out a report.

Keith told them he was unable to comply, because of the rash on his arms and face. In fact, he was later driven to the local doctor by his wife, where he learned that 15 other people had seen this object within a 20 mile radius, five of which sightings had occurred in the North London area.

Keith:

"All of us had to be taken to the Ministry of Defence, in London, to talk and sketch what we had seen, separated from each other.

Area roped off by the Civil Defence and Police

The results were exciting, because people had seen this object from different angles and all said it was pear-shaped. The area where I saw the 'craft' was roped off by the then Civil Defence and Police, for several days. Furthermore, the oak tree never grew again and three large holes were found in the ground below the tree, which I, and friends, went to see. The centre hole was about 18 inches in circumference; the two outer holes – one on either side – around 6 inches wide."

We contacted Colin, now living in Australia. During conversation about the incident, he explained how he had been asked by the Editor of *Flying Saucer Review* to interview the couple, after details of their experience were published in a local newspaper. We were, however, unable to track down this newspaper, or any record of the incident at the local library.

Colin confirmed *"having seen slight tanning of the skin on Keith's face – like sunburn. I also confirmed the discovery of holes in the ground, together with damage caused to a nearby oak tree by apparent burning".*

Sadly, he had no knowledge of the MOD and Police having cordoned-off the streets, and a letter sent to the Prime Minister.

MOD – No comment

When we asked the MOD if they had any information about the incident, following a request under the Freedom of Information Act (2006), they made no comment and advised us to go and search through Public Records.

Still classified?

What a pity we weren't able to speak to Keith personally. We would have liked to have learned more about what promised to be an exceptional incident, involving the landing of a UFO and the response of the authorities – matters, of course, which are no doubt still classified as Top Secret, irrespective of any records being declassified.

(Sources: As above/The *Sun*, 13.6.1967 – 'Take care – more Saucers'/The Wood Green UFO, *Flying Saucer Review*, Volume 12, No. 6, Nov/Dec. 1966)

At 11pm the same day, Mr D.R. Stones of Ryhill, Yorkshire, was on holiday in Scarborough, attending an open air theatre, one evening at about 11pm, when he saw:

"…what I took to be a meteor – dull orange in colour – but it didn't burn out and was far too slow to be one. I watched it for about two minutes, beginning in Ursa Major, then lost sight of it past Cygnus."

(Source: Letter to Mr A.W. Szachnowski, Anglo-Polish Research Club)

19th August 1966 – Domed 'disc' seen over Donnybrook, Dakota, USA

US Border Patrolman Don Flickenger was on duty at 4.50pm, when he saw:

"…a round white 'disc', with domed top, estimated to be 30 feet in diameter and 15 feet high, moving through the sky across a valley in the south-eastern direction. It then hovered over a reservoir and appeared to land in a small field, before rising upwards into clouds, five minutes later".

(Source: NICAP)

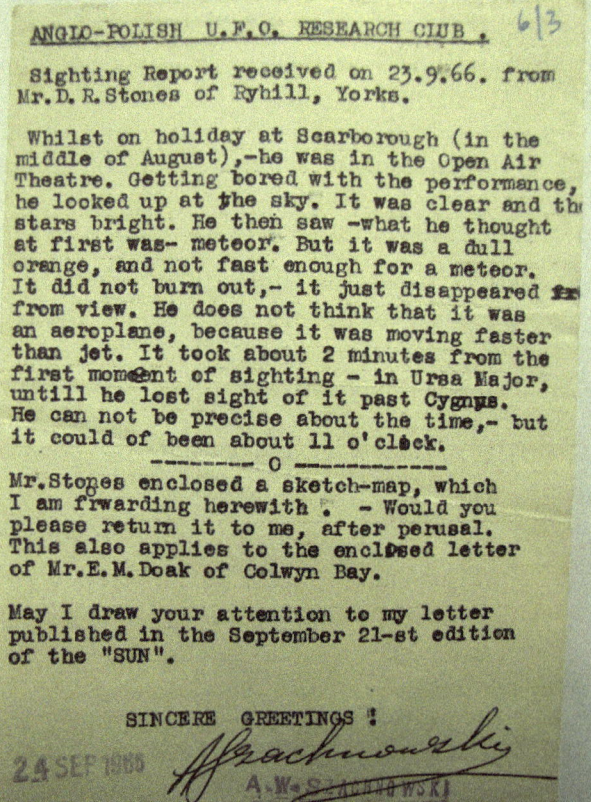

According to *The Hynek UFO report* following a visit to the location indentations were found in the field. Apparently the object was seen hovering 20-30feet over a reservoir, by the officer who was taking a prisoner to Canada. *"My first instinct was to pull out my revolver and empty it into the craft but fear of the unknown restrained me from doing so."*

20th August 1966 – Object, showing three lights

At 9.50pm, a bright red flashing light was seen in the sky over Wroxham. According to a number of people that witnessed its flight, the object changed in colour to yellow and amber and showed three small lights, while circling the sky over Sprowston and Crostwick.

Another couple – Mr and Mrs D. Blythe – told of watching what they took to be a red rocket rise up from the ground, over the Yarmouth road, and disappear from sight. Shortly afterwards, while walking home at 9.50pm, they noticed:

> *"...three pulsating red lights, in no particular sequence, were forming a flattened triangle, hovering over or near the Cathedral, before drifting northwards."*

(Sources: Isle of Wight UFO Society, John Feakins/*Eastern Daily Press*, 22.8.1966, 24.8.1966)

21st August 1966 – Strange object seen over Isle of Wight

At 1am, Jack Tait of Orchardleigh Road, Shanklin, Isle of Wight, was observing the night sky, facing westwards, when:

> *"I noticed a yellow or light coloured object – the size of a pinhead, at arm's length – crossing my field of vision, travelling in a north to south direction. I estimated its size was about six inches in diameter and felt it was only a hundred feet off the ground. I cannot be sure but also thought I heard a whistling noise as it went over, but that could have been my imagination."*

(Source: Aerial Phenomena sighting report)

21st August 1966 – 'Flying Saucer', Penge, Kent – Three strange noises heard

Gloria Blizzard (17) of Penge, Kent, was awoken at 4am on the same date, by three strange noises – described as like *"a jet engine starting up, a low whistle and hum"*.

On going to the window she saw:

> *"...a silver cigar-shaped object, approximately 25 yards in length, hovering silently above the house, 25 feet away, with light coming from it; on its side were what looked like three dark crevices, cut into the side of the body – not lights. The noise then started again and it took off, taking 20 minutes to completely disappear from view".*

(Sources: As above/*Gazette*, 8.9.1966 – 'Flying Saucer at Penge'/Anglo-Polish Club, Tony Szachnoswki and his wife, Stella)

23rd August 1966 – UFO splits into five over Ohio, USA

Mr Broomhall and Mr Gilpin reported having sighted a luminous white object over Columbus, Ohio, at 7pm, which was seen to split into five separate objects – all of them then heading away westwards, at high speed, fifteen minutes later. **(Source: NICAP)**

25th August 1966 – UFO interacts with US missile crew and then lands!

An Air Force Officer – in charge of a missile crew in North Dakota, United States, housed in a concrete capsule 60 feet below ground – found his radio transmission was being interrupted by static. While attempting to sort out the problem, Air Force personnel on the ground above reported sighting a bright-red light, high in the sky, which appeared to be alternately climbing and descending.

The object was tracked on radar and found to be at 100,000 feet. The Commander of Operations said:

'FLYING SAUCER' AT PENGE

Thurs. Sept. 8, 1966 — No. 8761 — 4d.

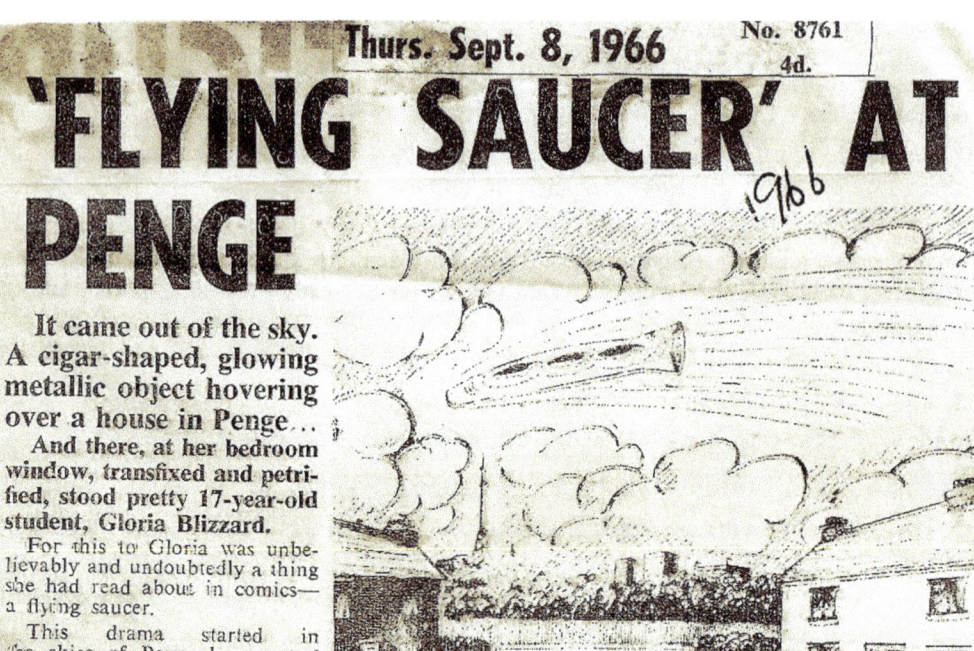

Our artist's impression of the U.F.O. described by Miss Gloria Blizzard.

It came out of the sky. A cigar-shaped, glowing metallic object hovering over a house in Penge...

And there, at her bedroom window, transfixed and petrified, stood pretty 17-year-old student, Gloria Blizzard.

For this to Gloria was unbelievably and undoubtedly a thing she had read about in comics— a flying saucer.

This drama started in the skies of Penge began at 4 a.m. on a clear morning on Sunday, August 21, when Gloria was wakened by three noises in one, a noise similar to a jet engine starting up, a low whistle and a low hum.

"I jumped out of bed and looked out the window", said Gloria, at her home in Kingswood Road, Penge, "and just couldn't believe my eyes".

"It was terrifying. It was a silver cigar-shaped object about 25 yards long and there was a light coming from it.

"On the side of the object were three dark crevices, which were certainly not windows".

Gloria went on: "It was about 25 feet above the house when the noise cut out and it hovered for approximately two minutes.

"The noise then began again and it started going round slowly.

MOTHER CAME TOO

"It then started off at a very fast rate and my mother, who had come into the room, and I, watched it go. It took exactly 20 minutes to disappear completely.

"There was a glimmer of light coming from it which was certainly not a reflection."

'A glowing cigar-shape says Gloria

Gloria added: "It was a most terrifying experience.

"I didn't want to say anything at first about the object, which I am now convinced was a flying saucer.

"But it got to such a state that I just had to tell someone.

"I have never really believed in flying saucers before, but now I think there is something in it".

EXPERT IN U.F.O.'s

And the person Gloria told her dramatic story to was 45-year-old writer and broadcaster, Mr. Antoni Szachnowski, founder and chairman of the Anglo-Polish U.F.O.—(Unidentified Flying Objects—as they are officially known) — Research Club, Oakfield Road, Penge.

Said Mr. Szachnowski, who is an expert of U.F.O.: "I have had a long talk with Miss Blizzard and I find she is very sincere in what she says.

"From what she told me, and the way she told it, I am certain her sighting was genuine. "She was also very terrified and tremely upset!"

Mr. Szachnowski added: "But I cannot say for sure whether it was an 'unidentified flying object' until I have checked all other possibilities, such as aircraft, weather balloons, airstreams, etc.

"If all these possibilities are out, I will certainly declare it an 'unidentified flying object'.

"I am hoping that other people in the road saw or heard the object. It was told that a neighbour of Miss Blizzard's did hear a noise on the morning of the incident, but I have not been round to see him yet."

"When the UFO climbed, the static stopped. The UFO began to swoop and dive; it then appeared to land 10-15 miles south of the area. A missile strike team – well armed Air Force guards – went out to investigate; when about 10 miles away, their radios were affected by static. A few minutes later, the glow diminished and the object took off. At this point, another object was tracked on radar and also visually sighted. The first object was seen to fly under the second and head away towards the North."

(**Source:** *Probe Phenomena Magazine,* **Spring 1967**)

26th August 1966 – Triangular formation of lights over Alabama, USA

At 8.30pm, Mr and Mrs Funk from Gaylesville, Alabama, along with their three children, sighted a cluster of four small glowing orange-yellow lights, moving across the sky in a triangular formation, heading in the east to west direction. The family watched them for forty-five minutes, ruling out any notion that this was space debris or natural phenomena. (**Source: NICAP**)

31st August 1966 – Two lights joined by a bar, seen over Lancashire

At 3.45am, a girl who was having trouble sleeping, looked out of her bedroom window of a fifth storey block of flats, situated off Littleton Road, Salford, overlooking playing fields, when she saw:

"...two salmon coloured diffuse lights, joined by a bar underneath a grey oval object, with a dome on top, moving through the air, 300 yards away, at a height of 25-30 feet off the ground, which passed over a block of flats in front of me and continued past me at a speed I estimated to be 80-100 miles per hour".

At 11.05pm, Kenneth Armin – a student at the local College of Science and Technology, Stockport, Cheshire – sighted *"two bright lights, travelling very fast through the sky, at high altitude"*, which he thought so unusual that he contacted Ringway Airport, who told him no aircraft were in the air.

Wrote to the MOD

He then wrote a letter to the Air Ministry, and received a reply to the effect that they believed the objects he had seen were the satellites 64/28A and 64/53A. This explanation was dismissed by DIGAP (to whom the matter was also reported) after some thorough research into the orbital movements of satellites in use, at the time, clearly shows this not to have been the explanation. (**Source: Joan Nelstrop, DIGAP**)

SEPTEMBER 1966

1st September 1966 – UFO over New York, USA

At 2.45pm over Willsboro, New York, an oval object, showing flashing red and white lights with an occasional flash of blue, was seen heading across the sky in a westwards direction, by Mr T.H. Ridman, who said:

"After disappearing downwards from sight, it returned several minutes later accompanied by a loud noise."

The entire sighting lasted 30 minutes. (**Source: NICAP**)

3rd September 1966 – Three circular objects seen over Leicester

On the late evening, *"three blue coloured, circular objects"* were seen in the sky over Leicester, by Alan Frost and his colleague – Tom Burnett – while repairing a street lamp by the side of the road. The objects then passed overhead and hovered for twenty minutes, until *"two of them drifted away, one after the other"*.

4th September 1966 – UFO display over Great Yarmouth

Police Constable 565 Alan .F. Delaney was on duty in Yarmouth, talking to Mr J. Abbot, fishing from the landing stage of the Yarmouth ferry, at 10.40pm, when he noticed a bluish-white 'light' moving towards the west, which he took to be either a star or aircraft.

"It wasn't an aircraft, as it was completely silent and the 'light' was not blinking. By the time we discussed it, the 'light' had returned to its original position near Lymington, having increased in brightness – now stationary in the sky. It then moved westwards again, getting dimmer, and faded once more, appearing over Lymington. I then drew a line between myself, a light on the mainland, and a star directly above the 'light', as a yardstick of reference. The 'light' moved backwards and forwards, seven or eight times, but didn't appear to pass the imaginary line of reference I had drawn. Suddenly, it began to adopt an erratic course through the sky. Each time it travelled westwards in a curved motion, towards the Isle of Wight, swung towards Fort Victoria and back to its starting place, before moving west again – now further out. It then came from Lymington and passed over Yarmouth, stopping in mid-air for a short time, went west again, and shot off through the sky at a speed far too fast to have been any aircraft." **(Source: Personal interview)**

At 10.45pm on the same date, Brian Wright from Waltham Cross, Hertfordshire, and a number of other people, sighted:

"…a large, cigar-shaped object, showing two orange lights moving across the sky."

(Source: International Sky Scouts Association)

6th September 1966 – Three objects sighted, resembling 'flying crosses'

At 11pm, three dull yellow objects, resembling 'flying crosses' were seen moving through the sky over Hebburn, County Durham. As they passed overhead, they appeared to change in shape to 'discs'. Ten minutes later, four more cross-shaped objects passed overhead. **(Source: TUFOS)**

6th September 1966 – UFO sighted over Suffolk County Air Force Base, USA

At 6.50pm on the same date (taking into consideration the time differences), a Mr Stahl and Ladesic sighted a white cylindrical light in the sky, moving at speed from the east, over Suffolk County Air Force Base, New York. It then halted in flight and hovered for a few minutes, turned, and slowly disappeared from view, eight minutes later. **(Source: NICAP)**

7th September 1966 – Rocket-shaped object, Leicestershire

Between the hours of 9.30pm and 11pm – a clear, moonlit night – an amateur astronomer from Braunstone, Leicestershire, was looking at the moon through his telescope, when he saw: *"what looked like a rocket, with what appeared to be a shadow underneath it"*, apparently stationary and silhouetted against the background of the moon, between the area of Tycho and Maurolycus. Excitedly, he summoned members of the family and the next door neighbour to come and view the object through the eyepiece, which remained in the same position for over an hour.

Could it have been a space rocket, launched by NASA, or Russia? – Extremely unlikely. Was there any connection with a three-day *Gemini 11* Mission, launched on 12th September 1966, and NASA's *Surveyor 11* spacecraft, which impacted after being launched on 22nd September 1966, on the moon, near the crater of Copernicus? – Highly unlikely, we would have thought.

(Source: *Leicester Mercury* – 'Saw moon rocket, says city man' [date not known])

8th September 1966 – Eight to twelve objects sighted over Leicester

At about 12.30am, between eight to twelve objects were seen moving across the sky over Leicester, heading eastwards.

(Sources: NICAP, Great Britain/*UFOLOG*/*Leicester Mercury* – 'We saw things in sky, say lamp men')

On the same date, at about 3.20pm, Mr Albert Baynton from Bradford-on-Avon, Wiltshire, was outside his home address, when he saw an object hovering in the sky, just below a layer of white cloud. Suddenly the object dived downwards, at terrific speed, disappearing from view behind the tower of Christ Church.

Mr Baynton described it as:

> "...saucer-like, with a dark coloured (probably black) dome, spanning about half of its surface, and that after hovering for a while, the 'saucer' flew off, making a deep vibrating droning noise, increasing into a high-pitched whine".

(Source: *Bath and Wiltshire Evening Chronicle,* **9.9.1966/Mary Baynton**)

9th September 1966 – Object seen over Franklin Springs, New York, USA

At 9pm, what appeared to be a solid object, larger than an army tank – according to the witness, Mr Jacobson – showing lights around it and making a humming noise, was seen to disappear into nearby woods 30 minutes later.

10th September 1966 – Halifax UFO Conference, Textile Hall, Westgate, Bradford – 8 shillings registration fee

The main lecture in the afternoon was given by Arthur Shuttlewood – it began at 2.30pm. 4pm: tea and biscuits, followed by a symposium on 'UFO investigation'. The Panel consisted of John Cleary-Baker, PhD., Editor of *BUFORA Journal,* John Leslie Otley, A.R.P.S., Hon. Secretary of Tyneside UFO Society and editor of *ORBIT,* Alan Sharp, B.Sc., B.Eng., F.G.S., F.R.A.S., and Stephen Smith, B.A., Hon. Sec. BUFORA.

Middle of September 1966 – Glittering red crescent-shaped object

A glittering red object was seen in the sky over Penge, south-east London, by local residents – Edward Homewood, and his wife. Through binoculars a crescent-shaped object could be seen. About 45 minutes later, the UFO moved away and was soon lost from sight in the direction of the north-east.

(**Sources:** Gordon Creighton, *Flying Saucer Review/Beckenham and Penge Advertiser,* **15.9.1966**)

13th September 1966 – UFO lands at North Dakota, USA

Mr Rotenberg of Gwinner, North Dakota, reported sighting a silvery-grey elliptical object with a clear 'bubble' protruding from its top, motionless in the sky, about half a mile away, accompanied by a low-pitched whining noise. It then landed within 300 yards away from him before taking off again, at speed, five minutes later. (**Source: NICAP**)

19th September 1966 – Strange object seen in the sky

At 7.15pm, a silent star-like object, reflecting the sun's rays, was observed moving slowly across the north-western part of the sky over Leadgate Catholic Junior School, County Durham, by three schoolboys. They saw it disappear from sight, a few minutes later.

Was this the same object seen at 10.30pm, on the same date, described as *"a bright 'dot of light', moving in jerks across the sky"* in an east-west direction over Rannoch Station, Perthshire, by TUFOS member – Frank Satterthwaite, and his cousin.

> *"It was like Venus in full aspect – no sound, showing a bright white colour, at an estimated height of 4-5,000 feet. It moved in a* **'W'** *shape across the sky and then turned southwards, before being lost in cloud cover."* (**Source: TUFOS/Isle of Wight UFO Society**)

Isle of Wight

At 10.35pm on 19th September 1966, Mr R. Corbett of Union Road, Cowes, on the Isle of Wight, was outside his house; it was a clear sky, with no moon. He noticed:

> "...a 'light', moving silently across the sky. At first I thought it was aircraft navigation light, but I couldn't see any green or red starboard/port lights – perhaps it was a satellite? It then veered to the

right, stopped and dropped, before continuing its flight – slow and gradual. I last saw it heading towards Lee-on-Solent. It is difficult to give any height or size ... maybe 3,000 feet."
(Sources: Aerial Phenomena sighting report/UFOLOG)

26th September 1966 – *Evening News* – 'The Z car and the thing in the sky' –
(Article regarding an investigation launched by Police, after a UFO was sighted in the sky over Eastleigh, Hampshire, at 11pm on 18th September 1966, moving at incredible speed)

County Durham

At 11pm, Mr Blamine and Miss Hanwell were walking along a road in Hebburn, County Durham, when they sighted four bright yellow 'discs' passing overhead, travelling in a south-west to north-east direction, which appeared to fade away.

They were not the only ones to sight something unusual that day. An unidentified flying object was seen in the western sky, over Southampton, described as *"flashing red, blue, and white lights, dropping purple flames"*.

Police officers, who attended at the scene, were unable to offer any explanation.
(Source: Isle of Wight UFO Society)

20th September 1966 – Pilot sights UFO over Florida
Former Army Security Investigator – Mr J.J. O'Connor (then a lawyer in Florida) – was piloting his plane near Sebring, Florida, at 9,500 feet, when a UFO hovered above him. As its shadow covered the aircraft, O'Connor reduced power and dived. He pulled out at 3,500 feet, and saw to his consternation that it was still with him. He reached for a .38 revolver he kept in the cockpit, but the size of the enormous object stopped him from firing it at the object. A few moments later, the UFO circled upwards and went out of sight. **(Source: NICAP)**

21st September 1966 – 'Thing' seen in the sky
Margaret Davies from Neath, Glamorgan, was trained in aircraft recognition and had been a member of a gun-sight crew during World War Two. During the late evening she was called outside by a group of schoolboys, after they had seen something strange in the sky.

"I rushed outside and saw this 'thing', stationary in the sky, constantly changing colour – blue, orange, and white.

All of a sudden, it went off at great speed, towards the sea."
(Source: Isle of Wight UFO Society)

22nd September 1966 – Chevron-shaped lights over Essex
At 8.30pm, Richard and Andrew Jones, of Debden Road, were in the back garden of their house at Saffron Walden, Essex, when they sighted a chevron-shaped cluster of lights moving across the sky, which was later explained away as being a flock of migrating birds, or the lights of an aircraft – which seems unlikely. **(Source: Mr H. Huxley, Cambridge University Investigation Group)**

24th September 1966 – UFO with 'fin', seen over Epping
In the evening, two schoolgirls were walking down Lindsey Street, past Shaftesbury Farm, Epping, when they heard a high-pitched whining noise. Looking around they saw *"an enormous silver-grey, cigar-shaped object, more pointed at one end than the other, showing what looked like a 'fin' at one end"*, a mile or so towards Epping Uplands, hovering above a water tower. The girls watched the object for a short while, before making their way back home. When they looked back, the object had gone and the whining noise was fading away. **(Source: *ORBIT*, Volume 7, December 1966)**

Wiltshire sighting

Was there a connection with what took pace at 9.20pm, on the same date, involving Mr T. Burwood, from London, who was driving along the A360 road between Tilshead and Shrewton on Salisbury Plain, accompanied by his wife, when his car engine failed?

Mr Burwood got out of the vehicle and opened the bonnet, in an attempt to locate the fault.

> *"We saw this red haze or 'mist' coming down from the sky, settling onto the road about 30 feet behind the vehicle, covering an area approximately the size of a car and some 6-7 feet tall. We were aware of a humming noise around us and became frightened when the 'mist' began to rise up and down, accompanied by a smell that reminded me of rotting flesh. Suddenly the glare of car headlights cut through the 'mist' and a Mini car roared past, hooting in protest, narrowly missing us. We looked around – the 'mist' had gone.*
>
> *When I operated the starter, the engine burst into life."*

(Source: Personal interview/Letter from Gordon Creighton)

September 1966 – Three UFOs sighted over Staffordshire

David Rayney contacted the *Stoke-on-Trent Sentinel* newspaper, after reading of our appeal, published by them on our behalf, seeking any information on local UFOs.

David:

> *"One of the strangest things I ever saw occurred just after midnight, in September 1966, when I was aged 19 and living at 1, Raglan Street (now known as Dimmelow Street, on the Coalville Estate, at Weston Coyney). The view from my upstairs front bedroom window looked out over Lavender Close and onto the fields, which led up to the Blythe Valley, marked by a long country lane called Handley Banks. In those days the BBC radio (then known as the Light Programme) used to close down at midnight. I remember preparing for bed, a few minutes past midnight, when the room was lit up by a powerful burst of light that shone like day. The radio, which was still on at the time, went mad with static. The light faded away, as did the static. All was now silent and dark. A few seconds later, the same thing happened again – the radio started whining. I went over to the window and pulled back the curtains, to be met by a powerful light that blinded with its intensity as it swung around towards me. As it moved away, the radio ceased its static. Slowly but surely, three luminescent blue glowing 'balls of light' then came from the position of the light – the right one near Caverswall, the centre one down towards the River Blythe, the left towards Sheepwash Lane – and glided silently over the fields. I saw a car going up Sheepwash Lane. One of the blue glowing spheres passed within a few hundred yards of the car. The driver must have seen it – then the beam went out, leaving darkness to return."* **(Source: Personal interview)**

28th September 1966 – 'Bar of orange light' seen in Worcestershire

At 6.30pm, a man from Halesowen, Worcestershire, arrived home after work. He was in the process of getting out of the car, when he noticed a large 'halo of light' behind the house. Wondering what was going on, he stopped to watch and saw:

> *"...a bright 'bar of orange light', flying 50-60 feet above the ground, pass overhead at about 20 miles per hour. From underneath it resembled an electric iron in shape, with flames coming out of the back. The flames or light flickered at three second intervals and were accompanied by a sound."*

It is reported that a neighbour also saw the object fly over, which turned back along its original course and headed westwards over the nearby park. Also on this date, a 'dustbin like' object was seen hovering over trees on the Cornbury Estate, Oxfordshire. **(Source: *UFOLOG*)**

Over Ohio

On the same date but this time over Wilmington, Ohio, was a report of three round aluminium coloured objects, with rotating rings around them, seen in the sky by a Mr Clarke. He said:

"Two of them remained stationary, while the third varied its height during the 90 second sighting."

(Source: NICAP)

OCTOBER 1966

October 1966 – 'Flying train' over Norfolk

At 9pm, in October 1966, Mr R.G. Warren – then a serving London Metropolitan Police Officer – was on his way to Cromer Railway Station, Norfolk. A few miles outside the village of Stiffkey, Mrs Warren brought her husband's attention to what she believed to be a railway train, passing through open countryside on their left.

Mr Warren:

"I looked out and saw what I took to be the lights of a two-coach train, moving very slowly in the darkness, about 150 yards away, diagonally to our position. I slowed down the Ford Zephyr car, at which point the 'train' passed across the front of us, no more than 30-40 yards away, at about the height of a two-storey house, which suggested the road we were travelling on was much lower than the railway track.

I noticed the 'train' was moving slowly, some ten miles per hour, and had a number of oblong windows set vertically into the side of the 'carriages', glowing a bright fluorescent green, with a red light showing at the rear of the 'train', as it headed silently away into the night."

When Mr and Mrs Warren reached Cromer Railway Station, a short time later, they were shocked to discover, during conversation with a railway porter, that the railway line ended a couple of hundred yards from the Railway Station.

Very curious about what they had witnessed, the couple returned to the locality where the sighting had taken place, the following day, but found only open fields and marshy land.

Mr Warren told us, a few weeks after the incident, that he came across an article in a local newspaper reporting the sighting of an unidentified flying object, resembling two brilliantly-lit coaches, seen over the seafront of Muddiford, Barnstaple, and UFOs reported over Eastbourne, at 9pm, the same evening.

(Source: Personal interview)

11th October 1966 – Oval object, showing lights

At 2.30am, *"an oval object with a number of lights around it, which became brilliant and then faded away and then brilliant again"*, was seen moving slowly towards the south, over Lidget Green, Bradford.

(Sources: BUFORA/*UFOLOG*)

14th October 1966 – *Evening News* – 'Do not scoff at things in the sky'

Interview with Gordon Creighton, President of BUFORA, and member of NICAP. Gordon, then living in Cedars Avenue, Rickmansworth – a distinguished diplomat – told the readers of sighting a 'flying disc' that took place in China, while retreating from the invading Japanese Forces.

15th October 1966 – Grey UFO seen in Warwickshire

At 8.50pm Mr Kerry Johnson, and his girlfriend, were standing by a gate leading into a field, at Evenlode (where strange marks in the crop had been found in 1960). They saw a grey object, zigzagging across the sky. Kerry told John 'Dennis' Llewellyn:

"At first I thought I had been mistaken, so carried on walking under some trees leading to the churchyard, when she looked back and screamed. I swung around and saw a grey shape in the sky. I grabbed hold of her and ran to a friend's house, where we recovered from the shock."

Mr Llewellyn, of Stratford-upon-Avon UFO Society, visited the couple concerned, who were still suffering from shock, and learnt that the object had been 'looping the loop' in the sky in *"fish-like movements"*.

(Source: John 'Dennis' Llewellyn)

17th October 1966 – UFO over Canterbury

A glowing saucer-shaped object, *"making a sound like a well kept lathe"*, was seen hovering over Sturry, near Canterbury, Kent, on the late evening, by 15 year-old schoolboys – Barry Neaves and John Binfield.

We contacted Barry, in 2006, who said:

"I remember it quite well, despite it being many years ago. I was with John Binfield, outside his dad's garage, when we saw three 'lights' moving over the sky from south-east to north-west, parallel to the coast, in a triangular formation, making a purring noise. Within fifteen seconds, they had gone out-of-sight. Although we were used to seeing many aircraft going over, including the Bristol freighter, this was so different. I can't remember the conversation with the RAF, whom I contacted, but they did tell me others had seen it."

(Source: The *Sun*, 19.10.1966 – 'Schoolboys see Flying Saucer'/Personal interview)

20th October 1966 – UFO over Bradford

A cone-shaped object, deep orange in colour, was seen over Bierley, Bradford, at 9.45pm, by a member of BUFORA and three members of his family. (**Sources: BUFORA/***UFOLOG*)

21st October 1966 – Isle of Wight UFO

Between 8pm and 8.15pm, local resident – Eric Clouston from Ryde, in the Isle of Wight – was walking along Ratcliffe Avenue, facing westwards, when he saw:

"...an 'orange light', which was moving across the sky over the Binstead area, towards the North. It then changed to white in colour, and something orange dropped vertically out of its underside and fell to the ground, leaving a sparkling trail behind it. I wondered if it was the power plant of something that had re-entered the Earth's atmosphere, discarded from a rocket."

Mr Clouston telephoned the *Evening News,* at Portsmouth, the *BBC* and *Niton Radio Station*, hoping they may have received other reports – but none had been received. (**Source: Isle of Wight UFO Society**)

Was this the same object seen by Keith Jones (15), from Binstead, Isle of Wight? He was walking home, at 10.15pm, with Karl Skoludick, Ian Kirkwood and Michael Newnham, when they heard a humming noise – like the sound of a spinning top. The noise was followed by the appearance of a bright red 'light', which rose up silently over a nearby golf course and continued with its upwards ascent. Almost immediately afterwards, a white 'disc of light' was seen heading across the sky, northwards, at fantastic speed – but was gone in seconds.

Keith dialled 999 for the Police. By the time the officers arrived, there was no sign of the UFO. Keith was then given a reprimand for using the Police 999 emergency call system!

(Source: Isle of Wight Society/Fred Smith, *UFOLOG*/Kath Smith)

22nd October 1966 – 'Solid white tube' moving over Lancashire

At 7pm, an elongated object – resembling a 'solid white tube' – was seen moving eastwards across the sky, over Unsworth, Bury, Lancashire. (**Source: NICAP, GB**)

23rd October 1966 – UFO display

Between 5.45pm and 6.15pm an object – *"four times brighter than any star"* – was sighted in the sky over Oldham, Lancashire, by Mr L. Price and his family, from Failsworth, who told of seeing it perform various manoeuvres across the sky, involving a series of 'stop and start' movements.
(Sources: *UFOLOG*/J.E. Knagg/Mrs J. Nelstrop, DIGAP)

Over power lines – Southampton, New York

On the same day – this time over Southampton, Long Island – was a report from a Mr Acquino, who told of sighting:

> *"...an object, with 'arms' in front of it, sparkling like an arc light, heading south over power lines. It was making a humming sound as it did so. It then turned south-west and was out of sight, four minutes later."* **(Source: NICAP)**

29th October 1966 – Red glow in the sky

Teenagers – Alan Hunter and David Wright – were on the way home from Brading Youth Club, Isle of Wight, at 7.30pm when they noticed:

> *"...a red glow in the sky, slightly north of east. Further scrutiny revealed a fuzzy oval patch, low down, behind some poplar trees, some considerable distance away. It reminded us of a sunset but in the wrong place. It turned white just before fading away."* **(Source: Isle of Wight UFO Society)**

31st October 1966 – Two 'discs' sighted over Lancashire

Draughtsman William Sinclair of Burlington Avenue, Oldham, was on his way home from work, at 5.35pm, when he noticed two *'bright disc-shaped objects'*, stationary in the sky, towards the North. After watching them for about ten minutes, the objects moved a few yards, gave off a red glow from the underside, and climbed upwards at speed. Ten minutes later the same, if not similar, objects were seen by Mr and Mrs Needham, who were driving along Broadway, when they saw two bright 'lights', motionless in the sky, over Oldham.

(Sources: *UFOLOG*/NICAP GB, Derek Samson/Mrs Joan Nelstrop, DIGAP)

NOVEMBER 1966

4th November 1966 – UFOs over Reading, Berkshire

At 10.45pm, a blue cylindrical object, *"with a piece cut out of it"*, was seen silently moving over the town, at a speed of 15-20 miles per hour.

7th November 1966 – Cigar-shaped UFO over Reading

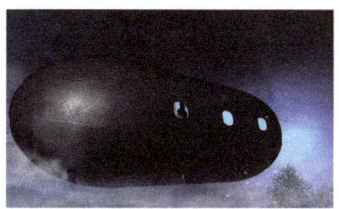

At 4am, Alan Prynn from Tilehurst Road, in Reading, was walking home after having finished work. As he neared his home address, he noticed a strange glow in the sky outside his house. Thinking something was on fire, he woke up his wife – Philomena. The couple then went outside to have a look around, to determine the cause.

> "I was shocked to see this dark, cigar-shaped object, hovering over trees at the end of the garden, about 60 feet away, accompanied by this crackling noise – like an arc welder's torch – coming from the rear of the UFO, glowing blue in colour. I could see portholes in the 'thing', with what looked like something, or someone inside, moving about. The birds in the trees, roosting, were squawking. All of the leaves came off the trees, which were blowing about everywhere. I shouted for my wife to fetch the camera. When she came back, there was no film in it! By this time the UFO was above us. My wife hid in the bed ... she was so scared. It then slid to the right and went off over woodlands at the end of the garden. That was the last I ever saw of it."
> **(Source: Personal interview)**

At 5.30pm on the same date, Peter Fredrick Flux – an engineer by occupation from Royston, Oldham, in Lancashire – was driving home near Werneth Fire Station, when he noticed:

> "...two white objects, motionless in the sky under cloud cover, approximately twice the size of stars."

Puzzled, he stopped the car in order to gain a clearer view – but a short time later, they disappeared.
(Source: Joan Nelstrop, DIGAP)

8th November 1966 – Schoolboys sight two objects

At 9.53pm, amateur astronomer schoolboys – Paul Harris and John McCue, from Middlesbrough – sighted two white, diffuse objects, heading silently across the sky towards the south-south-east direction.

8th November 1966 – Encounter with UFO, Shropshire

Following one of many visits to the National Archives in London, popular UFO author – Nick Redfern – came across a now declassified military document, which had been submitted to the Royal Air Force Provost and Security Services. It was dated November 1966, by a Corporal Rickwood, who told of being contacted by Flt. Lt. Williams, based at RAF Shawbury, following a telephone call received at the base from Mr Foulkes, on behalf of his daughter – then living in the Shropshire area.

The report, considered by Nick to be one of the strangest military documents he had ever come across, was of much interest to us – especially bearing in mind, first of all, the date (which was the day after the incident at Reading) and, secondly, the number of times we were to come across reports of UFO activity along the A5.

Burn marks left on the car

The gist of the complaint made to Flt. Lt. Williams by Mr Foulkes was that his daughter – Diana (22) – had been frightened by the appearance of an object in the sky, while driving along the A5, near Great Ness, at 11.55pm. Even more interesting was the disclosure of a 'burn mark' found on the car, after the event.

In late November, Diana was interviewed about the incident, after having received a letter, dated 11th November 1966, from a Flt.Lt. Penny, informing her that no aircraft had been flying over the locality at the time the UFO was seen.

She told the investigator of two other similar experiences; the first in November 1964, while driving along the A5, from Shrewsbury to her home address.

"As I neared the Montford Bridge, a brightly-lit, circular object appeared in the sky above the car and frightened me. I increased my speed but the object kept pace with me, remaining at the same height until I arrived home. I told my mother and father. They watched the object – now a stationary bright light in the sky – for about half an hour. It then rapidly diminished in size. The light was yellow in colour, but became red as it moved. The second incident occurred on the 8th November 1966. I was returning along the same stretch of road, when an object appeared at Montford Bridge – this time much lower in the sky and towards the North. I could see rays of light shooting from the object, which appeared to be keeping up with my car. At one point in the journey the object came close to the vehicle, rays of light striking the offside. I felt a bump against that side – as if they had struck it. I felt as though I had received an electric shock and experienced pain in my neck. The left-hand side headlight went out. I arrived home feeling very ill, and explained what had happened to my parents – the object still being stationary in the sky."

Diana mentioned she believed the appearance of these objects could be connected with a Mr Griffin, who lived in the local area, and had apparently made contact with the occupants of the UFOs at Montford Bridge. However, the grounds on which she supplied this information were not given. Attempts to trace her, or the mysterious Mr Griffin, were unsuccessful.

10th November 1966 – Sighting over Berkshire

Later that morning, Mr Leslie Bullen – Town Clerk for Wallingford District Council, Berkshire – and Didcot photographer, Mr A. Carpenter, visited Wittenham Clumps. This is an area of natural beauty, situated along the *River Thames*, between Abingdon and Wallingford, Berkshire, and is believed to be one of the oldest Iron Age settlements in Britain. Later it was a Roman Fort. Local myths claim the area is haunted by the 'white figure' of a lady. Other stories tell of the laughter of invisible children, heard at midnight.

The men, who were there to take photographs for a forthcoming Council guide book, noticed an object in the sky, at 11am,

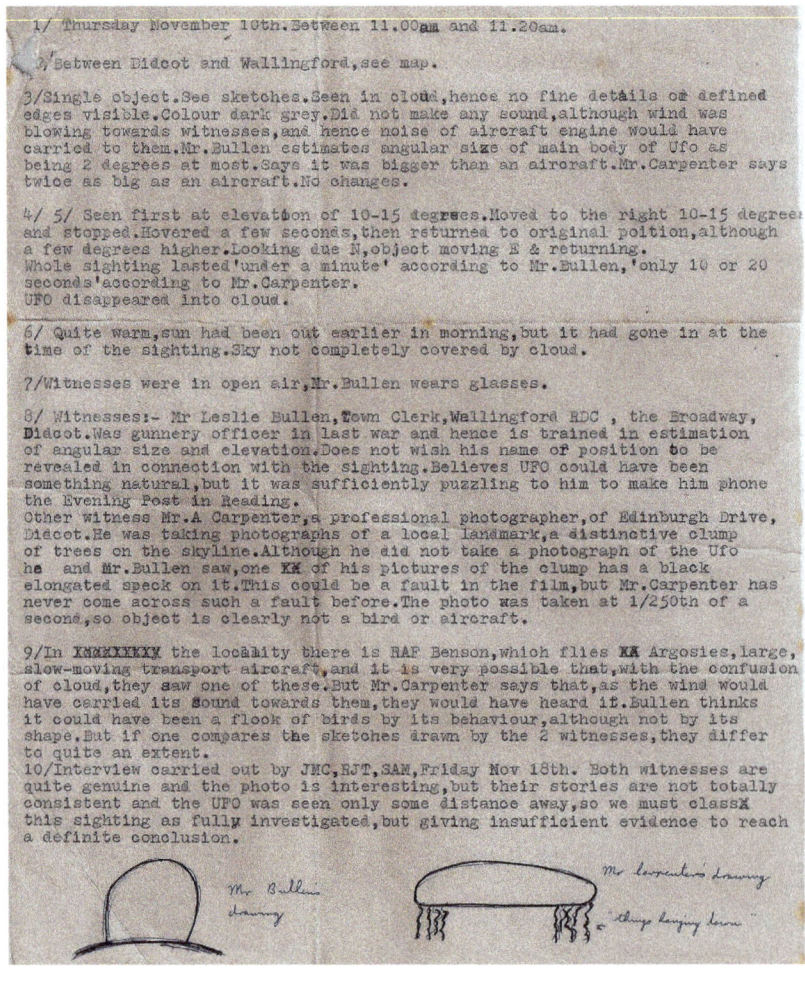

10/11/1966

Near Didcot

Two men were standing taking pictures of a local landmark, a prominent clump of trees between Didcot and Wallingford, at about 1110 am. One of them is a prominent person in a local town and is trained in the estimation of angular size, having been a gunnery officer in the war. The other is a professional photographer. However, despite their qualifications, the information gained by the three CUGIUFO members who interviewed them at length is inadequate to rule out, for example, a flock of birds as an explanation for this object. It was dark grey, of ill-defined shape, drawn by the two witnesses thus:

 or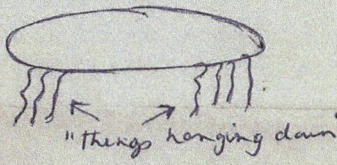

"things hanging down"

Its angular size was about 2° and its actual size probably bigger than an aircraft. No sound was heard and the wind was blowing from the object towards the witnesses. It was first seen 10° to 15° up in the North and then it moved some 10-15° to the East, stopped briefly and then returned until slightly above its formmer position. It disappeared into clouds. The whole sighting lasted less than one minute, maybe as little as 15 seconds. It was a warm November day, with the sun behind clouds at the instant of the sighting. CUGIUFO evaluate this as giving inadequate information for a definite conclusion, despite a full investigation.

When the photographer developed his film he found on one plate a very small black featureless elongated blip above the trees and to the right. There is a chance that this was the object described above, but it can hardly contribute much to an elucidation of its nature. The possibility of faking cannot seriously be entertained, and the photographer does not think that the image arises from a fault in the fiom, though this must remain a possibility. The interviewers examined the negative briefly, and CUGIUFO hope to borrow the negative for a more leisurely examination.

which they took to be an 'Argosy' aircraft, from RAF Benson. Further observations revealed *"an object, resembling an octopus in appearance, with 'legs' dangling from the outside edge, leaving a long plume trailing behind it, like the jet stream of an aircraft taking off"*, although Mr Carpenter described it as looking like a Portuguese Man-o'-War jellyfish, showing tentacles, moving backwards and forwards in flight.

(Sources: Cambridge University Group for the Investigation of UFOs [CUGIUFO]/*Flying Saucer Review*)
See sighting report for 29th June 1967.

Early November 1966 – Crater discovered at Chard, Somerset

Derek Samson, of NICAP GB, visited Chard, in Somerset, to investigate a report of a crater found in farmland at Long Lye, Bishopswood.

> *"The farmer – Harry Bickley – had reported the incident to the local police, who had called out the bomb disposal squad. They had examined the mark in the ground but found nothing, although they were puzzled about why it was more or less circular under the surface. One suggestion made was that it had been caused by an underground stream, although the River Yarty was some hundred yards from the hole. What I couldn't understand is that why it took the Army a month to finally arrive and look at the hole in the ground, found in a corner of the field with a depth of six feet."*

(Source: Derek Samson, NICAP, GB)

15th November 1966 – UFO with four antenna over Guildford, Surrey

At 1.35pm, *"a silvery-grey, or dark-blue 'double bubble', with four antennae protruding from its top, making a heavy buzzing sound"*, was seen descending through the sky, over Guildford, by at least five different witnesses. As it moved along, a jet of flame gushed out from one side – then pieces of the 'bubble' appeared to drop off. The whole object was enveloped in a 'ball of flame' as it disappeared up through the clouds.

One of the witnesses – ex-parachutist, Mr Seal – spoke of seeing a flashing orange light on the 'double bubble' as it descended through the clouds, with a sort of undercarriage gushing black smoke and flame. According to veteran UFO researcher – Omar Fowler, Mr Seal was 'still in an alarmed state' when interviewed by him, 24 hours later. Mr Brown, who was approximately 200 yards away from Mr Seal, standing at a nearby bus stop, spoke of seeing:

> *"...a gaseous flame in the sky, with what looked like a 'double bubble', with some sort of antennae in the centre, between two silvery-grey 'balls'."*

As the flame gushed out, it was impossible to see any reflection on the side of the 'bubble' before it disappeared into the clouds. Enquiries by Mr Fowler revealed no meteorological balloons had been launched in that area.

At 9pm on the same day, a large cigar-shaped object, emitting a high-pitched whine, was seen heading across the sky over North Wales. The same, if not similar, object was reported on the 2nd December 1966, at 00.20am. (**Source:** *UFOLOG*)

16th November 1966 – Blue object in the sky over Reading

At 10.45pm, Ascold Krushelnycky (12), was at his home address in Caversham, Reading, with his grandmother, when they saw a blue object in the sky, seen 'end on', before it turned sideways and headed in the direction of north-west, at an angle of 60 degrees off the horizon, moving at a speed of only 15-20 miles per hour. (**Source: Isle of Wight UFO Society**)

17th November 1966 – White UFO

At 3am, a white circular object was seen heading across the sky, over Middlesbrough, by Mr P. Harris, who was out watching the sky for any sign of the Leonid meteor shower. (**Source:** *UFOLOG*)

November 1966 – Strange phenomena over Essex

An odd shaped yellow cloud was seen moving slowly above mist over a field at Galleywood, Chelmsford, Essex, by teenager – Peter Day.

> *"Every few seconds, star-like objects shot out from the sides. It stopped, went a bit further, faded away and then repeated the process.*
>
> *We actually saw it over three nights' running. On the second occasion, it was making this rumbling noise."*

(**Source:** *Weekly News* – 'Youth tells of mysterious object in sky' – [date of publication not known])

21st November 1966 – 'Flying bomb' UFO

At 7pm, Mr and Mrs Bruce from Bishopston, near Stratford-upon-Avon, were on their way to visit a friend, when they saw a glowing red light, with a flickering tail, moving across the sky.

Mr Bruce:

> *"I stopped the van to obtain a better view. As I did so, the object – looking like a 'flying bomb' – silently passed slowly overhead. I gave chase and soon caught up, but then lost sight of it as it went behind some trees."*

(**Sources: Ken Rogers/John 'Dennis' Llewellyn**)

24th November 1966 – Pale yellow UFO and three 'stars' seen

At 7.55pm, Gwynn Jenkins and John Lowther of East Farm, Eaglescliffe, Stockton-on-Tees, sighted a pale yellow object moving rapidly across the sky, heading in a south-east direction, before exploding in mid-air, giving out a red glow. (**Source: TUFOS**)

At 8.05pm, four red objects were seen moving across the sky, by schoolboy Paul Joyce of Brambles Farm Hotel, Middlesbrough, who described them as being:

> "...as bright as a star, moving at a height of only 400 feet above the ground – then three of them appeared to collide and explode; the fourth vanished".

(**Sources:** *Evening Gazette,* **26.11.1966** – 'Young stargazer deepens the Saucer mystery'/*UFOLOG*)

24th November 1966 – Singer sights 'lights' in the sky

Popular music singer Mike Felix, formerly with *The Migil Five* Group, had just completed his act at the 'La Bamba' night club, Darlington, and was travelling towards Middlesbrough, when he noticed green and red 'lights' in the sky, which began to:

> "...stop, and move up and down. The taxi driver thought it came from a nearby Airport. Suddenly it curved around the sky, at fantastic speed, and was gone." (**Source:** *Evening Gazette,* **25.11.1966**)

Mike Felix

25th November 1966 – Strange pulsating light, over Yorkshire

At 6.40pm, *"a pale yellow light, showing a larger, pulsating, red light underneath"*, was seen in the sky over Shipley, near Bradford.

Thirty seconds later, the light on top disappeared and soon there was nothing to be seen.

DECEMBER 1966

3rd December – Drifting blue light and red light

At 5.15pm, a blue light and red light (apparently revolving) were seen drifting across the sky, before moving away in a different direction, descending, and rising upwards again.

4th December 1966 – Seen by motorist

At 3.15pm, an object – resembling sodium light in appearance – was sighted heading in a south-east direction, by a motorist driving along the A193 coast road, between Seaton Sluice and Blyth, Northumberland. (**Source: Tyneside UFO Society**)

10th December 1966 – Glowing object seen chasing another

At 8pm, a glowing object was seen apparently chasing another across the sky over Middle Wallop, Hampshire, before catching up with the first and then exploding in flames and tumbling down through the sky. (**Source: BUFORA**)

13th December 1966 – Star-like object over Isle of Wight

At 7.15pm, a star-like object – circular in shape and slightly smaller than a sixpence, held out at arm's length – was seen heading across the sky from west to east, by Miss Laurenson of Parkhurst, Isle of Wight.

14th December 1966 – Silver 'ball' seen over Isle of Wight

At 10.20am – a bright and sunny morning – an object, resembling a silver' ball of light', was seen moving across the sky over Newport, Isle of Wight, by Sandown resident – Jack Rumbold, and his companion – Mr T. Hoare, who were unloading pipes at the time.

"It gave off a puff of smoke before disappearing from sight, five to eight minutes later, as it headed towards the Portsmouth direction."

Interestingly, Mr Rumbold tells of another sighing which took place in November 1966.

"I awoke at 4.15am, and happened to look out of the window which overlooks the Prince of Wales car park, when I saw a brilliant 'light', hanging in the air. I got back into bed, thinking I might have imagined it, but curiosity got the better of me. I went to the window again and it was still there. I could not see any seats, or steering wheel. It was far too big to be a car.

When I told people about the sighting, they laughed at me."

Another witness was Mr Hayden, who sighted the same UFO *"hanging in the air over Sandown, at 10.20am; it then disintegrated and the white shape of the smoke from the object disappeared into a small patch of cloud."* **(Source: Kath Smith/John Feakins, UFOLOG)**

15th December 1966 – UFO captured on photograph, London

This was one of the shortest days of the year, with the sun setting at 3.53pm. It was a dull day, with drizzle and damp cloud.

At 2.30pm, Anthony Rider Russell (then aged 36) – a hairdresser by occupation – was standing by the window of his flat in Lewin Road, Streatham, which lies at the southern end of Streatham High Road, South West London. He was carrying out resolution tests on two new 2x converter lens (focal length increased from 135mm to 270mm by one converter) he had just purchased for his Zenith 35mm SLR camera, loaded with Gratispool colour film.

While aiming his camera at the gable of a house opposite, some 60 feet away, his attention was caught by a peculiar object dropping through the sky, which suddenly stopped dead in mid-air before slowly drifting downwards in a pendulum motion.

Tony managed to take the whole roll of film, after first setting the camera to infinity, before losing sight of it.

Although excited by what he had seen, he decided (as it was near the Christmas period) not to bother having the film developed, but to write down a report and send it to *Flying Saucer Review* (after finding their address in the telephone directory), relying on his memory of the events rather than what he had hopefully captured on film.

Anthony Rider Russell

After sending the letter off, he decided to have the film processed and was disappointed to find that only four of the photographic transparencies (out of 12 exposures) matched the image of the UFO, as seen through the lens of the camera, being convinced he had taken the whole roll of 12 exposures. In due course, he sent three of the exposures to Gordon Creighton, Editor of *Flying Saucer Review*, who asked his photographic expert – Mr Percy Hennell – to examine them (after taking prints from the negatives) and concluded that they were genuine. The first of the photos was depicted on the front cover of *Flying Saucer Review*, January/February 1967, Volume l3, No. 1 – *'UFO Photographed over London'*, accompanied with an article on page 29, as a late item – *'The Russell Photograph'*, which showed all three photos. The first was taken at 1/125 sec. f.5.6.focal length 270mm.

The second photo was taken at 1/125 sec. f5.6.focal length 270mm; the third at 1/25 sec. f11 focal length 540mm.

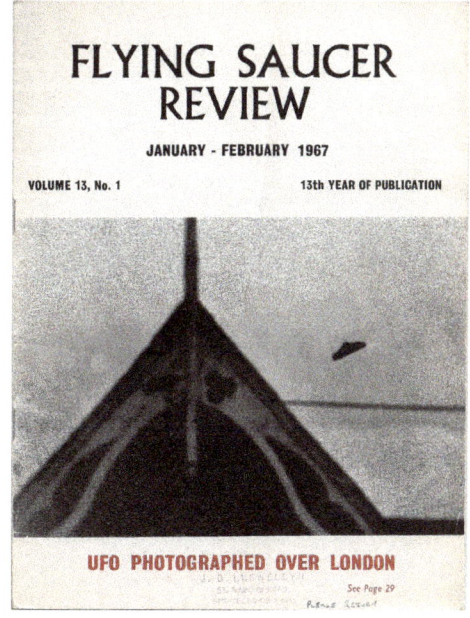

The incident and the three photos were shown again in the next edition of *Flying Saucer Review*, in March/April 1967 – *'The Tony Russell Photographs'* in an article 'written-up' by the editor of *Flying Saucer Review* – Mr Charles Bowen, following a visit made to Tony, accompanied by Mr R.H.B. Winder and Gordon Creighton. Comparisons were drawn between them and the illustration provided by P.C. Perks. © T. Russell, 2006.

We traced Mr Russell, who told us that his father – an artist by profession – had designed the cover for the first Adamski book, although it was later rejected for publication (but another one was approved and published).

> "I was sceptical of the existence of UFOs until December 15th, 1966, and decided to hang on to the fourth photo because of what it showed, feeling it to have been a very valuable photograph, as it showed a 'disc' or saucer shaped object, dark maroon in colour, with what appeared to be some lettering or marking on the underside. I would like to say I was upset to find the photos published in black and white, rather than colour, and although many magazines and books over the years have used the photos, I never gave anyone permission to publish them at all; worse, I never got my photos back from Flying Saucer Review."

Some time after the event Tony received a visit from two men, who showed him ID cards, identifying them as being from Home Office Security. They searched his house and found the fourth and best slide, after threatening him with the police. He did write to the MOD, some years later, asking for it back. They

LATE ITEM
THE RUSSELL PHOTOGRAPH

These spectacular photographs of a UFO were taken over a South London Suburb

AT about 2.30 p.m. on Thursday, December 15, 1966, Mr. Anthony Russell, a hairdresser, was standing at the open window of his flat testing for resolution two new 2 x converters for his ZENITH 3N camera (focal length 135 mm increased to 270 mm by one converter). During the testing, the camera, which was loaded with Gratispool colour film, was aimed at the gable of a house on the far side of the road.

The flat is in Lewin Road, Streatham, just to the west of Streatham Common, a grassy recreation area six miles due south from Charing Cross.

Mr. Russell was suddenly aware of an object plummetting from the sky, stopping dead, hovering, and then drifting slowly earthwards with a pendulum swinging motion. He had the good sense to 'slap the camera to infinity' and to take a series of photographs, the last two as the object moved away, at first slowly, and then with considerable speed.

The film was left in the camera so that the remainder could be used at Christmas, and it was then sent for processing after the holiday period. In the meantime, Mr. Russell had told a few friends who had laughed the incident off. Puzzled by what he had seen, he decided to try to find someone who might be interested, but decided against official bodies like the Royal Astronomical and Royal Aeronautical Societies. Glancing through the telephone directory under the word "flying" he chanced on the name of this REVIEW. He wrote to us, telling what he expected to be found on his film, and expressed surprise at the apparent changes of shape of the object he had witnessed.

The three transparencies which were successful (out of twelve exposures in all) have had prints taken from them: they are reproduced here and on the cover. Mr. Russell has been interviewed, and the photographs have been sent to Mr. Percy Hennell (the photographic expert who developed and examined the Cappoquin photograph). The prints which we have used were made by Mr. Hennell, who has indicated that they are genuine photographs of an object in the air, and (in the case of No. 1) some distance beyond the house opposite Mr. Russell's flat.

I understand that Mr. Russell's father, an artist, was asked to design a cover for the first Adamski book. Mr. Russell junior was not impressed by the book, and later, after meeting Mr. Adamski, thought even less of the subject of flying saucers. On December 15, 1966, his scepticism received a jolt.

From the sighting point the object appears to have been somewhere on a line which crosses Tooting Bec Common and Clapham Common, in other words NNW from the flat. The afternoon weather situation on December 15, 1966, over that part of London: *Misty, drizzle and rain. Low Cloud; cloudy, dull and damp. Visibility 2 miles. Ten knot wind.*

A full report will appear in our next issue.

CHARLES BOWEN

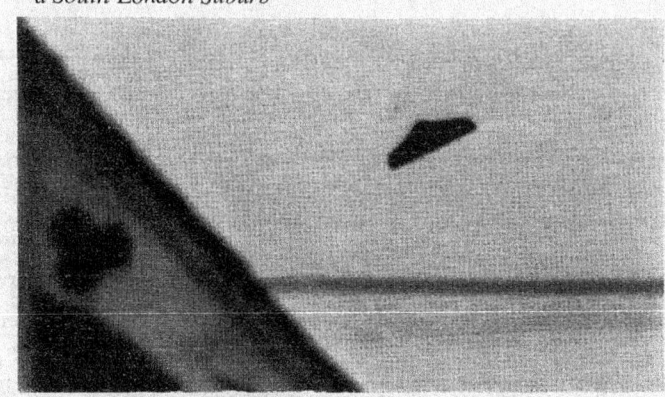

(1) 1/125 sec. f/5.6, focal length 270 mm.

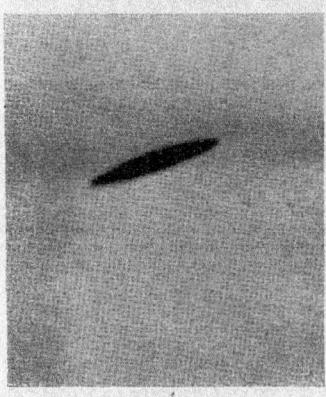

(2) 1/125 sec. f/5.6, focal length 270 mm.

(3) 1/25 sec. f/11, focal length 540 mm.

denied ever having been to his house or any knowledge of the UFO photos. Enquiries made with Anders and Clas at the excellent AFU Archives in Sweden, revealed they were in possession of three black and white images, copies of which were e-mailed to us and Tony Russell.

Another interested party that came to see Tony was Finnish film producer – Veikko Itkonen, (whom we were unable to find little about, other than that he was born on the 16th April 1919 and passed away in San Diego, California, on the 23rd March, 1990). Our attempts to track down any of his material relating to that interview, or the recovery of any of the colour photographs, was unsuccessful – despite Tony having seen them in a foreign magazine, many years ago. Unfortunately, he cannot remember the name of that magazine.

Tony replies to an Internet blog

Tony had this to tell the readers of an online forum, reiterating what he had told us:

> "I notice that you are discussing the Russell photographs taken in London in the 1960s. I am Anthony Russell, and I took the photographs in question and the facts as reported are not quite accurate. There were actually five photographs. Four went to the Flying Saucer Review and I have never had them returned! I then had a visit from three gentlemen, who had Home Office security I.D. cards, who systematically searched my picture files until they did find photograph number five. This was the most detailed of the pictures and I must be honest, I had kept it back because I thought that I could have made some money out of it. It was very detailed indeed, and showed part of the underside and a marking that was clearly visible. They took this away and, once again, it has never been seen or published since. Three months later, I had an unexpected visit from four men with cine camera and sound recording equipment, led by a man called Itkonen, and I got the impression that he was possibly Scandinavian. They filmed a long interview, which I have never seen. They had a very large amount of information, including the knowledge of the fifth photograph, so I assume they had been in touch with the Home Office." – Tony

Tony, with daughter, Janet

Sadly, Tony passed away in late May 2010, so we were never able to finally meet him face-to-face. However, we treasured the many conversations held with him not only about the UFO he photographed, but many other subjects that he showed lively interest in, and felt privileged to be invited to his funeral by his daughter, Janet. (**Source: Personal interviews, Tony Rider Russell**)

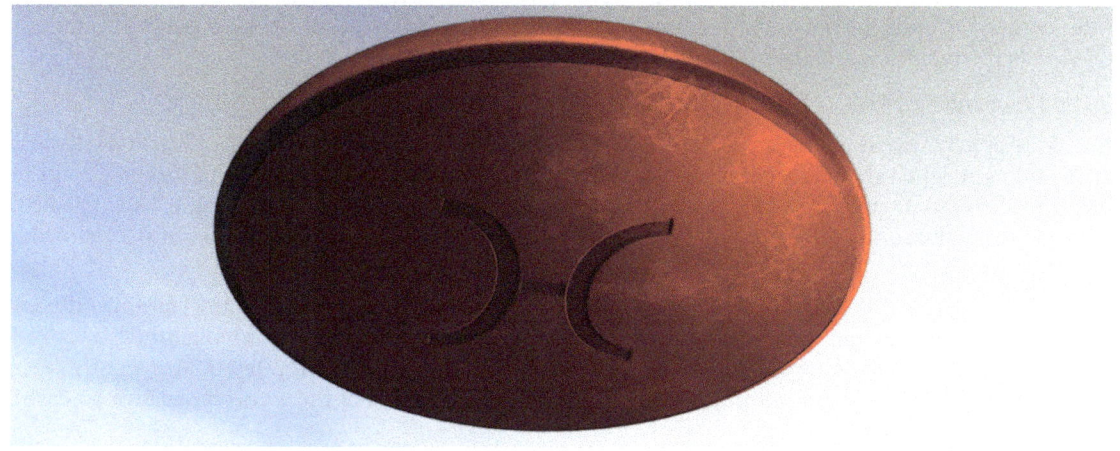

Tony Russell enjoying a family barbecue

20th December 1966 – Glinting UFO

At 3pm, three workmen, carrying out repairs to the roof at Plessey's factory at Titchfield, near Wareham – now the home of a trading estate, (previously a RAF Base, during the war) – noticed a bright object with a metallic glint moving overhead, giving off an occasional flash, resembling a 'tail' on its right-hand side – extremely unlikely to have been a weather balloon, according to one of the men, Mr R.V. Good, an ex-RAF Serviceman. **(Source: Isle of Wight UFO Society)**

25th December 1966 – 'Flying Cross' UFO

Mrs M. Appleby was standing at the window of her home in Sandyford, Newcastle-upon-Tyne, just after midnight, when she saw an object in the shape of *"a cross, displaying red lights"*, 20 degrees off the horizon, to the south-west, at a height of 50 feet above ground. Suddenly, it turned right and vanished. Was this the arrival of a 'species' of UFO that was to plague the County during autumn of the following year? **(Source: TUFOS)**

At 3am on the same date – this time over Monroe, Oregon, a number of both civilian and military witnesses reported having sighted three round objects, which were seen initially giving off what looked like vapour, before becoming visible as three bright reddish/orange coloured lights. Apparently their arrival during the 90 minutes' sighting was strong enough to push one of the witnesses against a nearby vehicle. **(Source: NICAP)**

CHAPTER 8 – 1967

UFO REPORTS INCLUDE:

JANUARY:
2nd January 1967 – Green 'ball of light' over Worcestershire
January 1967 – Close Encounter, North Wales
6th January 1967 – Strange lights over Sheffield, Yorkshire
7th January 1967 – Pair of 'lights' seen over Yorkshire
9th January 1967 – Three orange lights over Yorkshire,
11th January1967 – White 'light' moving over ground, Stockton-on-Tees, County Durham
17th January 1967 – Diamond-shaped UFO over Coventry
17th January 1967 – 'Flying Saucers' over Missouri, USA
22nd January 1971 – Mysterious diamond-shaped UFO over Ohio
25th January1967 – Cigar-shaped object over West Midlands
31st January 1967 – UFO splits into four separate objects, North Tyneside
Official figures from the MOD … their UFO figures for January 1967

FEBRUARY:
4th February 1967 – Strange 'patch' in the sky over Birmingham
6th February 1967 – Saturn-shaped object over Delaware
10th February 1967 – UFO over Warwickshire and Redditch
11th February 1967 – Black curved UFO, Tyneside
12th February 1967 – Over Michigan
13th February 1967 – Bright orange sphere over Tyneside
13th February 1967 – UFO over Birmingham, West Midlands – bone-shaped UFO seen
Northumberland – UFO sighted, then RAF Jet circles sky
February 1967 – Shiny object over Lancashire
18th February 1967 – Chromium plated UFO over Warwickshire
18th February 1967 – Isle of Wight 'Look into Space' Exhibition, held on Isle of Wight
21st February 1967 – UFO seen following aircraft – plotted on radar!
27th February 1967 – Cluster of 'lights' over Michigan

MARCH:
5th March 1967 – 'Flying Saucer' hovers over USA missile base
6th March 1967 – 'Flying Saucers' seen over Benton Harbor, Michigan, USA
9th March 1967 – Police Officer photographs UFO over Illinois
12th March 1967 – 'Fin' UFO in the sky over London
14th March 1967 – Square shaped object, with 'fin', over Greater Manchester
16th March 1967 – Oblong UFO over Glasgow
20th March 1967 – 'Flying tadpole', Reading, Berkshire
24th March 1967 – Three 'lights' seen in sky over Staffordshire
March 1967 – Green UFO over Bath, Somerset
March 1967 – 'Flying Saucer' over Didcot, Berkshire
March 1967 – Strange ghostly sightings, West Midlands
March 1967 – UFO landing in Illinois … giant circle in the crop found afterwards

APRIL:
17th April 1967 – Three 'lights' forming a triangle, Tyneside
19th April 1967 – 'Flying Saucer' over Sussex
20th April 1966 – Triangular object over Dorset
20th April 1967 – UFO over Heathrow Airport, London
27th April 1967 – Half-moon shaped objects seen over Tyneside
28th April 1967 – UFO over Devon, UFOs sighted over RAF Welford by US Servicemen

MAY:
1st May 1967 – Black boomerang-shaped UFO over Tyneside
10th May 1967 – Black 'disc' seen by Reading cyclist
12th May 1967 – Three round 'globes' seen over London
17th May 1967 – UFO seen in front of aircraft over Carolina, USA
19th May 1967 – Glittering 'disc', London
22nd May 1967 – 'Orange moon', County Durham
23rd May 1967 – 'Flying Saucer' takes-off, south-west Essex
24th May 1967 – Bright green UFO, Yorkshire Dales
26th May 1967 – Half-circle object in the sky over Somerset
MOD figures for May 1967

JUNE:
6th June 1967 – Dome-shaped UFO, Essex
8th June 1967 – A similar object was seen stationary in the sky, over marshes, at West Caistor
10th June 1967 – Six red lights and a white 'disc', Northampton

11th June 1967 – Humped UFO over Staffordshire
14th June 1967 – Three to five white dazzling 'bars' over Northumberland
15th June 1967 – UFO over Heysham, Lancashire
15th June 1967 – Flattened 'S' shape in the sky, Cornwall
19th June – Spinning UFO, Staffordshire
20th June 1967 – White 'ball of light', Northumberland
June 1967 – Police Officer sights six silver 'dots' in the sky, West Mercia
June 1967 – UFO detector comes under scrutiny by the GPO!
24th June 1967 – UFO display, triangular objects seen
25th June 1967 – Rotating UFO over Lancashire
27th June 1967 – Egg-shaped UFO over Woking, Surrey
29th June 1967 – 'Octopus' shaped UFO, Berkshire
29th June 1967 – Motorist followed by UFO over New Jersey, USA

JULY:

1st July 1967 – 'Jellybean' UFO, Yorkshire
2nd July 1967 – Strange light showing three 'prongs', seen over Leicestershire
3rd July 1967 – Orange 'disc' over Surrey
4th July 1967 – Green cylindrical object, Dorset
5th July 1967 – 'Flying Saucers' reported over Isle of Wight, 'Flying Saucers' over Nottingham
6th July 1967 – Orange 'ball of light' Hampshire, Police Officer sights UFO display over Poole, Dorset
7th July 1967 – Quarter-moon UFO and green flame, Cheshire
8th July 1967 – 'Spinning top' UFO over Nottinghamshire
10th July 1967 – Triangular UFO, Nottinghamshire, UFO landing, Isle of Wight
11th July 1967 – UFO over Warwickshire
13th July 1967 – Red 'Saucer', Sussex
14th July 1967 – Motorists followed by UFO at Essex and Northumberland
15th July 1967 – 'Flying Saucer' over Isle of Wight
15th July 1967 – Cyclists sight dome-shaped UFO at Sedalia, Missouri
16th July 1967 – White sphere with revolving lights, Tyneside
18th July 1967 – Clusters of objects over European airbases
19th July 1967 – Six bright 'discs', County Durham
20th July 1967 – Photograph taken of UFO, Cheshire
22nd July 1967 – Red 'disc', Newcastle-on-Tyne
23rd July 1967 – Pink halo hovering in the sky, Merseyside
30th July 1967 – Golden 'square' – MOD sightings not revealed to public

AUGUST:

2nd August 1967 – Flat, silver 'disc' and something strange at Birmingham
1st August 1967 – 'Figure of eight' movements, Lancashire
3rd August 1967 – UFOs over Berkshire
4th August 1967 – UFO display over Lancashire
5th August 1967 – UFOs over Mount Snowdon – Did RAF Jets respond?
5th August 1967 – 'Glowing mass' over Reading
6th August 1967 – UFO activity reported over Kent
7th August 1967 – Three red lights seen over Newark and flashing red light, Nottinghamshire
8th August 1967 – Lancashire Police Officers sight UFO
9th August 1967 – UFO over Hindley, Liverpool
10th August 1967 – UFO 'Triangle of lights', Northumberland
11th August 1967 – 'Red hot poker' seen in sky over Wolverhampton
14th August 1967 – Triangular UFO over Leeds
15th August 1967 – Cigar-shaped object in the sky over Cornwall
16th August 1967 – Silver, elongated, UFO over County Durham
16th August 1966 – UFO sighted by two schoolgirls over Cheshire
17th August 1967 – Silver metallic UFO, stationary in the sky over Harrogate
18th August 1967 – Pulsating UFO over Kent
19th August 1967 – Purple and green UFO over Liverpool
20th August 1967 – Two silver 'discs' over Manchester
22nd August 1967 – Bronze objects in the sky over Manchester
23rd August 1967 – Orange UFO on 'box-like structure' over South Shields
24th August 1967 – Pyramidal UFO over Cornwall
25th August 1967 – Mass of glowing lights, Staffordshire
27th August 1967 – Cigar-shaped UFO over Manchester
28th August 1967 – 'Flying Saucer', Shropshire
29th August 1967 – UFO, with orange centre, over Stoke-on-Trent
31st August 1967 – Red flare over the sea off Dorset coast
Late August 1967 – Close encounter, Essex, Alien beings seen inside craft
August 1967 – Humanoids seen at Chingford, Essex
August 1967 – Humanoid seen in Epping Forest
August 1967 – Glowing, triangular object seen by Cheshire motorist
1967 – Close Encounter, Hastings – Fact or Fiction?
August 1967 – Cheshire motorist confronted by triangular UFO

SEPTEMBER:

2nd September 1967 – UFOs land in car park, Staffordshire!
4th September 1967 – Close encounter with UFO, Reading
5th September – 'V' shaped UFO seen over Gateshead Power Station
6th September – UFO over Essex
9th September 1967 – Over Sussex Downs
11th September 1967 – 'Sky watch' held on the Sussex Downs
14th September 1967 – Rocket-shaped UFO over Manchester
15th September 1967 – Devon UFO sighted over the sea
18th September 1967 – UFO over the Cairngorm Mountains
19th September 1967 – Glowing objects seen in the sky at Merseyside
20th September 1967 – UFO seen over RAF tracking station
21st September 1967 – Strange 'star' over Par Sands Beach, Cornwall
22nd September 1967 – Splitting UFOs sighted over London

23rd September 1967 – UFO seen, showing 'portholes' and making a strange noise
25th September 1967 – Stationary UFO in sky over Newcastle-on-Tyne
26th September 1967 – Eight square lights, Scotland
29th September 1967 – A visit to the MOD
30th September 1967 – Three red 'globes' over County Durham
September 1967 – Close encounter for Essex schoolgirl

OCTOBER:
1st October 1967 – Red lights in the sky, South Yorkshire
2nd October 1967 – UFO over Wembley, London
4th October 1967 – Three 'red lights' seen, County Durham
5th October 1967 – Police Officer sights UFO over Newcastle-on-Tyne
6th October 1967 – Sighting of strange object by ex-RAF Radar technician
7th October 1967 – UFO sighted over Guildford
8th October 1967 – Metallic object sighted in sky at Hartlepool
10th October 1967 – Small domed object sighted, Staffordshire
13th October 1967 – Gold coloured 'cross' Birmingham
14th October 1967 – 'Flying Church Cross', Northampton
16th October 1967 – UFO over Suffolk
17th October 1967 – Lorry driver sights 'Flying Saucer' over M6, Staffordshire
18th October 1967 – Cigar-shaped UFO, Warwickshire
19th October 1967 – Brilliant pale blue light Northumberland
20th October 1967 – Cigar-shaped UFO over Devon
21st October 1967 – Saucer-shaped object, with dome, over Essex
23rd October 1967 – Yellow egg-shaped UFO over Yorkshire
24th October 1967 – 'Flying Crucifix', Watford, Hertfordshire
25th October 1967 – Sussex Police motorcyclist sights 'Flying Cross' UFO
30th October – Cigar-shaped objects seen, Kent
31st October – Eight objects seen in the sky over West Midlands

NOVEMBER:
1st November 1967 – 'Flying Cross' over Kent
2nd November 1967 – 'Flying Cross', Essex
3rd November 1967 – Oblong UFO, Northamptonshire
4th November 1967 – UFO over Staffordshire
4th November 1967 - Aircraft crashes with loss of all on board
6th November 1967 – Pulsating UFO over Yorkshire
6th November 1967 – UFO sighted over Morden (8 miles south-west of Central London)
6th November 1967 – UFO over Sopley, Hampshire
7th November 1967 – UFOs over Cheshire and Clacton
9th November 1967 – Cross-shaped UFO, Northamptonshire
11th November 1967 – UFO sightings over USAF Airbase
13th November 1967 – Incident at Winterfold Forest, in Surrey
14th November 1967 – Silver 'discs', Leamington Spa
15th November 1967 – UFO display, Kent
16th November 1967 – UFO over Sussex Downs
18th November 1967 – 'Flying Saucer', Northumberland
23rd November 1967 – Birmingham UFO, RAF Jets appear
25th November 1967 – Oval UFO, Northumberland
26th November 1967 – UFO display, Stratford-upon-Avon
27th November 1967 – Upside-down 'mushroom' seen in sky over Nottingham
29th November 1967 – Deflated balloon – explanation for UFO sightings!
November 1967 – Strange experience, Harrogate

DECEMBER:
3rd December 1967 – Nebraska Police Officer's Close Encounters
5th December 1967 – UFOs over RAF Welford, Berkshire
7th December 1967 – UFO showing dark 'patch', Sheffield
8th December 1967 – Three brilliant lights seen in the shape of a triangle
9th December 1967 – UFO meeting, London
10th December 1967 – 'Bowler hat' shaped UFO, Somerset
12th December 1967 – Glowing orange 'disc', Birmingham
27th December 1967 – Cigar-shaped UFO, Yarmouth
28th December 1967 – Pulsating UFO, Newcastle-on-Tyne
31st December 1967 – 'Close encounter', Wednesbury

JANUARY 1967

2nd January 1967 – Green 'ball of light' over Worcestershire

At 6.40am, a green 'ball of light' was seen over Easemore Road, Redditch, Worcestershire, by local resident – Kenneth Chillingworth.

> *"Suddenly it plummeted downwards, scattering a trail of silver particles, and disappeared behind nearby buildings."*

Was this a meteorite? (**Sources: NICAP, GB/***UFOLOG***)**

Over Dorset

At 4.15pm, two white flashes of intense light were seen in the sky due south of Crock Lane, Bridport, Dorset, 30 degrees off the horizon, followed by the appearance of eight grey objects, which were diamond in shape when viewed through binoculars. (**Source: Isle of Wight UFO Society**)

Isle of Wight

At midnight on the 2nd January 1967, *"a red-coloured semi-circular light, emitting a glow from its curved side nearest the ground – much larger than a full moon",* was seen travelling across the eastern part of the sky over Limerstone, Isle of Wight, by a couple out walking. They ran to the top of a hill overlooking Shorwell, but after feeling uneasy the girl decided to return home and drove back to Newport, with the object still visible in her rear view mirror – now hovering close to the ITV station mast, at Chillerton Down. **(Source: John W. Feakins, Isle of Wight UFO Society)**

January 1967 – Close Encounter, North Wales

On a visit to Abergele, North Wales, some years ago, to see our friend, Margaret Fry, Head of the Welsh Federation of Ufologists, we were introduced to Ernest Edwards – an affable man – who told us what he witnessed one evening, in January 1967.

Margaret Fry

It all started after Ernest's curiosity was aroused after hearing rumours of a ghostly lady seen along a stretch of road, between Cyffylliog and Bontuchel, and decided to go and have a look. While trudging along the moonlit road, passing familiar landmarks, such as the 'Old Smithy' at Boxers Corner, he said:

"I was shocked to see a large, black, silent mass, pulsating with lights, hovering over the 'gypsy caravan' used to advertise holidays, accompanied by a horrible smell – like a mixture of burning rubber and something rotting. I noticed the trees were swaying at the side of the road and then I saw, with some relief, the headlights of an approaching 'Guy Warrior' lorry, which came to a halt – its lights extinguishing. I ran over to the cab, opened the door, and jumped in next to the driver, who seemed mesmerized by the sight of this 'mass'. He kept shouting, 'What's that?' It then banked over to the left and took up a position over a nearby house. I asked the driver (who was very frightened) to drop me back home – which he did. When I arrived home, my mother took one look at me and asked if I had seen a ghost!

A short time later, after feeling sick, I noticed this rash all over my body, and had swollen eyes. I was taken to Ruthin Hospital by my mother, where the doctor examined me and suggested the allergy may have been caused by diesel, although I now believe my symptoms were caused by exposure to the fields of energy surrounding the UFO. Furthermore, I still suffer occasionally with a rash on my chest". **(Source: Personal interview)**

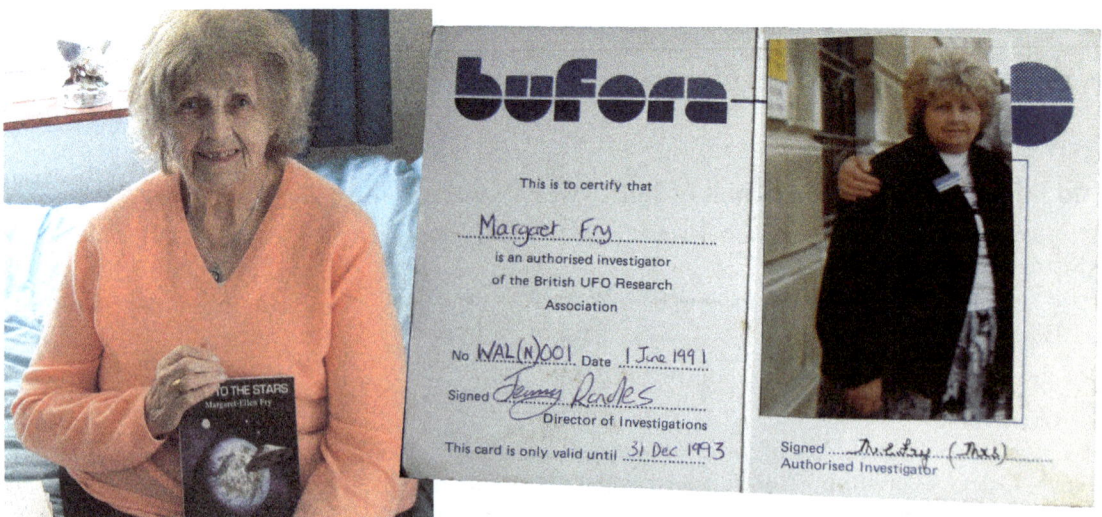

Margaret has been researching the UFO subject for over 50 years she is a credit to both BUFORA and Contact UK. We honour he commitment by showing some of her personal effects associated with various investigations, involving her husband Ron who was known to us personally.

*Margaret Fry with *Senator Roscoe Bartlett*

1st of May 2013 – *New York Daily News* **– WASHINGTON – What are a former U.S. senator and five former House members doing in a place like this? Quote:**

> *"The former lawmakers, including former Sen. Mike Gravel (D-Alaska), listened with "open" minds and full pockets for several hours Tuesday at a simulated congressional hearing taking testimony that extraterrestrials 'are here'.*
>
> *"I came here being very skeptical, but I also recognize that I don't know much about it,"* said former Rep. Darlene Hooley (D-Ore.)

---

*Roscoe Gardner Bartlett (born June 3, 1926) is an American politician who was U.S. Representative for Maryland's 6th congressional district, serving from 1993 to 2013. He is a member of the Republican Party and was a member of the Tea Party Caucus. At the end of his tenure in Congress, Bartlett was the second-oldest serving member of the House of Representatives, behind fellow Republican Ralph Hall of Texas.

Mr Bartlett and his wife Ellen have 10 children (of whom one, Joseph R. Bartlett, is a former member of the Maryland House of Delegates), 17 grandchildren, and 2 great-grandchildren. Following his defeat for re-election, Bartlett and his wife decided to live "off-the-grid" in the West Virginia Mountains. Their cabin is devoid of outside electricity, phone service, or municipal plumbing. Bartlett currently works as a senior consultant for Lineage Technologies, a cyber security group that seeks to protect supply chains. **(Source: Wikipedia)**

Haunted Skies Volume Two Revised

Paradigm Research Group at the National Press Club Building Washington

The six are being paid $20,000 each, plus expenses, by a group called the *Paradigm Research Group, which insists UFOs are real and the government has been covering up their existence.

The group's executive director, Stephen Bassett, told the Daily News that he initially contacted 55 former members of Congress with an offer of $10,000, among them former Rep. Dennis Kucinich (D-Ohio), who famously recounted a UFO sighting. After few responded, Bassett said he doubled the pay. That helped, he said.

The six former lawmakers are not exactly grilling witnesses in the faux hearing, being held at the National Press Club building. They spent the first two days of testimony asking questions that assumed accounts of UFO sightings from panel witnesses were true.

Witnesses Tuesday included retired U.S. Air Force members recounting first- or second-hand experiences with unidentified objects between the late 1960s through 1980 at U.S. nuclear facilities in England and western states. The sightings are cited by believers as evidence of alien interest in nuclear arms.

The members "swear-in" witness, announce "recesses" and assume other trappings of actual congressional hearings, minus staff and power. In the process they effectively act in a film produced by Bassett's nonprofit, Paradigm Research, that will use the footage to mimic an actual hearing.

The result is a motley crew. Gravel is best known for a long-shot presidential bid that made Kucinich's look moderate and pragmatic. Former Rep. Lynn Woolsey, (D-Calif.), 75, who said she was teased for being among Congress' "most left, progressive members" before retiring in 2011, on Tues. had noticeably slurred speak and struggled to complete some sentences."

*Stephen Bassett is the executive director of Paradigm Research Group founded in 1996 to end a government imposed embargo on the truth behind the so called "UFO" phenomenon. Stephen has spoken to audiences around the world about the implications of formal "Disclosure" by world governments of an extraterrestrial presence engaging the human race. He has given over 1000 radio and television interviews, and PRG's advocacy work has been extensively covered by national and international media. In 2013 PRG produced a *"Citizen Hearing on Disclosure"* at the National Press Club in Washington, DC. On November 5, 2014 PRG launched a Congressional Hearing/Political Initiative seeking the first hearings on Capitol Hill since 1968 regarding the extraterrestrial presence issue and working to see that issue included in the ongoing presidential campaign.

PRG has assisted numerous organizations and initiatives working to 1) raise public awareness of the both the extraterrestrial presence and the truth embargo, 2) convene open congressional hearings to take government and agency witness testimony, and 3) incite the political media to appropriately cover the attendant issues. There can be only one outcome to the Disclosure advocacy movement – the formal acknowledgement of the extraterrestrial presence by world governments.

7th January 1967 – Pair of 'lights' seen over Yorkshire

A pair of 'lights' – one red, the other green – was seen motionless in the sky above Sheffield, between midnight and 1.30am, by local resident – Nicholas Slater, who said:

> *"They seemed to be suspended at about 2,000 feet. I thought they were aircraft, but then the red 'light' began to zigzag across the green light. The 'lights' then began to move higher and were eventually lost from sight towards the south part of the sky."*

9th January 1967 – Three orange lights over Yorkshire

During the late evening, an object – described as being *"75-80 feet in length, showing three orange lights, approximately 100 feet up in the air"* – was seen stationary in the sky over Bradford, Yorkshire, by resident Colin Hall. (**Source: BUFORA**)

11th January 1967 – 'White light' moving over ground, Stockton-on-Tees, County Durham

At 1.25am, Mr B. Lister and Mrs M. Midgeley were travelling through Norton, Stockton-on-Tees, when they noticed:

"...a bright 'white light', approximately 1,500 feet off the ground, moving towards the north-west direction, which gradually descended to a few hundred feet above our position. The white tip on the UFO then turned red and it disappeared from view." (**Source: UFOLOG**)

17th January 1967 – Diamond-shaped UFO over Coventry

At 8.50pm, a rotating, diamond-shaped object of milky-white appearance, with a red light underneath, was seen over Radford allotments, Coventry, by local residents – Gerald Montague and Frank Earp – before accelerating away at speed. (**Source: Derek Samson – NICAP, GB**)

17th January 1967 – 'Flying Saucers' over Missouri, USA

The *Aurora Advertiser* of Missouri, in their edition published on the 20th January 1967, told of sightings of '*Flying Saucers*' over Exeter and Cassville, during the evening. City Patrolman – Allen Stubblefield – reported sighting an object flying over the town, at 8pm,

"...about five feet in diameter, with four 'horns' sticking out of it. It appeared as a bright light, to begin with, and after hovering for a period, departed towards the South direction."

A short time later, he overheard a Stone County radio report that an object had been sighted over Carr Lane, south-east of Cassville, in the Table Rock Lake country. (**Source: *Probe*, USA, Spring 1967**)

22nd January 1971 – Mysterious diamond-shaped UFO over Ohio

At least a dozen people living in the Tiro area rang the Huron County Sheriff's Department, reporting having sighted a UFO in the sky around 9pm. A deputy was quoted as saying:

"When you get a call like that you think it's from a drunk, or crackpot, but when you get many calls you begin to wonder."

Richard Williams was driving along Old River Road, north of Willard, with his wife and son, when they sighted a flying object.

"It looked like a bat, and was about 30 feet in diameter. The wings were wider than the plane, or whatever it was. On the middle of each wing there seemed to be an exhaust rocket engine, or jet engine. It had red lights on each of the wings and on the tails. I thought it was going to crash. It hovered about 100 feet above us, then took off again, went east, and circled around Willard. Some kind of creature was inside the UFO, because there appeared to be some kind of motion in the back of the cockpit; there was something flashing a light on and off."

The *Sandusky Register* reported that a woman was receiving treatment at a hospital for injuries sustained in an unrelated car accident, and that she had told law officers she had seen what she described as a *"flying school bus"*. Whether there was any connection between the accident and the UFO sighting can only be speculation. She wasn't the only one. A Huron County lawman, driving near Greenwich, saw the UFO – which was reported by another officer in the Willard area, moments later.

Diamond-shaped

Captain John Warner, Huron County Sherriff's Department, said that none of the witnesses has spoken to each other prior to the sightings, but they all described the same thing – diamond-shaped, with a glass globe in the front, with red and white lights at either point of the 'diamond' and two red exhausts in the middle of the underside.

Strange sound heard

Other witnesses included Mrs Skeans and her two sons – Bruce (12) and Mike (10) – of Akron, who were visiting Willard. They were skating on a large pond, at the time, with about 20 other children, when they saw a bright, oval, red light with several other lights of lesser intensity, pass through the sky at low altitude, and at an angle which allowed them to see wings which symmetrically formed a crescent shape, with the large oval light in the middle. The only sound heard came in three second intervals; it began at middle C and swung smoothly upward to D sharp, accelerating at the last and shutting off abruptly. The duration of each sound was a second, and they were heard five times. Oddly, during each sound, the object seemed to accelerate and glide in-between the sounds made.

(Sources: *Skylook/UFOLOG,* May 1971, Issue no. 82)

25th January 1967 – Cigar-shaped object over West Midlands

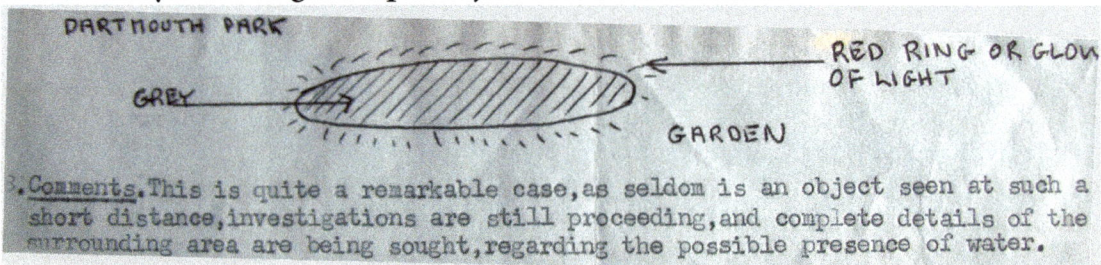

Housewife Mrs Waine and her daughter, Rosemary, from Beeches Road, West Bromwich, were in their garden, at 8.15pm, when they noticed:

> "…*a grey coloured, cigar-shaped object surrounded by a 'ring of light', hovering silently in the sky below roof level, about 30-40 feet away.*"

A short time later it rose upwards and flew off, southwards, across Dartmouth Park.

(**Source: Derek Samson, NICAP, GB**)

31st January 1967 – UFO splits into four separate objects, North Tyneside

At 4.20pm, a brilliant white object was seen in the sky over Smith's Dock, North Shields, by a number of people. It was seen to split into four separate objects, before disappearing from sight.

(**Source: Tyneside UFO Society**)

Official figures from the MOD … their UFO figures for January 1967

The MOD confirmed that during the period of January 1967, they received a total of eight UFO reports, of which they judged two to be aircraft, one meteorological phenomenon, one balloon, two satellites and two unidentified (insufficient information), but nothing earmarked for investigation. (**Source: TUFOS**)

FEBRUARY 1967

4th February 1967 – Strange 'patch' in the sky over Birmingham

At 8.30pm, "*a fuzzy dull red-orange 'patch' – totally unlike any cloud*" was seen by Philip Instone, and members of his family, heading south-east, across a clear, starlit, sky over Handsworth (a suburb to the North of Birmingham). (**Sources: NICAP, GB/*UFOLOG*)**

6th February 1967 – Saturn shaped object over Delaware

Over Odessa, Delaware, Donald and Marie Guseman sighted a large Saturn shaped UFO, 50 feet in diameter and 20 feet high in the sky, at 8.45pm.

> *"It had a green light on one side and a red on the other. It hovered over some trees before slowly moving northwards and out of view, two minutes later." (Source: NICAP)*

10th February 1967 – UFO over Warwickshire and Redditch

At Solihull, Warwickshire, *"a grey, oval object, with some kind of 'cabin' or 'dome', showing three lumps or projections underneath, and a revolving light inside, illuminated by a peculiar light"*, was seen at 7.15pm by Mr William Hunt, who estimated it to be 40 feet in diameter, moving at a speed of some 3-400 miles per hour in a south-easterly direction. Later the same day, some 10-12 miles away at Redditch, five schoolboys (aged between 8-12 years) were walking towards the town centre, at 8.25pm, when they saw:

> *"...four small objects, with bright flickering lights around their edges, accompanied by a larger object, in the north-west direction of the sky".*

According to UFO researcher Derek Samson, the locality was the scene of other UFO reports.
(**Source: Derek Samson, NICAP, GB**)

11th February 1967 – Black curved UFO, Tyneside

At 9.30pm, Mr and Mrs Jenkins were driving home from Acklington, Tyneside, when they saw:

> *"...a bright yellow, oval object, shoot across the sky at about 30 degrees elevation, before it dropped lower at an estimated height of only 50 feet above the car, enabling us to see a black curved object showing four square, dull yellow, windows".*

Within seconds, it was out of sight. (**Source: Tyneside UFO Society**)

12th February 1967 – Over Michigan

Over the Grand Rapids, Michigan, came a report of four dull-grey fluorescent shaped objects, seen heading across the sky in a rigid formation, at 3.40am, by Mr Lou Atkinson. They were last seen heading north-east, making a chirping noise, out of view seconds later. (**Source: NICAP**)

13th February 1967 – Bright orange sphere over Tyneside

At 12.30am, a stationary bright orange sphere was seen in the sky above the Rex Cinema, North Shields, before moving away in a gentle bobbing movement towards the coast.

13th February 1967 – UFO over Birmingham, West Midlands: bone-shaped UFO seen

Derek Samson, of NICAP GB, was driving along Redstone Farm Road, close to Robin Hood island, Hall Green, Birmingham, with his wife and children, at 6pm on the same date, when Mrs Samson brought her husband's attention to a 'bright light' in the eastern part of the sky. [Also close to another sighting of a saucer shaped object seen close to Robin Hood Cemetery in 1980]

> *Derek stopped the car and we all got out, obtaining a closer look at the object, clearly discernible as "somewhat bone-shaped, showing two white lights, with a third red one in the middle. The most remarkable thing was that each light in turn seemed to be trying to get in front of the other, in a 'paddling' effect."* (**Source: Personal interview**)

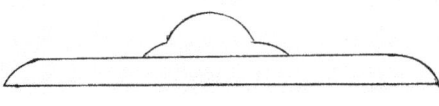

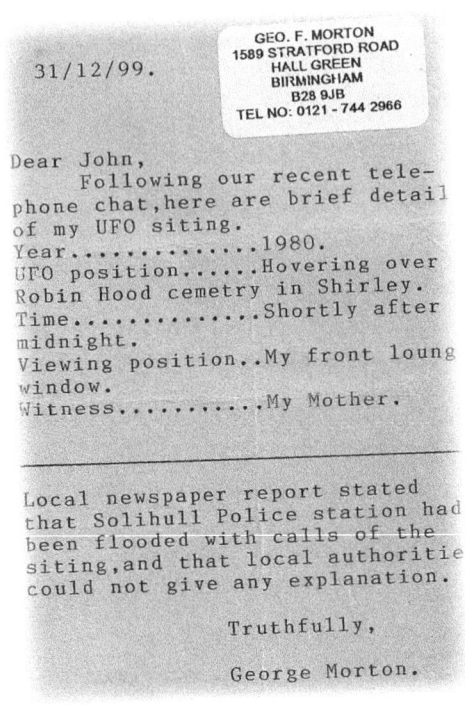

```
                    GEO. F. MORTON
                  1589 STRATFORD ROAD
31/12/99.              HALL GREEN
                      BIRMINGHAM
                        B28 9JB
                  TEL NO: 0121 - 744 2966

Dear John,
         Following our recent tele-
phone chat, here are brief detail
of my UFO siting.
Year................1980.
UFO position......Hovering over
Robin Hood cemetry in Shirley.
Time..............Shortly after
midnight.
Viewing position..My front loung
window.
Witness...........My Mother.

Local newspaper report stated
that Solihull Police station had
been flooded with calls of the
siting, and that local authoritie
could not give any explanation.

                    Truthfully,

                    George Morton.
```

Chased by a UFO!

At 10.55pm the same day, Mr Ronald Martino, of Blyth, was walking along the road from Ashington to Pegswood, when an amber 'ball of light' was seen circling the horizon. He said:

> "I watched it for a short while. It then dropped, as if examin-ing the ground (under which lays Pegswood mine). I felt frightened and began to run. It then turned towards me and started to follow at a distance of some fifteen yards behind me. It was about eight feet in diameter and the amber lights were pulsating outwards from the centre – like a huge eye staring right through me. I had the feeling it was interested in the static, produced by my nylon Mackintosh worn at the time. I felt it was keeping its distance to avoid harming me. I could feel icy 'pins and needles' down my back. I was hot and my 'Mac' was crackling. After a couple of minutes, a car approached and its headlights shone onto the object. I stopped and turned to examine it, but the amber glow contracted to nothing. After the car passed, the amber glow returned. This sequence of behaviour occurred six times over, as each car passed me on the road."

By this time Mr Martino had reached the main road and lights of Pegswood. He looked back but the UFO had gone, although a RAF jet fighter was seen circling the location. Enquiries with the RAF were made. They denied any knowledge of RAF response and suggested the witness might have seen the downward identification light of an aircraft.

(Source: *ORBIT,* Volume 8, Number 1, May 1967)

February 1967 – Shiny object over Lancashire

At 7pm, a mother and young son from Bickershaw Lane, Platt Bridge, Wigan, Lancashire, saw a bright object in the sky, while waving a relative off. The object then approached at terrifying speed and stopped over the top of a shop opposite, described as: *"...white shiny metal – as wide as two cars"*.

It then shot away into the sky and disappeared from view. **(Source: *UFOLOG*)**

18th February 1967 – Chromium plated UFO over Warwickshire

At 12.00 noon, a bright oval object – *"with a surface resembling chromium plating"* – was seen in the south-west direction of the sky, over the B4115 (near the A45) in Warwickshire, its brightness decreasing when clouds passed in front of it. **(Source: John 'Dennis' Llewellyn)**

18th February 1967 – Isle of Wight 'Look into Space' Exhibition, held on Isle of Wight

On the same day, the Isle of Wight UFO Society organised an exhibition, entitled '**Look into Space**', which was attended by over 400 people.

20th February 1967 – Truck driver paced by UFO, USA

Another example of UFO vehicle interaction took place at 3.10am, and involved USAF veteran (now truck driver) Stanton Summer from Oxford, Wisconsin. He reported seeing an orange-red object that paced his truck for two minutes. (**Source: NICAP**)

21st February 1967 – UFO seen following aircraft – plotted on radar!

At 11.05pm, a half oval, grey coloured, object was seen by Timothy Gardiner of Solihull, Warwickshire, apparently following a 'Viscount' Airliner, travelling south-east.

Enquiries made by Derek Samson, at Elmdon Airport, Birmingham, revealed *"nothing untoward had been plotted on radar".*

27th February 1967 – Cluster of lights over Michigan

Sheriff Grysen and his wife, with other witnesses, from Grand Haven, Michigan, sighted a large white 'light', accompanied by smaller red and green 'lights' in the sky, at 8.19pm, which then made an almost 90 degree turn and shot over the road in front of them before heading away, minutes later.

MARCH 1967

5th March 1967 – 'Flying Saucer' hovers over US missile base

During the evening, a UFO was tracked by radar from a tracking station at Minot, North Dakota, heading for one of the minuteman grids where the missiles are kept in deep pits, pointed upwards for launching. The alarm was raised and flashed to Minot Air Force Base and to the *'strike defenders'* – the men that defended the missiles. A minute later the UFO appeared – a metallic craft, over 100 feet in diameter. The guards watched as it descended; lights flashing around the rim shone onto a dome in the centre. The object turned towards the nearest missile site with three 'strike teams' in pursuit. Suddenly the UFO stopped and hovered about 500 feet off the ground, under the watchful eye of the guards below it, with their guns trained on it. The seconds ticked away; fighter pilots at NORAD had been scrambled and were awaiting take-off. A radio call was received from the base to say the UFO was circling the launch control. As the pilots readied to take off, the object swerved upwards and out of sight.

(**Source:** *Aliens from Space,* **Donald E. Keyhoe**)

6th March 1967 – 'Flying Saucers' seen over Benton Harbor, Michigan, USA

At 12.01am, Mr Jerome Wolanin (a former Police officer and the assistant director of a radio station), and his wife, sighted a saucer-shaped object, showing red, green, and yellow lights around the bottom rim, which pulsated red, making a hissing sound, heading in an east to west direction. A second object was then seen to appear from the east, after the top of the first object opened. This halted in mid-air for thirty seconds and disappeared from view. The duration of the sighting was forty minutes. (**Source NICAP**)

At 4.25am, Deputy Sherriff Frank Courson, from Illinois, saw:

> "...an object, shaped like a rubber cup – the type placed under legs of furniture – with a dome set in the 'cup', the bottom of which spun rapidly and pulsated red. It passed overhead making a hissing noise."

9th March 1967 – Police Officer photographs UFO over Illinois

Bill Fisher – then a Moline Police officer, [who was to serve 30 years in the Force] – had just parked his three-wheel patrol motorcycle on 16th Avenue across from *Sacred Heart* School, where his son William Jr. (11) was a student, when the nearby neighbours – several students and a couple - saw an unusual object in the northern sky. Reacting quickly, Bill took two minutes of cine film of the object. Interestingly, several UFO sightings were later reported from Moline to Galesburg over those few days in early March, 1967. Officer Fisher had a movie camera in a storage container on his motorcycle. He had put it there after hearing of the previous local UFO sightings.

"They were being viewed by a lot of people", Mr Fisher said. "There were stories all around. I was just naturally curious. I had my camera in there just in case."

Bill Junior:

"I looked up, and saw this big oblong wingless shape just hanging there. It was silvery-white, just reflecting sunlight. As soon as I looked up and saw it, my jaw dropped, wondering what this was."

Like his father, William Jr., to this day does not know what the object was.

"I've always said it was nothing but an unidentified flying object. The key word is unidentified. I've never made any conclusion about what we saw. We saw something bright and shiny in the sky we couldn't explain. That's all it was. It could be a lot of different things. What we don't know is way more than what we do know."

USAF investigates incident

Two USAF Captains – Edward Orenic and Anton Kato – arrived the next day and asked Bill a number of questions about the height and size of the object, before taking down a detailed two-page statement.

Following the sighting report and film taken, Mr Fisher found himself the subject of interest by a variety of UFO researchers, ranging from prominent Northwestern University astronomer – J. Allen Hynek, to a mysterious trio, dressed in black, who confronted him at the police station. Considerable publicity was given to this incident by the media; the story was reported in UFO magazines and even supermarket tabloids. Mr Fisher was also interviewed for a 1972 book, co-edited by astronomer – Carl Sagan, called *UFOs: A Scientific Debate*.

Bill Fisher

UFOs also sighted by other Police Officers

Mr Fisher was not the only Police Officer who saw a UFO during that period of 1967. In separate incidents, sheriff's deputies from Knox and Henry Counties also reported seeing strange and vivid objects in the sky, a couple of days before the sighting at Sacred Heart. [7th March 1967] One of them appears to have been Officer F.W. Courson, who described what he saw through binoculars:

"…an object, travelling directly overhead at 250 to 300 miles per hour; the bottom part of the object had a rim around it 5 or 6 feet thick, spinning at a terrific rate of speed. However, the bottom part of the object appeared to have vents in it – small narrow vents.

The top of the object, as much as I could make out, was kind of whitish, crystalline looking. As to the height of this object, I would estimate it at twenty-five hundred to three thousand feet. In referring to the white ray that emitted from the object, it looked more or less to me, the best way I can describe it, it looked like a sun ray."

Following the investigation by the USAF into these matters, and the production of a 94-page report, Captain Edward Orenic and Kato concluded that while all witnesses appeared reliable,

"what they had seen was very likely to be an object made on Earth; the sightings in rural areas were 'most likely' attributable to a couple of large balloons, with lights constructed out of plastic laundry

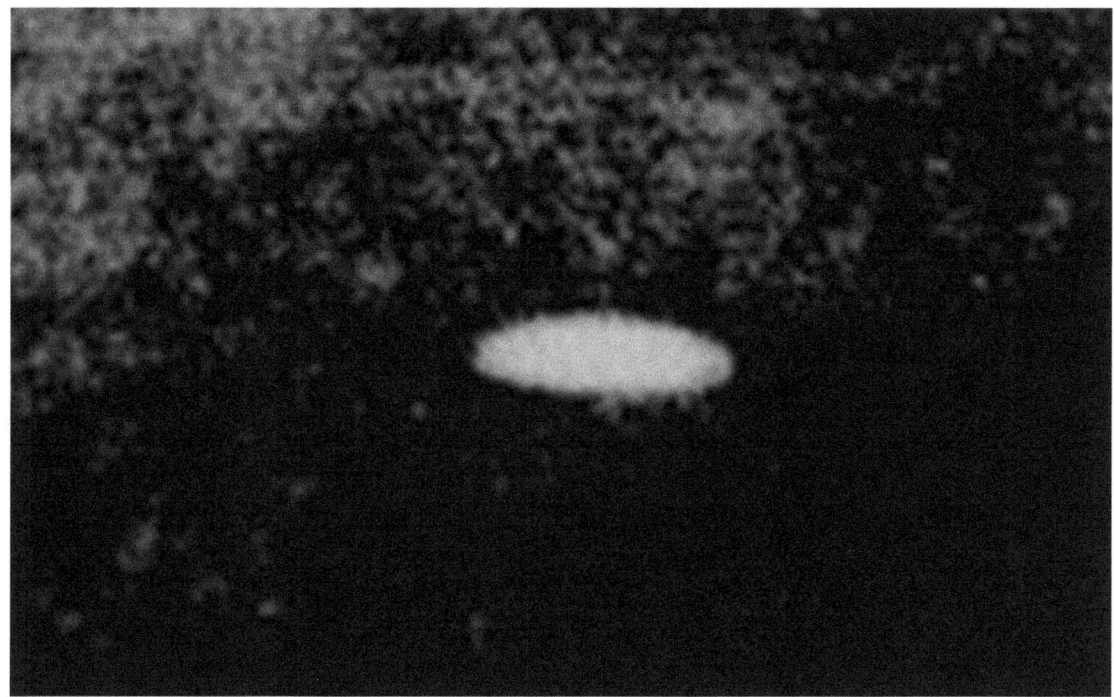

A still image from the two-minute cine film of the object that Mr Fisher witnessed over Moline, USA

bags found near Monmouth. However, we were unable to positively identify the object spotted by Mr Fisher, and others, from the area around Sacred Heart – most likely an air vehicle of some kind."

Other UFO sightings for this date included a report of a pulsating red object – shaped like a pancake, with a rounded top in the sky – seen to approach two housewives, at 7.10pm, over Galesburg, Illinois. According to them:

"...it seemed to explode with a brilliant-white light that lasted ten seconds, almost blinding us, before accelerating away northwards – soon lost from view."

At 9.05pm, a bright saucer-shaped object was seen heading eastwards across the sky, over Onawa, Iowa, by Jack Lindley – out of view two minutes later. (**Source: NICAP**)

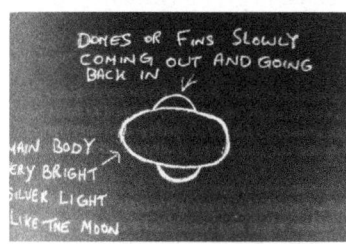

12th March 1967 – 'Fin' UFO in the sky over London

At 12.10am, Barry Panaretou, from London, was walking past Bouverie Gardens, Kenton, when he saw:

"...a narrow, elliptical object, with what looked like a 'hump' or 'fin' at the top and bottom, moving in and out of cloud cover over the suburb, showing a red and green light, at an estimated height of some 500 feet".

During conversation with Barry – now a successful businessman – (then over 35 years later) he told us he had no problem remembering the incident, as it was still crystal clear in his memory, and that enquiries made by him, through the local newspaper, had resulted in two other people coming forward to report having seen the object!

(**Sources:** *The Observer & Gazette*, 30.3.1967 – 'Did anyone else see this?'/Personal interview)

Over Northumberland

At 8.30pm, a glowing 'ball of fire', 30-40 feet in diameter, was seen hovering in the sky over Lynmouth Pit, Northumberland, by golfers on Newbiggin Golf Course. A short time later it was seen to head off eastwards, at speed, and soon out of sight.

At about the same time, Mrs A. Woodhouse sighted a flashing 'red light' hovering about 20 feet off the ground, only 30 feet away from her, over the centre of Wallsend shopping forum at Wallsend-on-Tyne.

"I watched for a few minutes – then it moved westwards, slowly, but returned to its original position before moving slowly northwards." (**Source: TUFOS**)

14th March 1967 – Square shaped object, with 'fin', over Greater Manchester

A strange square shaped object, with what looked like a 'fin' at either side, showing three red lights, was seen over Lancashire Hill, Stockport, and nearby Sandy Lane, flying in what was described as *"a clumsy, drifting, sideways movement"*, at an estimated speed of under a hundred miles per hour, making noise like a jet. Five minutes later, it was lost from view. (**Source: DIGAP**)

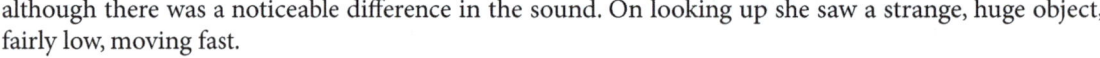

16th March 1967 – Oblong UFO over Glasgow

A woman was sat with her two year-old child in Ruchill Park, Glasgow, at 2.50pm, when she heard a noise resembling a plane, although there was a noticeable difference in the sound. On looking up she saw a strange, huge object, fairly low, moving fast.

"It was long, shaped like two oblong balloons, joined together, but hazy in the middle. I had the impression that there were one or two triangular shapes pointing up from the middle through the haze. It was unreal – like something out of a science fiction movie.

The object then went behind some cloud, dipping lower, before disappearing from sight."
(**Source: BUFORA, Mr T. O'Neil**)

20th March 1967 – 'Flying tadpole', Reading, Berkshire

At 4.30pm, a nurse and her companion were driving through Burghfield Common, Reading, when they saw an object they described as *"cigar-shaped, without wings or propellers, flying slowly over the ground"*.

Was this the same UFO seen a few hours later, at 7.30pm, by Mr Ronald Salisbury – an employee at the nearby Royal Ordnance factory (a locality to be the focus of many other UFO sightings)?

Mr Salisbury:

"I was finishing off the garden, at 7.30pm, when I happened to glance towards the Hatch Gate public house and see what I first took to be an aircraft vapour trail. A couple of minutes later, I looked up and was surprised to see it was still there in the sky, but flying from side to side in very strange movements. I called my neighbours and we watched it approach a little closer, when we were astonished to see it had no wings and resembled a carrot in appearance – thick at the front, tapering to a point at the other end. It was actually more like a 'flying tadpole', surrounded by a heat haze, hovering in the sky. I watched it for about 20 minutes before it flew away. I submitted a report to my supervisor at the factory, who later told me it had been sent to the Defense Department at Washington, in the United States. When I enquired some weeks later about any developments, I was told the report had been lost."

(**Source: Personal interview/*Reading Evening Post*, 21.3.1967**)

24th March 1967 – Three 'lights' seen in the sky over Staffordshire

At 6.30am, a large bright orange 'light', accompanied by two smaller ones, was seen hovering over a field just outside Hanley, Stoke-on-Trent, scattering particles of light across the early morning landscape.

(Source: Personal interview, *UFOSIS*)

On the same date was a report by Belt, Montana truck driver – Mr Ken Williams – who told of seeing a dome-shaped object, emitting a bright light at 9pm, which

". . . landed in a ravine. As I approached it took off and I lost view of it, several minutes later."

26th March 1967 – UFO over Ohio

A group of people from New Winchester, Ohio, were outside at 4pm, when they saw a copper or brass coloured object flying through the sky in a south-east to north-west direction, in tumbling movements – then out of view, thirty minutes later. **(Source: NICAP)**

March 1967 – Green UFO over Bath, Somerset

In the same month, British Rail fireman Chris Holder – then living in Whiteway Road, Kingswood, near Bristol – was walking downhill, towards a place known as 'The Hollow', at 2am, on his way to catch the train from Bristol Spa Station.

"As I reached the junction with Kelston View, overlooking Bristol, I noticed a green coloured object travelling from the direction of the City Centre, apparently following the course of the river. As it passed over Tiverton, I could see it just above the building line, occasionally dropping downwards in flight and then back up again for about 20 seconds, but lost view of it and continued on my journey. When I neared the bottom of the hill where the houses started, I was startled when the object – a round, pulsing, bright-green fluorescent 'ball', about 3 feet in diameter, with a row of smaller lights around its base (the colour of which 1 had never seen before in my life) – rose over the roof of a nearby house and dipped down to about two feet off the ground, before rising upwards over a large hedge, no more than l5 feet away. It then headed off over the gardens, where I lost sight of it."

The next day, Chris read in a local newspaper of a UFO having been sighted over Bath, on the other side of the city, although scant description was given. **(Source: Personal interview)**

March 1967 – 'Flying Saucer' over Didcot, Berkshire

Two brothers, and a friend, were walking across open farmland near Didcot, in Berkshire, when they noticed a 'flash of light' in the sky as the sun began to set. Looking up, they saw something drop downwards over the direction of the ESSO laboratories, and ran to gain a better position of observation, when they were shocked to see:

"...a silver 'flying saucer' shaped object of a diameter estimated to be 2-300 feet, hovering at a height of two miles off the ground.

A bright white light came on and the object shot up into the sky vertically, until just a tiny 'star' in the sky". **(Source: Mr Bennett)**

March 1967 – Strange ghostly sightings, West Midlands

A strange white 'ball' or 'globe' was seen dragging itself along the ground at Coldlands Wood, near Streetsbrook Road, Solihull, in the West Midlands. It was seen by a group of children, who apparently fled in fear after sighting the 'white bag-like object'. It apparently left tracks in the grass as it moved along. Details of the incidents were brought to the attention of the local newspaper, who published an account of what had taken place. However, they explained it away as an example of mass hysteria.

Haunted Skies **Volume Two Revised**

Coldlands Wood

Derek Samson, a NICAP, GB UFO investigator from Shirley (known personally to the authors) took an interest in this case and decided to conduct a vigil.

He said:

> "Unfortunately nothing was seen, although I did notice an area of grass laid flat, with many smaller branches broken off the tops of nearby trees."

An appeal, launched by us in the *Solihull Advertiser* to trace the children involved (some of whom were named), was unsuccessful.

Was there any connection with a report of a mysterious 'light' seen ascending into the sky from this area, in the same month?

During the time spent researching *Haunted Skies,* we were to come across many early UFO magazines, published by various organisations. They included the now defunct Isle of Wight Society (*UFOLOG*), which contained an extraordinary amount of information brought about through the dedication of just a few people. The team laboured for many hours to produce, print, and staple together, numerous sheets of typewritten news items and UFO reports, unaided by modern devices such as the Photostat machine and word processor. Even carbon paper was a rare commodity in those days!

UFOLOG was to produce over 80 of these 'magazines' – (if you can call them that, taking into consideration the glossy format of current day UFO Magazines) – thanks to the efforts of John Feakins, Fred Smith, Len Cramp and Pat and Kath Smith, who we feel privileged to have met.

The MOD confirmed that for the period of March 1967, they received a total of eight reports, of which they judged two to be satellites, one meteorological phenomenon, one unknown, two balloons and two unidentified (insufficient information), but nothing earmarked for investigation.

March 1967 – UFO landing in Illinois … giant circle in the crop found afterwards

Mrs Leona Boeving from *Mascoutah, Illinois, noticed a bright light outside her window. She awoke her daughter and the two of them watched a large moon-shaped object, showing a row of lights – mostly red with a very bright white one – about a quarter of a mile away. She said:

> "We tried to look at it through a pair of field glasses but the light was too intense. When we opened the window it immediately took off, heading east. Neighbours who visited the location, two days later, reported a large, precise, circle of brown and crumbly dead clover in the field, about 100 feet in diameter. The crop was growing normally in the rest of the field."

This was not the only occasion when UFOs were reported from that locality. On the 24th February 1967, the *Messenger* published details of a UFO sighting by Police Chief – Dave Geralds, who was out cruising at 4.45am, near the Wilmer Kunze farm, when he sighted a very bright object several miles away, in the east.

> "It moved slowly towards Marissa, stopped at Sam's Café, and awoke the owners – Sam Bilderback and his wife – to show them. I then drove to Dintelmann's Wye market and saw the object to be:…a 'disc' with red, green, and amber lights around the centre – now very difficult to look at – about a thousand feet up in the air and half a mile away. Within a short time it shot off northwards and out of sight." (**Source:** *Messenger* -24.2.1967 **'Flying Saucer again sighted in area'**)

*A small City in St. Clair County, Illinois, named for the Mascoutens – a tribe of Illinois Indians.

The officer was not alone; Police Chief Lorin Gregory also witnessed something very unusual in the same County, not dissimilar to what Dave Gerald described. The matter was brought to the attention of Scott Air Force Base, who said nothing had been tracked on radar.

APRIL 1967

17th April 1967 – Three 'lights' forming a triangle, Tyneside

Mr Frank Sattherthwaite was in Fenham, Newcastle-on-Tyne, at 11.08pm, when he saw a yellow 'light' travelling east. On looking through a telescope, he saw:

> "...three lights, forming a triangle, one of which pulsated once a second – the apex of the triangle pointing forwards".

19th April 1967 – 'Flying Saucer' over Sussex

At 2.15am, Judith Mosley – (whom, it appears, later adopted the title of Lady Judith Mosley, although – according to Arun District Council – she was not entitled to it) – and her husband from Worthing, Sussex, were awoken by what sounded like *"the noise of a child's humming top"*, but much louder. She looked through the window, wondering where the source of this noise was coming from, and saw:

> "...an oval 'globe of light' moving across the sky, which changed into a saucer-shaped object and dropped down behind Highdown Hill, leaving a glow in the sky marking where it was, accompanied by a humming noise.
>
> At about 4.30am, it rose upwards and vanished from sight." **(Source: Personal interview)**

20th April 1967 – Triangular object over Dorset

At 5.45am, Mr H. Hayes – a security officer, employed by the MOD at Portland Bill, Dorset – was driving to work along the coast road, close to the 'Bill', when he saw:

> "...a large, bright green, triangular object flash by and disappear towards the lighthouse".

He was not the only witness. A colleague, who was opening gates leading into a nearby factory, also saw it. (**Source:** Frank Marshall, BUFORA)

20th April 1967 – UFO over Heathrow Airport, London

Mr John Percy Thomas Greig was employed as a Chief Steward with British Airways, from 1958-1970. He was a member of Mensa, and in later life followed a career with the Diplomatic Service.

At 11.30am he was travelling back to Heathrow Airport, having been to Glasgow at 2pm on a crew bus, with a junior steward and air stewardess. He told us:

> "We drove through the tunnel under Runway 28R on the north side of the airport, heading towards the catering base. We then turned left out of the tunnel and began to drive up to ground level, when the steward sitting in front of me said 'Hey what is that?'
>
> I looked up, expecting to see an aircraft, but was astonished to see a dull aluminium coloured object, motionless in the sky over Ashford, Middlesex, some five miles away."

Somebody suggested to him that the object might have been a Boeing 707. However, he rejected this hypothesis, as there was no sign of any wings, or the black smoke – a characteristic trait of the early 707s.

A few hours later, it was still there – now prominent in the night sky, as aircraft flew in and out of the Airport – watched by a crowd of people. "*Suddenly, it tilted in the sky – now looking like Saturn, with a ring around it – and promptly vanished.*"

Haunted Skies Volume Two Revised

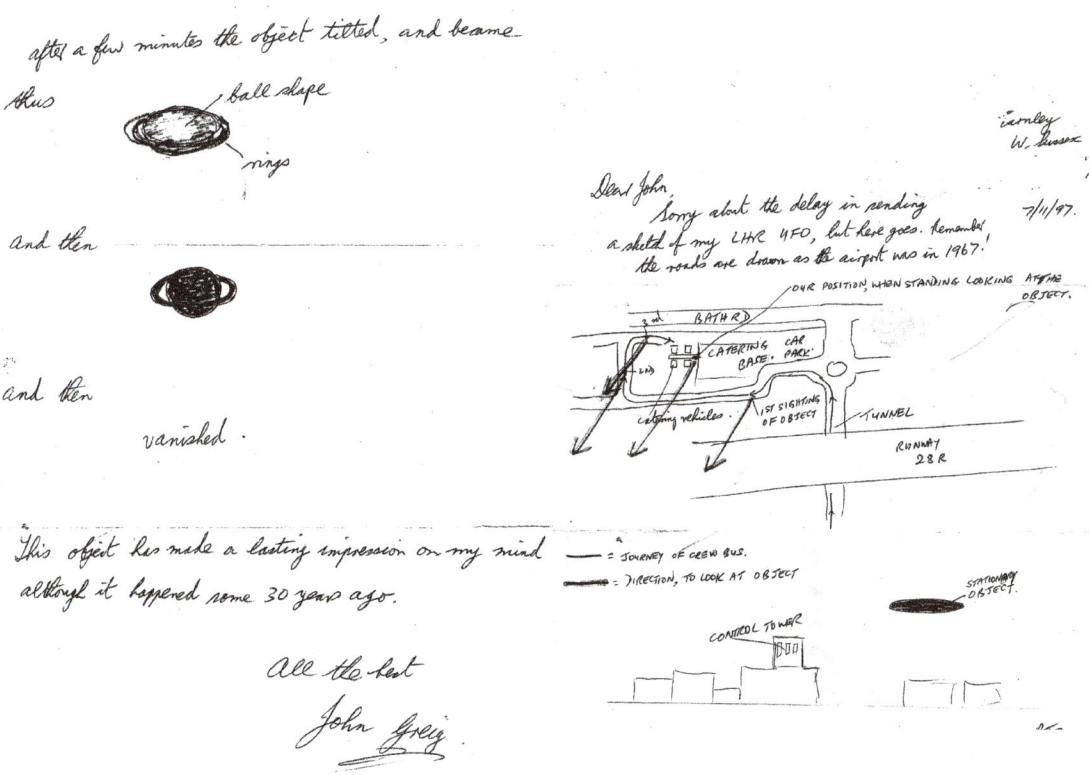

after a few minutes the object tilted, and became

thus — ball shape, rings

and then

and then

vanished.

"This object has made a lasting impression on my mind although it happened some 30 years ago.

All the best
John Greig

Crawley
W. Sussex
7/11/97

Dear John,
Sorry about the delay in sending a sketch of my LHR UFO, but here goes. Remember the roads are drawn as the airport was in 1967!

OUR POSITION, WHEN STANDING LOOKING AT THE OBJECT.
BATH RD
CATERING CAR BASE. PARK.
catering vehicles
1ST SIGHTING OF OBJECT
TUNNEL
RUNWAY 28R

— = JOURNEY OF CREW BUS.
━ = DIRECTION, TO LOOK AT OBJECT

CONTROL TOWER
STATIONARY OBJECT.

When Mr Greig contacted the control tower, asking for further information, they denied having seen it or any knowledge of the sighting.

> "Coincidently, a few days later, I happened to go to my mother-in-law's house in Hanworth, and was talking about what I had seen with her uncle, Richard, who was a Colonel at the Woomera Rocket Range, in Australia, attached to the Australian Air Force, on holiday in England. After some conversation, he went upstairs and brought a book down, showing photographs of UFOs seen in Australia, which contained an identical object as seen at the airport, a few days ago. I asked him what they were. He replied, 'nobody knew what these things were but that type of UFO had been seen many times in Australia. We have often sent jet fighters up, but never been able to catch them'."

This is, of course, not the end of the story. John was to experience other incidents, involving what he classed as psychic phenomena rather than sightings of UFOs, and has since joined the Unexplained Phenomena Research Society (run by Lucy Pringle) and the Havant Spiritualist Church, wishing to further his knowledge into the subject.

When we spoke to him in January 2011, he told us of a sighting that took place only a few weeks previously, when he and others witnessed the passage of what looked like a *'fiery red brick'* seen crossing the sky, over East Wittering. **(Source: Personal interviews)**

27th April 1967 – Half-moon shaped objects seen over Tyneside

At 10.40pm, a star-like object was seen to approach westwards, at fast speed in the sky, over Heaton, Newcastle-on-Tyne, before coming to a halt in mid-air and hovering for 20-30 seconds, then continuing on its journey.

At 11.55pm two, fuzzy, half-moon-shaped, objects with bright centre portions, were seen in the sky over Tilehurst, Reading, which changed colour every few seconds, from yellow to green. **(Source: BUFORA)**

28th April 1967 – UFO over Devon

Coastguard – Brian Jenkins – was on duty at Berry Head Coastguard Station, Brixham, in Devon.

> "It was the day of the annual inspection when I received a telephone call, at 11.20am, from the foreman of Berry Head Quarry, 200 feet below the cliff top, asking me if I could see a strange 'light' in the sky directly above the Coastguard Station. I went outside, looked through a pair of binoculars, and saw a large object with a glassy white dome atop a curtain-like structure, and what appeared to be a triangular opening, or door, in its side that disappeared as it rotated below thin cloud cover, at 20,000 feet. I continued to observe the object, now moving slowly north-west against the wind blowing from the east, at 40 knots. A short time later, I received a number of telephone calls from the public and the local Press, asking for information. When I told them what was happening, two or three reporters came to the lookout and watched the object through binoculars for themselves."

At 12.10pm Brian saw the condensation trail of a jet aircraft moving from east to north-east, towards the UFO, and presumed it was a RAF Lightning Jet, because of its speed.

> "I saw it fly over the top of the UFO and then underneath, before losing sight of the plane – by which time the UFO was rising upwards and passing through thin cloud. When I finished my shift at 1pm, it was still there. I later heard it was actually kept in view until 3pm, when visual contact became lost due to its height."

19 Venn Close
Stoke Fleming
Dartmouth
Devon TQ6 0QL

Tel 01803 770168

26.7.97

Dear John,
     I received your letter with interest, its a long time since I have been asked about the sighting.

I quite often think about it, especially now that there is a an increased interest in the subject.

  I am more than happy for you to use my sighting as you wish.

It is a long time ago that I read the account of what I saw so it is difficult to know if the full account was recorded.

I am quite happy to tell you the full story and let you decide if you want to use any additional info.

Firstly I must say that I have not seen anything since that I could say was a UFO.

  I was on the forenoon watch, 0700 to 1300, the weather was good, the wind was light from the NE, the cloud was thin cirrus at about 20,000 ft, a nice sunny day.
  The Chief Coastguard was making his annual inspection of the station, he left the Lookout, where I was on watch and was at the housing station a mile away, the time was approx 1120.
  The telephone rang and the caller, the foreman of the Berry Head Quarry, 200 ft below the cliff top where the lookout was situated, he asked if I knew what the light in the sky, directly above, was. I look out of my window and could see nothing, I went outside and looked up and could see a bright white light directly overhead, I returned to the phone and told the foreman that I could see the light but would need to take the large binoculars on its tripod outside to view the light. The foreman informed me that he and his men had been watching the light for about 20 mins and that it had remained stationary.
  I erected the large binoculars outside and viewed the light and what I saw startled me, the "light" was a very large object, glassy white dome with very white structure below which I can only describe as looking like a curtain.
  I estimated the height of the object to be just below the thin cloud, which was about 20,000ft. The object was slowly revolving, I could see the trianglar shape on the side moving around and disappearing behind the object. I estimated the size of the oblect to be about the size of three terraced houses on their end.

I telephoned the housing station and spoke to the station officer and informed him of what I saw, he informed the Chief. The station officer called me back and stated that they could also see the object and instructed me to inform the Met Office Plymouth and the RAF Controller SRCC
(Southern Rescue Control Centre).
The duty Met officer confirmed the height of the cloud as being about 20,000ft, as reported by aircraft, and that the wind at that height was from the east 40 knots (at sea level the wind was approx NE 15knots).The met officer ruled out the possiblity of the object being a met baloon, he stated that a met ballon would not be visible with the naked eye at that height and would not have remained stationary.

I reported the sighting to the RAF controller an he said he would pass the information on to the MOD.

I continued to observe the object which had started to move slowly NW (accross wind). I received a number of phone calls from the public and the local press asking about the object. Later 2 or 3 reporters came to the lookout and observed the object through the binoculars.

At about 1210 I observed the condensation trail of an an aircraft coming from ENE direction and flying towards the UFO, I watched the a/c through my hand held binoculars and thought that it must have been a Lightning, (the fast a/c at that time) as it was moving so fast. I followed the track of the a/c and observed that it flew over the top of the UFO and then down to pass below. By this time the UFO had risen and was passing through the thin cloud. I observed the a/c flying below the UFO and then it dissapeared.

I observed the UFO until I went off watch at 1300. My colleagues reported that the object was visible until about 1500.

I later learnt that a Station Officer travelling with the Chief Coastguard had made a drawing of the UFO, he stated that he was looking from directly below the UFO, I also learnt that a friend of mine, a Physics Master from the local Seconday School, with some of his pupils observed the UFO with a telescope until it dissapeared from view, he also saw the a/c and lost sight of it exactly as I had done.

The Controller SRCC reported later that he had passed the information to the MOD, who denied to the press that they had not received ant information about the sightings. The Sunday Express reported an explanation of the UFO, by the MOD, as being probably the reflection of car headlights in the sky!!!

That is how I remember it, if any of the above is any use to you, you are welcome to use it.

I would be interested to know the title of your book when it is published.

Best Wishes

(B F. JENKINS)

Round globe, with cross, sighted in the sky

During conversation, the following day, with the Station Officer – Harry Johnson – Brian discovered that he and the Chief Coastguard had seen the object from underneath, describing it as resembling a round globe with a cross on it.

Brian:

"I was able to make a detailed drawing of it, which I showed to an Air Vice Marshall who called at the station, a few days later; his only comment was 'most interesting'."

The *Sunday Express* published an article about the incident, which included an explanation given by the MOD, who mistakenly (believing it had happened at night-time), suggested that it was probably a reflection of car headlights in the sky! Mr Johnson said:

"It's just laughable for anyone to suggest to a body of highly trained observers that this was the reflection of car headlights. It was midday. The object was obviously made up of something very highly polished, and reflected the sunlight almost like a star".

The Meteorological Office ruled out the possibility of the object being a meteorological balloon because, if it had been at that height, it would have been visible with the naked eye and would not have remained stationary.

Site of an ancient Hill Fort

Berry Head Lighthouse was the site of an ancient Iron Age Hill Fort, which was mostly destroyed by construction between 1794 and 1804, when extensive fortifications were built to protect the Torbay naval anchorage against French invasion.

UFO researcher – Julian Hennessey

Julian Hennessey with co-author of 'Haunted Skies' Dawn Holloway

In 2005, we met up with Julian Hennessey – London-based UFO researcher and member of NICAP. In his own words, he was to become *"a veritable thorn in the side of the MOD"* with his determined attempts to obtain the truths which lay behind not only this but other UFO sightings, as can be seen from comments made in documents released some 30 years later. When he wrote to them, asking for details of the RAF Jet seen by the coastguards, much to his surprise, they were unable to identify where this aircraft had come from! This matter was also discussed during a visit to the MOD by Mr Hennessey, with Mr Cassells – then Head of S4f (Air) – who admitted some embarrassment over the matter, and that due to a 'mix up', the radar film of the object and the intercepting aircraft was destroyed before it could be examined! As Julian noted wryly, *"the film could not have shown anything untoward or it would have been retained."* If this was the case, then why didn't the MOD offer a substantial explanation as to what it was?

In October 1967, Mr W.F. Allen, of the Ministry, stated:

"as far as the Berry Head sighting is concerned, as we cannot positively state that the object was a balloon, its identity must obviously remain unknown".

In October 1969, Mr L.W. Akhurst wrote:

> *"We have received no further information about this report, and the position, as stated is in our letter of 4th October 1967."*

In May 1971, he wrote:

> *"The category in which a report is placed depends on the particular circumstances: this could mean that a report referred to as probably a weather balloon could be placed into the balloon category".*

The MOD confirmed that during the period of April 1967, they received a total of three reports, of which they judged two to be satellites, and one celestial object. Nothing at all was earmarked as being under investigation!

(Sources: Personal interviews/*Sunday Express,* 21.5.1967/*Space-link*/Isle of Wight UFO Society)

UFOs sighted over RAF Welford, by US Servicemen

We spoke to retired USAF Sergeant John Roger Artie (born 21st May 1935) – now living in Nevada – who was previously employed as a field investigator for the now defunct Aerial Phenomena Research Association (APRO). We were interested in a number of UFO sightings, witnessed by himself and other USAF security servicemen at RAF Welford, Newbury, Berkshire, during 1967.

He said:

> *"I was on duty in the 'Z' area, looking out over the interior road and fields when I noticed a security patrol vehicle – manned by Sergeants Nash and Brooks – slow down and stop. The two men then got out and looked up into the sky. I was later approached by the two men, who reported having seen a strange reddish glow in the middle of low hanging clouds, although I did not witness it myself."*

This was not to be the last time John was to become involved in sightings of UFOs at this base.

(Source: Personal interview)

UFO reported over RAF Lyneham Wiltshire 27 years later !

Another UFO incident happened while Malcolm Williams was working in air traffic control at RAF Lyneham in Wiltshire, on a night shift, just before Christmas in either 1994 or 1995, according to UFO investigator Phillip Mantle.

Mr Williams said he had nearly 20 years of experience at the time and was used to analyzing quirks that radar can sometimes produce such as bird activity and atmospheric variation. On the night in question, Mr Williams was guiding two C130 Hercules aircraft that were approximately three miles from touch down. But, he suddenly observed a very large "blob" on the radar screen that he has been unable to explain. Not knowing what it was, he contacted the pilots of the two Hercules aircraft and fed them around the target.

He said he then passed control of the inbound aircraft to a colleague and went upstairs to the visual control room.

Mr Williams was interviewed about the incident by UFO investigator Philip Mantle. Mr Mantle said:

> *"The room where he had been based had no windows so he wanted to see if he could obtain a visual sighting of this radar target.*
>
> *Mr Williams could not see anything but another radar called the DFTI (Distance from Touchdown Indicator) located in the visual control room also had this blob, which was stationary at the time, on its screen. He asked the visual controller if he had any idea what the target was but he replied*

that he didn't know what it was. Mr Williams returned to the radar room and the blob was still on the radar screen. He used the usual suppressors to try and eliminate it but all to no effect. After puzzling what this image might be for a while he decided that it must be a technical problem with the radar but after checking it all seemed to be functioning correctly.

Things took a decidedly different course when the radar blob on the screen suddenly seemed to 'burst' and shoot off at tremendous speed in all directions. Mr Williams had never seen anything like it and had never seen anything move so fast in all his life.

There was a brief discussion with a colleague but they had no idea what it was. The visual controller witnessed the same on the DFTI. Mr Williams was then telephoned by an agitated airman who was on guard duty on the base"

The airman said:

"Sir I have not been drinking, I am on guard duty and have just seen something that was very strange, but can't explain but thought that Air Traffic should be informed of it. I saw a bright light in the east which burst and shot off in all directions at speeds I could not believe."

Several minutes later another airman on guard duty on the perimeter of the base also telephone Mr Williams and reported the same thing. Mr Williams said this made the hairs on the back of his neck stand up. He then logged the details and telephoned the Ministry of Defence to report the incident.

MAY 1967

1st May 1967 – Black boomerang-shaped UFO over Tyneside

A black 'boomerang' shaped object was seen by at least eight people. It was hovering in the sky over Stella South Power Station, Gateshead – one of two power stations standing next to the *River Tyne* (demolished in 2006). After five minutes, a haze appeared to develop on and off around the 'craft', and smoke appeared at one end. It then shot off at high speed, towards the south-west. (**Source: Tyneside UFO Society**)

10th May 1967 – Black 'disc' seen by Reading cyclist

At 9.20pm, a black 'disc' shaped object, with a row of lighter 'blobs' around its edge and small central raised portion, was seen by a cyclist over Burghfield, near Reading, before it swerved and then climbed upwards.

12th May 1967 – Three round globes seen over London

Mr Steven Willey of Putney, London, was in the process of getting ready for bed, at 11.10pm, when he was called by his son – Leonard, to come and have a look at a UFO flying below the clouds, travelling south to north.

Mr Willey ran to the front door and saw a large 'bright star' heading silently towards London. His son passed him a pair of binoculars, through which he saw:

"...a large 'disc', that glowed with a bright golden light. On the underside I could see the outline of three round globes, spaced triangularly, which could have been landing gear. As it passed overhead we saw an aircraft flying below it, travelling towards London Airport, at around 3,000 feet. By comparison, the 'disc' was about the same size of the aircraft. Within four and a half minutes, it had gone out of sight."

One cannot deny the similarities between this sighting, involving three globes, set at equal distance from each other, forming a triangle, and many other sightings, indicating a commonality of description which can be traced back to the 1950s. (**Source: Letter to Gordon Creighton,** *Flying Saucer Review*)

17th May 1967 – UFO seen in front of aircraft over Carolina, USA

At 8.30pm, a round object – similar in size to a small aircraft – was sighted by Mr Red Ledford of Rural Hall, North Carolina, zigzagging across the sky, for five minutes, over a jet aircraft heading north-east.
(Source: Project Blue Book unknowns)

19th May 1967 – Glittering 'disc' London

At 4.20pm, a strange glittering 'disc' was seen hovering over Croydon Road, Penge, by a Beckenham man and his fiancée.

It moved away in a jerking motion across the sky, heading towards the south-east.

22nd May 1967 – Orange moon, County Durham

At 4am, a strange 'orange moon' was seen in the sky over Shotley Bridge, County Durham, by Mr R.W. Ferguson and his son – Dennis. As it approached closer, the two men were shocked to see a dome-shaped object, resembling a 'Flying Saucer', move across the sky and then hurtle off at speed.
(Source: Isle of Wight UFO Society)

23rd May 1967 – 'Flying Saucer' takes-off, south-west Essex

A married couple living near to Bush Road, on the edge of the forest in south-west Essex (the location is not clear) wrote a letter to BUFORA:

> "Last night, on 23rd May 1967, at approximately 9.20pm, my wife and myself observed from our flat, a 'Flying Saucer' about to take off from the roof of an unusual building, which is opposite us. This building is roughly half a mile away on the edge of the forest from Bush Road. The 'Saucer' slowly rose about 20 feet in the air and then moved slowly in the opposite direction, about 120 degrees south-east, till it diminished in the distance to approx 1/10th of its size – then coming into contact with another 'Saucer' in the same direction, which appeared to come from nowhere. One of the 'Saucers' came back and hovered above the building for a short period of time, and then slowly moved off into the distance and disappeared."

While the exact location of where this incident took place is not clear, we came across a footnote contained on the page:

> "The block of flats in question is only a couple of miles away from where an object – thought to have been a thunderbolt – plunged into the road, a year ago, leaving a hole wider underground with a horrible smell. Our investigator, visiting the top of the unusual building, was told that an unpleasant smell had been noticed there before, but it was presumed to be the urinals not working properly!"

An oval object *was* sighted over Burghfield, at 9.20pm, on the same date. It was moving up and down in the air. Was this merely a coincidence? **(Sources: *BUFORA Newsletter*/G.N.P. Stephenson/*UFOLOG*)**

At 10.25pm, a hazy, white, oval object, surrounded by a red haze, was seen in the sky over Burghfield. It was seen to move up and down in the air for two minutes, before vanishing from view. **(Source: Mr Eedle)**

24th May 1967 – Bright green UFO, Yorkshire Dales

A bright green object was seen moving slowly through the sky, over Malham, in the Yorkshire Dales.
(Source: *Craven Herald & Pioneer*, 2.6.1967)

26th May 1967 – Half-circle object in sky over Somerset

A resident of Withycombe, Somerset, described what he saw in the sky, at 12.50am.

> "It looked like a very large half-circle, darker than the surrounding sky, out of which long 'bars of

light' slanted down at an angle of 75 degrees – like the rays of the setting sun on a stormy afternoon. After ten minutes, the outer part of the half-circle began to glow pink, then fiery red, and drifted slowly over the hill, north-north-west, in single 'bars of light', leaving red streamers in the sky.

The whole lot then disappeared from sight, five minutes later." (**Sources: UFOLOG/BUFORA**)

MOD figures for May 1967

The MOD confirmed that during the period of May 1967, they received a total of **15 reports**, of which they judged four to be satellites, one celestial object, one balloon, 3 aircraft, one miscellaneous and four unidentified (insufficient information), but nothing earmarked for investigation.

JUNE 1967

6th June 1967 – Dome-shaped UFO, Essex

Geoffrey Tarbuck – a resident from Harold Hill, in Essex, – was having problems sleeping. He later said:

> "I glanced out of the window and saw this huge, bright, domed object, hovering in the sky, about 2,000 feet off the ground. I screamed out so loudly that the rest of the family came rushing into the room, wondering what was going on. They stood with me watching it.
>
> All of a sudden, in front of our eyes, it shot off across the sky – faster than anything we had ever seen move before." (**Source: Essex UFO Group**)

10th June 1967 – Six red lights and a white 'disc', Northampton

John Pickering, from Northampton, was looking out across the night sky, at 10.30pm, when he saw:

> "…six red lights (possibly more), in a rectangular formation, moving across the sky – gone out of sight in a few seconds."

11th June 1967 – Humped UFO over Staffordshire

This was followed by a report of "…*a white disc-shaped object, showing a slight protuberance or hump*", sighted moving through the sky over Aldridge, Staffordshire, at 3am on 11th June 1967, (close to electricity pylons).

According to Derek Samson, what was apparently the same object was later photographed over Erdington, Birmingham.

When Derek spoke to officials at Elmdon Airport, with a view to obtaining details of flight paths, they declined to assist him further. (**Source: Derek Samson – NICAP, GB**)

14th June 1967 – Three to five white dazzling 'bars' over Northumberland

At 3am, Mrs Marshall from the Westmoreland Estate, Wallsend, Northumberland, was getting ready for bed when she noticed what looked like:

> "three to five dazzling white 'bars' in the sky, surrounded by a magenta halo of light, 10 degrees off the north-north-east horizon – like iron filings under a magnet – probably over the sea."

(**Source: Tyneside UFO Society**)

UFO over Newcastle

At 8.55am, schoolboys – Keith Wilson and John Fairweather – were walking up the drive to school in Newcastle-on-Tyne, when they saw:

> "…a white, oval object, with a black band around its centre, flying from north-east, westwards, at about the speed of a jet aircraft; it entered a cloud and promptly disintegrated, leaving no trace of the UFO". (**Source: UFOLOG**)

Later the same day, at 10.45pm, five yellow, orange and white, 'lights' were seen moving around the sky over a railway bridge at Alderley Edge, Cheshire, by schoolboy – George Needham.

> *"They were in the eastern part of the sky until 1.30am, when a bright flash lit up the sky. During the observation, three of the objects formed a triangle. On another occasion, one of them split into two".* **(Sources: UFOLOG/Mr Moore, DIGAP)**

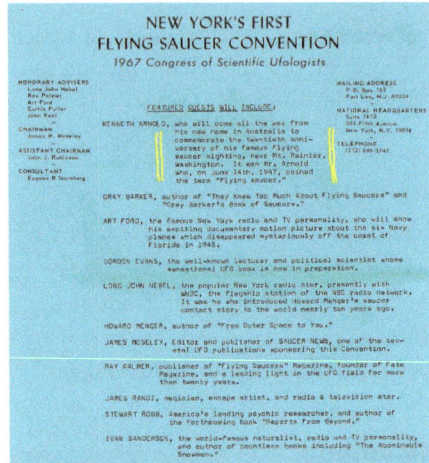

14th June 1967 – New York Flying Saucer Convention, USA

15th June 1967 – UFO over Heysham, Lancashire

At 8.50pm, Dennis Esplin (18) from Littledale Avenue, Heysham, Lancashire, happened to be looking out of his bedroom window, when he noticed a dark brown object above a field beyond a railway line, some 3-400 yards distance.

He rushed to a drawer in the bedroom and picked up his black and white Kodak 120 Halina camera, 6-4 fixed shutter speed, and without bothering to set any distances, took one photograph.

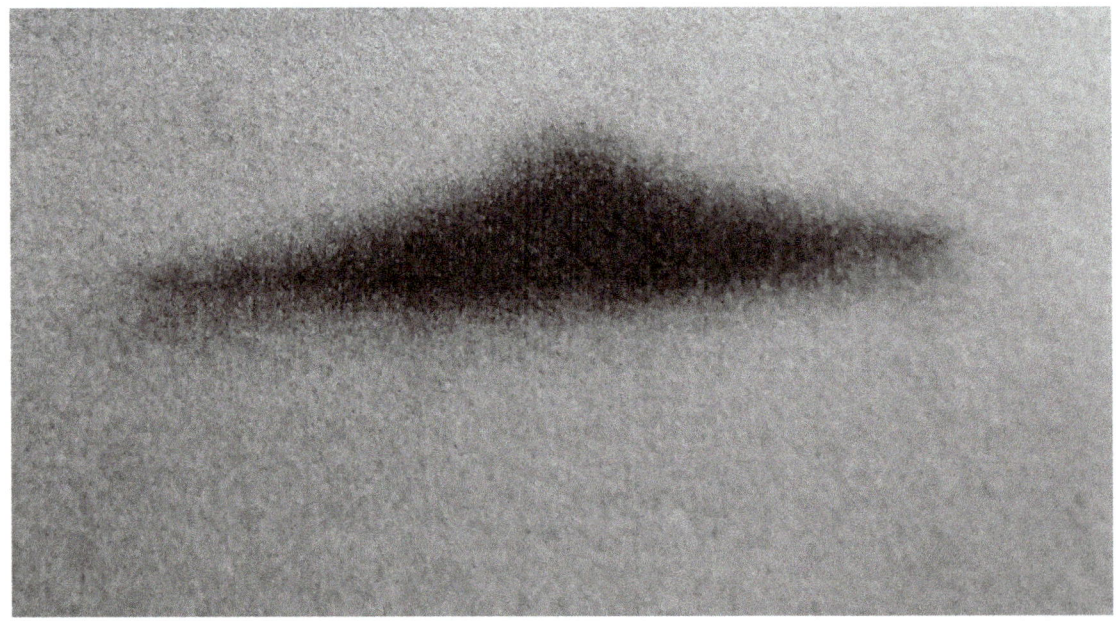

"About 20 seconds later it moved rapidly, vertically into the sky, and disappeared – soon just a tiny speck."

The film was taken to a local chemist in Morecambe, who didn't bother to print off the negative thinking it was faulty.

Dennis then sent the negative, together with a covering letter, to the local newspaper – *The Visitor*, where it was published.

Examined by *Flying Saucer Review* expert

The photograph and negative taken by Dennis (to whom we spoke in 2010), was examined by Mr Percy Hennell – the photographic expert for *Flying Saucer Review* – a short time after it was taken. He concluded, from his examination of the photo: *"Let me say at the outset that without committing me to any explanation of what the object is, in my opinion, the photograph has a genuine look about it and is, in every respect, consistent with the data supplied."* – a conclusion reached, from his observation, that the out of focus image (as opposed to a crisp image) was caused by the probable setting on the 120 camera, fixed for 10-15 feet – hence the presented image, understanding the object was 3-400 yards away when photographed. (We hope we have grasped what he meant!)

In 2010, we contacted Mr Esplin and spoke to him about the matter. He wrote back, offering us an image of the UFO, and assured us it was a genuine photo taken in genuine circumstances.

(Sources: Peter Haythornthwaite, BUFORA/Personal interview/*Space-link*, Volume 5, Number 2, March 1968/ *Flying Saucer Review*)

In the same month, Mr J. Harm of Whickham, Newcastle-upon-Tyne, was out walking on Fellside Road with his Kodak Instamatic camera. He noticed a dull-grey metallic, circular object, motionless in the north-western part of the sky, at an estimated height of 6-10,000 feet. Reacting quickly, he took a photograph of the UFO before it moved away, minutes later. The photograph was later sent to the Tyneside-based UFO Group for examination. Unfortunately this is the only information we have, apart from a sketch that was included in the sighting report. **(Source: TUFOS)**

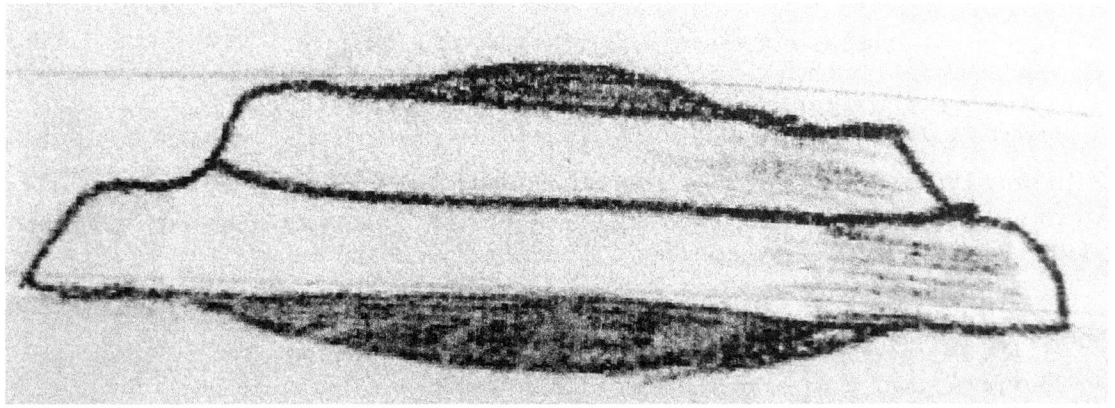

15th June 1967 – Flattened 'S' shape in the sky, Cornwall

On or about the 17th June, a number of tiny pinpoints of light were seen off the coast at Newquay, Cornwall, forming a flattened 'S' shape in the sky, ten degrees off the horizon.

Susannah Nicholls, living in the Solihull area of the West Midlands, close to Birmingham Airport (Elmdon), was in the garden at her home address, at 1am, when she saw *"an elongated object, shining like brass or shimmering, passing overhead"*.

According to Derek Samson, of NICAP GB, who forwarded details of this matter (albeit sparse ones) to the Isle of Wight UFO Society, while accepting the possibility that Mrs Nicholls may have seen an aircraft, he disclosed that:

"...there had been a number of other strange 'craft' seen flying over the area, brought to my attention."

(Source: Derek Samson – NICAP, GB)

19th June – Spinning UFO, Staffordshire

A silver-grey spinning object, with a pointed projection at its front, was seen flying through the air over Stoke-on-Trent. **(Sources: Tony Pace/Roger Stanway)**

20th June 1967 – White 'ball of light', Northumberland

Ex-World War Two RAF pilot, Mr Hamble from Whitley Bay – well acquainted with the passage of all manner of aircraft seen flying across the English skies – sighted a curious white 'ball of light'. It was moving through the sky, south to north, on a level flight path, at 11pm on 20th June 1967. He said:

"The object was twice as fast at the Echo 2 satellite and at least three times the size.

Five minutes later, a similar object appeared – this time in the eastern part of the sky – and promptly vanished."

June 1967 – Police officer sights six silver 'dots' in the sky, West Mercia

In June 1967, West Mercia Police officer – Philip Nuttall, was taking a rest from some physical work.

He was lying on his back, looking up into the sky and shielding his eyes from the sun, when:

"I saw what I first took to be an aircraft moving over. As my eyes became accustomed to the light, I was staggered to see a total of six silvery 'dots' passing overhead, at high altitude. I cannot say what they were, but I do know they weren't aircraft." **(Source: Personal interview)**

June 1967 – UFO detector comes under scrutiny by the GPO!

Following a documentary about an international 'sky watch', screened by BBC TV *Panorama*, one of the participants – Mr Colin McCarthy (known to us) received a visit from two representatives from the GPO Wireless Licensing Department, who expressed great concern about his attempts to communicate with UFOs by means of his electronic '*UFO Detector*', which was advertised for sale in UFO magazines. They pointed out that his attempts were contravening their regulations, as UFOs were not licensed by the GPO!

24th June 1967 – UFO display ... triangular objects seen

Mr George Needham was carrying out work underneath the Manchester-Crew railway bridge near Alderley Edge, at 10.45pm, when he saw, over a period of 3 hours, 45minutes:

"...five yellow and orange lights in the sky towards the east. Three of the objects formed a triangle and another two appeared high up. On another occasion, one split into three parts. At 1.30am a bright flash lit up the sky lasting a couple of seconds – then a blue light appeared from what seemed like two directions." **(Source: Derek Samson – NICAP, GB)**

On the same day, artist Roy Stanford of Austin, Texas, was up at 3.12am, when he saw:

"...a solid blue and white elliptical object, flying through the sky in a north-west to north-east direction.

Roy signalled with his flashlight, at which the object stopped (seemingly in response) and halted for 15minuites, before proceeding along its original path, at high speed, when it was then lost behind cloud cover, nine minutes later. **(Source: NICAP)**

25th June 1967 – Rotating UFO over Lancashire

At 12.15am, a dark, rotating, object was seen in the sky over Morecambe, Lancashire. It was followed, an hour later, by the appearance of a second object, described as:

"...elliptical, with a bright orange light in the centre, surrounded by a number of smaller brilliant lights, accompanied by a whirring noise – like the sound of an electric fan".

(Source: Birmingham University Group)

International 'sky watch'

On the 24th/25th June 1967, an international 'sky watch' was organised jointly by the International Sky Scouts (now Contact UK) and BUFORA, involving a total of twenty-three countries and over 40,000 observers. Although the results of that exercise are not fully known, we learnt that a cigar-shaped object was observed over Essex, from fifteen different locations, during the evening.

27th June 1967 – Egg-shaped UFO over Woking, Surrey

Squadron Leader Shipwright of Triggs Lane, Woking, Surrey, was walking with his wife along Albury Downs, at 12.30pm, near to Newlands Corner.

> *"We saw what we took to be a white horse, galloping in a field about half a mile away from Newlands Corner, but further scrutiny revealed an egg-shaped object moving rapidly backwards and forwards in a north-south direction. After about ten minutes it stopped and then slowly moved up to the hedge-line, before heading away in an eastwards direction. When it came up to a line of high trees it paused, before slowly rising over the tops of the trees, and then dropped down to the ground and continued at the same speed across the field – where we lost sight of it."*

(Source: Tape-recorded interview, Jimmy Goddard, Sky Scouts)

29th June 1967 – 'Octopus' shaped UFO, Berkshire

A bright and star coloured 'octopus'-shaped object was seen flying through the air over Wittenham Clumps, near Didcot, Berkshire – later explained away by the RAF as: *"searchlights being reflected from base of cloud"*. (Source: *Wallingford Herald*, 6.7.1967)

29th June 1967 – Motorist followed by UFO over New Jersey, USA

Truck driver Damon Brown was driving through Scotch Plains, New Jersey, at 1.30am, when he saw

> *"...an oyster-shaped object – 200 feet wide by 25-30 feet thick – showing a huge red light at each end and one on the bottom. It circled an aircraft in the sky before dropping down, and followed my car for about 500 feet, veering southwards, heading off at great speed ten minutes later."*

(Source: NICAP)

Prophecies that came true

In the spring of 1967, the late Dr. Olavo T. Fontes of Rio de Janeiro – a researcher of the UFO phenomena – predicted the autumn of that year would record more UFO sightings than any previous period in the 20-year history. This was due to UFO 'waves' occurring *"in cycles of every 26 months, with a peak period every five years"*, and that these 'two' would merge in late 1967 – Britain and Canada being selected as most likely to experience rises in UFO activity. How right he turned out to be!

JULY 1967

1st July 1967 – 'Jellybean' UFO, Yorkshire

Between 3am and 3.15am, a 'jellybean'-shaped object was seen hovering over houses in Brighouse, Yorkshire, by local resident – Mrs Sutcliffe – before disappearing from view, some minutes later.
(Source: Isle of Wight UFO Society)

2nd July 1967 – Strange light, showing three 'prongs', seen over Leicestershire

People living in the Knighton area of Leicestershire reported having sighted a 'bright light', with three 'prongs' sticking out of it, hovering in the sky over Carsibrooke Avenue.

Two 'bright lights' were seen in the sky over Cricket Hill, Woking, on the 2nd July 1967, before dimming and vanishing from view, and *"an enormous egg-shaped object was seen rising up and down in an uncanny manner in the sky"* over fields near Newlands Corner. (**Source:** *Woking News*, 7.7.1967)

July 1967

A silver disc-shaped object was sighted over South Wigston, Leicestershire, by local schoolboy – Steven Bull, and several others. (**Source:** *Unknown newspaper,* **14.7.1967** – 'Flying Saucer seen by a boy at South Wigston')

3rd July 1967 – Orange 'disc' over Surrey

At 1am, Mrs Harris from Bolding House Lane, Woking, in Surrey, was unable to sleep and went to the window.

> *"I saw what appeared to be a flashing aircraft light towards the direction of Woking. It then approached my position, allowing me to see a brilliant orange disc-shaped object – about twice the size of a dinner plate in the air – which passed over the house and flew silently away towards the Bagshot area."* (**Source: Jimmy Goddard, Sky Scouts Association**)

Over Leicestershire on the same date

A large silvery object, travelling at thousands of feet high in the sky (well above cloud cover) was seen by many people over Coalville, Leicestershire, heading towards Ashby, and was brought to the attention of Stratford-upon-Avon UFO researcher, John 'Dennis' Llewellyn, who had just returned from a debate held on UFOs at the *ATV TODAY* TV Studios, in Birmingham.

(**Sources: John D. Llewellyn/***Leicester Mercury*, **3.7.1967**)

Was this the same UFO seen by four teachers and 200 pupils hovering over Bearwood, near Birmingham, at high altitude, during the same day? According to the Meteorological Office at Birmingham Airport, it was *"unlikely to have been a weather balloon"*. (**Source:** *Birmingham Evening Mail,* **6.7.1967**)

4th July 1967 – Green cylindrical object, Dorset

During the late evening a green cylindrical object, resembling a telegraph pole, was seen moving across the sky over Weymouth, Dorset. (**Source:** *Dorset Evening News,* 7.7.1967)

Also on the same day, *"a fiery, egg-shaped object"* was seen hovering in the sky over Cromer, at a height of 1,000 feet, spilling out red and violet light, before 'swishing' away at terrific speed. As it did so lights showing on the side of the object were extinguished, although the 'front lights' stayed on.

(**Source:** *Eastern Evening News,* 12.7.1967)

Over York

Further sightings for this day included a report of *"a green glowing object with a white centre"* that appeared to land in the Melbourne area of York.

5th July 1967 – 'Flying Saucers' reported over Isle of Wight

Just after midnight – a clear night, with light fog patches in low lying areas – Mr R. Hall and Mr P. O'Brien from Cowes, Isle of Wight, sighted:

> *"...a round-like flare, or trail, which passed overhead, crackling and hissing like a firework rocket, then fizzled out over The Solent, between Fawley and Lymington – lighting up the surrounding countryside as clear as day with bluish light, scaring birds roosting in the neighbourhood. Ten seconds later, a rumble – like gunfire – was heard in the direction the object had gone."*

(**Source:** *UFOLOG*)

The same UFO (or a similar one) was seen moving over Scarborough, at high speed.

(**Source:** *Yorkshire Evening Post,* **6.7.1967**)

Clifton resident – Mr Barry Orme, told of having sighted *"...a white, oval 'thing', hanging in the sky over Castle Donnington"*, after his children brought the matter to his attention. He wasn't the only one. People living in Burton Joyce and East Leake also sighted the object, which was not believed to have been a weather balloon – although the RAF disclosed they had a single 'Vulcan' up in the air.

'Flying Saucer' over Nottingham

A 'Flying Saucer' was witnessed by dozens of people, during the same evening (5th July 1967). It was hovering low down in the sky over Clifton Estate, Nottingham. By the time police arrived in response to calls made to them, they found that over a hundred people had gathered on high ground next to Fareham Comprehensive School. However, the police saw no UFOs and suggested an 'optical illusion' as being the explanation. This was rejected by local resident – Mrs Marjorie Cowdell, who spoke of having seen *"a 'Flying Saucer'-shaped object swoop to the ground"*.
(Source: *The Daily Sketch*, 6.6.1967 – '100 say: we saw Flying Saucer land')

6th July 1967 – Orange 'ball of light', Hampshire

At 1.30am, *"a strange orange 'ball of light' was seen motionless in the sky"* over the New Forest, by a motorist.

He telephoned the Farnborough Police, and West Drayton, to report the incident. Unfortunately, the police refused to treat his complaint with any seriousness.

[The *Evening News* 6.7.1967 – 'Mystery of dancing lights in the sky' reported on this incident. They told of a police car crew having witnessed the orange lights 'looping the loop' and 'doing strange acrobatics'. The Officers had been called out by a member of the public to Stoney Cross Airfield, after a 'bright light' was seen hovering, about a hundred feet off the ground. By the time they arrived, the object had moved away towards the direction of Salisbury.]

Over Gateshead

Mr Foster from the Chandless Estate, Gateshead, was taking photographs of his children, at 7.30pm, when he noticed a dull red dome-shaped object, hovering over the *River Tyne*, at 15 degrees elevation, towards the north-east direction, estimated to be 50 feet wide by 15 feet high.

Mr Foster took a photograph of the UFO, which he sent to the Tyneside UFO Society. Once again, the whereabouts of this photo is not known. (**Source: Isle of Wight UFO Society**)

Over Bristol

At 8.35pm, a yellow and red circular object – the size of a golf ball in the air from the ground – was seen almost stationary in the sky over

Bedminster, Bristol. It was moving slightly up and down, and from side to side, until 9.30pm, when it dropped through the sky and disappeared from view. (**Source: UFOSIS, Birmingham**)

Police Officer sights UFO display over Poole, Dorset

Just before midnight, following a call from Mr N. Gallagher of Ashley Road, Poole, Police Constable D. Holloway, from Lyndhurst Police Station, arrived and watched the object, *"now moving up and down, forming a 'cross' in the sky, for over 20 minutes"*, before telephoning Police HQ, at Guildford, to explain what was happening.

In a letter sent to Fred Smith, of the Isle of Wight Society, dated 14th July 1967, PC Holloway had this to say:

"I have felt all along that what I saw was an object which could easily be explained by an astronomer, but not being in any way experienced with heavenly bodies, I just cannot offer any explanation.

I was called to the Stoney Cross area of the New Forest, at 02.30 hours on the night in question. I went as the result of an emergency call made to Police HQ by a Mr N. Gallagher of Ashley Road, Poole, who is an Auxiliary Officer in the RAF. I saw a bright object – the size of a large star – slightly orange in colour, positioned very high in the sky in a north-westerly direction from Stoney Cross. After remaining static for some time, the object would suddenly rise and then fall quite rapidly, then move around in a looping fashion, and return to static. It would then perform this all over again. We watched it for approximately 30 minutes. Before I returned to the Police Station, it flickered very much like a star, but did not change colour. I'm afraid that's all it is. I'm quite sure it can be explained away and the amount of publicity given to this sighting is out of proportion.

Yours faithfully,

D. Holloway"

(Sources: Isle of Wight UFO Society/*Evening News*, 6.7.1967 – 'Mystery of dancing light in the sky')

7th July 1967 – Quarter-moon UFO and green flame, Cheshire

At 1am, Michael Baker from Pine Road, Runcorn, Cheshire, was awoken by a whirring noise.

"I looked out and saw what looked like a moonbeam on the front path, which vanished but slowly reappeared resembling a 'bowl of fire'. I called out to the rest of the family to come and have a look. By this time the object was now looking like a quarter-moon, with the bottom cut-off. It then moved away, making a whining noise, leaving the sky a glowing pink in colour."

At about the same time, a green flame was seen descending through the sky over Burley, Hampshire, by an auxiliary coastguard based at Hengistbury Head, Dorset (the scene of a number of UFO reports over the years).

Later, the same morning, an object was seen high in the sky over Warminster, performing a number of what appeared to be complicated manoeuvres across the night sky.

(Sources: *Bournemouth Evening Echo*, 6.7.1967/John Hanley, MUFORG)

8th July 1967 – 'Spinning top' UFO over Nottinghamshire

Newark schoolteacher – Bernard Doy, and his wife, were driving through Wellow, near Ollerton, Nottinghamshire, at 9.10pm on Saturday, when they saw what looked like:

"...a child's spinning top, spinning in the air from one side to an upright position, for over forty minutes, surrounded by bright light.

I fetched Police Constable E. Holmes, from Welland Police Station, who had a look through binoculars and said, 'I wouldn't even be able to guess its identity. I'll have to inform Inspector R. Street. He will make some enquiries'."

(Sources: *Nottingham Evening Post*, 10.7.1967 -'Teacher saw spinning top in the sky'/Personal interview)

Over County Durham

At 9.30pm, two schoolgirls – Patricia Hewitt and Sheila Marshall – from Jarrow, County Durham, sighted a bright orange, cigar-shaped object, moving at the speed of a Jet aircraft. It was silently crossing the sky from south-east to north-west, at high altitude. By the time they ran in to alert the family, it had gone out of view. A grey coloured 'disc', surrounded by a silvery glow, was seen in the sky near Dungeness, Kent, on the same evening. (**Source:** *Newcastle Journal*, **10.7.1967** – '**Sky sight terrifies girls**')

10th July 1967 – Triangular UFO Nottinghamshire

At 8.30am, a triangular-shaped object, pure white in colour, was sighted over Radcliffe-on-Trent, Nottinghamshire. (**Source:** *Nottingham Evening Post,* **10.7.1967**)

UFO landing, Isle of Wight

At 8.45am, schoolboys queuing to go into school at Whippingham, near Newport, Isle of Wight, noticed:

> "...a milky-white 'disc' – resembling two saucers, joined together – hovering in the sky, framed by a line of trees in the distance, towards the north, over the Hovercraft Test Tank Research Establishment".

At 10.30am, two boys – John and Kenneth – came out at break time and saw:

> "...an object flying across the sky, then fall downwards, fluttering like a leaf, heading erratically towards the river – much larger than a double-decker bus."

On the same evening, one of the children was on his way home by local bus, when he noticed some strange marks in the barley crop in the field (covering nine fields) adjacent to the Newport-East Cowes road, owned by Farmer John Warne of Coburg Farm, and telephoned the police.

Leonard Cramp

They, in turn, contacted Leonard Cramp – an Aeronautical Engineer with the British Hovercraft Corporation and a member of the Isle of Wight UFO Society. Len carried out an investigation, together with Squadron Leader Bob Cox, Tom Pattison, David Crewman and John Feakins, which lasted over six weeks.

Leonard told us:

> "The first thing I noticed was the witnesses estimated the size of the object. To my question: 'was it a larger object, some distance away, or a smaller object, close up?' Both boys said, 'much larger than a double-decker bus and near the trees at the test tanks'. I later measured the distance from the school to the trees as being 530 yards, which suggests an approximate size of 37 feet – certainly bigger than a double-decker bus. At this point in the investigation I did not attach too much importance of the damage in the barley near the school, thinking

Leonard Cramp

it was more likely to be the result of schoolboys than 'little green men from Mars'! When I did commence an investigation of the field concerned, along with my friend – Bob Cox, he waited until the children had left before he asked me to 'come and have a look at this'. What we found in that field and subsequently in other fields, we did (until the time of writing) keep to ourselves, in order to ensure that the crop of barley would have been safeguarded."

Trail of damage found

"Unknown to the two boys – John and Kenneth – we found a trail which looked like 'a mad thing' had ploughed across the fields for over three quarters of a mile. I discovered a large area, up to six yards wide, of damage in the form of depressed and flattened stalks, which made an almost completely circular pattern. The damage had a very mechanical appearance in a vortex pattern, sometimes clockwise and sometimes anti-clockwise, but predominately clockwise. The centres of some of the vortices had tips with broken stalks and others had nothing. The roots and stalks had disappeared completely. The ears of the corn had been literally threshed and all the grains gone. I spoke with Farmer Warne about the matter. He felt the damage had been caused by something violent – more like a whirlwind – an opinion agreed by Farmer Thomas – an agricultural expert, who visited the area. Effects of a whirlwind just about describe what we found – a mobile whirlwind, a deep trough in the barley which was flattened to the ground in a whirligig pattern, hundreds of feet long and measuring up to 4 yards in width, which ran parallel to Mr Warne's little cart track, until it came to a little shed, where it narrowed somewhat, and then carefully skirted the little structure – as if to avoid knocking it down, despite the fact it was falling down anyway! The young witnesses had said the UFO had wobbled and fluttered. The marks in the barley looked just like that and where the maximum deviations from a straight flight path occurred, there were only baby troughs cut into the barley in semicircular patterns, which were only discernible as they left and re-entered the main troughs. When the corn was parted in one of these little lanes, the stalks were seen to be flattened, making a track several stalks wide only. The whole thing was too mechanic [sic]. One could easily imagine small stabilising verniers correcting the flight path of the UFO. In a word, this pattern was entirely consistent with the description given by the boys, who saw – at a certain position, framed by the reference point of the trees – the craft begin to rise. This exactly coincided with the point at which the track in the barley field narrowed and skirted around the little shed."

Wood pigeon found dead

"At the beginning of the trail, a small wood pigeon lay dead at the roadside; its feathers were scattered along the trail. I had noticed it a few days before when, unknown to me, this strange thing had happened. Following the trail of feathers, I began to find young feathers of a juvenile bird, one here and a few yards further another, sometimes impaled on a stalk, sometimes mingled in with it. I was able to establish that none of the feathers which I found spread over three-quarters of a mile of countryside were duplicated. (A total of 130 wood pigeon feathers were found in one of the troughs). In my opinion, all of the feathers came from the same bird. We also found dozens of large pieces of stone and concrete on top of the pressed barley, pieces of paper, and other material which shouldn't have been where we found it, as if it – along with the wood pigeon and barley – had been uplifted and borne along to be disgorged later. The trail looked as if a 'mad thing' had ploughed across the fields and the effect was similar to that created by a small whirlwind, travelling in a straight line; it was a deep trough in which the barley had been flattened to the ground in a whirligig pattern. In fact there were two layers, as though the leading part of the vortex had snatched the barley in one direction, and the tail had pulled it back the opposite way. The trough was almost straight, except for skirting a little hut. Every few yards there were twisted central tufts of barley, which were found to be numerically spaced, 7'-7'-10'-10'-10'-6'06'- etc.

We are forced to conclude that this was neither the result of a natural whirlwind nor fireball. For me this has been a somewhat awe inspiring experience, investigating what must surely rank as one of the most extensive and up-to-date ground effects on record."

Leonard: Not a whirlwind or fireball

On 2nd March 1968, Leonard gave a detailed account of the incident at Kensington Library. He showed many slides, including aerial stills, coloured stills of the ground, colour cine footage, and interviews recorded with Farmer Warne and the schoolboys involved. Sadly, the whereabouts of this historical material is not currently known.

(Sources: L.G. Cramp, *UFOLOG*, 1967/Personal interview/*Flying Saucer Review*, Volume 14, Number 3, May/June 1968/*Space-link*, Volume 5, Number 2, 1968)

11th July 1967 – UFO over Warwickshire

Mr Frank Rollett and his wife of Sibford Ferris, near Banbury, were driving along the Tredington to Shipston road, in Warwickshire. They saw what resembled: *"a stick of classroom chalk, with a thinner edge leading in the direction of* [sic] *travel across the sky in front of them."*

(Source: John 'Dennis' Llewellyn/*Stratford-on-Avon Herald*, 14.7.1967)

13th July 1967 – Red 'Saucer', Sussex

A red, saucer-shaped object, surrounded by a bright halo of light, was seen motionless in the sky over West Howes, Sussex.

Later, the same evening, a purple object was sighted in the sky over Wimborne, Dorset, and at Fair Oaks, in Hampshire, a brilliant orange, egg-shaped object, showing dark bands running along its face, was seen moving across the sky.

(Source: *Bournemouth Evening Echo*, 13.7.1967/*UFOLOG*)

14th July 1967 – Motorists followed by UFO at Essex and Northumberland

Essex man Edward Rouse (69) of 4, Rayleigh Road, Hillbridge, Essex, was driving his taxi home at 2.35am, along the A127. He said:

"Suddenly, this massive, flashing, dome-shaped object passed overhead. I swerved all over the road and found myself the wrong way around, facing the Southend-on-sea direction. It had a dome on top with white light, and red, green and yellow, smaller ones around the outside of the middle."

Mrs W. Potts from Morpeth, Northumberland, reported having been followed home by an orange 'disc', at 11pm. When her family rushed outside to have a look, they saw:

"...a large orange 'disc', moving across the sky 10 degrees above the horizon, apparently following overhead power lines". (Source: TUFOS/*UFOLOG*, August 1967, Issue 38)

15th July 1967 – 'Flying Saucer' over Isle of Wight

At 10.45am, an object resembling an Adamski-style 'Flying Saucer' was seen for twenty seconds in the sky over Carisbrooke, Isle of Wight. The witness was schoolboy John Smith, who was playing outside Carisbrooke Grammar School.

"The object was round in shape and not unlike the 'Adamski Saucer'. It was tilted at an angle of 45 degrees, heading from east to west, over Parkhurst Forest. It then seemed to hover over the centre of the forest for about five seconds, before carrying on. It was silver in colour and the size of a sixpence, held at arm's length."

(Source: Len Cramp Isle of Wight Society)

15th July 1967 – Cyclists sight dome-shaped UFO at Sedalia, Missouri

At Sedalia, Missouri, two people were out riding their cycles about a mile out of the town, as dusk fell [the sky was still well illuminated with clouds that were easily seen] when they saw:

> "...a grey, metallic 'disc' rise up from behind a cloud in the northern sky. It had a dull non-reflective surface, flattened at its base, domed on the top, and was about the size of a dime held at arm's length. It descended into or behind a cloud, then reappeared 30 seconds later. It rose to the same height as before, moved into the cloud again, and that was the last we saw of it." (**Source:** 'Skylook')

16th July 1967 – White sphere with revolving lights, Tyneside

At 8.25am, a bright white sphere with a number of red, green, yellow, and blue lights around its diameter – slightly larger than the moon – was seen in the sky over Newcastle-on-Tyne. This was followed by a report of *"a bright white sphere, with a number of lights revolving around its rim, slightly larger than the moon in size"*, seen motionless in the sky over Longbenton, Newcastle-upon-Tyne, at 10.35pm.

18th July 1967 – Clusters of objects over European airbases

Clusters of objects, streaming trails of light across the sky, were sighted by airline pilots over the Kent coast, English Channel, France, Germany and Switzerland, including the airbases of Ramstein, Spangdahlem and Sembach.

According to a USAF spokesman, *"they looked like they had flames coming out of them"*.

In Switzerland, many people told of sighting what looked like 'cylinders', or 'cigar-shaped lights' seen crossing over the country, leaving red luminous trails several miles long. Fifty seconds later they had gone. The authorities explained them away as being either a shower of meteorites, or the light of the moon descending across electrically charged clouds, or even a small comet passing close to Earth, whilst others favoured the re-entry of a satellite into the Earth's atmosphere.

(**Sources:** *Evening News*, 18.7.1967 – 'Pilots tell of mystery 'Fire Balls'/*Evening Standard*, 18.7.1967 – 'Riddle of the lights in the night sky')

UFOs over County Durham – RAF attempt intercept

At 10.30pm, a flickering red domed object, showing three white lights around its side, approximately 900 feet off the ground, was observed motionless in the eastern sky over Stanley, County Durham, by Mr R.K. Fallow. Within a short time it was seen to head away at speed, moving westwards. (**Source:** *UFOLOG*)

Another witness was Mr Brian Ford of Allendale Cottages, County Durham, who was sitting on a grassy slope, opposite Hedley on the Hill, watching out for foxes, at 10.30pm, when he noticed:

> "...six, grey 'disc-like' objects with flashing orange centres, hovering just above the brow of the hill."

Mr Ford rushed home and told his wife and neighbour – Mrs L. Reah, what he had seen. They laughed but, due to his insistence, decided to go and have a look themselves, accompanied by another neighbour – Mrs Richardson.

When they arrived at the location, at 11pm, the objects were still there.

> "Suddenly, they split up into smaller objects and began to move along the valley. A RAF jet fighter appeared and began to play what looked like a game of 'tag' with the UFOs, before disappearing from view." (The RAF later denied any knowledge of this incident.)

These sightings were subsequently explained away by the local newspaper as possibly being a cloud, catching the rays of the setting sun. At 1.30am, the flashing objects returned to the same position in the sky. At 2.30am all six of the objects flew away towards the direction of the new Derwent Reservoir, and were lost from view. (**Source:** TUFOS)

19th July 1967 – Six bright 'discs', County Durham

At 2am, *"six bright red 'discs', with deeper red pulsating centres, emitting yellow and orange flashes"*, were seen flying in 'stop and start' movements across the sky, north-west to west along the Derwent Valley, over Allendale Cottages, County Durham, by Mrs L. Reah.

(Sources: The *Stanley News*, 20.7.1967 – 'The Martians arrive'/*Newcastle Journal,* 11.8.1967 – 'Strangers in the night'/*Newcastle Journal,* 18.8.1967 – 'Flying Saucer seen again'/Personal visit to the location and interview of parties concerned by Tyneside UFO Society)

Over Scotland

"A silver 'ball', with red sparks trailing from it", was reported motionless in the sky over Carnoustie Golf Course, Scotland, at an estimated height of 20,000 feet. (**Source:** *Daily Record,* **20.6.1967**)

On the same day, Jessie Robley of Shotley Bridge, and Robert Telford, were walking towards Allendale Cottages, when they saw a 'silver disc' hovering over the valley. Frightened, the couple ran home.
(Source: TUFOS)

Andover 'Flying Saucer'

At 10.45pm, Andover couple – Tony and Ann Waters – happened to look out of the window of their flat, which overlooks the town towards St. Mary's Church:

> "My wife saw what she took to be a helicopter in the sky. I looked more closely, as it was totally silent, and saw a half-moon shaped object – like an upside-down crescent – its light pulsing brighter, then dimmer. It seemed to hover in two places at once. It's difficult to describe, but it was in one place one minute, then it moved a few feet to one side and continued to hover. It gradually moved to the right and seemed to come right round in a half circle, a bit closer, making this whining drone. It then moved slowly around and disappeared over the rooftops to my right."

Enquiries made with the police at Andover, and the Army Air Corps, revealed nothing that might have explained away what the couple had seen – although it was later established that a helicopter had been flying over the town, but this was unlikely to have been the answer.
(Sources: Andover Ufologists/*Andover Advertiser,* 21.6.1967 – 'UFO sighted over Andover')

20th July 1967 – Photograph taken of UFO, Cheshire

At 9.15pm, Kenneth Swain – a technical illustrator by occupation, from Alderley Edge (five miles north-west of Macclesfield, in Cheshire) – happened to sight something unusual in the sky. Reacting quickly, he picked-up his Yashica camera, loaded with film, and took a photograph at 130th of a second, at 45mm, F2.8. Unfortunately, the whereabouts of that photograph are not known, although we came across an illustration sent to the Isle of Wight UFO Society, which is intriguing, but sadly can only be taken on its own merits.

Over Trowbridge

At 9.45pm on the same day, an object – described as resembling a 'spinning top' – was sighted over Trowbridge, Wiltshire, moving at speed in a south-east to north-east direction.

At 10pm, an orange, domed, object was seen motionless in the sky over Cambois, Blythe, Northumberland, by Mr R. Jackson, who was with his daughter and three others, walking along the beach. After fifteen minutes, it gradually flattened to cigar in shape before disappearing. Was it a cloud, caught by the red rays of the sun?

Over London

At 10pm, a round bright 'light', with a 'ring' around the middle, was seen motionless in the southern sky over Finsbury Park, London. A few minutes later, it faded away from sight. **(Source: Ken Rogers)**

Andover sighting

At 11pm, a former member of the Royal Observer Corps, and his wife, saw what they first took to be a helicopter hovering over the Town Centre, at Andover. Closer inspection revealed:

> "...a half-moon shaped object – like an upside-down crescent – pulsating with light that dimmed and grew brighter, which gradually came around to the right and completed a half circle, moving a little closer – at which point a faint whining noise could be heard."

Ten minutes later it moved away over the nearby roofs, before being lost from view.
(Source: Andover Ufologists)

Darlington

At about the same time and date, three men – Mr Hetherington, Mr Hull and Mr Robinson – from Coronation Gardens, Staindrop, Darlington, sighted:

> "...a white/orange object moving through the sky, heading south-east, emitting flashes of light, which lasted at least ten seconds in duration, followed by a faint 'thumping' or 'banging' noise".

UFO over South Wales

Just before midnight, Clive Menadue – then living in Beech Road, Sunny Bank, Pyle, South Wales – was standing in the back garden of his house, on a warm, summer's evening. He saw what at first he took to be a reflection of light, fairly low on the horizon, followed by what appeared to be a red 'star' moving swiftly across the sky, which took up a position close to the source of light. He said:

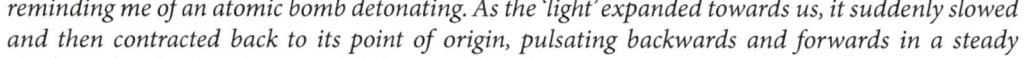

> "I shouted for my wife, Sylvia, to come and have a look at this 'red star', which was flashing red and white. At the same time, a flash of bright light silently exploded across the night sky – like a magnesium flare – reminding me of an atomic bomb detonating. As the 'light' expanded towards us, it suddenly slowed and then contracted back to its point of origin, pulsating backwards and forwards in a steady rhythm, illuminating the ground below and the sky above. In the centre of the light could be seen a huge circular cloud-like object, with a similar, smaller, one attached to its top right-hand corner. Both of the cloud-like objects then began to rotate in a clockwise direction; the smaller one moving away, leaving what looked like two thick 'smoke rings' in the sky. I saw the smaller object return to above dead centre of the larger one and appear to emerge with it – now resembling a 'potter's wheel' – before changing into a saucer-shaped image, with an opaque glassy surface reflecting the spinning light."

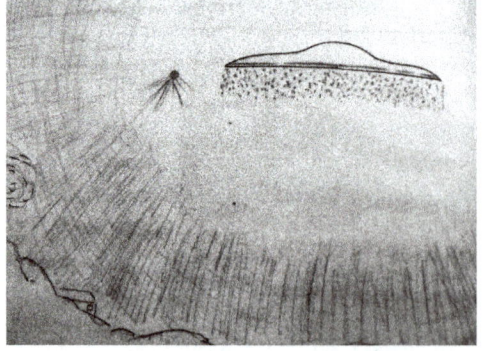

As a result of local newspaper publicity, Clive was contacted by a number of people, who suggested a variety of explanations, including misidentification of factory lights, the moon, a helicopter, or too much drink!

(Sources: Personal interview/*South Wales Echo*, 23.7.1970 – 'The night he thought an atom bomb had fallen')

22nd July 1967 – Red 'disc', Newcastle-on-Tyne

At 10.22pm, a red 'disc' shaped object, emitting yellow flashes, was seen in the sky over Newcastle-on-Tyne, for one minute, by Tyneside UFO Society member – Mr Frank Satterthwaite, and others. It disappeared into cloud cover.

23rd July 1967 – Pink halo hovering in the sky, Merseyside

A pink halo, surrounded by a broad band, was seen hovering in the sky over Prenton, near Birkenhead, before disappearing in a flash of light. **(Source:** *Birkenhead News, 23.8.1967)*

24th July 1967 – Questions in Parliament

An extract from Hansard tells of another question put to the Secretary of State for Defence – Merlyn Rees, by Edward M. Taylor, on the 24th July 1967, asking him,

> *"What information has he regarding reports of unidentified flying objects, in recent months, and if he will make a statement".*

Mr Rees:

> *"Such reports are investigated, but nothing of defence interest has been found."*

What would Mr Rees have made of an object seen to drop down from the sky over Walton, near Peterborough, on the same date?

It was described as a thirty feet silver sphere. Even if he had known about this, and the other hundreds of UFO sightings from that year, we cannot be that naïve to believe he would have admitted it to the public.

(Source: *Peterborough Evening Telegraph, 28.7.1967)*

July – UFO over Staffordshire

John Bradbury from Sneyd Green, Staffordshire, was playing with a friend and his dog, outside his house in Station Road, Mow Cop, near Kidsgrove, one afternoon in July 1967, when they noticed:

> *"…a yellow metallic spinning object, 30-40 feet across and 5-10 feet in height, rising above trees to their right, at an angle of 15 degrees off the horizon over the north-east direction. It rose to a great height – almost into the clouds – and then headed downwards, towards us, before shooting away over the Cheshire Plain to the right of Jodrell Bank, making this slight humming noise."*

(Source: Tony Pace)

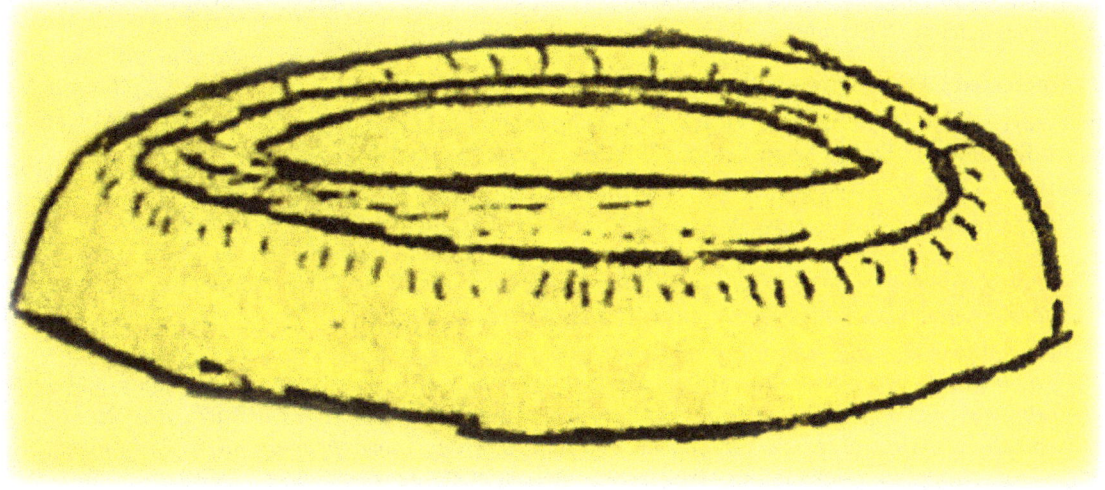

Letter from the Prime Minister

In July 1967, Julian Hennessey received a communication from The Rt. Hon. Harold Wilson, OBE, PC, MP – then Prime Minister of the United Kingdom, stating:

"As reports of these objects (UFOs) continue to appear from many parts of the world, it is quite understandable that there should be a growing interest in seeing some responsible effort made to seek explanations of these phenomena."

30th July 1967 – Golden 'square' – MOD sightings not revealed to public

At 2.30pm, a curious *"ten feet gold coloured 'square', with flashing white lights"*, was seen moving across the sky over Haywards Heath, Sussex, in short bursts of speed. It was close to the main flight corridor into Gatwick Airport. The witnesses – David and Patricia Wise – contacted the Sussex Police.

Eight hours later, at 10.45pm, a couple from Pease Pottage were driving home when they saw a pulsating 'white light', hovering overhead, near the Pease Pottage crossroads.

"We thought it was a helicopter, or plane, to start with. It didn't seem to be moving. All of a sudden, it then darted forwards at a rate of knots, and gradually faded away."

A MOD spokesman said:

"The incident would have been investigated, but results are never revealed to the public. In any case, we only investigate sightings to see if they are a defence threat and, if not, we lose interest. UFOs often turn out to be meteorological balloons, crop spraying airplanes or even a reflection of clouds or trees."

(Source: *Mid Sussex Times*, Haywards Heath, August 1967 – 'Flying Shreddie's second sightings')

30th July 1967 – Bell-shaped 'mass', three rows of 'portholes'

During the late night of the 30th July and the 1st August 1967, a bell-shaped mass, with lights shining from 'portholes' or 'windows', was seen in the sky over Bishopbriggs, by at least twelve people. It had a glowing red domed top, and a broad strip of white light around its base, and was accompanied by a humming noise – like a dynamo. One of the witnesses was George Jerritt – a night supervisor at a school. He said:

"I saw the object quite clearly. It was about two miles away and 500 feet up, moving slowly through the sky over Lambhill. It was shaped more like a bell than a saucer; at the top was a large circular dome, which glowed bright red. As I watched it, the part between the red dome and the base suddenly lit up. It looked like three rows of portholes. Prior to the sighting I would have said these things don't exist, but after seeing it I know they do."

Increased UFO activity – Letter to Ken Rogers

In a letter sent to Ken Rogers of Vicar's Lane, London, by Mr G.N.P. Stephenson – BUFORA's Central Co-ordinator, of 12 Dorset Road, Cheam, Surrey, we learn the following:

"We are now receiving reports of UFOs from all over the country, at a rate that has never been surpassed during the years we have existed. After a 'lull before the storm' from mid-March to mid-April, landings were reported on April 13th and from that date we have received on average one interesting report per day, which is exceptional, and since the middle of the month (July), the rate has stepped up to at least two interesting reports per day.

Like last summer, the tendency is for almost 50 per cent of reports received to be of interest to the extent that there is reason to consider the possibility of their representing unusual phenomena (although many of these are bound to have conventional explanations, while it is a matter of opinion as to what proportion of these do, in fact, represent unknown phenomena) and practically all these interesting observations take place at night, after 10pm.

There have also been a number of interesting daytime sightings this year, and several good photographs; unfortunately, it is difficult ever to be certain that a photograph is not a fake. All we can do is to decide on those that look as if they could quite easily be faked, or force a confession from the 'witness'. [Authors: Strong words, to say the least! Meant metaphorically rather than physical extraction, we presume!]

While it would be even more exceptional if the increase in reports built up still further, we hope people throughout the country, on seeing anything unusual, will report their observations immediately to the Press, national or local, or the police, who are requested in turn to pass on the information to us immediately, so that we may be quite up-to-date with the turn of events and ensure that all sightings, and particularly landing cases, are investigated with the minimum of delay."

July 1967 – Close encounter near RAF Lyneham

The wife of a RAF Officer, stationed at RAF Lyneham, contacted Leslie Harris – the Bournemouth-based UFO researcher – with a disturbing story. It took place while she was living (with her son, aged three) in a small caravan at Bradenstoke, near Lyneham, Wiltshire:

"One clear and calm night, I happened to look out of the window and notice an orange 'globe of light' stationary in the sky to the south-west, which then vanished but reappeared in another part of the sky – now much brighter and shining from inside a dark, cigar-shaped object. The 'light' then extinguished, leaving a faint line showing where the 'cigar' was. Over the next 20 minutes, the orange 'light' jumped about all over the sky, until darkness closed in, when I decided to draw the curtains and sit in front of the TV, meaning to bring the matter to my husband's attention when he arrived home. About an hour and a half later, I began to experience a peculiar sensation, like a physical pressing coming from the end of the caravan, which increased in strength, forcing my body against the wall of the caravan – so powerful I thought I was going to pass out – then it stopped."

According to Robert Webb, the investigator in this case, the witness was to experience similar sporadic 'bouts' of the uncomfortable sensations over the years, beginning a couple of weeks afterwards, usually lasting for between a few seconds, sometimes for up to a minute,

"...as if something was covering my body; when I get frightened the feeling switches off instantly. It's been happening about once a week, despite various house moves. My father, who is a doctor, was unable to diagnose the problem".

Previous to the incident, the woman had no interest in the UFO subject. However, after the event she spent some time visiting Cradle Hill, Warminster, with her husband. On one occasion she was interviewed by the *BBC Nationwide* camera team, who were visiting the location. Despite seeking further medical assistance, the doctors failed to discover the cause of the condition. (**Source:** *Scan*, **Number 17, January 1979**)

July – Five lights reported

An ex-Longley Junior School, Doncaster pupil – Graham Smith – wrote to us about what he saw, at the age of ten, while walking to school in July 1967:

"I noticed a group of five lights in the sky. Three of them then began to move in and out at different angles. I rushed home, very excited, and told my parents what had taken place. They just laughed at me, but I know what I saw and have never forgotten it."

Summer – 'Flying Saucer' over Lincolnshire

Mavis Sergeant, from Derbyshire, contacted us with regard to a mysterious encounter with a saucer-shaped object, while staying at Ingoldmells caravan site, Lincolnshire, in the summer of 1967 – an annual holiday made by the family, many times, throughout the years.

Haunted Skies Volume Two Revised

"As we approached the entrance to the caravan site, we noticed what appeared to be a fairground wheel, low in the sky at the site, accompanied by the sound of fairground music. At the time I didn't give it much thought, until about a week into the holiday, when, while strolling back to the caravan with my two young children, waiting for my husband to catch up, all of a sudden I experienced a strange sensation, as if someone, or something, was watching us.

I looked around and saw, with amazement, a small silver saucer-shaped object, about six feet in length, with lights on its base, hovering in the air approximately six feet above the line of caravans. I was so excited I could hardly get the words out. I pointed it out to the children, one of whom burst into tears, excitement turning to fear, and began to urge the children forward as it slowly descended into a field at the back, before being lost from sight. When my husband arrived, I told him what we had just seen, expecting him to laugh at me. Imagine my surprise when he told me he had sensed something which had made him feel very uneasy, although he hadn't been able to identify the source!"

Just before the family left the site, Mavis asked one of the holidaymakers, out of interest, what had happened to the fair? She was astonished to discover no fairs had ever been held at that site.

AUGUST 1967

1st August 1967 – 'Figure of eight' movements, Lancashire

Mrs I. Docherty of Heysham, Lancashire, happened to be looking out over Morecambe Bay, at 12.45pm, when she saw a round object flying over the bay, in a curious 'figure of eight' movement – *"like a wheel turning half left and then half right, zigzagging through the air"*.

(Source: *Milngavie and Bearsden Herald*, 6.8.1967)

2nd August 1967 – Flat silver 'disc' and something strange at Birmingham

In the early hours, a round, flattened, object was seen travelling across the night sky over Maidstone, Kent, leaving behind three or four shafts of light, which slowly faded away. At 6am, another white object was seen over Light Oaks, Stoke-on-Trent, followed by a report, thirty minutes later, of an object resembling *"a flat, silver 'disc',"* seen heading towards Bucknall, Derbyshire. Other UFO sightings told of *"a metallic 'disc', estimated to be 80 feet in diameter with a bright red dome"*, seen over Kidsgrove, Staffordshire, at an approximate height of 700 feet.

Later the same day, a glowing red domed object was seen flying over Arbroath, Aberdeen, followed by an interruption in the electricity supply. (**Source:** *Aberdeen Press and Journal,* 8.8.1967)

Close Encounter, Warwickshire

Something far more frightening happened to Birmingham couple – Terry Sproson, and girlfriend Christine Arkless – at 10.15pm, while parked in the Rubery area, a few miles from Frankley Beeches Reservoir.

Terry said:

> *"Something, or someone, came close to the car in which we were parked. It appeared to be looking in at the rear window on the driver's side and glided to the front side window. When I attempted to lock the car door, it moved back."* (**Source: Derek Samson – NICAP, GB**)

3rd August 1967 – UFOs over Berkshire

A 'bright rotating light', constantly changing colour from orange to red, was seen to pass through the sky over Abingdon, Berkshire.

4th August 1967 – UFO display over Lancashire

A 'bright light' was seen over Heysham, Lancashire, accompanied by a humming noise. Within seconds it had disappeared from view.

In addition to this sighting was a report of two bright 'lights', one of which constantly flickered, seen darting about in the sky over Lincolnshire, during the early evening.

Stoke-on-Trent

At 11.10pm the same evening, Mr and Mrs Brogan of Kidsgrove, Stoke-on-Trent, were bidding goodnight to their neighbours, Mr and Mrs Turner (who lived opposite), when they saw what at first they took to be a 'shooting star', moving northwards across the sky – until it changed direction and moved towards them.

> *"The object, approximately the size of two bungalows put together, possibly 80-90 feet across – now visible as a metallic 'disc', with a bright red dome on top and fifteen to twenty bright red lights revolving beneath – slowed down, descended, and almost came to a standstill above the bungalows at the top of Brieryhurst Road. After hovering for a few seconds, the object disappeared at a fantastic rate over the houses, on a westwards course. As it went, the lights stopped flashing."*

Tony Pace

(Sources: Tony Pace, Roger Stanway, BUFORA/*Morecambe & Heysham Visitor,* 9.8.1967/ Kath Smith, Isle of Wight UFO Society/*Reading Evening Post,* 7.8.1967)

5th August 1967 – UFOs over Mount Snowdon – Did RAF Jets respond?

A motorist driving past Capel Curig, in Gwynedd, sighted an object looking like *"two traditional Welsh hats, riveted together, travelling at an angle, approximately over Mount Snowdon – apparently following the contours of the valley – out-of-sight within 20 seconds"*.

Ten or fifteen minutes later, three English Electric Lightning RAF Jets were seen to shoot across the sky and head towards where the UFO had been seen. **(Source: Jenny Randles, UFOIN)**

5th August 1967 – 'Glowing 'mass' over Reading

"An orange 'disc', with sweeping searchlights dimming and then brightening alternatively", was seen swaying from side-to-side in the sky over Burghfield, near Reading, by Philip Bird – a schoolboy from The Willink School, (who first thought it to be factory lights in the distance, until it came closer). Another witness to this event was Peter Middleton, a resident of Tilehurst, Reading, who was driving home with his wife, Joyce, and daughter, Susan, towards Burghfield, at 11.30pm:

> *"We noticed this curious yellow glowing 'mass', hovering over a field, 2-300 yards away, close to the Royal Ordnance factory.*
>
> *I stopped the car and we watched – until it moved away. I have to admit that the hairs on the back of my neck stood up."*

An orange/white 'globe of light' was seen flying slowly in a 'stop and start' motion, south-east to North-north-west, at an elevation of 90 degrees across the sky, over Gateshead, at 11.50pm the same evening.

6th August 1967 – UFO activity reported over Kent

Two round, silver, objects were sighted in the sky close to the Medway Bridge, Chatham, in Kent.
(Source: *Chatham Observer*, **Kent, 11.8.1967)**

7th August 1967 – Three red lights seen over Newark, and flashing red light – Nottinghamshire

At 9.30pm on 7th August 1967, *"a small oval object, showing three red lights along its side"*, was seen passing through the sky over Shotley Bridge, County Durham, by local man Nigel McCann from Moorlands Road, Consett, before being lost from view as it dropped down below houses on the horizon.
(Source: TUFOS)

At 10.15pm, Dave Robinson from Newark, Nottinghamshire, was out walking with his girlfriend in a small clearing at the side of Stapleford Woods, about three miles away from the town, when his girlfriend brought his attention to two 'lights' in the sky.

Dave looked up and saw two round, or slightly oval 'lights', about half-a-mile away, resembling two pieces of yellow paper, 6 x 5 feet in diameter, hovering over a line of trees:

> *"Within minutes they disappeared, replaced by a flashing red light, which moved to our right, climbing up and over some trees.*
>
> *Five minutes later, we saw the lights again in the sky – now on our right – coming towards us, about a quarter-of-a-mile away. My curiosity aroused, I drove slowly towards the lights, losing sight of them as I drove around a bend. When I reached the spot where I had seen them, I flashed my headlights and this 'craft' appeared over the trees. Astonished, I stopped the car and listened – still no sound. We watched the 'craft' with amazement, as it hovered twenty feet away from us and about the same height off the ground, allowing us to see it had a curved base and top with three squared windows spilling out orange light, and a brilliant light projecting downwards from the top. As it moved overhead I became frightened and drove away, fearing what was going to happen next."*

(Source: Personal interview/William Blythe, Mansfield, Nottinghamshire)

Between the 6th and 9th August 1967, *"an eerie red light"* was seen in the sky on a number of occasions over Kidsgrove and Weston, Staffordshire, accompanied by a strange noise which continued to be heard into the night after the red light had gone. **(Source:** *Staffordshire Advertiser,* **10.8.1967)**

8th August 1967 – Lancashire Police officers sight UFO

At 12.43am, PC Lionel Haw, of the Lancashire Constabulary, was on foot patrol in Liverpool Road, Hindley, when he noticed a glowing object moving through the sky. A short time later, the officer was approached by PC Parsonage, who directed his attention towards *"an orange saucer-shaped object, estimated to be hundreds of feet in diameter, motionless in the sky"*. Within minutes, it was out of sight.

PC Haw was to write the following into his pocket book:

"12.43am. Liverpool Road, Hindley, saw an object in sky, high altitude, travelling east, fast speed, round shape, not plane or comet, also seen by PC Parsonage."

Shortly afterwards, PC Haw was contacted by colleagues – Police Constables Peter Morris and Robert Young, from Bredbury Police Station, Cheshire – who told him they had sighted:

"...a glowing white saucer-shaped object, stationary in the cloudless sky for about two minutes. It certainly wasn't any comet, weather balloon, plane, or trick of light. It was very high; we would say it looked to be about 100 feet in diameter. Seconds later, it disappeared from sight."

Inspector Albert Jordan, in charge of Hindley Police Station, later told reporters:

"Both men are very reliable and are trained observers; they would not say they had seen it if it was not true."

During the same morning, a similar object was seen over Farnworth – described as 80-100 feet in diameter, glowing pink and revolving. We were to come across many similar reports, involving a huge 'flash of light' which appeared to precede the appearance of a UFO, followed by its rapid disappearance to who knows where?

(Sources: *Daily Mail*, 17.8.1967/*The Times*, 16.8.1967/*Liverpool Echo/Western Daily Press* (Bristol edition) 17.8.1967, 18.8.1967,19.8.1967/*News of the World/Daily Mirror*, 16.8.1967)

9th August 1967 – UFO over Hindley, Liverpool

At 10pm Hindley, Liverpool, mechanic Michael Cox was indoors with his girlfriend – typist, Kathleen Mawdsley – watching, of all things, *My favourite Martian* on the TV, when his brother, Bernard, came in to tell them that the UFO he had seen, ten days previously, over Eckersley Avenue, Hindley, was back! They rushed outside to join neighbours already outside. The two boys went one way in their A35 car (striking some pit heaps, causing slight damage to the sump), leaving Kathleen to conduct her own search on foot. When they returned home, she told them she had seen:

"...a conical silver object, showing green and purple lights along the sides, with an orange dome on top, as it began to zigzag across the sky making a low humming sound as it moved away."

(Sources: UFOLOG/*South West News*, Lancashire – 'That Saucer over Hindley again and causes crash'/*Daily Mail* – 'Flying Saucer scout prangs an oil sump')

10th August 1967 – UFO 'Triangle of lights', Northumberland

At 11.30pm, 'a point of light' was seen moving through the sky over Cramlington, Northumberland, by Mr Middleton and his next door neighbour, before coming to a stop. This was joined by four others, at approximately five minute intervals, *"three of which formed a triangle"*, while the other two moved away in the north and west direction. By 12.10am on 11th August, they had all left – apart from one 'light', which continued to maintain its position in the sky.

Small objects were seen in the sky over Stafford around this date, showing blue lights and apparently rotating, accompanied by strange sounds. At Weston, a red glowing object was reported to have been seen moving up and down in the air.

(Sources: Wilfred Daniels/*Staffordshire Advertiser*, 10.8.1967)

11th August 1967 – 'Red hot poker' seen in sky over Wolverhampton

A crescent-shaped object, resembling *"a bent red hot poker"*, was seen in the sky over Blackheath, Wolverhampton.

Other witnesses told of seeing a strange orange 'ball', which split into two smaller parts, shrink in size, and then fade from view. (**Source:** *Wolverhampton Express and Star,* **10.8.1967**)

August 1967 – Cheshire motorist confronted by triangular UFO

A motorist, driving home at 60 miles per hour, near Northwich, Cheshire, during the early hours of one August morning, was shocked to see *"a triangular glowing object"*, estimated to be 60 feet in height, moving through the sky in front of him. He said:

"It then returned and cut across my path. I was so frightened that I stopped my car and awoke a man living in a nearby house, to prove to myself I wasn't imagining it. I asked him to look up into the sky – which he did. Clearly frightened, he told me to leave. As I continued on my journey it was still with me for about four miles, until it headed away northwards and disappeared from sight. I stopped off at a local police station and told them what I had seen."

(Sources: **Letter to Isle of Wight UFO Society**/*News of the World* – date not known)

14th August 1967 – Triangular UFO over Leeds

At 10pm – a clear, warm, still night – Carol O'Rourke and Harold Shaw from Leeds, in Yorkshire, were outside when they sighted a bright object in the south of the sky, heading east, described as *"triangular-shaped, like a 'V' bomber moving backwards."*

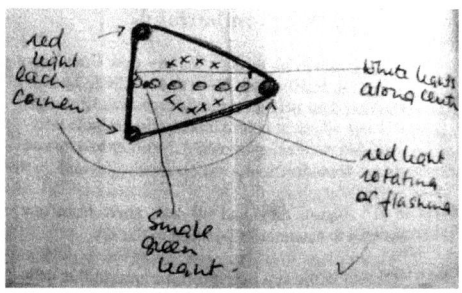

Was this an early arrival of the object, later labelled as the 'Triangular UFO', which was to make its debut on the European stage during the early 1980s, not forgetting the enormous number of previously unpublished sightings over Essex, during the mid 1990s?

'Flying Saucer' over Newcastle

At 11pm on the same date, Mr and Mrs Haines were walking down a steep hill, overlooking the Team Valley Trading Estate, when they saw *"a huge bright orange and black, dome-shaped craft"*, apparently revolving from right to left, hovering close to the Pontop Pike radio mast. After a few minutes, it disappeared from view.

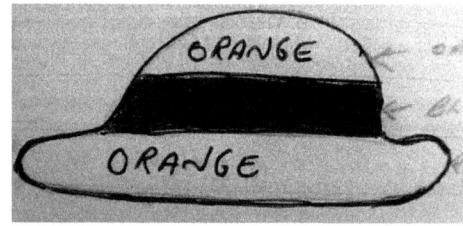

Other reports tell of two 'lights' seen hovering over a Lincoln housing estate, for 30 minutes, during the evening. (**Sources: Kath Smith, Isle of Wight UFO Society**/*Lincoln Daily Echo,* **15.8.1967**)

15th August 1967 – Cigar-shaped object in the sky over Cornwall

A cigar-shaped object, throwing off blue light, was seen in the sky over Cornwall, (**Source:** *Cornish and Devon Post,* **18.8.1967**), whilst, to the North, a curious 'red globe' was seen zigzagging across the sky over Wigan. (**Source:** *Daily Mail,* **Manchester, 18.8.1967**)

Over Stockport

At 10.45pm the same evening, a Mr Cunningham of Shaw Heath, Stockport, Cheshire, was with neighbours when they sighted *"two bright shimmering white lights, attached to a grey object"*, hovering over Cheadle Heath Reservoir, before being seen to head off towards the town centre at amazing speed. Later, the same day, a glowing pink revolving flat object, approximately 100 feet in diameter, was sighted over Farnworth, near Bolton. (**Sources:** *Space-link,* Edgar Hatvany/*Bolton Evening News,* 17.8.1967)

UFO over Reddish, Manchester

Between 11.45pm (15th August 1967) and 12.15am the following morning, Mr and Mrs Warburton, and her three daughters (then living in South Reddish) noticed a dome-shaped object, hovering just above the Dodge Hill flats.

> *"It moved up and down, then to the right-hand side of the flats, but could still be seen partially between the flats and adjacent buildings. I first thought the place was on fire. It was brighter than the moon, and giving off a colour resembling a magnesium flare.*
>
> *My daughters fetched the car to follow it, but by then it had moved away from us and was now near the tall chimney at Brinksway.* (**Source:** Mr A. Tomlinson, DIGAP)

The Warburton family were not the only ones to sight a UFO that day. Was there a connection with mystery power failures that affected several towns in the Yorkshire area, during this month? A Yorkshire electricity spokesman said:

> *"We are not sure what has caused the trouble. It could be that a transformer at the Sowerby Bridge Power Station has failed."*

16th August 1967 – Silver UFO over County Durham

At 4pm, Miss J. Robley of Shotley Bridge, County Durham, was walking towards Allendale Cottages, with a friend, when they sighted:

> *"...a silver, elongated object, with what appeared to be portholes along its side, flying through the air at treetop level, heading towards the direction of Newcastle."*

At 4.30pm, two cigar-shaped objects, moving in close formation, were seen in the sky above Weeton, Otley, Yorkshire, *"like an aircraft, without wings".*

Over Eccles, a spinning 'silver top' shaped object was seen, which became flatter before fading away.
(**Source:** *Bolton Evening News,* 17.8.1967)

16th August 1966 – UFO sighted by two schoolgirls over Cheshire

Another 'triangular object' was seen over Northwich, Cheshire, this time involving two schoolgirls – Christine Hardy and Linda Hardy, from Weaverham County Secondary School – who were returning home from a walk along Forest Street, at 9.30pm, when they saw:

> *"...a yellow glowing, triangular object, with a whiter light around its well-defined edges, moving horizontally slowly through the sky, low down, before disappearing vertically into the clouds. We were both frightened, we thought it may have been a new sort of Jet plane, but next day we saw in the newspapers that two policemen had sighted a similar object, near Manchester".*

At 9.15pm, Mr and Mrs Metcalfe from Harrogate, Yorkshire, were on holiday in Anglesey, close to RAF Valley, when they saw a cluster of red lights in the sky. Through binoculars, *"four cones or triangular-shaped lights could be seen changing colour from red to green, before heading westwards".* On the same day, an object – looking like a 'spinning top' – was seen over Eccles, Bolton.
(**Source:** *Bolton Evening News,* 17.8.1967)

UFO over Norwich

Kenneth Dutton – a Norwich fireman – was another witness to something inexplicable seen in the sky.

"It seemed to be spinning. Through night glasses, I could make out what appeared to be lights around the outside. They seemed to keep changing in colour from red, green and white, and gave off a yellowy glow. I watched the object for 45 minutes before losing sight of it."

17th August 1967 – Silver metallic UFO stationary in sky over Harrogate

A silver metallic object was seen stationary in the sky over Harrogate, followed by a brilliant white light seen over Hessle, near Hull, making a strange humming noise.

(Sources: *Harrogate Advertiser,* 26.8.1967/*Hull Daily Mail,* 18.8.1967/*Yorkshire Post,* 18.8.1967)

A dome-shaped UFO was seen over Hindley by at least thirty people, who came running out into the street to see the UFO pass overhead (which appears identical to what was seen over the locality, ten days later). (Source: *UFOLOG*)

18th August 1967 – Pulsating UFO over Kent

A pulsating black and orange cigar-shaped object, making a noise like a heavy transport aircraft, was sighted in the sky over Bromley, Kent, on the 18th August 1967. (Source: *Bromley & Kentish Times*, 25.8.1967)

19th August 1967 – Purple and green UFO over Liverpool

This was followed by reports of an unidentified flying object seen over Liverpool. It was described as being 2-300 feet across, showing windows and purple and green lights. The object was flying low, and it was hypothesised that it was the cause of interference with television reception which was reported in the area. Domestic animals were also said to be alarmed.

One of the witnesses was Bernard Cox from Hindley, near Wigan (then aged 17), who had no problem remembering the incident when we spoke to him, many years later.

"I was home with the family when we heard all the dogs in the locality barking frenziedly, accompanied by this strange humming noise – loud enough to wake-up my grandmother, who suffers from deafness. Wondering what was happening, we all rushed outside and were astonished to see a silver coloured object with violet lights around it. The top of the object had something resembling a red plastic surface and what appeared to be a strip of black windows inset".

(Source: *Liverpool Echo,* 22.8.1967)

20th August 1967 – Two silver 'discs' over Manchester

At 6.30pm, *"two silver 'discs', one above the other"*, were seen hovering in the sky for fifteen minutes, over Belle Vue, Gorton, Manchester, before moving off towards the City Centre. Later that evening, a bright red, huge, object was sighted moving at speed over Waterhead, near Oldham. Was there a connection with a report of a flat-bottomed object, with silver dome, seen in the night sky over Leeds? This was followed by a report of *"a spinning red circle, with flashing lights"*, seen during the early hours of the next morning. (Sources: *UFOLOG*/*Oldham Weekly Chronicle,* 26.8.1967/*Yorkshire Post,* 23.8.1967)

22nd August 1967 – Bronze objects in sky over Manchester

At 3am, *"two luminous, bronze coloured objects"* were seen flying across the sky over Denton, Manchester, by residents – Mr J. Pagan and Mrs Oldfield; the first being stationary in the air, while the second moved about in all directions, accompanied by a loud buzzing noise.

(Source: Arthur Tomlinson, DIGAP)

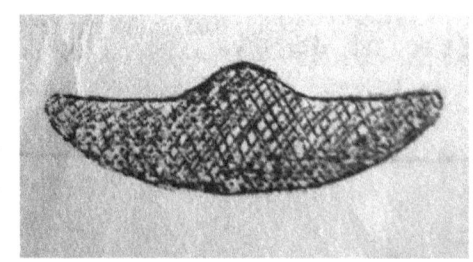

UFO over Reading

Later that day, at 8.45pm, Graham Hobbs (then aged 18) from Osborne Road, Reading, was out walking, with friends, when they saw 'flashing lights' over Southcote, followed by

"the appearance of a huge red shimmering 'disc', showing fourteen smaller white lights around its base, moving through the sky a few hundred feet above us. It went over towards the Burghfield area, where we lost sight of it due to a clump of trees."

(Sources: Personal interview/*Reading Evening Post*, 23.8.1967)

23rd August 1967 – Orange UFO on 'box-like structure' over South Shields

At 9.05pm, *"a large, orange, circular object, positioned on top of a silvery box-like structure resembling a torch in appearance"*, was seen over the north-east of South Shields, by Mr and Mrs A. Femandez. The object then faded away, *"like a TV being switched-off"*. (Source: Tyneside UFO Society)

24th August 1967 – Pyramidal UFO over Cornwall

An object, resembling *"a pyramid, with about three-quarters of the top chopped off and one corner longer than the others"*, was seen hovering over trees at St. Germans, on 24th August 1967. On (or about) the same day, *"a circle of orange lights"* were seen motionless in the sky over North Shields, Northumberland. (Source: *Newcastle Journal*, 25.8.1967)

25th August 1967 – Mass of glowing lights, Staffordshire

"A round, hazy, mass of glowing orange/red lights", some 60 feet in diameter, was seen hovering briefly at a height of 3-400 feet over Rising Brook, Staffordshire, at 11pm. It then moved southwards, where they stopped and moved back towards their original position.

Could this have been the same phenomena seen at Ramsbottom, in Manchester, the same evening?

(Sources: Tony Pace & Roger Stanway/*Manchester Evening News*, 25.8.1967)

What lay behind a brief report of a rectangular UFO, seen landing at Harold Hill, in Essex, on 25th August 1967? This was a locality which was to attract a number of UFO reports, over the years. It was allegedly witnessed by two Police Officers, and others.

(Sources: John Barklam, NICAP/Kath Smith, Isle of Wight UFO Society)

27th August 1967 – Cigar-shaped UFO over Manchester

At 3.05am, a cigar-shaped object – *"pointed at one end 'like a red hot poker', showing a white light, trailing what appeared to be a red-hot exhaust, making a noise like an electric train"* – was seen rushing through the sky over Crumpsall, Manchester. It was witnessed by local resident Larry Goldstone (an ex anti-aircraft bombardier), well-versed in aircraft recognition.

Later that day, three balloon-like objects were seen by many people – described as *"looking like electric lightbulbs, transparent on the top with an aluminium base, moving against the wind"*.

At the same time, in Torquay, flashing white lights were seen crossing the sky.

(Source: *Herald Express*, Torquay, 28.8.1967)

Over Gloucestershire

In Hucclecote, Gloucestershire, four children contacted the authorities after sighting *"an orange, domed, object with bright lights, which took aboard a smaller object and then disappeared across the sky making a 'whooshing' noise"*. (Source: *Gloucester Citizen*, 28.8.1967)

In addition to these sightings, we came across a number of reports of three objects – resembling silvery balloons – seen over the Lake District. During the same day, the police were being flooded with calls from the public; one was reported over the Langdale Valley, the second over Lake Windermere, the third over Kendal. A RAF spokesman said they *"had no knowledge of the objects"*.

28th August 1967 – 'Flying Saucer', Shropshire

Mr Edward Stokes – a local magistrate and farmer from Ellesmere, in Shropshire – was walking over fields near to the lake, during the afternoon of 28th August 1967, when he noticed:

> *"...rain, falling from a particularly darkened part of the sky, about seven miles away. All of a sudden a saucer-shaped object, looking like a monster jellyfish, appeared in the sky approximately three miles away. It then moved even closer, now at a height of about 500 feet above the lake, resembling a stationary central 'bubble' with an outer ring, which was spinning off mist around it – like a halo.*

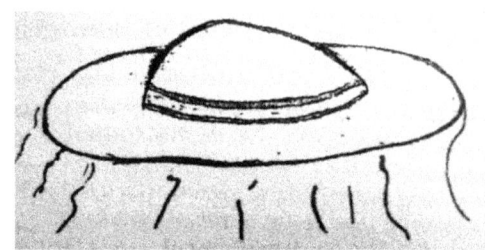

> *I remember thinking this can't be happening – 'Flying Saucers' don't exist! It then rose upwards a short distance, stopped briefly, and took off at fantastic speed."* **(Source: Personal interview)**

29th August 1967 – UFO with orange centre over Stoke-on-Trent

At 6.15am, an object – described as elliptical, with a bright scintillating orange centre, surrounded by a grey band and yellow outer ring – was seen over Shelton, Stoke-on-Trent. It was travelling towards London, at 6.16am. **(Sources: Tony Pace/Roger Stanway/*Evening Sentinel*, 28.8.1967/*Evening Sentinel*, 29.8.1967)**

At 10pm, Bernard Cox – a 15 year-old apprentice, living in Hindley (near Wigan) – was to find himself involved in a second UFO sighting within a couple of weeks, when his brother and girlfriend were told of a *"glowing spacecraft seen in the sky"*.

The three went outside and saw a number of neighbours gathered; unfortunately, by then, the object had gone.

The brothers drove off looking for the UFO while the girl ran down a nearby street, where she was surprised to see

> *"... a silver conical object, showing green and purple lights down the sides, with an orange glowing dome on the top. It hovered and zig-zagged through the sky".*

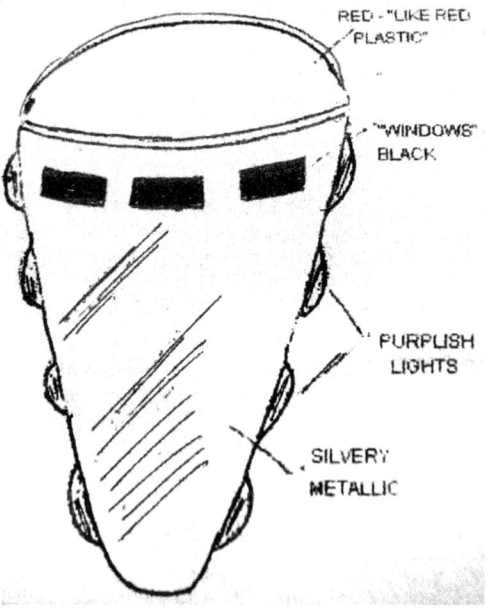

Mr Cox was not the only one; at least thirty other people living in the Hindley area contacted the authorities after seeing:

> *"... a conical, silvery object, showing green and purple lights down its side, with an orange dome, hovering and zigzagging across the sky"*, for ten minutes, at 10pm, before it moved away out of sight.

At 10.10pm on 29th August 1967, *"two bright red, cigar-shaped objects – one larger than the other"* were sighted heading towards the north-west direction, over Bradwell, Stoke-on-Trent. These objects passed behind a larger white object, which was star-shaped in image and apparently rotating, giving off a red and white light alternatively. Oddly, only one of the red objects emerged from behind the larger star-shaped object and continued on its journey, before disappearing into the distance.

White triangular UFO

A white triangular object, displaying a red flashing light on its front, was then observed approaching from the direction of Kidsgrove, and passed over the observers. As it did so, it flashed a bright light, or beam, from its front and headed off back towards Kidsgrove, after completing a semi-circle in the sky.

A few minutes later, the red cigar-shaped light appeared in the sky at the point where it had last been seen ten minutes ago. This returned along the path it had taken previously, and went behind the larger white object. When it emerged, there were now two red objects – last seen heading towards Newcastle-under-Lyme. (**Source: Tony Pace/Roger Stanway,** *Flying Saucer Report: UFOs Unidentified, Undeniable*)

30th August 1967 – 'Flying Saucer', Cheshire

At 8.30am, a domed object – *"through which the clouds could be seen with a very detailed underneath"* – was observed in the sky over the A530 road, just outside Crewe, before climbing upwards in a blur of speed. At about the same time, schoolboys – David Jones and Michael Hollander – were cycling along the Middlewich Road, in the direction of Crewe, after completing their newspaper rounds.

As they approached the road bridge across the valley stream, David (who was in front) brought Michael's attention to an object in the sky. It was to their left, and about a mile away. They took it to be an aircraft until it approached closer, when they realised from its shape that it was nothing of the sort. Within a short time it was motionless in the sky overhead. David rode into the kerb, and Peter collided into the back of him.

David said later:

"We were scared and dived under a hedge. On looking up, we could see bits of the underside and just stared. We got up and continued looking. Seconds later, it flew off fast. We couldn't keep track of it. It had a silver coloured outer perimeter, with an inner oval of what appeared to contain millions of black tubes, like wires, on a silver background. Along its centre was a silver rectangular section, containing three identical solid black circles."

BUFORA researchers – Tony Pace and Roger Stanway – visited the two boys and obtained a sketch of the UFO, which was published in their *Flying Saucer Report*.

(**Sources:** *Flying Saucer Report: UFOs Unidentified, Undeniable,* **Tony Pace, Roger Stanway, BUFORA/Personal interview/***Daily Mail* – 'Flying Saucer hovered over Crewe boys')

Seen over Nantwich, Cheshire

The boys were not the only people to witness UFO activity in the Cheshire area on this date.

At 8.55pm, a bright yellow-white object – resembling an elongated rugby ball in the sky – was seen by two people from Nantwich, in Cheshire.

"Through binoculars, a shallow dome – almost as bright as a full moon – could be seen. We first saw it in the North, about a mile away, at an angle of 25 degrees off the horizon, before passing in front of a dark cloud and later disappearing behind a low cloud, when a noise like a turbojet was heard."

At 9pm, a family of five from Sandbach (eight miles east of Nantwich), reported having sighted a shining white cigar-shaped object. It had blurred edges but was solid in appearance. They watched it passing in front of a 'black' cloud, before being lost from view.

UFOs over Stoke-on-Trent

At 10pm, a number of residents from Hethersett Walk on the Bentilee estate, Stoke-on-Trent, Staffordshire, sighted an object, *"...occasionally moving vertically and horizontally across the sky, changing in colour from* bright white or silver when stationary, to white, red, orange and green, before reverting to white again."

One of the residents – Mr Smith – initially thought that it was a star, but after looking through a telescope he described it as looking like *"...a teapot lid with the knob missing, and ping-pong balls around the leading edge".*

Mr Smith pointed out the lights to a neighbour – Mrs Hulme, who then alerted other people in the street as to what was being seen.

Within a short time, a number of residents had gathered. They included Doreen Harvey and her son, Alan, who was able to adjust the magnification on the small telescope by pulling out the eyepiece further. This enabled them to see:

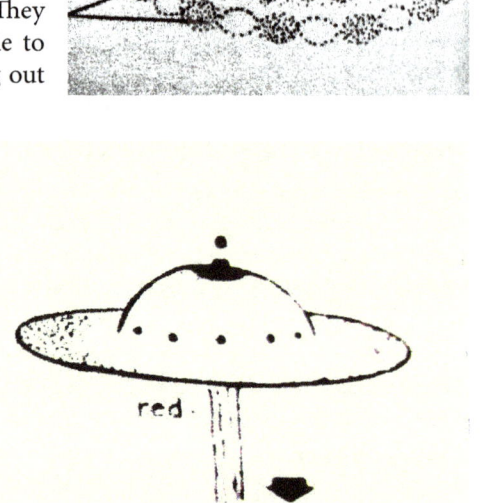

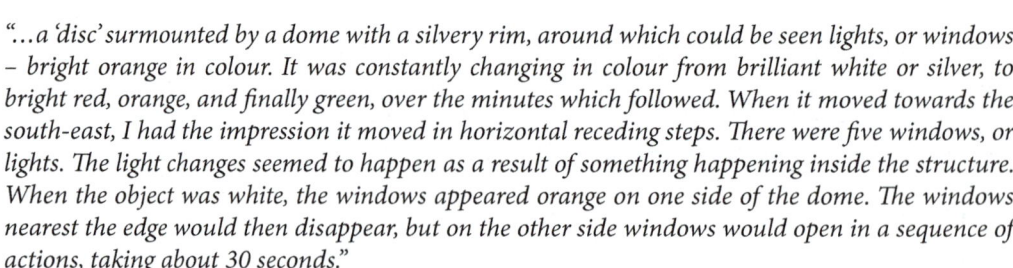

"...a 'disc' surmounted by a dome with a silvery rim, around which could be seen lights, or windows – bright orange in colour. It was constantly changing in colour from brilliant white or silver, to bright red, orange, and finally green, over the minutes which followed. When it moved towards the south-east, I had the impression it moved in horizontal receding steps. There were five windows, or lights. The light changes seemed to happen as a result of something happening inside the structure. When the object was white, the windows appeared orange on one side of the dome. The windows nearest the edge would then disappear, but on the other side windows would open in a sequence of actions, taking about 30 seconds."

At 10.10pm, Mrs K. Paszek from Whatmore Street, Smallthorne, saw a 'bright light' in the sky, which caught her attention.

"I stepped out into the street to get a better look and couldn't believe my eyes. It was hanging motionless in the sky, rotating and alternating between a vivid orange and deep red. It looked as big as the face on a small alarm clock in the sky. There was no sound.

It soon began to move slowly away, towards the south-east, over Sneyd Green, Birches Head, Hanley, and Bentilee direction."

At 10.15pm, a red 'flashing light' was seen heading across the sky from the direction of the Bentilee Estate, over Dresden Street, Hanley, Stoke-on-Trent, by at least three separate people. These included Miss B. Hemmings and Miss K. Price. Fifteen minutes later there was another sighting, when another bright red 'flashing light' was seen heading away from Smallthorne, towards the direction of London.

At 10.30pm, a 'bright light', flashing alternately vivid orange and deep red, was seen apparently motionless in the sky over Smallthorne, Stoke-on-Trent, towards the north-east. It then began to move south-east towards Hanley and Bentilee, where it became lost from view as it dropped below the horizon. According to Miss Hemmings and Miss K. Price:

"It was a different shape to the first one we saw. This was just like a spinning top, rotating across the clear night sky, heading towards the direction of Longton – unlike anything we had ever seen before in our lives".

At 10.30pm, Ernest White of Cleveland Gardens, High Heaton, was driving to Otterburn. He was accompanied by his son, David White (14), Judith Noble (17) and her sister, Susan (15), and Judith Strong (16). They were on the way back from a football match. When about three miles from Otterburn, they saw a large yellow 'ball of light' in the sky, which suddenly dropped down and swooped towards them, before shooting out of sight eastwards. (**Source:** *The Journal,* **31.8.1967 – 'Soccer fans spot the yellow ball')**

At 10.45pm, a bright red 'flashing light' was seen towards the south-east from Trowbridge Crescent, Bentilee, by Miss Ann Peters.

"It appeared to jerk, two or three times. It could not have been an aeroplane, as no sound was coming from it."

When Ann Peters and her brother went upstairs to get a better view, they saw a second object travelling south-east along the path taken by the previous object.

"It seemed bigger that the other light and larger, but still no shape could be seen as it travelled slowly over Hanley High School, facing Trowbridge Crescent. It then appeared to increase speed. I looked through binoculars and saw a flashing light coming from underneath the object. I also saw a square outline forming the top of the structure, beside the red light, and about a dozen spots of white light in one line that didn't flicker."

Also at 10.45pm, two or three bright orange 'flashing lights' were seen by Mrs Becanin and her son, Michael, from Ubberley Road, Bucknall. They were about half a mile away, in the fields opposite Hethersett Walk. They watched them until they faded away at 11.15pm.

31st August 1967 – Red flare over the sea off Dorset coast

At 2.29am, six coastguards on duty at St. Alban's Head Coastguard Station (south-west of Swanage, on the Dorset coast) were on alert following a search by the local lifeboat, after a red flare had been reported over the sea. Suddenly, the stillness of the night was broken by the sound of what was initially thought to be a helicopter, but much louder. One of the lookouts, situated at the base of a 300 feet cliff, heard a loud 'whooshing' noise, but was still unable to see anything. Enquiries made revealed that no aircraft were plotted in the vicinity. All that could be seen was a faint flickering, receding, orange glow.
(Source: Isle of Wight UFO Society)
On the same day, as a result of the considerable excitement generated by a number of reports of UFOs

Haunted Skies Volume Two Revised

being seen over the Bentilee estate, during the past few days, schoolgirls – Carole Marsden, Janet Brayford and Caroline Trotter – decided to make their way to Hanley High School, hoping to see something for themselves.

At 9pm, Janet was the first to sight an object approaching their direction from nearby fields, which halted in the air over the school clock – where it remained for about five minutes, accompanied by a loud 'whooshing' noise.

Carole Marsden told investigators:

> "We saw two of them in the air; one was about ten feet off the ground. It was round and a white-silvery colour, making this funny loud noise, with lights all around it. The colours were red, green, orange and white. The two in the air were going round and round, and looked more like the moon shining".

Anne viewed the object through a pair of 8 x 30 binoculars. She said:

> "The flashing light seemed to be coming from underneath the object. As it did so, I saw the outline of the top of the structure, which seemed to be square, but I couldn't see any other shape as the light was so bright". **(Source: Tony Pace/Roger Stanway)**

Late August 1967 – Close encounter, Essex, alien beings seen inside craft

In late August 1967, as twilight fell, Jim Fouche (then aged 15) from Grays, Thurrock, Essex, was out walking along a narrow footpath leading through Delafied playing field, off Dock Road, with a number of other schoolboys.

Jim said:

> "We saw this long yellow strip of light, about 75 feet in length, moving over the tops of trees lining the end of the nearby allotment. Within a few seconds it had drawn level with us, a few hundred feet away, allowing us to see what looked like four windows on the side, each separated by a vertical pillar about six inches thick. I was astonished to see a white woman, looking out of one of the windows at me, with long shoulder length hair flicked up at the end. When she turned her head to the right, the hair bounced gracefully to the opposite side and bounced back into position again. She had large but normal looking eyes, slanted like a Chinese person, with a thin pointed nose without any sign of nostrils. It then began to tilt and gradually moved away over Dock Road, and rose upwards, until a tiny dot of light in the sky."

Jim rushed to a telephone box, and asked the operator to put him through to the MOD.

After this was done he spoke to somebody at the other end, who listened to what he had to say and then suggested Jim must have seen a weather balloon, or aircraft. This was neither the first nor last time we were to come across close encounters involving the appearance of a 'Nordic' alien species.

(Source: Dan Goring)

August 1967 – Humanoids seen at Chingford, Essex

Barry Gates of Hackney, London – a bus Inspector by employment – was driving near Chingford Plain, during one weekend in August 1967, with his wife, at 11.45pm. They noticed a bright light, with a number of red lights, hovering in the air about 6 feet off the ground above a nearby bridle path, about 75 yards away from them. They first thought that they were fireworks and stopped the car. Mr Gates got out and was shocked to see what looked like two 'miniature men' – solid in appearance – next to the light source. Although we do not know what happened next (presumably either the couple carried on their journey or the 'beings' left) we learnt that an unidentified man and woman in the house, opposite, also witnessed this incident. **(Source: Barry King/Essex UFO Study Group**

August 1967 – Close Encounter, Shrewsbury

We spoke to Shropshire housewife Bridget Kelly, after learning of her remarkable experience which took place, late one evening in August 1967, while on her way home with her husband and three children.

> "We were driving along the road, when we saw what we took to be a 'shooting star', but realised it wasn't falling. It then hurtled towards the ground, as if about to crash, stopped, and hovered in front of us, allowing us to see a glistening silver metallic object with a bright light flashing on top and a lighted window to one side. The next thing I became aware of was standing outside the front door. We looked up and saw the 'craft' taking off across the rooftops. I had this feeling of sadness that whoever, or whatever, was on it was saying goodbye. The following day, I discovered a curious circle of dead skin on my stomach; if I had told anyone what had happened to us, they would have thought us mad."

Flashbacks

In 1992, she had a flashback of the experience and decided to contact the British UFO Research Association, who arranged for her to have hypnosis. After just one session, she became aware of having been the subject of some medical operation performed while aboard the 'craft'.

> "I could see faces around me, while something was done to my stomach. There was no pain – just faces, with large eyes. They looked like ordinary people, rather than anything alien in image."

Contacted BUFORA

In 1992, she contacted BUFORA and agreed to undergo hypnotic regression in an attempt to retrieve her subconscious memory of what had transpired during those 'abductions'. Under hypnosis she drew a tall muscular man in a grey jumpsuit, with reddish golden hair, standing at an instrument panel with a clipboard. He told her his name was *'Aplouff'*. Chillingly, she discovered a memory that they had performed an operation on her stomach. She said:

> "I could see faces around me; they were ordinary people, not alien beings".

Nordics

We were to come across other reports, over the years, involving the appearance of similarly described 'humanoids' that have been labelled as members of a *Nordic race, sometimes seen during an abduction experience, who are far more friendly and sympathetic to their human captors than the sinister 'Alien

Grey' species. Curiously, similar 'Nordic' beings have been seen by many people inside what is perceived to be an alien craft in daylight, while fully awake!

Called 'Nordics' because they appear similar to the Nordic races of our own species; those who live in Scandinavia and the Baltic states, and are blonde, tall, and often ruggedly handsome/glamorously beautiful.

Sadly, there is a wide gulf between stories like this – which appear genuine – and the way that the media and TV documentaries portray the role of the alleged abductees – often 'tongue in cheek', with no intention of treating such people seriously – and usually accompanied by men of science, who dismiss such 'interludes' as the product of overactive imaginations ... if only it was that easy!

People often ask us what we think of people who claim they have been abducted by Aliens and whether their experiences have any place in modern society.

Bridget Kelly

We tell them that while we are not qualified to judge the nature of the retrieved information, extracted by way of hypnotic regression (often pointed out now as an unreliable means of extraction), or cast any judgement on the abduction experience itself, we remain puzzled as to the cause of the physical marks and scars sometimes discovered on people who have been involved in a close encounter with a UFO.

Sadly, Bridget passed away in the autumn of 2006.

August 1967 – Humanoid seen in Epping Forest

Essex-based UFO researcher Barry King – who was to provide valuable assistance to the authors with regard to the many interesting incidents he had investigated, over the years – told of a sighting by a courting couple. They were parked at the end of a bridle path in Epping Forest, at 11.30pm one evening, in August 1967, off the main road to Chingford.

Small red light seen, then two 'figures' appear

"We noticed a small red light, which we thought might have been the reflection of our cigarettes in the windscreen – then what appeared to be a red firework shot upwards from the ground, about 75 yards away, in full view for about a minute. In the glare of these lights appeared to be what looked like two humanoid 'figures', clad in a flowing white mackintosh, which obscured the 'legs', estimated to be one and a half to three feet in height. This was followed by what looked like a bright lantern being waved in the air that moved closer, weaving from side to side about 6 feet off the ground. The object then passed underneath the headlight beam of the car."

Shocked, the couple decided to leave but had trouble starting the car. Eventually, when they did so, they made their way onto the road, where they met a man coming out of a nearby cottage. He told them that his terrified wife had locked herself in, after seeing strange lights in the woods.

Police informed

After driving to the local police station, the couple informed the officers that someone had been setting off fireworks in the wood, realising, by now, that it was unlikely the officers would have believed what they had really seen. A search of the area was later made by the police, but the results are not known.

This is an area which has been the source of numerous sightings of strange ghostly

'figures', some on horseback, some on the ground, as well as inexplicable noises. It was once a haven for highwaymen, robberies, and murders. We cannot say if there is any connection with either any UFO or paranormal matter in this instance, but no doubt the couple concerned will not be the last to experience something that many of us would find quite frightening, rather than exhilarating as some would believe.
(Source: *BUFORA Journal*, Vol. 5, No. 4, November/December 1976, interview with Barry King)

1967 – Close Encounter, Hastings – Fact or fiction?

While we had no compunctions about accepting Bridget's version of events, we weren't sure what to make of an encounter involving Mr Edwin Kembury – a retired audiologist from Sedlescombe, near Hastings. Mr Kembury was returning home, after taking his dog for a walk, when he saw the shape of a huge cannon shell heading towards him. He then became aware of two strange men at his side, each being about 5 feet tall, twittering like birds, moving up and down from the ground as they walked in a bouncing movement. He was then led gently back inside the bungalow, where he says he was able to see them more clearly:

> "They were identical, with deep set eyes, flat noses, thin lips, with three fingers on each hand. Their skin was dry, creamy – like parchment. They wore dull grey, tight, garments and a headpiece resembling a balaclava helmet with 'grids' for ears."

Edwin gave them cheese and biscuits and offered whisky, which they spat out. In return, they gave him some 'diamonds' (certified later to be rock crystals, and seeds) which, when later grown, sprouted caramel tasting berries on thin stems. These were sent to Stricklands, at Hastings (a seed and plant specialist), who were unable to identify them. Unfortunately, the plants died after being exposed to frost.

According to Edwin, he was visited at least six times over the following two months. He regarded them as benevolent rather than hostile, although this did not stop him reporting the matter to the police – who presumably dismissed him as a 'crank'.

We were unable to trace Mr Kembury (who appears to have passed away) or to discover further details about his allegations, absurd as they may seem at first glance. We did, however, establish that there had been a firm called Stricklands Ltd., (corn and seed merchants, in Hastings, who went out of business many years ago), but were unable to obtain any further information than was contained in a letter (sent to us, some years ago). What happened to the 'alien plant' if, in fact – like the sinister 'Aliens' – it existed at all? (Source: Unidentified newspaper, Kent area, 1967)

August 1967 – Glowing triangular object seen by Cheshire motorist

One early morning in the same month, a motorist was driving home from work at 50 miles per hour, in the Nantwich area of Cheshire, when he sighted *"a glowing, triangular object"*, moving across the sky in front of him, some 60 feet off the ground.

> "It made no sound; it was as big as a car. I was scared and wanted a witness to prove I wasn't imagining things, so I stopped and knocked on the door of a house and asked the man inside to have a look at the UFO – but he refused, clearly frightened, and told me to go. I watched it for about 5 minutes before it went out of sight, and then I went to a police station and told them what I had seen." (Source: DIGAP)

SEPTEMBER 1967

2nd September 1967 – UFOs land in car park, Staffordshire!

At 1.30am, Mrs Barbara Ward of Norwich Road, Bentilee, Staffordshire, was awoken by her crying baby. After attending to the baby, she happened to glance through the bedroom window, which overlooked fields, when something caught her eye.

"It was in the field below the house and shone a very bright yellow, with an orange light on top. I stood and watched it for about an hour. I didn't think it was anything and went back to bed."

Twenty-five minutes later, at 1.55am, Mrs Gillian Freakley of Nelson Place, Hanley, Stoke-on-Trent, was in the process of getting ready for bed, after having sat up late reading. After checking the security of the house, she opened the front door and stood looking outwards, when she noticed:

"...two, dark grey objects – like small armoured cars, facing each other – moving to and fro across the car park. The fronts of the 'cars' seemed to be merging into each other, or passing each other. There was only a small space between. The back half of the objects seemed nearly twice the height of the fronts. I couldn't see any windows, or lights, but they had an orange oval light on the outside, with yellow on the inside, flickering in and out as they moved. When the objects came together, the light flickered but came on again as they drew away from each other. I was fascinated – not scared, or even excited. I stepped back and called my husband, Gordon. When we looked back, the two small objects had moved to the top of the road."

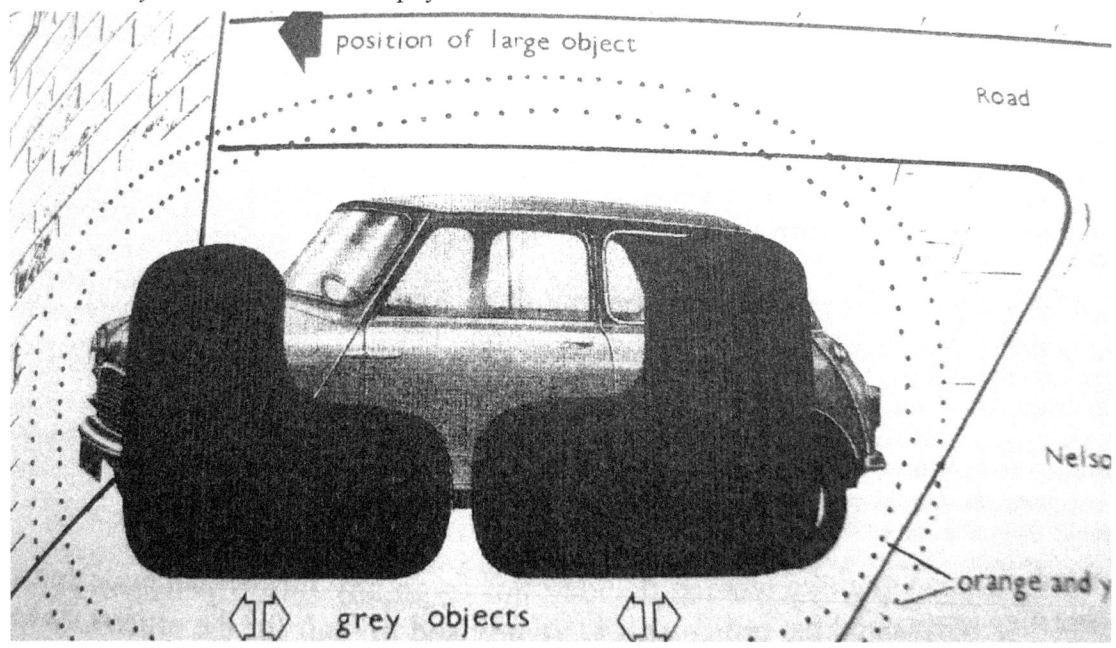

At 9.15pm, schoolchildren – Graham Teece, David McCue, Kenneth Harrington and Malcolm Bostock – were playing in Beverley Drive, opposite Wendoline Close on the Bentilee Estate, Stoke-on-Trent, in Staffordshire. Graham noticed:

"...an object travelling roughly parallel to Beverley Drive, heading north-west, which was seen to change direction at the top of the Drive, and then move over houses before heading north-east."

David shouted out, *"There's a 'flying saucer!"*, attracting the attention of the other children, who looked up into the sky to see *"a big red saucer-shaped light, shining brightly, with dull yellow glowing sides"*.

They brought the matter to the attention of Mrs Lilly Stevenson, who came out of her house and alerted the next door neighbour – Mrs Bowen – who described it as being *"dome shaped, and making a noise like the wind as it came over"*.

A group of six children made their way to the area, half a mile away, where – according to one of the boys – it was seen to drop down and then rise over a hedge, before ascending into the air.

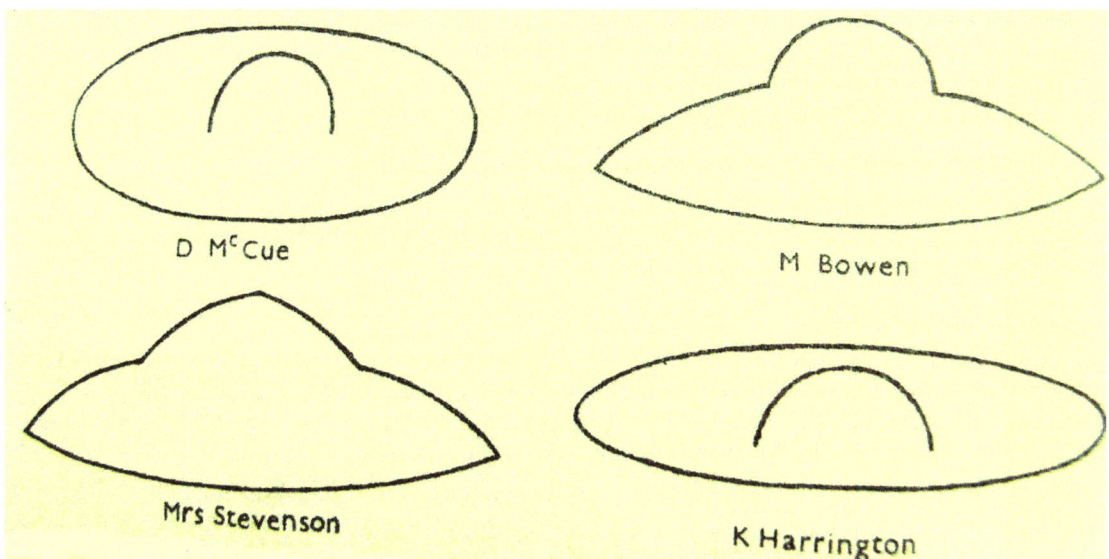

Mrs Stevenson said:

"The field looked like it was on fire – like a bonfire. You could see the leaves on the trees lit up by the red glow".

Due to the marshy ground, the two women decided not to go any further and made their way back to the road, where they telephoned the police and were advised to wait for the officers. As Kenneth Harrington and David McCue approached the area where the object was still glowing, the 'light' went out as it landed. The boys felt about in the darkness with their hands, but nothing was found.

Police attend the scene

At 9.20pm a police van arrived containing two constables and a sergeant. The policemen spoke to the boys and made a cursory search of the area. After seeing nothing, they instructed the children to go home but asked Malcolm Bostock to take them to where he had seen the UFO. After another fruitless search, the officers decided to withdraw. As they reached the road, one of the residents of Hethersett Walk, in an upstairs flat, shouted that he could see a 'bright light' moving up the field.

UFO takes off

Within seconds, a bright glowing object was seen by the officers and the others. When it reached a height of about 2-300 feet above the hill, it halted for an instant and then vanished. The police reluctantly admitted that they had seen the 'light' take off, but explained it away as being a car headlight!

At approximately 9.50pm, a group of other children – including Terry Bagnall and Philip Ball – were playing in the fields when a bright white cigar-shaped object was seen apparently motionless in the sky over the houses. It then brightened, faded, and in a 'flash of light' disappeared.

At 10.10pm, two bright red cigar-shaped objects – one larger than the other – were sighted heading towards north-west, over Bradwell, Stoke-on-Trent, and passing behind a larger white, rotating, object that resembled a star, flashing with red and white lights. Oddly, only one of the objects emerged from behind it. A white triangular object, displaying a red flashing light, was then observed approaching from the direction of Kidsgrove. As it passed over the heads of the observers it flashed a bright light, or beam, from the front, and headed off back towards Kidsgrove, after completing a semicircle in the sky. A few minutes later, a red cigar-shaped light appeared and returned along the path taken previously by the 'star', where it was seen to go behind it. When it emerged, there were now two objects – last seen heading towards Newcastle-under-Lyme.

(Source: Tony Pace/Roger Stanway, *Flying Saucer Report: UFOs Unidentified, Undeniable*)

4th September 1967 – Close encounter with UFO, Reading

At 7.25pm a silver, oval, object with a dome on top, moving much faster than an aircraft, was seen for a couple of minutes in the sky over Wellingborough, Northamptonshire, by Peter Smith, Robin Percival, David Calicott and A. Barker. **(Source: *UFOLOG*)**

UFO landing, Reading

Mr Arthur Eedle – a science teacher with an impressive list of scientific qualifications – was employed by Stoneham Grammar School, Tilehurst, Reading, during 1967. He decided to organise a 'sky watch', after learning of a number of UFOs seen in the locality, and invited Jane – a local reporter with the *Reading Evening News* – and Philip Bird, a local schoolboy who was interested, to attend.

Just before midnight on the 4th September 1967, a huge glowing object with revolving lights was seen to descend slowly over the Royal Ordnance factory at Burghfield Common, and drop down into a wooded area next to the side of the building. He said:

> *"Jane and Philip decided to go and have a closer look. Within ten minutes, they returned in a much shaken state. I asked them, when they had calmed down, what had happened. They told me, 'We were unable to get anywhere near it, because of what felt like an invisible force field preventing us from getting any closer'."*

Incident overshadowed by hoax 'Flying Saucers'

Although Jane was eager to publish what had happened, the event was overshadowed by much excitement in the National Press, the following day, when a number of 'Flying Saucers' were discovered all over the country – later established to have been elaborate hoaxes, planted by students, to promote their rag day celebrations … so the story was never told – until now. **(Source: Personal interview)**

5th September – 'V'-shaped UFO seen over Gateshead Power Station

At 10pm, Mr J. Patterson reported an odd group of stars, *"consisting of four 'stars' making a square, with ten or twelve others forming a rough 'V' shape inside"*. He saw them moving through the sky close to a power station in Leam Lane Estate, Gateshead, before being lost from view, ten minutes later. On the same day, a bright 'star', showing green flashes of light, was seen moving in and out of clouds over Worthing, Sussex, *"during gale force winds"*. **(Source: *UFOLOG*)**

6th September – UFO over Essex

Harold Hill, Essex, was the venue for the sighting of a white, oval, object, seen to fall from the sky at tremendous speed.

At 10.30pm, the object then turned sideways and disappeared from sight. **(Source: Tyneside UFO Society)**

9th September 1967 – Over Sussex Downs

Over the *Sussex Downs, *"a bright, saucer-shaped, object was seen hovering in the sky, projecting a beam of light across to another similar object, out of which were seen to fall a number of yellow 'cones of light'."* **(Source: *UFOLOG*)**

---

*The South Downs are a range of chalk hills that extends for about 260 square miles across the south-eastern coastal counties of England from the Itchen Valley of Hampshire in the west to Beachy Head, near Eastbourne, East Sussex, in the east.

TELESCOPES, cameras and patience help London Sky Scouts – at monthly watches at Alexandra Palace – in their quest for evidence to eradicate the "U" from UFOs.

11th September 1967 – 'Sky watch' held on the Sussex Downs

As a result of newspaper coverage of UFOs being seen over the Downs, a small group of people took part in a 'sky watch' on the 11th September 1967. At 2am a red light appeared, approaching the top of the Downs, about a mile away from them. Within 30 seconds, huge beams of light were seen spreading across the sky with what appeared to be answering flashes of light from above.

14th September 1967 – Rocket-shaped UFO over Manchester

Mr Arthur Tomlinson, B.Sc., of DIGAP (Direct Investigation Group on Aerial Phenomena), wrote to John Feakins of the Isle of Wight Society, in September 1967, with regard to an interview conducted with Miss Hilda Healey. Miss Healey was a music teacher, of Bury Road, Radcliffe, in Manchester. She was in the bedroom of her house, at 7.15pm, when she saw a dark coloured luminous object, moving slowly through the sky.

Miss Healey:

"It was cigar-shaped, to begin with, but when it tilted I saw a completely circular shape with central dome. On the front there was a star-like light and a small white trail of exhaust at the rear. The light 'winked' three times and paused, then again, following which the white trail ceased."

(Source: Arthur Tomlinson, DIGAP)

15th September 1967 – Devon UFO sighted over the sea

"A bright, luminous, orange 'ball', surrounded by blue/green haze", was seen moving up and down in the sky, out to sea, by three people walking up Hillhead, near Brixham, Devon. This was later suggested to have been ball lightning.

(Source: Richard Farrow, Torbay Astro-Research Association)

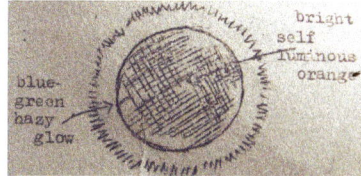

Haunted Skies **Volume Two Revised**

18th September 1967 – UFO over the Cairngorm Mountains
At 10pm, two Science University students, from Birmingham, were camping in the Cairngorm Mountains, a quarter of a mile east of Loch Morlich, Scotland. They reported seeing *"a dull red flattened ellipse, stationary in the south-east part of the sky"* (the moon had not yet risen), which grew brighter and larger before fading away. The incident was brought to the attention of Birmingham University UFO Group, who pondered if it could have been a paraselene (mock moon), formed in localised cloud, with the moon still below the horizon.
(Source: Richard Farrow/Mr T. Durham, Birmingham University Research Association)

19th September 1967 – Glowing objects seen in the sky at Merseyside
At 1.15pm, two glowing white objects – one round, and the other oval – were seen moving across the sky over Borough Road, Birkenhead, by two excited boys. The object then disappeared into a small cloud, towards the north-east, which broke up leaving nothing. **(Source: Mr T.C. Dixon, MUFORG)**

20th September 1967 – UFO seen over RAF tracking station
Chris Walker and Stuart Farr saw a red and white coloured object, stationary in the sky over Hack Green RAF tracking station, at Nantwich, in Cheshire, during the early evening of 20th September 1967.

> *"It followed the arrival of a pair of red flashing lights, a single white light and other red lights, which formed a triangle in the sky, and lasted a couple of minutes before moving away."*

(Source: NICAP, GB)

21st September 1967 – Strange 'star' over Par Sands Beach, Cornwall
Mr P. Bush, from London, was on holiday, sunbathing at Par Sands Beach, in Cornwall, at 1pm.

> *"To my surprise, an apparent solid looking rounded star-shaped object appeared high in the sky. After about half-an-hour, it moved very slightly towards the east. By 1.45pm it was out of view. I made some enquiries and discovered over two dozen others had also seen the UFO that day."*

22nd September 1967 – Splitting UFOs sighted over London
A bright, cigar-shaped, object was seen motionless in the sky over Peckham Rye, London, at 9.10pm.

"Ten minutes later it split into two round objects, one of which disappeared and reappeared further to the right of the sky after ejecting a 'light'." Both objects then vanished from view. **(Source: UFOLOG/BUFORA)**

23rd September 1967 – UFO seen, showing 'portholes' and making a strange noise
At 10.17pm, three people – including Francis James Shaw, from Liverpool – sighted a strange object in the sky. They described it as:

> *"...having no visible outline, with a row of five to seven 'portholes' visible along its side, making an intermittent 'brumming' noise. As it passed overhead, dogs in the area began to howl".*

Attempts to obtain the interest of the Press were unsuccessful.

The Meteorological Office suggested (yet again) that it was probably a weather balloon.
(Source: John W. Barklam, BUFORA)

25th September 1967 – Stationary UFO in the sky over Newcastle-on-Tyne
At 5.17am, a white, oval, object was sighted in the sky over Gosforth Road, Newcastle-on-Tyne, by Mr B. Swaddle.

> *"It was stationary in the east, at about 30 degrees elevation – completely silent. After about twenty seconds, it appeared to contract and grew dimmer. It then grew to its former size and brilliance and*

completed this sequence of action again, before finally vanishing from view about twenty seconds later." (**Source:** *UFOLOG*)

At 9pm, an orange coloured saucer-shaped object was sighted over Leeds, by a number of people – one of whom described seeing that *"...it tilted, showing a dome on top, before moving away faster than any Jet aircraft".*

26th September 1967 – Eight square lights, Scotland

At 6.45pm, five schoolboys living at the back of Warriston School, Moffat, Dumfriesshire, were preparing for bed when they noticed:

"...eight square 'lights' inclined at an angle of 25 degrees to the horizon, preceded by a brighter single 'light' moving from right to left over the sky, towards the north-east". (**Source: DIGAP**)

29th September 1967 – A visit to the MOD

BUFORA representatives – Tony Pace and Roger Stanway – visited the Ministry of Defence, Main Building, Whitehall; they were seeking advice on the large number of UFO sightings brought to their attention, and spoke to Mr Cassells of S4f.

Cassells was a man in his late twenties, who confirmed in conversation he wasn't a scientist but that all UFO reports were treated seriously. However, he wasn't able to supply them with any details adding:

"No person is employed full-time at the Ministry, due to lack of resources, and no one makes any 'on the spot' enquiries or field investigation when reports are received. The Ministry's function is to receive written reports and find explanation for them."

Mr Cassells firmly denied it was their policy to play down UFO sightings, and that no evidence had been found of any extraterrestrial connection. (**Source: Tony Pace and Roger Stanway**)

30th September 1967 – Three 'red globes' over County Durham

At 10.57pm, three boys out walking in Shotley Bridge, Consett, County Durham, sighted three 'red globes', moving through the sky. The objects then disappeared into a cloud, out of which emerged a much larger object that shot off at terrific speed, towards Consett Iron Works. (**Source:** *UFOLOG*)

MOD Declassified reports on UFOs

Declassified MOD documents AIR/19216-CO273876 informs us of the following factors for the increase in UFO sightings, during this period:

"First, the extended period of fine weather in the summer and early autumn months provided ideal conditions for intensive and extensive flying, gliding and ballooning activities, and they also caused a great many people to spend time outdoors and permitted those people to see much more of the aerial activity than usual.

Secondly, the planet Venus, which is extremely bright, was seen over the UK for an extended period from the beginning of October.

Thirdly, very wide publicity has been given in the press and on television to reports of Unidentified Flying Objects and this has encouraged the public to search the sky in the hope of seeing their own unidentified flying object.

It is significant that a large number of the additional reports received in recent months came from the London area and have proved to be aircraft or aircraft landing lights.

There has been nothing in the reports received in 1967 to indicate that they are in any way different from the reports received in earlier years. Apart from the frequent sightings of the planet Venus, especially by people in North Devon and Sussex, there have been no mass sightings".
(**Source: As above**)

September 1967 – Close encounter for Essex schoolgirl

In the same month, Brentwood, Essex schoolgirl – Barbara Major (aged 12), was on a break from class, after having had an argument with her German teacher. Walking down towards the sport field, she saw something glistening in front of her in the clear blue sky that caught her attention.

> "I wondered if it was hanging from a crane but then realised it was some distance away from the prefabricated school classrooms, which ruled out a prank being played."

Barbara felt herself unable to take her eyes off the half-moon shaped object, although eventually she was able to do so – at which stage she heard, telepathically, a female voice which said:

> "Don't worry, there is a purpose to your life but you wouldn't know it for some time."

The object then rotated slightly and an indentation appeared in the body, allowing her to see a 'beautiful female', who was moving very slowly yet precisely. "She was well proportioned but I don't remember her looks", she said.

The next thing that happened was that Barbara felt what she can only describe as a feeling of sympathy being expressed towards her, and an inclination that the 'woman' wanted her to go with her. A taller masculine 'being' appeared; he came to her side and told her: "We have to go now, so say farewell."

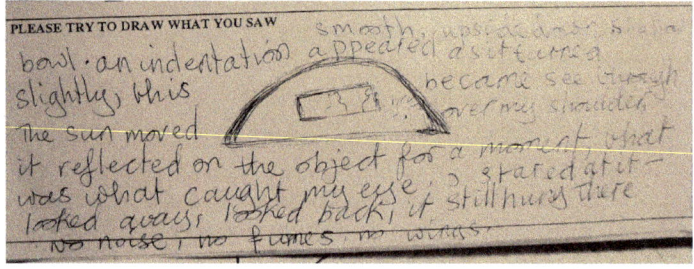

At this point Barbara heard the class bell go for morning break. She pleaded with the woman not to go but the craft began to rotate, the window becoming obscured and solid again. The next thing she became aware of was that her friend called out to her to tell her she had been looking for her. Barbara directed her friend's attention to the sky but the object was no longer there. Barbara was shocked when her friend told her that she had been out looking for her as she had been missing from class for 50 minutes, when Barbara thought the incident had only lasted ten minutes. Oddly her friend said she had been looking in the same place for here earlier, but had not seen her at all.

Barbara informed the investigating officer – Ron West, of the Essex UFO Society – that she suffered some discomfort in her muscles after having attended a school dance afterwards, which of course may have nothing to do with the 'close encounter'. Unfortunately, she now suffers from muscular disabilities and continues to have recurring dreams about the incident.

This interview took place in 1995. Obviously it would be beneficial to speak to her now over 20 years later, as there are a number of questions to be asked, one of which being where it happened. This is not given on the report form. As we have said before, if this was the only case ever brought to our attention, involving what appears to be some interaction with a non-human species, then our assessment might be different, rather than the opposite. Our heart goes out to people who have the misfortune to run into something that can be so life-changing, often in the face of disbelief by those that cannot accept the reality of what UFOs are all about.

OCTOBER 1967

1st October 1967 – Red lights in the sky, South Yorkshire

At 7.15pm, a retired miner – Harold Coles – was walking home along Low Road, Conisbrough, when he saw *"a bright red light"* in the sky, beneath heavy clouds, travelling slowly towards the direction of the castle, before losing view of it. He wasn't the only one to see something unusual. Local reporter – Stephen Kind – was walking through Thurnscoe, a quarter of an hour before, when he noticed *"two red lights"* in the sky. (**Source:** *South Yorkshire Times,* **14.10.1967, report of second sighting**)

2nd October 1967 – UFO over Wembley, London

Just before 10pm, Wembley resident – Mrs Ann Edward, and a friend, sighted:

> *"...a globe-shaped object, with four 'arms' jutting out of it, showing a bright 'spotlight', motionless in the sky."*

After some 30 seconds, it began to move slowly, at first, before circling the nearby railway station and then disappearing from view. (**Source:** *Wembley News,* **3.11.1967**)

4th October 1967 – Three 'red lights' seen, County Durham

At 8.45pm, an object showing *"three red lights"* was seen moving across the sky over Blackhill, Consett, County Durham, before being lost from view.

5th October 1967 – Police Officer sights UFO over Newcastle-on-Tyne

Police Constable Peter Dawson was patrolling Shields Road, Byker Bridge, in Newcastle-upon-Tyne (near the Apollo Cinema), during the early hours, (some accounts give the 3rd), when he sighted:

> *"...a bright grey 'light' in the sky, accompanied by a noise like a car with a loose fan belt. It was quite high and looked the size of a large lampshade. It then moved westwards and the sound faded. Other officers also heard the noise, as well as many people in the street."*

The witnesses included Mr G. Riley of Blackhill, Consett, who sighted two 'red lights' moving through the sky – one behind the other – followed by a third flashing one, some distance behind.

Another witness was local taxi driver Gordon Armstrong of Hotspur Street, Heaton, who was in his office when he heard a vibrating noise. On going outside to have a look, he saw:

> "...a strange grey object in the sky – then there was a flash and it accelerated away. The noise was like an uncoiled spring, unwinding. Several people came out to watch. The air was electric."

A police spokesman said, "Since Constable Dawson reported the matter, we haven't heard any reports of a landing, or aliens running about."

(Sources: Tyneside UFO Society/*The Journal*, 5.10.1967 – 'Dozens see Flying Saucer over Byker')

Over Cumberland

It appears a similar phenomenon was seen and heard on the same date – this time over Eden Valley, Cumberland.

A local woman, cycling along a country lane, at 10pm, reported having been

> "...followed by a UFO, which hovered twenty feet above my head, making a humming and bleeping noise".

According to Reverend Grant – the local vicar of Ainstable and Armathwaite parishes – he said:

> "There had been talk in the villages about this, but I wondered if there could be a connection with the railway in the valley." (**Source: Letter to Isle of Wight UFO Society**)

6th October 1967 – Sighting of strange object by ex-RAF Radar technician

The excellent *Flying Saucer Report: UFOs Unidentified, Undeniable*, compiled by Staffordshire amateur astronomers and UFO researchers – Tony Pace and Roger Stanway – tells of a sighting made by ex-RAF Radar serviceman, Mr Tunnicliffe, at 9.37pm, who had gone to pick up his motorcycle from the Midlands Electricity Board yard in Brunswick Terrace, Stafford, when he noticed an object resembling:

> "...a white parachute, carrying an orange light underneath it, at a height of between 5-10,000 feet. I thought it would come down but it carried on in a straight line over the houses, at about 35 miles per hour, until it disappeared northwards."

According to Mr Tunnicliffe, a number of young people near the railway bridge also witnessed the object's passage through the sky. (**Source: As above/***Stafford Newsletter*)

7th October 1967 – UFO sighted over Guildford

8th October 1967 – Metallic object sighted in the sky at Hartlepool

At 4.30pm, a metallic, elongated oval object, without any wings or propellers, was seen flying at an estimated height of 800 feet, heading westwards across the northern sky over Seaton Carew, Hartlepool.

10th October 1967 – Small domed object sighted, Staffordshire

At 7pm, two green and red lights were seen crossing the same county. Through binoculars, "*a small domed object could be seen, with a yellow light revolving around it*". Thirty minutes later, a second object appeared and joined-up with the other two before all moved away.

(Source: BUFORA, Tony Pace/Roger Stanway)

13th October 1967 – Gold coloured 'cross' Birmingham

Mrs Olive King from City Road, Edgbaston, was getting ready for work when she noticed some strange

lights in the sky, *"consisting of two small and a large one"*. She later reported her sighting to the local UFO organisation. They were unable to offer any explanation, although the British Astronomical Society suggested she may have seen the planets Venus and Jupiter, with Regulus underneath Jupiter.
(**Source: Birmingham Group, [UFOSIS]**)

14th October 1967 – 'Flying Church Cross', Northampton

A gold coloured object – described as *"resembling a Church Cross"* – was seen moving across the sky over Northampton, at 9.30pm. According to the witness, it was the most beautiful thing she had ever seen.

16th October 1967 – UFO over Suffolk

Bakery workers at Ipswich, in Suffolk, contacted the authorities after sighting *"a star-shaped object, with a red and blue light on either side, in the sky"*, at 1am.

Over Cumbria

On the same day, at 7.20pm, Mr G. Hampson of the *Swan Hotel*, Keswick, Cumbria, was looking out of his window, when he saw:

> *"...a white 'light' with a red tinge, moving three or four times the speed of a satellite, heading towards the south-east direction"*.

Worthing

Worthing residents – Ian Sheaf and Tony Whitlock – were out running, when they saw a peculiar shaft of light change shape, *"from rugby-ball to hemispherical, triangular and square"* in the sky, west of Worthing, on the early evening of 17th October 1967.

(**Source:** *Worthing Herald,* 22.10. 1967 – 'Joggers see weird UFO in the sky')

17th October 1967 – Lorry driver sights 'Flying Saucer' over M6 Staffordshire

Admittedly, while some of the sightings reported to the police and MOD may well have been misidentified stars, it could hardly have been the answer for what was seen by lorry driver J.D. Stotter, who had served in the RAF and was familiar with aircraft recognition. At 6pm, he was travelling southbound along the M6 Motorway, at 40 miles per hour, approaching the Holmes Chapel turn-off, when he experienced an eerie sensation that he was not alone.

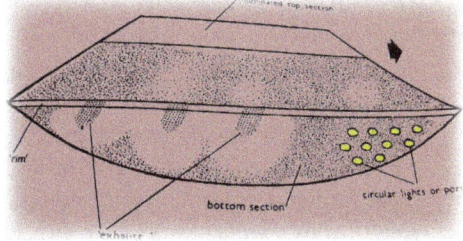

Glancing through the top left-hand corner of the windscreen, he was astonished to see a 'craft', resembling:

> *"...a large apple pie in a dish (but in need of a good coat of paint), with a curved underside, showing a group of white circular lights or portholes situated towards its front, with three mauve/blue flames coming out of three separate outlets – like exhausts – moving in the same direction along the left-hand side of the motorway, keeping pace with the lorry"*.

Shocked, Mr Stotter managed to pull up onto the hard shoulder, after having driven a total of five-and-a-half miles further along the road. He got out and watched the UFO for about ten minutes, during which time he heard a whining sound – like a Jet aircraft, but much higher in tone – emanating from the 'craft'. A short time after, the 'craft' swerved to the left and forward, nearly coming to a standstill, before moving sideways over the motorway and heading back along the path it had taken previously. A few seconds later, it disappeared.

(**Source: Tony Pace, Roger H. Stanway,** *Flying Saucer report: UFOs Unidentified, Undeniable*)

18th October 1967 – Cigar-shaped UFO, Warwickshire

At 4.15am, Mr Moseley from Coleshill, Warwickshire (near Birmingham), was awoken by his wife. She told him that she had sighted two very 'bright lights', one behind the other, moving across the sky. He said:

> "I went to the window and saw them motionless in the sky. They were approximately five or six times the size of Venus. I fetched a pair of binoculars and, looking through them, saw a cigar-shaped object with four darker patches along its length. The whole thing tilted at an angle of about 30 degrees above the horizon. We watched them until 5.15am, where they began to move rapidly away and out of sight." **(Source: Personal interview)**

19th October 1967 – Brilliant pale blue light, Northumberland

At 7pm, Mrs M. Downie from Killingworth, Northumberland, was waiting for a bus in West Moor, Newcastle-on-Tyne, and watching an aircraft coming in to land at Woolsington Airport, when she sighted:

> "…a brilliant pale-blue light in the eastern sky, at an estimated height of between 2-3,000 feet, brightening and dimming (which it did four times). Sixty seconds later it had gone."

(Source: Letter to Isle of Wight Society)

On the same day (time not given), an elongated object was seen hovering in the sky over Sowerby Bridge, near Halifax, by Mr T. Collins of Siddal, who later contacted the Halifax Branch of BUFORA.

20th October 1967 – Cigar-shaped UFO over Devon

At 2.50am, Mrs Small from Washington Station, County Durham, was awoken by *"a high-pitched buzzing sound, which increased in volume and tone, followed by a 'zooping' sound"*. Enquiries made, the next day, revealed that two other people had seen a UFO pass overhead, but they declined to be named.
(Source: TUFOS/*UFOLOG*)

Farmer's wife Lenore Coleen Bullock – then living at Metherell Moor Farm, Beaworthy, in Devon (off the B.3218 road, halfway between Okehampton and Holsworthy) – was finishing her chores, at 7pm, when her husband told her to look upwards into the sky.

> "I went outside and couldn't believe what I was seeing. I started to speak; my husband cut me short. He told me to make a very careful note of memory, so we wouldn't forget. It was cigar-shaped, with four oval lights circling around the main 'body'. The lights then began to move closer to the 'body'. All of a sudden, it just inexplicably vanished in front of our eyes. I suggested we should contact the police, but my husband advised me against it. 'Who would ever believe us?' he said.
>
> Two days later, we read about the 'Flying Cross' UFO, chased by the Devon and Cornwall police officers, near Hatherleigh, and wondered if what we saw was connected."

(Sources: Original, Eileen Buckle/Personal interview)

21st October 1967 – Saucer-shaped object, with dome, over Essex

At 4.30am, a UFO – described as *"saucer-shaped with a dome on the top, tapering to a point at the bottom"* – was seen in the sky over Ilford, in Essex, by a woman and her mother from Barking. After a while, it was joined by a second object.

> "The two just hung there in the sky", she said.

Ten minutes later, a mysterious bright *"pencil of light"* was seen passing across the sky by another resident.

Over South Shields – Triangular UFO sighted

At 7pm, a 'white light' was seen travelling through the sky over Lord Nelson Street, South Shields, by Police Constable D. Clough, and others, some of whom described seeing *"a triangular object, flying east to west"*. The RAF refused to confirm or deny having picked up the UFO on radar. (**Source: UFOLOG**)

Over Thirsk, Yorkshire

At 7.20pm, postman – Mr J. Cumberland, was out jogging between Sinderby and Thirsk (Grid Reference 353823). It was a pitch-black night, with heavy rain. He heard a noise and thought a car was approaching, when lights suddenly appeared through the roadside hedge. He stopped, looked behind, and was astonished to see *"a dazzling cross-shaped object, hovering about 1,500 feet in the sky, brighter than the sun"*, at an elevation of 30 degrees off the horizon. A few minutes later, it shot backwards into a cloud and vanished. (**Source: Tyneside UFO Society**)

Over Anglesey – UFO hovers over car

At 8.15pm, a huge 'star' was seen hovering above a car containing two women, travelling from Valley to Holyhead in Anglesey. It then raced away across the sky, at high speed. Enquiries with RAF Valley confirmed the last aircraft to use the runway had been at 7.10pm. Was this the same UFO seen by three members of the Royal Observer Corps, stationed at Longton, Stoke-on-Trent, the same evening? They watched an object, looking like *"a dinner plate, on edge"*, moving slowly across the sky, at an elevation of 60 degrees. To their astonishment the UFO returned a short time later, before heading off over power lines supplying the National Grid at Cavershall Woods.

UFO display, South Shields

On the same day, members of the Dudgeon family at Tyne Dock flats, South Shields, contacted the police after watching:

> *"…a formation of dazzling triangular objects, performing aerobatics in the sky". They observed it for several minutes.*

It was also witnessed by an attending police officer, whose account – together with those of other residents – was later dismissed by a police spokesman, who said,

> *"We are not making any enquiries; it appears it is not permissible to report about something that does not officially exist".*

23rd October 1967 – Yellow egg-shaped UFO over Yorkshire

At 3.25am a couple from Knottingley, in Yorkshire, sighted a bright yellow egg-shaped object, low in the sky, towards the direction of the south-eastern horizon. It was a *"football in size, compared to a pinhead of a star"*. From the rear of the object came a second, small, dull red object. It stopped in flight, leaving a dull red trail behind. Moments later, a third object came out. It was not quite as bright as the previous one. This object left a full-sized 'wake' of light – as big as the object itself.

Shortly afterwards, the third object returned along its own 'wake' to the larger UFO, and came back out. The second object then made its way back to the first one, still leaving a red glow or trail behind it. A few seconds later, the main UFO shot off at terrific speed across the sky (by now looking like a red hot cinder) and vanished, leaving a red glow behind in the sky. The whole performance was over in five minutes. It was later discovered that a similar UFO had been seen over Castleford, at 3.58am, six miles away.
(**Source: *UFOLOG*/BUFORA**)

24th October 1967 – 'Flying Crucifix', Watford, Hertfordshire

During the early hours, Michael Hurley – a resident of Bushy Heath, near Watford – was awoken by a brilliant 'light' flooding into his bedroom.

"I rushed to the window and saw what looked like a huge crucifix in the sky, just hanging there. A short time later, it moved away and out of sight."

Merseyside

At 3am, Joyce Hennesey from Huyton, Merseyside, was awoken by *"an intermittent whirring noise"*. On looking through the window, she saw an eerie glow heading across the sky over nearby rooftops.

Devon

At 4am in Sidmouth, Devon, as dawn approached, Evelyn Robinson awoke. She looked through the window and saw a bright flash in the sky over the nearby observatory. She thought that it might have been a star, *"...but then I realised, on closer inspection, the 'star' looked like a crucifix, flashing with lights. I watched it for about 10-15 minutes. Its lights kept dimming, going out, and then brightening again. It stayed in the same position until flying away."* (**Source:** *Pullman's Weekly News,* **31.10.1967**)

Police chase 'Flying Cross' UFO

At 4am, Police Constables Roger Willey and Clifford Waycott, of the Devon and Cornwall Constabulary, were on mobile patrol. They saw a *"star-shaped light"* at Anvil Corner, two miles east of Holsworthy. The officers attempted to give chase, but were unable to catch up with the UFO, which they estimated as being approximately four hundred yards away from the police car.

Media's reaction and response

On the 27th October 1967, the *Daily Mirror* (like so many of the newspapers around that period) published their account, but could not take this article seriously, quote: 'Grapefruit Joins The UFO'. A giant grapefruit – a saucer-shaped object, like a Maltese Cross were among the unidentified flying objects reported in Southern England yesterday. The 'GRAPEFRUIT' – reported by two policemen in a car at Holsworthy, near Okehampton, Devon – was seen at 2am.

Police Constable Roger Willey

One of the policemen – Constable Roger Willey (29), who reported a star-shaped object last Monday said:

> *"It looked bigger than an ordinary aircraft. The 'saucer' was spotted by my duty replacement – Constable Keith Droudge (24) and news agency reporter Ted Hines (22). The 'Maltese Cross' was reported at Middleton Cheyney, near Banbury, Oxfordshire."*

At a later Press conference, held by the Chief Constable of the Devon and Cornwall Constabulary, P.C. Waycott said: *"The light wasn't piercing, but it was very bright. It was star-spangled, just like looking through wet glass, and although we reached 90 miles per hour, it accelerated away from us."*

The *Times* reports on the incident!

The *Times* newspaper disclosed that Mr Peter Mills – Member of Parliament for Torrington, in Devon – intended to ask questions in Parliament about the recent spate of UFO activity. This statement appears to have galvanised the MOD into some action, judging from a report submitted on the 26th October by

Haunted Skies Volume Two Revised

the Head of S4 (Air), Mr I.E. Carruthers. This confirmed arrangements had been made with the Deputy Chief Constable of Devon and Cornwall for a MOD Officer (a member of the Defence Intelligence Service staff) to interview the police officers who had seen the UFO at Exeter Police Station.

On the 27th October, the Police Constables were interviewed by Mr J.C. Dickison from the MOD, (DI55), at Okehampton Police Station, who later 'wrote-up' the following report (now declassified):

> "The Police Constables first saw a bright light on the horizon shortly after 4am on 24th October. At this time they were sitting in a police patrol car. They decided to try and discover the source of the light and started to drive in what they believed to be the general direction of its source.
>
> The road, along which they were driving, from Holsworthy to Hatherleigh, near Okehampton, is a winding country road and, as they drove along, the light appeared to move. After driving some ten or twelve miles, the constables realised that they were no nearer the source of light and they stopped and got out of their car. The light no longer appeared to be moving. Shortly afterwards, it disappeared.
>
> From a scientific point of view, the observation of the light through the windscreen of a moving vehicle does not provide a sound basis for concluding whether the source of the light moved or not. It is possible that it was the movement of the car which gave an illusion that the light itself was moving. Although the planet Venus would have appeared over the eastern horizon between 3 and 4 o'clock, the police constables state that they observed their light to the north-east; therefore, it is not possible to state they observed Venus.
>
> When questioned about the disappearance of the light, one of the police constables indicated he had decided the light came from a spaceship. They did not see a spaceship but only saw a light, and his conclusion appears to have no factual basis.
>
> Signed,
>
> J.C. Dickison"

We chased it at 90 mph says P-cs

Western Daily Press Reporter

Two policemen in a patrol car chased a strange light in the sky at 90 mph at 4 a.m. yesterday.

Later an artist drew the picture reproduced above, as the two P-cs related their experience.

Driving the car was P-c. Roger Willey.

With him was P-c. Clifford Waycott, aged 33, father of two.

Between Okehampton and Holsworthy they saw what seemed to be like a flying cross.

'Bit sceptical'

Said P-c. Waycott: "I am normally a bit sceptical. You get like that in the police.

"It was a pleasant night and we were driving beside fields and trees. I saw a light in front of us.

"I thought what a funny place for a street lamp. It had a diffused light. It wasn't piercing, but it was very bright.

"It was star spangled just like looking through wet glass. Before I spoke, the driver saw the light and put his foot down.

"We reached 90 mph but the light accelerated away from us.

"I thought it might have been an aircraft in trouble. Then it seemed to drop. We gave chase again but it soared higher into the sky.

"We were in touch with HQ in Exeter all the time."

An official police announcement said the patrol car crew later saw a second light join the first.

The light was also seen by officers at Okehampton police station for nearly an hour before low cloud obscured their vision.

The patrolmen were so amazed by the sight that they woke a man sleeping in a Land Rover. He was Christopher Garner, of Marshwood Farm, Heatherleigh.

"I thought I am having a nightmare when they woke me up. I don't know what it was, but this object was much too bright for any star," he said.

At a press conference in Okehampton police station, the officers said it could not have been Venus. They saw the planet at the same time in another part of the sky.

'Motivated'

Mr. David Hill, chairman of the Exeter Unidentified Flying Objects research group said: "Assuming the police officers have given the correct description, this can only have been some sort of motivated vehicle.

"Their sighting coincides with a sighting by one of our own observers who described the same shape, brightness and movement at almost the same time."

IN BRISTOL Mr. Frank Dwyer, of Wellington Hill West, Henleaze, said he saw a similar obect while driving into Bristol on the M5 near Cribbs Causeway.

Further to the interview held with the officers, after investigations made into the matter by the MOD, it can be seen from the main body of a now declassified AIR/20.11612 MOD file that there was a concerted effort made to reinforce the official view held by the MOD that Venus was the explanation. In addition to this, the MOD suggested the following explanations for what the officers had seen: A light mounted on helicopter or aircraft, a light shone from a hill, Venus, or a balloon.

Although he conceded there was no record of any balloon, helicopter or aircraft, in the area at the time, Mr W.P. Cassell, the MOD official concerned, later 'wrote-up' the following con-clusion:

> *"In view of the attitude of mind of the two policemen during the interview, and the winding nature of the Holsworthy to Hatherleigh road, some doubt can be reasonably expressed about the absolute reliability and accuracy of their account; thus Venus is still the plausible explanation for what they saw. I think that it would be most unfortunate, in the light of conflicting conclusions of the policemen and of the departments, to make any 'off the record' statements which appear to brand the policemen as liars, or exaggerators. However, the USAF or the RAF might be able to find a way of suggesting to Mr Peter Mills, MP, that 'off the record' Venus remains the most likely explanation and that there are some grounds for believing that the policemen's account of what they saw **was** not 100% accurate.*
>
> *Signed, W.P Cassell"*

Room 2843, S4 Air, 19.12.67

The officers were also inter-viewed by John Cleary-Baker, Head of Investigations for BUFORA, during the same month.

Hansard tells us of another question put to Merlyn Rees, the Secretary of State for Defence, on the 25th October 1967, by Sir Eric Edward Bullus:

John Cleary-Baker

> "How many reports he has received in the last six months of the sightings of unidentified flying objects; what were the results of his investigations; and if he will make a statement."

Reply:

> "153 reports have been received in the MOD in the last six months. Some of these are still being investigated, but commonplace explanations have been found for the rest."

(Source: AIR21/19216)

PCs chase 'cross in the sky' at 80 mph

Two policemen in a patrol car today chased an unidentified flying object for about 12 miles.

The officers said it was "very large, bright and in the shape of a cross."

During the chase—at speeds of up to 80 mph—the object flew at about tree-top height virtually over the road.

Later the policemen reported seeing the object again, and this time it was joined by a second, similar object. They were in sight for about an hour.

PCs. Roger Willey and Clifford Waycott were in a patrol car at about 4 a.m. when they first saw the object on the Holsworthy to Hatherleigh road in Devon.

MARRIED

PC Willey is based at Okehampton, and PC Waycott at nearby Winkleigh. Both are family men in their 30's.

The nearest they got to the object was about 40 yards. A police spokesman said: "It left them. It appeared to stop in a field, and they stopped and got out, but it disappeared."

The constables were joined by a motorist, Mr. Christopher Garner, of Hatherleigh.

The police spokesman said: "He told the constables that he thought he was having a nightmare."

Police officers UFO sighting official explanation they had misidentified Venus!

Even now, over forty years later, one can still find allegations made on various websites, which claim that during a visit to the *BBC Plymouth* studios, in 1967, the two officers concerned admitted they had misidentified Venus. This is strenuously denied by Roger David Willey, who was known to us personally, and whose integrity – as far as we are concerned – has never been in question.

Roger told us:

"My regular observer was off that night, so I picked up Clifford Waycott – a county 'bobby'. I'd never thought about UFOs before, because it didn't concern or interest me up to then. I'd been in the Force for 12 years, but I do know that I saw something I couldn't explain. I drove at high speed to try and catch up with it, but it didn't make any difference. I stopped the car at Bassett's Corner and woke up a man, sleeping in a car, to show him the object (Chris Garner on holiday from Luton, in Bedfordshire). To actually pick up the microphone on the traffic car and tell traffic control that I was seeing something I couldn't explain in the sky, not unnaturally, attracted all manner of comments – as if I had been drinking. I admit I felt a proper 'Charlie' afterwards. When I returned to base, the Press were waiting for me.

When I woke up off nights, the Press were outside the house. This went on for a few days. I never described what we saw as a 'Flying Cross'. It didn't look like a cross, to begin with, but then neither was it globe or saucer-shaped. It was like looking through diffused glass."

On another occasion, shortly after the event being made public, PC Waycott was asked whether he could have seen an aeroplane or a helicopter, or perhaps a satellite:

"Absolutely not; it was unlike anything I had ever seen on Earth. It was terribly bright. In fact, it had a shattering effect, but wasn't glaring. We were about 400 yards away from it."

PC Willey added:

It seemed to be watching us and wouldn't let us catch up. It was at various altitudes all the time but mostly just above the trees. It had terrific acceleration. It seemed to

REPORT ON UNIDENTIFIED FLYING OBJECTS

Name: Roger David WILLEY
Address: 4, Police House, North Road, Okehampton.
Telephone: Okehampton 601
Date of observation: 24.10.67.

Place of Employment: Okehampton
Occupation: Police Officer
Education: Grammar School
Special Training: Advanced Police Driver
Time: 4.10 a.m.

Locality of Observations: A.3072 Holsworthy to Hatherleigh road, at Anvil Corner.

How long did you see the object. 30 minutes.

Please describe weather. Slight drizzly rain, nightime. Varying sky from cloudy to quite clear.

Position of the Sun or Moon in relation to the object seen and to you. Moon visible at times in southerly direction.

If seen at night, twilight or dawn were the stars or moon visible. At times.

Were there more than one object. Yes. If so, please tell how many and draw a sketch of what you saw, indicating direction of movement, if any. Two

Was the object brighter than the background of the sky? Yes.

If so compare the brightness with the Sun, Moon headlights etc. Liken to a fluorescant light.

Did the object.

    a. Appear to stand still at any time? Yes.
    b. Suddenly speed up and rush away at any time? Yes.
    c. Change shape. Yes, grew smaller with distance.

Was ther any wind. No.

Did you observe the object through an optical instrument or other aid, windshield windowpane, storm window, screening etc. That? Windshield and with the naked eye.

Did the object have any sound. No.

Please tell if the object was

    a. Fuzzy or blurred. Yes.
    b. Like a bright star. Yes.

Was the object self luminous. Yes.

Did the object rise or fall while in motion. Yes varying from treetop height to a high altitude.

The apparent size of the object when compared with the arms length. Larger.

How did you happen to notice the object. Driving along quiet country road with cloudy and starless sky the object suddenly appeared at treetop level

Where were you and what were you doing at the time? Driving a Police Vehicle.

How did the object disappear from view? Accelerated away to a pinpoint of light.

Compare the speed of the object with a piston or jet aircraft at the same apparent altitued. Faster; In the region of two or three thousand miles per hour.

Please estimate the distance of the object. Hard to define, but the nearest would be in the region of 400 yards.

Names and address of other witness if any. Constable Clifford Maycott and Christopher Thomas GARNER.

Is there an airport, military, government or research installation in the area: Nearest airport approximately 30 miles, nearest military approximately 10 miles.

Have you seen other objects of an unidentified nature? Yes.

know we were chasing it. It looked bigger than any aircraft. Later on it was joined by another similar shaped object – extremely bright and noiseless."

Ex-Devon and Cornwall Constabulary Police cadet – Brian Hagan, who was on the same initial police training course as Roger Willey, during 1957, from Droitwich, Worcestershire, contacted us in 2007.

"I ended up as a village 'bobby' but saw Roger frequently, who was on traffic. I remember the UFO incident, as it was the main talking point for some time. Knowing Roger and 'Cliff', I am certain this was not a hoax but a genuine happening, seen by these two experienced officers on night duty. It was general knowledge that there had been a number of unexplained UFO sightings over a period of a year in the Torbay area. Rumour had it there was a government directive, stating that on no account should UFO sightings by police officers be made public."

Over the years that have elapsed we have spoken to Roger on numerous occasions, and been to see him and his then partner – Michelle, who was devastated when he passed away a few years ago now. We also spent time with his son, Mark, who furnished us with many photographs of his father.

(Sources: *Daily Telegraph* – 'Police chase white flying light', 25.10.1967/*Daily Mirror* – 'Saucer led us a chase, say Police', 25.10.1967/*Daily Mirror* – 'PCs chase after mystery object', 26.10.1967/*Daily Mail* – 'Police car chases mystery light in the sky')

'Flying Cross', Surrey

A similar object was seen by Mrs F.M. Stead from Canterbury Road, Morden, Surrey, during the early hours of the same morning, described as being, *"a bright orange-red cross, spinning on a central axis, surrounded by a golden halo. Within a few seconds, it was gone"*.

At 4.40am, a woman living in St. Margarets Road, Edgware, London, was awoken by a bright light shining in her bedroom window, which faced northwards. She looked through it and saw, just above the rooftops, *"a bright silver 'cross', motionless in the sky, with a pale rainbow coloured centre"*, which she first took to be Venus, but then realised the planet was overshadowed by the brightness of the 'cross'. After watching it for 20 minutes, she went back to bed.

(Source: Gordon Creighton, *Flying Saucer Review*, Vol. 14, No. 2, March/April, 1968)

Brandis Corner

At about the same time, Stella Crocker from Goosemoor, Brandis Corner, also saw what she described as a *"starry cross"*, hovering in the sky under cloud cover. Shortly afterwards, Mrs Ursula Dommett from Caister-on-Sea, Norfolk, saw *"a cross-shaped object"*, with bright lights, heading out to sea over the coast. Although we do not know the exact time, we discovered that two police officers, from East Sussex Constabulary, had *"chased a 'Flying Cross' UFO in the Up Holland area, during the early hours of the same morning, before losing sight of it as it moved up and behind cloud."*

(Source: *Manchester Evening News Chronicle* – 'Police spot Flying Crosses')

Leicestershire

At 6am, a bright light was seen shining through the curtains of the Vicarage at Sheepy Magna, Leicestershire, by the rector's wife.

She drew the curtains and saw two mysterious objects in the sky; one resembled a large orange, hovering over the nearby church tower, the other was a little higher. (**Source:** *Leicester Mercury*, 25.10.1967)

Cheshire

At 7am, a blue, glowing, cross-shaped UFO was seen over Cheadle, in Cheshire, by paperboy Nigel Bailey. **(Source: DIGAP)**

Aldridge, Staffordshire

At 5.45pm, a 'yellow light' was seen circling high in the sky, for a couple of minutes, over Aldridge, in Staffordshire. **(Source: UFOSIS)**

Guildford

At 9pm, a glowing 'ring of fire' was seen to approach the ground over Wood Street Common, near Guildford. **(Source: SIGAP)**

Stockton-on-Tees

Stockton-on-Tees schoolgirls – Julie Hobday and Vicki Donaldson – were walking along Cotherstone Road, at 9.30pm, when they sighted what they described as *"a 'Flying Cross', covered with bright flashing lights around its centre, hovering about 30 feet in the air. Suddenly, it dropped downwards and disappeared from sight"*.

The girls, who admitted being frightened, had no knowledge of the incident which involved police officers from the Devon and Cornwall Constabulary, earlier that morning.
(Source: *North-Eastern Evening Gazette,* **26.10.1967 – 'UFO scared us stiff')**

Tyneside

"A cross-shaped object, with a flared end and irregular crosspieces", was seen hovering in the sky over some blast furnaces, between Stanley and Consett. It was seen by Miss Dodd and Alan Story, of Tyneside, at 9.30pm on 24th October 1967. **(Source: Tyneside UFO Society)**

Wing Commander Eric Cox

At 9.45pm Wing Commander Eric Cox, and his wife, sighted seven lights in a 'V' formation. It was north of their position, whilst they were driving along the B.3978, Cadnam to Fordingbridge Road, in Hampshire. Ironically, earlier in the evening, the couple (who were returning from visiting relatives) had watched a television interview held with the two Devon and Cornwall Police officers, regarding their chase of a 'Flying Cross'. This had led to Mrs Cox jokingly remarking to her sister, *"I'm going to look for lights in the sky tonight on my way home"*.

Ironically, this is exactly what happened, as she was the first to sight the strange lights in the sky and bring the matter to her husband's attention, whilst on the way home. Mr Cox initially dismissed her claim and continued to drive for a quarter of a mile, before his wife's insistence caused him to pull up the car in a lay-by.

As a result of what he and his wife saw, Mr Cox contacted the police and later wrote this detailed letter to the MOD, dated the 8th November 1967. It was eventually declassified, (Air 20/1 1889), over 30 years later:

"They appeared to be in a 'V' formation and stayed absolutely still for about three minutes, after which time the three on the right-hand side appeared to recede very rapidly, or the lights could have faded. The remaining four lights then formed into a perfect formation of a cross or plus sign. These remained for about three minutes, when they faded, or receded, rapidly. On looking around I noticed the following:

The clouds were 8/10ths.

The horizontal visibility was about 12 miles.

That the clouds to the north were visible, owing to the lights from Salisbury, eight miles distant, being reflected upon them, although not noticed at the time of the observation.

This was directly behind the observed lights at the time of the observation.

The moon was ascending towards the East, i.e. on our right, but was three parts obscured by cloud.

Our position was on top of a ridge and the objects appeared above an opposite ridge, about two miles distance, almost due north. I estimated that the height of the objects was about two hundred feet above the trees, which were faintly discernible against the light reflected onto the clouds from Salisbury.

The lights, in any opinion, could not have been due to reflection, refraction, nor were they anything to do with either Venus, or flight refuelling.

I inspected the site on the following day and could find nothing to account for the sighting of such bright and well defined lights.

Length of sighting: about six minutes; the objects did not change shape individually – colour whitish, sound none. No visible change of direction. The lights were bright, similar to a car's headlight but not dazzling. They were due north, at an elevation from the observation point of about 5 degrees from the horizontal. There was no wind, the temperature mild, the weather was dry. I hope that this information is satisfactory, but will gladly supply any further details if you care to visit me. I do not believe in 'little green men', or 'flying saucers', etc., but I am certain they cannot be dismissed as easily as authority would deem. I have never before seen anything like them and incidentally I am a teetotaller.

Yours faithfully,

A .Cox, Wing Commander, RAF, retired."

Wing Commander Cox, and his wife, was also interviewed by Mr Myers and NICAP UFO Researcher – Mr Julian J. Hennessey from Acton, in London.

We felt it served no useful purpose in presenting the full transcripts of the interviews, as much of it was already covered in the letter sent to the MOD by Eric Cox, but believe the following points of interest are worth bringing to the reader's attention:

Julian:
"What is your reaction to the possibility that these could have been flare illuminating projectiles of the type fired by 25 pounders?"

Eric Cox:

"If you fire any projectiles of any sort, you first of all have an upward movement, if you see the light as it lights, and then a slow descent. If it is on a parachute, it has a fast descent. This did neither. It could be either something going away from us, very fast indeed, so that the light disappeared, or it could be a powerful light being switched off."

Julian:

"You said that three of the lights departed, or seemed to fade first?"

Eric Cox:

"Yes that's right. They appeared to be a very good formation of lights and made me think of helicopters, because it was a very good formation, but they were a stationary formation. This is the thing that also made me think they were helicopters, when suddenly three on the right broke away as three and the lights went out."

Julian:

"When they broke away, did you actually see them move?"

Eric Cox:

"They moved away."

Julian:

"You actually saw them move away?"

Eric Cox:

"They moved away. They didn't move away all three together, they moved away in a higgledy-piggledy manner, as though they could have each been an individual something. If they had been flares, they would have fallen at the same rate."

The incident was later investigated by DI.55 Science 4 and 54 (Air) from the MOD, who sent a team of three men out to interview the Wing Commander, after making enquiries with a Major Avery, sub-district Salisbury Plain, who confirmed Larkhill Artillery was in use all evening, firing hard stuff, i.e. 25 pounders, 120 millimetres etc., which would light up the sky in a series of flashes, and that a check with the Range Officer at Larkhill Military, on 2nd January 1969, confirmed they were using illumination and flares that evening.

Accordingly, Mr L. Akhurst wrote to Wing Commander Cox:

"Dear Wing Commander Cox,

I am writing to let you know the results of our investigation of your report about unidentified flying objects, which you saw at 21.45hrs on 24th October. On the basis of the information you provided, we made a thorough examination of all activities in the area, which might have given rise to your observation.

Larkhill Artillery Range and Boscombe Down airfield are both close to the line of sight which you indicated to us and we found that both were in use at the time of your sighting.

Of course, both locations are rather further from your point of observation than the estimated position of the lights which you gave, but you will recall that our investigators discussed with you the difficulties of accurate estimation of range, particularly at night, and you accepted that the lights might have been further away than you first thought. Larkhill Artillery Range was in use all that evening until about midnight.

In addition to high explosive shells, illuminating flares were being fired. As I am sure you know these hang in the air for some time before expiring in a random manner. These flares were also observed by members of the Porton Down Establishment, which lies between your point of observation and the Range. It does seem probable, therefore, that 'your' UFO could have been a group of illuminating flares. Coincidentally, at the time of your observations, an aircraft was approaching to land at Boscombe Down and it is possible that you may have seen lights on this aircraft.

The variation in the appearance of the lights could then be explained by changes in altitude of the aircraft, as it made its circuit and final approach. However, the sight of aircraft lights will be familiar to you and, although even experienced pilots have been known to mistake the source of lights which they ought to recognise, this seems a far less likely explanation for your sighting.

You will be interested to learn that one of the officers who investigated your sighting, did himself subsequently see, by chance, an almost exactly similar series of lights, but was able, at the time, to identify them as lights of an aircraft. In this case, the explanation was immediately obvious, but it does mean that we cannot entirely disregard the possibility that you also saw the lights of an aircraft. In short, we cannot make a positive identification but we think you must have seen either illuminating flares above the Larkhill Artillery Range, or the lights of an aircraft landing at Boscome Down.

Yours faithfully

Signed... L.W. Akhurst"

The contents of this letter were brought to the attention of Julian Hennessey, who conducted another interview with

Wing Commander Cox. He was asked to comment on the conclusions reached by the MOD.

Julian:

"So as far as you are concerned, Larkhill and Boscombe Down are not visible. If they had any flares up at the time, would they not be in the direction that you had seen the objects?"

Eric Cox:

"I very much doubt it, but Boscombe Down is so laughable ... that it was an aircraft landing, is absolutely stupid. The clouds were low; although it is very clear up to whatever height the clouds were, because we could see the moon, but it was very low on the horizon over on the east, but you certainly would not have seen an airplane – that is absolutely certain."

Julian:

"The aircraft landed at 21.44hrs. (confirmed to me in writing, by the Senior Air Traffic Controller at Boscombe), and your sighting started at 21.46hrs, so the aircraft was not in the air at the time."

Eric Cox:

"I would not have seen that anyway."

Julian:

"What is your reaction to the Ministry's letter?"

Eric Cox:

"Well, I was going to write to them and say, lay this on this light business, the flare business, and get an aircraft to land at Boscombe Down, and come down here and I will accompany you to the spot. We will then have a look and see. Now that is a scientific check, in my opinion. If they say that this is so, well it is very easy for them to lay it on, no difficulty at all. We could have had a neutral observer as well. They have got my report, as you have, and they could say this is what you said then. You can't change that, this is what you are looking at now; we think it is similar or otherwise. I mean I am quite happy if they say 'there you are', but this is what they ought to do and, until they do, I think this is the biggest load of tripe that I've heard in a long time."

Julian visited the location, and retraced the steps taken by the couple. These included a visit to the police station at Fordingbridge, Larkhill School of Artillery, and Boscombe Down.

Like us, he is convinced that whatever the couple saw, it wasn't flares or the landing lights of a 'Hastings' aircraft.

If this had been the only incident of the late evening of 24th October 1967 (rather than the 25th October 1967, as incorrectly published in *some* UFO books), one might be tempted to accept the official explanation. However, as we have seen, it was no such thing.

In March 1968, Mr Hennessey – through Wing Commander Sir Eric E. Bullus, MP – submitted his findings to the

Ministry of Defence, and requested their comments. In May l968, the following reply was received from Mr Merlyn Rees:

> *"We have not heard from Wing Commander Cox since we told him of our findings in January. This exchange of views was, of course, a personal one between Wing Commander Cox and the department and, as Mr Hennessey has been told by the department, on a number of occasions, we do not discuss with third parties the detailed information included in such exchanges, without the consent of the member of the public concerned.*
>
> *However, l can tell you that in reaching our conclusions, we took into account all the information provided to us both in writing and verbally, by Wing Commander Cox, about the time and duration of the incident, the distance and bearings, and the description of the lights.*
>
> *We also took account of the experience in observation Wing Commander Cox must have accumulated over the years. Hennessey's personal assessment of the information, which he has obtained, doesn't give us cause to amend our views."*

According to *Penthouse* (UK), published in 1968 (Volume 3, Number 2), the MOD – when this matter had been brought to their attention – commented:

> *"It has been suggested that it might have been the planet Venus, which had been sighted in that area".*

When they once again asked the officers if this could have been the explanation, they were told:

> *"It was definitely not. Venus was north-east of the object and nowhere near it."*

Penthouse, in what appears to have been a dogged determination to get some answers, eventually received an explanation on the 9th November from the MOD's unidentified Press Officer, who told them:

> *"You won't approve of the explanation but it's an official one; the officers saw a light. We have complete radar coverage over the country and what they saw was not an alien object. There were many reports from that part of the country and most of them turned out to be Venus."*

Penthouse continued, asking:

> *"Do you mean to tell us that the two constables saw Venus come down to tree level, hover, and then take-off at supersonic speed?"*

The reply was: *"What do you want from me? I only work here!"*

25th October 1967 – Sussex police motorcyclist sights 'Flying Cross UFO'

At 4.45am, a police motorcyclist from Lewes, Sussex, reported having sighted a cross-shaped UFO travelling across the sky, over Halland, heading north-west. Although the officer was not named, we understand that a number of other officers also saw this object – some of whom attempted to give chase.

In Aberdeen, four flickering, yellowish 'lights' were seen high in the sky – one in front, with three others arranged behind in a semicircle, which slowly moved around it.

(Sources: *Aberdeen Press & Journal,* 26.10.1967/*Manchester Evening News,* 25.10.1967 – 'Police spot more Flying Crosses')

Over Birmingham

Mark Whittaker tells of a strange object he saw, while overlooking Perry Common playing fields, Birmingham (then in Warwickshire), at 6.45am:

> *"The sky was full of large black clouds that appeared not to be moving. A hundred feet below the clouds were two spheres, covered in a thin layer of 'mist', joined together. Around the right-hand sphere, this 'mist' formed a short stubby tail, about half the diameter of the sphere.*
>
> *I watched them for about 30 seconds as they moved away, heading in a north to south direction. Suddenly, they vanished from view."* **(Source: UFOSIS)**

At 7.15am, Mrs W. Hundell, her husband – Ray, and son – Andrew (15), of Goats Lane, Enfield, saw:

> *"...a round, orange 'ball of light' which grew quickly into a really big star. It hung in the sky in the west for about two minutes, before gradually decreasing in size then disappearing from view.*
>
> *Its place was now taken by a small black object, showing two pinpoints of light. These extinguished as the object headed away southwards, until I lost sight of it."*

(Source: *Evening Standard*, 26.10.1967 – 'Hotting up the trail of the Thing'/Unidentified newspaper, 26.10.67 – 'The Thing drops in at Enfield')

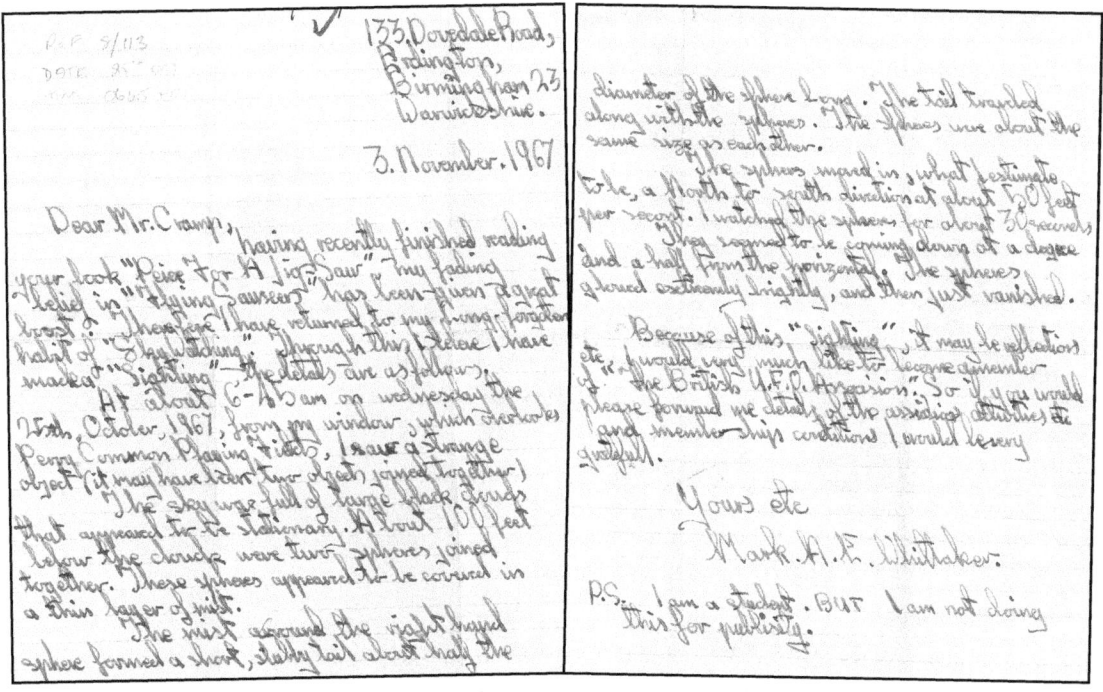

Over West Harrow

At 5.45pm, Mrs E. Rushton of 112, Welbeck Road, Harrow, saw a metallic object,

> *"...much smaller than a plane, heading south-west, about two miles away. It was globular at the rear and had what looked like the light from car headlamps at the front."*

(Source: *Harrow Observer*, 9.11.1967 – 'Another Thing')

Over County Durham

At 6.05pm, a brilliant red spherical object, *"twice as large as the moon"*, was sighted stationary in the sky, at an angle of 45 degrees off the horizon, over Old Hall, Washington, County Durham, by coal miners coming off shift. A short time later, it was seen to head north-east and lost from view, six to seven minutes later. (**Source: Leonard Cramp, Isle of Wight UFO Society**)

Over Sunderland

Schoolboys – John Reay, Kevin Pearson, Kevin Lynch and Ian Kent – were stargazing, at 7pm, on the Hill View Estate, Sunderland when they saw *"five red pea-sized objects"*, flying in a 'V' formation, travelling towards the north-east, before being lost from view as they headed out over the sea. On the same evening, a 'strange glow' was seen shooting backwards and forwards across the sky over Spalding, Lincolnshire. It was described as being round in shape, but not completely circular. When it turned in the sky, the witness saw it as long and slightly rounded in the middle. (**Source:** *Peterborough Evening Telegraph*, **28.10.1967**)

Lincolnshire

Mrs Christine Wilcox from Spalding, Lincolnshire, was driving along Barrier Cowbit Bank towards Crowland, with her friend Marlene Grant, at 8.30pm when they noticed: *"a strange glow in the sky moving in a crazy way – sort of shooting backwards and forwards, then fading away a few minutes later."* (**Source: South Lincoln UFO Study Group**)

Northamptonshire

At 8.45pm, a Northamptonshire resident was in his house when he was approached by one of his children, who told him to *"come and see the Sputnik"*.

The man went outside and saw:

> *"...a very big grey object, shaped like a boomerang, low down in the sky, showing four very bright orange lights on the front"*.

Malvern

Just before 9pm, Clive Robinson and Richard Corben – schoolboys from Chase School, Malvern – sighted *"a dome-shaped object, with a similar lump on the top"*. It descended over the girls' college playing field and landed behind a pavilion, a couple of hundred yards away, before taking off diagonally across the sky.

Clive told us:

> *"The object, in two halves, split vertically down the centre. The two halves then came together and it drifted to the ground. We went back to the field, a couple of days later, after a man called 'Tandy' came to see us. He showed us some triangular marks on the ground, two inches in size, in an arc."*

(**Source: Personal interview/***Malvern Gazette*, **2.11.1967**)

Wellingborough

At 9.30pm, Wellingborough School pupils – Peter Chapman and Timothy Pearce – sighted a bright glowing orange coloured 'sphere of light' in the sky and called out a number of other pupils to come and have a look at the object, which was now moving slowly away. Their curiosity aroused, the boys stopped outside scanning the sky. At 10pm, another strange object came into view.

Peter

> *"It was much higher and faster than the previous one; it then seemed to stop before fading away. At 11pm we saw another one, which stayed in view for about seven minutes."*

(**Source:** *Evening Telegraph*, **27.10.1967** – 'Schoolboys spot UFO over Wellingborough')

Devon

Although we were unable to identify the exact date, we learnt of a UFO sighting which took place towards the end of October 1967, involving Jack Prince – Chairman of Clovelly Parish Council, who was driving home between Okehampton and Torrington, in Devon.

"I had just left Hatherleigh, when I saw this 'light' in the sky, about the size of a helicopter, a hundred feet up in the air and some 80 yards away. I stopped the car at one stage, to obtain a closer look, and kept it in sight for about a mile, before it dropped downwards and out of view."

(Source: Isle of Wight UFO Society)

26th October 1967 – Surge in UFO activity

Police Constable Roger Willey was on night patrol with PC Keith Droudge, and parked on Southern Battle Camp – a high point, overlooking Dartmoor – at 2.50am; this time they were in possession of a camera.

Roger:

"A 'light' suddenly appeared in the sky over Bassett's Cross, exactly over the location where I and PC Waycott had seen the previous UFO, about seven miles away. This time it wasn't so well-defined. It appeared to head towards Jacobstowe, then dip down – as if about to land – and disappear in the same place we had seen it before. It happened so fast, we didn't have time to take a photo."

PC Keith Droudge was to witness something strange himself towards the early hours of the morning – as revealed in a police memo, left for PC Roger Willey.

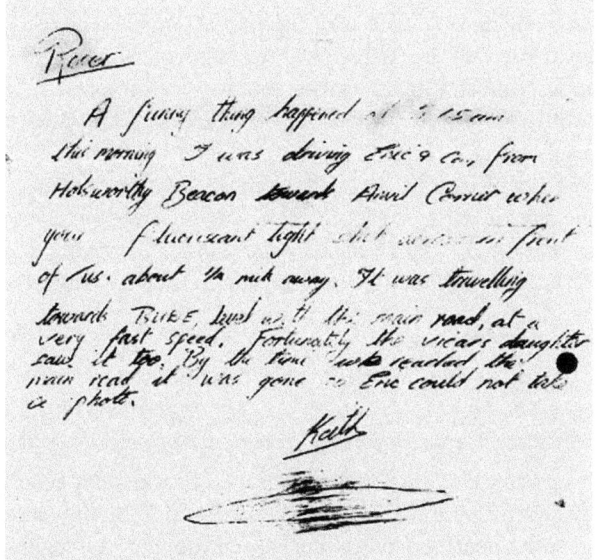

"A funny thing happened at 5.05am. I was driving Eric (Force photographer) from Holsworthy Beacon towards Anvil Corner, when your 'fluorescent light' shot across the front of us, about a quarter-of-a-mile away. It was travelling towards Bude, level with the main road, at a very fast speed. Fortunately, the vicar's daughter saw it as well. By the time we reached the main road, it was gone. Eric could not take a photo."

Wellingborough – Early morning

We also learnt that a Mr B. Spademan of Whytewell Road, Wellingborough, was outside during the early hours of the same morning, when he was fortunate to capture on photo what he described as:

"…something bigger than any mass of stars, and definitely not a planet or a star".

Mr Spademan then called the police, who arrived. One of them suggested it was Venus, and the other disagreed. **(Source:** *Evening Telegraph,* **27.10.1967)**

UFO over Hampshire

Mr W. Collett, from Sussex, was driving his Ford Transit van along the A32 in Hampshire, at 4.30am. He was heading towards Reading, after having just crossed the intersection with the A30, on what was a dry but not frosty morning – the road lit by a bright quarter moon. Suddenly, the electrical system on the van failed completely and the vehicle slowed to a halt.

Mr Collett alighted and had a look under the bonnet, thinking that a battery lead had come adrift. Finding nothing wrong, he was about to get back into the vehicle when he caught sight of a dark object, clearly outlined in the sky. It hung motionless over the road ahead, but Mr Collett thought no more of it, eager to retry the starter switch. At the first attempt, nothing happened. When he tried again, the engine burst into life. Breathing a sigh of relief, Mr Collett continued on his journey.

Triumph turned to failure when, a few hundred yards along the road, the engine cut out again. As he stepped out of the vehicle once more, he immediately noticed a change in air pressure and an all pervading, rather oppressive, smell – which he likened to that produced by an electric motor.

After examining the engine bay and finding nothing wrong, he straightened up – noticing the object was still in the same position as before, a few hundred yards away, 50-100 feet in the air. Mr Collett watched the object for several minutes, estimating it to be 60 feet wide, by 30 feet high, until it suddenly tilted before moving away – soon out of sight.

(Source: *Vehicle stoppage at Hook,* by R.H.B. Winder, *Flying Saucer Review,* Volume 13, No. 6, 1967)

Sunderland – 5.25am

At 5.25am, Mr J.D. Thatcher from Hillside, Sunderland, sighted *"a blue-white diamond-shaped object"* (estimated to be ten times the size of any star), apparently stationary in the sky. It was towards the south-east, at an elevation of 60 degrees, fading and brightening in luminosity at ten second intervals. It was not Venus, as that planet could be seen low in the sky towards the south. This was followed by the appearance of *"six to eight smaller objects",* forming a

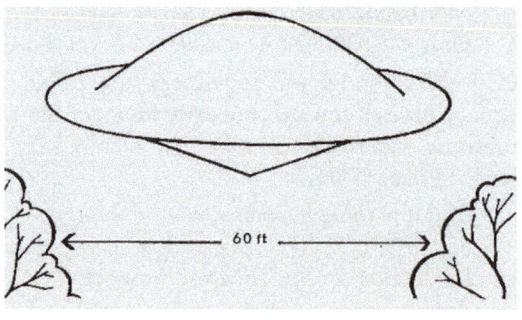

vertical oval-shaped formation, which took five minutes to pass from sight. (**Sources:** *UFOLOG/TUFOS*)

Meriden

At 6am, Meriden resident – Mr F. Woodcock, was awoken by a bright light. Rushing to the window he observed what looked like *"...a shining, cross-shaped, object with its upright 'arms' twice as long as its crosspiece. It was stationary for a couple of minutes, before accelerating away into the sky."*

It appears that the 'Flying Cross' UFO was next seen moving across the sky over the Daventry area, by several people, between 6.30am and 7am the same morning. This was accompanied by a report of an unidentified flying object seen moving in irregular jerks across the sky, over Warrington, at 6.30am, by teenager – Ray Spencer.

(Source: www.Magonia)

At 6.20am, two men were feeding the pigs on a farm at Southwick, near Trowbridge, when they sighted:

> *"...a diamond white coloured 'Flying Cross', accompanied by three other red objects, heading across the sky at fast speed, towards the direction of Bristol, at an angle of 45 degrees off the horizon".*

One of the workers was badly shaken by what he had witnessed.

(**Sources:** Ken Rogers/Trevor Selby, International Sky Scouts Association)

Lincoln

At 6.45am, Margaret Fenwick – a housewife from Sleaford, Lincoln – drew back her curtains and saw:

> "...a 'thing', shaped like the planet Saturn", heading south. "I wouldn't go as far as to say it was cigar-shaped. It was difficult to tell.
>
> I got the impression it was flashing and its behaviour certainly erratic."

Other witnesses to the passage of this object through the air included Mr Christopher Bird and several of his friends, who were leaving Westholme, when they saw something coloured orange or red – a little larger than a star – moving from north to south across the sky.

(Sources: *Sleaford Standard,* **3.11.1967 – 'Saucer shock for housewife'/South Lincolnshire UFO Study Group)**

Buckinghamshire

At 7am, a woman living in Buckinghamshire sighted a glowing 'ball of light' in the sky.

> "It was sort of silvery in the centre, surrounded by a white halo of light. It then seemed as though it started to spin and dipped lower, moving in a circle – as though inspecting something on the ground – before moving across the sky, northwards."

Stratford-upon-Avon

Was there any connection with what was seen at about the same time, over Stratford-upon-Avon? The witness was Susan Page (then aged 13), who happened to be looking out her bedroom window.

At around 7am, she noticed a couple of bright silver objects, moving north-east to south-west, above the scurrying clouds.

> "I called my mother and father, who stood with me watching them go over. To our surprise, three more identical objects appeared – not quite round, more like the baubles you get on a Christmas tree. What staggered us was they were only going slow – not as fast as an airplane. They took 10-15 minutes to pass over.
>
> After the first five came, there were two more identical objects – making seven in total – all travelling sideways. Strangely, we also saw two much smaller 'lights' heading the group. Unfortunately, we lost sight of the last two, as the sun was now rising."

In conversation with Susan, over 25 years later, she still considered the sighting the strangest thing she and her family had ever seen – something never to be forgotten.

Enquiries made with the police, at Leek Wootton, Warwickshire, revealed:

> "We have received a number of UFO sightings from several parts of the country, but not the War-wickshire area".

Details of the other reports were not disclosed. **(Source: Personal interview/ John D. Llewellyn)**

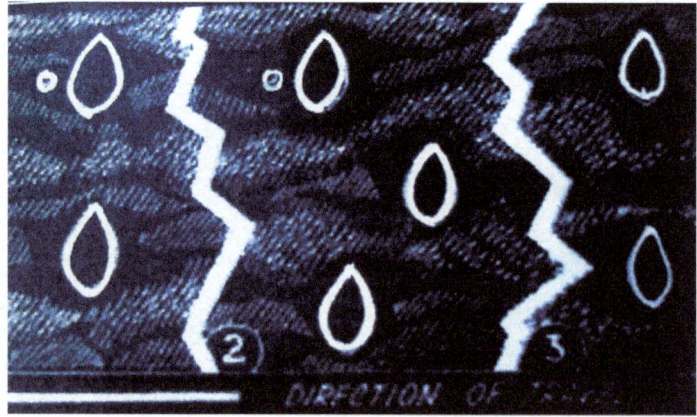

At 7.10am Gateshead

Six UFOs – described as fluores-cent green in colour – were seen crossing the face of the moon, at 7.10am, by three miners on their way to work at Springwell, near Gateshead.

"Four of them disappeared from sight; the other two remained stationary in the sky for five minutes, before vanishing into cloud." (**Sources:** *UFOLOG/TUFOS*)

A dimly-lit, green, circular, object was seen descending behind a group of trees over Hog's Back, Godalming, Surrey, by a newspaper boy out on his delivery. It was followed by the appearance of a brilliant white orb, which seemed to be circling over the ground – as if looking for something.
(**Source:** *Surrey Advertiser*, 28.10.1967)

7.10am – Birmingham

Another sighting around the same time took place over Tile Cross, Birmingham. It involved Mr Leonard Gain of 76, St Giles Road, and his colleague, who were waiting for a bus.

"We saw seven very bright lights crossing the sky, in the shape of a cross; we saw them for a few minutes."

At 7.30am

Mrs M. Jowett of Upper Norgrove, Alfrick, near Worcester, was awoken at this time by a brilliant light in the shape of an elongated star.

"It was high in the sky in the east, over Worcester. I woke my husband and we watched it for about five minutes."

(**Source:** *Birmingham Evening Mail*, 26.10.1967 – 'The bright lights seen over Birmingham')

'Flying Cross' UFO, Dorset

A remarkable UFO sighting occurred at Moigne Downs, halfway between Weymouth and Lulworth Cove, Dorset, at 11.25am, involving a former (now retired) British Overseas Airways Corporation (BOAC) Flight Administration Officer, Mr Angus Brooks, from Owermoigne Downs, Dorset, England. He was walking his dogs, when he decided to take shelter from the strong wind.

Almost immediately, he noticed a fine contrail, or the reflection of an aircraft, high up in the sky over Portland.

"This disappeared and into my view came this 'craft', descending at lightning speed, and levelled out approximately a quarter of a mile south of my position, 2-300 feet in height."

Three separate fuselages at rear

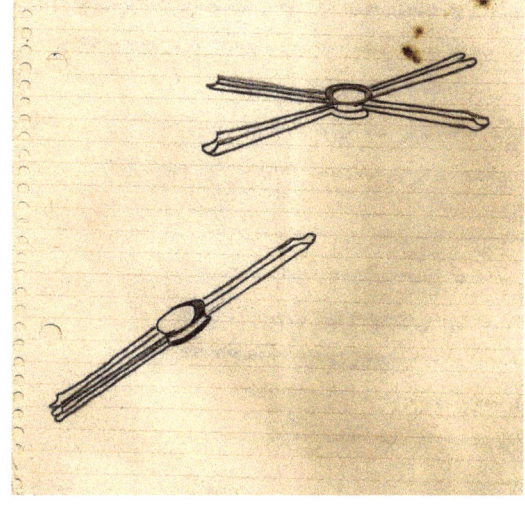

"The shape of the 'craft', prior to its levelling out to a hover position, was of a central circular chamber with a leading fuselage in the front and three separate fuselages together at the rear. On slowing to a 'hover' position, the two outer fuselages at the rear moved to position at the side of the 'craft' to form four fuselages at equidistance around centre chamber. There were no visible power units and no noise of applied power for reverse thrust, movement of fuselages, or for hovering. The 'craft' remained in the sky for the next 22 minutes and I remained rather apprehensive during this time. As seen from my horizontal position, the 'craft's' construction was of translucent material.

A II   26-10-67

Mr J.B.W. Brooks, a former Comet Flight Administration Officer with B.O.A.C.

Date of Observation: 26/10/67.
Time: 11.25 a.m. to 11.47 a.m. British Summer Time.
Position: Grid ref: 755833 ordnance survey map (1 inch/1 mile).
(Gt. Britain Sheet 178. (Dorchester.)

Weather at time: Clear sky with small amount of low cloud.
Wind: S.S.W. Force 8 (+ –)

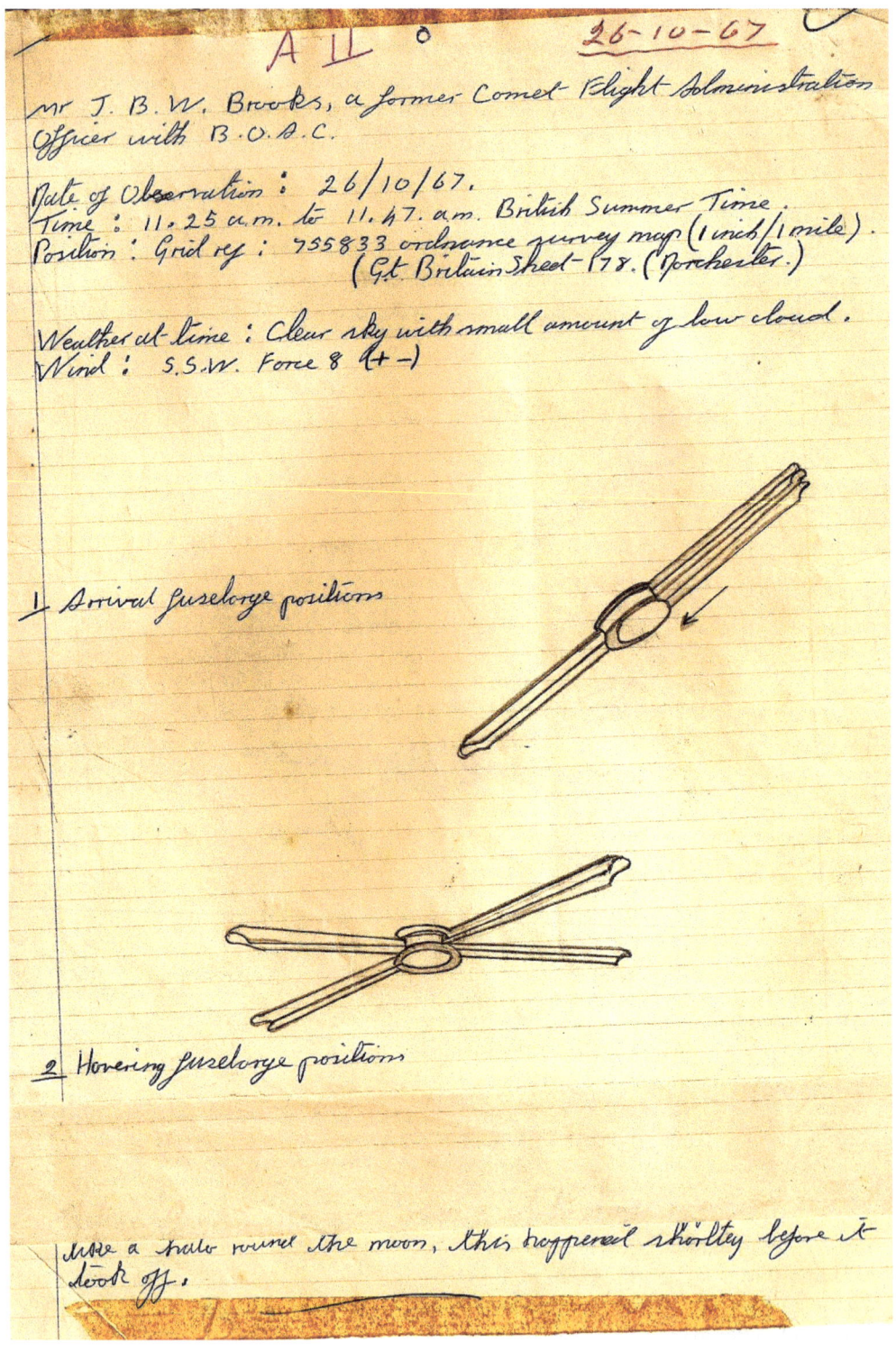

1 Arrival fuselage positions

2 Hovering fuselage positions

Also a halo round the moon, this happened shortly before it took off.

The colour of the 'craft' took on the colour of the sky above it, and changed with clouds passing over. It could have been a clear material at the top of the fuselage and centre chambers. There were dark centre shadows along the base of the fuselages and centre chambers. No movement was observed at any time of the operators and no portholes or crew viewing windscreens in the nose of fuselages. The nose cones of the fuselage were the reverse to our conventional types and the groove fins along the base of the fuselage did not open or close. The possibility of power passing through the construction material could not be considered.

The hover position was equidistant between Winfrith Power Station and the Portland Underwater Defence Station, about a mile inland from the USAF Communication Centre Unit at Ringstead Bay."

Movement occurs

"At 11.47am, two of the fuselages moved round to line up with a centre third fuselage. The 'craft' then climbed with increasing speed east-north-east over Winfrith. The lead fuselage on 'departure' was a different one to the 'arrival' lead. Dimensions – approx. centre chamber diameter, height 12-25 feet, length of fuselage 75 feet, height 7 feet, width 8 feet."

Receives a visit from the MOD

As a result of his letter sent to local newspapers, and the MOD, Mr Brooks received a visit from Dr. John Dickison, of the Royal Aircraft Establishment at Farnborough. He was accompanied by Mr Leslie Akhurst of S4 (Air) MOD, and Alec Cassie – a RAF psychologist, who interviewed him about the incident and later sent him the following letter, dated 5th April 1968. (Reference AF/509/10/56/Sf4 (Air):

"As promised at our meeting, I am writing to let you know the conclusions we have reached on your report about the object you saw at Owermoigne on 26th October. The information which you provided both in your written report and our discussion has been most carefully checked. We have also examined all activities in the area which might have given rise to your sighting, but have been unable to trace any other evidence of unusual or unauthorised aerial activity. In addition, in spite of the extensive local publicity on the radio, TV and Press, no corroborating reports have been received. Whilst it is true that the spot from which you made the observation is relatively remote, we did see some human activity during our walk to and from it last month; a farm worker on a tractor and a van on the road on the opposite hillside.

It seems unlikely that an object, which you estimated as having an overall length of 150 feet, could have hovered above the horizon for 22 minutes unnoticed by anyone else.

We do not doubt that the experience which you describe was a very vivid one, nor have we overlooked your long association with aviation. However, we are unable to agree with your conclusion that you saw a controlled flying vehicle of unique design and performance. I know that this may seem to contradict you but I am sure you will understand that the information you have given us is capable of other interpretations, which we believe are the more likely of what you saw."

Explanation: dead cell in the eye!

The explanation is this: you have told us that you were walking with your dogs on Moigne Downs. There was a gale force wind blowing and you decided to shelter from it and at the same time look for something unusual in the sky; that is to say, a bright star you hoped you might see in daylight. You first saw a contrail which was the normal vapour trail produced by a high flying aircraft, but this had no physical connection with the subsequent sequence of events. The next thing you saw was a vitreous floater – a piece of loose matter – a dead cell floating in the fluid of the eyeball. Such objects which appear as rods and/or discs are present in most people's eyes and are more noticeable when one is looking at brightly lit source colouring, such as a clear sky. The fact that you had an eye injury some years ago, since repaired by a corneal transplant, makes it possible that there might have been some larger floaters than usual. There are several similarities between the object you described and the floater, particularly its translucency and the slightly darker centre line of the rod-like components. The downward and transverse movement of the object is compatible with the movement of the object when the eye is held stationary, and the direction and speed of the departure of the object match the movement of a floater when the eye is flicked upwards. However, it is unlikely that the floater would have remained stationary for 22 minutes, but you will recall that you had the impression that the sighting lasted for a much shorter period than the 22 minutes shown on your watch. **It seems possible therefore, on lying down, after walking over rough country in a force 8 gale, you were feeling a little tired and you fell asleep or entered a near sleep state. There had been a great deal of publicity in October about UFO sightings and this, the floater, and the fact that you had been looking for an object in the sky, could have triggered-off a dream in which the floater took on the more elaborate form you described.** *Your instant knowledge and certainty of its size and distance and intent are all suggestive of the immediate and inexplicable awareness which are characteristic of many dreams. The distress of your Alsatian could be explained by her finding you in an unusual state asleep in the open air, rather than by the presence of an unusual object. I recognise that you may find our conclusions unsatisfactory, but in the light of information available to us we must form our own judgement about the object. As I have said, we have no other evidence of any unusual air activity that day, nor – despite widespread publicity – has any other witness come forward. While it would be intellectually arrogant to dispute the hypothesis that in the infinity of space there could be other intelligent life, we have no proof* of this, neither have the reports of unidentified flying objects passed to us provided evidence that extraterrestrial craft have visited Earth. Our radar cover is such that we are also quite satisfied that there is no clandestine aerial activity over the United Kingdom under terrestrial control. With respect, your report does not give us cause to alter or amend these conclusions. Finally, I should like to thank you very much indeed for your extremely detailed and interesting report and the kind welcome and wholehearted co-operation you gave to Mr Dickison, Mr Cassie and myself, when we visited you in February.

Signed,

Mr L. Akhurst."

Mr Brooks' reply was:

"I propose to take your report by paragraph and comment,

Paragraph 2

Corroborative reports in the area were received; these were night sightings of 'star' and 'dart' shaped craft. Either format could be affected by the Moigne Downs UFO with its fuselage control.

On the day of your visit there was one farm worker on our side of the valley and one was passed along the far road on the other side. This confirms that the percentage of activity in such a large and remote area is so low that on the day of the sighting it was more than possible that I was alone in the area. This had been the case in the previous eight months.

Paragraph 3

The report of any one person's experience can open interpretation permutations covering the range from frank disbelief to establishment oriented conclusions and I cannot but think that your contradiction of my interpretation of the very vivid experience that you agree I had must stem from the latter. Your paragraph 4 only strengthens this thought.

Paragraph 4

The 'con' trail mentioned was not a normal vapour trail, as it disappeared almost at once and must have been the craft's angled reflection in the sun. Vapour trails as we know continue with the aircraft and produce lengthy 'streamer' effects.

The 'floater' theory (what an unfortunate choice of name) means: mistake, bloomer, (in dictionary slang!) The Musca Volant, my specialist informs me, moves upwards and downwards and as the craft entered the vision circle at 30 degrees, moved across, descending to centre of vision... hovered for 22 minutes...then exited vision at 320 degrees – this hardly conforms.

As my eyes were not stationary during the observation, the chances of the exact similar shaped Musca Volant being present in the eyes at the exact same time can be discounted. The corneal implant of two years before had only improved the vision and MVs had not been noticed in the eye concerned. I understand that rod like MVs are exceedingly rare and seldom if ever linked.

In our discussion, my comment was not that my impression of the observation was shorter than the elapsed time, but that, after a period, I had lost the feelings of time due to the intense interest and admiration I was feeling for the craft's construction and of its non-aggressive appearance.

I walk daily for around two hours, over rough country, in all conditions and wind forces. I do not stop for rest, as I look at this walk in the same way I used to run each morning for exercise, when at the office, and as for sleeping en route...please!!! The fact that the gale was howling and my Alsatian was painfully par-clawing me to leave the spot, was hardly conducive of 'dropping off'.

Paragraph 5

It is normally contended that dream 'triggers' are of more personal evolvement than everyday news and I had not been particularly interested in the UFO 'splashes' at the time.

My instant knowledge, certainty of size, distance and intent, are indeed suggestive of the immediate awareness of the existence of the craft.

The Alsatian would not obey spoken or physical orders to remain still on the day, and on the two following days (with witnesses) at the site, showed distress which could only be attributable to having been pained or frightened at the craft's appearance. She could have received high VHF signal.

Paragraph 6

In your conclusions your disadvantage is, of course, that I was there at the time and any Investigation Commission can only work on the creditability of second hand report details combined with technical, medical and scientific assistance, so with reciprocal respect, your conclusions have not given me cause to alter my opinion of the Moigne Down UFO. Although, at the start of this experience, I had no wish to become involved in the UFO story, I now find I am interested enough to be doing some think tank work on this. May I suggest that 'fatigue mirages' and 'ghosting' be given some lateral thought by your department and on completion of my studies, I will pass on my results for discussion between us.

We should be happy to see you any time you are in the area; I enjoyed our meeting, next time who knows, the Moigne Down UFO may give you the doubtful privilege of seeing it.

My best regards to John Dickison and Alex Cassie and, of course, yourself.

Yours, Angus Brooks"

Dated: April 28th, 1968

It is difficult to accept the explanation given by the MOD as having any credibility. We do not believe this was any *'floater in the eye,'* or that it was manufactured by human hands ... absolute rubbish!

Whether 'it' was representative of some alien intelligence, who had acquired the knowledge to cross the enormous distances involved, is of course, a matter of speculation. We tend to believe it was (and most probably still is) indigenous to our planet.

Was there a connection with the flying cross-shaped objects that were seen by the police and other members of the public, during this month, or did this structure comprise part of a much larger object?

Frank Marshall – Letter to *Dorset Evening Echo*

Following the release of the MOD's explanation to the public, Frank Marshall felt it was necessary to write a letter to the *Dorset Evening Echo*, which was published on the 17th May 1968.

'Imagination' of Ministry of Defence:

Frank:

"With regard to the official explanation of the UFO seen by Mr A. Brooks of Owermoigne, last October, one has to admit that the Ministry has shown considerable imagination in conjuring up the explanation now given by them. However, the ingenuity of the explanation is somewhat dimmed when one recollects that Mr Brooks actually drew on a cigarette packet what he was witnessing at the time – no mean feat when one is asleep! Also, having visited the site where the incident occurred and finding it to be on the slope of a hillside, together with a force 8 gale, one feels it to have been one of the least likely spots for a mid-morning nap.

*Nevertheless, it now transpires that our Mr Brooks has been joined in this floating optical images by Mr James – a Reading student, who in late 1967 reported and drew an object which looks to be the twin of the Holwell sighting, with a central chamber and protruding arms, and which also folded up before taking leave of us. I suppose we, the believers in unknown aerial intruders in our skies, should be grateful for the efforts of the MOD for their efforts to unravel the mystery, but if we now (on top of trying to evaluate the flood of reports which will surely follow in the months ahead) have also to allow that our witnesses may be only people whose eyes need bathing or, as has just been put forward, are deep trance hypnotical subjects, many new and interesting possibilities are opened up. It will of course be a welcome respite from **blaming poor old Venus**, weather balloons and conventional aircraft doing unconventional things!*

I saw no reason to disbelieve the account given by Angus, of what appeared to be something highly unusual having entered our airspace, rather than the ludicrous explanation offered by the MOD."

Frank Marshall

(Source – *Dorset Evening Echo,* **9.3.1968 – 'Official Investigation of Dorset's aircraft mystery'/***Dorset Evening Echo,* **9.5.1968 – 'How Ministry discount Dorset man's sighting of a UFO/ /***Dorset Evening Echo,* **17.5.1968)**

Over Sunderland, 3.25pm – Anchor-shaped object

At 3.25pm, a huge sparkling blue-white anchor-shaped object, pulsating every ten seconds, was seen over Sunderland, at 60 degrees elevation in the south-east. It was separate from Venus (prominent in the night sky) and followed by the appearance of 6-8 smaller objects seen moving across the sky in an oval-shaped formation. **(Source: Tyneside UFO Society)**

Maidenhead, 5.30pm – Silver UFO

At 5.30pm a silver, oval, object was seen in the sky over Maidenhead, apparently following the M4 Motorway. It was then seen splitting into six separate fragments of light.
(Source: *Slough Observer,* **3.11.1967)**

UFO over Enfield, 7.15pm – Small black 'disc' with three lights

Andrew Hindle (aged 15) – then a member of the local Air Training Corps and versed in aircraft recognition – was at his home address in Goat Lane, Enfield, at 7.15pm. He heard his parents (who were upstairs), shouting out in alarm.

"I rushed upstairs, wondering what was happening. They directed my attention towards what looked like the Nativity Star, motionless in the sky, about two miles away. It then began to decrease in size and disappeared from view, leaving a small black 'disc' with three lights at the end and a line across the centre. This then shot off westwards and was gone out of view. […] I still don't know to this present day what it was we saw, but I do know that it wasn't Venus, a B52 Bomber refuelling, or mass hysteria, as suggested to us in the months afterwards."

At exactly the same time, three people saw a circular, revolving, 'globe of light', which gradually changed colour from yellow to red, to silvery-white in the sky, which was sighted moving south-east over the Hill View Estate, Sunderland.

(Source: *Evening Standard,* **27.10.1967 – 'The thing drops into Enfield')**

Darlington, 7.30pm – Flashing lights

At 7.30pm, three schoolboys – S. Birkby, C. Taylor, and M. Robinson, from Alderman Leach School, Darlington – sighted *"four bright flashing lights in a square formation"*, flying through the sky. They were travelling west to east, and were out of sight in five minutes. Later that evening, other strange objects were seen in the night sky over the same locality. These were described as *"looking like squashed triangles"* – orange in colour. (**Source:** *Surrey Advertiser,* **28.10.1967/UFOLOG**)

Canterbury, 8pm – Red flashing lights

At 8pm, *"a cigar-shaped object, showing a dozen red flashing lights"*, was seen heading across the sky over the University of Kent, at Canterbury. It was later explained away by the authorities as being an American aircraft, refuelling. Many hundreds of miles away, a doctor and his wife contacted the police, after having sighted:

> *"...a number of circular red and white flashing objects in the sky, towards the North, over the Spadeadam Rocket Establishment, near Carlisle".*

This establishment had been opened in the late 1950s, as a test area for the British Intermediate Range Ballistic Missiles.

At 8.30pm, two unidentified lights were seen moving at great speed over Letchworth, North Hertfordshire, followed by the ejection of a third object – which made off in the opposite direction, trailing flames like a rocket engine. A short time later, an object, six or seven times the size of a rugby-ball, was seen over Hawick, Scotland. It showed a brilliant light in its centre, and headed towards the direction of Carlisle. (**Source:** *Kent Messenger,* 3.11.1967/*Hertfordshire Express,* **Hitchin, 2.11.1967**)

Cirencester, 8.50pm – Triangular UFO

At 8.50pm, Mr William Puffitt from Victoria Road, Cirencester, staying with his relatives – Mr and Mrs Joan Muller – contacted the police after sighting:

> *"...a triangular object in the sky, showing a white light at the front with two red lights at the rear passing over nearby rooftops".*

When consulted, experts at the observatory at Jodrell Bank suggested that the object may have been Venus, sighted at low elevation. (**Source: Personal interview**)

An illuminated 'saucer', projecting beams of light, was seen moving across the sky over Colchester United football ground, following an aircraft. It was then seen to stop in mid-air when reaching the aircraft, and head away at great speed, before disappearing from sight. Other reports told of star or cross-shaped objects seen over Alnwick, Northumberland, and a bright glowing green 'cigar', trailing sparks, over Brighton.

(**Source:** *Edinburgh Evening News,* 26.10.1967/*Nuneaton Evening News,* 27.10.1967/*Bournemouth Evening Echo,* **27.10.1967**)

Further reports were made of what looked like *"squashed triangles of brilliant orange light"* seen moving through the sky, during the evening of the 26th October 1967, by people living in the Hog's Back area. (**Source:** *Surrey Advertiser,* **28.10.1967**)

Shropshire – Pear-shaped

A white-green pear-shaped object was seen rushing past a car, which was travelling between Edgmond and Crudgington, near Wellington, Shropshire. It was visible for 15 seconds – until it became lost from sight. (**Source:** *Shropshire Star,* **28.10.1967**)

We also discovered that an object – described as resembling a 'Maltese Cross' – was seen in the sky over

Banbury, during the evening of the 26th October 1967, by local residents – Mr and Mrs Baldwin.
(**Source: John 'Dennis' Llewellyn**)

Stretford (time not known) – Cigar-shaped

Roy Wellock (18) was in Wycliffe Road, Stretford, when his sister brought his attention to an object in the sky.

> "I looked up and saw a broad, cigar-shaped object, moving slowly across the sky, showing two lights at either end with a big red light in the middle, which was three or four times the size of the others and pulsing. I couldn't see any wings, but I could hear the sound of rotor blades. Within a few minutes it was out of sight."

(**Source: Roger Stanway/Tony Pace/*Flying Saucer Report/Lancashire Journal*, 1.11.1967**)

Merseyside, 11.25pm – Black shining object

At 11.25pm on 26th October 1967, Merseyside Police received a report from garage owner Peter Murphy. He had been driving along Croxteth Hall Lane, when *"a black shining object flashed past his car windscreen"*, before disappearing into a nearby field.

Police Constable Jackson attended at the scene, and made a search of the field, but found nothing untoward.

While talking to Peter Murphy, the officer saw an object in the sky over Norris Green. He described it as being:

> "…star-shaped; the size of a large plate showing a bright bluish light, hovering at a height of about 400 feet in the sky".

It then fell downwards and vanished. Another search carried out also proved unsuccessful. This was not the end of the story – a short time later the two men saw what they believed to be the same object over the East Lancashire Road, heading away at speed. (**Source: WWW. Magonia**)

County Durham, 11.55pm

Lanchester resident – Mr Allen Armstrong, was driving home from Stanley, County Durham.

> "I was startled by the appearance of a bright bluish light, pointed at the front with a flared rear, which travelled through about 40 degrees in seconds across the sky before going out of sight behind a row of houses." (**Source:** *Evening Chronicle*, 27.10.1967 – 'New sightings in great space mystery')

27th October 1967 – Another surge in UFO activity

A pulsating red object, surrounded by white fluorescent light, was seen over Hathershaw, near Oldham, in Lancashire, at 2am, heading northwards. It took 20 minutes to cross the sky.

At 2.25am, William Sharples, of Wavertree, recorded a mystery noise in the sky for 20 seconds, after having his sleep interrupted on previous occasions. The tape was later handed to the *Liverpool Echo*, who reported:

> "For about 20 seconds it gave out a high-pitched, continuous tone – similar in sound to what several other people who telephoned the Echo today have described."

One of them was Ken Rose, of Wavertree. His wife heard a strange whining noise in the early hours, at 2.30am, and awoke him to listen to the noise.

> "I went to the window, but could see nothing; the whining continued for about 40 seconds. There was no traffic anywhere in sight, and I am convinced that it did not come from the railway at Edge Hill. I have never heard anything like it in my life before."

Haunted Skies **Volume Two Revised**

They were not the only ones. Mr D.J. Furlong, of Liverpool, told of:

> "...an unearthly noise coming from the direction of the sky, which appears to resemble a high-pitched whistling sound and which, in some instances, is accompanied by a bleeping noise in the nature of some sort of signal. It gives the impression of something passing overhead, as the noise seems to start in the distance, pass overhead and then fade, as though going away. It is definitely not a train or an aeroplane, as these are quite common in my area and sound nothing like the noise we have heard".

(Source: *Merseyside UFO Bulletin,* Volume 1, Number 1, January-February 1968, Editor John Harney)

Northumberland, 2.45am – 'Flying Cross'

Richard Robinson and his wife, living at South Ouston, Northumberland, awoke at 2.45am on 27th October, and looked through the window, when they saw:

> "...a weird cross of diffused light, reminding us of a starfish with an elongated tail, travelling slowly, southwards across the sky, 30 degrees off the horizon – much brighter than any star. It took 30 minutes for it to go out of sight."

Ouston, 3am – Brilliant cube

At 3am, an object – described as *"resembling a brilliant huge cube of ice, moving very quickly across the horizon"* – was sighted by a resident from Ouston.

Lancashire, 4.10a.m – Hoax

At 4.10am, PC Brian Earnshaw, of the Lancashire Constabulary, reported having sighted:

> "...a cigar-shaped object with a number of holes along its length, hovering over the transmitter aerial at Bacup Police Station".

Other witnesses included, PC Colin Donahue and Malcolm reader – -Unfortunately, it subsequently turned out that this was a hoax, perpetrated by Brian and the officers, who were later disciplined.

(Source: Personal interview/*Daily Express* **28.10.1967** 'P.C. sees UFO with portholes')

Gloucester, 4.15a.m – Cross-shaped

At 4.15am, Mrs Maureen Harrison of Church Down, Gloucester, was awoken by her youngest daughter. On going to the window, Mrs Harrison saw two UFOs in the sky.

> "The larger one moved up to join the smaller one, forming a cross shape. You could see faint lines across its surface, some of the time. The larger one then became bright and dimmed again."

At the same time, six police officers from the Cheshire Constabulary sighted a UFO moving from side-to-side, over Glossop, Derbyshire, before heading into a misty cloud. (**Source:** *Derby Evening Telegraph*)

Redditch, 4.30a.m – 'Flying Saucer'

At 4.30am, workers at a local factory in Hewell Road, Redditch, in Worcestershire (a few miles from Birmingham, West Midlands), were taking a break from work, when a huge 'flying saucer', displaying a green light at each tip, passed overhead. It was travelling towards Birmingham, enabling them to see what looked like:

> "...two girders, projecting out of a middle that retracted as it continued on its journey".

Newcastle, 4.40a.m – Blue 'cone'

At 4.40am, *"a dazzling electric-blue cone-shaped UFO, with an orange periphery, making a sound like a high revving car engine"*, was seen motionless in the sky over Dunston Power Station, near Newcastle-on-

Tyne, by Mrs M. McLaughlin and her daughter – Deidre. It then developed a haze, changed its shape to oval, and disappeared. **(Source: UFOLOG)**

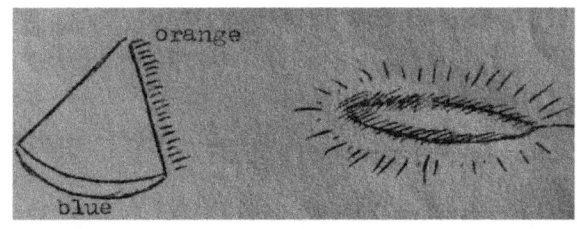

Wallsend, 5.48p.m – Cigar-shaped object

Mrs Craig and her friend – Mrs Brennan – were walking to work, at 5.48am. As they neared the Civil Defence Centre, at Wallsend, they saw:

> "...a cigar-shaped object with a spike at each end, revolving in the centre of a halo of light, which was flying vertically in the sky and moving northwards".

Meriden – 6am – 'Flying Cross'

At 6am, a *"flying cross of light"* was seen in the sky over Meriden, illuminating the ground and bedrooms of houses in the village as it headed towards Daventry. Could this have been the same UFO, sighted over the East Birmingham Hospital by two hospital staff, porters – Norman Holder (59) and George Munford (50) – which they described as a yellow glowing cylinder in the sky?

(Source: *Birmingham Evening Mail*, 27.10.1967 – 'Now Birmingham sees things in the sky')

This was followed by a sighting over Shrewsbury at the same time. Whether this was before or after the previous sighting is something we shall never know. However, it involved a triangular-shaped object sighted just under the moon, and was accompanied by several glowing 'lights' in the sky.

> "It stayed there for a few seconds and then turned over and disappeared – then a 'ball of light' appeared in the sky, followed by a 'bright light', which came up on top of the moon with a smaller 'light' close to it. The smaller 'light' then broke into two, and they all moved away until out of sight."

(Source: *Shropshire Star*, 31.10.1967)

Despite attempts made by the authorities to explain away sightings of the *'Flying Cross'* as being Venus, it is obvious that this could not be the answer for many of the sightings concerned, which involved what appeared to be structured objects.

Newcastle-on-Tyne – Structured UFO

At 9pm, an object *"looking like a tennis ball in the sky, with some sort of structure on top of it"* was seen over Newcastle-on-Tyne.

Sunderland – Shining UFO

At 11.35pm, Mrs Carroll of Jackson Street, Sunderland, was walking along the beach at Seaburn, near her home. She was with her two children when she noticed a circular shining object, showing a red tinge at its outer edges, flying eastwards over the sea. It faded away, leaving a wisp of smoke. **(Source: UFOLOG)**

Cheshire – Two 'lights'

John Goodman (aged 19) of Appleton, and his girlfriend, were at Appleton Reservoir, south of Warrington, in Cheshire. They were looking westwards, when they saw two lights in the sky; one red, and the other white.

> "They were close together and directly in front of us. They then travelled swiftly towards Fiddler's Ferry, at a height of about 100 feet, and then stopped, without turning around, and remained in the same position before reversing and travelling backwards in a straight line, for about five miles, and disappearing from view behind a wood." **(Source: *Liverpool Echo*, 28.10.1967)**

28th October 1967 – Red pulsating 'ball of light'

At 12.20am, a red pulsating 'ball of light', surrounded by a white glow, was seen heading in a north to south direction over Hathershaw, near Oldham, in Lancashire. It made no sound, and was witnessed by two people, who then saw it stop and reverse back along its route. It was then accompanied by a heavy burst of interference on the portable radio during the sighting. (**Source: DIGAP**)

12.25am Andover, Hampshire – Three 'patches of light'

Mrs V. Combes from Andover (head of the Andover UFO Group) was awoken by gale force winds coming down the chimney.

While checking the room, she looked out of the window and saw:

"...two whitish-grey 'patches' in the sky, over Andover, one above the other. I immediately called my husband, who came to the window and looked out. I then opened the window to make sure it wasn't any illusion. During the course of the next half an hour or so, we observed a constant variation in the lights, Sometimes three 'patches of light' would appear – then they would merge into a long vertical line of light, which itself contracted into one large 'patch of light', about the size of a full moon. There didn't seem to be any particular order to the various formations – all the time brightening and fading, sometimes completely disappearing but reappearing seconds later. I looked at the 'lights' through a pair of binoculars, but couldn't see further detail than one could see with the naked eye. After becoming cold we eventually went to bed, leaving the 'lights' still out there."

(**Source: Letter to the Isle of Wight UFO Society**)

5.30am – Mr F. Smith, living near the Shoreham area, was awoken by a lorry passing the house.

"I noticed a bright light in the sky and watched it through the window first. Curious, I got out of bed and opened the window which faces east. I looked out and saw – much higher in the sky – an object in the shape of the Lorraine Cross. I awoke my wife and she saw it as well. It was a wonderful sight. I estimated its height as being 2-3,000 feet. I watched it for about ten minutes – then it disappeared out of sight." (**Source: letter to Kath Smith, Isle of Wight UFO Society**)

7.40am – Staines, Two white 'lights'

Two brilliant white 'lights' were observed hovering below a bank of deep cloud, near Staines. A minute later they were seen to climb upwards, at fantastic speed, and disappear from view.
(Source: *Staines and Egham News*, 3.11.1967)

South Shields, Durham – Bullet-shaped object in the sky

A bullet-shaped object was seen hovering for a few seconds over an electricity substation, near South Shields, Durham, by three boys, who described it as being

"...eight feet in length with a glowing green outline, showing a white glowing spot on its underside as it silently rose upwards and disappeared."

The boys claimed some brown lines, believed to be burn marks, were left on the roof.
Source: *Shields Gazette*, **30.10.1967/TUFOS**)

6.30pm Warrington – 'Golden Cross' sighted

A bright, golden, cross-shaped object was seen in the Warrington area, hovering over fields adjoining the motorway. A piece of what appeared to be metal was seen to drop from the object, showing two cross-shaped projections, before promptly vanishing from view. (**Source:** *Liverpool Daily Post*, **30.10.1967**)

6.45pm Kent – Triangular object reported

A triangular object – composed of six very bright lights, shaped like a church steeple – was seen in the sky over Tunbridge Wells, in Kent. The witnesses were the occupants of a vehicle which inexplicably cut out and stalled. (**Source:** *Tunbridge Wells Advertiser,* **1.11.1967**)

A huge object with flashing lights, hovering over trees at Southend, was seen by a taxi driver. Five minutes later, it dipped down and rose up again, showing a single red light, before moving up into the sky – where it became lost in cloud. (**Source:** *Southend Standard,* **2.11.1967**)

8.30pm – County Durham, Green 'Triangle' seen

A bright green triangular object was seen stationary in the sky over South Shields, County Durham, by E. Watson, T. Robinson and K. Burnett – schoolboys from Horsley Hill Junior School. It was hovering over playing fields in South Shields, and was estimated to be:

> "...seven to eight feet long, by three feet wide. After about ten seconds, it shot upwards, a few hundred feet, and moved away discharging red sparks, showing a prominent white dot in the centre of its bottom edge". (**Source: TUFOS**)

29th October 1967 – Family sights UFO

Mr William Greenwell of Partridge Green, Sussex, was in the process of retiring to bed, at 12.30am, along with other members of the family, when they noticed a lighted object, *"like the 'Prince of Wales' feathers', showing a green, red, and white light, hovering over Cowfield".*

It is still remembered by him as being the strangest thing they had ever seen. (**Source: Personal interview**)

Hove, 1a.m – 'Flying Cross'

Jonathan Bennett and his sister – Wendy Szqarga, from Cliftonville Court, Goldstone Villas, Hove, watched a strange object in the sky. They saw it for over an hour, and said that it resembled,

> "...the 'Cross of Lorraine', which kept changing colour from red to green, blue to gold, splitting in the middle and rejoining itself".

They called the police, and a patrol car arrived with two officers, who seemed sceptical until they saw it for themselves.

A police spokesman later explained it away as being Venus (once again!) – An explanation rejected by the witnesses.

Lancashire, 1.30a.m – 'Flying Cross'

During the same morning, a mysterious 'Flying Cross', estimated to be 750 feet in length and moving at 1,000 miles per hour, was seen heading northwards, over St. Annes, Lancashire. According to the witness, it tilted and took-off at high speed. (**Source:** *Lancashire Evening Gazette,* **30.10.1967**)

In the early hours of this day, an astronomer from Hartlepool, Durham, was looking through his telescope when he saw two white objects travelling across the sky, followed by a third. Seconds later, they moved away in a 'V'-shaped formation across the sky, stopped still, and then started to zigzag towards the position of the moon, changing colour from green to blue, to red. Inexplicably, they then vanished from sight. (**Source:** *Northern Daily Mail,* **31.10.1967**)

Shrewsbury, 6a.m – Triangular object

Just after 6am a triangular object, accompanied by several glowing lights, was seen in the sky over Shrewsbury, 'under the moon', before disappearing completely from view. As it did so, a 'ball of light' appeared in the sky. Immediately following this, a light flashed on from an object 'over the top of the moon', next to which a second object was seen. It then moved away and out of sight.

(**Source:** *Shropshire Star,* **31.10.1967**)

Northampton, 4.45pm – Orange 'cigar'

At 4.45pm, two teenage girls from Northampton were out playing, when they saw an object resembling *"a flying orange 'cigar'"*, approaching their position. To their surprise, it flew around them before descending a few feet off the ground, constantly changing colour from orange to yellow, to white and dull grey. It was surrounded by a fuzzy green haze, which disappeared when the object took-off a few minutes later.

(**Source:** *Northampton Chronicle,* **30.10.1967**)

Was there any connection with the next sighting, of a peculiar *"orange and golden object, showing three long trails of what appeared to be vapour behind it",* seen flying over the London area at the same time and date as above?

Other reports of the same UFO described it as being cigar-shaped. (**Source:** *Western Mail,* **30.10.1967**)

UFO over West Sussex, 6.45pm

At 6.45pm, Paul Quick (then aged 21) was pushing his broken-down motorcycle two miles towards his home at Lobelia Cottage, Hampers Lane, Storrington. As he walked the machine through a thickly wooded estate, he looked upwards and saw an object – like a rugby-ball – silently floating towards him, at an estimated height of 250 feet. He said that it was about one-and-a-half times the size of a double-decker bus.

After calling at his mother's house at Longberry Hill, he told her and his sisters – Leone and Michelle – what had taken place.

They rushed to the window with their mother – Suzette – to look out, and saw the object apparently in the process of landing on Chanctonbury Downs, about two miles away.

Mrs Quick described seeing:

The Quick family

> "...what looked like an upside-down horseshoe-shaped object. Its colour changed from white to a glowing deep ruby-red, and then it began to flutter and flicker. Suddenly, it broke into what seemed to be three separate parts; the red part remaining stationary, while the other two objects – one blue, the other green – moved to the left. The three parts remained separate for a minute and then joined up again, reforming the upside-down horseshoe".

The three of them ran over to a clearing, fifty yards from the house, to obtain a closer look. They saw an object, resembling:

> "...a giant ice-cream cornet; the part where the ice-cream would be was bigger than a lorry. It kept fluttering – as if wanting to attract attention – and then began to slide downwards and out of sight".

The family decided against getting any closer, for fear of what might happen. Now feeling cold, after being outside for over half-an-hour, they returned to their house. They telephoned the police at Steyning, who attended and made a search of the area with police dogs. Unsurprisingly, they found nothing.

Further enquiries into this matter revealed another witness – Mr N.E. Satterly, from Brighton – who saw what appears to have been the same object, at 6.50pm. It was apparently following the power lines across the Downs. He later said:

> "I watched it through my binoculars, for a few minutes, before it went out of sight".

In an interview conducted with *Penthouse* (Volume 3, Number 2), published in 1968, we learn that Mrs Quick told of having received a visit from four men, *"waving official looking credentials"*, who warned her not to say anything about the incident.

(Source: *The Storrington Reports*, 'Landing in Sussex', **Charles Bowen and Gordon Creighton**, *Flying Saucer Review*, Volume 14, No. 2, March/April 1968/Omar Fowler, SIGAP/PRA/*Worthing Herald*, 3.11.1967/*Brighton Evening Argus*, 30.10.1967/*The Sun*, October 1967 – 'Police dogs hunt Flying Saucer')

Burnley – Bright 'light'

At 7pm, a bright red, irregular object (twenty times the size of a star) was seen in the sky over Burnley, in Lancashire, heading towards the town centre. (**Source:** *Lancashire Evening Telegraph,* **30.10.1967**)

Northumberland

Between 10.30pm and 11pm, a shimmering blue and white object was seen in the eastern sky over Rothbury, Northumberland. It was slowly moving upwards, from side-to-side, and then became lost from sight as it entered cloud cover. (**Source:** *Northumberland Gazette,* **3.11.1967**)

30th October – Cigar-shaped objects seen, Kent

An object, looking like a *"greyish vacuum cleaner"*, was seen passing over Ashford, Kent, on 30th October, heading in an east to west direction. (**Source:** *Kent Messenger,* **3.11.1967**)

Durham City – Cigar-shaped object

Other witnesses to strange phenomena on this date included a sighting by schoolgirl Catherine Day, from Newton Hall School (Bluecoat), near Durham City, at 8.50am, who told of sighting *"a cigar-shaped object, trailing a vapour from its rear"*.

Was this the same cigar-shaped object sighted by two Devon schoolboys, on the same date? It was travelling through the sky over Exmouth, showing two large red lights, during the same morning.

West Yorkshire – Cigar-shaped

At 7.30pm, *"a cigar-shaped object was seen hovering in mid-air, with sparks falling from it"*. It was reported over Halifax, West Yorkshire, by Mr Robert Brown of Weatherhouse Terrace, Pellon, near Halifax.
(**Source:** *Halifax Courier & Guardian,* **31.10.1967** – 'Man reports 'mystery' object over Halifax)

31st October – Eight objects seen in the sky over West Midlands

At 2am, teacher Mr B.M. Goldrick of Sharmans Cross School, Shirley, Solihull, was driving along the Yorkshire Moors, six miles west of RAF Fylingdales Early Warning Station, when he saw:

> *"…eight white objects, low down in the sky. One appeared to be at ground level, the others were higher up in the sky. The lower one projected a beam of light skywards, flashing on and off intermittently, before disappearing from view."* (**Source:** J.W.B. Barklam, NICAP, GB)

Sussex – Like red-hot coals

At 2.30am, *"a luminous object, glowing like red-hot coals, resembling a rugby football in shape with a white perimeter and sparks ejecting from its rear, accompanied by a suction noise"*, was seen over Midhurst, Sussex. (**Source:** *Brighton Evening Argus,* **1.11.1967**)

Cumbria – Red 'cross' seen

Mrs P. Alexander, and her two sons from Denton Mill, Brampton, Cumbria, saw *"a bright red, cross-shaped, pulsating object"*, moving through the sky, at 6pm, which disappeared behind trees after 30 seconds. Five minutes later, a bright orange 'light' was sighted over Blyth, by five people. *"It was moving at twice the speed of an aircraft, heading westwards."*

Devon – Rough 'cross' sighted in sky

At 6.15pm, an orange object was seen in the sky over Sidmouth, Devon. It was shaped like a rough 'cross', surrounded by an oval ring, approximately one thousand feet off the ground.
(**Source:** *Exeter Express and Echo,* **2.11.1967**)

Also on this date, two light-grey spinning 'flying saucers' were sighted over Great Yarmouth, before disappearing upwards into cloud. (**Source:** *Western Mail,* 1.11.1967)

10pm – Kirkby Underwood, Erratic UFO

At 10pm, an unusual 'light' was seen in the sky, apparently just above tree tops, over the village of Kirkby Underwood. It was witnessed by a number of customers from the *Three Tuns* Public House, who described it as:

"...moving erratically, upwards, right to left before disappearing completely".

(**Source:** *Stamford Mercury,* 3.11.1967)

MOD

UFO statistics released by the MOD for the 12 month period for 1967 reveals that for the month of October 1967 they received 89 reports, made up of seven unexplained, eleven miscellaneous, eleven celestial phenomena, six balloons, five satellite debris and 49 aircraft. With all due respect to the MOD, it is painfully obvious, bearing in mind the nature of the sightings outlined by us, that these figures appear flawed.

UFO over Lychett Minster

One evening in October 1967, Bournemouth resident Lance Druce, and his brother-in-law – Brian George, were driving home by car, after a fishing trip to Weymouth. As they approached Lychett Minster, close to the *St. Peter's Finger* Public House, at 5.30pm, Brian shouted out, *"What's that?"*, and pointed upwards. As he did so, the engine of the Austin Cambridge A60 began to splutter.

"I looked through his side window and saw a huge dark brown cigar-shaped 'thing', about 150 feet in length, with yellow lit portholes, stationary above St. Peter's Finger Garage, without any sound. We stopped the car and got out, soon joined by other road users, who stood with us watching the object. By this time, we were feeling nervous and decided to report the matter to a police house, situated a mile or so up the road".

The two men set off to alert the police. On glancing behind them, they were astonished to see that the UFO was following.

When they reached the *Oasis Café*, further along the road, they stopped the car again and were amazed to see that the object was now hovering about 200 feet in the sky over the police house.

Lance:

"I knocked on the door and a woman opened it. I blurted out, 'There's a strange spaceship above your house'. The look on her face clearly implied she thought me mad. I persisted and she called her husband, who looked at it, and then asked another officer to fetch a pair of binoculars. At this point, a strange thing happened. The object began to fade, becoming nearly invisible, and suddenly split into two. One section went beneath the other and then rejoined, forming the 'cigar', before completely disappearing from sight."

After obtaining written statements from the men concerned, the police promised to get in touch – but nothing further was heard.

Enquiries made into the incident by UFO researcher – Mr Leslie Harris, revealed that the two police officers had been moved out of the district.

Mr Harris wrote to the Chief Constable, asking for an interview with the two police officers, and was told the officers had declined any further contact.

End of October – Three 'lights' seen

Towards the end of October 1967, Jacqueline Frostrick (aged 17) from Moordown, near Bournemouth, was walking home. It was 8.30pm, and she was near to her house, when she saw:

> "...a large, dull metallic silver object – like an inverted saucer or dish, showing three lights – one brilliant white, two dimmer red ones – making a 'slashing' sound, hovering approximately 2-300 feet off the ground" between her house and the next door neighbours.

She rushed indoors to tell her mother. By the time they came outside, the object was racing off towards the New Forest.

(Source: *Flying Saucer Review,* **Volume 15, Number 6, November-December 1969/***Scan* **– 'Shape changing UFO', Leslie Harris)**

Flying 'box' UFO over Kent

Mr A.J. White and his wife, Della, were returning home to Westhill Drive, Dartford, in Kent, one early morning in the autumn of 1967. They noticed a red glowing 'ball of light' in the sky above them, a couple of hundred feet off the ground.

> "It appeared to pulsate with an irregular beat. As the red glow diminished, we could see a black object, resembling a box kite, appearing. This then disappeared, replaced by a saucer, or cigar-shaped object. At this point we were in Dartford Road, about 200 yards from where we lived. I decided to stop and put out the car lights. The 'ball of light' also stopped still, hovering above us."

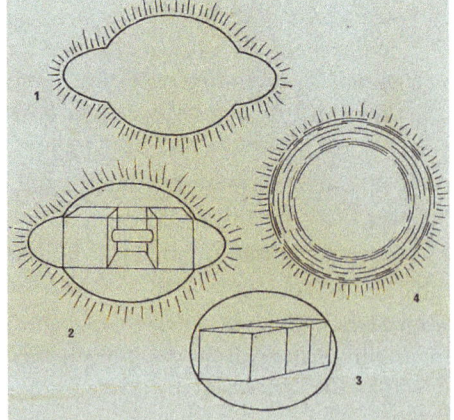

After a few minutes, Mr White started up the car and began to move forward – so did the UFO! He stopped the vehicle and tried again, determined to make the safety of the house, with the UFO pacing alongside the car. When he arrived at the house, he dashed in to fetch binoculars and a camera. By the time he reached the window and looked out, the UFO was already rushing upwards into the sky at speed.

(Source: Steven John Hall, Kent UFO Group)

Three hundred reports logged for October 1967

There was a marked increase in UFO activity beginning in early October 1967, and peaking towards the end of the month. While there are many who suggest the explanation for this rash of sightings was the planet Venus, at the time, Venus was visible at a crescent stage, looking like a parachute in the sky, at an elevation of 40 degrees off the horizon. It seems incomprehensible to accept this to be the answer for sightings of cross-shaped craft, observed at close quarters and moving fast through the sky.

Incredibly, we discovered there had been a total of over 750 separate sightings of UFOs logged for 1967, with over 300 reports of UFOs recorded for the month of October alone. But out of these, only sixty-four related to the appearance of what became labelled as the 'Flying Cross'. (**Source: Gordon Emery**)

October 1967 – UFO over Romford, Essex

Cyril William Eden, previously with the Air Cadets (18) of Wednesbury Road, Harold Hill, Romford, Essex – a telephone engineer by occupation – was stood in St. Neot's Road, in October 1967, with a friend (a RAF Jet Pilot, who subsequently died in a mid-air collision) when they noticed a red, watery, round 'blob of light' in the sky. The two men discussed it and wondered if it could have been a 'Nova'.

Cyril:

> "It became brighter and our curiosity got the better of us. We ran down St. Neot's Road to my home in Wednesbury Road, some 40 yards away, and fetched a telescope – as the object was now bright-red and moving. As it passed overhead we noticed a yellowish light, about the size of Jupiter, to the rear of the main object. It then went out of sight, over the tops of nearby houses.
>
> We were amazed by what we had seen, knowing it wasn't any aircraft. To our astonishment we saw it (or another) appear in the sky, heading in a NW to NNW direction, about 20 degrees off the horizon; this one appeared smaller than the first."

Bill, as he is known to us, is sure that this was no satellite, balloon, meteor, or aircraft – which we concur. He later joined the Essex UFO Study Group and was responsible for many investigations into reported UFO activity around that period of time. We were very impressed by his professional approach and wish him the best. (**Source: Bill Eden/Dan Goring**)

NOVEMBER 1967

1st November 1967 – 'Flying Cross' over Kent

At 3.15am, workmen from Fordwich, in Kent, sighted an object resembling a 'Flying Cross', motionless in the sky. As dawn approached, it disappeared from view. (**Source:** *Kent Messenger,* **3.11.1967**)

On the same day *"a 'Sputnik'-shaped object, with a white antennae"*, was seen in the sky over Midhurst. It continually changed shape from round to oval, altering in colour from red, green, to white.

(**Source:** *Hampshire Telegraph,* **9.11.1967**)

2nd November 1967 – 'Flying Cross', Essex

At 6am, a 'Flying Cross' – its edges blurred by light emanating from it, showering sparks like a firework – was seen moving through the sky over the local Police Station at Billericay, in Essex.

(**Source:** *Basildon Standard,* **3.11.1967**)

Over Guildford, in Surrey, *"two mysterious bright yellow lights"* were seen to arrive from opposite directions in the sky and halt close to each other, before separating, closing-up again, and heading off at fantastic speed. (**Source:** *Surrey Mirror,* **3.11.1967**)

Exmouth

At 7.40pm, a bright golden coloured object – about the size of a grapefruit – was sighted in the sky over Exmouth. It was then seen to blink on and off every few seconds, and become redder in colour, before climbing rapidly upwards into the starlit sky. (**Source:** *Exmouth Journal,* 4.11.1967)

Flintshire

At 7.45pm, a number of schoolgirls playing in the street at Rhuddlan, in Flintshire, noticed an object hovering in the sky. They described it as being, *"bright oval, with a white middle and flashing red ends".* Suddenly it shot upwards and out of sight. (**Source: Isle of Wight UFO Society**)

November 'Flying Saucer', Lowestoft

John Rand, from Aldeby, was walking home near Lowestoft. As he approached a disused railway line, he heard a heavy vibrating noise. Thinking it was a train approaching on the Beccles line, over the river, he glanced around and saw:

"…a huge 'flying saucer', about 20 yards away, hovering over an apple tree orchard; it was dark in colour, with a bulge at the top and bottom, with a number of slits of light running around a dome at the top, illuminating nearby trees. The vibration changed to a high-pitched screeching noise. It then took off, leaving me very frightened." (**Source:** Ivan W. Bunn, *'The Lantern'* series)

Early November – Oldbury

Mrs Joan Baxter, whose house overlooks the Old Park Steel Works, in Oldbury, spoke of what she saw, one evening.

"I was astonished to see a huge, dark-red 'ball of light' hovering over the buildings of the Steel Works – bright enough to flood the area with light. I shouted for my son to come quickly, but it suddenly flipped over and completely disappeared before he had time to see it."

(**Source: Personal interview**)

3rd November 1967 – Oblong UFO, Northamptonshire

At 6.15pm, a bright object was seen flying through the sky over Peterborough, in Northamptonshire. Through a telescope, an oblong yellow-white object, surrounded by several smaller ones, was seen. Enquiries with RAF Wittering revealed no aircraft were in the locality at the time.

Source: South Lincolnshire UFO Study Group)

Police Officers told they had seen Venus!

In addition to this, during the same period (early November, 1967) *"a silver-grey cigar-shaped object"*, was reported hovering above Burgh le Marsh, Skegness.

The Chief Constable of East Sussex summoned all the night crew officers to the Police Head Quarters, in order to persuade them they had seen the planet Venus!

(**Source:** *Kent Messenger,* **Editor Oliver Petts**)

4th November 1967 – Surrey, Five 'bright lights'

At 8pm, a retired engineer from Reigate, Surrey, sighted five 'bright lights' moving horizontally across the sky. He thought that they may have been a mirage, caused by a row of streetlights.
(**Source: Personal interview**)

At 9.30pm, Mr Michael Chadd, (20) – a plumber of Park Barn Drive, Guildford – and his girlfriend, Linda, were driving past Cut Mill, in Surrey, (ten miles from Haslemere) when they saw a glowing object, hovering in mid-air, approximately ten feet above nearby trees.

Michael:

"It was hovering there for 15 minutes; it looked like a spaceship."

He later reported this sighting to Omar Fowler – then Chairman of the Surrey UFO Group.

4th November 1967 – 10.02pm, Aircraft crashes with loss of all on board

At 10.02pm, a Caravelle Airliner, No. ECBDD, owned by Iberia Airlines, Spain, named *Jesus Gurudi,* under the command of Captain Hamando Maura (37), was flying from Malaga, Spain, to Heathrow – estimated time of arrival at 10.10pm.

On entering UK airspace, the aircraft had been reported at 31,000 feet and was cleared to descend to 21,000 feet and then 11,000 feet. The crew reported passing through 14,500 feet and were then cleared to the Epsom beacon at 6,000 feet. The weather at this time – low cloud and rain

– would mean that the pilots had no outside reference as to their height.

Sadly, the airplane crashed at Blackdown Hill, Sussex, (902 feet above sea level) (map reference 919289). This was a slightly misty night with intermittent drizzle, but with reasonable visibility. The wreckage was spread in a narrow swathe, 800 yards long, and was compatible with the aircraft having struck in a near level altitude at high forward speed. At first it broke through a large hedge causing parts to break away before damaging parts of the roof of Upper Blackdown House – and then disintegrated.

Haslemere Fire Brigade attended within minutes of the crash and was later joined by fire services from Grayshott and Liphook.

Aviation fuel had caused small fires to break out on the densely wooded hillside. Debris was scattered over the whole 355 yards of its passage. The Villagers and WRVS (Women's Royal Voluntary Service) came out to assist, and helped provide food and drink for the emergency services from the youth club behind the *Spread Eagle* Public House. The Village Hall was turned into a temporary mortuary.

Police Constable Barry Siviers:

"I was the night turn car driver on Juliet 1, running out of Godalming. My companion on that night was PC1075 Higginson, when we were called by Control, who told us there was a loud explosion in the hills to the south of Haslemere and could we check it out. We were on the way from Godalming, when we were told that a plane had failed to land at Gatwick and there was a possibility that the explosion was a plane hitting the ground. When we arrived at the scene, four miles south of Haslemere, at Fernhurst, we made our way up a narrow lane to the left of the main road and it was total devastation, with remains of the plane all over a large area. The area was completely destroyed and no survivors were found alive; in fact, all we found was pieces of body lying all over the ground and in the trees. We had to secure the site, along with other officers who arrived from Surrey and Hampshire. I remember staying there the whole night and the following morning. I remember a vast number of air cadets and suchlike attending, and was told to assist in collecting the body parts from the area. The cadets were only in their early teens and distraught to say the least. They were not able to conceal their feelings and indeed their stomach contents".

Analysis of the wreckage showed the aircraft was flying normally in the cruise configuration. All the major components were accounted for at the scene of the incident and examination of the engines showed they were both turning under power, at high speed on impact.

(**Source:** KSH History Boards, www.internet, April 2017)

'SAUCER' RIDDLE OF JET DISASTER

Did a flying saucer have anything to do with the Caravelle plane crash in Sussex in November?

This is the startling question which members of the Surrey investigation group on aerial phenomena are trying to answer.

For a sighting of a luminous oval-shaped object which hovered over trees at Cutmill, Surrey, 30 minutes before the crash, has just come to light.

It was seen by 20-year-old Michael Chadd, a plumber, of Park Barn Drive, Guildford, and his girl friend Linda.

Cutmill is about 10 miles from the scene of the crash near Haslemere.

Michael said: "The object was visible for about 15 minutes. It looked just like a space ship."

Mr. Omar Fowler, chairman of the Surrey UFO group, said: "If anyone in the vicinity of Cutmill or Haslemere on November 4 saw anything unusual in the sky, would they please contact us immediately at Guildford 63381."

The Iberian Airways Caravelle crashed into Blackdown Hill at Fernhurst, Sussex, killing 37 passengers and crew. Among the dead was June Thorburn, the actress.

Board of Trade investigation

The report from The Board of Trade investigators states that no evidence was found of any pre-crash failure or defect in either the airframe, engines, or of any faulty workmanship. Thirty passengers and seven crew died, which included Coventry City Football Club vice-president John Clarkson Donald 'Doc' Campbell of the Campbell Aircraft Company, and June Thorburn (actress), who was five months pregnant. In addition 88 sheep were killed. Our condolences to the families of those involved.

Appeal for any other witnesses by Omar Fowler

Whether there was any connection with the sighting of a UFO reported by Michael Chadd and his girlfriend half an hour before the air crash, a short time later, followed by an article published locally on the 30th December 1967, under the headlines – 'Saucer riddle of Jet Disaster', we cannot say, as there is no direct evidence and it would be highly inappropriate to make this association, but if the presence of UFOs in our airspace can and have caused interference with motor vehicles (and on occasion aircraft), then it would be wrong to completely dismiss out of hand any possibility however remote, although we shall never know. (**Source:** Omar Fowler, SIGAP/PRA)

Encounters between motorists and UFOs will always be the source of much interest. Over the years we have come across many cases involving vehicle interference, ranging from dimming lights and spluttering engines at one end of the scale, to a complete breakdown at the other. Whilst we were aware that diesel engines seem to remain unaffected by the putative presence of UFO fields of energy, we often wondered how many times aircraft engines were rendered inoperable (albeit for a short period), during an encounter with a UFO. Oddly, and rather fortunately, such incidents seem very rare, although there have been claims, from other parts of the world, that some aircraft attempting to intercept UFOs have crashed.

6th November 1967 – Pulsating UFO over Yorkshire

Wilfred Heaton from Hebden Bridge, near Halifax, West Yorkshire, was driving home (after completing a night shift), along the moorland road between Burnley and Heponstall, at 6.15am.

> "I had just passed the Kettledrum Inn on the outskirts of Burnley, going up Wicket Hill, when I saw a thin object came [sic] up from behind me in the sky from northwards, on my left-hand side, and it looked like a football – the same colour as the moon. It raced across the front of my car at an elevation of 30 degrees and stayed in the sky relative to the movement of the car. It was no longer round but had a flattened top and bottom, surrounded by a halo which was pulsating regularly. At the end of the stretch of road, known as Long Causeway, I turned into a horseshoe bend and saw the lights of a car in front of me, which I knew belonged to a workmate. By this time the object was now over his car. I flashed my headlights to try and gain his attention, but was unsuccessful. I saw the car accelerate up to a speed of about 65 miles per hour; the object now more or less on his side. Suddenly, the object shot away and went in front of his car again, until it reached a place where the road turns to the left, to skirt around a hollow. It stopped at a point across where the old road would have gone down the hollow. When my car drew level with it, it started to move forward again – now appearing to increase in size. Thinking it was getting closer, I slowed down but it looked to go higher again. As it descended over Oak Mount Garage, before rising upwards, another similar object appeared in the sky – the two of them now flying in front of the car all the way home."

When Wilfred arrived home, he fetched his wife to come and have a look. The couple then stood watching the two objects over Eastwood, for about ten minutes, until they climbed up into the sky and out of sight.

(**Source:** Trevor Whittaker/Malcolm Bull, BUFORA/*Halifax Evening Courier*, 7.11.1967 – 'UFO followed his trip home')

6th November 1967 – UFO sighted over Morden (8 miles south-west of Central London)

Although we cannot be 100 per cent sure of the date, it appears that the following sighting took place during the evening of the 6th November 1967, according to the *Merton Berry* Newspaper (7.11.1967 – 'Eight people watch UFO over Morden').

The object was first sighted by Christine Branch (15) of Bordesley Road, who was in the front garden of her friend's house – Pat Payne (15) at Haigh Place, Green Lane, when she saw:

> "…what looked like two stars in the sky, one hanging on top of the other; then the lower moved alongside the other. You could see a bright beam of light coming from the top with two smaller ones lasting only a few seconds coming out of the sides. We called the neighbours out and six people came out and watched the object as it hovered at varying speeds over the tops of houses for more than ten minutes."

6th November 1967 – UFO over Sopley, Hampshire

One of the most publicised accounts of a UFO incident, involving a complete disablement of the vehicle's electrical equipment, necessitating replacement of the batteries and considerable work required to repair the damage, occurred at 1am on the 6th November 1967, involving lorry driver Carl Beverley Farlow.

Haunted Skies Volume Two Revised

David Sankey, his partner – Erica, and us, met Mr Farlow, in 2006, whilst we were attending the Cornish UFO Lectures, organised by Dave Gilham.

Carl – then living in Dawley, in Shropshire – was driving his Leyland Power plus 401 six-wheeler Lorry along the main A338 road through the New Forest, four miles from Ringwood. He was on his way to deliver a cargo of Aga cookers to Christchurch, Hampshire – a regular night-time journey, made two or three times a week. As he neared the humpback bridge, close to the Sopley turn-off, the lights and radio of his lorry failed (although the engine kept running). He saw an egg-shaped object, with a whitish area at the bottom, moving slowly across the road from his right, at a height of about 20 feet. He said:

> "I shall remember it to the day I die. It was sort of magenta in colour – beautiful. The smell was like ozone – very strong. It came across and stopped, contrary to what people have said happened. I could hear a light humming noise and, from part of it (might have been the bottom or the side) there were lights that came off it which travelled over the top of the cab, like 'balls of light'. After it had gone, I sat there petrified. I mean I hadn't long come out of the Army. I thought I was a tough guy."

Using the nearby bridge as a 'yardstick', Carl was able to judge the length of the object as 80 feet. It was hovering motionless, above wasteland to his left, completely obscuring a view of the road ahead. The top of the telegraph pole stuck out incongruously from behind the UFO.

Tony Pace, BUFORA

According to Tony Pace, who investigated the incident for BUFORA, Carl got out of the lorry and noticed a battleship-grey Jaguar, parked facing him, about a hundred yards away, driven by Robert Carslake – a local veterinary surgeon. Carslake was apparently accompanied by a *"screaming and near hysterical"* female passenger, named Annette. Robert walked over and suggested they call the police from a nearby telephone box, after explaining his engine and lights had also failed. When they went over to the telephone box, the interior light was not working and a torch supplied by Bob failed to work, although it had been working earlier that evening.

PC Nineham attends

At some stage, a *Brooke-Bond* tea van pulled up behind Carl and, after asking Carl what was going on, *"turned around and left"*.

Carl telephoned the police, and reported the incident. A police sergeant arrived with a constable, who introduced himself as PC Nineham. The PC took Carl to one side near the parapet on the bridge, and asked him what had happened, while the police sergeant spoke to Bob. After some conversation, in which Carl formed the impression that the officer knew the vet, Bob went back to his car and drove away. Another Jaguar car arrived at the scene. This one was cream coloured, with a female driver. She got out and went over to comfort the girl, who was still in *"quite a state"*.

Carl Beverley Farlow.

Christchurch Police Station

The PC then offered to take Carl to Christchurch Police Station, as the lorry was completely devoid of any electrical power.

When Carl arrived there, he was asked to wait in the front office and noticed a woman, whom he presumed may have been another witness. However, it turned out that she was with the police. A plain clothes officer then asked him if he had been drinking, or was on medication.

"He asked me to touch my nose and walk in a straight line, which I did. I told him I hadn't touched a drop. I asked him about the lorry. He said it had been towed to the yard at the police station. He asked me to go through the story again, which I did, and then asked him to drop me off at my regular lodgings, 'Fairways', run by Miss Reynolds, at about 3.15am."

MOD arrive, Mr Perks and another man

At about 10am, Carl received a visit from two men (who showed him their ID), announcing themselves as MOD officials. One of them – Mr Perks – asked him a number of questions about what had taken place.

Carl told us:

"The one [sic] never said a word; the other did all the talking. He was the youngest [sic] and had a grey briefcase. After 15-20mins, I'd had enough. I was tired with lack of sleep. I told them to leave, suggesting if they wanted more to check with the police who had taken my statement."

Carl contacted the police and was told the lorry was being examined by Old Christchurch Commercials. He was astounded to discover the four 6v batteries were dry. Every fuse had blown; it needed a new starter dynamo and wiring harness. The lorry was then towed back to Shropshire by Carl, in the daylight, where it eventually cost £400 to put right.

Repairs to the road being carried out

"When I drove past the scene, the next day, I noticed they were putting chippings onto a newly covered strip of tarmac, by using a black tar barrel, mounted on a trolley, traffic being restricted to one lane with a 'stop and go' board in operation. There was a bulldozer doing something to the ground at the side of the road, with workmen washing down the telephone box."

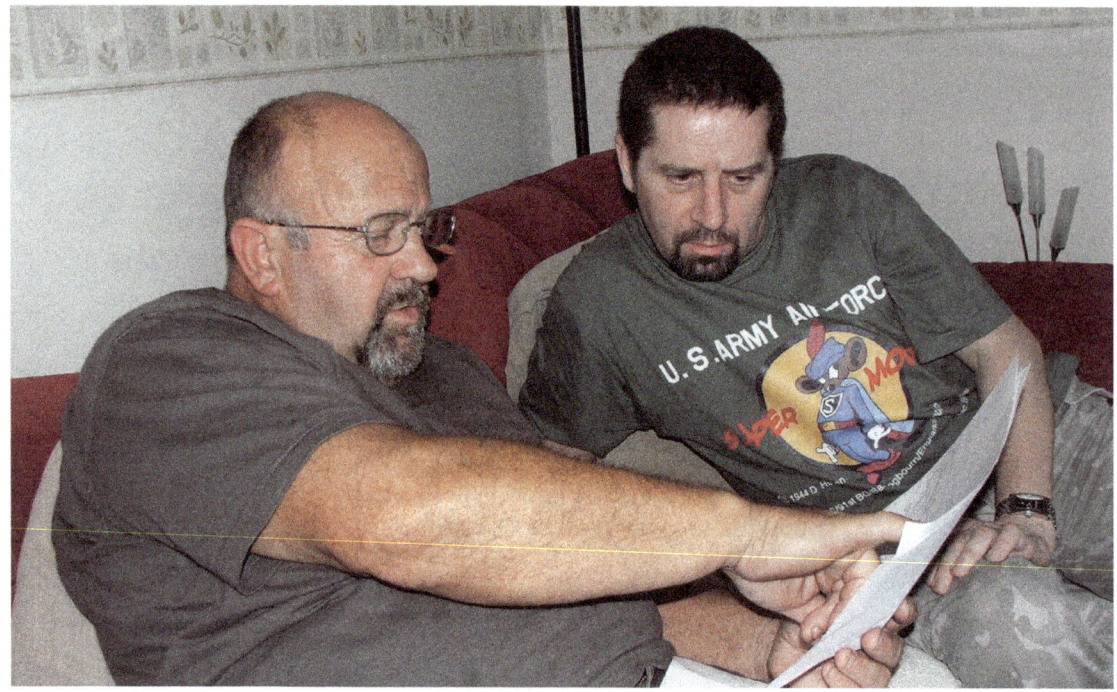

Carl Farlow and David Sankey

Carl confirmed that he had also received a visit from Tony Pace, of BUFORA, approximately a week after the event, following details of the incident having appeared in various newspapers.

Fridays People

Carl was to take part in an ATV documentary entitled, *Friday's People*, transmitted in October 1971 – the producer being Valerie Lewis. We met Valerie, many years later, through our sadly departed friend – Sheila Watkins. The programme dealt with reports of UFOs, and was one of the earliest sources of UFO information to us.

David Haith, Journalist

Following an appeal in the local Hampshire newspaper, attempting to track down any further witnesses to this event, we spoke to David Haith – a journalist – who had some knowledge of the matter. He had spoken to Carl shortly after the incident, when pertinent information (which was never released by the larger newspapers) was brought to his notice. This involved *"strange spheres, looking like mines with spikes, which came out from underneath the UFO and flew over the cab of the lorry"*. This information, never brought into the public domain, was confirmed by Carl during our visit to him.

David Haith

We contacted PC Roy Nineham (now retired) about the incident. He had no recollection of any damage caused to the road, or of taking Carl to the police station. However, he remembered attending the incident and speaking to Mr Farlow – whom he described as a *"genuine man"*, who was *"clearly shaken by what had taken place"*. Unfortunately he was unable to remember the name of the other police officer involved, but confirmed that the telephone box had been removed from its location some considerable time after the incident, but felt this was due to its isolated position and little use by the public rather than anything sinister.

Vet, Bob Carslake

Carl told us that, a few weeks after the incident, he received a letter from Bob Carslake – the other witness of that night's strange events. He had become firm friends, and the friendship has lasted to the time of writing (2008), despite Bob having immigrated to South Africa. Frustratingly, although we wrote to Bob and left telephone messages at his house, hoping he would be prepared to assist us, we never received any answer. We believe that this was clearly a matter he wanted to put behind him – an opinion reinforced by Carl's wife, Sue, who emailed us in March 2008, telling us that Carl had contacted Bob in South Africa with regard to the UFO incident, and was told, rather tersely, he (Bob) didn't want to suffer the ridicule he had experienced many years ago.

Rest in peace Carl

Sadly, in May 2017, Carl Farlow passed away. We offer our condolences to his wife, Susan, who we have spoken to over the last few weeks. We hope to meet up with Susan soon and share a glass of wine to the memory of Carl, whom she married on the 29th July 1988. Carl was a former serviceman and now missed very much by the family who adored him. His personal eyewitness account of what took place – now nearly 50 years ago – is preserved for future posterity – thanks, Carl our condolences are offered to her and his family.

Carl and Sue at an adventure park in Cornwall, some years ago

RAF Sopley – was it tracked on Radar?

Reflecting on the event we wondered if the UFO had been tracked on radar by nearby *RAF Sopley, taking into consideration the interest displayed by the MOD who interviewed Carl. One presumes that this may have been the case, but there would be no way of finding out because of the length ot time involved. not forgetting we are told that the records for this period were destroyed.

Just a few years later, in the summer of 1971, RAF Sopley Wing Commander Alan Turner (68) was the duty military supervisor at RAF Sopley – a joint military/civil air traffic control radar unit. He said:

> *"I saw a series of radar blips, one at a time, travelling south-east, at regular six or seven mile intervals, climbing fast for about 40 miles before disappearing. I calculated their height at 3,000 feet, climbing to in excess of 60,000 feet; the instrument wouldn't read any higher. I knew I was not watching military aircraft. The only craft with that rate of climb were supersonic 'Lightnings', but they wouldn't have held such perfect formation. They're also noisy."*

The phenomenon was also witnessed by four civil and six military controllers. Afterwards, everyone had to write a report.

---

*World War II station, codenamed *Starlight,* near the village of Sopley in Hampshire. The Radar Station was opened in December 1940. In 1959 it became an air traffic control radar station, and finally closed on 27th September 1974. Nearby Sopley Camp was built in the early 1950s as a domestic site for the radar station, and is probably best known as the initial home of the Vietnamese Boat People, in 1979. The camp was sold in 1993 to a local partnership under the name Merryfield Park. Most of the old barracks site had been redeveloped as housing, but the two-storey building at the Sopley end has been converted into a museum/education centre by Friends of New Forest Airfields. The museum opened in May 2016..

Wing Commander Turner says six military radars in southern England picked up the craft, as did operators at Heathrow. He also instructed a 'Canberra' aircraft, returning from Germany, to turn around and investigate.

"There was something about a quarter-mile away from him which, to quote him, 'was climbing like the clappers', but he didn't see anything really, nor did his crew."

Wing Commander Turner seen here to the far right of the group

Wing Commander Turner plotted the course of the UFOs. They travelled from near Marlborough, in Wiltshire, to near Alton, Hampshire, before disappearing. He said, a few days later, that they were interviewed by two anonymous men and told not to talk about the incident. He kept quiet until 11 years ago. Was it UFOs? He said:

"They were unidentified, they were flying, and they were objects. I've got to keep an open mind. It's arrogant to believe that we're the only ones in this universe.

During a visit to the United States to see his son, Carl met Michael Wallace, from NASA – engineer of Apollo Space Missions.

> "I just wanted to set the record straight. I know what I saw to this day. It wasn't ball lighting, or anything I could explain. I can't say it was any alien spaceship. All I know is what I saw. The 'Mickey taking' that went with it was unbelievable. I thought long and hard before I even spoke to anybody. There have been many things published about it. Why it's stirred up so much interest I don't know."

Valerie Lewis

In April 2007, we met up with Valerie Lewis –then retired and living in Wythall, Worcestershire. Valerie – then employed by Sandwell College to run a TV Studio as part of a training programme to teach Bachelor of Technology students, and others, who wished to train for a career in television – was most helpful and surprised us with her vivid recollection of her meeting with Carl Farlow, whom she regarded as,

> "...one of the most believable people I had ever met, although he was clearly very nervous, not because of taking part in the programme (Friday's People) – a documentary about UFO sightings – but because he had been 'leaned on' by someone, presumably because he had agreed to take part in the programme. I seem to remember he told me he had signed the Official Secrets Act and that he thought I might have to do the same, but I wasn't asked. Rather oddly, when I contacted the Home Office to speak to a Government representative about the programme and what it entailed, the man told me that 99.9% of UFO reports could be explained. When I asked about the point one per cent he admitted to me that he had sighted something he couldn't explain in the sky, but, if I quoted him, he would deny the conversation".

BUFORA member, Roy Winstanley

Somebody else, who interviewed Carl Farlow shortly after the event, was BUFORA member – Roy Winstanley, quote:

> "At about 10.30pm in early November 1967, Carl Farlow was driving his lorry down the A338 towards Bournemouth. Between Avon and Sopley, he saw a pale green light, about a quarter-of-a-mile away, above the trees, which was coming towards the road. He continued towards Sopley, keeping watch on the object. When he came to the straight part of the road, he saw the object hovering about 10 feet over the centre. About 20 yards from the UFO his radio stopped and all the lights went out, but the diesel engine continued running. Farlow described the UFO as glowing a brilliant pale green, about 15-20 feet in diameter, 10-15 feet high, with a circular top and parabolic base. A small semicircle in the base, glowing white, then opened. Immediately, a low-pitched noise came from the machine and a spherical object at the end of a 3 inch pipe appeared. Hanging from its underside were four smaller pipes, with a trumpet end. The pitch of the noise rose, as the spherical object came out further. Farlow heard a sound – like air rushing through a vacuum cleaner – and the object appeared to be 'searching for something'. It went to the side of the road and started to suck up leaves, dust and grass, and then went to the other side of the road and sucked

up twigs, more grass, soil, and little stones, for about 30 seconds, before returning to the UFO. The high-pitched noise changed to low-pitch and the 'hatch' closed. The UFO then rose slightly in the air, heading east for about a quarter of a mile, before climbing upwards and out of sight. As it did so, the lights and radio came back on again."

According to Roy Winstanley, Carl (judged by him as *"being quite sensible, rather than a man of imagination"*) saw the white Jaguar in front of him – still without lights – and went over to the vehicle, where he discovered the battery had been flattened, and then contacted the police who arrived and re-started the Jaguar by towing it.

Carl Farlow was also interviewed by Tony Pace – then the Director of Investigations for BUFORA – a keen amateur astronomer, whose knowledge of astronomy and the UFO subject is second to none.

(Unfortunately the original tape-recorded conversation of an interview conducted with Mr Farlow was mislaid, although a transcript of the interview was later published by BUFORA).

Wrote to the MOD

We wrote to the MOD, in 2007, asking them if they had any knowledge of any former employee – Mr Perks. Mr P.S. Webb, DAS-FOI, replied as follows:

'The Ministry of Defence does not hold any detailed information relating to UFO sightings for the year 1967 – Files for 1967 are available for examination at the National Archives. As for the role of Mr Perks, I am afraid that without more detail, such as a first name, or initial, any attempt to identify him is likely to exceed the £600 permitted by the Freedom of Information Act 2000 and as provided by Section 12 of the Act, the MOD is not obliged to comply with your request. That having said I would have thought that if, as you believe, his name would appear in the UFO files for that period. Again I would direct you to The National Archives.'

In 2009 we contacted Sue, after hearing that Carl was recovering from a stroke.

"He now tells our grandchildren of his UFO happening, as he calls it – something he never did before, as he took 'a lot of stick', over the years, from people who used to take the 'Mickey' out of him, although people now seem to be more inclined to believe such stories. Carl always says human beings laugh at things they are afraid of, or don't understand. I only know that after 21 plus years, my man saw something that night, long ago, which has stayed with him all these years."

(**Sources:** Personal interview/*Southern Evening Echo*, 6.11.1967/*Daily Express*, 7.11.1967/David Haith/Roy Winstanley/BUFORA *Vehicle Interference Project*, Geoff Falla, p.44-45, *Flying Saucer Review*, Volume 13, No. 6, Page 4/*New BUFORA Journal*, Issue 13, January 2005)

Over Bradford

At 4pm, a mysterious yellow 'cross' was seen over Bradford. After a few seconds it seemed to shudder, diminish in size, and disappear.

Birmingham

The Isle of Wight UFO Society tells of a UFO seen over Birmingham on the 6th November 1967, of which a number of photographs were taken. The whereabouts of these are unknown.

Reading

At 8.55pm the same day, a bright object – like a *"distorted Mercedes' three pronged emblem"* – was seen in the sky, by two men, over Reading. When it was nearly overhead, something seemed to drop from it and burn up. (**Source:** *Reading Evening Post*, 7.11.1967)

Leeds

In the evening, a bright object, flickering like a star, was seen in the west, over Bramley, Leeds – the direction taken with a hand-held compass. Suddenly, the UFO veered north, causing the needle on the compass to swing violently to and fro. (**Source:** *Yorkshire Evening Post,* 7.11.1967)

7th November 1967 – UFOs over Cheshire and Clacton

At 1.30am on 7th November 1967, night shift workers at a plastic coatings factory, situated at Winsford, Cheshire, sighted a strange object moving across the sky. According to Mr Colin Hawkins – a production manager at the works – he said that it resembled an elongated star, similar to that seen by a local butcher the week before. (**Source:** Joan Nelstrop, DIGAP/*Manchester Evening News,* 7.11.1967)

At 4.30am, Fred Bissell was awoken by a bright light shining into his home at Walton, near Clacton-on-Sea. He looked out of the window and saw an object, resembling:

> *"...a dustbin lid, hovering over Walton Pier, moving backwards and forwards, shining a light downwards. Suddenly, it shot off at terrific speed, towards Harwich – now looking like a 'cigar' – but returned and again hovered over the Pier, before shooting off northwards".*

Two police officers at Clacton, reported seeing *"orange lights"* at about the same time – a sighting backed up by four yachtsmen, at Clacton, who gave similar descriptions.

At the same time as Mr Bissell's sighting was a report from Mrs Mabel Allan, who was awoken by a terrific roaring noise. Looking out, she saw a huge light in the sky, very high up. She awoke her husband, who fetched his binoculars. Through the lens was seen *"a saucer-shaped object, with lights all around it",* which *"then rose higher, and vanished from sight".*

Hampshire – Grey, triangular UFO

Martin Challis – an apprentice engineer at Plesseys, Titchfield, Hampshire – and his friend, Gary Coomer, were travelling in a car, at 8pm, when they saw:

> *"...a light grey, triangular object, surrounded by an orange glow, emitting beams of light thousands of feet in height towards the south.*
>
> *After a few minutes it slowly descended behind the clouds".* (**Source: Southern Evening Echo,** **8.11.1967**)

Middlesbrough

At 10.45pm on the same evening, an orange coloured object, resembling *"what looked like a darning needle – round at one end, with a point at the other",* was seen hovering in the sky over Green Lane, Acklam, Middlesbrough, 45 degrees off the horizon, by Mr D. Bayliss, and his colleague – Mr T.R. Grief. (**Source:** *UFOLOG*)

Questions in the House

On the 7th November 1967, Dr. Bennett asked the Secretary of State for Defence:

> *"What organisation Her Majesty's Government has for the analysis and valuation of reports of flying objects not identified as aircraft?"*

Answer: Mr Rees

> *"The Ministry of Defence examines these reports in the light of their possible defence implications; and it obtains advice as necessary from Governmental and other scientific and technical organisations. The adequacy of our arrangements can be judged from the fact that between 1st January 1959 and 30th September 1967,* **625** *reports were examined and* **555** *were found to have*

*mundane explanations. The remaining **70** reports contained insufficient data for evaluation but there was nothing to suggest that they related to incidents materially different in kind to those which were explained."* (**HANSARD**)

As a result of several sightings of alleged UFOs seen over Southern England, particularly in Devon, during October 1967, Mr R. Peter Mills (C. Torrington), spoke in the House on 8th November 1967, *"of some concern, as well as considerable interest, in the South-West, about the sighting of the low flying star-shaped cross"*.

Mr Merlyn Rees, Under-Secretary for the RAF, replied:

"The objects in the sky over North Devon last month had been proved on investigation to be either aircraft, or lights. Of the lights, the majority were the planet Venus, but the source of a few lights has not been positively identified. I can say, however, that none of these unidentified lights was an alien object. There are standing arrangements for RAF stations to report unusual objects and for the investigation of such reports.

I do not think that any further action is necessary. None of the reports over recent years leads me to suspect that alien spaceships were overhead ...we have complete radar coverage to a very great height over these islands and over Europe. Eminent scientists and psychologists have been consulted on all these matters. As it is clear that the Government consistently denies there is any evidence to support the view that UFOs exist, it seems relevant to consider the possible reasons for this. We think that there may be five possible reasons.

Firstly, *it is possible that the Government does not treat UFO reports seriously, investigates them properly, but simply give the impression that it does so. This may be due to a preconceived policy that all UFO reports have a natural explanation.*

Secondly, *it is possible that their present policy is based on owing to the fact that instead of scientifically investigating unexplained reports, the Government assumes that reports of UFOs can be explained by natural phenomena, if more precise information were contained in reports. This ignorance probably stems from the fact that the Ministry of Defence is inadequately prepared and ill-equipped to make the necessary scientific investigations.*

Thirdly, *it is possible that the Government merely considers UFO reports to be 'red herrings' and the subject itself to be, at times, an embarrassing nuisance.*

Fourthly, *it may be that the Government already fully recognises the existence of the phenomenon, but for various reasons, it has decided not to inform the British public of the fact.*

Fifthly, *it is 'possible that the Government are correct in their belief' that the UFO phenomenon does not exist.*

We are of the opinion that the governmental policy at present is unrealistic and inherently dangerous. It is not out of the question to consider this policy to be jeopardizing World Peace."

Mr Wall asked the Secretary of Defence:

"...if he will make a statement on unidentified flying objects sighted over Great Britain, during the past 2 years".

Mr Rees:

*"From 1st January 1966 to 30th September 1967, **274** reports were found to have mundane explanations. The remaining **37** reports remain unexplained, because the information provided was so inadequate that no conclusive investigation was possible. The detailed analysis of these reports against the background of reports since the beginning of 1959 is set out as below."*

9th November 1967 – Cross-shaped UFO, Northamptonshire

At 5.30pm, *"an unidentified flying object in the shape of a cross"*, that was seen to change colour from white to tangerine, was observed travelling very fast across the sky over Great Billing, Northamptonshire. It was seen to slow down and halt in mid-air. (**Source:** *Coventry Evening Telegraph,* **10.11.1967**)

Lancaster

Ten minutes later, at 5.40pm, William Gardner of Mount Avenue, Skerton, Lancaster, (whose home overlooked the *River Lune*), saw what appeared to be an enlarged 'star', stationary in the sky over Halton. He called his wife, and they stood watching.

Seconds later, another one came from the opposite direction, *"about 300 feet off the ground, orange-red in colour and clear shaped, with what appeared to be windows inset, moving slower than an aircraft and silent".*

Surrey

At 7.15pm, a bright cross-shaped 'star' was seen moving slowly across the sky, south to north, over Woking, in Surrey. It then changed course, from west to east, in irregular and occasional 'stop' movements in the air. (**Source: SIGAP**)

Stoke-on-Trent

At about the same time, an object – alternating in colour from bright red to green – was seen over Stoke-on-Trent, moving northwards, accompanied by a humming noise. One hour later, a second UFO was seen over the same locality – this time described as having a small dome on top, showing a red flashing light underneath. (**Source: Tony Pace**)

Another tantalising report involved a woman motorist, who complained to the Thames Police that the engine of her car had stopped, after an object showing a blue light had passed overhead. In early November 1967, a Police Officer (who later examined the vehicle) could find no reason for the interference.
(**Source:** *Perception,* **November/December 1971, No. 26**)

During the same part of the month, people living in Marlow, in Buckinghamshire, sighted what looked like a four pointed 'bright star' in the sky, as dusk fell. Suggestions that it was Venus were rejected – as it was raining at the time, with heavy cloud.

Kent

Later the same evening, following reports of UFOs sighted over Tenterden, Kent, David King (aged 19) decided to carry a camera with him, should he see anything unusual. His patience was rewarded when, while walking home, he noticed a dazzling 'bright light' hovering over the town. After taking a number of photographs, he rushed to the local police station and reported the incident to Police Constable Pucker, who still remembers the incident to this present day.

Mr Pucker:

> *"I admit I was sceptical, to begin with, but decided to go and have a look, as Mr King was so excited.*
>
> *He pointed out a 'light', stationary in the sky, which I took to be the planet Venus. However, to my surprise, after a couple of minutes, it began to move off towards the North in a straight line."*

We were unable to obtain the whereabouts of the original photographs; enquiries made with the newspaper who had published the photograph were unsuccessful. They denied any knowledge of having published the article or photograph!

We don't believe that there was anything sinister about this. There was no cover-up. It was, after all, over 35 years ago! (**Source:** *Kent Messenger,* **10.1.1967 – 'David photographs UFO')**

11th November 1967 – UFO sightings over USAF Airbase

At 8.32pm, a *"glowing orange object"* was sighted moving across the face of the moon in the Berkshire area, travelling west to east across the clear night sky, which suddenly split into two separate parts; the top half disappearing, leaving the bottom half to continue on its journey.

At 8.45pm, a similar object was seen approaching from the same direction – this time travelling southwards, under the moon, in a series of jerky movements.

Between 9pm and 10pm on the same date, (a clear and bright night, with little or no cloud), USAF Security personnel Sergeants Coleman, Bean, Winston, Strickland, Knott, McDonald and Lane – all from 'B' flight 7551st Support Police Squadron – were on duty at RAF Welford, when they sighted *"a number of lights, moving erratically in the sky over the Base"* – a matter that was reported to Sergeant John Roger Artie, then assigned in charge of quarter duties that night.

Artie told us:

"I later learned that a report of the incident was written into the desk blotter – an official USAF document – and submitted, although I do not know the outcome of any investigations, but can tell you there was rumour going around that the night shift on the following night, the 12th November, also witnessed a similar phenomenon."

13th November 1967 – Incident at Winterfold Forest, Surrey

At 12.30am – a cold damp morning – Philip Freeman and his friend, Angela Carter, were travelling towards Woking, Surrey, in a red Triumph Vitesse. They decided to stop on the side of the road, about two miles from Cranleigh, near Pitch Hill, to demist the windscreen. They left the engine running, with the side lights on. As Philip cleaned the windscreen, he became aware of a very unpleasant odour – as if someone had let off a stink bomb. As he returned to the driver's seat, he was shocked to see:

"...a face, staring in through the near side passenger window, with no visible features like eyes or mouth, and what looked like an arm reaching up to the top of the car's hood".

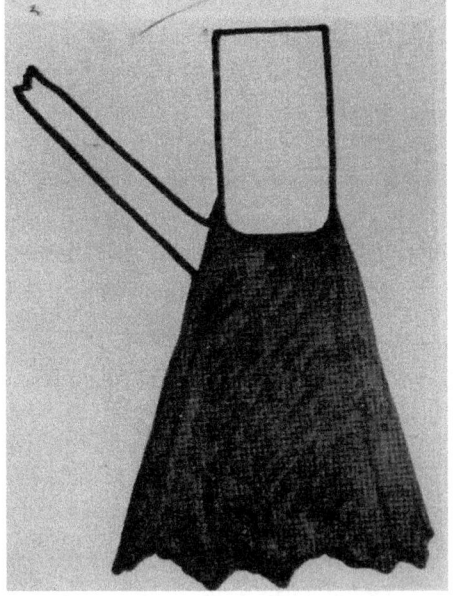

The apparition as sketched by Mr Freeman

Angela saw, from the horrified expression on Philip's face, that something was happening and, without looking around, urged him to drive away. In the time it took Philip to perform this operation, the 'being' had apparently moved to the rear of the vehicle. Philip switched on the headlights and started the car, *"seeing the same white face"* close to the Perspex back window. As he drove away, he had an impression of a dark bell shape, surmounted by two white or luminous parts. He cannot recall seeing any legs. As they recommenced their journey, the smell dissipated.

(**Sources:** Charles Bowen, *Flying Saucer Review,* Jan/Feb.1968, Vol. 14, Page 15-16 – 'The Spectre at Winterfold'/ *Woking Review*/SIGAP)

14th November 1967 – Silver 'discs', Leamington Spa

Amateur astronomer Brian Moore, from Leamington Spa, was a regular visitor to the Warminster area. On the late evening, along with his friend – Tony Bagnall, he was observing the night sky.

> "It was a clear and frosty evening. I was studying the constellation of Taurus, with its prominent red star, when I noticed a faint 'misty patch' moving slowly across the sky, heading west to east. I picked up the binoculars and was surprised to see the 'misty patch' consisted of five smaller silvery 'discs' – one of which actually broke away from the main body, and moved southwards."

(**Source: Personal interview**)

15th November 1967 – UFO display, Kent

Two red 'lights' were seen moving across the sky over West Wickham, Kent, before stopping briefly and heading south. A few minutes later, they reappeared – this time pulsing with light, accompanied by a third 'light'. They then performed various aerobatics across the sky, until 6pm when they faded away. We were puzzled about the purpose of these UFO displays, and felt it was extremely unlikely they were performing aerial acrobatics to impress. Was it possible they were energising themselves, in order to achieve the metamorphosis from swirling lights to something apparently far more structured?

16th November 1967 – UFO over Sussex Downs

Mrs Suzette Quick was walking towards the Downs with a friend, as the sun was setting, at 5pm, when she noticed an object on the horizon. She said that it resembled a 'steamroller'.

Her curiosity aroused, she went back inside her home and fetched a pair of opera glasses. Looking through them she saw:

> "…a trumpet-shaped object, with what appeared to be a gunmetal grey front, with a dome-shaped centre and two 'tails' from the right-hand side. I guessed its length to be about 25-30 feet. It swivelled several times, before disappearing over the Downs for at least ten minutes, reappearing and continuing the same movement. After the sun had set, behind the Downs, a flickering light appeared in front of the 'craft' – then diminished brightness followed by an extremely deep red glow coming from the object, which finally took off at incredible speed, towards the sea. Ten minutes later, it reappeared but disappeared behind a clump of trees."

This was the last she and her unnamed female companion saw of it, as they decided to go home, feeling rather nervous. Mrs Quick, in an interview with well-respected UFO researcher Omar Fowler, spoke of having seen a 'dark figure' approaching the 'craft' in a sort of *"gliding manner, slightly larger than a human being"*, which then suddenly disappeared. The description provided bears an uncanny resemblance to the object seen by scientist – Peter Wroath, in June 1966. (**Source: Omar Fowler/SIGAP/PRA**)

Over Alderney on the same date

Alderney residents – Brigadier P.G. Preston, D.S.O, and his wife – sighted a cross-shaped UFO. He thought, at first, that it was a distress or parachute flare, and went onto the cliff top to have a look.

> "The colours shown were alternating red and yellow. It was just after dark and there was too much cloud for any stars to be in view. The UFO made off at a very fast speed in a direction to the Sark side of Jersey. The object was stationary for at least 7-8 minutes and was very clear through field glasses. Before disappearing, it kept on a straight course without any pitching and very little rolling. The object was estimated to have been 500 feet above sea level, and about a mile to the south-east of Essex Castle. It seemed to be about 15-20 feet in length vertically and very thin, with the cross portion about 5 feet across and 5 feet from the top."

(**Source: Personal interview by Geoff Falla/*Guernesey Press*, 24.11.1967**)

18th November 1967 – 'Flying Saucer', Northumberland

Mr E. Hindmarsh of College Road, Ashington, (17 miles north of Newcastle-on-Tyne, Northumberland), was told of a strange object circling the moon. It had been seen by local boys, at 7am. On going out to look for himself, he was surprised to see:

> "...an oval object, dull grey in colour – the top part of which appeared to be rotating, with a white flashing light underneath – flying anticlockwise around the moon, 10 to 15 degrees off the horizon".

Five minutes later, it vanished from view. (**Source: Isle of Wight UFO Society**)

19th November

At 8.30pm, a peculiar moving light was seen passing through the sky, over Birmingham, by a university employee and his colleagues – observed for 15 minutes, and last seen heading northwards.
(**Source: John 'Dennis' Llewellyn**)

23rd November 1967 – Birmingham UFO, RAF Jets appear

At 4.45pm, an ex-RAF Bomber pilot was driving his car along the Rubery by-pass (A38), just outside Birmingham, when he noticed what he took to be the sun's rays, reflecting off the wings of an aircraft, but then realised this was not the case and stopped his car to watch it. After a couple of minutes it moved away slowly, towards the east (at one point changing direction), before being lost from view.

Within a few minutes two RAF Jets appeared and proceeded to fly underneath where the object had been seen. (**Source: Birmingham University Group**)

25th November 1967 – Oval UFO Northumberland

At 6.45am, *"a fuzzy, rotating, oval object, changing colour from red, white, blue, green, to orange"*, was seen moving slowly northwards through the sky over Bolam Drive, Ashington, Northumberland, by resident – David Turner. Five minutes later it became lost from view. (**Source: *UFOLOG***)

At the same time, a fuzzy object, spinning in the sky, flashing various colours, was sighted over Ashington, Northumberland, by at least six people. They told investigators from the Tyneside UFO Society that, *"whatever it was* [it] *seemed solid and was last seen heading northwards"*.

Another sighting on this day involved Bristol Police Constable Underwood, who was one of a number of people who saw *"a cylindrical object, with a protuberance on top"*, pass over the Clifton area of Bristol.

At 5.55pm, a spinning yellow and silver coloured 'disc' was seen stationary in the sky over Linthorpe, Middlesbrough, which constantly changed brightness. A short time later, it was seen to move southwards – and was out of view in 15 minutes. (**Source: *UFOLOG***)

26th November 1967 – UFO display, Stratford-upon-Avon

At 7am, a glowing 'ball' of silvery light, surrounded by a white halo, was seen motionless in the sky just before sunrise, over Suters stores Tower, Slough. The witness – Christine Deuchort, watched it *"begin to spin and dip lower in the sky, as if inspecting the tower, then head northwards"*.
(**Source: Letter to Slough Anomalous Phenomena Research Association, [SAPRA]**)

Stratford-upon-Avon

On the late afternoon, a woman motorist was driving along Shipston Road (A3400), near Alderminster, close to Stratford-upon-Avon, when she noticed *"a square object in the sky, between gaps in the trees, the base of which was jutting out a little, with two rounded corners at the top"*. After passing the line of trees, she looked out over open countryside and saw *"what looked like the wingspan of a large bird in the sky; within seconds, it was out of sight"*. (**Source: John 'Dennis' Llewellyn, Stratford-upon-Avon Group**)

Slough

Miss Patricia Gainer was travelling by bus from Maidenhead to Slough, at 5.30pm, when she saw a silver, oval, object in the sky towards the south.

"All of a sudden it split into six smaller objects, which moved away as if following the M4 Motorway. I kept them in view for 15 minutes, until I got off at Slough Town Hall. I didn't tell anyone at the time, as I felt rather silly, but I did contact the police, later, and tell them what I had seen. I couldn't have been the only one who saw the UFOs, as I saw a news item on the TV about similar objects seen above the M4 Motorway by others."

(Source: Isle of Wight UFO Society/Slough Anomalous Phenomena Research Association)

Birmingham

At 6.35pm on the same date, estate agent Eric Hanson of Radford Road, Erdington, Birmingham, and his ten year-old son, Paul, were walking near their home on the north-east side of the city. They saw what appeared to be:

"...a 'Shooting star', rising quickly above the rooftops, but soon had second thoughts when 'it' began to loop around the sky in a clockwise circle in front of the constellation Ursa Major, for about thirty minutes, before heading off in a straight line, where it halted in mid-air with the constellation Auriga, behind it, for a further 45 minutes. It then started its clockwise circling behaviour again around two of the stars that formed Auriga, for another 45 minutes, before finally heading southwards, at 10pm."

Solihull

Was there a connection with a report of *"a small bright 'fish'-shaped object"* seen moving across the sky over Solihull, Warwickshire, by a couple, at midnight? **(Source: Birmingham University Group)**

27th November 1967 – Upside-down 'mushroom' seen in sky over Nottingham

Paul Kenny (aged 13) was playing in the street at Clifton, Nottingham, when he noticed a saucer-shaped object, hovering above the ground over houses in Midhurst Way. Excitedly, he telephoned the police, but by the time they arrived there was nothing to be seen.

"After hovering for a while, it went away with a whooshing noise, leaving green smoke coming from it. It was a flat circle of light, with an oblong about 15 feet high. It looked like an upside-down mushroom."

Another witness was aircraft fitter – Mr J. Irwin. He said:

"It appeared to be rotating, with a red glow coming from it, and was moving at about 4,000 miles per hour. I've been in the aircraft industry for 25 years, but I've never seen anything like it before."
(Source: UFOSIS)

November 1967 – Strange experience, Harrogate

Olga Atherton from Crab Lane, Colgate, Yorkshire, was walking along Hill Top Road, one Sunday morning in November 1967, when she heard a roar of wind, *"like a hurricane"*, coming from behind her from the direction of the west. As it grew nearer, she detected a mechanical noise and wondered if it was an aircraft, making a crash-landing. By this time, the 'craft' (or whatever it was), hovered overhead.

Miss Atherton peered into the fog now enveloping the landscape, wondering if it was a 'flying saucer', and noticed a slight vibration all around her. Within seconds the noise ceased, leaving her shaken by the experience rather than distressed. In a letter written to Gordon Creighton, of *Flying Saucer Review*, she had this to say:

> *"A few weeks afterwards, I began to have some strange symptoms – a sickly feeling, which lasted about a fortnight, and an intense thirst, late at night, which meant drinking lots of water instead of my customary cup of cocoa. I think my mental processes were quite normal. I could concentrate on reading and writing, but was apathetic about things in general; worse, I lost weight, but in time recovered."* **(Source: Gordon Creighton)**

29th November 1967 – Deflated balloon – explanation for UFO sightings!

The police disclosed that a huge American scientific balloon, with a metal attachment in the shape of a cross, had been found in a field at Knightcott, near Barnstaple. The balloon, when deflated, occupied half the size of a football field. Also recovered, half a mile away, were two boxes – one fitted with a flashing red light. Packaging on the container identified the balloon as originating from the United States Department of Commerce, Environmental Science Services Administration, Boulder, Colorado (21.11.1967), asking for the package to be sent back to the Director of Magnetic Observatory, Alaska, USA.

Chief Inspector I. Lewis, of the Devon and Cornwall Constabulary, told the Press:

> *"This balloon could be the explanation for the mysterious 'flying cross' UFO sightings, made by police officers, although we don't know if balloons with this type of cross arrangement were in the area at the time of the sightings."*

November 1967 – UFO over Heathrow

Derek Dorman was another witness to something strange, during October or November 1967 (he cannot be sure of the date). He was living near Heathrow Airport, London.

Derek, a keen 'plane-spotter, was with two other people at the time. It was an early evening, and they were talking outside, when they noticed an object approaching their position. It was 3-4,000 feet above the ground, and about a mile away.

> *"If you can imagine half the length of a box – flat at the back but rounded at the front – this would be a good visual. The whole thing seemed composed of energy, like a whole load of disco lights all clumped together, each pulsating in a random manner. As the object flew overhead, passing over a cloud, it lit up – as if full of lightning. It seemed alive and was half the size of a jumbo jet, but twice as wide."*

The men watched it for about 10-15 seconds, as it moved away towards the north-east – then out of view.

Derek later discovered, from reading the national newspapers, the next day, that thousands of people living in the north-east had telephoned the newspapers and local authorities, after sighting a UFO crossing the sky. **(Source: Personal interview)**

DECEMBER 1967

3rd December 1967 – Nebraska Police Officer's Close Encounters

On 3rd December 1967, around 2.30am, in the vicinity of Ashland, Nebraska, police sergeant Herbert Schirmer, 22, noticed some red lights along Highway 63. Thinking that it was a stopped truck he approached and shown his high beams on it. Soon he realized it was no truck. Instead it was a disc-shaped object with a shiny, polished aluminum looking surface, and a catwalk that went around it. The red lights, which were

Herbert Schirmer

Haunted Skies Volume Two Revised

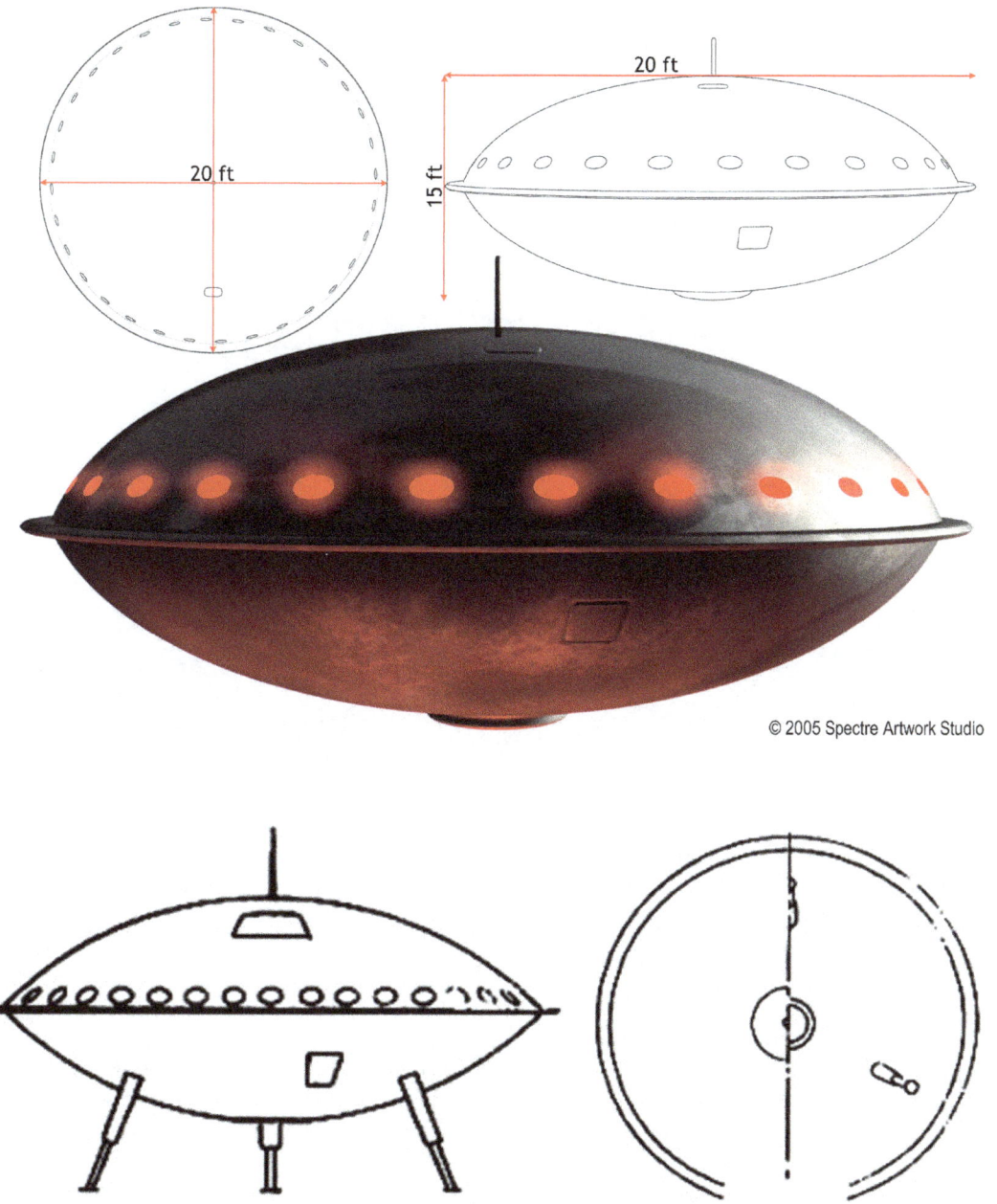

© 2005 Spectre Artwork Studio

blinking, were shining out from windows in the object. The UFO appeared to be a mere 6 to 8 feet above the road, and was hovering in the air with a slight tilt. Then the object began to slowly ascend, making a siren kind of noise and issuing a flame-like display from the underside. Sticking his head out the window, Sgt. Schirmer watched the UFO pass nearly overhead before it Schirmer then got out of the police car

Haunted Skies Volume Two Revised

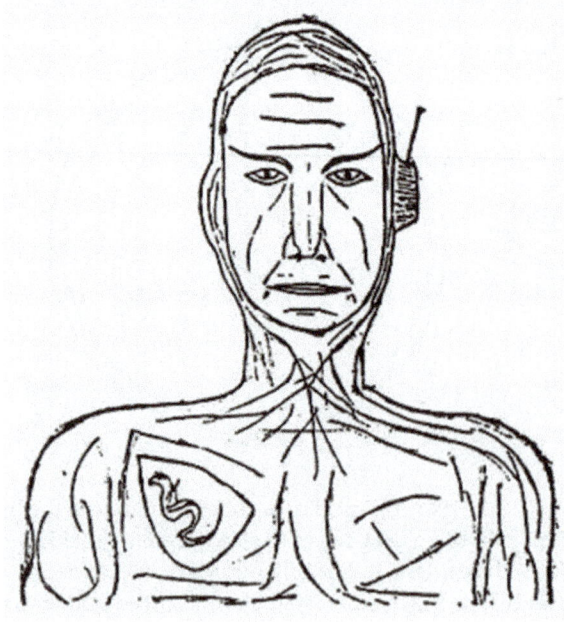

and, with a flashlight in hand, inspected the surface of the road where the object had hovered so low to the ground. After this he drove to the police station and wrote in the log book, *"Saw a flying saucer at the junction of highways 6 and 63. Believe it, or not!"* He was puzzled to notice that it was now 3am, as the sighting seemingly lasted no more than ten minutes. As the morning wore on, Schirmer was to suffer a headache, a "weird buzzing" in his head, and would discover that he had a "red welt" on his neck. It was about two inches long and approximately half an inch wide, and was located on the "nerve cord" below one of his ears.

Hypnotic sessions revealed that the occupants of the landed craft came and took Schirmer aboard, and communicated with him through some form of mental telepathy. They told him that they would visit him twice more and that some day he would "see the universe".

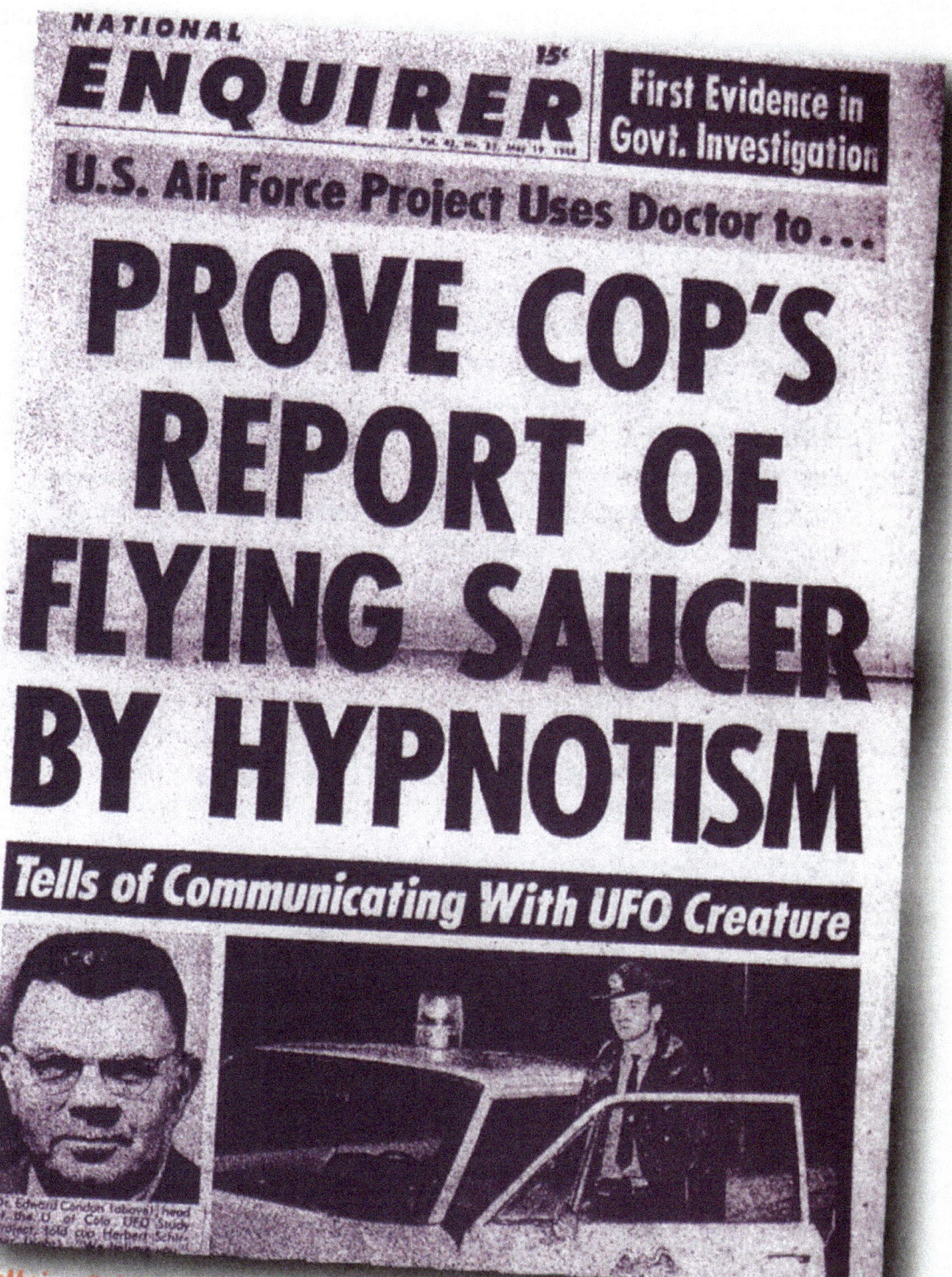

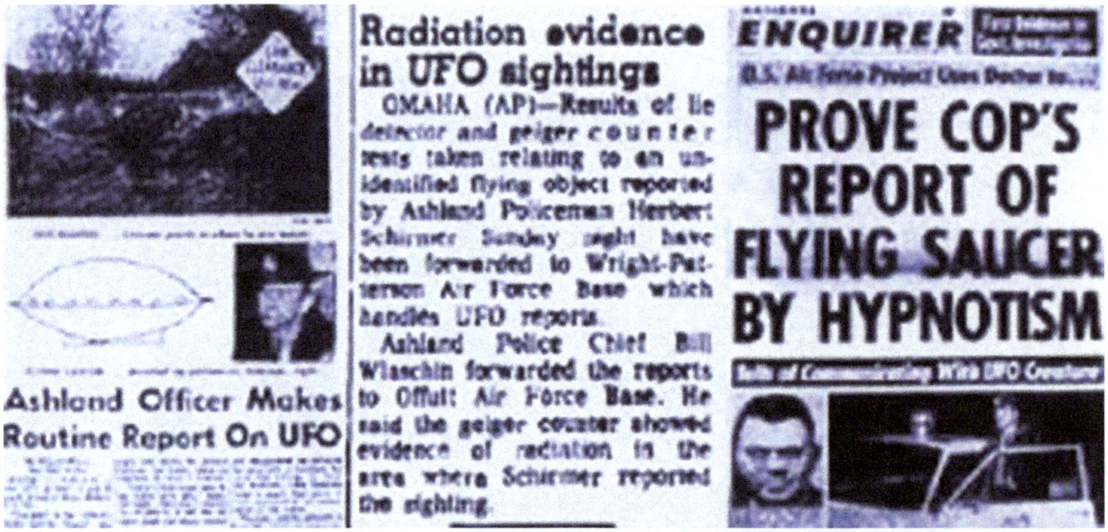

Haunted Skies Volume Two Revised

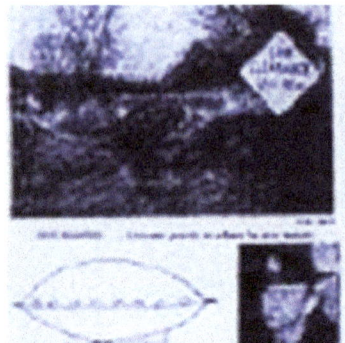

Herbert Schirmer

5th December 1967 – UFOs over RAF Welford, Berkshire

At approximately 8.30pm, USAF Security patrolmen Sgt. Coleman and Sgt. John Roger Artie were on duty at RAF Welford, when they sighted:

> "...an orange circle of light, moving high up in the north-western sky; within two minutes, it was gone from view".

On this occasion, no report was submitted.

At 8.30pm the following evening, an orange circular 'disc', showing a light on top, blinking erratically, was seen hovering approximately 30 feet above trees, in the vicinity of RAF Welford railhead gate. It was reported by two security personnel – Sergeants Coleman and Strickland.

As the men made their way towards the UFO, it dropped downwards, behind trees, east of the railway embankment.

The men then drove towards a wooded area, close to building F-99, and alighted from the vehicle. By this time the object was now out of sight. Sgt. Strickland flashed his lights, several times, following which the UFO reappeared, rising straight up from a position estimated to be a couple of miles away, in the vicinity of Rowbury Farm. It then gained altitude in an arc of movement across the sky, and flew over RAF Welford, passing along 'H' Row before turning up along an area known as 'Z', near the E3 complex.

Coleman got out of the vehicle and saw the UFO – now displaying an erratic yellow light – heading southwards, towards the direction of Welford gate, once again. It then flew over the gate and vanished from view. After about 45 minutes, the two men made their way back to the wooded area by the railhead gate. They parked up by building F-99.

At about 11.30pm., Sgt. Strickland looked through a pair of binoculars and saw:

> "...a 'glowing white mist' in the sky over the Rowbury hill area – which I thought strange, as it was a clear bright night, with no sign of any fog, or mist, elsewhere. The 'mist' appeared to shroud an object shaped like an 'evergreen', or something like that. Coleman suggested we wait until day shift to check it out. Whatever it was I don't know, but it wasn't the same object we had seen earlier.
>
> Suddenly, I noticed the 'yellow light' (only visible through binoculars) was back in the sky over the direction of Rowbury Farmhouse, possibly much further away – perhaps the A34 Oxford-Newbury road, in the direction of Chieveley. It moved backwards and forwards in a north, then south, direction across the sky, for a few minutes, and then disappeared, leaving the other object still visible in the 'mist'. At this point, we were called away. When we retuned to the scene, just under an hour later, there was no sign of anything untoward in the sky."

The next night, John Roger Artie happened to be on duty and was discussing the events with an RAF constable, known as 'Lofty'. He learnt that the officer had sighted a peculiar 'orange light' in the sky earlier in the week, while guarding the crash site of an RAF helicopter of the Queen's Flight, which had crashed at Bright Walton. Whether there was any connection can, of course, be only speculation.

7th December 1967 – UFO showing dark 'patch', Sheffield

At 5.10pm, Mrs Wilson and her daughters, of Woodland View, Sheffield, were standing on the drive of their house, when they noticed a red, circular, object – brighter than the moon – *"as big as a football in the air, with a dark patch on top"*, moving slowly through the sky, heading south-east to north-west.

8th December 1967 – Three brilliant lights seen in the shape of a triangle

The *Harrow Observer and Gazette* newspaper (Friday, 8th December 1967) told its readers about three brilliant lights, in the shape of a triangle, seen moving eastwards, towards Watford, at l0pm, by Harrow Weald resident – Michael Redman, and his wife Pamela.

NATIONAL INVESTIGATION COMMITTEE FOR AERIAL PHENOMENA - NICAP/GB

87, Morris Road,
Ward End,
Birmingham, 8,
Warwickshire,
England.

continued/...

The next incident took place on December 12th 1967, and was witnessed by Mrs Powell, a housewife; Anne and Susan who are schoolgirls; all of whom live at 25 Holloway, Northfield, Birmingham 31. The time was 10:10 P.M.

The object. seen through a bedroom window was visible for 4 mins 30 secs approx. It was a clear night with a few stars and a dull moonlight. The object seemed to change in brightness. Its colour was of an orange glow with a brilliant red core and a fuzzy outline.

The object eventually disappeared behind some houses.

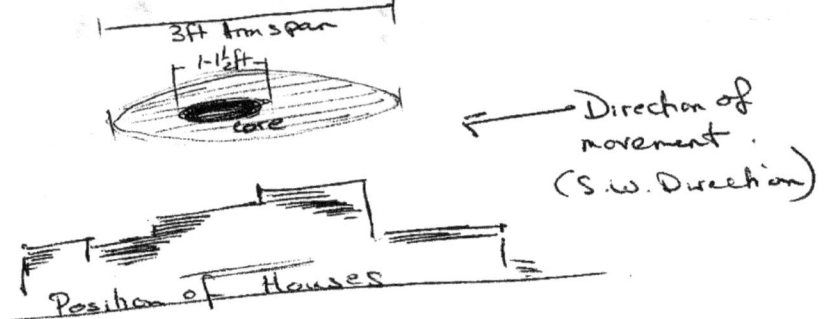

Any other reports will be immediately forwarded as they come in.

Fraternally yours,

J.W.B. BARKLAM.
N.I.C.A.P. FILES & RECORDS OFFICER

"Believe me! I hadn't been drinking that night! The lights were seen at tree level and maintained their triangular formation, the apex facing Earth, as they moved across the sky."

9th December 1967 – UFO meeting, London

At a meeting of Contact UK, held at Caxton Hall, Desmond Leslie said that he planned to turn part of his estate at Castle Leslie, County Monaghan, Eire, into a holiday camp for people interested in UFOs. **(Source: *Space-link,* 1968)**

10th December 1967 – 'Bowler hat' shaped UFO, Somerset

Minehead resident – Dennis Brewin, has held a private pilots' licence for a number of years.

On the 10th December 1967, he and his wife – Jean, were in the process of going into the house, after an afternoon drive. He said:

"We saw this large, white, object flying overhead, at 3-400 miles per hour, heading north-east in strange jerky movements, about 12,000 feet off the ground, before we lost sight of it in the haze. The most noticeable thing about the object, which I estimated was about 100 feet in diameter, was a large bowler hat shaped object beneath." **(Source: *Western Mail,* 11.12.1967)**

12th December 1967 – Glowing orange 'disc', Birmingham

At 10.10pm, a glowing orange 'disc' with a brilliant oval, surrounded by a fuzzy outline, was seen hovering over houses in Holloway, Northfield, Birmingham, for four minutes and thirty seconds, by Mrs Powell and her two young daughters – Anne and Susan. **(Source: John Barklam – NICAP, GB)**

26th December 1967

At 5.30pm, a brilliant-white, hazy, object was seen over Nantwich, Cheshire, flying near the Wardle tracking station. **(Source: NICAP, GB)**

27th December 1967 – Cigar-shaped UFO, Yarmouth

At 9pm, Miss J. Elliot was sitting in her car, parked at the Civil Service Sports Ground, Old Coast Road, Yarmouth, waiting for her fiancé – Mr M. Peddie, when she saw a large, white, cigar-shaped object, flying quickly across the sky.

"It hovered and rotated, for a few seconds, before moving silently off, very fast, towards the direction of the south-west. As it did so, it ejected a smaller 'disc' from its underside. Both objects then disappeared out of sight, in 60 seconds."

Five minutes later, the couple were surprised to see a rod-shaped object fly across the sky, stop and hover for a short time, before making off towards the south-west. This object was described as much duller than the first one and had ragged edges.

According to Miss Elliot, she thought there may have been something behind this less substantial object.

(We should consider the possibility that this may have been the original object, returning along its course.) **(Source: Letter to Isle of Wight UFO Society)**

28th December 1967 – Pulsating UFO, Newcastle-on-Tyne

At 9.30pm, an apparently 'solid', silver-coloured, pulsating object with blurred edges, changing shape in flight, was seen flying southwards over Newcastle-on-Tyne, by Mr and Mrs Moffat, who observed it for ten minutes before going to bed.

Upton by Chester

At about 7pm, Judith Craine (aged 18) of Upton by Chester, was returning home from work with her friend – Mrs Pat Perry (aged 19), when they saw 'strange lights' hovering over a house in Weston Grove, Upton. The girls ran across the road to get a closer look at the object, which was making a strange throbbing noise. It then appeared to rise, and move off slowly in the direction of the Chester by-pass.

Judith said:

"I began to run after it, trying to get a closer look, but when I reached the corner of St. James's Avenue, it suddenly shot off at a tremendous speed. The light we noticed first was a very bright orange, but as the thing began to move upwards it seemed to turn, showing other green and orange lights. Although it was dark and I couldn't make out any exact shape, it was easy to tell from the noise – like a ship's engine – and the way it moved, that it was not a plane."

Pat told researchers:

"I was scared out of my wits. When Judith ran after the object, my legs wouldn't move. I just stood rooted to the spot."

After the first sighting the girls continued on their way home, when they saw another 'set of lights'.

Pat added:

"Whatever it was seemed to stop, turn round in its own circumference, and shoot off in another direction." (**Source:** *Liverpool Echo,* **29.12.1967/***Liverpool Daily Post,* **29.12.1967**)

31st December 1967 – 'Close encounter', Wednesbury

At 2.30am, a man was walking along Woden Road, Wednesbury, after having just left his girlfriend's house. As he passed Wednesbury Youth Centre, on the right, a bright object dropped down from the sky in front of him. It was three or four yards away and moving at a fantastic speed.

"It was the most amazing and terrifying thing that had ever happened to me. I saw what appeared to be hundreds of green lights flashing together, like a beacon. A bright red glow appeared from the top of the object and I had a feeling I was being watched. Seconds later, it floated above my head and settled in a field to my left. I ran and never looked back, feeling very frightened by what had taken place." (**Source: Letter to Isle of Wight UFO Society**)

766 sightings for 1967 – 64 'Flying Cross's' reported

Mr Gordon Emery published a 16-page catalogue of brief UFO sightings for 1967, *The Great Wave of '67*, which listed 766 separate sightings for this year, 317 of which took place in October 1967, 64 of these being described as 'flying crosses'

CHAPTER 9 – 1968

UFO REPORTS INCLUDE:

JANUARY:
1st January 1968 – UFO over *River Exe* Devon
5th January 1968 – UFO over Belfast Northern Ireland
7th January 1968 – Red 'ball of light' over Birmingham
10th January 1968 – Silver UFO over Lake District
14th January 1968 – Cigar-shaped object follows motorist in Norfolk
15th January 1968 – Cigar-shaped UFO over Walsall
16th/17th January 1968 – Chevron formation of UFOs over London
18th January 1968 – Four 'red lights' over North Tyneside
23rd January 1968 – UFO over Buckinghamshire
Statement from MOD – 19 reports

FEBRUARY:
4th February 1968 – UFO over Derby
7th February 1968 – Egg-shaped UFO sighted by lorry driver
9th February 1968 – UFO, seen hovering above ground
27th February 1968 – Police report of 'close encounter' in Devon

MARCH:
3rd March 1968 – UFO, with 'tails', over the Isle of Wight
12th March 1968 – Pink UFO over Glasgow
19th March 1968 – Two UFOs sighted, Newcastle-on-Tyne
19th March 1968 – UFO over Nottingham
21st March 1968 – UFO sighted again over Belfast
UFO seen over the A31 road, Dorset
28th March 1968 – Devon and Cornwall Police sight UFO.

APRIL:
Hampshire Fisherman sight UFO
4th April – Flashing 'light' over Surrey
7th April 1968 – *Sunday Express* 'Buzz Flying Saucer'
9th April 1968 – Oblong UFO over London
13th April 1968 – 'Dumb-bell' UFO over South Lincolnshire
16th April 1968 – US Aircraft paced by UFO over Texas
23rd April 1968 – 'Tea cosy' UFO, Newport, South East Wales
24th April 1968 – 'Strange lights' over Leicestershire
April – Police Sergeant encounters UFOs over Derbyshire

27th April 1968 – Domed object, Arnos Park, Bristol
30th April 1968 – Pulsating UFO over Warwickshire
Isle of Wight UFO Society – sightings between April and June 1968

MAY:
5th May 1968 – Rugby-ball shaped UFO over Bedfordshire
13th May 1968 – UFO over Scotland
14th May 1968 – Kent Motorist encounters UFO
17th May 1968 – Thrumming noise UFO
18th May 1968 – Swansea man's close encounter with a 'cloud'
Summer 1968 – Kent Police sight red flashing light while on observations

JUNE:
4th June 1968 – Red fireball, Merseyside
6th June 1968 – Bright UFO, Surrey
9th June 1968 – UFO over Raynes Park, Merton, London
10th June 1968 – Flattened dome-shaped UFO over Liverpool
14th June 1968 – Luminous object, Newcastle-on-Tyne,
19th June 1968 – Silvery-white object sighted, North Yorkshire
25th June – UFO over Isle of Wight

JULY:
3rd July 1968 – Roger Stanway receives a letter from the MOD
4th July 1968 – Two 'Flying Saucers' over Devizes
5th July 1968 – Close encounter, Surrey
9th July 1968 – Black 'disc' seen, Lincolnshire
10th July 1968 – Cone-shaped UFO, Hertfordshire
14th July 1968 – UFOs over Coventry
15th July 1968 – BUFORA 'sky watch', Surrey
17th July 1968 – Red light, with 'bump' on top, over Berkshire
25th July 1968 – Teacher sights UFO over Shropshire
24th July 1968 – UFO display over Surrey
26th July 1968 – UFO over Warwickshire

AUGUST:
2nd August 1968, – 'D'-shaped object, Warwickshire
3rd August 1968 – Pencil-like object seen Gower, Wales
4th August 1968 – Horrifying 'close encounter', Warwickshire
11th August 1968 – UFO over Llandudno

Haunted Skies Volume Two Revised

15th August 1968 – Circular object showing orange lights over Coventry factory
19th August 1968 – Glowing UFOs, Warwickshire
20th August 1968 – UFO over Cheshire
23rd August 1968 – Cigar-shaped UFO reported by the BBC
28th August 1968 – Children sight four luminous objects over York
31st August 1968 – Cross-shaped UFO over Heathrow Airport, London

SEPTEMBER:
1st September 1968 – Horizontal line of four 'lights' seen, Hampshire
UFO landing 1968 – 'Keyhole' impression found in the crop
Surrey, 5th September 1968 – Brilliant 'light' over Essex
6th September 1968 – 'Disc' UFO over Chew Reservoir, Somerset
Early September 1968 – Wing-shaped UFO Bristol
8th September 1968 – Vehicle interference, Dorset
11th September 1968 – Splitting UFOs, Surrey
15th September 1968 – US Pilot encounters UFO display
17th September 1968 – 'Catherine wheel' UFO Coventry
September 1968 – The *Condon Report*
19th September 1968 – 'Flying Saucer' seen by passengers on South Devon ferry
21st September 1968 – Motorist encounters weird mass, Bedfordshire
September 1968 – UFO crash-lands at Wiltshire
24th September 1968 – Lecture by Coventry factory Boss, Mr. Wilf Grunau.

OCTOBER:
3rd October 1968 – UFO over Royal Albert Docks, London
12th October 1968 – Silver 'discs' seen over London
14th October 1968 – UFO over RAF Wittering, Cambridgeshire
18th October 1968 – Kent workmen sight UFO
21st October 1968 – Smoke Ring, Warwickshire,
22nd October 1968 – Triangular UFO, Surrey
30th October 1968 – 'Flying Saucer' over Harlow, Essex

NOVEMBER:
4th November 1968 – 'Flying Saucer' over Henley-on-Thames
7th November 1968 – Orange 'disc', Harlow, Essex
9th November 1968 – Bell-shaped UFO, Rugby
15th November 1968 – Blood-red object, Greater Manchester
20th November 1968 – Bell-shaped UFO, Cheshire
20th November 1968 – 'Flying Saucer' over Staffordshire

DECEMBER:
8th December 1968 – Three luminous 'discs' seen over Birmingham
15th December 1968 – Black object seen, with white halo, Shirley, Solihull
18th December 1968 – Three shining objects, Halifax, Yorkshire
21st December 1968 – Four shining 'lights' seen over Cheshire
25th December 1968 – 'Flying Saucer' sighted, Leicestershire
28th December 1968 – Red 'light' over Paignton, Devon

JANUARY 1968

1st January 1968 – UFO over *River Exe*, Devon

At 5am, *"a glowing yellow spinning 'disc', with a dark dome on top, accompanied with a sound like a swarm of bees"*, was seen moving low in the sky over the *River Exe*, in Devon, by a resident who had been awoken by the noise.

> *"It continued to make a buzzing noise and move from side to side, for some ten minutes, before shooting upwards into the sky at terrific speed."*
> **(Source:** *UFOLOG*/BUFORA**)**

Exebridge, River Exe and The Anchor *Inn*

5th January 1968 – UFO over Belfast Northern Ireland

A curious grey coloured object was sighted over the City by two men during the day. It was estimated to be moving at a height of between 8-10.000feet and moving at about 900 miles an hour.

(Source: *UFOLOG*)

7th January 1968 – Red 'ball of light' over Birmingham

At 5.30pm, two paper boys – John Smith and Robert Hughes – were on their round in Ward End, Birmingham, when they noticed:

> "…a red 'ball' of flickering light, with a yellow 'tail' behind it, appearing and disappearing into the sky".

Enquiries made at Elmdon Airport, Birmingham, revealed no other reports had been made to them. They suggested the boys may have seen an aeroplane. **(Source: Derek Samson – NICAP, GB)**

London

At 10.15pm, teenager Rebecca Smith from Kenilworth Road, Penge – a suburb of London, in the London Borough of Bromley – happened to look out of the bedroom window and see:

> "…a bowler hat shaped object, at least 25 yards long in size, dimly lit, showing red and white lights around it, about a thousand feet away, heading from the Elmers End area, moving towards Crystal Palace at the speed of an aircraft".

(Source: Mr Antonio Szachnowski, Anglo-Polish UFO Research Club/ *Advertiser and News*, 11.1.1968 – 'Flying Saucer seen over Penge. Girl, 9, draws bowler hat shaped UFO')

9th January 1968 – Two orange 'lights'

At 7pm, two bright orange 'lights' were seen in the sky over London, close to London Airport, by local resident – Mr French.

Two hours later, amateur astronomer – Richard Selmes of Catford, London, was watching the sky at 9pm, when he saw:

> "…about a dozen orange/brown cigar-shaped objects, tipped at an angle, travelling in a perfect 'V' formation and pass across the face of the moon, due south".

By the time Richard rushed in to fetch his parents, the UFOs had gone.

(Source: Letter to Isle of Wight UFO Society, from Norman Oliver, BUFORA/Richard Farrow)

10th January 1968 – Silver UFO over Lake District

At 10.30pm, a silver object, *"glittering like a star, rising and descending through the sky – the size of a small moon"*, was sighted over the summit of Barf Fell, by Mrs Coward and her charwoman.

(Source: Letter to Isle of Wight UFO Society)

Penthouse Magazine – their investigation

In 1968, *Penthouse* Magazine published various articles relating to UFOs. This followed what they termed as *'The biggest operation in its history'* by their special *Penthouse* research team. This had been set-up, six months previously, to consider and evaluate the immense literature available on the subject of UFOs, after the 'wave' of UFO activity which had occurred during the autumn 1967 period.

It may seem rather unusual for a men's magazine to publish well-researched and unbiased articles of the UFO subject alongside photographs of scantily clad ladies. They certainly made an impressive job, and included in-depth interviews held with people such as Gordon Creighton – then Chief Consultant of *Flying Saucer Review* and President of BUFORA. Creighton had served an illustrious career with the Foreign Service as British Consul in Antwerp, New Orleans, China and Pernambuco, and spoke fluent Chinese, Mongolian, Russian, and several oriental languages.

Contacted the Air Ministry

Previously to the publication of articles relating to their investigation into reports of UFO activity, a member of *Penthouse* contacted the Air Ministry, during September 1966 of the previous year and asked to be *'connected with someone in charge of investigating Flying Saucers'*. They were told that there was no such person, and were transferred to a Press Officer, who was unable to assist them with their enquiry. The Press Officer did, however, offer to contact someone at the Ministry who would know all the answers, although he declined to identity that person. The following day they received a telephone call from a Mr W.F. Allen, who spoke to them.

During the October 1967 'wave' of UFO sightings, the Magazine contacted Mr W.F. Allen, at the Air Ministry, but was told: *'There is no such person listed'*. Another telephone call made, a few days later, found him! However, as soon as he discovered it was *Penthouse*, he transferred the call to a Press Officer, who said to them: *"How did you know about Mr Allen? He's not supposed to speak to the Press!"* In their 'summing up' *Penthouse* had this to say:

> *"Firstly there is ample evidence to support the case for 'Flying Saucers'. Secondly, the military and intelligence units of most of the world's governments are sufficiently concerned with this evidence to try and suppress all information related to it. Thirdly, to uphold the public's right not only to the explicit knowledge that's its government may be threatened, but to make all the emotional and intellectual preparation necessary should such a crisis arrive. If, as their avid supporters believe, UFOs are intelligently controlled spacecraft of extraterrestrial origin, then surely this is the greatest story of all time".*

It is clear now, with the benefit of over many years hindsight that we are dealing with something of a magnitude that defies comprehension. *Penthouse* Magazine is to be congratulated for conducting such an exhaustive enquiry into something we are told does not exist!

(Source: – Interviews by Albert Z. Freedman/*Penthouse*, Mr Bob Guccione/Personal interview with Gordon Creighton)

14th January 1968 – Cigar-shaped object follows motorist in Norfolk

Mr Barron and his wife of Loughton, Essex, were travelling home from Long Stratton, at about 10.30pm, in his Ford Anglia. As they passed through Garboldisham on a dark and cold night, suddenly, the car was caught in a huge gust of wind, which pushed him onto the grass verge.

> "I said to my wife, 'what the so and so was that?' She said there is something over the pylon. I looked and about a hundred feet above me was an object, roughly 100 feet long, with orange light power streaming out of the centre; it was like looking into a volcano. I suggested that we take the next turning right, so that we could face it, and asked her to describe it. We then saw a cylindrical object, with portholes to the side, but were unable to find the right turn."

To their surprise they realised they were being followed by the object, which at some stage illuminated the vehicle and the locality with a powerful orange light.

After about three-quarters of a mile had elapsed, the object shot off like a shooting star. Mr Barron reported the incident to the Enfield Police, after careful consideration. Within an hour of reaching home, he was telephoned by someone from Whitehall, London, and once again Mr Barron outlined what he and his wife had seen. He later received a letter telling him that they had seen a helicopter on exercise!

Mr Barron does not accept this as the explanation. It appears he wasn't the only one to sight it; a number of people contacted the authorities about this – enough for *Anglia TV* to announce details of the UFO sighting to their viewers.

15th January 1968 – England: Cigar-shaped UFO over Walsall

At 3.30pm, *"a bright, metallic, cigar-shaped, object"* was seen moving slowly through the sky over Wolverhampton Road, Walsall, by local residents – Charles Robinson and Joseph Westley – who reported seeing a dome shape on top of the UFO, before it vanished completely from sight.

(Source: John Barklam, NICAP)

16th/17th January 1968 – Chevron formation of UFOs over London

Civil servant Mrs June Rose Parish (31) of Coppermill Lane, Walthamstow, London – (ex-RAF WRAF) – wrote to Mr Doug Canning of Cheddington

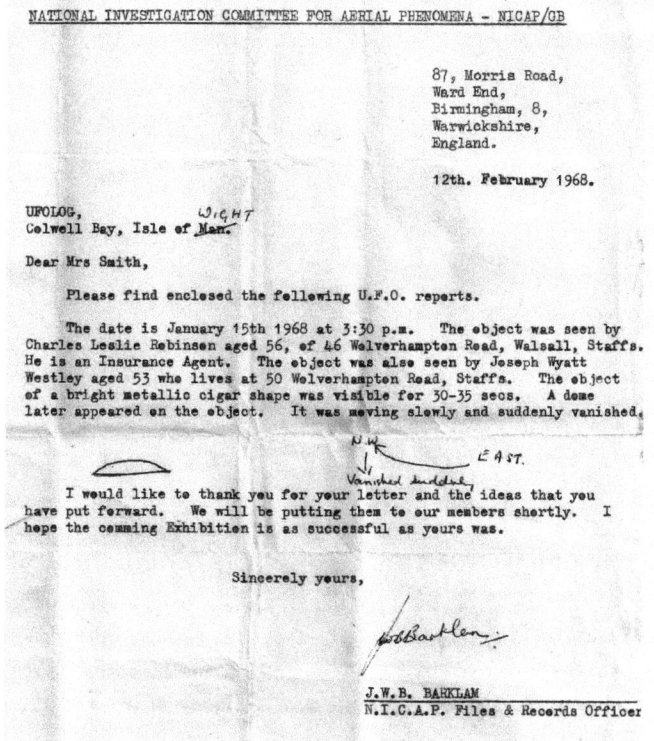

Haunted Skies Volume Two Revised

Road, Upper Edmonton, London – an investigator for the Essex UFO Study Group – about what she and her husband, Mr B. Parish, and mother and father, witnessed. Poignantly, she said in her letter:

"The other two witnesses were my Mum and Dad (he has since died). She (my Mum) – all I can get out of her is:

'They were like big stars – was scared'. I suppose her mind would go back to the bombings during the War and I have no doubt, by the way she acted at the time, that she thought we were going to be attacked. It was a marvellous thing to see a mystery."

The night was windy, with scattered clouds and some rain in the early morning of the next day.

June:

"I looked out from the back window at 11.45pm, and saw a whole formation of what looked like stars moving through the sky, like nothing I had ever seen before. There were six of them, moving westwards. While watching, they began to move about and the lead ones grew larger – they were about in the sky for several hours. We all had the distinct impression that we were being watched.

I believe I was the only one who noticed the noise. Whether it came from them, or the nearby railway or reservoir, I can't say."

June contacted the MOD and told them what they had seen. She received a letter back on the 7th March 1968 from Mr W.F Allen.

He said:

"I am writing to thank you for your report about the object you saw, just after midnight on the 17th January. From the description of the object, we think it was an aircraft, with cabin lighted, on the approach to London Airport. A BEA 'Comet' landed there at 0016hours on the 17th January and we think you must have seen the lights of this aircraft."

18th January 1968 – Four 'red lights' over North Tyneside

At 7.55pm, a cluster of four separate 'red lights' were seen crossing the sky, at an estimated height of 2,000 feet, over Monkseaton, by Mr Burgess and Mr Wellfield, before disappearing behind houses in the distance.

23rd January 1968 – UFO over Buckinghamshire

Mrs Leonora Wood, living in the small village of Old Faversham (15 miles from Northampton), awoke at 5am, for no apparent reason.

She immediately noticed a yellow and orange coloured object (which she took to be something on fire in the sky) seen through a gap between a clump of trees on the horizon, towards the direction of Newport Pagnell, over the motorway.

> "I sat watching the 'light' – now triangular in shape – for about ten minutes, and then awoke my husband, John, who described it as 'a glowing mass of light', approximately one and a half miles away."

The couple watched it for ten minutes, during which time it was seen to slowly rise towards the sky – at which point John fetched his Russian Zenith SLR camera, with a 300mm. lens, and looking through it saw:

> "...a traditional saucer-shaped object, with a raised central dome, the structure being white in colour, with what looked like red, orange, and white flames below it. I think it was these that we could see with the naked eye – then it changed shape to a perfect triangle".

John then took two photographs; the first did not turn out, the second (exposure time 8-11 seconds on 4.5f Kodachrome 2 film l9.Din 64 Asa.) was more successful. Unfortunately, the whereabouts of the original negatives and prints sent to *Flying Saucer Review,* many years ago, are not known. Invariably it was later suggested, in the absence of the planet Venus (which rose at 5.40am), that what the couple had seen was Antares – an explanation John rejects.

(**Source*: *Personal interview/*Flying Saucer Review,* 1968, by David Abbott – 'Buckinghamshire man photographs UFO')

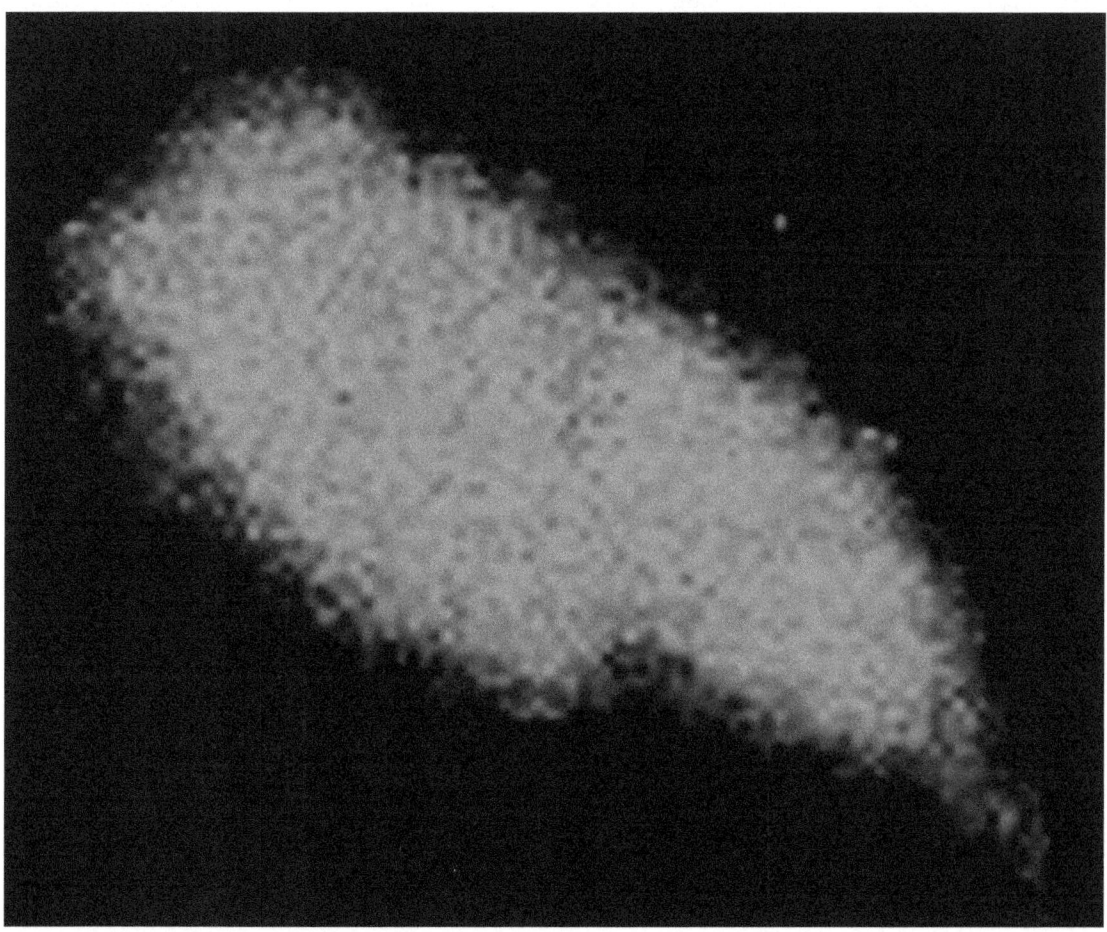

24th January 1968 – UFO reflection

At 4am, a mysterious 'light' was seen hovering over Bembridge Harbour, on the Isle of Wight – its reflection being caught in the water below, by a resident of St. Helens, who said:

> "It started to slowly waver, and halted in mid-air for a few minutes, before moving away towards Selsey Bill." **(Source: Isle of Wight UFO Society)**

At 8.15am a silver coloured pancake shaped object with what looked like 'pointers' around it was sighted moving through the sky over Belfast by a woman and her son (10) who was left very frightened.

Statement from MOD – 19 reports

The MOD confirmed that during the period of January 1968, they received a total of 19 reports, of which they judged four to be satellites, two celestial objects, 12 aircraft, one miscellaneous and one unexplained, under investigation.

FEBRUARY 1968

4th February 1968 – UFO over Derby

Assistant physiotherapist – Ann McDougal, was walking across the grounds at Manor Hospital, Derby, at 10.40pm, with her boyfriend, when they noticed a bright yellow spinning 'light' in the sky – larger than a full moon. Suddenly, it changed to:

> "...a crescent shape and emitted a dull glow. Several minutes later, it again altered shape to 'cigar' – now radiating a brilliant yellow light, no longer spinning, with dark spots appearing along its length, before moving to the left, forwards, and then backwards."

After watching the object for 20 minutes, the couple decided to leave, or they would have been late for work. **(Source: Kath Smith, Isle of Wight UFO Society/BUFORA)**

7th February 1968 – Egg-shaped UFO sighted by lorry driver

Mr Terrence King, from Norwich, was in a lorry being driven along the A361 road, on his way to the West Country, during the early hours (approximately 20 minutes from the town of Frome), when he noticed a large object, travelling a few feet off the ground.

> "I thought it was the moon, to start with – then it came down to nearly ground level. It was huge and egg-shaped. As it got closer to the ground, something seemed to come out of the top, until it was triangular. The driver thought it was a 'Sputnik'. It really shook us both up. It was in clear view for about a quarter of an hour, before vanishing from view." **(Source: *Western Gazette*, 9.2.1968)**

9th February 1968 – USA: UFO seen hovering above ground

Mr R.W. Bland from Groveton, Missouri, reported having sighted a UFO at 4.20am.

> "It was about 100 feet in diameter with concave sides, and had portholes in the centre of each, giving off a yellow-green light. It was hovering about 25 feet above the ground, before moving rapidly south-west. It made a pulsating sound – like wire being whirled at high speed – and was lost from sight, a few minuets later." **(Source: Project Blue Book unknowns)**

15th February 1968

At 5am, a curious 'patch' of triangular lights was sighted over Anna Valley, Andover. Within five minutes, it had gone. **(Source: *UFOLOG*)**

17th February

At 7am, a fiery, shimmering, orange object was seen silently crossing the sky over North Birmingham, heading north-west, at a height of approximately 1,000 feet. (**Source: Derek Samson – NICAP, GB**)

27th February 1968 – England: Police report of 'close encounter' in Devon

Derek Davis – a retired police sergeant from the Devon and Cornwall Constabulary – told us about a very peculiar incident. He was on duty at Crediton Police Station, at 7.20pm, and was approached by Police Constable 285 Herbert Edward Hawkins, who had been dealing with an enquiry from a member of the public in the front office, when lorry driver Andrew Norman Perry (37) of Adscombe Avenue, Bridgwater, came into the Station in a clearly agitated condition.

Andrew Perry

From copies of the original police statements, submitted to the Chief Constable and RAF, by Derek, PC Hawkins asked him what the problem was. He replied:

> "How long will you be with that chap, as I have something important and terrible to tell you?"

I asked him what he meant.

He said:

> "I have seen something, just now, which I never hope to see again."

PC Hawkins took him into another room and was then told by Mr Perry that he had seen a 'Flying Saucer', or similar object, at 6.55pm on the Crediton side of Winkleigh, in a field, with *"five or six 'figures', about 4 feet in height"*, stood near to the object.

the scene of the incident

PC Hawkins said:

> "Perry was clearly suffering from shock, and kept repeating how frightening it had been when he had seen the object and 'men' in the field".

At this point, PC 83 (Acting Police Sergeant) Derek Davis took over the enquiry. After being given the gist of what had transpired between PC Hawkins and Mr Perry, PC Davis said:

> "I went over to him and noticed how terrified he looked. His complexion was white. I went through the report again and was confident, in my opinion, that this was not a man who had been drinking and appeared to be a reasonable, unimaginative person of average intelligence."

The officer then asked Mr Perry if he would be willing to accompany him back to the scene and show him where it had happened.

After some perhaps understandable reluctance, Mr Perry then agreed.

His description of the area, as given to the officer, enabled the location to be found without any problem. It was at Blackditch Cross, between one and a half and two miles due south-west of Lapford, by the B3229 road and the North Tawton, Lapford district road, (Map reference 164/716061).

PC Derek Davis indicates the site of the incident

Police Constable Davis said:

> "The field was situated directly north of the crossroads, with its south-western side making the B3220 road side and south-eastern side making the road hedge of the Lapford to North Tawton district road."

A search was then made of the field with the aid of a torch, by the officer, but nothing of any significance was seen.

Police Statement of Andrew Norman Perry, 9.25pm – 27th February 1968:

"At about 6.55pm, today, Tuesday, 27th February 1968, I was driving my 'artic' lorry – SJL 97L, from Bideford, en route to Cullompton. Just before reaching Blackditch Cross, which is two miles from Lapford, I saw, on ascending a small hill, a very bright object away to my left, about a quarter of a mile distant. I didn't think much more about it at the time, but on coming over the crest I saw that the object had taken on the shape of a mushroom. It was a very brilliant silver colour, similar to the flashing one would get by flashing a mirror in the sun. I drove a bit further down the hill, until I was abreast of the object, and I would think, by then, it was about 300 yards distant.

I stopped the lorry and climbed out of my cab, leaving the engine running, and climbed onto the trailer to get a better view, and saw also what appeared to be five or six 'figures', about four feet in height, a dozen or so yards away from the object, and were spread around it. These 'figures' were brightly coloured in the same manner as described before. Almost immediately I stood up, the 'figures' seemed to scramble towards the object, and as soon as they reached it, they seemed to disappear inside. Immediately, the object climbed vertically and there was a high-pitched whining noise, which vibrated terribly. By this time my courage failed me and I became very frightened. I quickly jumped into the cab. I put the engine into gear and started to go down the road as fast as I could go.

The object had risen to about 200 feet and I travelled about a dozen yards. The noise from the object was so intense, I couldn't hear my engine running as it passed overhead. Suddenly, for no apparent reason, the engine cut out. I braked, stopped, and cradled my head in my arms, as I thought the object was coming right down on top of me.

A few seconds passed. The noise went, and when I looked up it was about the size of a football and was going away into the sun at a really fantastic speed. I pressed the starter button. The engine started and I went as fast as I could to the nearest police station – the rest you know."

Signed, A.N. Perry, Witnessed by: D.A. Davis, PC 83

Search of the area made

Shortly after first light, the following morning, PC Davis, accompanied by Police Sergeant McGregory, returned to the scene and conducted an examination of the ground, but found nothing untoward.

Derek Davis then contacted Sergeant Smiggs, of the MOD Police, in London, and was advised (after being admonished for his rather sceptical attitude towards the incident), to submit a full report, including statements taken from all parties, to the RAF and the MOD – which he did.

In 2008, we spoke to Andrew (the son of the witness) who told us his father didn't really want to get involved, for fear of attracting further ridicule, but he saw no reason to dispute what he believed was a genuine account given by his father, at the time, who has since passed away. **(Source: Personal interview)**

Cheltenham

An interesting footnote to this incident was a report from two unnamed schoolboys at Cheltenham, Gloucestershire, who reported having sighted a bright green, round object, falling through the sky from right to left, about 80 yards away from where they were standing, at 9.15pm on 27th February, 1968. *"It gave a off a deafening high-pitched whistling noise and also a curious smell"*.

In 2009 we emailed Cheltenham Library, asking them to check the local newspapers for any further information pertaining to this event, having regard to the previous incident at Devon.

(Source: Isle of Wight UFO Society)

MOD

The MOD confirmed that during the period of February 1968, they received a total of 18 reports, of which they judged nine to be satellites, one celestial object, 8 aircraft, and one under investigation. Was it the incident as above?

MARCH 1968

3rd March 1968 – UFO with 'tails', over the Isle of Wight

Miss N.B. Plumbe of Oak Dale, Cranmore – a village on the Isle of Wight (located about three miles east of Yarmouth, in the north-west of the island) – was outside her house when she saw a very bright object in the sky, at 10.15pm, which she described as:

> *"The first half was cream in colour; the second half, red. From the one end appeared cream coloured 'tails' – four or five of them, whirling around. This was no aircraft; it was silent and the sky clear. It wasn't any meteorite either. It was heading across the sky very fast, from east to west, about one third of the way up the horizon over The Solent. Suddenly, it vanished in the direction of Hurst Castle. I didn't see any sparks, or anything like that."*

(Source: Isle of Wight UFO Society/*County Press*, 8.3.1968)

12th March 1968 – Pink UFO over Glasgow

A large, round, pinkish object was seen in the sky over Glasgow, at 5.50am, by Glasgow resident – John Mortimer, close to where steelworks, lakes, and high tension pylons were situated. Ten seconds later, it had gone. **(Source: J.W. Barklam, NICAP)**

19th March 1968 – Two UFOs sighted, Newcastle-on-Tyne

At 6am, Mr J. Suley, from Newcastle-on-Tyne, was walking along West Road, when he saw a brilliant star-shaped object moving slowly across the sky, and dashed inside to fetch a telescope.

> *"Ten minutes later it began to zigzag across the sky and then stopped again. Suddenly, from the east direction, another object appeared. After a few seconds, the second object shot off across the sky, westwards, leaving the first one remaining in its position, showing green and blue flames projecting from its underside, for twenty minutes, until it moved away."* **(Source: TUFOS/*UFOLOG*)**

19th March 1968 – UFO over Nottingham

At 1.30am, an orange and silver coloured object – shaped like *"a train in the sky"* – was seen over Old Basford, Nottingham (four miles away from Hucknall Aerodrome), by Mrs J. Green.

> *"The object made a noise – like engines being forced to function at maximum speed. It had a silver pipe running down one side. At one stage it stopped, to avoid striking a TV aerial on a rooftop, then moved upward and to one side."*

UFO seen over the A31 road, Dorset

It appears this may well have been the same object seen at 3pm, on the same date, by Sam Richards – a member of the Isle of Wight UFO Group – who was travelling home from Dorchester, along the A31, as a passenger in the front seat of a car, heading towards Southampton, when he noticed a strange 'light' in the sky. Further observation revealed:

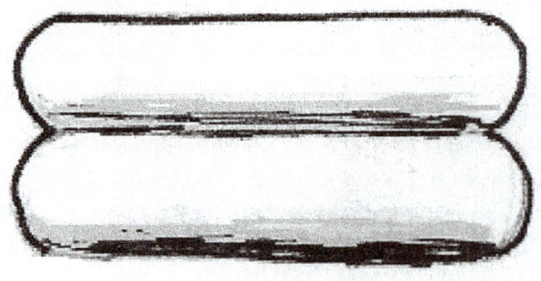

"...two horizontal cylinders, silver in colour showing a definite shadow on the lower edge. Suddenly, within seconds, it vanished from sight".

The driver of the car, also having witnessed the event, stopped the car but there was nothing to be seen. **(Source: Kath Smith, Isle of Wight UFO Society)**

Bristol

At 6.45pm, Jenny Casey, a member of Contact UK, Bristol, sighted a silver coloured object of solid appearance – the size of a 'florin', when held at arm's length – apparently rotating as it flew southwards across the sky. Was this the UFO seen previously by Sam Richards? **(Source: Contact UK, Bristol)**

21st March 1968 – UFO sighted again over Belfast

At 4.15pm Michael Browne was out walking in the outskirts of the City, when he was astonished to see a most unusual object flying through the sky at a height of about 2000 feet.

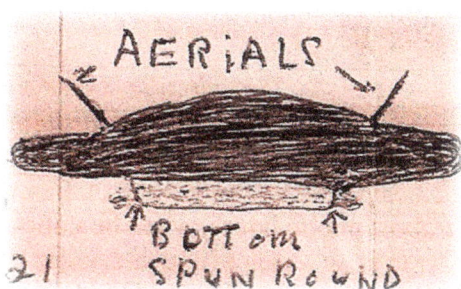

28th March 1968 – Devon and Cornwall Police sight UFO

Police Constables Michael Kirby and Basil Warren were driving along Union Street, Torquay, in Devon, at 3.15am, when they saw an object, resembling a flying railway carriage in the sky, with *"a line of illuminated portholes down the one side, clearly visible"*.

(Source: *News of the World,* **31.3.1968)**

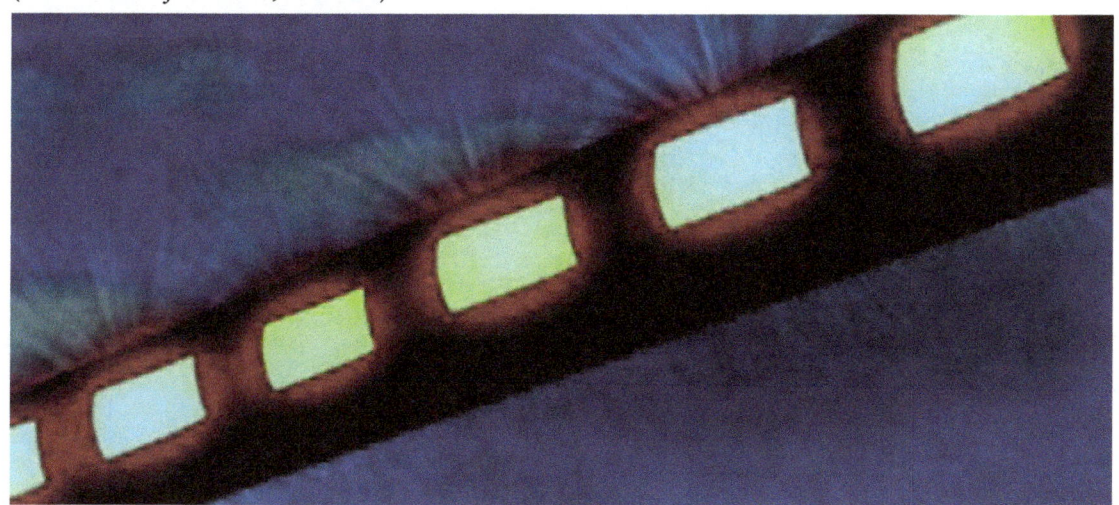

31st March 1968 – UFO display, Birmingham

At 11.50pm, a couple from Hall Green, Birmingham, noticed a 'bright light' in the sky,

"...executing an erratic motion, following a vertical anticlockwise ellipse about 20-30 degrees off the horizon, towards the south-west.

Ten minutes later, it shot off straight and to the right, covering several tens of degrees of arc in seconds, before halting in mid-air and then returning to its original position, where it began the process again."

Haunted Skies Volume Two Revised

The couple decided to go to bed but awoke at 3am, and looked out of the window, when they saw the object still in the sky. **(Source: Birmingham University Group)**

APRIL 1968

2nd April 1968 – Hampshire fishermen sight UFO

A mysterious object was seen in the sky over Hengistbury Head, in Hampshire, by three fishermen, during the evening, described as: *"...round and brilliant-white in colour, which suddenly changed to a flowing pink – then headed off towards the Isle of Wight."* **(Source: *UFOLOG*)**

SOUTHERN TELEVISION LIMITED
SOUTHERN INDEPENDENT TELEVISION CENTRE
NORTHAM · SOUTHAMPTON · SO9 4YQ.
Telephone: Southampton 28582   Telex: Southtel 47503

9th April 1968

K. Smith, Esq.,
Ringlemere,
Colwell Road,
Colwell Bay,
Isle of Wight.

Dear Mr. Smith,

The mystery object to which you refer was seen off the Hampshire coast on April 2nd.

The details are: Mystery object seen in sky over Hengistbury Head at Bournemouth on 2.4.68. Seen by three fishermen who were netting in Christchurch Harbour. They described it as round and brilliant white suddenly changing to a flowing pink. It headed off at a fast speed towards the Isle of Wight.

Thank you for writing in. I cannot promise to let you know when we do report such sightings in future bulletins but I will certainly bear your request in mind.

Yours sincerely,

Selwyn Valters
News Editor.

DIRECTORS:
JOHN H. DAVIS, Chairman · C. D. WILSON MC, Managing Director · Prof. ASA BRIGGS · The Rt. Hon. LORD CORNWALLIS OF LINTON KBE, MC
G. R. DOWSON · R. F. HAMMOND · The Hon. V. H. E. HARMSWORTH · B. G. HENRY · Sir ROBERT PERKINS · R. M. SHIELDS
BERKELEY SMITH · B. H. THOMSON TD · D. B. THOMSON · W. H. THOMSON · Capt. H. TUPPER MC · Sir DAVID WEBSTER

4th April – Flashing 'light' over Surrey

"A bright red-orange coloured 'ball of fire', flashing on and off", was seen high in the sky above Surbiton, Surrey, at midnight, for a few minutes, before moving away. (**Source: SIGAP**)

7th April 1968 – *Sunday Express* 'Buzz Flying Saucer'

This newspaper proclaimed that *John Betjeman's daughter had installed a 'flying saucer' detector at the family home in Kensington, London.

Candida:

"It cost £6 and is worth every penny. I bought it from a Flying Saucer Club to which I belong. Nearly every member has one. It's certainly catching; it detects very strong magnetic fields. When a 'Flying Saucer' appears in the sky, it buzzes loudly".

**Candida, wife of Rupert Lycett – owner of a Mayfair tailors', was asked if she had spotted a 'Flying Saucer', to which she replied:

"The machine buzzed the other day, but I was out. My husband, who had scoffed a lot at it, rushed outside and saw a bright object move across the sky. It couldn't have been anything other than a 'Flying Saucer', because the machine doesn't react to man-made objects."

Candida Lycett / Sir John Betjeman

*Sir John Betjeman, CBE, 28th August 1906 – 19th May 1984) was an English poet, writer, and broadcaster, who described himself in *Who's Who* as a "poet and hack". He was Poet Laureate of the United Kingdom from 1972 until his death.

He was a founding member of the Victorian Society and a passionate defender of Victorian architecture. He began his career as a journalist and ended it as one of the most popular British Poets Laureate and a much-loved figure on British television.

Candida Rose Lycett Green, (née **Betjeman**; 22nd September 1942 – 19th August 2014) was a British author who wrote sixteen books including *English Cottages, Goodbye London, The Perfect English House, Over the Hills and Far Away* and *The Dangerous Edge of Things*. Her television documentaries included *The Englishwoman and the Horse*, and *The Front Garden*. *Unwrecked England*, based on a regular column of the same name she wrote for *The Oldie* since 1992, was published in 2009.

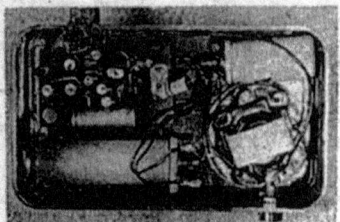

BAILEY'S LITTLE BLACK BOX

Daily Mirror, Mon April 15 1968

ONE OF the nation's most secret electronic devices, a flying-saucer detector, fell into my hands the other day, and five minutes later, I had the back off it.

This wasn't so very difficult as this mini-Jodrell Bank is housed in a Woolworth's sandwich box. Nevertheless, the array of coils and transistors (right) was an impressive sight to any believer.

The detector is made by electronics engineer Colin McCarthy, who has sold more than 250 at five guineas a time. You're no one these days if you don't have a flying-saucer detector. David Bailey has one. Mick Jagger has one. So has John Betteman's daughter, Candida Lycett comic (Dan Dare, the Mekon, Treens, etc.), spends his evenings by his, anxiously waiting for the alarm to go off.

The detectors sound a loud buzzer when there is a change in pulsating magnetic fields—such as only an Unidentified Flying Object can cause, I am told.

Unfortunately they have not produced quite the hoped-for results.

Candida's sounded the alarm the other day, but she was out shopping.

Bailey's house was fairly swarming with UFOs, but his detector remained silent. The battery, it seems, had run down.

In case you, too, want to join the Flying Saucer Set, I think I ought to tell you that no more of these delicate instru-

UFO detector: A must for

9th April 1968 – Oblong UFO over London

At 1am, *"a huge oblong object, showing a vivid white light tinged with blue"*, was seen travelling at great speed over London, before halting abruptly in mid-air. A vivid orange glow then appeared from underneath, as it descended towards the ground and out of sight.

(Source: Surrey Investigation Group on Aerial Phenomena, [SIGAP])

13th April 1968 – 'Dumb-bell' UFO over South Lincolnshire

At 3.15pm, on a fine sunny day, two people were walking across a field when they saw a silvery object, appearing and disappearing in the sky, apparently circling over the signals of a nearby railway junction of the Lincoln-Sleaford railway line. Through binoculars, *"a dumb-bell shaped object"* was seen.

(Source: Richard Thompson, South Lincolnshire UFO Study Group)

16th April 1968 – US Aircraft paced by UFO over Texas

Henry Ford the 2nd was aboard a Jetstar plane, accompanied by his executives, flying at 35,000 feet en route from San Antonio to Detroit. While near Austin, the pilots (and passengers) sighted a huge, round, object overhead. They thought, initially, that it might have been an unusually large research balloon – until it began to move with them.

A few minutes later it was still there, pacing the aircraft at 616 miles per hour. The senior pilot said:

> *"It looked twice the size of the DC-8, and was 5-600 feet in diameter. No protrusions or windows could be seen."*

During the hour long sighting, Mr Ford asked the pilot to radio the Air Force and send up a Jet fighter to intercept. The pilot, fearing ridicule, declined to do so. **(Source: NICAP)**

18th April 1968

At 11.30pm, a painter and decorator – Mr Thomas Frederick Moss from Lozells, Birmingham – sighted:

> *"...two circular silver objects moving across the sky, before merging into one another and disappearing two minutes later."* **(Source: NICAP)**

23rd April 1968 – 'Tea cosy' UFO, Newport, South-East Wales

At 2am, a man was out walking along Stow Hill, Newport, in the direction of the *Hardpost* public house, when he noticed a brilliant 'white light' moving towards the east.

> *"It moved in a series of bizarre pendulum, zigzag and curved, actions across the sky. After watching it for a short time, I was able to make out a 'tea cosy' shape, with a light on top and underneath. Along the perimeter of its base was a deep-red band. It eventually faded away in the distance, behind the glare of Newport's lighting complex.'* **(Source: SIGAP)**

Haunted Skies Volume Two Revised

At 7am, a silver, round, globe – about the size of a football in the sky – was seen flying westward, in daylight, over Low Fell, Gateshead, County Durham, by Mrs J. Montgomery. **(Source: TUFOS)**

Over Staffordshire

At 10.10pm, an odd looking 'star' was seen in the sky over Stoke-on-Trent, Staffordshire, by Mr Lister, who was in the process of putting his car away. After fetching a pair of binoculars, he saw a silvery object heading towards him.

> "It silently flew around the house, twice, and hovered in the sky for a few minutes. It then dived towards me and passed over the house, enabling me to see a grey 'disc' with a dome on top, and the outer edge rotating, leaving a long trail behind it."

Teesside – Two 'triangles', forming a cross

At 11.08pm a whitish-blue UFO (similar to a St. Andrew's cross) was seen in the sky over Billingham, Teesside, by Mr D. Lewis.

> "It passed through 15 degrees of arc in one minute. Through a telescope, two 'triangles' forming a cross of what appeared to be some sort of framework, with vapour around, could be seen. Two minutes later, it was gone." **(Source: UFOLOG)**

24th April 1968 – 'Strange lights' over Leicestershire

A number of 'lights' were seen in the sky over Wigston, Leicestershire, by Mr A. Payne, Manager of Holdings (Yarmouth) – believed to be stars – until examination through a telescope revealed at least *"twenty separate white lights, with a red and green light attached to each one"*.

Another witness was John Blondeau (a ex-RAF Air Traffic Controller), who sighted a number of green spheres, forming a triangle in the sky, and believed they were neither aircraft, nor stars – particularly after one of them split away while in flight.

It appears he was not the only one to sight this phenomenon over the Leicester area. The *Leicester Mercury* published a letter from a reader, who suggested they had seen navigation lights and the afterburner of an Avro Vulcan Bomber, flying at 625 miles per hour, at 40,000 feet.

Oddly, it was claimed the phenomenon had been seen on a number of previous occasions in the locality, going back some years.

(Source: *Leicester Mercury*, 24.4.1968, 29.4.1968, 2.5.1968/South Lincolnshire Study Group/*UFOLOG*)

April – Police Sergeant encounters UFOs over Derbyshire

Retired Police Sergeant Sidney Earnshaw, of the Derbyshire Constabulary, who was to see more than one example of inexplicable phenomena while on duty, still ponders as to the answer to what he saw, one evening, while ferrying prisoners to Buxton Police Station along the A619, Chesterfield to Baslow road.

"It was a fine evening, with a few scattered clouds. I was chatting away to my mate, when, all of a sudden, we saw a large green coloured object, travelling at about 1,000 feet off the ground, heading east to west. We watched as the object – approximately l50 feet in length – passed over the top of us, before being lost from view (map reference273723). My impression of this thing was that it seemed to be constructed, rather than anything organic or natural in origin."

When the officers arrived at Buxton Police Station, they discovered that there had been a number of telephone calls from the public, reporting having seen a UFO pass over the county. This was later explained away as being a meteorite that later landed in a bog in Northern Ireland.

"I couldn't believe this was the case, as the thing we saw was large and travelling horizontally, rather than straight down."

We learnt that at 9.22pm on 25th April 1968, a 'fireball' was tracked, travelling south-east to north-west over the British Isles, described as being blue/green in colour by observers on the ground, before crashing to Earth at Bovedy, County Antrim. Could this have been what Sid had seen? This is, of course, accepting that he was unable to identify the exact date when it happened. However, it must have been around the date when the object landed, although Sid would have none of it. He refused to believe he and the other officer had seen a meteor passing through the air.

Police officers sight UFO

Although there may be ample grounds for believing there was a rational explanation for what Sid and his colleague saw, the same could not be said for the next incident brought to our attention. One night while Sid and another officer were on patrol, driving along the Buxton to *Ashbourne road, Derbyshire, they came across an abandoned car. It was parked on the grass verge, about two miles north of Newhaven (map reference 156629). Sid contacted the Police controller and asked him to check out a driving licence found in the unlocked vehicle. Whilst waiting for a reply, another police car pulled up behind them.

"While talking, I noticed a bright luminous object in the sky and took it to be the lights of an aircraft en route to Manchester Airport. I pointed it out to the other officers, by which time it was very low in the sky, making me think it was a helicopter. I switched off the car's engine and listened intently, but could hear no sound, so switched on the blue flashing light. There was an immediate response. It became much brighter, as if about to land. After a few seconds, it started to move slowly towards us – now about thirty feet off the ground. When it was a few hundred feet away, I switched-off the blue beacon. Whatever it was, shot up into the sky and disappeared. I've often wondered what would have happened if I hadn't switched the light off."

Enquiries made into other reports of UFO activity around the Ashbourne area, revealed the following incidents:

At 9.30pm on **2nd August 2010,** Sheena Lindores of Ashbourne said:

"I was sitting alone having a cigarette outside the Miraj Hotel in Ashbourne, Derbyshire, when I saw a huge bright object (no idea how far away) above the houses there. It was bright golden/orange and I was very drawn to it. It moved very slowly across the sky and was oblong shaped. It had no flashing lights and made no sound. I watched it for approximately one minute and it began to fade in front of my eyes when other people came outside laughing and joking. It seemed to be influenced by this and started to fade slowly, until it turned into the brightest golden star I have ever seen – then it just disappeared completely in the night sky. I know what Chinese Lanterns look like, as I have watched many over the skies in Thailand, but this object was about three times larger than a Jumbo Jet and was nothing like I had ever seen before. My father also had a strange thing happen to him 15 years ago, when driving through quiet roads of East Lothian, but that's another story. Hope this helps. I have checked the internet and lots of other people saw UFOs in Derbyshire that night, around the same time."

At 2am on the **5th November 2013,** Roston resident John Preston said:

> "I opened my bedroom curtain to see if it was raining. There was a light – like a searchlight – from ground to cloud. It was straight; you could see that it went through the cloud. It was wide (wider than a car) and of course white. I only saw it for about 30 seconds – then it cut out. There's a farm and open fields across from my house. The light seemed to be in the field opposite, but I could not see the ground due to the hedge being in the way." (**Source www.uk-ufo.co.uk**)

27th April 1968 – Domed object – Arnos Park, Bristol

The Reverend Anthony G. Millican, who was to be later known for his staunch stand (again the evils of UFOs on the community), was walking through Arnos Park with his wife, when they noticed a small yellow glow on the ground, about 75-100 yards away.

> "We saw a 'light' that grew larger and larger, for more than 20 seconds. We clearly saw a transparent dome-shaped object that hovered above the grass and appeared to pulsate; it was about 15 feet in height and we did not approach it because, quite frankly, we were rather frightened."

Mr Millican reported the matter to his bishop and the police, who carried out a search of the area, at 10pm, but found nothing.

On a visit made to the scene, some days later, it is alleged a depression was found in the ground. It was fifteen feet in diameter. However, we have come across no evidence to support this or, indeed, any evidence of a 'figure' seen within the dome – as given in some accounts.

A decade later, the Reverend Millican erected a stall in the foyer of the Bristol Odeon cinema, during the showing of *Close Encounters of the Third Kind,* in order to persuade people that the UFOs were coming here to seduce us into the forbidden world of the occult.

In a letter he wrote to the *Bristol Evening Post* on 17th April 1968, he had this to say:

> "Beware: the film Close Encounters of the Third Kind, *now showing to capacity houses at the Odeon, is attractively deceptive; its authenticity is ensured by Dr. Hynek, a foremost authority on Unidentified Flying Objects. What the film doesn't show is their source purpose and nature.*
>
> *Dr. Hynek now discounts their extraterrestrial origin and says, 'If one wishes to postulate worlds other than physical, astral or etheric, one can easily satisfy and explain virtually all of the reported antics of the UFOs.*
>
> *Leading researchers Dr. Carl Jung and John Keel support demonic hypotheses as the data on UFOs that most accord with it. This is confirmed because occultists resist and pervert the gospel. These demonic 'angels' of light emanate from a parallel world in the unseen – St. Paul's cosmic powers and superhuman forces of evil in the heavens. Jesus warned that in the Last Days there would be 'in the sky terrors and great portents'. The demons appear to transmute themselves into UFOs for many testify. You know I don't think the thing I saw was mechanical at all. I got the distinct impression it was ALIVE, and my own*

close encounter in Arnos Park confirms that it was evil too. It is possible that by the temporary manipulation of energy matter, demons can conjure up UFOs as well as induce hallucinations, possession and suicide. Their aim is to change the collective psyche of mankind, so preparing the gullible for the Antichrist that supernaturally gifted World ruler prophesised in Scripture."

Signed, Anthony G. Millican, (Reverend),

St Christopher's Vicarage, 29, Runswick Road, Bristol BS4 3HY

We spoke to Mrs Millican about the matter in 2005. Her husband had died a few years before, and she was now remarried. She appeared very reluctant to discuss what she and her late husband had seen over 30 years before, and expressed the opinion that she now believes it was a pocket of gas released from the ground. This is extremely unlikely, bearing in mind the illustration obtained and the comments made by Tony Millican in his letter to the newspaper.

[Apparently a group of teenagers saw a similar object to that seen by the Reverend Millican, five years previously (1963), in the same place and time and also on a Saturday.]

The incident was also described in *Flying Saucer Review*, Volume 14, No. 4, July/August 1968, the 'object' shown on the front cover.

(**Source:** *Daily Mirror,* **16.5.1968** – 'Vicar sees Flying Saucer on his stroll'/*New Observer Newspaper,* **2.5.1968**)

30th April 1968 – Pulsating UFO over Warwickshire

A pulsating red and white coloured object was sighted in the sky over Sutton Coldfield, Warwickshire, at 8.50pm by David John Harris, for ten minutes – until it abruptly left. (**Source: NICAP**)

Isle of Wight UFO Society – sightings between April and June 1968

Isle of Wight resident – Steven Briscoe – wrote to Kath Smith, of the Isle of Wight UFO Society, in April 1968, describing a number of sightings of UFOs seen between the period 28th April and 10th June 1968, after seeing:

"...a 'bright light' moving eastwards across the sky, at 9.45pm, taking five minutes to cross over; I decided to continue my observations, beginning with a watch on the 30th April, when I saw an identical object to the one seen two nights previously – this time at 9.10pm."

In their summary of the events outlined by Steven, the Isle of Wight Society felt that some of the objects may have been satellites. However, the duration of observation suggests otherwise. Even if we give them the benefit of the doubt, there doesn't appear to be a rational explanation for the sighting of the 10th June 1968.

MAY 1968

5th May 1968 – Rugby-ball shaped UFO over Bedfordshire

At 10pm, Mr Douglas Wooley from the Silver Birch Caravan Site, Stotfold, Bedfordshire observed a red glow through the trees, hovering over the site.

"It moved away towards Astwick. I chased it on foot and knocked on someone's door to let them know what was happening. It looked like a rugby football, with a red pulsating light on top and a kind of rig around the middle. I later went to Biggleswade Police Station to report the matter."
(**Source:** *UFOLOG*/**Contact UK, Bristol**)

In the same month (exact date not known) ex-glider pilot – Michael Carey of West Park Avenue, Preston, told of having sighted a fairly small but elliptical black object, travelling swiftly in a westerly direction. It was at a height of 18,000 feet across the sky.

(**Source:** *Lancashire Evening Post,* **Preston, 28.5.1968/Contact UK/***UFOLOG*/**J. Barklam, NICAP**)

On the same day during the afternoon a Bristol woman saw what looked like: *"...a bright lemon coloured 'flying tadpole' pass slowly through the sky, heading towards the Arnos Park direction".* (Source: Squadron Leader Alastair Prevost)

13th May 1968 – UFO over Scotland

At 10.30pm, at least fourteen people sighted a round, glowing, object in the night sky over Coatbridge, Scotland. Dogs around the vicinity set up a howling protest, clearly agitated. Several minutes later, the object – which caste an eerie glow on the area – vanished inexplicably from sight. Similar objects were reported several weeks previously, at Kirkshaws and Sykeside.

(Source: Contact UK, Bristol/*UFOLOG*/*Airdrie and Coatbridge Advertiser*)

14th May 1968 – Kent motorist encounters UFO

We discovered details of an incident which took place at 10.12pm, involving a motorist who was driving along a country lane in Culverstone, Kent. It was on a low, overcast evening – no stars visible, with a cloud ceiling of 600 feet – when *"a large star like object shot over the top of the car and disappeared from sight"*. It was visible for a few seconds only. On reaching an intersection, about 200 yards away, the driver stopped to see if a better view could be obtained of the object. However, there was nothing to be seen.

On arriving home, a few minutes later, the driver switched off the engine and listened intently, but only heard the sound of a large Jet in the distance. **(Source: Isle of Wight UFO Society)**

17th May 1968 – 'Thrumming noise' UFO

At 4pm, two boys were walking along Wilmingham Lane, Freshwater, Isle of Wight, as part of a sponsored walk. They sighted an elliptical object, hovering in the sky over a line of fir trees. It made a 'thrumming noise' – like wind rushing through telephone wires. It then disappeared but appeared again, a short time later – this time accompanied by two other objects, one above the other, before finally vanishing from sight. **(Source: Kath Smith, Isle of Wight UFO Society)**

18th May 1968 – Swansea man's close encounter with a 'cloud'

Even stranger and certainly 'well out of the normal' is, perhaps, the best way to describe what happened to Swansea man – Mr Bellenger, who decided to get a breath of fresh air on what was a sunny afternoon. As he stepped out of his front door, he noticed:

> *"...what looked like a patch of fog, or a puffy white cloud, about two feet by one foot, moving over the buildings towards me, about two feet off the ground. It came towards me and 'touched' my left side. I felt a stabbing pain in the left-hand side of my stomach and the cloud disappeared.*
>
> *I staggered back into the house, panting for breath. The pain, which felt like a knife going through me, lasted for several minutes.*

I later went to see the doctor, who gave me some medicine which cleared up the problem."

Could this have been some sort of chemical inadvertently released from a factory, rather than the manifestation of any UFO or ghostly presence? **(Source: BUFORA)**

Summer 1968 – Kent Police sight red flashing light while on observations

On a clear night during the summer of 1968, Detective Constable Terry Lynch, of the Kent Constabulary, was on a night-time surveillance operation with another colleague, in Pilgrims Way, near Brasted.

As they sat in an unmarked police car, facing east, with the Weald of Kent on their right-hand side to the south, they noticed a flashing red light, about a thousand feet high above the top of the hills. Thinking it was a reflection, they got out of the vehicle and watched it for a few seconds, but were surprised to see a cigar-shaped object moving from the south direction, which then passed overhead.

> "I had never seen anything like this before in my life. It wasn't as high as the flashing red light and was completely silent, but left a trail in the sky which looked like smoke but wasn't."

Police cars in pursuit

Terry decided to 'give chase' to the cigar-shaped object – now moving at about 60 to 70 miles per hour – and followed it north to Bromley, in the Metropolitan Police District, after contacting the police control room and explaining what he was doing. He was then relieved by a police traffic car from Bromley subdivision, which took over the pursuit.

Upon their arrival back at Sevenoaks Police Station, amidst much 'leg pulling', he made a note of what had happened in the station minor occurrence book.

> "When I later made enquiries, I discovered the unidentified object had been followed by a number of police vehicles right up the country. Unfortunately, I have no idea how the pursuit finally ended.

BBC Panorama Documentary

> *The next day, I was told that BBC television, 'Panorama', were going to produce a documentary about the incident. We were told no police officers were to be allowed to take part in this programme. When the programme eventually went out, with bus conductors and housewives giving their witness statements, the presenter treated them with scorn."*

Terry believes if he and the other officers had been allowed to take part in the programme, a much more balanced view of what had taken place would have been presented – which, of course, is probably the reason why they were not allowed to participate.

We contacted the BBC, but were unable to obtain any information on the programme.

JUNE 1968

4th June 1968 – Red fireball, Merseyside

At 4.30pm at Wirral, Liverpool, a housewife was watching work in progress on Queens Drive, when she noticed:

> "...a red fireball, trailing a plume of thick black smoke, which appeared in the sky at about 25 degrees off the horizon, and descended vertically through the air – until lost from view behind the roofline of the Queens Drive's Baths."

According to the *Merseyside UFO Bulletin*, the object was also sighted by a number of other people.

6th June 1968 – Bright UFO, Surrey

At 10.40pm a stationary, bright object, showing golden yellow light, was seen in the sky over East Horsley, in Surrey, by motorist – Mr L. Dover, and his wife – *"bright enough to read the dial on the my watch"*.

Suddenly the 'light' extinguished, and it was gone. (**Source: Brinsley Le Poer Trench**)

9th June 1968 – UFO over Raynes Park, Merton, London

At 8pm, Mr C. Endfield, from London, was stuck in a traffic jam on the A3 at Raynes Park, with his wife and three children, when they noticed what they first thought was a child's black balloon – until they saw that it consisted of two domes, cupped together, with the axis of the join parallel to the Earth.

> "The object, made up of the most absorbent black we had ever seen, surrounded by a haze the same diameter as itself, came to within 50 feet off the ground, close to a tree, about 75 feet away from us, before moving upwards again. Its aerodynamic movements were wholly inexplicable in terms of any object known to us."

(Sources: Letter to *Flying Saucer Review*, Vol. 14, No. 5, September/October 1968/Brinsley Le Poer Trench)

10th June 1968 – Flattened dome-shaped UFO over Liverpool

At 8pm, an object with a flattened dome shape – as big as the moon – glowing red-orange, was seen moving slowly through the sky over Liverpool. It then appeared to change shape to something resembling a rectangle, then a triangle, before vanishing. There were three other witnesses to the sighting.

(Source: Steven Briscoe/*Liverpool Daily Post*/*Liverpool Echo*)

14th June 1968 – Luminous object, Newcastle-on-Tyne

Mr G.M. Kynman and Mr D. Wallace – residents of Kenton, Newcastle-on-Tyne, and engineers by occupation – sighted:

> "...a bright, oval, luminous object, reflecting light, like aluminium, three to four miles away, hovering in the sky at about 1,500 feet off the ground".

It was visible for a couple of minutes, at 5.30pm, before it, too, vanished from sight.

(Source: Tyneside UFO Society)

15th June 1968 – BUFORA 'sky watch'

June 15th 1968 BUFORA Skywatch Pewley Downs Guildford Surrey copyright Omar Fowler. – From *Spacelink* July 1968 BUFORA Field Unit in background

19th June 1968 – Silvery-white object sighted, North Yorkshire

At 3.15am, a mysterious glow was seen towards the east, behind a cloud in the sky, over Copmanthorpe, ten degrees off the horizon, by local resident – Mrs M. Satterthwaite.

> "The brilliant glow changed into a blurred silvery-white object, which grew from a point source to a crescent in fifteen seconds – then vanished. Later, I saw another glowing 'light source', at a higher altitude, before it also vanished from sight." (**Source: Tyneside UFO Society**)

June – Another visit to the MOD

Following publication of Roger Stanway and Tony Pace's report into the 1968 Staffordshire UFO sightings, entitled *Flying Saucer Report: UFOs unidentified, undeniable,* in April 1968, a complimentary copy was sent to Mr L.W. Akhurst, at the MOD in London. A month later, Her Majesty's Stationery Office ordered three copies of the booklet. The request came from the MOD!

In June 1968, Stanway and Pace contacted Mr Akhurst again, and arranged a visit for the 20th June 1968. Roger Stanway told us:

> "I arrived at 2.45pm and was escorted to the 6th floor, where I introduced myself to Mr Akhurst, who looked to be in his late forties or early fifties. A short time later, two of Mr Akhurst's colleagues from the Royal Aircraft Establishment entered the room; one was Mr Cassie – a senior psychologist in the MOD; the other a Mr Dickinson, who described himself as a scientific consultant to the MOD.
>
> I asked if I could tape-record the conversation and was told this would not be allowed, as it might pick up certain sounds from other parts of the building which were of a classified nature. The meeting lasted more than an hour. I found all three gentlemen friendly, helpful, and as frank as they could be under the circumstances. I must admit to being surprised when Mr Cassie made a reference to the exact page number at which the Bentilee account started – even I didn't know that offhand. I must confess, when we left, I felt relief and frustrated perplexity."

25th June – UFO over Isle of Wight

At 9pm, a black object was sighted over the Isle of Wight, just after the sun had set, described as *"cigar-shaped, with squared off ends"*, moving in the south-west direction. (**Source:** *UFOLOG*)

Early summer 1968 – High strangeness at Whipps Cross, London

In early summer 1968, Charles and Beryl Taylor (30) from Whipps Cross, North London, popped in for a drink at the *Rising Sun* Public house. They left thirty minutes later, at 10pm, and decided to cut across the rear of the churchyard of St Peters. While walking through a wooded area, they both felt that someone was behind them. They looked around and thought they could make out a dark shape, close to a nearby tree. Suddenly a shaft of green light fell around them. Frightened, they ran away and found themselves in a clearing. They felt uncomfortable and made their way out into the open at the other end of the wood.

The next day, in daylight, they made their way back into the wood but found no trace of the mysterious clearing.

This matter was reported to Andrew Collins, of the Dagenham Paranormal Research Group, who made his way to the scene on the 5th May 1976, and took photographs of the area. Although a vigil was conducted, nothing untoward was experienced.

Your Ref. AF/CX38/67/S4f (Air)

8th August, 1968

L.W. Akhurst, Esq.,
S4 f (Air),
Ministry of Defence,
Main Building,
Whitehall,
London. S.W.1.

Dear Mr. Akhurst,

Thank you for your letter of 23rd July and for the kind sentiments which you expressed.

Although the contents of your letter were not unexpected, Anthony Pace and myself were nevertheless disappointed that your letter did not tell us anything that we did not know already. We are surprised that you have made no reference to the fact that certain events described in our Report appear to be without explanation in terms of natural or man-made phenomena, especially as Mr. Cassie, Mr. Dickinson and yourself were unable to offer any explanation for the events that took place on Saturday, 2nd September 1967. We can understand Mr. Cassie's reaction when he said that he thought it was rather worrying that no explanations could be found for 2nd September sightings, but we fail to see why you should then say that the Ministry is unable to find any new scientific evidence in our Report. Also, we submit that the presence of unidentified flying objects in the vicinity of Stoke-on-Trent on 2nd September 1967, and directly under the Amber 1 air route has definite air defence implications and at least warrants a full scale investigation to discover why it is not possible to identify these "unknown aircraft". We appreciate that at the time of the sighting it would have been difficult to locate and identify these objects by means of our air defence system, as for most of the time the objects appeared to be no higher than a few hundred feet from the ground, and therefore, well under our radar detection network in this country. We are sure that the Ministry is aware of the danger inherent in the false assumption that unknown flying machines cannot possibly exist if they are not detected by this country's radar network and defence system.

We also consider that steps should be taken to find the owners and pilots of these "unidentified aircraft" as it does appear that prosecutions should be brought for apparent breaches of a considerable number of air laws and flying regulations. However, the fact that there were no identification markings or signs on most of the flying objects described in our Report does present problems.

Normally the lapse of time between reports and the investigation into them does materially effect the possibility of finding explanations. However, in our case, we must again confirm that our Report only contains the salient details of sightings, and on our files, we have the very fullest accounts and detailed drawings made by witnesses within days and sometimes hours of their sightings. Therefore, we must stress that investigations were made as soon as possible, and naturally, we should be very pleased to give you any further information that you may require. We must again confirm that a personal visit was made to a member of your department on 29th September 1967, when the events of the previous month were fully described to him. We were told that even if the Ministry wanted to interview witnesses and make its own field investigations, it could not possibly do so, as the Ministry did not have the necessary money, facilities, equipment or personnel to carry out such investigations. We are very worried about this inability to make the necessary investigations, and that is one of the reasons why we visited you on the 20th June this year.

We hoped to persuade the Ministry to change its policy by releasing all information relating to unexplained reports to the scientific world in general so that some serious research could be done at universities and scientific colleges. Naturally, we were dismayed that the Ministry's policy is one of treating all reports as confidential and that there appears to be a complete reluctance to investigate and solve scientific mysteries of this nature.

However, we hope that we may be able to interest various scientific bodies in the subject, and if you have any further information or advice that may assist us in our investigations, we should be very pleased to hear from you.

Yours faithfully,

p.p. A.R. PACE & R.H. STANWAY.

In a conversation held with a friend – Paul Rochford (now living in Canada) – they were surprised to learn that he had experienced an identical incident. After having been to a local cinema, he decided to walk home through the woods. This would have been around 1968/69, between 10.45pm-11pm.

JULY 1968

3rd July 1968 – Roger Stanway receives a letter from the MOD

Roger Stanway received a letter, showing the same inflexible attitude towards reports of UFOs – which still continues to this present day, despite the overwhelming evidence proving to the contrary.

As a result of further correspondence between the parties concerned, at the end of August 1968, Roger received a letter from 10, Downing Street, epitomising once again, the rigidly entranced attitude now synonymous with the Ministry of Defence's reaction towards the UFO subject.

BUFORA Personalities   No. 3

ROGER STANWAY

Born in 1944 at Stoke-on-Trent, Staffordshire, Roger was educated at Repton in Derbyshire, specialising in the sciences and served two years as Secretary of the School's Astronomical Society which was the relatively proud possessor of a 6" refracting telescope.

On leaving school he entered Articles of Clerkship with a firm of Solicitors in Stoke-on-Trent, and following attendance at the College of Law in Guildford, qualified as a Solicitor in 1969. After spending a further period with the same firm of solicitors he decided to embark upon a postgraduate course in Business Administration at the Cranfield School of Management in Bedfordshire, from where he eventually received his Master's degree in 1971.

Since leaving Cranfield, he has been working with the Industrial and Commercial Finance Corporation where he now holds the position of Legal Adviser to its Mergers and New Issues Department in the City of London. He married his wife Diane in 1972 and they are now living in Barnes, London.

Besides Astronomy and the study of UFOs, Roger's interests include athletics (javelin), hockey, amateur operatics and an occasional strum on his battered guitar. Societies of which he is a member include The Law Society: Business Graduates Association: Assoc. Royal Aeronautical Society: Royal Astronomical Society: British Astronomical Association: National Investigations Committee on Aerial Phenomena and the Society for Psychical Research.

Publications Roger has been associated with include UFO'S UNIDENTIFIED, UNDENIABLE which he co-authored with Anthony R. Pace, F.R.A.S.: this was published privately in 1968 and, now in its second edition, this book covers the UFO wave in Central England of 1967: THE PROSPECTIVE LAWYER— BLUEPRINT FOR THE FUTURE, published in 1969 by the Associate Members Group of the Law Society, of which the author was first Hon. Secretary and then Chairman: and, LAWYERS IN COMMERCE AND INDUSTRY which, published privately in 1972, contains the results of a survey and investigation into the role and status both of solicitors and barristers in Commerce and Industry which was conducted by the author as part of his thesis work at the Cranfield School of Management.

APPENDIX 2

Copy of the letter from L.W. Akhurst to R.H. Stanway dated 23rd July 1968.

MDL/24/16 - 4

MINISTRY OF DEFENCE
Main Building, Whitehall, LONDON S.W.1
Telephone: 01-930-7022

Our reference: AF/CX38/67/S4f(Air)
Your reference:

23 July 1968

Dear Mr Stanway,

When we met last month I promised to write to you about your Flying Saucers Report.

First I should like to say that those of us in the Department who read the report were very impressed by the amount of time, effort and enthusiasm put into the project by you and Mr Pace. Since we covered the ground fairly extensively at our meeting, I hope you will forgive me if I set down our views fairly briefly.

The Ministry of Defence's approach to the question of unidentified flying object reports is quite straightforward. Each report we receive is fed into our air defence system and we are able to call on the highest scientific and technical advice within the Department. We also take advice, where necessary, from other government departments and outside bodies such as the Royal Observatory, the Meteorological Office and the British Museum. Reports are examined in sufficient depth to establish that there are no air defence implication and that they can be reasonably related to known phenomena. But we do not undertake to pursue each report until we have established an indisputable correlation with a known object. So far we have found no evidence of air defence implications or of craft under extra terrestrial control.

We have an open mind on the possibilities of new evidence and are interested to see the results of serious studies such as yours. Your report has been examined carefully and although we have found much of interest, we are unable to find any new scientific evidence in it.

I am sure you will have found from your own investigations, that prompt reporting is often a prerequisite of positive explanation. The sightings covered by your report were between eight and sixteen months old when we received them. In view of this lapse in time we do not feel that an examination in depth by the Department at this stage would be likely to produce positive explanations. We are, of course, ready to look at any new reports from your area, but I must emphasise again the virtues of promptitude in these matters.

Finally, may I thank you personally and on behalf of Mr Cassie and Mr Dickison, for taking the trouble to come to see us.

Yours faithfully,

(L.W. AKHURST)

Mr R.H. Stanway
Dunwood Edge
LONGSDON
Stoke-on-Trent

4th July 1968 – Two 'Flying Saucers' over Devizes

At 10.15pm, two silver 'Flying Saucers' were seen over Great Cheverell, near Devizes, Wiltshire, by local women – Mabel Wilshin and Constance Williams, who reported:

> "A third 'saucer' then appeared. As it did so, the first two disappeared, leaving the third to divide into two. To our amazement, a similar but much lighter object appeared in the sky".

We were unable to speak to either of the women concerned, as they had passed away, but we did speak to Mabel's son, who told us he had no reason to disbelieve his mother's word and that prior to her death, at the age of 90, the sighting was occasionally the subject of conversation.

5th July 1968 – Close encounter, Surrey

Wanborough is a small hamlet consisting of a few tiny cottages on the edge of the North Downs, overlooking a range of hills known as the Hog's Back. It is approximately 6km west of Guildford, near the villages of Puttenham and Christmas Pie.

At 12.30am, Wanborough resident – Mr Langley, was in the process of getting ready for bed. As he entered the bedroom where his wife was asleep, he noticed a reflection of light. At first he thought it was the landing light behind him, but as he turned around he saw no sign of any light. Curious, he walked over to the window, expecting to see the lights of a parked car.

Mabel Lower with son and daughter-in-law

> "I peered through and was shocked to see a bright orange, shining 'ball of light', hovering outside in the darkness. It was difficult to judge its size but it looked about five feet in diameter. The outsides were bright orange but the centre was more opaque; its edges were jagged in appearance. It was

moving slowly at a walking pace over the top of the nearby cottages – then it stopped. My wife, who had awoken and was watching it, said 'It's a Flying Saucer', as it started to descend towards the ground next to the barn."

Mr Langley telephoned the police at Farnham and spoke to the officer, telling him what was occurring. However, he gained an impression they may have thought he had been drinking.

Mr Langley then went back to the window and saw that the 'object' was still there – hovering in the air, close to the old barn – and decided to go into the garden to obtain a better look.

"We noticed a dark band around the centre of the object, accompanied by a faint whistling noise. Its light was not brilliant and got fainter towards the middle, creating an impression 'like a pearl, or light, inside a ball'. It then started to move away from the old barn, the light taking on a darker hue as it headed across the adjoining field towards the direction of the 'Hog's Back'. The 'globe' then became more elongated and bullet-shaped. You could also see a misty cloud formation surrounding the light, which increased in brilliance as it moved further away up towards the summit of the ridge. The light approached the main road – the A31 Guildford to Farnham Road. In the distance we could see a car approaching and we thought the object would collide with the car, but instead it flew over the top of the car, which stopped; presumably the driver had seen it."

At this point the couple thought that their experience had come to an end. However, they were further surprised when Mrs Langley brought her husband's attention to five bright yellow star-like lights, about six feet apart, that were seen on the ground in a nearby field.

Mr Langley told Omar Fowler – then of SIGAP (Surrey Investigation Group of Anomalous Phenomena):

"I set off to investigate and had only gone a short distance, just past an adjoining house, close to the bend in the road, when I became aware that there was something in the darkness behind us. It was a vehicle of some kind. I could just make out a grey shape. I thought to myself, what could it be? There were several lights in a row and not even a coach could account for that pattern, sitting in the middle of the field."

Mr Langley decided to return to the house, where he and his wife continued watching the lights – until, finally, they went out, leaving the landscape in darkness. Later in the interview he mentioned a sighting by his wife, a few nights previously, when she had been disturbed by the dog barking, at 2.40am. On looking outside she saw a similar 'bank of lights' on the side of the hill, close to some nearby trees, but didn't wake him up – although, the next morning, she and her husband examined the area but found nothing untoward.

(Source: Omar Fowler, *UFOs: Guardians of the Planet Earth*)

9th July 1968 – Black 'disc' seen, Lincolnshire

The late Omar Fowler

A black 'disc'-shaped UFO was sighted above rooftop level over Bourne, Lincolnshire, by a local resident, who described what he saw to local UFO researcher – Richard Thompson.

"After a short while, a smaller object appeared behind the black 'disc', initially as an outline, then 'filled in with black'. Incredibly, four or five other UFOs arrived and formed a line behind each other. The first UFO then vanished."

(Source: Richard Thompson, Lincoln)

10th July 1968 – Cone-shaped UFO, Hertfordshire

At 9am over Bessemer School, Hitchin, in Hertfordshire, caretaker – Jack Fairweather, and two pupils, sighted a cone-shaped object, with a sphere suspended beneath it, dropping down through the sky over the Willian area. Enquiries made with the Meteorological Office, at Royston, revealed it was unlikely to have been a weather balloon. According to a spokesman: *"They don't look like that; they are wire mesh, with a cylinder underneath."* (**Source:** *Hertfordshire Express,* **11.7.1968**)

14th July 1968 – UFOs over Coventry

At 2am, Mr J. Mead was returning home from a night out with his girlfriend, when they saw a red glow above a layer of thin cloud towards the west of Coventry, *"which slowly increased in brightness, until a prominent red light in the sky. A few seconds later, it went out".*

On the same day, Mr N. Willis of Willenhall Wood, Coventry (close to the A46) was waiting outside the house for the electricity to come back on, after a power cut, when he noticed a 'red indefinable shape' crossing the sky.

At 11.15pm, a curious 'red light' was seen by Cheylesmore resident – Mr Tulley, just above cloud cover, constantly changing from red to orange, to white, before being lost from view. Similar objects were reported over Leamington and Coundon, attracting a comment by a spokesman from the local airport, who suggested they were seeing the moon behind cloud!

Over Doncaster

Barmaids – Daisy Coote and Mary Mawford – of Intake, Doncaster, who were on their way home at 11pm on 14th July, also saw something strange:

> *"...an object, like a child's humming top, hovering in the sky above houses in Westminster Crescent. It seemed to get bigger and nearer and gave us a considerable fright."*

(**Source:** *Doncaster Evening Post,* **15.7.1968**)

15th July 1968 – BUFORA 'sky watch', Surrey

BUFORA organised a national 'sky watch' with over 29 watching points; one was at Pewley Down, in Surrey, and involved the assistance of SIGAP, which had been formed with ten members in 1967.

17th July 1968 – Red light, with 'bump' on top, over Berkshire

Thomas Rodney Joynes of Old Windsor, Berkshire, was driving his A35 van along the outskirts of the town, during the evening, when he noticed:

> *"...a red light, flashing on and off, above a 'bump' on top of an elliptical dark-shaped object in the distant sky, 30 degrees off the horizon, at an estimated size of 200 feet in length, moving at about 500 miles per hour, before disappearing in the eastern direction."*

(**Source: Mrs S.G. Salter, Slough Aerial Phenomena Research Association**)

24th July 1968 – UFO display over Surrey

At 10pm, a yellow glowing object was seen performing a series of strange movements across the sky. It was seen behind trees at Addlestone, Surrey, by six schoolchildren. The object was then seen moving away but it returned along its original path and finally left, a short time later. Other witnesses came forward to back up what the children had seen. One couple spoke of having sighted an object, with flashing red and white lights, hovering over their caravan site. A saucer-shaped object, with a central dome and flashing red light on top, was clearly seen silhouetted against the horizon, flying at a height of 200 feet off the ground. (**Source:** *Surrey Herald/SIGAP/UFOLOG*)

25th July 1968 – Teacher sights UFO over Shropshire

Jerry Richmond – a science teacher living in Sparkhill, Birmingham – was returning home from Bridgnorth, at 1.30am. As he neared Hilton, on the Bridgnorth to Wolverhampton road, he saw an ellipse-shaped object. He estimated it to be one hundred feet long, and later described how it rose up into the air from behind a clump of trees (by a low fence on the left-hand side of the road, about 30-40 yards away), for a few hundred feet, before dropping downwards.

> "The object shot across the road and then started to zigzag towards me, a thousand yards in front, leaving no trail. It looked like a projectile of some sort. I put my hand on the outside of the windscreen to make sure the object was not a reflection. I didn't feel courageous enough to stop the car and increased speed, keeping a lookout for someone on the road or a house I could stop at. After 5 miles had elapsed, it disappeared over a hill. I then saw the lights of a car approaching, so flashed my lights and sounded the horn as it came closer. I think it was a Ford 'Zephyr', or 'Zodiac', but he didn't stop. The 'thing' then came back again, appearing on my left, travelled towards me over the top of the car, turned, and went ahead. I could see what looked like some sort of 'tail' at the rear – a bit like a helicopter in shape, when viewed from underneath. After repeated zigzags, the object – now cigar-shaped, with a light on top – stopped and hovered over a clump of trees on my right-hand side, a hundred yards away. By now, I was panic-stricken. All of a sudden it shot into the distance and disappeared – the whole incident having taken 9 miles and 10-15 minutes in duration."

(**Source: Personal interview/***Bridgnorth Journal***, 2.8.1968/Gordon Creighton,** *Flying Saucer Review***/UFOSIS/ Isle Wight UFO Society)**

[Could there be a connection with what was reported, the following year, (1969) when a schoolteacher sighted a landed object in the town]

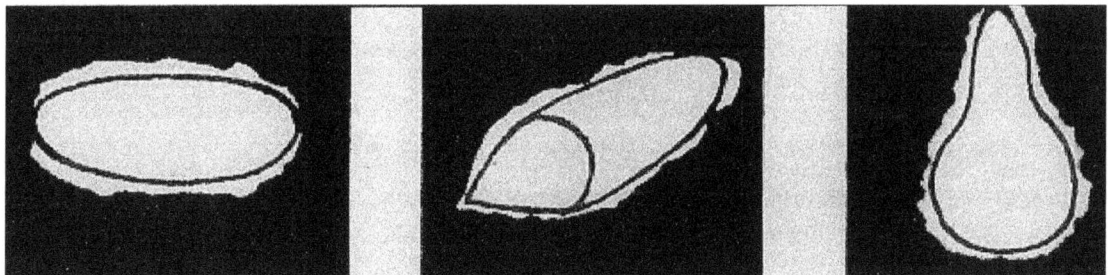

26th July 1968 – UFO over Warwickshire

At 9.45pm, a red/gold, circular or egg-shaped object, with a solid centre and pulsating outline, was seen stationary in the sky over Warwickshire, by Nigel Coupland, Howard Roy Crockford and George Webb, according to the men, who were later interviewed by NICAP representative – Derek Samson.

> "The object had a solid centre and pulsating outline, and was stationary in the air despite a breeze."

The incident was later reported to the Coventry Police. Was it a weather balloon seen by the men?

Over Coventry

At 10pm the same day, an orange/red oval object was seen in the sky over Coventry. After flashing four or five times, it shot off at high speed. Other reports told of a *"red diamond-shaped object, with a long tail"*. By an amazing coincidence, Bob Tibbitts' grandparents, then living in Foleshill (north of Radford), reported having sighted *"three red lights moving over the sky, in a triangular formation"*.

(**Source: Bob Tibbitts, CUFORG/***Coventry Evening Telegraph***, 27.7.1968/Derek Samson – NICAP, GB)**

Haunted Skies **Volume Two Revised**

AUGUST 1968

2nd August – 'D'-shaped object, Warwickshire

In 2006, we spoke to retired nurse Margaret 'Nan' Gellion – then living at Wood End Cottage, near Solihull, West Midlands – about what she and her sister saw, while driving home along the A34, at Shirley (just outside Birmingham) at 10.15pm.

> "We noticed a glowing half-moon shaped object in the sky, which I took to be the moon – until I realised the quarter moon was in another part of the sky. By the time we reached our house, in Wood End, the object was now 'D'-shaped and low down in the sky.
>
> It was one of the strangest things I have ever seen. I still occasionally think about it to this present date."

In 2017 we caught up with her again and asked if she had seen anything else since then? She replied in the negative. (**Source: Personal interview**)

Waterloo

At 10.45pm on the same date, Tony Sutcliffe (17) and Brian Ormsby, from Waterloo, were astride a motorcycle, driving along Little Crosby Road, Crosby, in Lancashire, when they saw a cigar-shaped object, surrounded by a white glow, with window like markings on it, hovering over nearby fields, approximately 400 feet above the ground.

They stopped and watched with amazement as it moved off, westwards, towards the direction of the *River Mersey* – in view for a total of 15 minutes.

Tony said later:

> It moved slowly, at first, and then seemed to accelerate away. It was not an aircraft, because there was no noise or vapour trail, and it was too low for a satellite. We lost sight of it near Mariners Road. I've never seen anything like it before."

(**Source:** *Merseyside UFO Bulletin,* **John Harney/***Liverpool Daily Post,* **3.8.1968**)

3rd August 1968 – Pencil-like object seen, Gower, Wales

At 5.15am, Mr C.W. Bell of Darras Hall, Newcastle, was on Rhossili beach, Gower, when he saw:

> "...a dark, pencil like object – as thick as a pin and one third as long – seen at sea level height, to begin with. It then moved northwards through the sky, at high speed, and slowed down as cloud closed around it, before veering upwards at 30 degrees elevation from the ground and vanished from sight, covering three miles in fifteen seconds". (**Source: Tyneside UFO Society**)

Later, the same evening, a cigar-shaped object, bathed in light, was seen slowly crossing the sky over Leamington Spa by a number of people, including Mr and Mrs Atwood.

4th August 1968 – Horrifying 'close encounter', Warwickshire

Was there any connection between the previous sighting and a frightening experience which befell retired teacher – *Harry Marlow from Snitterfield, near Stratford-upon-Avon?

---

*Harry Marlow – Snitterfield, Warwickshire's own poet laureate, and very much a well-loved character in the village, died in February 2015 – sadly missed by family, friends and neighbours. Harry lived in Snitterfield for 57 years with his wife, Val, and family, and was a familiar sight walking up Smith's Lane to the shop in his trademark beret. A former schoolteacher, Harry was an award-winning and published poet, who often contributed to *Snipe* – the village Magazine.

At 11.30pm, he had a most out of character vivid dream (?)

"...in which a person unknown to me was seated in a chair within a chamber-like compartment, a short distance away from me, directing a powerful beam of light towards me. Suddenly, I awoke in a heavy sweat and experienced something even more frightening and horrific than the dream itself. Wide awake now, and with a reality more empirical than a road accident in the middle of a city at noon, I realised there was something out there, seemingly just beyond the open window, with its curtain stirring gently in the breeze. My body was held completely rigid and I was unable to move, apart from being free to manipulate my head from side to side. To convince myself I was no longer dreaming, I made a point of noticing the strange way in which the curtains were blowing into the room and the exact time on the illuminated face of my watch, showing 2.45am. Without any warning, I was suddenly gripped by the most intense discomfort – a highly-pitched but hardly audible oscillation, which caused such an acute pain within my head that I wanted to scream. My body was, however, helpless and I was unable to use my vocal chords.

Mesmerized and perspiring heavily, I stared beyond the window. I saw nothing unusual, yet from just beyond came a soft, strange 'swishing' sound – like the noise made by a helicopter blade, rotating, without the engine noise. This sound, superimposed on the excruciating high frequency range vibrations,

Poet, Harry Marlow

produced 'the most weird' phenomenon imaginable. I had read of high-range sound vibrations beyond the range of human hearing being produced by jet aircraft which disturbed cattle, causing them to stampede, and I am now convinced this is the sort of thing I was experiencing at that terrifying moment, but what was the cause of the engineless blade 'swishing' noise?

As the noise and physical effect faded, my head was released from the severe grip of the force field, or whatever was creating the influence, and dripping all over with perspiration, together with understandable palpitations, I examined the whole house from top to bottom, creeping from room to room, observing that all four children were soundly asleep, as was my wife who had slept undisturbed throughout. For the remainder of the night I lay awake, puzzled and frightened. I was accustomed to odd nocturnal sounds, living as we did in an old country house, but this was in a quite different category.

I was astonished to read in a newspaper, a few days later, that people had reported seeing UFOs over the Leamington Spa area, which I believe was connected with my experience."

Dr. Susan Blackmore

Harry was not inclined to accept the opinion of Dr. Susan Blackmore – a specialist in the field of Parapsychology, at Bristol University (to whom he had written) – that his experience could be explained away as sleep paralysis.

Dr. Blackmore told us:

"I think people often get totally wrong what I am trying to do. I am not interested in UFOs or abductions, per se, in the sense whether there are people actually being abducted. I don't have the expertise to answer that question. What I do have expertise and interest in is all the strange psychological experiences that people have. I am fairly sure that a large proportion of abduction experiences are actually sleep paralysis and

Dr. Susan Blackmore

another whole lot are hallucinations, brought about by excessive firing in the temporal lobes of the brain, situated above the ears on either side of the head, particularly on the verges of sleep. Now I am really interested in these, because I have studied so many weird experiences in my life and they fit in with a pattern with similarities to near-death experiences and out-of-body experiences, and so on. I am fascinated by these."

Dr. Blackmore pointed out that many people who have more or less stable temporal lobes are very much down-to-earth, described as non-imaginative, uncreative people. These people are unlikely to become involved in weird experiences, and that people who have very unstable temporal lobes – like herself – are far more likely to have experiences of a mystical nature.

She claims that a small study found that people who claimed to have been abducted are also more likely to suffer from sleep paralysis, and believes abduction experiences are a form of borderline sleep phenomenon.

She points out that in 25 years of research, she has never come across any evidence of the existence of a paranormal or unexplainable phenomenon, but has come across examples of fraud, people being misled, and really sloppy experiments, following on from which her own research into those experiments failed to obtain results. She said:

"I accept there may or may not be real abductions but I can't give an opinion, having insufficient expertise on this subject".

We accept, on occasion, experiences like Mr Marlow's could fall into the category of sleep paralysis, which is the body's way of stopping itself from 'acting out its dreams'. However, we are mindful of the fact that identical experiences of strange audio vibrations, reported by people, have taken place *when they were awake,* accompanied by *sightings of UFOs,* which may rule out sleep paralysis as being the answer in Mr Marlow's case, but believe the presence of UFO activity, reported around the country, should be taken into consideration. (**Source: Personal interview**)

Humour – mixing alcohol with bell ringing!

Harry:

"As the organist and occasional bell ringer at St James's Church, Snitterfield, I was having a few beers with members of the choir in the village pub before returning late on New Year's Eve, 1962, to place the microphone of my old reel-to-reel tape recorder outside the window for the recording of the bells ringing in the New Year. I had just settled down at home when a knock came at the door. 'Would you please come and ring with us tonight as we are one short?' What could I do?

I went reluctantly off to the church, my wife promising to switch on the recorder at the appropriate moment in the belfry; even with my beery head, we got off to a good start. However, unfortunately for me, during a break in the activities, the vicar appeared suddenly with a tray of glasses and a large bottle of port! The occasion was duly toasted and I imbibed willingly, along with the others, thereby mixing the grape with the grain – which in my case proved not to be a good idea.

When we resumed, I soon forgot the sequence of changes, making a real mess of 'Grandsire' – but the worst moment came as all six of us were on the back stroke, arms poised aloft. My indecision about the next sequence confused the others with the result that several bells then came crashing down at the same time, causing fearful vibration in the tower. The villagers must have thought that Armageddon had arrived for 1963!

I shamefacedly left the other five ringers to finish the job as best they could, and headed home in the early hours to listen to it all over again on the tape."

On another occasion, after winning First Prize in a Warwickshire literary competition, he was asked what had inspired him to send it in to *Snipe*. He recalled it was conceived whilst observing an elderly man wearing an RAF Aircrew Association tie shopping in a Stratford-upon-Avon supermarket.

Tragedy ... the grim reality of airborne warfare
Harry:

"At the age of sixteen, during the Second World War, I was a member of the ATC at Corby in Northamptonshire. I hadn't been a cadet for very long before we were sent to Waddington, in Lincolnshire, which was an established Lancaster bomber base. On arrival we camped in tents quite close to the runways to begin a week of intense activity.

I was offered my first flight in an aircraft when I was directed to one of the famous bombers by a perky little man who was its rear-gunner. Laughingly he put me into his turret where, sitting backwards, I could see nothing of the plane except the two tail fins, one on either side; I was looking at ninety percent sky. Needless to say, I was glad when it was all over as we landed and I was rescued from my very excruciatingly painful position by the smiling little gunner. I did my best to thank him.

That night six bombers took off for Germany to bomb Essen. All six returned in the early dawn and we cadets got as close as we could to see them. Two of the Lancasters were badly shot up. I asked a RAF policeman standing nearby 'What are they doing?', as a hosepipe was being directed into one of the aircraft's tail. 'They are removing the rear-gunner' was the reply. I was not able to find out whether or not it was the amusing gunner who put me into his turret a few hours earlier; the incident affected me for a long, long time. On seeing the elderly ex-RAF man in the Stratford supermarket, I mused 'had he been a tail gunner like the airman who had made such an impression on me at Waddington, all those years ago and managed luckily to survive?' I did not get the chance to ask him."

(Source *Snipe* Magazine, Issue 28 and 38)

In the same month, a mother and daughter living in Whitley Bay, Northumberland, sighted a cigar-shaped object moving over the sea, north to south, passing in front of two ships on the horizon (approximately two miles away), at 4pm. **(Source: TUFOS)**

11th August 1968 – UFO over Llandudno

Mrs G. Thornton from Keresley, Coventry, was on holiday, at Llandudno, with her husband and son. They were watching over the sea, as the sun set, when she noticed a bright semi-curved object to the left of the sun in the sky.

"I thought it might have been the new moon – then realised it was much larger and brighter, moving in a northerly direction.

A few seconds later, it just melted away. By the time I had alerted my husband and son, it was too late."

Over Surrey

At 11.30pm, a luminous *'sausage'*, or cigar-shaped object, was seen in the sky over Earslwood Lakes, Redhill, in Surrey, by the occupants of a parked car. This was later explained away by a spokesman from Gatwick Airport, as having been likely to have been a weather balloon.

This was not the only report for this date. Over Yorkshire, a blue metallic object, resembling a silver 'three-penny bit', was seen heading in a south to south-east direction, at 2pm, one afternoon in August 1968, crossing the blue sky at an estimated height of 3,000 feet, by Mrs E. Thompson.

(Source: *UFOLOG*/BUFORA)

15th August 1968 – Circular object showing orange lights over Coventry factory
Ex-Special police constable Tommy Gardner – caretaker of the Awson Motor Carriage Company, Coventry – was checking the factory for flood damage after a recent storm, when he happened to look up into the sky and see:

> "...a huge circular 'thing' with two orange lights on its side, hovering in the clear blue sky. Ten seconds later, it just disappeared from sight. I told my boss – Wilfred Grunau, who was interested in UFOs. He actually constructed a cardboard model of the UFO, from which he calculated it to be a mile in length." (**Source: Bob Tibbitts, CUFORG**) See 24th September 1968

Yorkshire
At 10pm, the same day, a large bright orange 'light' with fuzzy edges was seen moving across the sky, over Liversedge, Yorkshire, at the side of a sharply-defined, smaller, silver-grey object, by Mr Haigh and his sister. The orange 'light' then disappeared over a hill, leaving the other object to hover a while in the sky, before it, too, disappeared from sight. According to the witnesses concerned, they believed the objects were fairly low in the sky, as the light given off from the orange object lit up the fields and surrounding area.

19th August 1968 – Glowing UFOs, Warwickshire
Brian Underhill and his friend – Derek, from Coventry, in Warwickshire, watched with amazement, as two glowing red objects circled the sky above their heads, during the late evening – apparently the same UFOs seen by Anne and Hazel Lewis, who were driving home from Walsgrave to Canley.

During the same month (date not known), Mrs A. Shaw and her daughter of Low Fell, Gateshead, County Durham, sighted:

> "...a cigar-shaped object moving at great speed, at sea level, about two miles away from us, heading silently in a south to north direction. It then passed in front of two ships on the horizon and disappeared from view – seen for fifteen seconds, or so." (**Source: Tyneside UFO Society**)

20th August 1968 – UFO over Cheshire
At Openshaw, Cheshire, a man was still awake at 3.30am, after having problems sleeping. On glancing through the bedroom window, he saw

> "...a rough cigar-shaped object in the night sky – brilliant-white and shimmering, and was at an elevation of some 30 degrees. The weather was cold and overcast. Suddenly, the silent object vanished from sight." (**Source: DIGAP**)

23rd August 1968 – Cigar-shaped UFO reported by the BBC
On this day, the *BBC News, South-West*, told in a newsflash of *"...a cigar-shaped object, with blue light, sighted by seven people (including a RAF photographer), moving across the sky over Bournemouth, at an estimated speed of 200 miles per hour."*

August 1968 – Cone-shaped UFO, Lincolnshire
During a visit to veteran UFO researcher – Richard Thompson, at his home address in Saxilby, Lincolnshire, he generously allowed us access to a number of UFO reports brought to his attention, over the years. One of them involved George Allan Brewitt (then aged 55) living in Trent View, Ermine East, West Lincoln – who was looking out of his front room window, one early evening in August 1968.

> "It was a warm, dry, evening – no wind, with a few scattered clouds about – when I noticed an object that seemed to come out of nowhere, hovering between two trees about a mile away, towards the north-east direction. It was triangular in shape and reminded me of an upside-down ice-

cream cornet, hovering a few feet off the ground, displaying all the colours of the rainbow – sort of interlocked together. After gazing at it for a few minutes, I was obliged to look away – the light was so dazzling. About ten minutes later, it just disappeared in front of my eyes, leaving me very bewildered by what had occurred." (**Source: Richard Thompson**)

28th August 1968 – Children sight four luminous objects over York

Several children sitting on the roof of an electricity sub-station, near York, heard a humming noise and saw:

"...four luminous objects, flying through the air towards them; the first described as bright-white and dome-shaped; the others, grey 'discs', showing bright lights around the outer edges".

The children watched as the objects began to circle the field, before shooting upwards into the sky leaving a rush of wind. (**Source: Richard Farrow**)

31st August 1968 – Cross-shaped UFO over Heathrow Airport, London

At 8.35pm, a peculiar 'light' was sighted hovering over Heathrow Airport, described as resembling *"a fireball, with a distinctive cross design",* before making a sharp right-hand turn and fly across the sky in a triangular pattern of movement, flashing red and blue lights.

The official explanation offered was that it was a Board of Trade aircraft, calibrating radar installations.
(**Source: Society for the Investigation of UFO Phenomena [SIGAP]**)/*Daily Mirror* (date not known)/*UFOLOG*, **October 1968, No. 51**)

SEPTEMBER 1968

1st September 1968 – Horizontal line of four 'lights' seen, Hampshire

A horizontal line of three or four white 'lights' were seen in the sky over Eastleigh, Hampshire, moving towards the direction of Southampton, at 11.45pm, which occasionally expanded to five in the formation. Within a few minutes, they had passed out of sight. (**Source: Isle of Wight UFO Society**)

Over Surrey

It appears this was not the only sighting which took place on that late evening. According to the Surrey Investigation Group on Aerial Phenomena, a bright star-like object (initially believed to be a satellite) was seen moving through the sky, westwards, over Guildford and Worplesdon, Surrey, at midnight, until...

"...it stopped briefly and then moved back the way it had come, stopping every two seconds, occasionally flickering and dimming".

The witnesses jumped into their van and gave chase, when they were able to discern that the object consisted of *"two domes, one upside-down, joined at their bases".*

By 1.10am the object had moved out of sight, towards the north-east. (**Source: Omar Fowler, SIGAP**)

UFO landing 1968 – 'Keyhole' impression found in the crop, Surrey

Winchester-based freelance science journalist and photographer – Ron Toft, told us of an incident that happened at a farm owned by the then 75 year-old Mr George Graham, in the village of Woodmansterne, near Banstead, Surrey, one night during either the last week of August, or the first week in September 1968 (exact date unknown).

Mr Graham was out, one evening, looking for marauding foxes, when his attention was caught by a strange glow – described as being dark blue and 'acetylene-like', about a hundred yards away – which he took to be his neighbour, working on a lorry. He paid no more attention, until he heard a loud 'whoosh', ten or fifteen minutes later, followed by a dark circular shape rising into the sky close to where he had seen the glow.

The next morning, Mr Graham was surprised to find:

> "...a huge 'keyhole'-shaped impression on the ground resembling a big horseshoe, with a heel on it (the length being 40 feet by 20 feet in width, with an inner band some 8 inches wide). All the grass (blades and roots) had been neatly plucked out of the 'band', as if a giant vacuum cleaner had been applied – the impressions left as if a knife had been used."

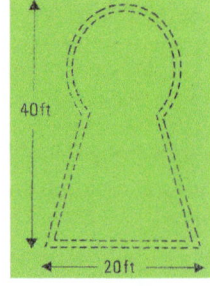

Mr Graham told Ron that two girls had seen a strange object in the same field, a week previously, while taking a short cut through with their dogs. Apparently the dogs had bolted, refusing to go anywhere near the field.

(Source: *Flying Saucer Review Case Histories,* supplement three, February 1971/Ron Toft, SIGAP – 'Farmer sees UFO take off')

5th September 1968 – Brilliant 'light' over Essex

A brilliant 'light' was seen in the sky over Baddow Hall Crescent, Chelmsford, Essex, at 7.45pm, by a number of people, before inexplicably disappearing five seconds later.

6th September 1968 – 'Disc' UFO over Chew Reservoir, Somerset

At 9.30pm, a party of four teenagers were driving along the B3114 (which skirts the Chew Reservoir, North Somerset), in a Morris traveller van, when they noticed a bright glowing object, high in the sky over the water, apparently moving parallel to them.

They stopped and watched the object drifting across the sky in a north-south direction. After a few seconds it halted, now increasing in size and brightness, allowing them to see it was tubular or 'disc'-shaped with an upturned 'lip' at its northern facing end, glowing with yellow-orange light. Along its length were brighter spots which streamed along the object from the upturned 'lip' to its right-hand end.

About five minutes later the object tilted upwards, allowing them to see it was disc-like in shape – the bright yellow-orange rotating around the rim. The rear section then tilted, rose upwards into the sky, and disappeared from sight approximately ten seconds after 'tilting'.

(Source: Peter Tate, Contact UK, Bristol/*UFOLOG*)

Same week

During the same week, a glowing orange-red object, initially seen as *"two big 'stars', continually changing shape"*, was sighted over Boreham, Essex, by schoolgirls Joanna Portray and her sister – Lisa, of The Chase, Boreham. The objects were flickering with red and gold light as it moved across the skyline – matters which they brought to the attention of their mothers, Mrs Shirley Portway and Mrs Penny Cansell. Apparently this sighting was just one of a number that had taken place around the Essex area over the last two weeks. (**Source:** *Essex Chronicle,* **13.9.1968/Ron West**)

Early September 1968 – Wing-shaped UFO, Bristol

A householder and his wife from St. George, Bristol, were standing outside their house, at 3.40pm, when they noticed a wheeling body of squawking seagulls passing over the clear blue sky above, which at first glance they took to be a buzzard. Further inspection revealed

> ". . . a wing-shaped object – flat, off-white colour, apparently solid looking with an almost imperceptible depression running down its centre. The object was tilted on its left-hand side and

travelling at great height, towards the north-east direction. At a point where the object was barely visible above the rooftops, we saw it tilt its left-hand 'wing' to a much more inclined angle and travel sideways in a westerly direction over the city." (**Source: Peter Tate, Bristol**)

8th September 1968 – Vehicle interference, Dorset

Another sighting we discussed with veteran UFO investigator Frank Marshall, from Weymouth, in Dorset, in 2006, was his involvement in a most peculiar incident, brought to his attention. This involved three cars being driven on the old Roman road, between Askerswell and Beaminster, at 9pm, which inexplicably came to a halt after an interruption in their power supply.

According to an interview conducted with Mr Paul Redshaw – driver of a Vauxhall Victor car, the second in a line of three vehicles, accompanied by passenger – Ernie Goldsworthy:

"Thunder and lightning occasionally flickered overhead. The rain was falling. We were only going at about 30 miles per hour, when the engine stalled for no apparent reason. We got out, investigating. The compass in the lead car, a Rover 2000, began to spin and continued spinning. My watch stopped at 9pm; the thermometer in the car dropped to zero. Ernie's watch also stopped. The boot of the Vauxhall and the bonnet of the third car refused to open. The drivers of the other two cars tried unsuccessfully to open the windows. I put a wire across the battery terminals. There was nothing. I began to feel dizzy and a headache came on, which was still there, hours later."

Mr Goldsworthy told the same story, but added he had seen a couple of black marks on the road behind the cars. These marks were about two feet long by one foot wide, which he didn't believe were skid marks. Thirty minutes later, all power came back on.

Mr Marshall – a radio engineer by profession – visited the scene and checked out the locality for any sign of radiation with a Geiger counter. He still remains perplexed to this present day as to the cause of the interference, which stopped three vehicles 'dead' in their tracks.

Rather disturbingly we were to learn from Frank, two years later, in 1971, that Paul was found to be suffering from a stomach bowel disorder – a condition the specialists were unable to diagnose. Paul's father told Frank he was asked if his son had ever been exposed to any form of radiation, or X-rays, which was rather worrying, because we were to come across the same thing in many others who were to be asked the same questions, following exposure to the fields of electromagnetic radiation surrounding UFO 'craft'.

Was there a connection with Eggardon Hill – (the scene of other similar strange incidents) – involving UFOs being observed and other electrical malfunctions experienced by vehicles, reported over the years, some ten miles away?

Other likely considerations were a nearby post office, radio station, and a large BBC transmitting station at Rampisham, broadcasting on 100 kilowatts on the overseas service. Enquiries made with a number of authorities, which included the police, revealed no interruptions with radio transmissions had occurred that Sunday evening. The incident happened on a narrow country road, roughly two miles from the BBC's Rampisham Down transmitting station and four miles from Beaminster, Dorset – a place known locally as the 'Knights in the Bottom'.

We were intrigued to come across a possible explanation, during February 2006, when the MOD admitted, quote: *'A fault at their Trimingham radar dome on the North Norfolk coast had been responsible for causing electrical problems with dozens of cars, causing engine failure (although they initially denied this at the time), attributed to a type 93 radar spinning inside a dome that had been out of alignment, between November 2005 and February 2006'.*

(**Source:** *Daily Sketch,* 11.9.1968 – 'Three lonely road drivers find that time stands still'/*Western Gazette,* 13.9.1968 – 'Motorists dead half-hour mystery')

11th September 1968 – Splitting UFOs, Surrey

At 7.30pm, a bright, apparently stationary 'light' in the sky, with two or three others close to it, was seen by members of the Guildford's Friary Sports Ground. Suddenly, three other 'lights' split away from the middle object and moved around in the air, before eventually ascending upwards and being lost from view. (**Source: SIGAP**)

Over Bristol – At 11.05pm, a bright star-like object, constantly changing colour from red to silver, was seen moving across the sky over Bristol, before being lost from view as it went behind clouds.
(**Source: Contact UK, Bristol**)

15th September 1968 – US Pilot encounters UFO display

At 9.30pm, missionary pilot – Mr Jay Cole, was flying his *Beech C-45* twin-engine aircraft near Ocala, in Florida, when a 'light' was seen in the sky performing acrobatics. After this vanished a second 'light' appeared, made a 90 degree turn, and was also then lost from view 15 minutes later. A check with Radar, made later, revealed the 'target' had been following the plane. (**Source: Project Blue Book unknowns**)

17th September 1968 – 'Catherine wheel' UFO, Coventry

Mr A.G. Vanveen of St. Andrew's Road, Coventry, was in Beechwood Avenue, Earlsdon, at 9.15pm, when he saw:

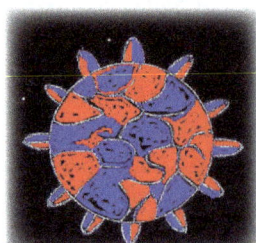

> "…what looked like a Catherine wheel, or twelve pointed star, showing red and blue lights, moving silently across the sky, heading towards the direction of Canley at about the speed of a light aircraft. It reminded me of a Belisha beacon, but more red in colour rather than orange."

At 10pm, Mr K. Parsons from Stoke Aldermoor, Coventry, was waiting for a bus in Quinton Road, when he saw a 'light' appear over nearby rooftops.

> "It was about 50 feet off the ground and projected a beam of light onto the ground, while it hovered for a short time – then it headed off towards Baginton, at tremendous speed."

Another witness was Derek Warren – then employed as a photographer for the local *Coventry Standard* – who saw:

> "…a red/orange glow in the sky, moving over the rooftops; by the time I reached for my camera, it had gone." (**Source: Bob Tibbitts, CUFORG**)

Over Surrey

At 10.50pm, a brilliant white light – "…*bigger than any star, but smaller than the moon*" – was seen oscillating from circular to bone-shaped in the sky, over the tops of houses, opposite, at West Ewell, in Surrey, before zigzagging out of sight.
(**Source: Society for the Investigation of UFO Phenomena/*UFOLOG*, 1968**)

September 1968 – *The Condon Report*

In September 1968, Dr. Edward Uhler Condon, Director of the University of Colorado – who had been given £208,000 pounds by the USAF to research into the subject of UFOs, 16 months before – finally published his report, which ran to 1,485 pages in hardcover and 965 pages in the *Bantam* paperback edition. He made no secret of his opinion even at the outset that no substantive evidence for extraterrestrial visitation was liable to result. It divided UFO cases into five categories:

1 Old UFO reports (from before the Committee convened); 2 New reports; 3 Photographic cases; 4 Radar/visual cases; 5 UFOs reported by astronauts (some UFO cases fell into multiple categories)

In the second paragraph of his introductory "Conclusions and Recommendations", Condon wrote:

"Our general conclusion is that nothing has come from the study of UFOs in the past 21 years that has added to scientific knowledge. Careful consideration of the record as it is available to us leads us to conclude that further extensive study of UFOs probably cannot be justified in the expectation that science will be advanced thereby."

An endorsement of the report by the National Academy of Sciences took place following an unusually rapid review, and the Air Force quickly used the report as a justification to terminate any further public involvement with the topic of UFOs.

The report was made the subject of various newspaper articles, published in the UK, which contained a plethora of headlines and included: ***Daily Mail***, 9.1.1969 – 'Flying Saucers don't exist say Scientists'/ ***Daily Express***, 10.1.1969 – 'US report upsets the UFO Spotters'/***Daily Mail***, 18.12.1969 – 'Hunt for Flying Saucers'/***Daily Mail***, 10.1.1969/13.1.1969 – 'There are no little green men')

Fortunately, *The Times* (11th January 1969), in their article – 'UFO study starts new controversy', adopted a far more sensible attitude, declaring that in spite of all the money spent, the controversy will not die down and that, according to the study, it was recommended, *"...some schoolchildren are being educationally harmed by absorbing unsound and erroneous accounts, and teachers should stop giving them credit for reading books on the subject"*, and that nine out of ten sightings can be explained. This attracted a letter from BUFORA representative – Norman Oliver, which appeared in the *Mail* on the 13th January 1969:

"The University of Colorado's report on 'Flying Saucers' concluded as anticipated. There is no evidence to justify a belief in 'Flying Saucers'. We are told that nine out of ten sightings can be plausibly explained. What about the rest? One aspect of the report is alarming the recommendation that teachers should stop students reading about 'Flying Saucers'. Where would this sort of thing stop?"

19th September 1968 – 'Flying Saucer' seen by passengers on South Devon ferry

Mr Philip Taylor was on holiday in South Devon, with other family members, when they saw:

"...a silver 'flying saucer' shaped object, approximately 30 feet in diameter, with two square illuminated panels, hovering above the Dartmouth ferry on which we were travelling."

(Source: Richard Farrow/BUFORA)

21st September 1968 – Motorist encounters weird mass, Bedfordshire

Mr E. Bennett, and his daughter, was driving to their home at Hill Grove, Whipsnade, and nearing the bottom of Bison Hill.

"A conical mass, six feet tall, rose out of the grass verge, 25 yards ahead, and vanished into the hedge." **(Source: *Dunstable Borough Gazette*, 27.9.1968)**

September 1968 – UFO crash-lands at Wiltshire

Mrs Helen Baston wrote to both the MOD and the Isle of Wight UFO Society, explaining what she had witnessed towards the end of September 1968, which took place along Bath Road, Warminster, in Wiltshire.

"We had just passed Minster Church and were walking along Gas House Lane, close to a local garage, next to a small cottage, when my companion said, 'Look, there's a lot of UFOs about tonight'. I replied, 'They're shooting stars'. She insisted and remarked that the 'starship' was moving. I explained to her that if you looked long enough at it you would form that impression. I said (and I shall never forget the words) 'What's the good of them looking down at us, down here, and us looking at them, up there?', followed by what looked like a 'shooting star' that streaked across the sky. My companion shouted 'It's a meteorite!' Then a very odd thing happened. The 'meteorite'

stopped still in the sky over some woods (Norridge Wood) – then it streaked past us – now a long object – burst into white light, and came lower and lower in the sky (all the time revolving) before landing onto the ground behind some trees, causing us to lose our view of it. There was a very strong smell in the air of burning sulphur, mixed with creosote.

A man shot out of the cottage, jumped into his car and drove off, but returned a short time later and ran into the cottage, completely ignoring us. We heard some footsteps around the bend, but saw nothing. My companion urged me to go and have a look but I refused, now frightened. Suddenly a blaze of light appeared behind where the object had gone down, accompanied by a humming noise, and whatever it was rose upwards, revolving and coming towards us, gaining height as it did so. It then moved back along the path it had taken originally and was soon lost from sight in the sky."

Helen told of having contacted Bill Horhler, from the Warminster area, after learning of his 'close encounter' (see sighting of 10th December 1967), and felt comparisons could be drawn between what they had both seen, after discovering the two incidents had occurred in more or less the same place.

(Source: Isle of Wight UFO Society)

24th September 1968 – Lecture by Coventry factory boss, Mr Wilfred Grunau

The *Coventry Evening Telegraph* published an article about a UFO lecture given by Managing Director of the Awson Motor Carriage Company, Mr Wilfred Grunau, at the Nuneaton Rotary Club.

Wilfred:

"Mankind has been seeing strange things in the sky since the beginning of recorded history, but in the last 20 years more strange sights have been recorded than in the previous 20 Centuries."

Wilfred also said that he had spoken to 13 Rotary clubs on the subject and seven had produced someone who believed he had seen a UFO.

Wilfred:

"I have sighted UFOs on two occasions and, as a result, believe in their existence."

(Source: *Coventry Evening Telegraph*, 24.9.1968 – 'Flying Saucers not a load of tripe – director')

OCTOBER 1968

3rd October 1968 – UFO over Royal Albert Docks, London

At 10.58am, NICAP, GB. UFO researcher Derek Samson from Wildmoor Road, Shirley, Solihull – employed as a goods driver – was delivering to the Royal Albert Docks, London.

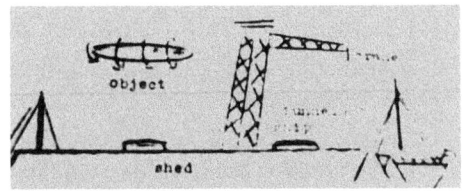

"It was a dry and cool day, with hazy clouds and slight breeze, when I saw a grey cigar-shaped object towards the south. Its apparent size, in comparison, was 4 inches on a ruler, held at arm's length. I watched in excitement, as it slowly climbed upwards into the sky – all the time spinning. As it entered a cloud, it appeared to split into two halves and disappeared from view."

12th October 1968 – Silver 'discs' seen over London

At 4.30pm, *"a silver 'disc', with a dome on top"*, was sighted over Greenwich, London, by a man on his way home. Four minutes later, it disappeared from view.

The *Sun* newspaper (12.10.1968) told its readers of a gleaming 'disc' seen by members of the public, and Police Sergeant T. Blenkinsop and WPC Z. Bradshaw, over Okehampton, in Devon, who strongly rejected suggestions put to them that they had seen either a weather balloon, or satellite, which had gone astray. A spokesman at RAF Chivenor, 30 miles from Okehampton, confirmed that *"a report had been sent to the MOD and RAF Fighter HQ, where a photographer was on standby should the UFO be seen again."*

It appears, from a letter sent to Frank Marshall from Michael Hunt, of the Weymouth News Agency, that another two witnesses to UFO activity were Trevor Mathews, and his girlfriend. Unfortunately, we were unable to trace any of the persons named in the letter, but judged the letter to be of interest.

BUFORA NORTHERN CONFERENCE IN MANCHESTER, 12th October 1968

The conference was hosted by the Direct Investigation Group on Aerial Phenomena and took place in the well-appointed Friends Meeting House near the centre of Manchester. The large reception area was well-filled with a display of UFO material, including numerous photos, press cuttings and sighting reports. Special features included a display of paintings and local material by S.I.G.A.P. a model of Newchapel Observatory together with a case of meteorites supplied by Messers Stanway and Pace, and a display of magnetic detectors together with a Geiger-Mueller radiation detector.

After coffee, the main programme started at 11.30 with DIGAP Chairman, Bill Moore, introducing BUFORA Executive member, Norman Oliver. At the start attendance was 80 with only six ladies present (two of whom, Mrs.Jean Stott and Mrs.Joan Nelstrop, were organisers). Norman gave an interesting and amusing talk entitled "Experiences of Contact Claims", and mentioned cases where telepathic contact was claimed. He explained his reasons for establishing COS-MOS, which will be dedicated to the investigation by all means, of all types of 'Contacts'; and this includes the aspect of sex which "was a pretty hot potato".

Attendance for the afternoon session rose to about 120, but the organisers were embarrassed by apologies from scheduled speakers, John Cleary-Baker and Leslie Otley. However Roger Stanway and Omar Fowler (SIGAP Chairman) filled the gap remarkably well. Roger went over the history of the Stanway and Pace "Flying Saucer Report" which led to some revealing discussion about the Ministry of Defence's approach to UFO investigation, commented on in the last article. Omar talked on "UFOs over Surrey" with the aid of Dan Butcher's very graphic paintings (later used at the New Year Show). Ample teas were then partaken of. oo

Bill Moore, DIGAP and Conference Chairman, with Roger Stanway and Anthony Pace, outside Friends Meeting House, Manchester.

The evening session commenced with Tony Duncan Wedd's standard "Skyways and Landmarks" lecture illustrated with colour slides. The question period for this dragged somewhat, and the evening concluded with a short session of badly edited slides and film material.

In comparison the Bristol Conference run by the British Flying Saucer Bureau in July 1968, reached and maintained a higher practical and technical level. However the diversity and quantity of the supporting exhibition at Manchester was far more impressive. DIGAP members are to be congratulated for their good all round organisation.

Lionel Beer.

14th October 1968 – UFO over RAF Wittering, Cambridgeshire

Declassified documents released by the MOD, over 30 years later, reveal that at 12.41pm, an object was picked-up by the Airfield Approach Radar at RAF Wittering, at a height of 19,000 feet. A report of the incident, witnessed by Flight Lt. M. Galbauer, was submitted by M/Sig. C.L. Goldsmith, along with information obtained from the duty controller on Northern Radar, which tells of an object plotted,

"...travelling at a speed of 1,800 miles per hour; heading 240 degrees at a range of 32 miles. It appeared to become stationary and overturned, for approximately one minute, before moving west at orthodox speed – until no longer visible on radar at a range of 40 miles".

Lincolnshire 1968 – Cross-shaped UFO

At 7.35pm, a bright, stationary object was seen in the sky over Saxilby, Lincolnshire, by a man driving home. His curiosity aroused, he got out taking a closer look.

> "I was staggered to see a brilliant cross-shaped object, with bright edges, suspended in the sky. Its brightness then dimmed and it increased in size, altering in appearance to saucer-shaped – now orange in colour – before vanishing from view."

(Source: Richard Thompson, South Lincolnshire UFO Study Group)

18th October 1968 – Kent workmen sight UFO

At 2am, three workmen – employed on the 60 feet Essen flare stack at Hythe, in Kent, working 60 feet off the ground – sighted a light-grey object in the sky, travelling south to north, at a height of about 1,600 feet.

> "It then passed over the top of the flare stack, showing the reflection of the flame on its underside, before passing over the chimney of the Styrene plant under construction."

(Source: Fred O. Gardner, F.R.G.S.)

21st October 1968 – Smoke ring, Warwickshire

Mr A. Marvin from Crick, near Rugby, was driving from Yelvertoft to Lilbourne, when he noticed a 'dark shadow' in grey cloud, about two miles ahead of him.

> "The 'dark shadow' moved to the edge of the cloud and became clearer, at first looking like a smoke ring. On emerging into clear air, it became immediately apparent that it was 'disc' shaped – perfectly circular, and on a declining flight path of 20-30 degrees – allowing me to see an orifice set into the underside of the object, which was oscillating gently. A second or two later, two more 'discs' appeared either side of the first – identical, apart from an absence of the orifice. All three remained in view for five seconds, before moving into cloud cover."

Over Kent

At 10.50pm, a 'golden ball' was seen hovering halfway up a group of trees at Meopham, in Kent, by a housewife.

> "Suddenly, an aircraft passed overhead. Immediately the 'ball' shot backwards and hung in the air over a nearby farm, eventually returning to its original position after the plane had gone."

(Source: *UFO Chronicle*)

22nd October 1968 – Triangular UFO, Surrey

At 7.40am, a triangular object – 'nearly as bright as the sun', with a small globe to its right – was seen stationary in the south-east sky, between Ewell and Cheam village, in Surrey. Several seconds later it vanished, to be replaced by two similar objects, *"weaving to and fro in the sky, but continuing to maintain its shape all the time"*.

(Source: Society for the Investigation of UFO Phenomena/*UFOLOG*, December)

30th October 1968 – 'Flying Saucer' over Harlow, Essex

Dennis Norris and his wife, of Harlow, Essex, were reading in bed, at 12.30am, when Mrs Norris noticed a large white 'light' shining on the bedroom window, and brought it to her husband's attention. By the time he looked, there was nothing to be seen.

A short time later, Mr Norris noticed a red glow coming through the bedroom window and got out of bed to take a look.

After opening the window, he glanced outside and saw an orange/red 'light' hovering in the sky, at an undetermined distance.

They watched the 'light' for twelve minutes, trying to work out what it could be.

> "It started to recede and swing from side to side, each swing being twice the length of the object, actually passing in front of the third storey windows of a 14 storey block of flats. On the next 'swing' it passed behind the flats, which gave some idea of distance and height."

It then accelerated away out of sight and was gone.

From calculations obtained – taking into consideration the flats were 150 feet high, by 60 feet wide, and half a mile away from the witnesses – it was ascertained that the unidentified 'light' was estimated to be 60 feet long, by 25 feet thick, and 150 feet off the ground. **(Source: Richard Farrow, BUFORA)**

A number of zigzagging objects were seen in the sky over High Wycombe Beacon and Gerrards Cross. According to a witness, one showed a hoop around its centre and stopped in mid-flight, before accelerating across the sky. It was later explained away by the MOD as being the lights of aircraft from London Airport – which was rejected by the parties concerned.

(Source: *The Evening News,* 31.10.1968 – 'Mystery of lights are not planes')

NOVEMBER 1968

4th November 1968 – 'Flying Saucer' over Henley-on-Thames

At 7.25am, a 'Flying Saucer' was seen hovering in the sky over Henley-on-Thames, in Surrey, by an employee of the UK Atomic Energy Authority, who was driving between Wargrave to Henley-on-Thames.

> "Dawn had almost broken, when I noticed a saucer-shaped object, glowing like a fluorescent strip light on the windscreen. I thought that it was a reflection of some sort, but then realised it wasn't. I lost sight of it as I went past some trees. When I cleared them, the object had gone."

(Source: Surrey Investigation Group, [SIGAP])

7th November 1968 – Orange 'disc', Harlow, Essex

In the early hours, a man and his wife from Harlow, Essex, saw what they first believed to be torchlight being shone onto their bedroom window, in Westfield. Wondering if there was some sort of emergency, they went to the window to look out and saw:

> "...a large orange coloured 'disc', estimated to be 200 feet in length, hovering over open ground at the rear of their house, before suddenly shooting upwards into the sky at a phenomenal speed."

Source: Contact UK, Bristol)

Rotherham 1968 – Three red lights

At 7pm, a triangular flare-like object, showing three red lights, was seen by a motorcyclist travelling home to Rotherham, moving 40 to 50 yards in front of him, at just a few miles an hour.

> "It was moving about 30 feet off the ground. The bottom two lights on its base were projecting out much more than the one above it; as I neared a railway bridge I saw it go in-between a bungalow, banking, then head off into the distance." **(Source: Flying Fact Investigation Society/UFOLOG)**

9th November 1968 – Bell-shaped UFO, Rugby

Paula Hollis was one of a group of children that rushed to the window at Dunsmore School, Rugby, after a report of three bright red and yellow 'Flying Saucers' seen circling the sky, at 4pm. Another witness to this

Haunted Skies Volume Two Revised

incident was local insurance agent – Mr John Knee, who told Coventry UFO researcher, Bob Tibbitts:

> "I was looking out of my office window, at 4.14pm; it was still daylight, when I noticed a light travelling northward across the sky. It was too far away to see any detail, but it wasn't any aircraft as there was an absence of any superstructure. It also displayed this uncanny light."

Just over an hour later, at 5.15pm, a boy (13) was exercising his family dog in the Lincolnshire area, as dusk fell, when he saw a bright, stationary object in the sky. A few minutes later, it vanished from sight.

(Source: South Lincolnshire UFO Study Group)

15th November 1968 – Blood-red object, Greater Manchester

At 7.07am, Mrs P. Bolton, from Flixton, was looking out of her front bedroom window, when she noticed a blood-red coloured object, which dimmed slightly as it pulsated, heading on a steady course across the sky in a south-east to west direction. Was this the same object seen just seven minutes later? **(Source: D. Tomlinson, DIGAP)**

Three men working at a steelworks in Port Talbot, Glamorgan, Wales, sighted a bright revolving light,

> "...like a large star, moving across the sky from the east, which came to a halt in mid-air over a corner of the steel yard – its light going out, leaving a barely discernible dark shadow in the sky showing where it was. Out of this 'shadow' emerged nine grey objects, shaped like television tubes in appearance, which went off in different directions. As dawn rose, at 8.10am, the 'patch' faded away from sight." **(Source: BUFORA/UFOLOG)**

20th November 1968 – Bell-shaped UFO, Cheshire

At 8.05am, Mrs N.J. Dugdale of Matlock Avenue, Flixton, Cheshire, was seeing her husband off to work on a dry, fairly clear day, when she sighted a bell-shaped object hovering in the northern part of the sky. Seconds later, it changed to 'cigar' in shape, moved to the left, and vanished from sight.

(Source: Mrs Nelstrop, DIGAP)

20th November 1968 – 'Flying Saucer' over Staffordshire

At 5.50pm the same day, Mr and Mrs Milakovic from Hednesford, near Cannock Chase, Staffordshire, were driving home with their small child, past Hanbury Hall, when their attention was caught by a number of rabbits running across the road in front of their car – as if frightened by something – followed by the appearance of a brilliantly lit object, which rose slowly upwards from the field on their left, passing over the car.

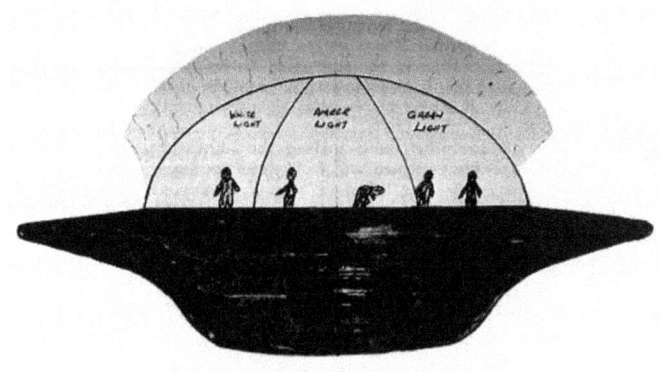

Mr Milakovic slammed on the brakes. The family watched, as the UFO headed towards a nearby house, some 100 yards away, where it took up a stationary position above it, appearing to be:

> "...quivering, like a jelly. We felt warm, although this soon passed when the object moved away. It was as big as a house in size and silent. We couldn't see anything rotating on the object, although we

did see several 'figures' – 'human', from their silhouettes – walking backwards and forwards across the brilliantly lit top portion. Occasionally, some of the 'figures' would bend down – as if looking for something in the object below the rim. Except for the three lights and the 'figures', nothing else was visible in the upper part of the craft. The object then began to move away in a series of pulsating, jerky movements, shining with light so intense that it hurt the eyes to look at it for too long."

After details of the incident were later published by the *Wolverhampton Express and Star* newspaper, the family were contacted by Stafford UFO researcher Mr Wilfred Daniels, who conducted a search of the area where the incident had taken place but was unable to identify the whereabouts of a distinctive house seen by the witnesses prior to the appearance of the UFO, although the absence of this building did not detract from what Mr Daniels believed to be a very genuine account.

The scene

(Source: Wilfred Daniels/NMH Turner, *Flying Saucer Review,* **The Milakovic Report,** **1968/***Flying Saucer Review,* **Volume 15, No. 1)**

At 7pm the same evening, a 'string' of strange lights was seen crossing the sky over England, travelling north-west to south-east, described as looking like formations of multicoloured objects with short tails – later explained away as being the *Russian Cosmos rocket 253* re-entering the atmosphere. These were also seen over north-western Europe.

One witness was Commander V.J. Chown of Woodford, Essex, who described seeing:

"...*a number of lights, assembled around an invisible tube – like the old Graf Zeppelin shape. They remained in rigid formation like warships.*"

Enquiries made with the Russian Embassy, at the time, revealed they had no such knowledge.

1968 – England: Alien 'figures', Devon

In the same year, a man was driving along the A38, in Devon, just after midnight. It was a journey he made regularly, although he was startled to see four 'figures' standing by the roadside. However, he dismissed them from mind, knowing that deer were often seen roaming at the side of the road. While negotiating Haldon Hill and keeping a watch out for deer, his attention was caught by a small group of 'figures', standing on a grass verge at the side of the road.

> *"Three of them stood together, while a fourth was some distance away. I was able to see them as I drove past. They were no more than three feet in height, and were a dark chocolate colour all over. I would describe them as having small upturned noses, with sharply pointed ears and peculiar necks, which appeared exceptionally thick at the back."*

What a pity we do not know the identity of the man, who expressed an opinion to researchers from 'Zenith' Contact UK Bristol Group that he could not be 100% sure of what he had seen, but nevertheless it remains an interesting sighting – especially bearing in mind other sightings of 'strange figures' seen in the Devon and Cornwall area, over the years. (**Source: Contact UK, Bristol**)

DECEMBER 1968

8th December 1968 – Three luminous 'discs' seen over Birmingham

At 6.20pm, retired RAF Meteorological Officer – Mr A.S. Rattray, B.Sc., from Erdington, Birmingham, was walking through Wylde Green, when he heard the faint whisper of what he took to be a jet aircraft, flying at 30,000 feet.

> *"After seven years in the RAF as a Meteorological Officer, I still instinctively look upwards whenever I hear an aircraft. Instead of seeing nothing, as I had expected, I was staggered to see three large luminous 'discs' gliding through the sky, positioned in the form of a perfect equilateral triangle, with one 'disc of light' at each apex. One was leading, with the other two in perfect formations to the rear. I first sighted them at an elevation of about 45 degrees, but was unable to obtain a height against the black, cloudy sky. The light from each 'disc' was equal and of a golden hue. They were heading on a constant direction of 315 degrees and visible for about 20-30 seconds, before being lost from view when entering lower broken cloud. The Meteorological Office, at Birmingham Elmdon Airport, were giving 8/8 stratus, at 980 feet, with 2/8ths at 800 feet. The three luminous 'discs' were evidently moving between the two cloud layers, at approximately 730 feet above ground level, when I saw them. Visibility was 3.8km or 2.4 miles, and their speed from simple calculations would have been about 150 miles per hour."* (**Source: Derek Samson – NICAP, GB**)

15th December 1968 – Black object with white halo, Shirley, Solihull

At 2.30pm, Adrian P. Clews (10), and his friend – Nicholas (15), were in Ralph Road, Shirley, when they noticed a white object, motionless in the sky between two houses. Through the telescope they saw a round, black object, with a white halo around it.

Shortly afterwards, it moved away and out of sight. (**Source: Derek Samson – NICAP, GB**)

18th December 1968 – Three shining objects, Halifax, Yorkshire

At 12.30am, three shining circular objects, resembling smaller versions of the full moon, were seen crossing the sky in broad daylight. (**Source: BUFORA, Halifax**)

21st December 1968 – Four shining lights seen over Cheshire

At 2.45pm, four shining objects were seen moving across the sky over Brereton, in Cheshire, by two men, out walking, described as:

> "...spherical in shape; the bottom half dark and solid, the upper part looked like a bubble. They changed their direction four times, until we lost sight of them about six minutes later."

(Source: BUFORA)

On the early evening of 21st December 1968, the authorities were flooded with calls reporting a UFO seen in the sky over the UK – later explained away as being the *Apollo 8* spacecraft, launched from the Kennedy Space Center, Florida, at 7.51am (Eastern Standard Time), venting off non-propulsive hydrogen, covering about two degrees of the sky.

A photo taken at the time, by an astronomer (published in many newspapers), shows a crescent-shaped object with a smaller luminous object next to it. Even accepting the four-hour time difference between Eastern Standard Time and Greenwich Mean Time, it appears that what Joan Bradbury saw from her house at Gosford Green, Coventry, at 6.35am (the same date), appears unlikely to be attributed to the sighting of *Apollo 8*.

In an interview conducted with Bob Tibbitts, from Coventry UFO Research Group, she had this to say:

> "I was in bed when a light flashed across the room. I first thought it was a passing motor vehicle but decided to have a look outside, when I was astonished to see a silver 'ball of light' rushing across the sky, followed by a red cigar-shaped object." **(Source: Bob Tibbitts, CUFORG)**

25th December 1968 – 'Flying Saucer' sighted, Leicestershire

At 10.30pm, two bright objects were seen passing through the sky over Wigston, Leicestershire, by a woman resident and her husband, who fetched a pair of binoculars.

> "The first object still appeared as a bright light; the second looked like one of those 'Flying Saucers' you see in children's comics, 'disc' shaped, with a raised dome in the centre – its outer part apparently revolving. An orange/red glow then appeared around the outer periphery of the object – as if an engine had been fired up. The object tilted slightly and the glow died away, followed by a silver flickering effect. Prior to this sighting, I had actually been sceptical of the existence of UFOs and only went out into the garden to please my partner." (**Source: Isle of Wight UFO Investigation Society**)

BUFORA Exhibition

Between the 28th December 1968 and 11th January 1969, an exhibition took place at the Empire Hall, Olympia, London, organised by BUFORA representatives, attracting (it was estimated) a total of 230 thousand people, who passed by the stand. What a golden opportunity to see 'UFO history in action' involving UFO researchers, such as Lionel Beer, Ivar Mackay (chairman), Richard Farrow (report co-coordinator), Norman Oliver, and many others, who contributed their money and time to making this a popular event. (**Source:** *Space-link*, **Volume 5, No. 4, February 1969/Omar Fowler/Lionel Beer**)

28th December 1968 – Red 'light' over Paignton, Devon

At 3am, Paignton resident – Martin Waterhouse, was awoken by a brilliant 'flash of light'. He rushed to the window, wondering what was going on, and was shocked to see:

> "...a large red 'disc', travelling slowly through the sky, at a height estimated to be 150 feet. After several minutes, flames and smoke started to emerge from the object, followed by it changing to bright silver. I called for my father to come and have a look and we watched it for eight minutes. We later found out that the Brixham Lifeboat was called out after somebody had contacted them, after seeing a light off the Paignton coast – but they found nothing."

The *Sunday Express* newspaper, in its edition of 29th December 1968, told of an unsuccessful search made by the Brixham Lifeboat being launched, after receiving a call of a red 'light' seen in the sky off the coast of Paignton, during the early morning of the 29th December 1968.

UFO activity was so intense for this period that the BUFORA Committee had to suspend their contract to an agency which supplied them with UFO newspaper cuttings, after having received 790 separate items, and appealed directly to their members to send them to their BUFORA Information Officer, Mr Richard Farrow – then living in North Wembley, Middlesex.

1968

Date not ascertained. Mrs Murray and four members of her family from Carrshield, in Northumberland, sighted three silver 'Flying Saucers', heading north, on a cold, frosty night, accompanied by what appeared to be a bright light. (**Source:** *UFOLOG*)

CHAPTER 10 – 1969

UFO REPORTS INCLUDE:

Postscript to August 1968 – Update on Harry Bowden Marlow

JANUARY:
1st January 1969 – 'Finned UFO' over Herefordshire
5th January 1969 – Cigar shaped UFO over Staffordshire
11th January 1969 – Motorist sights inverted 'saucer'
15th January 1969 – Motorcyclist encounters strange light
17th January 1969 – Cone-shaped object sighted
17th January 1969 – US mechanic sights amber lights in formation
25th January 1969 – Three lights seen over Lancashire
27th January 1969 – UFO over Stratford-upon-Avon
31st January 1969 – 'Orange light' over the Downs

FEBRUARY:
1st February 1969 – Seven luminous objects
2nd February 1969 – Coastguards sight UFO
3rd February1969 – Shimmering UFO
6th February 1969 – UFO disrupts TV signals
11th February 1969 – UFO over Kent
18th February 1969 – UFO over Doncaster
21st February 1969 – Cylindrical UFO seen
22nd February 1969 – UFO sighted over Yarmouth, Isle of Wight

MARCH:
2nd March 1969 – 'Flying Saucer' over Gloucestershire showing three red lights
4th March 1969 – Bright orange object over Staffordshire
6th March 1969 – UFO over Gloucestershire
7th March 1969 – Green UFO over Gloucestershire
23rd March 1969 –Charles Bowen writes to Frank Marshall
28th March 1969 – UFO over Lincoln Air Base
29th March 1969 – UFO sighted over Hampshire
30th March 1969 – Strange sounds, Coventry

APRIL:
3rd April 1969 – Pear-shaped object sighted by reporter
4th April 1969 – Landed UFO, Leicester
5th April 1969 – Massive cigar-shaped UFO seen Andover UFO Group

9th April 1969 – Star-shaped object over Yorkshire
12th April 1969 – UFO landing, Bridgnorth . . . Alien beings seen
16th April 1969 – UFOs making a hissing sound
20th April 1969 – Egg-shaped UFO over Yorkshire
24th April 1969 – 'Flying Saucer' paces car, Sheffield
25th April 1969 – Fireball over England
26th April 1969 – Orange 'ball' sighted
27th April 1969 – Pulsating object over London
30th April 1969 – Air Marshall Sir Victor Goddard speaks at Contact UK meeting in London

MAY:
2nd May 1969 – UFO landing, Exmouth
12th May 1969 – Glowing objects, Hampshire
13th May 1969 – Strange 'lights' in the sky
14th May 1969 –UFO over Kent
24th May 1969 – Orange UFO over Cumbria
May 1969 – UFO display, Devon

JUNE:
5th June 1969 – 'lights' over Enfield
12th June 1969 – Police sight UFO
15th June 1969 – Silver 'disc' over Birkenhead
18th June 1969 – UFO with three 'lumps', photographed at Birmingham
20th June 1969 – 'Chinese lantern' in the sky
21st June 1969 – Cigar-shaped object hovering above trees at Ayrshire
25th June 1969 – Triangular shaped UFO
26th June 1969 – Orange 'Flying Saucer' Hants
29th June 1969 – 'Full Moon' over Bristol
'Flying Saucer' over Nuneaton

JULY:
4th July 1969 – Three 'bright lights' seen over County Durham
12th July 1969 – Will-o'-the-wisp …?
13th July 1969 – UFO display over Glastonbury
July –UFOs over Gloucestershire
20th July 1969 – Silver object seen by schoolgirls
22nd July 1969 – Three 'bright lights' over Isle of Wight

Haunted Skies Volume Two Revised

23rd July 1969 – Bedfordshire Police chase UFO
25th July 1969 – Crimson sphere over Staffordshire
27th July 1969 – Three 'Flying Saucers' over Hertfordshire
Summer 1969 – Black triangular UFO over West Midlands
Summer 1969 – 'Doodlebug' UFO, London

AUGUST:
5th August 1969 – Silver UFO over Carmarthen
7th August 1969 – Silver cylindrical UFO
August 1969 – Warwickshire motorist encounters UFO
15th August 1969 – UFO landing, Stourbridge
19th August 1969 – Bright yellow UFO over Liverpool
20th August 1969 – UFO display Leicestershire
23rd August 1969 – UFO over Leicester
24th August 1969 – Triangular UFO, Nottingham
25th August 1969 – Triangular UFO, Bolton Lancashire
28th August 1969 – Bolton Lancashire firemen sight UFO
UFO over Great Yarmouth

SEPTEMBER:
6th September 1969 – UFO over Reading

OCROBER:
1st October 1969 – Size of a football
2nd October 1969 – Three pulsing 'red lights' over Devon
5th October 1969 – 'V'-shaped formation of UFOs Kent
21st October 1969 – UFO over Bournemouth

NOVEMBER:
5th November 1969 – 'T'-shaped UFO over Dorset
26th November 1969 – UFO over East Ham

DECEMBER:
5th December 1969 – 'Floating ballroom' over London
17th December 1969 – *Project Blue Book* closed!

Postscript to August 1968 – Update on Harry Bowden Marlow of Snitterfield

During the time spent writing up these intriguing, sometimes very personal, experiences into *Haunted Skies* Volume 2 Revised, cataloging UFO activity for the 1960s (when records for this period, previously kept on file by the MOD, were destroyed), we continually updated the work as we went on, wherever possible.

On the 7th July 2017 (Harry's Birthday!) we met up with Harry's wife – Valerie (85), now living in Stratford-upon-Avon – following conversation held with her recently, that in fact she remembered with great clarity the events of that night, which took place at the family home – 'Avebury' in Snitterfield.

Valerie:

> "Having read the account, I would like to point out that I did not sleep throughout what Harry told me later what had taken place. I do distinctly remember waking up suddenly and see Harry standing up out of bed, looking through the window mullion panes of glass, one of which was opened slightly about a foot through which he was looking out of. I asked him 'What are you doing?'
>
> He didn't reply. I must have dropped off. The next morning, when he told me about it, he said 'something happened in there – just over there', although I didn't hear anything myself."

The location was identified as being a children's playground and a nearby pylon (often associated with UFO sightings, although this would be only conjecture on this occasion).

Having said that, the 'swishing' noise described by Harry is unusual but not rare to the background of other reports we have come across over the years. We enjoyed our time spent with Valerie and wish her the best of luck. She is a lovely lady and was only too willing to let us have some photos of Harry, which we felt should be included, as it forms additional information not made available during the first interview, when, as we recall, Valerie was not present.

The family home

Valerie Bowden Marlow

Harry Bowden Marlow

Hazel Bowden Marlow

Hazel Marlow, RIP.

Sadly, we were once again reminded of the couple's tragic loss of their daughter, Hazel, who tragically died in a road accident.

Hazel had served in Bosnia on a six-month tour of duty, as apart of the British peacekeeping force with the Chelsea branch of the Territorial Army. After this she returned home and went to work with the Royal Shakespeare Company.

Poignantly, Hazel wrote a poem about Bosnia and another, about the family home.

> A BOSNIAN BATTLEFIELD
> AUTUMN 1996
>
> Kupres, a wasteland of slow-changing light,
> Hangs lost in a lonely charred graveyard.
> Dead, blistered houses lie empty of life,
> Walls furrowed by mortars and hate.
> On a stark and high hill tidy stones
> Line up, parading lost souls to the heavens.
> From shy misty dawn with its sad silver tones
> Lacing slaughtered flat plains with cold dew,
> To the gloaming deep night, angry whispers
> Cry out from the souls of dead soldiers in pain.
> Whole families fled, babes in arms, to escape,
> But no mortal release from Hell's work
> Saved these ghosts in the ground on the top of the hill
> From desolate death in Kupres.

> FOREVER AVEBURY
>
> Whatever marks the track of time
> In city-bursting space
> However cohorts tangle
> At their hellish workland pace
> When reason shouts that
> Silence dwells outside the walls of town
> Then Home lies close at Avebury
> Where breathes the homely ground.

Haunted Skies **Volume Two Revised**

JANUARY 1969

1st January 1969 – 'Finned UFO' over Herefordshire

At 11.20am, a silver football-shaped object – slightly pushed out of shape with 'fins' on either side – was seen flying through the sky over Ross-on-Wye, Herefordshire. According to eye-witness accounts:

> "…it was estimated to be moving at 45 miles per hour, travelling in a tumbling sort of motion, until disappearing out of sight, southwards, three minutes later."

(Source: South-west Unidentified Aerial Phenomena Investigations Group)

At 7.57am, Frank Satterthwaite – an amateur astronomer – was in his garden at Copmanthorpe, York, when he saw a stationary 'light' to the right of the moon, which grew progressively fainter during the two minutes he observed the object, described as:

> "…being pale silver in colour, the same size as the moon but with a bar of light crossing it, at an angle of 19 degrees above the horizon".

(Source: Tyneside UFO Society/Isle of Wight UFO Society)

Frank Satterthwaite

5th January 1969 – Cigar-shaped UFO over Staffordshire

A cigar-shaped object, lit up at both ends, was seen moving quickly across the sky over Brown Edge, Staffordshire, by several people. (**Source: John 'Dennis' Llewellyn**)

6th January 1969 – UFO with occupants sighted Spain

While we appreciate that we don't have the space to include sightings from Spain France, Germany, Italy etc…we thought it seemed appropriate to include this cutting from *FSR* which may, or may have nothing to do with what Mr Milakovic sighted at Hanbury during 1968, but is still intriguing…

January 6, 1969 (21.00)
Pontejos (Santander, Spain). Four persons were inside the kitchen of a small cafe across the street from the Pedrosa Sanitarium. Through a large window they saw an illuminated yellow rectangle about 30 metres away

Pontejos: January 6th, 1969

and 5 m. above ground, where the figure of a man walking back and forth was clearly noted. Other figures appeared, behaving similarly, and they met in the centre, then were lost to sight. The main luminosity was extinguished, and the outline of a large gray object, shaped like an inverted bowl on a plate, was discernible. It rose lightly and flew out of sight, illuminating the grass and the trees. (Prof. Pedrejo, first-hand report.)

UFOs in Two Worlds

11th January 1969 – Motorist sights inverted 'saucer'

At 9.30am, four women from Leeds, in Yorkshire, were driving to work when they noticed:

"…a glowing, bright red object in the east, shaped like an inverted saucer, travelling parallel to the road we were on at the time".

(Source: BUFORA)

Over Northamptonshire

Later the same day, at 5pm, two brothers had a terrifying encounter, which took place at a farmyard in Northamptonshire (four miles from Kettering), when they heard a loud continuous wailing, or swishing noise, above a bank of heavy fog, about a hundred feet above their heads. Further inspection revealed 'something' inside it moving around and around in zigzags and tight circles.

(Source: Society for the Investigation of UFO Phenomena/*UFOLOG*)

15th January 1969 – Motorcyclist encounters strange light

A motorcyclist riding along the A38 near Poole, in Dorset (close to Poole crossroads), saw what he took to be the light of an approaching motorcyclist on the other side of the road, coming towards him.

"As the white shape, with an off-white halo neared me, it tilted (as if going into a skid), came right across my path, and disappeared completely in front of my eyes." (**Source: Contact UK, Bristol Group**)

17th January 1969 – Cone-shaped object sighted

Following severe storms which struck the locality, an unidentified cone-shaped object, flashing red, green, and orange lights, was seen in the evening sky over Street, Somerset.

17th January 1969 – US mechanic sights amber lights in formation

At 3.24am, Mr Roman Lupton – a test facility mechanic from Crittenden, Virginia – reported having sighted several amber lights moving in formation across the sky, one of which was blinking.

"They moved slowly in an up and down movement, making a humming noise, before disappearing from view a couple of minutes later."

25th January 1969 – Three lights seen over Lancashire

At 10.58pm, Michael Merron of Crosby, in Lancashire, reported having sighted three 'lights' moving in line astern formation across the sky.

"During the ten seconds they were seen, the right-hand one flew off in a different direction, several times while in flight, and returned to the other two." (**Source: John 'Dennis' Llewellyn**)

27th January 1969 – UFO over Stratford-upon-Avon

At 7.30pm, schoolgirls – Linda and Aileen Ashby of Masons Road, Stratford-upon-Avon – were out playing in Baker Avenue school playground, with other children, when they sighted a small star-like object (later established to be Venus), circling a larger star, over the town.

At 9.15pm the same day, a Stratford-on-Avon housewife – Rita Duffy – was walking home when she saw a white object, low down in the sky, with rays of light emanating from it. In an interview with local UFO investigator John 'Dennis' Llewellyn, she had this to say:

"I know it sounds silly and if I'd been the only one to see it I may have thought I was dreaming. It was lower than a plane, white, with rays coming from it. I was really frightened when it followed me home. My husband and at least five of the neighbours watched it for about an hour."

(**Source:** *Stratford-upon-Avon Herald*, 31.1.1969 – 'UFO story seems silly'/John D. Llewellyn)

31st January 1969 – 'Orange light' over the Downs

At Chale, on the Isle of Wight, Norman Parr was walking to use the telephone, near Chale Church, at 11.15pm, when he noticed an 'orange light' that appeared to be moving back and forth in a zigzag manner along the Downs, where his daughter kept a pony.

Another witness to the phenomena was Mr A. Rostron – also a resident of Chale. He described seeing a spluttering 'ball of fire', at 1,000 feet over the sea, travelling towards Freshwater, at 11.15pm.

(**Source: Isle of Wight UFO Society**)

FEBRUARY 1969

1st February 1969 – Seven luminous objects

A woman living at East Stoke, in Hayling Island, went into the garden to call her dog, when she sighted:

"...seven luminous objects, flying slowly in formation across the sky".

Excitedly, she called her mother and the two women then watched the objects for thirty minutes, until lost from view. (**Source: BUFORA**)

2nd February 1969 – Coastguards sight UFO

It appears that the same or a similar UFO was seen later that evening, over the Isle of Wight, by a number of coastguards on duty there, who logged an 'unidentified light' between 11.08pm and 11.15pm. It began when Kenneth Newnham – an auxiliary coastguard from Atherfield – telephoned his colleague, Stan Lence, at Brook, asking him if he could see a strange 'light' in the sky.

Mr Lence told Kath Smith:

"At first I wrote it off as a star, but Ken insisted this was not the case, so I took bearings on a saucer-shaped object, which was green/white, about five times the size of a star, apparently 2,000 feet up in the sky over the Bournemouth/Swanage area, and showing a number of lights on its top half. It then turned a bright red and kept changing colour, and was on a bearing of 270 degrees but altered to 280 degrees, moving at the speed of an aircraft. Suddenly, whatever it was went over the horizon at colossal speed." (**Source: Isle of Wight UFO Society**)

3rd February 1969 – Shimmering UFO

At 10.45pm, Yarmouth resident – Mrs Pauline Raddings, was in the process of preparing a room for a guest at Buxton Lodge, Yarmouth, in the Isle of Wight. It was a clear night, with many stars visible. Suddenly her attention was caught by a brightly-lit object, moving in the south-west direction.

"It was seen as a shimmering background of gold and silver, with intermittent outbursts of brilliant red. I watched it for a few minutes, until it appeared to stop at a position of 280 degrees, at an angle of 20 degrees to the horizon. At this point my interest increased, so I asked someone to fetch a pair of binoculars. By this time, the brilliance had increased to such intensity that I was unable to discern the colouring of the object. I continued to observe for a further 3-4 minutes. After readjusting my position, I looked through the binoculars again at 11.10pm – there was nothing to be seen."

(**Source: Isle of Wight UFO Society/*UFOLOG*/*County Press* Newspaper, 8.2.1969 – 'Coastguard reports UFO'**)

6th February 1969 – UFO disrupts TV signals

At 8.08pm, an 'orange light' was seen travelling in a north-east direction over Wandsworth, London, which then turned sharply south-east and moved horizontally across the sky, before being lost from view over rooftops – apparently the cause of severe disruption to television signals.

(**Source: *UFOLOG*/BUFORA**)

11th February 1969 – UFO over Kent

Duncan Baxter – a photographer (whom we were unable to trace) for the *Tonbridge News* (a *Kent Messenger* newspaper) – was out in the 'field', carrying out his own investigation, after having received a report of UFO activity from a family in the Hildenborough area.

"Between 7.15pm and 10pm, I and seven other witnesses sighted a large, bright, object in the sky. The object appeared to pulsate, changing from bright to very dull at irregular intervals. At 9pm, the object had risen to such a height that no shape was visible. Our attention was drawn to a smaller star-like object, which shot over our heads, travelling in a north to south direction, before disappearing into distant cloud. We all agreed this was no aircraft.

At 9.45pm the small object appeared as though from the larger one, and moved slowly and erratically southwards, occasionally stopping at regular intervals of about ten seconds, and was out of view in ten minutes. At one time during the sightings, an airliner flew overhead en route to Heathrow. As it did so, the object dimmed until the aircraft had passed."

(**Source: *Kent Messenger*, exact date not known**)

18th February 1969 – UFO over Doncaster

At 5.30pm, scores of people – including two Meteorological Officers from RAF Finningley – watched a shiny object over the town, described (through telescopes and binoculars) as looking like:

> "…a translucent bullet-shaped object – flat at the back, round at the front – drifting slowly northwards, at a height of about 10,000 feet, before being eventually lost behind cloud cover".

The Meteorological Office denied it was a weather balloon.

(Source: Isle of Wight UFO Society/Richard Farrow)

At 7.55pm on the 21st February, a bright 'white light' was seen moving slowly through the sky over Ryde, in the Isle of Wight, heading eastwards. **(Source:** *The County Press,* Isle of Wight, 20.2.1969**)**

21st February 1969 – Cylindrical UFO seen

At 10.15pm, a cylindrical object with a cream-coloured front half, red rear, and showing four or five 'twirling tails' with several red star-like objects rising from the rear, was seen over *The Solent,* Great Yarmouth. **(Source: Isle of Wight UFO Society)**

22nd February 1969 – UFO sighted over Yarmouth Isle of Wight

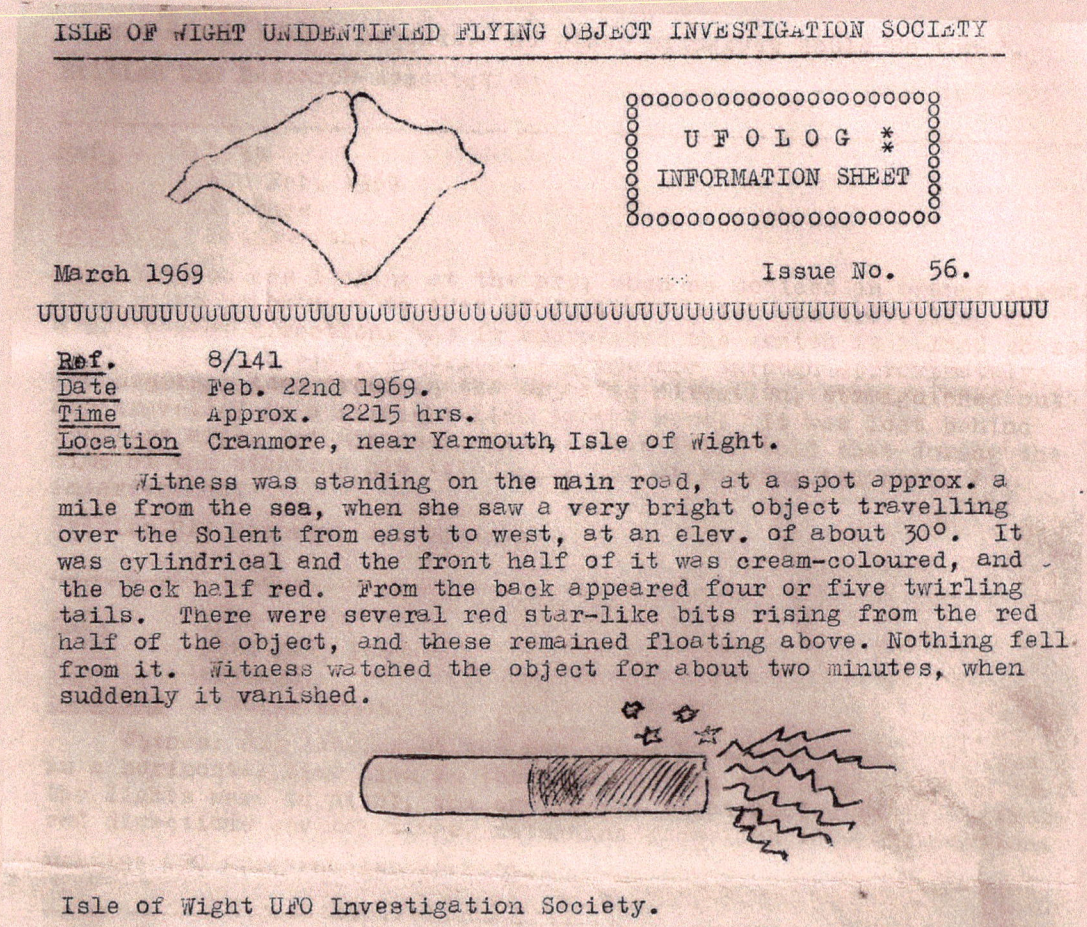

MARCH 1969

2nd March 1969 – 'Flying Saucer' over Gloucestershire showing three red lights

At 9.20pm, a draughtsman cycling home to Cam, in Gloucestershire, was astonished to see a 'sphere of light' travelling through the sky, at tremendous speed, in a wave like motion.

"It appeared to come to a halt over the Woodfield area of Cam, glowing bright green, disappearing from sight over the River Severn, in view for a few minutes. It had a strip of pink light on top, which contained three bright red lights. Below this, I could see the black shape of a solid object."

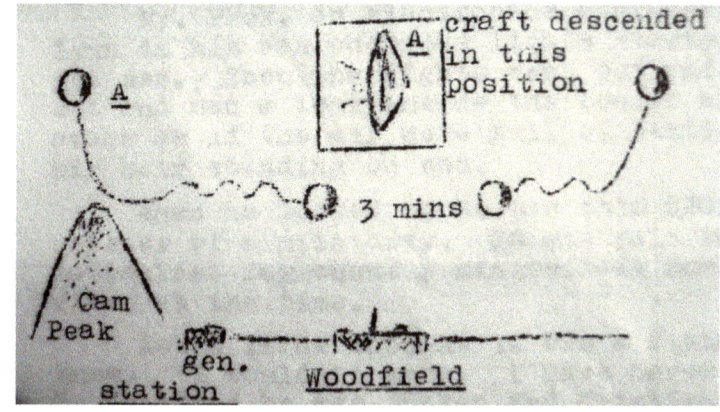

According to the investigators, the witness told of waking up at 3am, four nights in a row, unable to sleep after the incident had taken place, with a strange feeling that someone was in the room, although nobody else was seen.

(**Source:** Contact UK, Bristol/*UFOLOG*)

4th March 1969 – Bright orange object over Staffordshire

At 9.10pm a bright orange object, resembling a 'disc, on-edge', was seen stationary in the sky over Leek, in Staffordshire

By 10.15pm, it had gone from view.

(**Source:** John 'Dennis' Llewellyn)

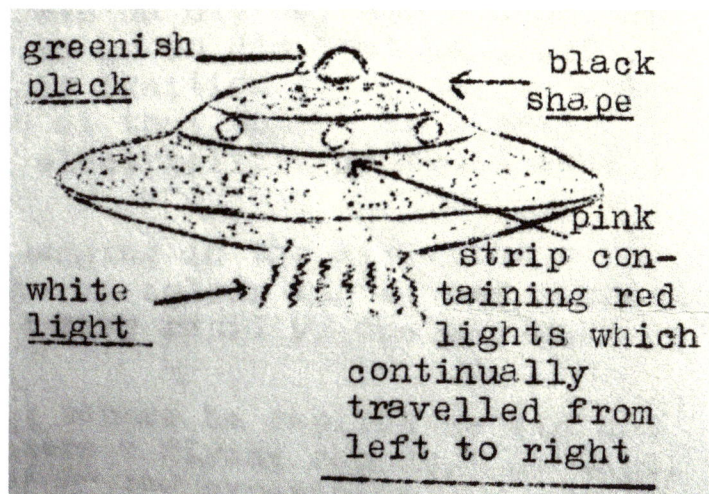

6th March 1969 – UFO over Gloucestershire

In the late evening, a young couple was travelling in a car towards Uley, in Gloucestershire, when they noticed:

"...a strange cluster of lights in the sky. We stopped the car and saw an object with a glowing orange top, and several smaller lights evenly spaced around it; after hovering for a while over Cam Long Down, it suddenly shot off at great speed towards Wiltshire, changing altitude frequently, as if manoeuvring around the surrounding hills".

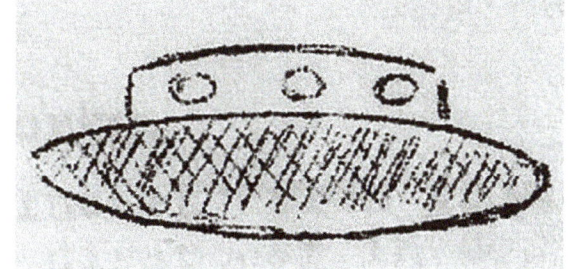

7th March 1969 – Green UFO over Gloucestershire

A green fluorescent object, showing two 'tails of light', was seen passing slowly through the sky over Dursley, Gloucestershire, at approximately 9.45pm, by a group of people, including a Methodist lay preacher, his son, brother-in-law, and two small boys. (**Source:** *UFOLOG*/Contact UK, Bristol)

23rd March 1969 – Charles Bowen writes to Frank Marshall

FLYING SAUCER REVIEW
A FLYING SAUCER SERVICE LIMITED PUBLICATION

Editorial
21 Cecil Court,
Charing Cross Road,
London, W.C.2. England
Subscriptions:
49a Kings Grove,
London, S.E.15.
Telephone:
NEW Cross 0784

19th March 1969

F.E. Marshall, Esq.,
8 Reap Lane,
Weston,
Portland,
Dorset.

Dear Mr. Marshall,

Thank you for your letter of 27th February, and for the newspaper cutting. I had, in fact, been holding the case of the three stopped cars as a possible item in a half-planned special issue concentrating on British sightings. I had no intention of overlooking the case. Recently, however, I have heard something from a source which I consider reliable which casts a tinge of doubt on the story. This was that the witness in question had in fact been showing an interest in EM effect cases prior to the alleged incident. Perhaps you could shed some light on this.

Thirty-two pages, six times a year, is not an adequate vehicle for the volume of material we are now receiving. The task of an editor of a journal like ours is to balance the material in his publication between reports, investigations, hypotheses, technical matters, historical cases and peripheral topics so that the whole is a readable document which holds the interest of people whose tastes are widely different. You may not like the 1897 case, but there are thousands of readers who do, including Dr. J. Allen Hynek. As for <u>BUFORA</u> Journal and <u>Spacelink</u>, just look through our issues and see what we have carried that they have not.

Just one more point. I'm glad you have got your indignation off your chest, but put yourself in my position. Lots of bits and pieces all to be gathered together, all to be written up (believe you me, I'm <u>very</u> glad when investigator send in completed articles of cases), all in my spare time from a normal nine-to-five job; at the same time I am involved in lectures, books, and heaven knows what else. So please be patient.

Yours sincerely,

Charles Bowen
Editor.

Directors: C. A. Bowen (Editor)   G. W. Creighton   D. D. Dempster   C. H. Gibbs-Smith   The Hon. Brinsley le Poer Trench   R. H. B. Winder

28th March 1969 – UFO over Lincoln Air Base

At 2.35am, Saxilby night shift worker – John Horton, was on his way to work when he saw what he took to be a 'Vulcan' bomber on its final approach to RAF Scampton Airbase, but then realised, as the base was in darkness, that it could not have been an aircraft.

> *"The lights were pulsating in a manner that reminded me of radiation, glowing from dim to bright. I watched it for about 30 seconds, able to obtain a clear view of a saucer-shaped object before it climbed away, towards the north, at a rate of speed, disappearing from view in one minute. It was like nothing I had ever seen before in my life. It shook me up. I had butterflies in my stomach, remindful of when the air raid sirens went off in the Second World War, and a feeling of misapprehension that has persisted ever since."* **(Source: Richard Thompson, South Lincolnshire UFO Study Group)**

29th March 1969 – UFO sighted over Hampshire

At 8.05pm, a 'bright light' was seen in the sky over Titchfield, Hampshire, by a number of people. Through binoculars a circular object, showing red lights around its perimeter and yellow lights in the centre, could be made out. By 8.50pm it had faded from view.

30th March 1969 – Strange sounds, Coventry

A terrified householder, living in Cross Road, Foleshill, Coventry, contacted the police, who were unable to offer an explanation for an incident later brought to the attention of Bob Tibbitts and Gary Ashby, of the Coventry UFO Research Group, who met up with the resident – Mrs P. Hughes.

> *"We had been out visiting friends and went to bed feeling tired. My husband dropped off to sleep straightaway. I lay there quite comfortable, looking at the drawn curtains, when I became aware of a high-pitched whirling sound – so loud I had to keep moving my head and mouth to correct my fast deafening ears. It increased in volume, as if coming closer. I felt myself perspiring heavily, with a prickling sensation on the back of my neck. A strange pale pink light then entered the bedroom from the top of the curtain, flooding the room with light. I wanted to get out of bed and have a look, but found myself unable to move. As the light and noise began to diminish, I managed to wake up my husband – Peter, who confirmed he could hear the noise, already now fading away."*

Out of character

Over the next few days, Mrs Hughes developed a slight earache and, out of character, an enormous appetite. One may be inclined to believe the witness had suffered a nightmare, if it wasn't for the startling discovery that a number of other people, living in the same street, had also suffered similar experiences, involving a feeling of being paralysed after a 'light' lit-up the bedroom, and unable to eat for a number of days.

'SAUCER' OVER CITY, SAY WOMEN

Evening Telegraph Reporter

TWO COVENTRY women believe there may have been a flying saucer over the city during the weekend, after they were woken by an "unearthly" high-pitched whining accompanied by a glowing light.

"I have been over all the possibilities and that is the only explanation I can think of," said 28-year-old Mrs. Patricia Hughes of 109, Cross Road, Foleshill.

"I heard a shrill, shrieking sound which grew in intensity and as it reached its peak the room was filled with a pink light," she said.

Her friend, Mrs. Maureen Iarrobino, also aged 28, of 96, Cross Road, was awakened by exactly the same noise, but she thought the light was red rather than pink.

"It only lasted about ten seconds, but I was really frightened, and my friend spent most of the night awake she was so upset," said Mrs. Hughes.

31 MAR 1969

Bob and Gary felt (quite rightly) there was no evidence, contrary to contemporary newspaper reports, that a 'Flying Saucer' was responsible for the sightings and effects sustained by the women concerned, although we could not help wondering if there was any connection with what happened to Mr Harry Marlow, in the previous year. **(Source: Bob Tibbitts)**

At 8.38pm, John Piper – a reporter for the *Angler's Mail* – was out fishing on the coast, twenty miles from Southampton, when he sighted:

> "...a pear-shaped, glowing object, approximately a couple of hundred yards away, with a jagged tail of white fire streaming from its rear, a hundred yards or more, pass through the sky and disappear over nearby cliffs".

Upon his arrival home, he switched-on the TV and learnt from a *Southern TV* broadcast that a number of people, living in the Southampton area, had reported seeing a glowing red, football-sized, object pass through the sky.

During the same evening, a mysterious red and white object was seen shooting across the sky over Leicestershire, by several people, including Melbourne Road resident – Rodney Bishop.

> "I first saw it at 8.30pm, as a huge 'ball' of mingled red and white colours, travelling high in the sky, leaving a bright trail behind it." **(Source: *Leicester Mercury*, 4.4.1969)**

APRIL 1969

4th April 1969 – Landed UFO, Leicester

At 10.45pm, Mr and Mrs E. Neale of Thurlaston, Leicester, had just got into bed when they noticed a pulsating 'white light' moving up and down, low down in the sky.

> "We thought this was peculiar and went to the window. On looking out, we saw a stationary bright 'pillar-box red', dome-shaped object, slightly taller than broad, apparently on the ground, 2-300 yards away. We carried on watching the 'white light' and the object on the ground when, to our astonishment, the red object rose upwards into the sky, heading towards the south-east, now looking like an elongated triangle – the smaller triangle ahead, followed by the 'white light'."

(Source: Stratford-on-Avon UFO Group)

5th April 1969 – Massive cigar-shaped UFO seen

At 6.30am, a greengrocer – John Twist from Banks, Southport – was driving towards Tarleton with his wife, Jean, and son Tony, to pick up some deliveries, when they noticed an object in the sky. He said:

> "At one angle it looked like a massive cigar. I've never seen anything like it before in my life."

The sighting was later explained away by Preston Control Centre as, *"possibly being the sun's refection on a dark cloud"*. **(Source: DIGAP/*Manchester Evening News*, 5.4.1969 – 'Supersonic cigar riddle')**

At 12.40pm, a silver object was seen in the sky over Chorlton-cum-Hardy. **(Source: DIGAP)**

Andover UFO Group

The Andover UFO Group, run by Valerie Combes and her husband, aided by Chairman John Ledner (who was to later become involved with the running of the Bournemouth-based group, run by Leslie Harris), told of being contacted by Steven Tidy of Stockbridge, Hampshire.

He told them he was travelling from Stockbridge to Andover, at Red Rice, at 10.30pm on 5th April 1969.

> "I noticed an abnormally large 'red star' in the sky, which dropped downwards and divided into two bright red ruby coloured parts. These moved at right angles, forming a 'W' in the sky, before stopping in mid-air – then moving away at high speed, vertically, into the sky. At this point, our car went past an avenue of trees. When we had cleared them, I looked around – there was nothing to be seen."

9th April 1969 – Star shaped object over Yorkshire

At 8.39pm, a pale yellow star-shaped object was sighted in the sky over Halifax, Yorkshire, by Mr P. Davidson, from Kings Cross, and a friend, before being lost from view as it dropped over the horizon.
(Source: Halifax Branch, BUFORA)

12th April 1969 – UFO landing, Bridgnorth ... Alien beings seen

A retired schoolmistress, living a few miles from Bridgnorth, in Shropshire, was exercising her dog – Stanley, a short distance from the house. She picked up a stick and threw it over a nearby hedge. The dog ran after it but came straight back, yelping, and clearly distressed. Thinking someone had thrown something at the dog, the woman barged through a narrow gap in the fence. Her annoyance changed to excitement, then fear, when she saw the amazing sight of an object resembling a spinning top in appearance, with three legs, around which stood three 'figures', bending down, picking something up from the ground and placing whatever it was into an object that looked like a large mirror, situated beneath or close to the front of the 'craft' – which she estimated to be approximately the length of two cars.

Fearing for her safety, the woman ran back to the house with the dog and, after a sleepless night, packed her suitcase and went to stay with friends, in London, for a few days.

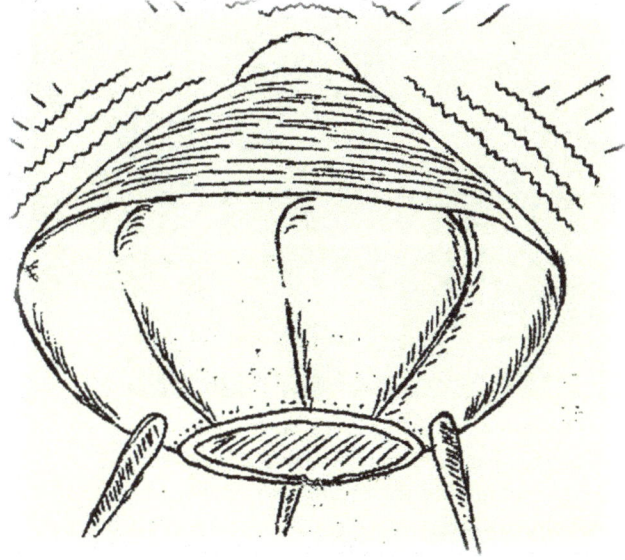

Following her arrival back home, she contacted Derek Samson – an investigator for NICAP, living in Shirley, Solihull, in the West Midlands – and told him what had happened. Derek decided to pay her a visit and arrived at the house, two weeks after the incident.

"I found her to be a charming, capable lady, who took me to where it had happened, 25 yards away from a group of trees. I searched the area and found no definitive landing marks, although I did discover three small holes, each having a circumference of seven inches, to a depth of five inches. The distance between each hole was three, four, and five yards, in a triangular shape. If these were made by the landing legs of a craft, then the vehicle was very light. I took some soil samples – (nothing untoward was found). After more thorough investigation, I was convinced an area of some several feet in diameter had been used, or trodden down. This area seemed devoid of the longer blades of grass and plant life. When viewed from a short distance away could be seen as a little clearing."

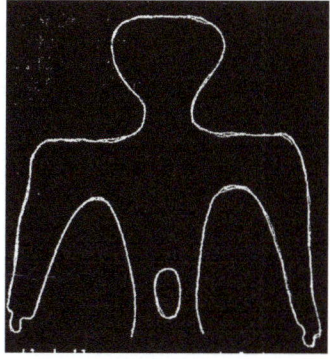

We spoke to Derek about this incident, hoping to discover where this had happened and, possibly, obtain details of the witness. Unfortunately, owing to his deteriorating health, Derek was unable to assist further – although he saw no reason to treat this woman's extraordinary account as being anything other than genuine.

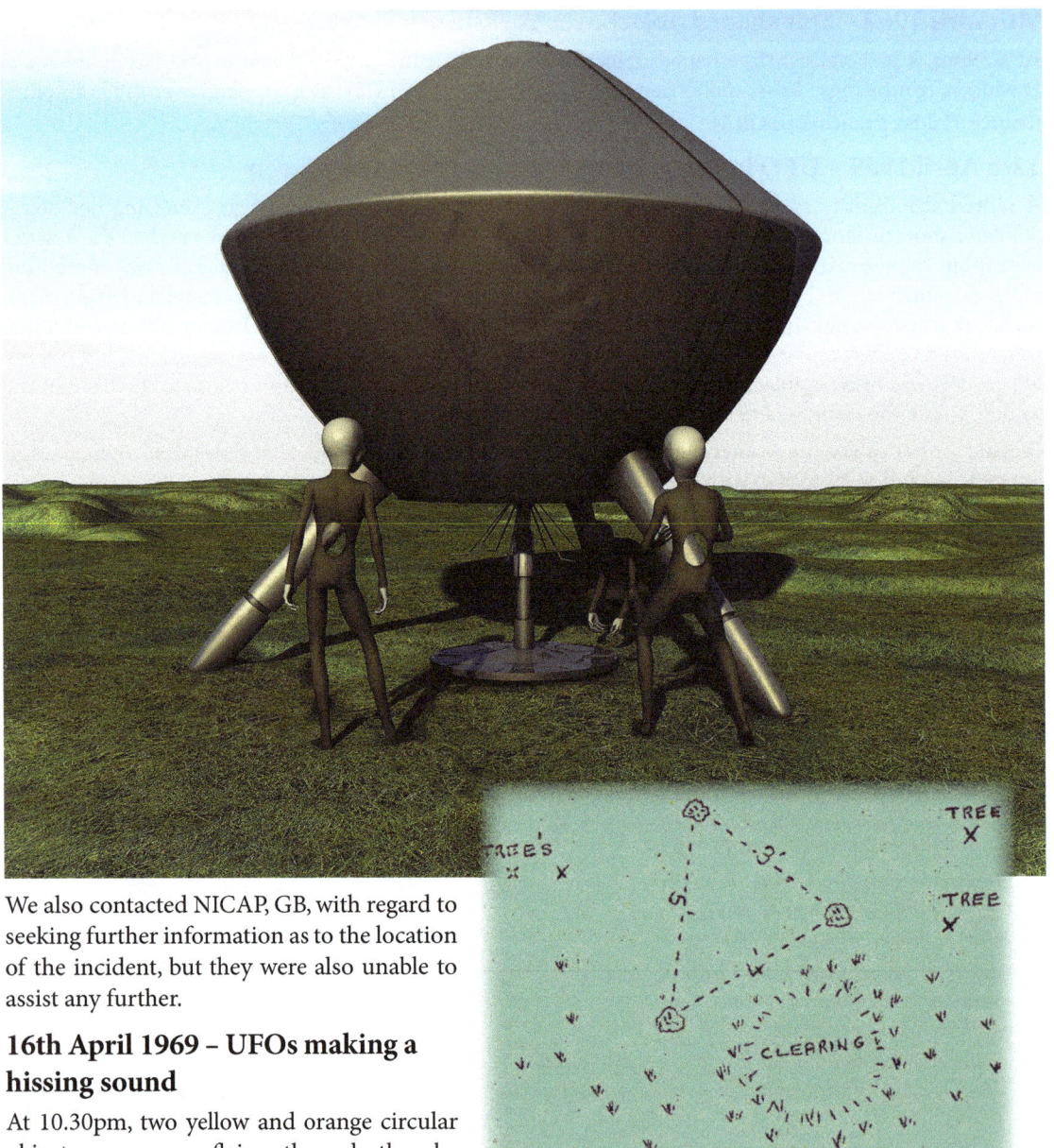

We also contacted NICAP, GB, with regard to seeking further information as to the location of the incident, but they were also unable to assist any further.

16th April 1969 – UFOs making a hissing sound

At 10.30pm, two yellow and orange circular objects were seen flying through the sky over Thurmaston, Leicestershire, by Mr and Mrs D. Belcher. As they passed overhead, a hissing sound could be heard. The incident was brought to the attention of RAF Cottesmore, who promised that an investigation would be made into the matter. **(Source: NICAP, GB)**

20th April 1969 – Egg-shaped UFO over Yorkshire

At 4.30am, a bright egg-shaped object was seen hovering in the sky over Halifax, Yorkshire, next to a smaller object, before eventually moving slowly away and out of sight. **(Source: *UFOLOG*/BUFORA)**

24th April 1969 – 'Flying Saucer' paces car, Sheffield

At 3am – a clear moonlit night – a couple was driving home, after having been to a wedding reception. As they passed through the small village of Whiston, they noticed an unusual orange light in the sky, and began to slow down to get a closer look. At approximately 40 degrees elevation, they saw:

"...*a fluorescent orange 'saucer' with fuzzy edges, with smoke and sparks coming from its underside*".

The man wanted to stop, but his wife (now terrified) urged him to continue on their journey. As they drove on, they realised the object was apparently following them – which proved to be the case, as it appeared in front of them after negotiating bends in the road.

As they neared their home at Dinnington, it suddenly shot off upwards into the sky, at fantastic speed – never to be seen again. (**Source:** *UFOLOG*)

25th April 1969 – Fireball over England

The switchboards of the emergency services and newspapers were swamped with calls from the public all over the country, after reports of a 'ball of fire', 'shining flying saucer', or 'green rocket-shaped object', followed by an 'orange flame', were sighted flying across the blue sky.

The Royal Ulster Constabulary, in Belfast, confirmed this had been a meteorite, after fearing, initially, that the loud bangs and flashing green lights in the sky was the work of terrorists, blowing up the water pipelines. Other explanations included a Russian satellite – *Cosmos 265* – burning up and fragmenting into the atmosphere.

At the Welsh village of Rowen, in the Conwy Valley, fire engines raced to the Parish Church, after an object crashed to the ground in flames from the sky.

(**Source:** *Daily Telegraph*, 26.4.1969 – 'Sky fireball scare jams switchboards'/Isle of Wight UFO Society)

Surrey

At 9pm, a mysterious object, looking like a 'steely moon', was seen over Fetcham, in Surrey, by a housewife, who thought it was the moon – until she realised it was still in the sky and much higher up. When she returned to the area, an hour later, the object – bright enough to make the street lamps look dim with its brilliance – had gone. (**Source:** SIGAP)

Newcastle-on-Tyne

At 9.20pm, Miss. J. Counsell from Gosforth, Newcastle-on-Tyne, was out walking when she saw:

"...*a 'disc'-shaped object, green in colour, with fuzzy edges, leaving a trail of green light behind as it headed in a south to north direction. Twenty seconds later, it had gone.*"

She was not the only one. At 10pm, a man and his wife were driving towards Sherburn village, in County Durham, when, through the windscreen of their car, they saw:

"...*what appeared to be a large bird – dark grey in colour, with wings outstretched – motionless in the sky, unsupported by anything like trees or wires, as it was in a clearing; it was more like an owl, but it never moved at all. My wife continued to watch it through the rear window as we resumed our journey. The whole thing was very uncanny*". (**Source:** TUFOS)

26th April 1969 – Orange 'ball' sighted

At 9.24pm, a bright orange 'ball' was seen travelling at considerable speed across the sky over Birstall, Leeds, heading in a north-east direction, by Mr and Mrs W.J. Newsome.

27th April 1969 – Pulsating object over London

At 8.30pm, a large 'bright light', with a slowly pulsating centre, was seen in the sky over London, by a man awaiting a taxi; ten seconds later, it vanished from sight. (**Source:** BUFORA)

30th April 1969 – Air Marshall Sir Victor Goddard speaks at Contact UK meeting in London

"I'll Tell Flying Saucer Secrets Says Air Chief 30 April 1969. London"

Evening News Reporter

Air-Marshal Sir Victor Goddard whose true-life air drama, The Night My Number Came Up, became a classic film, is to tell "some secrets" about Unidentified Flying Objects on Saturday.

After 23 years investigating flying saucers, Sir Victor has promised to uncover "certain unrevealed aspects" to a meeting of Contact, the International Society of UFO followers.

Members of the society believe Sir Victor will reveal information he learned when he was in Washington for the RAF in the mid-40s—when the U.S. Air Force first began investigating reports of flying saucers.

Sir Victor, who retired from the RAF in 1951, said at his Brasted, Kent, home: "I think people have been misled over this subject.

"My lecture will be the result of my own thoughts and investigations. It shows I believe in the phenomenon."

Did he really learn something in 1946 which has never been made public?

"There was something which did not come to light. Beyond that I am not prepared to say any more at this stage. It is for the people at the meeting to hear the story first."

The Hon. Brinsley Le Poer Trench, International Chairman of Contact, said: "For UFO believers it will be a wonderful and unique moment.

"I am sure Sir Victor will be able to throw some new light on the whole question. But it would be wrong of me to say how."

The meeting is at Caxton Hall beginning at 7.30 p.m. "The hall takes 400 but I expect a full house and now feel we should have booked a larger hall," said Mr. Le Poer Trench.

Sir Victor was chief of the Royal New Zealand Air Force and principal of the College of Aeronautics.

Sir Victor was at a party in Shanghai just after the war before flying to Tokio. He overheard a guest say: "This party was meant for Air Marshal Goddard — but he was killed in a plane crash."

The guest described the plane, the crew and the passengers—two men and a woman—in detail. "The plane iced up in heavy mists and snowstorms and crash landed on a pebbled beach somewhere in China or Japan," said the guest.

"That's all right then," said Sir Victor. "I'm flying in a Dakota and to Tokio, but there won't be any passengers."

But by the end of the evening Sir Victor had been persuaded to take passengers—two men and a woman. The plane did ice up and was forced to crash land on a pebbled beach by mountains described by the party guest. But despite the aircraft being smashed to pieces, no one was killed.

The story became the basis for the film, The Night My Number Came Up. see cluster

Air Marshal Sir Victor Goddard

MAY 1969

2nd May 1969 – UFO landing, Exmouth

Bread rounds man – Michael Sparkes, was delivering in Hamilton Lane, Exmouth, when he saw a green coloured object, heading low over the nearby river estuary, before striking a piece of waste ground about a hundred yards away. When he arrived at the spot, he saw what he took to be a meteorite – about the size of a grapefruit – which he described as:

Photo: Edward Lucas, of Exmouth

"...exactly round, ash colour, with little brown streaks running through and a dark-grey inside; I didn't dare touch it, because it might have been radioactive".

When Michael returned to the same place, later that day, he saw two men, dressed in white smocks, carrying what looked like a Geiger counter and mine detector. They were removing the 'meteorite' to a dirty grey van, parked at the side of the road, fitted with some unusual aerials. He asked them who they were. They declined to tell him!

According to the *Exmouth Journal* (3rd May, 1969) who covered this story ('Was ball of green light from Outer Space?'), some of the minutely honeycomb chippings (almost white in colour) recovered from the object, with the exception of a few (showing light-brown markings), were forwarded to Mr Howard Miles – Director of Artificial Satellite Section of the British Astronomical Research Association – who told the reporter:

"The pieces you describe bear no resemblance to anything I have come across before and do not sound as if it has any connection with a large meteorite which crossed Northern Ireland, the previous evening."

Letters sent to the British Astronomical Research Association, in 2008, asking for any further information on the 'artifact', remain unanswered.

12th May 1969 – Glowing objects, Hampshire

A glowing 'ball of light' was seen in the sky over Yateley, and the surrounding district of Hampshire. It was described as looking like a white saucepan, without a handle, hovering just above some trees. Another witness told of seeing a fluorescent 'white light' cross the sky – much bigger than a star – which suddenly shot off at speed, shrinking in size to that of a pinhead. **(Source: *UFOLOG*)**

13th May 1969 – Strange 'lights' in the sky

At 2.25am, two night shift workers were standing outside the factory, near Devizes taking a break, when a star-like object was seen travelling towards them in the night sky. They described it as increasing in brightness as it moved closer. When about a half-a-mile away, it stopped still – then began to move up and down, looking like a series of headlights, or floodlights, 150 feet above the ground.

A few seconds later it turned, silhouetting the trees with a yellow glow, before accelerating away. **(Source: *UFOLOG*)**

An even stranger story came from a Surrey housewife, who was awoken by the sound of her Bull Terrier wanting to go outside. On going into the kitchen, she was surprised to see a 'beam of white light', six inches wide, shining onto the floor – like a searchlight.

"I looked through the window and noticed a red 'ball of light' in the sky nearby. I tried in vain to rouse my 17 year-old son, and then let the dog outside. Almost immediately, it ran back in and jumped onto the table, keeping its gaze on the red 'ball of light' – clearly frightened. The 'red light' then headed off towards the direction of Blackwater." **(Source: DIGAP)**

14th May 1969 – UFO over Kent

At 10.12pm, a large star-like object was seen in heavy overcast conditions in the sky over Culverstone, in Kent, by a motorist; the man said the sighting was accompanied by the sound of a large Jet.
(Source: *UFOLOG*)

24th May 1969 – Orange UFO over Cumbria

A large orange object appeared in the sky over Keswick, Cumbria, in front of a motorist and his four passengers, before halting in mid-air. The motorist stopped, and he and the passengers got of the car.

"After a few minutes it appeared to move back along the route it had taken, and we commenced our journey. To our surprise, as we neared the Cockermouth area, it appeared again and headed towards us, hovered, and stopped again. Several minutes later, it finally moved away."

(Source: *West Cumberland Times*, 31.5.1969)

May 1969 – UFO display, Devon

Joyce Prior (now passed away) wrote to us about what she and her family had witnessed, while travelling to Devon in May 1969.

> "We pulled off the road, deciding to take a break in the journey at Meare, near Glastonbury. We were settling down for the night, when my husband drew my attention to six or seven 'lights', moving horizontally in the sky. Within seconds they formed a circle, then a triangle, before commencing what we can only refer to as a fantastic display, rushing all over the sky – like nothing we had ever seen before in our lives."

Listening to this account, one is reminded of what appears to be an identical phenomenon reported at Hartcliffe, near Bristol, Harston Hill, Cambridge, Harborne Golf Course, Birmingham, Ullenhall, Warwickshire, and many others, involving displays of UFO behaviour. For what purpose we can only guess, but hardly likely for our entertainment!

JUNE 1969

5th June 1969 – 'lights' over Enfield

An object was seen moving through the sky over Enfield, Middlesex, between 10.05pm and 11.10pm, by Mr L.R. Staines, who wrote to Kath Smith (of the Isle of Wight UFO Society) about the matter.

> "I first put it down as a red star with a green light, moving north-east. A short time later it appeared again, low down in the sky towards the east – now green, slightly longer than its width, followed by a red flashing light. Suddenly it appeared as five distinct red lights, changed direction, and was gone from sight."

12th June 1969 – Police sight UFO

UFO RIDDLE OF A LIGHT IN THE SKY

S. MIRROR JUNE 15 1969

CONSTABLE Sydney Edwards stood by his police car watching a mysterious light moving across the night sky.

Calmly, he reported over his radio: "It's bright and pulsating—travelling north. It is flickering like a star."

Then PC Edwards shouted excitedly: "It's stopped... and vanished."

So another "sighting" was added to the growing list of U F Os — unidentified flying objects — that are baffling scientists throughout the world.

The drama began at 1.30 a.m. on Thursday when retired police inspector Alan Machin went into his garden in Farrington-road, Winwick, near Warrington, to check that his greenhouse was locked. He glanced up and saw the light "travelling slowly across the sky, I reckon about 1,500 ft. up, with a jerky movement. It was bright and white with no shape at all—just like a big star."

Listening

Mr. Machin, 51, called his wife and then telephoned Warrington police.

P C Michael Conduct, 21, was in the Orford area of Warrington when he spotted the light while listening to PC Edwards' radio description.

He, too, is baffled: "I've never seen anything like this before and can't offer any explanation."

Air Traffic Control centres at Ringway, Manchester and Preston are equally baffled. The only aircraft flying in their territory was as far away as Lichfield, Staffs.

Was God an astronaut?— Page Ten.

15th June 1969 – Silver 'disc' over Birkenhead

On 15th June 1969, security officer Neil Piper was patrolling along Noctorum Lane, Birkenhead, with Tex his guard dog, when he heard a swishing sound – like a generator humming. Looking upwards, he was astonished to see a glowing silver 'disc' heading from the direction of Woodchurch housing estate, towards Moreton. The dog, clearly frightened, began to yelp in distress.

(Source: *Liverpool Echo,* **16.6.1969 – 'UFO shock for Tex and his master'**)

18th June 1969 – Smoke ring with three 'lumps', photographed at Birmingham

At 9.10pm, a photographer – Mr Carl Robbins of Iris Grove, Chelmsley Wood – was driving along Charles Road, Bordesley Green, near Birmingham.

> "A huge ring of smoke came into view ahead of me. It was almost a perfect circle, at times, but distorted slightly in the breeze as it rolled slowly over the sky – like a large rubber band. At a very rough estimate, I would say that it was 50 feet in diameter. It appeared as a thick ring of black oily smoke, having some sort of inner core around which it was burning. There were three equally spaced 'lumps' around the ring, which appeared to be burning a little more fiercely than the rest. After about five minutes, the smoke started to burn away form one of these 'lumps' in each direction towards the next – then the smoke between these last two 'lumps' burned away, leaving a thin ring of what appeared to be smoke or gas. It reminded me of some sort of fuse burning down. The thin ring remained for another three or four minutes, with smoke still lingering around the three 'lumps'. Then the whole lot faded away."

The *Birmingham Post* published two photos, taken within a few minutes of each other, together with a quote from Professor John Fremlin of The Applied Radioactivity Centre, at Birmingham University, who said:

> "It was difficult to establish what it had been, apart from pranks".

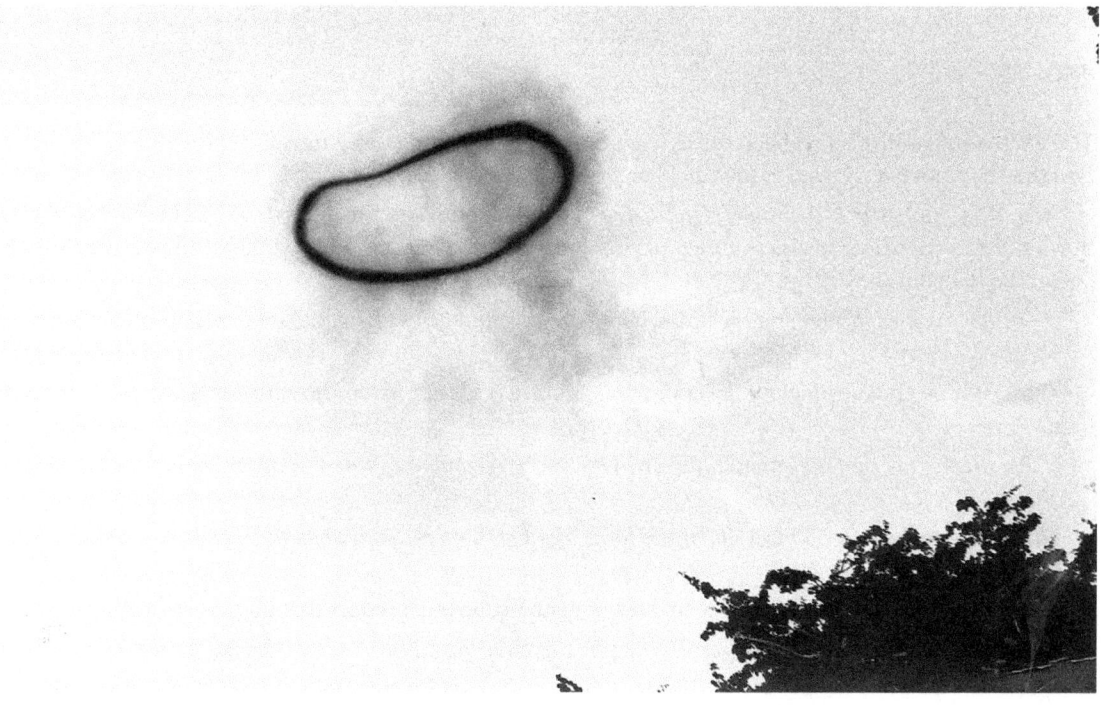

There was a suggestion it had been caused by a fire, but the Birmingham Fire Service told the *Birmingham Post* they had not been called to any incidents in that road on that morning.

On the 20th June 1969, the *Birmingham Evening Mail* published a letter from Rebecca Harvey, of Bordesley Green, who explained it away as being caused by children, throwing petrol or paraffin onto one of the fires on a refuse tip.

> *"There was an explosion and big mushroom of smoke and bright flames. As the smoke went higher, it developed into a thick black ring."*

On the 21st June, the *Birmingham Evening Mail* published a letter from Mr Ashby of Ward End, Birmingham.

> *"The smoke ring that appeared in the sky was observed from my garden as descending from a great height, at a fairly rapid rate.*
>
> *It disappeared about 500 feet up, in the form of a black smoke similar to that emitted from diesel engine vehicles."*

A police spokesman, at Bordesley Green, said they had received a report that it was

> *"...a gaggle of Canadian black geese, flying in a circular formation".*

(Source: Bob Tibbitts/*Birmingham Post*, 19/20.6.1969/*Birmingham Evening Mail*, 21.6.1969/John D. Llewellyn)

19th June 1969 – Mushroom-shaped UFO over West Newton, Norfolk

Mr. Robin Peck, of Docking, who saw a U.F.O. in the early hours of this morning over Bircham. "It was a terrifying experience," he said.

At 12.25am, Robin Peck – an electronics engineer by profession (then 23 years of age) – was on his way home from King's Lynn to Docking, when the light on the van he was driving began to fail, followed by the engine cutting out. Robin got out and looked under the bonnet, when he became aware of the air around him being full of static – powerful enough to make his hair stand on end.

Glancing around him, he saw an object resembling an inverted mushroom – pale blue in colour, surrounded by orange light – motionless in the sky, about 150 feet off the ground, about a quarter-of-a-mile away. A minute or two later it took off, heading towards the direction of King's Lynn. Mr Peck got back into the van and smoked a cigarette to calm his nerves. When he tried the starter knob, linking a cable from the solenoid to the battery, the engine burst into life.

Mr Peck discussed the incident with a colleague, the following morning, and subsequently made a full statement to the police, who then contacted the Press. A spokesman, at RAF West Raynham, said:

"There was no flying from the base last night. We don't fly UFOs from here!"

Mr Peck then took reporters to the location and pointed to a group of trees at the farm of Mr Harry Bennion, where he said the UFO had been seen.

As a result of the sighting being made public, he was visited by a number of UFO researchers, including BUFORA representative, ex Second World War RAF radar operator – Peter F. Johnson from Sheringham, Norfolk, who was involved in many UFO investigations around the East Coast. Peter worked for the Anglia Water Board for over 40 years, until retiring in 1977, and was a BUFORA regional Coordinator for five years, until passing away in August 1988, leaving a wife, Rachel, and young son.

Peter F. Johnson

Museum that never was to be

This knowledgeable man had, over the years, amassed a huge amount of information, which he hoped would form the foundation of a museum at the house, so that people could see for themselves, the work carried out by him and others. Sadly, this was not to be.

(Source: *Flying Saucer Review* Case Histories Supplement, 5.6.1971 – 'Auto stop near Docking'/Peter Johnson/ Ivan W. Bunn, *'The Lantern'* series/*Eastern Evening News*, 19.6.1969 – 'Flying mushroom mystery')

20th June 1969 – 'Chinese lantern' in the sky

An elderly woman living in Bridport, Dorset, saw what looked like a Chinese lantern hanging in the sky, below heavy cloud, near the Portland coast. Later, the same morning, two objects – described as 'flare like' – were seen hovering over Chew Magna, Somerset, by the unnamed crew of a police car.

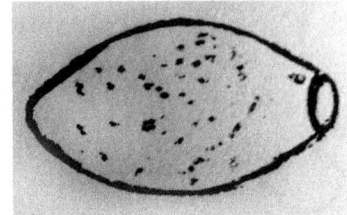

(Source: South-west Unidentified Aerial Phenomena Investigation Group)

21st June 1969 – Cigar-shaped object hovering above trees at Ayrshire

A taxi driver was travelling home along Shewalton Road, Irvine, Ayrshire, when he saw what he took to be a clump of trees on fire. As he approached closer, he was astounded to see a cigar-shaped object, apparently on fire, hovering above the trees. Suddenly, it shot upwards into the night sky and disappeared from view, leaving him very frightened.

25th June 1969 – Triangular shaped UFO

At 12.30am, an orange/gold coloured, triangular-shaped, object was sighted over Southowram, near Halifax, by Miss A. Conway, who watched it for five minutes – until lost from view.

(Source: BUFORA, Halifax)

26th June 1969 – Orange 'Flying Saucer' Hants

During the early hours, Mrs Neill of Christchurch, Hampshire, sighted:

> "...a brilliant orange 'light' – flying low and rising in the sky, resembling a 'flying saucer' – visible for half-an-hour, until it disappeared into a cloud."

(Source: *Bournemouth Evening Echo*, 26.6.1969)

29th June 1969 – 'Full Moon' over Bristol

At 10.50pm, five people from the Bristol area, living in separate parts of the City, sighted an object looking like a full moon – electric-blue in colour – which was seen to disappear abruptly, as if 'switched off'.

'Flying Saucer' over Nuneaton

At 11.47pm, Mr Jack Cook from Jodrell Street, in Nuneaton – employed as a kiln firer at the Midland Brick Company, Ansley Hall – was working a hundred feet up, on the firm's chimney, when he was astonished to see an object, resembling:

> "...an oval 'butter dish' with a bright yellow top, showing dark vertical lines running down the side of the craft's exterior vivid green base, and smoke or steam pouring out from the underside, making a noise like the 'hiss' from a boiler valve being released, flying low over the brickyard at an estimated speed of between 4-500 miles per hour. I was very frightened but drew what I had seen on a matchbox. I showed it to my mates, but they didn't believe me."

Jack was not the only one to see it. His sighting was corroborated by at least four other people in the Nuneaton area, including Mrs Davies of Bedworth, William Thompson from Atherstone, Mr and Mrs

Kenneth Painter, and Mr S. Caney from Bedworth, who told of seeing it cross Heath Road, heading towards the direction of Ansley.

(**Source:** *Nuneaton Evening Tribune,* 30.6.1969/2.7.1969/Geoffrey Coxon, BUFORA/Mrs Kath Smith, Isle of Wight UFO Society)

Was this the same cigar-shaped UFO seen resting in a field at Frome, in Somerset, by a Bristol lorry driver, the following day (30th June 1969), who told of watching it start to spin and rise upwards, and move away towards the direction of Bristol? (**Source:** *Zenith* Newsletter/*UFOLOG*)

```
                          U.F.O. REPORT

Name:  John H. Cook                    Age:  61 years.
Address:  28 Jodrell Street, Nuneaton, Warwickshire.
Occupation:  Kiln Burner.
Date:  June 1969 (On a sunday).
Time:  11:47 P.M.                      Duration:  2 mins. approx.
Exact Location:  Object seen over Ansley brickyard, Coleshill Rd.,
                                       Nuneaton.
Reported to:  Witness has been interviewed by the Press ( Nuneaton
              Tribune) on Monday 30th. June.
Weather:  Scattered cloud and no wind.  Dry and warm.
Number of objects:  One                Colour:  Dark yellow, surrounded by
                                                green light.
Shape:  Like an oval shaped butter dish with a cover on top, with black
        vertical markings. (Approx 100 ft. up over brickyard).
Sound:  Terrific sound like steam escaping from a boiler.
Estimated speed:  Very fast - 500 m.p.h. approx.
Markings:  Vivid green lights with an orange coloured flame from the rear.
           Also clouds of white smoke.
Flight Path:   A straight line.
Physical Effects:  Very startled and worried.
Sketch:
```

[Handwritten sketch: Clouds of white smoke, orange flame, oval UFO with vertical markings and displayed green lights]

```
Further Comments:   "When the U.F.O. was passing over the brickyard two
                    cars were going along the Coleshill Road, one with
                    dark red headlights, followed by a car with bright
                    headlights.
                    When the object was over Ridge Lane two more cars
                    came  by with identical headlights (One red and
                    then one bright).
(This information was volunteered by Mr. Cook.).
```

JULY 1969

4th July 1969 – Three 'bright lights' see County Durham

Three 'bright lights' were seen in the northern sky over Darlington, during the evening, by a married couple. The wife said:

> "There was a red one, blue one, and a bright white one. They rose up into a cloud and came down again. The white one seemed to be rocking backwards and forwards, while the others flickered around it."

The sighting was explained away by a spokesman from Catterick Army Base as being aerial night-time photography. (**Source: Anglo-Polish UFORC/*UFO Chronicle*/*UFOLOG***)

12th July 1969 – Will-o'-the-wisp …?

At 2.30am, a peculiar orange 'light', with a long tail, was seen hovering several feet above the ground near Borth Bog, Cardiganshire, Wales, until 4am. Was this an example of 'Will-o'-the-wisp' – also known as Ignis Fatuus, or 'Jack-o'-lantern' – a natural phenomenon occurring when methane gas ignites, and rumoured to have lured travellers to their deaths in marshy graves? (**Source:** *UFOLOG*)

13th July 1969 – UFO display over Glastonbury

At 2.30am, night shift workers at a Glastonbury factory were smoking a cigarette by the front gate, when a round 'ball of white light' appeared in the sky over the Tor. According to witnesses:

> "…it turned a fiery red and flew around the sky in a series of complicated patterns of movement, backwards and forwards, as well as up and down, before flying out of sight".

(**Source:** *Link-Up* newsletter)

Over the years we were to come across others who had experienced strange sightings of UFOs over the Tor; a 500 feet high conical hill – an inspiring landmark, believed, by many, to have magical powers. It is sometimes referred to as 'magic mountain', 'faeries' glass hill', 'spiral castle', 'a Grail castle', 'a Druid initiation centre', 'an Arthurian hill fort', 'a magnetic power-point', 'a crossroads of leys', 'a centre for Goddess fertility rituals and celebrations' – and now, also, 'a possible converging point for UFOs'.

A Photograph taken of the area showed what appears to be a red streak of energy.

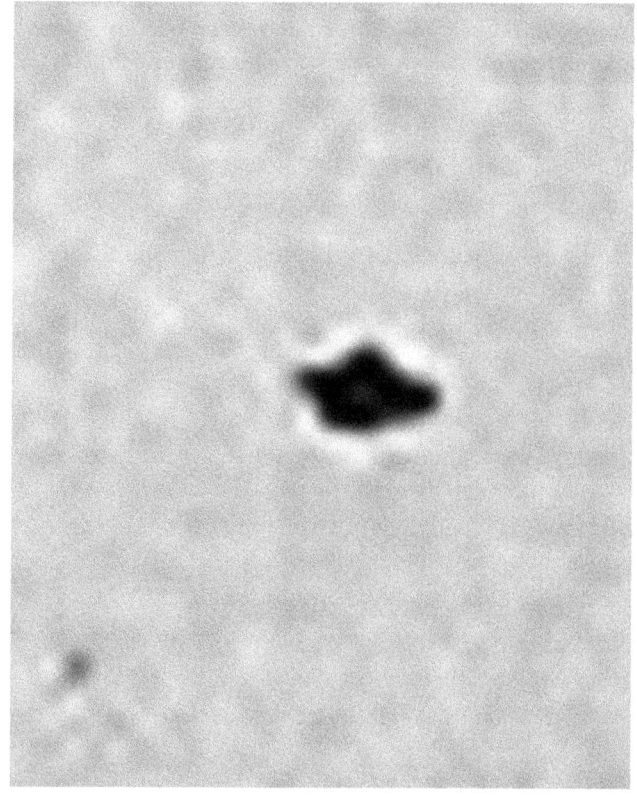

July – UFOs over Gloucestershire

Mr Harold Wilson – landlord of *The Holford Arms,* Sherston, Gloucestershire, sighted:

> "…two objects, bobbing about in the sky after closing time, about 5,000 feet high, like a couple of butterflies". **(Source: *Bristol Evening Post,* 16.7.1969)**

20th July 1969 – Silver object seen by schoolgirls

On the afternoon, schoolgirls – Jacqueline Dolley and Jennifer Johnson – were playing on the swings in the local park at Unsworth, Bury, when they saw:

> "…a small silver coloured object, moving from side-to-side in the sky, before it dropped down behind the school building".

(Source: Mr A. Tomlinson, DIGAP)

22nd July 1969 – Three 'bright lights' over Isle of Wight

At 10.30pm, Mr George Rushton from Yarmouth, Isle of Wight, who had always considered the question of the existence of UFOs to be nonsense, was in the back garden looking at the sky with his two sons, a few days after the moon landing, when they noticed:

> "…three 'bright lights' – flashing red and green – which appeared to be attached to an object of indiscernible shape".

George went into the street and stopped two young men who were passing, and showed them the object, which they took (after some conversation) to be a helicopter. Suddenly, ten or fifteen minutes later, it flashed across the sky like a rocket going off, and disappeared over the western horizon. Almost immediately, it returned to its original position in the sky – now accompanied by three similar objects.

Mr Rushton was so excited that he dashed down the street and into the local public house, where he persuaded some of the customers to go outside and have a look; unfortunately, by then, there was no sign of the UFOs. **(Source: Isle of Wight UFO Investigation Society)**

23rd July 1969 – Bedfordshire Police chase UFO

During the evening, a number of people – including Police Sergeant Martin Burgess – chased a UFO for some distance, before losing sight of it at Brickhill, Bedford.

> *"When we first saw the object, it seemed quite high up and then dropped rapidly – until it was floating a few hundred feet in the air. The 'light' was very bright, so it was impossible to gauge its size accurately, but I would say it was between six to eight feet across. It looked like it was coming down over the centre of Brickhill, but then veered off towards Manton Heights. We chased after it, but lost it amongst the houses. I don't know what we would have done if we had seen 'little green men' coming out of the thing – either breathalysed them, or run away, I suppose."* **(Source: DIGAP)**

Another witness was Mr Jack Cowan of Haylands Way. He thought it was an aircraft with its engine on fire, flying at 30,000 feet over Bromham, but lost sight of it as it entered clouds.

Somebody else who saw it was Michael Burke and Steve Bartlett, who described it as:

> "…being the shape of a rugby football, or thick 'cigar', lit by a bright orange light seen coming from the Bedford area, before stopping dead in the sky for several minutes, some 400 yards away, and then disappearing from sight at an amazing speed".

A police spokesman said no official report was made of the incident.

(Source: *The Bedford Record,* 29.7.1969 – 'UFO chased by Police patrol')

25th July 1969 – Crimson sphere over Staffordshire

At approximately 9.30pm, a bright red light with fuzzy edges was seen descending through the sky in angles from right to left, over Stone, in Staffordshire, by four boys. The boys were not the only ones to see something strange. At least six other people saw what they described as:

> "...a brilliant crimson sphere slowly descending from the sky, resembling a football – brilliant as tin foil and spinning. It was then lost from sight behind rising ground, but reappeared a couple of minutes later, straight up and levelled off, before travelling horizontally, and dropped out of sight. We noticed a light grey puff of vapour behind it – like a short aircraft condensation trail."

About twenty minutes later, a mother and daughter saw the object rise up again into the sky.
(Source: *UFOLOG/Space-link*)

North of London

On the same date, Mr Barry Snixhall from Eversholt (ten miles north of London) was on his way home on his moped, at 10.15pm, when he noticed *"a bright yellow 'light' hovering in the sky, over the Woburn Animal Kingdom"*.

He stopped near to Stumps Cross hill and watched the 'light' (from which could be heard a faint humming sound) for about five minutes, until it suddenly shot off across the sky at terrific speed.

Barry continued on his journey, but noticed that the 'light' was now apparently over Woburn Town Hall.
(Source: Personal interview)

27th July 1969 – Three 'Flying Saucers' over Hertfordshire

At 3am, three 'flying saucers' were seen hovering in the sky over the village of Willian, in Hertfordshire, by Letchworth artist – David James, and his Californian girlfriend – Dana Cousins, who were walking home along Letchworth Lane, near to the Golf Club.

Dana said later:

> *I thought it was a star, at first, but then I noticed the colouring. It was made of extremely bright silvers and gold. I've never seen such a beautiful thing. It was hovering above a tree. It started to move towards us. We panicked. Dave tried to flag a car down, but they wouldn't stop. The object then moved back up to its original position, above the tree. I looked up and saw two other similar objects in the sky, but at a much higher altitude. After a couple of hours, the three objects moved away and out of sight."*

(Source: *Hertfordshire & Bedfordshire Citizen*, 1.8.1969 – 'Three Flying Saucers')

Summer 1969 – Black Triangular UFO over West Midlands

In the summer, Philip Gwynne – a long-term resident of the Princess Estate, Tipton, West Midlands – was walking home at 10pm, one evening, as dusk was falling, when he happened to glance upwards into the sky and see:

> "...a massive, shiny black, triangular object, motionless in the sky above me, about a few thousand feet off the ground. I could see a circle in the middle, with a cross design inset. I've never seen anything like it before in my life. A short time later, it headed away and was soon out of sight."

(Source: Personal interview)

Summer 1969 – 'Doodlebug' UFO, London

Mrs Phyllis Moonie from Romford Road, Forest Gate – a shy, retiring woman, with no particular interest in the UFO subject – was to find her outlook on life irrevocably changed one day, when, while hanging out the washing, she heard a noise in the distance – like an engine, labouring. Thinking it was an aircraft in trouble, she looked upwards and saw:

> "...an object, shaped like a bomb, with a rounded wing on each side of the body – pitted like a poker, left too long in the fire. As it flew overhead, it made a horrible noise, reminding me of the 'Doodlebugs' which rained down on London, during the Second World War".

The sighting was to trigger an extreme interest in the UFO subject and lead to Phyllis contacting London-based UFO Researcher, Dan Goring – Head of the Essex UFO Group, Editor of *Earth-link* – who asked her to investigate reports of UFO activity around the Essex and London areas. Thanks to access to the *Earth-link* magazines, we were able to examine for ourselves some spectacular reports of UFO activity, which were thoroughly investigated by people such as Phyllis Moonie and Bill Eden.

(**Source: Personal interview**)

AUGUST 1969

5th August 1969 – Silver UFO over Carmarthen

Farmer John Moffat Bailey – a former RAF Radar operator, five miles from Carmarthen – was repairing his television aerial, when he sighted:

> "...a silver UFO, with a sort of undercarriage, making a peculiar whistling or buzzing noise as it hovered up and down in the sky, at a height of between 5-20,000 feet."

The object was also observed by John's wife and other relatives, including his brother-in-law – Mr Angelo Van Der Tupe, from Belgium, who was staying at the farm.

John telephoned the police at Ammanford Division of the Carmarthen and Cardigan Constabulary, who sent a motorcycle officer and confirmed the sight of the silver object – now stationary in the sky – although his identity was never disclosed.

(**Source:** *The Times,* 7.8.1969 – 'Aerial object unexplained'/Margaret Fry, Welsh Federation of Ufologists)

7th August 1969 – Silver cylindrical UFO

"A silver cylindrical object – about the size of a Jet and at the same height" – was sighted hovering in the sky, between Tunbridge Wells and Wadhurst, just after 6pm, by local commuter – Joan Fuller, from Bexhill-on-Sea, who was travelling home on the train. (**Source: Kent & Sussex Courier, 15.8.1969**)

August 1969 – Warwickshire motorist encounters UFO

John and Denise Howarth from Redditch, Worcestershire, were travelling along the B4085, towards Bidford-on-Avon, Warwickshire, at 11.30pm, in August 1969.

John Howarth told us:

> "I saw what I first took to be the moon – perfectly round, deep orange in colour, and looking like a car headlight – low down in the sky. I kept my eye on it as we drove along from my position in the front seat of the mini-van, bringing it to the attention of Denise, when I realised it was not the moon as it was apparently following us on a parallel course to our vehicle – occasionally moving forwards and backwards while in flight. Suddenly, it moved away from us. We were so relieved, but then it rushed at us – as if on a collision course. We swerved to avoid it and came off the road into a ditch. When we regained our composure and looked out across the night sky, there was nothing further to be seen." (**Source: Personal interview**)

15th August 1969 – UFO landing, Stourbridge

Over the years we heard rumours of an alleged UFO landing at a timber yard, in the Stourbridge area, but it wasn't until some years later that we spoke to the witness – Mr Ken Hughes, who told us what he saw, while working at Bateman's Wood Yard, in Union Street, during the morning.

> "I was in the office, when I saw this steely-grey coloured egg-shaped object, with a wide 'cushion'

around it, descending downwards – like a silent hovercraft, onto a high pile of wood, about 50 yards away. It hovered about 9 inches off the wood, then frighteningly, what looked like curved doors (about 5 feet high) opened, but nothing came out of the 'craft'. I estimated it to be 6 feet high, 4-5 feet long and 12 feet high. It then rose upwards and, when 20 feet in the air, disappeared."

Another workman – Ralph Attwood – also witnessed the incident. Unfortunately, he only caught a brief glimpse of the UFO before it vanished from sight.

At the end of Union Street is a hexagonal-shaped cemetery, adjoining an allotment, which seems rather bizarre ... growing food next to deceased people who may have died from all sorts of diseases?

19th August 1969 – Bright yellow UFO over Liverpool

Many people contacted the *Liverpool Daily Post*, and Airport, after sighting a bright yellow object, stationary in the sky at 8.20pm, showing orange flares around its outer edge, at an estimated height of about 1,000 feet.

One witness, who was an experienced pilot and trained in aircraft recognition, said:

"At one point it seemed to change to a cluster, with a bright yellow centre, with smaller orange lights around it. Suddenly, after 45 seconds, it vanished from sight".

(Source: Bob Tibbitts, CUFORG/*UFOLOG*, 1969)

20th August 1969 – UFO display Leicestershire

A weird flashing object was seen at 9.45pm on 20th August 1969, by student Robert Jordan, who was walking home with his girlfriend through Sileby, Leicestershire, pointing out the 'The Plough' asterism to her, when he saw what he thought to be a 'shooting star' moving fairly slowly in the sky, heading towards the City of Leicester. As it disappeared behind cloud, another one appeared in the sky.

Somebody else who saw it was Mark Fenn (then a 17 year-old apprentice) who described seeing:

"...a red and white object, wandering to and fro across the sky, in set patterns, at around 10pm".

Enquiries into the incident revealed that a Russian satellite was launched at 9.31 BST, followed by a second satellite – probably a *Cosmos* – on a parallel path to that seen by the witnesses. Could this have been what they saw? **(Source: Mr Geoffrey Coxon/*Leicester Mercury*, 21.8.1969)**

At 10.40pm the same evening, a red flashing light, with a larger green one underneath it, was seen motionless in the sky over Enfield, Middlesex, by at least four separate witnesses, who judged it to be about one hundred feet off the ground.

23rd August 1969 – UFO over Leicester

At 12.25am, Mr and Mrs Black were preparing to go to bed, when they saw what they took to be the moon through the bedroom window – but then realised this could not be the case, as it was lying on its side.

In an interview conducted with UFO Investigators – Geoffrey Coxon and Janet Gregory (now Janet Bord), of the Fortean Picture Library, the couple told of seeing *"a bright orange crescent-shaped object, with a blurred or shimmering outline – like the setting sun"*, hovering silently, low down in the sky over

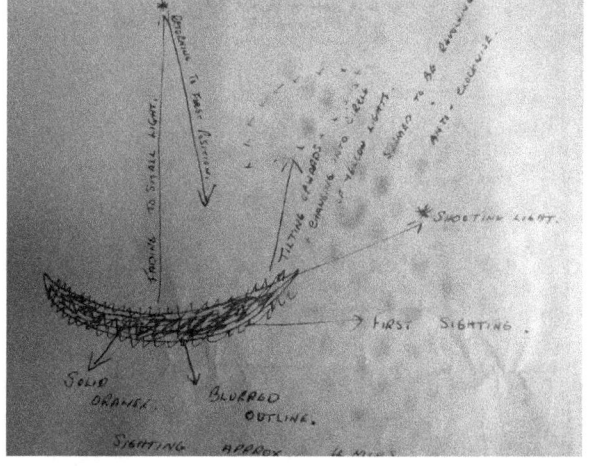

the City of Leicester, some miles away. As it moved, a 'white light' shot upwards from the side, like a 'shooting star', before reducing in size. Immediately, the object shot off into the sky – soon a tiny 'point of light' – but returned to its original position. Moments later, it tilted upwards to the right and, to the astonishment of Mr and Mrs Black, changed into a circle of 20-30 yellow lights, slowly rotating in an anticlockwise direction. At this point, Mr Black went and summoned the next door neighbour, while Mrs Black continued to watch the object, which once more travelled across the sky in a similar sequence of action as before, but now no longer visible. **(Source: Isle of Wight UFO Investigation Society)**

24th August 1969 – Triangular UFO, Nottingham

At 4.30am, a bright triangular object, changing colour in the cloudless sky towards the north-east, was seen over Mansfield, Nottingham, by Police Constable Page, who was on patrol near Mansfield Hospital.

> *"After stopping, it moved to the right and became stationary. I contacted other officers, who confirmed they could see it – now brilliant and distinct in the night sky, moving upwards. By 6am it was gone from view."*

25th August 1969 – Triangular UFO, Bolton Lancashire

Mrs Ann Unsworth, and her daughter – Carol, were looking out of their back bedroom window in Morris Green Lane, Bolton, as dusk fell.

They saw:

> *"...a huge, triangular object, surrounded by green flickering lights, with one red and two green oval lights, 'burning at the corners', hovering over nearby chimneys. It looked as if it was going to land on the nearby concourse. I will never forget those colours. I hoped it wouldn't land on our shed. It looked like it was taking flash photos of us. I wondered if it was trying to communicate. Ten seconds later, it flew away. My legs turned to jelly. I could hardly walk, never mind speak. I will never forget the look on my daughter's face as long as I live."*

(Source: *Lancashire Evening Post, 26.8.1969/Bolton Evening News,* 26.8.1969/Anthony Wiseman, BUFORA/Janet Gregory**)**

28th August 1969 – Bolton Lancashire Firemen sight UFO

Bruce Robinson was one of several firemen fighting a blaze on an estate near Raikes Lane, Bolton, which included Sub-Officer Eric Dyer.

> *"We saw an oval object, with green and red lights, flash across the sky in full view, for several seconds, and thought it was going to crash, but it then flew off towards Great Lever."*

(Source: Personal interview)

UFO over Great Yarmouth

In the same month, John Child – a pupil at Peterhouse Junior School, Gorleston, Great Yarmouth (aged 10) – was looking out over a block of flats, when he heard the sound of Jet engines.

> *"I looked around and saw what I thought was a De Havilland 'Comet' flying across the sky, leaving a vapour trail, then I noticed two peculiar objects moving northward, unlike any aircraft I had ever seen before – still as sharp in my memory, over 30 years later."* **(Source: Personal interview)**

6th September 1969 – UFO over Reading

Mrs Gloria Bomford from Abingdon, Berkshire, decided to visit her sister living in Northumberland Avenue, Reading, together with her two young daughters and mother. After arriving, Gloria and her sister stood on the balcony overlooking John Rabson Park, chatting, on what had been a warm day – the setting sun glowing through the slight evening haze.

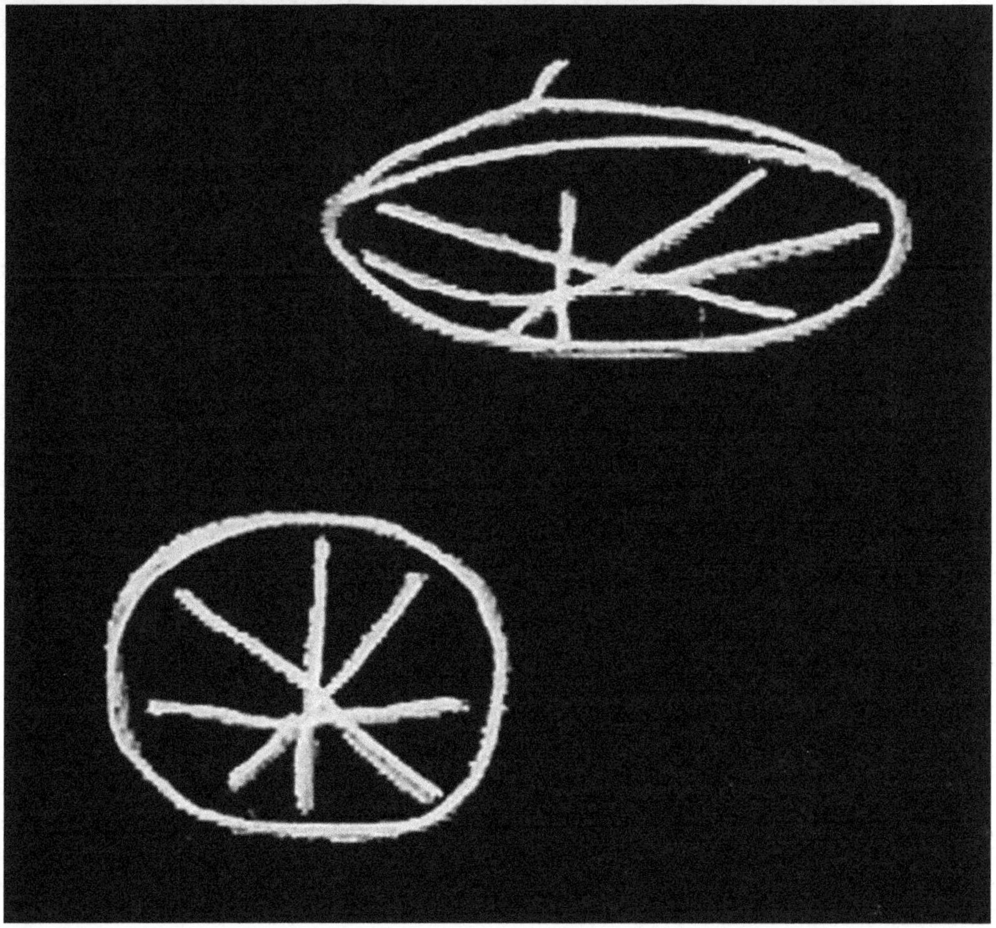

Haunted Skies Volume Two Revised

At 7pm, Gloria collected the children, playing a few hundred yards away in the park. She started walking back to the flat when she saw a flock of geese passing overhead, at which point Gloria noticed:

> "...a 'speck of light', in the sky. As it came closer, it looked like a biplane – then began to move along a steadily descending path, as though intending to land in the park. I could see this was no conventional aircraft. Intrigued, we ran towards the object to get a closer look. Suddenly, it stopped – now stationary – hovering a few hundred feet in the sky. It looked like two grey metallic saucers, joined at the rims. There were markings, like radial lines on its underside, dividing it into six equal segments, about 30-40 feet in diameter. I had the feeling it was observing us"

A couple of hundred yards away, a group of young boys, playing football, stopped and pointed upwards at the object. Gloria rushed inside to tell her mother. When she returned, it had gone.

In interviews later held with the children, they told of seeing:

> "...three or four black knob-like protuberances – darker than the radial lines on the underside – emerge on the right-hand side of the 'craft', before it rose vertically into the sky at a fantastic speed".

We contacted scientist – Peter Wroath, who had investigated this matter. He felt there was no reason to doubt the genuineness of the witnesses involved and was unable to explain what had been seen.

Mrs Bomford wrote a letter to the *London Evening News*, which was published on 24th May 1970, asking for any of the 'schoolboys' to contact her, quote: *"The incident made such a strong impression on me that I feel I must get corroboration and have the fact placed on record. I was very sceptical about 'flying saucers' until this happened."* (**Source: Peter Wroath**)

OCTOBER 1969

1st October 1969 – Size of a football

Two brothers were out golfing at Bude, in Cornwall, when they saw a bright object – the size of a football – in the south-east part of the sky, approaching their position, at 7.15pm, as dusk fell. It stopped in mid-air, giving off an intense white shimmering light, for a few minutes, before heading away out of sight – now moving south-west. (**Source: South-west Unidentified Aerial Phenomena Investigations**)

2nd October 1969 – Three pulsing 'red lights' over Devon

A small 'red light' was seen in the sky over Brixham, at 10.10pm, at an estimated height of 2-3,000 feet. As it approached closer, now flying over the harbour, the witness (a local housewife) saw:

> "...three pulsing 'red lights', illuminating, quite clearly, what looked like a fuselage without any wings, making a thudding noise.
>
> It then moved away towards the direction of Dartmouth and I lost sight of it."

(**Source: Fred O'Gardner, F.R.G.S.**)

5th October 1969 – 'V'-shaped formation of UFOs Kent

At 9.43pm, seven to ten vague fluorescent 'discs', flying in a 'V'-shaped formation, were sighted over Greenhithe, in Kent, at an estimated height of 3-400 feet, moving rapidly from north to south, by Mr Brian Slade, F.R.A.S. – an amateur astronomer, who was looking through an 8-inch reflector telescope.

> *"At least six of them maintained the basic 'V' formation, while one or two 'discs', at the rear section of the 'fork', behaved in an erratic fashion, darting to and fro across the rear of the 'V' – like sparks from a bonfire. It was an amazing sight, quite unlike anything I had ever seen before."*

In October 1969, a housewife from Alum Bay, near Freshwater, Isle of Wight, was awoken by a loud clattering noise. When she went to the bedroom window and looked outside, she saw two or more red glowing 'lights' darting about in the sky over the sea, accompanied by a noise, which sounded like several dustbins being rattled. Minutes later, they vanished from sight, leaving darkness and tranquility to settle down onto the landscape once more. (**Source: Isle of Wight UFO Society**)

21st October 1969 – UFO over Bournemouth

Retired Lieutenant Commander Alastair G. Mackenzie was with his wife, Olga, mother-in-law Peggy Beatty, and family – Sarah (11), and brother, Ian (18) – talking, after the evening meal in their private quarters of the Suncliff Hotel, East Overcliff Drive, at 7.45pm, when a member of the family directed his attention to something fluttering outside the window. Thinking it to be a piece of burnt paper, the Lieutenant Commander asked Sarah to open the door leading out onto the sun balcony, so they could investigate further.

In an interview later conducted with John Feakins, of the Isle of Wight UFO Society, he had this to say:

> *"It was a foggy night, with visibility right down, although there was some illumination from the moon and the Hotel's floodlights. We looked out and upwards and saw an object, circular in shape, 9-12 inches in diameter, translucent greyish/white in colour, with a blue pulsating centre, darker in the middle than the outside rim, approximately 30 feet high in the air – like a jellyfish – although Sarah said it looked like an octopus in image.*
>
> *It then moved from what had been a stationary position, towards the building, and headed southwards, slowly to begin with, at walking speed, then 'running', then moving much faster. I formed the impression there was immense power behind the movement of whatever it was that left no trail in the sky."*

Haunted Skies Volume Two Revised

The Lieutenant Commander telephoned the police, who checked with the coastguards. They confirmed they had received no other reports from the public.
(**Source:** *Bournemouth Evening Echo*, 22.10.1969 – '**When a flying jellyfish dropped in for coffee**'/Frank Marshall, BUFORA)

Surrey

At 10.35pm, a couple were walking home in Richmond, Surrey, when they noticed a 'light' in the sky approaching them, from the west-south-west, which they took to be a helicopter. As it passed silently overhead they saw some sort of balloon-shaped structure, with yellow flickering lights above, before it vanished over the horizon. (**Source:** *UFOLOG/Space-link*)

NOVEMBER 1969

5th November 1969 – 'T'-shaped UFO over Dorset

During the early morning, retired RAF Radar operator Alan Christopher from Parkstone, Dorset, was driving to work with a colleague, towards Wyke Regis, when they noticed a peculiar 'light' in the sky and decided to stop and have a closer look.

> "We saw this sausage-shaped object, some 1,200 feet in the air, which began to flow outwards, forming the shape of a 'T', with a noticeable black spot at each point – then it changed into a brilliant white cross, showing the dark spots on the end of its 'arms'. It changed again into what looked like a dog's bone in the sky, with a very black base – still showing the black spot at each end – before altering in image to a squared look, out of which emerged what looked like two teeth descending out of the underneath." (**Source: Personal interview**)

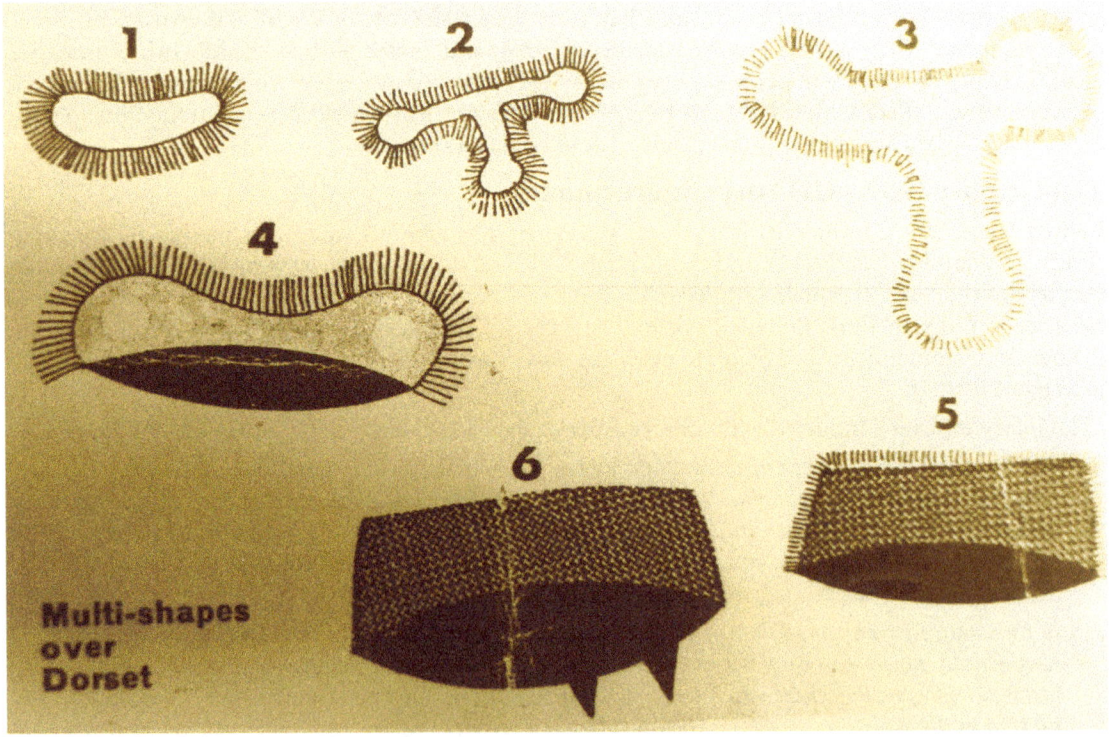

Multi-shapes over Dorset

Leighton Buzzard

At 7.45pm, the same day, a man was driving to work near the A5, at Leighton Buzzard, when he saw a conical object flying through the sky. It was at a high altitude, and the front portion was orange in colour, tapering to a conical tail. Enquiries carried out by the Bedfordshire UFO Society at the nearby Air Force Base, at Chicksands, revealed *"the object had been tracked on radar"*, although they refused to disclose any further details.

In the same month, Jack Zetter, from Westcliff-on-Sea, claimed he and his wife saw a UFO from Sutton Road, and followed it in their car – until losing sight of it, five minutes later.

"At first I thought it was the top of a building, with silvery lights on it, but then it kept moving and stopping – just like a giant kite.

I'm sure it wasn't any aircraft, or balloon." (**Source:** *Southern Evening Echo***, date not known**)

26th November 1969 – UFO over East Ham

We spoke to Michael Oram (then living in Raynham, Essex, but now living in Cumbria) about what he saw, at 6am, while delivering bread in East Ham.

"A week before the sighting, I felt a premonition that I would see a UFO and wondered whether I should carry a camera with me.

I was parked in my van at the end of St. Albans Road, East Ham, overlooking the recreation ground and Beckton Gasworks, having a drink from my flask, when I noticed a bright yellow cigar-shaped object, apparently over the gasworks, about a mile away. I watched the object for approximately 15 minutes, as it moved from left to right and then stopped. I jumped out of the van, still holding my cup, staring at this 'thing'.

A short time later, a local Co-op milkman went past. I wanted to tell him what I was seeing, but I felt struck dumb – unable to speak. By 8.45am, it was out of view."

Michael continued on his round in such a shocked state that he was unable to deal properly with the transactions which took place, but managed to telephone the *Daily Mirror* newspaper to report the matter. He was later relieved by his concerned employees, after a woman customer contacted them as to his demeanor. The incident was to provide the catalyst of what turned out to be a lifelong interest in the UFO subject, culminating in the publication of his autobiography, entitled: *Does it Rain in Other Dimensions?* (John Hunt 'O' Books)

Michael Oram (left) with Wendelle C. Stevens

DECEMBER 1969

5th December 1969 – 'Floating ballroom' over London

At 7.40am, a row of 'powerful lights' – as large as several airliners – moving at 400 feet above the ground, resembling a 'floating ballroom', was seen over Leyton, London, by housewife – Ethel Smith, who told of watching it through binoculars before it moved away towards the south-west, at incredible speed.

Mrs Smith disclosed, in a letter sent to the MOD, that this was the third occasion when she had seen something like this in the sky. She also mentioned that for several days after the sighting, the airspace towards the west-north-west was abnormally crowded with smaller aircraft – as if looking for the object.

(**Source: Air/2/18565 – declassified document, 2006/J. Matson, forwarded to Arthur Shuttlewood**)

17th December 1969 – Project Blue Book closed !

On this day, the American Air Force closed *Project Blue Book* – the agency officially investigating unidentified objects, since 1947 – pointing out that neither scientific value, nor National Security warranted continuation of the Project.

American Association for the Advancement of Science

1515 MASSACHUSETTS AVENUE, NW, WASHINGTON, D.C., 20005

(Sheraton-Boston Hotel)   29 December, 1969

The Hon. Robert Seamans, Jr.
Secretary of the Air Force
Washington, D.C.

Dear Mr. Secretary:

The scientists listed below, convened at a General Symposium during the Annual Meeting of the Association, understand that USAF Project BLUE BOOK has been discontinued in accordance with Dr. E. U. Condon's recommendation in the Colorado Study of Unidentified Flying Objects. We know that Project BLUE BOOK accumulated, over the past two decades, irreplaceable data of great historical interest and potential value to physical and (particularly) behavioral scientists.

After two days' discussion of the data involved, the Colorado Study, and several proposed studies by sociologists and psychologists, we formally request that you, Mr. Secretary

(1) Ensure that *all* of the material, both classified and unclassified, be preserved without alteration or loss,

(2) Declassify promptly all documents filed by the Aerial Phenomena Section of the Wright-Patterson Air Force Base which are classified by virtue of AFR 200-17 and AFR 80-17,

(3) Make all the unclassified documents available to qualified scientific investigators at a more suitable location than the USAF Archives (we recommend a major university in the mid-west), and

(4) Order an annual review of the remaining classified documents in the present file to determine when they can be declassified without alteration in accordance with current USAF security procedure.

My twelve colleagues, who receive copies of this letter, would appreciate your favouring us with a reply. I can distribute it to the others if you address it to Dr. Page, 18639 Point Lookout Drive, Houston, Texas 77058.

Sincerely,

Thornton Page (Wesleyan University)
Chairman, AAAS Special Committee, for

Walter Orr Roberts, Retiring President, AAAS	Douglass Price-Williams, Rice University
Franklin E. Roach, University of Hawaii	J. Allen Hynek, Northwestern University
William Hartmann, University of Arizona	James McDonald, University of Arizona
Lester Grinspoon, Harvard University	Carl Sagan, Cornell University
Robert Hall, University of Illinois	Walter Sullivan, The New York Times
Philip Morrison, Mass. Inst. of Technology	George Kocher, University of S. California

BOSTON MEETING   ..   DECEMBER 26-31, 1969

Flying Saucer Review -July-August 1965 - Volume 11 No 4

U.S.A.F. issues secret warning

The radiation hazard from close proximity to UFOs is very real. Accordingly we reprint this item from the March/April issue of THE UFO INVESTIGATOR, by kind permission of the National Investigations Committee on Aerial Phenomena (NICAP) of Washington D.C.

IN a startling report just received, a former Navy pilot has revealed an Air Force warning that he might become seriously ill after three UFOs closely circled his plane. During an interview with an Air Force major at Kirtland Air Force Base, strict secrecy was imposed on the pilot. Except for his wife, who had to be prepared if he were suddenly stricken, he was ordered not to tell anyone about the encounter or the radiation hazard.

Believing this possibly serious danger should not be hidden, the pilot has given NICAP a signed confidential report, with sketches of the UFOs, a map of the sighting area, and confirmation of the secrecy order. The report was secured by Paul Cerny, chairman of the Bay Area (San Francisco) NICAP Sub-committee. Members of the Board of Governors have photo-copies and will if necessary certify the existence of the report.

The pilot, who served in the Navy in World War II, is now a service engineer for a large tool company. He has a B.Sc. degree in mechanical engineering. He uses a private plane in business; to date, he has logged over 6,000 flying hours. Following is his report of the incident which occurred on August 13, 1959:

Flying a Cessna 170, en route from Hobbs to Albuquerque, New Mexico, he was holding a course of 313 degrees, at 8,000 feet altitude. Suddenly he was amazed to see his Magnesyn electric compass revolving instead of indicating the course. Thinking the Magnesyn must be 'haywire', he looked at the standard magnetic compass.

"It was spinning so crazily I couldn't read it." the pilot reports.

A moment later, he was startled to see three oval-shaped devices in close echelon formation pass directly in front of the Cessna. They were grey in colour and identical in shape—like two bowls face to face (one inverted on the other) but with bottoms rounded instead of flat. The pilot estimated their diameter at about eight feet, but they could have been considerably larger.

Since the UFOs were circling the plane at nearly 250 m.p.h., no other details could be noted, except that they left a short, wispy trail.

As the strange objects circled the Cessna, the Magnesyn compass continued to revolve, precisely indicating the UFOs' bearing. Holding the same tight formation, the unknown devices finished another circle, passing in front and then disappearing to the rear. The Magnesyn then came to rest near its original heading, and the standard magnetic compass finally stopped its 'crazy spinning' and returned to normal.

[NICAP note: The abnormal compass actions obviously were caused by the electromagnetic effect reported by other responsible observers.]

Upon landing at the base, states the report, he was "hustled to an office and interrogated for about two hours by an Air Force major—the UFO Officer at the field."

Then came the statement that in the pilot's words "raised the hair on the back of my neck." The Air Force major told him that if anything unusual happened, or if he had any unusual illness in the next six months, he was to get to a government hospital straight away. The Air Force, the major said, would take care of him.

Some years ago, Capt. E. J. Ruppelt, former Chief of Project Blue Book, confirmed that Air Force instrumentation had recorded high radioactivity when UFOs passed over the test area. Also, several apparently genuine cases of illness from UFO radiation are on record.

In the case of the former Navy pilot, the fear injected by the Air Force warning kept him and his wife in a state of apprehension until six months had passed, and he decided the Air Force was wrong to conceal the facts.

If the Air Force knows a UFO-radiation hazard exists, a nationwide warning should have been broadcast. Many planes have been circled or closely approached by UFOs—Service aircraft, private planes, airliners. If this danger is real, then not only pilots and crews but hundreds of airline passengers could be exposed. And since most airplane encounters are kept from the Air Force, to avoid public ridicule, crews and passengers would be unaware of their possible danger.

4

June Thorburn – A little more on this famous lady [see page 449]

At the end of the day we cannot categorically prove a connection with the sighting of a UFO and the tragedy which unfolded, a short time later. The loss of this talented woman and her unborn child, along with the death of other passengers, should not be forgotten.

Here is some additional information about June.

June Thorburn was born in Karachi, British India. She was the eldest of three children, including her sister, Diana, and her brother Keith. Her full name was Patricia June Thorburn Smith. She spent most of her schooldays in boarding schools in India, since her father was a colonel in the Indian Army and therefore her parents travelled a lot. When he retired from the military, they moved back to Britain

June began writing plays from about the age of seven. Her grandfather (Sydney Thubron) who had also spent many years in India as a design engineer, building many important bridges, made early 'movies' and she was the star in several, the first being "Her Second Birthday", when she was only two years old.

When she was 20 she left home and moved to London to pursue her career, where she met and married her first husband, Aldon Richard Bryse-Harvey. During their short and stressful marriage she bore one daughter in 1953, named Heather-Louise June. The marriage ended in divorce and June moved back to Hampshire, close to her family, for a couple of years until her career started to take off.

In 1957 she moved back to London, where shortly thereafter she met Morten Smith-Petersen, who subsequently became her second husband. She was married to him until her death in 1967. Together with Morten, she had a second daughter named Inger-Sheleen Christabel.

She appeared in her first commercial film in 1952, and began to win leading roles, in British costume dramas such as *Fury at Smugglers' Bay* (1961) and *The Scarlet Blade* (1963). Her most notable film appearance was as the Forest Queen in *Tom Thumb* (1958). During the early 1960s, she also appeared regularly on British television.

She was pregnant with her third child when returning to London from Spain on Iberia Airlines Flight 062 when it crashed at Blackdown Hill, Sussex, killing all 37 people on board. RIP June and your fellow passengers…

Catch-up with updated reports and further information

As we reach the final part of another monumental book, incredibly – despite the passing of now nearly 50 years later – reports still continue to be brought to our attention either from external sources or sifting through ancient newspaper cuttings and files from the huge archives now in our possession.

1961

5th-7th February 1961 – UFO display, Maine

Numerous reports were made of strange lights, which were seen flashing around in the sky over Maine. Some blinked and moved up and down; others lit up like a ball of fire, heading at speed over Portland. Unidentified shapes, showing green, yellow and red, lights were seen to hover over Brunswick – then dart away at unbelievable speed. (**Source:** *Portland Press Herald* editorial, 9th February 1961)

9th February 1961 – Mysterious flash in the sky over Ohio

During the early morning, a mysterious flash of blue light lit up the sky south of Cleveland, Ohio. This was followed by a vibration that was strong enough to rock the car of John Lengel, Deputy Sheriff on patrol in Geuga County. The 'flash' was also seen by two pilots approaching Cleveland Hopkins Airport in their planes, separately. Enquiries made revealed no trace of any satellite launched on that day as being responsible, or in orbit, over the locality.

11th February 1961 – *The Brains Trust*, Caxton Hall, London

This consisted of a panel of five people, who met to discuss the 'Flying Saucer' subject. They were Reginald Dutta – Director on the board of *Flying Saucer Review*, Desmond Leslie – author, Dr. Bernard Finch – investigator into the widely publicised 'Ring Angels', Leonard Cramp – author, and Eric Smith – researcher in Physics and Fellow of the British Interplanetary Society.

One of the questions put to the panel was: *"Are Space people friendly and, if so, what are we are doing about it?"*

Desmond Leslie replied:

> *"There have been few hostile incidents, apart from the Captain Mantell case and the various small incidents which have been cooked up for publicity purposes, and that the Space people are just as curious about us as we them at this critical stage in the evolution of mankind."*

Leonard Cramp made reference to a sighting recorded in Captain Cook's logbook:

> *"Two small clouds approached each other at great speed; there was the sound of gunfire, then a gigantic flash, at which one disappeared."*

Following some discussion, the panel agreed that approximately 10 per cent of UFO sightings were caused by temperature inversion, and that many such sightings could be explained away as meteorological in origin. They were then asked for their opinion on the infrared photographs taken in the sky by Trevor James [Constable], which appeared in his book – *They Live In The Sky*. Reginald Dutta, in answer, believed they were forms that fringed on a fourth dimensional state, while Desmond Leslie felt that the 'gaseous caterpillars' were elementals and it was difficult to draw the line between these and UFO sightings.

2nd September 1961 – UFO display over New Mexico

At Albuquerque, New Mexico, at about 4.50pm, a Mr Ziegler (no other details) saw an object reflecting the sun from its surface, moving erratically west to east across the sky. It stopped and ejected several smaller, silvery, objects about 1/6th the size of the main object, then continued on its flight towards the south-east where it stopped once more and ejected for the second time, once again, several silvery similar objects, before moving away and climbing to about elevation 50 degrees, until lost from view.
(Source: Project 1947; McDonald list; FUFOR Index) [See 1st September 1961, UK, page 41]

13th September 1961 – Orange UFO over Indiana

At 4am, at Crawfordsville, Indiana, three people sighted an orange-shaped UFO moving across the sky rapidly, in an east to west direction. It then stopped and hovered for 5 minutes, before accelerating rapidly and disappearing into the distance. **(Source: NICAP UFOE, XII.)**

19th September 1961* – UFO traced on Radar

At 5.22am, North Concord Air Force Station, Vermont, height finder radar tracked an object at a height of 62,000 feet, 196° distance, 84 miles. The target was the size of a large aircraft and appeared as a normal target. Contact was lost at 199° at 80 miles, going north-west, then south. Length of observation was

*(See Page 41, Betty and Barney Hill sighting later that day)

18 minutes. The target moved at a low speed on an erratic course. The location of observers was at 5 miles east of Claremont, New Hampshire. Pease Air Force Base also had an unidentified radar contact at 2.14am. (**Source: Dan Wilson, Vallée Magonia, NICAP UFOE, XIV**)

1962

December 1962 – Sir Gilbert Samuel Inglefield's comments on UFOs

Champions of the UFO cause come from every section of society. One unlikely supporter, whose role in this subject is hardly common knowledge to this present day, was *Sir Gilbert Samuel Inglefield (1909-1991) – a British architect and Lord Mayor of London, from November 1967 to November 1968. The Honourable Gentleman spent considerable time tracking people down and interviewing them from far off places such as Spain and Portugal, during the 1960s, after they reported having seen a UFO.

During an interview with reporter Neil Jones of the *Daily Sketch*, following the extraordinary sighting involving Bedfordshire motorist Ronald Wildman, [see page 75]

He commented:

> "Why are 20 per cent of UFO sightings unexplained? – If there are such things are 'flying saucers', what are they, where do they come from? Why do they come?"

Questions that we would all like the answer to, over 50 years later!

1963

18th July 1963 – Mystery animal seen, Shooters Hill, Greenwich, London

At 1am on this date, lorry driver David Back was driving up the west side of Shooters Hill and stopped to assist what he thought was an injured dog. As he approached, it got up and ran off into the woods.

> "It was not a dog; it had long legs and a long pointed tail that curled up. It appeared to have a mouth full of food."

He reported it to the local police station. This sparked off a hunt that eventually included extra police from other stations, (British Army) troops and sixth-formers from the local grammar school!

On the south-eastern side of Shooters Hill, near Welling Way, searchers found claw marks on a tree and, in the mud of a dried-up stream 'a number of prints, several inches across, with the

---

*The son of Admiral Sir Frederick Samuel Inglefield, KCB, FRGS, DL, and Millicent Evelyn Cecilia Crompton, the heiress of the Derbyshire banker, John Gilbert Crompton. Sir Gilbert appeared as a "castaway" on the BBC Radio programme *Desert Island Discs* on 1st July 1968. On 23rd September 1968, he laid the foundation stone of the relocated London Bridge, at Lake Havasu City, Arizona, United States. Inglefield was a Knight Commander of the Order of the Bath and a Knight Grand Cross of the Order of the British Empire. From 1950 to 1976 he lived at Eggington House, the manor house of the village of Eggington, near Leighton Buzzard, Bedfordshire. Gilbert Inglefield Middle School at Leighton Buzzard was named in his honour. (**Source: Wikipedia**)

THE IVINGHOE SAUCER INCIDENT ENGLAND 1962

At 3am on the morning of February 9th 1962, Mr. Ronald Wildman was driving a Vauxhall car from Luton to Cardiff, as he was driving along the Ivinghoe road the headlights of his car lit up a large saucer shaped object which had port holes around its rim, the engine slowed down and the speed of the car dropped to 20 mph although the accelerator pedal was hard down. As the car came within 25yds the object seemed to shine very brightly around the rim, like a halo, it then sped off into the night at a terrific speed sucking the frost from the ground and trees with it. Investigators later found that the area was slightly radio/active.

marks of claws clearly visible'. Three-quarters of an hour before dawn, on the 23rd July 1963, at *Johnson and Phillips'* sports grounds, Kidbrooke (about a mile south-west of Shooters Hill), Head Groundsman Jim Green was awoken by loud snarling noises, starting near Kidbrooke Park Road, and moving along the course of the *River Quaggy,* a stream running behind bushes and trees along one side of the sports ground. A security sergeant from the nearby RAF station also heard the snarls and investigated with a constable. As dawn broke, they saw a big dark animal, between 18 and 19 inches (45 and 47.5 centimeters) high, silhouetted against a white cricket screen, which then walked off into the bushes. Five carloads of police arrived, by which time, naturally, the beast had disappeared. (**Source:** *The Daily Mirror*, **19.7.1963**)

27th July 1963 – Flamborough coastguard sighting

Another fascinating sighting came from our colleague *Paul Sinclair, who recently wrote *Truth Proof* – a well recommended book now on sale on Amazon, which is attracting 5 star reviews.

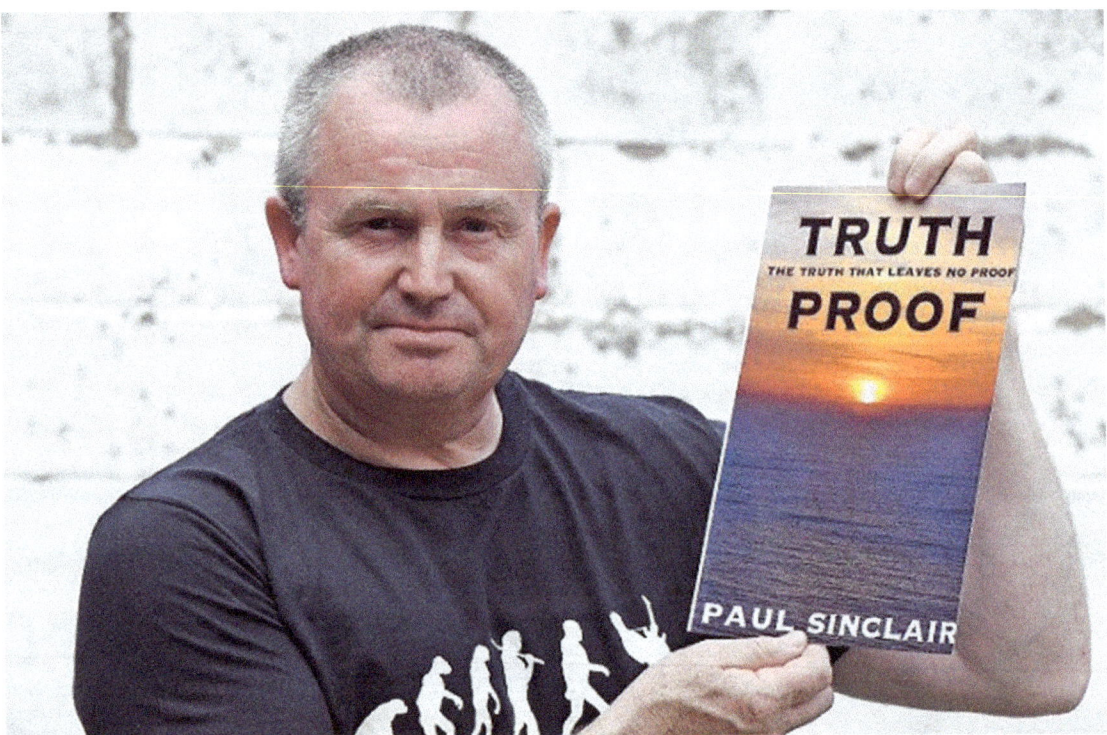

*Paul Sinclair lives with his wife and family in the UK seaside town of Bridlington, on the east coast of Yorkshire. He began his research in 2002 after creating the ILF-UFO sightings website and is a most thorough researcher, who is not content with hearsay or rumours. He studies and investigates his subjects to the tiniest detail, then seeks out documented evidence to back up his work. He has interviewed witnesses to events far stranger than anything reported worldwide. Some are recent, some are historical, but they are all mysterious and fascinating. Published in 2016, Paul's first book entitled *Truth-Proof,* is a collection of first-hand accounts and recollections of local UFO activity, missing people, alien big cats, missing aircraft and other anomalous phenomena. Paul is well known locally for his work and has made many friends who rely on his credibility and confidentiality. *Truth-Proof* is his first published work, which show-cases his efforts to collate the strange truths that surround him every day...…from the 'intelligent' light forms that are seen by many, both on land and out to sea, to the mysterious disappearances of ordinary men around the cliff-tops of nearby Flamborough and Bempton. His fascination with the mysterious activities surrounding nearby Air Force bases is included in *Truth-Proof,* together with reports of tragedies out to sea which leave the reader wanting to know more... *Truth-Proof* also contains reports of strange creatures seen locally, including small humanoid beings stalking farmland, giant cats on the Yorkshire Wolds and even werewolves! Paul Sinclair not only presents this amazing collection of accounts in a logical, yet down-to-earth way, he provides his own theories in an attempt to understand them.

Paul:

> "This report is of great interest, due to the length of time the object was observed and that it was taken very seriously at the time, plus the fact that it just happens to have been reported around the same location as the 'Hood Farm crater', reported on the 19th July – so we seem to have a double mystery."

On Saturday, 27th July 1963, The *Bridlington Free Press* and *Chronicle* announced: *"Coastguards See Mystery Object in Sky"*, which tells of an unidentified object seen in the eastern part of the sky, at 5.20am, by Flamborough coastguards.

COASTGUARDS SEE MYSTERY OBJECT IN THE SKY

THROUGHOUT Saturday morning coastguards at Flamborough kept track on an unidentified object in the sky at about 40,000 ft. Shortly before noon the object was north-west of the look-out station at Flamborough and appeared to be over Filey.

A Free Press reporter also watched it. Once spotted, the object could be easily picked out in the sky without the aid of a telescope. To the eye it looked like a white star. When looked at through a telescope the object seemed to change its shape as it moved. At one time it looked like a white triangle, with a deep white line running along one side. At another time it looked something like a shortened bullet.

The object was first seen at Flamborough coastguard lookout station at 5.20 a.m. It was then to the east of the station. It then moved overhead and was lost for a time. Later it was seen to the north-west over Filey, shining white in the sky. The object was last seen by the Flamborough coastguards at 12.30 p.m., north-west of Flamborough.

A coastguard said: "There were a considerable number of aircraft taking part in an exercise in this area this morning. They seemed to be at about 30,000 ft., and the object was well above them. It must have been about 40,000 ft. The object moved against the direction of the wind at ground level."

When the object was first sighted by the coastguards they informed R.A.F. Leconfield and R.A.F. Preston. They were told that it might be a large meteorological balloon which would expand until it had a diameter of a quarter of a mile and then burst into fragments.

An R.A.F. spokesman at Leconfield said: "The exercise this morning was not connected with the report on the sighting at Flamborough."

THING IN THE FILEY SKY

Throughout this morning coastguards at Flamborough kept track on an unidentified object in the sky at about 40,000 ft. Shortly before noon the object was north-west of the look-out station at Flamborough and appeared to be over Filey.

An Evening News reporter also watched it. Once spotted, the object could be easily picked out in the sky without the aid of a telescope. To the eye it looked like a white star. When looked at through a telescope the object seemed to change its shape as it moved. At one time it looked like a white triangle, with a deep white line running along one side. At another time it looked something like a shortened bullet.

The object was first seen at Flamborough coastguard lookout station at 5.20. It was then to the east of the station. It then moved overhead and was lost for a time. Later it was seen to the north-west over Filey, shining white in the sky.

A coastguard said: "There were a considerable number of aircraft taking part in an exercise in this area this morning. They seemed to be at about 30,000 ft, and the object was well above them. It must have been about 40,000 ft. The object moved against the direction of the wind at ground level."

When the object was first sighted by the coastguards they informed R.A.F. Leconfield and R.A.F. Preston. They were told that it might be a large meteorological balloon which would expand until it had a diameter of a quarter of a mile and then burst into fragments.

An R.A.F. spokesman at Leconfield said: "The exercise this morning was not connected with the report on the sighting at Flamborough."

Early this afternoon Scarborough coastguards had not received any reports of unidentified objects in the sky.

It was then observed to move overhead, at an estimated altitude of around 40,000 feet, when it was lost from view for a short time before noon, and then sighted north-west of their lookout station, shining bright white in the sky over the coastal town of Filey, at 12.30pm, some five hours later.

One of the newspaper's reporters stated he had also seen the object, describing it as

"... easy to pick out in the sky without the aid of a telescope, with the naked eye; it resembled a bright star, but when viewed through a telescope it seemed to change shape as it moved. At one moment, it appeared to look like a triangle with a deep white line running along one side and then at another moment, it resembled something like a shortened bullet."

Paul:

"The coastguard commented that a considerable number of military aircraft were taking part in an exercise that morning, which were observed to be at an altitude of about 30,000 feet. They noted that the object looked well above them and that it moved against the wind direction at ground level."

Enquiries were made with both RAF Leconfield and RAF Preston, and it was suggested that they might have been seeing a meteorological balloon, which could have expanded until it reached a diameter of a quarter of a mile, then burst into fragments.

Paul:

"Personally, I would like to see a balloon that resembles a huge triangle one moment, and then morphs into the shape of a bullet the next!" [See page 121 for other sightings around this month]

Paul:

"During research into my second book Truth Proof 2 'I was told an incredible story that tied in with many of the things I came across when researching the first book. I was fortunate enough to interview a former lighthouse keeper from Flamborough, who told me something that tied in with other events from July 1963."

The former lighthouse keeper told Paul he came to Flamborough in the 1960s and during that time he collected a small folder containing many of his own sightings of UFO activity seen while in service – matters that he decided never to report due to the position his job carried, taking into consideration it would hardly enhance any subsequent career move, because of the ridicule attached to the subject.

Paul:

*"He told me about a sighting that was said to have taken place shortly before he arrived in the area. It also appears to coincide with a mysterious crater that appeared from out of nowhere on the cliff tops at Flamborough, known locally as the **Hood crater** due to its sudden discovery on Hood farmland, in July 1963, which also coincided with the coast guard sighting in the same month.*

If you believe in coincidence then these two incredible accounts are nothing unusual, but commonsense sometimes dictates differently as I have discovered during my research into this enigmatic subject! –

UFO landing

"The retiring lighthouse keeper spoke about contact with a silver UFO which had actually landed in fields at Flamborough, on T.W Waines farmland, and told the new lighthouse keeper this had occurred in July 1963. I had already found a witness to a second 'crater' which appeared around the same time that the 'Hood crater' was discovered in addition to the information from the coast guard regarding the UFO sighting in the same month.

These other sources appeared to corroborated the report of the UFO said to have landed at the back of the former RAF base, understanding I wasn't prepared to accept wholeheartedly, without fear of conviction, matters of great importance like this as being 100% genuine without conducting further research into the matter – the new information given to me by the retired lighthouse keeper adds more credibility to the landed UFO story.

Now all these years later, these five unexplained events have come to the surface, and all within the same time frame in 1963; unfortunately no one realised the significance at the time, which shows in part how easily the public can be fooled. The MOD sent the army in to investigate all of the craters that appeared around the UK in 1963 and I am sure they must have been aware of the coast guard sighting. Yet these events were never put together and presented to the public. We must ask ourselves why? Why send in the army to investigate something of no significance?

And then we have the 'Hood crater' and the coast guard sighting, both close to where the former lighthouse keeper claims a UFO landed. RAF Bempton was just a stone's throw away from all of the sightings. Is it possible they were unaware that such amazing things were happening within a stone's throw of the base? I don't think so. I believe the RAF knew all about the UFOs and the appearances of the craters."

4th October 1963 – UFO over Ohio

At 3.32pm, Beford, Ohio, resident – Mr Robert Carpenter – sighted an intense 'light', oblong in shape, showing tapered end stationary in the sky, surrounded by a green haze. It flashed and flickered for about 15 seconds, before moving away. (**Source: Project Blue Book**) [See page 140 for UK report also]

1964

18th May 1964 – Splitting UFO sighted

At Mount Virginia, a civil engineer was on duty at 5.15pm when he saw a small, glowing white, oval object in the sky, which was seen to split on two occasions, moving from right to left of the moon, over a period of 17 minutes observation. (**Source: Project Blue Book**)

18th August 1964 – UFO over Atlantic Ocean

Major D.W. Thompson and First Pilot 1st Lt. J.F. Jonke were aboard a USAF C-124 transport plane, 200 miles east of Dover, Delaware, at 12.35am, when they sighted a round, blurred, reddish-white object on a collision course with the aircraft.

The airplane evaded the object, which was out of sight a couple of minutes later.

(**Source: Project Blue Book**) [See page 179 for UFO sighting over UK on same date)

14th November 1964 – Three objects sighted

Three dim reddish 'lights' were seen flying through the sky in an arc of movement that lasted a few seconds, over Menomonee Falls, Wisconsin, at 9.40pm, by two girls.

(**Source: Project Blue Book**) [See page 195]

1965

4th April 1965 – Black oval object with light seen

At 3:30am, two Naval Air Cadets, at Ellyson Naval Air Station, sighted a 'ball of flame', approximately 16 feet long, from which two objects appeared to emerge. Earlier, Brookley Air Force Base was made aware of a UFO report but the report was classified.

Keesler Air Force Base

At 4.05am, A/2C Corum of Keesler Air Force Base, Biloxi, Mississippi, was on duty in the weather observation tower, when he sighted a black oval object, estimated to be 40 feet long, approximately 45 degrees elevation in the south-western sky, at a height of 800 feet and some 500 feet away. The silent object, moving at an estimated speed of 500mph, passed overhead (under cloud layer of 1,200 feet) and headed north-east and then faded into the clouds 15-20 seconds later, at approximately 30-45 degrees elevation.

(**Source: Dan Wilson (UFOE II, Section I, Berliner)** [Further to brief details contained on page 206.]

23rd April 1965 – Landed UFO with occupant!

At Rivesville, West Virginia, a woman was up at 8am when she saw a 25 feet object land near her house, while in the kitchen.

> "It was shaped like a disk, with portholes, from a cylinder about 3 feet high; a sliding door opened, out of which a small being, about three feet tall, wearing white clothing, emerged and jumped to the ground. Its face was not clearly visible but it had pointed ears, a sort of tail, and was linked to the main object by a cable. It picked up something from the ground, then re-entered the cylinder, which slid up into the larger white disk. The outside rim of the object started spinning in a counter clockwise motion – then with a soft whistling sound, it rose straight up out of sight."

(**Source: Vallée Magonia 644**)

1966

5th April 1966 – Cone-shaped UFO seen over Tennessee

At 11.55pm over Alto, Tennessee, a Mr Smith reported having sighted an oval object with a dark top, (cone-shaped when moving), making a high-frequency noise during the two and a half hours observation. Whether there was any connection with an object – described as resembling a 'vapour like sphere' seen by Lillian Louis to hover and spin in the sky over Lycoming, New York, at 3am, discharging its 'exhaust' onto the ground below, for about a minute – can only be speculation. (**Source: Project Blue book**)

1967

8th March 1967 – UFO causes interference with motor vehicle

Mr and Mrs William Wallace from Leominster, Massachusetts, were out in their car observing the snow-covered landscape, after a storm at 1.05am.

"We noticed a large white 'light', hovering and swaying gently in the air over St. Leo's cemetery. I stopped the car and got out, pointing to the object. The car stalled, the lights went out, and the radio stopped playing. I was unable to move; my wife was in panic. We stood there, frozen to the spot for about half a minute, then the light moved away emitting a humming noise. Our reactions afterwards were slow and sluggish. We felt like we had been given an electric shock; it took us 15-20 minutes to recover. The car worked perfectly after the object left."

(Source: *UFO Investigator*, Volume 3, No. 12) [See page 347 for other accounts in this month]

10th July 1967 – Domed UFO seen over Lizelia, Mississippi

At 5.50pm golf professional Harold Washington (Retired Captain, USMC) sighted a domed object in the sky.

"The top was gunmetal blue in colour; the bottom resembling old lead, which moved eastwards. It then crossed the highway, tilted upward, moved to the right, accelerated and disappeared into the clouds after 3-5 seconds, making a swishing sound." [See page 373]

1968

18th October 1968 – Close Encounter, Florida

At 7.30pm on this date, members of the McMullen family living in Medulla, in Florida, went outside to see what was causing their dog to become very agitated. They were surprised to see a purple-red object, about thirty feet wide, hovering in the air about ten feet off the ground.

"It was completely transparent. Inside it could be seen what appeared to be two normal sized men, pumping a horizontal bar up and down. It then slowly ascended into the sky."

Enquiries made later revealed that a 'bright light' had been seen previous to the incident, rising up from the grounds of the Medulla school, situated close to the property of the McMullen family.

(Source: John Keel, *Operation Trojan Horse*, Souvenir Press London 1971) [See page 518 re UK UFO sighting for same day]

Obituaries

Obituary – Mrs Jessie Roestenberg – Rest in Peace

In May 2017, Mrs Jessie Roestenberg, from Stafford, passed away.

Irrespective of the fact that she was in her early 90s, we were mortified on hearing the news some weeks later. Over the years we had visited her on a number of occasions. One of those was by *Haunted Skies* artist David Sankey and partner Erica Williams. David still laughs at the memory of when she despatched him off to the local shops to buy some cigarettes! This good hearted-sincere woman, with a sense of humour, was always eager to tell of what she sighted in 1954, while living at Ranton, Staffordshire, when a saucer-shaped object, with occupants, took up a position above the house. Full details of this have been fully covered in the recently published Revised Volume 1 of *Haunted Skies* (1939-1959).

The value of meeting people like Jessie and listening to their extraordinary accounts, told with honesty and sincerity, cannot be measured. The pleasure she gave us and the warmth of friendship is one of heartfelt nature. Thank you, Jessie, for allowing us the privilege of meeting you….and we sadly miss you.

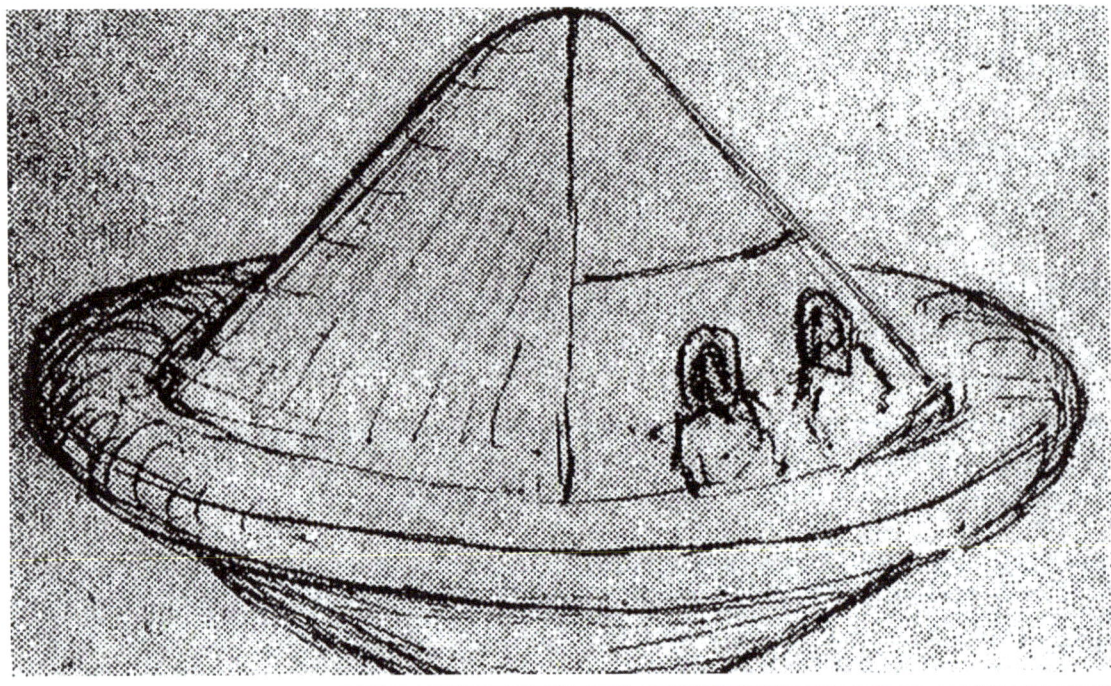

Rest in Peace Jess'

Obituary – Omar Frederick Fowler, by David Sankey & Erica Williams

After a period of illness, Omar Frederick Fowler (born 5th January 1931) – founder of PRA (Phenomenon Research Association) – sadly passed away on the 8th June 2017.

David Sankey and Erica Williams attended the funeral and paid their respects to a true gentleman of Ufology.

> "The service was held in The Round Chapel at Derby Crematorium on Thursday, 22nd June, at 11am. Those that attended included a small group of close friends and family.
>
> All were privileged to hear a brief narrative from his cousin, some six years younger than he, relating to their childhoods, growing up in the turbulent times of World War Two.

Erica and David

Stories were related by both friends and family, and all conveyed the inspiration, generosity and sincerity, of a man that had briefly touched all our hearts along his life's journey. He was a rare jewel within the ufological circle, and his integrity and memory will be a constant reminder that we should all follow our hearts to seek truth and understanding – wherever that should lead. God bless you and may you rest in peace Omar."

David Sankey, June, 2017

Another attendee was club secretary Karen Richardson.

> It is with recent sadness that we heard of the death of Omar Fowler, Group Leader of the Phenomenon Research Association, on the 8th June.
>
> He was a leading and respected expert, and well-known worldwide for his investigations of anomalous aerial craft, and more recently the Flying Triangle mystery.
>
> He founded the Surrey Investigation Group on Aerial Phenomena in 1967, and he moved to Derby in 1990, and set up the P.R.A. in his Sinfin home. For many years, he was a director of the acclaimed "Flying Saucer Review", and acted as a consultant on the Japanese magazine Mu.
>
> His expertise, and calm unassuming manner, together with his openness and acceptance, that the UFO subject had progressed significantly since the "Nuts and Bolts" theories of the 1950s & 1960s, was welcomed, and actively discussed by us all.
>
> He will be greatly missed.

Colin Saunders, June 2017 – death of good friend, Omar

"It is with great sadness that I heard of the death of my good friend, Omar Fowler. On reflection I should be pleased that he reached such a grand old age and to the very end was heavily involved in the UFO world, still chairing his local UFO meetings in Derby and driving himself there at the age of 86.

I first met Omar after my own close encounter with a 'triangle', back in 1999. It was Omar who helped me come to terms with what I had experienced ... a true friend in need. Omar was a softly spoken gentleman, reassuring in his calm, collective way. Over the following years Omar introduced

Haunted Skies Volume Two Revised

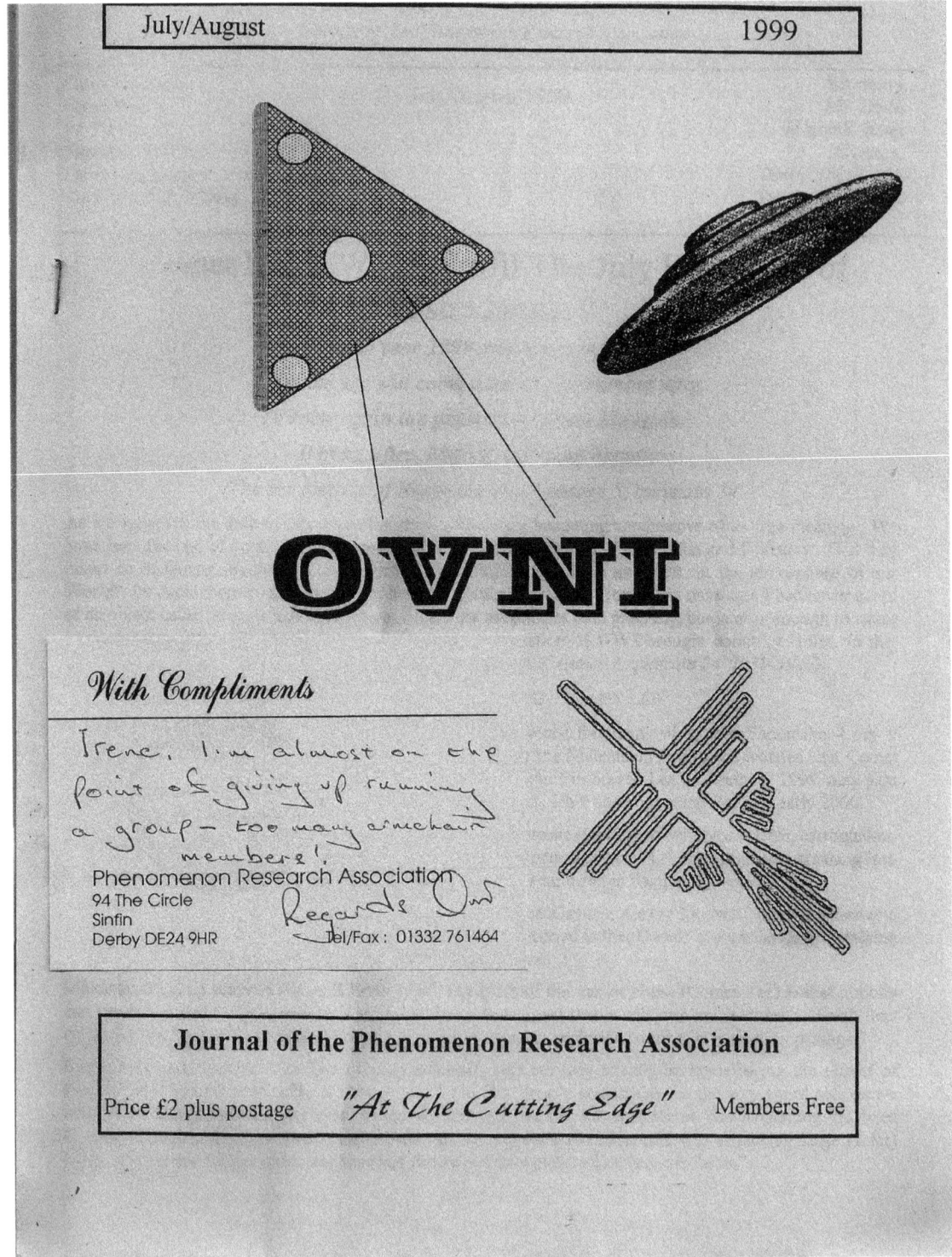

TALE ENDERS

ALL UFO GROUPS ARE INVITED TO PARTICIPATE IN "PROJECT FT". At present there are 33 UFO groups assisting in this 'Flying Triangle' research and the database (Director: Victor J.Kean) has over 7,000 FT sighting reports (Aug.1942 - to the present day).

See: http://ourworld.compuserve.com/homepages/Tspurrier/ufosight.html. **Send your data to: Tony Spurrier, 18 Argyle Road, Edmonton, London. N18 2PP**, or E-Mail Victor J.Kean: *100545.1505@Compuserve.com*

NUMEROUS UFO REPORTS continue to flow into our office, but due to lack of space, we are unable to give full details in this issue.

BRIERLEY HILL (Staffs.) was the scene of an unusual sighting by Mr Ray Leyen, a retired technical sales engineer at 9.30pm on the 1st May 1999. Mr Leyen supplied us with a sketch of what could be described as an upside-down straw hat, with portholes clearly visible around the object. "It could have been about 10,000ft high, but I estimated it to be about 40ft long with lighted portholes. I could not tell whether it was round or square, but it moved very slowly."

BELPER (Derbys.) continues to be the scene of numerous FT sightings, according to PRA member Melanie Cunningham. The PRA recently supplied Melanie with an 8mm movie camera in the hope that valuable FT footage may be obtained. Several of Melanie's sightings will be included in the next issue of the OVNI.

WARP SPEED AHEAD. In 1994 Miguel Alcubierre then at the University of Wales in Cardiff, startled physicists by showing that Starship Enterprise's "Warp Speed" might not be so ludicrous after all. Although the theory has had its critics, Chris VanDen Broeck of the Institute for Theoretical Physics in Belgium, has recently resurrected the idea, but by using a "bubble" to warp space.

LATE OVNI APOLOGIES to our members. The delay in this month's OVNI production has been entirely due to family sickness problems, entirely out of our control.

HUMAN ERROR...Earth's first radio message for extra-terrestrials in 25 years has an all-too-human failing. It contains two errors. The message 23 pages long is to be aimed at four Sun-like stars about 60 light years away. It is written in code devised to make it readable even if the signal becomes degraded across distance.

However, its authors, the Canadian Astrophysicists Yvan Dutil and Stephen Dumas were mortified to be told by a Dutch computer programmer that they had used the wrong symbol for an equals sign in a page devoted to geometry. Source: The Times 24-5-99

THE ROTARY CLUB OF BLACKFRIARS (Newcastle-under-Lyme) gave a great vote of thanks for a talk on UFO's by your Editor Omar Fowler, on the night of 19th July. Two Rotary Club members admitted that they too had seen a glowing cigar in Cheshire a few months ago.

NEXT MEETING

Will be held at the Allenton, Derby. Royal British Legion at 8pm on Tuesday 27th July
A visit by **Diane Shepherd,** Leader of the Northampton UFO Society. Diane was recently featured in a Sky TV programme on **abductees.** Diane will relate her experience that took place while driving late at night!
Non-members welcome: £1 on the night.
(Please note: NO SMOKING in the meeting room).

OVNI articles may be reproduced by other organisations, with due credit to the source.
Articles and opinions printed in the OVNI journal do not necessarily reflect the views of the P.R.A.

me to many great names in the world of UFOs – Stanton Friedman, Dr. Roger Leir, to mention but a few. We also appeared on TV together on more than one occasion, never seeking fame or fortune for himself in his relentless search for truth. I know he will be sadly missed by many people, but especially by me. RIP Omar, until we meet again."

Ron West
95 Chilburn Road
Great Clacton, Essex
CO15 4PE
Tel 01255 431391

EUFORG

Member's Name *Barbara Beckensal* No. 48

The Colchester Group meets at The Quaker Meeting House, Church Street, Colchester on the Fridays below. Doors open at 7pm. Sightings 7.45pm, Speakers 8pm and open discussions from 10-10.30pm,.

Jan 19/1996 ~ Tom Perrott on Ghosts
Feb 16 ~ Mike Bennett on UFOs
Mar 15 ~ Busty Taylor on Crop Circles
Apr 19 - Ken Phillips on UFO witnesses
May 17 ~ Omar Fowler on Crop Circles
June 21 ~ Wesley Downes on the Paranormal
July 19 ~ Paul Fuller on the Roswell autopsy
Aug 16 - Terry Johnson on UFOs
Sept 20 - George Wingfield on UFOs
Oct 18 - Roy Banks the club sceptic !
Nov 15 - Peter Hebden on Crop Circles
Dec 6 - AGM, Christmas get together & sightings

NEW OVNI

BI-MONTHLY JOURNAL OF THE PHENOMENON RESEARCH ASSOCIATION

Omar Fowler – his first allegation of Alien abduction

Omar had been a font of fascinating information and unrivalled knowledge of the UFO subject in particular. He was an authority on sightings of what became refered to as the *'Flying Triangle'* – a mysterious object that was to plague the Derbyshire area in the mid- 1990s. he was also a long standing Consultant for *Flying Saucer Review*. I remember speaking to him some years ago when he was very upset after loosing his dog 'Pup' and suggested as a thank you for his assistance over the years to include a photo of his departed companion.

Omar was responsible as Consultant for *FSR* (a privilege both Dawn and I shared) for the submission of various articles over the years. One of them involved what Omar labelled the "First claim of alien abduction" that he personally investigated, although he had heard of at least one other in the Nottingham area, following an interview on 13th September 1998.

On the 3rd July 1996, a resident of Bilton (a small village near Harrogate, in Yorkshire) referred to as Miss M.F., was out walking in the nearby countryside during the early morning on what was a warm sunny day.

Black Triangular UFO hovers overhead

"Suddenly I was aware of a large shadow moving overhead. I looked up and saw a large, completely silent, black triangular craft – twice the size of an aircraft – showing a white light at each corner. Near it could be seen other lights flashing on and off. A beam of blue light shot down. The next thing I was aware of was going upwards, very fast, and I felt really sick. My nose was hurting and I'm scared of heights; I seemed to black out. The next thing was being in a strange building. Everything was very bright white – so bright I couldn't see anything – and there was this funny smell to it. I felt myself laid on something but I don't know what it was."

Strange beings seen – one taller alien appears to be in charge

(Reluctantly she continues)…

> "There were strange small beings around me; they were doing something down near my legs. I know that people see these drawings of aliens on T-shirts and other things, but they weren't like that. They had black eyes, no whites to the eyes, no eyebrows, no eyelashes, no cheekbones, no ears and no mouth or facial hair, or anything like our skin. Theirs was one skin tone, translucent white. There was a taller alien. He seemed to be in charge and looked the same as the others, but was about six feet tall. I say 'he' 'it'. I don't know what 'it' was. He stood over me and then stared into my eyes and I felt euphoria and happiness – which was odd. I thought he would communicate, because I'm sure that he could see what I was seeing and I had a feeling that I should be at peace, which is not a normal reaction. That was the last thing I remember … the next thing waking up in the field, but in a different spot."

Finds herself back in the field – many hours of missing time

The woman searched around and found her book in the hedge. She looked at her watch; it had stopped (although she didn't notice this at the time), and then discovered a rash on her arm. When she arrived home, she realised five-and-a-half hours had elapsed. The five family dogs cowered and whimpered in fright – totally unlike their usual behaviour. She felt an enormous headache and found her nose was bleeding. The witness told Omar that she had also suffered from an epileptic fit and believes she may have M.E.

Not surprisingly, she revealed a history of previous sightings since the age of six. On another occasion it appears that she was taken while asleep in bed – apparently confirmed by her partner, who awoke and found her gone! A short time later she awoke in bed and ended up in a row with her partner, who accused her of having been elsewhere – possibly with another man – which she vehemently denied.

(Source: *FSR*, Volume 43/3, autumn 1998, 'A "Flying Triangle" Abduction case, North Yorkshire, 1996)

RIP Zigmund, 'Ziggy'

Bob Tibbitts:

> "Ziggy kept me company during many hours working on Haunted Skies, sitting in a chair next to me while I worked on the computer. A sad moment today (30-7-17) when, as a result of being hit by a vehicle, Gabby and I reluctantly decided – as his quality of life was going to be far less than before the accident – that he should be allowed to pass away. 'Sleep tight little man'. Our home is empty without him. God Bless."

Eugene Keher Photograph

At the end of July 2017, as we were in the throes of completing the final text (as you can see from above) we received a copy of *Contact UK Magazine*, sent to us by our colleagues, Geoff Ambler, Mike Soper, Francis Copeland, and Bill Foley, not forgetting our friend – Margaret Fry, who is an honourable lifelong member.

We noticed on page 27 a letter to the editor from Eugene Keher (59), from Wilmslow, Cheshire. Eugen's letter caught our attention, as the three UFO photographs which accompanied the report reminded us not only of the Tony Russell UFO photos, but of the image sketched by Cheshire Constabulary Police Constable Colin Perks, following his sighting of what appears to have been a landed UFO in Wilmslow shopping centre in January 1966. (See page **256** for further details).

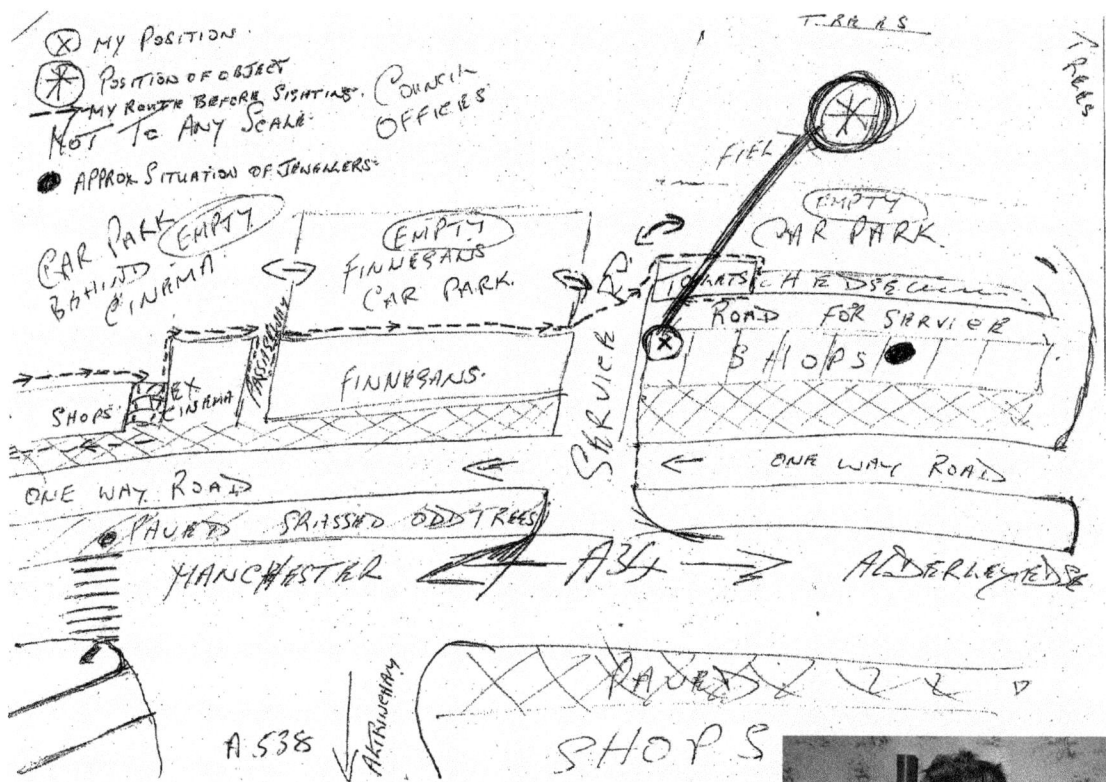

Claims of a UFO shot down by the RAF

This article was accompanied by a letter in which Eugene made references to his photographs – the subject of publicity by a local newspaper.

Eugene also mentioned a conversation with a colleague next door to where he lived in Handforth, Wilmslow, concerning a report on the internet, involving two RAF Pilots who were alleged to have shot down a UFO over the English Channel (as witnessed by some Spanish fishermen), which was withdrawn from the internet some 24 hours later. In addition, Eugene made the following comment:

Police Constable Colin Clive Perks

> "The night MH370 airplane went missing, I was watching Sky News when they went over to a live conference about the missing plane. The first question asked by an American journalist was 'What more can you tell us about a report that the plane was involved in an incident with a UFO?' The reply was never given.
>
> The next second we were back to the Sky Studios in London, suggesting that someone had pulled the plug on that one."

[Authors: The Internet can often prove to be an unreliable source of information, especially relating to the presentation of UFO imagery, which is still treated with ridicule by the National media and fake news rules.

I (John) had not heard of a UFO connection with the demise of the missing aircraft, although Dawn

UFO hunter snaps close encounter

by Karen Britton

YOU MAY think you're as likely to see a flying pig as you are to spot an alien ship in the sky - but one space-mad Handforth UFO-spotter believes the skies above his house are rife with alien activity.

Eugene Keher, 54, of Sandiway Road, says that Handforth is a UFO hotspot and he's seen a host of flying saucers himself - and now he proudly claims he has the photographic evidence to prove he's not totally spaced-out.

After snapping his sightings from afar, Eugene had his photos blown up - and when he picked up the enlarged images he was delighted to see the objects are spaceship-like in shape.

Eugene, a volunteer for Barnados, said: "I'm amazed to see my photos blown up, the objects in the sky are exactly the shape of flying saucers!

"You can't argue with the photos."

Eugene spends a lot of time studying the sky from his garden and thinks there is something unexplained going on up there.

The former sports centre manager, who also writes poetry, said: "I'm always seeing UFOs, they seem to come from the same place in the sky

"I believe there are alien craft entering our skies all the time and there are conspiracies to cover it up."

Wilmslow's UFO sightings have included policeman Barrie Hawkyard's "close encounter" with a UFO 30 years ago at the end of the airport runway, which sparked an international investigation.

EUGENE with his unexplained photograph

And PC Colin Perks spotted a craft in 1966 behind Hoopers on Alderley Road.

Another sighting of "unexplained lights in the sky" by a Handforth resident last August was explained away as a group of chinese lanterns.

With the close proximity to Manchester Airport, Eugene may have a job on his hands persuading people that his "UFOs" are anything other than planes.

He added: "I know there are sceptics but I believe what I am seeing are alien ships."

His best bet is to show his spaceship snaps to someone who will take them seriously - and Dave Sadler from the Congleton-based Unknown Phenomena Investigation Association may be his man.

Dave, who works for BA systems in Woodford and has just been interviewed by TV's Richard and Judy about paranormal activity, said he'd be happy to have a look at Eugene's photos.

He said: "We would look at them in depth as there are a lot of fraudulent pictures out there.

"We would need to see the original shots and breakdown the photos to check they came from the originals and nothing has been added.

"And we would need as much information as possible about the circumstances."

Dave and his team would then contact the people with the sky know-how, namely the Ministry of Defence, the Civil Aviation authority, Jodrell Bank and meteorological agencies which could identify weather conditions that explain Eugene's sightings.

Dave added: "There are lots of things which can explain UFO sightings but we will always take a look at a person's claims."

Contact Dave via his website www.upia.moonfruit.com.

remembers specifically this comment was made, in agreement with Eugene. UFO does, of course, mean Unidentified Flying Object, which could relate to anything!

A personal visit

We decided it was well worth going to see Eugene after initially speaking to him about the photographs, curious as to whether there could be any connection with what Colin Perks had seen – apart from that, we wanted to examine for ourselves the location drawn by Colin Perks.

We made our way up along the torturous M6 Motorway on the 5th August 2017, only to find that junction 19 was closed due to an accident. This meant taking the A34 road from junction 16 and heading towards Manchester, as Eugene lives a short distance from the airport.

Eugene Keher displaying one of his photographs of the UFO

After arriving we introduced ourselves to Eugene – a single man who is very interested in horse racing, with many paintings depicting famous jockeys sitting astride their mounts from many years ago, adorning the wall of his humble residence. He made us welcome and spoke at length about his interest in the UFO subject. We found him likeable and believe him to be genuine. He showed us the intriguing photo taken by him from the back of his garden, facing east to north-east, with a Canon Sureshot 115 non-digital, using standard Kodak film last year of an object – apparently a regular visitor to the sky.

The location. The view from Eugene's back garden

The next photograph (bottom left on the Contact UK page, as above) according to Eugene *"...was completely silent – about the size of a car – and brown in colour"* and was taken by him at 6.15pm over Cleeve Hill, Cheltenham, on the 18th March 2004, when *'Best Mate'* won the Cheltenham Gold Cup for the third consecutive time.

[Authors: this area is well known to us and is where the GCHQ transmitters are situated. In the mid 1970s, Police Officers sighted a huge triangular object hovering over the masts.]

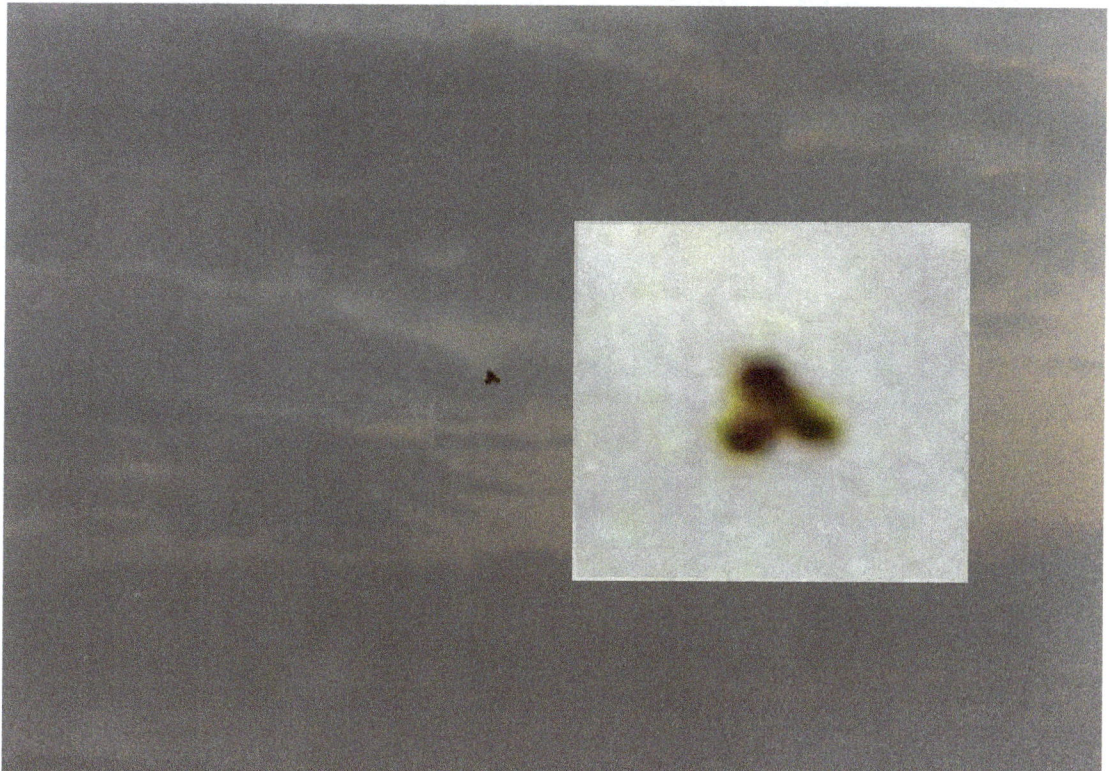

Object photographed above Cleeve Hill, Cheltenham

The saucer-shaped UFO depicted on the other photo was given to him by a member of Wildings photographic shop on the Alderley Road, where Eugene took his films to be processed. The firm closed in July 2011. The man who took it asked that his name not be revealed. Again this is an interesting photo but we can only take such images on face value, taking into consideration that there is no knowledge of the manner in which it was obtained or even an interview with the witness.

The entrance to the town.

Hoopers (formerly Finnegans)

Haunted Skies Volume Two Revised

The area where the UFO was seen to the far left of Dawn, marked accordingly. Below, the location.

Haunted Skies Volume Two Revised

Rather incongruously, a squirrel ran across the car park and posed for us!

INDEX

A

The Brains Trust' panel – 64
A32, Hampshire – 425
A34, Stratford Road, Shirley – 506
Aaron, Mrs – 20
Abbots Langley, Hertfordshire – 240, 252
Abbotsinch Airport, Glasgow – 174
Abbott, Pauline – 150
Abell, Richard – 165
Aberdeen collier, *Thrift* – 142
Abergele, North Wales – 342
Abilene, Texas – 30
Accrington, Lancashire – 126
Acklam, Middlesbrough – 459
Acklington Meteorological Office – 191
Acklington, Tyneside – 347
Ackroydon Estate, Wandsworth – 136
Adamski, George – 104
Adamski-style 'Flying Saucer' – *375*
Addlestone, Surrey – 504
Adkins, Eric – 103
Aerial Phenomena Research Association – 164, 362
Aetherius Society – 82
Afton Down, Isle of Wight – 127
AFU Archives, Sweden – 337
Air Historical Branch – 306
Air Ministry – 1, 8, 20, 34, 64, 82, 100, 107, 129, 321
Air Traffic Control, Elmdon Airport – 307, 349
Air Traffic Control, Gaydon – 67
Air Training Corps – 226
Albert and Edward Dock, *Gateshead* – 263
Alcester Road, Hollywood – 178
Alderley Edge, Cheshire – 366, 368, 377
Alderman Leach School – 436
Alderminster, Stratford-upon-Avon – 464

Aldridge, Staffordshire – 365, 418
Alexander, P. – 444
Alfrick, Worcestershire – 429
Alien 'Aplouff' – 395
Allan, Mabel – 459
Allen, Graham – 159, 179
Allen, W.F. – 361
Allendale Cottages, County Durham – 376, 377, 387
Allinson, Joan – 138
Allpress, Monica – 149
Allpress, Sarah – 149
Alnmouth, Northumberland – 138
Alnwick, Northumberland – 436
Alveston, Warwickshire – 119
American Horror Story: Asylum – 60
Anchorsholme – 126
Anderson, Rosalind – 69
Andover UFO Group – 440, 536
Andover, Hampshire – 229, 337, 378
Andrews, Colin – 16
Andrews, Mark – 156
Andrews, Shirley – 309
Angela House School, Nottinghamshire – 214
Angler's Mail – 536
Anglesey – 116, 409, 487
Anvil Corner – 410
Apollo 8 spacecraft – 523
Apollo Space Missions – 457
Appleby, M. – 328
Appleton Reservoir, Warrington – 439
Arbroath, Aberdeen – 383
Arkless, Christine – 383
Armin, Kenneth – 321
Armitage, Robert – 126

Armstrong, Gordon – 406
Arnold, Kenneth – 98
Arnold, Monroe – 12
Arnold, Nottinghamshire – 209
Arnos Park – 494
Ashby, Aileen – 530
Ashby, Gary – 535
Ashby, Linda – 530
Ashby, Mr. – 544
Ashford, Kent – 444
Ashington, Northumberland – 464
Astle, Elizabeth – 186
Aston Clinton, Buckinghamshire – 75
Atherton, Olga – 465
Atkin, Ronald – 136
Atomic Energy Research Establishment – 307
Attwood, D. – 96
Attwood, Ralph – 553
ATV 'Friday's People' – 454
ATV TODAY TV Studios, Birmingham – 370
Atwood, Mr. and Mrs. – 506
Auld, Mr. G. – 230
Austin, Orval – 133
Austin, Ronnie – 133
Avon Canal – 39
Awson Motor Carriage Company – 510, 516

B

B.3978, Hampshire – 418
Babylon 5 – 60
Baddeley Green, Stoke-on-Trent – 183
Badger, Ray – 221
Baggart, John, Major – 101
Baginton Airfield – 316
Bagnall, Terry – 399, 463
Bailey, Gillian – 186
Bailey, Moffat, John – 552
Bailey, Nigel – 418
Bainbridge, George – 40
Bainbridge, Northumberland – 262
Baker, David – 59
Baker, John – 140
Baker, Michael – 372
Baldwin, Mr. and Mrs. – 437
Ball, Philip – 399
Bamber, B. – 278
Barf Fell – 478
Barnes, C. – 110
Barnett, Toby – 41

Barnsley, Yorkshire – 305
Barron, Mr. – 479
Barry, O'Dowd – 129
Bartlett, Steven – 550
Bashford, M. – 104
Basingstoke, Hampshire – 226
Bassett, Stephen – 344
Basterfield, Keith – 291, 293
Baston, Helen – 515
Bateman's Wood Yard, Stourbridge – 552
Bath – 214
Baxter, Duncan – 531
Baxter, Joan – 448
Bayliss, D. – 459
Baynton, Albert – 322
BBC news item – 99
BBC News, South-West – 510
BBC Plymouth studios, – 415
BBC programme 'Today' – 64
BBC Round-up programme – 149
BBC Sutton Coldfield – 214
BBC television, 'Panorama' – 496
BBC transmission mast – 28
BBC transmitting station – 513
Bearwood, Birmingham – 370
Beather, A.V., Captain – 37
Beatty, Peggy – 557
Bebington 1123 Air Training Corp – 119
Becanin, Ann – 393
Becanin, Michael – 393
Bedminster, Bristol – 371
Beechdale Estate – 131
Beer, Lionel – 39, 8, 131, 133
Belcher, D. – 538
Belfast Corporation – 188
Belgrade, Montana – 115
Bell Raymond – 165
Bell, Christine – 196
Bell, Jennifer – 75
Bell, Keith – 165
Bell, W.C. – 506
Bellenger, Mr. – 495
Bembridge, Isle of Wight – 230, 482
Bennett, Charles – 110
Bennett, D. – 255
Bennett, Dr. – 459
Bennett, E. – 515
Bennett, Jonathan – 441

Bennion, Harry – 545
Bentilee Estate, Staffordshire – 391, 392
Bentilee, Staffordshire – 397
Bentley, Warwickshire – 40
Berry Head Coastguard Station, Brixham – 358
Berry Head Lighthouse – 361
Berry Mound – 178
Berry, J. – 41
Berry, Jim – 165
Berson, Dr. – 114
Berson, Dr. F.A. – 290
Bessemer School, Hertfordshire – 504
Betjeman, Candida – 488
Betjeman, John – 488
Betz, R.J. – 164
Bexhill-on-Sea – 552
Bickley, Harry – 331
Bidford-on-Avon, Warwickshire – 552
Bierley, Bradford – 326
Biggin Hill Aerodrome, Kent – 193
Billingham, Teeside – 491
Bills, Dennis – 179
Binfield, John – 326
Birch, Alexander – 80, 101
Bird, Mr. – 205, 268
Bird, Philip – 384, 400
Birdsall, Graham – 146
Birkby, S. – 436
Birkenhead – 402
Birkenhead – 543
Birmingham – 40, 219, 405, 477
Birmingham Elmdon Airport – 303, 365, 366, 370, 477, 522
Birmingham University – 543
Birstall, Leeds – 539
Bishop, Rodney – 536
Bishopbriggs, Scotland – 19, 380
Bishopton, Stratford-upon-Avon – 332
Bison Hill – 515
Bissell, Fred – 459
Bissett, Alan – 164
Black, J.W. – 213
Black, Mr. and Mrs. – 553
Blackburn, Lancashire – 117
Blackditch Cross – 484
Blackdown Hill, West Sussex – 448
Blackgang, Isle of Wight – 251
Blackheath, Wolverhampton – 386

Blackhill, Consett, County Durham – 405
Blackmore, Susan, Dr. – 507
Blake, Michael – 137
Blamine, Mr. – 324
Blanchard, Roy – 121
Blanchflower, Agnes – 104
Bleakley, David, MP – 188
Bletchley – 252
Blizzard, Gloria – 319
Blondeau, John – 491
Bloom, Harvey – 239
Blow, Graham – 226
Blythe, D. – 319
Bolton Royal Infirmary – 74
Bolton, Lancashire – 75, 314, 554
Bolton, P. – 520
Bomb Disposal Squad – 154
Bomford, Gloria – 554
Bontuchel – 342
Book: *Aliens from Space* – 202, 204
Book: *Birth of a Beam* – 34
Book: *By Space Ship to the Moon* – 69
Book: *Cosmic Crashes* – 146
Book: *Danger from the Skies* – 211
Book: *Flying Saucer Report: UFOs Unidentified, Undeniable* – 406
Book: *Meole Brace Through the Centuries* – 69
Book: *Our Forbidden Moon* – 21, 212
Book: *Piece for a Jigsaw* – 40
Book: *Piece for a Jigsaw* and *UFOs and Anti-Gravity* – 40
Book: *Science Was Wrong* – 63
Book: *Space, Gravity and the Flying Saucer* – 36
Book: *The A.T. Factor* – 40
Book: *The Alien Abduction Files* – 63
Book: *The Chronologies of Babylon 5* – 60
Book: *The Coming of the Space Ships* – 69
Book: *The Coming of the Spaceships* – 69
Book: *The Cosmic Matrix* – 40
Book: *The Great Flying Saucer Hoax* – 164
Book: *The Interrupted Journey* – 41
Book: *They Rode in Space Ships* – 69
Book: *Trains Under the Channel* – 69
Booth, Anita – 195
Booth, John – 21
Bootle, Merseyside – 261
Bordesley Green, Birmingham – 543
Boreham, Essex – 512
Borehamwood, Hertfordshire – 20

Borrows, Alice – 189
Borrows, Frank – 189
Bosnia – 527
Bostock, Malcolm – 398, 399
Boston Traveler – 58
Bott, Irene – 159, 179
Bourne, Lincolnshire – 503
Bournemouth – 110, 261
Bouverie Gardens, Kenton – 351
Bovedy, County Antrim – 492
Bowden, Nigel – 12
Bowden, Vera – 12
Bowen, Charles – 303
Bowen, Charles – 335
Bowen, Mrs. – 398
Bowling green, Jubilee Park, Liverpool – 168
Bowyer, Barbara – 31
Boxers Corner – 342
Boyce, Olivia, R. – 39
Bradbury, John – 379
Bradford, Yorkshire – 345, 458
Bradford-on-Avon, Wiltshire – 322
Bradwell, Stoke-on-Trent – 390
Bramley, Leeds – 459
Branch, Christine – 451
Brandis Corner – 417
Brands Hatch, Kent – 98
Braunger, F. – 67
Braunstone, Leicestershire – 322
Brayford, Janet – 394
Breakwell, H. – 314
Brecon – 174
Brentwood, Essex – 404
Brew, Charles – 112
Brew, Trevor – 112
Brewin, Dennis – 473
Brewitt, Allan, George – 510
Brian Underhill – 510
Brickhill, Bedford – 550
Bridge, Eric – 180
Bridgnorth – 505, 537
Bridport, Dorset – 546
Brighouse, Yorkshire – 369
Brighton – 35
Briscoe, Steven – 494
Bristol – 128, 308
Bristol Odeon cinema – 494
Britannia Barracks, Norwich – 117

British Astronomical Research Association – 541
British Flying Saucer Bureau – 308
British Transport Police – 258
British trawler, *Lepanto* – 41
British trawler, *St. Chad* – 115
British UFO Association Conference – 101
Britland, Robert – 192
Brixham, Devon – 400
Broad Street, Birmingham – 177
Broadwater – 255
Broadwater Lake – 12
Brockton, Stafford – 190
Brogan, Mr. and Mrs. – 383
Bromley, Kent – 388
Brooke, James – 140
Brooks Edwin – 306
Brooks, Angus – 429
Brough, Westmorland – 218
Brown, Geoffrey – 205
Brown, George – 18
Brown, James – 123
Brown, Robert – 134, 444
Browne, Thompson – 191
Brownlow, David – 80
Bruce, Mr. and Mrs. – 332
Bruce, Phyllis – 133
Bryant, David – 210, 212
Bryant, Linda – 210
Buck, Cornelius, Captain – 124
Buckingham Palace – 36
Buckinghamshire – 189, 428
Bucknall, Derbyshire – 383
Buffey, T. – 205
BUFORA – 39, 156, 454
BUFORA UFO Handbook No.1 – 195
Bull, Malcolm – 195
Bull, Steven – 370
Bullen, Leslie – 330
Bullock, Coleen, Lenore – 408
Bullus, Edward, Eric, Sir – 414
Bunting, Harold – 38, 69, 80, 142
Burgess, Mr. – 480
Burgh Le Marsh, Skegness – 448
Burghfield Common, Reading – 352, 363, 364
Burghfield, Reading – 384
Burke, Michael – 550
Burn, E. – 102
Burnett, K. – 441

Burnett, Tom – 321
Burnham-on-Sea – 128
Burnley, Lancashire – 444
Burrows, Frank – 67
Burson, Michele – 66
Burton Joyce – 371
Burwood, T. – 325
Bush, P. – 402
Bushy Heath – 409
Butcher, Harold – 219
Butcher, William – 219
Butler, Robert – 65

C
Cady, Ronnie – 156
Cairngorm Mountains – 402
Caister-on-Sea, Norfolk – 417
Calicott, David – 400
Calverton, Nottinghamshire – 223
Cam, Gloucestershire – 533
Cambois, Blythe, Northumberland – 377
Cambridge University Group – 262, 305
Campbell Aircraft Company – 450
Caney, S. – 547
Canning, Doug – 479
Cannock, Staffordshire – 179
Cansell, Penny – 512
Canterbury, Kent – 326
Capel Curig, Gwynedd – 383
Capon, Brian – 239
Caravelle Airliner 'Jesus' – 448
Cardoza, Julia – 33
Carey, Michael – 494
Carisbrooke Grammar School – 375
Carisbrooke, Isle of Wight – 299, 375
Carlisle, Cumbria – 255, 276
Carmarthen – 552
Carnoustie, Scotland – 377
Carpenter, A. – 330
Carr, Colin – 90
Carr, John – 90
Carroll, 'Des' – 290
Carroll, Mrs. – 439
Carrshield, Northumberland – 524
Carslake, Robert – 452, 455
Carter, Angela – 462
Carter, C. – 299
Carter, D. – 316
Casey, Jenny – 487

Cash, Alan – 173
Cassidy, Bill – 110
Castle Donnington – 371
Castle Leslie, County Monaghan, Eire – 473
Catterick Army Camp – 203, 209
Caversham, Reading – 332
Caxton Hall, London – 64
CERN, Geneva – 308
Chadd, Michael _ 448, 450
Chale, Isle of Wight – 530
Chalker Bill – 291
Challenger, J. – 135
Challis, Martin – 459
Chanctonbury Downs – 443
Chandler, Raymond – 150
Chapman, John – 104, 168
Chapman, Peter – 424
Chard, Somerset – 331
Charlton crater – 40
Chase School, Malvern – 424
Cheadle Heath Reservoir – 387
Cheadle, Cheshire – 128, 140, 332, 418
Cheam, Surrey – 518
Chelston, Torquay – 37
Cheltenham Echo – 10
Chester-le-Street, County Durham – 316
Chesters, Christopher – 315
Chew Reservoir, North Somerset – 512
Child, Joan – 140
Child, John – 554
Chillingworth, Kenneth – 341
Chingford – 396
Chingford Plain – 395
Chiswell, Alice – 128
Chiswick, South London – 19
Chitterne – 303
Cholmondeston – 315
Chorlton-cum-Hardy – 195
Christchurch, Hampshire – 546
Christmas Island – 301
Christopher, Alan – 558
Church, May – 161
Cirencester – 436
Civil Defence – 317
Civil Defence Centre, Wallsend – 439
Civil Service Sports Ground, Yarmouth – 473
Clacton-on-Sea – 128, 459
Clapton, T.G. – 241

Clark, Jerome – 225
Clark, Mrs. M. – 12
Clarke, Arthur, C. – 20
Clarke, Belinda – 218
Clarke, Dorothy – 305
Clarke, James – 314
Clarke, Kathleen – 251
Clarke, Terry – 164
Clarkson, John, Donald – 450
Clayton, Melbourne – 278
Cleary-Baker, John, Ph.D. – 151, 195, 323, 414
Cleckheaton, Yorkshire – 227
Cleethorpes – 241
Clews, Adrian – 522
Clift, R.G. – 37
Clifton Estate, Nottingham – 371
Clifton, Nottingham – 465
Closeburn, Dumfries – 314
Clouston, Eric – 326
Clovelly Parish Council – 425
Clyde Airport – 65
Coatbridge, Lanarkshire, Scotland – 22, 127
Coatbridge, Scotland – 495
Coburg Farm – 373
Colchester – 35
Colchester United football ground – 436
Coldlands Wood – 353
Coldrige, Andrew – 174
Cole, Harold – 405
Cole, Josephine – 35
Coles, Mr. – 15
Coleshill, Warwickshire – 408
College of Science and Technology, Stockport – 321
Collett, W. – 425
Collins, Andrew – 498
Collins, Frank, Major – 151
Collins, Stephanie – 218
Collins, T. – 408
Colt Crag Reservoir, Northumberland – 142
Colwyn Bay, North Wales – 304
Comber, Norman – 263
Combes, V. – 440
Combes, Valerie – 536
Conarski, S.W., Dr. – 133
Coning, Peter – 228
Conisbrough – 405
Connolly, Cathie – 62

Constable (Parks Police) James Nolan – 169
Constance, Arthur – 10
Contact International UK – 156, 369
Conway, A. – 546
Cook, D. – 141
Cook, Jack – 546
Cooke, Mr. and Mrs. – 23
Coomer, Gary – 459
Cooper, Douglas – 86
Cooper, H.G. – 241
Coote, Daisy – 504
Cope, G. – 130
Copmanthorpe – 498
Corben, Richard – 424
Corbett, R. – 323
Corns, Michael – 303
Cosmos, 'Encyclopedia Galactica' – 60
Cotton, Angela – 312
Coulthard, M. – 209
County Durham – 242, 300, 324
Coupland, Nigel – 505
Cousins, Dana – 551
Coventry – 25, 98, 110, 345, 504, 510
Coventry City Football Club – 450
Coventry Standard – 514
Coventry UFO Research Group – 62, 535
Coventry, C. – 12
Cowan, Jack – 550
Cowdell, Marjorie – 371
Cowes, Isle of Wight – 323, 370
Cox, Barry – 215
Cox, Bernard – 385, 388, 390
Cox, Gladys, Sarah – 418
Cox, Janet – 305
Cox, Michael – 385
Cox, W.J. – 89
Coxon, Geoffrey – 553
Cradle Junior School, Fforestfach, Swansea – 142
Craine, Judith – 473
Cram, J. – 258
Cramlington, Northumberland – 385
Cramp, Leonard – 35, 81, 82, 101, 262, 303, 373
Cranmore, Isle of Wight – 486
Cransford, Suffolk – 10
Creighton, Gordon – 257, 308, 326, 335, 478
Crewman, David – 373
Criccieth, Wales – 118

Cricket Hill, Woking – 369
Crisp, Alfred – 110
Crocker, Stella – 417
Crockford, Howard, Roy – 505
Cromer – 370
Cromwell Street, Middlesbrough – 25
Cropper's Paper Mill, Burneside – 106
Crosby – 506
Crosby, Lancashire – 530
Crowhurst, Roger – 19
Crowley, Susan – 203
Croydon, Surrey – 136, 161
Crump, Peter – 38
Crumpsall, Manchester – 389
Crystal Palace – 477
Culverstone, Kent – 541
Cumberland, J. – 409
Cumberlidge, William – 182
Cunningham, Mr. – 386
Cupar, Fife – 141
Cut Mill, Surrey – 448
Cwmbran, Monmouthshire – 241

D

D'Alessandro, S.F. – 179
Dagenham Paranormal Research Group – 498
Dale, Stephen – 242
Daniels, Wilfred – 71, 143, 521
Darby, P. – 251
Darlington, County Durham – 205
Darlington – 548
Darrel, L. – 226
Dartford, Kent – 446
Data-Net – 86
David, Kenneth – 230
David, Michael – 230
Davidson, P. – 537
Davies, Margaret – 324
Davies, Mrs. – 546
Dawson, J. – 74
Day, Catherine – 444
Day, David – 13
Day, Peter – 332
Declassified MOD-AIR/19216-CO273876 – 403
Delafied playing field – 394
Demant, David – 191
Dempster, Derek – 36
Denton Mill, Brampton, Cumbria – 444
Denton, Manchester – 388

Depledge, Walt – 192
Derry, John – 139
Desert News and Telegram – 65
Deuchort, Christine – 464
Devizes, Wiltshire – 502
Devizes – 541
Devon – 37
Dewey, Gordon – 24
Dexter family – 264
Dickenson, Mr. and Mrs. – 126
Dickinson, John, Dr – 431
Dickson, Kathleen – 276
Didcot, Berkshire – 353
DIGAP (Direct Investigation Group on Aerial Phenomena) – 38
Diglis Wier – 221
Dixon, Stuart – 80
Docherty, I. – 382
Dodd, Miss – 418
Doel, D.G., Dr. – 82, 101, 150, 160, 195
Doel, Diana – 150
Dolley, Jacqueline – 550
Dommett, Ursula – 417
Donaldson, Vicki – 418
Doncaster – 504
Dorman, Derek – 466
Dover – 204
Dover Gaswork – 116
Dover, L. – 496
Downie, M. Mrs. – 408
Downing College, Cambridge – 118
Doy, Bernard – 372
Druce, Lance – 445
Drummond, Pete – 222
Dubuque, Iowa – 11
Duckworth, C. – 218
Duckworth, Mary – 218
Duffield, I. – 117
Duffy, John – 126
Duffy, Rita – 530
Dufton Fell, Westmorland – 123
Dumfries, Scotland – 33, 89, 213
Dundee Courier & Advertiser – 12
Dunford, Tommy – 17, 18
Dungeness, Kent – 373
Dunn, E. – 130
Dunsmore School, Rugby – 519
Dunston Power Station, Newcastle-on-Tyne – 17, 438

Dursley, Gloucestershire – 534
Durward, Eric – 102
Dutton, Kenneth – 387
Dyer, Eric – 554

E

Eaglescliffe, Stockton-on-Tees – 333
Earls Barton – 239
Earlsdon – 514
Earp, Frank – 345
East Anglian Daily Times – 10, 19
East Belfast – 188
East Birmingham Hospital – 439
East Hagbourne – 223
East Horsley, Surrey – 496
East Leake – 371
East London – 260
Eastleigh, Hampshire – 511
Eastwood, Marilyn – 289
Eaves, Myrtle – 204
Eaves, Reginald – 204
Eccleston, Lancashire – 110
Echo 2 satellite – 241
Eden Valley – 405
Eden, Cyril, William – 447
Edgware, London – 417
Edinburgh – 134
Edward O'Dowd – 129
Edward, Ann – 405
Edward, O'Dowd – 129
Edwards, Bill – 13, 15
Edwards, Ernest – 342
Edwards, Kathleen – 13
Eedle, Arthur – 400
Eggardon Hill – 513
Ellesmere, Shropshire – 390
Elliott, John – 89
Ellis, Evan – 306
Ellwood, Douglas – 213
Elrick, William – 173
Elwood, Douglas – 314
Emery, Gordon – 474
Empire Hall, Olympia, London – 524
Endfield, C. – 497
Enfield – 423, 251, 542
Enfield UFO Investigation Society – 255
English, B.L. – 167
Epping – 234
Epping Forest – 396

Erdington, Birmingham – 465
Ermine East, West Lincoln – 510
Esplin, Dennis – 366
Essex UFO Society – 405
ESSO laboratories – 353
Estop, Maurice – 23
Evans, Cecil – 143
Evenlode – 326
Ewing, Robert – 150
Exeter – 170
Exeter Airport – 34
Exmoor – 204
Exmouth – 444

F

Fair Oak, Hampshire – 375
Fairbrother, Mr. – 252
Fairweather, Jack – 504
Fairweather, John – 365
Fall, Bob – 160
Fallow, R.K. – 376
Fareham Comprehensive School – 371
Farlow, Beverley, Carl – 451
Farnworth, Bolton – 387
Farr, Stuart – 402
Feakins, John – 35, 373, 401, 558
Fearon, Banks – 38
Felix, Mike – 333
Felixstowe – 230
Femandez, A., Mr. and Mrs. – 389
Fenham, Newcastle-upon-Tyne – 355
Fenn, Mark – 553
Fenwick, Margaret – 428
Ferguson, Dennis – 364
Ferguson, W.R. – 364
Fetcham, Surrey – 539
Fielding, Bruce – 241
Film: *Close Encounters of the Third Kind* – 71, 494
Film: *The Great Escape* – 133
Finlay, Peter – 118
Finsbury Park, London – 378
Fishel, Aubrey, C. – 69
Fisher, William – 349
Flamborough Head, Yorkshire – 125
Flixton – 520
Flux, Peter, Fredrick – 329
Flying Disk Press – 60, 278
Flying Saucer Review – 36, 81, 257, 303, 316, 335
Foleshill, Coventry – 535

Foley, Mr. – 104
Foley, Mrs. – 104
Ford, Brian – 376
Fordwich, Kent – 447
Forfar, Scotland – 313
Forsyth, Mavis – 230
Fort Mead Missile Master Center, Maryland – 31
Foster, Carol – 150
Foster, Mr. – 371
Foster, Susan – 237
Foster, Valerie – 307
Fouche, Jim – 394
Foulkes, Diana – 329
Fowler, Omar – 332, 448, 503
Fox, Celia – 41
Foy, Donald – 126
Francis, V. – 241
Frankley BeechesReservoir – 383
Franklin, Louise – 172
Freakley, Gillian – 398
Freakley, Gordon – 398
Freeman, Arthur – 98
Freeman, Philip – 462
Freitag, L.W. – 214
Fremlin, John, Professor – 543
Freshwater, Isle of Wight – 557
Frimley, Surrey – 117
Frodsham Marshes – 192
Frome, Somerset – 546
Frost, Alan – 321
Frost, Joan – 219
Frostrick, Jacqueline – 446
Fry, Margaret – 104, 156, 342
Fryer, Maurice – 22
Fuller, Grant, John, Jr. – 41, 42
Fuller, Joan – 552
Fuller, John, G. – 225
Furkenhoff, J.B. – 37
Furlong, D.J. – 438

G

Gain, Leonard – 429
Gainer, Patricia – 465
Galbraith, Jay – 65
Gallagher, John – 127
Gallagher, N. – 371
Gallimore, Mr. and Mrs. G. – 203
Garboldisham – 479
Gardiner, Timothy – 349

Gardner, Tommy – 510
Garlington, Lee – 60
Garner, Chris – 415
Gates, Barry – 395
Gateshead – 102, 165, 191, 195, 239, 371, 428
Gatwick Airport – 22, 208, 380, 509
Gellion, 'Nan', Margaret – 506
Gemini 11 Mission – 322
Gemini IV – 209
George, Brian – 445
Gibbons, Gavin – 69
Gibbons, Margaret – 69
Gibbons, Robin – 69
Gibbs, Brian – 209
Gibbs-Smith, Charles, H. – 64
Gilham, Dave – 452
Gilkicker Point – 237
Gillingham, Kent – 129
Gilmore, R.S., Dr. – 308
Girvan, Waveney – 145, 146, 192
Glasgow – 486
Glasson, near Lancaster – 38
Glastonbury – 548
Glazier, R.M. – 172
Glenn, John – 86
Glossop, Cheshire – 150
Gloucester – 136, 438
Godalming – 12, 429
Goddard, A. – 21
Goldrick, B.M. – 444
Goldstone, Larry – 389
Good, Timothy – 130
Goodfellow, B.D. – 100
Gooding, Barry – 18
Gooding, Judy – 19
Goodman, John – 439
Gordon Kinsey -34
Goring, Dan – 552
Gorseinon, South Wales – 230
Gosforth, Newcastle-upon-Tyne – 104, 539
Government Establishment, Larkhill – 260
Graham, George – 511
Grant, Marlene – 424
Grant, Reverend – 406
Grassgarth Cottages, Kendal – 104
Gray, D. – 219
Grays, Thurrock, Essex – 394
Great Billing, Northamptonshire – 461

Great Corby – 208
Great Yarmouth – 237, 445
Green, Barry – 146
Green, J. – 486
Green, Jeffrey – 119
Green, Paul – 228
Green, Steven – 255
Greenwell, William – 441
Greenwich, London – 516
Greenwood, Andrew – 282, 284, 285, 290
Gregory, Janet – 553
Greig, Miss – 12
Greig, Thomas, Percy, John – 356
Grief, R.T. – 459
Grunau, Wilfred – 516
Guildford, Surrey – 332, 418, 447, 514
Gulley, K.R. – 262
Guseman, Donald – 347
Guseman, Marie – 347
Gwynne, Philip – 551

H

H.R.H. The Queen – 71
Haigh, Mr. – 510
Haines, Mr. and Mrs. – 386
Haith, David – 455
Haldon Hill – 522
Halifax Branch of BUFORA – 408
Halifax UFO Conference, Bradford – 323
Halifax, West Yorkshire – 188, 205, 228, 444, 522, 537, 538
Hall Green, Birmingham – 487
Hall, Avis – 106
Hall, Colin – 345
Hall, R. – 370
Hamble, Mr. – 368
Hammersmith Hospital – 20
Hampson, G. – 407
Hanbury Hall, Worcestershire – 52
Hancock, C.L. – 142
Handforth, Cheshire – 196
Hankinson, Mr. and Mrs. – 182
Hanley High School – 393, 394
Hanley, Stoke-on-Trent – 398
Hansard – 378
Hanson, Eric – 465
Hanson, John – 16
Hanson, Paul – 465
Hanwell, Miss – 324

Hardman, Beatrice – 203
Hards, Margaret – 260
Hardwick, James – 102
Hardy, Christine – 387
Hardy, Linda – 387
Harlow, Essex – 22, 518, 519
Harm, J. – 366
Harman, Evelyn – 213
Harold Hill, Essex – 365, 389, 400
Harper, C.O. – 18
Harper, Denise, Roberta – 75
Harrington, Kenneth – 398
Harris, John, David – 494
Harris, Leslie – 445, 536
Harris, Mrs. – 370
Harris, P. – 219
Harris, Paul – 329
Harris, Waldo, J. – 64
Harrison, Ivy – 187
Harrison, M. – 178
Harrison, Maureen – 438
Harrison, Percy – 187
Harrison, V.W. – 204
Harrogate – 141, 388, 465
Harrow – 423
Harry, Cyril – 179
Harvey, Alan – 392
Harvey, Doreen – 392
Harvey, Eddy – 227
Harwood Forest – 173
Haslemere Fire Brigade – 448
Hastings – 175
Hastings, G. – 190
Hatch, Helen – 67
Hathershaw, Oldham – 437
Haugham, Mrs. – 255
Havant Spiritualist Church – 358
Hawick, Scotland – 436
Hawker factory, Whitley, Coventry – 316
Hawkins, Colin – 459
Hayes, H. – 356
Haywards Heath, Sussex – 380
Healey, Denis, The Right Honourable – 304
Healey, Hilda – 401
Heathrow Airport – 251, 356, 466, 511
Heaton – 405
Heaton, Wilfred – 451
Hebburn – 322

Heightley, Freda – 90
Heim, G., Mr. and Mrs. – 203
Hemmings, B. Miss – 393
Hempnall, Norfolk – 106
Henderson, L. – 15
Henderson, S. – 262
Henderson, W. Paul, Major – 49
Hengistbury Head – 372, 488
Henley-on-Thames, Surrey – 519
Hennell, Percy – 335, 366
Hennessey, Joyce – 410
Hennessey, Julian – 361, 380, 419
Hensall, Hilda – 305
Henson, Anne – 99
Heppell, Olivia – 195
Hertfordshire – 208
Heseltine, Gary – 258
Hetherington, C. – 127
Hetherington, K. – 299
Hetherington, Mr. – 378
Hewitt, Patricia – 372
Heysham, Lancashire – 366, 383
Hicken, Mr. – 214
Highdown Hill – 355
Highway 168 – 148
Hill View Estate, Sunderland – 424
Hill, Mike – 134
Hill, Norman – 156
Hill, Ronny – 116
Hilley, Nannette – 37
Hindle, Andrew – 435
Hindley, Liverpool – 385, 388
Hindmarsh, E. – 464
Hines, 'Ted' – 410
Hirst, Robert – 165
Hoare, T. – 333
Hobbs, Graham – 389
Hobday, Julie – 418
Hodgson, Rita – 102
Holberton, Jennifer – 69
Holden, E. – 208
Holden, Frank – 227
Holden, John – 240
Holder, Chris – 353
Holder, Norman – 439
Holford Arms, Sherston – 550
Holiday, Frederick, 'Ted' William – 258
Holland, William – 125

Hollander, Michael – 391
Holler, 'Dub' – 30
Holliday, Mr. and Mrs. – 223
Hollis, Paula – 519
Holman, E. Robert – 54
Holmes, L. – 11
Holton Airfield – 91
Holton, Chris – 147
Home Office Security – 335
Homer, P.J. – 175
Homewood, Edward – 323
Honeycombe, Gordon – 93
Honolulu – 117
Hopkins, Ernest, David – 175
Horse, 'Leberstram' – 150
Horsham Bomb Disposal Unit – 123
Horsley Hill Junior School – 441
Horton, John – 535
Houghton Lake, Michigan – 173
Houghton, Ian – 297
Hove – 441
Hovercraft Test Tank Research – 373
Howard, Peter – 220
Howarth, Denise – 552
Howarth, John – 552
Hucclecote, Gloucestershire – 389
Hucknall Weather Station – 188
Huddersfield, Yorkshire – 140, 174
Hudson, Faith – 263
Hudson, Pauline – 263
Huey, Captain – 11
Hughes, Ken – 552
Hughes, P. – 535
Hughes, Robert – 477
Hull, Mr. – 378
Hulme, Mrs. – 392
Hundell, Andrew – 423
Hundell, Ray – 423
Hundell, W. – 423
Hunt, Michael – 517
Hunt, William – 347
Hunter, Alan – 328
Hurley, Kevin – 290
Hurley, Michael – 409
Hurst, Mr. and Mrs. – 174
Hussey, Miss – 251
Huyton, Merseyside – 410
Hyde, Andrew – 315

Hyde, Joseph – 241
Hynek, Allen, J. – 350
Hythe, Kent – 518

I

Iberia Airlines, Spain – 448
Ibstone House, Hertfordshire – 258
Ilford, Essex – 408
Inglesby, E.V. – 71
Inglesby, Paul, Reverend – 71
Ingoldmells caravan site, Lincolnshire – 381
Instone, Philip – 346
International Sky Scouts Association – 306, 369
Ipswich, Suffolk – 141, 407
Irvine, Ayrshire – 546
Irving, Maud – 208
Irwin, J. – 465
Isle of Wight – 35, 118, 141, 148, 167, 205, 213, 218, 241, 306, 328, 342
Isle of Wight UFO Society – 35, 110, 149, 155, 303, 348, 371
Isles, Harold – 24
Itkonen, Veikko – 337
ITV Midlands News – 13
Ivy Chimneys Riding School, Epping – 150

J

Jackson, D.C. – 5
Jaffe, Mike – 86
James, David – 551
Jamieson, Mr. and Mrs. – 219
Jarrow – 219, 226, 241, 372
Jarvis, Jean – 170
Jefferson, William – 115
Jenkins, Brian – 358
Jenkins, Gwynn – 333
Jenkins, Mr. and Mrs. – 347
Jerritt, George – 19, 380
Jersey – 174
Jodrell Bank – 203, 299, 436
John Rabson Park – 554
Johnson, Colin – 34, 208
Johnson, Harry – 361
Johnson, Jennifer – 550
Johnson, Kerry – 326
Johnson, Michael – 230
Johnson, F., Peter – 545
Jones, Andrew – 234
Jones, Brian – 169

Jones, C.H. – 220
Jones, David – 13, 15, 391
Jones, Earl, James – 60
Jones, Keith – 326
Jones, Myra – 100
Jones, Peter – 134
Jones, Richard – 234
Jones, Robert – 306
Jordan, Ellen – 100
Jordan, Robert – 553
Journal of Transient Aerial Phenomena – 195
Jowett, M. – 429
Joy, Paul – 175
Joyce, Paul – 333
Joynes, Rodney, Thomas – 504

K

Karslake, Cornwall – 184
Kelly, Bridget – 395
Kelman, Allan – 208
Kembury, Edwin – 397
Kennedy Space Center, Florida – 523
Kenny, Paul – 465
Kensington Central Library, London – 101, 375
Kent, Ian – 424
Kent, Peter – 37
Kenton, Newcastle-upon-Tyne – 497
Kerfoot, Keith – 125
Kerrison, S. – 195
Kettering, Northamptonshire – 297
Kettledrum Inn, Burnley – 451
Kidderminster – 222
Kidsgrove – 379, 383, 391
Kilworth, John – 92
Kimber, John – 141
Kimberley, Kenneth – 229
Kind, Stephen – 405
King, Barry – 396
King, David – 461
King, John, T. – 263
King, Olive, Mrs. – 406
King, Terrence – 482
Kingswinford, West Midlands – 205
Kingswood, Bristol – 353
Kirkby Industrial Estate, Liverpool – 17, 165
Kirkby Underwood – 445
Kirkham, Harry – 74
Kirkwood, Ian – 326
Knee, Charles, Jr. – 202

Knee, John – 520
Knewstub, G.F.N. – 64
Knight, Robert – 206
Knightcott, Devon – 466
Knottingley, Yorkshire – 409
Komiske, C.A. – 20
Kosmos 96 – 246
Krushelnycky Ascold – 332
Kynman, M.G. – 497

L

Laban, Raymond – 136
Ladderedge, Staffordshire – 448
Lake Llyn Celyn – 306
Lake Windermere – 390
Lakeside Ty-Nant Farm – 306
Lamb, J. – 212
Lambert, W.R. – 172
Lamorna Cove – 17
Lancashire Hill, Stockport – 352
Langdale Valley – 390
Langenhoe Hall – 228
Langford-Holt, Sir John – 312
Langland, Swansea – 136
Langley, Mr. – 502
Langley, Robert – 255
Lansdowne, Bournemouth – 220
Lapalme, Mrs. – 31
Larsen, Mr. and Mrs. E.I. – 12
Laurenson, Miss – 333
Lawson, W.E. – 268
Lawton, J., Reverend – 172
Le Page, Doris – 220
Leadgate Catholic School, County Durham – 323
Leam Lane Estate, Gateshead – 400
Leam Lane Farm – 166
Leam Lane, Gateshead, County Durham – 165, 300
Leamington Spa – 506
Leather, Peter – 309
Leaworthy, Betty – 170
Lee, Michael – 126
Leeds, Yorkshire – 80, 403, 386
Leek, Staffordshire – 533
Leicester – 103, 321
Leicestershire – 369, 370
Leighton, R. – 263
Lence, Stan – 531
Leslie, Desmond – 36, 64, 473
Letchworth, North Hertfordshire – 436

Lewis, Anne – 501
Lewis, Eric – 28
Lewis, Hazel – 510
Lewis, Valerie – 454
Leyton, London – 559
Liberal Airport – 95
Lidget Green, Bradford – 326
Lightfoot, Paul – 125
Lilly, M.A. – 220
Lindores, Sheena – 492
Linfield College – 149
Linnet, J. – 204
Lister, B. – 345
Little Hulton – 276
Little, P. – 276
Littlehampton, – 175
Liverpool – 193, 206, 388, 402, 497
Liversedge, L. – 74
Liversedge, Yorkshire – 510
Llandudno – 509
Llangeinor Mountain – 91
Llewellyn, Dennis, John – 15, 16, 66, 70, 75, 93, 210, 211, 370, 530
Llewellyn, Ruby – 15, 66
Lloyd, Donald – 127
Lobelia Cottage, Hampers Lane, Storrington – 443
Lockhart, Douglas – 22
Locklear, Mr. C. – 67
Loftus, Judith – 102
London Airport – 477
London Evening News – 34
London UFO Research Organisation – 98, 101
Long Lye, Bishopswood – 331
Longbenton, Newcastle-upon-Tyne – 376
Longley Junior School, Doncaster – 381
Longshaw, Mr. and Mrs. – 106
Longton, Stoke-on-Trent – 409
Look Magazine – 42
Lord Nelson Street, South Shields – 409
Lord, Harry – 124
Lorenzen, Coral – 164
Lovell, Bernard, Sir – 299
Low Fell, Gateshead – 510
Lowdenson, Mr. and Mrs. – 258
Lowdon, A. – 213
Lowestoft, – 104, 106, 314, 448
Lowther, John – 333
Ludlow Museum, Shropshire – 314

Luisi, Mario – 106
Lulsgate Bottom, Somerset – 229
Luton, Bedfordshire – 80
Luttrell, John H. – 58, 59
Lychett Minster – 445
Lynch, Kevin – 424

M

M6, Holmes Chapel – 407
Macclesfield – 175, 182
Mackenzie, Alastair – 557
Mackenzie, Olga – 557
MacLean, Ogilvy, Charles, – 313
Madams Wood – 261
Maddison, R. – 300
Maddocks, John – 316
Maddocks, Stanley – 316
Madge, W.A. – 170
Maidenhead – 435
Maidstone, Kent – 139, 383
Mains, T.F. – 203
Major, Barbara – 404
Malpos, Pete – 223
Malvern – 127
Malvern Hills – 206
Manchester – 182, 189, 203, 388
Manchester Airport – 140
Manchester Evening News – 67
Manchester Meteorological Office – 23
Mandham, Paula – 100
Mann, Mr. and Mrs. – 107
Manor Farm, Charlton, Wiltshire – 121
Manor Hospital, Derby – 482
Mansfield, Nottingham – 554
Mantle, Philip – 60, 278, 362
Mardle, Stewart – 229
Margate – 149
Marlow, Buckinghamshire – 461
Marlow, Harry – 506
Marlow, Valerie – 526
Marlow-Hazel – 527
Marr, Hector – 95
Marsden, Carole – 394
Marsden, Kathleen – 63
Marshall, Frank – 513, 517
Marshall, Sheila – 372
Martin, R. – 131
Martino, Ronald – 348
Martyn, C.M.W. – 251

Marvin, A. – 518
Maskey, Geoffrey – 230
Mathews, Trevor – 517
Maura, Hamando, Captain – 448
Mawdsley, Kathleen – 385
Mawford, Mary – 504
Mayhew, Harold – 106
McCann, Nigel – 384
McCarthy, Colin – 316, 318, 368
McCerlane, J. – 226
McCue, David – 398, 399
McCue, John – 329
McCutcheon, Margaret – 165
McDonald, Professor James – 290
McDougal, Ann – 482
McDougall, Stuart, John – 193
McFarlane, J. – 261
McGill, James – 90
Mckean, Miss H. – 10
McKeown, Betty – 89
McKeown, John – 89
McKinley, Don – 168
McLean, A. – 141
McLean, G. – 141
Mead J. – 504
Medway Bridge, Chatham, Kent – 384
Melbourne, Victoria, Australia – 278
Melton, Homer – 30
Menadue, Clive – 378
Meopham, Kent – 518
Mercury capsule – 86
Meriden – 426, 439
Meridian, Ohio – 141
Merron, Michael – 530
Merseyside – 69
Metcalfe, Mr. and Mrs. – 387
Meteorological Office – 37, 402
Meteorological Officer, *RAF Mildenhall* – 22
Metherell Moor Farm, Devon – 408
Metzger, Captain – 95
Middle Moneynut Farm, Edinburgh – 123
Middle Wallop, Hampshire – 333
Middlesbrough – 333
Middleton, Joyce – 384
Middleton, Peter – 384
Middleton, Susan – 384
Mills, Peter, MP – 460
Middlewich Road, Crewe – 391

Midgeley, M. – 345
Midland Brick Company, Ansley Hall – 546
Midland Planetary Association – 255
Milakovic, Mr. and Mrs. – 520
Miles, Howard – 541
Miller, Alfred – 21
Miller, Stewart – 305
Millican, Anthony – 494
Milligan, Claudine – 117
Mills, Brian – 175
Mills, Pete – 223
Ministry of Aviation – 257
Ministry of Defence – 317, 403
Miskin, Remolds – 66
Mitchell, Susan – 118
Mobberley, Cheshire – 182
MOD – (DI55) Mr. J.C. Dickison – 412
MOD – 260
MOD – 361, 458
MOD – *Dorset* – 356
MOD – Gaynor South – 147
MOD – Head of S4 (Air) *Mr. I.E. Carruthers* – 412
MOD – Mr. Cassie – 498
MOD – Mr. L.W. Akhurst – 260, 362, 498
MOD – Mr. P.S. Webb – 458
MOD – Mr. Perks – 453
MOD – Mr. W.F. Allen – 478, 480
MOD – Officer, Defence Intelligence Service staff – 412
MOD – Police Sergeant Smiggs – 485
MOD – R.A. Langton – 182
Moe, Victoria, Australia – 112
Moffat, Dumfriesshire – 20
Moffat, Mr. and Mrs. – 473
Mohan, David, Anthony – 136
Moigne Downs, Dorset – 429
Mole, Commander – 36
Monkseaton – 480
Montague, Gerald – 345
Montebello – 110
Moonie, Phyllis – 551
Moor House Inn, Seaton Burn, Northumberland – 168
Moorabbin Airport – 286
Moordown, Bournemouth – 446
Moore, Brian – 463
Moore, T. – 190
Morden, Surrey – 417, 451
Moreau, Richard – 226

Morecambe Bay – 382
Morecambe, Lancashire – 263, 368
Morpeth, Northumberland – 25, 375
Morris, H. – 237
Mortimer, John – 486
Morton-Sooley, G. – 191
Mosborough incident – 80
Moseley, Mr. – 408
Mosley, Judith – 355
Moss, Frederick, Thomas – 490
Motor vessel, *Azmaut* – 156
Moule, R. – 205
Mount Vernon Airport – 133
MUFON – 85
Muir, Bill – 124
Muir, Jeanette – 282
Muir, Marion – 196
Muir, Mrs. – 262
Muir, William – 116
Muller, Joan – 436
Mumbles Head – 17
Muncy, C.F. – 69
Munford, George – 439
Murphy, Alan – 89
Murphy, John – 89
Murphy, Peter – 90, 437
Murray, Captain – 142
Murray, Mrs. – 524
Muscarello, Norman – 223
Myers, W.J. – 69

N

Nantwich, Cheshire – 473
NASA – 457
NASA, Cape Kennedy – 264
Nastoff, T. – 220
National Archives, London – 329
National Institute for Research in Nuclear Science – 308
Neale, Mrs. and Mr. – 536
Neaves, Barry – 326
Needham, George – 366, 368
Needham, Mr. and Mrs. – 328
Neill, Mrs. – 546
Nelson, Lancashire – 100
New Forest – 371
Newcastle Arts Festival – 204
Newcastle-upon-Tyne – 90, 91, 169, 195, 205, 209, 365, 402, 405, 473

Newlands Corner – 369
Newnham, Kenneth – 531
Newnham, Michael – 326
Newport, Isle of Wight – 220, 333
Newsome, J. – 539
Newton Aycliffe, County Durham – 252
Newton Hall School, Durham – 444
NICAP – 49, 54, 65, 202, 204, 206, 361, 537
Nicholls, Mr. – 209
Nightingale, John – 129
Noble, Judith – 393
NORAD – 34
Norman, Paul – 290
Norris, Dennis – 518
Norris, Peter – 290,
North Shields – 389
North Yorkshire – 205
Northampton – 365, 407, 442
Northfield, Birmingham – 473
Northumberland – 89, 116, 173, 179, 268, 352
Northwich, Cheshire – 309, 386, 387
Norton, W.J. – 314
Nottingham – 4, 92, 104, 139, 189, 220
Nottinghamshire – 178
Nubel, Basil – 98
Nuneaton Rotary Club – 516

O

O'Brien, P. – 370
O'Flynn, Gerard – 156
Oakley, Dave – 290
Ochsner, W.B. – 161
Ocker Hill Power Station – 136
Odd, Stephen – 255
Oddotte, Ben – 127
Oddy, Stephen – 226
Old Basford, Nottingham – 486
Old Christchurch Commercials – 453
Old Faversham – 480
Old Park Steel Works, Oldbury – 448
Old Trafford, Manchester – 195
Old Windsor, Berkshire – 504
Oldfield, Mrs. – 388
Oldham, Lancashire – 191, 328, 440
Olive, W.G. – 220
Oliver, Norman – 195, 524
Ollerton, Nottinghamshire – 372
Onslow, Ken – 103
Openshaw, Cheshire – 510

Oram, Michael – 559
Oregon – 204
Orme, Barry – 371
Ormsby, Brian – 506
Otley, Jean – 21
Otley, Lesley – 102, 104, 142, 165, 323
Otley, Yorkshire – 204, 387
Otterburn – 393
Ovenden, Halifax – 208

P

Pace, Tony – 391, 403, 405, 452, 454, 498
Pagan, J. – 388
Page, Martin – 189
Page, Sandra – 251
Page, Susan – 428
Paignton – 524
Painter, Kenneth – 547
Palmer, Keith – 316
Panaretou, Barry – 351
Panther, John – 297
Par Sands Beach, Cornwall – 402
Parish, Rose, June – 479
Parker, Frederick – 138
Parker, W.H. – 305
Parkhurst Forest, Isle of Wight – 237
Parkhurst, Isle of Wight – 333
Parkinson, John – 173
Parks, A. – 252
Parkstone, Dorset – 125
Parr, George – 38
Parr, Norman – 530
Parry-Jones, Elizabeth – 226
Parsons, Estelle – 60
Parsons, K. – 514
Partridge Green, Sussex – 441
Paszek, K., Mrs. – 392
Patterson, J. – 400
Pattison, Tom – 373
Payne, A. – 491
Payne, Pat – 451
Peach, Roy – 154
Peacock, Bob – 297
Peake, Frank – 177
Pearce, Timothy – 42
Pearson Frank – 128
Pearson, Kevin – 424
Pearson, P. – 214
Peck, Robin – 545

Peckham Rye, London – 402
Peddie, M. – 473
Pellegrina, Greta – 96
Pelsall, West Midlands – 174
Pendleton, Gordon, Captain – 90
Penge, Kent /London -319, 323, 477
Penkridge, Staffordshire – 157
Penny, Mr. and Mrs. – 30
Penthouse Magazine – 478, 479
Pentre Meyrick – 37
Penybont Common, Llandrindod Wells – 314
Percival, Robin – 400
Perry Common playing fields – 423
Perry, Norman, Andrew – 483
Perry, Pat – 474
Peterborough – 448
Peters, Ann – 393
Pewley Down, Surrey – 504
Philpot, Janet – 236
Phipps, Tom – 37
Pickering, Brian – 91
Pickering, John – 365
Pilgrim, S. – 92
Pinkney, John – 291
Piper, John – 536
Piper, Neil – 543
Plumbe, B.N. – 486
Plunkett, Denis – 308
Pogostin, S., Lee – 60
Police – *Bacup* – 438
Police – *Biggleswade* – 494
Police – *Billericay,* – 447
Police – *Bredbury* – 385
Police – *Buxton* – 491
Police – *Cheshire Constabulary* – 438
Police – Chief Constable – 483
Police – Chief Constable of East Sussex – 448
Police – Chief Constable of St. Helens, Mr. A. Atherton – 304
Police – Chief Inspector I. Lewis – 466
Police – *Christchurch* – 453
Police – Constable 285 Herbert Edward Hawkins – 483
Police – Constable 565 Alan .F. Delaney – 321
Police – Constable Anthony Penny – 123
Police – Constable Barry Siviers – 450
Police – Constable Basil Warren – 487
Police – Constable Brian Earnshaw – 438
Police – Constable Brian Fenlon – 261
Police – Constable Clifford Waycott – 410, 415
Police – Constable Colin Clive Perks – 256
Police – Constable Colin Donahue – 438
Police – Constable D. Clough – 409
Police – Constable D. Holloway – 371
Police – Constable David F. Smith – 193
Police – Constable David Harris – 91
Police – Constable E. Holmes – 372
Police – Constable Fox – 75
Police – Constable Gordon Cameron – 304
Police – Constable Harwood – 252
Police – Constable Higginson – *450*
Police – Constable Jackson – 437
Police – Constable John Williamson – 89
Police – Constable Keith Droudge – 41, 415
Police – Constable Lionel Haw – 385
Police – Constable Malcolm Reader – 438
Police – Constable Michael Kirby – 487
Police – Constable Parry – 75
Police – Constable Parsonage – 385
Police – Constable Peter Buford – 37
Police – Constable Peter Dawson – 405
Police – Constable Peter Morris – 385
Police – Constable Philip Nuttall – 368
Police – Constable Pucker – 461
Police – Constable R.G. Warren – 326
Police – Constable Robert Young – 385
Police – Constable Roger Willey – 410, 415, 417, 425
Police – Constable Roy Nineham – 453, 455
Police – Constable Underwood – 464
Police – Constable William Donovan – 154
Police – Constable Z. Bradshaw – 516
Police – *Coventry* – 505
Police – *Crediton* – 483
Police – Deputy Chief Constable of Devon and Cornwall – 412
Police – *Derbyshire Constabulary* – 491
Police – Detective Constable Terry Lynch – 496
Police – *Devon and Cornwall Constabulary* – 410, 466, 483
Police – Ex-Devon and Cornwall Constabulary cadet, Brian Hagan – 417
Police – *Farnborough* – 37
Police – *Farnham* – 503
Police – *Glamorgan* – 37
Police – *Hampshire Constabulary* – 193
Police – Inspector Albert Jordan – 385
Police – *Inspector R. Street* – 372

Police – *Kent Constabulary* – 496
Police – *Lancashire Constabulary* – 385, 438
Police – *Leek Wootton* – 428
Police – *Lyndhurst* – 371
Police – *Merseyside* – 437
Police – *Okehampton* – 412
Police – Sergeant Derek Davis – 483
Police – Sergeant McGregory – 485
Police – Sergeant Sidney Earnshaw – 491
Police – Sergeant T. Blenkinsop – 516
Police – *Sevenoaks* – 496
Police – *Steyning* – 443
Police – *Sussex* – 380
Police – *Thames Valley* – 461
Police – *Ventnor* – 154
Police – *Welland* – 372
Police – *Carmarthen and Cardigan Constabulary* – 552
Police – Constable Page – 554
Police – Sergeant Martin Burgess – 550
Polperro, Cornwall – 149
Pontop Pike radio mast – 386
Poole – 227, 529
Poplar Farm, Evenlode – 13
Port Talbot – 67, 520
Portchester, Hampshire – 31
Portsmouth – 189
Portway, Joanna – 512
Portway, Lisa – 512
Portway, Shirley – 512
Potts, W. – 375
Poulton, James – 138
Powell, Anne – 473
Powell, Brian – 165
Powell, Catherine – 213
Powell, F. – 230
Powenall, Anne – 189
Powenall, Valerie – 189
Poyser, Pete – 223
Pratt, Kevin – 269-275
Pratt, Stephen – 269-275
Preston Control Centre – 536
Preston, G.P., Brigadier – 463
Price, K., Miss – 393
Prime Minister Harold Wilson, OBE – 313, 316, 380
Prime Minster's Question Time – 306, 309
Prince, Jack – 425
Pringle Lucy – 358

Prior, Joyce – 542
Project Blue Book – 560
Proton Linear Accelerator – 307
Prynn, Alan – 329
Pryor, G.H. – 91
Puckwell Farm, Isle of Wight – 154
Puffitt, William – 436
Pulham Market, Norfolk – 37
Pursey, F. – 204
Putney, London – 363
Pyle, South Wales – 378
Pyle, Sylvia – 378

Q

Quick, Leone – 443
Quick, Michelle – 443
Quick, Paul – 443
Quick, Suzanne – 443, 463

R

R. Peel Junior School, Manchester – 261
RAAF – Flight Lieutenant N. Hudson – 112
RAAF – Squadron Leader A.F. Javes – 112
Radcliffe, Manchester – 401
Radcliffe-on-Trent – 373
Raddings, Pauline – 531
Radio station *WTOD* – 167
Radiosonde Station, Liverpool – 263
RAF – *Air Vice Marshall* – 361
RAF – *Barton Hall, near Preston* – 126
RAF – *Benson* – 331
RAF – *Bentwaters* – 34
RAF – *Boulmer* – 118
RAF – *Bovingdon* – 34
RAF – *Chivenor* – 99, 517
RAF – *Church Lawford* – 98
RAF – *Corporal Rickwood* – 329
RAF – *Cosford* – 142
RAF – Cosford, Flight Lt. Stevens – 143
RAF – Cosford, Flt. Lt. Reverend Brian George Henry – 145
RAF – Cosford, Flying Officer Robert Alan Roberts – 143
RAF – Cosford, Wing Commander Wolsey – 143
RAF – *Farnborough* – 431
RAF – Farnborough Air Show – 100
RAF – *Finningley* – 532
RAF – Flight Lieutenant Anthony Bardsley (Air Intelligence department) – 82

RAF – Flight Lieutenant R.H. White of S6 – 82
RAF – Flight Lt. M. Galbauer
RAF – Flt. Lt. Penny – 329
RAF – Flt. Lt. Williams – 329
RAF – *Fylingdales Early Warning Station* – 444
RAF – *Hack Green Radar* – 402
RAF – *HQ Shinfield Park* – 12
RAF – *Kidbrooke* – 226
RAF – *Lyneham* – 362
RAF – M/Sig. C.L. Goldsmith
RAF – *Manston* – 116
RAF – *Markham, Norfolk* – 22
RAF – Merlyn Rees, Under-Secretary – 460
RAF – *Mount Batten, Plymouth* – 17
RAF – Officer Mr. W.D. Evans – 136
RAF – Officer Ernest Scott – 91
RAF – Pilot Officer Terrence Jones – 306
RAF – Provost and Security Services – 99, 329
RAF – Psychologist, Alec Cassie – 431
RAF – *Scunthorpe, Lincolnshire* – 85
RAF – Sergeant J.W. Scott – 99
RAF – *Shawbury* – 13, 329
RAF – Squadron Leader Bob Cox – 373
RAF – Squadron Leader Shipwright – 369
RAF – *Valley* – 306, 387, 409
RAF – *Waddington, Lincoln* – 121
RAF – *Welford, Newbury, Berkshire* – 362, 462
RAF – Wing Commander C.M. Gibbs – 99
RAF – Wing Commander Eric Alfred Cox – 418, 419, 420, 421, 422
RAF – *Wittering* – 448, 517
RAF – *Woodbridge* – 34
RAF – *Cottesmore* – 538
RAF – *Scampton* – 535
RAF – *West Raynham* – 545
RAF – Wing Commander V.J. Chown – 521
Raikes Lane, Bolton – 554
Ramsbottom, Manchester – 389
Ramstein – 376
Rand, John – 448
Rand, M.W., First Lt. – 33
Randall, D., Robert – 123
Rannoch Station, Perthshire – 323
Rattray, S.A., B.Sc. – 522
Rawden, A.J. – 118
Raynes Park, Merton, London – 497
Rayney, David – 325
Reading Evening News – 400

Reading, Berkshire – 242, 329, 389, 458
Reay, John – 424
Reddish – 182
Redditch, Worcestershire – 341, 347, 438
Redfern, Nick – 146, 158, 257, 329
Redgrave, Vanessa – 93
Redhead, B. – 209
Redhill, Surrey – 509
Redman, Michael – 471
Redman, Pamela – 471
Redmarley – 23
Redmond, Virgil S. – 65
Redshaw, Paul – 513
Reed, Colin – 175
Rees, Merlyn – 306, 309, 379, 414
Reigate, Surrey – 100, 448
Retford, Nottinghamshire – 16
Revill, Walter – 96
Rex Cinema, Cheshire – 257
Rex Cinema, North Shields – 347
Reynolds Chains, Coventry – 62
Rhossili beach, Gower – 506
Rhuddlan – 448
Richard, S. – 255
Richards, M. – 242
Richards, Sam – 486
Richardson, Bill – 123
Richardson, Stanley – 139
Richmond, Jerry – 505
Ridgeway, Christopher – 195
Riley, G. – 406
Rising Brook, Staffordshire – 389
Rising Sun, public house – 498
River Exe, Devon – 476
Robbins, Carl – 543
Roberts, A.C. – 101
Roberts, Thelma – 20
Robin Hood Island, Hall Green – 347
Robinson, Bruce – 554
Robinson, Charles – 479
Robinson, Clive – 424
Robinson, Dave – 384
Robinson, Derek – 301
Robinson, Evelyn – 410
Robinson, M. – 436
Robinson, Mr. – 378
Robinson, Richard – 438
Robinson, T. – 441

Robley, Jessie – 387
Rochford, Paul – 498
Rockinghams Farm, Layer Marney – 213
Roe, Ruby – 175
Rogers, Ken – 133, 255, 303, 380
Rogers, Marie – 136
Rollett, Frank – 375
Rollington, John – 140
Romford, Essex – 140, 447
Rookley Farm – 149
Rose, Ken – 437
Roslin, Midlothian – 127
Ross-on-Wye, Herefordshire – 528
Rostron, A. – 530
Rothbury, Northumberland – 118, 444
Rotherham – 519
Round, Frank – 263
Roundhay Park Wood – 126
Roundway Hospital, Devizes – 141
Rouse Edward – 375
Roush, F.E. – 139
Rowlands Gill, County Durham – 258
Rownhams Mount – 124
Royal Albert Docks, London – 516
Royal Observer Corps – 378, 409
Royal Ordnance factory – 352, 384, 400
Royal Shakespeare Company – 527
Rubery bypass – 464
Ruchill Park, Glasgow – 352
Rudd, John – 123
Rumbold, Jack – 333
Runcorn, Cheshire – 372
Rushton E. – 423
Rushton, George – 550
Rushton, Peter – 301
Russell Hotel, Bloomsbury, London – 82
Russell, Janet – 337
Russell, John – 193
Russell, Rider, Anthony – 334, 335
Rutherford High Energy Laboratory – 308
Ruthin Hospital – 342
Ryan, Shane – 278, 294
Ryde – 118
Ryhope General Hospital – 102
Ryton, County Durham – 223

S

Sachs, Norman – 149
Saddleworth, Lancashire – 263

Sadler, R. – 208
Saffron Walden, Essex – 234
Sagan, Carl – 60, 350
Salford, Lancashire – 168, 187
Salisbury Plain – 325
Salisbury, Ronald – 352
Salisbury, Wiltshire – 260
Samblebe, Mr. – 288
Samson, Derek – 179, 202, 206, 213, 307, 331, 347, 354, 365, 366, 505, 516, 537
Sanderson, Albert – 173
Sanderson, Linda – 96
Sandwell College – 457
Sankey, David – 125, 452
Satterly, N.E. – 443
Satterthwaite, Frank – 124, 262, 323, 355, 379, 528
Satterthwaite, M. – 498
Saucer Forum – 69
Saundersfoot – 258
Savage, Suzanne – 290
Savoy, H.J., Captain – 33
Sawtry – 301
Saxilby – 518
Scarborough – 318, 370
Scott, A.P. – 219
Scott, Ruth – 127
Scowl, Margaret – 96
Seaburn – 439
Seal, Mr. – 332
Seaton Carew, near Hartlepool – 405
Secretary of State for Defence – 306, 379, 459
Sedgley, Wolverhampton – 135
Sedlescombe, near Hastings – 398
Seighford Aerodrome – 75
Self's Garage, Denton Burn, Newcastle-upon-Tyne – 18
Selmes, Richard – 477
Selwood, Frank – 125
Sembach – 376
Sergeant, Mavis – 381
Shakespeare, John – 74
Shanklin, Isle of Wight – 219
Shard, Kathleen – 182
Sharman, James – 192
Sharmans Cross School, Shirley, Solihull – 444
Sharp, Alan, B.Sc., B.Eng., F.G.S., F.R.A.S. – 323
Sharp, Mary – 110
Sharples, William – 437
Shaw, C.H., Reverend – 165

Shaw, James, Francis – 402
Sheaf, Ian – 407
Sheepy Magna, Leicestershire – 417
Sheffield Star – 98
Sheldon, Birmingham – 226
Sheldrick, A. – 214
Shelton, Derek – 65
Shelton, Stoke-on-Trent – 390
Shepherd, Edgar – 252
Shepherd, Gerry – 287
Shepperton – 33, 241
Ship, *British Cavalier* – 306
Shoreham, Sussex – 30, 219
Shotley Bridge, Consett, County Durham – 364, 377, 403
Shrewsbury – 441
Shuttlewood, Arthur – 304, 323
Sibford Ferris, Banbury – 375
Sidmouth, Devon – 410, 444
Sileby, Leicestershire – 553
Silloth, near Carlisle, Cumbria – 278
Silver Birch Caravan Site – 494
Simonton, Joe – 32
Simpson, N. – 38
Sinclair, Duane – 65
Sinclair, William – 328
Sirisena, Ananda L. – 170
Skerton, Lancaster – 461
Skywatch International – 85
Slade, Brian – 557
Sleaford, Lincoln – 428
Slough – 464
Small, Mrs. – 408
Smethwick – 92
Smith, C. – 35
Smith, Ethel – 559
Smith, Fred – 35, 110, 155, 371
Smith, Graham – 381
Smith, John – 375, 477
Smith, Kath – 35, 214, 531, 542
Smith, Keith – 40
Smith, N. – 220
Smith, Pat – 35, 110
Smith, Peter – 400
Smith, Rebecca – 477
Smith, Reginald – 172
Smith, Robert, John – 220
Smith, Stephen, B.A. – 323

Snitterfield, near Stratford-upon-Avon – 506
Snixhall, Barry – 551
Solihull – 242, 347, 349, 465
Solway Firth – 90
Sopley, Hampshire – 452
South Devon – 515
South Ouston – 438
South Reddish – 387
South Shields – 208, 389, 409, 440, 441
South, Harold – 159
Southampton – 101, 193, 137, 220, 324
Southampton Docks – 75
Southend-on-Sea – 35
Southern Television – 36
Southwick, Sussex – 255
Southwick, Wiltshire – 426
Southwold, Suffolk – 239
Sowerby Bridge – 408
Space Review – 100
Space Rocks UK – 210
Space-link Books – 39
Space-link Magazine – 36, 98
Spadeadam Rocket Establishment, Carlisle – 436
Spademan, B. – 425
Spalding, Lincolnshire – 424
Spangdahlem – 376
Sparkes, Michael – 540
Spencer, Ray – 426
Spielberg, Steven – 71
Spotwood, Teresa – 96
Spread Eagle, public house – 450
Sproson, Terry – 383
St. Alban's Head Coastguard Station – 393
St. Austell, Cornwall – 142
St. Chad's, Liverpool – 172
St. Germans – 389
St. Helens, Lancashire – 125, 304
St. Mary's Industrial School – 19
St. Peter's Finger, public house – 445
Stafford – 405
Staffordshire – 33, 35, 100
Staffordshire UFO Group – 159
Staindrop, near Darlington – 378
Staines, R.L. – 542
Stalker, Harry – 127
Stamford, Lincolnshire – 121, 315
Stanford, Ray – 82
Stanford, Rex – 82

Stanley, County Durham – 376, 437
Stanway, Roger – 391, 403, 405, 498, 500
Stapleford Woods – 384
Stead, F.M. – 417
Stebbing, R., Susanne – 100
Steel, Andrew – 205
Steel, Eileen – 21
Stella South Power Station, Gateshead – 363
Stephens, Dr. – 58
Stephenson, Nigel – 101, 121, 19, 195, 380
Stevens, S. – 124
Stevenson, D. – 226
Stevenson, Lilly – 398, 399
Stickland, Charles – 12, 195
Stiffkey, Norfolk – 326
Stirling, Josephine – 193
Stockport – 23, 104, 386
Stockton, Cheshire – 190
Stockton-on-Tees – 345, 418
Stoke-on-Trent – 368, 383, 461
Stokes, Edward – 390
Stone, Staffordshire – 551
Stoneham Grammar School, Reading – 400
Stonehenge – 219
Stones, D.R. – 318
Stoney Cross Airfield – 371
Story, Alan – 418
Stotfold, Bedfordshire – 494
Stott, John – 190
Stotter, J.D. – 407
Stow Hill, Newport – 490
Strange Aerial Sights Information Organisation – 66
Stranraer Corporation – 11
Stratford-upon-Avon – 93, 530
Stratford-upon-Avon UFO Society – 326
Streatham, London – 334
Street, Somerset – 530
Streetsbrook Road, Solihull – 353
Stricklands, Hastings – 397
Strong, Judith – 393
Strood – 126
Stroud, Gloucestershire – 251
Suffolk Square, Cheltenham – 10
Sujka, Bernard – 196
Suley, J. – 486
Suncliff Hotel, Bournemouth – 557
Sunday Dispatch – 11

Sunday Post – 104
Sunderland – 219, 426, 439
Surrey – 12
Sussex Downs – 400
Sutcliff, Tony – 506
Sutcliffe, Mrs. – 369
Sutton Coldfield – 74, 182, 205, 215, 307, 494
Swaddle, B. – 402
Swain, Kenneth – 377
Swan Hotel, Keswick, Cumbria – 407
Swansea Bay – 67
Swansea man – 495
Swindale, F.L. – 104
Szqarga, Wendy – 441

T

Taber, K.J. – 80
Tait, Cecily – 215
Tait, Jack – 215, 219, 319
Tarbuck, Geoffrey – 365
Tarleton – 536
Taunton – 99
Taylor, A.W. – 35
Taylor, Beryl – 498
Taylor, C. – 436
Taylor, Charles – 498
Taylor, Edward – 379
Taylor, Philip – 515
Taylor, Richard – 306
Taylor, Vivienne – 138
Team Valley Trading Estate – 386
Teece, Graham – 398
Telford, Robert – 387
Telstar – 241
Tenterden, Kent – 461
Territorial Army – 527
Testwood – 191
Thatcher, D.J. – 426
The Dandenong Journal – 290
The Lizard – 17
The Migil Five Group – 333
The Outer Limits 'The Bellero Shield' – 59
The Wheatsheaf Hotel, Newport – 303
The X-Files episode, Jose Chung's *'From Outer Space'* – 60
Thomas, Elgar – 188
Thomas, George A. – 30
Thompson, Richard – 220, 503, 510
Thompson, William – 546

Thorburn, June – 450
Thornlow School, Weymouth, Dorset – 261
Thornton, G., Mrs. – 509.
Three Tuns, public house – 445
Threkeld, Harold – 104
Thurlaston, Leicester – 53
Thurmaston, Leicestershire – 538
Thurnscoe – 405
Tibbitts, Bob – 25, 62, 98, 111, 201, 215, 314, 316, 505, 520, 523, 535, 536, 544, 553
Tidy, Steven – 536
Tighe, Joy – 290
Tile Cross, Birmingham – 429
Tilehurst, Kent – 12, 358
Till, Mabel – 183
Tilt, Dennis – 303
Tilt, Jean – 303
Tintagel Castle – 99
Tipping, Mr. – 10
Tipton – 128
Tipton, West Midlands – 551
Tiro, Ohio – 345
Tisbury – 121
Titchfield, Hampshire – 535
Toft, H. – 304
Toft, Ron – 511
Tomlinson, Arthur – 401
Tosh, Ramsay – 208
Trent Bridge – 129
Trevor, J. – 212
Trewyddfa, Swansea – 241
Trotter, Caroline – 394
Trowbridge, Wiltshire – 377
Truro, Cornwall – 91
Tryweryn Reservoir – 306
Tucker, Martin – 141
Tulley, Mr. – 504
Tunbridge Wells, Kent – 441
Tunnicliffe, Mr. – 406
Tupe, Der, Van, Angelo – 552
Turleigh, near Bradford-on-Avon, Wiltshire – 39
Turnbull, Olive – 191
Turner, David – 464
Turner, M. – 251
Twist, John – 536
Tyneside UFO Society – 21, 89, 102, 124
Tyneside Unidentified Flying Objects Society – 204

U

UFO film, *Phenomena – Seven Point Seven* – 252
UFO Magazine – 146
UFO Times – 195
UFOLOG – 35
Uley, Gloucestershire – 533
Unexplained Phenomena Research Society – 358
Union Club, Cheltenham – 95
Unitarian Church Hall, Newport, Isle of Wight – 36, 262
Unsworth, Ann – 554
Unsworth, Bury – 550
Unsworth, Carol – 554
Uphoff, Chauncey – 134
Uplands, Gloucestershire – 24
Upshire, Essex – 237
Upton – 474
Upton, J.H. – 41
USA – Lupton, Roman – 530
USA – University of Colorado – 514
USA – Acquino, Mr. – 328
USA – Air Force, Major George A. Filer – 85
USA – American Embassy – 210
USA – Ann Arbor – 67
USA – Area 51 – 148
USA – Ashland, Nebraska – 466
USA – Astronaut, Edgar Mitchell – 210
USA – Atkinson, Lou – 347
USA – Austin, Texas – 368
USA – Baker, Kimberley – 300
USA – Baker, Max – 307
USA – Bangor, Maine – 263
USA – Beer, P.N. – 268
USA – Belt, Montana – 353
USA – Benton Harbor, Michigan – 349
USA – Bingham, Maine – 300
USA – Bland, W.R. – 482
USA – Boeving, Leona – 354
USA – Bonenfant, Richard – 301
USA – Bonny Spring Ranch, near Las Vegas – 37
USA – Border Patrolman Don Flickenger – 318
USA – Broomhall, Mr. – 320
USA – Brown, Damon – 369
USA – Burns, Horace – 196
USA – Burnsville, North Carolina – 308
USA – California – 12, 22, 23, 33
USA – Cape Canaveral, Florida – 30, 32, 117
USA – Capital Beltway, Washington – 315

USA – Carolina – 261
USA – Cassville – 345
USA – Cherry Creek, New York – 219
USA – Chesterton, Indiana – 262
USA – Chippewa State Police – 299
USA – Chisholm, Minnesota – 230
USA – Cole, Jay – 514
USA – Columbus, Ohio – 320
USA – Commander R.W. Corson – 197
USA – Department of Commerce – 466
USA – Detroit Press Club – 267
USA – Dexter Police Chief Robert Taylor – 265
USA – Dintelmann's Wye Market – 354
USA – Director of Magnetic Observatory, Alaska – 466
USA – Dover – 225
USA – Eagle River, Wisconsin – 32
USA – Edwards, Frank – 239
USA – El Sobrante, California – 117
USA – Elyria Fire Department, Kecksburg – 243
USA – Empire Film Studio, Hollywood – 252
USA – Erie Peninsula – 315
USA – Exeter – 345
USA – Fairfield, Illinois – 133, 134
USA – Federal Aviation Administration – 247
USA – Florida – 67
USA – Florida Air Force Base – 33
USA – Forest Service – 138
USA – Franklin Springs, New York – 323
USA – Freedom, Pennsylvania – 299
USA – Funk, Mr. and Mrs. – 321
USA – Galesburg, Illinois – 351
USA – Gannett Publishing Company – 300
USA – Gatty, Robert – 246, 250
USA – Gaylesville, Alabama – 321
USA – Gilpin, Mr. – 320
USA – Glassboro, New Jersey – 186
USA – Glendale Shopping Center – 239
USA – Gordon, Stan – 244, 245, 246, 250
USA – Grand Haven, Michigan – 349
USA – Grand Rapids, Michigan – 347
USA – Gray, Dorothy – 307
USA – Greensburg Radio Station WHJB – 243
USA – Grewe, Donald, Martin – 239
USA – Grewe, Retha, Ann – 239
USA – Groveton, Missouri – 482
USA – Hastings, Robert – 310
USA – Hawthorne, Charles – 310

USA – Hays, John – 244
USA – Helfrich, Lee E. – 250
USA – Henry Ford the 2nd – 490
USA – Higgins, Bruce – 300
USA – Higgins, Wendy – 300
USA – Highway 150 – 223
USA – Hill, Barney – 41, 42, 44, 46, 49, 60
USA – Hill, Betty – 41, 42, 44, 46,
USA – Hynek, Allen, J. Dr. – 267, 268
USA – Illinois – 117, 203
USA – Indianapolis, Indiana – 12, 238
USA – Jamestown, New York – 315
USA – Johnson, L., Nicholas – 246, 247
USA – Jones, Fred – 95
USA – KALG Radio, Alamogordo – 164
USA – Kalp, Frances – 242
USA – Kalp, Nadine – 242
USA – Kalp, Nevin – 242
USA – Kansas – 37, 307
USA – Kean, Leslie – 247, 250
USA – Kecksburg – 242
USA – Keyhoe, Donald – 49, 202, 204
USA – King, Allie – 300
USA – Kirksville Air Force Station, Missouri – 22
USA – Landsman, Larry – 250
USA – Las Vegas – 37
USA – Ledford, 'Red' – 364
USA – Lexington, Kentucky – 25
USA – Lindley. Jack – 351
USA – Littleton, Illinois – 173
USA – Long Island, New York – 276
USA – Manor, Frank – 265
USA – Manor, Leona – 265
USA – Manor, Robert – 265
USA – Mascoutah, Illinois – 354
USA – Matheson, Paul – 300
USA – McConnell, Steve – 247
USA – McDonald, James, Dr. – 114
USA – McMinnville, Oregon – 149
USA – Merkle, Donald – 265
USA – Miami – 264
USA – Michigan – 31, 37, 208
USA – Michigan College – 267
USA – Missile site, Charlottesville, West Central Virginia – 110
USA – Missouri – 345
USA – Mohall, North Dakota – 311
USA – Monroe, Oregon – 328

USA – Montana – 12
USA – Monticello, Wisconsin – 161
USA – Murphy, John – 243
USA – Naperville, Illinois – 117
USA – NASA Johnson Space Center – 246
USA – NASA public liaison officer – 247
USA – National Press Club building, Washington – 344
USA – Naval Air Station Patuxent River – 197
USA – Nederland, Texas – 261
USA – New Hampshire – 225
USA – New Jersey – 369
USA – New Winchester, Ohio – 353
USA – New York – 161, 179, 321
USA – New York State Department of Health – 301
USA – New York, Rome Air Force Base – 11
USA – Niles, Michigan – 276
USA – North Dakota – 320, 323
USA – Northern Air Service – 173
USA – O'Connor, J.J. – 324
USA – Ocala – 514
USA – Odessa, Delaware – 347
USA – Ohio – 37, 202
USA – Old River Road, Willard – 345
USA – Onawa, Iowa – 351
USA – Panzenella, Frank – 299
USA – Paradigm Research Group – 344
USA – Patrolman N.G. Lee – 265
USA – Pennsylvania – 242
USA – Pleasant View, Pennsylvania – 165
USA – Police California Highway Patrol Officer, Charles A. Carson – 33
USA – Police California Highway Patrol Officer, Stanley Scott – 33
USA – Police Captain John Warner – 346
USA – Police Chief Dave Geralds – 354
USA – Police Chief Richard Crawford, *Elmore, Ohio* – 167
USA – Police Deputy Carl Soenichsoen – 167
USA – Police Deputy J. Foster – 263
USA – Police Deputy Sheriff Arthur Strauch – 239
USA – Police Deputy Sheriff B. Bushroe – 263
USA – Police Deputy Sheriff Dale Spauer – 297
USA – Police Deputy Sheriff Harry Lee – 134
USA – Police Deputy Sheriff David Fitzpatrick – 266
USA – Police Deputy Sheriff Frank Courson – 349
USA – Police Deputy Wilbur 'Barney' Neff – 297

USA – Police Huron County Sheriff's Department – 345, 346
USA – Police Lt. Joseph McCarthy – 225
USA – Police Officer Bill Fisher – 349
USA – Police Officer Robert Adams – 225
USA – Police Officer Wayne Huston – 298
USA – Police Patrolman Allen Stubblefield – 345
USA – Police Patrolman Lonnie Zamora – 161
USA – Police Sergeant Herbert Schirmer – 466, 468, 469
USA – Police Sergeant Hollis Whalen – 225
USA – Police Sgt. Merill Rinfret – 226
USA – Police Sheriff Grysen – 349
USA – Police, Edmund Bressler – 226
USA – Police, *Exeter Station* – 225
USA – Police, James Gatcomb – 226
USA – Police, Louis Spence – 225
USA – Police, Washtenaw County Sheriff – Douglas J. Harvey – 266, 268
USA – Police, Washtenaw Deputy Sherriff – Ford Bushroe – 266
USA – Portville, New York State – 19
USA – Presque Isle State Park – 315
USA – Prince George County, Maryland – 315
USA – Project Blue Book – 141, 251
USA – Qualtrough, H.P., Major – 123
USA – Ravenna, Ohio – 297
USA – Red Bluff, California – 12, 20
USA – Ridman T.H. – 321
USA – Rodeo, New Mexico – 236
USA – Romansky, James – 243, 244, 246
USA – Route 4a – 202
USA – Rural Hall, North Carolina – 364
USA – Russian space probe – 247
USA – Rutledge, W.K. – 30
USA – Sacred Heart School, Illinois – 349
USA – Salt Lake City – 64
USA – Salt Lake City Tribune – 65
USA – Sam Bilderback – 354
USA – Sebring, Florida – 234
USA – Sedalia, Missouri – 376
USA – Sheriff's Deputy, Billy E. McCoy – 225
USA – Sheriff's Deputy, Robert Goode – 225
USA – Sibley County, Minnesota – 239
USA – Simon, Benjamin, Dr. – 42, 55, 58
USA – Sioux City, Iowa – 67
USA – Skeans, Bruce – 346
USA – Skeans, Mike – 346
USA – Skeans, Mrs. – 346

USA – *Sky & Telescope* – 249
USA – Socorro Police Department – 161
USA – Southampton, Long Island – 328
USA – Spooner, Wisconsin – 307
USA – Stanford, Roy – 368
USA – State Trooper Richard Gidcumb – 134
USA – Steitz, David – 247
USA – Strauch, Katherine – 239
USA – Strauch, Martin, Gary – 239
USA – Stringfield, Leonard – 158
USA – Susanville, California – 138
USA – Swett, H., Benjamin – 54
USA – Tampa, Florida – 104
USA – Taylor, Douglas, Robert – 266
USA – Temple, Oklahoma – 268
USA – Texas – 30, 37
USA – Texhoma, Texas – 268
USA – The *Sandusky Register* – 345
USA – Toledo, Ohio – 167
USA – Topeka, Kansas – 203
USA – Treml, Bill – 268
USA – *Tribune-Review* – 246
USA – Twin Mountain – 42
USA – Two State UFO Study Group, Massachusetts – 55
USA – Tyndale Air Force Base, Florida – 33
USA – Union, Pennsylvania – 310
USA – Urbana, Ohio – 220
USA – Utah Central Airport – 64
USA – Uzunoglu, Vasil, Dr. – 315
USA – Vanceboro, North Carolina – 314
USA – Vandalia, Ohio – 139
USA – Virginia – 196, 203
USA – Condon, Uhler, Edward, Dr. – 514
USA – Crittenden, Virginia-530
USA – Washington DC – 276
USA – Washtenaw County Sheriff's Department – 264
USA – Wesley, Joyce – 300
USA – White Mountains of Hampshire – 42
USA – White River Elementary School – 238
USA – Wichita, Kansas – 20
USA – Williams, Ken – 353
USA – Williams, Richard – 345
USA – Wilmer Kunze Farm – 354
USA – Wilmington, Ohio – 326
USA – Wolanin, Jerome – 349
USA – Wood, Carl – 310
USA – Wright-Patterson Air Force Base – 158

USA – Yosemite National Park, California – 179
USA – Wallace, Michael – 457
USAF – 'B' flight, 7551st Support Police Squadron – 462
USAF – Andrews Air Force Base – 315
USAF – Anton Kato – 350
USAF – Barksdale Air Force Base – 116
USAF – Captain B.C. Jones – 178
USAF – Captain David D. Schindele – 310
USAF – Captain Edward Orenic – 350
USAF – Communication Centre Unit, Ringstead Bay – 431
USAF – First Lt. H.J. Cavender – 178
USAF – Goodfellow Air Force Base, Texas – 304
USAF – Holloman Air Force Base – 164
USAF – Kessler Air Force Base, Mississippi – 206
USAF – Major Gordon Cooper – 119
USAF – Major H. Quintanilla – 141
USAF – Major James McDivitt – 209, 210, 211
USAF – Major Robert White – 95
USAF – Minot Air Force Base – 310, 349
USAF – Pease Air Force Base – 49
USAF – Police Officer F.W. Courson – 350
USAF – Reserve Major K.C. Smith – 264
USAF – Scott Air Force Base – 133, 355
USAF – Security personnel, Sergeant Bean – 462
USAF – Security personnel, Sergeant Coleman – 462, 471
USAF – Security personnel, Sergeant John Artie – 462, 471
USAF – Security personnel, Sergeant Knott – 462
USAF – Security personnel, Sergeant McDonald – 462
USAF – Security personnel, Sergeant Strickland – 462, 471
USAF – Security personnel, Sergeant Winston – 462
USAF – Selfridge Air Force Base – 263, 267
USAF – Sergeant John Roger Artie – 362
USAF – Suffolk County Air Force Base, New York – 322
USAF – Village Marshal, George Sexton – 134
Usworth Colliery – 212

V

Vanveen, G.A. – 514
Varty, Raymond – 165
Venables, David – 98
Vessey, David – 24
Vickers Evelyn – 191

Vickers, Carol – 314
Victorian Flying Saucer Research Society – 290
Vince, Colin – 17, 90
Vincent, Joan – 184
Vincent, Roy – 184
Vipond, Edwin – 168
Vipond, Elaine – 168

W

Waddell, Doreen – 119, 167, 214
Waine, Roesmary – 346
Wake Island – 178
Wakefield, Ron – 214
Wales – 90
Wales Fellowship of Independent Ufologists – 156
Walker, Amy – 256
Walker, Anthony, John – 121
Walker, Chris – 402
Walker, Joseph (NASA Pilot) – 89
Walker, Tom – 148
Wallace, Basil – 60
Wallace, D. – 497
Wallasey Coastguard Station – 172
Wallingford District Council, Berkshire – 330
Wallsend, Northumberland – 365
Wallsend-on-Tyne – 242
Walsall, West Midlands – 130, 479
Walsh, Catherine – 174
Waltham Cross, Hertfordshire – 322, 316
Walthamstow – 160, 209
Walton Pier – 459
Walton, George, Dr. – 236
Walton, Peterborough – 379
Wanborough – 502
Wandsworth, London – 531
Warburton, Mr. and Mrs. – 387
Ward, Barbara – 397
Wardle, Ray – 146
Warminster, Wiltshire – 23, 303, 372
Warne, John – 373, 375
Warren, Derek – 514
Warrington – 426, 440
Warriston School, Moffat – 403
Warwickshire – 505
Washington – 69
Washington Station, County Durham – 408
Washington, County Durham, 213, 258, 424
Waterhouse, John, Michael – 97
Waterhouse, Martin – 524

Waters, Ann – 377
Waters, Tony – 377
Watford – 471
Watkins, Sheila – 454
Watkinson, Harold, M.P. – 117
Watson, C. – 204
Watson, E. – 441
Watson, Mr. and Mrs. – 20
Watters, Phyllis – 119
Watts, Alan – 81
Weaverham County Secondary School – 387
Webb, George – 505
Webb, Paul – 151
Weber, G. – 69
Webley, Mrs. – 230
Wedgewood, J. – 208
Wednesbury – 38, 220
Wednesbury Youth Centre – 474
Wellfield, Mr. – 480
Wellingborough, Northamptonshire – 400, 425
Wellington, Shropshire – 436
Wellock, Roy – 437
Wembley – 405
Werner, Laurie – 36
Werneth Fire Station – 329
West Bromwich – 346
West Freugh, Scotland – 11
West Howes, Sussex – 375
West Mersea – 228
West Midlands – 202
West Moor, Newcastle-upon-Tyne – 408
West Wickham, Cambridgeshire – 305
West Wickham, Kent – 463
West, Rebecca, Dame – 258
West, Ron – 405
Westall High School – 278, 290
Westcliff, Southend -16
Westcliff-on-Sea – 559
Western Mail – 258
Westgarth, Martin – 237
Westley, Joseph – 479
Westmoreland Estate – 365
Weymouth News Agency – 517
Weymouth, Dorset – 370
Wharton, Henry – 99
Whickham, near Newcastle-upon-Tyne – 366
Whippingham, Isle of Wight – 373
Whipps Cross, North London – 498

Whipsnade – 515
Whiston – 539
White John – 128
White, A.J. – 446
White, David – 393
White, Della – 446
White, Ernest – 393
Whitlock, Tony – 407
Whittaker, Doreen -188
Whittaker, Mark – 423
Whittaker, Trevor – 188
Whittingham – 118
Whybrow, Violet – 20
Whyteleafe, Surrey – 119
Wigston, Leicestershire – 491, 524
Wilcox, Christine – 424
Wildman, Ronald – 75
Willey, Leonard – 363
Willey, Mark – 417
Willey, Steven – 363
Williams, Alan – 67
Williams, Constance – 502
Williams, Erica – 452
Williams, Howard – 128
Williams, Jennifer – 237
Williams, Kenneth – 237
Williams, Malcolm – 362
Willian, Hertfordshire – 551
Willis, N. – 504
Wilmslow, Cheshire – 118, 256, 260
Wilshin, Mabel – 502
Wilson, Brian – 263
Wilson, David – 166, 168
Wilson, Harold – 550
Wilson, Keith – 365
Wilson, Mrs. – 471
Wimbledon County Boys Secondary School – 171
Wimborne, Dorset – 375
Winder, R.H.B. – 257
Winfrith Power Station – 431
Winkle, J.J. – 173
Winsford, Cheshire – 459
Winstanley, Christopher, Roy – 131, 457
Winstanley, E. Mrs. – 131
Wisbech, Cambridgeshire – 191
Wise, David – 380
Wise, L.J. – 261
Wise, Patricia – 380

Withrow, Dwight – 134
Withycombe, Somerset – 364
Wittenham Clumps – 330
Woburn Animal Kingdom – 551
Woking, Surrey – 370
Wolverhampton – 37
Wontoon, Jeffrey – 261
Wood Green, London – 316
Wood, Alan – 149
Wood, Leonora – 480
Wood, Rita – 65
Woodcock, F. – 426
Woodhouse, A. – 352
Woodmansterne, Surrey – 511
Woods, Alan – 119
Woods, Derek – 257
Woofferton Railway Station, Shropshire – 28
Wooley, Douglas – 494
Woolford, Mrs. – 260
Woolsington Airport – 230, 408
Woomera Rocket Range, Australia – 358
Worcester Park, London – 251
Worthington, Jane – 101
Worthington, Sandra – 191
Wrangle Mudflats – 220
Wright, Brian – 322
Wright, Colin – 140
Wright, David – 328
Wright, Dennis – 116
Wright, John – 260
Wright, Yvonne – 205
Wroath, Dowling, Peter – 307, 556
Wroxham – 319
Wylde Green, Birmingham – 522

Y

Yardley Hastings – 242
Yarmouth, Isle of Wight – 255, 473, 531
Yateley, Hampshire – 541
Yates, Dudley – 228
York – 511
Yorkshire Dales – 364
Yorkshire Moors – 444
Yorkshire Post – 83
Young, C. – 251

Z

Zeta Reticuli incident – 41
Zetter, Jack – 559

Haunted Skies **Volume Two Revised**

DISCLAIMER

Should we have inadvertently missed anybody, we unreservedly apologise and will credit the copyright in *Haunted Skies*, Volume 12.

Thanks go to many people who assisted us with putting this book together. They include Nick Pope for the foreword, David Sankey, Steven Franklin, David Bryant and Wayne Mason for their illustrations. Bob Tibbitts for the design and typesetting of this volume. Phil Mantle for his assistance. Not forgetting those whose sightings and reports are contained within the pages of this book, some of whom have sadly left us.

All statements made by the people in the book involved are opinions expressed by them and should be treated as such.

The publisher/author John Hanson and the co-author Dawn Holloway do not accept liability or responsibly for statements made by the participants involved. All rights are reserved. This book or parts thereof may not be reproduced in any form, stored in any retrieval system or transmitted in any form by any means – electronic, mechanical, photocopy, or otherwise – without permission from the publisher or co-authors.

These books have cost us a great deal of money to produce, but we strongly believe that this information forms part of our social history and rightful heritage. It should therefore be preserved, despite the ridicule still aimed at the subject by the media.

If anyone is willing to assist us with the preparation of any illustrations, it would be much appreciated. We can be contacted by letter at **31, Red Lion St, Alvechurch, Worcestershire B48 7LG**, by telephone **0121 445 0340**, or email: **johndawn1@sky.com** • Website: **www.hauntedskies.co.uk**

Volumes 1 to 6 *not* currently available – Being Revised and Updated

Volume 1 of *Haunted Skies* **1940-1959** *(Foreword by Timothy Good)*

We present sightings from the Second Word War. They include many reports from allied pilots, who describe seeing unidentified flying objects, while on bombing missions over Germany. Some pilots we interviewed told of being ordered to intercept a UFO; one pilot was even ordered to open fire! In addition to these are reports of early close encounters, involving allegations of abduction experiences.

Another report tells of strange 'beings' seen outside an RAF Base. We also outline a spectacular sighting, in 1957, that took place in Bedfordshire, which appears identical to that seen over Oregon by employees of the Ames Research Laboratory, San Francisco. There are also numerous reports of 'saucer', 'diamond' and 'cigar-shaped' objects seen during these years.

Volume 2 of *Haunted Skies* **1960-1965** *(Foreword by Jenny Randles)*

We re-investigated what may well be one of the earliest events, involving mysterious crop circles discovered in June 1960, at Poplar Farm, Evenlode. A 'V'-shaped UFO over Gloucestershire, and an example of a early 'Flying Triangle' over Tyneside in early September 1960. This type of object attracted much media interest in the early 1980s, following attempts by the Belgium Air Force to intercept what became labelled as 'Triangular' UFOs. This book contains many reports of saucer-shaped objects, and their occasional effect on motor vehicles. We also, wherever possible, include numerous personal letters and interviews with some of the researchers. We should not forget the early magazines, such as UFOLOG, produced by members of the (now defunct) Isle of Wight UFO Society.

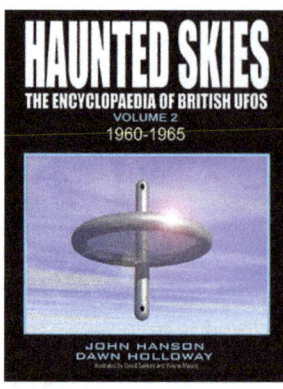

Volume 3 of *Haunted Skies* **1966-1967** *(Foreword by Nick Redfern)*

This was two years before manned landings took place on the Moon. In October 1967, there was a veritable 'wave' of UFO sightings which took place in the UK, involving cross-shaped objects, reported from Northumberland to the South Coast, with additional reports from Ireland and the Channel islands. (The police in the USA also reported sightings of 'Flying Crosses'). The sightings took place at various times, mostly during the evening or early morning hours, and involved an object which was manoeuvrable, silent – and at times – apparently flying at a low altitude. Attempts were made by the police and various authorities to explain away the sightings as Venus, based on the fact that the planet was bright in the sky during this period, which is clearly, in the majority of sightings, not the answer.

Volume 4 of *Haunted Skies* **1968-1971** *(Foreword by Philip Mantle)*

This book begins with a personal reference to Budd Hopkins, by USA researcher – Peter Robbins.

We outline a close encounter from Crediton, in Devon, which was brought to the attention of the police. Further police sightings of UFOs have been tracked down from Derbyshire, and a police chase through Kent. Multiple UFO sightings occur over the Staffordshire area, which are brought to the attention of the MOD. UFO researchers – Tony Pace and Roger Stanway – travel to London to discuss the incidents with the MOD. Close encounters at Warminster are also covered. A domed object at Bristol and further UFO landings are covered. They include a chilling account from a schoolteacher, living near Stratford-upon-Avon, and a 'flying triangle' seen over Birmingham.

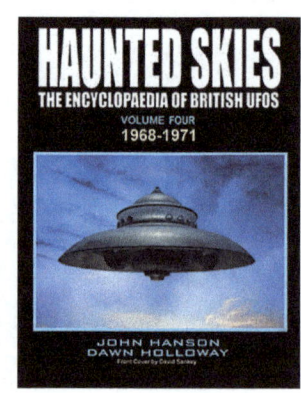

Volume 5 of *Haunted Skies* 1972-1975 *(Foreword by Matt Lyons, Chairman of BUFORA)*

Further examples of UFO activity at Warminster, involving classic 'sky watches' from such locations as Cradle Hill, was the focus of worldwide attention during this period. In addition to this are reports of mysterious footsteps heard. A visit from the 'Men in Black', and other amazing stories, form just a tiny part of some amazing material collected by us, over the years, during personal interviews with the people concerned. UFO fleets are seen over Reading, and a landed saucer-shaped object is seen at Lancashire.

A UFO, containing aliens, is seen at close range over Worcestershire. A local councillor also described seeing what he believes was an alien spaceship, with occupants. There is also an investigation into the famous Berwyn Mountain incident, when it was alleged, by some, that a 'craft' had landed.

Volume 6 of *Haunted Skies* 1976-1977 Jubilee edition *(Foreword by Kevin Goodman)*

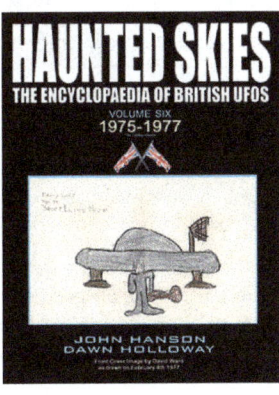

Strange globes of light, seen moving in formations of three (often referred to as triangular in overall shape). Warminster, Wiltshire – reports of mysterious black shadows, flying globes of light and a triangular-shaped UFO seen over Cleeve Hill, near Cheltenham by police officers. There is also an investigation into a number of reported landings of alien craft around the Dyfed area, in February 1977. We present some original illustrations, drawn by children at the local school (which will be reproduced in colour, in a later edition of Haunted Skies). A triangular UFO is seen over Stoke-on-Trent. Comprehensive details were also obtained, regarding Winchester woman, Joyce Bowles – who was to report many encounters with UFOs and their alien occupants.

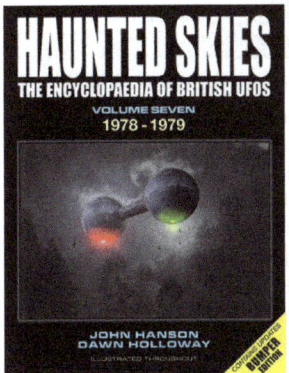

Volume 7 of *Haunted Skies* 1978-1979 *(Foreword by David Bryant)*

The famous debate into UFOs, held at the United Nations, is covered. A UFO landing at Rowley Regis, West Midlands – involving housewife Jean Hingley – labelled by the Press as the 'Mince Pie Martian' case. Many original sketches and additional information supporting her claims are offered. Another classic UFO sighting is re-investigated, following interviews held with Elsie Oakensen – a housewife from the Daventry area – who sighted a dumb-bell shaped UFO while on the way home from work. Thanks to Dan Goring, editor of EarthLink we were able to include a large number of previously unpublished sighting reports from Essex and London. We also include a close encounter from Didsbury, Manchester involving Lynda Jones, who is known personally to us.

Volume 8 of *Haunted Skies* 1980 *(Foreword by Philip Mantle)*

This book covers the period of just one year and is now, for the first time in the *Haunted Skies* series of books, published in colour. Unfortunately, due to the increase in pagination and the use of colour, the price has been raised, but still represents extremely good value. The first part of the book covers the period from January to November 1980. This includes numerous reports of UFO sightings and encounters. In addition to this, we outline our investigation into the Zigmund Adamski death, and the UFO sighting involving Todmorden Police Constable Alan Godfrey. In the second part, which covers December 1980, we present a comprehensive overview of the events that took place in Rendlesham Forest, thanks to the assistance of retired Colonel Charles Halt and long-standing UFO researcher, Brenda Butler.

Volume 9 of *Haunted Skies* 1981-1986 *(Foreword by Nick Redfern)*
Over 450 pages, many in colour

The authors point out that the majority of the information contained within the *Haunted Skies* series of books will not be found in declassified UFO files, catalogued in the Public Records Office, Kew, London.

This book contains:

UFO sightings over RAF Woodbridge, Suffolk – the scene of much interest during the previous month; a landed UFO at South Yorkshire; UFOs seen over Kent – harrowing close encounters between UFOs and motorists are outlined. These include a report from three women, driving home along the A5 in rural Shropshire (UK), which can be contrasted with a similar allegation made by three women from Kentucky, USA. A close encounter over the M50 Motorway, Gloucestershire; a couple from Hampshire tell of their roadside encounter – which left the husband with some strange marks on his body; a man out fishing, in Aldershot – who was approached by aliens; mysterious apports of stones that occurred, over a number of years, at Birmingham, West Midlands, involving the police – who staked out the locality in a bid to catch the offender. In addition to this, falls of coins and stones in other parts of the world are also outlined.

Although primarily covering British UFO sightings – wherever space permits (always in short supply) – we now include other forgotten worldwide cases of interest, brought to the attention of the reader. One such incident tells of a triangular UFO, seen over Arizona; another of a UFO sighted by a Russian astronaut.

A bizarre story involving David Daniels, who approached a number of prominent worldwide UFO researchers during the early 1980s – he alleged he was from the Pleiades and claimed to be able to metamorphosise from a human body to a reptilian. While it is difficult to believe rationally that this could be true, the authors tell of visits made to influential people, such as the head of the MOD, and The Lord Hill-Norton. Fact is stranger than fiction!

Volume 10 of *Haunted Skies* 1987-1988 *(Foreword by Nick Pope)*
632 pages, many in colour

Includes a focus on UFO cases reported from USA, Australia and New Zealand, 1940-1962.

Volume 10 of *Haunted Skies* catalogues the results of over 20 years research into reported UFO activity by the authors. The majority of those sightings and personal experiences will not be found in any declassified MOD files. Despite promises by their department to release specific individual files from 1971 (which we brought to their notice), the situation remains unchanged.

This volume covers the period of 1987-1988; which documents not only British UFO activity but also UFO activity from New Zealand, Australia and the United States, and

forms an ongoing process by the authors to document such matters. In addition, a number of historical UFO cases between the periods 1940 and 1962 is also presented.

The book contains over 600 pages – many in colour – including numerous original illustrations relating to increased UFO activity over the Essex area. In addition to this, the authors outline a mysterious incident in 1987, involving claims of a UFO crash-landing in Nottinghamshire, and a spectacular sighting of goblin-like creatures that invaded a farm in Kentucky. A number of thought-provoking images, captured on camera, are shown from locations such as Cumbria, Rendlesham Forest and the Sedona area of the United States.

Volume 11 of *Haunted Skies* 1989-1990 *(Foreword by Charles I. Halt, USAF Col. Ret.)*
756 pages, many in colour

Includes a focus on UFO cases reported from UK, USA, Australia and New Zealand, 1963-1964.

Volume 11 contains over 750 pages with a foreword written by retired USAF Colonel Charles Halt – then the Deputy Base Commander of RAF Woodbridge – during the now famous UFO incident that has attracted worldwide attention, which took place in late December 1980. In this Volume the the authors continue their examination of further chronological reports of UFO activity over Great Britain, USA, Australia, New Zealand and Tasmania, for the period 1989-1990.

They also include previously unpublished material from the late Essex UFO researcher Ron West, which shows that the Essex area, like its Belgium and European counterparts, was the source of much UFO activity involving sightings of the Flying Triangle .

There is also an examination of historical UFO reports covering the period of 1963-1964, which includes sightings from the archives of Project Blue Book for the first time. In addition, the Volume outlines the valuable commitment made by the researchers themselves and their efforts to preserve what forms part of our important social history, rather than relying on other dubious sources of information.
The authors point out that very few of the UFO sighting reports published in the *Haunted Skies* books will be found in any declassified MOD files.

Volume 1 Revised – *Haunted Skies* 1939-1959 *(Foreword by Timothy Good)*
628 pages, many in colour

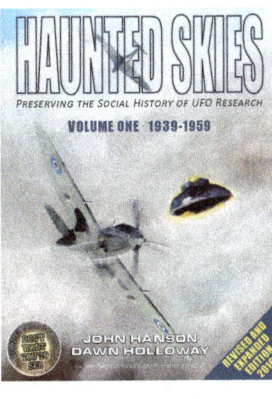

The original Volume 1 of *Haunted Skies* (320 pages) covered the period 1940-1959, with a foreword submitted by Timothy Good, and was published in 2010.

Due to the early books being removed from sale in late October 2015 by our ex-publisher, we were obliged to republish the book ourselves, which then gave us full control – now the volume has twice as many pages as the early one.

This is not a reproduction of the original black and white book. It includes many additional UFO reports from RAF servicemen, accompanied by photos and images, wherever possible, in colour.

We have now gone even further into the past and presented sightings of strange objects from the turn of the Century.

In this unique book you will read of numerous inexplicable close encounters, some involving humanoid figures, red glowing objects, ghostly figures, a number of reports of landed 'craft', allegations of abduction, dogfights with UFOs, gremlins – and our review is only up to the first 100 pages!

People asked us to publish in colour; we have done that. People asked us to document as much as we could; we have also done this to the best of our ability.

No one else (as far as we know) has ever compiled such an incredible amount of UFO social history – which should be preserved for posterity. Make of it what you will.

Haunted Skies Wiltshire *(Foreword by Nick Pope)*
Over 700 pages, many in colour

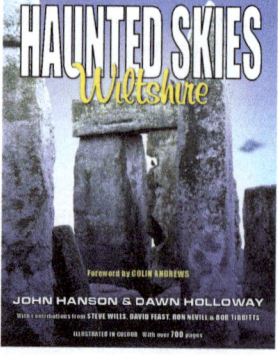

Haunted Skies Wiltshire is another in a series of unique books on the UFO subject, co-written by retired Police Officer John Hanson and his partner – Dawn Holloway. The couple have made many personal visits, over a period of 20 years, to interview members of the public living in the Wiltshire area, in order to preserve the history of reported UFO activity.

This volume contains approximately 1,000 images in over 700 pages – in colour and black and white. They include photographs, sketches, private letters and illustrations, many of which have not been previously published.

Whether it's 'sky watching' from the now famous Cradle Hill, outside the lovely town of Warminster – host to some incredible UFO sightings back in the halcyon days of the 1960s/1970s, recorded by local journalist Arthur Shuttlewood – or perhaps a visit to the famous *Barge Inn* at Honey Street, Alton Barnes, overlooking the famous 'White Horse', or the magic of nearby ancient sites, such as Silbury Hill, Avebury Stone Circle, Adam's Grave, West Kennet Long Barrow, or Stonehenge, the authors have been there and enjoyed every fascinating moment.

Whatever the reason, no one can deny the breathtaking beauty of what this wonderful magical county has to offer in exceptional landscapes, and the possibility that strange objects may be captured on film or photograph.

The locality is rich with not only legends and myths but reports of UFO sightings – along with their occasional occupants – and a huge number of mysterious crop circles which abound each year, attracting tourists from all over the world, eager to see for themselves the intricate, dazzling formations which have been the subject of so much media interest over the years.

We hope you enjoy this book, as much as we have putting it together.

John & Dawn
www.hauntedskies.co.uk

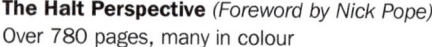

The Halt Perspective *(Foreword by Nick Pope)*
Over 780 pages, many in colour

Over three nights running, in December 1980, a series of UFO encounters occurred at RAF Bentwaters and United States Air Force Woodbridge – twin bases, in Suffolk.

"As the Deputy Base Commander in a senior management position, I knew most of the main witnesses to the reported sightings, and was involved in investigating these incidents. Additionally, as many of the readers will know, I was a witness myself to UFO activity taking place in the nearby forest. I wasn't sure what to make of what I and the other airmen saw. Other than briefly reading a book as a teenager, I never gave any thought to UFOs, although I had read one or two out of interest.

I asked UK retired Police Officer, John Hanson, to assist me with the publication of this book in order to set the record straight, instead of relying on the continuing rumours about what did or didn't take place. Ironically, when initially confronted with the unexplained, I did everything in my power to keep the events quiet. Over the years there has been so much rubbish and sensational accounts given in the media surrounding the allegations made, who talk of missing time, alien beings meeting with the base commander, and so forth – more in keeping with science fiction than reality! I decided it was time to let people know exactly what took place and then make up their own minds, rather than trusting assessments made by people who weren't there and continuing publication of so much misinformation over the last 36 years. My own personal perspective on what took place needs to be told for posterity's sake." **Colonel Charles I. Halt USAF Retired**

RECOMMENDED READING

http://flyingdiskpress.blogspot.co.uk

Lightning Source UK Ltd.
Milton Keynes UK
UKHW051018051121
393433UK00003B/6